Decisions of the
Federal Constitutional Court

Volume 6:
General right of personality

Edited by the
Federal Constitutional Court

Karlsruhe 2022

 Nomos Verlagsgesellschaft
Baden-Baden

Die Deutsche Nationalbibliothek verzeichnet diese Publikation in
der Deutschen Nationalbibliografie; detaillierte bibliografische
Daten sind im Internet über http://dnb.d-nb.de abrufbar.

The Deutsche Nationalbibliothek lists this publication as part of
the national bibliography; detailed bibliographic data
is available at http://dnb.d-nb.de.

ISBN 978-3-8487-8585-8 (Print)
ISBN 978-3-7489-3000-6 (ePDF)

1. Auflage 2022
© Nomos Verlagsgesellschaft, Baden-Baden 2022. Gesamtverantwortung für Druck und Herstellung bei der Nomos Verlagsgesellschaft mbH & Co. KG. Alle Rechte, auch die des Nachdrucks von Auszügen, der fotomechanischen Wiedergabe und der Übersetzung, vorbehalten. Gedruckt auf alterungsbeständigem Papier.

This work is subject to copyright. All rights are reserved, whether the whole or part of the material is concerned, specifically those of translation, reprinting, re-use of illustrations, broadcasting, reproduction by photocopying machine or similar means, and storage in data banks. Under § 54 of the German Copyright Law where copies are made for other than private use a fee is payable to »Verwertungsgesellschaft Wort«, Munich.

PREFACE

Continuing the series of Federal Constitutional Court decisions in English translation, this sixth volume is devoted to the general right of personality and thereby addresses one of the cornerstones of the Basic Law's fundamental rights architecture.

The current wording of Article 2(1) of the Basic Law stems from the well-known formulation that appeared in the Basic Law's original draft following the Constitutional Convention at Herrenchiemsee in 1948: "Every person shall be free, within the limits of the legal order and morality, to do anything that does not harm others." As the legislative history shows, this fundamental right guarantees freedom of individual action in a broad sense. This means that there is no area of life that does not fall under the fundamental rights protection afforded by the Basic Law. Where the Basic Law's more specific freedoms are not directly applicable, the general freedom of action may thus be invoked. But constitutional protection reaches even further. Building on Article 2(1) of the Basic Law in conjunction with the guarantee of human dignity enshrined in Article 1(1), it protects the free development of one's personality. Like all fundamental rights in the Basic Law, the general right of personality is not guaranteed without limitation. But because of its foundation in the right to human dignity as well, there are especially high hurdles to take. Due to the seamless nature of fundamental rights protection, any state activity that curtails individual freedoms must be justified. It is a key achievement of the state based on freedom and bound by fundamental rights that in conflicts with the individual, it is the *state* that must justify its actions, not the individual.

The general right of personality is also open to new developments, the extent of which can be seen in the decisions chosen for the present volume. The Federal Constitutional Court has derived various manifestations of this right from the Basic Law, each one defining its particular substance and significance in a different type of case. The best known of these manifestations is probably the right to informational self-determination – the core fundamental right pertaining to data protection in Germany. This is accompanied by rights of the individual to protection against false, distorting or unsolicited portrayals by others – including the right to one's own image, the right to one's own speech and a right of reply. Beyond that, the private sphere is itself protected in a manner comparable with the right to privacy under Article 8 of the European Convention on Human Rights and Article 7 of the Charter of Fundamental Rights of the European Union – this being relevant in cases involving the use of diary-like notes as criminal evidence, the monitoring of postal correspondence, or the interception of communications in private spaces used for retreat and refuge, for example. The general right of personality furthermore guar-

Preface

antees the individual's right to self-determination in the most private aspects of personal life. It also guarantees criminal offenders a right to social reintegration and it ensures that individuals cannot be subjected to medical treatment against their will. The rapid progress of technological development and the possibilities for monitoring and surveillance arising therefrom are reflected in the right to protection of the confidentiality and integrity of information technology systems – sometimes known as the 'computer fundamental right'.

Technological advances and the resulting global interconnectivity – which make practically all the information about an individual that has ever been published anywhere on the Internet readily available at all times from anywhere on the planet – are amongst the most salient new challenges facing the general right of personality. The same can be said regarding new technical possibilities for state surveillance. In our globally interconnected world, these challenges no longer affect individual states alone but also arise in the European Union or at the international level.

It is therefore immensely gratifying both for the Federal Constitutional Court and for me personally that the Court's case-law on the general right of personality is being made more easily accessible to an international audience with this English-language volume. International cooperation is now more important than ever for tackling global challenges such as data protection. Given the need for concerted action, effective communication within the multi-level cooperation of European constitutional courts and clear dialogue with academia have a vital role to play in facilitating the development of common approaches.

May this volume contribute to the international fundamental rights discourse on the protection of personality rights.

Professor Dr. Stephan Harbarth, LL.M. (Yale)
President of the Federal Constitutional Court   Karlsruhe, November 2021

ACKNOWLEDGMENTS

This volume is the result of a collaborative effort. Members of the legal translation unit of the Federal Constitutional Court – Wiebke Ringel, Stefanie Schout and Aileen Doetsch – coordinated this project, translated and edited the collection. Claudia Baumann, Dr. Margret Böckel (head of unit), Astrid Heine-Regenberg, Fiona Kaltenborn, Wilf Moss, Ennid Roberts, Wiebke Schierloh and Hedwig Weiland contributed to this endeavour in many ways, as did many judicial clerks. Chairing the working group for translation and internationalisation at the Federal Constitutional Court, Justice Prof. Dr. Susanne Baer, LL.M. (Michigan) as well as Vice-President Prof. Dr. Doris König provided guidance and support. We are grateful to all those who contributed to this continuation of comparative conversations in constitutional law.

CONTENTS

Table of Abbreviations ... XIII

Table of Court Names Cited ... XVI

Table of Legal Acts Cited ... XVII

Introductory Remarks ... XXII

Foundations

1. BVerfGE 27, 1	**Microcensus** - disclosure of personal data for statistical purposes (1969)	1
2. BVerfGE 34, 238	**Secret Tape Recordings** - admissibility as evidence in criminal proceedings (1973)	6
3. BVerfGE 34, 269	**Soraya** - damages for false press reports on personal life (1973)	14
4. BVerfGE 49, 286	**Transsexuals I** - legal sex (1978)	26
5. BVerfGE 54, 148	**Eppler** - statements falsely attributed to one's person (1980)	34
6. BVerfGE 65, 1	**Census** - informational self-determination and modern data processing (1983)	41

Self-Determination and Limits to Personal Choice

7. BVerfGE 35, 202	**Lebach** - prisoner's right to social reintegration (1973)	69
8. BVerfGE 75, 201	**Foster Parents** - child custody (1987)	86
9. BVerfGE 78, 77	**Public Announcement of Legal Incapacitation** (1988)	94
10. BVerfGE 117, 71	**Life Imprisonment** - prospect of release (2006)	100

CONTENTS

11. BVerfGE 128, 282	**Coercive Treatment in Psychiatric Confinement under Criminal Law** (2011)		116
12. BVerfGE 142, 313	**Coercive Medical Treatment** (2016)		127
13. BVerfGE 153, 182	**Assisted Suicide*** - right to a self-determined death (2020)		140

Name and Identity

14. BVerfGE 97, 391	**Sexual Abuse Allegations** - victim's right to state their own name (1998)		166
15. BVerfGE 115, 1	**Transsexuals V** - change of first name (2005)		175
16. BVerfGE 147, 1	**Third Gender Option** - civil register entry for intersex persons (2017)		185

Image

17. BVerfGE 87, 334	**Honecker** - TV broadcasting of criminal proceedings (1992)		196
18. BVerfGE 99, 185	**Helnwein/Scientology** - imputed group membership (1998)		201
19. BVerfGE 119, 309	**TV Broadcasting from the Courtroom** (2007)		212
20. BVerfGE 120, 180	**Caroline III** - celebrities' right to their image (2008)		222

Speech

21. BVerfGE 63, 131	**Right of Reply** - right to defend oneself against negative media portrayals (1983)		242
22. BVerfGE 114, 339	**Stolpe/Stasi Dispute** - injunctive relief against ambiguous defamatory statements (2005)		250
23. BVerfGE 119, 1	**Esra** - prohibition of a literary work (2007)		262

CONTENTS

Privacy and Intimacy

24. BVerfGE 80, 367	**Diary-Like Notes** - admissibility as evidence in criminal proceedings (1989)	289
25. BVerfGE 90, 255	**Monitoring of Correspondence** - screening of prisoners' personal mail (1994)	300
26. BVerfGE 109, 279	**Surveillance of Private Homes** - inviolable core of private life (2004)	307
27. BVerfGE 128, 109	**Transsexuals VIII** - no surgery requirement (2011)	338
28. BVerfGE 138, 377	**False Paternity** - former legal father's right to information (2015)	350

Health Data

29. BVerfGE 44, 353	**Addiction Counselling Agency** - seizure of client records (1977)	358
30. BVerfGE 89, 69	**Mandatory Medical-Psychological Assessment** - conditions for retaining driving licence (1993)	367
31. BVerfGE 103, 21	**DNA Fingerprinting** - databases of DNA profiles (2000)	376

Data Protection and Virtual Identity

32. BVerfGE 27, 344	**Divorce Files** - sharing personal data in disciplinary proceedings (1970)	388
33. BVerfGE 56, 37	**Bankruptcy Proceedings** - compulsory disclosure (1981)	393
34. BVerfGE 113, 29	**Seizure of Electronic Data** - search warrant for entirety of law firm's hardware and files (2005)	401
35. BVerfGE 152, 152	**Right to Be Forgotten I*** - name searches in online press archives (2019)	415
36. BVerfGE 152, 216	**Right to Be Forgotten II*** - claim for dereferencing against search engine operator (2019)	438

CONTENTS

Informational Self-Determination and Security

37. BVerfGE 100, 313	**The Article 10 Act** - telecommunications surveillance by intelligence services (1999)	455
38. BVerfGE 115, 166	**Telecommunications Surveillance** - covert investigation of a judge (2006)	483
39. BVerfGE 115, 320	**Profiling** - electronic databases for profiling and searches (2006)	506
40. BVerfGE 120, 274	**Remote Searches** - covert searches of private computers (2008)	534
41. BVerfGE 125, 260	**Data Retention** - service providers' obligation to retain telecommunications traffic data (2010)	565
42. BVerfGE 129, 208	**The Telecommunications Surveillance Revision Act** (2011)	606
43. BVerfGE 133, 277	**Counter-Terrorism Database Act I** - sharing of data between police and intelligence services in a joint security database (2013)	626
44. BVerfGE 141, 220	**The Federal Criminal Police Office Act** - counter-terrorism surveillance powers (2016)	662
45. BVerfGE 154, 152	**Surveillance of Foreign Telecommunications*** - Federal Intelligence Service's powers to intercept communications of foreigners abroad (2020)	712
Appendix - Basic Law of the Federal Republic of Germany		762
Index		851

All texts have been abridged. The paragraph numbers refer to the numbering used in the *juris* database.

* *longer version available on the Court's website at*
www.bundesverfassungsgericht.de/EN

TABLE OF ABBREVIATIONS

A-Drucks	*Ausschussdrucksache*	*Bundestag* committee document
ARD	*Arbeitsgemeinschaft der öffentlich-rechtlichen Rundfunkanstalten der Bundesrepublik Deutschland*	ARD broadcasting corporation
AVR	*Archiv des Völkerrechts*	(law journal)
BAG	*Bundesarbeitsgericht*	Federal Labour Court
BGBl	*Bundesgesetzblatt*	Federal Law Gazette
BGH	*Bundesgerichtshof*	Federal Court of Justice
BGHSt	*Entscheidungen des Bundesgerichtshofes in Strafsachen*	Decisions of the Federal Court of Justice in Criminal Matters
BGHZ	*Entscheidungen des Bundesgerichtshofes in Zivilsachen*	Decisions of the Federal Court of Justice in Civil Matters
BND	*Bundesnachrichtendienst*	Federal Intelligence Service
BR	*Bayerischer Rundfunk*	BR broadcasting corporation
BTDrucks	*Bundestagsdrucksache*	*Bundestag* document
BTPlenarprotokoll	*Plenarprotokoll des Bundestags*	Plenary minutes of the *Bundestag*
BVerfG	*Bundesverfassungsgericht*	Federal Constitutional Court
BVerfGE	*Entscheidungen des Bundesverfassungsgerichts*	Decisions of the Federal Constitutional Court
BVerwGE	*Entscheidungen des Bundesverwaltungsgerichts*	Decisions of the Federal Administrative Court
CDU	*Christlich Demokratische Union Deutschlands*	(German political party)

Table of Abbreviations

CJEU	*Gerichtshof der Europäischen Union*	Court of Justice of the European Union
CMLR	--	Common Market Law Review
CRPD	*Übereinkommen über die Rechte von Menschen mit Behinderungen (VN)*	Convention on the Rights of Persons with Disabilities (UN)
DM	*Deutsche Mark*	(former German currency)
ECtHR	*Europäischer Gerichtshof für Menschenrechte*	European Court of Human Rights
ERPL	--	European Review of Private Law
EU	*Europäische Union*	European Union
EuGRZ	*Europäische Grundrechte-Zeitschrift*	(law journal)
EuZW	*Europäische Zeitschrift für Wirtschaftsrecht*	(law journal)
FDP	*Freie Demokratische Partei*	(German political party)
GDR	*Deutsche Demokratische Republik*	German Democratic Republic
GVBl HH	*Gesetz- und Verordnungsblatt Hamburg*	Hamburg Law and Ordinance Gazette
GVBl NRW	*Gesetz- und Verordnungsblatt Nordrhein-Westfalen*	North Rhine-Westphalia Law and Ordinance Gazette
GVBl RLP	*Gesetz- und Verordnungsblatt Rheinland-Pfalz*	Rhineland-Palatinate Law and Ordinance Gazette
HR	*Hessischer Rundfunk*	HR broadcasting corporation
HRLR	--	Human Rights Law Review
IDPL	--	International Data Privacy Law
MDR	*Mitteldeutscher Rundfunk*	MDR broadcasting corporation

Table of Abbreviations

MHP	*Milliyetçi Hareket Partisi*	(Turkish political party)
NDR	*Norddeutscher Rundfunk*	NDR broadcasting corporation
NJW	*Neue Juristische Wochenschrift*	(law journal)
NRW	*Nordrhein-Westfalen*	North Rhine-Westphalia
OJ L	*Amtsblatt der Europäischen Union, Reihe L*	Official Journal of the European Union, L series
ORB	*Ostdeutscher Rundfunk Brandenburg*	ORB broadcasting corporation
PKK	*Partiya Karkerên Kurdistanê*	(Kurdish political party)
RDP	*Revue de droit public*	(law journal)
RTDE	*Revue trimestrielle de droit européen*	(law journal)
SDR	*Süddeutscher Rundfunk*	*SDR broadcasting corporation*
SPD	*Sozialdemokratische Partei Deutschlands*	(German political party)
SWR	*Südwestrundfunk*	SWR broadcasting corporation
UN	*Vereinte Nationen*	United Nations
WDR	*Westdeutscher Rundfunk*	WDR broadcasting corporation
ZDF	*Zweites Deutsches Fernsehen*	ZDF broadcasting corporation

TABLE OF COURT NAMES CITED

Federal Constitutional Court	*Bundesverfassungsgericht*	BVerfG
Local Court	*Amtsgericht*	AG
Regional Court	*Landgericht*	LG
Higher Regional Court	*Oberlandesgericht* (in Berlin: *Kammergericht*)	OLG
Federal Court of Justice	*Bundesgerichtshof*	BGH
Administrative Court	*Verwaltungsgericht*	VG
Higher Administrative Court	*Oberverwaltungsgericht*	OVG
Federal Administrative Court	*Bundesverwaltungsgericht*	BVerwG
Supreme Court of Bavaria	*Bayerisches Oberstes Landesgericht*	BayObLG

TABLE OF LEGAL ACTS CITED

Accompanying Act to the Telecommunications Act	*Begleitgesetz zum Telekommunikationsgesetz*	BegleitG
Act Amending the Basic Law (Article 13)	*Gesetz zur Änderung des Grundgesetzes (Artikel 13)*	--
Act Criminalising Assisted Suicide Services	*Gesetz zur Strafbarkeit der geschäftsmäßigen Förderung der Selbsttötung*	--
Act Improving Hospice and Palliative Care in Germany	*Gesetz zur Verbesserung der Hospiz- und Palliativversorgung in Deutschland*	--
Act on Administrative Offences	*Ordnungswidrigkeitengesetz*	OWiG
Act on Consent by a Custodian to Coercive Medical Treatment	*Gesetz zur Regelung der betreuungsrechtlichen Einwilligung in eine ärztliche Zwangsmaßnahme*	--
Act on the Surveillance of Foreign Telecommunications by the Federal Intelligence Service	*Gesetz zur Ausland-Ausland-Fernmeldeaufklärung des Bundesnachrichtendienstes*	--
Act Revising Parental Care Law	*Gesetz zur Neuregelung des Rechts der elterlichen Sorge*	--
Act to Amend Civil Status Law	*Personenstandsrechts-Änderungsgesetz*	PStRÄndG
Act to Reform Civil Status Law	*Personenstandsrechtsreformgesetz*	PStRG

Table of Legal Acts Cited

Art Copyright Act	*Kunsturhebergesetz*	KunstUrhG
Article 10 Act	*Artikel-10-Gesetz*	G 10
Atomic Energy Act	*Atomgesetz*	AtG
Bankruptcy Code	*Konkursordnung*	KO
Basic Law	*Grundgesetz*	GG
Census Act	*Volkszählungsgesetz*	VZG
Civil Code	*Bürgerliches Gesetzbuch*	BGB
Civil Partnerships Act	*Lebenspartnerschaftsgesetz*	LPartG
Civil Status Act	*Personenstandsgesetz*	PStG
Code of Civil Procedure	*Zivilprozessordnung*	ZPO
Code of Criminal Procedure	*Strafprozessordnung*	StPO
Counter-Terrorism Database Act	*Antiterrordateigesetz*	ATDG
Courts Constitution Act	*Gerichtsverfassungsgesetz*	GVG
Criminal Code	*Strafgesetzbuch*	StGB
Custodianship Act	*Betreuungsgesetz*	--
DNA Identification Act	*DNA-Identitätsfeststellungsgesetz*	DNA-IFG
Equal Rights Act	*Gleichberechtigungsgesetz*	--
European Convention on Human Rights	*Europäische Menschenrechtskonvention*	ECHR
Federal Constitutional Court Act	*Bundesverfassungsgerichtsgesetz*	BVerfGG
Federal Criminal Police Office Act	*Bundeskriminalamtgesetz*	BKAG

Table of Legal Acts Cited

Federal Data Protection Act	*Bundesdatenschutzgesetz*	BDSG
Federal Intelligence Service Act	*Gesetz über den Bundesnachrichtendienst*	BNDG
Federal Police Act	*Bundespolizeigesetz*	BPolG
Federal Statistics Act	*Bundesstatistikgesetz*	BStatG
Fight Against Organised Crime Act	*Gesetz zur Verbesserung der Bekämpfung der Organisierten Kriminalität*	--
Fight Against Crime Act	*Verbrechensbekämpfungsgesetz*	--
Framework Act on Civil Registration	*Melderechtsrahmengesetz*	--
Hamburg Act on the State Treaty of the *Länder* on the North German Broadcasting Corporation	*Hamburgisches Gesetz zum Staatsvertrag über den Norddeutschen Rundfunk*	--
Hamburg Press Act	*Hamburgisches Pressegesetz*	--
Introductory Act to the Courts Constitution Act	*Einführungsgesetz zum Gerichtsverfassungsgesetz*	EGGVG
Joint Databases Act	*Gemeinsame-Dateien-Gesetz*	--
Lower Saxony Public Security and Order Act	*Niedersächsisches Gesetz über die öffentliche Sicherheit und Ordnung*	--
Microcensus Act	*Mikrozensusgesetz*	MZG
Narcotics Act	*Betäubungsmittelgesetz*	BtMG

Table of Legal Acts Cited

North Rhine-Westphalia (NRW) Constitution Protection Act	*Verfassungsschutzgesetz Nordrhein-Westfalen*	VSG-NRW
NRW Police Act	*Polizeigesetz des Landes Nordrhein-Westfalen*	PolG NRW
Ordinance on the Competences of the Federal Police Authorities	*Verordnung über die Zuständigkeit der Bundespolizeibehörden*	BPolZV
Prevention of Sexual Offences and Other Dangerous Criminal Offences Act	*Gesetz zur Bekämpfung von Sexualdelikten und anderen gefährlichen Straftaten*	SexualdelBekG
Prison Act	*Strafvollzugsgesetz*	StVollzG
Residence Act	*Aufenthaltsgesetz*	AufenthG
Rhineland-Palatinate Act on Psychiatric Confinement of Criminal Offenders	*Rheinland-Pfälzisches Landesgesetz über den Vollzug freiheitsentziehender Maßregeln*	MVollzG
Road Traffic Act	*Straßenverkehrsgesetz*	StVG
Statistics Act *see Federal Statistics Act*		
Telecommunications Act	*Telekommunikationsgesetz*	TKG
Telecommunications Surveillance Revision Act	*Gesetz zur Neuregelung der Telekommunikationsüberwachung*	--
Transsexuals Act	*Transsexuellengesetz*	TSG
Treaty on European Union	*Vertrag über die Europäische Union*	TEU

Table of Legal Acts Cited

Treaty on the Functioning of the European Union	*Vertrag über die Arbeitsweise der Europäischen Union*	TFEU
Vehicle Registration and Licensing Ordinance	*Straßenverkehrs-Zulassungs-Ordnung*	StVZO
Weimar Constitution	*Weimarer Reichsverfassung*	WRV
Youth Courts Act	*Jugendgerichtsgesetz*	JGG

INTRODUCTORY REMARKS

What is a 'general right of personality'? Constitutional and human rights catalogues traditionally address liberty and integrity of the person, often explicitly guaranteeing political freedoms such as free speech or assembly as well as privacy interests like those associated with the home or communication. But how does constitutional law handle conflicts around deeply personal issues? How does it handle the individual's interest in being and living the way they define themselves? And how does constitutional law address data privacy and protect the integrity of one's data devices in a world that framers of constitutions did not even imagine? In German constitutional law, the Federal Constitutional Court has developed a doctrine – based on general provisions on dignity and freedom in the Basic Law – to protect a 'right of personality' in order to meet these challenges. This volume presents the leading cases in English.

The Issue

The German doctrine of the right of personality is legally complex as such, and also presents the translator with significant challenges, for several reasons. The development of this right is a rather recent phenomenon, as it is not based on long-standing, centuries-old tradition in many jurisdictions. It does not always have equivalents in other legal systems, and unlike rights like freedom of assembly or freedom of the press, the essence of the right of personality is not intuitively obvious. Even where aspects of the right of personality are recognised in national, international or European law, as in Article 8 of the European Convention on Human Rights or in Articles 7 and 8 of the Charter of Fundamental Rights of the EU, the English terminology may invoke notions of 'privacy' or a 'private life' which do not convey what is covered by the general right of personality under the German Basic Law.

Against this backdrop, translating a thematic collection of decisions offers a major advantage. With consistent terminology and the presentation of distinct lines of case-law within a broader context, it allows the reader to see the otherwise hidden DNA that informs this jurisprudence, in terms of overarching principles, themes and doctrine. The collection furthermore illustrates how legal concepts evolve over time. For instance, the notion of 'informational self-determination' emerged to address a classic conflict around census data, balancing the state's interest in collecting data against privacy interests of citizens. Today, it is a key point of reference in decisions on digital data, especially in the balancing of privacy and

Introductory Remarks

security, concerning a broad range of state powers from profiling and data retention to transnational surveillance practices. As such, what seems to be a fairly recent topic can actually be traced back to much earlier lines of legal argument. Today, the general right of personality confers upon individuals the authority to decide for themselves to what extent and to whom they wish to disclose aspects of their personal life.

Translating Law

The present volume not only presents the leading cases on a foundational theme in German constitutional law. It is also a result of a formative phase in the translation work undertaken by the Federal Constitutional Court. Faced with growing interest in translations of landmark decisions, the Court initially relied almost exclusively on freelance translators. Yet to ensure consistency and to contextualise doctrinal developments in a comparative understanding of constitutionalism, the Court created a translation unit. Here, trained translators and lawyers work together and liaise closely with the Justices and their judicial clerks. The unit also meets regularly with two Justices, from both Senates of the Court, in a working group that plays a pivotal role in conceptualising translation projects. This group has produced a glossary on terminology of constitutional law that is now used in translations by the Court and beyond, since the Court actively networks with translation units of other courts, parliaments and government institutions.

One important element of the Court's efforts to translate its work into English are thematic collections of its decisions. In 1992, European and international law was an obvious choice for the first volume of a series catering to an international audience, and it proved all the more timely the year in which Germany and other European countries signed the Treaty of Maastricht establishing the European Union. Just two years earlier, in 1990, Germany had achieved national unity based on then Article 23, which thus became obsolete. In 1992, when a new Article 23 was inserted into the Basic Law to affirm the commitment to a united Europe and lay down a constitutional basis and requirements for Germany's participation in the development of the European Union, it also became clear that doctrine shapes constitutional law in many ways. Today, the wording of Article 23 reflects the principles laid down in the *Solange I* and *II* landmark decisions, both to be found in the first volume of translations published by the Court.

The subsequent volumes of thematic compilations focused on freedom of expression (volume 2, 1998), constitutional issues arising from German reunification (volume 3, 2005), freedom of religion and the law on state-church relations (vol-

Introductory Remarks

ume 4, 2007) and constitutional aspects of family matters (volume 5, 2013). With its focus on the general right of personality, the sixth instalment circles back to a central notion informing the Federal Constitutional Court's mandate as a citizens' court: protecting individual self-determination and the free development of one's personality.

Mapping Personality

This volume presents 45 decisions to map the right of personality as a fundamental guarantee in constitutional law. It covers a variety of issues, requirements and standards arising from the general right of personality. Again, all decisions have been abridged in order to highlight seminal parts of the Court's reasoning, and cross-references are indicated by case names in italics (e.g. BVerfGE 65, 1 – *Census*; BVerfGE 100, 313 – *The Article 10 Act*). Yet slightly different from its predecessors, this volume does not present the translated decisions in strict chronological order. Instead, it is organised into **chapters** dedicated to a specific aspect and manifestation of the right of personality. This is not an exhaustive categorisation. As readers will quickly realise, a rigid approach would not be compatible with the Court's doctrinal concept of the general right of personality itself. Rather, the decisions each touch on several aspects of the right of personality yet are assigned to one specific chapter to best illustrate a particular issue. For instance, the three decisions concerning transsexual persons (*Transsexuals I, V, VIII*) are presented in different chapters because of their respective focus. Also, in *Caroline III*, the applicable standards regarding the protection of celebrities' private life vis-à-vis the media are consolidated on the basis of other decisions rendered by this Court as well as by the German Federal Court of Justice and by the European Court of Human Rights, interpreting Article 8 of the Convention. Overall, the chapters aim to provide a more systematic way of accessing the case-law, and guide further research.

The Starting Point: Foundations

The first chapter, entitled **Foundations**, traces the origins of the general right of personality. It derives from two fundamental rights expressly guaranteed in the German Constitution, the Basic Law. There is the general freedom of action, in Article 2(1) of the Basic Law, which is then read in conjunction with the guarantee of human dignity in Article 1(1) of the Basic Law. The underlying notion is that these guarantees interact, that they are interconnected. Indeed, such a holistic reading of the Constitution, rather than an approach that treats rights as isolated guarantees, is

Introductory Remarks

a staple of constitutional interpretation by the Federal Constitutional Court, which has repeatedly recognised that fundamental rights intersect and can be mutually reinforcing. As such, the doctrine of a right of personality is a case in point.

In addition, both human dignity and the general freedom of action are central pillars of the Basic Law's fundamental architecture. Human dignity is declared inviolable in Article 1(1) of the Basic Law, meaning that it is absolutely, unequivocally and unconditionally protected. Already the message of placing this guarantee at the very beginning of the Constitution is remarkable – before laying out what the state *can* do in terms of its powers, competences and authority, the Basic Law spells out what the state *cannot* do under any circumstances: violate human dignity. While dignity is sometimes seen as just a principle, or a black box for fundamental precepts, the decisions in this volume show that it is a right, yet one of specific dimensions.

The constitutional promise behind the general freedom of action under Article 2(1) of the Basic Law provides quite the contrast. As a catch-all fundamental right, the general freedom of action in principle protects any kind of human behaviour, no matter how trivial, random, undesirable or irrational, according to an early decision by the Court which also established its power to accept challenges to any law that at least potentially violates this general right (*Elfes*). Yet as a subsidiary right, it is only applicable in cases that do not fall within the scope of the more specific freedoms listed in the Basic Law. And very much unlike human dignity, this freedom does not enjoy absolute protection. Generally speaking, limitations may derive from the constitutional order, which in this context refers to the entirety of laws and rules that make up the legal order, and from the rights of others or moral law. Nevertheless, this right to freedom of action ensures that no area of human life is excluded from fundamental rights protection per se, and that the burden of justification rests firmly with the state. The Federal Constitutional Court combined these two rights to conceptualise the general right of personality. It is based on the notion that human dignity and the free development of one's personality lie at the centre of the Basic Law's system of values. As an additional, 'non-listed' freedom, the general right of personality affords protection to certain domains of personal life not covered by the specific guarantees in the fundamental rights norms beyond Article 2.

This rationale underpinning the relevant case-law is outlined in the **Foundations** chapter. The Court held early on that the Basic Law recognises, for each individual, an inviolable part of private life that is beyond the reach of public authority (*Microcensus*). This inviolable core of private life reflects the human dignity dimension.

Introductory Remarks

As summarised in *Eppler*, the general right of personality further guarantees the personal sphere close to the core of private life, as well as its basic conditions, which are not entirely protected by the traditional and 'listed' specific freedoms. Most notably, the Court saw the need for more comprehensive protection with regard to developments in media and technology that pose new risks to one's personality. The link to human dignity implies that the domains protected are defined more narrowly than those covered by the general freedom of action. As protected domains, the Court recognised the private and intimate sphere (*Transsexuals I*), one's own image and one's own speech (*Secret Tape Recordings*) as well as one's portrayal in public and the protection against false or fabricated statements being attributed to one's person (*Eppler, Soraya*). Moreover, the risks associated with data processing have led the Court to recognise the right to 'informational self-determination'. In its *Census* decision of 1983, the Court held that the almost unlimited potential of data processing technologies must not result in the unlimited registration, cataloguing and profiling of one's personality or life; and this caveat still stands today.

Titled **Self-Determination and Limits to Personal Choice**, the second chapter focuses on how the right of personality protects interests that are specifically essential to the free development of one's personality. To begin with, every person has a right to be valued and respected as a person in society. Based on the idea of dignity, the individual may not be turned into a mere object of state action, and no one may be treated in a way which calls into question their quality as a conscious subject – a human being (*Life Imprisonment, Assisted Suicide*). Moreover, every person is guaranteed an autonomous domain of private life. This includes the right 'to be left alone', 'to be oneself' and to be free from intrusion or inspection by others. Yet at the same time, the individual is always connected to and bound by the community, since the development of one's personality takes place within the social community and through interaction with others. Therefore, and from the very start, tension may arise between the right to self-determination on the one hand and the interests of the community or the rights of others on the other hand. The decisions selected for the second chapter illustrate how the Court strikes a balance to reconcile these interests.

One seminal decision is the *Lebach* case, which concerns a TV documentary on a violent crime that had attracted an unusual amount of public attention. The documentary was scheduled to air shortly before one of the offenders, convicted on a charge of accessory to murder, was set to be released on probation. Was this compatible with his fundamental rights? The Court had to balance his rights against the freedom of broadcasting and the public's interest in information. It held that the offender has a right to reintegration into society, derived from the general right of personality, given that living in liberty goes beyond the freedom of action, as dignity has to be taken into account, too.

As another seminal case, the decision on *Life Imprisonment* illustrates how high-ranking constitutional interests are actually capable of justifying very severe restrictions of personal liberty, self-determination and freedom, but can never strip anyone of their right to be recognised as a human being. The Court argued that where the actions of individuals bring danger and harm to others or the community, society has a right to protect itself. Yet the human dignity guaranteed to *every* person demands that even those convicted of the most serious crimes must retain at least the chance of regaining liberty at some point.

Beyond imprisonment and its limits, other decisions in this chapter touch on the difficult question of whether and to what extent coercive measures such as involuntary medical treatment may be administered against a patient's will. This is especially controversial in cases of persons who have limited capacity for insight and self-determination, and the Court again emphasised that no one ever loses the right to respect for their dignity (*Coercive Medical Treatment, Coercive Treatment in Psychiatric Confinement under Criminal Law*). In the recent decision on *Assisted Suicide*, the Court held that the general right of personality also encompasses the right to a self-determined death, which includes the freedom to take one's own life and to use assistance freely offered by others for this purpose. The Court also emphasised that where an individual decides to end their own life, based on an informed decision taken of their own free will, this decision must in principle be respected by state and society as an act of personal autonomy and self-determination. Thus, the state must take measures to protect life and personal autonomy, yet it may not impose restrictions that would effectively vitiate the right to a self-determined death in certain constellations.

The third chapter on **Name and Identity** explores the right of personality in relation to respect for and protection of one's personal identity. Where does the right to assert one's identity within society start, what are its limits? In *Sexual Abuse Allegations*, the Court held that a survivor of sexual abuse has the right to state their own name when they decide to tell their story in public. This includes a right to use their name on TV, even though disclosure of a family name could allow identification of the alleged abuser. In other instances, legal categorisations may impede or conflict with one's personal identity, and a right to one's chosen name may be a constitutional issue, as *Transsexuals V* regarding the official change of name and *Third Gender Option* on the civil register entry for intersexual persons illustrate.

The fourth and fifth chapters cover **Image** and **Speech** respectively. They take a closer look at the right of individuals to determine their public portrayal. Basically, individuals do in fact have the freedom to decide how they wish to present themselves to third parties or the public, and thus how they wish to define their social image. In turn, they also have a right to define whether and to what extent third parties may disclose aspects of their personality or life, including personal information, statements or images, with some limits already mentioned above and others covered in these chapters. In addition, individuals may also want to decide whether or not to be the subject of public discussion, especially on platforms with extensive reach such as mass media or social media. In these contexts, constitutional and human rights law is increasingly concerned with the conduct of private, non-state actors. Overall, in these cases, the Court must reconcile and balance conflicting fundamental rights related to communication, information and artistic creation with the right of personality, based on freedom and dignity of all.

Such conflicts arise in many settings. Specifically, the selected decisions illustrate the protection of the right of personality in relation to audio-visual recordings produced by broadcasting media in court proceedings (*Honecker, TV Broadcasting from the Courtroom*) and in relation to images published as part of entertainment media coverage regarding celebrities' private and everyday life (*Caroline III*). In addition, the chapter includes a seminal decision on conditions for exercising a *Right of Reply*, and cases on the right of individuals to defend themselves against alleged group membership that affects their public image (*Helnwein/Scientology*), against ambiguous and possibly defamatory statements (*Stolpe/Stasi Dispute*) and against the portrayal of intimate personal matters in literary fiction (*Esra*).

Privacy and Intimacy are the focus of the sixth chapter. The intimate sphere is where the right of personality is strongest – but what matters must be considered intimate? According to the Court, these are matters related to one's sexuality, as well as expressions of one's inner self and innermost thoughts or feelings. Therefore, protection extends to conversations with close family members or trusted confidants, which may set limits for police surveillance, including in the context of counter-terrorism-measures. In this manifestation, the significance of recognising a right of personality based on human dignity, with its absolute protection of the inviolable core of private life, is particularly telling: An interference is generally impermissible and cannot be justified, not even on the basis of proportionality, not even when balanced against exceptionally significant interests like national security. Yet this also means that delimiting the scope of the inviolable core is extremely difficult. The Court thus emphasises that not every measure that is unlawful, harmful or despicable amounts to an attack on human dignity. Similarly, not every matter that individuals might understandably wish to keep private and confidential falls within the innermost domain of one's private life. This is discussed in *Surveillance of Private Homes*, where the Court had to specify the inviolable part of private life with regard to a constitutional amendment of Article 13 of the Basic Law that curtailed the inviolability of the home. Since the human dignity core of fundamental rights is protected under the eternity clause in Article 79(3) of the Basic Law, it is beyond the reach of constitutional amendment.

Regarding **Privacy and Intimacy**, there is also the question of what protection is afforded private messages and diaries. In *Diary-Like Notes,* the Court discussed whether personal notes can be introduced as criminal evidence if written, on the suggestion of a therapist, as a personal diary, documenting violent-aggressive impulses. In *Monitoring of Correspondence*, the issue was whether private letters sent by the sister of a prison inmate containing derogatory remarks about prison staff may be grounds for a conviction on insult charges. In *False Paternity*, the question arose whether the mother of a child can be compelled to disclose information on her sexual relations to enable the legal father to seek compensation for child support payments from the biological father. Finally, the protection of intimacy extends to one's gender identity and sexual orientation (*Transsexuals VIII*). In a series of decisions, the Court explained that if a transsexual person's felt gender is lastingly in conflict with the official sex assigned to them, the fundamental right to one's personality requires that their self-determination be taken into account, and that their internally felt gender identity be officially recognised. The Court stated that the legal order must be designed in a manner that allows individuals to live in accordance with their felt gender, which requires measures to ensure that their intimate sphere is not exposed when the felt gender and the legal status collide. In *Transsexuals VIII*, the Court added that the right of personality also protects transsexuals with a homosexual orientation from a requirement to undergo surgery before seeking legal recognition of their relationship with a partner.

Finally, three chapters on **Health Data**, **Data Protection and Virtual Identity**, **Informational Self-Determination and Security** explore the risks and vulnerabilities arising from the increased availability, recording and sharing of personal data. To begin with, the Court emphasises that the general right of personality imposes strict limits on data access by the state. Notably, it is not sufficient that state authorities deem certain data to be useful, helpful or 'worth having just in case'. Even where the state pursues legitimate aims, such as law enforcement or public security, it must strictly adhere to the principle of proportionality. Therefore, data access by the state is limited to what is suitable and necessary for achieving a legitimate aim, based on specific reasons, and appropriate in the individual case. Yet neither the right to informational self-determination nor conflicting rights take general precedence. Data access is only impermissible where it would affect the inviolable core of private life or result in disproportionate impairments.

Health Data is a particularly sensitive area. The cases presented in this chapter concern access to information like treatment and therapy records relating to one's health, biology, physiological and psychological condition. In *Addiction Counselling Agency*, the Court discusses the seizure of client records from a drop-in centre for counselling and treatment of persons struggling with drug addiction. In another case, the focus is on *Mandatory Medical-Psychological Assessment* and the obligation to disclose the findings to road traffic authorities in order to prove fitness to drive. In *DNA Fingerprinting*, the Court deals with the conditions under which DNA samples may be collected from criminal offenders in order to create and store DNA profiles in a law enforcement database.

Another key issue is **Data Protection and Virtual Identity.** Drawing on the early *Census* case presented in the first chapter, the Court continues to specify basic data protection requirements deriving from fundamental rights. Namely, the 'right to informational self-determination' requires that the individual be protected against the unlimited collection, storage, use and sharing of their personal data. In particular, this serves to prevent a 'chilling effect': it could impair the exercise of other fundamental rights if individuals were no longer able to tell who has obtained what kind of personal information about them and when. The Court argues that this could greatly impede one's freedom and self-determination and that such a deterrent effect would affect the common good, since self-determination is a fundamental prerequisite for the functioning of a free and democratic society, which relies on agency and active participation of its citizens. Against this backdrop, the general right of personality, together with privacy guarantees regarding telecommunications (Article 10 of the Basic Law) and the inviolability of the home (Article 13 of the Basic Law), forms part of a comprehensive framework of protection. In addition, the Court understands the collection, storage, use and sharing of personal data as each constituting separate (new) interferences with self-determination. Thus, every measure of this type requires a statutory basis and must be justified in each individual case, again measured against the principle of proportionality, and the inviolable part of private life must always be respected (*Divorce Files*).

Introductory Remarks

This is particularly relevant in light of new technical possibilities, such as the automatic processing and linking of data, and is thus reflected in an increased level of fundamental rights protection. For instance, it is not permissible for law enforcement authorities to seize a law firm's entire digital records and storage devices in a criminal investigation against one of the law firm's partners (*Seizure of Electronic Data*). Unrestricted state access to the law firm's data records would be excessive and jeopardise the right of clients to informational self-determination and to a fair trial, violating the rule of law. Therefore, authorities must take reasonable measures to prevent access to data that is not relevant, and procedural safeguards must be in place to prevent violations. Such safeguards may include a prohibition to share data with other authorities or use data as evidence in criminal proceedings (*Bankruptcy Proceedings*).

Moreover, the chapter on **Data Protection and Virtual Identity** addresses impairments of the right of personality in the context of Internet communication. In *Right to Be Forgotten I* and *II*, both also known for the Court's new concept of fundamental rights protection in the European Union, conflicts arose around old press articles and a broadcast segment stored in online archives that may, with the help of search engines, lead to new and much larger exposure of an individual to the public than the original publication. Therefore, fundamental rights require a balance between personality interests on the one hand and the interests of media, publishers, search engine operators, Internet users and the general public on the other. Again, these cases concern relationships between private actors, which is why constitutional protection differs from the direct effect of fundamental rights vis-à-vis the state. Yet even in such cases, fundamental rights do not leave the individual without protection. Where such conflicts arise between private actors, the general right of personality provides the individual with the possibility of influencing the context and manner in which their data is accessible to and can be used by others. This is not a right to demand that all information relating to one's person be deleted from the Internet. Yet in *Right to Be Forgotten I* and *II*, the Court acknowledges that the possibility of matters being forgotten is a temporal dimension of freedom. Therefore, the legal order must protect the individual against the risk of being indefinitely confronted in public with their past, as this would deprive them of the chance to start afresh. This notion was already recognised by the Court in the *Lebach* case presented in the second chapter, which exemplifies how doctrine evolves over time.

The decisions on **Informational Self-Determination and Security** trace an important line of case-law dealing with the protection of individuals against particularly intrusive and often covert state action. The decisions selected here deal with the use of targeted surveillance in domestic criminal investigations (*Telecommunications Surveillance, The Telecommunications Surveillance Revision Act*) and with the much broader surveillance of international and foreign telecommunications by the intelligence services (*The Article 10 Act, Surveillance of Foreign Telecommunications*). When the Court was called upon to assess new powers of the Federal Criminal Police Office to fight international terrorism (*The Federal Criminal Police Office Act*), it clarified the relevant constitutional standards, and later applied them in its decisions on remote searches of private computers (*Remote Searches*), on the creation and use of databases for facilitating electronic profiling and search measures (*Profiling*) and on inter-agency data sharing, a sensitive issue in a country which in the past has seen the abuse of police powers in collusion with security forces (*The Counter-Terrorism Database Act I*). Like many courts in other jurisdictions, the Court also assessed the constitutionality of the precautionary retention of telecommunications traffic data (*Data Retention*) based on the specific protection afforded by intersecting fundamental rights, namely dignity and freedom, as well as those expressly listed in the Basic Law, privacy of telecommunications (Article 10) and the inviolability of the home (Article 13). These decisions also demonstrate how new risks have led to the recognition of a right to informational self-determination, and how protection was eventually extended to the integrity and confidentiality of information technology systems like computers or smartphones (*Remote Searches*).

While the powers of the state at issue are considered necessary to address security threats, and while new powers may be needed in order to allow law enforcement to adapt to new technologies and globalisation, the Court has also emphasised the fact that new security and surveillance powers expose the individual to unprecedented risks and intrusions. Constitutional law requires the Court to reconcile these interests. But since the inviolability of human dignity is at stake, even the pursuit of exceptionally significant aims – such as the protection of life, limb and liberty or the existence and security of the state – does not give authorities carte blanche. Here as well, limitations set by constitutional and human rights law must be respected, including in relation to foreigners abroad (*Surveillance of Foreign Telecommunications*). Stringent requirements apply to any covert collection and use of personal data and the sharing of such data with domestic and foreign bodies, which presupposes procedural safeguards and oversight regimes.

Introductory Remarks

Towards Consensus on Fundamental Rights

The world we live in has changed in many ways since the adoption of the Basic Law in 1949 and the establishment of the Federal Constitutional Court in 1951. The decisions presented in this volume are testimony to this – with a marked contrast between cases from an era of print publications as the dominant source of information and more recent decisions that address the Internet and global telecommunications. The Court's mandate has remained the same: to uphold the Basic Law and give effect to its guarantees, most notably the fundamental rights enshrined therein. The evolution of the general right of personality may thus serve to illustrate how fundamental rights can be interpreted in a manner that preserves established principles while adapting to changed circumstances. The case-law presented in this book shapes the interpretation and application of fundamental rights today. We hope that others will benefit from the translations provided and that the present volume, like its predecessors, will invite and promote a broader dialogue on fundamental rights, shared legal traditions and future challenges.

Prof. Dr. Susanne Baer, LL.M. (Michigan), Justice of the First Senate
Vice-President Prof. Dr. Doris König, Justice of the Second Senate
and the Legal Translation Unit of the Federal Constitutional Court

Karlsruhe, November 2021

No. 1

BVerfGE 27, 1 – Microcensus

HEADNOTE

to the Order of the First Senate of 16 July 1969
1 BvL 19/63

On the constitutionality of a representative statistical survey conducted by the state (microcensus).

FEDERAL CONSTITUTIONAL COURT
- 1 BvL 19/63 -

IN THE NAME OF THE PEOPLE

In the proceedings
for constitutional review of

§ 2 no. 3 of the Act on Conducting a Representative Statistical Survey on Population and Occupation (Microcensus Act) of 16 March 1957 – BGBl I, p. 213 – in the version of the Act of 5 December 1960 – BGBl I, p. 873

– Order of Suspension and Referral of the Fürstenfeldbruck Local Court of 30 October 1963 - Gs 168/63 -

the Federal Constitutional Court – First Senate –
with the participation of Justices

> President Müller,
> Stein,
> Haager,
> Rupp-von Brünneck,
> Böhmer,
> Brox,
> Zeidler

held on 16 July 1969:

§ 1 and § 2 no. 3 of the Microcensus Act of 16 March 1957 (BGBl I, p. 213) in the version of the Act of 5 December 1960 (BGBl I, p. 873) [no longer in force] were compatible with the Basic Law insofar as they provided that the survey pursuant to § 1 of the Act contained questions on holiday and recreational travel.

REASONS:

A.

1-6 [...]

B.

I.

7 1. The plaintiff in the initial proceedings lives in a region [...] where all residents were to be surveyed under the Microcensus Act. She refused [...] to answer all 60 questions [...]. At the request of the Bavarian Statistical Office (*Bayerisches Statistisches Landesamt*), the Fürstenfeldbruck Administrative District Office (*Landratsamt*) [...] imposed a fine of DM 100 [...], against which she sought recourse to the courts. By Order of 30 October 1963 - Gs 168/63 - the Fürstenfeldbruck Local Court suspended the proceedings and referred to the Federal Constitutional Court the question whether Art. 1(2) no. 2 of the Amending Act of 5 December 1960 was compatible with the Basic Law.

8 2. The Local Court submitted the following reasons for the referral: Art. 1(2) no. 2 of the Amending Act of 5 December 1960 contradicted Art. 1 and Art. 2 of the Basic Law to the extent that the survey subjects were obliged to disclose information on holiday and recreational travel. [...]

9 3. The questions on holiday and recreational travel that the plaintiff in the initial proceedings refused to answer read as follows:

10 Who has travelled for holiday and recreational purposes for 5 or more days, including in connection with business travel,
   a) during the period from 1 October 1961 through 30 September 1962 and/or
   b) before 1 October 1961?
   Which members of the household participated in the travel?
   What kind of travel was it? (individual trip (privately organised), package tour for single traveller, organised group tour, health retreat)
   When did the travel begin, and how long did it last?

No. 1 – Microcensus

Where did the traveller primarily stay (in Germany or abroad)? (in Germany: indicate city; abroad: indicate country)
What means of transport were primarily used for the outbound and inbound journey?
What type of accommodation was primarily used? (tourist accommodation, private rental, free accommodation (provided by relatives, acquaintances), health resort or sanatorium, holiday retreat or resort, children's home, campground, youth hostel).

II.

The Federal Minister of the Interior considers the challenged provision to be constitutional. 11
[…] 12-13

C.

I.

The referral is admissible. 14
[…] 15-16

II.

The questions on holiday and recreational travel as part of the representative survey pursuant to the Microcensus Act violated neither Art. 1(1) and Art. 2(1) of the Basic Law nor any other provisions of the Basic Law. 17
1. a) According to Art. 1(1) of the Basic Law, human dignity is inviolable and must be respected and protected by all state authority. 18
Human dignity is the highest value within the system of values of the Basic Law (BVerfGE 6, 32 <41>). This commitment to human dignity informs all provisions of the Basic Law, including Art. 2(1) of the Basic Law. The state may not violate human dignity through any measure, not even a law, or otherwise infringe on the essence (*Wesensgehalt*) of personal freedom beyond the limits established in Art. 2(1) of the Basic Law. Thus, the Basic Law recognises, for each citizen, an inviolable part of private life which is beyond the reach of public authority (BVerfGE 6, 32 <41>, 389 <433>). 19
b) In light of this conception of human nature, all persons, as members of the community, enjoy a right to be valued and respected as a person in society (*sozialer Wert- und Achtungsanspruch*). Treating a person as a mere object of the state would 20

be a violation of human dignity (cf. BVerfGE 5, 85 <204>; 7, 198 <205>). It would be incompatible with human dignity if the state claimed for itself the power to subject the individual to compulsory registration and cataloguing of their entire personality, thereby treating them as a commodity that can be analysed in every respect; this applies even in the context of statistical surveys where data is rendered anonymous.

21 [...]

22 c) However, not every statistical survey of personality-related or biographical data violates the dignity of one's person or affects the right to self-determination within the innermost domain of private life. As a citizen connected to and bound by the community (cf. BVerfGE 4, 7 <15 and 16>; 7, 198 <205>; 24, 119 <144>), everyone must to a certain extent tolerate necessary statistical surveys collecting personal data, for example for census purposes, as a prerequisite for planning government action.

23 A statistical survey on one's personal circumstances may be perceived as degrading, and as a risk to the right to self-determination, where it captures the domain of personal life that is secret by its very nature, thus turning this innermost domain into a matter that can and must be analysed by means of statistics. In this regard, the state in a modern industrial society must respect limits to administrative 'depersonalisation'. However, where a statistical survey only relates to a person's conduct in the outside world, it does not typically affect one's personality to an extent that amounts to a 'capturing' of the inviolable part of private life. This applies at least if the collected data is stripped of its connection to an individual person through anonymous data processing. This in turn requires sufficient safeguards ensuring that the data is indeed rendered anonymous. [...]

24 d) Based on this, the survey questions on holiday and recreational travel did not violate Art. 1(1), Art. 2(1) of the Basic Law.

25 While this survey did concern a certain part of private life, it did not compel the survey subjects to disclose information from their intimate sphere, nor did it grant the state access to individual relationships that would not normally be disclosed to the outside world, and that are by their very nature secret. [...]

26 2. With regard to the principle of the rule of law, the survey does also not raise constitutional concerns. In particular, it neither violated the requirement of legal clarity (cf. BVerfGE 20, 150 <158 and 159>; 21, 245 <261>) nor the principle of proportionality (cf. BVerfGE 17, 306 <313>; 19, 342 <348 and 349>).

27 a) § 2 no. 3 of the Microcensus Act satisfies the constitutional requirement of legal clarity regarding the questions on holiday and recreational travel. [...]

28 b) According to the official explanatory memorandum to the Microcensus Act, the documentation of data concerning holiday and recreational travel was intended to

No. 1 – Microcensus

provide information about the economic and social significance of such travel, and about the means of transport used. [...]

Given that the results of the representative survey could already be undermined if only a few survey subjects refused to provide information, it did not amount to an excessive burden on the individual that the Microcensus Act in conjunction with § 10(1) and § 14 of the Statistics Act made answering the questions mandatory, with non-compliance punishable by sanctions. [...]

3. Finally, there are no constitutional objections regarding the design of the microcensus as a representative survey with a sampling rate of 1% of the total population of the Federal Republic of Germany, as laid down in § 1 of the Microcensus Act.

In particular, a representative survey for statistical purposes in which only a group of persons determined by a randomised procedure is subjected to the obligation to provide information does not violate the right to equality. The right to equality bars the legislator from treating citizens unequally only in cases where a provision must ultimately be considered arbitrary because, in light of the requirement of fairness, no reasonable grounds for the statutory differentiation are ascertainable; such grounds may derive from the inherent nature of the matter at hand or from other objective factual reasons (cf., e.g., BVerfGE 1, 264 <276>; 18, 121 <124>). Therefore, the legislator has wide latitude in determining which group of persons to subject to the legal framework (cf. BVerfGE 9, 20 <32>; 11, 245 <253>; 17, 1 <33>; 23, 12 <28>).

§ 1 of the Microcensus Act did not exceed these limits. The fact that the burden on citizens resulting from statistical sampling varies randomly is inherent in such a representative survey. Moreover, the legislative decision to conduct a representative survey, rather than a census of the entire population, can be justified by objective factual reasons. In comparison to a full census, a representative survey provides information to the state in a cost-efficient and quick manner, while affecting only a small share of the population.

Justices: Müller, Stein, Haager, Rupp-von Brünneck, Böhmer, Brox, Zeidler

No. 2

BVerfGE 34, 238 – Secret Tape Recordings

HEADNOTES

to the Order of the Second Senate of 31 January 1973
2 BvR 454/71

1. The fundamental right under Article 2(1) of the Basic Law also protects legal interests that are essential to the development of one's personality. Subject to certain limitations, this fundamental right also includes the right to one's own speech, just as it includes the right to one's own image. Therefore, every person may, in principle, determine for themselves who may record their speech, and for whom, if at all, their voice recorded on a sound recording device may be played.
2. However, this does not rule out that in cases where overriding public interests imperatively require it, the interest – meriting protection – of the accused to have secret tape recordings excluded from use as evidence at trial must stand back.

FEDERAL CONSTITUTIONAL COURT
- 2 BvR 454/71 -

IN THE NAME OF THE PEOPLE

In the proceedings
on the constitutional complaint of

Mr V...,
– authorised representative: ...

against the Order of the Osnabrück Regional Court of 3 May 1971 - 12 Qs 86/71 - the Federal Constitutional Court – Second Senate –

No. 2 – Secret Tape Recordings

with the participation of Justices

> Vice-President Seuffert,
> Rupp,
> Geiger,
> Hirsch,
> Rinck,
> Rottmann,
> Wand

held on 31 January 1973:

The Order of the Osnabrück Regional Court of 3 May 1971 - 12 Qs 86/71 - violates the complainant's fundamental right under Article 2(1) in conjunction with Article 1(1) of the Basic Law. The decision is reversed insofar as the court dismissed the complaint against the judicial order to use the tape recording handed over to the police as evidence (record entry no. 10319/70). To this extent, the matter is remanded to the Osnabrück Regional Court.

[...]

REASONS:

A.

I.

The constitutional complaint concerns the admissibility as evidence of a secretly made private tape recording in the criminal investigation of the complainant on suspicion of tax evasion, fraud and the falsification of documents.

1. In essence, the facts of the case are as follows:

a) On 11 May 1970, Mr and Mrs B. sold to the complainant a residential and commercial building in the city of Osnabrück. [...]

b) On 14 December 1970, Mr B. brought criminal charges against the complainant. He explained that the parties had verbally agreed on a sales price of DM 495,000 for the building and DM 20,000 for fixtures. At the complainant's request, in order to reduce the amount of real property transfer tax due, a sales price of only DM 425,000 had been attested by the notary. On 11 May 1970, at 6:45 p.m. and before the attestation of the sales contract, the complainant had paid him the difference of DM 70,000 in cash 'under the table', and had asked him and his wife to sign a prepared receipt. According to Mr B., this document stated the following:

	Receipt
5	
6	We hereby confirm having received an interest-free loan of DM 70,000 – seventy thousand – in cash from Herbert V.

7   Mr B. said that he was the only one to sign this receipt. They had agreed that the complainant would destroy it upon conclusion of the notarised contract. On the evening of 11 May 1970, the complainant had, in his presence, torn a document to pieces. But Mr B. was not sure whether it had been the original receipt. There were fragments of the receipt's text on the scraps of paper that the complainant had handed him, but not his signature.

8   The day the last instalment was due, the complainant showed him a receipt for a loan of DM 70,000 and said he would set off this sum against the remaining balance of DM 70,000. This receipt, which is included in the case file, reads as follows:

	Receipt
9	
10	We hereby confirm having received an interest-free loan of DM 70,000 – seventy thousand – in cash from Herbert V. The loan can be terminated with 3 months' notice. Set-off = upon payment of balance of sales price/fixtures at the latest.

11   Next to the date, 11 May 1970, it bears the signatures "Erwin B." and "Anni B.".

12   However, Mr B. claims that neither he nor his wife signed a loan document in this form and that the document is a forgery.

13   During his interrogation by the police, the complainant stated that the sales price attested by the notary was the price the parties had in fact agreed upon. He claimed not to know anything about a verbal agreement on a payment 'under the table'. At the request of Mr B., he had supposedly granted him an interest-free loan of DM 70,000 in cash on 11 May 1970, at 8:00 p.m. in Mr B.'s flat. The receipt on file was issued in this context, he claimed.

14   c) The relevance of the tape recording mentioned above is as follows:

15   Purportedly, the tape recording is of a conversation between the complainant and Mr and Mrs B. in August 1970, i.e. after the attestation of the building purchase, and was made without the complainant's knowledge. Mr B. claims that at the time of the recording, he was not yet aware of the existence of the loan receipt that was presented to him later. The recorded conversation had taken place because the complainant had indicated that he wanted to pay a lower price due to a mortgage rate increase. In the recorded conversation, they had, among other things, discussed

No. 2 – Secret Tape Recordings

the adequacy of the sales price, 'under the table' payments and a corresponding receipt.
On 23 February 1971, Mr B. handed the tape recording over to the police for investigation. [...]
2. On 10 March 1971, at the request of the public prosecution office, the Osnabrück Regional Court ordered, pursuant to §§ 94, 98 and 110 of the Code of Criminal Procedure, the seizure of some of the documents secured during a search of the complainant's flat on 3 March 1971. In addition, it ordered the use of the tape recording handed over to the police as evidence, on the grounds that it might be of significance for the investigation.
The complaint filed by the complainant against that order was only partially successful. [...] In its order, the Regional Court observed the following on the admissibility of the tape recording as evidence:
While the use of a secretly made tape recording as evidence is, in principle, impermissible because the secret nature of the recording violates the speaker's right to the free development of their personality (Art. 2(1) of the Basic Law), [...] in the absence of other appropriate evidence, the recording is potentially the only proof that the complainant has committed a criminal offence. [...]

II.

1. The constitutional complaint is directed against this order. The complainant claims a violation of his fundamental right under Art. 2(1) of the Basic Law [...].
[...]
2. The Federal Minister of Justice, who submitted a statement on behalf of the Federal Government, considers the constitutional complaint to be admissible and well-founded.
[...]

B.

I.

The constitutional complaint, lodged within the statutory time-limit, is admissible.
[...]

II.

The constitutional complaint is well-founded.

29 By allowing, without the complainant's consent, the use of the secret tape recording in the criminal proceedings against him, the challenged order violates the complainant's fundamental right under Art. 2(1) in conjunction with Art. 1(1) of the Basic Law.

30 1. In its established case-law, the Federal Constitutional Court has affirmed that the Basic Law recognises, for each citizen, an inviolable part of private life which is beyond the reach of public authority (BVerfGE 6, 32 <41>, 389 <433>; 27, 1 <6> – *Microcensus*; 27, 344 <350 and 351> – *Divorce Files*; 32, 373 <378 and 379>; 33, 367 <376>). The constitutional requirement to respect this core that encompasses the intimate sphere of the individual is based on the right to the free development of one's personality, as guaranteed by Art. 2(1) of the Basic Law. When determining the content and scope of this fundamental right under Art. 2(1) of the Basic Law, it must be taken into account that, according to the fundamental precept in Art. 1(1) of the Basic Law, human dignity is inviolable and must be respected and protected by all state authority. Moreover, under Art. 19(2) of the Basic Law, the essence (*Wesensgehalt*) of the fundamental right under Art. 2(1) of the Basic Law may also not be infringed upon (BVerfGE 27, 344 <350 and 351> – *Divorce Files*; 32, 373 <379>). The core of private life enjoys absolute protection, and even overriding public interests cannot justify an interference; this protection is not subject to a balancing of interests under the principle of proportionality.

31 However, not the entire domain of private life enjoys the absolute protection afforded by the fundamental right under Art. 2(1) in conjunction with Art. 1(1) of the Basic Law (BVerfGE 6, 389 <433>; 27, 1 <7> – *Microcensus*; 27, 344 <351> – *Divorce Files*; 32, 373 <379>; 33, 367 <376 and 377>). Rather, as a citizen connected to and bound by the community, every person must tolerate state measures that serve overriding public interests and that strictly adhere to the requirement of proportionality, unless these infringe upon the inviolable part of private life. In this respect, the principles which the Federal Constitutional Court has developed in its case-law on the constitutional permissibility of interferences with physical integrity apply accordingly (BVerfGE 16, 194 <201 and 202>; 17, 108 <117 and 118>; 27, 211 <219>; 27, 344 <351> – *Divorce Files*; 32, 373 <379>).

32 2. Art. 2(1) of the Basic Law guarantees every person the right to the free development of their personality, insofar as they do not infringe the rights of others or violate the constitutional order or moral law. This fundamental right also protects legal interests that are essential to the development of one's personality. Subject to certain limitations, this fundamental right also includes the right to one's own speech, just as it includes the right to one's own image. Therefore, every person may, in principle, determine for themselves who may record their speech, and for whom, if at all, their voice recorded on a sound recording device may be played.

No. 2 – Secret Tape Recordings

On a tape recording, a person's speech and voice are detached from this person and become objects at the disposal of others. The inviolability of someone's personality would be seriously curtailed if others could freely use words spoken in private, without the consent of the person concerned or even against the person's will. Human communication free from fear or worry would be largely impossible if everyone were aware that one's every utterance – a remark that might be unreflected or intemperate, a tentative opinion expressed in an unfolding conversation, or an expression comprehensible only in this context – could be brought up on another occasion and in a different context to bear witness against the person using the content, expression, or tone of the statement. Every person should be able to conduct a private conversation without the suspicion or fear that a secret recording of it could be used without their consent or even against their declared will. § 298 and § 353d of the Criminal Code for substantive criminal law, [...] and the case-law of the Federal Court of Justice on the general right of personality for private law, [...] have long reflected this concern.

3. The conversation between Mr and Mrs B. and the complainant was confidential. It was recorded secretly. The complainant opposed the use of the recording as evidence. Under these circumstances, such use in the criminal investigation constitutes an interference with the constitutionally guaranteed right to one's own speech.

There are indeed cases in which a tape recording made without the speaker's knowledge does not fall within the scope of protection of Art. 2(1) in conjunction with Art. 1(1) of the Basic Law from the outset because, in such situations, it is generally agreed that the right to one's own speech is inapplicable. [...] But this is not the case here. The conversation took place between three persons. They were discussing a contractual agreement. The complainant did not have to expect that his words were being recorded. He is therefore entitled to invoke the right to one's own speech guaranteed by Art. 2(1) in conjunction with Art. 1(1) of the Basic Law.

4. Whether a secret tape recording affects the absolutely inviolable part of private life or merely the part of private life where state interference may be permissible under certain circumstances is difficult to determine in the abstract. This question can be answered satisfactorily only on a case-by-case basis, taking into account the particularities of each situation.

The present case concerns a business conversation. Partners to a transaction were discussing their differences in respect of the purchase of a building and the adequacy of the agreed price. They did not discuss any highly personal matters that could be attributed to their inviolable intimate sphere.

5. Since this is not a matter of an intrusion of public authority into the absolutely protected part of personality, the use of the tape recording would be permissible if it were justified by an overriding public interest. This is, however, not the case.

39 a) The Basic Law attributes high standing to the right to the free development of one's personality. State measures that impair it are, if at all, allowed only if the requirement of proportionality is strictly observed. However, the Basic Law also attaches particular importance to the effective administration of justice. [...]

40 There are many ways in which the constitutionally guaranteed right to the free development of one's personality and the effective administration of justice can come into conflict with one another. A fair balance to resolve these tensions can only be found if the protection requirement under Art. 2(1) in conjunction with Art. 1(1) of the Basic Law is used as an ongoing corrective to the interferences that seem necessary for the effective administration of justice (cf. BVerfGE 19, 342 <347>; 20, 45 <49>, 144 <147>). This means that it must be determined in every case which of these two constitutionally significant principles carries greater weight.

41 b) In such a balancing, the interest – meriting protection – of the accused is taken into account by the Code of Criminal Procedure, by way of its protection *inter alia* against self-incrimination (§ 136(1) second sentence of the Code of Criminal Procedure). Beyond this specific safeguard, the accused also requires protection when a statement recorded on tape without their knowledge is used against them in criminal proceedings.

42 c) However, this does not rule out that in cases where overriding public interests imperatively require it, even the protected interest of the accused to have secret tape recordings excluded from use as evidence must stand back.

43 Thus, generally, constitutional objections will not arise in cases involving serious crime – be it against life and limb, against the existential foundations of the free democratic basic order, or against other legal interests of comparable magnitude – where the law enforcement authorities, as a last resort, have used tape recordings secretly made by a third party to establish the identity of offenders or to exculpate persons wrongly accused of a criminal offence. [...]

44 Yet here – as in all cases – it is crucial that such an interference be compatible with the principle of proportionality in a balancing that takes all the circumstances of the case into account. This means that on the one hand, it must be determined how seriously the intended use of a specific tape recording – in view of its content and form – would interfere with the right to the free development of the personality of the affected person. On the other hand, when balancing the thus determined severity of the interference with the right to the free development of one's personality against the legitimate requirements of the criminal justice system, the focus must be not only on the charged offence in its abstract constituent elements, but on the specific wrongdoing considered in the case at hand. Otherwise, a proper and fair

No. 2 – Secret Tape Recordings

balancing would be impossible, given the multitude of possible acts that may in fact be constituent elements of many offences.

In addition, it is relevant to consider, when all other legally permissible possibilities have been exhausted, whether the use of the tape recording is the only means of convicting the offender of a serious crime or of exculpating the accused.

Finally, it is important to take into account whether and to what extent there is a legal and factual guarantee that knowledge of the statements recorded on the tape, which may possibly not be relevant to the criminal proceedings, will be restricted to those persons that are directly involved in the proceedings – e.g. through a non-public hearing to discuss the contents of the tape recording (cf. BVerfGE 32, 373 <381>).

6. The challenged order does not meet these constitutional standards. The order to use the tape recording upheld by the Regional Court allows the investigating law enforcement authorities to listen to the secretly made tape recording without the complainant's consent, and to use its contents against him. This interference cannot be justified by the interest in investigating the offences referred to by the Regional Court. The challenged order does not demonstrate that the offence is so serious, or that public interests are affected to such an extent, that the complainant's fundamental right under Art. 2(1) in conjunction with Art. 1(1) of the Basic Law must stand back. Therefore, the order is reversed.

III.

[…]

The decision was taken with 6:1 votes.

Justices: Seuffert, Rupp, Geiger, Hirsch, Rinck, Rottmann, Wand

No. 3

BVerfGE 34, 269 – Soraya

HEADNOTE

to the Order of the First Senate of 14 February 1973
1 BvR 112/65

The case-law developed by the civil courts according to which financial compensation may also be claimed for non-material damage is compatible with the Basic Law.

FEDERAL CONSTITUTIONAL COURT
- 1 BvR 112/65 -

IN THE NAME OF THE PEOPLE

In the proceedings
on the constitutional complaint of

1. *Die Welt* publishing company, represented by its Managing Director..., 2. Mr V...,
- authorised representative: ...

against   a) the Order of the Federal Court of Justice of 8 December 1964
- VI ZR 201/63 -,

b) the Order of the Karlsruhe Higher Regional Court of 3 July 1963
- 1 U 7/63 -,

c) the Order of the Mannheim Regional Court of 24 August 1962
- 7 O 73/61 -

the Federal Constitutional Court – First Senate –
with the participation of Justices

        President Benda,
        Ritterspach,
        Haager,
        Rupp-v. Brünneck,

No. 3 – Soraya

Böhmer,
Faller,
Brox,
Simon

held on 14 February 1973:

The constitutional complaint is rejected.

REASONS:

A.

1. Pursuant to § 249 of the Civil Code, a person liable for damages must restore the injured person's position to the position that would have existed had the circumstances giving rise to such liability not occurred. This principle of 'natural restitution' (restitution in kind) also applies to the compensation of non-pecuniary, 'non-material' damage. In the case of violation of a person's honour, for instance, the insulted person's loss of reputation may be redressed by retraction or by publication of a judgment requiring retraction of the insulting statement.

However, restitution in kind requires that restoration to the former position is possible. If, for factual reasons, such restoration leads to no or to insufficient compensation for damage, the injured party may request financial compensation pursuant to § 251(1) of the Civil Code. In respect of non-material damage, however, this principle is limited by § 253 of the Civil Code: According to this provision, financial compensation may only be requested in the cases specified by law, which are mainly damages for pain and suffering (*Schmerzensgeld*) [...]. Beyond the scope of the Civil Code, specific grounds for non-material damage are set out in other legislation [...].

2. [...]
3. [...]

There was [...] general approval in 1954 when the Federal Court of Justice first recognised the general right of personality (BGHZ 13, 334 <337 and 338>). The court held that the right to human dignity and to the free development of one's personality protected by Arts. 1 and 2 of the Basic Law is also a right under private law, which must be respected by everyone in private legal transactions. According to the court, the general right of personality is protected under § 823(1) of the Civil Code [which lists the rights and interests whose injury can lead to liability for damages]; however, the assessment of whether this right was violated requires a thorough and detailed balancing of the legal interests involved. In its later decisions, the Federal Court of Justice sought to specify the blanket-clause-like scope of the general right of personality (cf. BGHZ 15, 249; 20, 345; 26, 52; 27, 284; 31, 308).

7   4. While the general right of personality as such was quickly accepted by courts and legal scholars, the question whether applicable law allowed affected persons to claim financial compensation for non-material damage in case of violation of the right of personality remained controversial.

8-11   [...]

12   5. The courts did not wait for the legislator to enact statutory provisions on the protection of one's personality. In 1958, the Federal Court of Justice first granted financial compensation to a person whose right of personality had been violated through non-pecuniary damage in the so-called *Dressage Rider* judgment (*Herrenreiter-Urteil*) [...]. [...]

13   In a number of further decisions, the Federal Court of Justice confirmed and developed the standards laid down in that judgment. [...]

14   [...]

15   6. The civil courts and legal scholarship largely followed the view of the Federal Court of Justice [...]. The Federal Labour Court and the Federal Finance Court also adopted it.

16   [...]

B.

17   1. The complainant in the present proceedings is the publishing company *Die Welt*, which is part of the Axel Springer Group. In the past, it also published the weekly magazine *Das Neue Blatt mit Gerichtswoche*, which was sold all over Germany. Until June 1961, complainant no. 2 was the managing editor of that magazine, which mainly entertained readers with its sensational reporting on societal matters. In 1961 and 1962, the magazine repeatedly ran illustrated articles on the Shah of Iran's divorced wife, Princess Soraya Esfandiary-Bakhtiary. On the first page of the 29 April 1961 issue, a so-called special report was published [...], which included an 'exclusive interview' that Princess Soraya was supposed to have given to a journalist. The report contained statements by the princess about her private life. The interview had been sold to the magazine by a freelancer; it was purely fictional. In its 1 July 1961 issue, the magazine published a brief correction by Princess Soraya, indented within a new report [...]. In this correction, she stated that the interview had in fact not taken place.

18   The Regional Court granted Princess Soraya's action for damages on the basis of the violation of her right of personality and declared the complainants jointly

and severally liable for DM 15,000. The complainants' appeals were unsuccessful. The Federal Court of Justice held the dissemination of the fictional interview on Princess Soraya's private life to be an unlawful violation of her right of personality. [...]

Based on its earlier decisions (BGHZ 35, 363 and 39, 124), the Federal Court of Justice set out that financial compensation could be demanded in respect of severe violations of personality rights if there were no other way to properly redress the non-material damage caused by the interference. According to the court, these requirements were met here. When assessing the interference with the right of personality, the fact that the fictional interview had been disseminated widely and the fact that it had been published in pursuit of purely commercial interests carried particular weight. The court held that publishing the correction did not redress the damage inflicted.

2. In their constitutional complaint, the complainants claim a violation of their fundamental rights under Art. 2(1) in conjunction with Art. 20(2) and (3), Art. 5(1) second sentence and (2) and Art. 103(2) of the Basic Law; as a "precautionary" challenge, they also claim a violation of their fundamental rights under Arts. 3, 12 and 14 of the Basic Law. [...]

[...]

C.

The constitutional complaint is unfounded.

I.

1. The court case that led to the challenged decisions is a private law case. It is not for the Federal Constitutional Court to review the interpretation and application of private law as such. However, the objective system of values enshrined in the fundamental rights provisions of the Constitution also guide the interpretation of private law; as fundamental decisions enshrining constitutional values they are applicable to all areas of law. It is incumbent upon the Federal Constitutional Court to ensure that this permeating effect of fundamental rights on other areas of law (*Ausstrahlungswirkung*) is observed. Therefore, the Court reviews whether the civil courts' decisions are based on a fundamentally incorrect understanding of the scope and impact of a fundamental right or if the outcome of a decision violates the fundamental rights of one of the parties (in this regard, cf. in general BVerfGE 7, 198 <205 *et seq.*>; 18, 85 <92 and 93>; 30, 173 <187 and 188, 196 and 197>; 32, 311 <316>).

25 In the case at hand, the complainants not only object to the outcome of the civil court decisions; they primarily challenge the method the courts used to reach that outcome. The complainants dispute that judges, being bound by law, are allowed to grant financial compensation in such cases. […].

26 2. In the private law case at hand, the statutory basis for the claim was § 823(1) of the Civil Code. The Federal Court of Justice also includes the "general right of personality" in the rights listed in that provision, citing its established case-law, in particular the detailed reasons given in its decision of 25 May 1954 (BGHZ 13, 334); it holds the complainants' behaviour to be a violation of this right. It is not for the Federal Constitutional Court to evaluate the 'correctness' of this case-law insofar as its reasons and development adhere to private law doctrines. It is sufficient to establish that the general right of personality – still rejected by the drafters of the Civil Code – has asserted itself over the course of decades of debate in legal scholarship, finally attaining recognition in the above-mentioned decision of the Federal Court of Justice, which has allowed it to become an integral part of private law […].

27 There is no reason for the Federal Constitutional Court to object to this case-law of the Federal Court of Justice on constitutional grounds. The free development of human personality within the social community and its dignity lie at the core of the system of values of the fundamental rights (BVerfGE 6, 32 <41>; 7, 198 <205>). It must be respected and protected by all state authority (Arts. 1 and 2(1) of the Basic Law). In particular the individual's private sphere is afforded such protection. This is the domain in which individuals wish to be left alone, make their own decisions for themselves and not be disturbed by interferences of any kind (BVerfGE 27, 1 <6> – *Microcensus*). In private law, the general right of personality also serves to ensure this kind of protection; it fills gaps in the protection of one's personality, which have persisted despite the recognition of individual personality rights and have become ever more noticeable over time for different reasons. Therefore, the Federal Constitutional Court has never objected to the recognition of a general right of personality in the case-law of the civil courts (see especially BVerfGE 30, 173 <194 *et seq.*>; 34, 118 <135 and 136> and BVerfGE 34, 238 <246 and 247> – *Secret Tape Recordings*).

28 3. § 823(1) of the Civil Code is a general law within the meaning of Art. 5(2) of the Basic Law (BVerfGE 7, 198 <211>; 25, 256 <263 *et seq.*>). Given that the general right of personality, according to the interpretation that is not objectionable under constitutional law, is to be included in the rights listed in that provision, the Constitution affords it the ability to restrict the fundamental right to freedom of the press invoked by the complainants. The potential impact of the general law is constitutionally reinforced, as established above, by the mandate of protection

under Arts. 1 and 2(1) of the Basic Law. However, the fundamental importance of freedom of the press for the free democratic order must not be ignored. It retains its weight in the balancing that is required in case of conflict between the parties' constitutionally protected interests in a private law relationship (BVerfGE 25, 256 <263>; 30, 173 <196 and 197>). When balancing these interests, the general right of personality cannot claim precedence *per se*; depending on the specific case, freedom of the press may have a restrictive effect on the right of personality (BVerfGE 7, 198 <208 and 209>).

4. The challenged decisions gave precedence to the protection of the personal sphere of the initial proceedings' plaintiff over freedom of the press This approach does not raise any constitutional concerns, given the established facts of the case. According to these, the complainants published a fictional interview with the initial proceedings' plaintiff in an entertainment magazine in which events from the plaintiff's private life were depicted as though she had described them herself. The courts considered this an unauthorised interference with the plaintiff's private life, given that it is for her to decide whether and how she wishes to disclose parts of her private life to the public. 29

Indeed, in this situation, the complainants cannot invoke freedom of the press to justify their actions. It would be going too far if the entertainment and sensational press were generally denied the protection of this fundamental right, as decided by the Regional Court based on individual views in legal scholarship. The term 'press' must be interpreted broadly and formally; irrespective of which standards are applied, it must not hinge upon an assessment of the individual press product. Freedom of the press is not limited to the 'serious' press ([…]; see also BVerfGE 25, 296 <397> and – for radio – BVerfGE 12, 205 <260>). However, this does not mean that the protection derived from the fundamental right must be granted to any press medium in any legal context and for any statement in the same way. When balancing freedom of the press against other constitutionally protected legal interests, it can be taken into account whether the press discusses a public interest matter in a serious and fact-based way in a specific case, thus satisfying the readership's need for information and contributing to the formation of public opinion, or whether it merely satisfies the need of a more or less broad readership for superficial entertainment. 30

In the case at hand, the need for protection of the private sphere of the plaintiff in the initial proceedings was not countered by an overriding public interest in public discussion on the matters covered in the interview. Readers do not have a right to be 'informed', by way of fictional reports, about the private life of a person who has been of public interest at some point. And even if such an interest were recognised as justified in this area, a fabricated interview cannot contribute to true 31 opinion-forming. Ultimately, the protection of the private sphere must thus take precedence over press statements of this kind.

II.

32 If a general law potentially restricts freedom of the press, the manner in which such a restriction applies is solely determined by the content of that specific law. This primarily means that only sanctions authorised by the law may be imposed on the press and effectively restrict its freedom. On that basis, the complainants claim there was no general law that provides for financial compensation for non-material damage when the right of personality is violated and that in fact, § 253 of the Civil Code even explicitly excluded such a claim. According to the complainants, when the courts granted such compensation claims, they thus crossed the boundary within which it was constitutionally permissible to restrict freedom of the press; furthermore, the courts imposed a sanction that violated freedom of the press in substantive terms, because it was directed one-sidedly against the press and imposed an unpredictable risk which would threaten its existence in the long run. This, they claim, fundamentally failed to recognise the essence and significance of freedom of the press in a free and democratic state.

33 As regards these submissions, too, it must be highlighted that the Federal Constitutional Court is not competent to decide whether the legal consequence that the Federal Court of Justice derived from the presumed violation of the general right of personality can be justified on grounds of private law doctrine, i.e. whether it was possible and advisable, from a private law perspective, to pursue the recognition of the general right of personality thus far, and to grant this right the protection provided by similar constituent elements set out in § 847 of the Civil Code by granting a claim for compensation.

34 In respect of this question, too, the Federal Constitutional Court must limit itself to reviewing the constitutional aspects of the case-law. In doing so, the following questions arise: First, does the substantive outcome of the decisions as such already violate the fundamental right to freedom of the press? Secondly, is it compatible with the Basic Law to bring about this outcome by way of judicial decision despite the lack of an unequivocal basis in written law?

35 An assessment of both questions does not raise any constitutional concerns in relation to the case-law of the Federal Court of Justice insofar as it forms the basis for the decisions challenged here.

III.

It is only natural that violations of the general right of personality are mainly committed by press organs as they possess the technical means for obtaining and disseminating information, which makes it relatively easy for them to intrude into the private sphere of individuals. However, examples from the case-law show that the civil courts also apply the rules they developed for the protection of the general right of personality to areas other than the press (cf., e.g., BGHZ 26, 349; 30, 7; 35, 363). For that reason alone, this is not a case of "special rights against the press".

Imposing excessively strict sanctions, including unpredictably large claims for damages, would indeed restrict freedom of the press in an unconstitutional manner, in particular if the legal requirements for such claims were not clearly defined. However, this is not the case here. Financial compensation for non-material damage is not a sanction that is generally alien to our legal order, as demonstrated by § 253 of the Civil Code. It is laid down in § 847 of the Civil Code for a violation of other legal interests specified in § 823 of the Civil Code, as well as certain other statutes. Over the course of the development of the relevant case-law, the groups of cases in which compensation must be paid for non-material damage have taken clear shape. The claim for compensation is subsidiary in nature; the courts only grant financial compensation if natural restitution, for instance in the form of injunctive relief or an order of retraction, is not possible or not sufficient in light of the facts of the case; it is out of the question to see a "commercialisation of honour" in this matter. Given the prerequisites of serious impairment to the personal sphere and serious misconduct, it is ensured that the duty of care imposed on a responsible press organ is not too strict and that liability is not incurred for any inaccuracy or objectively incorrect information. Finally, the relevant case-law shows that – just like in the case at hand – compensation payments granted remain within reasonable limits, particularly when taking into account that the press behaviour leading to the claims for compensation is usually guided by commercial interests. The risks faced by the press due to this case-law thus do not exceed the limits of what is reasonable (*zumutbar*). In the case at hand, this is particularly evident; the degree of care necessary to prevent a fabricated interview from being disseminated is never unreasonable.

IV.

1. Judges are traditionally bound by the law; this is an integral part of the principle of the separation of powers, and thus the rule of law. This principle is modified in the Basic Law, at least in respect of its wording, in that the judiciary is bound

by "law and justice" (Art. 20(3) of the Basic Law). The general view is that this indicates a rejection of narrow legal positivism. The wording makes it clear that law and justice are generally but not necessarily always aligned. Justice is not identical to the entirety of written laws. Beyond the positive statutes adopted by state authority, there may exist further law that finds its source in the constitutional legal order as a meaningful whole and may act as a corrective to written law; it is the judiciary's duty to find and implement it in its case-law. Under the Basic Law, judges are not obliged to apply legislative instructions within the limits of their literal meaning to individual cases. Such an obligation would require there to be no gaps in the positive legal order of the state, which may be defensible as a postulate of legal certainty in principle, but is unattainable in practice. Judicial activity does not merely consist in identifying and pronouncing legislative decisions. In particular, judicial activity may require that values inherent in the constitutional legal order but which are not, or only incompletely, expressed in written law be brought to light and manifested in decisions in an act of evaluative assessment, which does not lack elements of will. In doing so, judges must remain free from arbitrariness; their decisions must be based on rational argument. It must be reasonably laid out how the written law at issue does not serve its function of solving a legal problem justly. The judicial decision then closes this gap in accordance with the standards of practical reason and "the community's established general notions of justice" (BVerfGE 9, 338 <349>).

39 A judge's responsibility and authority for "constructive development of the law" has never been called into question in principle – in any case not under the Basic Law [...]. The highest federal courts have claimed this authority from the beginning (cf., e.g., BGHZ 3, 308 <315>; 4, 153 <158>; BAG 1, 279 <280 and 281>). The Federal Constitutional Court has always recognised it (cf., e.g., BVerfGE 3, 225 <243 and 244>; 13, 153 <164>; 18, 224 <237 and 238>; 25, 167 <183>). The legislator itself has expressly assigned the task of "development of the law" to the Grand Senates of the highest federal courts (cf., e.g., § 137 of the Courts Constitution Act). In some areas of the law, such as labour law, judicial development of the law has taken on particular significance as legislation has lagged behind social developments.

40 It is only the limits of such constructive development of the law that may be controversial, considering the principle that the judiciary be bound by law, which is indispensable for rule-of-law reasons. These limits cannot be standardised for all areas of law or all legal relationships arising from or governed by these.

41 2. For the purposes of this decision, the relevant issue can be limited to the area of private law. In this area, judges have at their disposal the grand codification of the Civil Code, which has been in force for more than 70 years. This is important in

two respects: Firstly, the more "codifications age" [...], that is to say the more time has elapsed between the adoption of a law and the judicial decision on an individual case, the more a judge's freedom for constructive development of the law must necessarily grow. The interpretation of a legal provision cannot forever hold on to the meaning assigned to it when it was drafted. It must be considered what reasonable purpose it may serve at the time of its application. The provision is always situated in the context of the social conditions and the socio-political views upon which it is to have an effect; its content can, and possibly must, change as they do. This applies in particular when living conditions and legal views have changed as profoundly between the time of drafting and the application of a law as they have in this century. If a conflict arises between a provision and the substantive ideas of justice of a changed society, judges cannot withdraw from it by pointing to the unaltered wording of the law; they must handle legal provisions more freely in order not to fail at their task of administering justice. Secondly, experience has shown that legislative reforms encounter particular difficulties and obstacles when they attempt to change one of the grand legislative works that characterise the legal order as a whole, the way the codification of the Civil Code has impacted private law.

3. As stated above, the question that is the subject of the case-law challenged here was already controversial during the preparatory work on the Civil Code [...]. The criticism that immediately followed the legislative solution – initially without taking into consideration constitutional aspects – did not die down with time. Critics invoked the development of the law in other Western countries, which, to a far greater extent, recognise the option of financial compensation for non-material damage, too [...]. Thus, the critics could argue that nowhere in the West did an unlawful act remain without private law sanctions as frequently as in Germany on the grounds that it 'only' caused non-material damage. The limitation of financial compensation for non-material damage to a few explicitly specified particular cases – with a certain "lack of clear direction" – was characterised as "legislative failure" [...]. This criticism became harsher once the civil courts proceeded to recognise the general right of personality under the influence of the "power of the Basic Law in shaping private law" [...]. This recognition revealed a gap in view of the sanctions to be imposed when the right of personality was violated. The significance of this problem was not foreseeable at the time of development of the Civil Code, but it urgently required a solution when changed legal views and the moral concept of the new Constitution emerged; no such solution could be derived from statutory law given the enumeration clause in § 253 of the Civil Code [listing non-material damage in respect of which compensation can be claimed].

42

43 The judiciary was faced with the question of whether to close this gap with available means or to wait for the legislator to intervene. When courts chose the former option, their decisions were affirmed by important voices in the legal discourse […]. Relevant decisions by the Federal Court of Justice and other courts thus met with broad approval in legal scholarship from the outset […]. This reveals that the case-law was in line with general notions of justice and was not considered an unacceptable restriction of freedom of expression or freedom of the press. Deliberations at the 42nd and 45th (1957 and 1964) German Jurists' Convention (*Deutscher Juristentag*) as well as the explanatory memorandum to the draft act by the Federal Government (BTDrucks III/1237) show how strongly the need for effective protection of one's personality under private law, and specifically by way of awarding non-material damages, was perceived. Therefore, the criticism was not directed so much against the outcomes of the judicial decisions as against the methodological and doctrinal considerations used by the courts to justify the chosen approach. To the extent that methods of private law are concerned, it generally does not fall to the Federal Constitutional Court to review the validity of objections presented in that context. However, it cannot be overlooked that the majority of scholars in private law apparently also do not see a problem with the courts' considerations in doctrinal terms […]. In the context of the negotiations of the Expert Group for Comparative Private Law of the Society for Comparative Law (*Fachgruppe für Zivilrechtsvergleichung der Gesellschaft für Rechtsvergleichung*) in Mannheim in 1971 (*Arbeiten zur Rechtsvergleichung*, vol. 61 (1972)), the case-law of the Federal Court of Justice was seen as having brought about a legal situation largely in line with international legal developments […]. An outcome resulting from an approach that is at least acceptable in private law, and which in any case does not obviously run counter to the rules of private law hermeneutics, is not objectionable under constitutional law if it serves to enforce and effectively protect a legal interest which the Constitution itself regards as the centre of its system of values. This outcome reflects 'justice' within the meaning of Art. 20(3) of the Basic Law – not in contradiction to written law, but as a supplement and further development of it.

44 As things stand, the alternative option – to wait until the legislator settles the matter – cannot be considered to be required by constitutional law. […]

45 Furthermore, the method of developing the law applied by the Federal Court of Justice is not objectionable under constitutional law given that it edges away from written law only to the degree that is indispensable for manifesting justice in the specific case. The Federal Court of Justice neither held that § 253 of the Civil Code is non-binding in its entirety, nor did it seek to designate it as unconstitutional (an option that would have been available to the court, given that the provision is pre-constitutional). The court left the principle of enumeration expressed in the

provision untouched and merely added another case to those in respect of which the legislator had already mandated compensation for non-material damage; the development of social realities, but also *jus superveniens* of higher rank, namely Arts. 1 and 2(1) of the Basic Law, urgently required this addition. In recognising this addition, the Federal Court of Justice and the courts following it have not abandoned the legal order or imposed their own will regarding legal policy; rather, they have merely resorted to means inherent in the system to further develop fundamental notions of the legal order shaped by the Constitution [...]. The legal principle thus discovered is therefore a legitimate component of the legal order and, as a general law within the meaning of Art. 5(2) of the Basic Law, it serves as a limitation to freedom of the press. Its goal is to guarantee, also in private law, effective protection of human personality and of human dignity, which are at the centre of the system of values of the Basic Law, and thus strengthen the applicability of fundamental rights in one area of law. For these reasons, the complainants' constitutional objections are without merit.

V.

[...] 46-47

Justices: Benda, Ritterspach, Haager, Rupp-v. Brünneck, Böhmer, Faller, Brox, Simon

No. 4

BVerfGE 49, 286 – Transsexuals I

HEADNOTE

to the Order of the First Senate of 11 October 1978
1 BvR 16/72

Article 2(1) in conjunction with Article 1(1) of the Basic Law requires that a transsexual's male sex entry in the birth register be corrected, at least in cases where transsexualism is irreversible according to medical findings and gender reassignment surgery has been undergone.

FEDERAL CONSTITUTIONAL COURT
- 1 BvR 16/72 -

IN THE NAME OF THE PEOPLE

In the proceedings
on the constitutional complaint of

H…,
– authorised representatives: …

against   the Order of the Federal Court of Justice of 21 September 1971
- IV ZB 61/70 -

the Federal Constitutional Court – First Senate –

with the participation of Justices

President Benda,
Haager,
Böhmer,
Simon,
Faller,
Hesse,

No. 4 – Transsexuals I

Katzenstein,
Niemeyer

held on 11 October 1978:

The Order of the Federal Court of Justice of 21 September 1971 - IV ZB 61/70 - violates the complainant's fundamental right under Article 2(1) in conjunction with Article 1(1) of the Basic Law. It is reversed. The matter is remanded to the Federal Court of Justice.

[…]

REASONS:

The complainant is one of the persons who were assigned male at birth because of their visible sexual characteristics, but later felt they belonged to the female gender in every respect and – after adjusting their appearance – now live as women, but are legally treated as men (male transsexuals). With his constitutional complaint, he challenges the refusal to change his official sex entry in the birth register from 'male' to 'female'. 1

A.

I.

On the basis of current findings, as set forth in a publication published by the German Society for Sexology (*Deutsche Gesellschaft für Sexualforschung*) from 1974, the key characteristic of transsexualism is the complete psychological identification with the other gender, i.e. the gender that contradicts that of one's body. […] 2
[…] 3-4
According to the scientific findings at hand, attempts to change the basic psychosexual structure of transsexuals by means of psychotherapy or hormone treatment have failed so far. According to scientific opinion, the only effective and helpful treatment is to adapt the transsexual's body to the gender identity they experience as far as possible. Only this way can the danger of self-mutilation and suicide, to which transsexuals are always exposed, be averted. However, the medical experts argue that for a transsexual full recognition of the new gender role is only achieved when their first name and civil status are changed. 5

II.

6 Pursuant to § 1(2) of the Civil Status Act in the version officially published on 8 August 1957 (BGBl I, p. 1125), the registrar is responsible for keeping a birth register. In this respect, the law provides in its current version:

§ 21

7 (1) The following information is entered in the birth register:
1. - 2.(...)
3. the child's sex
4. the child's first and last name
5. (...)
(2) (...)

8 Entries may be amended or corrected by the registrar.
9-11 [...]
12 The registrar is also authorised to enter margin notes.
13 [...]

14 § 47

(1) For the rest, a final entry may only be corrected by a court order. The same applies if a registrar has doubts as to whether they can correct an entry.
(2) (...)

III.

15 1. The complainant, who was born out of wedlock as the son of a seamstress, was raised first by foster parents, and later grew up in an orphanage in Silesia led by nuns. [...]

16 The complainant married in 1953. His marriage ended in divorce in 1964. In 1961, his wife had a baby. Following the complainant's action for annulment, a judgment was issued in 1965 declaring that it was not his legitimate child. From about 1960, serious disturbances to the complainant's general well-being became apparent, as he increasingly identified with the female gender. Already in 1962, his left testicle was removed because of a contusion. In 1963, his right testicle was removed as an undescended testicle. After having been treated with female sex hormones, the complainant underwent gender reassignment surgery at a German university hospital in 1964.

No. 4 – Transsexuals I

Today, the complainant works as a nurse at a university hospital.

2. In 1968, the Berlin-Schöneberg Local Court granted the complainant's request to officially recognise him as a woman under civil status law, and instructed the responsible registrar to correct the complainant's entry in the birth register with the following margin note: "The child designated here is female." The court order was based on several medical reports, each of which diagnosed the complainant with an irreversible case of transsexualism. It also pointed out that a refusal to change the civil status could lead to unpredictable contradictions and interpersonal and social difficulties for the complainant.

3. Following the complaint of the *Land* Minister of the Interior, the Regional Court reversed the Local Court's order and rejected the application for correction of the entry in the birth register. […]

4. The complainant immediately filed a further complaint against this decision. The Higher Regional Court referred this complaint to the Federal Court of Justice for decision:

The Higher Regional Court argued that assigning the male sex was correct at the time of the entry. However, according to the court, it should now be considered established medical fact that gender is not determined by the sexual organs and characteristics alone, but also by the human psyche. […]

[…]

5. The Federal Court of Justice did not concur with the Higher Regional Court and rejected the immediate further complaint […]. According to the court, certain basic experiences have been taken for granted so far when assigning persons to the respective sex categories. The court held that in addition to the finding that there are no sexless persons, but that all persons can be assigned to the alternative categories of 'male' and 'female', there is the experience that a person's sex may be and must be determined based on physical sexual characteristics, which are innate and unchangeable. This principle not only governs all of social life, but the entire legal order. Occasional difficulties when assigning hermaphrodites to a sex cannot be considered a disruption of these principles.

The court held that this was not a failure to recognise that a transsexual who by fate has an irresistible urge to convert to the other gender may have a recognisable need to also be officially assigned to this sex. It held, however, that this was not possible without the corresponding legal provisions. […]

IV.

1. The treatment of transsexuals under civil status law has repeatedly been debated in the German *Bundestag*. […] A draft "Act on Changing Officially Assigned Sex

in Certain Cases" [...] provides for a 'small' and a 'big' solution. According to this draft, transsexuals of legal age who are unable to reproduce and have felt compelled to belong to the other gender for at least three years may assume a first name corresponding to this gender, if their identification with the other gender is highly likely to no longer change. [...]

27 2. In order to at least somewhat accommodate the difficult situation of transsexuals even before legislation is put in place, and in order to avoid causing undue hardship, the *Länder* and the Federation have agreed that transsexuals may assume a so-called gender-neutral first name [...] in addition to the first name they have had so far. This new first name may then be stated on their identity card as their only first name without any additional gender markers. Accordingly, the complainant's male first name was changed to Helge.

V.

28 With his constitutional complaint, the complainant claims a violation of Art. 1(1) and (3) and of Art. 2(1) of the Basic Law. [...]

VI.

29 1. The Federal Minister of Justice considers the constitutional complaint to be admissible, but unfounded. [...]
30 [...]
31 2. The President of the Federal Administrative Court stated that the court merely decided that a person who could be considered as transsexual may not have a female first name as long as they have a male sex entry in the birth register. [...]

B.

32 The constitutional complaint is well-founded.
33 The challenged decision violates the complainant's fundamental right under Art. 2(1) in conjunction with Art. 1(1) of the Basic Law.

I.

34 1. According to the medical reports submitted, the complainant is female in psychological terms and his physical appearance was adapted to this gender as far as medically possible by way of hormone treatment and surgery. Legally, however, the complainant is treated as a man against his will. He is thus denied the opportunity

of leading an ordinary and assimilated life as a woman. The inconsistency between appearance and civil status is illustrated by the simple fact that he cannot legally have a female first name. Given that the Civil Status Act clearly assumes that the first name must indicate the sex of the name bearer […], the complainant can only change his name once the sex entry in the birth register has been changed. In this respect, even a gender-neutral first name does not entirely rule out contradictions for the complainant. The sphere affected by these belongs to the most intimate part of personality, which is in principle beyond the reach of the state and where in any case interference is only permissible if special public interests exist (cf. BVerfGE 47, 46 <73>).

2. a) Art. 1(1) of the Basic Law protects human dignity, the way persons understand themselves as individuals and become aware of themselves. This includes the right to determine one's own being and to take one's destiny into one's own hands. Art. 2(1) in conjunction with Art. 1(1) of the Basic Law guarantees the free development of the abilities and strengths inherent in a human being. Therefore, human dignity and the fundamental right to the free development of one's personality require assigning persons the civil status of the gender they identify with on the basis of their psychological and physical constitution. In this context, our legal order and our social life are based on the precept that humans are either male or female, independent of possible anomalies in the genital area. However, it is doubtful whether the hypothesis of an unchangeable identity based on sex, as determined at birth by way of external sexual characteristics, is still tenable in the absolute terms described by the Federal Court of Justice in its challenged decision. Science shows that there are various forms of somatic intersexuality. Based on studies on hermaphrodites, medical research has also pointed out that dissociation between body and psyche may occur, which is particularly pronounced in transsexuals according to established scientific findings.

The "basic experience" that a person's gender is determined by their physical sexual characteristics, and that it is innate and unchangeable, is seriously challenged by the medical findings concerning psychosexual development as the product of hereditary and external environmental factors […]. In any case, irrespective of remaining doubts as to the origins and causes of transsexualism, the transsexual complainant does not identify as a man, and according to the submitted medical reports, there are no external indications of male sex. In addition, his social behaviour is adapted to that of a woman, as his work as a nurse also indicates.

b) However, the right to the free development of one's personality is only guaranteed within the limits of moral law. Yet moral law is not violated in the case at hand. It is not within the scope of the current proceedings to decide whether gender reassignment surgery that is not required from a medical perspective would be contrary to moral law. According to the medical reports submitted here, surgery was medically indicated. Based on established scientific findings, transsexuals do not seek to manipulate their gender. Their focus is not sexuality, but rather achieving an alignment of body and psyche, and thus surgery must be considered necessary for realising this goal. The suffering of transsexuals described in the medical literature is strikingly confirmed by the medical reports regarding the complainant. Based on these reports, the complainant's process of gender change cannot be considered immoral. In the order challenged by the constitutional complaint, the Federal Court of Justice also denied the immorality of genital corrective surgery that aims to avoid severe psychological and physical damage.

38 The fact that the complainant, as a result of the correction of the complainant's sex entry, is able to marry a person of his former sex is not contrary to moral law either.

39 No further consideration is needed regarding the fact that a man's reproductive capacity and a woman's ability to give birth are not a precondition for marriage. Under the Basic Law (Art. 6(1) of the Basic Law) marriage is the union of a man and a woman in a partnership that is in principle inseparable (BVerfGE 10, 59 <66>). It is up to the spouses to shape this partnership according to their wishes. [...]

40 c) According to the case-law of the Federal Constitutional Court, restrictions to an individual's exclusive right to determine their domain of private life may follow from their co-existence with others, insofar as this domain does not belong to their inviolable innermost domain (BVerfGE 35, 202 <220> – *Lebach;* with further references). Yet in the complainant's case, no public interest in refusing to change his sex entry in the birth register is apparent which might justify an interference with the fundamental right of Art. 2(1) in conjunction with Art. 1(1) of the Basic Law.

II.

41 Since the refusal to correct the sex entry in the birth register is therefore incompatible with Art. 2(1) in conjunction with Art 1(1) of the Basic Law, the obligation of the courts to act in a manner compatible with fundamental rights cannot be denied merely because a legal provision is lacking.

42 1. [...] Of course, the legislator is free [...] to create a legal basis for correcting transsexuals' sex entries in the birth register. However, as long as it has not specified the requirements for such a correction, the obligation that follows directly from Art. 2(1) in conjunction with Art. 1(1) of the Basic Law can be met by means of an interpretation of § 47(1) of the Civil Status Act in conformity with the Constitution.

43 2. [...]

a) It is true that case-law and legal scholarship have developed the view that § 47(1) of the Civil Status Act only allows for the correction of entries in the birth register that were false from the outset. […] The Federal Court of Justice concurred with this view in the challenged decision.

b) However, the term 'correction' does not necessarily require information to have been false originally. It may also refer more generally to the subsequent rectification of incorrect information. […]

As far as the legislator's intent is concerned, it must be taken into account that § 47(1) of the Civil Status Act […] not only […] does not preclude corrections to transsexuals' sex entries, but also stipulates the procedural conditions for making such corrections.

3. The Federal Court of Justice is of the opinion that the legal problems associated with gender reassignment cannot be solved by way of judicial development of the law. This view fails to recognise that while there may be a legal gap in this respect, this gap cannot be considered a general lack of legal regulation in light of the constitutional law described above, according to which the fundamental right of Art. 2(1) in conjunction with Art. 1(1) of the Basic Law directly results in an obligation upon the courts. In the interest of legal certainty, it is indeed for the legislator to resolve the civil status issues arising from gender reassignment and its consequences. However, as long as such legislation is not in place, the task incumbent upon the courts is the same as it was in the case of equality between men and women before the Equal Rights Act entered into force (BVerfGE 3, 225 <239 *et seq.*>, cf. also BVerfGE 37, 67 <81>). The courts cannot be denied this responsibility, given that the judiciary is directly bound by the fundamental rights (Art. 1(3) of the Basic Law).

Moreover, the complainant's case does not raise most of the legal problems which, according to the Federal Court of Justice, can only be solved by the legislator itself. The complainant is divorced, does not have any children, underwent gender reassignment surgery as early as 1964, and is 46 years old. Insofar as it is necessary to determine the time at which gender reassignment attains legal validity, the view that entries in the birth register are merely declaratory does not have to be upheld given the applicable constitutional law. For instance, a solution that is not objectionable under constitutional law would be giving *ex nunc*, and thus constitutive effect, to the margin note of a change of a person's sex entry after birth.

However, it is not for the Federal Constitutional Court to decide on this matter. Therefore, the matter is remanded to the Federal Court of Justice.

Justices: Benda, Haager, Böhmer, Simon, Faller, Hesse, Katzenstein, Niemeyer

No. 5

BVerfGE 54, 148 – Eppler

HEADNOTES

to the Judgment of the First Senate of 3 June 1980
1 BvR 185/77

1. The general right of personality, as constitutionally guaranteed by Article 2(1) in conjunction with Article 1(1) of the Basic Law, also protects individuals from having statements falsely attributed to them that impair their right to maintain a self-defined social image.

2. As long as the defendant has a procedural obligation to cooperate, there is no constitutional requirement to deviate, in cases of this nature, from the general rule of civil procedure that the plaintiff must provide proof of the factual circumstances giving rise to their claim [for injunctive relief].

FEDERAL CONSTITUTIONAL COURT
- 1 BvR 185/77 -

IN THE NAME OF THE PEOPLE

In the proceedings
on the constitutional complaint of

Dr. E…,

– authorised representatives: …

against   the Judgment of the Stuttgart Higher Regional Court of 9 February 1977
 - 4 U 117/76 -

the Federal Constitutional Court – First Senate –
with the participation of Justices

President Benda,
Böhmer,
Simon,

Faller,
Hesse,
Katzenstein,
Niemeyer,
Heußner

held on 3 June 1980:
The constitutional complaint is rejected.

REASONS:

A.

I.

1. The complainant is the chairperson of the Baden-Württemberg regional branch of the *Sozialdemokratische Partei Deutschlands* (SPD political party); the defendant in the initial proceedings was the Baden-Württemberg regional branch of the *Christlich-Demokratische Union* (CDU political party). As a campaign service for the 1976 state parliament elections [...], the defendant provided a model speech to its district speakers titled "The Socialist Agenda", excerpts of which read as follows:

"It is particularly disastrous that the social and economic policy ideas of the SPD are clearly informed by Socialist ideology, framing *economic policy and social policy as polar opposites*. Given such a political narrative, demands for the *nationalisation* of banks and key industries flourish, as do calls for state control over *economic investments*, and for *co-determination*, which in reality is nothing other than *external control*. The intention here is ultimately – as E. and S. have put it – to test the economy's resilience, as though industry were an engine which could be pushed until it chokes, and then re-started at will".

2. The complainant contended that this violated his right of personality and lodged an application for injunctive relief; he claimed that he had never said, either verbatim or in spirit, that the economy's resilience should be tested. The Regional Court rejected the application; the appeal on points of fact and law (*Berufung*) to the Higher Regional Court was unsuccessful. The Higher Regional Court gave the following reasons for its decision:

It was not possible for the court to determine whether the complainant had in fact said that one should test the economy's resilience. The court also affirmed that it would generally be for the defendant to bear the consequences of this procedural *non liquet* (inconclusive evidence) [...]. However, the court held that this rule of evidence [placing the burden of proof on the defendant] was not applicable in the case at hand on the grounds that the defendant could invoke the defence of having pursued legitimate interests. It thus concluded that the burden of proof fell on the complainant, who was not able to demonstrate that he had not made the disputed statements. [...]

5 The court also concluded that the assertion challenged by the complainant did not amount to defamation in any case [...]. [...]

II.

6 1. With his constitutional complaint, the complainant challenges a violation of his fundamental rights under Art. 1(1), Art. 2(1), Art. 3(1) and Art. 3(3), Art. 4 and Art. 5 of the Basic Law. [...]

7 2. The Ministry of Justice of the *Land* Baden-Württemberg considers the constitutional complaint to be unfounded. [...]

B.

8 The constitutional complaint is unfounded.

I.

9 The constitutional complaint is directed against a court decision in civil proceedings regarding a claim for injunctive relief under private law. It is incumbent upon the ordinary courts to interpret the applicable legal provisions, taking into account the influence of fundamental rights on private law in their decisions. The Federal Constitutional Court is only called upon to ensure that the ordinary courts observe fundamental right guarantees and standards; in this respect, the Court must review whether a challenged decision shows any errors of interpretation that are based on a fundamentally incorrect understanding of the significance of a fundamental right, in particular of its scope of protection, and whether these deficits are of considerable weight in the case at issue (BVerfGE 42, 143 <147 *et seq.*> with further references). [...]

II.

Having regard to these limits of constitutional review, the challenged judgment cannot be held to violate fundamental rights.
1. The complainant claims a violation of his right of personality, which he asserts is guaranteed by Art. 1(1) and Art. 2(1) of the Basic Law; in addition, he invokes the specific fundamental rights set out in the constitutional complaint. It is correct to assume that within their respective scope, the specific fundamental rights also serve the protection of one's personality. However, neither the complainant's submissions nor other evidence provides any indication of a violation of the specific fundamental rights under Art. 3(1) and (3), Art. 4 or Art. 5 of the Basic Law. [...]
2. a) Given that a violation of specific fundamental rights can thus be ruled out, the applicable basis for review is the general right of personality, which is constitutionally guaranteed by Art. 2(1) in conjunction with Art. 1(1) of the Basic Law.
While the specific ('listed') freedoms of the Basic Law, such as freedom of conscience or freedom of expression, also protect fundamental aspects of one's personality, the general right of personality supplements these guarantees as a 'non-listed' freedom. Affirming "human dignity" (Art. 1(1) of the Basic Law) as the supreme constitutive principle, the general right of personality serves to guarantee the personal sphere that is closer to the core of private life (*engere persönliche Lebenssphäre*) as well as its basic conditions, which cannot be entirely protected by the traditional specific freedoms guaranteed in the Constitution; most notably, this need for more comprehensive protection arises with regard to modern developments that pose new risks to the protection of one's personality. As the link to Art. 1(1) of the Basic Law reveals, the general right of personality under Art. 2(1) of the Basic Law comprises an element of "free development of one's personality", which manifests as a right to respect for a certain protected domain, and that differs from the 'active' element of this development guaranteed in the form of general freedom of action (cf. BVerfGE 6, 32). Accordingly, the constituent elements of the general right of personality must be defined more narrowly than those relating to the general freedom of action: the former may only come to bear on interferences that are capable of impairing one's closer personal sphere (cf. BVerfGE 34, 238 <247> – *Secret Tape Recordings*; BGHZ 24, 72 <81>; 27, 284 <287>).
Given the particularities of the general right of personality set out above, neither the case-law of the Federal Constitutional Court nor the case-law of the Federal Court of Justice has exhaustively defined the substance of this protected right; rather, the various manifestations of this right have been developed on a case-by-case basis. Legal interests that have thus been recognised as protected by the general right of personality include the private sphere, the secret sphere and the intimate sphere

(cf., e.g., BVerfGE 27, 1 <6> – *Microcensus*; 27, 344 <350 and 351> – *Divorce Files*; 32, 373 <379>; 34, 238 <245 and 246> – *Secret Tape Recordings*; 47, 46 <73>; 49, 286 <298> – *Transsexuals I*), personal honour, the right to determine the portrayal of one's person (BVerfGE 35, 202 <220> – *Lebach*), the right to one's own image and to one's own speech (BVerfGE 34, 238 <246> – *Secret Tape Recordings*) and, under certain circumstances, the right to be protected against fabricated comments attributed to one's person (cf. BVerfGE 34, 269 <282 and 283> – *Soraya*). These manifestations of the constitutionally protected right of personality must be observed by the courts when they assess conflicting interests under provisions of private law in their decisions (cf. BVerfGE 35, 202 <221> – *Lebach*).

15 b) The factual circumstances underlying the constitutional complaint do not fall within any of the manifestations of the right of personality protected by Art. 2(1) of the Basic Law that have been recognised in case-law so far. Neither the complainant's private sphere nor his secret or personal sphere are affected. The assertion challenged by the complainant also does not constitute an attack on his honour; […]. Calling for the economy's resilience to be tested does, by itself, not amount to dishonourable conduct; nor does it constitute incitement to unconstitutional action […]. […] Finally, the complainant cannot directly invoke the right to one's own speech (cf. in this regard BGHZ 13, 334 <338 and 339>). The case at hand specifically concerns a statement that has been attributed to, yet – according to his own submission – was never made by the complainant [and thus does not qualify as his own speech]; the statement in dispute also does not result in an incorrect portrayal of the complainant's personality by way of misquoting comments he made in the past.

16 The general right of personality guaranteed by Art. 2(1) of Basic Law may, however, also be invoked where statements are falsely attributed to one's person. This requires the challenged conduct to amount to a violation of a legal interest that has been recognised as protected by the right of personality, such as the private sphere; this is the case, for instance, where a fabricated interview is spread that concerns the private life of the affected rights holder (BGH, NJW 1965, p. 685; cf. also BVerfGE 34, 269 <282 and 283> – *Soraya*). Even if the impairment of a protected interest is not ascertainable, an interference with the general right of personality may be found where statements attributed to a person who did not actually make these statements impair that person's right to maintain a self-defined social image (*selbst definierter sozialer Geltungsanspruch*). This follows from the notion of self-determination, which underlies the protection of the general right of personality: individuals should generally – not just in relation to their private life – be afforded the right to decide how they wish to present themselves vis-à-vis third

parties or the public, and whether and to what extent third parties may determine or control aspects of their personality; this particularly includes the decision on whether and how the individual wishes to share their own statements with others. [...] In this context, it is only for the individual person to determine what should constitute their self-defined social image; to this end, the substance of the general right of personality is primarily informed by the self-perception of the rights holder (cf. for freedom of worship BVerfGE 24, 236 <247 and 248>).

Thus, it would be incompatible with Art. 2(1) of Basic Law if the assessment of whether a statement falsely attributed to a person impaired their general right of personality were based on how the person is – justifiably or not – perceived by others, instead of giving consideration to the self-perception of the rights holder. [...]

3. a) Seen this way, the constitutional guarantee of the general right of personality could only be significant for the assessment of the merits in the initial proceedings if the complainant did not make the statement about testing the economy's resilience. If the Higher Regional Court had considered this to be true but nonetheless found no interference with the complainant's right of personality, it would not only have failed to give sufficient consideration to the substance of this right as set out above, but the court itself would have violated Art. 2(1) of the Basic Law by setting its own perception of the complainant's personality as the relevant standard for assessing whether the statement that was attributed to the complainant distorted the portrayal of his personality. In that scenario, the social image of the complainant would have been defined not by the complainant himself, but by the court. Despite the fact that the court did refer to comments made by the complainant in different contexts, such an approach is incompatible with Art. 2(1) of the Basic Law.

b) These considerations, however, would only have been relevant for the challenged judgment if it had been established as fact that the complainant did not make the statement in dispute. In this regard, the Higher Regional Court concluded that the evidence was inconclusive with regard to establishing the truth of the defendant's assertions. The evaluation of the evidence presented that led to this conclusion is not subject to review by the Federal Constitutional Court. [...]

[...] The Higher Regional Court correctly assumed that the statement in dispute was not capable of disparaging the complainant or negatively affecting public opinion of him. The only open question is whether the Higher Regional Court's view that it was incumbent upon the complainant to demonstrate and prove the alleged unlawful violation of his right of personality resulted in a violation of constitutional law. Ultimately, this view is not objectionable under constitutional law.

A facet of constitutional law that would require a deviation from the general evidentiary rules of civil procedure applicable in cases of this kind is not discernible.

The rules of evidence provide that the burden of proof regarding the elements of the claim rests with the injured party; in this regard, evidence might indeed be difficult to obtain if the injured party must prove that it did not make a disputed statement. However, this does not impose an undue burden on the injured party, given that the defendant is under an obligation to cooperate: the defendant must substantiate the contention that the plaintiff made a certain statement; thus, the defendant must specify, in particular, when and how the statement was made and to whom it was addressed. These assertions may be refuted by the plaintiff. In the case at hand, the defendant had indeed specified the relevant circumstances, and the information provided in this regard was thoroughly examined and assessed. [...] In a case like this, constitutional law does not require [...] a departure from the general rules of civil procedure in respect of the burden of proof.

22 c) Based on the factual findings of the Higher Regional Court, which were established without any violation of constitutional law, it is not ascertainable that a statement was falsely attributed to the complainant in violation of his right to a – self-defined – social image. In order to assert an interference with the complainant's right of personality, it would have been necessary for the complainant to first establish that a statement had been falsely attributed to him. [...]

Justices: Benda, Böhmer, Simon, Faller, Hesse, Katzenstein, Niemeyer, Heußner

No. 6

BVerfGE 65, 1 – Census

HEADNOTES

to the Judgment of the First Senate of 15 December 1983
1 BvR 209, 269, 362, 420, 440, 484/83

1. In the context of modern data processing, the general right of personality under Article 2(1) in conjunction with Article 1(1) of the Basic Law encompasses the protection of the individual against the unlimited collection, storage, use and sharing of their personal data. This fundamental right confers upon the individual the authority to, in principle, decide themselves on the disclosure and use of their personal data.
2. Restrictions of this right to 'informational self-determination' are only permissible if they serve an overriding public interest. They require a statutory basis that must be constitutional and must satisfy the requirement of legal clarity under the rule of law. In the design of the statutory framework, the legislator must furthermore observe the principle of proportionality. It must also provide for organisational and procedural safeguards that counter the risk of violating the general right of personality.
3. As for the constitutional requirements applicable to such restrictions, a distinction must be made between personal data that is collected and processed as individualised information and not rendered anonymous, and data intended for statistical purposes.
   Where data is collected for statistical purposes, requiring a strict and specific purpose limitation would not be feasible. However, to compensate for the lack of such a purpose limitation, the collection and processing of such information must be subject to other adequate limitations within the relevant information system.
4. The data collection provided for under the 1983 Census Act (§ 2 nos. 1 to 7, §§ 3 to 5 of the Act) does not amount to the registration and cataloguing of the data subjects' personality in a manner that would be incompatible with human dignity; the relevant provisions also satisfy the requirements of legal clarity and proportionality. However, it is imperative that additional

procedural safeguards be put in place in order to ensure that the right to informational self-determination is respected in the implementation and organisation of the census data collection.

5. The legal provisions governing the transfer of data under § 9(1) to (3) of the 1983 Census Act (including the comparison of census data with civil registry records) violate the general right of personality. However, the sharing of data for scientific purposes (§ 9(4) of the 1983 Census Act) is compatible with the Basic Law.

FEDERAL CONSTITUTIONAL COURT
- 1 BvR 209, 269, 362, 420, 440, 484/83 -

IN THE NAME OF THE PEOPLE

In the proceedings
on the constitutional complaints of

a) Mr von M…,
   - 1 BvR 209/83 -,
b) 1. Dr. W…, 2. Ms S…,
   – authorised representative: …,
   - 1 BvR 269/83 -,
c) Prof. Dr. M…,
   - 1 BvR 362/83 -,
d) 1. Prof. Dr. B…, 2. Prof. Dr. Dr. P…, 3. Prof. Dr. S…, 4. Ms W…,
   – authorised representative: …,
   - 1 BvR 420/83 -,
e) 1. Dr. H…, 2. Mr B…, 3. Mr F…, 4. Mr G…, 5. Ms M…, 6. Mr O…, 7. Mr S…, 8. Mr S…, 9. Mr W…, 10. Ms W…, 11. Ms B…, 12. Ms B…, 13. Mr D…, 14. Ms H…, 15. Mr J…, 16. Ms K…, 17. Ms M…, 18. Mr R…, 19. Ms S…, 20. Ms S…, 21. Ms Z…,
   – authorised representative: …,
   - 1 BvR 440/83 -,
f) Ms F…,
   – authorised representative: …,
   - 1 BvR 484/83 -

No. 6 – Census

directly against the Act on a Census Surveying Population, Occupation, Housing and Workplaces of 25 March 1982 (BGBl I, p. 369)
the Federal Constitutional Court – First Senate –
with the participation of Justices

>President Benda,
>Simon,
>Hesse,
>Katzenstein,
>Niemeyer,
>Heußner,
>Niedermaier,
>Henschel

held on the basis of the oral hearing of 18 and 19 October 1983:

JUDGMENT

1. § 2 nos. 1 to 7 and §§ 3 to 5 of the Act on a Census Surveying Population, Occupation, Housing and Workplaces (1983 Census Act) of 25 March 1982 (BGBl I, p. 369) are compatible with the Basic Law; however, the legislator must ensure that additional organisational and procedural rules for the census be put in place in accordance with the reasons set forth in this judgment.
2. § 9(1) to (3) of the 1983 Census Act is not compatible with Article 2(1) in conjunction with Article 1(1) of the Basic Law, and is thus void.
3. To the extent set out in nos. 1 and 2 above, the Census Act violates the complainants' fundamental rights under Article 2(1) in conjunction with Article 1(1) of the Basic Law.

For the rest, the constitutional complaints are rejected.
[...]

REASONS:

A.

The constitutional complaints directly challenge the Act on a Census Surveying Population, Occupation, Housing and Workplaces (1983 Census Act) of 25 March 1982 (BGBl I, p. 369).

2   The data collection prescribed by the challenged Act has sparked concern among the general public, even among law-abiding citizens who recognise the power and duty of the state to gather the information necessary for rational and well-planned government action. In part, this may be attributable to wide-spread misconceptions regarding the scope and purposes of the survey; due to new developments in automatic data processing, the general perception of such measures has changed significantly since the microcensus data collections from 1956 to 1962 were carried out (cf. BVerfGE 27, 1 – *Microcensus*). It was not recognised early enough that it would be necessary to provide reliable information to the census subjects concerning the envisaged collection of their data. Nowadays, only experts can fully grasp the possibilities of modern data processing, which may prompt citizens to fear that personality profiles are being compiled beyond their control, even if the legislator limits their obligation to provide information to what is necessary and reasonable (*zumutbar*). [...]

I.

3   1. The 1983 Census Act, in its §§ 1 to 8, specifies the data collection framework and its implementation. § 9 further specifies the regime governing the use and sharing of the collected data. The key provisions read:

4-5   [...]

§ 2

6   The population and occupation census shall record:

7   1. given names and surnames, address, telephone number, sex, date of birth, marital status, legal membership (or lack thereof) in a religious community, nationality;

8   2. use of dwelling as exclusive, primary or secondary residence (§ 12(2) of the Framework Act on Civil Registration);

9   3. primary source of income;

10 4. participation in the workforce, status as housewife, pupil or student;

11 5. professional qualifications, duration of vocational training, highest qualification obtained in general education, highest qualification obtained in vocational or higher education, including the major field of study in which the most recent qualification was obtained;

No. 6 – Census

6. regarding the working population, pupils and students: name and address of the workplace or training facility, primary means of transport used and time spent getting to and from work or education;

7. regarding the working population: line of business of employer, professional position, type of occupation carried out, working hours, secondary occupations (agricultural and non-agricultural);

8. regarding detention facilities and institutions: status as inmate or staff member or staff family member.

§ 3

(1) The building-related survey shall record the address, type and year of construction as well as ownership information for residential buildings or buildings in permanent residential use [...].

(2) The dwelling-related survey shall record:

1. type, size, fixtures and fittings, intended use, type of heating and heating supply, year of taking up residence, living arrangements, subsidies received under affordable housing programmes as well as number and usage of individual rooms;

2. regarding rented apartments: amount of monthly rent;

3. regarding vacant apartments: duration of vacancy.

§ 4

The workplace census shall record:

1. regarding non-agricultural workplaces and companies:

    a) name, designation, address, telephone numbers and number of telephone stations, type of establishment, type of activities or tasks performed at the workplace or company, start of business operations (year), information on (new) establishments or relocation, the responsible body for workplaces in facilities or institutions of public authorities or of social insurance providers, as well as of churches, associations or other organisations,

23   b) number of staff disaggregated by sex, company position, number of part-time employees as well as number of foreign employees disaggregated by sex,

24   c) total amount of gross wages and salaries paid in the preceding calendar year;

25   2. regarding main establishments and single-location establishments:

26   a) registration of the company in the register of craft businesses,

27   b) legal form of the company;

28   3. regarding main establishments, in addition to nos. 1 and 2 above, information for each branch establishment on:

29   a) names, designation, address, type of activities or task performed,

30   b) number of staff,

31   c) total amount of gross wages and salaries paid in the preceding calendar year.

32-46   [§§ 5-7…]

§ 9

47   (1) Census data collected pursuant to § 2 nos. 1 and 2 may be compared with the civil registers and used for the purposes of correcting the latter. The information obtained from this data may not be used for taking measures against the individual census subject.

48   (2) In relation to the census elements listed in §§ 2 to 4, the statistical offices of the Federation and the *Länder* may transfer individual data, excluding names, to the competent highest federal and *Land* authorities pursuant to § 11(3) of the Federal Statistics Act of 14 March 1980 (BGBl I, p. 289) to the extent that the relevant information is necessary for the lawful exercise of functions conferred upon the respective authorities. With the exception of information on legal membership (or lack thereof) in a religious community collected pursuant to § 2 no. 1, and on the census elements listed in § 4 no. 1 lit. c and § 4 no. 3 lit. c, the first sentence of this subsection also applies to the transfer of data to authorities designated by the competent highest authorities of the Federation or the *Länder* and to other public and non-public bodies, to the extent that the data transfer is necessary for the lawful exercise of functions conferred upon the

No. 6 – Census

competent highest authorities of the Federation or the *Länder*. In this regard, the second sentence of subsection 1 applies accordingly.

(3) With the exception of information on legal membership (or lack thereof) in a religious community collected pursuant to § 2 no. 1, and on the census elements listed in § 4 no. 1 lit. c and § 4 no. 3 lit. c, the statistical offices of the *Länder* may transfer to municipalities and municipal associations individual data, excluding names, of the census subjects residing in the relevant jurisdiction for purposes relating to regional planning, surveying, municipal planning and environmental protection. [...]

(4) For scientific purposes, the statistical offices of the Federation and the *Länder* may transfer individual data, excluding names and addresses, on the census elements listed in §§ 2 to 4, with the exception of information on legal membership (or lack thereof) in a religious community collected pursuant to § 2 no. 1, and on census elements listed in § 4 no. 1 lit. c and § 4 no. 4 lit. c, to public officials and persons of equivalent status.

(5) Individual data transferred pursuant to subsections 2 to 4 may only be used for the purposes for which it was transferred.

(6) Individual data contained in statistical results and concerning information on legal membership (or lack thereof) in a religious community pursuant to § 2 no. 1 disaggregated by age and sex, and on the census elements listed in § 4 no. 1 lit. b disaggregated by the type of activity carried out by the workplace or company, as well as on the census elements listed in § 4 no. 3 lit. b, may be disclosed by the statistical offices of the Federation and the *Länder*.

[(7)-(8)...]

[...The Federal Statistics Act is also applicable to the proposed type of statistical data collection. Relevant provisions are:]

§ 10

(1) All natural persons and legal persons incorporated under private law, commercial partnerships, and bodies, institutions and foundations incorporated under public law, and authorities and other public bodies of the Federation, the *Länder*, the municipalities and municipal associations, as well as their subordi-

nate bodies, institutions and foundations incorporated under public law over which they exercise regulatory oversight, are obliged to answer lawfully submitted questions except where answering is expressly declared optional.

57 (2) The obligation of census subjects to provide the requested information applies vis-à-vis the bodies and persons officially tasked with carrying out federal statistical surveys.

58 (3) Answers must be provided in a truthful and complete manner, within the stipulated time period and free of charge (including postal fees).

59 (4) Where official survey sheets to be filled in by the census subjects are provided, the requested information must be submitted on these forms. If indicated on the survey sheet, the accuracy of the information provided must be confirmed by signature.

§ 11

60 (1) In the absence of provisions to the contrary, individual data on personal and material circumstances provided for federal statistics purposes must be treated confidentially by the public officials, or persons of equivalent status, that are tasked with carrying out federal statistical surveys, unless the persons concerned expressly consent, in the individual case, to the sharing and disclosure of their personal data. […]

61 (2) The sharing of individual data between persons and bodies tasked with carrying out federal statistical surveys is permissible to the extent that is necessary for the purposes of compiling the federal statistics in question.

62-65 [(3)-(6)…]

66 (7) Data collected for the purposes of identifying the respective census subjects, especially names and addresses, shall be deleted as soon as knowledge of such data is no longer necessary for carrying out the relevant tasks pertaining to statistics compiled for federal purposes. Names and addresses must be stored separately from the rest of the data, and must be subject to special confidentiality protection.

No. 6 – Census

[... The Federal Data Protection Act also applies in the absence of more specific provisions. Relevant provisions are:]

§ 5

Data confidentiality

(1) Without authorisation, persons employed in data processing pursuant to § 1(2) of this Act or acting under instruction of the persons and bodies listed in § 1(2) of this Act are prohibited from processing, disclosing, providing access to or using protected personal data for purposes other than the designated purpose pertaining to the lawful exercise of their respective functions.

[(2)...]

§ 13

Information to be provided to the data subject

(1) Upon request, the data subject concerned shall be provided with information on personal data stored about them. The request should specify the type of personal data on which information is sought. The body controlling the relevant data shall exercise due discretion in determining the applicable procedure and, in particular, the manner in which the requested information is to be provided.

(2) (...)

(3) The request by the data subject shall not be complied with if

1. providing the information sought would jeopardise the lawful performance of tasks for which the body controlling the data is responsible,

2. providing the information sought would pose a danger to public security and order, or otherwise impair legitimate interests of the Federation or a *Land*,

3. a legal provision or the nature of the data requires that the personal data in question, or the fact that it is stored, be kept confidential, especially on grounds of overriding legitimate interests of third parties,

4. (...)

(4) (...)

78 2. After the initial attempt to introduce draft legislation on a census failed during the 8th legislative period, due to disagreement regarding costs, the Federal Government re-submitted essentially the same census draft law in early 1981. The key considerations put forward in the explanatory memorandum attached to the draft can be summarised as follows (BTDrucks 9/451, p. 7 *et seq.*):

79 Population, occupation and workplace censuses are integral to collecting statistical data. Data on updated population figures, including on regional distribution, demographic composition and social indicators as well as economic activity, is vital to decision-making on social and economic policies at the level of the Federation, the *Länder* and the municipalities. Various legal provisions make reference to census results. Similarly, political parties, trade unions and employers' organisations, business and professional associations, science and research, and other relevant groups of public life rely on census results. Moreover, census results serve as the basis for updating information on ongoing developments and as the selection basis for random sample surveys provided for in other legislation. The results of the last census, which took place on 27 May 1970, are outdated. The Federation, *Länder* and municipalities, but also numerous social and business organisations believe that their work may be seriously impaired in the foreseeable future, and fear miscalculations in planning and investment decisions. The data to be collected for the purposes of updating existing records is limited to what is absolutely necessary, in order to ease the burden on the census subjects and to minimise costs.

80 The population and occupation census will provide a comprehensive overview of population structures, including a detailed regional breakdown. The results of the census will be used for numerous administrative purposes. Population figures, for example, are significant for determining the votes allocated to each *Land* in the *Bundesrat*, for delimiting constituencies for *Bundestag* elections, for determining the size of municipal councils and for many other matters. The Free State of Bavaria counted more than one hundred legal provisions that make reference to population figures. Comparing the residential address data collected in the census with the data of the civil registers will ensure that the population figures produced by the census, and updated continuously on its basis thereafter, will largely be identical to the content of the civil registers.

81 The building-related survey is primarily needed for the purposes of analysing regional and urban development, which is relevant for the entire federal territory, and will serve as a basis for the statutorily required update of housing stock records. The dwelling-related survey aims to provide a detailed regional

breakdown of the volume and structure of the housing stock. This serves to establish essential indicators for evaluating the housing stock regarding, for instance, occupancy levels, or information on vacant apartments and rent to income ratios. At the same time, such data provides the basis for statutorily required updates of housing stock records.

As an umbrella survey, the workplace census covers all economic sectors, except for the agricultural sector. Breaking down the data by sector and region, the census will provide an overview of the number and size of workplaces and companies and their respective legal forms. The results of the census will provide valuable information, most notably in relation to spatial, *Land* and regional planning, as well as in relation to structural, labour and transport policies. 82

[...] 83-86

[Upon receiving the legislative draft adopted by the *Bundestag*], the *Bundesrat* requested, firstly, that § 5(2) of the 1983 Census Act be inserted into the draft law; according to this provision, neither an objection in administrative proceedings nor a rescissory action before the administrative courts (*Anfechtungsklage*) upon receiving the official demand to provide information has suspensive effect. In its reasoning, the *Bundesrat* submitted that the costs of the census would only be justified if complete data were available within the shortest time possible. This objective would be jeopardised if legal remedies were to have suspensive effect. It would be difficult to establish sufficient grounds for issuing orders for immediate execution in each individual case [in accordance with the general rules of administrative procedure]. The *Bundesrat* stated that this uncertainty could be avoided if the law itself prescribed that the suspensive effect of legal remedies did not apply. 87

In addition, the *Bundesrat* submitted that it was necessary to include, in its entirety, all data obtained pursuant to § 2 nos. 1 and 2 of the 1983 Census Act in the envisaged comparison of census data with civil register records. [...] 88

[...] 89-91

II.

The complainants claim a violation of their fundamental rights under Art. 2(1) in conjunction with Art. 1(1), Art. 4(1), Art. 5(1), Art. 13 and Art. 19(4) of the Basic Law as well as a violation of the principle of the rule of law (Art. 20(3) of the Basic Law). [...] 92

93-100 [...]

III.

101 [...]
102 In respect of the constitutional complaints and the questions posed by the Federal Constitutional Court in these proceedings, the Federal Minister of the Interior submitted a statement on behalf of the Federal Government; further statements were submitted by the *Land* Government of Baden-Württemberg, the Government of the Free State of Bavaria, the Government of the Free and Hanseatic City of Hamburg, the *Land* Government of Lower Saxony, the *Land* Government of North Rhine-Westphalia, the *Land* Government of Rhineland-Palatinate and the *Land* Government of Schleswig-Holstein. In addition, statements were submitted by the Federal Data Protection Officer as well as by the Data Protection Officers of the *Länder* Baden-Württemberg, Bavaria, Berlin, Bremen, Hamburg, Hesse and North Rhine-Westphalia and by the Data Protection Commission of the *Land* Rhineland-Palatinate.

103-123 [...]

IV.

124 The complainants [and the other parties to the proceedings as well as experts] were heard in the oral hearing.
125 [...]

B.

126 The constitutional complaints are, for the most part, admissible.
127 In accordance with established case-law, a universally applicable legal provision may be challenged directly by individual citizens only in the event that the relevant legal provision affects them individually, presently and directly with regard to their

No. 6 – Census

fundamental rights (BVerfGE 40, 141 <156>; 43, 291 <385>; 50, 290 <319>; 58, 81 <104>; 59, 1 <17 and 18>; 60, 360 <370>).

I.

[…] 128-130

II.

To the extent that the complainants are individually affected by the 1983 Census Act, they are also directly and presently affected. 131

According to the case-law of the Federal Constitutional Court, a complainant is not directly affected by a challenged law if implementation of the law requires specific measures to be taken by the administrative authorities. This is because the interference with the citizen's legal sphere only occurs through the relevant implementation measure; legal recourse against this interference also allows for a challenge of the constitutionality of the law on which the measure was based (BVerfGE 58, 81 <104>; cf. BVerfGE 59, 1 <17>; 60, 360 <369 and 370>). 132

In order to implement the 1983 Census Act, a demand to provide information would have had to be issued; the legal sphere of the complainants would only have been affected upon receiving such a demand […]. At that point, recourse to the administrative courts against this implementation measure would have become possible. Yet this does not rule out the admissibility of the constitutional complaints in the current proceedings. 133

In certain constellations, the Federal Constitutional Court has, by way of exception, accepted constitutional complaints directly challenging a law as admissible even though specific implementation measures had yet to be taken; this requires that the law itself already compels the persons concerned to presently make decisions that cannot be reversed at a later date, or to make arrangements with consequences that cannot be undone once the implementation measures provided for under the relevant law have been carried out (BVerfGE 60, 360 <372> with further references). Accordingly, the constitutional complaints that directly challenge the 1983 Census Act are admissible by way of exception even though specific implementation measures have yet to be taken. 134

Notably, the Act was supposed to be enforced vis-à-vis all citizens within a very short period of time. […] 135

C.

136 To the extent that they are admissible, the constitutional complaints are in part well-founded.

I.

137 Insofar as § 5(1) of the 1983 Census Act directly imposes an obligation upon the complainants to provide information on specific subject matters enumerated in §§ 2 to 4 of the Act, there is no violation of the complainants' fundamental rights under Arts. 4, 5 and 13 of the Basic Law.

138 1. The obligation to provide truthful information [...] on legal membership (or lack thereof) in a religious community [...] does not violate the complainants' fundamental right to freedom of faith (Art. 4(1) of the Basic Law). Freedom of faith encompasses not only the right to profess one's religious beliefs, but also the right not to disclose one's beliefs, as is specifically recognised in Art. 140 of the Basic Law in conjunction with Art. 136(3) of the Weimar Constitution. The negative freedom not to profess a belief is limited, however, by the exception set forth in Art. 136(3) second sentence of the Weimar Constitution: according to this provision, authorities have the right to inquire about a person's membership in a religious community to the extent that citizens' rights or duties depend on it or that a statutorily mandated statistical survey so requires. Given that the census constitutes a statutorily mandated statistical survey for federal purposes (Art. 73 no. 11 of the Basic Law), the prerequisites of a permissible exception are met in the present case.

139 [...]

140 2. Moreover, the 1983 Census Act does not violate the fundamental right to the inviolability of the home (Art. 13(1) of the Basic Law).

141 Contrary to what some of the complainants submitted, the obligation imposed on them to disclose information on their private housing situation, as provided for in § 3(2) in conjunction with § 5(1) no. 3 of the 1983 Census Act, does not violate this fundamental right. For the purposes of Art. 13 of the Basic Law, the term 'home' refers only to the sphere of private space within one's home (BVerfGE 32, 54 <72>). This fundamental right subjects public authority to a general prohibition barring officials from entering a private home, and from being present there, against the will of the resident. This prohibition covers, for example, the installation or use of listening devices within private homes; however, it does not extend to collecting or requesting information where such information is obtained

No. 6 – Census

without entering or being present in the home. In such cases, Art. 13 of the Basic Law is not applicable. [...]
3. The obligation to provide information on the subject matters listed in §§ 2 to 4 of the 1983 Census Act also does not violate the fundamental right to freedom of expression (Art. 5(1) first sentence of the Basic Law).
[...]
For determining whether a statement qualifies as an opinion and thus falls within the scope of protection guaranteed by that fundamental right, the decisive issue is whether the statement contains elements of taking a position, of condoning or of opining as part of an intellectual discourse; the value, accuracy or reasonableness of the statement in question is irrelevant. [...] By contrast, information provided for statistical purposes such as the collection of data under the 1983 Census Act contains mere factual statements that bear no relation to the formation of opinions.

II.

The applicable standard of review here derives primarily from the general right of personality protected under Art. 2(1) in conjunction with Art. 1(1) of the Basic Law.
1. a) The value and dignity of the person, acting in free self-determination as a member of a free society, are at the centre of the Basic Law. In addition to the constitutional guarantees laid down in specific freedoms, the general right of personality, guaranteed in Art. 2(1) in conjunction with Art. 1(1) of the Basic Law, serves to protect these interests; this protection may gain even more significance in light of modern developments that pose new risks to one's personality (cf. BVerfGE 54, 148 <153> – *Eppler*). The different dimensions of the right of personality that have so far been recognised in the Court's case-law do not exhaustively define the substance of this right. In the *Eppler* decision (BVerfGE 54, 148 <155>), which draws on earlier cases (BVerfGE 21, 1 <6>; 27, 344 <350 and 351> – *Divorce Files*; 32, 373 <379>; 35, 202 <220> – *Lebach*; 44, 353 <372 and 373> – *Addiction Counselling Agency*), it was already implied that, based on the notion of self-determination, the general right of personality confers upon the individual the authority to, in principle, decide themselves whether and to what extent to disclose aspects of their personal life (cf. also BVerfGE 56, 37 <41 *et seq.*> – *Bankruptcy Proceedings*; 63, 131 <142 and 143> – *Right of Reply*).
Given the present and future realities of automatic data processing, this authority conferred upon the individual merits special protection. Most notably, risks arise because decision-making processes that in the past required records and files to be compiled manually can now rely on automatic data processing. As a result, specific information concerning the personal or material circumstances of an identified or

identifiable individual (i.e. personal data, cf. § 2(1) of the Federal Data Protection Act) can be stored indefinitely, from a technical perspective, and retrieved at any time within seconds, without distance being an issue. In addition, the data in question can be compared with data collected from other sources, especially by creating integrated information systems, and can be compiled into partial or practically complete personality profiles, leaving the person concerned without sufficient control over the accuracy or use of the data stored on them. This has expanded possibilities of gaining and influencing information to unprecedented levels, so that even the mere psychological pressure created by public perception may potentially impact individual behaviour.

148 Yet it is a prerequisite for individual self-determination – especially in light of modern information technology – that the individual be afforded the freedom to decide whether to take or refrain from certain actions, including the possibility to actually conduct themselves in accordance with this decision. If individuals cannot, with sufficient certainty, determine what kind of personal information is known to certain parts of their social environment, and if it is difficult to ascertain what kind of information potential communication partners are privy to, this could greatly impede their freedom to make self-determined plans or decisions. A societal order, and its underlying legal order, would not be compatible with the right to informational self-determination if citizens were no longer able to tell who knows what kind of personal information about them, at what time and on which occasion. Individuals who worry that non-conformist behaviour could be recorded at any time and that such information could permanently be stored, used or shared will try not to draw attention to themselves by not engaging in such behaviour. If individuals anticipate that participation in an assembly or a citizens' initiative, for instance, was going to be recorded by the authorities and could thus expose them to certain risks, they might decide to forgo the exercise of their respective fundamental rights (Arts. 8 and 9 of the Basic Law). Not only would this impair opportunities of personal development for the individual, it would also affect the common good because self-determination is a fundamental prerequisite for the functioning of a free and democratic society which relies on the agency and participation of its citizens.

149 In the context of modern data processing, the free development of one's personality therefore requires that the individual be protected against the unlimited collection, storage, use and sharing of their personal data. Consequently, the fundamental right of Art. 2(1) in conjunction with Art. 1(1) of the Basic Law encompasses such protection. In this regard, the fundamental right confers upon the individual the authority to, in principle, decide themselves on the disclosure and use of their personal data.

No. 6 – Census

b) The right to 'informational self-determination' is not, however, guaranteed without limitation. It does not afford the individual absolute or unlimited control over 'their' personal data; rather, the individual develops their personality within the social community, and is dependent on communication with others. Any information, including personal data, mirrors social reality and thus cannot be attributed exclusively to the person concerned. As repeatedly emphasised in the Court's case-law, the Basic Law resolves the tension between the individual and the community by endorsing the notion that the individual is connected to and bound by the community (BVerfGE 4, 7 <15>; 8, 274 <329>; 27, 1 <7> – *Microcensus*; 27, 344 <351 and 352> – *Divorce Files*; 33, 303 <334>; 50, 290 <353>; 56, 37 <49> – *Bankruptcy Proceedings*). The individual must therefore accept that the right to informational self-determination is, in principle, subject to restrictions serving overriding public interests. 150

Pursuant to Art. 2(1) of the Basic Law [...] such restrictions require a (constitutional) statutory basis specifying the prerequisites and scope of the restrictions in a manner that is clear and recognisable to citizens in accordance with the principle of legal clarity deriving from the rule of law (BVerfGE 45, 400 <420> with further references). Furthermore, when enacting restrictions, the legislator must observe the principle of proportionality. This principle, which enjoys constitutional status, derives from the essence of fundamental rights; it is a manifestation of the general claim to freedom that citizens have vis-à-vis the state; public authority may only restrict such freedom to the extent that is absolutely necessary for protecting public interests. In view of the risks arising from the use of automatic data processing outlined above, it is incumbent upon the legislator to provide for organisational and procedural safeguards that counter the risk of violating the right of personality (cf. BVerfGE 53, 30 <65>; 63, 131 <143> – *Right of Reply*). 151

2. In the present constitutional complaint proceedings, there is no need to discuss the right to informational self-determination in an exhaustive manner. The Court is only called upon to decide on the scope of this right in relation to interferences that arise when the state demands that citizens disclose personal data. In this context, it is not sufficient to simply assess what kind of information is being demanded. The decisive factor is how the data may be used, and for what purposes. On the one hand, this depends on the purposes for which the data is collected; on the other hand, the unique possibilities created by information technologies with regard to the processing and linking of data must be taken into account. Therefore, data that by itself appears insignificant may gain new relevance; in the context of automatic data processing, it can therefore no longer be assumed that any data is insignificant. 152

Qualifying data as sensitive is not solely dependent on whether the relevant data concerns intimate matters. Rather, knowledge of the relevant context in which 153 the data will be used is necessary to determine its significance for the right of personality: whether a restriction of the right to informational self-determination is permissible can only be assessed once it is clear for what purposes the relevant information has been demanded and what possibilities exist with regard to using and linking the data obtained. In this regard, a distinction must be made between personal data that is collected and used in the form of individualised information that has not been rendered anonymous (see a below), and personal data that is intended for statistical purposes (see b below).

154 a) It is well-established that the mandatory collection of personal data is only permissible within certain limits; this applies, most notably, if the data is collected for purposes pertaining to the exercise of public functions (for instance concerning taxes or social benefits). In this regard, the law has already put in place various mechanisms for the protection of the persons concerned [...].

155 Imposing an obligation to provide personal data requires that the legislator specify precisely, for each subject matter, the purposes for which the data may be used; furthermore, the information obtained must be suitable and necessary for achieving these purposes. The gathering and retention of data that has not been rendered anonymous for undefined or yet to be defined purposes would not be compatible with these principles. In addition, it is imperative that data collected by public bodies for the purpose of exercising their functions be limited to what is necessary for achieving the objective pursued.

156 Data may only be used for statutory purposes. Not least in light of risks arising from automatic data processing, it is necessary to provide protection against use of the data for other purposes, by way of statutory prohibitions regarding data sharing and further use, including protection against use of the data in the context of inter-agency administrative assistance (*Amtshilfe*). Other essential procedural safeguards include notification, information and deletion requirements.

157 Due to the lack of transparency regarding data storage and use from a citizen's perspective in the context of automatic data processing, it is particularly important to involve independent data protection officers in order to ensure effective protection of the right to informational self-determination; this also serves to ensure preventive legal protection by means of timely precautions.

158 b) With regard to the collection and processing of data for statistical purposes, constitutional review must not disregard the specific nature of statistics.

159 aa) Statistics play a pivotal role in ensuring that public policy remains committed to the principles and rationale of the Basic Law. The availability of comprehensive, continuous and regularly updated information on economic, ecological and social factors is a prerequisite for pursuing economic and social development as a lasting [state] responsibility, as opposed to surrendering to the perceived inevitabilities

of fate and happenstance. It is only through knowledge of the relevant data and through the possibility of using the information obtained from it – and the advantages automatic data processing offers – for statistical purposes that a basis for action is created which is indispensable for public policy guided by the principle of the social state (cf. BVerfGE 27, 1 <9> – *Microcensus*).

The collection of data for statistical purposes cannot be subject to a strict and specific purpose limitation. It is inherent in the nature of statistics that data processed for statistical purposes is intended to be used for a variety of tasks that cannot necessarily be determined in advance; therefore, it is necessary to retain certain data. The requirement that the purposes of data collection and use be precisely defined, as well as the strict prohibition on retaining personal data, are both applicable to data collection for non-statistical purposes; however, they do not apply to the collection of census data which, by producing reliable data on population and social demographics, serves to establish a verified data pool as the basis for further statistical analysis and political planning processes. The population census must necessarily allow multi-purpose data collection and multi-purpose data use, i.e. the gathering and storage of data for further retention, so as to not leave the state utterly unprepared to face new developments within an industrial society. Similarly, in relation to statistical data, statutory prohibitions on data sharing and other uses would undermine the purpose of statistics. 160

bb) Accordingly, it is inherent in the nature of statistics that the numerous possibilities of how such data can be used and linked are not ascertainable in advance. Therefore, the collection and processing of information within such information systems must be subject to certain limitations. Clearly defined conditions for the processing of data must be established in order to ensure that the individual is not reduced to a mere information object, given the realities of automatic collection and processing of their personal data. [...] It is precisely because data collected during population censuses is not from the outset restricted by purpose-related limitations that censuses tend to entail a risk, as already emphasised in the *Microcensus* decision (BVerfGE 27, 1 <6>), of registering and cataloguing the individual in a manner that violates personality rights. Therefore, data collection and processing for statistical purposes must be subject to specific requirements to protect the right of personality on the part of citizens obliged to provide information. 161

Notwithstanding the fact that data collection and processing for statistical purposes inherently have multiple functions, they may only be employed as a means to facilitate the exercise of public functions. Even then, not any type of information may be requested. Also, when imposing obligations to provide specific information needed for statistical purposes, it is incumbent upon the legislator to assess, in particular, whether this could create a risk of social stigmatisation for the persons 162 concerned (e.g. by branding people as drug addicts, convicts, mentally ill, social misfits), and whether the statistical objective could just as well be achieved by means of collecting anonymous data. [...]

163 Furthermore, in order to ensure that the right to informational self-determination is respected, specific safeguards must be put in place concerning the implementation and organisation of data collection and processing. This is due to the fact that at the stage of collection – and in part also during storage – such data can still be attributed to individual persons. It is also necessary to impose statutory deletion requirements with regard to data collected as auxiliary information (identification markers) such as name, address, identification number and census list number that would easily allow for anonymisation to be reversed (cf. also § 11(7) first sentence of the Federal Statistics Act). In respect of statistical surveys, an effective regime on shielding data against external access is of particular importance. As long as the relevant data is still attributed or attributable to a person, it is indispensable for the protection of the right to informational self-determination that individual data collected for statistical purposes be treated as strictly confidential (principle of statistical confidentiality), even at the stage of data collection; the same holds true for the requirement that data be rendered (effectively) anonymous as soon as possible and that safeguards against reversing anonymisation be put in place.

164 Statutory requirements that data be rendered anonymous and, as long as the information is still attributable to individuals, treated confidentially derive from the right to informational self-determination and must be laid down in the law; only once data has been shielded in this manner may state organs access the information that is necessary for carrying out public planning functions. An obligation to provide the requested information may be imposed on citizens only where these requirements are met. If personal data collected for statistical purposes could be shared against the will or without the knowledge of the affected person, this would restrict the constitutionally protected right to informational self-determination in an impermissible manner; it would also jeopardise the official statistics provided for in Art. 73 no. 11 of the Basic Law, which that provision recognises as an interest meriting protection. It is imperative for the proper functioning of official statistics to ensure a high level of accuracy and veracity. This objective will only be achieved if citizens obliged to provide information can trust that their personal data collected for statistical purposes will be sufficiently shielded; otherwise, citizens might not be inclined to provide truthful information [...]. If state practice did not endeavour to build the necessary public trust by ensuring transparency in data processing procedures and strict data protection regimes, distrust among the general public would eventually lead to a decline in the willingness to cooperate. [...] It follows that the state can only carry out its policy planning function properly if statistical

data is sufficiently shielded; accordingly, the principle that the relevant data be treated confidentially and rendered anonymous as soon as possible is integral not only to protecting the right to informational self-determination afforded individuals under the Basic Law but also to the functioning of statistics as such.

cc) If the requirements set out above are met in an effective manner, then based on the current state of knowledge and experience, the collection of data for strictly statistical purposes is not objectionable under constitutional law. It is not ascertainable that the citizens' right of personality would be impaired if statistics offices shared data with state organs or other public bodies [...] after the relevant data has been rendered anonymous or processed for statistical analysis.

Yet particular problems arise if personal data is transferred (data sharing) before such data has been either rendered anonymous or processed for statistical analysis. The collection of data for statistical purposes includes individualised information on individual citizens that is not specifically required for the relevant statistics but merely serves as an auxiliary means to facilitate the data collection process – and citizens must be able to trust that this data will indeed only be used in that auxiliary capacity. [...] Where data collected for statistical purposes is shared with other authorities for the purposes of carrying out administrative functions, and such transfer occurs before the data has been rendered anonymous or processed for statistical analysis, this may [...] unlawfully interfere with the right to informational self-determination (cf. also C IV 1 below).

III.

For the most part, the data collection framework provided under the Census Act satisfies the constitutional requirements set out above. [...] The provisions are compatible with the general right of personality under Art. 2(1) in conjunction with Art. 1(1) of the Basic Law, provided that the legislator enacts additional organisational and procedural rules for the protection of fundamental rights in order to remedy the existing deficits; this is necessary to ensure that the constitutional requirements applicable to the type of full census envisaged under the 1983 Census Act are adhered to.

1. The 1983 Census Act imposes an obligation [...] on the complainants [...] to provide information regarding [specific] census elements [...] and makes non-compliance punishable by fine. The Census Act thus interferes with the general right of personality guaranteed under Art. 2(1) in conjunction with Art. 1(1) of the Basic Law. The data to be collected in the census is intended to be used for future tasks that are not foreseeable at the time the census takes place. The resulting interference [with informational self-determination] must be tolerated by the census

subjects. The interference serves an overriding public interest and satisfies the requirements of legal clarity and proportionality.

169 a) The data collection framework laid down in the 1983 Census Act does not amount to the registration or cataloguing of full or partial personality profiles in a manner that is incompatible with human dignity.

170 According to the explanatory memorandum attached to the Federal Government's draft law, the envisaged population, housing, occupation and workplace census [...] is intended to provide up-to-date information on the population as well as on its regional, demographic and social breakdown and on economic activity; in consequence, the census is ultimately designed to produce de-personalised data.

171 While the envisaged data collection may provide insights into certain aspects of citizens' lives, such as their housing situation, the collected data cannot be used to compile personality profiles. A different assessment would only be merited if it were possible to link the collected data to (in part rather sensitive) data records maintained by other administrative authorities, or if it were possible to establish such a data network by way of introducing a uniform system of personal identifiers or some other kind of structural markers; even where data collected for statistical purposes is rendered anonymous, it is still not permissible to carry out a comprehensive registration and cataloguing of individuals' personality by means of compiling personality profiles of the citizens concerned on the basis of their biographical and personal data (BVerfGE 27, 1 <6> – *Microcensus*). [...]

172 The compilation of data collected for the 1983 Census and its comparison with information that is already available to the statistical offices does not enable the creation of partial personality profiles in a manner that is incompatible with human dignity. [...]

173 b) Moreover, the data collection framework of the 1983 Census Act satisfies the requirement of legal clarity.

174 A law is sufficiently specific if its purpose is ascertainable from the text of the law read together with the relevant legislative materials (BVerfGE 27, 1 <8> – *Microcensus*); in this respect, it is sufficient if the purpose of the law can be discerned from the relationship between the legal text and the factual context of its subject matter (cf. BVerfGE 62, 169 <183 and 184>). The descriptions contained in the 1983 Census Act regarding the census elements on which data is to be collected satisfy these requirements; it is possible for citizens to identify the basic type of information on social structure they will be required to answer. The main purposes of the Act can be derived with sufficient certainty from the nature of the envisaged data collection – a census of population, occupation, housing and workplaces – as well as from the data collection framework and the relevant legislative materials. [...]

No. 6 – Census

c) To the extent that the data collection framework laid down in the 1983 Census Act is subject to review in the current proceedings, it satisfies the principle of proportionality. Under the principle of proportionality, a measure must be suitable and necessary for the purpose pursued; the intensity of the interference which it entails may not be disproportionate to the importance of the matter and the burden imposed on the individual (cf. BVerfGE 27, 344 <352 and 353> – *Divorce Files*; established case-law). 175

The 1983 Census Act aims to provide the state with the information required for future planning and action. By ensuring that state action can be properly planned (cf. BVerfGE 27, 1 <7> – *Microcensus*), the 1983 Census Act pursues a reasonable purpose that serves the exercise of legitimate state functions. 176

By choosing to conduct the population census in the form of a full census (complete data collection), and with the envisaged catalogue of survey questions [...], the Federal Republic of Germany fulfils its obligation arising from the Directive of the Council of the European Communities of 22 November 1973 on the synchronisation of general population censuses – 73/403/EEC [...]. The data collection method and framework are suitable and necessary to achieve the purpose pursued; moreover, they do not impose unreasonable burdens on the census subjects. 177

aa) At present, it is not objectionable that the legislator assumed that neither the collection of data by way of a sample survey conducted on a strictly voluntary basis nor a combination of a full survey and a sample survey could adequately substitute a population census in the form of a full census. These alternatives to full census surveys still entail too many sources of error. [...] 178

This assessment is based on the current state of knowledge and experience. [...] The methods used in official statistics and social sciences are constantly evolving. The legislator must take account of these developments. [...] When circumstances change, the legislator may be required to amend provisions that were previously considered constitutional (cf. BVerfGE 56, 54 <78 and 79> with further references). Thus, when prescribing the collection of statistical data, the legislator must assess, based on available information, whether a full census can still be considered proportionate despite possible advances in the methods used in statistics and social sciences. 179

[...] 180-184

bb) Retrieving data from existing administrative records is also not a viable alternative to the envisaged full census. Using data contained in different registers and records would require technical, organisational and legal measures to allow the compiling of data relating to specific persons or institutions. [...] In light of this, linking existing data would also not constitute a less restrictive means. 185

186 cc) Similarly, using data collection methods that are commonly employed for electoral and voting purposes, i.e. methods that are modelled on postal voting procedures and thus provide a higher level of anonymity, do not generally provide an alternative to the envisaged census.

187-189 [...]

190 dd) The census elements [...] are also necessary in their entirety in order to achieve the purpose pursued. The census is intended to provide, in a detailed and coordinated manner, a comprehensive statistical assessment of society and the economy. To this end, it is necessary to obtain and link data from each census segment, i.e. the population census and the occupation census as well as the building, dwelling and workplace censuses. [...]

191 2. At the same time, in order to ensure protection of the right to informational self-determination, it is imperative that additional procedural safeguards be put in place concerning the implementation and organisation of the data collection. The data collection envisaged under the 1983 Census Act only in part satisfies the constitutional requirements (see C II 2 bb above). It is true that the Census Act sets out provisions on the requirement that data collected for statistical purposes be treated confidentially, protecting the fundamental right to informational self-determination. Moreover, the Act requires that any data used to identify census subjects be deleted as soon as it is no longer needed for federal statistical purposes. [...] These provisions do not suffice, however, to ensure that the data collection and processing in the envisaged census is carried out in line with constitutional requirements. Rather, it is incumbent upon the legislator to amend the existing framework by putting in place necessary safeguards for the protection of the right to informational self-determination. While the legislator is not required to determine all the details itself, it must nevertheless ensure that the necessary measures are taken. In particular, the following measures are required to ensure fundamental rights protection:

192 a) Census subjects must be notified and informed of their rights and duties. As the law stands, they can object to having their data collected jointly with other persons living in the same household; if they prefer, they may request that their data be collected on a separate survey sheet [...]. In addition, the census subjects have the right [...] to give a sealed envelope containing the completed survey sheet to the census officials, submit it to a census office, or send it in by post. In case of mass surveys like the envisaged census, however, it is generally difficult for citizens to know their rights [...]. Therefore, it is incumbent upon the legislator to ensure that citizens are informed about their rights in writing. It must also be clearly indicated that certain types of information (telephone numbers, for instance) are merely collected on a voluntary basis.

No. 6 – Census

b) Information used to identify census subjects (especially name, address, identification number and census list number) must be deleted as soon as possible; prior to deletion, this data must be treated confidentially and kept separate from the rest of the data. The application of these rules [...], which serve to protect fundamental rights, may not be left entirely to the discretion of the administrative authorities. It must also be ensured that the responsible data protection officer exercise effective oversight. [...]

c) Data subjects interact with census officials, who may obtain knowledge of the information provided in the census documents if the survey sheet is not sealed in an envelope. Therefore, measures must be taken to prevent conflicts of interest to the greatest possible extent. [...] Data protection officers have rightly [...] pointed out that officials should not be assigned census duties when a conflict of interest cannot be ruled out. As an additional measure of protection, the law must state that census officials [...] may not be deployed in the immediate proximity of their homes so as not to affect residents' willingness to cooperate in the relevant neighbourhoods.

d) Finally, the legislator must ensure that the contents of the questionnaire used in the census actually comply with the statutory framework. [...]

IV.

1. As set out above (see C II 2 cc), data collected for statistical purposes that has not yet been rendered anonymous and thus still qualifies as personal data may only be shared if there is a statutory basis expressly authorising such data sharing. Furthermore, the sharing of such data is only permissible for the purposes of statistical processing by the receiving administrative authority and on condition that necessary safeguards for protecting the right of personality have been put in place. In this respect, it must be effectively ensured that the receiving authority observes the requirements that data collected for statistical purposes be treated confidentially and rendered anonymous as soon as possible; the level of protection required of the receiving authority must be equal to the level of protection required of the statistical offices of the Federation and the *Länder*. By contrast, it would constitute an unjustifiable interference with the right to informational self-determination if personal data collected for statistical purposes in accordance with the relevant statutory basis were to be shared, without being rendered anonymous, for purposes pertaining to the exercise of administrative functions (use of data for unauthorised purposes). [...]

A legal framework [...] designed to simultaneously achieve both statistical and other purposes is in any case unsuitable and unconstitutional where it seeks to combine what is generally incompatible. Where a census law combines statistical purposes with purposes of exercising administrative functions, this may undermine its legal clarity and comprehensibility; it also renders the relevant law disproportionate. If data is not collected exclusively for statistical purposes, it is imperative that the sharing and use of such data be subject to strict and specific purpose limitations (see C II 2 a above). In addition, the principle of legal clarity is of particular importance. The applicable legal provisions must make it clear to citizens that their data will not be used exclusively for statistical purposes; that their data will be used for other specific purposes related to the exercise of administrative functions for which use of their data is necessary; that use of their data will remain limited to the specified purposes; and that the law affords them protection against self-incrimination in this context.

198   2. The envisaged combination of collecting census data for statistical purposes and for comparing it with civil register data [...] does not meet these constitutional requirements.

199-200   a) [...]

201   b) § 9(1) of the 1983 Census Act violates the right to informational self-determination guaranteed under Art. 2(1) in conjunction with Art. 1(1) of the Basic Law, given that the provision seeks to combine what is generally incompatible; the provision is therefore unsuitable to the purpose pursued and lacks legal clarity regarding its content so that, from the perspective of citizens, its implications are not fully comprehensible.

202   § 9(1) first sentence of the 1983 Census Act authorises municipalities to compare the data provided in the census documents with the data contained in their civil register records and to then use the census data to correct the latter. Selected personal data collected in the 1983 Census may thus not only be used for statistical purposes but also for purposes related to the exercise of administrative functions, which means that no specific purpose limitations apply. [...] Due to the fact that the registration offices are in turn obliged [...] to share their data with other authorities, [...] it is not foreseeable for which specific purposes and by which public authorities the data would be used. [...]

203   The legislator was aware of the degree to which combining the two different purposes could significantly jeopardise the proper functioning of official statistics, which is essential for statistical data collection [...]; consequently, the legislator laid down an express prohibition in § 9(1) second sentence of the 1983 Census Act against using individual information collected for statistical purposes as the basis for state measures directed against the relevant census subject. Yet this prohibition against using data to the detriment of census subjects falls short. It cannot compensate the deficits in the proper functioning of official statistics and in the protection

of the persons concerned that result from the combination of statistical purposes and purposes of exercising administrative functions. [...]

3. § 9(2) of the 1983 Census Act also violates Art. 2(1) in conjunction with Art. 1(1) of the Basic Law. This provision authorises the transfer of certain personal data to the competent highest administrative authorities at the level of the Federation and the *Länder*, as well as to other public bodies designated by such authorities, to the extent that the receiving body requires the relevant data for the lawful exercise of its respective official functions. The data sharing authorised under the Census Act exceeds the scope of [existing statistics laws], as it allows all data to be shared, excluding only names [...] and information on membership in religious communities (or lack thereof); in consequence, there is little difficulty in attributing the relevant data to the individual concerned. In this respect, the Census Act does not specify whether the sharing of data is only allowed for statistical purposes or also permissible for exercising administrative functions. [...] In any case, § 9(2) of the 1983 Census Act already violates the right to informational self-determination of citizens because it is not clearly ascertainable whether the provision even authorises the data sharing for administrative purposes, nor does the law set out clearly defined purposes for the use and sharing of the collected data, despite the fact that this would be required under constitutional law as long as the relevant data has not been rendered anonymous. [...]

4. Similarly, § 9(3) of the 1983 Census Act violates Art. 2(1) in conjunction with Art. 1(1) of the Basic Law.

a) This provision provides that personal data (excluding names) collected with the help of municipalities may be shared for certain administrative purposes at the municipal level. The provision permits the sharing of specific (personal) data that is required [...] for purposes relating to regional planning, surveying, municipal planning and environmental protection. It is not sufficiently clear, however, for what specific purposes data may be shared; it is unclear, in particular, whether these purposes are limited to statistics or also extend to the exercise of administrative functions. [...] Consequently, § 9(2) of the 1983 Census Act already violates the general right of personality guaranteed under Art. 2(1) in conjunction with Art. 1(1) of the Basic Law due to the fact that the provision clarifies neither whether personal data that is shared may also be used for the purposes of exercising administrative functions nor what specific and clearly defined purposes would be concerned. [...]

b) [...]

[...]

5. In contrast, § 9(4) of the 1983 Census Act does not violate the general right of personality. This provision states that certain personal data may, for scientific purposes, be shared with public officials or persons of equivalent status. The data

shared for scientific purposes must be limited to what is necessary; under no circumstances may the data include names or addresses. The provision thus recognises that in most fields of research it is not necessary to directly link the relevant data to a specific person, as scientists are generally not interested in the individual person [...].

V.

210-214 [...]

VI.

215   1. Given that § 9(1) to (3) of the 1983 Census Act is not compatible with the Basic Law and violates the complainants' fundamental rights under Art. 2(1) in conjunction with Art. 1(1) of the Basic Law, these provisions are declared void pursuant to § 95(3) first sentence of the Federal Constitutional Court Act. Exceptional grounds on the basis of which it would be permissible to forgo declaring the relevant provisions void are not ascertainable in the current proceedings.

216-217   2. [...]

Justices: Benda, Simon, Hesse, Katzenstein, Niemeyer, Heußner, Niedermaier, Henschel

No. 7

BVerfGE 35, 202 – Lebach

HEADNOTES

to the Judgment of the First Senate of 5 June 1973
1 BvR 536/72

1. A radio or television broadcasting corporation may, in principle, invoke the protection of Article 5(1) of the Basic Law for every broadcast. Freedom of broadcasting covers both the selection of the material presented and the choice of the way in which it is presented, including the form chosen for the programme.
Only in cases where freedom of broadcasting conflicts with other legal interests do the interest pursued with the specific programme, the design of the programme and its achieved or foreseeable effect become relevant.
2. §§ 22 and 23 of the Art Copyright Act provide enough scope for a balancing of interests to sufficiently take into account the permeating effect of freedom of broadcasting under Article 5(1) first sentence of the Basic Law on all other areas of law on the one hand, and the protection of one's personality under Article 2(1) in conjunction with Article 1(1) of the Basic Law on the other hand.
In such a balancing, neither of the two constitutional values can generally claim to take precedence. Rather, the intensity of the interference with the personal domain must be balanced against the interest of the public in obtaining information in the individual case.
3. In respect of current events coverage of serious crimes, the interest of the public in obtaining information generally takes precedence over the protection of the offender's personality interests. Yet both life's inviolable innermost domain and the principle of proportionality must be respected; thus, it is not always permissible to name, portray or otherwise identify the offender.
However, the constitutional protection of one's personality does not allow television to report on the offender and their private sphere indefinitely, beyond news coverage, for example in the form of a docudrama.

Later coverage is in any case not permissible if it might have a significantly new or an added adverse effect on the offender, especially if it might jeopardise their social reintegration. Social reintegration will frequently be jeopardised where a TV programme about the crime identifying the offender is broadcast shortly before or after the offender's release from prison.

FEDERAL CONSTITUTIONAL COURT
- 1 BvR 536/72 -

IN THE NAME OF THE PEOPLE

In the proceedings
on the constitutional complaint of

Mr W…,

authorised representative: …

against a) the Judgment of the Koblenz Higher Regional Court of 5 October 1972 - 9 U 552/72 -

b) the Judgment of the Mainz Regional Court of 8 June 1972 - 1 O 128/72 -

the Federal Constitutional Court – First Senate –

with the participation of Justices

President Benda,
Ritterspach,
Haager,
Rupp-v. Brünneck,
Böhmer,
Faller,
Brox,
Simon

held on the basis of the oral hearing of 2 and 3 May 1973:

JUDGMENT

1. The Judgments of the Mainz Regional Court of 8 June 1972 - 1 O 128/72 - and the Koblenz Higher Regional Court of 5 October 1972 - 9 U 552/72 - violate the complainant's fundamental rights under Article 2(1) in conjunction with Article 1(1) of the Basic Law. They are reversed.

No. 7 – Lebach

2. By way of preliminary injunction and on pain of a fine of an unlimited amount to be determined in case of non-compliance, the ZDF broadcasting corporation is barred from broadcasting the docudrama *Der Soldatenmord von Lebach* ("The murder of soldiers in Lebach"), insofar as the applicant and complainant is named or portrayed therein, before a final judgment has been rendered with regard to the action brought in the principal proceedings.
[…]
3. […]

REASONS:

A.

The constitutional complaint is directed against the civil courts' rejection of the complainant's application for a preliminary injunction to bar the ZDF broadcasting corporation from broadcasting its own docudrama production insofar as the complainant is named or portrayed therein.

I.

The complainant, born in 1945, was involved in a serious crime, known as the murder of soldiers in Lebach. This crime was dealt with in proceedings before the competent court. The two main offenders were friends with each other and with the complainant; the relationships were partly of a homosexual nature. The three young men sought to establish a community outside of society, which they rejected. They planned to raid an ammunition depot of the *Bundeswehr* (German Federal Armed Forces) in order to get hold of weapons, with the help of which they wanted to commit other crimes in order to realise their dream of life on an ocean-going yacht in the South Seas. In January 1969, the two main offenders carried out the attack: they killed four soldiers of the guard team who were asleep, seriously injured another soldier and stole weapons and ammunition. Later, they tried to extort money from a financial broker by threatening similar acts. During the planning stages, the complainant had repeatedly stated that he was incapable of carrying out the crime; therefore, he had not participated in the attack.

On 7 August 1970, the competent court sentenced the two main offenders to life imprisonment and the complainant to a total of six years' imprisonment on a charge of accessory [to murder]. […]

4 By now, the complainant has served almost two-thirds of his sentence; execution of the remainder of the prison sentence will likely be suspended on probation in July of this year in accordance with § 26(1) of the Criminal Code. The complainant intends to return to his hometown.

II.

5 1. The violent crime of Lebach attracted an unusual amount of attention from the German public, in part because the search for the perpetrators lasted several months. The crime, the extensive investigations and the criminal proceedings were widely covered in the press, on the radio and on television.

6 Even before the judgment in the criminal proceedings became final, the head of the ZDF docudrama department, Jürgen Neven duMont, and the chief criminal investigator of the Federal Criminal Police Office (*Bundeskriminalamt*), Karl Schütz, in collaboration with Rainer Söhnlein, published a book about the case.

7 Furthermore, Neven duMont and Söhnlein wrote the script for a TV docudrama *Der Soldatenmord von Lebach*, directed by Söhnlein and completed in the spring of 1972. According to the – undisputed – facts ascertained by the Higher Regional Court, the docudrama is to be featured on ZDF presumably on a Friday night as a two-part programme, with a break for news headlines, running to a total of 2 hours and 40 minutes. The first part of the docudrama portrays the relationships within the group of friends and shows how the attack was planned and carried out. The second part primarily deals with the search for and identification of the perpetrators and with the attempted blackmail. Photographs of both the complainant and the main offenders are shown at the beginning of the docudrama; the complainant is played by an actor thereafter. His name is mentioned repeatedly throughout the docudrama.

8 2. The complainant argues that the planned broadcast of the docudrama constitutes an unlawful violation of his right of personality, his right to his own name and his right to his own image. In the challenged decisions, the Regional Court and the Higher Regional Court rejected his application for a preliminary injunction to bar the ZDF from broadcasting the docudrama insofar as he is named or portrayed therein. Both judgments are based on §§ 22 and 23 of the Art Copyright Act of 9 January 1907.

No. 7 – Lebach

[…] 9-12

III.

1. With his constitutional complaint, the complainant claims that the challenged decisions violate his fundamental rights under Art. 1(1) and Art. 2(1) of the Basic Law. […] 13
[…] 14
2. […] 15-17
3. […] 18
4. […] 19-23
5. […] 24-29

IV.

1. The Federal Constitutional Court issued a preliminary injunction on 13 March 1973 barring the ZDF from broadcasting the docudrama insofar as the complainant is named or portrayed therein until a decision on the constitutional complaint is rendered. 30
2. The Federal Constitutional Court has examined the docudrama. […] 31
[…] 32-40

B.

The constitutional complaint is well-founded. 41

I.

The constitutional complaint is directed against court decisions rendered in civil proceedings that are based on the application of private law provisions. In such cases, it neither falls to the Federal Constitutional Court to review the interpretation and application of the relevant legal provisions as such, nor is it for the Court to review the related determination and assessment of the facts. However, it is subject to review by the Federal Constitutional Court whether the permeating effect (*Ausstrahlungswirkung*) on private law of decisions on constitutional values is sufficiently reflected in the decisions of the ordinary courts. The Federal Constitutional Court must therefore review whether the challenged decisions are based on a fundamentally incorrect understanding of the scope and impact of one of the fundamental rights asserted here, or whether the outcome of the decision in itself 42 violates such a fundamental right (cf. BVerfGE 7, 198 <206 and 207>; 21, 209 <216>; 30, 173 <187 and 188>; 32, 311 <316>). [...]

II.

43 In the case at hand, the Higher Regional Court correctly recognised that several fundamental rights affect the application of ordinary law, and that they in fact pull in opposite directions: The protection of one's personality guaranteed by Art. 2(1) in conjunction with Art. 1(1) of the Basic Law conflicts with freedom of reporting by the broadcast media under Art. 5(1) second sentence of the Basic Law.

44 1. A TV programme of the type at issue here, i.e. a programme that deals with the planning, carrying out and prosecution of a criminal act and depicts, portrays and names the offender, necessarily affects the scope of the offender's fundamental rights guaranteed by Art. 2(1) in conjunction with Art. 1(1) of the Basic Law. The right to the free development of one's personality and human dignity guarantee everyone an autonomous domain of private life in which they can develop and protect their individuality. This includes the right "to be left alone", "to be oneself" within this domain of one's private life [...], and to be free from intrusion or inspection by others (cf. BVerfGE 27, 1 <6> – *Microcensus*; 33, 367 <376>; 34, 238 <245 et seq.> – *Secret Tape Recordings*). It also encompasses the right to one's own image and the right to one's own speech (cf. BVerfGE 34, 238 – *Secret Tape Recordings*), and especially the right to determine the portrayal of one's person. In principle, every person has the right to determine for themselves whether and to what extent others may portray their biography or certain incidents from their life in public.

45 According to the Federal Constitutional Court's established case-law, however, not the entire domain of private life enjoys the absolute protection afforded by the above-mentioned fundamental rights (cf. BVerfGE 6, 389 <433>; 27, 1 <7> – *Microcensus*; 27, 344 <351> – *Divorce Files*; 32, 373 <379>; 33, 367 <376 and 377>; 34, 238 <245> – *Secret Tape Recordings*). Where an individual communicates with others as a member of the community or influences them by way of being or behaviour and thereby affects the personal sphere of others or interests of the common good, the exclusive right to decide on one's private domain may be subject to limitations as long as the inviolable innermost domain is not affected. Any such bearing on social relations – provided it is sufficiently strong – may justify measures taken by public authorities to protect interests of the general public, for example, the publishing of images of suspects for the purpose of law enforcement (§ 24 of the Art Copyright Act). However, neither the state's interest in investigating crimes nor any other public interest *per se* justifies an intrusion into

the personal domain (cf. BVerfGE 32, 373 <381>; 34, 238 <248> – *Secret Tape Recordings*). Rather, the high standing of the right to the free development of and to respect for one's personality that follows from its close connection to human dignity, the Constitution's highest value, mandates that the protection requirement under Art. 2(1) in conjunction with Art. 1(1) of the Basic Law be used as an ongoing corrective to the interferences that seem necessary to give effect to such interests. Accordingly, the affected rights and interests must be balanced in each case to ascertain whether the public interest pursued should take precedence in general and under the particular circumstances, whether the intended interference with the private sphere is required in view of its nature and scope, and whether the interference is appropriate in light of the significance of the matter (cf. BVerfGE 27, 344 <353 and 354> – *Divorce Files*; 32, 373 <381>; 34, 238 <248> – *Secret Tape Recordings*).

These principles, developed in the case-law on measures by public authority, must also be observed accordingly in judicial decisions on conflicting interests under private law. Yet this does not preclude taking into account the special status of radio and television given their organisation under public law and their public function. 46

2. In this respect, […] it is a significant factor here that the disputed broadcast serves a function the free exercise of which is itself directly protected in the Constitution by a fundamental right. Just like freedom of the press, freedom of expression and freedom of information, freedom of reporting by the broadcast media enshrined in Art. 5(1) second sentence of the Basic Law (freedom of broadcasting) is a constitutive element of the free democratic basic order (cf. BVerfGE 7, 198 <208>; 10, 118 <121>; 12, 205 <259 *et seq.*>; 20, 56 <97 and 98>; 20, 162 <174 *et seq.*>; 27, 71 <81 and 82>). 47

Like the press, radio and television are indispensable means of mass communication. They have a decisive impact both on the link between the people and state organs and on the scrutiny of such state organs, as well as on the integration of the community in all areas of life. They provide individuals with the necessary comprehensive information on current affairs and political and social developments. […] Despite the narrow wording [in the Basic Law] ("reporting"), in its essence, freedom of broadcasting does not differ from freedom of the press; it applies to both broadcasts with a focus on reporting and other broadcasts. Information and opinions can be conveyed through a TV docudrama or a music programme just as well as through news or political commentary; to some extent, each broadcasting service shapes opinions simply through its selection of broadcasts and the presentation of its programmes (cf. BVerfGE 12, 205 <260>; 31, 314 <326>). Furthermore, from the outset, freedom of broadcasting also does not permit differentiating between 48 programmes on the basis of the interests pursued or the quality of the respective format; ultimately, a restriction to 'serious' productions that serve a commendable private or public interest would amount to rating and control by public authorities, which would contradict the very essence of this fundamental right (cf. BVerfGE 25, 296 <307>; 34, 269 <281 and 282> – *Soraya;* with further references). Accordingly, a broadcasting or TV corporation may, in principle, invoke the protection of Art. 5(1) second sentence of the Basic Law for each broadcast, irrespective of whether political broadcasts, critical discussions of other questions of general interest, radio plays, cabaret programmes or other entertainment programmes are concerned. The applicability of the constitutional guarantee is thus not dependent on a demonstrated 'justified' or 'legitimate' interest in the broadcast concerned [...]. Correspondingly, freedom of broadcasting covers not only the selection of the material presented, but also the decision on the way in which it is presented, including the right to determine which of the various forms of programmes to use for this purpose.

49 Yet the interest pursued with the specific programme, the design of the programme and its achieved or foreseeable effect do become relevant where the exercise of freedom of broadcasting conflicts with other legal interests. The Constitution handles the potential conflict between freedom of broadcasting and the interests of individuals, groups or the community affected by this freedom by referring to the general legal order: pursuant to Art. 5(2) of the Basic Law, broadcasts are subject to the limitations that result from general laws. However, according to the established case-law of the Federal Constitutional Court, the respect for other legal interests as required by law may not relativise freedom of broadcasting; rather, laws restricting freedom of broadcasting must be interpreted in light of the constitutional guarantee and, where necessary, must be restricted themselves in order to ensure adequate realisation of freedom of broadcasting (cf. BVerfGE 20, 162 <176 *et seq.*>; 7, 198 <208 *et seq.*>). This requires a general and specific balancing of the conflicting legal interests in the individual case.

III.

50 1. General laws within the meaning of Art. 5(2) of the Basic Law also include the provisions on which the challenged decisions are based, namely §§ 22 and 23 of the Art Copyright Act [...]. These statutory provisions, which, according to their wording and their original meaning, only relate to the right to one's own image, have long been interpreted in the case-law and in legal scholarship as applying to the image of a person, regardless of whether their name is mentioned, and to the representation of a person by an actor on stage, in film or on television [...].

No. 7 – Lebach

These provisions are not objectionable under constitutional law; their relatively flexible design provides sufficient scope for application in conformity with the Constitution. [...]

2. In cases of conflict of the kind at hand, the general principle applies that the application of §§ 22 and 23 of the Art Copyright Act to television broadcasts must not excessively constrain freedom of broadcasting. Yet in contrast to other general laws within the meaning of Art. 5(2) of the Basic Law, this constellation is special in that the restriction of freedom of broadcasting itself serves to protect a constitutional value of high standing: the interest of the affected person opposing portrayal or representation, which must be taken into account pursuant to § 23 of the Art Copyright Act, is directly strengthened by the constitutional guarantee of the protection of one's personality.

The resolution of this conflict must reflect that, according to the Constitution's intent, both constitutional values constitute essential elements of the free democratic order of the Basic Law, which is why neither can claim to take general precedence. [...] Thus, in case of conflict, a balance must be struck between both constitutional values where possible; if this cannot be achieved, the specific circumstances and nature of the case must be taken into account in order to decide which interest must stand back behind the other. In this respect, both constitutional values must be viewed in light of their connection to human dignity as the centre of the Constitution's system of values. Accordingly, freedom of broadcasting may result in restrictive effects on rights derived from the right of personality; however, any loss in personality resulting from a portrayal in public must not be disproportionate to the significance of the public portrayal for free communication [...]. Furthermore, this benchmark requires, on the one hand, that the necessary balancing of interests take into account the intensity of the interference with the personal domain resulting from the programme at issue. On the other hand, the specific interest which the programme serves to satisfy and is suited to satisfy must be assessed, and it must be reviewed whether and to what extent this interest can also be satisfied without impairing the protection of one's personality, or at least without impairing it to the same extent.

IV.

1. The following constitutionally relevant criteria can be derived from these general principles for the purpose of assessing TV programmes like the one at issue here.

a) Public reporting of a crime that depicts, portrays and names the offender will always constitute a severe impairment of their personal domain, given that it publicly discloses that person's wrongdoings and, from the outset, conveys a negative image of the person to the audience. […]

56 b) Notwithstanding the possibility that the respective presentation (polemics, falsification) may amount to an additional impairment, even television coverage that aims for objectivity and fact-based reporting usually entails a far greater interference with the private sphere than spoken or written coverage on the radio or in the press. This follows from the greater intensity of the visual impression and the combination of image and sound, but especially from its far greater reach, which is a particular feature of television also when compared with film and theatre. Therefore, it is especially important "to ensure that the limitations set by law are adhered to and to prevent abuse of the right of personality, which has become more vulnerable. In this respect, the law must not defer to technical development" (BGH, NJW, 1966, p. 2353 <2354>).

57 It is of course important to differentiate according to the types of programme. The present case concerns a production that belongs to the genre of TV docudramas developed by the ZDF. According to the former head of the ZDF Department of TV Docudramas, Dr. Wolfgang Bruhn, this type of programme, in which an authentic incident is enacted in an equally authentic manner, has quickly become one of the most popular types of programme and is more popular with the audience than feature films and entertainment shows (cf. Bruhn, Fernsehen in Deutschland, 1967, p. 157 *et seq.* <157, 160>). […].

58 c) For these reasons alone, there is already a particular need for protection against violations of the right of personality resulting from television programmes with such a reach. In addition, the docudrama broadcasting format entails specific risks with regard to aspects that are relevant here. It combines catchy information with intriguing entertainment; it re-enacts an actual event, including its development and its course, without distorting or disguising it, and it shows or represents the persons involved therein as realistically as possible. For example, almost all names of places and persons remained unchanged in the programme at issue; some of the actual protagonists of the events presented, such as some minor characters, play themselves in the docudrama […]. If the casting of the main characters is convincing, such a docudrama has a "fascinating effect on the audience. It evokes significantly greater intellectual, emotional and thus active awareness than even the best documentary or so-called feature would be able to achieve. […]" (cf. Bruhn, *loc. cit.*, p. 160).

59 Such a vivid portrayal of a serious crime, emphasising emotional components in particular, will usually incite stronger and more lasting reactions in the audience against the portrayed offenders compared to simple spoken or written coverage. In addition, a docudrama, even if it restricts itself to portraying the events as

realistically as possible, cannot do without narrative features [...]. Another striking characteristic of such docudramas is that the concentration that is necessary for dramaturgic reasons, including temporal synopsis and an accelerated depiction of the course of events, leads to a portrayal of the offenders' person that is linked exclusively to the offence and its interpretation by the screenwriter and director. Since the programme creates the 'illusion of authenticity', the audience thinks that they are provided a comprehensive view of the offender's real personality. In fact, such docudramas reduce the portrayal to the negative dimension of the offender's personality, without showing fine nuances or highlighting the person's positive or neutral traits and behaviour.

d) [...] 60

Finally, the problem of selective perception, which also occurs with regard to other means of communication, is especially prevalent in television. Selective perception means that the audience tends to be unaware of the fact that it selects and perceives the statements provided in line with its own opinions or bias. [...] In the present context, this means that the portrayal of criminal or homosexual persons in a docudrama can reinforce a prevailing general disapproval of such social outsiders and, as a result, may also lead to an unfavourable overall assessment of the portrayed individuals. 61

In summary, it follows that television coverage of a crime – and in particular a docudrama – in which the offender is depicted, portrayed and named will usually result in serious interference with his personal sphere. 62

2. Nevertheless, there are important reasons for comprehensively informing the public about crimes and the events leading up to them, including information on the offender. Crimes are also an element of contemporary society, the presentation of which is one of the basic tasks of the media. Furthermore, the violation of the general legal order, the impairment of the legal interests of affected persons or the community, sympathy for the victims and their families, fear of similar crimes being committed and the endeavour to prevent them give rise to a legitimate interest in obtaining further information about the crime and the perpetrators. The importance of this interest increases the more the offence at issue stands out when compared to ordinary crime, because of the special nature of its target, the way in which the crime was committed or the severity of its consequences. Thus, in respect of serious violent crime like the criminal act at issue in the present case, there are serious reasons – i.e. reasons beyond general curiosity and sensationalism – for the interest in obtaining information about who the perpetrators were, what motives they had, what was done to identify and punish them and how to prevent similar offences. [...] Furthermore, the legitimate democratic need for the scrutiny of state organs and of authorities responsible for public security, of law enforce- 63

ment authorities and of criminal courts is significant. Finally, there is no need to further explain that television broadcasts are specifically suited to meeting such information needs, precisely because of their reach.

64 3. When balancing this interest in obtaining information through suitable television reporting with the necessary intrusion into the offender's personal domain, the interest in obtaining current information about crimes must generally take precedence. If someone violates the peaceful legal order (*Rechtsfrieden*) and attacks or injures fellow citizens or legal interests of the community through a criminal act or its consequences, that person must not only accept the criminal punishment imposed by the legal order, but they must also, in principle, accept that the crime itself attracts the interest of the public in obtaining information, which the public will satisfy by resorting to the normal channels in a community living in accordance with the principle of free communication. In fact, the scrutiny of law enforcement authorities and criminal proceedings that such reporting entails also benefits the offenders.

65 The precedence of the interest in obtaining information is not absolute. One limitation to this right is the general right of personality; the central constitutional importance of this right requires, in addition to respect for life's inviolable innermost domain (cf. BVerfGE 32, 373 <379>), strict adherence to the principle of proportionality. The intrusion into the personal sphere may not extend further than necessary to adequately satisfy the interest of the public in obtaining information; furthermore, the disadvantages inflicted upon the offender must be appropriate to the severity of the crime or to its relevance to the public based on other reasons. Accordingly, it is by no means always permissible to name, portray or otherwise identify the offender. In practice, the media mostly adhere to these general principles in cases of so-called petty crime or if juveniles are involved. [...].

66 The presumption of innocence that applies in favour of the accused until their final conviction (cf. Art. 6(2) ECHR, BGBl 1952 II, p. 686) also requires restraint, and at least an appropriate consideration of the facts and arguments put forward in their defence. It is self-evident that the right of personality only stands back in case of factual reporting and serious interpretation of the facts, but not in case of sensational, deliberately one-sided or distorting coverage; in that respect, reference can be made to the principles developed in legal scholarship and case-law on § 23 of the Art Copyright Act in respect of how information is presented. [...].

67 On the other hand, news coverage of a serious crime is justification not only for naming, portraying or otherwise identifying the offender; in principle, it also extends to coverage of their personal life insofar as it is directly linked to the crime committed, provides information on the motives or other preconditions of the crime and appears essential for assessing the culpability of the offender from

a contemporary criminal law perspective. Where to draw the line with regard to the generally prevailing interest in information from news reporting can only be decided in consideration of the particular circumstances of each case. [...]

4. However, the permeating effect on private law of the constitutional protection of one's personality does not permit the media to indefinitely cover the personal life and private sphere of the offender beyond news reporting. Instead, as soon as the interest of the public in obtaining current information on the crime has been satisfied, the offender's "right to be left alone" gains significance and sets limits to the mass media's desire for, and the public's interest in, discussing the offender's individual domain; this applies all the more to turning their individual domain into an object of entertainment. Even an offender who has attracted the interest and disapproval of the public by committing a serious crime still remains a member of this community and has a constitutional right to the protection of their individuality. If the crime that attracted the interest of the public was prosecuted in criminal proceedings, and thus punished as required by the common good, and if the public was adequately informed, any further or repeated interference with the offender's personal domain will generally not be justified; it would impose a renewed social sanction on the offender, especially in the case of television broadcasts.

5. a) It is impossible to determine a general rule applicable in every case stating after how many months or years one would have to draw the line between news coverage, which is in principle permissible, and a later portrayal or discussion, which is in principle impermissible. The decisive criterion is whether the respective broadcast, as weighed against the current level of information available to the public, might have a significantly new or an added adverse effect on the offender. [...]

b) The offender's interest in rehabilitation into society, i.e. their interest in social reintegration, can be a significant benchmark for a more precise determination of such a time limit. In recent decades, the significance of this objective has been increasingly acknowledged in criminal law; according to the prevailing opinion, the offender's social reintegration or socialisation is the primary objective of prison sentences (cf. also BVerfGE 33, 1 <7 et seq.>). Prisoners should be imparted with the ability and the will to lead responsible lives. They are to learn how to assert themselves in a free society without breaking the law, to make use of its opportunities and conquer its risks. [...]

[...]

Under constitutional law, this principle reflects the self-perception of a community with human dignity at the centre of its system of values that is committed to the principle of the social state. As holders of fundamental rights that follow from human dignity and ensure its protection, convicted offenders must be given the opportunity to reintegrate into the community after having served their sentence. From their point of view, the interest in social reintegration derives from their fundamental right guaranteed by Art. 2(1) in conjunction with Art. 1(1) of the Basic Law. From the community's point of view, the principle of the social state requires that the state provide care and support to those social groups whose personal or social development is impeded due to personal weaknesses or fault, inability or social disadvantage, including prisoners or persons released from prison. Not least, social reintegration serves to protect the community itself; it has a direct interest in preventing the offender from reoffending and from harming fellow citizens or the community.

73 c) […] Practical experience has shown that social reintegration often fails because of the community's contempt for and rejection of the person released from prison, even if preconditions were relatively favourable and forensic therapy had been successful. This kind of isolation can destroy the courage especially of unstable persons to start afresh, and throw them back on the same path that had already previously led them to crime.

74 d) In line with the considerations outlined above (see B IV 1 above), there is no need to further discuss that the attitude of the community towards released former prisoners can be negatively influenced by television coverage of the crime, especially by coverage in the form of a docudrama. In addition, large parts of the population still do not sufficiently recognise and accept the need for the community to help those released from prison reintegrate into society. Therefore, the adverse effects of the television programme in question are in fact reinforced by the existing generally defensive attitude towards former prisoners. At the same time, such a television programme can also destroy or call into question the internal stabilisation offenders have achieved – perhaps painstakingly – in prison: The renewed graphic confrontation with the crime effectively throws them back to their state at the time of the crime and discourages them, making them believe that the community still sees them as the offender from that time, despite all their efforts. Based on this insight, the German Press Council (*Deutscher Presserat*), upon the suggestion of the Federal President, made the following recommendations on 28 September 1971:

75 "not to publish names of prisoners or details that allow drawing conclusions about released prisoners, their families or the place of their release from prison" (Activity Report 1971, p. 102).

76 e) In sum, repeated television broadcasts about a serious crime that are no longer justified by the interest of the public in obtaining information on current events will

in any case not be permissible if they jeopardise the offender's social reintegration. [...]

Social reintegration will regularly be jeopardised where a television programme identifying the offender and covering their crimes is broadcast shortly before or after their release from prison. In that respect, it must be taken into account that a fixed-term prison sentence may be suspended on probation pursuant to § 26(2) of the Criminal Code as soon as prisoners have served half the sentence, and that their sentence must be suspended on probation in accordance with the conditions set out in § 26(1) of the Criminal Code after they have served two-thirds of the sentence.

V.

When reviewed in light of the constitutional criteria developed above, the challenged decisions cannot be upheld.

1. [...]

2. An assessment sufficiently giving effect to the impact of the relevant fundamental rights on ordinary law requires the granting of the complainant's application.

As noted in the challenged decisions, it can be assumed that the specifics of the case – namely the attack on a *Bundeswehr* facility, the heinous way the crime was carried out, the number of victims, and the unusual, largely incomprehensible motivation – attracted great interest among the population in further information and investigation. This must be taken into consideration when balancing the right of the ZDF to portray events significant for contemporary society within the meaning of § 23(1) no. 1 of the Art Copyright Act – a right that is strengthened by freedom of broadcasting – against the complainant's interest in preventing the portrayal of the events – a right that is strengthened by the fundamental right to the free development of one's personality and human dignity. It must also be taken into account that the docudrama at issue seeks to be as realistic as possible and that the portrayal of the relationship between the perpetrators is not offensive.

However, for the above-mentioned reasons (see B IV 1 above), the broadcasting of the docudrama would result in a serious interference with the complainant's right of personality given the programme's reach, the chosen docudrama form and its anticipated impact. To the extent that the ZDF argued that the drama should, among other purposes, also serve to promote understanding for the complainant, the courts in the initial proceedings already held that this submission is irrelevant because the docudrama's content and design do not reveal any such tendency. In fact, the chosen interpretation of the crime that emphasises homosexual grouping has [...] the opposite effect insofar as it conveys the impression that the criminal act is not really much less attributable to the complainant than to the main offenders and in that it suggests that he only remained in the background due to his cowardliness while aggressively encouraging the others in their endeavours. This does not match the assessment of the court of first instance, which came to the conclusion that the complainant's contributing role was much smaller than that of the main offenders.

84 This serious interference with the complainant's personal domain cannot be justified by the interest in the coverage of the crime as a current event, which generally takes precedence. This interest has been satisfied by the extensive information provided to the public in all media immediately after the crime was discovered, during the search for the perpetrators and especially over the course of the criminal proceedings. In comparison, the portrayal in a docudrama that no longer has a direct temporal link to the criminal proceedings amounts to a new impairment of the protection of the complainant's personality […].

85 This new interference […] might seriously jeopardise the social reintegration of the complainant; the broadcast would adversely affect, first and foremost, the community's attitude towards the complainant, but also his internal stabilisation. To have such an impact, temporal proximity of the new broadcast to the forthcoming release from prison is required; this would be the case here, irrespective of the potential date of release the assessment is based on. Given that the ZDF suggested to hear other expert opinions with regard to the personality assessment of the complainant, and thus apparently questioned the success of social reintegration in general but also the complainant's social reintegration in particular, it must be highlighted that it is not for the civil or constitutional court proceedings to replace with their own prognosis the assessment of the primarily competent criminal court and of the authorities responsible for the carrying out of the sentence. In addition, the success of social reintegration always depends on the interaction of various factors, which can never be foreseen with complete certainty. As far as the assessment under constitutional law is concerned, what matters is merely that the complainant retain his chance of reintegrating into society – a chance that the competent authorities found to exist.

86 […]

87 It is not ascertainable that the public has an exceptionally significant interest in forming opinions, which could justify such a serious infringement of personality in exceptional cases (cf. also BVerfGE 7, 198 <211 and 212>; 12, 113 <126 *et seq.*>; 25, 256 <264>; BGHZ 45, 296 <308>; BGH, NJW 1965, p. 1476 <1477>). […]

88 As a result, when interpreting § 23 of the Art Copyright Act in accordance with the values enshrined in the Constitution, the complainant's interest in preventing the broadcasting of the docudrama must take precedence. This interest would not be satisfied if, as suggested by the Federal Government, the broadcast were prohibited only insofar as it depicts and names the complainant. Even if the complainant were

not depicted or named in the broadcast, the remainder of the portrayal would be sufficient to identify the complainant and thus could adversely affect his social reintegration; in fact, the audience might be tempted to decipher the secret, which could specifically direct the interest of the audience to the complainant – especially in the relevant local area.
[…]

3. There is no need to decide whether the disputed docudrama that aims to realistically reproduce an actual event should also be recognised as a work of art within the meaning of Art. 5(3) of the Basic Law. Even if this constitutional provision were applied, it should be noted that freedom of the arts, although it is not subject to the limitations set out in Art. 5(2) of the Basic Law, does not have a higher standing than the protection of one's personality guaranteed by Art. 1 and Art. 2(1) of the Basic Law (cf. BVerfGE 30, 173 <193 *et seq.*>).

VI.

Therefore, the challenged decisions violate the complainant's fundamental rights under Art. 2(1) in conjunction with Art. 1 of the Basic Law and must be reversed pursuant to § 95(2) of the Federal Constitutional Court Act. Remanding the case to another court with jurisdiction in civil proceedings would not do justice to the particularities of the case. These constitutional standards and the evidence compiled by the Federal Constitutional Court leave no latitude for a new decision by the courts in the present case; rather, the complainant's application must be fully successful. […]
[…]

Justices: Benda, Ritterspach, Haager, Rupp-v. Brünneck, Böhmer, Faller, Brox, Simon

No. 8

BVerfGE 75, 201 – Foster Parents

HEADNOTE

to the Order of the First Senate of 14 April 1987
1 BvR 332/86

§ 1632(4) of the Civil Code must be interpreted in conformity with the Basic Law to the effect that a request by the parents or by one parent for the surrender of their child – not with the aim of reuniting the family but of achieving a change in foster parents – may only be granted if endangerment of the child's physical, mental or emotional well-being can be ruled out with reasonable certainty.

FEDERAL CONSTITUTIONAL COURT
- 1 BvR 332/86 -

IN THE NAME OF THE PEOPLE

In the proceedings
on the constitutional complaint of

the child L..., represented by its supplementary curator,
– authorised representatives: ...
against   a)   the Order of the Supreme Court of Bavaria of 14 January 1986
   - BReg. 1 Z 99/85 -
   b)   the Order of the Aschaffenburg Regional Court of 13 November 1985
   - T 180/85 -
   c)   the Order of the Obernburg Local Court - X 12/85 - issued on 30 July 1985

the Federal Constitutional Court – First Senate –
with the participation of Justices

President Herzog,
Simon,

No. 8 – Foster Parents

Hesse,
Niemeyer,
Henschel,
Seidel

held on 14 April 1987:

The Orders of the Obernburg Local Court - X 12/85 - issued on 30 July 1985, the Aschaffenburg Regional Court of 13 November 1985 - T 180/85 - and the Supreme Court of Bavaria of 14 January 1986 - BReg. 1 Z 99/85 - violate the complainant's fundamental right under Article 2(1) in conjunction with Article 1(1) of the Basic Law. The decisions are reversed. The matter is remanded to the Local Court.
[...]

REASONS:

A.

The constitutional complaint concerns court decisions ordering the complainant's foster parents to surrender the complainant to her father.

I.

The legal care responsibility for a minor includes the right to demand from anyone who unlawfully withholds a child from the parents or one parent that the child be surrendered (§ 1632(1) of the Civil Code). If the child has been in foster care for a longer period of time, the family court can, however, in accordance with § 1632(4) of the Civil Code, order *ex officio* or at the foster carer's request that the child remain with them if and as long as the requirements of § 1666(1) first sentence of the Civil Code are met, particularly regarding the reasons for or duration of foster care. According to the provision's wording, this is the case where, for example, the child's physical, mental or emotional well-being is endangered by the abusive exercise of parental custody, neglect of the child, or failure of the parents through no fault of their own.

II.

1. The complainant was born in wedlock on 22 November 1983 as the daughter of an inland skipper. She has two older sisters, one of whom is raised by their grandmother. The other – born in 1980 – was removed from her mother's household at

the age of three months in a neglected state and brought to her step-aunt, where she still lives today. The children's mother had been suffering from addiction for years and had repeatedly been treated in hospitals for that reason. Husband and wife have been living separately since May 1984.

4   In mid-December 1983, the district youth welfare office (*Kreisjugendamt*) informed the family court that the mother had abused the complainant and that the father hardly took care of the child. Thereupon, the court temporarily withdrew parental custody from the parents, ordered guardianship over the child and appointed the district youth welfare office as legal guardian. The authorities first placed the complainant in a children's hospital, and in January 1984 into the care of a married couple who had no children of their own.

5   Custody was initially withdrawn from both parents permanently, but the father regained custody following his successful complaint. Since January 1985, he has been demanding that the foster parents surrender the complainant in order to place her with his step-sister as well.

6   2. In January 1985, the foster parents attempted to obtain a judicial order from the family court for the child to remain with them (§ 1632(4) of the Civil Code). The father, however, applied [to the Local Court] for an order obliging the foster parents to surrender the complainant. The court granted his request. […]

7-8   […]

9   3. a) The foster parents filed a complaint against the decision of the Local Court [at the Regional Court] […].

10   b) The complaint was unsuccessful.

11-14   […]

15   4. The Supreme Court of Bavaria affirmed the Regional Court's decision, holding that it was free of legal error.

16-18   […]

III.

19   With the constitutional complaint filed against these court decisions, the complainant claims that her fundamental rights under Art. 1(1) and Art. 2(1) of the Basic Law as well as Art. 103(1) of the Basic Law are violated. In addition, she claims that her constitutional right to remain in the foster family (Art. 6(3) of the Basic Law) was disregarded.

No. 8 – Foster Parents

[…] 20-21

IV.

[…] 22-29

V.

[…] 30-38

B.

The constitutional complaint is, for the most part, admissible. […] It is inadmissible only insofar as the complainant claims a violation of her right to be heard (Art. 103(1) of the Basic Law). 39

I.

[…] 40-43

II.

[…] 44-50

C.

To the extent that the constitutional complaint is admissible, it is also well-founded. The challenged decisions violate the complainant's fundamental right under Art. 2(1) in conjunction with Art. 1(1) of the Basic Law. 51

I.

§ 1632(4) of the Civil Code must be interpreted in conformity with the Constitution to the effect that a request by the parents or by one parent for the surrender of their child – not with the aim of reuniting the family but of achieving a change in foster parents – may only be granted if endangerment of the child's physical, mental or emotional well-being can be ruled out with reasonable certainty. 52

1. The decisions challenged in the constitutional complaint are based on the application of § 1632(1) and (4) of the Civil Code. Pursuant to § 1632(1) of the Civil 53

Code, parents with custody have the right to demand from anyone who unlawfully withholds their child that the child be surrendered. This follows from the right to determine the child's place of residence under § 1631(1) of the Civil Code […]. This right to have the child surrendered is modified by § 1632(4) of the Civil Code in the sense that removing the child from a foster family at an unsuitable time should be avoided in order to not jeopardise their personal, and especially their emotional well-being (cf. BTDrucks 8/2788, pp. 40, 52). The provision does not contain any systematic restriction of parental rights, but rather makes the courts' decisions dependent upon the circumstances of the individual case. The provision is thus informed by the principle that individual measures to prevent the endangerment of children take precedence over general rules (cf. BVerfGE 24, 119 <145> with further references).

54 2. As the highest-ranking domestic law, the Basic Law is not only the standard against which the validity of domestic legal provisions is measured. All such legal provisions must also be interpreted in accordance with the Basic Law. […]

55 Decisions under § 1632(4) of the Civil Code are taken in the case of a conflict between the interests of the parents, or of one parent with sole custody, in having the child surrendered to them, on the one hand, and the child's best interests, on the other hand. The Constitution requires that this provision be interpreted so that both the parental rights under Art. 6(2) first sentence of the Basic Law as well as the child's fundamental rights arising from Art. 2(1) in conjunction with Art. 1(1) of the Basic Law are taken into account. When interpreting provisions that fall within the scope of Art. 6(2) of the Basic Law, just like when interpreting legislative decisions, the required balancing of interests must take into account the fact that ultimately, the child's best interests must be decisive (cf. BVerfGE 68, 176 <188>).

56 a) The relationship between parental rights and the child's right of personality is shaped by the particular structure of the parental right. It is essentially a right in the child's interest, as already follows from the wording of Art. 6(2) first sentence of the Basic Law, which refers to the parental right to care for and raise the child and thus incorporates the child's interest into the parental right (cf. BVerfGE 59, 360 <382>). Generally, it is in the best interest of the child to be in its parents' care, given that the likeliest way to ensure that the child grows up to become a self-reliant person is if it is raised and cared for by its mother and father in harmonious community (cf. BVerfGE 56, 363 <395>). However, it is not always possible to achieve this ideal state, for instance when children grow up in a foster family. A foster care relationship might arise from a voluntary decision by the parents or the parent with sole custody; more frequently, however, it is ordered by the authorities. Regardless of how it came about, and in accordance with Art. 6(2) first sentence of the Basic Law, the aim should be not to allow the foster care

relationship to become so strong that the natural parents must in almost every case fear that the child will permanently remain in the foster family. This does not mean, however, that § 1632(4) of the Civil Code cannot allow for decisions that the parents find inacceptable because they feel that their parental rights have been impaired (cf. BVerfGE 68, 176 <189 and 190>).

b) It follows from the expert opinions by Fthenakis and Lempp that new research in the field of child psychology and child psychiatry challenges formerly established notions as to the effects of a separation of infants from their immediate caregivers. Nevertheless, it is still beyond dispute that such an event causes severe psychological stress for a child, and that how well the child deals with this challenge depends on its personality and the circumstances of the change. [...] When balancing parental rights and the best interests of the child in decisions pursuant to § 1632(4) of the Civil Code, it is [...] important to consider whether the surrendering of the child is meant to enable the child's return to its family or whether only a change of its foster family is intended. This distinction determines what degree of uncertainty regarding possible negative effects on the child is acceptable when taking into consideration the child's fundamental rights. In general, a greater risk may be acceptable if the natural parents themselves, or one parent, want to care for the child again. However, the situation is different where the child is not meant to return to its father's and mother's household, but is supposed, without any significant grounds related to the child's best interests, to move to a new foster family. In such a case, asserting the right of care for a minor pursuant to § 1631(1) of the Civil Code, in the form of the right to determine its place of residence, is only compatible with Art. 2(1) in conjunction with Art. 1(1) of the Basic Law if it can be ruled out with reasonable certainty that the child's separation from its foster parents will cause psychological or physical harm.

3. This interpretation of § 1632(4) of the Civil Code, which follows from Art. 2(1) in conjunction with Art. 1(1) of the Basic Law, does not contradict the legislative history of § 1632(4) of the Civil Code, which was incorporated in the Civil Code through Art. 1 no. 8 of the Act Revising Parental Care Law of 18 July 1979 (BGBl I, p. 1061). The aim of the revision of the law on parental custody was to take on board the demands of professional associations and experts in the field, and to grant the child a stronger legal position in the family [...]. Referring to the Federal Constitutional Court's case-law, it was stressed during the legislative process that, when assessing the scope of parental responsibilities, one had to consider that every child is a person with its own human dignity and its own right to develop its personality ([...]). This is in line with an interpretation of § 1632(4) of the Civil Code pursuant to which, if the person who has custody of the child does not exercise the right to determine the child's place of residence in order to

reunite it with its parent or parents, the child may only be separated from its foster parents if there is no reason to fear for its well-being.

II.

59 It is not ascertainable from the challenged decisions that the courts, in interpreting § 1632(4) of the Civil Code, sufficiently took into account the requirements resulting from Art. 2(1) in conjunction with Art. 1(1) of the Basic Law.

60 1. The Federal Constitutional Court does not review the interpretation and application of statutory law as such. The Court is only called upon to review whether the competent courts have properly assessed the scope and impact of fundamental rights in the area of private law. However, the limits of the Federal Constitutional Court's capacity to intervene when carrying out this task cannot be inflexible and rigid; the Court needs some degree of latitude in order to consider the specific situation of the individual case. The extent of the impairment of fundamental rights is of particular significance in this context (cf. BVerfGE 42, 163 <168> with further references).

61 Surrendering the complainant to her father who has custody entails separating her from her foster parents, after which she is to be placed with other persons. This measure is of existential significance for the complainant's future. Thus, such an interference is only constitutional subject to strict requirements: Aside from the question of whether errors are discernible in the challenged decisions that are based on a fundamentally incorrect understanding of the significance of a fundamental right in general, and in particular its scope of protection, individual errors of interpretation must also be considered (BVerfGE 54, 129 <136> with further references).

62 2. When interpreting and applying § 1632(4) of the Civil Code, none of the courts that dealt with the matter deemed it relevant to consider whether the complainant, after being surrendered by the foster parents, is meant to grow up with her father or in a family she does not know. In this context, the Supreme Court of Bavaria only stated that the frequent and long absences of the complainant's father, which mean that he would have to place the child into care elsewhere, did not raise any concerns about his suitability for being fully responsible for her care.

63 It is true that negative conclusions concerning the exercise of parental custody cannot be drawn from the father's work-related absences. However, this does not answer the question about what constitutes a reasonable (*zumutbar*) future risk for the complainant if she is uprooted to live in a new foster family. To the extent that the courts considered that the disadvantages of this measure may be compensated by reuniting the complainant with her sister, this argument must be dismissed, in

accordance with the Lempp expert opinion. This consideration must be accorded at least less significance than was done by the Regional Court and the Supreme Court of Bavaria when assessing its importance for the complainant's physical and psychological development upon her removal from the foster family. As a result, the experts' statements to the effect that no one can say with reasonable certainty whether the complainant's removal from the foster family would cause her permanent harm take on additional significance. Based on the expert opinion it had obtained, the Regional Court stated that it could not conclude that a change in the child's place of residence would result in non-negligible physical or emotional harm for the complainant. In addition to this, the Supreme Court of Bavaria points to case-law that has been recognised for decades (BGHZ 6, 342 <347 and 348>), according to which it cannot generally be assumed that living at a different place would permanently harm a child's psychological development. In doing so, the courts fail to appropriately interpret § 1632(4) of the Civil Code in conformity with the Constitution, as is warranted in cases such as the one at hand. In fact, such consequences for the complainant when changing the foster family must instead be ruled out with reasonable certainty.

Justices: Herzog, Simon, Hesse, Niemeyer, Henschel, Seidl

No. 9

BVerfGE 78, 77 – Public Announcement of Legal Incapacitation

HEADNOTE

to the Order of the First Senate of 9 March 1988
1 BvL 49/86

The public announcement of legal incapacitation on the grounds of profligacy or alcoholism (§ 687 of the Code of Civil Procedure) is incompatible with the general right of personality (Article 2(1) in conjunction with Article 1(1) of the Basic Law).

FEDERAL CONSTITUTIONAL COURT
- 1 BvL 49/86 -

IN THE NAME OF THE PEOPLE

In the proceedings
for constitutional review of

§ 687 of the Code of Civil Procedure
– Order of Suspension and Referral of the Detmold Local Court of 28 July 1986 (15 C 8/83) –

the Federal Constitutional Court – First Senate –
with the participation of Justices

President Herzog,
Niemeyer,
Heußner,
Henschel,
Seidl,
Grimm,
Söllner,
Dieterich

held on 9 March 1988:

No. 9 – Public Announcement of Legal Incapacitation

§ 687 of the Code of Civil Procedure is incompatible with Art. 2(1) in conjunction with Art. 1(1) of the Basic Law and void.

This does not apply to the public announcement that a legal incapacitation is lifted if such announcement is made with the affected person's consent and the incapacitation itself had previously been publicly announced.

REASONS:

A.

The referral concerns the question of whether § 687 of the Code of Civil Procedure, which orders the public announcement of a person's legal incapacitation on the grounds of profligacy or alcoholism, is compatible with the Basic Law.

I.

According to § 6(1) of the Civil Code, persons may be declared legally incapacitated if they are unable to manage their affairs on the grounds of mental illness or mental deficiency (no. 1), if they expose themselves or their family to the risk of indigence as a result of profligacy (no. 2) or if, as a result of alcoholism or drug abuse, they cannot manage their affairs or expose themselves or their family to the risk of indigence, or endanger others (no. 3). The essential effects of legal incapacitation are set out in §§ 104 *et seq.* of the Civil Code. A person who has been declared legally incapacitated on the grounds of mental deficiency, profligacy, alcoholism or drug abuse has limited capacity to contract pursuant to § 114 of the Civil Code. Legal incapacitation on grounds of mental illness brings about the incapacity to contract, pursuant to § 104 no. 3 of the Civil Code. A legally incapacitated person who has reached the age of majority is assigned a legal guardian under § 1869 of the Civil Code.

The proceedings for incapacitation are governed by §§ 645 to 687 of the Code of Civil Procedure. The wording of the provision in question […] reads:

§ 687

The legal incapacitation of a person on the grounds of profligacy or alcoholism as well as the lifting of the incapacitation is to be announced publicly by the Local Court.

5 The general view is that the public announcement of legal incapacitation is intended to protect third parties who may be engaged in legal transactions with the incapacitated person. It is intended to protect them from any losses they may incur because they were unaware of the limited contractual capacity of the person concerned. Furthermore, some consider § 687 of the Code of Civil Procedure to also have an instructional function. According to this view, the announcement is intended to influence legally incapacitated persons and motivate them to behave in a socially adequate manner.

6 Public announcement is only mandatory in cases of legal incapacitation on the grounds of profligacy, alcoholism and – according to prevailing opinion – drug addiction, as well as for the lifting of the incapacitation orders. However, § 687 of the Code of Civil Procedure does not require public announcements for legal incapacitation on the grounds of mental illness or mental deficiency. The original reasoning for this distinction was that no warning was necessary in the case of mentally ill persons because their condition was obvious to third parties anyway.

7 The public announcement has no legal effect on incapacitation. Its sole purpose is to serve as a warning.

II.

8 The person concerned in the initial proceedings was declared legally incapacitated on the grounds of alcoholism. The Local Court suspended the legal incapacitation proceedings in respect of the still outstanding public announcement, and referred to the Federal Constitutional Court the question of

9 whether the mandatory public announcement of legal incapacitation on the grounds of alcoholism as required by § 687 of the Code of Civil Procedure is compatible with the requirement to protect the general right of personality enshrined in Art. 1(1) and Art. 2 of the Basic Law.

10 The Local Court considers the provision to be unconstitutional. [...]
11 [...]

III.

12 Statements on the referral were submitted by the Federal Ministry of Justice on behalf of the Federal Government, the President of the Federal Court of Justice, data protection officers and the German Head Office for Addiction Matters (*Deutsche Hauptstelle gegen die Suchtgefahren e. V.*).

No. 9 – Public Announcement of Legal Incapacitation

[...] 13-19

B.

The referral is admissible. [...] 20
[...] 21-24

C.

§ 687 of the Code of Civil Procedure is incompatible with Art. 2(1) in conjunction 25
with Art. 1(1) of the Basic Law.
1. The general right of personality guaranteed by Art. 2(1) in conjunction with 26
Art. 1(1) of the Basic Law encompasses the authority of the individual to decide
themselves on the disclosure and use of their personal data (right to informational
self-determination – cf. BVerfGE 65, 1 <41 *et seq.*> – *Census*). The act and the
status of legal incapacitation as well as the personal circumstances that led to the
incapacitation also constitute protected data.
[...] Because it is rooted in the general right of personality, the right to informa- 27
tional self-determination provides general protection against the collection and
processing of personal data by the state [...]. A public announcement of the kind
provided for by § 687 of the Code of Civil Procedure with regard to certain cases of
legal incapacitation is merely a special form of data sharing by the state. The effect
of the announcement is to share personal data with an unspecified and unspecifiable
group of recipients, both within and beyond administrative authorities and other
public bodies, in what is assumed to be the legitimate interest of the recipients. It
does so without imposing any restrictions on the use of the data and without any
additional procedural safeguards.
[...] 28
2. The right to informational self-determination is not guaranteed without limita- 29
tion. The individual must accept that this right is subject to restrictions serving
overriding public interests. However, in accordance with Art. 2(1) of the Basic
Law, such restrictions require a statutory basis and must satisfy the requirements
of proportionality. The principle of proportionality requires that a restriction of
fundamental rights be sufficiently justified by the common good; that the chosen
means be suitable and necessary for achieving the intended purpose; and that the
limits of what is reasonable (*zumutbar*) must be respected in an overall balancing
of the severity of the interference on the one hand, and the weight of the reasons
invoked to justify it on the other hand (cf. BVerfGE 71, 183 <196 and 197> with

further references). § 687 of the Code of Civil Procedure does not meet these requirements.

30 a) The main purpose of the provision is to protect legal relationships by informing participants in transactions of the limited contractual capacity of the legally incapacitated person, so that they may protect themselves against losses incurred in legal transactions concluded without the necessary approval or consent of the guardian. The legislator may pursue such a purpose in the interest of reliably functioning legal relationships.

31 [...]

32 b) It is true that the public announcement of legal incapacitation can only fulfil its warning function to the extent that participants in legal relationships actually become aware of it and know that the legally incapacitated person is identical with their potential contractual partner. However, given today's anonymous lifestyles, the mobility of the population, the reach of publishing institutions and the plethora of available information, this will only seldom be the case. On the other hand, automatic data processing provides new possibilities for storing and retrieving such information centrally, which can be used to this end if there is a legitimate interest (cf. § 32(2) of the Federal Data Protection Act), as is increasingly the case. That is sufficient to make the provision suitable for achieving its intended purpose.

33 [...]

34 c) To achieve the legislative purpose, it is indeed necessary that the information be publicly accessible. [...]

35 d) Balancing the severity of the interference and the reasons invoked to justify it leads to the conclusion that the limits of what is reasonable have been exceeded. On the one hand, it must be taken into account that the public announcement has no legal effect, and instead serves solely to issue a general warning with no specific objective. Furthermore, the legislator has itself refrained from requiring an announcement in the great majority of legal incapacitation cases (fewer than 10% concern cases of profligacy, alcoholism and drug abuse – cf. BTDrucks 10/5970, pp. 7 and 8). On the other hand, the public announcement of legal incapacitation on the grounds of alcoholism or profligacy constitutes a severe restriction of a person's fundamental right to decide themselves on the disclosure and use of their personal data. The severity of the interference follows from the contents of the announcement. It is not only a statement on contractual capacity, which is a status relevant to legal relationships, but also affects the person as a whole. As such, it can give rise to the risk of social exclusion and hamper measures taken under the principle of the social state to help a person overcome their addiction and to reintegrate them into society. As has been shown, the public announcement addresses an unspecified and unspecifiable group of persons and thus reaches an indeterminable number of

No. 9 – Public Announcement of Legal Incapacitation

individuals in addition to those whose interests it is meant to serve. Under these circumstances, it is not possible to limit the use of the data to the verification of contractual capacity. [...]

[...] 36

However, in cases in which legal incapacitation has already been announced publicly, the person concerned must retain the possibility of making the lifting of their legal incapacitation publicly known as well. § 687 of the Code of Civil Procedure is incompatible with the Basic Law, subject to the above-mentioned exception regarding cases of prior announcement. 37

D.

[...] 38

Justices: Herzog, Niemeyer, Heußner, Henschel, Seidl, Grimm, Söllner, Dieterich

No. 10

BVerfGE 117, 71 – Life Imprisonment

HEADNOTE

to the Order of the Second Senate of 8 November 2006
2 BvR 578/02, 2 BvR 796/02

Enforcing a sentence of life imprisonment beyond the time required on account of particularly aggravated guilt on the grounds that a criminal offender is particularly dangerous violates neither the guarantee of human dignity (Article 1(1) of the Basic Law) nor the fundamental right to liberty of the person under Article 2(2) second sentence of the Basic Law. The decision whether to suspend a life sentence must strictly adhere to the principle of proportionality in order to maintain the specific and, in principle, also realistic chance for the convicted person to regain their liberty.

FEDERAL CONSTITUTIONAL COURT
- 2 BvR 578/02 -
- 2 BvR 796/02 -

IN THE NAME OF THE PEOPLE

In the proceedings on
the constitutional complaints of

1. Mr W...,
   – authorised representative: ...

against   a) the Order of the Hamm Higher Regional Court of 27 July 2006
            - 1 Ws (L) 5/05 -,
          b) the Order of the Aachen Regional Court of 1 August 2005
            - 33 StVK 306/04 K -,
          c) the Order of the Hamm Higher Regional Court of 23 April 2002
            - 1 Ws (L) 5/02 -,

d) the Order of the Düsseldorf Regional Court of 20 February 2002
   - StVK 202/00 K (72) -,
e) indirectly against § 57a(1) first sentence no. 3 in conjunction with § 57(1) first sentence no. 2 of the Criminal Code,
   - 2 BvR 578/02 -,

2. Mr B...,
   – authorised representative: ...

against a) the Order of the Koblenz Higher Regional Court of 22 July 2002
   - 2 Ws 308/02 -,
b) the Order of the Koblenz Higher Regional Court of 8 July 2002
   - 2 Ws 308/02 -,
c) the Order of the Koblenz Higher Regional Court of 22 April 2002
   - 2 Ws 308/02 -,
d) the Order of the Koblenz Regional Court of 29 January 2002
   - 7 StVK 583/98 -,
e) indirectly against § 57a(1) first sentence no. 3 in conjunction with § 57(1) first sentence no. 2 of the Criminal Code
   - 2 BvR 796/02 -

the Federal Constitutional Court – Second Senate –

with the participation of Justices

Vice-President Hassemer,
Broß,
Osterloh,
Di Fabio,
Mellinghoff,
Lübbe-Wolff,
Gerhardt,
Landau

held on 8 November 2006:

1. The constitutional complaint of complainant no. 1 is rejected as unfounded.
2. a) To the extent that they did not decide on the merits of the formal complaint against court delay that is contrary to the rule of law, the Orders of the Koblenz Higher Regional Court of 22 April 2002 and of 22 July 2002 – both 2 Ws 308/02 – violate complainant no. 2's fundamental right to effective legal protection under Article 2(1) of the Basic Law in conjunction with the principle of the rule of law (Article 20(3) of the Basic Law). They

are reversed in this respect. The matter is remanded to the Koblenz Higher Regional Court for a decision on the formal complaint against court delay.

    b) For the rest, the constitutional complaint of complainant no. 2 is rejected as unfounded.

3. [...]

REASONS:

A.

1   The constitutional complaints, which are combined for joint decision, concern the question whether the legal provisions on suspending the remainder of a life sentence and their application by the courts are compatible with the Basic Law if particularly aggravated guilt (*besondere Schwere der Schuld*) no longer requires its continued enforcement (§ 57a(1) first sentence no. 3 in conjunction with § 57(1) first sentence no. 2 of the Criminal Code).

I.

2   The suspension of the remainder of a life sentence is governed by § 57a of the Criminal Code. [...]

3-12 [...]

13   If fifteen years have been served and if the particularly aggravated guilt of the convicted person no longer requires continued enforcement of the life sentence, the provision requires that the conditions of § 57(1) first sentence nos. 2 and 3 of the Code of Criminal Procedure must be satisfied in order to suspend enforcement of the sentence. Following its amendment by the Prevention of Sexual Offences and Other Dangerous Criminal Offences Act of 26 January 1998 (BGBl I 1998, p. 160), § 57(1) of the Criminal Code reads as follows:

§ 57

14   Conditional early release – fixed-term imprisonment

15   (1) The court suspends enforcement of the remainder of a fixed-term sentence of imprisonment on probation if

16   1. two-thirds of the imposed sentence, but at least two months, have been served, and

17

No. 10 – Life Imprisonment

2. this can be justified having regard to public security interests, and

3. the convicted person consents thereto.

The decision must, in particular, take into consideration the convicted person's character, previous history, the circumstances of the offence, the significance of the legal interest at risk should the convicted person re-offend, the convicted person's life circumstances and conduct whilst serving the sentence imposed, and the effects that such suspension is expected to have on the convicted person. (2) (...)

II.

1. a) Complainant no. 1, born in 1940, was convicted by the competent criminal chamber of the Düsseldorf Regional Court of murder under specific aggravating circumstances [pursuant to § 211 of the Criminal Code] together with attempted rape, committed in a single crime (*Tateinheit*), and sentenced to life imprisonment on 31 October 1974. [...]
[...]
In an order of 16 December 1992, upheld by the Higher Regional Court on 11 May 1993, the Regional Court determined that the continued enforcement of the life sentence was no longer required on account of particularly aggravated guilt, but that the offender continued to be dangerous. The courts competent for the enforcement of sentences (*Vollstreckungsgerichte*) refused to suspend the remainder of the life sentence. They held that there was a residual risk that the complainant might commit another homicide offence.
b) [...]
c) [...]
d) [...]
e) [...]
f) [...]
g) [...]
2. a) Complainant no. 2, who was born on 18 June 1944, is serving a life sentence imposed by a judgment of the competent criminal chamber of the Mainz Regional Court of 19 July 1972 for two counts of murder.
[...]
b) The complainant had been in remand detention and subsequently served a prison sentence from June 1970 onward. In November 1997, the criminal chamber competent for the enforcement of sentences determined that the continued enforcement

of the sentence was no longer required on account of particularly aggravated guilt. At the same time, it rejected the first application for suspension of the sentence. According to all experts involved in the proceedings, there was a residual risk that the complainant might commit other homicide offences.

33 c) […]
34-35 d) […]
36-37 e) […]
38-39 f) […]
40 g) […]
41 h) […]

III.

42 The complainants both filed constitutional complaints against the orders of the courts competent for the enforcement of sentences which refused to suspend the remainder of their life sentences. […]

43 The complainants claim a violation of their rights under Art. 1(1), Art. 2(1) and (2) first and second sentence, Art. 3(1), Art. 19(2) and (4) and Art. 103(2) and (3), Art. 104(1) as well as under Art. 2(2) second sentence in conjunction with Art. 20(3) of the Basic Law; they indirectly challenge life imprisonment as the legal consequence of § 211 of the Criminal Code as well as of § 57a(1) first sentence no. 3 and second sentence in conjunction with § 57(1) first sentence no. 2 and second sentence of the Criminal Code.

44-53 […]

IV.

54 Statements on the constitutional complaints were submitted by the Federal Ministry of Justice on behalf of the Federal Government, the First, Second, Third and Fifth Criminal Division of the Federal Court of Justice, the Public Prosecutor General (*Generalbundesanwalt*) and the Bavarian Ministry of Justice. […]

55 […]

B.

56 The constitutional complaints are admissible.

No. 10 – Life Imprisonment

[…]

C.

The provisions on the suspension of the remainder of a life sentence in cases where the enforcement of the sentence is no longer required on account of particularly aggravated guilt (§ 57a(1) first sentence no. 3 and second sentence in conjunction with § 57(1) first sentence no. 2 and second sentence of the Criminal Code) are compatible with the Basic Law if the principles of interpretation set out below are taken into account. The constitutional complaints against the challenged decisions are unfounded to the extent that they challenge the courts' rejection of the complainants' conditional release. The enforcement orders do not affect the complainants' human dignity. They do not violate their right to liberty of the person, given that they satisfy both the principle of proportionality and the procedural requirements that must be observed in decisions on the suspension of a life sentence.

[…]

I.

Applicable law provides that the remainder of a life sentence be suspended at the earliest when fifteen years of the sentence have been served (§ 57a(1) first sentence no. 1 of the Criminal Code). In addition, § 57a(1) first sentence no. 2 of the Criminal Code provides that suspending the remainder of a life sentence is only permissible if its continued enforcement is not required on account of particularly aggravated guilt. With this provision, the legislator intended to provide a specific time for the possible suspension of the remainder of a sentence, taking into account the wrongfulness and culpability associated with the criminal acts that resulted in the conviction (cf. in this respect BVerfGE 86, 288 <314>). However, the legislator retained life imprisonment as such, and, even in the case of a favourable criminal prognosis, it did not intend any kind of "automatic release" (BVerfGE 86, 288 <321>). When the period of imprisonment required on account of particularly aggravated guilt has been served, a life sentence may be conditionally suspended if this can be justified in consideration of the security interests of the general public, and if the convicted person consents thereto (§ 57a(1) first sentence no. 3 in conjunction with § 57(1) first sentence nos. 2 and 3 of the Criminal Code). The circumstances listed in § 57(1) second sentence of the Criminal Code must be taken into account in the decision (§ 57a(1) second sentence of the Criminal Code). The two constitutional complaints [challenging life sentences] enforced for more than thirty years respectively show that the requirement of § 57a(1) first sentence no. 3

of the Criminal Code may result in extraordinarily long deprivation of liberty – in some cases until the end of one's life.

65 The enforcement of a life sentence beyond the time required on account of particularly aggravated guilt on the grounds that the offender continues to be dangerous does not violate the guarantee of human dignity (Art. 1(1) of the Basic Law) or the fundamental right to liberty of the person (Art. 2(2) second sentence of the Basic Law).

66 1. Human dignity is the highest legal value within the constitutional order (cf. BVerfGE 27, 1 <6> – *Microcensus*; 30, 173 <193>; 32, 98 <108>). No one may be deprived of it (cf. BVerfGE 109, 133 <150>). Respect and protection of human dignity are among the constitutive principles of the Basic Law (cf. BVerfGE 45, 187 <227>; 87, 209 <228>; 96, 375 <398>; 102, 370 <389>; 109, 133 <149>). This means that every person has a right to be valued and respected as a person in society (*sozialer Wert- und Achtungsanspruch*); this right precludes turning a person into a mere object of state action or exposing them to treatment which generally calls into question their quality as a conscious subject (cf. BVerfGE 27, 1 <6> – *Microcensus*; 45, 187 <228>; 109, 133 <149 and 150>).

67 The individual's personality develops within the social community. The guarantee of Art. 1(1) of the Basic Law is based on the idea of human beings as intellectual-moral beings with the inherent aspiration to be free to determine their own being and to develop (BVerfGE 45, 187 <227>). The Basic Law resolves the tension between the individual and the community by endorsing the notion that the individual is connected to and bound by the community, insofar as the individual must accept that their fundamental rights are subject to restrictions serving interests of the common good (cf. BVerfGE 65, 1 <44> – *Census*; 109, 133 <151> with further references).

68 a) In view of these contents of Art. 1(1) of the Basic Law, the enforcement of a life sentence is, in principle, compatible with the Basic Law, including when it serves to protect the general public.

69 State and society are not barred from protecting themselves against criminal offenders who are dangerous to the public, even by way of a long period of deprivation of liberty (cf. BVerfGE 45, 187 <242>).

70 In addition, the enforcement of a life sentence beyond the time required on account of particularly aggravated guilt does not violate the principle of *nulla poena sine culpa* (the punishment must be appropriate in relation to culpability), which enjoys constitutional status and is derived from Arts. 1(1) and 2(1) of the Basic Law, and from the principle of the rule of law (cf. BVerfGE 20, 323 <331>; BVerfGE 25, 269 <285>).

Insofar as the legal provisions on the suspension of the remainder of a life sentence provide that, under certain conditions, the enforcement of the sentence may continue although it is no longer required on account of particularly aggravated guilt, this does not constitute the enforcement of a sentence irrespective of culpability, which would fall short of the requirement that punishment be appropriate in relation to culpability.

It is permissible under constitutional law to enforce a sentence of life imprisonment beyond the time required on account of particularly aggravated guilt on the grounds that the convicted person continues to be dangerous, thus ruling out a suspension of the sentence. Already in its judgment of 21 June 1977 concerning the constitutionality of life imprisonment, the Federal Constitutional Court concluded that life imprisonment, as a necessary and appropriate punishment for the most serious homicide offences, does not violate the constitutional requirement that all punishment be adequate and measured (cf. BVerfGE 45, 187 <253 to 259>). Accordingly, the principle of proportionate punishment that is appropriate in relation to culpability is not violated even where a life sentence, as the punishment imposed, is enforced [without suspension] if this is necessary on the grounds that the prisoner continues to be dangerous (cf. BVerfGE 45, 187 <242>).

b) The possibility of further enforcing a life sentence irrespective of particularly aggravated guilt also does not violate constitutional law on the grounds of the potentially damaging effects of imprisonment [...]

Long-term deprivation of liberty does not inevitably result in irreversible damage (cf. BVerfGE 45, 187 <237 *et seq.*>). Recent research, too, [...] does not prove that irreversible psychological or physical damage necessarily results from long-term deprivation of liberty (cf. BVerfGE 109, 133 <153>).

aa) Nevertheless, health impairments as a result of a prolonged period of imprisonment cannot be ruled out. In order to address this problem, constitutional law mandates that a life sentence must be complemented by adequate treatment programmes (cf. BVerfGE 45, 187 <238>; 64, 261 <272>; [...]). Prisons are obliged, even in respect of persons sentenced to life imprisonment, to work towards their social reintegration, to maintain their ability to cope with life and to counter the damaging effects of the deprivation of liberty (cf. BVerfGE 45, 187 <238>). The protection of human dignity imposes an obligation on the community to ensure that convicted persons are prepared for release from prison, so that after a prolonged period of deprivation of liberty, they can, at least to some extent, begin to orient themselves towards a normal life (cf. BVerfGE 35, 202 <235 and 236> – *Lebach*; 45, 187 <238 and 239>; [...]). [...]

bb) In the Prison Act, the legislator also laid out a treatment and social reintegration concept in respect of life sentences. The provisions on the prison regime (§ 3 of the

Prison Act) and on the objective of imprisonment (§ 2 first sentence of the Prison Act) apply to persons sentenced to life imprisonment, just as they apply to persons sentenced to fixed terms of imprisonment. The enforcement measures are also guided by the objective of social integration, and they must thus prepare prisoners for life in liberty. The provisions regarding the relaxation of imprisonment measures (§§ 10, 11 and 13 of the Prison Act) serve the purpose of reintegrating offenders into society. Apart from the provision on prison leave in § 13(3) of the Prison Act, the Act contains no particular provisions for persons sentenced to life imprisonment that set out different arrangements than for persons sentenced to fixed terms.

77 Applying the provisions of the Prison Act in conformity with the Constitution helps avoid the damaging effects of imprisonment, which is also in the public interest. Successful tests on probation considerably increase the prospects of release and may protect prisoners against resignation and depression. Therefore, even if persons are sentenced to life imprisonment, prisons are explicitly obliged to work towards their social reintegration in order to maintain prisoners' ability to cope with life and to counteract the damaging effects of imprisonment, thus also and primarily counteracting distorting changes to their personality. [...]

78 cc) In addition, the current legal provisions set out treatment measures in order to counter potential damage to prisoners' physical condition to the greatest possible extent or to treat them in the specific case. [...]

79-80 [...]

81 2. The guarantee of human dignity and the principle of the rule of law require that the convicted person have a specific and, in principle, also realistic chance of regaining liberty at a future point in time (see a below). When deciding on continued deprivation of liberty, the chance of regaining liberty must be guaranteed by strict adherence to the principle of proportionality in consideration of the fundamental right to liberty of the person under Art. 2(2) of the Basic Law (see b below). Finally, specific procedural requirements in respect of the long-term deprivation of liberty follow from the Basic Law; these must take into account the great significance of the right to liberty (see c below).

82 a) The possibility of enforcing a life sentence beyond the period during which particularly aggravated guilt precludes the suspension of the sentence sufficiently takes into account Arts. 1(1) and 2(2) of the Basic Law.

83 aa) Under Art. 1(1) of the Basic Law and the principle of the rule of law, the humane enforcement of a sentence requires that a person sentenced to life imprisonment must in principle retain a chance of regaining liberty at a future point in time (cf. BVerfGE 45, 187 <245>; 64, 261 <272>). [...]

84 bb) The decision on the continued enforcement of a life sentence should not only take into account the inviolability of human dignity. Such a decision primarily

No. 10 – Life Imprisonment

concerns the deprivation of the prisoner's personal liberty, and thus affects liberty of the person guaranteed under Art. 2(2) of the Basic Law (cf. BVerfGE 29, 312 <316>; 86, 288 <326>). The fundamental right to liberty under Art. 2(2) of the Basic Law enjoys high standing. It may only be restricted for particularly weighty reasons and subject to strict formal guarantees (Arts. 2(2) and 104(1) of the Basic Law; BVerfGE 86, 288 <326>). Given this particular significance, the constitutional principle of proportionality governs the sentencing to and enforcement of measures of deprivation of liberty to a particularly high degree (established case-law; cf. BVerfGE 19, 342 <349>; 20, 45 <49 and 50>; 20, 144 <148>; 29, 312 <316>; 35, 5 <9>; 36, 264 <270>; 70, 297 <311>; 90, 145 <172>; 109, 133 <156 *et seq.*>).

If a court rejects conditional suspension of the remainder of a sentence because the prisoner remains dangerous, this may result in deprivation of liberty for life in the individual case. However, under no circumstances may this infringe on the essence (*Wesensgehalt*) (Art. 19(2) of the Basic Law) of the fundamental right to liberty of the person. The inviolable essence of a fundament right must be determined in respect of each one based on its particular significance in the overall system of fundamental rights (cf. BVerfGE 22, 180 <219>). [...] In the field of criminal law and the law of criminal procedure, deprivation of liberty primarily serves to protect the general public (cf. BVerfGE 22, 180 <219>; 45, 187 <223>; 58, 208 <224 and 225>; 70, 297 <307>). According to these principles, interferences with liberty of the person are generally permissible if, taking into account the principle of proportionality, the protection of others or of the general public requires them.

b) The legal provisions on the suspension of a life sentence (§ 57a(1) first sentence no. 3 and second sentence in conjunction with § 57(1) first sentence no. 2 and second sentence of the Criminal Code) are also not objectionable under constitutional law insofar as they require that security interests of the general public be taken into account in the decision on suspending the remainder of the sentence, thus serving to protect the general public from dangerous offenders. The deprivation of liberty, potentially for life, constitutes a serious interference with the right to liberty of the person; yet this interference does not violate the guarantee that the essence of a fundamental right be protected as long as this is mandated by higher-ranking protected interests of others [...].

The prognosis of the danger posed by the convicted person provides a sufficient basis upon which to decide on the deprivation of liberty beyond the time during which particularly aggravated guilt precludes an earlier release (see aa below). In such cases, however, the Basic Law requires strict adherence to the principle of proportionality; in this context, the general public's need for security may take precedence over the convicted person's right to liberty (see bb below). [...]

88 aa) It is not objectionable under constitutional law if the legislator requires the suspension of a life sentence to be based on a prognosis of danger in order to achieve the desired protection. This applies irrespective of the uncertainties involved in having a prognosis serve as the basis for the long-term deprivation of liberty (cf. BVerfGE 109, 133 <157>). A perfect prediction of human behaviour is ultimately impossible, given that there are no criteria that could provide, on the basis of past and present observations of human behaviour, an absolutely reliable prognosis of a person's likelihood to reoffend.

Nevertheless, an expert opinion on the prognosis of danger posed by a convicted person is a necessary aid to the judicial decision on whether to suspend the remainder of a sentence or on relaxing imprisonment measures [...].

89 bb) Constitutional limits in respect of the particularly serious interference arising from the potentially life-long deprivation of liberty follow, in particular, from the prohibition of excessive measures (*Übermaßverbot*). [...] The longer the deprivation of liberty lasts, the stricter the proportionality requirements in respect of the depriving measures (cf. on confinement in a psychiatric hospital BVerfGE 70, 297; on preventive detention BVerfGE 109, 133 <159>; [...]). [...]

90 When interpreting § 57a(1) first sentence no. 3 in conjunction with § 57(1) first sentence no. 2 of the Criminal Code, the courts and legal scholarship have sufficiently taken into account this fact [...].

91 On the one hand, the convicted person's general right to liberty carries great weight, given the long prison sentence that has typically been served (cf. BVerfGE 70, 297 <315>; [...]). That is why the clause on the defensibility of the suspension of a sentence "having regard to public security interests" also implies that an acceptable residual risk is taken [...]. To what extent a residual risk is acceptable depends not only on the legal interests threatened in case of a relapse, but also on the degree of likelihood of recidivism. Therefore, even in cases of serious violent or sexual offences, the mere hypothetical possibility of a relapse, which can never be ruled out with certainty due to the limits of any prognosis, does not rule out the suspension of a sentence from the outset [...]. Rather, the decision to reject a suspension must be supported by specific facts that make the risk appear unacceptable.

92 On the other hand, the prognosis to be made in the context of the decision on suspension requires the suspension to be defensible in light of the recidivism that is to be expected under certain circumstances (cf. BVerfGE 86, 288 <327>). The higher the threatened legal interest ranks, the lower the risk of recidivism required. In respect of offences that carry a life sentence, such as murder under specific aggravating circumstances (§ 211 of the Criminal Code), the general public's need for security is, by its nature, of particular significance for determining whether it is

No. 10 – Life Imprisonment

defensible to test on probation if the convicted person will not commit any further criminal offences once released from prison [...]. In cases such as the one at hand, conditional release from life imprisonment can therefore only be considered under strict conditions given the nature of the offences to be feared if it fails [...].

Life imprisonment, which is very onerous for the convicted persons, can thus be justified by the particularly high value placed on life and the corresponding increased need on the part of the general public for security, which must also be a decisive factor in any decision on conditional early release. When weighing the risks, the increasing length of imprisonment must be taken into account in favour of the convicted person. A certain risk of offences of merely medium or low weight does not stand in the way of a suspension of the remainder of a life sentence [...]. In contrast to fixed-term imprisonment, which is followed by release notwithstanding a negative prognosis, the longer the continued enforcement of a life sentence goes on for, the more likely it would be to violate the prohibition of excessive measures, if the only offences the prisoner was expected to commit were medium-level. [...] 93

If it is positively established that the convicted person remains dangerous, the continued enforcement of a life sentence is necessary in order to protect the general public. In addition, however, the particularly high value placed on life justifies the continued enforcement of a life sentence also where, upon satisfaction of the constitutional requirement for adequate judicial investigation of the facts, it is impossible to give a favourable prognosis of danger. Even though life imprisonment was imposed as the appropriate sentence in relation to the offender's culpability, it is not objectionable under constitutional law that the doubts that remain in these cases with respect to a sufficiently favourable prognosis are held against the convicted person [...]. 94

cc) [...] 95-96

c) The principle of proportionality also gives rise to procedural requirements in respect of particularly long periods of deprivation of liberty. Procedural safeguards must sufficiently reflect the great significance of the right to liberty (cf. BVerfGE 86, 288 <326>). 97

Given that the duration of a life sentence is indefinite, its continued enforcement must be reviewed regularly [...]. The longer the deprivation of liberty continues, the stricter the requirements for the courts to investigate the facts [...]. The conditions for suspension must be reviewed early on in order to allow time for an appropriate preparation for release. In this context, a relaxation of imprisonment measures is particularly important [...]. The increasing weight of the right to liberty in case of very long periods of deprivation of liberty also affects the requirements pertaining to the substantiation of the judicial decision [...]. As a rule, a public 98 defender must be assigned to the convicted person [...]. If the deprivation of liberty is essentially justified on the basis of the security interests of the general public, it is necessary to examine whether the prisoner can be granted privileges to compensate for the particular burdens of the long period of deprivation of liberty [...].

99-113 [...]

II.

114 The legal provisions pertaining to the enforcement of a life sentence once fifteen years have been served (§ 57a(1) first sentence no. 1 of the Criminal Code) and possibly after a longer minimum period of imprisonment to be served on account of particularly aggravated guilt (§ 57a(1) first sentence no. 2 of the Criminal Code) on the basis of § 57a(1) first sentence no. 3 and second sentence in conjunction with § 57(1) first sentence no. 2 and second sentence of the Criminal Code satisfy the constitutional specificity requirements.

115 1. The provisions regarding the suspension of a life sentence must be measured against Art. 104(1) first sentence of the Basic Law in conjunction with the principle of the rule of law. [...]

116 2. § 57a(1) first sentence no. 3 and second sentence in conjunction with § 57(1) first sentence no. 2 and second sentence of the Criminal Code define a sufficiently precise standard of review for the decision on suspension. The constituent elements upon which the decision on reviewing a suspension of life imprisonment is based are sufficiently specific, also with regard to the serious interference with fundamental rights that is associated with imprisonment potentially for life.

117 a) When reviewing criminal law provisions, the requirement of specificity serves to safeguard freedom (cf. BVerfGE 75, 329 <341>; 96, 68 <97>; 105, 135 <152 and 153>). In the context of deprivations of liberty, the Basic Law requires statutory provisions that fulfil particular formal requirements and procedural guarantees (cf. Art. 2(2) third sentence and Art. 104(1) and (2) of the Basic Law). The more serious the interference with a fundamental right that a law provides for, the stricter the requirements with respect to its specificity (cf. BVerfGE 59, 104 <114>; 75, 329 <342>; 86, 288 <311>). The degree of specificity required under constitutional law depends on the specific constituent elements and on the circumstances that result in the application of the law (cf. BVerfGE 28, 175 <183>; 86, 288 <311>). The requirement of specificity deriving from the rule of law only mandates that the legislator must draft laws as specifically as possible, taking account of the particular nature of the underlying subject matter and the purposes pursued (cf. BVerfGE 49, 168 <181>; 78, 205 <212>; 102, 254 <337>; 110, 370 <396>). It is sufficient that

No. 10 – Life Imprisonment

the constituent elements of a statutory provision can be determined by interpreting the relevant provisions by means of the recognised rules of interpretation (cf. BVerfGE 21, 209 <215>; 79, 106 <120>; 102, 254 <337>; 103, 332 <384>). [...]

b) § 57a(1) first sentence no. 3 and second sentence in conjunction with § 57(1) first sentence no. 2 and second sentence of the Criminal Code, which governs suspension, satisfies these requirements. The constituent elements concerning the decision on suspending the enforcement of the remainder of a life sentence beyond the time required on account of particularly aggravated guilt are sufficiently specific.

[...]

c) The requirement of specificity does not require that legal provisions establish an absolute maximum period for enforcing a life sentence.

Where fifteen years of a life sentence have been served and continued enforcement is not required on account of particularly aggravated guilt, the continued deprivation of liberty will be primarily based on the prognosis that the convicted person remains dangerous to a degree that justifies the continued enforcement of a life sentence. It is in the very nature of such a judicial decision, which depends on a prognosis, that its outcome in a given case cannot be determined with certainty in advance. Many different aspects must be taken into account in the assessment, which are all subject to dynamic processes. The offender's personality usually continues to develop. It is only natural that predictions on the degree of the future danger posed by convicted persons present factual difficulties, yet this does not necessarily lead to an unconstitutional lack of specificity in the requirements laid down by the legislator. Indeed, an absolute maximum time limit for the enforcement of a life sentence would contradict the purpose of § 57a(1) first sentence no. 3 of the Criminal Code. The danger posed by a person cannot be determined in abstract and general terms by a maximum time limit. The offender does not necessarily cease posing a danger to the general public after a certain time.

III.

[...]

IV.

1. The orders challenged by complainant no. 1 meet the constitutional requirements set out above. They do not violate his human dignity, they are in accordance with the principle of proportionality and they satisfy the procedural requirements that must be observed when deciding on the suspension of a life sentence.

130 a) Each of the four decisions rejecting suspension that are challenged here took into account the constitutional standards set out above regarding respect for human dignity under Art. 1(1) of the Basic Law.

131 [...]

132 b) The challenged orders do not definitively deny complainant no. 1 the opportunity of ever being able to live in liberty again, and they stand up to constitutional review with regard to the prohibition of excessive measures in the context of liberty-depriving measures.

133 The ordinary courts plausibly held that conditional release was not tenable because the complainant's conduct in open detention had shown that he remains dangerous. The chance to regain his liberty may be realised in the future when imprisonment no longer appears necessary to protect the higher-ranking interest of others. In particular, the complainant's conduct in the event of potential relaxations of imprisonment measures will be of considerable significance.

134 aa) The outcome of the challenged orders remains within the margin of appreciation laid down in the Basic Law. The courts competent for enforcement assessed the continued danger posed by the complainant and, on the basis of new and up-to-date information, concluded that the prognosis of danger must be to his disadvantage.

135-138 [...]

139 bb) The ordinary courts based each of their decisions on an up-to-date and detailed opinion submitted by an external expert regarding the danger posed by the complainant. The expert opinions, prepared promptly before their decisions and by experts they knew to be experienced, provided a sufficient basis for the courts' decisions. In the second suspension proceedings of 2005/2006, the Higher Regional Court obtained a new and up-to-date prognosis so that it had an expert opinion available on the development of the complainant's personality since the last assessment. Independently of each other, the external experts concluded that the complainant had a tendency to react in ways that gave rise to the assumption that he remained dangerous. They substantiated this conclusion. No further measures were necessary to satisfy the requirement to investigate the facts as thoroughly as possible. The courts competent for enforcement also sufficiently observed the stricter substantiation requirements applying to cases of long-term deprivation of liberty and assigned a public defender to the complainant.

140 c) The next decision on suspension will have to take into account that the expert, in her last opinion of 10 May 2006, considered a relaxation of imprisonment measures to be generally tenable and even indispensable in preparation for release. The fact that the complainant has now been in closed detention for six years without any relaxations gives rise to the concern that his right to liberty is not being sufficiently

No. 10 – Life Imprisonment

respected. In the context of a relaxation of imprisonment measures, it will be possible to gain some indications for further assessing whether the complainant remains dangerous. In addition, both the prohibition of excessive measures inherent in the fundamental right to liberty, and the requirements to be observed in suspension proceedings that arise from the fact that the prognosis of danger is only valid for a limited period require the courts competent for enforcement to regularly review their decisions on suspension.

In their decisions hereafter, the courts competent for enforcement will also have to take into account that the right to respect for human dignity requires that the complainant be permitted to visit his mother, who is ill and elderly, at appropriate intervals. Direct contact to his only surviving and closest relative is an integral part of the complainant's remaining quality of life. 141

2. The challenged decisions on suspending the remainder of complainant no. 2's life sentence also satisfy the constitutional requirements (see a below). [...] 142

a) In their decisions, the courts competent for enforcement sufficiently reflected the increasing weight of the convicted person's right to respect for his human dignity and of his right to a realistic chance of regaining liberty. 143

[...] 144-149
b) [...] 150-161
c) [...] 162
d) [...] 163
[...] 164-165

Justices: Hassemer, Broß, Osterloh, Di Fabio, Mellinghoff, Lübbe-Wolff, Gerhardt, Landau

No. 11

BVerfGE 128, 282 – Coercive Treatment in Psychiatric Confinement under Criminal Law

HEADNOTES

to the Order of the Second Senate of 23 March 2011
2 BvR 882/09

1. Medical treatment of persons in psychiatric confinement against their natural will constitutes a serious interference with the fundamental right under Article 2(2) of the Basic Law; this interference may be justified if it aims to achieve the confinement's objective.

2. Coercive medical treatment administered to achieve the confinement's objective is only permissible if, due to illness, the confined person lacks the mental capacity for insight into the necessity of medical treatment or for acting upon this insight. Coercive medical treatment may only be used as a last resort, and only if the prospects of success in respect of the objective of the treatment justifying the measures are good and if it does not burden affected persons disproportionately to the benefit that can reasonably be expected. In order to protect the fundamental rights of confined persons, specific procedural safeguards are necessary.

3. A clear and specific statutory framework must set out the essential requirements, including procedural requirements, under which coercive medical treatment is permissible.

No. 11 – Coercive Treatment in Psychiatric Confinement under Criminal Law

FEDERAL CONSTITUTIONAL COURT
- 2 BvR 882/09 -

IN THE NAME OF THE PEOPLE

In the proceedings
on the constitutional complaint of

Mr P...,

– authorised representative: ...

against a) the Order of the Palatinate Higher Regional Court Zweibrücken of 18 March 2009 - 1 WS 365/08 (Vollz) -,

b) the Order of the Landau Regional Court of 16 October 2008 - 2 StVK 255/06 -,

c) the notification of coercive medical treatment of the complainant by letter from the Klingenmünster Hospital of 28 September 2006 - Dr. Atm./Zs. -

the Federal Constitutional Court – Second Senate –

with the participation of Justices

> President Voßkuhle,
> Di Fabio,
> Mellinghoff,
> Lübbe-Wolff,
> Gerhardt,
> Landau,
> Huber,
> Hermanns

held on 23 March 2011:

1. § 6(1) second sentence of the Rhineland-Palatinate Act on Psychiatric Confinement of Criminal Offenders of 23 September 1986 (GVBl RLP p. 223), last amended by the Act of 22 December 2004 (GVBl RLP p. 571), is incompatible with Article 2(2) first sentence in conjunction with Article 19(4) of the Basic Law, and void.

2. The Orders of the Landau Regional Court of 16 October 2008 - 2 StVK 255/06 - and of the Palatinate Higher Regional Court of 18 March 2009 - 1 Ws 365/08 (Vollz) - violate the complainant's fundamental right under Article 2(2)

first sentence of the Basic Law. The Orders are reversed. The matter is remanded to the Landau Regional Court.

3. [...]
4. [...]

REASONS:

A.

I.

1   The constitutional complaint concerns coercive medical treatment of a person confined in a psychiatric hospital on the basis of § 6(1) second sentence, first half-sentence of the Rhineland-Palatinate Act on Psychiatric Confinement of Criminal Offenders.

2-10 [...]

II.

11 1. The complainant is confined in the Klingenmünster Hospital following the Judgment of the Frankenthal Regional Court of 16 December 1999. As a result of a delusional disorder exempting him from criminal responsibility, he had beaten his sleeping wife with a wine bottle and attempted to suffocate her. Subsequently, with another wine bottle, he had beaten his daughter, who was lying in bed.

12 From the end of December 1999 to the end of February 2000, the complainant was treated with an atypical neuroleptic drug. The complainant refused further treatment due to side effects. In 2005, in the context of the annual review of continued confinement, Prof. Dr. N., an external expert, stated that the paranoid psychosis which had triggered the act for which he was confined persisted. According to the expert, the only way to improve the complainant's mental health was to treat him with neuroleptic agents. [...]

13 2. In the letter dated 28 September 2006 challenged by the complainant, the hospital notified the complainant of treatment "with a suitable neuroleptic drug administered by intramuscular injection – if necessary against your will". [...]

14 3. a) The complainant lodged a "complaint" and requested external medical evaluation by a specialist. He stated that the planned treatment was associated with significant health risks and therefore not permitted against his will. These risks included the possibility of blood count changes and impaired liver function, as

pointed out by the hospital itself. He claimed that the drugs also had personality-changing effects. [...]
b) [...] 15
c) By its challenged Order of 16 October 2008, the Regional Court [...] dismissed 16 the application and ruled that coercive drug treatment with atypical neuroleptic agents was permissible for a period of six months. [...]
[...] 17-20
4. a) [...] 21
b) By its challenged Order of 18 March 2009, the Higher Regional Court dismissed 22 the complaint on points of law as unfounded. [...]

III.

In his constitutional complaint, challenging the orders of the Regional Court and 23 the Higher Regional Court as well as the notification letter of the hospital, the complainant asserts a violation of his rights under Art. 2(2) and Art. 1(1) of the Basic Law, Art. 3 of the European Convention on Human Rights as well as of his right to a fair trial. [...]
[...] 24

IV.

Statements on the constitutional complaint were submitted by the Federal Government, the *Land* Government and the *Land* Parliament of Rhineland-Palatinate, the Federal Court of Justice, the German Association for Psychiatry, Psychotherapy and Psychosomatics (*Deutsche Gesellschaft für Psychiatrie, Psychotherapie und Nervenheilkunde*) as well as by the Federal Association of Users and Survivors of Psychiatry (*Bundesverband Psychiatrie-Erfahrener*). [...]
[...] 26-35

B.

The constitutional complaint is admissible to the extent that the complainant challenges the orders of the Regional Court and the Higher Regional Court. [...] 36
To the extent that the constitutional complaint is admissible, it is well-founded. 37 The orders of the Regional Court and the Higher Regional Court, which confirm the lawfulness of the announced coercive treatment, violate the complainant's fundamental right under Art. 2(2) first sentence of the Basic Law. [...]

38 [...]

I.

39 1. The medical treatment of confined persons against their natural will interferes with the fundamental right to physical integrity (Art. 2(2) first sentence of the Basic Law). This fundamental right protects the physical integrity of holders of fundamental rights and thus also their right to self-determination related to it. Traditionally, this includes protection against coercive treatment by the state (cf. BVerfGE 79, 174 <201>).

40 2. Coercive treatment amounts to an interference, including where it is carried out for curative purposes. [...]

41 Even if the affected person does not put up any physical resistance, any treatment administered against their will amounts to an interference. Merely desisting from a certain type of protest cannot be interpreted as consent. The only scenario in which medical treatment of a confined person, which affects the fundamental right to physical integrity, might not be an interference is where the affected person gives voluntary and informed consent. That requires that the confined person be capable of giving consent (cf. BGHZ 29, 46 <51>; 154, 205 <210>) and that they not be subjected to undue pressure, such as threats of disadvantages, in case of refusal of treatment that are not simply necessary consequences of the person's condition that are to be expected if the person is left untreated or if treatment is refused.

42 A confined person's lack of mental capacity on grounds of illness does not render treatment against their natural will and affecting their physical integrity any less of an interference with the scope of protection of Art. 2(2) first sentence of the Basic Law. Affected persons may even, because of their lack of mental capacity, perceive the interference as particularly threatening, which increases its weight (see 3 below). Lack of mental capacity does not, from the outset, rule out that protection is afforded by Art. 2(2) of the Basic Law [...]. Even with the consent of a custodian appointed for a confined person who lacks mental capacity and is unable to consent, the measure still amounts to an interference given that it is carried out against the natural will of the affected person [...].

43 3. Coercive medical treatment of a confined person with neuroleptic agents constitutes a particularly serious interference with fundamental rights.

44 The substantive guarantees of freedom and liberty in Art. 2(2) of the Basic Law – including the right to physical integrity – carry special weight among the fundamental rights enshrined in the Constitution (cf. BVerfGE 65, 317 <322>). Coercive medical treatment of confined persons, especially surgery and coercive drug treatment, constitutes a particularly serious type of interference with the right to

physical integrity [...]. Affected persons are coerced into tolerating a measure that fits the classification of bodily harm [...] and is generally only permissible with the consent of the affected person justifying such a measure under criminal law. The interference that is coercive medical treatment not only affects physical integrity as such, it also, in a particularly severe way, affects the related right to self-determination, which is protected under Art. 2(2) first sentence of the Basic Law. A deliberate interference with physical integrity carried out by others will be perceived as all the more threatening the more the affected person feels helpless and at the mercy of others. In addition, treatment in psychiatric confinement often affects persons who, due to their psychological condition, will have particularly sensitive reactions both to the horror of the coercive invasion of their physical integrity and to their will being disregarded, as well as to the fear of these intrusions. When assessing the severity of the interference, subjective feelings are relevant, too (cf. BVerfGE 89, 315 <324>). Finally, administering neuroleptic drugs to patients against their natural will constitutes [...] a particularly serious interference with fundamental rights also with regard to the effects of these drugs, not least given the possibility of serious, irreversible and life-threatening side effects, which cannot be ruled out [...]. In addition, psychotropic drugs are intended to change mental processes. Therefore, their administration against the natural will of the affected person, regardless of physical coercion, especially affects the core of personality.

II.

1. Despite the weight of this interference, the legislator is not generally precluded from allowing coercive treatment of a confined person. This also applies to treatment that serves to achieve the confinement's objective (§ 136 of the Prison Act, § 1(2) of the Rhineland-Palatinate Act on Psychiatric Confinement of Criminal Offenders), i.e. that aims to prepare the confined person for release.

a) However, the necessary protection of third parties from offences that confined persons might commit after their release cannot be considered a justification in this regard. Such protection can also be achieved by keeping confined persons in a psychiatric hospital without providing treatment. [...]

b) The interference may be justified, however, on the basis of the confined person's own liberty interest (Art. 2(2) second sentence of the Basic Law) if they are not able to exercise this interest as a result of their lack of mental capacity due to illness.

aa) The fundamental freedoms [enshrined in the Basic Law] encompass the right to exercise the liberties and freedoms in a way that is – at least in the eyes of third parties – contrary to the seemingly best interests of the fundamental rights holder. Therefore, it is generally for individuals to decide whether they wish to undergo therapeutic measures or other treatment that solely serve to 'better' them (cf. BVerfGE 22, 180 <219 and 220>). This constitutionally protected freedom also encompasses the 'freedom to be ill', and thus the right to refuse curative treatment, even if it is urgently indicated according to current medical findings (cf. BVerfGE 58, 208 <226>; 30, 47 <53>; 22, 180 <219>).

49 bb) When balancing the restricted fundamental right against those fundamental rights interests which the interference with that right seeks to protect, the weight of the restricted fundamental right cannot be considered completely independently of the actual ability of its holder to reach a decision informed by their free will (cf. BVerfGE 58, 208 <225>). Therefore, the legislator is entitled to allow treatment measures against the natural will of the holders of fundamental rights as an exception and subject to strict conditions if, due to illness, they lack the mental capacity for insight into the severity of their illness and the necessity of treatment measures, or for acting upon such insight. The Federal Constitutional Court has held that, subject to these conditions, the serious interference with fundamental rights that is deprivation of liberty may be justified to protect the affected persons themselves; it accepted the possibility of confinement for treatment purposes as provided for by *Land* confinement law in respect of such cases (cf. BVerfGE 58, 208 <224 *et seq.*> [...]).

50 Nothing fundamentally different applies with regard to the interference that is medical treatment of confined persons against their natural will. [...]

51 If a confined person, due to illness, lacks the mental capacity for insight into the illness that makes their confinement necessary, or if they cannot appreciate or act upon the fact that the only chance of a cure lies in treatment, the state is not obliged, on grounds of some principle of the primacy of an illness-induced expression of will, to abandon them to a life of permanent confinement. An interference aiming to restore the factual preconditions for the free self-determination of the confined person may be permissible under these circumstances [...]. The lack of mental capacity, due to illness, precludes affected persons from exercising their fundamental rights as far as regaining their liberty is concerned. As the affected persons are vulnerable in that respect (cf. BVerfGE 58, 208 <225>), the state may – in consideration of the principle of proportionality – interfere with those fundamental rights to which the affected persons, only on account of illness, attribute too much weight.

52 cc) The UN Convention on the Rights of Persons with Disabilities (CRPD), which has the force of law in Germany [...] and serves as an interpretive guideline for determining the content and scope of fundamental rights (cf. BVerfGE 111, 307 <317 and 318>), does not suggest a different conclusion [...].

Persons with disabilities to whom the guarantees of the Convention apply include persons with mental illness if they have a long-term impairment that may hinder their full, effective and equal participation in society (Art. 1(2) CRPD [...]). The Convention, and in particular its Art. 12(2) and Art. 12(4), aims to protect and strengthen the autonomy of persons with disabilities. In Art. 12(2) CRPD, States Parties recognise that persons with disabilities enjoy legal capacity on an equal basis with others in all aspects of life. Art. 12(4) CRPD obliges States Parties to respect the rights, will and preferences of the persons concerned when taking measures relating to the exercise of legal capacity. Yet these provisions do not generally prohibit measures relating to a limited capacity for self-determination due to illness to be carried out against the natural will of affected persons. This clearly follows, *inter alia*, from the regulatory context of Art. 12(4) CRPD, which expressly relates to measures restricting the legal capacity of affected persons. The Convention does not prohibit such measures in general; rather, it limits their permissibility, including by obliging States Parties to the Convention under Art. 12(4) CRPD to provide for appropriate safeguards against conflicts of interest, abuse and disregard, and to ensure proportionality.

2. Coercive medical treatment aiming to secure the eventual release of the affected person is only permissible under constitutional law if they, due to illness, lack mental capacity to appreciate their situation in a way that leads to their taking action (lack of mental capacity due to illness) [...].

While it must be acknowledged that these conditions constitute exceptional authorisation for the state to "protect individuals from themselves" (cf. BVerfGE 58, 208 <224> [...]), this does not establish the 'sovereignty of reason' (*Vernunfthoheit*) of state organs over fundamental rights holders in such a way that their will is set aside merely because it differs from average preferences or appears to be unreasonable from an outside perspective [...]. The lack of capacity for free self-determination, which would justify an interference, cannot be inferred from the mere fact that the affected person refuses medical treatment that is necessary from a medical point of view and has risks and side effects that, according to prevailing opinion, are tolerable with respect to the benefits that can reasonably be expected. Rather, a lack of mental capacity for insight due to illness or for acting upon such insight is necessary (cf. BVerfGE 58, 208 <225>).

3. Further requirements, in addition to the necessary lack of mental capacity due to illness, result from the principle of proportionality. In light of the particular severity of the interference, coercive medical treatment aiming to achieve the confinement's objective is only permissible under strict conditions.

a) aa) In substantive terms, it follows from the principle of proportionality that measures of coercive treatment may only be applied if their prospects of success are good in regard to the objective of the treatment justifying the measures [...]. This also limits the permissible duration of their use. [...]

58 bb) Furthermore, coercive measures may only be taken as a last resort, where less intrusive measures are unlikely to be successful [...]. In relation to coercive drug treatment administered to achieve the confinement's objective, this means, firstly, that less intrusive treatment must be futile. Secondly, to the extent that the affected persons are able to communicate, coercive treatment must be preceded by serious attempts, taking the necessary time and without impermissible pressure, to obtain their agreement based on trust (see B I 2 above) [...]. This applies independently of whether confined persons have mental capacity, including the capacity to consent, since coercive treatment constitutes an interference regardless of mental capacity or capacity to consent (see B I 2 above).

59 Even if a person lacks capacity to consent, appropriate disclosure by a physician of information on the intended measure cannot be dispensed with from the outset. It is true that informing a person who lacks capacity to consent cannot serve as a basis for the consent justifying the measure [...]. Regardless of whether effective informed consent can be obtained by providing information on the intended measure, even persons lacking capacity to consent may not be left wondering whether and how they will be subjected to treatment [...]. Informing the affected persons about the intended treatment and its effects in accordance with their cognitive abilities is therefore still required (cf. also UN Principles for the Protection of Persons with Mental Illness, Principle 11(9)).

60 The principle that an interference may not exceed the limits of what is necessary must also guide the decision on which specific measures to take [...].

61 cc) Beyond the requirements of suitability and necessity, for the coercive medical treatment to be justified, it must also not entail burdens on the affected persons that are disproportionate to the benefits that can reasonably be expected. [...] This requirement will generally not be met in cases of coercive treatment administered to achieve the confinement's objective if the treatment is associated with a more than insignificant residual risk of irreversible damage to health [...].

62 b) The fundamental rights give rise to procedural requirements for authorities and courts (cf. BVerfGE 52, 380 <389 and 390>; 101, 106 <122>; 124, 43 <70>; established case-law). Persons confined in closed facilities are particularly dependent on such safeguards.

63 aa) Certainly in respect of scheduled treatments, and thus also of treatments administered to achieve the confinement's objective, notice must be given to affected persons where a measure is to be performed even though the necessary efforts to obtain consent (see B II 3 a bb above) have failed, so that the affected person has time to seek legal protection. [...]

No. 11 – Coercive Treatment in Psychiatric Confinement under Criminal Law

[...] 64-65

bb) In order to ensure proportionality, it is indispensable that coercive drug treatment be ordered and supervised by a physician. [...] 66

cc) The advance effects (*Vorwirkung*) of the fundamental rights guarantee of recourse to the courts (see B II 3 b aa above) make it necessary to document treatment measures administered against the will of the confined persons, including their coerciveness, how they were administered, the relevant reasons therefor as well as the monitoring of their effects [...]. 67

dd) Furthermore, specific procedural safeguards follow from Art. 2(2) of the Basic Law to protect against the particular risk to fundamental rights posed by the situation where the decision ordering coercive treatment is made solely by the institution where the person is confined [...] (cf. BVerfGE 52, 391 <407 and 408>; 53, 30 <60 *et seq.*>; 113, 29 <57 and 58> – *Seizure of Electronic Data*; 124, 43 <70>; established case-law). [...] 68

[...] 69

The above considerations give rise not only to specific constitutional requirements for potential court proceedings. [...] It must also be ensured that, prior to coercive treatment, a review is carried out that is entirely independent of the institution where the person is confined. [...] 70

[...] 71

4. a) Like any other interference with fundamental rights, coercive treatment of a confined person is only permissible on the basis of a statutory provision that sets out the permissibility requirements for the interference. This applies to both requirements for justifying the interference and procedural requirements. The essential questions regarding how to give effect to fundamental rights must be addressed through the enactment of legal provisions on procedural matters, just as with substantive matters (cf. BVerfGE 57, 295 <320 and 321>; 73, 280 <294, 296>; 82, 209 <224 and 225, 227>; 120, 378 <429>). 72

The requirements subject to which an interference is permissible must be set out in a sufficiently clear and specific manner [...]. 73

III.

According to these standards, § 6(1) second sentence, first half-sentence of the Rhineland-Palatinate Act on Psychiatric Confinement of Criminal Offenders does not constitute a sufficient statutory basis for coercive treatment. The requirements of legal clarity and specificity, which are applicable in the context of a particularly serious interference with fundamental rights, are not satisfied by this provision (see B I 3 above). [...] 74

75-76 1. [...]
77 a) Thus, in particular, there is no statutory provision setting out that lack of mental capacity due to illness is an indispensable prerequisite that must apply in cases of coercive treatment administered to achieve the confinement's objective (see B II 2 above). [...] § 6(5) first sentence of the Rhineland-Palatinate Act on Psychiatric Confinement of Criminal Offenders, which lays down that measures must be reasonable (*zumutbar*) with respect to the confined patient and may not be disproportionate to the success that can be expected, does not sufficiently specify the substantive permissibility requirements for the interference.
78 To the extent that the Act contains a provision specifying the efforts, required by the principle of proportionality, to obtain the consent of the affected person, it is [...] insufficient because it only requires such efforts if the affected person has comprehensive capacity for insight [...] (see B II 3 a bb above).
79 b) In addition, there is no legal provision setting out further essential procedural prerequisites for interference necessary for protecting fundamental rights. [...] Furthermore, requirements relating to the documentation of treatment are lacking (see B II 3 b cc above), as are [...] the necessary procedural safeguards to ensure that, prior to coercive treatment [...], a review that is entirely independent of the institution is carried out (see B II 3 b cc above). [...]
80 2. The shortcomings of the provision cannot be remedied by interpreting it in conformity with the Constitution. The constitutional shortcomings can only be resolved by the legislator.

C.

81 The violations of constitutional law found here concern § 6(1) second sentence of the Rhineland-Palatinate Act on Psychiatric Confinement of Criminal Offenders in its entirety [...]. Therefore, the entire § 6(1) second sentence of the Act must be declared void.
82-83 [...]

Justices: Voßkuhle, Di Fabio, Mellinghoff, Lübbe-Wolff, Gerhardt, Landau, Huber, Hermanns

No. 12

BVerfGE 142, 313 – Coercive Medical Treatment

HEADNOTES

to the Order of the First Senate of 26 July 2016
1 BvL 8/15

1. The state's duty of protection following from Article 2(2) first sentence of the Basic Law requires that, under certain narrow conditions and as a last resort, where there is imminent risk of considerable impairments to their health, persons under custodianship who lack mental capacity be provided medical treatment even if that treatment is against their natural will.

2. a) Judicial review proceedings pursuant to Article 100(1) of the Basic Law may also concern provisions that, according to the plausible view of the referring court, lack elements that would be required by a specific constitutional duty of protection.

    b) If there is a weighty and objective need to clarify a question of constitutional law raised by a referral, the referral may remain admissible even if the initial proceedings have become moot because of the death of one of the main parties.

FEDERAL CONSTITUTIONAL COURT
- 1 BvL 8/15 -

IN THE NAME OF THE PEOPLE

In the proceedings
for constitutional review of

whether § 1906(3) of the Civil Code in the version of the Act on Consent by a Custodian to Coercive Medical Treatment of 18 February 2013 (BGBl I, p. 266) is compatible with Article 3(1) of the Basic Law to the extent that, as a precondition to the custodian's consent to in-patient coercive medical treatment, it requires the treatment to be conducted in a setting of confinement pursuant to § 1906(1) of the Civil Code, even in cases where affected persons do not intend to remove themselves from the site of treatment, or are physically unable to do so

– Order of Suspension and Referral of the Federal Court of Justice of 1 July 2015
  - XII ZB 89/15 -

the Federal Constitutional Court – First Senate –

with the participation of Justices

> Vice-President Kirchhof,
> Gaier,
> Eichberger,
> Schluckebier,
> Masing,
> Paulus,
> Baer,
> Britz

held on 26 July 2016:

1. It is incompatible with the state's duty of protection following from Article 2(2) first sentence of the Basic Law that, where there is imminent risk of considerable impairments to their health, persons under custodianship who lack the mental capacity for insight into the necessity of needed medical treatment or for acting upon this insight cannot, under any circumstances, receive medical treatment against their natural will if they are receiving in-patient treatment but cannot be confined in an institution because they do not intend to remove themselves from the site of treatment or are physically unable to do so.

2. The legislator is obliged to enact provisions covering this type of case without undue delay.

3. Until such provisions are enacted, § 1906(3) of the Civil Code, in the version of Article 1 no. 3 of the Act on Consent by a Custodian to Coercive Medical Treatment of 18 February 2013 (BGBl I, p. 266), also applies to persons under custodianship who are treated as in-patients and are unable to remove themselves from the site of coercive medical treatment.

REASONS:

A.

1 The Federal Court of Justice referred to the Federal Constitutional Court the question whether § 1906(3) of the Civil Code […] is compatible with the Basic

No. 12 – Coercive Medical Treatment

Law to the extent that, as a precondition to in-patient coercive medical treatment, it requires the treatment to be conducted in a setting of confinement pursuant to § 1906(1) of the Civil Code, even in cases where affected persons do not intend to remove themselves from the site of treatment, or are physically unable to do so, i.e. where ordering confinement is impermissible according to established case-law.

I.

1. a) The objective of the [...] Custodianship Act [...] is to improve the legal status of adults with mental illness or disability taking into account their individual needs and abilities.

If adults, due to mental illness or physical, mental or psychological disability, are unable, entirely or in part, to attend to their affairs, the custodianship court appoints a custodian for them on their application or *ex officio* (cf. § 1896(1) of the Civil Code). The Civil Code governs the appointment of a custodian (§§ 1896 *et seq.* of the Civil Code), the extent of custodianship (§§ 1901 *et seq.* of the Civil Code), and makes certain measures subject to the approval of the custodianship court (§§ 1904 *et seq.* of the Civil Code).

To the extent that custodianship pursuant to § 1896 of the Civil Code is ordered for tasks relating to health matters, the custodian must arrange for the necessary measures to be taken and, where required, consent to necessary medical treatment (§ 1901 of the Civil Code). The custodian must attend to the affairs of the person under custodianship in their best interests. These best interests include the possibility to live their lives according to their own wishes and ideas, within the limits of their abilities (§ 1901(2) of the Civil Code). [...] As far as it is possible to ascertain – e.g. on the basis of an advance healthcare directive pursuant to § 1901a of the Civil Code – the free will of the person under custodianship in respect of whether and how they would want specific treatment measures to be carried out, this will is also binding on the custodian.

[...]

Medical treatment against the natural will of persons under custodianship who, due to mental illness or mental or psychological disability, lack the mental capacity for insight into its necessity or for acting upon such insight is only permissible on the basis of § 1906 of the Civil Code, and thus only in cases in which persons under custodianship are confined in an institution pursuant to § 1906(1) of the Civil Code. In the past, it was controversial whether coercive medical treatment was also permissible, on the basis of §§ 1896 and 1901 of the Civil Code, in cases in which persons under custodianship are not confined in an institution and where the custodian consented [...]. By order of 11 October 2000 [...], the Federal Court of Justice held that this was impermissible [...].

7 [...]
8-9 b) [...]
10-12 2. [...]
13-14 3. [...]
15 4. [...]
16-17 5. [...]

II.

18 1. The person concerned in the initial proceedings, who was 63 years old, suffered from schizoaffective psychosis. For this reason, she had been under custodianship for, *inter alia*, tasks relating to care and health matters, including consent to medical measures and treatment, as well as for determining her place of residence, including decisions on confinement or similar measures, since the end of April 2014.

19 In early September 2014, the person concerned was briefly admitted to a care facility. While there, she refused to take the medication prescribed to treat an autoimmune disease, refused to eat and expressed the intent to commit suicide. From mid-September 2014, she was confined in a dementia unit at a hospital, a measure approved by a judge. On the basis of several orders of the custodianship court, she was subject to coercive medical measures for medicating her autoimmune disease, hypothyroidism and mental illness. The medication – as well as food – was administered via stomach tube, the insertion of which also constituted a coercive medical measure. In addition, further examinations (punch biopsy) were carried out with regard to suspected cancer. They confirmed the suspicion of breast cancer, which had not yet broken through the skin.

20 At that time, she was severely weakened physically and could no longer walk or move herself around in a wheelchair. However, mentally, she was able to express her natural will. In response to a judge's questions, she repeatedly stated that she did not wish to be treated for cancer. She wanted neither surgery nor chemotherapy.

21 2. In a letter dated 20 January 2015, her professional custodian applied for authorisation to extend the patient's confinement, and to carry out coercive medical measures, to treat the breast cancer in particular [...], but also to continue the treatment of the other conditions with medication.

22 3. The Local Court rejected the application for confinement and coercive treatment. While the person concerned was suffering from a mental illness preventing her from consenting to the necessary medical treatment, confinement was not necessary

given that the requested treatment and medical interventions could also be carried out in an open institution.

4. The Regional Court rejected the custodian's complaint but admitted the complaint on points of law. 23

[...] 24-27

5. On behalf of the person concerned, the custodian filed a complaint on points of law before the Federal Court of Justice. 28

III.

1. The Federal Court of Justice suspended the proceedings pursuant to Art. 100(1) first sentence of the Basic Law and referred to the Federal Constitutional Court the question whether § 1906(3) of the Civil Code in its version of 18 February 2013 is compatible with Art. 3(1) of the Basic Law to the extent that, as a precondition to the custodian's consent to in-patient coercive medical treatment, this treatment must be conducted in a setting of confinement pursuant to § 1906(1) of the Civil Code, even in respect of cases where the persons concerned do not intend to remove themselves from the site of treatment, or are physically unable to do so. 29

[...] 30-37

2. [...] 38

IV.

Statements in the referral proceedings were submitted by the Federal Association of Notaries (*Bundesnotarkammer*), the Federal Association of Persons with Physical and Multiple Disabilities (*Bundesverband für körper- und mehrfachbehinderte Menschen e.V.*), the Federal Association of Families of People with Mental Illness (*Bundesverband der Angehörigen psychisch Kranker e.V.*), the Federal Association of Professional Custodians (*Bundesverband der Berufsbetreuer/innen e.V.*), the Association of German Notaries (*Deutscher Notarverein e.V.*), the Initiative for Persons with Mental Illness – Association for Reforming the Care of Persons with Mental Illness (*Aktion psychisch Kranke Vereinigung zur Reform der Versorgung psychisch Kranker e.V.*), the German Association for Psychiatry, Psychotherapy and Psychosomatics (*Deutsche Gesellschaft für Psychiatrie und Psychotherapie, Psychosomatik und Nervenheilkunde e.V.*), the Federal Workers' Welfare Association (*AWO Bundesverband e.V.*), the Federal Bar Association (*Bundesrechtsanwaltskammer*), the German Caritas Association, the Federal Working Group of Users and Survivors of Psychiatry (*Bundesarbeitsgemeinschaft Psychiatrie-Erfahrener* 39

e. V.) and the Federal Association of Users and Survivors of Psychiatry (*Bundesverband Psychiatrie-Erfahrener e. V.*).

40-51 [...]

B.

I.

52 The referral is admissible.
53-58 1. [...]
59 2. [...]
60 3. The referral was not rendered inadmissible by the fact that the affected person in the initial proceedings died in the course of the referral proceedings.
61 a)
62-63 [...]
64 b) Despite the death of the affected person in the initial proceedings, a weighty objective need persists for clarifying the question of constitutional law referred by the Federal Court of Justice.
65 [...]

II.

66 It constitutes a violation of the state's duty of protection, which follows from Art. 2(2) first sentence of the Basic Law, that persons under custodianship who cannot reach a decision informed by their free will are – regardless of the risks involved in the treatment and of the extent of the risk to their life or physical integrity – entirely excluded from necessary medical treatment if that treatment is against their natural will, yet they cannot be confined in an institution because the requirements for such confinement are not met (see 1 below). There is no need to decide here whether this is also incompatible with the right to equality (see 2 below).

67 1. It follows from Art. 2(2) first sentence of the Basic Law that the state is obliged to provide protection to vulnerable persons who are under custodianship for health matters and who lack the mental capacity for insight into the necessity of medical treatment where there is imminent risk of considerable impairment to their health, or for acting upon such insight; where necessary, the state must provide this protection, in the form of medical care, even against the vulnerable person's natural will (see a below). Such coercive medical treatment is also compatible with Germany's obligations under international law (see b below). The fact that, under the law as it

No. 12 – Coercive Medical Treatment

currently stands, vulnerable persons who are in-patients in an open institution and are unable to move about without assistance cannot, even when urgently necessary, be treated against their natural will constitutes a violation of the duty of protection following from Art. 2(2) first sentence of the Basic Law (see c below). [...]

a) [...] 68

aa) The fundamental right to life and physical integrity not only guarantees the individual a defensive right against state interference with these legal interests, but also constitutes an objective decision on constitutional values that establishes duties of protection on the part of the state. Accordingly, the state is obliged to protect and defend the individual's right to life (cf. BVerfGE 39, 1 <42>; 46, 160 <164>; 90, 145 <195>; 115, 320 <346> – *Profiling*). Art. 2(2) first sentence of the Basic Law also encompasses protection against impairments to physical integrity and health (cf. BVerfGE 56, 54 <78>; 121, 317 <356>). 69

[...] The Federal Constitutional Court can only find a violation of such a duty of protection if safeguards have either not been put in place at all, or if the provisions enacted and measures taken are evidently unsuitable, entirely inadequate, or fall significantly short of achieving the required aim of protection (cf. BVerfGE 56, 54 <80>; 77, 170 <215>; 92, 26 <46>; 125, 39 <78 and 79>). 70

bb) Accordingly, in respect of persons under custodianship who, due to mental illness or mental or psychological disability, lack the mental capacity for insight into the necessity of medical treatment, or for acting upon such insight, the general duty of protection consolidates, under certain narrow conditions, into a specific duty of protection. It follows from Art. 2(2) first sentence of the Basic Law that the legislator is obliged to provide a system of assistance and protection for persons under custodianship who lack the mental capacity for insight into the necessity of medical treatment to prevent or fight serious illnesses, or cannot act upon such insight. In serious cases, it must be possible, as a last resort, to carry out medical examination and treatment measures, even if this entails having to override the opposing natural will of persons under custodianship. 71

[...] 72

(1) Under narrow conditions, Art. 2(2) first sentence of the Basic Law gives rise to a constitutional duty to protect certain persons under custodianship, even by way of coercive treatment measures where necessary; this duty follows from the specific need for assistance of these persons. If, due to illness, they lack the capacity for insight into the medical necessity of an examination or curative treatment or to act upon such insight, they are unprotected and vulnerable given that they are exposed to risks to their life and physical integrity without being able to ensure their protection themselves (cf. BVerfGE 58, 208 <225>; 128, 282 <304 *et seq.*> – 73

Coercive Treatment in Psychiatric Confinement under Criminal Law). The state and society may not simply abandon helpless persons.

74 (2) Nonetheless, every coercive treatment measure interferes with the fundamental right to the free development of one's personality because under the Basic Law everyone is in principle free to decide on interferences with their physical integrity and to deal with their health as they see fit. This freedom is a manifestation of one's personal autonomy, and as such is protected by the general right of personality under Art. 2(1) in conjunction with Art. 1(1) of the Basic Law (for the same outcome, referring to Art. 2(2) first sentence of the Basic Law, cf. BVerfGE 128, 282 <302> – *Coercive Treatment in Psychiatric Confinement under Criminal Law*; 129, 269 <280>; 133, 112 <131 para. 49>). An individual is not required to follow a standard of objective reasonableness when deciding whether and to what extent to seek diagnosis and treatment. The state's duty to "protect individuals from themselves" does not establish the 'sovereignty of reason' (*Vernunfthoheit*) of state organs over fundamental rights holders in such a way that their will is set aside merely because it differs from average preferences or appears to be unreasonable from an outside perspective (cf. BVerfGE 128, 282 <308> – *Coercive Treatment in Psychiatric Confinement under Criminal Law*). The fundamental freedoms [enshrined in the Basic Law] encompass the right to exercise the liberties and freedoms in a way that is, in the eyes of third parties, contrary to the seemingly best interests of the fundamental rights holder. Therefore, it is generally for individuals to decide whether they wish to undergo therapeutic measures or other treatment, even if these serve to preserve or improve their health. This constitutionally protected freedom also encompasses the 'freedom to be ill', and thus the right to refuse curative treatment, even if it is urgently indicated according to current medical findings (cf. BVerfGE 128, 282 <304> – *Coercive Treatment in Psychiatric Confinement under Criminal Law*; with further references).

75 To the extent that the affected persons are able to decide on medical treatment to preserve or improve their own health on the basis of their free will, there is no need for protection and assistance; in this case, the state's duty of protection following from Art. 2(2) first sentence of the Basic Law must stand back. Coercive medical treatment against a person's free will is then ruled out.

76 If the affected persons are unable to reach a decision informed by their free will on how to deal with an illness because, due to illness, they lack the mental capacity for insight into the necessity of medical treatment, or for acting upon such insight (on this requirement cf. BVerfGE 128, 282 <304 and 305> – *Coercive Treatment in Psychiatric Confinement under Criminal Law* as well as § 1906(3) first sentence no. 1 of the Civil Code), a potentially existing natural will relating to their illness is still, under constitutional law, an expression of the right to self-determination

that is protected by the right to the free development of one's personality; even under these conditions, coercive medical treatment is an interference with this right. However, the natural will opposed to necessary medical treatment does not alter the fact that the affected persons need special help and protection.

(3) If a medical measure cannot be justified through the consent of the affected person given of their own free will, and coercive medical treatment is imposed against their natural will, this also conflicts with that person's fundamental right to physical integrity (cf. also BVerfGE 128, 282 <300 and 301> – *Coercive Treatment in Psychiatric Confinement under Criminal Law*). This applies to both diagnostic and therapeutic measures.

(4) If there is a risk of serious impairment to the health of persons under custodianship who lack the mental capacity for insight into their illness, and if, in a balancing of the prospects of curing them against the burdens imposed on them through medical treatment, the former prevail, the state's duty of protection prevails over the conflicting freedoms. In that case, it is incumbent on the state to open up the possibility of medical treatment even against the natural will of the persons under custodianship. Strict substantive and procedural requirements regarding such coercive treatment must ensure that the affected freedoms are taken into consideration to the greatest possible extent.

(a) Where the state's duty of protection following from Art. 2(2) first sentence of the Basic Law requires that medical treatment be administered against the natural will of persons under custodianship, this conflicts with their right to self-determination and their fundamental right to physical integrity. In this case, the duty of protection does not lapse merely because the risk of a fundamental rights violation does not stem from third parties, but because measures based on that duty of protection conflict with opposing fundamental rights of the affected persons. [...]

(b) In cases in which serious health impairment, including a danger to one's life, can be averted through treatment measures that do not amount to an excessively intrusive interference and that have good prospects of success, the legislator must provide for the possibility of coercive medical treatment of persons who, due to illness, lack mental capacity and therefore, of their natural will, oppose such treatment. [...]

In fulfilling this duty of protection, the legislator has latitude in setting out the details of specific protective measures. In particular, the legislator has latitude to set out the substantive requirements for curative treatment and the procedural rules safeguarding the self-determination and physical integrity of the affected persons. However, where a duty of protection is already established, the legislator's latitude only relates to the question of how – but not whether – medical treatment of persons under custodianship for health matters should be regulated.

82 (c) Given that in the cases described above the specific duty of protection ultimately prevails over the right to self-determination and physical integrity of the affected persons, the legislator is, in the interest of the greatest possible respect for the fundamental freedoms that must stand back in such cases, obliged to provide for stringent and sufficiently specific substantive requirements supplemented by procedural ones in respect of coercive medical treatment (regarding the justification of coercive medical treatment as an interference, cf. already BVerfGE 128, 282 <308 et seq.> – *Coercive Treatment in Psychiatric Confinement under Criminal Law*). In this regard, the legislator must take into account that this is not a matter of ensuring medical protection according to standards of objective reasonableness; rather, the free will of persons under custodianship must be respected. This also applies where the free will can only be determined on the basis of indications – especially by drawing on earlier statements or on how and to what extent the natural will is expressed. Only where this is not possible can the opposed natural will formed due to illness be overridden as a last resort.

83 (d) [...]

84-85 (e) [...]

86 The Basic Law calls for the autonomous self-determination of the individual to be respected. This requires the legislator to put in place the necessary provisions to ensure that, before specific examinations of their state of health, curative treatment or medical interventions are performed, it is established whether persons under custodianship for health matters have sufficient mental capacity for insight and agency with regard to these measures to reach a decision informed by a free and thus decisive will. In this respect, an advance healthcare directive or prior statements on desired treatment in a situation such as the one in question can be decisive, as already provided for by law (cf. § 1901a(1) and (2) of the Civil Code). Where the natural will of persons under custodianship who lack the mental capacity for insight opposes such measures, it is necessary to first try and convince them of the necessity and reasonableness of the intended treatment (cf. already § 1906(3) no. 2 of the Civil Code), before coercive treatment may be carried out as a last resort.

87 b) International law obligations do not stand in the way of the state's duty to protect persons under custodianship who are vulnerable and unable to form a free will, and if necessary, to subject them to coercive medical treatment under the conditions set out above (see a bb, para. 71 *et seq.* above).

88 aa) In its order of 23 March 2011, the Federal Constitutional Court held that the UN Convention on the Rights of Persons with Disabilities (CRPD), which has the force of law in Germany [...] and serves as an interpretive guideline for determining the content and scope of fundamental rights (cf. BVerfGE 111, 307 <317 and 318>),

does not suggest a different conclusion (cf. BVerfGE 128, 282 <306 and 307> – *Coercive Treatment in Psychiatric Confinement under Criminal Law*). The Court did not infer from the provisions of the Convention that aim to safeguard and strengthen the autonomy of persons with disabilities, in particular from Art. 12 CRPD, a general prohibition of measures carried out against the natural will of persons with disabilities, where such measures are grounded in their limited capacity for self-determination due to illness. […].
[…] 89-91

bb) The state's duty following from Art. 2(2) first sentence of the Basic Law to protect vulnerable persons under custodianship who lack the capacity to reach a decision informed by their free will and, where necessary, to subject them to coercive medical treatment under the conditions set out above (see a bb, para. 71 *et seq.* above), is also in conformity with the European Convention on Human Rights and the case-law of the European Court of Human Rights. 92

According to the case-law of the European Court of Human Rights, Art. 8 of the European Convention on Human Rights provides for a right to conduct one's life in a manner of one's own choosing. That also includes the opportunity to pursue activities that are physically harmful or dangerous. Medical treatment against the will of mentally competent adult patients would interfere with their physical integrity, and therefore with the rights protected under Art. 8 of the Convention, even if refusal of the treatment might lead to a fatal outcome (cf. ECtHR (GC), *Lambert v. France*, Judgment of 5 June 2015, no. 46043/14, § 120 *et seq.*; ECtHR, *Pretty v. the United Kingdom*, Judgment of 29 April 2002, no. 2346/02, §§ 62 and 63). In this respect, however, the states have a margin of appreciation (ECtHR (GC), *Lambert v. France*, Judgment of 5 June 2015, no. 46043/14, § 148). 93

However, the state and society are only required to accept decisions which by objective standards are unreasonable and may possibly lead to death where that decision is based on the free will of a mentally competent adult. Where a person does not make such a decision freely and with full understanding of what is involved, the European Court of Human Rights assumes that the state has a duty, derived from Art. 2 of the Convention, to prevent such persons from endangering their own lives (cf. ECtHR (GC), *Lambert v. France*, Judgment of 5 June 2015, no. 46043/14, § 140; ECtHR, *Haas v. Switzerland*, Judgment of 20 January 2011, no. 31322/07, § 54; ECtHR, *Arskaya v. Ukraine*, Judgment of 5 December 2013, no. 45076/05, §§ 69 and 70). Where a patient refuses medically indicated treatment and thereby endangers their life, the European Court of Human Rights holds that the state must sufficiently provide for a duty upon attending physicians to establish the decision-making capacity of the person concerned where there are indications that 94 free will may be lacking (cf. ECtHR, *Arskaya v. Ukraine*, Judgment of 5 December 2013, no. 45076/05, §§ 62, 69, 70, 88).

95 Thus, it cannot be found that there is a contradiction between the European Convention on Human Rights, in particular Arts. 2 and 8 of the Convention, as interpreted by the European Court of Human Rights, and necessary coercive medical treatment, under the conditions set out above (see a bb, para. 71 *et seq.* above), of vulnerable persons under custodianship as mandated by Art. 2(2) first sentence of the Basic Law.

96 c) According to these considerations, it constitutes a violation of the state's duty of protection following from Art. 2(2) first sentence of the Basic Law that, under applicable custodianship law, persons under custodianship who lack mental capacity, who are at risk of considerable health impairments due to illness and who can be treated with good prospects of success by a measure that entails only relatively minor burdens cannot under any circumstances be treated against their natural will, if they are in-patients, but are unable to remove themselves from the site of necessary treatment and can therefore not be confined in an institution.

97 Custodianship law in the Civil Code only provides for coercive medical treatment in respect of persons under custodianship who are confined in an institution pursuant to § 1906(1) of the Civil Code (§ 1906(3) first sentence no. 3 of the Civil Code). […]

98 Persons under custodianship who are treated as in-patients and who […] are *de facto* unable to remove themselves from the site of treatment cannot be confined in an institution pursuant to § 1906(1) no. 2 of the Civil Code, and therefore cannot be subjected to coercive treatment pursuant to § 1906(3) of the Civil Code. Thus, even if these persons under custodianship unquestionably fit all the substantive conditions that would give rise to a constitutional duty of protection on the part of the state, and all procedural requirements were satisfied, they would still not receive the required protection following from Art. 2(2) first sentence of the Basic Law. In this respect, the legal situation for persons under custodianship does not satisfy the constitutional requirements.

99 […]
100 d) […]
101 2. […]

No. 12 – Coercive Medical Treatment

C.

[…]

Justices: Kirchhof, Gaier, Eichberger, Schluckebier, Masing, Paulus, Baer, Britz

No. 13

BVerfGE 153, 182 – Assisted Suicide

HEADNOTES

to the Judgment of the Second Senate of 26 February 2020
2 BvR 2347/15, 2 BvR 651, 1261, 1593, 2354, 2527/16

1. a) As an expression of personal autonomy, the general right of personality (Article 2(1) in conjunction with Article 1(1) of the Basic Law) encompasses a right to a self-determined death.

   b) The right to a self-determined death includes the freedom to take one's own life. Where an individual decides to end their own life, having reached this decision based on how they personally define quality of life and a meaningful existence, their decision must, in principle, be respected by state and society as an act of personal autonomy and self-determination.

   c) The freedom to take one's own life also encompasses the freedom to seek and, if offered, make use of assistance provided by third parties for this purpose.

2. Even state measures that only have indirect or factual effects can amount to impairments of fundamental rights and thus require constitutional justification. The criminalisation of assisted suicide services in § 217(1) of the Criminal Code renders it *de facto* impossible for persons wanting to commit suicide to make use of assisted suicide services as their chosen form of suicide.

3. a) The prohibition of assisted suicide services must be measured against the standard of strict proportionality.

   b) When reviewing whether the provision in question is reasonable, it must be taken into account that suicide assistance is subject to various conflicting protections under constitutional law. Respect for the fundamental right to self-determination, encompassing self-determination in decisions regarding the end of one's life, of a person making the free and voluntary decision to end their life and seeking assistance to this end collides with the state's duty to protect the autonomy of persons wanting to commit suicide and, additionally, its duty to protect life, a legal interest of high standing.

4. The high standing the Constitution accords to autonomy and life can in principle justify effective preventive protection of these interests, including by means of criminal law. If the legal order criminalises certain forms of suicide assistance that jeopardise personal autonomy, it must ensure that suicide assistance provided voluntarily can in practice still be accessed in the individual case.
5. The prohibition of assisted suicide services in § 217(1) of the Criminal Code reduces the options for assisted suicide to such an extent that there is *de facto* no scope for the individual to exercise their constitutionally protected freedom.
6. No one can ever be obliged to assist in another person's suicide.

FEDERAL CONSTITUTIONAL COURT
- 2 BvR 2347/15, 2 BvR 651, 1261, 1593, 2354, 2527/16 -

IN THE NAME OF THE PEOPLE

In the proceedings
on the constitutional complaints of

I.	1. Mr F..., 2. Dr. L...,
	– authorised representatives: ...
	- 2 BvR 2347/15 -,
II.	registered association S..., represented by its board members, Chairman Dr. K...,Vice-Chairman B..., and Secretary S...,
	– authorised representative: ...
	- 2 BvR 651/16 -,
III.	1. D..., represented by its Secretary M..., 2. registered association D..., represented by its board members L... and M..., 3. Mr M..., 4. Ms L..., 5. Ms G..., 6. Mr G...,
	– authorised representatives: ...
	- 2 BvR 1261/16 -,
IV.	Dr. med. d. R...,
	– authorised representatives: ...
	- 2 BvR 1593/16 -,
V.	1. Dr. med. B..., 2. Dr. med V..., 3. Dr. med. S..., 4. Dr. med. V...,
	– authorised representatives: ...
	- 2 BvR 2354/16 -,

VI. 1. Mr A..., 2. Dr. med. P..., 3. Prof. R..., 4. Ms S..., 5. Mr S...,
– authorised representative: ...
- 2 BvR 2527/16 -

against § 217 of the Criminal Code as amended by the Act Criminalising Assisted Suicide Services of 3 December 2015 (BGBl, p. 2177)

the Federal Constitutional Court – Second Senate –

with the participation of Justices

President Voßkuhle,
Masing,
Huber,
Hermanns,
Kessal-Wulf,
König,
Maidowski,
Langenfeld

held on the basis of the oral hearing of 16 and 17 April 2019:

JUDGMENT

1. The proceedings are combined for joint decision.
2. § 217 of the Criminal Code, as amended by the Act Criminalising Assisted Suicide Services of 3 December 2015 (BGBl I, p. 2177) violates the fundamental right under Article 2(1) in conjunction with Article 1(1) of the Basic Law of the complainants in proceedings I. 1, I. 2, and VI. 5, the fundamental right under Article 2(1) of the Basic Law of the complainants in proceedings II. and III. 2, the fundamental rights under Article 2(1) and Article 2(2) second sentence in conjunction with Article 104(1) of the Basic Law of the complainants in proceedings III. 3 to III. 5 and VI. 2, and the fundamental rights under Article 12(1) and Article 2(2) second sentence in conjunction with Article 104(1) of the Basic Law of the complainants in proceedings III. 6, IV., V. 1 to V. 4 and VI. 3. The provision is incompatible with the Basic Law and void.
3. The constitutional complaints of the complainants in proceedings VI. 1 and VI. 4 have been rendered moot by their death.
4. The constitutional complaint of the complainant in proceedings III. 1 is dismissed as inadmissible.
5. [...]

No. 13 – Assisted Suicide

REASONS:

A.

I.

The constitutional complaints directly challenge § 217 of the Criminal Code, as amended by the Act Criminalising Assisted Suicide Services of 3 December 2015 (BGBl I, p. 2177).

The complainants are seriously ill persons who want to end their lives with the help of assisted suicide services provided by third parties, as well as associations based in Germany and Switzerland providing such suicide assistance, the associations' representatives and employees, doctors working in outpatient or inpatient care and lawyers providing legal advice on and arranging suicide assistance.

In their constitutional complaints, the complainants who want to make use of suicide assistance derive a right to a self-determined death in particular from the general right of personality (Art. 2(1) in conjunction with Art. 1(1) of the Basic Law). They claim that, as an expression of personal autonomy and self-determination, the general right of personality also encompasses the right to use suicide assistance provided by third parties and that this right is violated by § 217 of the Criminal Code. They assert that their chosen form of suicide assistance is no longer available to them given that providing assisted suicide services (*geschäftsmäßige Förderung der Selbsttötung*) was made a punishable offence.

[...]

II.

1. § 217 was introduced into the Criminal Code by the Act Criminalising Assisted Suicide Services of 3 December 2015 (BGBl I, p. 2177) with effect from 10 December 2015.

a) The provision reads as follows:

Assisted suicide services

(1) Whoever, with the intention of assisting another person to commit suicide, provides, procures or arranges the opportunity for that person to do so as a professionalised service incurs a penalty of imprisonment for a term not exceeding three years or a fine.

(2) A participant whose actions are not provided as a professionalised service and who is either a relative of or is close to the person referred to in subsection (1) is exempt from punishment.

10-14 b) [...]
15 c) [...]
16 2. When the Act Criminalising Assisted Suicide Services was adopted, certain instances of participation in the suicide of a person acting on their own initiative were made a punishable offence for the first time since a uniform criminal law system was introduced in Germany in 1871.
17-22 [...]
23 3. [...]
24-25 4. [...]

III.

26 Most European countries prohibit and criminalise suicide assistance [...]. Switzerland, the Netherlands and Belgium have more liberal regimes. In Switzerland, only suicide assistance is permissible, whereas in the Netherlands and Belgium, termination of life on request (*Tötung auf Verlangen*), if it is performed by doctors, is exempt from punishment under certain conditions, too. Outside Europe, the US state of Oregon and Canada exempt medical assistance in dying from punishment under certain conditions.
27-32 [...]

IV.

33-87 [...]

V.

88 1. The German *Bundestag*, the *Bundesrat*, the Federal Government (the Federal Chancellery and the Federal Ministry of Justice and Consumer Protection) as well as all *Land* Governments were given the opportunity to submit a statement pursuant to § 94(4) in conjunction with § 77 no. 1 of the Federal Constitutional Court Act.
89-123 [...]
124 2. [...]
125-141 3. [...]

No. 13 – Assisted Suicide

4. Furthermore, statements pursuant to § 27a of the Federal Constitutional Court Act were submitted by the Commissariat of German Bishops (*Kommissariat der deutschen Bischöfe*), the Protestant Church in Germany (*Evangelische Kirche in Deutschland*), the Central Council of Jews in Germany (*Zentralrat der Juden in Deutschland*), the German Medical Association (*Bundesärztekammer*), the doctors' association *Marburger Bund*, the German Nurses Association – National Office (*Deutscher Berufsverband für Pflegeberufe – Bundesverband e.V.*), the German Association for Palliative Medicine (*Deutsche Gesellschaft für Palliativmedizin e.V.*), the German Palliative Care Foundation (*Deutsche PalliativStiftung*), the German Patient Protection Foundation (*Deutsche Stiftung Patientenschutz*), the German Association for Hospice and Palliative Care (*Deutscher Hospiz- und PalliativVerband e.V.*) and the Humanist Union (*Humanistische Union*), the German Humanist Association – National Office (*Humanistischer Verband Deutschland – Bundesverband e.V.*) as well as the German Lawyers Association (*Deutscher Anwaltverein e.V.*). 142

[...] 143-173

5. In addition, the G. B. Foundation, the F. ideological community, the E. and the K. Working Groups submitted briefs on their own initiative, and practitioners and academics submitted specialist articles. 174

[...] 175-177

VI.

[...] 178-180

B.

I.

1. The complainant in proceedings VI. 1 died on 12 April 2019. Therefore, his constitutional complaint has become moot (cf. BVerfGE 6, 389 <442 and 443>; 12, 311 <315>; 109, 279 <304> – *Surveillance of Private Homes*). [...] 181

[...] 182

2. The same applies to the constitutional complaint of the complainant in proceedings VI. 4, who has also died since. 183

II.

The constitutional complaint of the complainant in proceedings III. 1, an assisted suicide association based in Switzerland, is inadmissible. The complainant cannot 184 assert that § 217 of the Criminal Code violates its fundamental rights or rights that are equivalent to fundamental rights. [...]

185-191 [...]

III.

192-199 [...]

C.

200 To the extent that the constitutional complaints are admissible, they are well-founded.

201 § 217 of the Criminal Code violates the right to a self-determined death deriving from the general right of personality (Art. 2(1) in conjunction with Art. 1(1) of the Basic Law) of the complainants in proceedings I. 1, I. 2 und VI. 5 (see I below). In respect of the other complainants, the prohibition of assisted suicide services violates their fundamental right to occupational freedom (Art. 12(1) of the Basic Law), insofar as they want to provide suicide assistance in the context of their professional activities and are German nationals, and, for the rest, their general freedom of action (Art. 2(1) of the Basic Law). By providing for the possibility of a prison sentence, § 217 of the Criminal Code also violates the right to liberty under Art. 2(2) second sentence in conjunction with Art. 104(1) of the Basic Law of the complainants in proceedings III. 3 to III. 6, IV., V. 1 to V. 4 as well as VI. 2 and VI. 3. As the criminalisation of assisted suicide services may lead to administrative fines being imposed on the complainants in proceedings II. and III. 2 under § 30(1) no. 1 of the Act on Administrative Offences, § 217 of the Criminal Code also violates the fundamental right of these associations under Art. 2(1) of the Basic Law (see II below). § 217 of the Criminal Code cannot be interpreted in conformity with the Constitution (see III below). Therefore, the provision is incompatible with the Basic Law and void (see IV below).

I.

202 The prohibition of assisted suicide services set out in § 217 of the Criminal Code violates the general right of personality (Art. 2(1) in conjunction with Art. 1(1) of the Basic Law) in its manifestation as a right to a self-determined death of persons who decide to end their own life. Even if the provision were interpreted strictly to the effect that it only applied to suicide assistance rendered with the intention to

offer such services on a recurring basis to persons taking their own life themselves, such interpretation does not lead to a different conclusion.

Art. 2(1) in conjunction with Art. 1(1) of the Basic Law guarantees the right to choose, in self-determination, to take one's own life based on an informed and deliberate decision and to make use of the assistance of third parties when doing so (see 1 below). § 217 of the Criminal Code interferes with this right (see 2 below). This interference is not justified (see 3 below). The recognition of a right to suicide and the limits to how far it can be restricted set out here are in accordance with the European Convention on Human Rights (see 4 below). 203

1. The right to take one's own life of persons capable of self-determination and personal responsibility forms part of the guarantees deriving from the general right of personality (Art. 2(1) in conjunction with Art. 1(1) of the Basic Law). 204

a) Respect for and protection of human dignity and freedom are fundamental principles of the constitutional order, informed by the central notion that human beings are capable of self-determination and personal responsibility (cf. BVerfGE 5, 85 <204>; 45, 187 <227>). As a 'non-listed' freedom, the general right of personality protects aspects of one's personality that are not covered by the specific freedoms of the Basic Law, but are equal to these freedoms in terms of their constitutive significance for one's personality (established case-law, cf. BVerfGE 99, 185 <193> – *Helnwein/Scientology*; 101, 361 <380>; 106, 28 <39>; 118, 168 <183>; 120, 274 <303> – *Remote Searches*; 147, 1 <19 para. 38> – *Third Gender Option*). 205

The protective guarantee of the general right of personality is determined by its specific link to Art. 1(1) of the Basic Law: when determining the content and scope of the protection afforded by the general right of personality – which is not defined exhaustively –, it must be taken into account that human dignity is inviolable and must be respected and protected by all state authority (cf. BVerfGE 27, 344 <351> – *Divorce Files*; 34, 238 <245> – *Secret Tape Recordings*). Rooted in the notion that personal autonomy and the development of one's personality are integral to human freedom (cf. BVerfGE 45, 187 <227>; 117, 71 <89> – *Life Imprisonment*; 123, 267 <413>), the guarantee of human dignity encompasses in particular the protection of one's individuality, identity and integrity (cf. BVerfGE 144, 20 <207 para. 539>). This implies that every person has a right to be valued and respected as a person in society (*sozialer Wert- und Achtungsanspruch*); this right precludes turning a person into the "mere object" of state action or exposing them to treatment which generally calls into question their quality as a conscious subject (cf. BVerfGE 27, 1 <6> – *Microcensus*; 45, 187 <228>; 109, 133 <149 and 150>; 117, 71 <89> – *Life Imprisonment*; 144, 20 <207 paras. 539 and 540>). Thus, inalienable human dignity means that any human being is unconditionally 206 recognised as an individual with personal responsibility (cf. BVerfGE 45, 187 <228>; 109, 133 <171>).

207 The specific guarantees deriving from the general right of personality give effect to the notion of autonomous self-determination that is rooted in human dignity (cf. BVerfGE 54, 148 <155> – *Eppler*; 65, 1 <41, 42 and 43> – *Census*; 80, 367 <373> – *Diary-Like Notes*; 103, 21 <32 and 33> – *DNA Fingerprinting*; 128, 109 <124> – *Transsexuals VIII*; 142, 313 <339 para. 74> – *Coercive Medical Treatment*). This right guarantees the basic conditions enabling the individual to find, develop and protect their identity and individuality in self-determination (cf. BVerfGE 35, 202 <220> – *Lebach*; 79, 256 <268>; 90, 263 <270>; 104, 373 <385>; 115, 1 <14> – *Transsexuals V*; 116, 243 <262 and 263>; 117, 202 <225>; 147, 1 <19 para. 38> – *Third Gender Option*). Notably, the self-determined protection of one's personality requires that the individual can control their life on their own terms and is not forced into ways of living that are fundamentally irreconcilable with their idea of self and their personal identity (cf. BVerfGE 116, 243 <264 and 265>; 121, 175 <190 and 191>; 128, 109 <124, 127> – *Transsexuals VIII*).

208 b) As an expression of personal autonomy, the general right of personality encompasses a right to a self-determined death, which includes the right to suicide (see aa below). The protection afforded by fundamental rights also encompasses the freedom to seek and, if offered, make use of assistance provided by third parties for this purpose (see bb below).

209 aa) (1) In terms of human personality, the decision to end one's own life is of the most vital significance to one's existence. It reflects one's personal identity and is a central expression of the person capable of self-determination and personal responsibility. For the individual, the purpose of life, and whether and for what reasons they might consider ending their own life, is a matter of highly personal beliefs and convictions. The decision to commit suicide concerns fundamental questions of human existence and has a bearing on one's identity and individuality like no other decision. Therefore, the general right of personality in its manifestation as right to a self-determined death is not limited to the right to refuse, of one's own free will, life-sustaining treatments and thus let a terminal illness run its course (cf. in terms of the outcome BVerfGE 142, 313 <341 para. 79> – *Coercive Medical Treatment*; BGHSt 11, 111 <113 and 114>; 40, 257 <260, 262>; 55, 191 <196 and 197 para. 18, 203 and 204 para. 31 *et seq.*>; BGHZ 163, 195 <197 and 198>). The right to a self-determined death also extends to cases where the individual decides to take their own life. The right to take one's own life guarantees that the individual can determine their fate autonomously in accordance with their ideas of self and can thus protect their personality […].

No. 13 – Assisted Suicide

(2) The right to a self-determined death, as an expression of personal freedom, is not limited to situations defined by external causes. The right to determine one's own life, which forms part of the innermost domain of an individual's self-determination, is in particular not limited to serious or incurable illness, nor does it apply only in certain stages of life or illness. Restricting the scope of protection to specific causes or motives would essentially amount to an appraisal of the motives of the person seeking to end their own life, and thereby a substantive predetermination, which is alien to the Basic Law's notion of freedom. Such a restriction would lead to considerable difficulties in drawing distinctions; furthermore, it would come into conflict with the concept of human dignity and the free development of one's personality in self-determination and personal responsibility, which is fundamental to the Basic Law (cf. BVerfGE 80, 138 <154> regarding general freedom of action). The right to a self-determined death is rooted in the guarantee of human dignity enshrined in Art. 1(1) of the Basic Law; this implies that the decision to end one's own life, taken on the basis of personal responsibility, does not require any explanation or justification. Art. 1(1) of the Basic Law protects human dignity, the way humans understand themselves as individuals and become aware of themselves (cf. BVerfGE 49, 286 <298> – *Transsexuals I*; 115, 1 <14> – *Transsexuals V*). What is decisive is the will of the holder of fundamental rights, which eludes any appraisal on the basis of general values, religious precepts, societal norms for dealing with life and death, or considerations of objective rationality (cf. BVerfGE 128, 282 <308> – *Coercive Treatment in Psychiatric Confinement under Criminal Law*; 142, 313 <339 para. 74> – *Coercive Medical Treatment*; regarding medical treatment). Self-determination regarding the end of one's own life forms part of the "most foundational domain of human personality", in which the person is free to choose their own standards and to decide accordingly (cf. BVerfGE 52, 131 <175> dissenting opinion of Justices Hirsch, Niebler and Steinberger regarding medical treatment). This right is guaranteed in all stages of life. Where an individual decides to end their own life, having reached this decision based on how they personally define quality of life and a meaningful existence, their decision must, in principle, be respected by state and society as an act of autonomous self-determination.

(3) The right to end one's own life may not be denied on the grounds that a person committing suicide forfeits their dignity given that, by ending their life, they also give up the very basis of self-determination and thus their quality as a conscious subject […]. While life is the fundamental basis of human dignity (cf. BVerfGE 39, 1 <41 and 42>; 88, 203 <252>; 115, 118 <152>), it cannot be inferred that committing suicide of one's own free will is contrary to human dignity guaranteed by Art. 1(1) of the Basic Law. Where persons are capable of free self-determination

and personal responsibility, human dignity, which guarantees the individual personal autonomy, does not conflict with the decision to end one's own life. Rather, the self-determined act of ending one's life is a direct, albeit final, expression of the pursuit of personal autonomy inherent in human dignity. A person committing suicide of their own free will makes the decision to die as a conscious subject (cf. BVerfGE 115, 118 <160 and 161>). They give up their life in self-determination and in pursuit of their own goals. Thus, human dignity does not limit a person's self-determination, but rather is the very reason for self-determination: The person only remains an individual with personal responsibility, and thus a conscious subject, and their right to be valued and respected can only be upheld if they can determine their existence based on their own, self-defined standards […].

212 bb) The right to take one's own life, protected by Art. 2(1) in conjunction with Art. 1(1) of the Basic Law, also encompasses the freedom to seek and, if offered, make use of assistance provided by third parties for this purpose.

213 The development of one's personality, as guaranteed by the Basic Law, also protects the freedom to engage with others, who, for their part, are also acting freely. Therefore, the constitutionally protected freedom also includes the possibility of approaching others, seeking their assistance and accepting the assistance they offer in the exercise of their own freedom. In particular, this also applies to persons who consider taking their own life. Especially those persons often only feel they are in a position to take such a decision, and, as the case may be, put it into practice in a manner that is reasonable (*zumutbar*) to them, if they receive expert help provided by competent and willing third parties, especially by doctors. Where the exercise of a fundamental right depends on the involvement of others, and the free development of one's personality hinges on the participation of another person […], the general right of personality also provides protection from restrictions that take the form of prohibiting this other person from offering such assistance in the exercise of their own freedom.

214 2. § 217 of the Criminal Code interferes with the general right of personality of the complainants in proceedings I. 1, I. 2 and VI. 5, even though the provision is not directly addressed to them (see a below). The effects of the provision are not merely a reflex of a law serving other objectives (see b below).

215 a) Fundamental rights protection is not limited to interferences that are directly addressed to the persons affected by them. Even state measures that only have indirect or factual effects can amount to impairments of fundamental rights and thus require sufficient constitutional justification. […]

216 The criminalisation of assisted suicide services in § 217(1) of the Criminal Code renders it *de facto* impossible for the complainants to make use of assisted suicide services as their chosen form of suicide because providers of such services have

No. 13 – Assisted Suicide

ceased their activities after § 217 of the Criminal Code came into force so as to avoid sanctions under criminal law and under the law on administrative offences. [...]

b) [...]

The indirect interference arising from § 217 of the Criminal Code objectively has the effect of restricting the freedom to commit suicide. Individuals wanting to end their life in self-determination with the help of others who are providing assisted suicide services are forced to resort to alternatives, with the considerable risk that they cannot realise their decision given that other reasonable options for a painless and safe suicide are not actually available (see also para. 280 *et seq.* below). The interference with the complainants' general right of personality is particularly serious given the vital significance that self-determination in decisions about one's own life carries for personal identity, individuality and integrity and given that the provision at least considerably impedes the exercise of this fundamental right.

3. The interference with the general right of personality is not justified.

Restrictions of the general right of personality require a constitutional legal basis (see a below). The prohibition of assisted suicide services in § 217 of the Criminal Code must be measured against the principle of proportionality (see b below). § 217 of the Criminal Code does not satisfy the requirements arising from this principle (see c below).

a) The general right of personality is not completely beyond the reach of public authority. Every person must tolerate state measures that serve overriding public interests or the interests of others protected by fundamental rights where these measures strictly adhere to the requirement of proportionality (cf. BVerfGE 120, 224 <239> with further references). As regards proportionality, interferences with the general right of personality are subject to stricter justification requirements than interferences with the general freedom of action protected under Art. 2(1) of the Basic Law. Justification requirements are particularly strict for guarantees that have a specific link to the guarantee of human dignity under Art. 1(1) of the Basic Law. These guarantees are more extensive the more the individual is within their closest private sphere; they diminish the more the individual interacts with the outside world within a social context [...].

The free decision to end one's life with the help of third parties does not exclusively fall within the closest private sphere. While it is a highly personal decision, it also depends on the conduct of others [...]. When a person wants to realise their decision to end their life by making use of assisted suicide services provided by others and requests such assistance, this person interacts with the public. Assisted suicide services therefore not only affect the relationship between the person who has made a voluntary decision to commit suicide and the person providing suicide assistance. Assisted suicide services also have advance effects and consequences that include considerable risks of abuse and risks to the autonomous self-determination of others.

223 b) The prohibition of assisted suicide services must be measured against the standard of strict proportionality (cf. BVerfGE 22, 180 <219>; 58, 208 <224 *et seq.*>; 59, 275 <278>; 60, 123 <132>). A law restricting fundamental rights only satisfies this standard if it is suitable and necessary for achieving its legitimate purpose, and reflects an appropriate balance between the purpose pursued and the restrictions of the freedom afforded by the respective fundamental rights (cf. BVerfGE 30, 292 <316>; 67, 157 <173>; 76, 1 <51>). When reviewing whether the provision is reasonable, it must be taken into account that a legal framework on suicide assistance must reflect various conflicting facets of protection under constitutional law. Respect for the fundamental right to self-determination, encompassing self-determination in decisions regarding the end of one's life, of a person who makes the free and voluntary decision to end their life and seeks assistance to this end (see para. 208 *et seq.* above), conflicts with the state's duty to protect the autonomy of persons wanting to commit suicide and, additionally, its duty to protect life, a legal interest of high standing. These legal interests must be kept free from undue influence and pressure that could result in affected persons having to justify why they do not want to make use of suicide assistance.

224 It generally falls to the legislator to resolve these conflicts. The state's duty of protection must be given more specific shape (cf. BVerfGE 88, 203 <254>). In this respect, the legislator has a margin of appreciation and evaluation as well as latitude (cf. BVerfGE 96, 56 <64>; 121, 317 <356>; 133, 59 <76 para. 45>). The scope of this latitude depends on various factors, including in particular the specific nature of the matter in question, the ability to make a sufficiently certain assessment, especially regarding future developments and the effects of a provision, as well as the significance of the affected legal interests (cf. BVerfGE 50, 290 <332 and 333>; 76, 1 <51 and 52>; 77, 170 <214 and 215>; 88, 203 <262>; 150, 1 <89 para. 173>).

225 Constitutional review also extends to whether the legislator has sufficiently taken into account these factors and has exercised its margin of appreciation in a tenable manner (cf. BVerfGE 88, 203 <262>). The legislator must have adequate regard to the conflict between the freedom granted by the fundamental right on the one hand, and the protection it affords on the other.

226 c) The prohibition of assisted suicide services in § 217 of the Criminal Code does not satisfy these requirements. It is true that it serves legitimate purposes in the interest of the common good (see aa below) and is suitable for achieving these purposes (see bb below). While it has not been definitively determined whether the

prohibition is necessary (see cc below), it is in any case not appropriate (see dd below).

aa) With the prohibition of assisted suicide services, the legislator pursues a legitimate purpose. The provision serves to protect the individual's self-determination over their life and hereby to protect life as such (see 1 below). This purpose is tenable under constitutional law. It is within the mandate of protection that is incumbent upon the legislator under constitutional law (see 2 below). The legislator's assumption that it is precisely the absence of legal restrictions on assisted suicide services that could result in risks to self-determination and to life is sufficiently tenable (see 3 below). 227

(1) The legislator intended the prohibition in § 217 of the Criminal Code as a measure to curb assisted suicide services in order to protect self-determination and the fundamental right to life (cf. BTDrucks 18/5373, pp. 2 and 3). 228

One aim of the law is to prevent suicide assistance from becoming a "regular service in the healthcare system" that could prompt people to end their life (cf. BTDrucks 18/5373, p. 2). [...] 229

The other aim of the law is to counter "conflicts of interest jeopardising autonomy" so as to protect integrity and personal autonomy (cf. BTDrucks 18/5373, p. 17) and to prevent the risk, generally arising from such conflicts of interest, of "undue outside influence in situations where self-determination is jeopardised" (cf. BTDrucks 18/5373, p. 11). [...] 230

(2) In aiming to protect autonomy and life, the prohibition in § 217 of the Criminal Code serves to fulfil the state's duty of protection arising from constitutional law and thus pursues a legitimate purpose. 231

(a) Under Art. 1(1) second sentence of the Basic Law in conjunction with Art. 2(2) first sentence of the Basic Law, the state has a duty to protect the individual's autonomy in deciding whether to end their own life, and hereby to protect life as such. The Basic Law calls for the autonomous self-determination of the individual to be respected (cf. BVerfGE 142, 313 <344 para. 86> – *Coercive Medical Treatment*), which requires free and autonomous decision-making on the part of the individual. Given that the realisation of a decision to commit suicide is irreversible, the significance of life as one of the highest values within the constitutional order (cf. BVerfGE 39, 1 <42>; 115, 25 <45>) requires that suicides be discouraged if they are not based on free self-determination and personal responsibility. The state must ensure that the decision to commit assisted suicide is really based on the free will of the affected person. Thus, the legislator pursues a legitimate purpose in seeking to counter risks to the free will and its free formation as prerequisites of autonomous self-determination in decisions regarding one's own life. 232

233 (b) In fulfilling this duty of protection, the legislator may not only act to protect personal autonomy against impending risks in the specific case arising from the conduct of others. In aiming to prevent assisted suicide from becoming recognised by society as a normal way of ending one's life, the legislator also pursues a legitimate purpose.

234 However, preserving an existing or implied consensus on values and moral principles may not be a direct aim of criminal legislation (cf. BVerfGE 120, 224 <264>, dissenting opinion of Justice Hassemer). Therefore, it is not a legitimate legislative aim to prohibit suicide assistance merely on the grounds that suicide and suicide assistance contradict the majority opinion in society regarding how to handle one's own life, particularly for old and ill people. A prohibition of assisted suicide services merely for the purpose of keeping the number of assisted suicides low is therefore impermissible; likewise, it is impermissible to pursue the aim of disapproving, placing under a taboo or framing as inferior in any other way the decision of a holder of fundamental rights, who acts of their own free will and in personal autonomy, to deliberately end their own life with the assistance of others.

235 However, the legislator may intervene to counteract developments that potentially create social expectations which might pressure individuals in certain situations to take their own life, for example based on what is considered expedient. Even in the absence of specific influence exercised by others, individuals must not be exposed to certain expectations held by society. The free will is not the same as the complete freedom from any outside influence when making decisions. Human decision-making is typically influenced by social or cultural factors; self-determination is always understood to be relative. The Constitution guarantees the individual protection of life as an intrinsic value which does not require justification; this protection is based on the unconditional recognition of the person and their existence as such. Therefore, the legislator may, and must, effectively counteract social influences which might amount to pressure and make it appear necessary that affected persons explain their refusal of suicide services. The legislator can thus take precautions ensuring that persons in difficult stages of life do not face a situation where they have to consider such services in detail or have to take an explicit position on them.

236 (3) The legislator assumes that the availability of assisted suicide services poses risks to self-determination in end-of-life decision-making, which must be countered to fulfil the state's duty of protection. The basis of this assumption is not objectionable under constitutional law.

237 (a) It must be reviewed under constitutional law whether the assessment and prognosis of impending risks to the individual or the public has a sufficiently sound basis (cf. BVerfGE 123, 186 <241>). […]

No. 13 – Assisted Suicide

[…] 238

(b) The risk assessment conducted by the legislator satisfies these constitutional standards. The legislator tenably assumed that assisted suicide services pose risks to autonomous self-determination in decisions regarding one's own life. 239

(aa) A decision to commit suicide is based on an autonomous and free will if the individual has made this decision on the basis of a realistic weighing of the pros and cons that is determined by their idea of self. 240

Thus, a free decision to commit suicide requires the ability to freely form one's will, without being influenced by an acute psychological disorder, and to act accordingly. […] 241

Moreover, the affected person must be aware of all aspects that are relevant for the decision. […] 242

It is also required that affected persons not be subject to undue influence or pressure (cf. BVerfGE 128, 282 <301> – *Coercive Treatment in Psychiatric Confinement under Criminal Law*; regarding consent to medical treatment). 243

Finally, it can only be assumed that a person made the decision to end their life of their own free will if the decision is "lasting" to some degree and based on "a certain internal stability" (cf. BGH, Judgment of 3 July 2019 - 5 StR 132/18 -, NJW 2019, p. 3092 <3093 and 3094> with further references). […] 244

(bb) According to the expert third parties, psychological conditions seriously jeopardise a free decision to commit suicide. […] Especially among persons who are elderly and seriously ill, the share of persons committing suicide who suffer from depression is high; their risk of suicidal thoughts increases when they suffer from depression. 245

Insufficient information provided to affected persons also seriously jeopardises a free decision to commit suicide. […] 246

Finally, according to the expert third parties, a free decision to commit suicide can also be jeopardised by forms of influence other than coercion, threats or deception (cf. BGH, Judgment of 3 July 2019 - 5 StR 132/18 -, NJW 2019, p. 3092 <3094> with further references), where these are likely to prevent or significantly impair an informed and considered decision in line with one's idea of self. […] 247

(cc) In light of the foregoing, the legislator's assumption that in the absence of legal restrictions, assisted suicide services jeopardise the autonomy and thus the life of affected persons is sufficiently tenable […]. The same applies to the legislator's assessment that assisted suicide services could become recognised as a normal way of ending one's life, especially for elderly and ill persons, which might create social expectations and pressure endangering personal autonomy […]. 248

249-259 […]
260 bb) As a criminal law provision, § 217 of the Criminal Code is in principle a suitable means for protecting the affected legal interests, since the criminalisation of dangerous acts can at least further the aim of protection (cf. BVerfGE 90, 145 <172>; regarding the criterion of suitability in general BVerfGE 30, 292 <316>; 33, 171 <187>).
261-262 […]
263 cc) In view of the lack of empirical findings regarding the effectiveness of alternative and less intrusive measures of protection, such as those considered in the legislative procedure, it may be doubtful whether § 217 of the Criminal Code is necessary to achieve the legislator's legitimate aim of ensuring protection (cf. […] BTDrucks 18/5373, pp. 13 and 14). Yet there is no need to make a decision on this issue in the present proceedings.
264 dd) The restriction of the right to a self-determined death resulting from the provision is in any case not appropriate. Restrictions of individual freedom are only appropriate if the burden imposed on the individual is in reasonable proportion to the benefits arising for the common good (see 1 below). The burden that § 217 of the Criminal Code imposes on persons wanting to die goes beyond what is reasonable. The criminalisation of assisted suicide services causes the right to suicide, as a manifestation of the right to a self-determined death, to effectively be largely vitiated in certain constellations. This suspends self-determination in a key part of end-of-life decision-making, which is incompatible with the vital significance of this fundamental right (see 2 below).
265 (1) Restrictions of freedom are only appropriate if the burden imposed on the individual is in reasonable proportion to the benefits arising for the common good (cf. BVerfGE 76, 1 <51>). In order to establish whether this is the case, the interests of the common good that the interference with fundamental rights serves to protect must be balanced against the effects on the legal interests of persons affected by the interference (cf. BVerfGE 92, 277 <327>). The more severely individual freedom is restricted, the weightier the pursued interests of the common good must be (cf. BVerfGE 36, 47 <59>; 40, 196 <227>; […]). Yet the need to protect the common good becomes all the more pressing, the greater the detriment and dangers that would potentially arise if the exercise of fundamental rights were free of any restriction (cf. BVerfGE 7, 377 <404 and 405>). In the context of such a review based on the standard of the prohibition of excessive measures, the protection which, as such, has been sought in a legitimate manner may have to stand back if the means chosen led to an impairment of the rights of affected persons that is not appropriate. […]

No. 13 – Assisted Suicide

Where the legislator's decision involves serious interferences with fundamental rights, as is the case with the prohibition of assisted suicide services under review here, it is subject to a strict standard of review (cf. BVerfGE 45, 187 <238>). The vital significance attached to self-determination, in particular for protecting personal individuality, identity and integrity in decisions regarding one's own life (see para. 209 above), imposes strict limits on the legislator when designing a legal framework for protection in the context of suicide assistance.

(2) When enacting the prohibition of assisted suicide services by way of § 217 of the Criminal Code, the legislator exceeded the limits for restricting the right to self-determination, which follow from its vital significance. § 217 of the Criminal Code is aimed at protecting autonomy and life, which are recognised as constitutional interests of high standing. In principle, it may thus be legitimate to use criminal law – including offences based on an abstract danger – as a means for protecting these interests (see a below). However, the exemption of suicide, and of suicide assistance, from punishment reflects the – constitutionally mandated – recognition of individual self-determination; as such, it is not at the legislator's free disposal (see b below). The prohibition of assisted suicide services under criminal law reduces the possibilities for assisted suicide to such an extent that, regarding this aspect of self-determination, there is *de facto* no scope for the individual to exercise their constitutionally protected freedom (see c below).

(a) The high standing that constitutional law accords to autonomy and life, and which § 217 of the Criminal Code aims to protect, may, in principle, warrant the use of criminal law for protecting these interests.

Criminal law serves an indispensable function when it comes to fulfilling the state's responsibility to establish, safeguard and enforce a rule-based social co-existence by protecting the fundamental values of the community (cf. BVerfGE 123, 267 <408>). In certain cases, the state's duty of protection may indeed require the state to provide for a legal framework designed to reduce even the risk of fundamental rights violations (cf. BVerfGE 49, 89 <142>).

[...]

The high standing the Constitution accords to life and autonomy can in principle justify effective preventive protection of these interests, especially given that suicide assistance poses particular risks to them. Empirical findings support the conclusion that a decision to commit suicide is fragile [...], and the fragility of such a decision is a particularly weighty consideration given that a decision to end one's own life is, by its nature, irreversible once acted upon.

(b) However, where criminal law no longer protects free decisions of the individual but renders such decisions impossible, it exceeds the limits of what constitutes a legitimate means for protecting personal autonomy in the decision on ending one's life.

274 The exemption of suicide, and of suicide assistance, from punishment reflects the – constitutionally mandated – recognition of individual self-determination; as such, it is not at the legislator's free disposal. At the heart of the Basic Law's constitutional order lies a central notion of human beings informed by human dignity and the free development of one's personality through self-determination and personal responsibility (cf. BVerfGE 32, 98 <107 and 108>; 108, 282 <300>; 128, 326 <376>; 138, 296 <339 para. 109>). This notion must be the basis of any legislative framework.

275 It follows that the state's duty to protect self-determination and life can only take precedence over the individual's freedom where the individual is exposed to influences that endanger their self-determination over their own life. The legal order may counteract these influences through preventive measures and safeguards. Beyond this, however, an individual's decision to end their own life, based on their personal understanding of what constitutes a meaningful existence, must be recognised as an act of autonomous self-determination.

276 Recognising the right to a self-determined death does not bar the legislator from taking general measures to prevent suicide. In particular, the legislator may take measures to expand and strengthen palliative care in order to counter wishes to commit suicide born out of illness. The state does not fulfil its duty to protect personal autonomy by merely preventing threats to autonomy posed by other persons. It must also counter risks to autonomy and life arising from current and foreseeable life circumstances that are capable of influencing an individual to choose suicide instead of life (cf. BVerfGE 88, 203 <258> regarding unborn life).

277 Yet the legislator must not evade its social policy obligations by trying to counteract risks to autonomy through the complete suspension of individual self-determination. The legislator may not set aside the constitutionally protected right to self-determination altogether in response to developments that prompt fears of a loss of self-determination and may lead to decisions to commit suicide, such as deficiencies in healthcare services and social infrastructure or negative aspects of overtreatment. The individual must still be afforded the freedom to refuse life-sustaining treatment and to act upon a decision to end their own life with the assistance of others based on their personal understanding of what constitutes a meaningful existence. Where the protection of life undermines the protection of autonomy, it contradicts the central understanding of a community which places human dignity at the core of its order of values and thus commits itself to respecting and protecting the free human personality as the highest value of its Constitution. Given the vital significance for self-determination and respect for one's personality that can be attached to the freedom to commit suicide, it must always be ensured that

realistic possibilities of committing suicide are available (see para. 208 *et seq.* above).

(c) The prohibition of assisted suicide services violates constitutional law insofar as it fails to leave the required scope for the pursuit of autonomous self-determination. § 217 of the Criminal Code in principle recognises the constitutionally mandated exemption from punishment of suicide and suicide assistance by merely criminalising professionalised assisted suicide services, which the legislator considers a form of suicide that poses particular risks to personal autonomy (cf. BTDrucks 18/5373, p. 2). However, the prohibition is not an isolated legal act (see aa below). As the law stands, the introduction of the provision criminalising assisted suicide services causes the right to suicide to effectively be largely vitiated because the resulting restriction of constitutionally protected freedom cannot be compensated by the continued exemption from punishment of suicide assistance that is not offered as a professionalised service, by the expansion of palliative and hospice care mandated by law or by the availability of suicide assistance in other countries. Where the choice of the individual is limited to these alternatives, their right to self-determination is violated (see bb below). 278

(aa) In providing protection through an absolute prohibition of assisted suicide services, § 217 of the Criminal Code suspends individual self-determination in the domain covered by the provision given that it places any decision to commit suicide under an irrefutable blanket suspicion of lacking freedom and reflection. This upends the Constitution's central notion of human beings as free beings capable of self-determination and personal growth (cf. BVerfGE 32, 98 <107 and 108>; 108, 282 <300>; 128, 326 <376>; 138, 296 <339 para. 109>). [...] 279

It is true that the prohibition set out in § 217 of the Criminal Code is limited to assisted suicide services, i.e. a specific form of suicide assistance. However, the resulting loss of autonomy is disproportionate insofar as and as long as the remaining options available to the individual provide only a theoretical but no actual prospect of self-determination. The detrimental effects on personal autonomy brought about by § 217 of the Criminal Code are further aggravated precisely because in many situations, individuals will be left with no actual, reliable options to act upon a decision to commit suicide if assisted suicide services are not available. 280

(bb) Under a strict interpretation of § 217 of the Criminal Code, the option of providing suicide assistance in an isolated case remains exempt from punishment (see α below); other options include palliative care (see β below) and suicide assistance provided in other countries. Yet all of these options fail to give sufficient effect to self-determination regarding the end of one's life as required under constitutional law. 281

282 (α) The legislator deems the prohibition of assisted suicide services to be appropriate on the grounds that providing suicide assistance in an isolated case in a manner that is not professionalised remains exempt from punishment. Thus, within its own legislative concept, it accords decisive importance to the option of making use of such suicide assistance in an isolated case for upholding and realising the right to self-determination (cf. BTDrucks 18/5373, pp. 2, 13, 14).

283 Yet in tacitly assuming that options for suicide assistance other than professionalised assisted suicide services are actually available, the legislator fails to consider the legal order as a whole. If the legislator excludes specific ways of exercising freedom with reference to remaining alternatives, these remaining courses of action must be actually suitable for ensuring the effective exercise of the fundamental rights in question. In particular in the context of the right to suicide, such alternatives must really exist. In this respect, the individual's knowledge of actually being able to act according to their own wishes is in itself a crucial element of asserting one's identity. [...]

284 Consequently, if the legal order criminalises certain forms of suicide assistance that jeopardise personal autonomy, especially assisted suicide services, it must be ensured that suicide assistance provided voluntarily can in practice still be accessed in the individual case. The fact that the legislator chose not to criminalise all forms of suicide assistance unconditionally does not, by itself, satisfy this standard. In the absence of professionalised assisted suicide services, the individual largely depends on the willingness of doctors, either their treating physician or another doctor, to provide assistance at least in the form of prescribing the substances necessary to commit suicide. Realistically, a doctor will only be willing to do so in exceptional cases. This is precisely why associations providing suicide assistance offer their services. Firstly, doctors can never be obliged to provide suicide assistance (see αα below); secondly, the prohibitions of providing suicide assistance, which have largely been incorporated into the laws and codes governing the medical profession, at least guide doctors' actions in practice (see ββ below).

285-288 (αα) [...]

289 Individuals must generally accept the decision of an individual doctor, protected by their freedom of conscience, not to provide suicide assistance. The right to a self-determined death does not give rise to a claim vis-à-vis others to be assisted in one's plan to commit suicide (see already paras. 212 and 213 above).

290 (ββ) The laws and codes governing the medical profession set further limits to doctors' individual willingness to provide suicide assistance that go beyond or even disregard what individual doctors decide in accordance with their conscience. [...].

No. 13 – Assisted Suicide

[...]

(β) Improvements in palliative care [...] mandated by the Act Improving Hospice and Palliative Care in Germany, which accompanied the introduction of the prohibition of assisted suicide services, cannot compensate for the disproportionate restriction of the individual's self-determination. They may well remedy existing deficiencies in palliative care services, in quantitative and qualitative terms, and thus be a suitable means for reducing the number of cases in which terminally ill patients wish to die as a consequence of such deficiencies. [...]
No one is obliged to make use of palliative care. [...]
(γ) The state may also not simply refer the individual to the option of using suicide assistance offered in other countries. Under Art. 1(3) of the Basic Law, the state must guarantee the necessary fundamental rights protection within its own legal order (cf. BVerwGE 158, 142 <158 para. 36>).
(cc) Finally, the restriction of individual self-determination resulting from § 217 of the Criminal Code cannot be justified by the protection of others. Given that the individual is connected to and bound by the social community, they must accept those restrictions of their constitutionally protected freedom that the legislator, within the limits of what is reasonable in the relevant circumstances, imposes for the purposes of maintaining and fostering social co-existence. However, the individual autonomy of the person must be upheld (cf. BVerfGE 4, 7 <15 and 16>; 59, 275 <279>). Measures of suicide prevention can be justified by the aim of protecting others – e.g. by seeking to prevent assisted suicide services from prompting copycat behaviour or to curtail a strong pull on persons that are fragile in terms of self-determination and thus vulnerable. However, the aim of protecting others does not justify forcing the individual to accept that their right to suicide is effectively vitiated (see para. 273 *et seq.*, in particular para. 281 *et seq.* above)
4. This assessment is in accordance with the European Convention on Human Rights, which serves as a guideline for interpretation when determining the content and scope of fundamental rights (cf. BVerfGE 111, 307 <317 and 318>; 149, 293 <328 para. 86>), and with the interpretation of the Convention set forth by the European Court of Human Rights (cf. BVerfGE 148, 296 <354 para. 132, 379 and 380 paras. 173 and 174>).
The European Court of Human Rights recognises the right of the individual to choose when and how to die as a manifestation of the right to respect for private life under Art. 8(1) of the Convention; the Court holds that, while this right may be restricted to protect the life and autonomy of others, it must not be completely vitiated.
According to the case-law of the European Court of Human Rights, Art. 8(1) of the Convention encompasses the right to live one's life in self-determination and

in a manner of one's own choosing. In its decision *Pretty v. the United Kingdom*, which raises the question whether a person suffering from a severe physical illness has a right to assisted suicide, the Court emphasises that the notion of personal autonomy is an important principle underlying the interpretation of the guarantees of Art. 8 of the Convention (cf. ECtHR, *Pretty v. the United Kingdom*, Judgment of 29 April 2002, no. 2346/02, § 61). Having regard to the very essence of the Convention – respect for human dignity and freedom – the European Court of Human Rights holds that notions of the quality of life take on significance under Art. 8 of the Convention. According to the Court, in an era of growing medical sophistication combined with longer life expectancies, nobody should be forced to linger on in old age or in states of advanced physical or mental decrepitude which conflict with strongly held ideas of self and personal identity. State and society must respect the decision to end physical and mental suffering through assisted suicide (cf. ECtHR, *Pretty v. the United Kingdom*, Judgment of 29 April 2002, no. 2346/02, §§ 64 and 65). In *Haas v. Switzerland*, a case concerning a mentally ill complainant, the European Court of Human Rights further specified its case-law, expressly holding that an individual's right to decide by what means and at what point their life will end, provided they are capable of freely reaching a decision and acting in consequence, is one of the aspects of the right to respect for private life within the meaning of Art. 8 of the Convention (cf. ECtHR, *Haas v. Switzerland*, Judgment of 20 January 2011, no. 31322/07, § 51).

305 However, the European Court of Human Rights also recognises that restrictions of this right may be necessary for the protection of the life of others under Art. 8(2) of the Convention. In balancing the individual's right to self-determination against the state's duty to protect life derived from Art. 2 of the Convention, the Court acknowledges that the Contracting States have a significant margin of appreciation in this sensitive area (cf. ECtHR, *Pretty v. the United Kingdom*, Judgment of 29 April 2002, no. 2346/02, §§ 70 *et seq.*; *Haas v. Switzerland*, Judgment of 20 January 2011, no. 31322/07, §§ 53, 55; *Koch v. Germany*, Judgment of 19 July 2012, no. 497/09, § 70). Thus, it is primarily for states to assess the risk and the likely incidence of abuse arising from suicide assistance (cf. ECtHR, *Pretty v. the United Kingdom*, Judgment of 29 April 2002, no. 2346/02, § 74). Where a country adopts a liberal approach, appropriate implementing measures for such an approach and preventive measures are necessary; such measures must also prevent abuse (cf. ECtHR, *Haas v. Switzerland*, Judgment of 20 January 2011, no. 31322/07, § 57). Art. 2 of the Convention obliges the national authorities to prevent an individual from taking their own life if the decision has not been taken freely and with full understanding of what is involved. The right to life guaranteed by Art. 2 of the Convention obliges states to protect vulnerable persons, even against actions

No. 13 – Assisted Suicide

by which they endanger their own lives, and to establish a procedure capable of ensuring that a decision to end one's life does indeed correspond to the free will of the individual concerned (cf. ECtHR, *Haas v. Switzerland*, Judgment of 20 January 2011, no. 31322/07, §§ 54, 58). On the other hand, the European Court of Human Rights also emphasises that the right to choose the time and manner of one's death must not be merely theoretical or illusory (cf. ECtHR, *Haas v. Switzerland*, Judgment of 20 January 2011, no. 31322/07, §§ 59 *et seq.*).

II.

The constitutional complaints lodged by the other complainants are also well-founded. The restrictions of their occupational freedom (Art. 12(1) of the Basic Law), and, subsidiarily, their general freedom of action (Art. 2(1) of the Basic Law) that result from § 217 of the Criminal Code are not constitutional (see 1 below). The provision violates the right to liberty under Art. 2(2) second sentence in conjunction with Art. 104(1) of the Basic Law of the complainants who are natural persons and thus face a possible prison sentence (see 2 below). § 217 of the Criminal Code also violates the fundamental right under Art. 2(1) of the Basic Law of the complainants in proceedings II. and III. 2 as the criminalisation of assisted suicide services may lead to administrative fines being imposed on these associations under § 30(1) of the Act on Administrative Offences (see 3 below). […]

306

307-333

III.

§ 217 of the Criminal Code cannot be interpreted in conformity with the Constitution. An interpretation restricting its scope of application, which declared assisted suicide services to be permissible under certain circumstances, would contradict the legislative intent and thus amount to outright judicial law-making that would be incompatible with the requirement of sufficient specificity (Art. 103(2) of the Basic Law) (cf. BVerfGE 47, 109 <120>; 64, 389 <393>; 73, 206 <235>; 105, 135 <153>).
[…]

334

335-336

IV.

1. Due to the violations of constitutional law set out above, § 217 of the Criminal Code must be declared void (§ 95(1) first sentence of the Federal Constitutional Court Act). The requirements for a mere declaration of incompatibility are not

337

met (cf. BVerfGE 128, 282 <321 and 322> – *Coercive Treatment in Psychiatric Confinement under Criminal Law*; 129, 269 <284>).

338 2. The fact that § 217 of the Criminal Code is unconstitutional does not mean that the legislator must completely refrain from regulating suicide assistance. It is not objectionable under constitutional law that the legislator derived a mandate to take action from its duty to protect personal autonomy in end-of-life decision-making (see para. 231 *et seq.* above). However, any legislative concept of protection must be guided by the notion – which is at the heart of the Basic Law's constitutional order – of human beings as intellectual-moral beings with the inherent aspiration to determine their own being and to develop (cf. BVerfGE 32, 98 <107 and 108>; 108, 282 <300>; 128, 326 <376>; 138, 296 <339 para. 109>). The constitutional recognition of the individual as a being capable of self-determination requires that state intervention be strictly limited to measures protecting self-determination, which may be complemented with elements ensuring medical or pharmaceutical quality assurance and protecting against abuse.

339 In the context of organised suicide assistance, a wide array of options is available to the legislator for ensuring protection of self-determination in decisions regarding one's own life. These include enacting procedural safeguards such as statutory obligations to provide information or to observe waiting periods; requirements to obtain administrative approval, which ensure the reliability of the assisted suicide services offered; as well as the prohibition of particularly dangerous forms of suicide assistance in accordance with the legislative intent underlying § 217 of the Criminal Code. In view of the importance of the legal interests these options serve to protect, the legislator may also resort to the use of criminal law, or at least provide for criminal sanctions in case of breaches (see already para. 268 *et seq.* above).

340 Given that the right to suicide, including the motives underlying an individual decision to commit suicide, is recognised under constitutional law and these motives thus elude any appraisal on the basis of objective rationality standards (see para. 210 above), the permissibility of suicide assistance may not be linked to substantive criteria, e.g. by requiring a diagnosis of incurable or terminal illness. Nonetheless, different requirements may be set, depending on the relevant life circumstances, for establishing that an individual's decision to commit suicide is serious and lasting. The legislator is free to develop a framework of procedural safeguards.

341 However, any legislative restriction of assisted suicide must ensure that sufficient scope remains in practice for the individual to exercise their constitutionally protected right to depart this life based on their free decision and with the assistance of others. This not only requires legislative coherence in the design of the legal

No. 13 – Assisted Suicide

framework applicable to doctors and pharmacists, but potentially also adjustments of the law on controlled substances.

[…] Regardless of all the foregoing, no one can ever be obliged to assist in another person's suicide. 342

D.

[…] 343

Justices: Voßkuhle, Masing, Huber, Hermanns, Kessal-Wulf, König, Maidowski, Langenfeld

No. 14

BVerfGE 97, 391 – Sexual Abuse Allegations

HEADNOTE

to the Order of the First Senate of 24 March 1998
1 BvR 131/96

The protection of freedom of expression and the general right of personality also apply to saying one's own name when making a statement protected by Article 5(1) first sentence of the Basic Law.

FEDERAL CONSTITUTIONAL COURT
- 1 BvR 131/96 -

IN THE NAME OF THE PEOPLE

In the proceedings
on the constitutional complaint of

Ms K…,
– authorised representatives: …

against the Judgment of the Celle Higher Regional Court of 22 November 1995 - 13 U 84/94 -

the Federal Constitutional Court – First Senate –
with the participation of Justices

Vice-President Papier,
Grimm,
Kühling,
Seibert,
Jaeger,
Haas,

No. 14 – Sexual Abuse Allegations

Hömig,
Steiner

held on 24 March 1998:

The Judgment of the Celle Higher Regional Court of 22 November 1995 - 13 U 84/94 - violates the complainant's fundamental rights under Article 5(1) first sentence and Article 2(1) in conjunction with Article 1(1) of the Basic Law insofar as it requires her to refrain from naming herself when stating that the plaintiff in the initial proceedings sexually abused her. To this extent, [...] the judgment is reversed. The matter is remanded to the Higher Regional Court.
[...]

REASONS:

A.

The constitutional complaint challenges a civil court decision ordering the complainant to refrain from making any statement in which she names her father or herself.

I.

1. The complainant is the daughter of the plaintiff in the initial proceedings. According to the findings of the Regional Court and the Higher Regional Court, the plaintiff sexually abused her from a young age over a period of many years.

The complainant, who is now 41 years old and [...] still uses her maiden name, first revealed the abuse to her friends in 1973. In 1977, she told one of her superiors about it. In 1986, she confided in several doctors [...]. [...] In addition, she notified the youth welfare office of the abuse in order to protect her sister's daughter, for whom [her father] occasionally baby-sat [...].

[...] In January 1991, she stated on a TV show that she had been abused by her father as a child. [...] In 1992, she once again approached the youth welfare office. Soon afterwards, she spoke of the abuse on the TV show *Schreinemakers Live* and offered, to the magazine *Emma*, to write an article on claims for damages against the person responsible for long-term psychological effects of sexual abuse.

Citing the renewed notification of the youth welfare office, the plaintiff in the initial proceedings requested that the complainant refrain from accusing him of sexual abuse in the presence of others. The complainant refused to comply with this request. Thereupon, the plaintiff sought injunctive relief. [...]

6   2. The Regional Court dismissed the action for injunctive relief. [...]
7   a) [...]
8   b) Upon the plaintiff's appeal on points of fact and law (*Berufung*), the Higher Regional Court ordered the complainant to refrain from accusing the plaintiff of having sexually abused her, if in doing so she states either the plaintiff's or her own name.

9-11   [...]

II.

12   The complainant challenges that judgment with her constitutional complaint, claiming a violation of Art. 5(1) first and second sentence and Art. 2(1) of the Basic Law insofar as she is required to refrain from stating her own name when discussing the sexual abuse. [...]

13-17   [...]

III.

18-22   [...]

B.

23   The constitutional complaint is well-founded. The judgment of the Higher Regional Court violates Art. 5(1) first sentence and Art. 2(1) in conjunction with Art. 1(1) of the Basic Law.

I.

24   These fundamental rights are affected by the challenged decision.
25   1. Naming one's own name in a statement is protected by freedom of expression.
26   The fundamental right to freedom of expression protects any expression of opinion and factual assertion as well as other types of statements if these are required for forming an opinion (cf. BVerfGE 61, 1 <8>; 85, 23 <31>). Mentioning one's own name in a statement does not amount to a separate type of statement, nor is it, strictly speaking, an inherent part of the statement. [...] However, this does not mean that mentioning one's name does not fall within the scope of protection of this fundamental right. On the contrary, the name is of great significance not only in respect of the statement itself, but also as part of an individual's or the general public's opinion-forming process, as it contributes thereto.

The free expression of opinion is "the most direct form of expression of an individual's personality in society" (BVerfGE 7, 198 <208>). When the person making the statement is named, the connection between the person and the statement becomes manifest. When a person making a statement adds their name to the statement, they express that the statement is their personal opinion or view, and that they are prepared to back it up and, if their statement is a factual assertion, to personally vouch for its veracity. Naming one's own name is thus one of the prerequisites for conveying the intended meaning of the statement, particularly in respect of statements with which the speaker strongly identifies or which describe their own story. 27

Moreover, the name of the person making the statement can also convey a message that goes beyond the mere content of the statement. It is possible, for instance, that a personal account of painful experiences encourages other affected persons to break their silence. Such a message could not be conveyed in the same way without stating one's own name given that, in doing so, the person making the statement reveals that they are personally affected. This applies particularly when communication on certain occurrences is treated as a taboo. [...] 28

[...] Art. 5(1) first sentence of the Basic Law [...] protects statements not only with regard to dissemination, but also with regard to their impact (cf. BVerfGE 7, 198 <210>). Freedom of expression also encompasses the speaker's right to choose to deliver their statement in precisely the form and under the circumstances that will ensure the greatest possible impact (cf. BVerfGE 93, 266 <289>). However, the impact of a statement on others largely depends on whether or not the person making the statement can be identified. Anonymous statements often lack the degree of authenticity and credibility that brings about the desired effect or produces the desired response. 29

[...] 30

2. Furthermore, stating one's own name falls within the scope of protection of the general right of personality under Art. 2(1) in conjunction with Art. 1(1) of the Basic Law. 31

A person's name not only serves to organise [society] and distinguish [persons from one another], it is also an expression of one's identity and individuality. Individuals have the right to demand that the legal order respect and protect their name. In certain contexts, this protection [...] also encompasses the desire to withhold one's undisputed name, or to replace it with a pseudonym. A name, as an expression of one's identity and individuality, cannot be exchanged at will. [...] Thus, refraining from stating one's name is not without adverse effects on one's personality. 32

The same applies in respect of naming one's own name in a statement. Statements do not consist solely of the transmission of specific communication contents. They 33 are also an expression of the personality of the person making a statement. Through their statements, those concerned present themselves to others as a person. These statements allow others to perceive their identity. When persons making a statement name their own name, others can not only associate the statement with the person, they can also integrate this statement into their image of the person's personality. At the same time, they are able to assess not only the contents of the statement, but also the person making the statement. Thus, if persons are obliged to refrain from naming their own name when making statements which they expressly regard as personal, and where it is important to them that such statements are associated with them, such an obligation must also be measured against the standards of Art. 2(1) in conjunction with Art. 1(1) of the Basic Law.

34 3. By contrast, the fundamental right to freedom of the press is not relevant here. [...]

35 4. Obliging the complainant to refrain from saying her name when publicly discussing that she was sexually abused by her father restricts her fundamental right to freedom of expression and her right of personality. The fact that the statement may be further disseminated in public does not change this, because the use of one's name falls within the scope of protection of both fundamental rights.

II.

36 The challenged decision is incompatible with the fundamental right to freedom of expression and the general right of personality.

37 1. Both fundamental rights are, of course, subject to statutory limitations. Pursuant to Art. 5(2) of the Basic Law, freedom of expression is only guaranteed within the limits of the provisions of general laws, of provisions for the protection of young persons, and of the right to personal honour. Under Art. 2(1) of the Basic Law, the development of one's personality is bound by the limits set by the constitutional order. This includes all legal provisions that are compatible with the Basic Law in terms of both their form and substance (cf. BVerfGE 6, 32 <41>). Among these are the provisions of §§ 823, 1004 of the Civil Code, on which the Higher Regional Court based the challenged judgment.

38 2. However, the application of these provisions in the present case does not meet the fundamental rights requirements.

39 a) The interpretation and application of private law falls to the civil courts, just as it is also their task to establish the facts of the case and to evaluate the evidence. However, when, in the course of applying constitutionally unobjectionable provisions of private law, legal interests that are protected by fundamental rights are affected, the civil courts must be guided by the significance and scope of the

affected fundamental rights to ensure that the values enshrined therein are upheld when applying the relevant statutory provisions (cf. BVerfGE 7, 198 <205 *et seq.*>; established case-law). This generally requires a balancing, during the usual course of the civil proceedings, between the significance of the restricted fundamental right for its holders in the specific case and the extent of their impairment, on the one hand, and the importance of the legal interest protected by the applied law and the severity of its impairment through the exercise of fundamental rights, on the other hand. In doing this, the courts must have sufficient regard to both interests and must balance them in such a way that both are adequately taken into account. In particular, where a civil court fails to consider the impact of the fundamental rights altogether or incorrectly appraises it, and where the decision is grounded in this disregard for the impact of fundamental rights, this amounts to a violation of fundamental rights, which the Federal Constitutional Court must then remedy (cf. BVerfGE 95, 28 <37>).

b) On the complainant's side of the balancing, it is particularly significant that, in respect of freedom of expression and the right of personality, the disputed statement is closely related to the complainant's personality and she would be largely deprived of the desired impact of her communication process if she were prohibited from stating her name. 40

The complainant is only permitted to publicly make the statement in question if she refrains from disclosing her name; yet this statement relates not to some distant subject but to one that concerns her highly personal story. On the basis of the facts established by the civil courts, which the Federal Constitutional Court must accept, this is an experience with far-reaching consequences that is significant to her physical and psychological development. Every person is free to decide whether to share experiences of this type with others at all, and whether to do so publicly. Yet if the person concerned decides to do so, a prohibition on personally describing this highly personal story generally amounts to a severe impairment to one's means of communication and the development of one's personality. 41

This finding is not altered by the fact that the challenged judgment does not prevent the complainant from discussing her abuse experience using her own name in the context of private conversations or therapy sessions. That is because she is prevented from discussing it beyond her personal circle of acquaintances or the persons professionally concerned with her personality development. The complainant cannot make a public appearance as an identifiable person, vouch for her story with her name and receive direct reactions to her story from others. 42

This also reduces the impact of her story on persons in a similar position, or on members of the general public who are concerned by the issue of sexual abuse of 43 children, as there is a danger that the credibility and authenticity of the description generally associated with the use of one's name may be lacking. [...]

44 The life-changing experience about which the complainant wishes to speak publicly is, however, inextricably linked to her father. While this relationship demands a certain degree of restraint, it must be taken into account that the complainant speaks about the plaintiff in the initial proceedings from her perspective as a victim of his actions. [...] The fact that the complainant is a victim, as established by the courts, would be re-emphasised if the victim were denied the chance to present her story in a personalised form. [...]

45 c) In the balancing, on the side of the plaintiff in the initial proceedings, significance must be accorded to his right of personality, which is protected as a fundamental right and reflected in private law in §§ 823 and 1004 of the Civil Code. [...] However, personality interests must generally stand back behind freedom of expression when the disputed statement concerns facts that must be considered true.

46 There are, however, some exceptions to this principle. True reports may constitute a violation of the right of personality of the person concerned, particularly when the portrayal would have serious consequences for the development of their personality, and if the need for protection outweighs the interest in making the statement. Thus, in its *Lebach* decision (BVerfGE 35, 202) the Federal Constitutional Court accorded personality interests precedence over freedom of broadcasting [...].

47 The present case is indeed different, given that not media reports but a report by the victim are at issue. [...]

48 Notwithstanding this, the consequences for the plaintiff in the initial proceedings are serious given that he is accused of having sexually abused his own child, which is considered a particularly heinous crime. Reports of such conduct usually lead to the stigmatisation of the perpetrator. Due to societal judgment and behaviour mechanisms, i.e. patterns that are not within the control of the affected person, stigmatisation can result in a loss of social acceptance and lead to social isolation and to fundamental insecurity and loss of self-worth on the part of the affected person in numerous areas of life. The free development of one's personality is thereby rendered considerably more difficult [...].

49 The protection afforded by Art. 2(1) in conjunction with Art. 1(1) of the Basic Law does not require the statements about a person to be false. In fact, the protection also applies in cases in which the statements are true and may therefore result in social exclusion and isolation. [...]

50 [...] The right to the protection of one's personality applies [...] also with regard to the consequences of this allegation becoming information for others. That is why the information and the means of identification that the addressees of the statement are provided with are relevant. The possibility that an allegation may be taken to

refer to a certain person who will have to bear the consequences – consequences against which the constitutional right of personality grants protection – thus arises not only when the person's name is mentioned, but also when other details make their identification possible.

Nevertheless, the weight of the impairment of the fundamental right depends on how far-reaching the discriminatory effects are. This can vary depending on how well-known the person concerned is. Furthermore, it must be taken into account whether the effects of the statement are limited due to the name's frequency. If the name is very common, the statement will only have an effect in respect of those persons who know the speaker and their family and who can therefore draw conclusions as to the identity of the perpetrator from a public appearance of the speaker using her own name. In the case of a television appearance, the statement of the speaker's name gives rise to an even less serious impairment of the right of personality, as much of the speaker's identity is revealed even if the name is not disclosed. 51

d) In its balancing of interests, the Higher Regional Court did not sufficiently take into account these aspects, although mandated to do so by fundamental rights. 52

The Higher Regional Court, in accordance with the civil courts' case-law, did affirm a pillorying effect by the complainant's statement on the plaintiff in the initial proceedings, with serious consequences for the development of his personality, and held that this could therefore only be tolerated if it were matched by important reasons for publishing the allegation in such a form that would allow for his identification. There are no constitutional objections to this reasoning. 53

However, the Higher Regional Court failed to attribute sufficient weight to the arguments in favour of making a statement using one's own name. Its judgment raises doubts as to whether the court was aware of the fact that the complainant, in using her name when making her statement, is protected by freedom of expression and by the general right of personality. In any event, the complainant's interests protected by these fundamental rights were not sufficiently taken into account in the court's balancing. [...] 54

[...] 55-56

As the Higher Regional Court failed to sufficiently address the specific interests that are relevant with regard to freedom of expression and the right of personality, it also failed to properly attribute weight to the necessary elements in the balancing of interests. [...] 57

[...] 58

e) [...] 59

Justices: Papier, Grimm, Kühling, Seibert, Jaeger, Haas, Hömig, Steiner

No. 15

BVerfGE 115, 1 – Transsexuals V

HEADNOTE

to the Order of the First Senate of 6 December 2005
1 BvL 3/03

In respect of homosexual transsexuals, § 7(1) no. 3 of the Transsexuals Act violates the right to one's name protected under Article 2(1) in conjunction with Article 1(1) of the Basic Law, as well as the right to the protection of one's intimate sphere, insofar as a legally protected partnership is not available to homosexual transsexuals without having to give up their first name, which had been changed to correspond to their internally felt gender.

FEDERAL CONSTITUTIONAL COURT
- 1 BvL 3/03 -

IN THE NAME OF THE PEOPLE

In the proceedings
for constitutional review of

§ 7(1) no. 3 of the Act on the Change of First Names and of Officially Assigned Sex in Special Cases of 10 September 1980 (BGBlI, p. 1654)
– Order of Suspension and Referral of the Itzehoe Regional Court of 26 March 2003 (4 T 497/02) –

the Federal Constitutional Court – First Senate –
with the participation of Justices

President Papier,
Haas,
Hömig,
Steiner,
Hohmann-Dennhardt,
Hoffmann-Riem,

Bryde,
Gaier

held on 6 December 2005:
1. § 7(1) no. 3 of the Act on the Change of First Names and of Officially Assigned Sex in Special Cases (Transsexuals Act) of 10 September 1980 (BGBl I, p. 1654) is incompatible with Article 2(1) in conjunction with Article 1(1) of the Basic Law insofar as a legally protected partnership is not available to homosexual transsexuals who have not undergone gender reassignment without them having to give up their first name, which had been changed pursuant to § 1 of the Transsexuals Act.
2. § 7(1) no. 3 of the Transsexuals Act is not applicable until a legal provision has been enacted that enables homosexual transsexuals who have not undergone gender reassignment to enter into a legally protected partnership without having to give up their first name.

REASONS:

A.

1   The referral concerns having to give up, by reason of marriage, the first name that had previously been changed to express the gender a transsexual person identifies with.

I.

2   The Act on the Change of First Names and of Officially Assigned Sex in Special Cases of 10 September 1980 (BGBl I, p. 1654) was enacted following the foundational decision by the First Senate of the Federal Constitutional Court of 11 October 1978 (BVerfGE 49, 286 – *Transsexuals I*) to accommodate the special situation of transsexuals. In addition to a procedure that, following gender reassignment surgery, establishes a change of officially assigned sex and allows first names to be changed (the so-called big solution), the Act provides for an option for transsexuals to change their first names upon application without first having to undergo surgery (the so-called small solution).

3   1. § 1 of the Transsexuals Act sets out the requirements for a change of first names without gender reassignment […].

No. 15 – Transsexuals V

[...]

[...] A change of first names concluded this way [...] may become void under certain circumstances. This is laid down in § 7 of the Transsexuals Act [...]:

§ 7

Voidness

(1) The decision that changes the first names of the applicant shall become void if

1. within a period of three hundred days after the decision has attained legal validity, a child is born of the applicant, effective from the day the child is born, or

2. (...), or

3. the applicant enters into marriage, effective from the declaration [before the registrar] under § 1310(1) of the Civil Code

(2)-(3) [...]

[...] However, in the case of the birth of a child, but not in the case of marriage, § 7(3) of the Transsexuals Act provides those concerned with the option of reverting to their changed first name under the circumstances specified therein. [...] In addition, a married transsexual can obtain a change of first name under § 1 of the Transsexuals Act without consequences for their marriage. [...]

2. [...]

II.

[...]

III.

The plaintiff in the initial proceedings is male. His first name Kai was changed to Karin Nicole by order of the Hamburg Local Court of 9 July 1997 pursuant to § 1(1) of the Transsexuals Act. He did not undergo gender reassignment pursuant to §§ 8 and 10 of the Transsexuals Act, which requires surgery among other things. After the plaintiff had married, on 5 April 2002, the woman with whom he is, in his view, in a same-sex relationship, the registrar noted in the birth register that the plaintiff was from now on once again named Kai.

27 The plaintiff then initiated two legal proceedings in order to regain his female first name of which he had been deprived. Firstly, he invoked the provisions of the Transsexuals Act. His application to reinstate his changed first name, which is the subject matter of the constitutional complaint 1 BvR 2201/02 lodged by the plaintiff, was unsuccessful in all instances. Secondly, the plaintiff applied for his birth register entry to be corrected by means of a further margin note pursuant to § 47 of the Civil Status Act declaring the registrar's note of 19 September 2002 to be void. The Itzehoe Local Court rejected this application by order of 28 October 2002. [...]

28 By order of 26 March 2003, the Itzehoe Regional Court suspended the proceedings concerning the plaintiff's immediate complaint (*sofortige Beschwerde*) against the order of the Itzehoe Local Court; it referred to the Federal Constitutional Court the question whether § 7(1) no. 3 of the Transsexuals Act is unconstitutional. In the referring court's view, § 7(1) no. 3 of the Transsexuals Act violates Art. 1(1) in conjunction with Art. 2(1) of the Basic Law as well as Art. 3(1) and Art. 6(1) of the Basic Law. Moreover, the court has doubts as to the provision's compatibility with Art. 2(2) first sentence of the Basic Law.

29 [...]

IV.

30 Statements on the referral were submitted by the Federal Ministry of the Interior on behalf of the Federal Government, the German Conference of Family Courts (*Deutscher Familiengerichtstag*), the German Society for Sexology (*Deutsche Gesellschaft für Sexualforschung*), the Lesbian and Gay Association (*Lesben- und Schwulenverband*), the Ecumenical Working Group 'Homosexuals and the Church' (*Ökumenische Arbeitsgruppe Homosexuelle und Kirche*), the German Society for Trans Identity and Intersexuality (*Deutsche Gesellschaft für Transidentität und Intersexualität*) and the *sonntags.club*.

31-44 [...]

B.

45 The Transsexuals Act is not compatible with Art. 2(1) in conjunction with Art. 1(1) of the Basic Law insofar as, on the basis of § 7(1) no. 3 of the Transsexuals Act, it does not provide homosexual transsexuals who have not undergone gender reassignment with the option of a legally protected partnership without giving up their changed first name.

No. 15 – Transsexuals V

I.

1. a) Art. 1(1) of the Basic Law protects human dignity, the way humans understand themselves as individuals and become aware of themselves (cf. BVerfGE 49, 286 <298> – *Transsexuals I*). Art. 2(1) of the Basic Law, as the fundamental right to the free development of one's personality in conjunction with Art. 1(1) of the Basic Law, protects the personal sphere that is closer to the core of private life (*engere persönliche Lebenssphäre*), which also encompasses intimate sexual matters (cf. BVerfGE 96, 56 <61>), comprising sexual self-determination and thus also the finding and recognising of one's gender identity and sexual orientation.

In this context, Art. 2(1) in conjunction with Art. 1(1) of the Basic Law protects a person's first name, firstly as a means of forging identity and developing one's own individuality (cf. BVerfGE 104, 373 <385>), and secondly as an expression of the gender identity felt or attained by that person (cf. BVerfGE 109, 256 <266>). Individuals have the right to demand that the legal order respect their first names, so that these names can develop their function of forging and expressing one's identity. In this respect, the general right of personality protects name bearers from deprivation or forced change of their first names (cf. BVerfGE 109, 256 <267>).

b) However, the protection of names is not guaranteed unconditionally. The right to one's name must be designed so that it can fulfil the social function that names take on as a distinguishing feature (cf. BVerfGE 78, 38 <49>). This also applies to first names, which, in our legal system, serve to express the name bearer's gender. Having a person's gender identity correspond to the gender expressed in their first name reflects the desire, protected by the general right of personality, to express one's gender identity through one's name, and serves to protect the best interest of the child when choosing a name.

c) Gender identity cannot be determined exclusively on the basis of physical sexual characteristics. It also greatly depends on a person's psychological condition and their lastingly felt gender. § 1 of the Transsexuals Act takes this scientifically proven fact into account. Under certain conditions specified in the Act, persons who, based on their transsexualism, no longer identify with the sex stated in their birth entry but rather with the opposite gender are given the option of changing their first name in order to establish a link between their felt gender and their name. The gender identification that is reflected in the first name that is thus chosen and borne belongs to a person's most intimate part of personality, which is in principle beyond the reach of the state. Therefore, interference with the right to one's first name, which is the result of a person's own search for gender identity and reflects this, is only permissible if there are particularly weighty public interests justifying it (cf. BVerfGE 49, 286 <298> – *Transsexuals I*).

50 2. § 7(1) no. 3 of the Transsexuals Act interferes with this right to a first name chosen under § 1 of the Transsexuals Act which expresses the name bearer's felt gender identity, and which is protected under Art. 2(1) in conjunction with Art. 1(1) of the Basic Law. In case of marriage, the provision deprives the name bearer of the first name chosen and borne, and imposes on them the reversion to their previous first name, which is in conflict with their felt gender. At the same time, depriving a person of their first name also affects that person's intimate sexual matters which are protected by fundamental rights; the obligation to give up one's first name and to revert to one's former name renders it obvious that the name bearer's gender identity is in conflict with the name they are required to bear and which expresses a different gender.

51 It cannot be presumed that the name bearer consented to this interference with their right to their name and with their intimate sphere [...]

52 This holds true in particular if, as in the case of the applicant in the initial proceedings, no option other than marriage is available to the person concerned for legally protecting their relationship. The applicant is a transsexual who identifies as female, but who has not undergone surgery to change the external sexual characteristics. In addition, his sexual orientation is homosexual. § 1 of the Transsexuals Act provides him the option of adapting his first name to his felt female gender, but in terms of civil status law, he is still treated as a man. If he wants to legally protect a homosexual relationship with a woman, the option of a civil partnership is not available to him, as only two persons of the same sex may enter into a civil partnership under § 1(1) first sentence of the Civil Partnerships Act. [...] Therefore, the only option available to a homosexual transsexual who has not undergone gender reassignment, such as the applicant, to legally protect his partnership, is marriage. [...] If he decides [to enter into marriage] [...], this does not constitute a voluntary abandoning of his name.

53 3. This interference cannot be justified with the assumption that by entering into marriage, transsexuals show that they once again identify with the sex stated in their birth entry [...]. This assumption, which the legislator used to justify depriving the persons concerned of their first names, is no longer supported by current findings in sexology. It has been proven by now that a large proportion of male-to-female transsexuals in particular is gynephile, i.e. with a homosexual orientation, and that this is the case irrespective of whether they have undergone gender reassignment surgery [...]. Accordingly, a person's internally felt gender cannot be deduced from their sexual orientation. [...]

54 Thus, the legislative purpose of achieving a realignment of assigned sex and first name, by way of the obligation to revert to the previous first name, cannot be

No. 15 – Transsexuals V

considered a weighty public interest that could justify an interference with the right to one's first name under Art. 2(1) in conjunction with Art. 1(1) of the Basic Law.

4. Depriving the persons concerned of their first names under § 7(1) no. 3 of the Transsexuals Act does pursue the legitimate public interest of avoiding the impression that same-sex couples may enter into marriage as well. 55

a) [...] 56-58

b) The legislator pursues a legitimate objective in avoiding the false impression that marriage is also available to same-sex couples. 59

When shaping marriage, the legislator must take into consideration its essential structural principles that are informed by pre-existing realities of marriage as a form of living on which Art. 6(1) of the Basic Law builds in line with the freedom dimension of this fundamental right and other constitutional guarantees (cf. BVerfGE 31, 58 <69>; 105, 313 <345>). It is part of the core content of marriage, which has been preserved irrespective of social change and the associated changes in its legal design, and which has been shaped by the Basic Law, that marriage is the union of a man and a woman in a long-term partnership, established of their own free will with the participation of the state (cf. BVerfGE 10, 59 <66>; 29, 166 <176>; 62, 323 <330>; 105, 313 <345>). It is compatible with this core content of marriage, which follows from Art. 6(1) of the Basic Law, that the legislator may prevent same-sex couples from entering into marriage. In this context, the legislator obviously looks to the official sex assigned under civil status law. In order to emphasise this and to distinguish marriage from other legal institutions, it is also legitimate to enact provisions with which the legislator seeks to avoid even the impression that marriage might also be available to same-sex couples. [...] 60

5. Likewise, revoking the first name pursuant to § 7(1) no. 3 of the Transsexuals Act is suitable and necessary to avoid the false impression that marriage is also available to same-sex couples. [...] 61

6. However, the interference of § 7(1) no. 3 of the Transsexuals Act with transsexuals' right to their name protected under Art. 2(1) in conjunction with Art. 1(1) of the Basic Law and with their right to protection of their intimate sphere is unreasonable (*nicht zumutbar*) for the persons concerned given its interactions with the provisions of the Transsexuals Act, civil status law and the provisions of marriage law and the Civil Partnerships Act. As long as the law does not provide homosexual transsexuals who have not undergone gender reassignment with the option of entering into a legally protected partnership without giving up the first name that corresponds to their felt gender identity, it is unconstitutional that they must give up their first name when entering into marriage under § 7(1) no. 3 of the Transsexuals Act. 62

63 a) The assumptions on transsexuality underlying the Transsexuals Act have become scientifically untenable in essential aspects.

64 The Transsexuals Act was enacted in 1980, following the foundational decision of the Federal Constitutional Court of 11 October 1978 (BVerfGE 49, 286 – *Transsexuals I*). In that decision, the Court held that Art. 2(1) in conjunction with Art. 1(1) of the Basic Law requires that a transsexual's male sex entry be corrected if transsexuality is irreversible according to medical findings and if gender reassignment surgery has been carried out. The legislator satisfied these requirements by way of provisions on the 'big solution', in §§ 8 to 12 of the Transsexuals Act. Under the circumstances specified there, these provisions not only provide transsexuals who have undergone gender reassignment surgery with the option of choosing a first name corresponding to their felt gender, but they also provide them the option of being treated, in civil status law, in accordance with their felt gender. In addition, the legislator introduced the 'small solution', in §§ 1 *et seq.* of the Transsexuals Act, to enable transsexuals to adapt their first name to their felt gender without undergoing gender reassignment surgery, but also without any change in civil status.

65 aa) Based on the scientific findings at the time, the legislator assumed that the 'small solution' would only be a temporary stage for transsexuals, until they transition to the 'big solution'. According to the explanatory memorandum to the Act, the 'small solution' was meant to give those concerned the opportunity of changing their first name and thus of taking on the role of the other gender early on (cf. BTDrucks 8/2947, p. 12). This was based on the assumption, which was also cited by the Federal Constitutional Court at the time, that transsexuals considered their sexual organs and characteristics that do not match their felt gender to be an error of nature and therefore sought to correct them, by any means available, through gender reassignment (cf. BVerfGE 49, 286 <287 and 288> – *Transsexuals I*). […]

66 In the meantime, these assumptions on transsexuality which underlie the Transsexuals Act have proven untenable in light of new scientific findings. In cases of a largely certain diagnosis of transsexuality, today's experts no longer consider it right to always recommend gender reassignment measures. Rather, it must be determined individually and over the course of treatment whether gender reassignment surgery is recommendable. In addition, the 20 to 30% share of lasting transsexuals without gender reassignment out of the total number of transsexuals […] shows that the assumption that transsexuals seek to change their sexual characteristics by any means is not true. Thus, the hypothesis of a temporary stage in which transsexuals with the 'small solution' find themselves before transitioning to the 'big solution' is no longer tenable. Expert literature does not see justifiable reasons

for treating transsexuals who underwent gender reassignment surgery differently than transsexuals who did not [...].

bb) Also, the fact that a significant share of – particularly male-to-female – transsexuals are homosexual, as current research indicates [...], did not play any role when the Transsexuals Act came about. [...] It is not only well-known today that there is homosexuality also among transsexuals, but it has also been proven that even among transsexuals who have undergone gender reassignment a sizeable number are homosexual. Thus, it can no longer be assumed that transsexuality is called into question when transsexuals opt for same-sex relationships.

b) The legal consequences that the legislator derived at the time from the now outdated scientific findings, to define the civil status of transsexuals and the possibility of their entering into legally protected partnerships, are, given the new findings, no longer justified. This is because, in interaction, these provisions unreasonably require homosexual transsexuals to give up a first name that expresses their felt gender identity when entering into a legally protected partnership.

aa) As such, the Transsexuals Act is based on the necessity, recognised by the legislator, of providing transsexuals with the option of having a first name that corresponds to their felt gender identity, thus contributing to the development of an identity-building effect on the name bearer. However, the legislator has attributed different consequences under civil status law to the change of first names depending on whether or not transsexuals had previously undergone gender reassignment surgery. Only if they had done so did the legislator provide for official recognition of the felt gender following the name change. [...] [By contrast,] the felt gender expressed in the first name diverges from the sex officially assigned under civil status law in respect of transsexuals who have not undergone gender reassignment. [...] Thus, a [...] male-to-female transsexual must be addressed by his female first name, but continues to be considered male under civil status law.

bb) Both the legal institution of marriage, protected under Art. 6(1) of the Basic Law, and the institution of civil partnership, created by the legislator, refer to the sex of the partner, and not to their sexual orientation, to limit who may legally unite. Marriage is thus a union between a man and a woman, while a civil partnership is established by two persons of the same sex, pursuant to § 1(1) of the Civil Partnerships Act. [...]

cc) Both the fact that sex assigned under civil status law is determined by external sexual characteristics, as well as the fact that legal forms of partnership are linked to this officially assigned sex under civil status law result in the situation that a homosexual male-to-female transsexual who has not undergone gender reassignment and who wants to establish a union with a woman cannot enter into a civil partnership, because he is considered male under civil status law. The only option for a long-term legal union available to him is marriage. However, this gives the impression of a same-sex marriage, specifically not intended by the legislator, and he is also forced to give up his first name, which expresses his felt gender identity, in order to rule out that such an impression is created by the first names of the spouses. Even though the person concerned acts in conformity with the only option to enter a union that is legally available to him, a sanction is imposed on him as he must give up the first name that had been recognised in a legal procedure and expresses his gender identity. This interaction of different rules violates a transsexual's right to protection of their intimate sphere and of their gender identity expressed in their first name, protected under Art. 2(1) in conjunction with Art. 1(1) of the Basic Law.

II.

72-73   1. This violation of the Constitution does not result in specific provisions of the Transsexuals Act being declared void. The legislator must ensure that homosexual transsexuals who have not undergone gender reassignment have the option of entering into a legally binding partnership without having to give up their first name. In this respect, there are several options for new provisions. […]

74   2. As long as the legislator has not enacted provisions allowing homosexual transsexuals who have not undergone gender reassignment to enter into a legally protected partnership without having to give up their first name, § 7(1) no. 3 of the Transsexuals Act is to be declared not applicable by way of an order pursuant to § 35 of the Federal Constitutional Court Act.

Justices: Papier, Haas, Hömig, Steiner, Hohmann-Dennhardt, Hoffmann-Riem, Bryde, Gaier

No. 16

BVerfGE 147, 1 – Third Gender Option

HEADNOTES

to the Order of the First Senate of 10 October 2017
1 BvR 2019/16

1. The general right of personality (Article 2(1) in conjunction with Article 1(1) of the Basic Law) protects gender identity. It also protects the gender identity of those who cannot permanently be assigned either the male or female sex.
2. Article 3(3) first sentence of the Basic Law also protects persons who do not permanently identify as male or female against discrimination on the basis of sex.
3. Both of these fundamental rights of persons who do not permanently identify as male or female are violated if civil status law requires that sex be registered but does not allow for a further positive category other than male or female.

FEDERAL CONSTITUTIONAL COURT
- 1 BvR 2019/16 -

IN THE NAME OF THE PEOPLE

In the proceedings
on the constitutional complaint of

K...,
– authorised representatives:...
1. directly against
    a) the Order of the Federal Court of Justice of 22 June 2016 - XII ZB 52/15 -,
    b) the Order of the Celle Higher Regional Court of 21 January 2015
       - 17 W 28/14 -,
    c) the Order of the Hanover Local Court of 13 October 2014 - 85 III 105/14 -

2. indirectly against

§ 21(1) no. 3 of the Civil Status Act in the version of Article 1 of the Act to Reform Civil Status Law of 19 February 2007 (BGBl I, p. 122),

§ 22(3) of the Civil Status Act in the version of Article 1 no. 6 lit. b of the Act to Amend Civil Status Law of 7 May 2013 (BGBl I, p. 1122)

the Federal Constitutional Court – First Senate –

with the participation of Justices

> Vice-President Kirchhof,
> Eichberger,
> Schluckebier,
> Masing,
> Paulus,
> Baer,
> Britz,
> Ott

held on 10 October 2017:

1. § 21(1) no. 3 of the Civil Status Act in the version of Article 1 of the Act to Reform Civil Status Law of 19 February 2007 (BGBl I, p. 122) in conjunction with § 22(3) of the Civil Status Act in the version of Article 1 no. 6 lit. b of the Act to Amend Civil Status Law of 7 May 2013 (BGBl I, p. 1122) is incompatible with Article 2(1) in conjunction with Article 1(1) and Article 3(3) first sentence of the Basic Law insofar as it imposes an obligation on persons to state their sex and does not allow for a positive entry other than 'female' or 'male' for persons whose gender development deviates from female or male and who permanently identify as neither male nor female.

   The legislator must enact provisions that are compatible with the Constitution by 31 December 2018.

2. The Orders of the Federal Court of Justice of 22 June 2016 - XII ZB 52/15 -, of the Celle Higher Regional Court of 21 January 2015 - 17 W 28/14 - and of the Hanover Local Court of 13 October 2014 - 85 III 105/14 - violate the complainant's fundamental rights under Article 2(1) in conjunction with Article 1(1) and Article 3(3) first sentence of the Basic Law. The Orders of the Federal Court of Justice of 22 June 2016 - XII ZB 52/15 - and of the Celle Higher Regional Court of 21 January 2015 - 17 W 28/14 - are reversed. The matter is remanded to the Higher Regional Court. The proceedings must be suspended until new provisions have been enacted.

3. [...]

No. 16 – Third Gender Option

REASONS:

A.

The constitutional complaint concerns the question whether the challenged decisions and the underlying provisions of § 21(1) no. 3 in conjunction with § 22(3) of the Civil Status Act violate the complainant's fundamental rights. At birth, the complainant was assigned the female sex and registered as a girl in the birth register. The complainant has an atypical set of chromosomes (so-called Turner syndrome) and permanently identifies neither as female nor as male. The complainant filed an application for a positive entry as "inter/diverse", or alternatively as "diverse", in the birth register. The registry office rejected the application, claiming that § 21(1) no. 3 and § 22(3) of the Civil Status Act did not permit such an entry. The complainant considers the provisions to be unconstitutional.

I.

1. a) When a child is born, its sex, too, must be documented in the birth register under German civil status law. The child must be assigned either the female or male sex. If this is not possible, the entry is left blank. [...]
b) [...]
c) [...]
d) [...]
e) [...]
2. [...]
3. [...].
4. [...]

II.

[...]

III.

With the constitutional complaint, the complainant claims a violation of their general right of personality under Art. 2(1) in conjunction with Art. 1(1) of the Basic Law, discrimination on the basis of sex under Art. 3(3) first sentence of the Basic Law and a violation of the right to equal treatment under Art. 3(1) of the Basic Law.

16-17 [...]

IV.

18 Statements on the constitutional complaint were submitted by the *Land* Government of Thuringia, the German Ethics Council (*Deutscher Ethikrat*), the German Medical Association (*Bundesärztekammer*), the German Institute for Human Rights (*Deutsches Institut für Menschenrechte e.V.*), the Federal Association of German Registrars (*Bundesverband der Deutschen Standesbeamtinnen und Standesbeamten e.V.*), the German Society for Sexology (*Deutsche Gesellschaft für Sexualforschung e.V.*), the Professional Association of German Psychologists (*Berufsverband Deutscher Psychologinnen und Psychologen e.V.*), the German Society for Psychology (*Deutsche Gesellschaft für Psychologie e.V.*), the German Society for Trans Identity and Intersexuality (*Deutsche Gesellschaft für Transidentität und Intersexualität e.V.*), the Association for Intersexual Persons (*Intersexuelle Menschen e.V.*), the German Lesbian and Gay Association (*Lesben- und Schwulenverband in Deutschland e.V.*), the Central Committee of German Catholics (*Zentralkomitee der deutschen Katholiken*), the Study Centre of the Protestant Church in Germany for Gender Issues in Church and Theology (*Studienzentrum der EKD für Genderfragen in Kirche und Theologie*), the Trans* Federal Association (*Bundesvereinigung Trans* e.V.*), the Trans-InterQueer Association (*Trans-InterQueer e.V.*) and, on their own initiative, by the Association for Lesbian, Gay, Bisexual, Trans*, Intersexual and Queer Persons in Psychology (*Verband für lesbische, schwule, bisexuelle, trans*, intersexuelle und queere Menschen in der Psychologie e.V.*) and the Free Association of Student Unions (*freier zusammenschluss von studentInnenschaften e.V.*).

19-34 [...]

B.

35 The constitutional complaint is admissible and well-founded. § 21(1) no. 3 in conjunction with § 22(3) of the Civil Status Act is unconstitutional insofar as § 21(1) no. 3 of the Civil Status Act requires a sex entry under civil status law, but § 22(3) of the Civil Status Act does not allow for a further positive entry for persons whose gender development deviates from female or male development and who permanently identify as neither male nor female. The decisions challenged with the constitutional complaint are based on these provisions. They violate the complainant's general right of personality (Art. 2(1) in conjunction with Art. 1(1) of

No. 16 – Third Gender Option

the Basic Law) and the prohibition to disadvantage a person on the basis of their sex (Art. 3(3) first sentence of the Basic Law).

I.

§ 21(1) no. 3 in conjunction with § 22(3) of the Civil Status Act violates the general right of personality (Art. 2(1) in conjunction with Art. 1(1) of the Basic Law) in its manifestation as protection of one's gender identity. The general right of personality also protects the gender identity of persons who can be assigned neither the male nor the female sex (see 1 below). There is an interference with their fundamental right because current civil status law requires that sex be registered, but does not allow an entry other than female or male (see 2 below). This interference with fundamental rights is not justified (see 3 below).

1. The general right of personality protects the complainant's gender identity.

a) Art. 2(1) of the Basic Law grants every person the right to the free development of their personality. This fundamental right encompasses both the general freedom of action and the general right of personality (Art. 2(1) in conjunction with Art. 1(1) of the Basic Law). As a 'non-listed' freedom, the general right of personality supplements the specific ('listed') freedoms, which also protect fundamental aspects of one's personality (cf. BVerfGE 54, 148 <153> – *Eppler*). One of the purposes of the general right of personality is to guarantee the basic conditions enabling the individual to develop and protect their individuality in self-determination (cf. BVerfGE 35, 202 <220> – *Lebach*; 79, 256 <268>; 90, 263 <270>; 117, 202 <225>). However, the general right of personality only protects those aspects of the development of one's personality, which – without already being covered by the specific freedoms guaranteed under the Basic Law – are equal to these freedoms in terms of their constitutive significance for one's personality (cf. BVerfGE 79, 256 <268>; 99, 185 <193> – *Helnwein/Scientology*; 120, 274 <303> – *Remote Searches*; established case-law). Thus, it does not afford protection against anything that could in any way impair the self-determined development of one's personality; in any case, no person is able to develop their individuality independent of external conditions and affiliations. Yet where the self-determined development of and respect for one's personality is specifically jeopardised, this is covered by the protection of the general right of personality, which serves to fill gaps in protection (BVerfGE 141, 186 <201 and 202 para. 32>).

b) Accordingly, the general right of personality also protects one's gender identity (cf. BVerfGE 115, 1 <14 et seq.> – *Transsexuals V*; 116, 243 <259 et seq.>; 121, 175 <190 et seq.>; 128, 109 <123 et seq.> – *Transsexuals VIII*), which is usually a constitutive aspect of an individual's personality. Under the given circumstances, the official assignment of sex is of paramount importance for one's individual identity; it typically occupies a key position both in a person's self-image and in the way this person is perceived by others. Assigned sex plays an important role in everyday life: in part, sex determines entitlements and obligations provided for by law; it also often forms the basis for identifying a person, and, beyond legal provisions, assigned sex is also significant in everyday life. To a large extent it determines, for instance, how persons are addressed or what is expected of them in terms of their appearance, upbringing or behaviour.

40 The gender identity of persons who can be assigned neither the male nor the female sex is protected as well. These persons might be able to develop their personality more freely if less significance were attributed to the assigned sex in general. Yet under the given circumstances, assigned sex is a particularly relevant factor for how persons are perceived by others and for how they see their own personality. The complainant, too, emphasises the practical importance of assigned sex and argues that under these circumstances, gender identity is a constitutive aspect of their personality.

41 2. § 21(1) no. 3 in conjunction with § 22(3) of the Civil Status Act interferes with the general right of personality in its manifestation as protection of one's gender identity (see a below) and specifically jeopardises the development of and respect for the complainant's personality in their gender identity (see b below).

42 a) The provisions that are indirectly challenged interfere with the general right of personality in its manifestation as protection of one's gender identity. Civil status law requires that sex be registered, but does not allow the complainant, whose gender development deviates from female or male development and who permanently identifies as neither male nor female, an entry under civil status law that corresponds to their gender identity (on the qualification as interference cf. BVerfGE 49, 286 <298> – *Transsexuals I*; 60, 123 <132 *et seq.*>; 116, 243 <259 *et seq.*>; 121, 175 <190 *et seq.*>; 128, 109 <124> – *Transsexuals VIII*). Under civil status law, a person's sex must be documented in the birth register pursuant to § 21(1) no. 3 of the Civil Status Act. The only positive categories available for this are 'female' and 'male'; there is no further category. This follows from § 22(3) of the Civil Status Act ("no entry"), according to which the entry in the birth register should be left blank if the child can be assigned neither the female nor the male sex. In this case, no positive entry can be made in the birth register. Accordingly, the complainant must tolerate an entry that does not correspond to their constitutionally protected gender identity.

43 Pursuant to § 22(3) of the Civil Status Act, the complainant has the option of deleting their female entry in the birth register. However, this does not eliminate the interference with fundamental rights: The complainant's gender identity is not

only impaired by their incorrect assignment of the female sex, but also by the legal alternative "no entry" under current law (§ 22(3) of the Civil Status Act). "No entry" would not show that, while indeed not identifying as a man or a woman, the complainant does not identify as without gender either, and sees themselves as gendered beyond male or female. The "no entry" option does not alter the exclusively binary pattern of assigned sex; it gives the impression that official recognition of another gender identity is ruled out and that the sex entry has simply not been clarified yet, that a solution has not been found yet or even that it has been forgotten. This does not amount to official recognition of the complainant in their felt gender. From the complainant's view, the entry remains inaccurate, because merely deleting a binary sex entry creates the impression that they are not gendered at all ([...]).

b) If civil status law requires a sex entry, but at the same time denies persons recognition of their gender identity under civil status law, it specifically jeopardises the self-determined development of and respect for these persons' personality.

aa) Under the given circumstances, the official recognition of sex under civil status law has an identity-building and expressive effect. Civil status is not a marginal issue; rather, it is the "position of a person within the legal system", as stated by the law (§ 1(1) first sentence of the Civil Status Act). Civil status measures a person according to statutory criteria; it defines the central aspects of the legally relevant identity of a person. Thus, denying the recognition of felt gender identity under civil status law in itself, i.e. irrespective of the consequences associated with the sex entry outside of civil status law, specifically jeopardises the self-determined development of and respect for one's personality.

The entry under civil status law in itself only takes on specific significance for gender identity because civil status law requires that a sex be stated in the first place. If it did not require a sex entry, it would not specifically jeopardise the development of and respect for one's personality as the assigned sex of a person would not be registered under civil status law. [...]

However, pursuant to § 21(1) no. 3 of the Civil Status Act, civil status currently includes a person's sex. Despite several reforms of civil status law, the legislator has maintained the registration of sex as an identifying feature under civil status law. Given that the legislator regards sex as so crucially important for describing a person and their legal status in civil status law, the recognition of a person's specifically assigned sex under civil status law has an identity-building and expressive effect in itself, regardless of the substantive legal consequences of the civil status entry outside of civil status law (on the independent relevance for fundamental rights of the register entry in the case of transsexuality cf. BVerfGE 49, 286 <297 and 298> – *Transsexuals I*; on naming see also BVerfGE 104, 373 <385>; 109,

256 <266>; 115, 1 <14> – *Transsexuals V*). If, under these circumstances, the gender identity of a person is not recognised under civil status law, it specifically jeopardises the self-determined development of and respect for their personality.

48 bb) In particular, the requirement of a sex entry under civil status law combined with the limited entry options make it difficult for affected persons to move about in public and be seen by others as the persons they are with regard to their gender identity. Yet the way a person is depicted and perceived in public and by others is significant for the free development of their personality and may result in specific risks [to fundamental rights] (cf. BVerfGE 99, 185 <193> – *Helnwein/Scientology*; 114, 339 <346> – *Stolpe/Stasi Dispute*; 119, 1 <24> – *Esra* […]). Civil status law requires a sex entry, but does not allow affected persons an entry in the birth register that is in line with their self-image. This contributes to the fact that their individual identity is not perceived and recognised in the same way and as naturally as that of female or male persons. The complainant plausibly argues that an individual often cannot just pass over their sex entry under civil status law when appearing in public.

49 3. The interference is not justified. The court decisions are based on an unconstitutional legal provision, because compelling persons to have a sex entry under civil status law while denying them a further positive entry other than 'female' or 'male' is not based on a legitimate purpose for which the provision would be suitable, necessary and appropriate.

50 a) The Basic Law does not require that civil status be exclusively binary in terms of sex. It neither requires that sex be governed by civil status law, nor is it opposed to the civil status recognition of a third gender identity beyond male and female. It is true that Art. 3(2) first sentence of the Basic Law refers to "men" and "women". However, this does not amount to a conclusive determination that the term 'sex' only means men and women. It follows from the requirement of equal rights under Art. 3(2) of the Basic Law that existing social disadvantages between men and women should be eliminated. The aim of this provision is mainly to eliminate discrimination against women based on sex (cf. BVerfGE 85, 191 <207>; […]), but its aim is not to enshrine assigned sex in civil status law or to rule out introducing another category in addition to 'male' and 'female'. To the extent that the Federal Constitutional Court did state in the past that our legal order and our social life are based on the principle that every person is either male or female (cf. BVerfGE 49, 286 <298> – *Transsexuals I*), even then this was not a finding that the Constitution prescribes sex as being binary. Rather, it was a mere description of the social and legal notion of gender prevailing at the time.

51 b) The interests of third parties cannot justify that § 22(3) of the Civil Status Act does not offer a third option allowing for a positive entry in the birth register. The

status of men and women under civil status law remains unaffected by a further entry category. [...]

c) The fact that the introduction of a third positive entry may be associated with bureaucratic and financial costs during a transitional period does not justify denying the option of a further entry. [...]

d) Organisational interests of the state cannot justify the denial of a third standardised and positive entry option either. [...]

Allowing a positive entry for a third gender with a standardised third designation [...] does not result in any difficulties in assigning sex that do not already exist under current law anyway. Uncertainties may occur where a provision outside of civil status law is linked to sex and presumes that a person is either female or male. In that case it would indeed be unclear how a person officially assigned a third gender should be treated. However, the same issue exists already under current law if the sex entry is left blank pursuant to § 22(3) of the Civil Status Act. In this case, assigning a person the male or female sex is not possible either. In this respect, substantive law neither sets out which sex-based provisions apply, nor has the legislator created specific provisions for persons without a sex entry. If a further positive entry is allowed, the questions to be clarified are thus the same as those that already arise when opting for the no sex entry, which is possible *de lege lata*. In fact, the positive entry of a third gender could provide greater clarity given that – unlike a sex entry that is permanently left blank – it does not convey the wrong impression that the entry was left blank inadvertently.

The permanent nature of civil status is also not affected by the option of a third gender entry, because the mere creation of another entry option does not say anything about the requirements for changing one's civil status.

II.

Insofar as § 21(1) no. 3 in conjunction with § 22(3) of the Civil Status Act excludes an entry other than 'male' and 'female', it also violates the prohibition of discrimination of Art. 3(3) first sentence of the Basic Law. The provisions that are indirectly challenged disadvantage persons who are neither male nor female and who permanently identify with another gender. Article 3(3) first sentence of the Basic Law not only protects men and women against discrimination on the basis of sex, but also protects persons who do not permanently identify with these two sex categories. The disadvantaging is not justified.

57-64 [...]

C.

I.

65 If a statutory provision indirectly challenged by constitutional complaint is unconstitutional, the provision is typically declared void (§ 95(3) second sentence of the Federal Constitutional Court Act). However, in this case, the provision can only be declared incompatible with the Basic Law given that the legislator has several options for remedying the disadvantaging of affected persons (cf. BVerfGE 133, 59 <99 para. 106>; established case-law). For instance, the legislator could dispense with a sex entry under civil status law altogether. The legislator could also create a standardised and positive entry for affected persons other than male or female – in addition to the existing alternative "no entry" (§ 22(3) of the Civil Status Act). There are different options available for designing such a further entry. [...]

II.

66 To the extent that the challenged provisions are incompatible with the Basic Law, the courts and administrative authorities may no longer apply them. The legislator must enact new provisions by 31 December 2018. [...]

III.

67 The decisions of the Federal Court of Justice, of the Celle Higher Regional Court and of the Hanover Local Court are based on the provisions that have been declared incompatible with the complainant's fundamental rights as set out above. The decisions of the Federal Court of Justice and of the Celle Higher Regional Court are reversed. The matter is remanded to the Higher Regional Court. The proceedings must be suspended until new provisions have been enacted.

IV.

68 [...]

D.

69 This decision was taken with 7:1 votes.

No. 16 – Third Gender Option

Justices: Kirchhof, Eichberger, Schluckebier, Masing, Paulus, Baer, Britz, Ott

No. 17

BVerfGE 87, 334 – Honecker

FEDERAL CONSTITUTIONAL COURT
- 1 BvR 1595/92 -
- 1 BvR 1606/92 -

IN THE NAME OF THE PEOPLE

In the proceedings
on the constitutional complaints of

1. the ZDF broadcasting corporation, ..., represented by its Director General ...,
   - 1 BvR 1595/92 -,
2. a) the BR broadcasting corporation, ...
   b) the NDR broadcasting corporation, ...
   c) the SDR broadcasting corporation, ...
   d) the SWR broadcasting corporation, ...
   e) the HR broadcasting corporation, ...
   f) *Radio Bremen*, ...
   g) *Sender Freies Berlin*, ...
   h) the SR broadcasting corporation, ...
   i) the WDR broadcasting corporation, ...
   k) the MDR broadcasting corporation, ...
   l) the ORB broadcasting corporation, ...
   m) the *RTL plus* broadcasting corporation, ... represented by its Managing Director ...
   n) the *SAT 1* broadcasting corporation, ... represented by its Managing Directors ...
   - 1 BvR 1606/92 -,

– authorised representatives: ...

against the Order of the Presiding Judge of the 27th Criminal Division – sitting as court of assize with lay judges – of the Berlin Regional Court issued pursuant to

No. 17 – Honecker

§ 176 of the Courts Constitution Act, published on 3 November 1992, amended by the Order of the Presiding Judge of 9 November 1992,
here: application for preliminary injunction
the Federal Constitutional Court – First Senate –
with the participation of Justices
> President Herzog
> Henschel,
> Seidl,
> Grimm,
> Söllner,
> Dieterich,
> Seibert

held, on the basis of § 32 of the Federal Constitutional Court Act, on 11 November 1992:

The presiding judge of the 27th Criminal Division of the Berlin Regional Court is instructed to issue the necessary orders so that a TV team representing a pool of public or private TV broadcasters (so-called media pool solution) is permitted, from 12 November 1992, to film for a reasonable time period – before and after the hearing – in the courtroom where the trial hearing in the criminal proceedings against [former political leader of the GDR] Erich Honecker and others is taking place. Before the hearing, filming shall also be permitted with the accused present in the courtroom. To this extent, the Order of the Presiding Judge published on 3 November 1992 and amended on 9 November 1992 is suspended. For the rest, the application for a preliminary injunction is rejected.

REASONS:

A.

The constitutional complaints and applications for preliminary injunction concern judicial orders, issued in exercise of the presiding judge's powers to maintain order in court (*sitzungspolizeiliche Maßnahmen*), regarding the permissibility of TV recordings in the criminal proceedings against Erich Honecker [and other high-ranking representatives of the GDR]. 1

1. [...] The complainants wish to report on the proceedings [in the broadcasting media]. Given that the proceedings were expected to attract a large number of camera teams and media representatives, the complainant in proceedings no. 1 proposed that the presiding judge opt for the so-called media pool solution for film 2

recordings in the courtroom [...]. Under the pool solution, only a three-person camera team of one broadcaster is granted access to the courtroom. This broadcaster must then make the film material available free of charge to all other interested radio and TV broadcasters. [...]

3   On 3 November 1992, the trial court's press office published the decision of the presiding judge of the 27th Criminal Division, according to which TV recordings would not be permitted in the courtroom, but only in the adjacent security area outside the courtroom.

4   2. On 8 November 1992, the complainant in procceedings no. 1 lodged a constitutional complaint [and an application for a preliminary injunction] against this order [...].

5   By order of 9 November 1992, amending his initial order, the presiding judge permitted film recordings without a microphone on the first day of the trial hearing in the courtroom for approximately five minutes before the hearing, made by a three-person camera team.

6   On 9 November 1992, the complainants in proceedings no. 2 also lodged a constitutional complaint and an application for a preliminary injunction against the order of the presiding judge.

7   All complainants claim that the exclusion of their camera teams from the courtroom violates their fundamental right to freedom of broadcasting under Art. 5(1) second sentence of the Basic Law. [...]

8-11   [...]

12   3. [...]

B.

13   The application for a preliminary injunction is well-founded. In the necessary weighing of consequences, which must weigh the reasons supporting a preliminary injunction against the reasons opposing it, the reasons in favour of the injunction sought by the complainants prevail.

14   1. Pursuant to § 32 of the Federal Constitutional Court Act, the Federal Constitutional Court may provisionally decide a matter by way of a preliminary injunction if this is urgently required to avert severe disadvantage or for other important reasons in the interest of the common good. In the context of this decision, the reasons submitted for the unconstitutionality of the challenged act of public authority are generally not to be taken into account, unless the constitutional complaint is inadmissible from the outset or clearly unfounded. In case the outcome of the constitutional complaint proceedings cannot be foreseen, the Federal Constitutional Court must in principle only weigh the consequences that would arise if the prelim-

inary injunction were not issued but the constitutional complaint were successful in the principal proceedings, against the disadvantages that would arise if the preliminary injunction sought were issued but the constitutional complaint were unsuccessful (cf. BVerfGE 85, 94 <95 and 96>; established case-law).

2. The constitutional complaints are neither inadmissible nor manifestly unfounded. 15
[...] 16
The constitutional complaints raise the question whether and to what extent the 17 fundamental right to freedom of broadcasting also protects film recordings in courtrooms for television purposes, a matter not yet decided by the Federal Constitutional Court. [In its case-law], the Court did, however, decide that with regard to the presence of press journalists at trial hearings, the protection afforded by freedom of the press also encompasses free access to information (cf. BVerfGE 50, 234 <240 and 241>). Since freedom of broadcasting serves the same purpose as the other guarantees enshrined in Art. 5(1) of the Basic Law, it cannot be ruled out from the outset that it also guarantees TV journalists access and filming rights. Freedom of broadcasting must therefore be adequately taken into consideration when interpreting and applying §§ 169 *et seq.* of the Courts Constitution Act.

3. In essence, the outcome of the required weighing of consequences is in favour of 18 the complainants.

a) If the preliminary injunction were not issued but the constitutional complaints 19 proved to be well-founded in the principal proceedings, TV reporting of the trial hearing would be insufficient. Due to the restrictions imposed by the challenged order, documentation of the way in which the accused present themselves [in the courtroom] at the beginning of the trial hearing – an aspect the complainants correctly consider to be of historic significance – would not be ensured. The possibility of actually documenting, by means of film recordings, the further course of the proceedings would be lost irreversibly, at least until the Federal Constitutional Court rendered its decision in the principal proceedings.

b) If the preliminary injunction were issued but the constitutional complaints later 20 proved to be unfounded, film recordings of the accused in the context of the trial hearing would already have been made and disseminated, even though neither the complainants nor the public would have been entitled to receive such footage.

However, it can be virtually ruled out [at this point] that allowing recordings 21 would compromise the orderly course of the trial. With the media pool solution proposed by the complainants, under which only a three-person camera team would be granted access to the courtroom, and a limitation of recording time to reflect the interests of both sides, it is not ascertainable that order in the courtroom could be compromised and that the hearing could therefore be adversely affected.

22 Nevertheless, this solution could impair the general right of personality of the accused, specifically their right to one's own image. Even if the film recordings were destroyed afterwards, the dissemination of the images could not be undone. In that respect, it is significant that, even at the present time, the accused clearly qualify as figures of contemporary society '*par excellence*' within the meaning of § 23(1) no. 1 of the Art Copyright Act; images of such persons may be disseminated without their consent, which would otherwise be required under § 22 of the Art Copyright Act. The media pool solution prevents a possible crowding of the courtroom by a large number of camera teams, which could significantly impair the right of the accused to respect for their person (*Achtungsanspruch*).

23 It also appears unlikely that the TV recordings would adversely affect the physical or mental health of the accused and thereby significantly increase the burden already placed on them by the trial hearing as such. In that respect, it must be taken into account that the media pool solution is relatively unintrusive, accommodating the health interests of the accused.

24 c) Based on these considerations, the disadvantages that would very likely occur if the preliminary injunction were not issued but the constitutional complaints later proved to be well-founded outweigh the disadvantages that would occur if the preliminary injunction were issued but the constitutional complaint later proved to be unfounded. However, it is sufficient, for now, to permit film recordings in the courtroom before and after the hearing for a reasonable time period. Given that the situation in the courtroom, including organisational aspects, and the changing circumstances on different days of the hearing must be taken into consideration, no fixed time period can be set in advance. Rather, it is incumbent upon the presiding judge to determine the time period during which broadcast recording is permitted, in consideration of the public interest in obtaining information and the technical requirements of TV broadcasting. [...]

Justices: Herzog, Henschel, Seidl, Grimm, Söllner, Dieterich, Seibert

No. 18

BVerfGE 99, 185 – Helnwein/Scientology

HEADNOTES

to the Order of the First Senate of 10 November 1998
1 BvR 1531/96

1. The general right of personality (Article 2(1) in conjunction with Article 1(1) of the Basic Law) also protects the individual against falsely imputed membership of an association or group where such imputed membership has a certain significance for their personality and public image.
2. It is incompatible with the general right of personality that a person adversely affected by a factual assertion is completely barred from refuting that assertion as false in court proceedings on the grounds that the person making the assertion already presented circumstantial facts supporting the assertion.

FEDERAL CONSTITUTIONAL COURT
- 1 BvR 1531/96 -

IN THE NAME OF THE PEOPLE

In the proceedings
on the constitutional complaint of

Mr H…,
– authorised representative: …

against   the Judgment of the Frankfurt am Main Higher Regional Court of 20 June 1996 - 16 U 163/95 -

the Federal Constitutional Court – First Senate –
with the participation of Justices

Vice-President Papier,
Grimm,
Kühling,

BVerfGE 99, 185

Jaeger,
Haas,
Hömig,
Steiner

held on 10 November 1998:

The Judgment of the Frankfurt am Main Higher Regional Court of 20 June 1996 - 16 U 163/95 - violates the complainant's fundamental right under Article 2(1) in conjunction with Article 1(1) of the Basic Law insofar as it rejects his action for injunctive relief. To that extent, the judgment is reversed together with the decision on costs and the matter is remanded to the Higher Regional Court.

[...]

REASONS:

A.

1   The constitutional complaint challenges the rejection of an action under private law seeking injunctive relief against defamatory statements.

I.

2   The complainant, a well-known Austrian artist living in Germany, had been studying the works and teachings of Scientology since 1972 and had also attended courses offered by this organisation. Since 1975, he was referred to as a Scientologist in various magazines or associated with Scientology in other contexts.

3   [...] In 1989, the magazine *Celebrity*, published in the United States by the 'Church of Scientology – Celebrity Centre International', [...] ran an article about the complainant. The article was illustrated with pictures of the complainant and the first part of the text provided information on his biography and career. The article stated *inter alia* that the complainant had joined Scientology in 1973, that he was an 'OT® V' and had attended the 'Academy Levels' at the 'Celebrity Centre' in Düsseldorf.

4   'OT' is short for 'Operating Thetan'; according to the teachings of Scientology, this term designates a person who has attained the state of total spiritual freedom through a series of gradient steps of salvation, is committed to social causes and actively contributes to solving social problems and grievances. The 'Academy Levels' are Auditor training courses. In Scientology terminology, an 'Auditor' is roughly equal to a priest.

No. 18 – Helnwein/Scientology

The second part of the article featured questions asked by *Celebrity* and corresponding answers. The answers conveyed the impression that they were actual statements by the complainant, since the entire article was presented as an interview with the complainant and the text referred to him by his first name. The interview included the following statements:

> I overheard other artists talking about Scientology in Vienna in 1973. (...) Together with an artist friend of mine, I attended the Communications Course. [...] All my old problems disappeared. (...) I think that artists need Scientology to survive. (...) The Celebrity Centre in Düsseldorf is the best. (...) I love being there. (...)
>
> [*translator's note: the English magazine excerpts were retranslated from the German text used in the decision of the Federal Constitutional Court. The original English text is no longer available to the Court.*]

[...]

In Issue 262 of 1993, *Celebrity* presented five celebrities in an advertising campaign featuring 'answers' to the headline question "Why should you train?". The caption under a picture of the complainant read "H., Class IV Auditor, world-renowned artist". The corresponding 'answer', set in inverted commas, included *inter alia* the following statements [...]:

> In my view, the artist is the most vulnerable person in the world. (...) If you make a great impact through music or paintings, you will be in trouble, since there are certainly people in this world who are opposed to this and will do everything they can to suppress your work. (...) I think that artists need Scientology to survive. Scientology training is the best. (...)

[...]

2. In Germany, a private initiative had successfully campaigned for the site of the former concentration camp *Neue Bremm* in Saarbrücken to be transformed into a memorial site based on an artistic concept. The complainant was among the artists considered for this project and was asked to create a model [of his proposed design]. His involvement was opposed by two private associations committed to the fight against religious cults, which sent an open letter to the media and politicians. Excerpts from the letter read as follows:

> (...) The fact that Austrian artist H., who promotes the criminal and totalitarian Scientology Church all over the world, was asked to create a model for the memorial site's new artistic concept (...) is absolutely appalling.

15-18 [...]
19 The complainant was ultimately not chosen for the project.
20 3. a) Upon an action brought by the complainant [...], the Regional Court ordered the defendants [...] to refrain from making or disseminating the following assertions, either verbatim or in spirit:
21   1. The Austrian artist H. calls himself a priest.
22   2. The Austrian artist is an Auditor IV of the Scientology Church.
23   3. H. is part of a group that works to destroy people's minds by using lie detectors and forced hypnosis for brainwashing purposes.
24   4. [...]

25 [...]
26 b) Following the defendants' appeal on points of fact and law (*Berufung*), the Higher Regional Court reversed the decision by the court of first instance [...] [and] rejected the complainant's action. [...]
27-31 [...]

II.

32 In his constitutional complaint, the complainant claims a violation of his general right of personality under Art. 2(1) in conjunction with Art. 1(1) of the Basic Law.
33 He asserts that he is not a Scientologist, that he has neither received training as a priest nor assumed the role of a priest, and that he has never referred to himself as a priest. [...] While he did study Scientology in the 1970s and 1980s and [...] attended classes during this time, he claims to have distanced himself from Scientology since 1992 and to have sought recourse before the courts against the assertions that he was a member of Scientology.
34 [...]

III.

35 The defendants in the initial proceedings submitted a statement in the constitutional complaint proceedings. The Working Group for Mental and Psychological Freedom (*Arbeitsgemeinschaft für Geistige und Psychische Freiheit, AGPF*), an umbrella association of initiatives working against cults, which one of the defendants in the initial proceedings is a member of, submitted a statement on its own initiative.

No. 18 – Helnwein/Scientology

[...]

B.

The constitutional complaint is well-founded. The challenged decision violates the complainant's general right of personality under Art. 2(1) in conjunction with Art. 1(1) of the Basic Law insofar as it rejects his action for injunctive relief. [...]

I.

The challenged decision affects the complainant's general right of personality.
1. The general right of personality affords protection against being falsely portrayed as the member of a group if such imputed membership has a certain significance for one's personality and adversely affects one's public image.
The general right of personality protects aspects of one's personality that are not covered by specific freedoms, but are equal to these freedoms in terms of their constitutive significance for one's personality (cf. BVerfGE 54, 148 <153> – *Eppler*; established case-law). One such aspect is the social recognition of the individual. Therefore, the general right of personality encompasses protection against statements which are capable of tarnishing one's public image. Such statements jeopardise the free development of one's personality guaranteed under Art. 2(1) of the Basic Law because they damage the affected person's reputation in society, weaken their social relations, and as a result may undermine their self-esteem. However, the protection afforded by this fundamental right does not go so far as to grant individuals the right to be portrayed in public only as they see themselves or as they wish to be seen by others. Yet the general right of personality does protect individuals from skewed or distorted portrayals of their person whose significance for the free development of their personality is not entirely negligible (cf. BVerfGE 97, 125 <148 and 149>; 97, 391 <403> – *Sexual Abuse Allegations*).
Membership in a particular group or association generally affects one's personality in this sense. For most people, being affiliated with a group through birth or socialisation influences how their identity forms and develops. Where individuals join a group or association of their own free will, it generally means that they strongly identify with the aims and activities of said group or association, which may be determinant for their personality. As the case may be, people will more or less associate an individual with the groups or organisations the individual identifies with. The individual's reputation no longer depends solely on their own characteristics and achievements as an individual, but also on how the groups they belong to are perceived (cf. BVerfGE 93, 266 <299>). This applies in particular

to groups or associations whose self-defined mission is informed by religious or ideological beliefs; it is especially true for groups or associations falling outside the traditional religious or ideological communities that represent a minority and are viewed critically or even rejected by society.

44 2. The challenged decision impairs the complainant's fundamental right under Art. 2(1) in conjunction with Art. 1(1) of the Basic Law.

45 However, the constitutional protection against negative assertions cannot directly be invoked against third parties. Like other fundamental rights, the general right of personality is only directly applicable vis-à-vis the state. Yet it does give rise to a duty of the state to protect individuals against risks to their personality originating from third parties (cf. BVerfGE 73, 118 <201>; 97, 125 <146>). When applying legal provisions that give effect to such protection, the ordinary courts must take into account the relevant constitutional standards. According to the Federal Constitutional Court's established case-law, failure on the part of ordinary courts to meet these standards not only violates objective constitutional law, but also the individual fundamental rights of affected persons (cf. BVerfGE 7, 198 <206 and 207>).

46 Therefore, where individuals challenge statements affecting their personality on the grounds that these statements are false, yet the courts find the statements to be permissible, these court decisions impair the general right of personality. This holds true for the court's rejection of the complainant's action seeking injunctive relief against the assertion that he is a member of Scientology, that he had referred to himself as a Scientology priest and that he was indeed a priest. The assertion that he had close ties to Scientology could negatively influence his public image. This is especially true in the present case given that Scientology is extremely controversial in society and has often been the subject of warnings by state officials and of critical press reports. It cannot be ruled out that the assertion that the complainant is a leading Scientologist makes his work as an artist more difficult, since damage to his reputation could adversely affect commissions or purchases of his art.

II.

47 The challenged decision violates the general right of personality.

48 1. The general right of personality is not guaranteed without reservation. Under Art 2(1) of the Basic Law, it is limited by the constitutional order, including the rights of others. These rights include freedom of expression guaranteed to everyone by Art. 5(1) of the Basic Law. Yet just like the general right of personality, freedom of expression is also not guaranteed without reservation. Pursuant to Art. 5(2) of the Basic Law, it may be limited *inter alia* by the provisions of general laws and

by the right to personal honour. Private law actions for injunctive relief may be based on § 1004(1) and § 823(2) of the Civil Code in conjunction with § 186 of the Criminal Code. The Higher Regional Court based its judgment on these provisions. By contrast, § 193 of the Criminal Code primarily gives effect to interests relating to freedom of expression (cf. BVerfGE 12, 113 <125 and 126>; 93, 266 <290 and 291). This provision contains an exemption from liability for defamation where the respective statement seeks to safeguard legitimate interests. This also applies in private law relations, either by directly invoking § 823(2) of the Civil Code or by invoking the general precept underlying it.

The interpretation and application of these provisions falls to the competent [ordinary] courts. The interpretation adopted by the ordinary courts, however, must be guided by the affected fundamental rights to ensure that the values enshrined therein are upheld when applying the relevant statutory provisions (cf. BVerfGE 7, 198 <205 et seq.>). This generally requires that the severity of a statement's adverse impact on an individual's personality be balanced against the curtailing of freedom of expression that prohibiting the statement would entail. This balancing must be undertaken in respect of the constituent elements set out in statutory law that lend themselves to interpretation, taking into account the specific circumstances of the case.

The outcome of the balancing can generally not be determined in the abstract, given that the balancing is contingent upon the circumstances of the individual case. Yet over time, certain rules have emerged from the case-law that guide the determination as to which legal interest takes precedence. Where statements containing value judgments are concerned, protecting the right of personality usually takes precedence over freedom of expression if the relevant statement amounts to an attack on human dignity, calumny (*Schmähkritik*) or profanity (*Formalbeleidigung*) (cf. BVerfGE 93, 266 <293 and 294). Where statements containing factual assertions are concerned, the outcome of the balancing depends on their truthfulness. Generally, true statements must be tolerated, even where they adversely affect the person concerned. Untrue statements do not have to be tolerated (cf. BVerfGE 97, 391 <403> – *Sexual Abuse Allegations*).

However, this formula requires further differentiation. In exceptional cases, even where statements are true, interests relating to one's personality may take precedence over freedom of expression, which must then stand back. In particular, this is the case if the statements relate to the intimate, private or confidential sphere and cannot be justified by a legitimate interest of the public in obtaining information (cf. BVerfGE 34, 269 <281 et seq.> – *Soraya*; 66, 116 <139>) or if they are likely to impair one's personality to a degree that is disproportionate to the interest in disseminating the truth (cf. BVerfGE 35, 202 <232> – *Lebach*; 97, 391 <403 *et seq.*> – *Sexual Abuse Allegations*).

52 By contrast, there is generally no justification for disseminating untrue factual assertions. However, this does not mean that all untrue factual assertions are, from the outset, excluded from the scope of protection of freedom of expression. While the Federal Constitutional Court has established that incorrect information is not a value meriting protection under freedom of expression (cf. BVerfGE 54, 208 <219>), only deliberately untrue factual assertions and assertions that are demonstrably false at the time they are made are excluded from the scope of protection of Art. 5(1) first sentence of the Basic Law. All other factual assertions bearing a connection to freedom of expression enjoy fundamental rights protection, even if they later turn out to be untrue (cf. BVerfGE 61, 1 <8>; 90, 1 <15>; 90, 241 <254>).

53 Whether and to what extent a statement is true is a significant factor for the required balancing of interests (cf. BVerfGE 94, 1 <8>). In principle, when untrue assertions are made, freedom of expression stands back behind the right of personality. It must, however, be taken into account that the truth is often uncertain at the time a statement is made and can only be determined through discussion or judicial review (cf. BVerfGE 97, 125 <149>). Given these circumstances, imposing sanctions in all cases where statements turn out to be untrue in retrospect could jeopardise the culture of communication, as the only statements that could be made safely would be statements of irrefutable truths. This would have a deterrent effect on the exercise of fundamental rights, which must be avoided for the sake of freedom of expression (cf. BVerfGE 43, 130 <136>).

54 Therefore, the case-law of the civil courts has sought to achieve a balance between the requirements deriving from freedom of expression and the protection of one's personality by imposing duties of care on those making negative statements about others. In the specific case, the exact nature of such duties is determined by the means available for establishing the truth; they are stricter for the media than for individuals (cf. BGH, NJW 1966, p. 2010 <2011>; NJW 1987, p. 2225 <2226>). There are no constitutional objections to the recognition of such duties (cf. BVerfGE 12, 113 <130>). On the contrary, they may be seen as a manifestation of the duty of protection deriving from the general right of personality. Ultimately, what matters under constitutional law is that the duty to be truthful does not become excessive in scope, hampering free communication, which Art. 5(1) of the Basic Law seeks to protect (cf. BVerfGE 54, 208 <219 and 220>; 61, 1 <8>; 85, 1 <15, 17>).

55 The outcome of the balancing depends on whether these duties of care were observed. Where an assertion is completely unfounded or purely speculative, freedom

of expression does not take precedence over the right of personality. Moreover, the duties of care derived from constitutional law and their specific scope are significant in this respect. If the applicable duty of care has been observed yet the statement subsequently turns out to be untrue, the statement must be qualified as lawful at the time it was made, so that no punishment, retraction or damages may be imposed. By contrast, there is no legitimate reason for upholding an assertion after it has been proven false (cf. BVerfGE 97, 125 <149>). If there is a danger that the statement will nevertheless be upheld in the future (so-called risk of first infringement – *Erstbegehungsgefahr;* cf. BGH, NJW 1986, p. 2503 <2505>), a court can order the person making the statement to refrain from doing so. If the statement continues to impair the person affected by it, they may request that the statement be corrected (cf. BVerfGE 97, 125 <149>).

Determining the truthfulness of factual assertions is often extremely difficult; therefore, the civil courts place an extended burden of substantiation on persons making negative statements about third parties, which requires them to substantiate circumstantial facts supporting their assertions (*Belegtatsachen*) (cf. BGH, NJW 1974, p. 1710 <1711>). This extended burden of substantiation is the procedural equivalent of the substantive law principle that – in the case of speculative assertions – the protection afforded freedom of expression must stand back behind the protection of one's personality. If the person making an assertion is unable to substantiate it with supporting facts, the assertion will be treated as false. 56

This standard [developed by the ordinary courts] is not objectionable under constitutional law, provided that the requirements derived from the burden of substantiation are not overly strict to the detriment of freedom of expression. [...] Where individuals make factual assertions that are not based on events that they have personally witnessed, it is usually sufficient to use uncontested press reports as references that are capable of supporting the assertions in order to satisfy the burden of substantiation. Otherwise, it would hardly ever be possible for persons voicing individual opinions to invoke press reports containing negative statements about others despite the influence of the media on the opinion-forming process (cf. BVerfGE 85, 1 <22>). 57

However, satisfying the burden of substantiation does not render establishing the truth obsolete. Rather, it is necessary to distinguish, at the procedural level, between the rules of substantiation and the rules of evidence. Even where the person making an assertion substantiates facts supporting the assertion, it can still be false. For that reason, it would be incompatible with the general right of personality if the person adversely affected by a factual assertion could no longer challenge that assertion as false because they are procedurally barred from doing so in the event that the person making the assertion already satisfied the burden of substantiation. 58

The truthfulness of the disputed statement may only be presumed [under procedural law] if the affected person fails to refute the facts submitted to substantiate the assertion. In all other cases, the truthfulness of the statement must be determined in accordance with the general rules of evidence.

59 This applies even where the factual assertions originate from press reports. [...]

60 2. The Higher Regional Court did not satisfy these requirements arising from the general right of personality.

61 a) The refusal to grant the injunctive relief sought in respect of statement no. 1 does not meet constitutional standards.

62 This notwithstanding, it is not objectionable under constitutional law that the Higher Regional Court qualified statement no. 1 (that the complainant described himself as a Scientology priest) as a factual assertion. [...] However, the court erred when it held that it was not necessary to assess the truthfulness of this assertion. In the case at hand, the court would have been obliged to take into account the complainant's submission that he had not approved the article in which he supposedly called himself a priest; that the contents of this article were untrue, at least with regard to the assertion that he had served as an Auditor; and that he had distanced himself from Scientology in 1992.

63 In particular regarding the submission that the complainant had distanced himself [from Scientology], the Higher Regional Court should have taken into account that changing one's view and endorsing new positions is also an expression of one's personality. In this case, third parties can be expected to respect the new self-image that arises when individuals have seriously and publicly distanced themselves from an organisation they used to be involved with. Third parties may then only impute past membership in this group. As the challenged statement is expressed in the present tense, the decisive factor for upholding the disputed statement is not just whether the complainant had indeed referred to himself [as a priest of Scientology] in the past but also whether he had later distanced himself from Scientology, as he claims.

64 b) The Higher Regional Court's decision furthermore violates the complainant's general right of personality by refusing the injunctive relief sought in respect of statement no. 2. The Higher Regional Court [...] erred in finding that in light of the *Celebrity* articles, it was not necessary to determine whether it is true or false that the complainant was an "Auditor IV" [...]. Instead, the court would have been required to take into account that the complainant denies having been trained or having served as an Auditor, and that he had submitted declarations from the Church of Scientology in Germany to support his claim. Moreover, the court should have assessed whether and how seriously the complainant had made efforts to distance himself from Scientology, as he claims he did.

c) Finally, the Higher Regional Court's decision violates the complainant's general right of personality by refusing to grant injunctive relief in respect of statement no. 3.

It is true that the Higher Regional Court did not leave open the question whether the complainant was a Scientologist, as it actually found this to be a proven fact. It is also true that the court qualified this assertion and the statements about the organisation's activities as derogatory. Yet it also held that freedom of expression takes precedence over the protection of the complainant's personality. In doing so, the court failed to take into account that the complainant had objected to the defendants' assertions by claiming to have distanced himself from Scientology. As this disregard [for the complainant's submission] is rooted in an incorrect understanding of the scope of protection afforded by the general right of personality, the shortcomings of the decision that have been established in respect of statements nos. 1 and 2 apply accordingly in respect of statement no. 3 [...].

3. The challenged decision is based on a violation of a fundamental right. [...] It cannot be ruled out that the Higher Regional Court would have reached a different conclusion, one that would have been more favourable for the complainant, if it had taken into consideration the requirements deriving from Art. 2(1) in conjunction with Art. 1(1) of the Basic Law.

Justices: Papier, Grimm, Kühling, Jaeger, Haas, Hömig, Steiner

No. 19

BVerfGE 119, 309 – TV Broadcasting from the Courtroom

HEADNOTE

to the Order of the First Senate of 19 December 2007
1 BvR 620/07

On the significance of the fundamental right to freedom of broadcasting under Article 5(1) second sentence of the Basic Law for judicial orders, issued in exercise of the presiding judge's powers to maintain order in court, with regard to audio and film recordings immediately before and after oral court hearings as well as during recesses.

FEDERAL CONSTITUTIONAL COURT

- 1 BvR 620/07 -

IN THE NAME OF THE PEOPLE

In the proceedings
on the constitutional complaint of

the …,
an institution established under public law,
represented by its Director General
– authorised representatives: …
against the Order of the Presiding Judge of the Eighth Grand Criminal Division of the Münster Regional Court of 21 February 2007
- 8 KLs 81 Js 1837/04 (25/05) -

the Federal Constitutional Court – First Senate –
with the participation of Justices

President Papier,
Hohmann-Dennhardt,

No. 19 – TV Broadcasting from the Courtroom

Hoffmann-Riem,
Bryde,
Gaier,
Eichberger,
Schluckebier

held on 19 December 2007:

The Order of the Presiding Judge of the Eighth Grand Criminal Division of the Münster Regional Court of 21 February 2007 - 8 KLs 81 Js 1837/04 (25/05) - violates the complainant's fundamental right to freedom of broadcasting under Article 5(1) second sentence of the Basic Law.
[...]

REASONS:

A.

The constitutional complaint concerns the permissibility of filming in the courtroom before and after the trial hearing in criminal proceedings.

I.

1. The complainant is a public broadcasting corporation. It had planned to report on a trial hearing before [...] [the] Münster Regional Court scheduled to begin on 19 March 2007.
In the indictment, [...] officers of the *Bundeswehr* (German Federal Armed Forces) were charged with physical abuse and degradation of recruits. [...]
Print and broadcasting media had [...] repeatedly reported on the incidents and the opening of criminal proceedings [...].
[...]
2. On 21 February 2007, the presiding judge of the Eighth Grand Criminal Division of the Münster Regional Court ordered the following restrictions on media reporting pursuant to § 176 of the Courts Constitution Act to maintain order in the upcoming trial hearing:

> Audio and film recordings and the taking of photographs in the courtroom and in the foyer leading to the courtroom (in the access-restricted security area) are permitted until 15 minutes before the beginning of the hearing and for 10 minutes after the end of the hearing. For the rest, audio and film recordings

and the taking of photographs are not permitted in the courtroom or the foyer leading to the courtroom.

8 [...]
9-10 3. [...]
11 4. [...]

II.

12 The complainant asserts that its fundamental rights under Art. 5(1) second sentence and Art. 19(4) of the Basic Law have been violated [...].
13-15 [...]

III.

16 Statements on the constitutional complaint were submitted by the Federal Ministry of Justice on behalf of the Federal Government, the Ministry of Justice of the *Land* North Rhine-Westphalia, the President of the Federal Court of Justice and the President of the Federal Administrative Court. Moreover, the presiding judge of the Eighth Grand Criminal Division of the Münster Regional Court was given the opportunity to submit a statement on the application for a preliminary injunction and on the constitutional complaint.
17-21 [...]

B.

I.

22 The constitutional complaint is admissible.
23-25 [...]

II.

26 The constitutional complaint is well-founded. The Order of the Presiding Judge of the Eighth Grand Criminal Division of the Münster Regional Court of 21 February 2007 restricts media reporting on a trial hearing in criminal proceedings by prohibiting audio and film recordings immediately before and after the hearing. This violates the complainant's fundamental right to freedom of reporting by the broadcast media guaranteed under Art. 5(1) second sentence of the Basic Law.

No. 19 – TV Broadcasting from the Courtroom

1. Freedom of reporting by the broadcast media (Art. 5(1) second sentence of the Basic Law) protects [the entire journalistic process], from the gathering of information to the creation of broadcast contents and their dissemination (cf. BVerfGE 91, 125 <134 and 135>; established case-law). Insofar as the media partake in access to a source of information that is open to everyone, access for both the media and the public is protected by the general right to freedom of information under Art. 5(1) first sentence of the Basic Law. By contrast, the use of broadcast-specific means for recording, in particular audio and film recordings, falls under freedom of broadcasting under Art. 5(1) second sentence of the Basic Law, which is applicable in such cases as the more specific fundamental right (cf. BVerfGE 103, 44 <59>). Its scope of protection covers the right to use the means of presentation specific to broadcasting for reporting purposes, including sound and images, which convey, in particular, the impression of authenticity and of witnessing an event first-hand (cf. BVerfGE 103, 44 <67>). This also applies to media reporting on a public court hearing.

2. However, neither freedom of broadcasting nor freedom of information generally give rise to a right to be granted access to a source of information [that is not already open to the public]. A right of access vis-à-vis the state may, however, arise in cases where the state does not grant sufficient access to a source of information within its sphere of responsibility, even though the relevant source is statutorily defined as publicly accessible (cf. BVerfGE 103, 44 <59 and 60>). These conditions are met if permission to make audio and film recordings in the context of a court hearing is denied in cases where the public interest in the dissemination of such recordings outweighs conflicting interests.

a) [...]

In principle, constitutional law recognises an objective mandate, deriving from the principles of the rule of law and democracy, to guarantee the opportunity for the public to observe and possibly monitor court proceedings. To that end the media may report on proceedings, and broadcast stations may make audio-visual recordings, unless a specific prohibition applies that imposes a general ban or a prohibition is merited in the individual case to protect conflicting interests. [...]

In general, media presence in the courtroom and media reporting promote public scrutiny of court hearings (cf. BGH, Order of 10 January 2006 - 1 StR 527/05 -, NJW 2006, p. 1220 <1221>). Satisfying the interest of the public in obtaining information about court proceedings not only serves the general objective of contributing to the formation of individual and public opinion; it also serves the interest of the judiciary in raising public awareness of judicial proceedings and decisions [...]. Pursuant to § 169 second sentence of the Courts Constitution Act, audio and film recordings of the hearing itself are not permitted, in line with constitutional law (cf. BVerfGE 103, 44 <66 *et seq.*>); rather, public scrutiny of court hearings is achieved by the principle of public court sessions and by media reporting on the events in the courtroom [without direct recordings]. Nevertheless, using footage of a courtroom and the persons acting within it may provide the general public with a clearer impression of court proceedings, which serves to satisfy the information interest.

32 [...]

33 b) The law governing the organisation of courts does not prohibit broadcast reporting that takes place right before or after the hearing; it also does not prohibit broadcasting during recesses, which are part of the court session but not of the actual hearing within the meaning of the law (cf. BGHSt 23, 123 <125>). However, further restrictions may be imposed by judicial orders issued in exercise of the presiding judge's powers to maintain order in court (*sitzungspolizeiliche Anordnung*) under § 176 of the Courts Constitution Act (cf. BVerfGE 91, 125 <136>).

34 aa) Insofar as procedural law does not provide otherwise, the presiding judge has discretion as to the conduct of the court hearing and as to orders in exercise of the powers to maintain order in court [...]. When exercising this discretion, the presiding judge must have regard to the importance of broadcasting for ensuring public awareness and scrutiny of court proceedings, as well as to interests that oppose such broadcasting. The presiding judge must also ensure that the principle of proportionality is observed. If the interest in reporting by means of audio and film recordings outweighs other interests that must be taken into account in the exercise of the presiding judge's discretion, the opportunity to make such recordings must be provided (cf. BVerfGE 91, 125 <138 and 139>).

35 (1) In assessing the interest of the public in obtaining information, the subject matter of the court proceedings in question is a significant factor. In criminal proceedings, factors that must be taken into account include, in particular, the seriousness of the charges, but also the level of public attention the case has attracted, for instance due to special circumstances or the context of the crime, the identity of the persons implicated in it, fear of similar crimes being committed or sympathy for the victims and their families. The weight and importance attached to the information interest generally increase the more the charges at issue stand out when compared to ordinary crime, for example because of the way in which the crime was committed or the special nature of its target (cf. BVerfGE 35, 202 <231> – *Lebach*). A weighty interest [of the public] in obtaining information may also result from the nature of the court case as such even if the accused themselves are not considered figures of paramount significance for contemporary society [...].

36 The interest of the public in obtaining information is generally not limited to the accused and the charges laid against them, but also extends to the persons who,

No. 19 – TV Broadcasting from the Courtroom

as members of the adjudicating body or the public prosecution office, partake in administering justice in the name of the people. Furthermore, legitimate information interests may, in principle, be directed at lawyers [...] or other persons involved in the proceedings, such as witnesses.

(2) In the presiding judge's exercise of their discretion and the balancing of interests it entails, the judge must take into account legitimate interests opposing the creation and dissemination of audio and film recordings. These include, in particular, the protection of the general right of personality of the persons involved in the proceedings, i.e. of the accused and the witnesses, and their right to a fair trial (Art. 2(1) in conjunction with Art. 20(3) of the Basic Law), as well as the proper functioning of the administration of justice, in particular ensuring that the process of finding truth and justice is not disturbed (cf. BVerfGE 103, 44 <64>). In this context, the interests opposing broadcast recordings have special weight in cases where they fit the statutory requirements for completely excluding the public from the courtroom on the basis of typifying person-related grounds set out in procedural law (cf., e.g., § 48, § 109(1) fourth sentence of the Youth Courts Act, § 171a, § 172 no. 1a, no. 4 of the Courts Constitution Act).   37

(a) The protected interests [that possibly oppose the interest in broadcasting] include the general right of personality of persons involved in the proceedings (cf. BVerfGE 103, 44 <68>).   38

(aa) The right of the media to obtain and disseminate footage of persons present in the courtroom during a hearing must be measured against the affected persons' right to their own image, as a specific manifestation of the right of personality. This right guarantees that affected individuals have the authority to influence and decide not only whether photographs and recordings of their person may be used by others, but also whether such photographs and recordings may be produced in the first place (cf. BVerfGE 101, 361 <381>).   39

The constitutional standards applicable to the dissemination of one's image by the mass media without one's consent (cf. in this regard BVerfGE 35, 202 <224 *et seq.*> – *Lebach*; 101, 361 <387 *et seq.*>) must also be observed when deciding whether to allow the depiction of specific persons, for the purposes of dissemination in the mass media, in connection with a criminal trial hearing. Since court hearings that give rise to a particular interest of the public in obtaining information are events of significance to contemporary society, the protection of the general right of personality of persons involved in such proceedings does not require an absolute ban on filming in the courtroom (cf. BVerfGE 87, 334 <340> – *Honecker*; 91, 125 <137 and 138>).   40

However, when determining the scope of protection of the right to one's own image, it must be taken into account that at least some of the persons involved in   41 the proceedings typically find themselves in an unfamiliar and stressful situation. In many cases, their presence in the courtroom is mandatory – for instance as a witness or the accused in criminal proceedings. Regarding the accused, consideration must be given in particular to a possible pillory effect and to possible impairments of their right to be presumed innocent or of their interest in future social reintegration, as these rights and interests might be affected by media coverage identifying the accused (cf. BVerfGE 35, 202 <226 et seq.> – *Lebach*; 103, 44 <68>). The risk of biased media reporting regarding the culpability of the accused must also be taken into consideration, not least in light of the powerful influence of TV broadcasting. With regard to witnesses, it must be taken into account that they are subjected to a high level of stress, for instance if they are victims of the crime for which the accused was indicted.

42 Persons who attract public attention in court proceedings […] in their capacity as organs serving the administration of justice (*Organe der Rechtspflege*) are not afforded the same level of protection of their personality rights as private individuals involved in the proceedings (cf. BVerfGE 103, 44 <69>), or as members of the audience. Nevertheless, persons involved in the proceedings as judges, public prosecutors, lawyers or judicial staff are also entitled to a certain level of protection; their interest may outweigh the publication interest, for instance, in the event that publishing their images would result in significant harassment or threats to their safety due to attacks on their person by third parties […]. […]

43 (bb) […]

44 (b) The right of the persons involved in the proceedings to a fair trial (Art. 2(1) in conjunction with Art. 20(3) of the Basic Law) and the proper functioning of the justice system, in particular the unimpeded process of finding truth and justice in the case on trial, are less affected by audio and film recordings outside the hearing than by direct recordings of the hearing itself […]. However, adverse consequences cannot be ruled out entirely. If there are film and audio recordings of events accompanying the hearing, the knowledge that they may be disseminated might influence individuals involved in the proceedings in such a way that it adversely affects the course of the hearing and the objective of finding truth and justice. One of the main objectives of criminal trial hearings is to obtain, from all persons giving testimony, truthful and complete information of forensic value. This requires a setting that helps avoid inhibition and anxiety, in particular for persons not experienced in dealing with the media. […]

45 Likewise, audio and film recordings of the events accompanying the hearing may adversely affect the right of the accused to unfettered communication with their defence lawyer, as guaranteed under § 148(1) of the Code of Criminal Procedure. This may in turn impact their right to a fair trial (cf. BVerfGE 49, 24 <55>). […]

No. 19 – TV Broadcasting from the Courtroom

(3) The presiding judge's discretionary decision on orders issued in exercise of the power to maintain order in court must satisfy the principle of proportionality and strike a balance between the conflicting interests. Restrictions imposed by the presiding judge on access to information relating [not to the actual court hearing itself but] to events accompanying the hearing must have regard, in particular, to the principle of necessity (cf., e.g., BVerfGE 50, 234 <241>; 91, 125 <137>). 46

A ban on audio and broadcast recordings is not necessary if the protection of conflicting interests can already be ensured by imposing restrictive conditions, requiring, in particular, that the footage obtained be rendered anonymous by suitable technical means if the depicted persons are entitled to special protection. If the risk that the depicted person could be identified by the general public can be ruled out by such restrictions, the risk that the person concerned could still be recognisable to their personal acquaintances can be tolerated, provided that the conflicting information interests of the public are sufficiently weighty and that the person concerned does not face severe disadvantages resulting specifically from being recognised by acquaintances. However, imposing such anonymisation requirements [on the media] also constitutes a significant restriction of the public's access to information, and thus requires specific justification based on the circumstances of the individual case. 47

Restricting the place, time, duration and type of recordings may be a suitable means where recordings could potentially harm the persons concerned by depicting them in a particularly detrimental or embarrassing situation; where the making or duration of the envisaged recordings adversely affect the course of the proceedings; or where persons involved in the proceedings wish to speak confidentially with their lawyer when the hearing is not in progress. Imposing such conditions may avoid the need for further restrictions such as a complete ban on audio and film recordings (cf. BVerfGE 91, 125 <138 and 139>). It is for the presiding judge to ensure an appropriate balance between the interest [of the public] in obtaining information and conflicting interests […]. […] 48

The risk of disturbance to the proper conduct of the hearing that arises, for instance, due to the limited space available in the courtroom, can be mitigated or avoided by opting for a so-called media pool solution [where only one camera team representing a media pool is admitted], rather than several individual camera teams (cf. BVerfGE 87, 334 <340> – *Honecker*; 91, 125 <138>; […]). The requirement that all other broadcasters receive access to the material may be satisfied, for instance, by imposing an obligation to share the recordings with any interested press representative on condition that any resulting expenses be reimbursed. 49

bb) […] 50

51 c) As audio and film recordings immediately before or after a hearing and during recesses fall under the freedom of broadcasting, an order prohibiting or restricting such recordings requires that the presiding judge disclose the reasons for their decision in order to ensure an effective protection of substantive fundamental rights; this allows the persons concerned to ascertain that all significant circumstances have been taken into account in the balancing of interests.

52 3. The challenged Order of the Presiding Judge of 21 February 2007 restricting the time for audio and film recordings and for the taking of photographs does not meet these constitutional requirements.

53 a) To the extent that the order was aimed at protecting the accused, it is not sufficient to simply state in the reasons attached to the order that most of the accused did not have a criminal record and that the charges against them did not stand out from ordinary crime. The assessment of the public interest in court cases is not subject to the same standards as its classification under criminal law. Even a charge that is considered minor under criminal law may affect weighty information interests of the public; this may be the case, for instance, where the matter touches on possible deficits of the state system. The proceedings at hand concerned allegations of abuse of *Bundeswehr* recruits by the officers and non-commissioned officers responsible for their training, which led to widespread public discussion. As the circumstances clearly set the case apart from what is considered ordinary crime, the investigation of the incidents attracted considerable public interest, too.

54 The presiding judge could not simply rely on the generalised assumption that visual courtroom recordings outside the trial hearing would cause the accused to feel inhibited and anxious, and that this would make it more difficult for the court to try the case. Rather, it would have been incumbent upon the judge to establish, in a comprehensible manner, specific indications to support such concerns. It is not immediately obvious from the specifics of the case nor from the identity of the accused, who are all experienced *Bundeswehr* officers and non-commissioned officers, that such concerns were indeed justified.

55 b) [...]

56 To the extent that the order was aimed at protecting the defence lawyers, the underlying balancing of interests does not sufficiently take into consideration that lawyers, acting as authorised representatives in court, perform their duties as organs serving the administration of justice. [...]

57 c) The challenged order was also not justified by the interest in protecting lay judges (*Schöffen*). [...] In the absence of specific indications, it is not tenable to assume adverse effects on the functioning of the court. [...] The legal order builds on the legitimate presumption that lay judges are, in principle, capable of meeting

the expectations linked to their function, including in proceedings that attract public attention, even if the media disseminate footage of the proceedings.

d) [...] 58

e) Even if there actually had been indications in the case at hand that broadcast recordings would adversely affect the right of personality or the impartiality of persons involved in the proceedings, it would have been necessary to clarify, prior to banning broadcast recordings, whether the expected adverse effects could have been averted by imposing specific restrictions, such as anonymisation requirements regarding footage depicting the persons concerned or requirements that filming of the entry of the judges be kept to a wide angle, without close-ups of individual faces. [...] 59

III.

[...] 60

IV.

[...] 61-62

Justices: Papier, Hohmann-Dennhardt, Hoffmann-Riem, Bryde, Gaier, Eichberger, Schluckebier

No. 20

BVerfGE 120, 180 – Caroline III

HEADNOTE

to the Order of the First Senate of 26 February 2008
1 BvR 1602, 1606, 1626/07

On the scope of the fundamental right to the protection of one's personality under Article 2(1) in conjunction with Article 1(1) of the Basic Law in respect of photos of celebrities published as part of entertainment media coverage concerning their private and everyday life.

FEDERAL CONSTITUTIONAL COURT
- 1 BvR 1602, 1606, 1626/07 -

IN THE NAME OF THE PEOPLE

In the proceedings
on the constitutional complaint of

1. E... GmbH & Co. KG,
   – authorised representative: ...
   against a) the Judgment of the Federal Court of Justice of 6 March 2007
   - VI ZR 51/06 -,
   b) the Judgment of the Hamburg Regional Court of 1 July 2005
   - 324 O 873/04 -,
2. K... GmbH & Cie., represented by its directors
   – authorised representative: ...
   against a) the Judgment of the Federal Court of Justice of 6 March 2007
   - VI ZR 51/06 -,
   b) the Judgment of the Hamburg Higher Regional Court of 31 January 2006 - 7 U 88/05 -,

No. 20 – Caroline III

3. Princess von H...
   – authorised representative: ...
   against a) the Judgment of the Federal Court of Justice of 6 March 2007
   - VI ZR 51/06 -,
   b) the Judgment of the Hamburg Higher Regional Court of 31 January 2006 - 7 U 88/05 -

the Federal Constitutional Court – First Senate –

with the participation of Justices

President Papier,
Hohmann-Dennhardt,
Hoffmann-Riem,
Bryde,
Gaier,
Eichberger,
Schluckebier,
Kirchhof

held on 26 February 2008:

1. The constitutional complaints are combined for joint decision.
2. The constitutional complaints of complainants nos. 1 and 3 are rejected as unfounded.
3. The Judgment of the Federal Court of Justice of 6 March 2007 - VI ZR 51/06 - and the Judgment of the Hamburg Regional Court of 24 June 2005
   - 324 O 869/04 - violate complainant no. 2's fundamental right under Article 5(1) second sentence of the Basic Law. The Judgment of the Federal Court of Justice is reversed. The matter is remanded to the Federal Court of Justice for a new decision.
4. [...]

REASONS:

A.

The constitutional complaints concern the permissibility of publishing photos in reports on the private and everyday life of celebrities. 1

The initial proceedings concern actions under private law by which complainant no. 3 sought injunctive relief against the publication of photos in a magazine. The actions were brought after the European Court of Human Rights, in a judgment 2 of its Third Section of 24 June 2004 (Application no. 59320/00, *von Hannover v. Germany*, Reports and Decisions 2004-VI, p. 1 *et seq.*; [...]) held that the Federal Republic of Germany was in breach of its obligations under Article 8 of the Convention for the Protection of Human Rights and Fundamental Freedoms, given that the German courts had, in several earlier decisions on the permissibility of disseminating photos of complainant no. 3, repeatedly failed to provide protection against the publication of photos in the press. The individual application submitted by the applicant to the European Court of Human Rights concerned, in particular, a landmark decision by the Federal Court of Justice (BGHZ 131, 332), which complainant no. 3 had challenged at the time by way of constitutional complaint. In its Judgment of 15 December 1999 (BVerfGE 101, 361), the First Senate of the Federal Constitutional Court had partly granted the relief sought, but only in respect of aspects that were immaterial to the decision of the European Court of Human Rights.

I.

Complaint proceedings 1 BvR 1602/07 and 1 BvR 1626/07

1. Complainant no. 3 is one of the daughters of the now deceased Prince Rainier of Monaco and is married to Prince Ernst August von Hannover. The initial proceedings concerned a photo report on the private and everyday life of complainant no. 3 and her husband, which was not related to the exercise of their official duties.

a) Complainant no. 1 publishes the weekly magazine *Frau im Spiegel*. In issue no. 9/02 of 20 February 2002, the magazine reported that the father of complainant no. 3, the reigning Prince of the State of Monaco, had fallen ill [...] under the headline: "Prince Rainier – Not Alone at Home". The article stated:

> The whole country is concerned, as are his children. Prince Albert (presently in Salt Lake City as a member of the Olympic team), Princess Caroline (on holiday in St. Moritz with Prince Ernst August von Hannover) and Princess Stephanie take turns caring for their father. [...].

The article also included a photo showing complainant no. 3 together with her husband on a street in the Swiss winter sport resort of St. Moritz.

In issue no. 9/03 of 20 February 2003, the same magazine ran an article entitled: "St. Moritz – Royal Fun in the Snow" concerning the stay of complainant no. 3 and other well-known members of the European aristocracy at this winter sport resort. The article was accompanied by a photo of complainant no. 3 and her husband on one of the resort's streets. [...]

In issue no. 12/04 of 11 March 2004, the magazine reported under the headline "Princess Caroline – Monaco Awaits Her" that complainant no. 3, who had not appeared in public for some time, was expected to attend the Rose Ball held annually in Monaco. A photo accompanying the article [shows complainant no. 3] with her husband in a ski lift; the caption under the picture reads: "Cosy chat in a chair lift". [...]

b) Complainant no. 3 sought injunctive relief against complainant no. 1 regarding the publication of these photo reports.

aa) [...]

bb) [...]

cc) In its judgment [...], the Federal Court of Justice rejected complainant no. 3's appeal on points of law (*Revision*), thus upholding the appellate court's rejection of complainant no. 3's action insofar as it was directed against the publication of a photo in an article on her father's illness. With regard to the two remaining photos, the Federal Court of Justice reversed the judgment delivered upon the appeal on points of fact and law (*Berufung*) and, by rejecting complainant no. 1's appeal, reinstated the prohibition ordered by the Regional Court.

[...]

2. a) Complainant no. 1 claims [...] that the decisions of the Regional Court and the Federal Court of Justice violate its fundamental right to freedom of the press guaranteed by Art. 5(1) second sentence of the Basic Law to the extent that they prohibited it from disseminating photos of complainant no. 3. [...]

b) [...] Complainant no. 3 claims a violation of her right of personality guaranteed by Art. 2(1) in conjunction with Art. 1(1) of the Basic Law to the extent that the Higher Regional Court and the Federal Court of Justice held that publishing a holiday photo in the report on her father's illness was permissible.

[...]

II.

Complaint proceedings 1 BvR 1606/07

1. Complainant no. 2 publishes the weekly magazine *7 Tage*. In issue no. 13/02 of 20 March 2002, under the headline "Sleeping in Princess Caroline's Bed – A Dream That Could Come True! – Caroline and Ernst August Rent Out Their Dream Villa", it reported that the husband of complainant no. 3 owned a holiday villa in Kenya, which the couple rents out when they are away. The headline contains the clearly highlighted subtitle "Even the rich and beautiful are frugal. Many rent their villas out to paying guests."

29 The article listed the names of several private individuals besides complainant no. 3 – Hollywood stars and members of the aristocracy – who had "developed an inclination for thinking economically" and also rented out their palaces or houses when not using them themselves. [...]

30 In addition to several photos of the holiday villa and its surroundings, the article included a photo showing complainant no. 3 and her husband on a street during a holiday visit. The caption reads "Holidaying – Caroline and her husband".

31 2. The Regional Court prohibited [...] any renewed publication of this photo. [...]

32 3. The Higher Regional Court reversed the decision of the Regional Court [...] and rejected the action brought by complainant no. 3. [...]

33 4. The Federal Court of Justice [...] reversed the judgment delivered upon the appeal on points of fact and law and upheld the prohibition issued at first instance, rejecting complainant no. 2's appeal. [...]

34 5. Complainant no. 2 claims that the decision of the Regional Court and its affirmation by the judgment delivered upon the appeal on points of law rendered by the Federal Court of Justice violates freedom of press reporting guaranteed by Art. 5(1) second sentence of the Basic Law. [...]

35 [...]

III.

36 Complainants nos. 1 and 3 submitted statements on the constitutional complaint lodged by the respective defendants in the initial proceedings.

37-38 [...]

B.

39 The constitutional complaints of complainants nos. 1 and 3 are unsuccessful. The injunctive relief, upheld by the Federal Court of Justice, prohibiting renewed dissemination of the photos challenged [by complainant no. 3] does not violate the fundamental right to freedom of the press under Art. 5(1) second sentence of the Basic Law. Complainant no. 3's fundamental right to the protection of her personality under Art. 2(1) in conjunction with Art. 1(1) of the Basic Law is also not violated by the fact that the Federal Court of Justice and the Higher Regional Court did not object to the dissemination of a photo of complainant no. 3.

40 However, the order requiring that complainant no. 2 in complaint proceedings 1 BvR 1606/07 refrain from publishing the report with photos violates the fundamental right to freedom of the press. The Judgment of the Federal Court of Justice is reversed.

No. 20 – Caroline III

I.

The orders issued against complainants nos. 1 and 2 in complaint proceedings 41
1 BvR 1602/07 and 1 BvR 1606/07 interfere with the fundamental right to freedom of the press under Art. 5(1) second sentence of the Basic Law since the publication of certain photos [in their magazines] was prohibited by the courts.

At its core, the fundamental right to freedom of the press guarantees the right 42
to freely determine the type and focus, contents and form of a publication. This includes the decision on whether and how a printed product is to be illustrated. Images are covered by the constitutional protection of the report they serve to illustrate […]. Notably, the protection afforded by freedom of the press also covers publishing photos of persons (cf. BVerfGE 101, 361 <389>; […]). The protection does not depend on the type or quality of the printed product or the coverage (cf. BVerfGE 34, 269 <283> – *Soraya*; 50, 234 <240>). The press has the right to decide according to its own journalistic criteria what it considers worthy of public interest (cf. BVerfGE 97, 228 <257>; 101, 361 <389>). The protection afforded by freedom of the press may not be made contingent on an assessment of the printed product – irrespective of the standards that are applied for such an assessment (cf. BVerfGE 66, 116 <134>). Entertainment media reports, too, including articles on celebrities, are covered by the protection afforded by freedom of the press (cf. BVerfGE 101, 361 <390>). The informative value and the extent to which the coverage is relevant to questions of significant concern to the public only begin to matter where the courts are called upon to balance [such reporting against] opposing personality rights (cf. BVerfGE 34, 269 <283> – *Soraya*; 101, 361 <391>).

II.

The decisions of the civil courts challenged in complaint proceedings 43
1 BvR 1626/07 impair complainant no. 3's fundamental right to the protection of her personality under Art. 2(1) in conjunction with Art. 1(1) of the Basic Law insofar as the prohibition on publishing certain photos sought by complainant no. 3 was not granted.

1. The fundamental right to the protection of one's personality serves to guarantee 44
the basic conditions of social relationships between the holders of the fundamental right and the world around them (cf. BVerfGE 54, 148 <153> – *Eppler*; 97, 391 <405> – *Sexual Abuse Allegations*; 114, 339 <346> – *Stolpe/Stasi Dispute*). By protecting freedom of conduct and privacy, this fundamental right safeguards aspects of the free development of one's personality that are not covered by the

specific freedoms guaranteed in the Basic Law, but are equal to these freedoms in terms of their significance for the individual's personal sphere that is closer to the core of private life (*engere persönliche Lebenssphäre*) as well as for maintaining its basic conditions (cf. BVerfGE 99, 185 <193> – *Helnwein/Scientology;* 118, 168 <183>; 119, 1 <23 and 24> – *Esra*). Determining what specific legal protection is invoked in relation to the various manifestations of the protection of one's personality is mainly guided by the type of risk to one's personality at play. It will depend on the circumstances of the specific case and its anticipated impact on fundamental rights, particularly on the development of one's personality and the private life of the persons concerned (cf. BVerfGE 101, 361 <380>; 106, 28 <39>; 118, 168 <183 and 184>).

45   2. Court decisions on the permissibility of publishing photos showing the subject in private or everyday contexts may touch upon different aspects of the protection of one's personality, in particular the guarantee of the right to one's own image and the guarantee to respect of one's private sphere (cf. BVerfGE 101, 361 <380 *et seq.*>).

46   a) Art. 2(1) in conjunction with Art. 1(1) of the Basic Law does not provide for a general, let alone comprehensive, right to determine the portrayal of one's person (cf. BVerfGE 101, 361 <380>). The right to one's own image does, however, grant individuals the possibility of influencing and deciding on the creation and use of images of themselves by others. The need for protection mainly arises from the possibility that the image of a person in a particular context may be taken out of that context and reproduced by third parties at any time under circumstances which the affected person cannot control (cf. BVerfGE 101, 361 <381>). The easier this is, the greater the need for protection may be. Thus, advances in the field of image technology increase the possibility of risks to personality rights (cf. BVerfGE 101, 361 <381>). The growing availability of small and portable cameras, such as digital cameras built into mobile phones, for instance, exposes celebrities to the increased risk of being photographed in practically any situation without warning and without their knowledge, and of the photos being published in the media. A particular need for protection can further arise in the case of covert or surprise photography (cf. BVerfGE 101, 361 <394 and 395>). In assessing the need for protection, the situation in which the affected persons are shown is also significant; for instance, they may be photographed while going about their usual routines or in situations in which they relax after work and away from everyday life and in which they may reasonably assume that they will not be exposed to photographers.

47   b) The fundamental right to the protection of one's personality encompasses both the right to one's own image and the protection of one's private sphere (cf. in this respect BVerfGE 101, 361 <382>). The protection of the private sphere has several dimensions. Thematically, it affects those matters in particular that holders

of the fundamental right tend to withhold from public mention or display. Spatially, the private sphere includes a person's refuge, the place where, particularly in their home but also outside, they can clear their mind and relax (cf. BVerfGE 101, 361 <382 *et seq.*>) and where they can satisfy their need "to be left alone" (cf. BVerfGE 27, 1 <6 and 7> – *Microcensus*; see additionally on Article 13 of the Basic Law BVerfGE 32, 54 <75>; 51, 97 <107>). The boundaries of the protected private sphere cannot be established in general and abstract terms (cf. BVerfGE 101, 361 <384>).

More extensive protection may follow from Art. 6(1) and (2) of the Basic Law, which provides for stronger protection of one's personality in situations where parents are in public places with their minor children (cf. BVerfGE 101, 361 <385>; 119, 1 <23 and 24>). 48

III.

The fundamental rights to freedom of the press and to the protection of one's personality are not guaranteed without reservation. Freedom of the press can be limited in the form of general laws pursuant to Art. 5(2) of the Basic Law. Such laws include § 22 *et seq.* of the Art Copyright Act, but also Art. 8 of the European Convention on Human Rights (see 1 below). At the same time, the Art Copyright Act and freedom of expression guaranteed by Art. 10 of the Convention restrict the protection of one's personality, as part of the legal order under the Constitution pursuant to Art. 2(1) of the Basic Law (see 2 below). The interpretation and application of such limitations and their balancing against one another by the ordinary courts must be guided by the significance of the fundamental rights interests affected by the limitations and take into account the relevant guarantees of the European Convention on Human Rights. Review by the Federal Constitutional Court is limited to the question whether the impact of German fundamental rights – with due regard to the guarantees of the Convention – on the interpretation of private law provisions as well as on the balancing of conflicting interests was sufficiently observed [...] (see 3 below). 49

1. Pursuant to Art. 5(2) of the Basic Law, freedom of the press can be limited through provisions of general laws. The category 'provisions of general laws' encompasses all laws that are not directed against the freedoms guaranteed by Art. 5(1) first sentence of the Basic Law themselves, but which serve to protect a legal interest *per se*, irrespective of specific opinions. Such a legal interest must be generally protected within the legal order and thus regardless of whether it can be violated by expressions of opinion or in any other manner (cf. BVerfGE 117, 244 <260>). 50

51 a) §§ 22 *et seq.* of the Art Copyright Act and the legal principles on the protection of one's personality under private law enshrined in § 823(1) of the Civil Code are general laws within this meaning (cf. BVerfGE 7, 198 <211>; 25, 256 <263 *et seq.*>; 34, 269 <282> – *Soraya*; 35, 202 <224 and 225> – *Lebach*). […]

52 b) Another general law within the meaning of Art. 5(2) of the Basic Law that limits freedom of communication is the right to respect for one's private life enshrined in Art. 8 of the Convention. In domestic law, the Convention has the rank of ordinary federal law (cf. BVerfGE 74, 358 <370>; 82, 106 <114>; 111, 307 <316 and 317>). Additionally, in constitutional law, the guarantees of the Convention and the case-law of the European Court of Human Rights serve as guidelines for interpretation for determining the content and scope of fundamental rights, provided this does not restrict or lower the level of fundamental rights protection afforded under the Basic Law (BVerfGE 111, 307 <317, 329>), which is not intended by the Convention (cf. Art. 53 of the Convention).

53 The protection of private life guaranteed by Art. 8(1) of the Convention, just like the protection of one's personality guaranteed by the Constitution, also encompasses all personal, social and business relationships that form an integral part of the private life of every individual […]. In determining the scope of such protection, the extent of the individual's legitimate expectations of privacy in a given situation must be taken into account […]. The guarantee of Art. 8(1) of the Convention may also include a right to be protected by the domestic courts against the publication of images of individuals from their everyday life (cf. ECtHR (Third Section), *von Hannover v. Germany*, Judgment of 24 June 2006, no. 59320/00, §§ 50 *et seq.*, […]). The scope of this right in a specific case is to be determined by balancing it against freedom of expression guaranteed by Art. 10 of the Convention and the limitations thereto listed in Art. 10(2) of the Convention (cf. ECtHR (Fourth Section), *Minelli v. Switzerland*, Judgment of 14 June 2005, no. 14991/02; ECtHR (Second Section), *Gourguenidze v. Georgia*, Judgment of 17 October 2006, no. 71678/01, § 38 *et seq.*).

54 2. The fundamental right to the protection of one's personality derived from Art. 2(1) in conjunction with Art. 1(1) of the Basic Law is subject to the limitations of Art. 2(1) second half-sentence of the Basic Law.

55 a) The fundamental rights, such as Art. 5(1) of the Basic Law, constitute one limitation that derives from the legal order under the Constitution; other limitations include, in particular, the provisions in § 22 *et seq.* of the Art Copyright Act, which govern the publication of photos of persons (cf. BVerfGE 101, 361 <387>). These provisions set out a multi-tier system of protection, which accommodates both the portrayed person's need for protection and the general public's interest in obtaining information as satisfied by the media (cf. BVerfGE 35, 202 <224 and

225> – *Lebach*; 101, 361 <387>). This multi-tier system of protection comprises a requirement of consent to the dissemination of photos of persons in § 22 first sentence of the Art Copyright Act, an exception to this requirement in particular for images portraying an aspect of contemporary society as set out in § 23(1) no. 1 of the Art Copyright Act, and an exception to this exception laid down in § 23(2) of the Art Copyright Act for cases in which the legitimate interests of the portrayed person are violated (cf. BVerfGE 35, 202 <224 and 225> – *Lebach*; 101, 361 <387>).

b) Besides these provisions, the freedom to express, disseminate and receive opinions and information, as guaranteed by Art. 10 of the European Convention on Human Rights, restricts the protection of one's personality.

Press activity is covered by freedom of expression guaranteed by Art. 10(1) first sentence of the European Convention on Human Rights, and by freedom to hold opinions and to receive and impart information and ideas guaranteed by Art. 10(1) second sentence of the Convention. The protection afforded by Art. 10(1) of the Convention extends, in particular, to the publication of photos to illustrate a media report (cf. ECtHR (First Section), *Verlagsgruppe News GmbH v. Austria* (no. 2), Judgment of 14 December 2006, no. 10520/02, § 29; ECtHR (Third Section), *von Hannover v. Germany*, Judgment of 24 June 2004, no. 59320/00, § 59, […]; ECtHR (Second Section), *Gourguenidze v. Georgia*, Judgment of 17 October 2006, no. 71678/01, § 55). According to the case-law of the European Court of Human Rights, the question whether restrictions of this right through measures ordered by domestic courts to protect the private life of the portrayed person are permissible must also be decided by balancing this right against the right to respect for one's private life guaranteed by Art. 8 of the Convention (cf. ECtHR (Second Section), *Gourguenidze v. Georgia*, Judgment of 17 October 2006, no. 71678/01, § 37 with further references).

In cases where press reporting contributes "information and ideas on all matters of public interest", freedom of expression guaranteed by Art. 10(1) of the Convention must be accorded special weight (cf. ECtHR (Fourth Section), *Karhuvaara and Iltalehti v. Finland*, Judgment of 16 November 2004, no. 53678/00, § 40; ECtHR (First Section), *Tønsbergs Blad and Others v. Norway*, Judgment of 1 March 2007, no. 510/04, § 82) when balancing it against conflicting legal interests, in consideration of the presumption, enshrined in Art. 5(1) of the Basic Law, of the permissibility of press coverage intended to contribute to the formation of public opinion (cf. BVerfGE 20, 162 <177>).

c) aa) The right to one's own image, the scope of which is set out in § 22 *et seq.* of the Art Copyright Act and the protection of which is strengthened by the fundamental right under Art. 2(1) in conjunction with Art. 1(1) of the Basic Law, is influenced by whether information is conveyed to the wide audience reached by the mass media and thus does not remain limited to a narrow group of persons ([...]; see also ECtHR (Second Section), *Gourguenidze v. Georgia*, Judgment of 17 October 2006, no. 71678/01, § 55).The weight of freedom of the press, which may restrict personality rights, depends on whether the coverage concerns a matter which significantly affects the public (cf. BVerfGE 7, 198 <212>; established case-law).

60 According to the case-law of the Federal Constitutional Court, when the media covers celebrities, it is not only the revealing of discrepancies between celebrities' public self-portrayal and their private life that is of public interest. Celebrities can also provide orientation for shaping one's own way of life and serve as role models, or negative examples (cf. BVerfGE 101, 361 <390>). Legitimate interests of the public in obtaining information would be defined too narrowly if they were restricted to behaviour that is scandalous or morally or legally questionable. Normal everyday life and the unobjectionable conduct of celebrities, too, may be brought to the attention of the public if this serves the formation of public opinion on matters of public interest (cf. BVerfGE 101, 361 <390>).

61 The entertainment value of media content or the way it is presented is often important for attracting public attention and thus also for contributing to the formation of public opinion. If an article was deemed insignificant for the formation of public opinion merely because of its entertaining presentation, this might also violate the content of the guarantee under Art. 10 of the Convention (cf. ECtHR (Fourth Section), *Wirtschafts-Trend-Zeitschriften-Verlagsgesellschaft mbH v. Austria*, Judgment of 13 December 2005, no. 66298/01 *inter alia*, §§ 49-50).

62 Even in respect of 'mere entertainment', its relevance to the formation of opinions cannot be denied from the outset. Entertainment is an essential part of media activity that is covered by the protection afforded by freedom of the press in its subjective and objective legal dimensions (cf. BVerfGE 35, 202 – *Lebach* <222>; 101, 361 <390>). The journalistic and commercial success of a printed product that competes with other available media and entertainment offers can hinge on its entertaining content and corresponding photos. In fact, the significance of visuals for press reporting has even increased in recent years (cf. BVerfGE 101, 361 <392>).

63 It would be one-sided to assume that the public's interest in entertainment is always focused exclusively on satisfying a desire for amusement and relaxation, a departure from reality and distraction. Entertainment can also convey images of reality and provide subjects for debate that may spark a process of discussion relating to life philosophies, values and habits; it thus serves an important purpose in society. For this reason, entertainment in the press is not insignificant, let alone

without value, with regard to the interests that freedom of the press aims to protect (cf. BVerfGE 101, 361 <390>).

The scope of protection of freedom of the press also includes entertainment media coverage on the private and everyday life of celebrities and their social relationships, particularly persons who are close to them. Restricting all coverage of these persons to their exercise of official functions would constrain freedom of the press to a degree that is incompatible with Art. 5(1) of the Basic Law.

bb) However, particularly where contents are entertaining, the conflicting legal interests must be taken into account and balanced. When the interest in obtaining information is weighed against the conflicting interest of the protection of one's personality, the subject matter of the reporting has decisive significance – for instance, it is crucial to examine whether private matters are covered merely to satisfy curiosity (cf. BVerfGE 34, 269 <283> – *Soraya*; 101, 361 <391>). Where photos are concerned, the occasion and the circumstances under which they were obtained are significant, too.

cc) It does not automatically follow from the recognition of the importance of press reporting for the formation of public and individual opinion that the special protection of one's own image afforded the portrayed persons that is derived from the right of personality must always stand back, and thus that any illustration of media products is protected under constitutional law.

(1) The balancing must take into account the right of the press to decide in accordance with its journalistic criteria what attracts public interest; this right falls within the scope of protection of Art. 5(1) second sentence of the Basic Law (cf. BVerfGE 101, 361 <392>). However, this right of the press to self-determination does not also include the decision on how to weigh the interest in obtaining information when balancing it against conflicting legal interests and on how to reconcile the legal interests concerned [...]. When deciding to print an image of a person and to use it as part of a particular report, the mass media use their constitutionally protected right to decide themselves what they consider worthy of coverage. In so doing, they must take into account the protection of personality rights of affected persons. In the event of a dispute [...], it is incumbent upon the courts to carry out the decisive balancing of the [public's] interest in obtaining information against the conflicting interests of the affected persons. [...] When weighing the interest in obtaining information, however, the courts must refrain from assessing the contents of the coverage in question as to its value and seriousness; they have to limit themselves to reviewing and determining to what extent the coverage might contribute to the formation of public opinion.

To the extent that the image as such does not contain a significant message for the formation of public opinion, its informative value must be derived from the accompanying written article (cf. BGHZ 158, 218 <223>; Federal Court of Justice, Judgment of 19 October 2004 - VI ZR 292/03 -, NJW 2005, p. 594 <595 and 596>). Thus, images can complement an article and serve to expand on its message, for example by confirming its authenticity. Another purpose of information protected by Art. 5(1) of the Basic Law might consist in drawing the reader's attention to the article by adding images of the persons involved in the reported event. Where it is also permitted to use images that were not taken in the context of the reported event, this can help prevent those disturbing effects on the affected celebrities that might arise if the article could only be illustrated with images obtained in the context of the reported event [...]. However, if [the purpose of] the accompanying article is solely to furnish some occasion for publishing a celebrity photo, then a contribution to the formation of public opinion is not ascertainable. In such cases, constitutional law does not require giving the interest in publication precedence over the protection of an individual's personality.

69 (2) In order to determine the weight of the interest in protection of an individual's personality, the situation in which they are photographed and how they are portrayed is also significant, as are the circumstances under which the photo was taken, for instance in secret or as a result of persistent tracking. The impairment of personality rights resulting from the publication of the photos is more severe where the visual portrayal affects the private sphere by disseminating details of the [subject's] private life which are usually beyond the reach of public debate. The same holds true if the affected person, in the circumstances under which the photo was taken, could in general reasonably expect not to be shown in the media, for instance because they are in a private space, especially in a particularly protected space (cf. BVerfGE 101, 361 <384>). The need to protect the general right of personality can, however, take on greater weight even if affected persons are not in a secluded space, with, for instance, media coverage showing the subject relaxing or letting go outside the context of professional or everyday life.

70 [...]

71 dd) It is for the ordinary courts to determine the informative value of coverage with photo illustrations in the specific case on the basis of its relevance to the formation of public opinion, and to balance freedom of the press against the impairments of the right of personality resulting from taking and disseminating the photos. In such decisions that require a balancing, the courts have a margin of assessment. In accordance with these considerations, the case-law of the European Court of Human Rights recognises that domestic courts have an independent margin of appreciation also with regard to the requirements of the European Convention on Human Rights that are relevant to interpreting German fundamental rights (cf.

ECtHR (Grand Chamber), *Dickson v. the United Kingdom*, Judgment of 4 December 2007, no. 44362/04, §§ 77 *et seq.*).

The courts must take into account that the guarantee of freedom of the press serves not only to uphold the subjective rights of the press, but equally protects the process of public opinion-forming and thus individuals' freedom to form opinions (cf. BVerfGE 20, 162 <174 *et seq.*>; 66, 116 <134>; 77, 346 <354>). Statements in or by the press generally seek to contribute to the formation of public opinion; therefore, the initial presumption is that they are permissible, even if they affect the sphere of other persons' rights (cf. BVerfGE 20, 162 <177>). According to the case-law of the European Court of Human Rights, too, there is only little scope for subordinating the guarantee of Art. 10(1) of the Convention [to other interests] if a media report is relevant to a debate in matters of public interest (cf. ECtHR (Grand Chamber), *Lindon and Others v. France*, Judgment of 22 October 2007, no. 21279/02 *inter alia*, § 45; ECtHR (Grand Chamber), *Pedersen and Baadsgaard v. Denmark*, Judgment of 17 December 2004, no. 49017/99, §§ 68 and 69).

Yet the fundamental right in Art. 5(1) of the Basic Law does not prescribe that any visual depiction taken from the private and everyday life of celebrities is generally assumed to contribute to the formation of opinion, and is in itself sufficient to justify its precedence over the interest in protection of one's personality. The Federal Constitutional Court has thus far not recognised that the press may unrestrictedly take photos of figures of contemporary society; rather, it has only considered the publication of photos to be justified to the extent that the general public would otherwise be deprived of opportunities to form opinions, for example, on whether persons who are regarded as idols or role models can convincingly reconcile their official and private conduct (cf. BVerfGE 101, 361 <393>). However, constitutional law does not guarantee that figures of contemporary society may be photographed at any time without restriction for media purposes in all situations except when they are in a secluded space.

3. In interpreting and applying the private law provisions on the balancing of different interests protected by law, it primarily falls to the civil courts to have regard to the fundamental rights laid down in the Basic Law while also taking into account the requirements of the European Convention on Human Rights. […]

The role of the Federal Constitutional Court is limited to reviewing whether the ordinary courts, in interpreting and applying ordinary law provisions, particularly when balancing conflicting legal interests, have sufficiently taken into account the impact of fundamental rights (cf. BVerfGE 101, 361 <388>). The same applies to the review by the Federal Constitutional Court of whether the ordinary courts have fulfilled their duty to integrate the decisions of the European Court of Human Rights into the respective part of the domestic legal order.

76 The fact that different conclusions could be reached in the balancing of legal positions in complex cases of conflicting legal interests, particularly in multipolar ones, is not sufficient to justify a correction of the ordinary courts' decisions by the Federal Constitutional Court. [...] A violation of the Basic Law, which renders a challenged decision objectionable under constitutional law, exists where the scope of protection of a relevant fundamental right was incorrectly or incompletely determined, or where its weight was not accurately established and it was thus not correctly taken into account in the balancing, or where the balancing ran counter to other requirements of constitutional law, in particular where the standards of the Convention, which must also be observed under constitutional law, were not sufficiently taken into account.

IV.

77 The Judgment of the Federal Court of Justice (VI ZR 51/06) challenged in proceedings 1 BvR 1602/07 and 1 BvR 1626/07 satisfies the constitutional requirements. [...] By contrast, the decision of the Regional Court challenged by complainant no. 2 in complaint proceedings 1 BvR 1606/07 and the related judgment delivered upon the appeal on points of law by the Federal Court of Justice (VI ZR 52/06) do not satisfy the constitutional requirements.

78 1. It is not objectionable under constitutional law that the Federal Court of Justice carries out the legal assessment of the requirements of § 22 *et seq.* of the Art Copyright Act on the basis of a concept of protection it developed for this purpose. [...]

79 [...]

80 a) In particular, constitutional law does not prevent the Federal Court of Justice from dispensing with the application of the legal concept of figures of contemporary society that was previously developed by the court with reference to legal scholarship. It was within its powers to instead seek a solution to the case purely in the context of a balancing and weighing of interests [...].

81 Doing away with the concept of figures of contemporary society *'par excellence'* or 'relatively' public figures does not contradict the previous case-law of the Federal Constitutional Court. The Federal Constitutional Court, however, did not object to the use of such a legal concept for the purposes of determining the weight to be attributed to the informative value of celebrity photos for the public, which is important for the balancing to be conducted [...].

82 As the concept of figures of contemporary society is not laid down in constitutional law, the ordinary courts are free under constitutional law not to make use of the term at all in future or to only make limited use of it, and to decide instead by

means of a balancing on a case-by-case basis whether the image concerned belongs to the "domain of contemporary society" (§ 23(1) no. 1 of the Art Copyright Act). [...]

b) The general standards on which the challenged decisions of the Federal Court of Justice are based [...] are not objectionable under constitutional law.

Just as in the proceedings leading to the landmark decision of 15 December 1999 (BVerfGE 101, 361), the present constitutional dispute does not concern the permissibility of the written report as such. [...] In the present case, it must only be decided to what extent [...] articles may be illustrated using photos showing celebrities in their private life.

aa) In its balancing of the interest of the public in obtaining information against the legitimate interests of the portrayed person, the Federal Court of Justice attributes the images to the "domain of contemporary society" – in accordance with the constituent elements of § 23(1) no. 1 of the Art Copyright Act – in a manner that is in principle not objectionable under constitutional law. In doing so, it must be ensured that the right to obtain information guaranteed by Art. 5(1) of the Basic Law is comprehensively taken into account in the context of "images from the domain of contemporary society" (§ 23(1) no. 1 of the Art Copyright Act) (cf. BVerfGE 101, 361 <391>; [...]). The other element which may be affected by fundamental rights is the "legitimate interest" of § 23(2) of the Art Copyright Act, which, from the outset, relates only to figures of contemporary society and thus cannot sufficiently incorporate the interests of freedom of the press if these were not taken into account at the earlier stage where the group of persons concerned was delimited (cf. BVerfGE 101, 361 <391 and 392>).

bb) In the challenged decisions, the Federal Court of Justice noted that a possible basis for assessing informative value is whether a report contributes to a debate of general interest or portrays events of general interest. In doing so, it indicated in the constitutionally required manner that the interest in protecting one's personality may be outweighed by an interest in obtaining information not only in respect of spectacular and unusual events, but also in the context of circumstances typical of the times and of life situations, and that the portrayal of the private and everyday life of celebrities outside the realm of state and political functions does not have to be excluded from this context if it is of public interest.

cc) [...]

2. In accordance with the standards set out above, the constitutional complaints of complainants nos. 1 and 3 in proceedings 1 BvR 1602/07 and 1 BvR 1626/07 are unfounded. In its decision, which was challenged by both parties to the initial proceedings (VI ZR 51/06), the Federal Court of Justice balanced the affected interests in a manner that is unobjectionable under constitutional law and also took

into account the relevant requirements arising from the case-law of the European Court of Human Rights.

90 a) Complainant no. 1's fundamental right under Art. 5(1) of the Basic Law is not violated by the Judgment of the Federal Court of Justice of 6 March 2007 (VI ZR 51/06), in which it found, in accordance with constitutionally tenable standards, that the dissemination of the photo of complainant no. 3 as part of a report on her winter holiday in the 9/03 issue of the magazine *Frau im Spiegel* was impermissible.

91 The Federal Court of Justice took into account the fact that complainant no. 3 had been photographed during an appearance in public and not in a secluded space. [...] It was within its margin of assessment to accord significance to the fact that complainant no. 3 was exposed to photojournalists on a holiday during which she wanted to relax. The Federal Court of Justice, in a manner which is not objectionable under constitutional law, concluded that in respect of the report there was no public interest in obtaining information that went beyond the satisfaction of mere curiosity about the private affairs of complainant no. 3.

92 [...]

93 b) [...]

94 c) The decision of the Federal Court of Justice (VI ZR 51/06) which held that the photo story published in issue no. 9/02 of the magazine *Frau im Spiegel* was not objectionable, and which is challenged in complaint proceedings 1 BvR 1626/07, did not fail to recognise the significance of complainant no. 3's fundamental right to the protection of her personality guaranteed by Art. 2(1) in conjunction with Art. 1(1) of the Basic Law. [...]

95 The Federal Court of Justice did not fail to recognise the constitutional requirements relating to the weight of the informative value of a report needed to justify the publication of an image when it held that the illness of the reigning Prince of Monaco constitutes an event of public interest and that the press should be allowed, in connection with such an event, to also report on the way his children, including complainant no. 3, managed to reconcile their family duties with the legitimate needs of their own private lives, including the desire to go on holiday. [...]

96 The Federal Court of Justice took into account that the interest in protection of one's personality may take precedence [over freedom of the press] in cases where the photo was taken under particularly burdening circumstances, for instance in secret or as a result of persistent tracking by photographers. [...] Complainant no. 3, [however,] [...] did not assert that the photo she objected to had been taken under circumstances which had constituted a burden for her.

97 d) The claim by complainant no. 3 that the Federal Court of Justice disregarded or did not sufficiently take into account the case-law of the European Court of Human

Rights in its decision does not hold. While such a claim – based on the relevant domestic fundamental right – can be brought before the Federal Constitutional Court (cf. BVerfGE 111, 307 <323 *et seq.*, 329 and 330>), it is unfounded in the proceedings at hand.

The Federal Court of Justice took into account both the Judgment of the European Court of Human Rights of 24 June 2004, and another decision of the Court of 16 November 2004 (*Karhuvaara and Iltalehti v. Finland*, no. 53678/00 [...]). In interpreting this case-law, the Federal Court of Justice recognised that there is scope for a differentiated assessment of the photos. There are no indications to suggest that, in its assessment, the Federal Court of Justice breached its obligation to observe the standards of the European Convention on Human Rights. 98

aa) The European Court of Human Rights, too, considers it necessary that a decision concerning the permissibility of the publication of images of persons for the purpose of press reporting must balance the interest in protection of the private sphere against freedom of expression, which essentially corresponds to the protection afforded the press guaranteed in Art. 5(1) of the Basic Law. According to the European Court of Human Rights, the decisive element is to what extent the photo and the other information provided contribute to the formation of public opinion (cf. ECtHR (Second Section), *Gourguenidze v. Georgia*, Judgment of 17 October 2006, no. 71678/01, § 59). The Court distinguishes between politicians and other public figures and the ordinary person in order to set out standards for the balancing. It emphasises that reporting on ordinary persons is subject to greater restrictions than reporting on public figures, with the protection of politicians being weakest. According to this case-law, complainant no. 3 does not belong to the group of politicians, but to the group of public figures. In later decisions, the European Court of Human Rights cited the judgment of 24 June 2004 on the protection of the image of complainant no. 3 as an example of a decision on public figures (cf. ECtHR (Second Section), *Gourguenidze v. Georgia*, Judgment of 17 October 2006, no. 71678/01, § 57; ECtHR (Fourth Section), *Sciacca v. Italy*, Judgment of 11 January 2005, no. 50774/99, §§ 27 *et seq.*). 99

bb) According to the case-law of the European Court of Human Rights, belonging to this group of persons makes it possible for the press to publish photos of the subject where there is a public interest in the report, even if they are taken in the context of public everyday life. According to its case-law, in particular reports facilitating public scrutiny also of the private conduct of influential persons, for instance from the commercial, cultural or media sector, may amount to a report of public interest protected by Art. 10 of the European Convention on Human Rights (cf. ECtHR (First Section), *Tønsbergs Blad and Others v. Norway*, Judgment of 1 March 2007, no. 510/04, §§ 87 and 88; ECtHR (First Section), *Verlagsgruppe* 100

News GmbH v. Austria, Judgment of 14 December 2006, no. 10520/02, § 35 *et seq.*; ECtHR (Fourth Section), *Minelli v. Switzerland*, Judgment of 14 June 2005, no 14991/02). The European Court of Human Rights has objected to decisions by domestic courts that apply a standard that is too strict with regard to the question whether media reporting on the private life of a person that is not part of official or political life is of public interest (cf. ECtHR (First Section), *Tønsbergs Blad and Others v. Norway*, Judgment of 1 March 2007, no. 510/04, § 87). In accordance with this case-law, it is sufficient that the report deal with political or other significant questions at least to some degree (cf. ECtHR (Fourth Section), *Karhuvaara and Iltalehti v. Finland*, Judgment of 16 November 2004, no. 53678/00, § 45).

101 cc) The Federal Court of Justice specifically assessed the informative content of the relevant article and concluded that it dealt with factual topics of relevance for a democratic society. [...] It is not objectionable under constitutional law that the Federal Court of Justice found, in the context of the balancing and weighing of interests incumbent on it, and in taking into account and specifying the case-law of the European Court of Human Rights, that the informative value was sufficient in the present case.

102 3. However, the decisions of the Regional Court and of the Federal Court of Justice challenged by complainant no. 2 violate the fundamental right to freedom of the press under Art. 5(1) second sentence of the Basic Law.

103 a) The proceedings concerned a photo of the plaintiff in the initial proceedings, complainant no. 3, and her husband in the context of a report on their renting out their villa in Kenya. [...] The Federal Court of Justice limits itself to the finding that the article concerning the dwelling and its renting out is not an event of public interest, even if broad standards are applied – here, it cites the decision of the European Court of Human Rights of 24 June 2004 – and does not concern an event of contemporary society [...].

104 The challenged decisions failed to assess the article more closely as regards its informative content. The relevant article did not describe the scene of a holiday as part of private life. Rather, it was reported that complainant no. 3 and her husband rent out a villa on an island in Kenya, which they occasionally use for holidaying, to third parties. This fact was commented with value judgments that could give rise to social criticism on the part of readers. The thrust of the article is summed up in the words that were highlighted in bold print and at the centre of the article: "Even the rich and beautiful are frugal. Many rent their villas out to paying guests." [...]

105 Where readers are thus provided information in an entertainment media report on changing behaviour patterns within a small group of affluent celebrities, who in other contexts are the focus of public attention through their own efforts and consequently serve as role models for a large part of the population or in fact

display a lifestyle others may object to, this may spark a factual debate that is of interest to the general public in a democratic society and it can also generally justify showing an image of the celebrity landlords of the property who are the subject matter of the article.

b) The Federal Court of Justice's blanket statement to the effect that the, in principle, protected core of the private sphere of celebrities – complainant no. 3 included – also encompasses holidays is not conducive to making clear the overriding interests in the protection of the right of personality. Complainant no. 2 used a small photo to illustrate the article which, according to its caption, shows complainant no. 3 and her husband "holidaying" in casual clothing and among other people and portrays them at a location that cannot be identified by readers. [...] The situation shown, being together with other people, does not suggest [...] that complainant no. 3 was photographed in the course of an activity that is particularly typical of relaxation and consequently requires a greater degree of protection from media attention and portrayal. Such greater need for protection is not derived from the holiday as such, but must be derived from and specified by the circumstances of the situation shown. Ordinary courts cannot simply refrain from specifying this need for protection by reason of the margin of appreciation and assessment granted to them in the context of balancing the circumstances of the case; in the interests of a substantive fundamental rights protection, it must be ascertainable from their decisions that they considered the decisive circumstances in their balancing by disclosing the reasons decisive for its outcome. Neither the considerations of the Federal Court of Justice nor those of the Regional Court satisfy these requirements.

c) The prohibition on disseminating the photo, upheld by the Federal Court of Justice, must therefore be reviewed again in light of the constitutional aspects set out above. It cannot be ruled out that a review of the publication of the photo on the basis of these standards in consideration of the accompanying article may lead to a different outcome.

The judgment of the Federal Court of Justice is thus reversed and the matter is remanded to it for a new decision.

[...]

Justices: Papier, Hohmann-Dennhardt, Hoffmann-Riem, Bryde, Gaier, Eichberger, Schluckebier, Kirchhof

No. 21

BVerfGE 63, 131 – Right of Reply

HEADNOTES

to the Order of the First Senate of 8 February 1983
1 BvL 20/81

1. Where a decision in preliminary proceedings before the ordinary courts regarding a right of reply in relation to allegations published in the press or in the broadcasting media will settle the matter in dispute in a definitive manner, the ordinary court can make a judicial referral to the Federal Constitutional Court pursuant to Article 100(1) of the Basic Law.
2. Making a right of reply in broadcasting media subject to the requirement that the request for a reply be made within two weeks of publication of the challenged broadcast is incompatible with the general right of personality guaranteed by Article 2(1) in conjunction with Article 1(1) of the Basic Law.

FEDERAL CONSTITUTIONAL COURT
- 1 BvL 20/81 -

IN THE NAME OF THE PEOPLE

In the proceedings
for constitutional review of

the Hamburg Act on the State Treaty of the *Länder* on the North German Broadcasting Corporation of 1 December 1980, to the extent that it refers to § 12(2) first sentence of the State Treaty of the *Länder*

– Order of Suspension and Referral of the Hamburg Regional Court of 29 July 1981 - 74 O 235-81 -

the Federal Constitutional Court – First Senate –
with the participation of Justices

President Benda,
Böhmer,

No. 21 – Right of Reply

Simon,
Faller,
Hesse,
Katzenstein,
Niemeyer,
Heußner

held on 8 February 1983:

The Hamburg Act on the State Treaty of the *Länder* on the North German Broadcasting Corporation of 1 December 1980 (GVBl HH p. 349), to the extent that it refers to § 12(2) first sentence of the State Treaty of the *Länder* on the North German Broadcasting Corporation (GVBl HH p. 350), is incompatible with Article 2(1) in conjunction with Article 1(1) of the Basic Law, and thus void, insofar as it provides that a right of reply must be requested within two weeks after the challenged programme was broadcast.

REASONS:

A.

The proceedings concern the question whether it is compatible with the Basic Law that a right of reply (*Gegendarstellung*) in relation to radio and TV programmes can only be requested within two weeks after the challenged programme was broadcast.

I.

Until 1980, § 11 of the Hamburg Press Act of 29 January 1965 provided the legal basis for a right of reply on the part of persons affected by a broadcast of the NDR broadcasting corporation [...]. Pursuant to § 11(2) fifth sentence of the Hamburg Press Act, affected persons could demand the publication of a reply if the responsible editor or publisher received the request "without undue delay and within three months of publication".

On 20 August 1980, the Free and Hanseatic City of Hamburg, the *Land* Lower Saxony, and the *Land* Schleswig-Holstein concluded a new State Treaty on the NDR (*Staatsvertrag über den Norddeutschen Rundfunk*) [...]. The NDR State Treaty replaces the previous regime, providing as follows.

4 § 12 Right of Reply

5 (1) (…)
(2) The right of reply must be requested in writing, without undue delay and at the latest within two weeks after the challenged programme was broadcast; the reply must be signed by the person concerned or their legal representative (…)
(3)-(6) (…)

II.

6 1. On 1 June 1981, the news programme *Tagesthemen*, produced by the NDR and broadcast on the ARD television network, included a segment titled "Turks in the City of Bingen". In the segment, it was suggested, *inter alia*, that the Turkish-Islamic Cultural Association headquartered in the German city of Bingen was part of the Turkish Federation in Frankfurt and considered by the Turkish authorities as the foreign arm of the MHP, a criminal terrorist organisation.

7 By letter […] of 12 June 1981, the plaintiff in the initial proceedings, the Registered Federation of the Turkish Democratic Associations of Idealists in Europe, requested a copy of the broadcast transcript from the defendant, the NDR. On 15 June 1981, the plaintiff received the transcript. By letter of 22 June 1981, the plaintiff demanded that the defendant broadcast a reply to the segment in dispute, which the defendant refused.

8 The plaintiff then sought a preliminary injunction from the referring court ordering the defendant to broadcast the reply. It withdrew the application after the court indicated concerns regarding its merits. On 9 July 1981, the plaintiff demanded that the defendant broadcast an amended version of the reply. When this demand was rejected yet again by the defendant, the plaintiff applied for a preliminary injunction the following day ordering the defendant to broadcast the [amended] reply […]. The defendant requested that the application be rejected, on the grounds that the limitation period pursuant to § 12(2) first sentence of the NDR State Treaty had expired and that the reply was manifestly false.

9 2. Even though the Regional Court considered the plaintiff's application to be admissible and well-founded, it found that it could not issue a preliminary injunction due to the statutory limitation period. It suspended the proceedings and referred to the Federal Constitutional Court the question

10 whether § 12(2) first sentence of the State Treaty of the *Länder* on the North German Broadcasting Corporation of 20 August 1980, in conjunction with the Act on the State Treaty of the *Länder* on the North German Broadcasting Corporation of 1 December 1980, is incompatible with the Basic Law, and therefore

No. 21 – Right of Reply

void, to the extent that it provides that the publication of the reply must be requested within two weeks after the challenged programme was broadcast.

[…] 11-15

III.

1. In consultation with the Governments of the *Länder* Lower Saxony and Schleswig Holstein, the Ministry of Justice of the Free and Hanseatic City of Hamburg submitted a statement on behalf of the Hamburg Government, contending that § 12(2) first sentence of the NDR State Treaty was compatible with the Basic Law. […] 16
[…] 17
2. […] 18-21
3. The ARD concurred with this statement. 22
4. […] 23

B.

I.

The referral is admissible. 24
[…] 25-27

II.

The provision referred for review is not compatible with Art. 2(1) in conjunction with Art. 1(1) of the Basic Law. 28

1. In light of the realities of modern mass communication, the right of reply is specifically recognised in media law as a means of protecting individuals from the media intruding into their personal sphere (cf. BGHZ 66, 182 <195> with further references). Anyone whose personal matters are publicly discussed in the media is granted the right to present their own account in the same forum, with the same publicity and before the same audience; it allows them to defend themselves in a timely manner, significantly increasing the effectiveness of their reply. By contrast, other legal remedies for the protection of one's personality under private and criminal law would generally only provide relief once the principal proceedings have been concluded, i.e. at a time when the public has long forgotten about the incident. 29

30 a) While the right of reply is not directly set out in the Constitution itself, recognising such a right serves to protect the right of individuals to determine the portrayal of their person, which is covered by the constitutional guarantee of the general right of personality under Art. 2(1) in conjunction with Art. 1(1) of the Basic Law (cf. BVerfGE 54, 148 <153> – *Eppler*, with further references). Individuals must be able to decide for themselves how they wish to present themselves vis-à-vis third parties or the public, how they wish to define their social image (*sozialer Geltungsanspruch*), and whether and to what extent third parties may determine the portrayal of their person by making it the subject of public discussion (BVerfGE 35, 202 <220> – *Lebach*; 54, 148 <155 *et seq.*> – *Eppler*). Accordingly, individuals affected by a media portrayal of their person must have a legally guaranteed right of reply to counter this portrayal; otherwise, they would be degraded to mere objects of public discussion.

31 The procedure governing the right of reply must be designed in line with objective demands ensuring that this right can be exercised effectively. Just as the right of reply itself serves to safeguard the general right of personality, procedural law plays a significant role in ensuring effective protection of the general right of personality; procedural law, too, must conform to the demands of such protection (cf. BVerfGE 53, 30 <65> with further references, and the dissenting opinion ibid. p. 71 *et seq.*). If procedural law does not fulfil its purpose or if it obstructs the exercise of the right of reply to such an extent that there is a risk of undermining substantive fundamental rights, it is incompatible with the fundamental rights it is meant to protect in the first place. Thus, the procedural provisions governing the right of reply must themselves be measured against the right of personality guaranteed by Art. 2(1) in conjunction with Art. 1(1) of the Basic Law.

32 b) When specifying the right of reply in relation to the broadcasting media, the legislator must take into consideration not just the general right of personality of affected persons, but also the fundamental freedom of broadcasting (Art. 5(1) second sentence of the Basic Law). This freedom guarantees the right to determine the form and content of broadcasting programmes (BVerfGE 35, 202 <223> – *Lebach*; 59, 231 <258>). Regardless of the content of the reply, this freedom is impaired – albeit only marginally – by the fact that the broadcasting media are legally obliged to broadcast a reply. In terms of content, the obligation to publish a reply may indeed run counter to freedom of broadcasting if the reply conflicts with the broadcasting media's duty to provide comprehensive and accurate information, or – as seems possible in the present case – if the reply is broadcast so late that it lacks topicality, i.e. that the link to the originally published information that it now aims to correct is no longer clear to the audience.

No. 21 – Right of Reply

Both the general right of personality and freedom of broadcasting are essential elements of the constitutional order of the Basic Law (BVerfGE 35, 202 <225> – *Lebach*), which is why neither can claim to take general precedence. Thus, in case of conflict, a balance must be struck, where possible, with the principle of proportionality serving as the applicable constitutional standard for weighing the conflicting interests (cf. BVerfGE 44, 353 <373> – *Addiction Counselling Agency*). According to this principle, measures restricting a fundamental right must be suitable and necessary to achieving the purpose pursued, without placing an excessive burden on affected persons, which means the measures must be reasonable (*zumutbar*). 33

2. The provision referred for review violates the principle of proportionality. The referring court assumes correctly that the provision excessively restricts the constitutionally guaranteed right of personality: even when taking into account the protected interests of the broadcasting media, the provision unduly impedes the exercise of the right of reply as a means of effectively protecting the personality rights of individuals affected by a broadcasting programme. 34

a) The legislator is not barred from subjecting a request to publish a reply to a time limit, in keeping with the purpose of the right of reply; this applies all the more since affected persons can still invoke other claims under private law to protect their right of personality. The legislator has considerable latitude in setting such a time limit. It may, for instance, opt for a shorter period than the three months specified in most other comparable provisions concerning a right of reply. However, the time limit set out in § 12(2) first sentence of the NDR State Treaty is so short that it renders the exercise of the right of reply considerably more difficult, if not impossible, in more than just exceptional cases. The time limit starts to run on the date of the broadcast, regardless of whether the affected person listened to or viewed the programme, and regardless of when they learned about it from a third party. If the person concerned neither followed the programme themselves nor learned about it [from other sources] within two weeks, they have virtually no possibility – through no fault of their own – of protecting their personality rights by publishing a reply. Given the number of radio and television programmes available, this is not an unlikely scenario. Even if the person concerned followed the programme themselves – that is, in the best case, which was apparently the assumption on which the *Länder* based the treaty provision in question – there is a risk, not just in individual cases, that the persons concerned will be unable to meet the two-week time limit. In the case of radio and television programmes, a reply that satisfies the strict statutory prerequisites necessarily requires the affected person to first obtain the transcript of the programme. The postal delivery times alone, first for requesting the transcript and then for submitting one's reply, already 35 take up some time. In addition, it will take time for the broadcasting corporation to process the request. The person concerned has no influence over when the broadcaster will send the transcript; the transcript might be sent with some delay, even if just for technical reasons, and it may thus arrive only shortly before the two-week limit expires. In the remaining time, the person concerned must decide on their approach, possibly seek legal advice and draft a reply that does not raise legal objections. Where the contested media publication is complex and broad in scope, more time may be needed to draft a reply that satisfies legal requirements. These aspects may prevent the person concerned from exercising their right of reply, even if they become aware of the programme within the two-week time limit but only so late that they cannot submit a reply to the broadcaster in due time.

36 In light of these consequences, § 12(2) first sentence of the NDR State Treaty does not satisfy the principle of proportionality, specifically the element of necessity. It is not discernible what protected interests of the broadcasting media were capable of establishing the need for such a short limitation period, giving rise to such serious consequences [for the other party]. Notably, the interest in ensuring that replies are published in a timely manner does not require that replies can generally only be requested within two weeks after the programme at issue was broadcast. The interests of the broadcasting media can generally be accommodated by way of the less restrictive requirement that replies be requested without undue delay. Such a requirement is also contained in § 12(2) third sentence of the NDR State Treaty, which provides that the right of reply be exercised without any delay attributable to the person concerned. This allows for the circumstances of the individual case to be taken into account, while ensuring that the reply, at the time it is disseminated, has not lost its relevance. […]

37 b) […]

38 3. The referring court correctly pointed out that the unequivocal wording of the State Treaty does not allow for an interpretation of the provision in conformity with the Basic Law, for instance to the effect that the limitation period could begin not at the actual time of the broadcast, but only at the time when the broadcast comes to the attention of the person concerned (cf. BVerfGE 54, 277 <299>). Since § 12(2) first sentence of the NDR State Treaty is thus incompatible with Art. 2(1) in conjunction with Art. 1(1) of the Basic Law to the extent that it requires that the right of reply be exercised within two weeks after the challenged programme was broadcast, the Hamburg Act on the NDR State Treaty is declared void pursuant to § 82(1) in conjunction with § 78 first sentence of the Federal Constitutional Court Act.

No. 21 – Right of Reply

Justices: Benda, Böhmer, Simon, Faller, Hesse, Katzenstein, Niemeyer, Heußner

No. 22

BVerfGE 114, 339 – Stolpe/Stasi Dispute

HEADNOTE

to the Order of the First Senate of 25 October 2005
1 BvR 1696/98

Where an ambiguous statement of opinion violates another person's right of personality, an action for injunctive relief against any future repetition of the statement is not ruled out just because the statement could also be interpreted in a different manner that would not impair another's personality. The standard in injunctive relief proceedings differs from the standard applicable when courts hold a person liable for past statements, for instance by imposing punishment, damages or an obligation to retract.

FEDERAL CONSTITUTIONAL COURT
- 1 BvR 1696/98 -

IN THE NAME OF THE PEOPLE

In the proceedings
on the constitutional complaint of

Dr. S...,
– authorised representatives: ...
against   the Judgment of the Federal Court of Justice of 16 June 1998
    - VI ZR 205/97 -
the Federal Constitutional Court – First Senate –
with the participation of Justices

    Vice-President Papier,
    Haas,
    Hömig,
    Steiner,

No. 22 – Stolpe/Stasi Dispute

Hohmann-Dennhardt,
Hoffmann-Riem,
Bryde,
Gaier

held on 25 October 2005:

The Judgment of the Federal Court of Justice of 16 June 1998 - VI ZR 205/97 - violates the complainant's fundamental right under Article 2(1) in conjunction with Article 1(1) of the Basic Law. It is reversed and the matter is remanded to the Federal Court of Justice.

[...]

REASONS:

A.

The constitutional complaint concerns claims for injunctive relief against the dissemination of disparaging factual assertions. 1

I.

The complainant had served as chairperson of the executive committee (*Konsisto-* 2 *rialpräsident*) of the Berlin-Brandenburg Protestant Church in the GDR. After German reunification, he became Minister-President of the *Land* Brandenburg. From 1969 to 1989, in his capacity as a church representative, he had maintained contacts with officials at the Ministry of State Security (*Ministerium für Staatssicherheit*). He was listed in the Ministry's internal files as an unofficial collaborator (*inoffizieller Mitarbeiter* – IM) under the code name *IM-Sekretär*.

The defendant in the initial proceedings (hereinafter: the defendant) is a lawyer, no- 3 tary and former deputy chairperson of the CDU parliamentary group in the Berlin state parliament. On 2 April 1996, during a ZDF television broadcast discussing public opinion in the build-up to the referendum on merging the *Länder* Berlin and Brandenburg into one federal state, he made the following comments about the complainant:

> I have a massive problem with the fact that Mr S. – who as we all know served 4 the GDR Ministry of State Security for over 20 years under the code name *IM Sekretär* as an unofficial collaborator – that this man has now been given the chance, in 1999 here in Berlin, to become Berlin's Minister-President, meaning

that he could become *my* Minister-President, that he could be Minister-President over the people of Berlin.

5   The complainant is seeking injunctive relief against the defendant. The assertion that he served the GDR Ministry of State Security for over twenty years is defamatory, he claims. He contends that he never worked as an unofficial collaborator in the service of the Ministry of State Security and that the defendant's assertion – emphasised by the words "fact" and "as we all know" – is capable of disparaging and demeaning him in public opinion.

6   The Regional Court rejected the complainant's action for injunctive relief primarily on the grounds that the statement was covered by the fundamental right to freedom of expression.

7   The Higher Regional Court reversed the Regional Court's judgment and ordered the defendant, on pain of an administrative fine, to refrain from disseminating or repeating the assertion that the complainant had "served the GDR Ministry of State Security for more than 20 years under the code name *IM-Sekretär*". In its reasoning, the court in essence stated that the defendant had made and disseminated a factual assertion disparaging and demeaning the complainant. The court found that, based on normal language usage, the meaning of the challenged statement was that someone, based on an explicit or implicit 'undertaking' (*Verpflichtungserklärung*), had collected or obtained information about third parties at the request of the Ministry of State Security and had passed this information to their 'employers' for them to exploit.

8   The Higher Regional Court further held that pursuant to § 823(2) of the Civil Code and § 186 of the Criminal Code, it would have been incumbent upon the defendant to prove the truthfulness of his assertion, but that he had failed to do so. According to the court, the fact that the complainant had been kept on file by the GDR Ministry of State Security as *IM-Sekretär* was not sufficient proof that he had actually been in the service of the Ministry. It was not known whether there had been any written undertaking, the court found. The file kept on the complainant by the Ministry of State Security had been destroyed. [...]

9   Following the defendant's appeal on points of law (*Revision*), the Federal Court of Justice reversed the Higher Regional Court's judgment (BGHZ 139, 95) and rejected the complainant's initial appeal on points of fact and law (*Berufung*) against the Regional Court's judgment. This decision is now being challenged in the constitutional complaint proceedings. The Federal Court of Justice held that the Higher Regional Court had wrongly granted the injunctive relief sought by the complainant.

It further held that the challenged statement contained factual assertions whose truthfulness could be ascertained by means of evidence. Yet the Higher Regional Court had wrongly interpreted the meaning of the statement in one very specific sense only, without even discussing other possible interpretations. The reference to activities 'serving' the GDR Ministry of State Security did not necessarily mean that the complainant had carried out such activities on the basis of an undertaking that recognised the Ministry as his employer. Rather, that part of the statement in question could also be understood as meaning that the complainant, who was listed as *IM-Sekretär* in the relevant files, had provided services to the Ministry of State Security – without having been obliged to do so on the basis of any undertaking – by intentionally and deliberately providing the Ministry of State Security (for whatever reasons) with information about third parties or specific events in the context of his (undoubtedly close) relations with the Ministry, thereby meeting the latter's expectations. In doing so, one could say that he had indeed acted as an agent in the sense that he knew the information he provided served (i.e. was useful to) the Ministry of State Security. The Federal Court of Justice found that such an interpretation could in any case not be ruled out. It held that where it was possible to attribute different meanings to a statement, and where these different interpretations were not mutually exclusive, the legal assessment had to be based on the interpretation that was more favourable for the party against which injunctive relief is sought and less intrusive for the affected person. In this case that would be the second interpretation.

[…]

II.

The complainant claims a violation of his general right of personality (Art. 2(1) in conjunction with Art. 1(1) of the Basic Law), and of procedural fundamental rights guarantees (Art. 2(1) in conjunction with Art. 20(3) and Art. 103(1) of the Basic Law).

He claims that the Federal Court of Justice's decision violates his general right of personality by assigning to the defendant's assertion a new meaning that has no tenable basis. […]

16-17 […]

III.

18-21 […]

B.

22 The constitutional complaint is admissible and well-founded.

I.

23 The Federal Court of Justice's decision violates the complainant's general right of personality under Art. 2(1) in conjunction with Art. 1(1) of the Basic Law.

24 1. The decision affects the scope of protection of the complainant's general right of personality.

25 a) The general right of personality enshrined in Art 2(1) in conjunction with Art. 1(1) of the Basic Law supplements the freedoms laid down in the Basic Law and protects the personal sphere that is closer to the core of private life (*engere persönliche Lebenssphäre*) as well as its basic conditions (cf. BVerfGE 54, 148 <153> – *Eppler*). The substance of this right has yet to be comprehensively and exhaustively defined. Its recognised protected elements include the right to determine the portrayal of one's person, to social recognition and to personal honour (cf. BVerfGE 54, 148 <153 and 154> – *Eppler*; 99, 185 <193> – *Helnwein/Scientology*). Notably, it guarantees protection against statements which could tarnish a person's reputation, especially their public image. In particular, the general right of personality protects individuals from skewed or distorted portrayals whose significance for the free development of their personality is not entirely negligible (cf. BVerfGE 97, 125 <148 and 149>; 99, 185 <193 and 194> – *Helnwein/Scientology*).

26 b) The constitutional protection of the right of personality under Art. 2(1) in conjunction with Art. 1(1) of the Basic Law mandates that the state protect individuals against risks to this right originating from third parties. When applying provisions of private law that give effect to such protection, the courts must take into account the relevant constitutional standards. Failure to meet these standards not only violates objective constitutional law, but also the individual fundamental rights of affected persons. Therefore, where individuals challenge statements affecting their personality on the grounds that these statements are false, yet the courts find the statements to be permissible, these court decisions affect the general right of personality (cf. BVerfGE 99, 185 <194 and 195> – *Helnwein/Scientology*).

This is the case here. The Federal Court of Justice rejected the complainant's application for injunctive relief regarding the statement that he had served the Ministry of State Security as *IM-Sekretär* for more than twenty years. Given that the statement was capable of damaging the complainant's social and political reputation, the Federal Court of Justice's decision affects his general right of personality.

2. The Federal Court of Justice's decision violates the complainant's general right of personality. The defendant's statement, which adversely affects the complainant, is not covered by the fundamental right to freedom of expression under Art. 5(1) first sentence of the Basic Law.

a) Private law gives effect to the general right of personality by allowing claims for injunctive relief against adverse statements on the basis of § 1004(1) and § 823(2) of the Civil Code in conjunction with § 186 of the Criminal Code. By contrast, § 193 of the Criminal Code primarily gives effect to interests relating to freedom of expression. This provision contains an exemption from liability for defamation where the respective statement seeks to safeguard legitimate interests. This also applies in private law relations, either by directly invoking § 823(2) of the Civil Code or by invoking the general precept underlying it (cf. BVerfGE 99, 185 <195 and 196> – *Helnwein/Scientology*). These provisions recognise that the general right of personality is not guaranteed without reservation. Under Art. 2(1) of the Basic Law, it is limited by the constitutional order, including the rights of others. These rights include freedom of expression under Art. 5(1) first sentence of the Basic Law, which is also not guaranteed without reservation. Pursuant to Art. 5(2) of the Basic Law, it may be limited *inter alia* by the provisions of general laws and by the right to personal honour.

The interpretation and application of private law provisions by the competent [ordinary] courts must be guided by the affected fundamental rights to ensure that the values enshrined therein are upheld when applying the relevant statutory provisions in practice (cf. BVerfGE 7, 198 <205 and 206>; 85, 1 <13>; established case-law). The civil courts apply the general right of personality as a guarantee that is open to interpretation and that thus requires an appropriate balancing of interests in order to determine whether an unlawful violation has occurred (cf. BGHZ 45, 296 <307 and 308>; 50, 133 <143 and 144>; 73, 120 <124 and 125>). This is not objectionable under constitutional law. In cases of the present type, the severity of a statement's adverse impact on an individual's personality must be balanced against the curtailing of freedom of expression that prohibiting the statement would entail. This balancing must give consideration to fundamental rights requirements. When reviewing and deciding cases concerning statements of opinion, certain considerations and rules developed in the case-law for determining which legal interests take precedence must be observed to ensure that the conflicting fundamental rights are safeguarded to the greatest possible extent (cf. BVerfGE 61, 1 <8 *et seq.*>; 85, 1 <14 *et seq.*>; 93, 266 <293 *et seq.*>; 99, 185 <196 *et seq.*> – *Helnwein/Scientology*). The outcome of the balancing can generally not be determined in the abstract, given that the balancing is contingent upon the circumstances of the individual case.

31 b) When assessing whether a statement violates fundamental rights, it is imperative that the statement's meaning be properly determined. In particular, it is necessary to clarify how and to what extent the statement's objective meaning impairs the complainant's right of personality. In interpreting the statement, the courts may not rely on the subjective intention of the person making the statement, nor may they rely on the understanding of the person affected by the statement. Rather, it is necessary to determine how the statement would be understood by a neutral and reasonable audience (cf. BVerfGE 93, 266 <295>; BGHZ 95, 212 <215>; 132, 13 <19>). Far-fetched interpretations must be discarded (cf. BVerfGE 93, 266 <296>). If, based on this standard, the statement's meaning is unambiguous, the court must rely on this meaning in its assessment. However, if a neutral and reasonable audience perceives the statement to be ambiguous, or if a considerable number of persons representing such an audience understand the meaning in different ways, the court must presume the statement to be ambiguous for the purpose of its review.

32 In the case at hand, the Federal Court of Justice found the statement to be ambiguous. In this regard, it based its decision on the standards developed by the Federal Constitutional Court for reviewing criminal and private law sanctions for ambiguous statements of opinion made in the past. In doing so, however, the Federal Court of Justice did not take into account that these standards do not apply accordingly to actions seeking injunctive relief in respect of future statements. The basis of the legal assessment [in the challenged decision] was thus flawed from the outset (see aa below). The balancing carried out on this basis by the Federal Court of Justice also runs counter to constitutional requirements (see bb below).

33 aa) (1) When reviewing sanctions imposed under criminal or private law with regard to ambiguous statements made in the past, the Federal Constitutional Court presumes that, in principle, freedom of expression is violated if the lower court based its decision to find against the person making the statement on an interpretation that leads to a conviction, without having plausibly ruled out other possible interpretations that would not justify the sanction (cf. BVerfGE 82, 43 <52>; 93, 266 <295 *et seq.*>; 94, 1 <9>). According to this case-law, a criminal conviction, or a civil court order for damages or for retraction or correction of the statement, violates Art. 5(1) first sentence of the Basic Law if the wording of the contested statement or its context would also allow a different interpretation, one that does not violate the right of personality (cf. BVerfGE 43, 130 <136>; 93, 266 <296> –

regarding criminal sanctions; BVerfGE 85, 1 <18>; 86, 1 <11 and 12> – regarding private law sanctions). […] The potential chilling effect of state-imposed sanctions in such cases could have major adverse effects on freedom of speech, freedom of information and the free formation of opinion, striking at the heart of freedom of expression (cf. BVerfGE 43, 130 <136>; 54, 129 <136> 94, 1 <9>).

(2) By contrast, when courts decide on injunctive relief regarding future statements, 34 the individual exercise of fundamental rights or the functioning of the opinion-forming process is not in equal need of protection. When balancing freedom of expression against the protection of one's personality in such cases, it must be taken into account that the person making the statement has the possibility to express themselves more clearly in the future. They can therefore clarify the meaning of the statement on which the courts must base their legal assessment of whether the statement violates the right of personality. […] If the statement is a factual assertion, it is decisive whether the person making the statement can prove its truthfulness. If the statement is a value judgment, it is material whether it amounts to calumny (*Schmähung*), profanity (*Formalbeleidigung*) or an attack on human dignity, as this would already be sufficient for a claim to injunctive relief. Where this is not the case, it must be assessed whether the protection of the statement takes precedence over the protection of personality in the context of the necessary balancing (cf. BVerfGE 90, 241 <248 and 249>; 93, 266 <293 and 294>).

If the person making the statement is unwilling to clarify the intended meaning in 35 an unambiguous manner, there is no constitutionally sound reason to exempt them from liability in injunctive relief proceedings merely because the statement lends itself to several possible interpretations, including interpretations which would not (or only to a lesser degree) violate the right of personality. Rather, the balancing [of the interests on the part of the person making the statement] against the right of personality must take into account all possible interpretations that could impair this right, with the exception of far-fetched ones. Nothing prevents the person making the statement from expressing themselves in the future in a manner that is not ambiguous and – if an interpretation that would violate the right of personality does not actually correspond to the intended meaning – from clarifying how they want the statement to be understood. According to the case-law, the person making the statement can avoid an injunctive relief order issued by a civil court if they declare in a serious and sufficiently precise manner that they will not repeat the ambiguous statement that lends itself to an interpretation that would violate the right of personality, or that they will only do so on condition that the statement is adequately clarified […].

Unlike criminal or private law sanctions imposed retroactively with regard to 36 statements that have already been made, these requirements imposed on the person making the statement do not create a chilling effect on the process of free expression and formation of opinion. The right on the part of the person making the statement to determine the meaning of their statement is upheld. At the same time, the right of personality afforded individuals adversely affected by the statement is protected. The person making the statement can continue to pursue the interests advanced by the statement in free self-determination, albeit in a manner that does not violate another individual's right of personality. Where this is not possible, their freedom of expression stands back behind the limits deriving from the protection of personality.

37 (3) The Federal Court of Justice put forward an interpretation that differs from the one undertaken by the complainant and by the Higher Regional Court. It then carried out its legal assessment of whether the statement violated the complainant's personality solely on the basis of this interpretation. Its decision was not therefore guided by the standards applicable in injunctive relief cases.

38 The complainant and the Higher Regional Court interpret the defendant's statement as an assertion that the complainant had worked for the GDR Ministry of State Security based on an explicit or implicit undertaking and that he had passed information about third parties to his 'employers' for them to exploit. While the Federal Court of Justice considers this interpretation to be tenable, it put forward a different interpretation: namely that the statement suggested that the complainant, within the framework of his existing contacts with the Ministry of State Security, had provided a service to the latter by supplying information about third parties or specific events in line with the Ministry's expectations. In doing so, he had acted as an agent in the sense that he knew that this information would serve (i.e. be useful to) the Ministry. The Federal Court of Justice held that such an interpretation of the statement could in any case not be ruled out.

39 Applying the case-law developed by the Federal Constitutional Court for criminal and private law sanctions, the Federal Court of Justice based its decision regarding the claim for injunctive relief on this interpretation. In doing so, it failed to give consideration to the difference between claims for injunctive relief under private law, which pertain to future conduct, and sanctions under criminal or private law for statements made in the past. The court should instead have based its assessment on the interpretation that resulted in the more severe violation of the complainant's right of personality. The constitutional requirements have not been satisfied, since the basis of the legal assessment was flawed from the outset.

40 bb) The flawed basis of the court's assessment negatively impacted the balancing of the affected legal interests to the detriment of the complainant. The balancing itself also fails to fully satisfy the constitutional requirements.

No. 22 – Stolpe/Stasi Dispute

(1) The assertion that the complainant had been in the service of the Minister of State Security as *IM-Sekretär* is – as the Federal Court of Justice correctly found – a severe violation of the complainant's personality. Since this is an assertion of fact, it is possible to prove the truthfulness of the statement.

According to the ordinary courts' case-law, the burden of proof regarding truthfulness is on the person making a factual assertion that could violate another's personality (cf. BGHZ 132, 13 <23>). This is also in line with the legal precept reflected in § 186 of the Criminal Code, which is applied accordingly in private law cases concerning free speech in a manner that is not objectionable under constitutional law. There is generally no justification for disseminating untrue factual assertions (cf. BVerfGE 61, 1 <8>; 94, 1 <8>; 99, 185 <197> – *Helnwein/Scientology*). In principle, where factual assertions are deliberately untrue or proven to be false, freedom of expression stands back behind the right of personality (cf. BVerfGE 85, 1 <17>).

According to the findings of the Higher Regional Court, it is impossible to establish the truthfulness of the statement on the basis of the interpretation that is less favourable for the defendant, which is the interpretation the court's decision was based on. In the view of the Federal Court of Justice, the truthfulness of the statement when interpreted in the version that is more favourable for the defendant has also not been proven. Therefore, the courts had to presume a *non liquet* (inconclusive evidence) for both interpretations.

When reviewing the dissemination of factual assertions in cases where the truthfulness of the statement cannot be conclusively established, the civil courts determine the balance between the requirements of freedom of expression on the one hand and the interests in protecting one's personality on the other by examining whether the person making the statement has satisfied the requirements for justifying a dissemination of unverified factual assertions on the grounds of pursuing legitimate interests (§ 193 of the Criminal Code) (cf. BGH, NJW 1987, pp. 2225-2226 with further references). According to this case-law, at least in cases regarding matters that have a considerable bearing on public concerns, it is not permissible to bar someone from making or disseminating an allegation that might be untrue as long as that person conducted sufficiently diligent research regarding the truthfulness of the statement (cf. BGHZ 132, 13 <23 and 24>).

There are no constitutional objections to establishing such duties of care provided that the ordinary courts determine the scope of these duties in accordance with the constitutional requirements (cf. BVerfGE 99, 185 <198> – *Helnwein/Scientology*). On the one hand, to safeguard freedom of expression, the ordinary courts must ensure that the requirements they set regarding the duty to be truthful do not reduce the willingness to exercise this fundamental right and hence curtail freedom of expression in general (cf. BVerfGE 54, 208 <219 and 220>; 85, 1 <17>). On the other hand, however, they also have to take into account that the duty to be truthful is a manifestation of the duty of protection deriving from the general right of personality (cf. BVerfGE 12, 113 <130>; 99, 185 <198> – *Helnwein/Scientology*). If there is a serious interference with the right of personality, this gives rise to strict requirements regarding compliance with the duty of care (cf. BGHZ 95, 212 <220>; 132, 13 <24>). These requirements are not satisfied if the person making the statement solely bases the assertion on points which are negative for the affected person, doing so in a selective manner and without making this clear to the public, while failing to disclose aspects that could possibly refute the assertion (cf. BVerfGE 12, 113 <130 and 131>; BGHZ 31, 308 <318>).

46 (2) When determining the scope of the defendant's duty to be truthful and his duty of care, the Federal Court of Justice did not satisfy these requirements arising from the general right of personality – not even based on its own less intrusive interpretation of the statement. These requirements are most certainly not met if one takes the interpretation that should have been applied in the present case.

47 [...]

48 The Federal Constitutional Court has recognised that the extended burden of substantiation incumbent upon the person making defamatory statements, which applies in addition to their duty to be truthful and their duty of care, can be satisfied by using uncontested press reports as references (cf. BVerfGE 85, 1 <21 *et seq.*>). However, this presupposes that the referenced press reports are actually capable of supporting the statement in question (cf. BVerfGE 99, 185 <199> – *Helnwein/Scientology*). If the person making the statement is aware that the truthfulness of the assertion disseminated by the press is in doubt, they may not base their own statement on such reports [...]. The duty to be truthful thus goes beyond the obligation to exhaust all possibilities of research available to the person making the statement. If the person making the statement disseminates assertions which their own research was not able to confirm, they must disclose this fact. They may not portray as true what they know to be disputed or doubtful (cf. BVerfGE 12, 113 <130 and 131>; [...]).

49 In the case at hand, the nature of the complainant's activities in connection with the GDR Ministry of State Security [that the statement refers to] was disputed. This holds true even on the basis of the interpretation put forward by the Federal Court of Justice, which would have amounted to a less intrusive interference. Both the official statements published by the authorities and the media reporting on this matter were controversial. The case at hand did not concern the dissemination of a specific factual assertion on the basis of undisputed media reports, but rather a

selective account that endorsed one specific view of the reported facts as the only correct representation when in fact it was contested.

When making a statement that endorses a specific view of known facts, which results in a violation of the right of personality of the person affected by the statement, the person making the statement must make it clear that their view is controversial, and that the underlying facts are not sufficiently clarified, in order to ensure protection of the right of personality. [...] Should the defendant wish to make similar statements in the future, requiring him to disclose that his assertion is not supported by uncontested facts does not excessively stretch the duty to be truthful and is thus not incompatible with the presumption in favour of free speech. 50

II.

[...] 51-52

III.

It cannot be ruled out that the Federal Court of Justice would have reached a different conclusion if it had based its assessment on the interpretation of the statement that more seriously implicated the complainant's person, and had applied the requirements necessary for protecting the complainant's right of personality with regard to the defendant's duty to be truthful. The challenged decision must therefore be reversed and the matter remanded to the Federal Court of Justice (§ 95(2) of the Federal Constitutional Court Act). 53

[...] 54

Justices: Papier, Haas, Hömig, Steiner, Hohmann-Dennhardt, Hoffmann-Riem, Bryde, Gaier

No. 23

BVerfGE 119, 1 – Esra

HEADNOTES

to the Order of the First Senate of 13 June 2007
1 BvR 1783/05

1. In respect of court decisions banning a novel, which constitute particularly serious interferences with freedom of the arts, the Federal Constitutional Court reviews the compatibility of the challenged decisions with the constitutional guarantee of freedom of the arts based on the specific circumstances of the case.
2. Freedom of the arts requires that literary works presented as novels be considered from a specifically artistic perspective. In particular, it gives rise to the presumption that a literary text is fictional.
3. Freedom of the arts includes the right to draw inspiration from real life.
4. The degree to which an author creates an aesthetic reality detached from actual fact and the intensity of a violation of the right of personality are interrelated. The greater the similarity between the artistic portrayal and the original, the more serious the impairment of the right of personality. The more the artistic creation affects dimensions of the right of personality that are afforded special protection, the greater the fictional elements must be in order to rule out violations of the right of personality.

FEDERAL CONSTITUTIONAL COURT
- 1 BvR 1783/05 -

IN THE NAME OF THE PEOPLE

In the proceedings
on the constitutional complaint of

V… GmbH, represented by its directors …,
– authorised representatives: …
against   a)   the Judgment of the Federal Court of Justice of 21 June 2005

- VI ZR 122/04 -,
b) the Final Judgment of the Munich Higher Regional Court of 6 April 2004 - 18 U 4890/03 -,
c) the Final Judgment of the Munich I Regional Court of 15 October 2003 - 9 O 11360/03 -

the Federal Constitutional Court – First Senate –

with the participation of Justices

> Vice-President Papier,
> Steiner,
> Hohmann-Dennhardt,
> Hoffmann-Riem,
> Bryde,
> Gaier,
> Eichberger,
> Schluckebier

held on 13 June 2007:

1. The Judgment of the Federal Court of Justice of 21 June 2005 - VI ZR 122/04 -, the Final Judgment of the Munich Higher Regional Court of 6 April 2004 - 18 U 4890/03 - and the Final Judgment of the Munich I Regional Court of 15 October 2003 - 9 O 11360/03 - violate the complainant's fundamental right under Article 5(3) first sentence of the Basic Law, to the extent that the judgments granted plaintiff no. 2 the right to bar the complainant from publishing or having someone else publish, distributing or having someone else distribute, selling or having someone else sell and advertising or having someone else advertise the novel *Esra* in the version set out in the declaration of undertaking of 18 August 2003, making non-compliance punishable by a fine.

   For the rest, the constitutional complaint is rejected.

2. The Judgment of the Federal Court of Justice of 21 June 2005 - VI ZR 122/04 - is reversed to the extent of the violation of fundamental rights set out in no. 1 of this order. The matter is remanded to the Federal Court of Justice in this respect.

3. [...]

BVerfGE 119, 1

REASONS:

A.

I.

1 The constitutional complaint is directed against judgments of the Munich I Regional Court, the Munich Higher Regional Court and the Federal Court of Justice, which banned the publication, distribution and dissemination of the novel *Esra*, written by B. and published by the complainant, on the grounds that the novel violated the general right of personality of the plaintiffs in the initial proceedings.

2 1. The novel *Esra* was published by the complainant's publishing house in the spring of 2003. It tells the love story of Adam and Esra, an author and an actress. The intimate relationship between the two main characters is set in Munich-Schwabing and is described from the perspective of the first-person narrator Adam over a period of four years. The couple's relationship faces all sorts of obstacles: Esra's family, with her domineering mother in particular, Esra's daughter from her first, failed marriage, the daughter's father, and above all, Esra's own passive, fatalistic personality.

3 Although the author and the complainant argue that the characters of the novel are fictional, both conceded in the initial proceedings that the author was inspired by his intimate relationship with plaintiff no. 1. […]

4-6 […]

7 Plaintiff no. 1 was awarded the 1989 German Film Award. She got married at the age of 17 and has a daughter from this marriage. After the failure of her marriage, plaintiff no. 1 had an intimate relationship with the author for one and a half years. During this time, her daughter fell seriously ill. After her separation from the author, plaintiff no. 1 had a brief relationship with a former schoolmate. She has another child from this relationship, which later also failed. Plaintiff no. 2 is the mother of plaintiff no. 1. She received the 2000 Right Livelihood Award and owns a hotel in Turkey.

8 2. The Esra character is portrayed as a woman lacking independence who obeys her mother's will. In the latest version of the novel, she was awarded the [fictional] 'Fritz Lang Prize' for her acting performance in a film. Her relationship with the first-person narrator is marked by the constant switching between affection and rejection and by the disappointed love of the first-person narrator. It is doomed to fail since Esra is not able to free herself from the clutches of her mother, of her seriously ill daughter Ayla and of her daughter's father. The relationship of the first-person narrator to Esra is depicted in detail and on different levels, breaking up

the chronology with several flashbacks. This includes Esra contemplating having an abortion when she is pregnant with her second child; ultimately, she does not have the abortion, because – as readers can infer from the first-person narrator's thoughts – she wants to have this child to replace her terminally ill daughter. The novel contains several passages portraying sexual acts between Esra and the first-person narrator.

Esra's mother, the Lale character, owns a hotel on the Turkish Aegean coast. In the original version of the novel, she was awarded the Right Livelihood Award for her environmental activism; in the version that was revised following the parties' endeavours to settle and which is challenged here, she was awarded the [fictional] 'Karl Gustav Prize'. There are clear and prominent similarities between Lale's biography and that of plaintiff no. 2 (number of marriages and children, places of residence and action). In the novel, the failure of Adam and Esra's relationship is largely blamed on Lale; the novel paints a distinctly negative picture of her. According to the judgment of the Federal Court of Justice, she is portrayed as a depressed and mentally ill alcoholic who bullies her daughter and family.

II.

1. [...]	10
2. [...]	11-12
3. The Regional Court ordered the complainant to refrain from publishing or having someone else publish, distributing or having someone else distribute, selling or having someone else sell and advertising or having someone else advertise the novel *Esra*, with non-compliance punishable by a fine.	13
[...]	14
The Regional Court found that the plaintiffs were recognisable in the characters in the novel. [...]	15
[...]	16-19
4. The Higher Regional Court dismissed the complainant's appeal on points of fact and law (*Berufung*) against the judgment of the Regional Court. It found that the publication of the novel violated the plaintiffs' general right of personality.	20
[...]	21-26
5. The Federal Court of Justice dismissed the appeal on points of law (*Revision*) against the judgment of the Higher Regional Court.	27

28-35 [...]

B.

I.

36 In its constitutional complaint, the complainant claims *inter alia* that the challenged decisions violate its right under Article 5(3) first sentence of the Basic Law.

37-47 [...]

II.

48 Statements on the constitutional complaint were submitted by the Association of German Publishers and Booksellers (*Börsenverein des Deutschen Buchhandels*), the Association of German Writers in the United Services Union (*Verband deutscher Schriftsteller in der Vereinten Dienstleistungsgewerkschaft*), the German PEN Centre (*PEN-Zentrum Deutschland*) and the plaintiffs in the initial proceedings.

49-56 [...]

C.

57 The constitutional complaint is well-founded in part. The challenged decisions violate the complainant's fundamental right under Art. 5(3) first sentence of the Basic Law to the extent that they grant the injunctive relief sought by plaintiff no. 2.

I.

58 The decisions challenged with the constitutional complaint interfere with the complainant's fundamental right to freedom of the arts under Art. 5(3) first sentence of the Basic Law.

59 1. Notwithstanding the difficulties in conclusively defining the term 'art', which the Federal Constitutional Court has repeatedly emphasised (cf. BVerfGE 30, 173 <188 and 189>; 67, 213 <224 *et seq.*>), the challenged decisions correctly consider the novel *Esra* to be a work of art, namely a free creative composition that artists use to express what they have felt, learned or experienced, by means of a chosen medium – in this case a novel (cf. BVerfGE 30, 173 <188 and 189>; 67, 213 <226>; 75, 369 <377>). Even though the legal dispute that led to the constitutional complaint

mainly concerns the degree to which the author describes real-life persons in his work, it is clear that his aim is to present this reality through art.
[...]

2. Like all fundamental freedoms, freedom of the arts is primarily directed against the state. [...]

At the same time, this fundamental right is an objective decision in favour of freedom of the arts, which must also be taken into account in the relationship between private actors, particularly where individual rights are invoked in order to obtain bans on artistic works through the courts (cf. BVerfGE 30, 173 <187 *et seq.*>; 36, 321 <331>).

3. The guarantee of freedom of the arts equally covers both elements of artistic creation: the 'creative process' (*Werkbereich*) and the 'effect produced' (*Wirkbereich*). Not just artistic activity (the creative process), but also the presentation and dissemination of the work of art are necessary for the work to be perceived, which is also specific to the artistic process. This 'effect produced' is the basis upon which the guarantee under Art. 5(3) first sentence of the Basic Law has mainly taken effect so far (cf. BVerfGE 30, 173 <189>; 36, 321 <331>; 67, 213 <224>; 81, 278 <292>).

4. As a publisher, the complainant is also entitled to invoke this fundamental right.

Art. 5(3) first sentence of the Basic Law comprehensively guarantees freedom of artistic activity. To the extent that publishing media are needed in order to establish a relationship between artists and the public, persons acting as intermediaries between artists and the public are also protected by the guarantee of freedom of the arts (cf. BVerfGE 30, 173 <191>; 36, 321 <331>; 77, 240 <251, 254>; 81, 278 <292>; 82, 1 <6>).

5. Even where parties in a private law dispute involving a conflict between freedom of the arts and the right of personality have different positions that are protected by fundamental rights, this still constitutes a dispute between private actors, and it primarily falls to the civil courts to decide such disputes. In particular, civil courts are tasked with establishing the facts that are significant for finding a violation of the right of personality. However, banning a novel constitutes a particularly serious interference with freedom of the arts. Therefore, the Federal Constitutional Court cannot limit its review to whether the challenged decisions are based on a fundamentally incorrect understanding of the significance of Art. 5(3) first sentence of the Basic Law, and on an incorrect understanding of its scope of protection in particular. Rather, the Federal Constitutional Court must review the compatibility of the challenged decisions with the constitutional guarantee of freedom of the arts on the basis of the specific circumstances of the case (cf. dissenting opinion of Justice Stein, BVerfGE 30, 173 <201 and 202>).

II.

67   The ban of the novel interferes with the complainant's fundamental right to freedom of the arts, which is only partially justified.

68   1. Freedom of the arts is not subject to an express limitation clause. However, this does not mean that freedom of the arts is guaranteed without limitation; rather, it is directly limited by other provisions of the Constitution that protect other significant legal interests in the constitutional order of the Basic Law (cf. BVerfGE 30, 173 <193>; 67, 213 <228>).

69   Especially where, for the sake of protecting artistic self-determination, the term 'art' is broadly defined, and where no attempt is made to use a narrow definition of art to exclude, from the outset, artistic forms of expression that conflict with the rights of others from such constitutional protection (as is the tendency in the decision BVerfG, Order of the Preliminary Examination Committee (*Vorprüfungsausschuss*) of 19 March 1984 - 2 BvR 1/84 -, NJW 1984, p. 1293 <1294>), and where protection not only covers the creative process but also extends to the effect produced, it must be possible for persons whose rights are impaired by artists to defend their rights and obtain effective legal protection, all while freedom of the arts is taken into consideration. In such a situation, the courts are obliged to equally give effect to the fundamental rights of both sides. If private legal action results in an interference with freedom of the arts, this is not an instance of state 'censorship of art', but must be reviewed as to whether such interference equally balances the fundamental rights of the artist on the one hand and those of the person affected by a work of art on the other.

70   In particular, this applies to the right of personality protected by Art. 2(1) in conjunction with Art. 1(1) of the Basic Law (cf. BVerfGE 67, 213 <228>). This right enjoys a particularly high standing in the Federal Constitutional Court's case-law, especially with regard to its human dignity core (cf. BVerfGE 75, 369 <380>; 80, 367 <373 and 374> – *Diary-Like Notes*). The right of personality supplements the freedoms laid down in the Basic Law, and it serves to guarantee the personal sphere that is closer to the core of private life (*engere persönliche Lebenssphäre*) as well as its basic conditions (cf. BVerfGE 54, 148 <153> – *Eppler*; 114, 339 <346> – *Stolpe/Stasi Dispute*). Thus, it may also limit artistic creations.

71   The substance of this right has not yet been defined comprehensively and exhaustively. Its recognised protected elements include the right to determine the portrayal of one's person, to social recognition and to personal honour (cf. BVerfGE 54, 148 <153 and 154> – *Eppler*; 99, 185 <193> – *Helnwein/Scientology*; 114, 339 <346> – *Stolpe/Stasi Dispute*). Notably, it guarantees protection against statements which could tarnish a person's reputation, especially their public image. In particu-

lar, the general right of personality protects individuals from skewed or distorted portrayals whose significance for the free development of their personality is not entirely negligible (cf. BVerfGE 97, 125 <148 and 149>; 99, 185 <193 and 194> – *Helnwein/Scientology*; 114, 339 <346> – *Stolpe/Stasi Dispute*).
[...]

2. The right of personality of the plaintiffs in the initial proceedings is affected.

a) This requires that the plaintiffs be recognisable as the real-life inspiration for the characters in the novel, although this in itself does not yet constitute a violation of their right of personality.

The challenged decisions are based on the finding that the plaintiffs were recognisable as the real-life inspiration for characters Esra and Lale in the novel. This assessment and its underlying findings are not objectionable under constitutional law. In particular, the Federal Court of Justice correctly applied a standard requiring that they be recognisable by a more or less large circle of acquaintances. In its *Mephisto* decision, the Federal Constitutional Court reviewed the standard to be applied by the civil courts, according to which a non-negligible readership would easily recognise that the character Hendrik Höfgen in the novel was inspired by the dead actor Gustaf Gründgens, since Gründgens was a figure of contemporary society and the public's recollection of him was still quite vivid. The Federal Constitutional Court found that this standard was not objectionable under constitutional law (cf. BVerfGE 30, 173 <196>). This was based on the specific circumstances of that case, but does not define a necessary condition for determining the recognisability of characters in a novel that is relevant under constitutional law. Otherwise, the protection of the right of personality vis-à-vis works of art would be limited to celebrities, although it is precisely the recognition of persons by their immediate circle of acquaintances that can be particularly harmful for these persons (cf. on a press law case BVerfGK 3, 319, NJW 2004, p. 3619 <3620>).

However, such recognisability cannot be sufficiently established when the real-life inspiration for a character in a novel can only be proven by way of further clues. Since artists are often inspired by reality, a critic or literary scholar who researches carefully will in many cases be able to identify sources of inspiration for characters in a novel, or be able to name actual events that form the basis of a novel. Freedom of the arts would be far too limited if such a possible identification were sufficient to establish the recognisability of the person serving as real-life inspiration. Rather, the identification must suggest itself at least to readers familiar with the circumstances. This usually requires a large number of identifying features.

In the present case, the courts correctly found that the plaintiffs were recognisable according to this standard. With regard to the original version of the novel, there is no doubt in this respect, given the clear identification of the plaintiffs by way of the prizes awarded to them [...]. The courts also reasonably assumed that the plaintiffs are still identifiable in the latest version of the novel, which is the subject matter of the present proceedings, despite a renaming of the prizes, because the facts are still similar to reality [...] and there are many other recognisable details [...]. Given the combination and accumulation of numerous circumstances, the identification of the plaintiffs suggests itself. In this respect, it is primarily for the ordinary courts to establish the facts from which the recognisability of the affected persons can be deduced

78 b) The plaintiffs are also not affected to such a negligible degree that their right of personality must stand back, from the outset, behind freedom of the arts. Acts and characteristics that are recognisably inspired by the plaintiffs are attributed to the characters in the novel; if readers can link these acts and characteristics to the plaintiffs, this can seriously impair the plaintiffs' right of personality.

79 3. Yet freedom of the arts can, in turn, set limits to the right of personality. This is also the case because the enforcement of the right of personality vis-à-vis freedom of the arts is more likely to set substantive limits to the scope of freedom of the arts than to that of other individual rights asserted in respect of a work of art (cf. regarding property BVerfG, Order of the Preliminary Examination Committee of 19 March 1984 - 2 BvR 1/84 -, NJW 1984, p. 1293). In particular, there is a risk that invoking the right of personality may prevent public criticism and the discussion of topics important for the public and for society (cf. dissenting opinion of Justice Stein, BVerfGE 30, 200 <206 and 207>).

80 Therefore, in order to determine these limits in a specific case, it is not sufficient to establish, in court proceedings, that the right of personality has been impaired, without taking into consideration freedom of the arts. If it is established in a dispute that the exercise of freedom of the arts by a writer impairs the right of personality of third parties, freedom of the arts must be adequately taken into account in decisions on private-law claims to protection based on the general right of personality. Thus, it must be assessed whether the impairment is so serious that freedom of the arts must stand back. In view of the particular weight of freedom of the arts, minor impairment or the mere possibility of serious impairment are not sufficient. Yet where serious impairment of the right of personality is established with certainty, even freedom of the arts cannot justify it (cf. BVerfGE 67, 213 <228>).

81 In this respect, the severity of the impairment of the right of personality depends both on the degree to which the artist allows the reader to link the content of the work to real persons, and on the intensity of the impairment of the right of personality when the reader establishes this link.

82 a) A specific feature of narrative art forms such as novels is that they are often, or even regularly, based on reality, although the artist creates a new aesthetic reality.

This requires applying a specifically artistic perspective for determining whether the novel allows readers to establish a link to reality in each of its elements, in order to assess, on this basis, the severity of the impairment of the general right of personality.

A work of art seeks to create its own 'more real' reality independent of 'actual' reality, in which reality is experienced more consciously on an aesthetic level in a new relationship with the individual. Therefore, artistic creations cannot be measured against real-world standards, but only against specifically artistic and aesthetic standards (cf. dissenting opinion of Justice Stein, BVerfGE 30, 200 <204>). This means that the tension between the right of personality and freedom of the arts cannot be examined only in light of the effects of a work of art in the non-artistic social domain, but that specifically artistic considerations must also be taken into account. Therefore, a decision whether the right of personality is violated can only be made by balancing all the circumstances of the individual case. In this balancing, it must be considered whether and to what extent the artistic presentation of the material and its incorporation into the work of art as an organic whole have made the artistic portrayal independent of the original, by rendering objective, symbolical and figurative what was individualised, personal, and intimate (cf. BVerfGE 30, 173 <195>).

The guarantee of freedom of the arts requires that the reader of a literary work be considered capable of distinguishing literary work from an expression of opinion, and of differentiating between a description of actual facts and a fictional story. Therefore, a literary work presented as a novel should initially be seen as a work of fiction that does not purport to be factual. Without the presumption of a literary text's fictionality, the specific qualities of a novel as a work of art, and thus the standards of freedom of the arts, would be overlooked. At the outset, this presumption also applies where real-life people are recognisable as the originals that inspired the characters in a novel. Since freedom of the arts extends to inspiration drawn from such real persons, there can also be no right to determine the portrayal of one's person, analogous to the right to one's own image, if such a right were interpreted as the right not to serve as inspiration for a character in a novel. However, for this to apply, the publication in question must actually be literature that the reader can recognise as not purporting to be factual. A report falsely labelled as a novel would not enjoy the protection afforded by a specifically artistic perspective.

The more authors detach a character in a novel from its original, making it an independent fictional character ('altering' – *verfremden*; cf. BVerfGE 30, 173 <195>), the more their work will be measured against specifically artistic standards. In this context, fictionalisation does not necessarily mean that all traces of recognisability must be completely removed. Instead, it must be clear to readers that they should not assume the factuality of the text. It is true that a work of art not only has an effect on aesthetic reality but also on real-life facts. However, if due to this 'double effect' one were always obliged, in the context of balancing fundamental rights against one another, to only consider the possible effects on real life, freedom of the arts could never prevail in cases where a novel affects someone's personal sphere. It would be the opposite if one were to consider aesthetic reality alone. In that case, the right of personality could never prevail over freedom of the arts. Thus, this problem can only be solved by way of balancing both fundamental rights in a way that accommodates both.

86 b) In balancing these rights, it is the intensity of the effect on the right of personality that is decisive.

87 The substance of this right has yet to be comprehensively and exhaustively defined. Notwithstanding the great significance of this fundamental right, its individual dimensions carry differing weight as potential limits to freedom of the arts.

88 In its case-law, the Federal Constitutional Court has held that a core of private life is inviolable and subject to absolute protection, given its particular proximity to human dignity (cf. BVerfGE 6, 32 <41>; 6, 389 <433>; 27, 344 <350 and 351> – *Divorce Files*; 32, 373 <378 and 379>; 34, 238 <245> – *Secret Tape Recordings*; 35, 35 <39>; 38, 312 <320>; 54, 143 <146>; 65, 1 <46> – *Census*; 80, 367 <373 and 374> – *Diary-Like Notes*; 89, 69 <82 and 83> – *Mandatory Medical-Psychological Assessment*; 109, 279 <313> – *Surveillance of Private Homes*). The private sphere is afforded a lesser degree of protection than this absolutely protected core (cf. BVerfGE 32, 373 <379 *et seq.*>; 35, 35 <39>; 35, 202 <220 and 221> – *Lebach*; 80, 367 <374 and 375> – *Diary-Like Notes*), which also encompasses expressions of sexuality in particular (cf. BVerfGE 109, 279 <313> – *Surveillance of Private Homes*).

89 The different dimensions of the right of personality ought not to be understood as a schematic order of priority, but they do indicate the intensity of the impairment by the literary work.

90 c) The degree to which an author creates an aesthetic reality detached from actual fact and the intensity of the violation of the right of personality are interrelated. The greater the similarity between the artistic portrayal and the original, the more serious the impairment of the right of personality. The more the artistic presentation affects dimensions of the right of personality that are afforded special protection, the greater the fictional elements must be in order to rule out a violation of this right.

91 4. According to these standards, the courts did not fully satisfy the requirements of freedom of the arts in the present case. They fully granted the relief sought by both

plaintiffs, even though there are clear differences between the two cases with regard to balancing freedom of the arts and the right of personality.

a) In respect of plaintiff no. 2, the challenged decisions do not consistently apply the required specifically artistic perspective; they thus violate the guarantee of freedom of the arts under Art. 5(3) first sentence of the Basic Law.

However, it is not objectionable under constitutional law that the challenged decisions found the novel's Lale character only slightly altered in comparison to plaintiff no. 2, the real-life person on which she was based. In this respect, the courts found that plaintiff no. 2 was recognisable as the source of inspiration for the character in the novel, on the basis of a variety of biographical data, in particular the award of a prize. This finding is not objectionable under constitutional law.

Contrary to their own starting point, according to which a ban on publication requires a serious violation of the right of personality in addition to recognisability, the courts, and in particular the Federal Court of Justice, only held that the novel's Lale character was portrayed in a very negative light and saw this to be a violation of her right of personality. At the same time, they assumed that not everything written about Lale in the novel corresponded to the facts, and criticised the novel precisely for that reason. However, simply because plaintiff no. 2 is recognisable as the source of inspiration for Lale does not mean that the novel invites the reader to ascribe all of Lale's acts and characteristics to plaintiff no. 2.

In this respect, the court decisions do not sufficiently take into account that the novel must initially be regarded as a work of fiction. At the same time, it is not objectionable that the Federal Court of Justice considers that a disclaimer at the beginning or end of the novel stating that similarities with real people are purely coincidental and unintentional is insufficient to inform the assumption that a text is fictional. Instead, such an assumption must be evaluated on the basis of the text itself. If, according to this evaluation, a literary text turns out to be a mere retaliation against or calumny (*Schmähung*) of another person, the right of personality may well prevail.

However, this is not the case with regard to the novel in question. It is true that *Esra* is realistic literature in the sense that the novel is set at real-life locations and has main characters with realistic features. The author most certainly plays with the overlap between fact and fiction. To this extent he intentionally seeks to blur boundaries. Nonetheless, a reasonable reader will be able to recognise that the text is not merely a report-like account of real-life persons and events, but that there is a second level beyond this realism. [...] More precisely, it is raising the question of blame and the emphasis on the difficult relationship between a man and his lover's mother that indicates a second level to the novel.

97 This holds true with regard to the novel's Lale character, because unlike the author's portrayal of Esra, his portrayal of Lale predominantly does not stem from his own experience. Lale's biography is an extensive novel within the novel. In particular those elements of the novel challenged by plaintiff no. 2 are clearly narrative and are told, in part, with a certain detachment as retellings of other people's accounts, rumours and impressions.

98 The findings of the Federal Court of Justice regarding the portrayal of plaintiff no. 2 insufficiently reflect the required specifically artistic perspective: it is stated that plaintiff no. 2 is portrayed "as a depressed and mentally ill alcoholic" who "(appears) to bully her daughter and family, who is domineering and cantankerous, who neglected her children, used her prize money to prop up her bankrupt hotel, stole money from her parents and sent the mafia after them, only fought against gold mining because there was no gold on her own fraudulently acquired property, took out a high fire insurance policy before her hotel burned down, urged her daughter to have an abortion, was cheated on by her first husband and beaten by her second husband, who was also an alcoholic". This summary by the Federal Court of Justice blends statements that might even be permissible as facts in an autobiography or a critical article on the recipient of the Right Livelihood Award with fictional elements and the court's own pointed interpretation. In response to the objection that some of the incriminating passages were true, the Federal Court of Justice states that the complainant did not provide proof for that; yet in doing so, the Court expects the artist to do something that, based on his own understanding of his work, he cannot do because he himself considers the narrative to be fictional. Thus, if this approach were used, a work of art that draws on reality would be afforded less protection than a factual account that has not been proven true.

99 It is indeed characteristic of works of literature drawing on reality that they mix real and fictional accounts. Under these circumstances, the fundamental rights protection of such literature would be flawed if it were sufficient to show that the source of inspiration for the character in the novel was recognisable and that the character had negative traits in order to establish a violation of the right of personality. Such an understanding of the right to determine the portrayal of one's person would not accommodate freedom of the arts. Instead, it would be necessary to at least prove that an author made it possible for the reader to regard certain parts of the account as actual events, and that it was precisely these parts that violated the right of personality because they contained false and defamatory statements or because they had no place in the public domain at all since they affected the core of personality. There is no evidence for this in the challenged decisions. Instead, the decisions fail to recognise that freedom of the arts requires an initial assumption that a text is fictional.

b) By contrast, to the extent that the challenged decisions granted the injunctive relief sought by plaintiff no. 1, they are, ultimately, not constitutionally objectionable. Unlike in the case of plaintiff no. 2, the courts did not only find that plaintiff no. 1 was recognisable. They also established that certain accounts in the novel constituted specific serious violations of her right of personality, and based their decision in part on the violation of her intimate sphere and in part on the mother-daughter relationship in view of the daughter's life-threatening illness. Either aspect justifies the ban.

aa) As the courts correctly found, plaintiff no. 1 is not only recognisable in the novel's Esra character. Her role in the novel also relates to central events which occurred directly between her and the first-person narrator, who is easily recognisable as the author, during their relationship. As the courts correctly found, her intimate relationship with the author, her marriage, her daughter's illness and her new relationship were more or less directly based on reality so that – unlike in the case of plaintiff no. 2 – the novel does not invite the readers to infer that these events should be regarded as fiction, given that the novel is written from the perspective of a first-person narrator presenting his own experiences.

bb) The right of personality of plaintiff no. 1 is affected in a particularly serious manner precisely because of the realistic and detailed account of events stemming from the author's immediate experience. In particular, this concerns the exact account of some of the most intimate details of a woman who is clearly recognisable as an actual intimate partner of the author. This amounts to a violation of her intimate sphere and is thus a violation of a dimension of the right of personality belonging to its human dignity core (cf. BVerfGE 109, 279 <313> – *Surveillance of Private Homes*). In respect of this subject, neither she nor the author can provide evidence of the truth, nor would it be reasonable (*zumutbar*) to ask them to do so. Since the protection of the intimate sphere is of exceptional significance, plaintiff no. 1, who is clearly recognisable as Esra, does not have to bear readers asking themselves the obvious question whether the events reported in the novel really happened. Therefore, when the freedom of the arts of the publishing house that lodged the constitutional complaint is balanced against plaintiff no. 1's right of personality, the latter prevails (cf. also BVerfGE 75, 369 <380>).

cc) In addition, the account of the daughter's life-threatening illness also amounts to a serious violation of the right of personality of plaintiff no. 1. The daughter is also clearly identifiable to her social environment, for example to her classmates. In view of the special protection afforded children and the mother-child relationship (cf. BVerfGE 101, 361 <385 and 386>), the depiction of the illness and its effect on the mother-child relationship, with two clearly identifiable persons, does not belong in the public domain, as the Regional Court correctly found.

104 c) To the extent that the decisions granted the injunctive relief sought by plaintiff no. 1., they reasonably imposed a total ban on the novel. It is not objectionable under constitutional law that the courts, in the operative part of their judgments or in their reasons, did not limit the ban to those parts of the novel which specifically gave rise to the unjustified violation of the right of personality. In this respect, the Federal Court of Justice referred to an older decision (BGH, Judgment of 3 June 1975 - VI ZR 123/74 -, NJW 1975, p. 1882 <1884 and 1885>) and put forward its corresponding view that a total ban is not disproportionate if the challenged parts of the text are significant for the overall design of the work and for understanding its aim, which is also not objectionable under constitutional law. It is not for the courts to delete or modify certain parts of a novel so as to eliminate the violation of the right of personality, given that there are many possible ways to make such changes and the essence of the novel would be altered considerably through such interventions. However, freedom of the arts requires that the identification of the violation of the right of personality be so specific that the author and the publishing house are able to infer how they could remedy the shortcomings. This requirement was met with regard to plaintiff no. 1.

105 The above considerations show that the complainant and the author must be given the opportunity to find a solution that is in line with the Constitution by publishing a version of the novel which does not violate the right of personality of plaintiff no. 1. This could be achieved by making changes that reduce the identifiability of plaintiff no. 1 or by removing parts of the novel that violate her right of personality. Given that the degree to which an author creates an aesthetic reality and the intensity of the violation of the right of personality are interrelated, such changes do not mean that sexual matters become taboo, since the author can still depict intimate relations if they do not invite the reader to infer that such depictions refer to certain persons. Such changes also do not entail a prohibition on the use of biographical material such as in the work [by Goethe] *The Sorrows of Young Werther* (*Die Leiden des jungen Werther*), which is mentioned in one of the dissenting opinions. The author and publisher must accept that, as a consequence of a violation of plaintiff no. 1's right of personality which she was entitled to defend, the legal dispute surrounding the novel has made it harder, at least for the time being, to reduce the identifiability [of the real persons who inspired the characters].

III.

106 No other violations of constitutional law are ascertainable. Contrary to the complainant's view, the challenged decisions violate neither the prohibition of arbitrari-

ness (Art. 3(1) of the Basic Law) nor the right to be heard (Art. 103(1) of the Basic Law).

IV.

With regard to plaintiff no. 2, the challenged decisions are based on the constitutional shortcomings outlined above. It cannot be ruled out that the courts would have decided differently if they had taken into account the constitutional requirements set out above, and in particular the required specifically artistic perspective. The matter is remanded to the Federal Court of Justice pursuant to § 95(2) of the Federal Constitutional Court Act.

V.

[...]
The decision was taken with 5:3 votes.

Justices: Papier, Steiner, Hohmann-Dennhardt, Hoffmann-Riem, Bryde, Gaier, Eichberger, Schluckebier

Dissenting Opinion of Justices Hohmann-Dennhardt and Gaier

We do not agree with the decision of the Senate majority. In the Federal Constitutional Court's *Mephisto* decision (BVerfGE 30, 173 *et seq.*), it was still the civil courts who, in balancing freedom of the arts against the protection of the personality of a person who serves as inspiration for a novel, failed to recognise the necessity of applying a specifically artistic perspective to the novel and instead applied the unsuitable criterion of recognisability to measure the severity of an impairment of the right of personality; this was rightly criticised by Justices Stein and Rupp-v. Brünneck in their dissenting opinions. Now, the majority of this Court has adopted this criterion as their own standard in the case of the novel *Esra*. In doing so, it has restricted freedom of the arts, guaranteed under Art. 5(3) of the Basic Law, in an untenable manner (see I below) Furthermore, this standard is applied differently to the two plaintiffs in the initial proceedings whose right of personality was affected, leading to unacceptable results (see II below). In our opinion, from a specifically artistic perspective, the novel *Esra* does not violate the right of personality of the plaintiffs in the initial proceedings and thus must not be banned (see III below).

I.

111   1. We concur with the majority (which differs from the majority opinion in the *Mephisto* decision in this respect) that in reviewing civil court decisions that ban novels and thus constitute a particularly serious interference with freedom of the arts, the Federal Constitutional Court may not limit itself to the question of whether the challenged decisions are based on a general failure to recognise the significance and scope of protection of Art. 5(3) of the Basic Law. Rather, the Court must assess whether the decisions are compatible with the guarantee of freedom of the arts based on the specific circumstances of the case at hand. We also subscribe to the view that a conflict between the freedom of the arts afforded the author and his publisher on the one hand, and the protection of the right of personality on the other hand can only arise if it is not merely possible to guess the identity of a person serving as inspiration for a character, but if the person is actually recognisable as such; in this context, recognisability can be limited to a more or less large circle of acquaintances. The extent of recognisability is not a matter of whether a person is affected, but to what degree they are affected. Finally, we concur with the majority's considerations to the effect that a novel, even if it is based on reality, elevates this reality to a different aesthetic level, transforms it, further develops it, sets it in other contexts and thereby creates new realities; initially, a novel must thus generally be regarded as a work of fiction that does not purport to be factual. Given that the author used their imagination to create a new reality in the literary work, this work may not be measured against reality to establish whether the artistic portrayal could nevertheless amount to a serious violation of the right of personality. Rather, a specifically artistic standard is required in this respect; the Court also considered such a standard to be decisive for review in its *Mephisto* decision, although it was not applied in that decision after all (cf. BVerfGE 30, 173 <195>).

112   2. The majority rightly refers to this specifically artistic standard, but then ties this standard back to reality again. According to the majority, this standard should not be based on the type of literature, the specific genre of the novel, its forms of presentation or its thematic levels. Instead, authors should only benefit from this standard to the extent that they detach their characters from reality, i.e., alter them. In order to establish that a work of art, which is categorised and accepted as a novel, impairs the right of personality, it is ultimately significant, in the view of the majority, to what degree a person is recognisable therein and which protected

part of the personality of the person concerned is affected. According to this view, the greater the alteration, the higher the degree of art in a work; the greater the recognisability, the greater the impairment; and the more attention a person's intimate sphere receives, the more alteration is required. In our opinion, this leads to erroneous conclusions that do not adequately give effect to freedom of the arts.

It is contradictory to relativise the application of a standard which is itself based precisely on the fact that art transforms real-life facts into new realities by making this application contingent upon the degree to which the work of art is detached from real-life fact, thereby treating the artistically transformed reality as though it were real after all. Such an application of quantitative measures for comparing a novel with reality does not adequately take into account the qualitative dimension of the artistic processing of reality. [...] Art is not merely a subjective view of realities; rather, it takes these and forges own worlds from them, lending expression to the artist's concerns. 113

It is also not obvious how the degree of a person's recognisability in a novel can lead to the conclusion of a serious impairment of their right of personality. The only effect of recognisability is that the possibility of impairment cannot be ruled out. It cannot help distinguish between what is fact and what is fiction in a novel. [...] 114

Finally, in our view, it is not tenable to assume that merely because there are recognisable references to certain persons, their rights of personality have been impaired and to conclude from this that the more a novel affects the core of a person's private life, in particular their intimate and sexual sphere, the more a violation of the right of personality must be ruled out by fictionalising, i.e. altering, the source of inspiration. While it is true that a person's intimate sphere belongs to the core of personality affecting their dignity, and must therefore be protected, it is wrong to conclude solely based on the fact that a novel contains intimate scenes that these scenes tell of the true sex life of the person who inspired one of the characters in the novel involved in the scenes, and that they thus affect the personal sphere, which enjoys absolute protection. There is no basis for this at all, apart from the details that make the source of inspiration recognisable. In addition, the question arises how the author can alter the source so that they can rule out an impairment of fundamental rights. The intention certainly cannot be for the author to change the account so that it no longer reflects potential real-life facts. After all, readers are unable to discern if and how intimate relations occurred in reality, and if and how the author might already have altered them. Nor is the alteration of the details of affected persons helpful as long as these persons are recognisable as inspiration. The only alternative would be to refrain from using characters that are based on reality or not to portray the intimate and sexual sphere in the novel. And yet, the things to be portrayed in the novel are literature. The majority's consideration that 115 an author can still portray intimate relations if they do not invite the reader to think that these refer to a real person does not give rise to a different conclusion. This is because if a person remains recognisable in an intimate situation portrayed in a novel, they are necessarily connected with the situation – regardless of how many identifiable traits this recognition is based on. This also ultimately leaves an author with only two options: either they only portray intimate scenes with unrecognisable persons or they do not write about such scenes at all.

116 This approach limits freedom of the arts in an unacceptable manner given that artists are thus ultimately compelled to treat sexual matters as taboo because art thrives on its references to reality and there is thus always the risk that persons will recognise themselves or be recognisable to others.

117 It is doubtful whether a ban would not have to be imposed on Goethe's novel *The Sorrows of Young Werther* based on the majority's standards – even if the majority denies this. [...] In that novel, both criteria that the majority considers sufficient for establishing a serious violation of the right of personality – clear recognisability of the persons portrayed and scenes that are part of the intimate sphere – are met.

II.

118 In addition, the majority applies these standards, which do not adequately give effect to freedom of the arts, in different ways and uses additional criteria to assess whether the novel *Esra* violates the right of personality of the plaintiffs in the initial proceedings, who recognise themselves in the novel. It makes distinctions based on stylistic devices and uses these to assess the extent to which the author invites the reader to infer that parts of his novel correspond to reality. This approach, too, is unsuitable for distinguishing fact from fiction in a novel and for determining whether a description amounts to a violation of the right of personality so serious that it can no longer be justified by freedom of the arts.

119 1. In the case of plaintiff no. 2, who was the source of inspiration for the novel's Lale character, the majority concludes that the courts violated freedom of the arts by failing to consider the novel from a specifically artistic perspective. The majority holds that the negative portrayal of this character is not sufficient to establish a violation of the right of personality, given that fact and fiction overlap in reality-based literature, so that acts and character traits cannot readily be attributed to plaintiff no. 2. The majority states that the challenged court decisions did not sufficiently consider the fact that the novel is primarily a work of fiction. We fully support this view and the reasons given. The only question that remains is why the majority then fails, in this case, to apply the standard of recognisability developed above, which we consider to be wrong, and which will supposedly reveal the

violation of the right of personality and its extent. After all, plaintiff no. 2 is no less recognisable than plaintiff no. 1. [...]

2. In the case of plaintiff no. 1, however, the majority considers that the portrayal of the character Esra in the novel constitutes a serious violation of her right of personality. Unlike with plaintiff no. 2, there is no reference to a specifically artistic perspective here. Rather, the majority bases this finding, firstly, on the recognisability of plaintiff no. 1; secondly, on the fact that the account concerning Esra was based on the author's direct experience, was realistic and detailed, and precisely for these reasons constituted a particularly serious impairment of plaintiff no. 1's right of personality; and thirdly, on the fact that very intimate details are portrayed, which the plaintiff did not have to bear. Again, the majority makes assumptions regarding the degree of reality of the narration on the basis of the recognisability of the source of inspiration and the narrative style. In doing so, it fails to set out where it obtained the knowledge that the account depicts actual experiences and on what basis it makes this assessment. This may be the subjective impression of the Justices, but it could also be seen in a completely different light, in particular from a specifically artistic perspective, which is not applied here. According to the majority's opinion, the "truthfulness" of the account does not even matter with regard to the intimate scenes and those parts in which plaintiff no. 1's child appears to be recognisable as inspiration. In these instances, the majority invokes a categorical imperative – such depictions must not be tolerated and have no place in the public domain – to find that the right of personality has been violated and uphold the ban of the novel. Yet moral considerations alone, without any indication as to whether what is described occurred in the way described or even occurred at all, whether it is not simply a poetic way of expressing feelings and conflicts, or really is intended to portray plaintiff no. 1 after all, are not a yardstick that may be applied to art if art is to be free, as required by Art. 5(3) of the Basic Law.

3. Furthermore, in overall consideration of the outcome of the majority's decision, it is difficult to understand why in the same novel, with similarly many links to the lives of the plaintiffs, the depiction and portrayal of the characters should be considered fictional in one case and factual in the other. A novel is a complete work that is difficult to dissect into individual parts. Either the work as a whole is a novel and tells a fictional story or it is not a novel at all. Yet the majority does not deny that *Esra* is indeed a novel. Therefore, its content cannot be subject to double standards. Only if there were indications showing that the form of a novel is used to make someone the subject of calumny would a differentiated assessment be necessary. However, this is not the case in regard of *Esra*, particularly when the two characters in the novel are compared. [...]

III.

122 If one proceeds from the premise that literature should, for the sake of freedom of the arts, be reviewed based on a specifically artistic perspective – as the Senate majority actually rightly requires –, it is not sufficient to simply identify the genre of the narrative, even if the genre does give an indication of how the text should be understood. According to the majority's view, too, *Esra* is to be classified as a novel; this implies that the story told in the novel is fiction, even though it relates to real-life people or events. Yet this does not resolve conclusively whether the content of the narrative is novelistic and whether fact and fiction have formed a symbiotic relationship from which an independent story has arisen. However, such an assessment cannot be left to the much cited reader alone, who possesses more or less well-developed literary knowledge and their own view of the novel. [...] Instead, it is necessary to consult literary scholars.

123 Literary scholars unanimously hold that the novel *Esra* is about the relationship of the first-person narrator (whose details correspond to the author's) and the character Esra (who is in some respects based on plaintiff no. 1); yet this relationship is described from the author's own perspective and is not just used as a means of expressing subjective feelings, but also as a framework to address topics in a multifaceted way that are in turn reflected in the characters' utterances and behaviour and which characterise and guide them. For instance, literary scholars point out that even dialogues between Esra and the first-person narrator concern our way of perceiving reality, raising the question whether literature which deals with reality can be misunderstood as representing reality; the author thus provocatively questions himself and his work [...]. In view of the above, literary scholars unanimously conclude that the novel *Esra* neither re-creates experiences nor presents autobiographical material, but that it instead pursues a literary-aesthetic objective and that it is a narrative construction – a novel [...].

124 This not only confirms our understanding of the book, but also leads to the conclusion that in the case of plaintiff no. 1, too, a violation of her right of personality is neither ascertainable nor can it be presumed. [...] If an overall assessment of a novel leads to the conclusion that this art form is being abused, and is merely a sham, a device for insulting, defaming or denigrating certain persons, then it is no longer protected by freedom of the arts (cf. BVerfGE 30, 218 <224>). Neither we nor the literary scholars see any such intention on the part of the author in the *Esra* novel. This would make *Esra* a novel in which real-life fact has dissolved into art. Thus, it is impossible to distinguish between what is fact and what is fiction. We subscribe to Adorno's view: "For everything that artworks contain with regard to form and materials, spirit and subject matter, has emigrated from reality into the

artworks and in them has divested itself of its reality" [...]. The ban of the novel *Esra*, based on a violation of the right of personality of plaintiffs nos. 1 and 2 and imposed by the courts in the challenged decisions, is therefore an unconstitutional interference with the author's and the complainant's freedom of the arts, protected under Art. 5(3) of the Basic Law.

Justices Hohmann-Dennhardt and Gaier

Dissenting Opinion of Justice Hoffmann-Riem

This decision of the Court gives greater consideration to freedom of the arts than its *Mephisto* decision (BVerfGE 30, 173). While the Court held in its *Mephisto* decision that specifically artistic aspects must be taken into account when a legal assessment of the effects of a work of art is made, it did not establish sufficiently far-reaching consequences; in particular, the decision did not apply the now accepted presumption that a literary text is fictional. Furthermore, the Court now makes it clear that it is not sufficient that a person be recognisable in a novel, even if negative character traits are attributed to that person, to establish a violation of their right of personality. According to the Court's view, it must be shown, taking into account the presumption of fictionality, that the author invites the reader to infer that the events described actually happened or that a person actually had the traits attributed to them.

While it must be acknowledged that this constitutes a further development of the protection afforded by Art. 5(3) of the Basic Law, I am not convinced by certain aspects of the legal reasoning set out here (see 1 below) and by the application of the principles to the specific case (see 2 below). Following my questions and criticism, I try to explain why there is a risk that the starting point used by the majority could fail to take account of the special features of works of art and of their protection (see 3 below).

The majority is right to consider the judicial ban of the publication of the novel an interference with freedom of the arts. However, I do not think that the explanations for why this interference is partially justified are convincing under constitutional law. To supplement the dissenting opinion of Justices Hohmann-Dennhardt and Gaier, I would like to add the following:

1. a) The Federal Court of Justice considers it sufficient that a specific person be recognisable as the source of inspiration for a character in a novel for finding that this person's right of personality has been impaired (it uses the term "interfer-

ence"). By contrast, the majority correctly finds that such recognisability initially only indicates that a person is affected. Being affected – as the first step of review – is a necessary, but not a sufficient condition for a possible violation of the right of personality.

129 b) In cases where a person is recognisable, the majority calls for a second step in which it must be established that the degree to which a person is affected must not be so minor that freedom of the arts must prevail over the right of personality from the outset. This indicates a minimum threshold for the impairment of the right of personality: a restriction of freedom of the arts can only be based on impairments of the right of personality that attain a certain degree of severity.

130 c) Since the majority assumes that the minimum threshold has been crossed in the case at hand, they consider the interaction between freedom of the arts and the protection afforded by the right of personality in a third step. They again apply the formula used in the second step, holding that the impairment of the right of personality must be so serious that freedom of the arts cannot prevail. Thus, a more serious impairment than in the second step is obviously meant: its severity must be determined in a balancing against freedom of the arts in the specific case – and is thus, in principle, variable.

131 In this third step, a specifically artistic perspective is required (see C II 3 a above). In particular, its purpose is to determine what is within the realm of fiction. Accordingly, the majority finds that fictionality should be presumed when a literary work is presented as a novel and – even if it uses real-life persons as inspiration – when it is clear that it does not purport to be factual, i.e. if it is not simply a report falsely labelled as a novel. [...] In this context, the presumption of fictionality does not just relate to the persons portrayed, but also to events described, character traits and similar features.

132 d) However, the significance of the work being classified as fictional is partially undone by the majority in a fourth review step (see C II 3 c above). Where the violation of the right of personality is serious – in the case at hand, the descriptions of the intimate and sexual spheres as well as the illness of the child fall into this category (see C II 4 b above) – the presumption of fictionality no longer applies. Instead, the majority adds another requirement: the more extensive the protection afforded the affected dimension of the right of personality, the greater the need for efforts to fictionalise the source of inspiration. [...]

133 2. I certainly do not have any doubt that the right of personality is violated if someone realistically presents the most intimate details of their partner's sexual behaviour to others, let alone to the general public – regardless of whether it is based on direct experience or not. However, in the present case it is doubtful, and the author denies, that he wanted to describe past sexual activities or that he

wrote a report about them. In my opinion, the majority does not give sufficient consideration to this and instead simply upholds the factual findings of the ordinary courts, who for their part did not proceed from a presumption of fictionality.

a) To the extent that Art. 5(3) of the Basic Law requires a presumption of fictionality for the novel as an art form even where a specific source of inspiration is recognisable, and to the extent that it requires that this also apply to specifically described events, behaviour or character traits, it is not understandable why this should not also cover descriptions of the sexual sphere. However, if this presumption of fictionality is ultimately to be disregarded here, this signifies that the specifically artistic perspective is set aside in this respect. To put it differently, descriptions of sexuality will only be protected as art if their fictionality is more strongly substantiated than for other subject matters, and there will be no presumption of fictionality. [...] 134

Yet if the presumption of fictionality to which the required specifically artistic perspective gives rise were also applied here, this presumption would not already be rebutted by the detailed and realistic description of sexual intercourse given that such a description could also occur in a fictional account. The fact that an author [...] writes about the behaviour or character traits of a person from their own experience is not in itself an indication that they claim or that it must be presumed that what is described is a factual report about that person's sexual practices; this applies even if that person is recognisable as the author's intimate partner. [...] It is unfathomable how the author could rule out the possibility of a violation of the right of personality by "fictionalising the source of inspiration", as suggested by the majority. [...] 135

Unlike their approach in respect of the Esra character, the majority applies the presumption of fictionality with regard to the description of Lale and rejects the objection of the Federal Court of Justice that the complainant failed to provide any proof of its truthfulness, holding that expecting the artist to provide proof would mean expecting something from him that, based on his own understanding of his work, he could not do because he himself considers the narrative to be fictional. 136

b) Why this should apply in one case but not in the other is not understandable. [...] 137

c) Apparently, what the Court considers to be decisive is which dimension of the right of personality has been adversely affected. It is not apparent that the assertions made about Lale, including that she was a depressed, mentally ill alcoholic who neglected her children, bullied her family, and had been beaten by her husband, constitute less serious impairments of the right of personality than the portrayal of sexual practices, at least not to such a degree that the distinction would justify giving effect to freedom of the arts through a presumption of fictionality in one case but not in the other. 138

139 3. The difficulties experienced by the majority in giving shape to the specifically artistic perspective and in applying it in such a way that it is integrated into a coherent line of legal reasoning seem to stem from the majority's understanding of what constitutes a description of reality (real-life facts) and what constitutes processing it into art. In this context, the majority appears to assume that there is a distinction or even a conflict between empirical facts and artistic fiction. At the same time, the attempt to overcome the dilemmas arising from difficulties experienced in the balancing of interests by resorting to a presumption of fictionality may help obtain acceptable results in many cases; however, it does not always work, in particular not where the artist does not describe a product of their imagination, but instead artistically processes events that can be observed intersubjectively, as shown by the present case.

140-141 a) […]

142 The special protection afforded freedom of the arts by Art. 5(3) of the Basic Law is a protection of the freedom to construct reality in a "specifically artistic" way. In this respect, there are, however, no general rules or conventions regarding what is art or specifically artistic. Art keeps inventing new ways of constructing reality, challenges the aesthetic standard time and again and defines it variably. Many works of art aim to transcend established boundaries and artists are involved in unbounding and blending old or even newly developed categories.

143 b) Assuming, as even, in principle, the majority does, the necessity of applying a specifically artistic perspective to how artists construct reality in works of art, various phenomena of significance for jurists can be affected. For instance, occurrences which anyone, i.e. also everyday observers, can observe and discuss intersubjectively with other everyday observers may be observed and described in a completely different manner by artists in their field of reference. […]

144 This must be gradually, not principally, distinguished from an artistic presentation that does not at all aim to describe events that can also be observed by other persons or to depict them in a specifically artistic manner according to aesthetic principles, but that instead – as a product of the artist's imagination – is separate from things specifically observed, even if the artist, when processing and describing material, may make use of insights and experiences from previous observations and may create the impression that what is described could relate to an event that could also have been observed by others. This second type of art is meant when fictionality is discussed. […]

145 However, it is undisputed that freedom of the arts extends not only to presentations that are the products of a person's imagination, but also to artistic processing of real-life events that can be observed and communicated intersubjectively. Furthermore, it also extends to intermediate forms, i.e. combinations and blends of artistic

treatments of circumstances that can be observed intersubjectively together with products of the imagination.

c) It is easy to lose sight of this diversity in artistic creativity and the necessity for developing dimensions of protection that take into consideration this diversity if the protection of art is ultimately limited to fictional works and a work of art is assessed on the basis of the presumption that it is either fictional or empirical (real-life facts). In this context, there is a risk that the artist's independence regarding the use of their observations, i.e. the artistic construction of reality, will be lost. This risk cannot be avoided by making the scope of protection of freedom of the arts contingent on the degree of fictionality, as proposed by the majority. Making protection contingent on whether fictional elements prevail may be useful as a legal tool for distinguishing what can be observed intersubjectively from what are products of a person's imagination, but it is not suitable for taking into account the special way of artistically processing an event which can be observed intersubjectively. The artistic processing of such events in a novel – in the language of the majority by developing a "second level" – does not turn them into fiction, but it does turn them into a work of art. Accordingly, a presumption in favour of the arts must also apply in this respect. [...] The majority's understanding of fictionalisation is in any case not so clear as to allow authors to use it as a practical guideline. The majority is of the opinion that "the author could reduce the identifiability" of affected persons – yet the persons apparently still remain identifiable – and remove the parts of the novel that violate the right of personality; but under what circumstances can an "aesthetic reality" (understood as a specifically artistic construction of reality) even violate the right of personality at all?

d) If, despite these objections, the protection of freedom of the arts is made contingent on the degree of fictionality, this would require related evidentiary principles and principles for the rebuttal of presumptions. The majority recognises that the principles of legal proof are unsuitable to the extent that it holds, in the case of the portrayal of Lale, that the author has allowed distinctions to become blurred and played with the overlap between truth (apparently meant in the sense of an event that can be observed intersubjectively) and fiction (apparently meant as additions from the author's imagination); the majority also recognises that the principles of legal proof are unsuitable in its finding that the author could not reasonably be expected to prove something which he regarded as fictional if he did not set out to write a report. It may be added: a work that claims to be fictional cannot violate the right of personality of others.

A classification is more difficult where artists base their description on events that can also be observed by others, but where it is not recognisable to what extent they describe what can be observed and to what extent they make artistic additions imagined through their way of observing and describing or even through adding things they have come up with.

149 The majority did not make any attempt to make this type of distinction with regard to the portrayal of Esra. [...] Therefore, it is difficult to avoid the impression that it is the subject matter – in particular the description of sexual details – that rules out an assessment based on a specifically artistic perspective with regard to such descriptions in the novel in the context of a balancing of interests. The possibility that the author may also have "constructed" a specifically artistic, aesthetic reality in the case of this literary subject matter is quickly dismissed by the majority.

150 The author is not given the benefit of the presumption of fictionality. This presumption would, however, have to be understood in a broader sense to extend it to the constellation relevant here. If the presumption were to be applied, it would be necessary to raise the question (provided there were specific parallels between the events described in the novel and what can be observed intersubjectively) whether the artistic processing of these events had lifted them to the "second level" – which the majority has emphasised is decisive – to an extent that the artist could be said to have constructed a "new reality" following its own aesthetic rules. This question cannot be answered without the expertise of literary scholars.

151 An author can include a disclaimer in the novel making clear that readers should not assume that the story is factual (i.e. intersubjectively provable) (see C II 3 a above). A disclaimer will have its own significance if it corresponds to the content of the novel, i.e. if it does not appear to be false. However, if the disclaimer turns out to be false, i.e. if the author does not fulfil their claim to deal with a subject matter in artistic terms, they are not covered by the protection of freedom of the arts. In this context, it is unfortunate that the majority uses the term "calumny" to express the opposite of a work of art. The term 'calumny' is a technical term in connection with the principles governing Art. 5(1) of the Basic Law, which is related and limited to the legal categorisation of value judgments, and covers cases in which an evaluation has no basis in reality even from the point of view of the critic and is aimed at personal defamation. However, if, as in this case, the issue is whether the account can be categorised as an intersubjectively understandable description of events that have really occurred or as fiction or as a specifically artistic construction of reality, such categories are not suitable or may only serve as loose guidelines.

Justice Hoffman-Riem

No. 24

BVerfGE 80, 367 – Diary-Like Notes

HEADNOTE

to the Order of the Second Senate of 14 September 1989
2 BvR 1062/87

On the admissibility of diary-like notes of the accused as evidence in criminal proceedings.

FEDERAL CONSTITUTIONAL COURT
- 2 BvR 1062/87 -

IN THE NAME OF THE PEOPLE

In the proceedings
on the constitutional complaint of

Mr B...,
– authorised representative: ...
against a) the Judgment of the Federal Court of Justice of 9 July 1987
  - 4 StR 223/87 -
  b) the Judgment of the Dortmund Regional Court of 21 October 1986
  - Ks 9 Js 502/85 / 14 (Schw) B 3/86 -
the Federal Constitutional Court – Second Senate –
with the participation of Justices
  Vice President Mahrenholz,
  Träger,
  Böckenförde,
  Klein,
  Graßhof,
  Kruis,

BVerfGE 80, 367

Franßen,
Kirchhof

held on 14 September 1989:
The constitutional complaint is rejected. [...]

REASONS:

A.

1   The constitutional complaint concerns the question whether diary-like notes of the accused may be used as evidence in criminal proceedings.

I.

2   1. The Regional Court convicted the complainant of murder under specific aggravating circumstances [pursuant to § 211 of the Criminal Code] and sentenced him to life imprisonment, finding him guilty of having killed a woman in August 1985. The complainant had denied the charges; the trial court based the conviction on circumstantial evidence. It held, *inter alia*, that evidentiary indications could be drawn from the complainant's personality profile, as the complainant was found to have experienced strong aggressive resentments against women due to his inability to maintain a long-term relationship. These findings were in part based on the testimony of a court-appointed expert who had discussed certain diary-like notes with the complainant. According to the complainant, he had written the notes upon the recommendation of a psychologist. The notes had been secured by law enforcement authorities while investigating the room occupied by the complainant in his parents' house. The complainant [...] had not discussed the contents of his writings with anyone outside the criminal proceedings. From the numerous documents secured, the court – against the objection of the defence – introduced three notes as evidence at the trial, by way of hearing the testimony of the court-appointed expert [who had examined the notes].

3   In these notes, the complainant had written the following:
4   Note of 27 March 1984
> [...] I do admit that I have a problem. I can't find a woman as a partner for my love life. That kills me. I would understand if there was something wrong with me or my body. But I'm a complete man.

No. 24 – Diary-Like Notes

As it is, I would actually feel sorry for the girls if they were to suffer brutal rape. But I'm not sure how much longer this feeling will last...

Notes of December 1984

I'm at the outpatient clinic because I was about to take the final step (commit The Act). What I'm trying to say is that I would very likely commit a sex crime if I hadn't agreed to therapy. Any extreme situation could trigger me to carry out The Horrible Act.

Because I feel so much tension inside. The last extreme episode happened on Wednesday, 19 December 1984 at 7:00 p.m. I could practically feel how I had to fight, with every fibre of my being, the urge to commit The Act. Duration of the episode: 30 minutes – I don't know if the next episode will also end without harm, I actually don't think so. I think the surroundings prevented it, the car, the motorway.

Had I encountered a woman in a deserted place, The Act would have been triggered, I'm sure.

23 December...

I am thinking again ...

I saw a very beautiful girl, didn't feel my insecurities, would have actually spoken to her. But then there was, again, some other guy. Idiot. Smug guy. Rage, coming close to exploding aggression. I almost did it. I'm high. What I'm writing now doesn't count when I'm sober. I want to explain. I have a serious neurosis. At least that's what I think. It has to do with wanting a relationship with a woman. When I see a couple. Then I think, the next moment they're going to...

[...]

2. [...]

3. Upon the complainant's appeal on points of law (*Revision*), the Federal Court of Justice reversed the sentencing decision, and dismissed the appeal for the rest [...]. [...]

4. In the re-trial, the Regional Court sentenced the complainant to 14 years in prison, and ordered his confinement in a psychiatric hospital. The Federal Court of Justice dismissed the appeal on points of law lodged against this judgment as manifestly unfounded (§ 349(2) of the Code of Criminal Procedure).

II.

The constitutional complaint is directed against the initial judgment of the Regional Court and the first appellate decision of the Federal Court of Justice. [...]

III.

10 The Federal Minister of Justice and the Minister of Justice of the *Land* North Rhine-Westphalia submitted statements on the constitutional complaint.

11-12 [...]

B.

13 The constitutional complaint is unfounded.

I.

14 1. Based on the notion of self-determination, the general right of personality enshrined in Art. 2(1) in conjunction with Art. 1(1) of the Basic Law confers upon the individual the authority to, in principle, decide themselves whether and to what extent to disclose aspects of their personal life (cf. BVerfGE 65, 1 <41 and 42> – *Census*, with further references). However, this right is not guaranteed without limitation. Restrictions may arise from overriding public interests, in particular where an individual communicates with others as a member of the community or influences them by way of behaviour and thereby affects the personal sphere of others or interests of the common good (cf. BVerfGE 35, 35 <39>; 35, 202 <220> – *Lebach*).

15 2. Yet the Federal Constitutional Court does recognise an inviolable part of private life which is beyond the reach of public authority (cf. BVerfGE 6, 32 <41>; 389 <435>; 54, 143 <146>; established case-law). Even weighty public interests cannot justify an interference with this part of private life; its protection is not subject to a balancing of interests under the principle of proportionality (BVerfGE 34, 238 <245> – *Secret Tape Recordings*). This follows, on the one hand, from the guarantee of the essence (*Wesensgehalt*) of fundamental rights (Art. 19(2) of the Basic Law), and results, on the other hand, from the inviolability of human dignity, which protects the core of one's personality.

16 3. Where information or an action affects the personal sphere of another person, it gains social significance and thus becomes a matter that may be subject to legal rules. Nevertheless, even events that unfold through communication with others may still enjoy absolute protection from state interference. Human beings necessarily exist in social contexts, including within the core of their personality. Thus, for determining whether a matter falls within the part of private life that is inviolable or within the part of private life where state interference may be permissible under certain circumstances, it is not sufficient to simply assess whether the matter has

any kind of social significance or bears on social relationships at all; rather, the nature and intensity of this connection are decisive. This question is difficult to determine in the abstract; it can be answered satisfactorily only on a case-by-case basis, taking into account the particularities of each situation (cf. BVerfGE 34, 238 <248> – *Secret Tape Recordings*).

4. In the present case, the Court only has reason to determine the scope of the core of private life in the context of criminal proceedings. In this regard, it must take into account formal as well as substantive aspects.

a) First of all, it is relevant whether the affected person wishes to keep a matter of their personal life secret. Where the affected person themselves does not consider confidentiality to be important, the core of private life is generally not affected. Yet the determination of what constitutes the core of one's personality right cannot be based solely on that person's intention to keep a matter secret.

b) Qualifying a matter as falling within the core of private life furthermore depends on whether it is highly personal in terms of content, and on how and to what extent the matter affects the sphere of others or interests of the common good.

c) Therefore, the Constitution does not require that the use of diaries or comparable private notes as evidence in criminal proceedings be excluded *per se*. The mere fact that information is recorded in a diary does not mean that it is automatically beyond the reach of the state. Rather, the admissibility as evidence in court proceedings depends on the nature of the notes' contents and their significance. If diary-like notes contain information on the planning of criminal acts that are about to be or have already been committed, and are thus directly connected to specific criminal conduct, they do not fall within the inviolable part of private life. This also means that, in the context of criminal prosecution, constitutional law does not necessarily give rise to a procedural obstacle that would preclude an examination of such documents to determine whether they contain information that could be admissible as evidence in court proceedings. However, this is subject to the exercise of utmost restraint, which must be ensured by suitable measures. [...]

5. Where private notes do not partake in the absolute protection of the core of private life, their use as evidence in criminal proceedings still requires justification by an overriding public interest. In view of the notion of justice, the Basic Law attributes high standing to requirements relating to an administration of justice based on rule of law guarantees. The Federal Constitutional Court has repeatedly emphasised the undeniable need for effective law enforcement and the fight against crime; it has also repeatedly stressed the public interest in establishing the truth in criminal proceedings to the greatest extent possible, and has recognised the effective investigation of crimes, especially serious ones, as a fundamental responsibility of society under the rule of law (cf. BVerfGE 77, 65 <76> with further references).

However, the fundamental right to the free development of one's personality is no less important. A fair balance between these tensions can only be found if the protection requirement under Art. 2(1) in conjunction with Art. 1(1) of the Basic Law is used as an ongoing corrective to the interferences that seem necessary for the effective administration of justice. This means that it must be determined in every case which of these two constitutionally significant principles carries greater weight (cf. BVerfGE 34, 238 <249> – *Secret Tape Recordings*). If, based on these standards, the use of the notes as evidence is not excluded from the outset, a further assessment is necessary in the next step. It must then be determined whether, in the specific case, the use as evidence in criminal proceedings is suitable and necessary for investigating the relevant crime, and whether the resulting interference with the private sphere of the affected person is proportionate in relation to the aim pursued. […]

II.

22   Due to a tie in the Justices' vote, the Court cannot find a violation of the Basic Law (§ 15(3) third sentence of the Federal Constitutional Court Act) regarding the use of the complainant's notes as evidence in the criminal proceedings against him.

23   1. According to the view of Justices Träger, Klein, Kruis and Kirchhof, which carries this decision, the complainant's notes were, in principle, admissible as evidence in criminal proceedings. It is not objectionable under constitutional law that the Federal Court of Justice, in light of the criminal charges at issue, found it permissible to use the relevant notes as evidence in order to determine the question of guilt and to make an appropriate sentencing decision.

24   a) The notes do not fall within the inviolable part of private life. The opposing view is already called into question by the fact that the complainant has documented his thoughts in writing. In doing so, he released them from the domain of inner thought, which he alone controls, and exposed them to the risk of access by others […]. In any case, the contents of the notes extend beyond the author's legal sphere and substantially affect interests of the general public. It is true that the notes neither touch upon the specific planning of the crime nor describe the criminal act as such. However, the incidents reflected in the notes are connected to the crime in question in such a manner that they cannot be considered completely beyond the reach of the state.

25   […] [The notes] address matters that, according to the findings of the trial court, explain the events leading up to the crime, the underlying causes and triggers, thereby providing the key to understanding the actual act. The close connection of the notes' contents to the suspicion that the author has committed a very serious

No. 24 – Diary-Like Notes

crime implies that the notes cannot be regarded as belonging to the part of personal life that enjoys absolute protection, which is beyond the reach of the state. In addition, the notes indicate that the complainant's personality traits pose specific dangers to others; on these grounds, too, the notes are not beyond the reach of the state in the context of criminal proceedings.

As was demonstrated in the course of the trial, the notes provided important insights into the complainant's personality for the trial court, allowing the court to make findings that were indispensable for a fair assessment of the charges. The responsibility, deriving from the rule of law, to establish the truth in criminal proceedings to the greatest extent possible (cf. BVerfGE 77, 65 <76> with further references) applies not only to the investigation of the facts of the case; based on the constitutionally guaranteed principle of culpability (*Schuldprinzip*) (cf. BVerfGE 57, 250 <275>), the responsibility to establish the truth extends to all aspects that are relevant for assessing the culpability of the accused under criminal law and for the purposes of sentencing. This follows, most notably, from the constitutional requirement that criminal punishment be commensurate with the offence and the culpability of the offender, which is firmly rooted in the state's duty to respect human dignity (cf. BVerfGE 45, 187 <228 and 229, 259 and 260>). As a general rule, investigations must therefore not be limited to the factual circumstances of the crime on which the charges against the accused are based; in the interest of reaching a fair judgment, the criminal investigation and trial must take into account the personality of the suspect, their prior history and their conduct after committing the offence (cf. § 46(2) of the Criminal Code). Where specific grounds for suspicion indicate a link to criminal conduct, all these circumstances, and the facts necessary to evaluate them, are very closely related to the actual criminal act. The requirement of an administration of justice committed to the rule of law and the notion of justice lends constitutional weight to these aspects; the inviolable part of private life does not protect such information and thus neither excludes it from criminal investigations nor prohibits its use as evidence. The requirement, deriving from the rule of law, that all relevant circumstances be investigated to the greatest possible extent in order to ensure a fair trial serves a public interest; it is therefore generally not at the suspect's disposal. Even where such investigations seek to reveal only exonerating circumstances – regarding the suspect or third parties –, it is not for the suspect to prevent or effectively deny such investigations. Accordingly, the Federal Constitutional Court has held, in its case-law, that constitutional law does not generally prohibit non-negligible interferences with physical integrity against the will of the accused in the event that the measures are necessary, when investigating serious crimes, to establish any special circumstances relating to the

26

suspect's mental and emotional state that may be relevant for determining criminal responsibility (cf. BVerfGE 16, 194 <200 *et seq.*>; 17, 108 <117>).

27 Hence, allowing the use of private notes which contain information of the kind at issue in the present case in criminal investigations does not violate human dignity. This applies at least in cases where the documents in question can provide insight into the causes and context of the offence, thereby ensuring that the investigations – which are an indispensable part of criminal proceedings conducted in accordance with the rule of law – are carried out to the extent necessary to provide the basis for a fair assessment of the crime, as required by the substantive principle of culpability rooted in Art. 1(1) of the Basic Law.

28 b) However, the finding that the notes do not fall within the inviolable part of private life does not mean that the authorities are granted free access. The examination of private notes in the course of a criminal investigation, and their use as evidence, amount to an interference with the general right of personality of the suspect; these measures are therefore only permissible if they satisfy the requirements set out above (see I 5 above).

29 (1) Based on an overall assessment, and the required balancing between the effective administration of justice and the fundamental right deriving from Art. 2(1) and Art. 1(1) of the Basic Law (cf. BVerfGE 34, 238 <249 *et seq.*> – *Secret Tape Recordings*), it is in principle unobjectionable under constitutional law to use private notes as evidence in cases of serious crime in order to determine whether the accused is guilty or to exonerate them if they are wrongfully accused, and to assess the culpability and dangerousness of the accused. In this respect, limitations to the right of personality derive from the protection of the general public and of the victims of the crime the accused is charged with as well as possible future victims, but also from the right of the offender to a fair trial.

30 (2) In the present case, the criminal courts' interference with the complainant's fundamental right to the free development of his personality, which results from the use of the complainant's notes as evidence, satisfies the principle of proportionality given the evidence available in those proceedings. It is not for the Federal Constitutional Court to review the challenged decisions in all detail; rather, it only reviews whether the challenged decisions strike a balance between the special need for protection of intimate personal notes and the interest in prosecuting the murder charges at issue, and whether the assessment criteria applied by the criminal courts are compatible with the Constitution.

31 The Federal Court of Justice assumed that the use of the notes as evidence interferes with the part of the complainant's personality that is protected under Art. 2(1) in conjunction with Art. 1(1) of the Basic Law. It accorded particular weight to this interference due to the intimate nature of the notes, and balanced the

No. 24 – Diary-Like Notes

resulting adverse effects on the personal sphere against the interest in prosecuting the specific crime at issue. The Federal Court of Justice found that the principle of proportionality had not been violated in the present case because the notes substantially contributed to the successful investigation of [aggravated murder charges as] one of the most serious offences under the Criminal Code while also providing relevant information on exonerating circumstances; a violation of constitutional law is not ascertainable in this regard. In addition, the use of the notes as evidence not only served to prosecute the crime at issue, but also seemed to be indispensable for assessing the risk of the complainant committing other criminal acts in the future. This consideration, which is informed by the notion of preventive protection, supports the finding of the appellate court that the confidentiality interest of the individual, which in principle merits protection, must stand back behind overriding public interests (cf. BVerfGE 32, 373 <380 and 381>) in the present case.

2. The other four Justices [opposing the outcome of the decision] hold the view that the complainant's fundamental rights under Art. 2(1) in conjunction with Art. 1(1) of the Basic Law were violated by the challenged decisions. […] They contend that, in the context of the criminal proceedings against the complainant, his private notes do fall within the absolutely protected part of private life. For this reason, the notes should have been excluded from the reach of the state, except for a very preliminary examination to determine the notes' significance for the right of personality. 32

a) The manner in which the records were stored indicates that the complainant intended to keep them secret; in its judgment, the Federal Court of Justice presumed that the intention to keep the notes secret persisted, despite the fact that the complainant had agreed to the securing of the notes by law enforcement and to a discussion of their contents [with a court-appointed expert]. 33

b) The diary-like notes at issue here are, without exception, highly personal in nature. In the notes, the complainant provides an honest account of specific emotional stages he went through, without trying to paint himself in a positive light. In the notes, the complainant also reflects on his own personality profile, as he tries to gain a better understanding of himself through unsparing descriptions of his emotions, seeking to come to terms with the major problems that have caused him distress and, ultimately, to achieve peace of mind. This confrontation with his inner self occurred the way it did, and could only occur the way it did, because it unfolded in the isolation of an inner monologue, i.e. shielded from other people's sight and hearing, and it was supposed to remain there; this inner monologue did not lose its highly personal character simply because it was written down. There can be no doubt that thoughts are free – and that they must remain free from coercion and interference by the state so as not to affect individuals in the core 34 of their personality. It is equally clear that the same level of protection must be afforded to an inner monologue that is written down, giving the inner self a voice and thus gaining a better understanding by way of confronting oneself.

35 By themselves, the notes – which were written seventeen and eight months before the crime was committed – do not as such affect the sphere of others or the community. They merely describe inner perceptions and emotions, and do not contain any information on the specific criminal act the complainant was later charged with. Nor can it be argued that a substantial connection to the sphere of the general public arises on the grounds that the crime committed could only be understood in light of the complainant's personality profile revealed in the notes.

36 Following this line of argumentation would mean that a connection between the notes and interests of the general public – which did not exist from the outset, i.e. was not inherent in the notes as such – would be construed in retrospect and from the outside. If a person, frightened by impulses to commit a crime, addresses this in an intimate inner monologue and if then, after that person failed to overcome these impulses, their inner monologue could be linked to a criminal act and thus be excluded from the absolute protection of the part of private life for the purposes of criminal proceedings, this would grant others access to that person's inner self in a manner that the affected person could neither foresee nor control.

37 If the mere possibility of gaining knowledge on the suspect's personality were considered sufficient grounds for denying absolute protection to such private notes for the purposes of criminal proceedings, the differentiation between the core part [that is inviolable] and the part of one's personality in relation to which a balancing of interests is permissible would be practically eliminated in the context of criminal proceedings. Since, in principle, any insight into the psychological condition of a suspect may provide additional information on their criminal responsibility and on whether they committed the crime or not, this approach would mean that basically any suspicion against the affected person would be enough to eliminate the absolute protection of the core of private life.

38 These considerations also apply in cases where private diary-like notes are intended to be used exclusively as evidence in favour of the affected person. The accused has the unconditional, constitutionally protected right to remain silent when charged with a crime. To the same extent, constitutional law also protects the individual from being confronted in criminal proceedings, against their will, with a matter that touches on their innermost personal domain. This is imperative for protecting the right to self-determination regarding one's inner self, which is conferred upon every individual as part of human dignity. […]

No. 24 – Diary-Like Notes

C.

[…]

Justices: Mahrenholz, Träger, Böckenförde, Klein, Graßhof, Kruis, Franßen, Kirchhof

No. 25

BVerfGE 90, 255 – Monitoring of Correspondence

HEADNOTE

to the Order of the First Senate of 26 April 1994
1 BvR 1689/88

Where a statement made in confidential correspondence is covered by the protection of the private sphere (Article 2(1) in conjunction with Article 1(1) of the Basic Law), it does not lose its confidential nature simply because the correspondence is subject to monitoring by prison officers pursuant to §§ 29(3) and 31 of the Prison Act. By assuming the opposite, and, based thereon, convicting a person on insult charges, courts violate the fundamental right to freedom of expression (Article 5(1) first sentence of the Basic Law).

**FEDERAL CONSTITUTIONAL COURT
- 1 BvR 1689/88 -**

IN THE NAME OF THE PEOPLE

In the proceedings
on the constitutional complaint of

Ms K...,
– authorised representative: ...

against a) the Order of the Supreme Court of Bavaria of 17 November 1988 - RReg. 2 St 253/88 -,

b) the Judgment of the Nuremberg-Fürth Regional Court of 14 April 1988 - 4 Ns 283 Js 4207/88 -,

c) the Order of the Supreme Court of Bavaria of 20 January 1988 - RReg. 2 St 396/87 -,

d) the Judgment of the Ansbach Regional Court of 25 June 1987 - 1 Ns 3 Js 9665/86 -,

No. 25 – Monitoring of Correspondence

e) the Order of the Supreme Court of Bavaria of 29 April 1987 - RReg. 2 St 385/85 -,
f) the Judgment of the Ansbach Regional Court of 26 August 1986 - 2 Ns 3 Js 9665/85 -

the Federal Constitutional Court – First Senate –

with the participation of Justices

President Herzog,
Henschel,
Seidl,
Grimm,
Söllner,
Kühling,
Seibert,
Jaeger

held on 26 April 1994:

The Orders of the Supreme Court of Bavaria of 29 April 1987 - RReg. 2 St 385/85 -, of 20 January 1988 - RReg. 2 St 396/87 - and of 17 November 1988 - RReg. 2 St 253/88 - and the Judgments of the Ansbach Regional Court of 26 August 1986 - 2 Ns 3 Js 9665/85 - and of 25 June 1987 - 1 Ns 3 Js 9665/86 - and the Judgment of the Nuremberg-Fürth Regional Court of 14 April 1988 - 4 Ns 283 Js 4207/88 - violate the complainant's fundamental right under Article 5(1) of the Basic Law in conjunction with the general right of personality (Article 2(1) in conjunction with Article 1(1) of the Basic Law). The decisions are reversed. The matter is remanded to a different criminal division of the Nuremberg-Fürth Regional Court for a new hearing.

[...]

REASONS:

A.

The complainant was convicted of insulting prison officers through a statement she made in a letter to her brother, who is currently serving a prison sentence.

1

BVerfGE 90, 255

I.

2 1. The complainant's [...] brother was imprisoned at the Heilbronn Correctional Facility. He sent her a letter, telling her [...] about events that had occurred at the prison and affected him so severely that, as he implies in the letter, he was considering suicide. The complainant sent him a letter in return, in which she made the following statement:

3 And don't forget that almost all the people you're dealing with are cretins (imbeciles) who are hot to get promoted or who are simply perverts. Just think of concentration camp guards and you'll know what kind of people you are surrounded by. Keep that in mind, and hopefully you can maintain your normal life-affirming attitude and cheerful nature.

4 At that time, her brother was being transported from the Heilbronn Correctional Facility to the Ansbach Correctional Facility. In Ansbach, the prison administration confiscated the complainant's letter and filed a criminal complaint against her for insult because of the remarks she had made in the letter about the prison officers at the Heilbronn Correctional Facility. The Heilbronn Correctional Facility also filed a criminal complaint after obtaining knowledge of the letter.

5 2. The Ansbach Local Court convicted the complainant of insult and sentenced her to pay a fine.

6-11 [...]

12 [Following various appeal proceedings with different outcomes,] the Supreme Court of Bavaria rejected the complainant's final appeal on points of law (*Revision*) as manifestly unfounded.

II.

13 The constitutional complaint is directed against the final appellate decision and the previous decisions of the Regional Courts and the Supreme Court of Bavaria. The complainant claims violations of Art. 2(1), Art. 3(1), Art. 5(1), Art. 6(1), Art. 10(1) and Art. 14(1) of the Basic Law.

[...]

III.

[...]

B.

The constitutional complaint is well-founded.

I.

The challenged decisions violate the complainant's fundamental right to freedom of expression (Art. 5(1) first sentence of the Basic Law) in conjunction with the general right of personality (Art. 2(1) in conjunction with Art. 1(1) of the Basic Law).

1. The complainant was punished for a statement she made. The constitutional standards applicable to the legal assessment of such statements, and the permissibility of restrictions, derive from the fundamental right to freedom of expression. However, as this case concerns a statement made within the private sphere protected by Art. 2(1) in conjunction with Art. 1(1) of the Basic Law, this fundamental right [the free development of one's personality] also comes into play.

2. As a value judgment, the complainant's statement is protected under freedom of expression, irrespective of whether the statement is considered reasonable or unfounded (cf. BVerfGE 61, 1 <7>; 85, 1 <15>; established case-law). However, freedom of expression is subject to the limitations set out in law for the protection of personal honour. One of these limitations is laid down in § 185 of the Criminal Code, on which the conviction of the complainant is based. When interpreting and applying this provision, however, the significance and scope of Art. 5(1) first sentence of the Basic Law must be taken into account (cf. BVerfGE 7, 198 <208>; established case-law). The application of ordinary law requires a case-by-case balancing of the restricted fundamental right against the legal interest which the law restricting that fundamental right serves to protect. In that respect – at least where serious and baseless insults in the private domain are concerned – the protection of honour generally takes precedence over freedom of expression (cf. BVerfGE 54, 129 <137>).

3. However, this rule for balancing interests is not absolute. It is subject to the implicit condition that the offensive statement be directed at the affected individual or at third parties, and would unfold its disparaging effect in those relationships.

This is not the case where the statement is made within a sphere that is specifically shielded so as to prevent the affected person or third parties from obtaining knowledge thereof.

21. The general right of personality gives rise to such a protected sphere. Art. 2(1) of the Basic Law guarantees the free development of one's personality. The development of one's personality requires that individuals have a domain in which they are left alone and remain unobserved, and in which they can interact with persons they trust without having to consider social expectations regarding their conduct and without having to fear state sanctions. Given the significance attached to the possibility of refuge for the development of one's personality, it follows that the protection afforded by Art. 2(1) in conjunction with Art. 1(1) of the Basic Law encompasses the protection of one's private sphere (cf. BVerfGE 27, 1 <6> – *Microcensus*; established case-law).

22. The protection of the private sphere extends to confidential communication. Especially where statements are made vis-à-vis family members and confidants, the emphasis is often less on the expression of one's opinion with the aim to influence the opinion of others, and more on the development of one's own personality. Only in situations of particular confidentiality is it possible for individuals to express emotions without reserve, to reveal secret wishes or fears, to frankly state their opinion about certain matters and people, or to unburden themselves in their self-presentation. In such circumstances, individuals may be prompted to make statements which, either in terms of content or form, they would not make vis-à-vis outsiders or the public. Yet as an expression of and prerequisite for the development of one's personality, such statements enjoy protection under the general right of personality.

23. At the same time, confidential communication [meriting protection] is not limited to statements that aim to foster personal development. Statements made in the private sphere or to very close family members do not only serve the purpose of expressing one's own honest sentiments, or of finding relief by expressing one's discontent. Rather, statements made in that sphere may also be directed at family members or other confidants in order to help them through a personal or existential crisis, contributing to their mental and emotional balance or aiding their integration into society (cf. BVerfGE 57, 170 <178>). In such circumstances, too, individuals may be prompted to make statements or choose forms of expression that they would avoid under normal circumstances, but which nonetheless merit fundamental rights protection under Art. 2(1) in conjunction with Art. 1(1) of the Basic Law.

24. This is reflected in the case-law of the criminal courts and in legal scholarship through the recognition of a [protected] sphere in which defamatory statements about absent third parties made in the context of close personal relationships do not

constitute insults under criminal law if the statement is an expression of a special relationship of trust and if there is no reasonable possibility that it will be shared with others [...].

Contrary to the view of the criminal courts that dealt with the case at issue, however, the protection afforded within the confidential sphere is not lost simply because the state gains knowledge of statements made in confidence. This also applies to the monitoring of prisoners' correspondence pursuant to §§ 29(3) and 31 of the Prison Act. Such monitoring is, in principle, permissible under constitutional law to protect other significant legal interests. It serves to avoid endangering the objective of prison sentences and prison security and order, as well as to prevent the covering up of criminal acts already committed and the commission of new ones. It is also inevitable that in the course of monitoring correspondence, prison officers obtain knowledge of the entire contents of the monitored correspondence. Even where prison officers thus obtain knowledge of a statement, however, that statement still belongs to the private sphere that is protected by fundamental rights. By granting monitoring powers to authorities, the state may lawfully intrude on that sphere; however, by doing so it cannot redefine the private sphere as a public sphere. Rather, the fundamental rights protection afforded to that sphere requires that the confidential nature of the communication be upheld despite monitoring by the state. A statement is not stripped of its confidential nature merely because the person making the statement knows that the correspondence is being monitored (cf. BVerfGE 35, 35 <40>).

A different conclusion is only merited if the persons making such statements themselves set aside confidentiality; in this case, the possibility of third parties gaining knowledge of their statements is actually attributable to these persons, and does not result from state interference. This may, for example, be the case if the person making the statement disregards necessary precautions to shield the statement from third parties, or chooses transmission channels that are subject to monitoring even though they could easily have made contact using other channels. This applies all the more in case a statement is communicated to trusted persons for the sole purpose of hurting the person monitoring the correspondence or using the contacted person to hurt third parties. However, such an assumption requires the establishment of factual circumstances supporting it.

These standards apply irrespective of whether the statements at issue constitute incoming or outgoing prison communication. Likewise, it is irrelevant whether it is the person making the statement or the recipient who is serving a prison sentence or being held in remand detention. Finally, the group of potential confidants is not limited to spouses (BVerfGE 35, 35; 42, 234) or parents (BVerfGE 57, 170). The arguments set out in the latter decision (BVerfGE 57, 170 <178>) particularly show that, in light of its purpose, the protection of one's personality requires that this group be extended to other relationships of trust that are of similar quality.

28 4. Based on these standards, the challenged decisions do not stand up to constitutional review.

29 It is not objectionable under constitutional law that the criminal courts found the complainant's letter to constitute serious insult, lacking any factual basis, of the prison officers at the Heilbronn Correctional Facility. At the same time, the criminal courts based the complainant's conviction on the assumption that the monitoring of correspondence by the state sets aside a statement's confidential nature, finding that the person making the statement had to expect that their statement would become known to third parties due to the monitoring measures. This assumption, however, is incompatible with the protection of the private sphere under Art. 2(1) in conjunction with Art. 1(1) of the Basic Law, which supplements the protection afforded by freedom of expression. The criminal courts did not establish that the confidential nature of the statement was set aside by the complainant herself, rather than by the state's monitoring of correspondence. Nor do the established facts of the case support such an assumption.

II.

30 [...]

Justices: Herzog, Henschel, Seidl, Grimm, Söllner, Kühling, Seibert, Jaeger

No. 26

BVerfGE 109, 279 – Surveillance of Private Homes

HEADNOTES

to the Judgment of the First Senate of 3 March 2004
1 BvR 2378/98, 1 BvR 1084/99

1. Article 13(3) of the Basic Law in the version of the Act Amending the Basic Law (Article 13) of 26 March 1998 (BGBl I, p. 610) is compatible with Article 79(3) of the Basic Law.
2. With the guarantee of inviolable human dignity, Article 1(1) of the Basic Law recognises a core of private life, which enjoys absolute protection. Acoustic surveillance of private homes carried out for law enforcement purposes (Article 13(3) of the Basic Law) must not interfere with this core. This protection is not subject to a balancing of the right to the inviolability of the home (Article 13(1) in conjunction with Article 1(1) of the Basic Law) against law enforcement interests based on the principle of proportionality.
3. Not every instance of acoustic surveillance of private homes violates the human dignity dimension of Article 13(1) of the Basic Law.
4. Statutory authorisations to carry out surveillance of private homes must include safeguards to protect the inviolability of human dignity and must satisfy the prerequisites of Article 13(3) of the Basic Law as well as other constitutional requirements.
5. Where acoustic surveillance of private homes based on such a statutory authorisation nevertheless results in the collection of information that relates to the absolutely protected core of private life, it must be discontinued and any records must be deleted; any use of such information is impermissible.
6. The provisions of the Code of Criminal Procedure governing measures of acoustic surveillance of private homes for law enforcement purposes do not fully satisfy the constitutional requirements relating to the protection of human dignity (Article 1(1) of the Basic Law), the principle of proportionality following from the principle of the rule of law, effective legal protection (Arti-

cle 19(4) of the Basic Law) and the right to be heard (Article 103(1) of the Basic Law).

FEDERAL CONSTITUTIONAL COURT
- 1 BvR 2378/98 -
- 1 BvR 1084/99 -

IN THE NAME OF THE PEOPLE

In the proceedings
on the constitutional complaints of

1. a) Dr. N...,
   who died on 5 May 2001,
   continued by his heiress Ms N...,
   – authorised representative: ...
   b) Mr S...,
   – authorised representative: ...
   against Art. 13(3) to (6) of the Basic Law in the version of Art. 1 no. 1 of the Act Amending the Basic Law (Article 13) of 26 March 1998 (BGBl I, p. 610) and Art. 2 no. 2 lit. a and no. 5 of the Fight Against Organised Crime Act of 4 May 1998 (BGBl I, p. 845)

- 1 BvR 2378/98 -,

2. a) Dr. H...,
   b) Ms L...,
   c) Mr B...,
   d) Ms H...,
   e) Mr H...,

– authorised representative of complainants nos. 2b to e: ...

against a) directly
   the Fight Against Organised Crime Act of 4 May 1998 (BGBl I, p. 845),
   b) indirectly
   the Act Amending the Basic Law (Article 13) of 26 March 1998 (BGBl I, p. 610)

- 1 BvR 1084/99 -

the Federal Constitutional Court – First Senate –

No. 26 – Surveillance of Private Homes

with the participation of Justices
>President Papier,
>Jaeger,
>Haas,
>Hömig,
>Steiner,
>Hohmann-Dennhardt,
>Hoffmann-Riem,
>Bryde

held on the basis of the oral hearing of 1 July 2003:

JUDGMENT

1. The constitutional complaint of complainant no. 1a is rendered moot by his death.
2. The following provisions of the Code of Criminal Procedure in the version of the Fight Against Organised Crime Act of 4 May 1998 (BGBl I, p. 845), and in the version of later amending acts, are incompatible [with the following provisions of the Basic Law] as set out in the reasons attached to this judgment:

    - § 100c(1) no. 3, § 100d(3), § 100d(5) second sentence and § 100f(1) of the Code of Criminal Procedure are incompatible with Article 13(1), Article 2(1) and Article 1(1) of the Basic Law,

    - § 101(1) first and second sentence of the Code of Criminal Procedure is incompatible with Article 19(4) of the Basic Law,

    - § 101(1) third sentence of the Code of Criminal Procedure is incompatible with Article 103(1) of the Basic Law, and

    - § 100d(4) third sentence in conjunction with § 100b(6) of the Code of Criminal Procedure is incompatible with Article 19(4) of the Basic Law.

3. For the rest, the constitutional complaints of complainants nos. 1b and 2 are rejected.
4. [...]

BVerfGE 109, 279

REASONS:

A.

1   The constitutional complaints directly challenge Art. 13(3) to (6) of the Basic Law and provisions of the Code of Criminal Procedure that authorise acoustic surveillance of private homes for law enforcement purposes.

I.

2   1. The introduction of acoustic surveillance of private homes for law enforcement purposes was preceded by a longstanding controversy in the public; the measures were referred to as *Großer Lauschangriff* ("major eavesdropping").

3-4 [...]

5   2. In October 1997, the *Bundestag* parliamentary groups CDU/CSU, SPD and FDP jointly introduced draft legislation that ultimately resulted in the amendment of the Basic Law and in the introduction of [acoustic surveillance] powers in the Code of Criminal Procedure. [...] Sections (3) to (6) were inserted into Art. 13 of the Basic Law, while former section (3) became section (7).

6   a) Art. 13(3) of the Basic Law now allows for the acoustic surveillance of private homes for law enforcement purposes. Only a home in which the suspect is presumably present may be placed under surveillance. Furthermore, it is required that specific facts give rise to the suspicion of a particularly serious crime – that must be specifically defined by a law – and that alternative methods of investigating the matter would be disproportionately difficult or futile. The Constitution also sets out the requirement that the surveillance measures be limited to a specific time period. The surveillance measures require a warrant issued by a panel composed of three judges. The warrant may only be issued by an individual judge in cases of danger requiring immediate action (*Gefahr im Verzug*).

7-9 [...]

10 b) On the basis of the amended Art. 13(3) of the Basic Law, the Fight Against Organised Crime Act of 4 May 1998 (BGBl I, p. 845) was enacted. § 100c(1) no. 3 of the Code of Criminal Procedure is the central statutory provision that was enacted by Art. 2 of that Act. According to § 100c(1) no. 3 of the Code of Criminal Procedure, non-public speech in private homes of a person suspected of a criminal offence may be intercepted and recorded by technical means if specific facts give rise to the suspicion that this person committed one of the criminal offences listed in the statutory catalogue. The catalogue includes in particular offences that are typically associated with organised crime. In addition, the catalogue

comprises certain offences against the state. Surveillance measures for investigating the facts of a criminal case or for determining the whereabouts of an offender are only permissible if the investigation would be disproportionately difficult or futile otherwise. Pursuant to § 100c(2) first sentence of the Code of Criminal Procedure, the measures may only be directed against the suspects themselves. However, § 100c(2) fifth sentence of the Code of Criminal Procedure expressly states that homes of other persons may also be placed under surveillance if it can be presumed – with the same level of suspicion – that the suspect is present in those homes.
[...] 11-49

II.

[...] 50-66

III.

Statements on the constitutional complaints were submitted by the Federal Ministry of Justice on behalf of the Federal Government, the Government of the Free State of Bavaria, the Federal Data Protection Officer, the Data Protection Officers of the *Länder* Berlin, Brandenburg, Bremen, Hamburg, Hesse, Mecklenburg-Western Pomerania, Lower Saxony, North Rhine-Westphalia, Schleswig-Holstein, Saxony-Anhalt, the Federal Bar Association (*Bundesrechtsanwaltskammer*), the German Association of Judges (*Deutscher Richterbund*) and the Federal Working Group for Justice of the United Services Union (*Bundesfachgruppe Justiz der Vereinten Dienstleistungsgewerkschaft*). 67

68-85 [...]

IV.

86 [...]

B.

87 The constitutional complaints are for the most part admissible.

88-104 [...]

C.

105 To the extent that the constitutional complaints are admissible, they are in part well-founded. While the constitutional amendment in Art. 13(3) of the Basic Law satisfies the requirements of Art. 79 of the Basic Law, the challenged provisions of the Code of Criminal Procedure are not fully compatible with the Basic Law.

I.

106 Art. 13(3) of the Basic Law, which was inserted by way of constitutional amendment, is compatible with the Basic Law.

107 1. Art. 13(3) of the Basic Law allows restrictions of the fundamental right to the inviolability of the home under Art. 13(1) of the Basic Law. This fundamental right guarantees individuals an essential space of private life and affords them the right to be left alone there (cf. BVerfGE 32, 54 <75>; 42, 212 <219>; 51, 97 <110>). Art. 13(1) of the Basic Law protects the sphere of private space within one's home, in particular as a defensive right against state interference (cf. BVerfGE 7, 230 <238>; 65, 1 <40> – *Census*). The provision contains the general prohibition, directed at public authority, to enter and be present in a private home against the resident's will (cf. BVerfGE 76, 83 <89 and 90>), but also to install or use listening devices in the home (cf. BVerfGE 65, 1 <40> – *Census*).

108 When the Basic Law was first adopted, the fundamental right enshrined in its Article 13(1) primarily served to protect individuals against state representatives being present in their home against their will. New possible risks to this fundamental right have emerged since. With new technology available, there are now other ways for the state to reach into that sphere of private space [without physically entering it]. The protection intended by Art. 13(1) of the Basic Law would be undermined if this fundamental right did not afford protection against surveillance of the home

No. 26 – Surveillance of Private Homes

by technical means, even where they are used from outside the home. The newly inserted Art. 13(3) of the Basic lays down a constitutive limit to this fundamental right enshrined in Art. 13(1) of the Basic Law.

2. Art. 13(3) of the Basic Law was adopted in accordance with the formal requirements for constitutional amendments.

[…]

3. The Constitution-amending legislator also respected the substantive limits that the Basic Law imposes on constitutional amendments.

a) Art. 79(3) of the Basic Law prohibits constitutional amendments that affect the principles enshrined in Arts. 1 and 20 of the Basic Law. These include the requirement that human dignity be respected and protected (Art. 1(1) of the Basic Law), but also the commitment to inviolable and inalienable human rights as the basis of every community, of peace and justice (Art. 1(2) of the Basic Law). […]

[…]

b) Art. 13(3) of the Basic Law is compatible with the guarantee of human dignity enshrined in Art. 1(1) of the Basic Law.

The guarantee of human dignity, as the applicable constitutional standard, requires further elaboration with regard to the specific situations that may give rise to conflicts. Acoustic surveillance of private homes for law enforcement purposes does not generally violate the human dignity content of Art. 13(1) of the Basic Law and Art. 2(1) in conjunction with Art. 1(1) of the Basic Law. However, depending on how surveillance of private homes is carried out, it may lead to a violation of human dignity in certain constellations. To prevent this, Art. 13(3) of the Basic Law contains explicit safeguards, which are complemented by further requirements following from constitutional interpretation. Therefore, the insertion of Art. 13(3) into the Basic Law, which now allows for the surveillance of private homes, does not violate Art. 79(3) of the Basic Law as it requires a further statutory basis granting surveillance powers, in which the legislator can, and must, ensure that human dignity is not violated by surveillance measures in the individual case. Art. 13(3) of the Basic Law only authorises the legislator to enact such statutory provisions that ensure respect for human dignity.

aa) Human dignity is the supreme constitutive principle and the highest constitutional value of the Basic Law (cf. BVerfGE 6, 32 <36>; 45, 187 <227>; 72, 105 <115>). […]

(1) The Federal Constitutional Court has repeatedly emphasised that it is incompatible with human dignity to treat persons as mere objects of state authority (cf. BVerfGE 30, 1 <25 and 26 and 39 *et seq.*>; 96, 375 <399>). Thus, violations of criminal offenders' constitutionally protected right to be valued and respected as a person in society (*sozialer Wert- und Achtungsanspruch*) are impermissible as this

would turn them into mere objects in law enforcement and the fight against crime (cf. BVerfGE 45, 187 <228>; 72, 105 <116>).

121 [...] Human dignity is not violated merely because someone is targeted by law enforcement measures. However, it amounts to a violation of human dignity if the type of the measures taken generally calls into question their quality as a conscious subject. This is the case if public authorities fail to respect the value accorded to all human beings as such. Such measures are impermissible, even if they serve an effective criminal justice system and the establishment of the truth.

122 In this context, covert state action in itself does not result in a violation of the absolutely protected right to respect for one's person. If someone is placed under surveillance, this does not necessarily imply disregard for their value as a person. However, there is an inviolable core of private life that must be upheld in the context of surveillance measures (on the protection of this core cf. BVerfGE 6, 32 <41>; 27, 1 <6> – *Microcensus*; 32, 373 <378 and 379>; 34, 238 <245> – *Secret Tape Recordings*; 80, 367 <373> – *Diary-Like Notes*). If the state were to intrude upon this core, it would infringe the inviolable freedom, afforded every person, to develop freely in their highly personal domain. Even overriding public interests cannot justify an interference with this absolutely protected core of private life (cf. BVerfGE 34, 238 <245> – *Secret Tape Recordings*).

123 (2) The fundamental right under Art. 13(1) of the Basic Law gives specific shape to the protection of human dignity. The inviolability of private homes is closely linked to human dignity. At the same time, it is closely related to the constitutional requirement of absolute respect for a person's sphere of development that is strictly private – i.e. highly personal. Individuals must be guaranteed a right to be left alone, in particular in their private homes (cf. BVerfGE 75, 318 <328>; cf. also BVerfGE 51, 97 <110>).

124 The free development of one's personality within the core of private life encompasses the possibility of expressing internal processes such as emotions and feelings, as well as reflections, views and experiences of a highly personal nature. These must be possible without fear of surveillance by state authorities. The expression of feelings, of subconscious sentiments and of one's sexuality is protected as well. Free development in this sense is only possible if individuals have a space that allows them to express themselves in this manner. Confidential communication requires protected spaces, too, at least where the legal order affords special protection to the highly personal domain of private life and where citizens rely on this protection. Private homes, which can be closed to others, typically constitute protected spaces. Access to such a space allows individuals to just be themselves, in private, and to freely develop their personality in accordance with their own beliefs. Private homes as the last refuge are a means to safeguard human dignity.

No. 26 – Surveillance of Private Homes

What follows from this is not necessarily absolute protection of the rooms within a private home as such, but absolute protection of conduct that takes place in these rooms to the extent that it constitutes personal development within the core of private life.

(3) This protection cannot be made conditional upon a balancing against law enforcement interests under the principle of proportionality (cf. BVerfGE 34, 238 <245> – *Secret Tape Recordings*; cf. also BVerfGE 75, 369 <380>; 93, 266 <293>). There will always be forms of particularly serious crime, and suspicions thereof, which will make the public interest in an effective criminal justice system appear weightier to some than protecting the human dignity of a suspect. However, the state is barred by Art. 1(1) and Art. 79(3) of the Basic Law from making such an assessment.

bb) Where it fails to respect the core of private life, the acoustic surveillance of private homes for law enforcement purposes violates human dignity.

Qualifying a matter as falling within the core of private life furthermore depends on whether it is highly personal in terms of content, and on how and to what extent the matter affects the sphere of others or interests of the common good (cf. BVerfGE 80, 367 <374> – *Diary-Like Notes*). This assessment depends on the circumstances of the individual case (cf. BVerfGE 34, 238 <248> – *Secret Tape Recordings*; 80, 367 <374> – *Diary-Like Notes*). It must be determined whether there are either specific indications that the inviolable core of private life is affected, or whether the matter in question is one that typically affects the core, without any factual counter indications in the individual case suggesting otherwise, for instance where state observation encounters expressions of one's most intimate feelings or sexuality.

cc) The authorisation in Art. 13(3) of the Basic Law to enact legislation regarding acoustic surveillance of private homes does not violate Art. 79(3) in conjunction with Art. 1(1) of the Basic Law since it only allows for statutory provisions and, based thereon, surveillance measures that respect constitutional limits. Art. 13(3) of the Basic Law itself contains restrictions limiting the authorisation of surveillance under constitutional law; further restrictions follow from other constitutional guarantees that must be taken into account in the systematic interpretation of the Basic Law. While this may concern elements of the principle of proportionality, it does not call into question the absolute protection of human dignity. Rather, the principle of proportionality is only applicable, as a further restriction, in cases where surveillance measures do not violate human dignity [and are thus not *per se* impermissible]. This notwithstanding, the resulting limitation of the authorisation to carry out acoustic surveillance of private homes also serves to counter the risk of surveillance measures violating the human dignity dimension of Art. 13(3) of the Basic Law.

129 (1) Art. 13(3) of the Basic Law sets out substantive and formal requirements for lawful interferences.

130 Under Art. 13(3) first sentence of the Basic Law, acoustic surveillance is only permissible to prosecute particularly serious crime; relevant offences must specifically be listed in the law, and surveillance measures may only be carried out if there is a suspicion of relevant criminal conduct based on specific facts. [...]

131 In addition, Art. 13(3) of the Basic Law requires that an investigation of the matter by other methods would be disproportionately difficult or futile. Thus, the constitutional text itself states that the surveillance measures in question, which constitute particularly serious interferences with the fundamental right to the protection of the home, are only to be used as a last resort by law enforcement. Moreover, surveillance of a private home is from the outset only permissible when, and as long as, the suspect is presumably present in that home.

132 With the obligation to obtain a judicial warrant, the Constitution-amending legislator provided for a procedural safeguard to ensure that the surveillance measure satisfies constitutional requirements. In particular, the legislator provided that the warrant must generally be issued by a panel composed of three judges and that it must be limited in time.

133 (2) Not all limitations to acoustic surveillance of private homes for law enforcement purposes merited by the absolute protection of the inviolable core of private life are expressly laid down in Art. 13(3) of the Basic Law. As with other fundamental rights, further limits arise from other constitutional guarantees. Even when modifying fundamental rights provisions, the Constitution-amending legislator is not required to set out anew all rules of constitutional law that will in any case remain applicable. Thus, when reviewing whether Art. 13(3) of the Basic Law is compatible with Art. 79(3) of the Basic Law, Art. 13(3) of the Basic Law must be read together with other rules of constitutional law that are applicable as well.

134 (a) [...]

135 (b) [...]

136-137 [...]

138 (c) Art. 13(3) of the Basic Law must be understood in the sense that it requires implementing legislation to rule out the obtaining of information by way of acoustic surveillance of private homes in cases where the investigation measures would reach into the inviolable part of private life protected by Art. 13(1) in conjunction with Art. 1(1) and Art. 2(1) of the Basic Law.

139 dd) Surveillance powers require a statutory basis that ensures, in accordance with the principle of legal clarity, that the manner in which acoustic surveillance of private homes is carried out does not result in a violation of human dignity. Surveillance measures must be prohibited from the outset if there are indications that

the measures will violate human dignity. Moreover, if the acoustic surveillance of private homes unexpectedly results in the collection of information that is afforded absolute protection, the measures must be discontinued and the recordings must be deleted; any use of such absolutely protected data obtained in the context of law enforcement is impermissible.

(1) Safeguards to protect human dignity are not just required with regard to situations in which individuals are alone, but also when they communicate with others (cf. BVerfGE 6, 389 <433>; 35, 202 <220> – *Lebach*). Human beings necessarily seek fulfilment in social contexts, including within the core of their personality (cf. BVerfGE 80, 367 <374> – *Diary-Like Notes*). Thus, for determining whether a matter falls within the part of private life that is inviolable or – if this is not the case – within the social domain, where state interference may be permissible under certain circumstances, it is not sufficient to simply assess whether the matter has any kind of social significance or bears on social relationships at all; rather, the nature and intensity of this connection in the specific case are decisive (cf. BVerfGE 80, 367 <374> – *Diary-Like Notes*). 140

(2) In terms of their content, conversations that contain information on crimes that have been committed do not fall within the inviolable core of private life (cf. BVerfGE 80, 367 <375> – *Diary-Like Notes*). However, this does not mean that any link between the suspicion of criminal conduct and the [personal] utterances or expressions made by suspects is sufficient for attributing matters to the social domain. Notes or statements made in the course of a conversation that only reveal, for instance, inner impressions and feelings and do not contain any indications pointing to specific criminal acts do not simply become relevant to the public because they might reveal the reasons or motives for criminal conduct. However, a sufficient link to the social domain does exist where [personal] statements directly refer to specific criminal acts. 141

(3) In order to prevent interferences with the core of private life, the interception of non-public speech in private homes must be discontinued if the person [under surveillance] is by themselves or only in the company of persons to whom they have a special relationship of trust relating to the core of private life – for instance family members or other particularly close confidants – and if there are no specific indications that the content of the anticipated conversations is directly linked to criminal conduct. While not all conversations individuals have with their close confidants are part of the core of private life, a presumption applies to that effect in order to ensure effective protection of human dignity. Surveillance measures are impermissible if it is likely that conversations enjoying absolute protection would be intercepted. 142

143 (4) The content of a conversation is decisive for attributing the matter [to the different domains]. A final determination of whether information must be attributed to the highly personal domain or to the social domain can often only be made once the information has been collected. Yet the protection of the core of private life requires that, prior to carrying out measures of acoustic surveillance of private homes, there are factual indications suggesting, at least in a typifying assessment, that the conversation [to be intercepted] does not relate to the highly personal domain. Investigation measures may not be carried out in cases where intercepting non-public speech in private homes will likely lead to a violation of the core of private life.

144 Thus, prior to a surveillance measure, the law enforcement authorities have to make a prognosis regarding possible indications that the conduct within the home targeted by surveillance might relate to the core of private life. It is feasible [for law enforcement authorities] to make such a prognosis in practice.

145 (a) In this regard, the type of premises to be targeted by surveillance may provide preliminary indications for assessing the situation.

146 (α) For instance, conversations taking place on commercial and business premises are generally related to business and thus typically fall within the social domain (cf. BVerfGE 34, 238 <248> – *Secret Tape Recordings*). While conversations on premises used exclusively for commercial or business purposes partake in the protection under Art. 13(1) of the Basic Law, they generally do not affect the human dignity dimension of this fundamental right, unless the specific conversation in the individual case actually relates to the core of personality. It is the nature of business premises that they are characterised by greater openness to the outside world (cf. BVerfGE 32, 54 <75>). They generally lack the intimacy and safety of private homes. Therefore, it is justified to categorise them as being typically less protected than private premises. Where highly personal conversations do occur on business premises, however, they are afforded absolute protection once their highly personal nature becomes ascertainable in the specific case.

147 A different standard must be applied to premises used for both business and residential purposes. The presumption that conversations on business premises are generally of a business-related nature is not applicable in this case. The same holds true where premises are used for professional activities that require a special relationship of trust which falls within the highly personal domain.

148 (β) It must be presumed that conversations relate to the inviolable core if they occur on premises that typically serve as refuges of private life or that are used for that purpose in the individual case. Yet within private homes, it is generally not feasible to differentiate further between individual rooms. Even highly personal acts and conversations need not be limited to certain rooms within one's private home. In

general, individuals consider each room in their private homes as equally safe and feel equally unobserved in each room. Categorising actions [as typically belonging to different domains] depending on which room they occur in runs counter to the diverse individual uses of private homes. It is therefore impossible to limit the core of private space within one's home to certain parts of the home.

(b) It must also be taken into account that the likelihood of surveillance measures interfering with the core of personality depends on the persons who are present in the home under surveillance. 149

The presence of persons enjoying the highest level of personal trust is an important indication that conversations may relate to human dignity. Individuals primarily develop their personality in interaction with others, i.e. by communicating with them. In this respect, marriage and the family take on particular importance when it comes to communication regarding highly personal matters, in particular intimate matters. The intimacy of marriage allows for communication between spouses that may extend to virtually all subject matters, with no topics being off limits, based on the expectation that outsiders will not obtain knowledge of such conversations. The same holds true for conversations with other close family members, such as siblings or direct relatives, especially if they live in the same household. Art. 6(1) and (2) of the Basic Law is applicable in addition to Art. 13(1) of the Basic Law in such cases. 150

The protection of the core of private life also encompasses communication with other persons enjoying special trust (cf. BVerfGE 90, 255 <260> – *Monitoring of Correspondence*). This group only partially overlaps with persons entitled to refuse to give evidence under §§ 52 and 53 of the Code of Criminal Procedure. The scope of the prohibitions of acoustic surveillance following from [the constitutionally required protection of] the core of private life is not identical to the scope of the rights to refuse to give evidence under criminal procedural law. Accordingly, § 52 of the Code of Criminal Procedure does not serve to protect the relationship of trust between the family members mentioned therein and the suspect. Rather, the provision gives consideration to the predicament of witnesses, who have a duty to tell the truth but also have reason to fear that in complying with this duty they will compromise a family member. Moreover, the right to refuse to give evidence is linked to the formal criterion of a family relationship rather than a special relationship of trust, which may also exist between very close friends. 151

As for § 53 of the Code of Criminal Procedure, it is true that this provision aims to protect the [professional] relationship of trust between witness and suspect. However, not in all cases in which § 53 of the Code of Criminal Procedure applies is this protection afforded for the sake of safeguarding the suspect's human dignity or the dignity of their conversation partner. The assumption that communications 152 merit absolute protection does apply to conversations with clerics in their capacity as faith-based counsellors. The protection of confession, or conversations of a confessional nature, is part of the human dignity dimension of the freedom to practice one's religion under Art. 4(1) and (2) of the Basic Law. Conversations between a suspect and their defence lawyer also play an important role in protecting human dignity by ensuring that the suspect is not treated as a mere object in criminal proceedings. In the individual case, doctor-patient consultations, too, may relate to the core of private life (cf. BVerfGE 32, 373 <379>). By contrast, the rights to refuse to give evidence afforded members of the press and members of Parliament are not directly related to the core of private life. These rights are granted for the sake of safeguarding the proper functioning of Parliament and the media rather than for protecting the suspect's right of personality.

153 (5) Even where acoustic surveillance is not *per se* ruled out, the interception of conversations in private homes must nevertheless be limited to situations in which it is likely that contents of the conversation will be relevant to criminal proceedings. Where needed, suitable preliminary investigations through measures that do not affect the core of private life must be carried out to ensure that acoustic surveillance of private homes is limited to situations in homes that are relevant to the proceedings in question. It is impermissible to interfere with the absolutely protected core of private life for the purposes of determining whether the envisaged collection of information would affect this core.

154 Sweeping surveillance, in terms of both time and location, will generally be impermissible as this would almost invariably lead to the interception of highly personal conversations. Similarly, surveillance taking place over an extended period of time and covering almost every movement and expression of [private] life of the person under surveillance, which could be used as the basis for creating a personality profile, is incompatible with human dignity (cf. BVerfGE 65, 1 <42 and 43> – *Census*).

155 (6) To the extent that acoustic surveillance of private homes is not prohibited from the outset, because there are no sufficient external indications that absolutely protected conversations are likely to be recorded, conversations of the suspect may be intercepted for the purposes of determining whether they contain information that may be used in criminal proceedings. Under these circumstances, a preliminary screening to assess the contents of conversations, required by the protection of human dignity, is not objectionable under constitutional law. At the same time, suitable measures must be taken to ensure utmost restraint when carrying out such a preliminary screening (cf. BVerfGE 80, 367 <375, 381> – *Diary-Like Notes*). For instance, the protection of human dignity under Art. 1(1) of the Basic Law may require that conversations in private homes not be intercepted by means of

No. 26 – Surveillance of Private Homes

automatic recordings only, so as to ensure that the investigation measure can be discontinued at any time.
Where, in the context of surveillance of private homes, a situation unfolds that relates to the inviolable core of private life, surveillance must be discontinued. Where recordings were obtained despite intrusion into the core, they must be destroyed. Any sharing or use of the information thus obtained is prohibited. Art. 13(3) of the Basic Law must be interpreted to the effect that such recordings are subject to prohibitions to use data thus obtained as evidence (regarding the constitutional basis of such requirements cf. BVerfGE 44, 353 <383 and 384> – *Addiction Counselling Agency*; cf. also BVerfGE 34, 238 <245 *et seq.*> – *Secret Tape Recordings*).
c) [...]

II.

The statutory authorisation to carry out acoustic surveillance of private homes under § 100c(1) no. 3, § 100c(2) and (3) of the Code of Criminal Procedure and the framework regarding the prohibitions to collect and use the data as evidence under § 100d(3) of the Code of Criminal Procedure do not sufficiently give effect to the requirements arising from Art. 13(1) and (3) of the Basic Law and Art. 2(1) in conjunction with Art. 1(1) of the Basic Law with regard to the inviolable part of private life, with regard to the specific design of the catalogue of relevant criminal offences, and with regard to the principle of proportionality. They are only in part compatible with the Basic Law.

1. The standards for reviewing the constitutionality of the statutory provisions authorising acoustic surveillance of private homes in the Code of Criminal Procedure are, primarily, Art. 13(1) and (3) of the Basic Law and, additionally, Art. 2(1) in conjunction with Art. 1(1) of the Basic Law. Other fundamental rights, in particular Art. 4(1) and (2) and Art. 6(1) and (2) of the Basic Law, may also be affected by the surveillance measures authorised by the provisions.

a) However, the general right of personality following from Art. 2(1) in conjunction with Art. 1(1) of the Basic Law is not applicable in addition to Art. 13(1) of the Basic Law to the extent that interferences with the sphere of private space of residents are at issue.

Art. 13(1) of the Basic Law contains a more specific guarantee protecting the sphere of private space within one's home against acoustic surveillance by the state, which supersedes the general guarantee [of Art. 2(1) in conjunction with Art. 1(1) of the Basic Law] (cf. BVerfGE 100, 313 <358> – *The Article 10 Act* – regarding Art. 10 of the Basic Law). Given its broad scope of protection, Art. 13 of the Basic Law applies as the more specific guarantee not only with regard to the actual surveillance measures carried out by the state, but also with regard to any necessary preparatory measures, to information and data processing measures that follow data collection, and to the use of the information thus obtained (cf. BVerfGE 100, 313 <359> – *The Article 10 Act*).

166 Art. 13(1) of the Basic Law protects the right to be left alone and the right to private speech within one's home, which is precisely the part of the private sphere that would otherwise come under the protection afforded by the general right of personality. As a non-listed freedom, the general right of personality supplements the specific freedoms, which also protect fundamental aspects of one's personality (cf. BVerfGE 54, 148 <153 and 154> – *Eppler*); as such, the general right of personality is only applicable in cases that fall outside the specific freedoms' scope of protection.

167 b) Where persons affected by surveillance of a home cannot invoke Art. 13(1) of the Basic Law, they are protected by the general right of personality under Art. 2(1) in conjunction with Art. 1(1) of the Basic Law. Fundamental rights holders who can invoke Art. 13(1) of the Basic Law include all owners or residents of a home, irrespective of the legal relationships governing use of the home. Where several residents share a home, each resident can invoke this fundamental right, where a family shares a home, each family member can invoke this right. Yet surveillance of private homes may not only affect residents, but also persons who happen to be present in a home under surveillance. While those persons cannot invoke Art. 13(1) of the Basic Law, they are afforded protection under the general right of personality. However, the protection afforded by Art. 2(1) in conjunction with Art. 1(1) of the Basic Law cannot be more extensive than the protection afforded by Art. 13(1) and (3) of the Basic Law.

168 c) As the case may be, the protection afforded the sphere of private space within one's home and the general right of personality can also be supplemented by further fundamental rights guarantees. [...]

169 2. The challenged statutory provisions, which authorise the interception and recording of conversations in private homes, provide a basis for interferences with the fundamental rights under Art. 13(1) and Art. 2(1) in conjunction with Art. 1(1) of the Basic Law.

170 a) The physical intrusion into homes, the installation of technical devices on the protected premises and the acoustic surveillance of events unfolding in private homes by technical means all amount to interferences with the fundamental right to the inviolability of the home (see C I 1 above). These interferences are perpetuated when the information obtained is stored, used and shared with other bodies.

171 Any form of acoustic or visual surveillance of private homes constitutes an interference, regardless of whether the technical means used for surveillance are installed

on protected premises or used from outside the homes, such as directional microphones [...]. However, this only applies to the extent that surveillance from outside the homes records events inside the homes that cannot be naturally perceived from outside the protected area. [...]

b) Moreover, acoustic surveillance of private homes interferes with the general right of personality to the extent that persons are affected who happen to be present in a home under surveillance and who cannot invoke the more specific fundamental right under Art. 13(1) of the Basic Law (see C II 1 b above). 172

3. The statutory authorisation to carry out acoustic surveillance of private homes for law enforcement purposes is only in part constitutional. 173

a) Statutory provisions of this kind must include sufficient safeguards to prevent interferences with the absolutely protected core of private life, thus protecting human dignity. If this prohibition is violated or if a measure unexpectedly interferes with the absolutely protected core of private life, it must be discontinued. Deletion requirements and prohibitions to use the data must be put in place to ensure that the measure has no consequences for affected persons. § 100d(3) of the Code of Criminal Procedure does not sufficiently meet these requirements. 174

aa) The legislator failed to sufficiently specify the prohibitions to carry out surveillance measures and to collect data that are required under constitutional law in cases where the core of private life is affected. 175-176

(1) Art. 13(3) of the Basic Law only allows for statutory provisions authorising acoustic surveillance of private homes if the legislation in question ensures that the core of private life is not affected (see C I 3 b cc above). Therefore, these statutory provisions must prohibit any interception and recording of non-public speech in private homes if there are indications that absolutely protected conversations could be recorded. 177

[...] 178-179

(2) Based on these considerations, constitutional law requires that legislation authorising acoustic surveillance contain statutory restrictions, yet § 100d(3) of the Code of Criminal Procedure does not fully satisfy this requirement. While the provision reflects the general assumption that acoustic surveillance of private homes is not permissible if a matter relates to the inviolable part of private life, § 100d(3) of the Code of Criminal Procedure does not give sufficient effect to these constitutional limits. 180

(a) To the extent that surveillance of conversations between suspects and persons bound by professional confidentiality under § 53 of the Code of Criminal Procedure is prohibited under constitutional law, this is reflected in § 100d(3) first sentence of the Code of Criminal Procedure through a comprehensive prohibition to collect data. [...] 181

182 (b) However, § 100d(3) of the Code of Criminal Procedure does not ensure that surveillance remains impermissible in cases where suspects are in their home with only immediate family or other particularly close confidants present and there are no indications to suggest that those persons themselves committed or were complicit in a criminal act.

183 In this regard, the provision does not contain a general prohibition of surveillance measures affecting persons entitled to refuse to give evidence pursuant to § 52 of the Code of Criminal Procedure, which in particular includes immediate family; the provision only contains a prohibition to use data as evidence that is subject to the principle of proportionality. Regarding the surveillance of conversations with particularly close confidants who are not part of the group of persons entitled to refuse to give evidence, § 100d(3) of the Code of Criminal Procedure does not provide for any restrictions at all.

184 § 100d(3) second sentence of the Code of Criminal Procedure does not contain a sufficient prohibition to intercept conversations with particularly close confidants either. [...]

185 [...] Given that the legislator only prohibits acoustic surveillance of private homes in cases where all information obtained would be subject to a prohibition to use it as evidence, this provision does not satisfy the constitutional requirements. A restrictive interpretation that would bring the provision in line with constitutional law is precluded by the clear wording ("all information").

186 bb) The legislator also failed to include sufficient safeguards in § 100d(3) of the Code of Criminal Procedure to ensure that surveillance measures are discontinued if a situation unexpectedly arises which relates to the inviolable core of private life, even though continuing surveillance measures would be unlawful in such cases.

187 cc) There are also no sufficient provisions prohibiting the use of information obtained in violation of the core of private life and requiring that any collected data be deleted if such violations have occurred.

188 (1) In both respects, the Basic Law sets constitutional requirements for the legislator.

189 (a) Constitutional law requires that the legislator impose a prohibition to use data relating to the core of private life.

190 The risk of interfering with the core of private life that is associated with acoustic surveillance of private homes can only be tolerated under constitutional law if safeguards exist to ensure that violations that have occurred by exception do not have further consequences. It must be ensured that information obtained through such interferences not be used in any way, neither in the course of the criminal investigation nor in other contexts.

No. 26 – Surveillance of Private Homes

[...] 191-192
(b) To the extent that information relating to the core of private life has already been collected, it must be deleted without undue delay. [...] 193
[...] 194
(2) The current statutory provisions do not fully satisfy these constitutional requirements. 195
(a) It is true that § 100d(3) first sentence of the Code of Criminal Procedure could be interpreted to the effect that the use of data is prohibited if conversations with persons bound by professional confidentiality pursuant to § 53 of the Code of Criminal Procedure were intercepted and recorded in breach of the statutory prohibition [to carry out surveillance measures in such constellations] [...]; yet for other cases, absolute statutory prohibitions to use data are lacking. In this regard, the legislator did not provide for any restrictions other than emphasising the significance of the principle of proportionality when deciding on the use of information relating to conversations with persons bound by professional confidentiality pursuant to §§ 52 and 53a of the Code of Criminal Procedure. 196
(b) In addition, constitutionally mandated prohibitions to use data as evidence require supplementary procedural safeguards ensuring the enforcement of such prohibitions. Such safeguards are also lacking. 197
Given that legal recourse is typically not available to the affected persons, protection of the core of private life is only sufficiently guaranteed – unless data is deleted immediately – if it is not solely for the law enforcement authorities to assess whether the information obtained by them can be used [as evidence] in the criminal proceedings under way or even just as a basis for further investigations in other proceedings. Rather, this determination must be made by an independent body, taking into account the interests of affected persons. 198
§ 100d(3) fifth sentence of the Code of Criminal Procedure does not sufficiently provide for such procedural safeguards. [...] 199
[...] 200-201
(c) § 100d(1) second sentence in conjunction with § 100b(6) of the Code of Criminal Procedure does not provide for a requirement that collected data relating to the core of private life be deleted. These provisions only concern the deletion of lawfully obtained data when it is no longer needed for law enforcement (see C VIII below). As demonstrated in the oral hearing, the lack of a statutory requirement that data relating to the core be deleted immediately results in considerable uncertainties regarding data handling. As a consequence, the original recordings are often retained for long periods of time. These gaps in the statutory framework jeopardise fundamental rights protection. 202

203 (d) In this regard, it is necessary to enact statutory provisions [filling these gaps]. The legislator cannot forgo such provisions merely because the prohibition to use the data and the requirement that data be deleted derive from the Constitution. [...]

204 b) Where acoustic surveillance of private homes does not affect the absolutely protected core of private life, it is only constitutional if the principle of proportionality – a general principle that is specified in Art. 13(3) of the Basic Law – is observed. The challenged provisions do not fully satisfy the proportionality requirements. It is true that they pursue a legitimate purpose (see aa below) and are suitable (see bb below) and necessary (see cc below) for achieving this purpose. Yet when enacting § 100c(1) no. 3 of the Code of Criminal Procedure, the legislator did not fully take into account that Art. 13(3) of the Basic Law restricts the grounds for the use of acoustic surveillance of private homes to particularly serious criminal acts (see dd below). For the rest, the statutory provisions authorising surveillance do not raise constitutional concerns if interpreted restrictively (see ee below).

205-206 aa) The purpose pursued by the challenged provisions authorising acoustic surveillance of private homes is legitimate under constitutional law.

207 With this statutory authorisation, the legislator in particular aims to strengthen the legal instruments available to fight organised crime, in addition to pursuing the general purpose of investigating serious crime. [...]

208 [...]

209 bb) Acoustic surveillance of private homes on the basis of § 100c(1) no. 3 of the Code of Criminal Procedure is, in principle, suitable for prosecuting the crimes listed in that provision.

210 [...]

211 (1) There are ultimately no doubts under constitutional law that acoustic surveillance of private homes is, in principle, a suitable means for law enforcement.

212-215 [...]

216 (2) Yet with the statutory authorisation to carry out [surveillance] measures constituting interferences, the legislator also pursues the particular purpose of penetrating the inner sphere of organised crime. [...]

217 (a) Given the difficulties in capturing the phenomenon of organised crime, it is at present not possible to present reliable findings regarding the extent to which this particular aim pursued by the legislator can be achieved.

218-219 [...]

220 (b) Currently, it cannot be definitively determined whether the structures of organised crime are indeed of such nature that acoustic surveillance of private homes, as an instrument of law enforcement, could make a specific contribution to penetrating these structures. [...]

No. 26 – Surveillance of Private Homes

It is not objectionable under constitutional law that the legislator proceeded on the assumption [that this is the case]. The remaining uncertainties require that the legislator further monitor developments in this area and continually reassess whether that investigation instrument is really suitable for achieving its specific aim to a sufficient degree (regarding the monitoring of legal provisions cf. BVerfGE 33, 171 <189 and 190>; 37, 104 <118>; 88, 203 <310>). 221

The legislator did provide for mechanisms in this regard. A continual assessment is in particular guaranteed by the reporting obligations under Art. 13(6) of the Basic Law in conjunction with § 100e of the Code of Criminal Procedure. [...] 222

cc) The challenged law is necessary for achieving the purpose pursued. No other means are available that would be equally effective but less intrusive for fundamental rights holders (see 1 below). Moreover, the legislator linked the grounds for carrying out the measures constituting interferences to statutory prerequisites that sufficiently ensure that acoustic surveillance of private homes is only carried out if it is necessary [for achieving the law enforcement purpose pursued] (see 2 below). 223

(1) It is not ascertainable that other investigation measures would be generally less intrusive yet equally suitable for achieving the same investigation purpose. 224

When assessing the necessity of the means chosen to achieve the aims pursued, the legislator has a margin of appreciation, in respect of which the Federal Constitutional Court's powers of review are limited (cf. BVerfGE 90, 145 <173>). According to the legislator's assessment in the present case, there are no alternatives to acoustic surveillance of private homes that would be less intrusive for fundamental rights holders. In respect of organised gangs that almost completely isolate themselves from outsiders, the legislator believes that conventional investigation methods, including the surveillance of telecommunications, are usually not sufficient to allow investigations to reach into the core of organised crime. [...] This assessment is not objectionable under constitutional law, at least according to the current state of knowledge regarding existing forms of organised crime. 225-226

[...] 227

(2) Moreover, the legislator included statutory safeguards to ensure that acoustic surveillance of private homes is only used as a last resort. 228

Art. 13(3) of the Basic Law provides that acoustic surveillance of private homes may only be used if investigating the matter in question by other methods would be disproportionately difficult or futile. A corresponding subsidiarity requirement was inserted into § 100c(1) no. 3 of the Code of Criminal Procedure. Acoustic surveillance of private homes may thus only be used as a last resort by law enforcement. 229

[...] 230-233

dd) Insofar as acoustic surveillance of private homes does not affect the absolutely protected core of private life, the Constitution-amending legislator set out particular 234 requirements governing the lawfulness [of such surveillance measures] in Art. 13(3) of the Basic Law, further specifying the principle of proportionality. The catalogue of criminal offences set out in § 100c(1) no. 3 of the Code of Criminal Procedure does not satisfy these constitutional requirements in that it is not limited to particularly serious crime within the meaning of Art. 13(3) of the Basic Law.

235-251 [...]

252 ee) For the rest, the statutory provisions authorising surveillance give sufficient effect to the requirements set out in Art. 13(3) of the Basic Law and the principle of proportionality in the strict sense, at least if interpreted restrictively.

253 (1) With regard to the tension between the state's duty to guarantee an effective criminal justice system under the rule of law and the interest of suspects and third parties that their constitutionally guaranteed rights be respected, it is primarily incumbent on the legislator to achieve an abstract balance between the conflicting interests. Moreover, in interpreting and applying provisions that restrict fundamental rights, the courts have to ensure that their decisions are appropriate [in terms of proportionality]. The same applies to the authorities carrying out surveillance measures. In this regard, the principle of proportionality must be applied not least because Art. 13(3) of the Basic Law does not spell out explicit requirements for the design in the Code of Criminal Procedure of the statutory powers at issue here, nor does it provide for such requirements regarding their application in the individual case.

254 (2) Based on these standards, § 100c(1) no. 3 of the Code of Criminal Procedure is not objectionable under constitutional law if interpreted restrictively – except for the overly broad catalogue of criminal offences [which is unconstitutional].

255-259 [...]

260 (3) § 100c(1) no. 3 of the Code of Criminal Procedure also satisfies the requirements of proportionality to the extent that, in addition to the investigation of the facts of the case, it also permits surveillance measures to determine the whereabouts of the "offender".

261 [...]

262 (4) By interpreting § 100c(1) no. 3, § 100c(2) fourth and fifth sentence and § 100c(3) of the Code of Criminal Procedure restrictively, it can be ensured that third parties who are not themselves suspects are only affected by acoustic surveillance of private homes to an extent that is appropriate to the public interest in effective law enforcement, as the purpose pursued by the investigation measure. However, surveillance of third parties is – as always – impermissible from the outset with regard to communication relating to the core of private life. This is not the case if the suspect is in a private home rented by a third party for the purpose of conspiring [to commit a crime]. By contrast, the core of private life is more likely

No. 26 – Surveillance of Private Homes

to be affected if the suspect enters the home of a third party, for example a friend or a family member, only temporarily and as a visitor.

(a) The severity of interference is a decisive factor for determining whether a measure that restricts fundamental rights is appropriate. In this regard, it is significant how many persons are affected by impairments, how severe the impairments are and whether the affected persons have prompted them (cf. BVerfGE 100, 313 <376> – *The Article 10 Act*). The severity of the impairment depends on whether affected persons remain anonymous, what communication circumstances and contents can be intercepted, and what disadvantages the holders of fundamental rights might face or have reason to fear on account of the surveillance measures (cf. BVerfGE 100, 313 <376> – *The Article 10 Act*; 107, 299 <320>). It is also significant whether the investigation measures take place in a private home or on commercial and business premises and whether, and how many, non-suspects are affected. 263

(α) Acoustic surveillance of private homes is a particularly serious interference with fundamental rights. It can affect a considerable number of persons who have no connection to the criminal charges and who did not prompt the interference, but merely have some form of connection to the offender or happen to be in the same home. 264

Affected third parties in this sense are persons who are not themselves the target of the investigation measures. These include conversation partners of the suspect, other persons who are temporarily or permanently staying in the suspect's home, but also other persons affected by surveillance measures in offices and on business premises. Furthermore, apart from the suspect, persons are affected [as third parties] if their homes become the object of surveillance because the suspect is presumed to be present there. These persons, too, must be considered affected parties if they are in a home under surveillance at any time during the measure. Where communication of non-suspects is recorded, acoustic surveillance of private homes exposes them to the risk that they themselves may become the target of state investigations. This specific risk then aggravates the general risk of being falsely suspected of wrongdoing (cf. BVerfGE 107, 299 <321>). 265

[…] 266

The particular severity of the interference follows from the contents and the scale of communications intercepted in the context of acoustic surveillance of private homes, in addition to the large number of non-suspects affected by the measures. All aspects of everyday communication taking place during the surveillance period in the targeted home could be intercepted. Therefore, the share of conversations without any relevance whatsoever to law enforcement is likely to be high. 267

268 (β) Covert surveillance of non-public speech in private homes affects not only individuals but communication in society as a whole. The possibility that acoustic surveillance of private homes is carried out may have chilling effects, in particular on non-suspects, because the measures authorised by the statutory provisions could affect them at any time and without their knowledge. Simply the fear of being under surveillance may lead to communication no longer being free from fear or worry. Art. 13 of the Basic Law protects individuals against the state interfering with the sphere of private space within their home and thus guarantees, as an objective value, the confidentiality of communication, which is also significant for society as a whole. The constitutional and statutory safeguards put in place to protect individual holders of fundamental rights also foster the general public's trust in a surveillance practice that respects fundamental rights (cf. BVerfGE 107, 299 <328>).

269 (γ) Art. 13(3) of the Basic Law only sets out the requirement that the suspect must be presumed to be present in the home to be monitored: this constitutes a minimum requirement regarding the likelihood that the suspect is in the home. In light of the severity of the interference, acoustic surveillance of private homes is only appropriate if the surveillance measure from the outset exclusively targets conversations of the suspect, because only then can it be assumed that the intercepted conversations have a sufficient connection to the crime under investigation. Yet this means that acoustic surveillance of private homes is only permissible if the suspect is actually or, as the case may be, at least presumably present in the home under surveillance at the time in question. This requirement also serves to protect non-suspects.

270 (b) The statutory provisions satisfy these constitutional requirements as they sufficiently restrict interferences affecting non-suspects.

271-278 [...]

III.

279 The statutory design of the requirement of prior judicial authorisation (*Richtervorbehalt*) in § 100d(2) and (4) first and second sentence of the Code of Criminal Procedure does not violate the fundamental rights invoked by the complainants.

280 1. Art. 13(3) third and fourth sentence of the Basic Law subjects acoustic surveillance of private homes to a qualified requirement of prior judicial authorisation. The requirement of judicial authorisation aims to ensure prior review by an independent and neutral authority. The Basic Law rests on the presumption that judges can best and most reliably ensure that the rights of the affected person are respected in the individual case due to their personal and professional independence and the

No. 26 – Surveillance of Private Homes

fact that they are bound only by the law (Art. 97 of the Basic Law) (cf. BVerfGE 77, 1 <51>; 103, 142 <151>; 107, 299 <325>). [...]
[...] 281-282
2. The statutory provisions governing judicial warrants for the acoustic surveillance of private homes satisfy these requirements. 283
[...] 284-290
3. In § 100d(4) first sentence of the Code of Criminal Procedure, the legislator provided, in accordance with Art. 13(3) second sentence of the Basic Law, that a judicial warrant may be valid for a maximum of four weeks, which is not objectionable under constitutional law. This guarantees a regular judicial review of the surveillance measures that is appropriate to the severity of the interference. 291
[...] 292-294
4. [...] 295-297

IV.

§ 101 of the Code of Criminal Procedure, which governs the requirement to notify persons affected by acoustic surveillance of private homes, is only in part compatible with Art. 19(4) and Art. 103(1) of the Basic Law. 298
1. § 101(1) first sentence of the Code of Criminal Procedure is incompatible with Art. 13(1), Art. 19(4) and Art. 2(1) in conjunction with Art. 1(1) of the Basic Law to the extent that the notification of persons affected by acoustic surveillance of private homes is subject to the condition that notifying them does not pose a threat to public security or to the continued use of an undercover police investigator. In addition, the fact that a judicial decision is only required once to defer notification for six months after the measure has ended pursuant to § 101(1) second sentence of the Code of Criminal Procedure does not sufficiently guarantee adherence to the procedural notification requirement under constitutional law. 299
[...] 300-318
2. [...] 319
[...] 320-329

V.

Taking into account the above-mentioned requirements regarding notification, *ex post* legal protection of affected persons against acoustic surveillance of private homes is sufficiently ensured. 330

331-333 [...]

VI.

334 The challenges brought by complainants no. 2 regarding the legislative design of the Federal Government's reporting obligations are unsuccessful.

335-338 [...]

VII.

339 Regarding the use of personal data in other proceedings, § 100d(5) second sentence and § 100f(1) of the Code of Criminal Procedure are not compatible with Art. 13(1), Art. 2(1) and Art. 1(1) of the Basic Law to the extent that they lack an obligation to label the data to be shared as information [obtained through surveillance].

340-358 [...]

VIII.

359 Just like the provisions governing data sharing, the provisions on the destruction of data in § 100d(4) third sentence, § 100b(6) of the Code of Criminal Procedure must be viewed together with the provisions on data collection for the purposes of a constitutional assessment. In light of that, the provisions on the destruction of data violate Art. 19(4) of the Basic Law. [...]

360 The protection of Art. 13(1) of the Basic Law, which is also applicable in subsequent stages of data processing, requires that the lawfully obtained data be in principle destroyed as soon as it is no longer needed for the defined purposes (regarding Article 10 of the Basic Law, cf. BVerfGE 100, 313 <362> – *The Article 10 Act*). Yet at the same time, the provisions on data destruction must satisfy the requirement of effective legal protection. In this respect, specific conflicts may arise: On the one hand, deleting data that is no longer needed gives effect to data protection; on the other hand, deletion makes effective legal protection more difficult or even obstructs it altogether because judicial review of a surveillance measure is only possible to a limited extent once the records have been destroyed [...]. In light of the foregoing, in cases in which affected persons seek judicial review of information and data processing measures by the state, the obligation to destroy data must be balanced against the guarantee of legal protection so as to ensure that legal protection is not undermined or obstructed (cf. BVerfGE 100, 313 <364, 400> – *The Article 10 Act*).

No. 26 – Surveillance of Private Homes

[...]

§ 100d(4) third sentence and § 100b(6) of the Code of Criminal Procedure do not provide for [the required] safeguards. [...]

IX.

To the extent that the challenged provisions of the Code of Criminal Procedure are incompatible with the Basic Law, it is incumbent upon the legislator to bring the law in conformity with the Constitution by 30 June 2005 at the latest.

Until then, the challenged provisions may continue to be applied on condition that the protection of human dignity and the principle of proportionality are sufficiently observed. During this transitional period, the application of § 100d(3) fifth sentence of the Code of Criminal Procedure is subject to the condition that the court designated in § 100d(2) first sentence of the Code of Criminal Procedure *ex officio* decides whether information obtained by surveillance measures may be further used in criminal investigations. The court designated in § 100d(2) first sentence of the Code of Criminal Procedure remains competent to decide [on deferring notification] pursuant to § 100d(4) first sentence and § 101(1) second sentence of the Code of Criminal Procedure, including after the suspect has been formally indicted.

D.

[...]

Justices: Papier, Jaeger, Haas, Hömig, Steiner, Hohmann-Dennhardt, Hofmann-Riem, Bryde

Dissenting Opinion of Justices Jaeger and Hohmann-Dennhardt

We do not agree with the parts of the judgment set out under C I. In our view, the amended Art. 13(3) of the Basic Law as such is already incompatible with Art. 79(3) of the Basic Law and thus void. However, we concur with the parts of the decision set out under C II to IX to the extent that the statutory provisions governing acoustic surveillance of private homes by technical means for law enforcement purposes are declared unconstitutional.

I.

367 1. Art. 79(3) of the Basic Law bars constitutional amendments that affect the principles laid down in Arts. 1 and 20 of the Basic Law. These principles include the protection of private homes as domestic space for one's highly personal life, which is indispensable for upholding a legal order that observes the requirement to respect and protect human dignity. In this regard, we agree with the Senate majority's view that the right to the inviolability of the home under Art. 13(1) of the Basic Law also serves the protection of human dignity. The development of one's personality requires private refuges in which individuals can express themselves and communicate with confidants about their personal views and feelings without fear of being under surveillance. In particular in a world in which it has become technically feasible to observe and record almost everything a person does and says, private homes more than ever serve as a last refuge for individuals, where they may express their free thoughts without being monitored. Thus, homes provide a space that serves as a means of protecting human dignity.

368 2. We also agree with the Senate majority's assessment that the Constitution affords private homes absolute protection only to the extent that the behaviour occurring in them falls under the protection of human dignity; not every statement made in a private home is highly personal. Yet in order to safeguard human dignity, private homes enjoy absolute protection where they are used to express and exchange personal feelings and opinions.

369 However, it is precisely because private homes are closed to the outside world that it is not possible to determine in advance whether conversations taking place therein at a given moment are about highly personal matters or matters that affect the sphere of others or interests of the common good. As stated in the judgment, such a distinction can only be based on indications from which it can be inferred what presumably goes on within the home. For instance, it can be presumed that a situation relating to the highly personal domain is more likely to occur in private homes than on business premises, more likely to occur in conversations with close confidants than with business partners or acquaintances. Yet such presumptions can only be confirmed once the closed sphere of the home is intruded upon and information on what happens within it is obtained. At that point, the surveillance measure may already have interfered with intimate matters, which enjoy absolute protection especially within one's own home. Thus, if the attribution of a situation behind closed doors to the absolutely protected core of private life were contingent upon a specific determination in the individual case, this would imply that an interference with this core would always have to be tolerated initially – which is exactly what Art. 79(3) of the Basic Law seeks to prevent. For the sake of protecting the

possibility of free expression of one's personality, in order to safeguard human dignity, it must thus be presumed that at least private homes in which the suspect is alone, with family members or with persons who are evidently close confidants provide space and are used for highly personal communication. Therefore, they enjoy comprehensive protection under Art. 13(1) of the Basic Law.

II.

Art. 13(3) of the Basic Law, as amended, exceeds the substantive limits which Art. 79(3) of the Basic Law sets for interferences with the inviolability of the home protected by Art. 13(1) of the Basic Law. It authorises the creation of statutory powers for the acoustic surveillance of private homes by technical means for law enforcement purposes if a person suspected of a particularly serious crime is presumably present there. It thus also enables covert interception of highly personal conversations.

1. [...] The wording of Art. 13(3) of the Basic Law does not contain restrictions ensuring that the core of private life is protected when the investigation instruments in question are used.

2. [...]

It is true that in the later stages of the legislative process, a prohibition to collect evidence was ultimately introduced at the level of statutory law, in § 100d(3) of the Code of Criminal Procedure, regarding conversations with persons bound by professional confidentiality pursuant to § 53 of the Code of Criminal Procedure. Regarding conversations with family members, who are entitled to refuse to give evidence pursuant to § 52 of the Code of Criminal Procedure, however, only a prohibition to use data as evidence subject to a proportionality assessment was agreed upon in the end, while no further changes were made to Art. 13(3) of the Basic Law. Even if one presumes that the legislator based this modification at the level of statutory law on the assumption that an inherent limitation on acoustic surveillance measures targeting private homes was implied in Art. 13(3) of the Basic Law, the design of this constitutional provision by the Constitution-amending legislator in any case left highly personal conversations with family members and close confidants unprotected. It allows such conversations to be intercepted by technical means, as it only restricts the use of information thus obtained at the level of statutory law and on the basis of proportionality considerations.

As a consequence, family members' right to refuse to give evidence is in part undermined given that the protection afforded by the prohibition to use data as evidence is inadequate. Once obtained, knowledge of conversation contents cannot be erased, and it can in fact influence the conduct of law enforcement authorities in the proceedings against the suspect or even against third parties. Moreover, persons talking to the suspect become objects of law enforcement measures by the state, even though they do not themselves qualify as suspects. This is especially true if it is their home rather than the home of the suspect that becomes the target of surveillance, with the authorities exploiting their close personal relationship with the person under observation and the atmosphere of trust within their home.

III.

375 We cannot agree with the Senate majority that the constitutional shortcomings of Art. 13(3) of the Basic Law, which was inserted by constitutional amendment, can be remedied through an interpretation in conformity with the Constitution or through a systematic interpretation of the Constitution.

376 1. It is true that constitutional provisions in particular are open to interpretation, cannot be considered in isolation and must be interpreted in line with the fundamental principles of the Basic Law and its system of values (cf. BVerfGE 19, 206 <220>). However, the question to what extent Art. 79(3) of the Basic Law limits constitutional amendments is not about achieving equilibrium between existing fundamental rights guarantees, but about determining whether the amendment affects the principles laid down in Art. 1 and Art. 20 of the Basic Law. Thus, the constitutional amendment must be measured against these principles as such, and not be interpreted in a manner that, by invoking these principles and contrary to its wording, seeks to rephrase the amendment to bring it in conformity with the Constitution.

377 a) […]

378 b) […]

379 c) Art. 79(3) of the Basic Law serves to ensure not only that certain standards are observed within the legal order, but first and foremost that the principles laid down therein are upheld in the Constitution itself. […]

380-381 […]

382 2. The option, presumed to be feasible by the Senate majority, to render a Constitution-amending provision constitutional by interpreting it in conformity with the Constitution impermissibly limits the scope of application of Art. 79(3) of the Basic Law. […] Art. 79(3) of the Basic Law is designed to resist even the beginnings of any dismantling of such fundamental rights guarantees enshrined in the Constitution that are rooted in rule-of-law principles or serve to guarantee human dignity, rather than merely becoming applicable once the state under the rule of law has been completely abolished and human dignity has been stripped of any protection (cf. BVerfGE 30, 1; dissenting opinion, p. 33 <47>). Constitutional amendments

must be taken literally and the underlying legislative decisions must be measured against the principles laid down in Art. 1 and Art. 20 of the Basic Law, otherwise Art. 79(3) of the Basic Law cannot fulfil its purpose of counteracting any gradual chipping away at the cornerstones of our Constitution. If these principles are affected, Art. 79(3) of the Basic Law does not leave room for an interpretation in conformity with the Constitution that could retroactively render the impermissible constitutional amendment permissible after all.

[…]

Today, people seem to have become used to the reality that once the technical means become available, their unrestricted use must apparently be tolerated. Yet if even the personal intimate sphere, as manifested within one's own home, is no longer off-limits to satisfy security interests, we must ask ourselves, not least from a constitutional perspective, whether the conception of human nature reflected by such an approach is still in keeping with a free democracy under the rule of law. This is all the more reason to interpret Art. 79(3) of the Basic Law strictly and adamantly, not to resist the beginnings, but to resist a bitter ending.

Justices Jaeger and Hohmann-Dennhardt

No. 27

BVerfGE 128, 109 – Transsexuals VIII

HEADNOTE

to the Order of the First Senate of 11 January 2011
1 BvR 3295/07

It violates Article 2(1) and (2) in conjunction with Article 1(1) of the Basic Law that transsexuals who satisfy the requirements of § 1(1) nos. 1 to 3 of the Transsexuals Act may only enter into a registered civil partnership to legally protect their same-sex partnership if they have undergone surgery changing their external sexual characteristics pursuant to § 8(1) nos. 3 and 4 of the Transsexuals Act and if they are permanently infertile and have therefore been recognised in the gender with which they identify and in which they live under civil status law.

FEDERAL CONSTITUTIONAL COURT
- 1 BvR 3295/07 -

IN THE NAME OF THE PEOPLE

In the proceedings
on the constitutional complaint of

Ms Baroness...,
– authorised representative: ...
against   a)   the Order of the Higher Regional Court of 23 October 2007
- 1 W 76/07 -,
b) the Order of the Berlin Regional Court of 25 January 2007
- 84 T 442/06 -,
c) the Order of the Schöneberg Local Court of 30 August 2006
- 70 III 101/06 -
the Federal Constitutional Court – First Senate –
with the participation of Justices

No. 27 – Transsexuals VIII

>Vice-President Kirchhof,
>Hohmann-Dennhardt,
>Bryde,
>Gaier,
>Eichberger,
>Schluckebier,
>Masing,
>Paulus

held on 11 January 2011:

1. § 8(1) nos. 3 and 4 of the Act on the Change of First Names and of Officially Assigned Sex in Special Cases (Transsexuals Act) of 10 September 1980 (BGBl I, p. 1654) is not compatible with Article 2(1) and (2) in conjunction with Article 1(1) of the Basic Law as set out in the reasons.
2. § 8(1) nos. 3 and 4 of the Transsexuals Act is not applicable until new legal provisions have been enacted.
3. The Order of the Higher Regional Court of 23 October 2007 - 1 W 76/07 -, the Order of the Berlin Regional Court of 25 January 2007 - 84 T 442/06 - and the Order of the Schöneberg Local Court of 30 August 2006 - 70 II 101/06 - violate the complainant's rights under Article 2(1) and (2) in conjunction with Article 1(1) of the Basic Law. The Order of the Higher Regional Court is reversed and the matter is remanded to the Higher Regional Court.
4. [...]

REASONS:

A.

The constitutional complaint concerns the question whether a male-to-female transsexual having undergone the so-called 'small solution' may be denied entering into a registered civil partnership with a woman, on the grounds that they have the option of entering into marriage, given that a change in civil status must have taken place in order to enter into a registered civil partnership, which requires that the transsexual must be infertile and must have undergone reassignment surgery. 1

I.

2   1. To enter into marriage, spouses must be of different sex. By contrast, § 1 of the Civil Partnerships Act requires that persons entering into a civil partnership belong to the same sex. In both cases, sex under civil status law acts as a determinant.

3   2. a) The Act on the Change of First Names and of Officially Assigned Sex in Special Cases (Transsexuals Act) of 10 September 1980 (BGBl I, p. 1654) in the version of 17 July 2009 (BGBl I, p. 1978) provides for two procedures which aim to enable transsexuals to live in their felt gender.

4   The so-called 'small solution' allows for changing one's first name without first having to undergo gender reassignment surgery. The requirements for this are laid down in § 1 of the Transsexuals Act [...].

5-16   [...]

17   In order to establish that the requirements laid down in § 1(1) of the Transsexuals Act have been met, the competent Local Court (cf. § 2(1) of the Transsexuals Act) must obtain opinions from two experts sufficiently familiar with the particular problems of transsexualism on the basis of their training and professional experience and who work independently from one another (cf. § 4(3) of the Transsexuals Act).

18   § 8 of the Transsexuals Act sets out the requirements for the so-called 'big solution', which results in the recognition of the felt gender under civil status law [...].

19-25   [...]

26   If, following the procedure laid down in § 9 of the Transsexuals Act, the application is granted by a court, the applicant, pursuant to § 10 of the Transsexuals Act, is considered to belong to the other gender, from the moment the decision attains legal validity. From then on, the applicant's gender-dependent rights and obligations are, in principle, based on the new gender. However, pursuant to § 11 of the Transsexuals Act, the transsexual's relationship to their descendants and parents remains unaffected. Under § 9(3) of the Transsexuals Act, in conjunction with § 6 of the Transsexuals Act, civil status can be changed back to the sex registered at birth upon application.

27-28   b) [...]
29-30   3. [...]
31-33   4. [...]
34-40   5. [...]

II.

1. The complainant was born with male external sexual characteristics in 1948 and was named R. R. However, she feels she belongs to the female gender. She is homosexually oriented and lives with her female partner. Pursuant to § 1 of the Transsexuals Act, she changed her first names to L. I. and changed her title of nobility to its female form ('small solution'). There was no change in civil status pursuant to § 8(1) of the Transsexuals Act ('big solution'). However, she is receiving hormone treatment. In her birth certificate, the complainant is designated as "L. I. Baroness ..., male". 41

By application of 8 December 2005, the complainant sought the registration of a civil partnership with her partner at the T. registry office in Berlin. The registrar refused the application by notice of 2 February 2006, claiming that a civil partnership can only be registered for two persons of the same sex. In response, on 8 February 2006 the complainant applied for the registrar to be ordered to register the civil partnership with her partner. 42

The Local Court rejected this application in its order of 30 August 2006. It held that a civil partnership could only be established between two persons of the same sex. [...] The Regional Court rejected the complaint against this order in its order of 25 January 2007. A further complaint remained unsuccessful. In its order of 23 October 2007, the Higher Regional Court confirmed the legal view of the lower courts. 43

2. The complainant lodged a constitutional complaint against this decision on 28 December 2007. She claims a violation of her rights under Art. 2(1) in conjunction with Art. 1(1) of the Basic Law. She argues that she has a constitutionally protected right to live in a legally and socially recognised partnership with another person. 44
[...]
[...] 45
3. [...] 46

III.

Statements on the constitutional complaint were submitted by the Federal Ministry of the Interior on behalf of the Federal Government, the *Land* Berlin, the German Lesbian and Gay Association (*Lesben- und Schwulenverband Deutschland*), the German Society for Trans Identity and Intersexuality (*Deutsche Gesellschaft für Transidentität und Intersexualität*), the Ecumenical Working Group 'Homosexuals and the Church' (*Ökumenische Arbeitsgruppe Homosexuelle und Kirche*), the *sonntags.club* and the Transgender Network Berlin (*Transgender-Netzwerk Berlin*). 47

48-52 [...]

B.

53 The constitutional complaint is admissible. In particular, the complainant continues to have a recognised legal interest in bringing an action even though she has married in the meantime.

54 [...]

C.

55 § 8(1) nos. 3 and 4 of the Transsexuals Act is not compatible with Art. 2(1) and (2) in conjunction with Art. 1(1) of the Basic Law insofar as the requirements laid down therein indirectly prevent a homosexual transsexual who satisfies the requirements under § 1(1) nos. 1 to 3 of the Transsexuals Act from entering into a registered civil partnership.

I.

56 1. Art. 2(1) in conjunction with Art. 1(1) of the Basic Law protects the personal sphere that is closer to the core of private life (*engere persönliche Lebenssphäre*), which also encompasses intimate sexual matters, comprising sexual self-determination, and thus also the finding and recognising of one's gender identity and sexual orientation (cf. BVerfGE 115, 1 <14> – *Transsexuals V*; 121, 175 <190>). It is scientifically proven that a person's gender cannot be determined on the basis of the external sexual characteristics at the time of birth alone, but that it greatly depends on a person's psychological condition and their own internally felt genderedness (*selbstempfundene Geschlechtlichkeit*) as well (cf. BVerfGE 115, 1 <15> – *Transsexuals V*). If a transsexual's own felt gender is lastingly in conflict with their official sex assigned on the basis of external sexual characteristics, human dignity in conjunction with the fundamental right to the protection of one's personality require that the right to self-determination of the person concerned be taken into account, and that their internally felt gender identity be officially recognised. This allows the person to live in accordance with their felt gender without their intimate sphere being exposed by the contradiction between the person's appearance as adapted to their felt gender and their actual legal status (cf. BVerfGE 116, 243 <264>). It is for the legislator to structure the legal order in such a way that these requirements are satisfied and, in particular, that officially assigning the lastingly felt gender is not subject to unreasonable (*unzumutbar*) requirements.

No. 27 – Transsexuals VIII

2. It is not compatible with these principles that transsexuals with a homosexual orientation who wish to legally protect their partnership must either enter into marriage or must undergo surgery for gender reassignment and for inducing infertility in order to be recognised in their felt gender under civil status law and thus to be able to enter into a registered civil partnership corresponding to their relationship, which they themselves feel is a same-sex relationship. The recognition under civil status law of their felt gender must not be dependent on requirements that involve severe impairments to physical integrity and are associated with health risks, if these are not, according to current scientific findings, a necessary requirement for a lasting and recognisable change of gender.

a) The free development of one's personality, protected under Art. 2(1) of the Basic Law, includes the right of any person to enter into a long-term partnership with the person of their choice and to legally protect this partnership in one of the institutions provided for by law (cf. BVerfGE 115, 1 <24> – *Transsexuals V*). In accordance with the constitutional requirement [to protect marriage and the family] of Art. 6(1) of the Basic Law, it is, on the one hand, possible to enter into marriage, an option available to opposite-sex couples (cf. BVerfGE 105, 313 <344 and 345>). On the other hand, the legislator has created the institution of registered civil partnership for same-sex couples. In this respect, access to the respective institution under German law is currently determined by the gender constellation of the couple wanting to form a legal union, not by their sexual orientation, even though a person's decision for marriage or registered civil partnership is generally linked to their sexual orientation (cf. BVerfGE 124, 199 <221>). What is relevant here is the officially assigned sex under civil status law at the time of entering into the legal union. It is not objectionable under constitutional law that the two options provided by the legislator for couples to enter into a legal union are differentiated solely on the basis of the officially assigned sex of the persons concerned (cf. BVerfGE 115, 1 <23> – *Transsexuals V*; 121, 175 <195>). This allows for an objective and simple determination of the requirements for access to marriage and civil partnership, prevents partners from having to disclose intimate information about their gender identity or their sexual orientation before entering into marriage or civil partnership, and thus serves to protect their private sphere (cf. BVerfGE 107, 27 <53>).

b) However, the fact that a person's sex under civil status law is decisive for entering into marriage or civil partnership does affect the right to sexual self-determination under Art. 2(1) in conjunction with Art. 1(1) of the Basic Law if a person's officially assigned sex is based only on their external sexual characteristics and not on their felt gender as confirmed by expert opinions, and if an existing disparity between sex under civil status law and felt gender cannot be eliminated in a way that is reasonable (*zumutbar*) for the person concerned, so that this person would have to live in what they feel is the wrong gender if they wish to legally protect their union.

60 This is the case for transsexuals with a homosexual orientation who satisfy the requirements of § 1(1) nos. 1 to 3 of the Transsexuals Act but who have not undergone surgery changing their external sexual characteristics and bringing about infertility, which is required under § 8(1) nos. 3 and 4 of the Transsexuals Act in order to be recognised in one's felt gender under civil status law. Male-to-female transsexuals with the 'small solution', such as the complainant, feel themselves to be women and adapt their name and appearance to their felt gender, but continue to be treated as men under civil status law. In accordance with the current legal situation, the ordinary courts have found that the complainant was not able to enter into a registered civil partnership to legally protect her relationship to a woman, which she feels is same-sex, even though this form of partnership has been created by the legislator specifically for same-sex couples in order to reserve marriage as an opposite-sex union between a man and a woman (cf. BVerfGE 115, 1 <18> – *Transsexuals V*). If a male-to-female transsexual wants to enter into a legal union with her partner, she thus faces a choice between entering into marriage with her partner (see aa below) or subjecting herself to surgery for gender reassignment and for inducing infertility in order to obtain recognition of her felt gender under civil status law and thus satisfy the requirements for entering into a registered civil partnership which corresponds to her homosexual relationship (see bb below). Both options impair her right to sexual self-determination in an unreasonable way.

61 aa) By requiring a transsexual with the so-called 'small solution' and with a homosexual orientation to marry in order to legally protect their partnership, the transsexual is obliged to take on an official gender role that is externally perceptible and that contradicts their felt gender. At the same time, their transsexuality becomes apparent. This does not satisfy the requirement under Art. 2(1) in conjunction with Art. 1(1) of the Basic Law to recognise a person's felt gender identity and to protect their intimate sphere.

62 When marriage is available to both opposite-sex and same-sex couples, as is the case in several European countries […], no conclusions can be drawn from marriage as to the sex and sexual orientation of the partners. When, by contrast, the legal order provides for a second form of partnership besides marriage to protect a legally binding partnership – as is the case in Germany with registered civil partnerships – and when it distinguishes these two forms of partnership solely on the basis of the sex of the partners, reference to one such form of partnership also involves ascribing gender roles within the partnership. Thus, even the mere designation of spouse or civil partner influences how the respective partners per-

ceive themselves and how they and their relationship are perceived by others. If transsexuals with the 'small solution' and a homosexual orientation are required to marry in order to legally protect their partnership and they then marry out of necessity, because gender reassignment surgery is not an option yet they do not want to forgo a legal bond with their partner, this exposes them to a questioning of their gender identity as well as their sexual orientation. Not only does this create a contradiction between the impression that marriage conveys of their gender identity and their own opposite internally felt gender. Marriage, as a heterosexual union, also ascribes a role to the transsexual which runs counter to their sexual orientation. It is true that even when they marry, transsexuals may keep their name which they had changed pursuant to § 1 of the Transsexuals Act and which corresponds to their felt gender (cf. BVerfGE 115, 1 <24> – *Transsexuals V*). Yet precisely this name and their appearance adapted to the felt gender, which expose the relationship to their partner as a same-sex relationship, permanently contradict them and their partner in their status as a married couple. They are perceived as a couple for which marriage is actually not a suitable option. It becomes apparent that one of them must be a transsexual. Because of the discrepancy between their marital union and their noticeably same-sex relationship, they must always expect to be asked about their gender. While it may be possible in everyday life to avoid revealing one's status as a spouse, under constitutional law it is not reasonable to expect the persons concerned to keep their legal status secret in order to live in accordance with their felt gender roles. The intimacy of transsexuals and their partners, protected against involuntary disclosure by Art. 2(1) in conjunction with Art. 1(1) of the Basic Law, is thus not sufficiently safeguarded (cf. BVerfGE 88, 87 <97 and 98>). Therefore, it is not reasonable for transsexuals or their partners to be required to marry in order to legally protect their relationship. 63

bb) It is not objectionable under constitutional law that the legislator defines access to registered civil partnerships on the basis of the sex assigned to the partners under civil status law, even in the case of transsexuals with a homosexual orientation. Nor is it objectionable that the legislator sets objective requirements for the assignment of sex under civil status law. However, it does violate the right to sexual self-determination under Art. 2(1) in conjunction with Art. 1(1) of the Basic Law when the recognition of a transsexual under civil status law is subject to requirements which are too strict and thus unreasonable. 64

(1) A registered civil partnership is available to same-sex couples only. However, while homosexual transsexuals and their partners see themselves as same-sex couples, the relationship is not legally regarded as same-sex as long as the transsexual's felt gender is not recognised under civil status law. Transsexuals can only enter into a civil partnership that corresponds to their self-perception if they satisfy the 65

requirements for changing civil status as laid down by the legislator. The officially assigned sex in civil status law serves the purpose of unambiguously assigning a sex to the partners when reviewing whether they should be granted access to a registered civil partnership. In doing so, the legislator pursues a legitimate objective. By requiring proof of sex under civil status law, it seeks to ensure that a registered civil partnership is only available to partners who are officially recognised as same-sex (cf. BVerfGE 105, 313 <351 and 352>).

66 (2) In principle, the legislator may use the external sexual characteristics of a person at the time of birth as the basis for assigning sex. It may define certain requirements for the recognition under civil status law of the felt gender which is in contradiction with these characteristics. As sex is determinant for attributing rights and obligations and as family roles are dependent on it, it is a legitimate objective of the legislator to make civil status lasting and unambiguous, in order to avoid the divergence of biological sex and legal gender where possible, and to grant a change in civil status only if there are valid reasons for it and constitutionally guaranteed rights could otherwise not be sufficiently safeguarded. In order to rule out arbitrary changes of civil status, the legislator can request proof based on objective criteria that the felt gender, which is in contradiction with the officially assigned sex, is indeed lasting and its recognition is of existential significance to the person concerned.

67 Thus, for a change of sex under civil status law pursuant to § 8(1) no. 1 of the Transsexuals Act with reference to § 1(1) of the Transsexuals Act, the legislator requires persons who identify with the gender that is not their officially assigned sex to submit two opinions by independent experts with relevant professional knowledge and experience in the field of transsexuality. These expert opinions must establish that the persons concerned have felt compelled to live in their felt gender for at least three years. Furthermore, it must be highly probable that the felt gender will not change in the future. It is not objectionable under constitutional law that recognition under civil status law is subject to such requirements.

68 (3) The legislator can indeed determine in detail how to legally substantiate the stability and irreversibility of a transsexual's identification with and life in the other gender. It can even go beyond the requirements of § 1(1) of the Transsexuals Act to specify conditions, for instance, regarding medical care for transsexuals, their appearance, or the quality of expert assessments. However, the legislator's requirements for substantiating that a transsexual identifies with and lives in the other gender lastingly are overly strict and unreasonable for the persons concerned, and are thus incompatible with Art. 2(1) in conjunction with Art. 1(1) of the Basic Law, given that in § 8(1) nos. 3 and 4 of the Transsexuals Act the legislator requires unambiguously and without exception that transsexuals undergo surgery

that changes their sexual characteristics and results in infertility in order to obtain recognition of their felt gender under civil status law [...].

(aa) [...]

Surgery to largely eliminate a person's sexual characteristics or to reshape these in such a way that their appearance corresponds to the felt gender to the greatest extent possible is a severe impairment of physical integrity, protected under Art. 2(2) of the Basic Law, and involves considerable health risks and side effects for the person concerned. [...]

In its decision of 6 December 2005 (BVerfGE 115, 1 – *Transsexuals V*), the Federal Constitutional Court already held that in light of current scientific findings, it cannot be assumed that seriously and irreversibly felt transsexuality can only be determined where the person concerned seeks, by any means available, to correct, as an error of nature, their sexual organs and characteristics through gender reassignment. Indeed, since then, experts have reached the conclusion that gender reassignment surgery is not always recommendable, even if the diagnosis of transsexuality is largely definite. Whether gender reassignment is medically acceptable and advisable must be determined on an individual basis, in the context of a medical diagnosis (cf. BVerfGE 115, 1 <21> – *Transsexuals V*). The lasting and irreversible nature of a transsexual's felt gender cannot be measured by the degree to which their external sexual characteristics are adapted to the felt gender by way of surgery. Rather, it must be determined how consistently a transsexual lives in their felt gender and is at ease with it [...]. It is true that gender reassignment surgery is a clear indication of a person's transsexuality. Yet if it is turned into an absolute prerequisite for recognition under civil status law, this would require transsexuals to undergo physical surgery and to accept health impairments, even if in their case this were not advisable and not necessary for determining that their transsexuality is lasting. The legislator has thus set excessive requirements for substantiating the lasting nature of transsexuality. These requirements do not sufficiently take into account the fundamental rights of the persons concerned under Art. 2(1) in conjunction with Art. 1(1) and Art. 2(2) of the Basic Law, which must be protected.

[...]

(bb) Permanent infertility is another unreasonable requirement set by the legislator, in § 8(1) no. 3 of the Transsexuals Act, for recognition of a transsexual's felt gender under civil status law, insofar as surgery is required for permanent infertility. Exercising the right to sexual self-determination under Art. 2(1) in conjunction with Art. 1(1) of the Basic Law is thus made conditional upon abandoning the right to physical integrity, without sufficiently weighty reasons that could justify these interferences with the fundamental rights of the transsexuals concerned (cf. BVerfGE 121, 175 <202>).

74 A person's fertility is protected by Art. 2(2) of the Basic Law, and is part of the right to physical integrity (cf. BVerfGE 79, 174 <201 and 202>). If transsexuals are required to undergo surgery resulting in their infertility in order to obtain recognition of their felt gender under civil status law, they face a dilemma: they can either refuse surgery, but at the same time forgo official recognition of their felt gender, which forces them to permanently live in conflict with their officially assigned sex; or they can accept surgery with far-reaching consequences, entailing not only physical changes and loss of function, but also affecting their self-image as a person, given that this is the only way to obtain official recognition of their felt gender under civil status law. No matter the choice of the persons concerned, essential fundamental rights in respect of their psychological or physical personal integrity are always impaired.

75 The reasons given for this inescapable and serious interference with fundamental rights are not tenable. However, the legislator does pursue a legitimate objective when it makes permanent infertility a requirement for the recognition of felt gender under civil status law, because it seeks to prevent persons officially assigned the male sex from giving birth or persons officially assigned the female sex from fathering children, which would be contrary to our understanding of sex and would have far-reaching consequences for the legal order [...].

76 [...]

77 [...] It is a legitimate objective to officially assign children to their biological parents in such a way that their parentage is not attributed to two legal mothers or fathers, in conflict with their biological conception. As § 11 of the Transsexuals Act shows, such a clear official assignment of children to a father and a mother, corresponding to the biological circumstances, is already provided for by law. The provision sets out that the relationship of a transsexual recognised under § 8 of the Transsexuals Act to their children is not affected; for adopted children this only applies if they were adopted before the decision on the recognition of the new gender attained legal validity. [...] In this respect, when balancing, on the one hand, the reasons that led the legislator to make permanent infertility a requirement pursuant to § 8 of the Transsexuals Act for official recognition of the felt gender against, on the other hand, the serious interferences with transsexuals' fundamental rights arising from the fact that they only obtain official recognition of their felt gender when they undergo surgery that seriously interferes with their physical integrity, even if this is not medically justified and even though male-to-female transsexuals are often infertile anyway due to hormone treatment, the right of transsexuals to sexual self-determination while safeguarding their physical integrity carries greater

weight. This applies not least because there are legal options for ensuring that children who have transsexual parents are nevertheless officially assigned to their father and their mother. [...]

II.

The challenged decisions of the Higher Regional Court, the Regional Court and the Local Court are indirectly based on the unconstitutional provision and violate the complainant's fundamental right under Art. 2(1) and (2) in conjunction with Art. 1(1) of the Basic Law. The order of the Higher Regional Court is reversed pursuant to § 95(2) of the Federal Constitutional Court Act. The matter is remanded to the Higher Regional Court for a decision on procedural costs.

D.

§ 8(1) nos. 3 and 4 of the Transsexuals Act is unconstitutional, yet the provision is not declared void; it is only declared incompatible with Art. 2(1) and (2) in conjunction with Art. 1(1) of the Basic Law. This is because, as set out above, the legislator has the option to lay down requirements for substantiating the serious need to live in the other gender that are more specific than the requirements laid down in § 1(1) of the Transsexuals Act. Alternatively, the legislator can completely revise the law on transsexuals to bring it in conformity with the Constitution.

Given the severity of the impairment for transsexuals whose felt gender is not recognised under civil status law if they do not satisfy the requirements of § 8(1) nos. 3 and 4 of the Transsexuals Act and who therefore cannot enter into a registered civil partnership corresponding to their sexual orientation, § 8(1) nos. 3 and 4 of the Transsexuals Act is declared not applicable until new provisions have been enacted.

[...]

The decision was taken with 6:2 votes.

Justices: Kirchhof, Hohmann-Dennhardt, Bryde, Gaier, Eichberger, Schluckebier, Masing, Paulus

No. 28

BVerfGE 138, 377 – False Paternity

HEADNOTES

to the Order of the First Senate of 24 February 2015
1 BvR 472/14

1. The general right of personality following from Article 2(1) in conjunction with Article 1(1) of the Basic Law protects the private and intimate spheres, and thus also the right to decide oneself whether and how to disclose information relating to one's intimate sphere and one's sex life. This includes not having to disclose sexual relations with a specific partner.

2. A court decision obliging a mother to disclose information on the identity of her child's putative father in order to enable the former legal father to assert his claim to compensation (§ 1607(3) of the Civil Code) exceeds the constitutional limits of judicial development of the law since it does not have a sufficiently clear basis in statutory law.

FEDERAL CONSTITUTIONAL COURT
- 1 BvR 472/14 -

IN THE NAME OF THE PEOPLE

In the proceedings
on the constitutional complaint of

Ms M...,
– authorised representative: ...
against a) the Order of the Schleswig-Holstein Higher Regional Court of 28 January 2014 - 15 UF 165/13 -
b) the Order of the Bad Segeberg Local Court of 27 September 2013 - 13a F 40/13 -
the Federal Constitutional Court – First Senate –

with the participation of Justices

> Vice-President Kirchhof,
> Gaier,
> Eichberger,
> Schluckebier,
> Masing,
> Paulus,
> Baer,
> Britz

held on 24 February 2015:

1. The Orders of the Bad Segeberg Local Court of 27 September 2013 - 13a F 40/13 - and of the Schleswig-Holstein Higher Regional Court of 28 January 2014 - 15 UF 165/13 - violate the complainant's general right of personality (Article 2(1) in conjunction with Article 1(1) of the Basic Law) and her fundamental right under Article 2(1) of the Basic Law in conjunction with the principle of the rule of law (Article 20(3) of the Basic Law). The Order of the Schleswig-Holstein Higher Regional Court of 28 January 2014 - 15 UF 165/13 - is reversed and the matter is remanded to the Schleswig-Holstein Higher Regional Court.

2. [...]

REASONS:

A.

The constitutional complaint concerns the question whether it is compatible with the Basic Law that the courts obliged the complainant, as the mother of a child, to disclose, on the basis of § 1353(1) in conjunction with § 242 of the Civil Code, information on the identity of the putative biological father to the non-biological, former legal father (so-called *Scheinvater*) upon the latter's successful challenge to his paternity in order to enable the latter to assert his compensation claim under § 1607(3) of the Civil Code.

I.

If a paternity challenge is successful (§§ 1599 *et seq.* of the Civil Code), a retroactive declaration of non-paternity is issued. The child's maintenance claims against the legal father then also retroactively cease to exist. The child's maintenance claims vis-à-vis the biological father are vested in the former legal father (§ 1607(3) first and second sentence of the Civil Code) to the extent of the maintenance the latter actually previously paid. […]

3   The former legal father can, however, only assert a claim to compensation under § 1607(3) first and second sentence of the Civil Code if he knows the identity of the biological father. If he does not know who the biological father is, the question arises whether he can demand that the mother disclose information on the identity of the putative biological father. Such a right to information is not explicitly provided for by law.

4   In a decision dated 9 November 2011 (BGHZ 191, 259 *et seq.*), the Federal Court of Justice recognised the former legal father's right to information, following from the requirement of good faith under § 242 of the Civil Code. It held that, in cases where the mother brought the former legal father to acknowledge paternity, the mother's general right of personality, which is affected by her obligation to disclose information, does not carry more weight than the former legal father's claim to effective legal protection. […]

II.

5   The complainant, then 20 years old, had a relationship with the plaintiff in the initial proceedings (hereinafter: the plaintiff) – in respect of whom a declaration of non-paternity was later issued. During the course of this relationship, she became pregnant. […] The complainant and the plaintiff were married owing to her […] pregnancy. Their daughter […] was born in wedlock in October 1991, thereby making the plaintiff the legal father of the child pursuant to § 1592 no. 1 of the Civil Code. […] In a letter to the plaintiff in 1994, the complainant disclosed that he might not be the biological father. They were divorced in 1995. […]

6   […]

III.

7   1. The challenged order of the Local Court obliged the complainant to disclose to the plaintiff the identity of the putative father of the child. […]

8   2. The Higher Regional Court dismissed the complaint against this order. […]

No. 28 – False Paternity

[…] 9-12

IV.

[…] 13-17

V.

Statements in respect of the constitutional complaint were submitted by the Federal Court of Justice, the German Conference of Family Courts (*Deutscher Familiengerichtstag*), the Academic Society for Family Law (*Wissenschaftliche Vereinigung für Familienrecht*) and the association 'Alimony and Family Law' (*Interessenverband Unterhalt und Familienrecht*). 18

[…] 19-21

B.

The constitutional complaint is admissible and well-founded. 22

[…] 23

The challenged decisions violate the complainant's general right of personality under Art. 2(1) in conjunction with Art. 1(1) of the Basic Law since they fail to recognise the scope of the complainant's fundamental rights. In the initial proceedings, the civil courts did not correctly assess the impact of the fundamental rights, and based the challenged decisions on this flawed assessment (see I below). 24

Regardless of the circumstances of the case at hand, a court decision taken despite a lack of a clear statutory basis therefor and obliging the complainant to disclose information exceeds the constitutional limits of judicial development of the law, which also constitutes a violation of the complainant's rights (Art. 2(1) in conjunction with Art. 20(3) of the Basic Law) (see II below). 25

I.

Given the circumstances of the case at hand, the complainant's general right of personality protected by Art. 2(1) in conjunction with Art. 1(1) of the Basic Law has been violated. The courts did not correctly assess the significance to be attached to this fundamental right (see 1 below). It cannot be ruled out that the courts would have reached a different conclusion had they attributed to the complainant's fundamental right the weight required under constitutional law when balancing it 26 against the conflicting interest of her former husband to assert his compensation claim under § 1607(3) first and second sentence of the Civil Code (see 2 below).

27 1. The courts did not correctly assess the significance to be attached to the complainant's general right of personality.

28 a) Obliging the complainant to disclose the required information is a serious impairment of her general right of personality. By obliging her to provide information on the identity of the putative biological father, the decisions compel the complainant to disclose a sexual relationship with one particular man or several particular men. In doing so, the complainant must reveal very intimate matters of her private life. For most people, there are certainly very few matters that are as intimate and that they would wish to keep as confidential for the sake of their personal integrity as their sexual relations.

29 The general right of personality following from Art. 2(1) in conjunction with Art. 1(1) of the Basic Law protects a person's private and intimate spheres and thus also aspects of their sex life and the right to keep these private. The protection of the private and intimate spheres covers matters that, due to the information they convey, are typically regarded as private in particular because their discussion or display in public is regarded as unseemly, because they are regarded as embarrassing if they become known, or because they provoke negative reactions from one's social environment, which is particularly true when it comes to sexuality. Without any protection against others obtaining knowledge thereof, one's sexual development would be severely impaired even though it is protected by fundamental rights (cf. BVerfGE 101, 361 <382> with further references). The right to respect of one's private and intimate spheres specifically protects the right not to have to disclose sexual relations with a partner, but to decide oneself whether, how and to whom to disclose information relating to one's intimate sphere and sex life (cf. BVerfGE 117, 202 <233> with further references).

30 b) The courts correctly set this right against the former legal father's interest in asserting his statutory claim to compensation under § 1607(3) first and second sentence of the Civil Code. Even though the interest in deciding oneself whether and to whom one wishes to disclose information on one's sex life carries great constitutional weight, the mother's interest in confidentiality may in certain cases – on grounds, for example, of earlier conduct – merit less protection than the former legal father's interest in financial compensation [...]. Particularly in circumstances where, given her conduct, the mother is liable to compensate the former legal father for his payments made towards his former legal child pursuant to § 826 of the Civil Code [i.e. for intentional unconscionable damage] [...], it might be reasonable *(zumutbar)* under constitutional law to oblige her to disclose the information necessary for a claim to compensation under § 1607(3) of the Civil Code. Therefore, under

constitutional law, it cannot be ruled out from the outset that the mother may be required to disclose to the former legal father the identity of the actual father, even against her will, in order to enable him to assert his claim to compensation.

c) In the present case, however, the courts failed to correctly assess the significance of the complainant's right to decide for herself whether, how and to whom she wishes to disclose information on her intimate sphere and her sex life.

The Local Court did not attach any importance to the complainant's general right of personality solely on the grounds that she had not informed the plaintiff – who when they married assumed he was the child's biological father – that he was not the only possible biological father. Thereby, the court impermissibly curtailed the protection afforded to the complainant by the general right of personality and failed to balance her interest in not having to name the putative father against the plaintiff's financial interest in compensation on the basis of the specific circumstances of the case.

The Higher Regional Court, by contrast, found that obliging the complainant to disclose the identity of the putative father of her child affected her right of personality. Nevertheless, based on flawed considerations, the Higher Regional Court subsequently failed to address the impairment of the complainant's general right of personality and therefore did not further balance her fundamental right against the plaintiff's financial interest. Indeed, the court at first correctly asserted that the general right of personality protects the authority conferred upon the individual to, in principle, decide themselves to what extent and to whom they disclose aspects of their personal life. However, the court then assumed that there was no "such interference", since the successful paternity challenge had shown that the complainant had had sexual intercourse with another man around the time of conception; according to the court, the "only" remaining question was the identity of the father. In pursuing this line of argument, the court failed to recognise that the mother's constitutionally protected intimate sphere encompasses in particular information about the partner or partners with whom she had sexual relations. With regard to protecting the private sphere of the person concerned, the disclosure and naming of sexual partners is often even more sensitive than the circumstance that the child was conceived out of wedlock. When she disclosed that she had had other sexual relations, the complainant did not forfeit her right not to have to disclose information on sexual relations with a specific partner, which is specifically protected by the general right of personality; the courts should have continued to take this right into account in their balancing of interests.

2. The challenged decisions are founded on a failure to recognise the significance of the general right of personality, because the courts, precisely as a result of this failure, did not sufficiently consider the specific circumstances of the present

case that speak for or against the worthiness of protection of the parties to the proceedings and failed to include these in their decision. [...]

II.

35 A court decision obliging the mother to disclose information on the identity of the putative father of the child in order to enable the former legal father to assert his claim to compensation (§ 1607(3) of the Civil Code) exceeds the constitutional limits of judicial development of the law since it has no sufficiently clear basis in statutory law, regardless of the circumstances of the case at hand. Therefore, the complainant's fundamental rights have been violated (Art. 2(1) in conjunction with Art. 20(3) of the Basic Law).

36 [...]
37-38 1. [...]
39-42 2. [...]
43 3. [...]
44 a) The limits set by fundamental rights on judicial development of the law are narrower in this case because the obligation to disclose information considerably impairs constitutionally protected legal interests, while the reasons in favour of an obligation to disclose information are of minor weight under constitutional law.
45 The impairment of the complainant's fundamental rights resulting from the obligation to disclose the information sought is serious (see B I 1 a above). Furthermore, the complainant's obligation to disclose information indirectly impairs the general right of personality and the family life of a man to be named.
46 In the present case, this impairment is solely set against the former legal father's interest in asserting his claim to compensation under statutory law. The fact that the legislator designed the claim to compensation in a manner that makes it difficult to assert by not pairing it with a right to information does not require correction under constitutional law. The legislator was not constitutionally obliged to make it easier to assert the claim to compensation. [...]
47 In principle, by means of development of the law, civil courts can strengthen individual legal interests beyond the minimum level required under constitutional law. However, in the case of the claim to information under review here, the scope for judicial development of the law that reaches beyond what is necessary under constitutional law is narrower due to the mother's conflicting fundamental right.
48 b) Accordingly, the courts may not base an obligation on the mother's part to disclose information on the identity of former sexual partners for the purpose of asserting the claim to compensation under § 1607(3) second sentence of the Civil Code solely on the blanket provision of § 242 of the Civil Code. Rather, court

decisions obliging a mother to disclose information on a sexual partner or partners require a more specific statutory basis, from which an obligation to disclose information of the type in question can be derived.

[…] 49-51

Thus, given that there is no specific statutory basis, and regardless of the specific circumstances of the case, the courts cannot generally derive from § 242 of the Civil Code a right to information afforded a former legal father against the mother that serves to assert the compensation claim. Strengthening the former legal father's claim to compensation would require action on the part of the legislator. The legislator is not prevented from introducing a provision to protect the former legal father, even though it is not required to do so in order to fulfil its duty of protection following from fundamental rights. The legislator could provide for stronger protection than what the courts can grant through their application of existing blanket provisions (cf. BVerfGE 134, 204 <223 and 224 para. 70>). However, the legislator would have to take the mother's conflicting general right of personality into account, which carries great weight under these circumstances. 52

III.

[…] 53-55

Justices: Kirchhof, Gaier, Eichberger, Schluckebier, Masing, Paulus, Baer, Britz

No. 29

BVerfGE 44, 353 – Addiction Counselling Agency

HEADNOTES

to the Order of the Second Senate of 24 May 1977
2 BvR 988/75

1. The seizure of client records from an institution operating an addiction counselling agency recognised under public law within the meaning of § 203(1) no. 4 of the Criminal Code violates that institution's fundamental right under Article 2(1) of the Basic Law and the fundamental rights of its clients under Article 2(1) in conjunction with Article 1(1) of the Basic Law if it impairs public health interests to such a degree that the damage caused by the interference is disproportionate to the outcome that is intended and can reasonably be expected of the seizure.

2. The seizure of such records violates the principle of proportionality if it is merely based on the general suspicion that clients of the counselling agency may have committed criminal acts relating to the acquisition and possession of drugs and may have acquired such drugs illegally.

FEDERAL CONSTITUTIONAL COURT
- 2 BvR 988/75 -

IN THE NAME OF THE PEOPLE

In the proceedings
on the constitutional complaint of

1. the Caritas Association for the regions Aachen-Stadt and Aachen-Land e. V., represented by Father G… and Father L…, 2. Father G…, 3. Professor Dipl.-Psych. G…, 4. Ms G…, 5. Ms K…, 6. Ms K…, 7. Mr R…,
– authorised representatives: …
against

No. 29 – Addiction Counselling Agency

a) the Order of the Aachen Regional Court of 7 November 1975
- 15 Qs 32/75 -,
b) the Order of the Aachen Local Court of 29 October 1975
- 41 Gs 3446/75-,
c) the Order of the Aachen Local Court of 16 October 1975
- 41 Gs 3313/75 - and the applications for preliminary injunction

the Federal Constitutional Court – Second Senate –

with the participation of Justices

> Vice-President Zeidler,
> Rinck,
> Wand,
> Hirsch,
> Rottmann,
> Niebler,
> Steinberger

held on 24 May 1977:

1. The Order of the Aachen Local Court of 16 October 1975 - 41 Gs 3313/75 - violates the fundamental right of complainant no. 1 under Article 13(1) of the Basic Law in conjunction with the Basic Law's principle of the rule of law.
2. The Order of the Aachen Local Court of 29 October 1975 - 41 Gs 3446/75 - violates the fundamental right of complainant no. 1 under Article 2(1) of the Basic Law and the fundamental rights of complainants nos. 4 to 7 under Article 2(1) in conjunction with Article 1(1) of the Basic Law.
Insofar as the Aachen Regional Court rejected the appeal against that order, its Order of 7 November 1975 - 15 Qs 32/75 - also violates the above-mentioned fundamental rights; it is reversed. [...]
3. [...]
4. [...]

REASONS:

A.

The constitutional complaints concern the search of the premises of a drug counselling agency operated by the Caritas Association and the seizure of records from the premises for the purpose of criminal investigations.

I.

2   1. The Caritas Association for the Regions Aachen-Stadt and Aachen-Land e. V. (complainant no. 1) […] operates an addiction counselling agency […] in Aachen. The counselling agency is recognised as a model institution by the Federation and the *Land* and receives public subsidies […]. In 1975, it had 25 staff members, including two psychologists and five social workers, employed on a permanent basis. It has a 'tearoom' and other premises. Its objective is both to prevent drug abuse and to help drug users overcome their addiction. For these purposes, it offers different forms of assistance, such as outpatient counselling and treatment. The 'tearoom' serves as a gathering place where young people can meet each other and the counsellors several nights a week. It is intended to facilitate counselling and treatment. For every client, the counselling agency creates a record containing the counsellor's notes on conversations, tests and therapeutic measures, but also the client's own statements. A 'problem questionnaire' to be completed by the clients requests information on an array of personal circumstances. The counselling agency assures its clients that any information will be kept confidential.

3-4 2. […]

5   a) On 16 October 1975, the public prosecution office sent files to the Local Court requesting an order for the search of the drug counselling agency "pursuant to §§ 102, 103 and 105 of the Code of Criminal Procedure". […]

6-7 […]

8   The search took place on the evening of 24 October 1975. It began at 8:00 p.m. and ended at some point after 9:00 p.m. At the same time, the police raided the premises. […]

9-13 b) […]

14-17 c) […]

II.

18 The constitutional complaints […] are directed against the search and seizure orders as well as against the decision of the Regional Court upholding these orders. They are also directed against the police raid that – in the complainants' opinion – was carried out "under the protection and cover" of the search order, and against the time chosen to carry out the search. […]

No. 29 – Addiction Counselling Agency

[…] 19-25

III.

[…] 26-37

B.

The constitutional complaints are admissible to the extent that complainant no. 1 challenges the search order and complainants nos. 1 and 4 to 7 challenge the seizure order and the decision of the Regional Court upholding it. To the extent that the constitutional complaints concern the police raid and the time chosen for the search, there are considerable doubts as to whether they are admissible; however, the Senate does not need to address these given that the constitutional complaints are in any case manifestly unfounded in this respect. For the rest, the constitutional complaints are inadmissible. 38
[…] 39-52

C.

The constitutional complaints, which are admissible to the extent set out above, are well-founded, except where they are directed against the police raid and the time chosen for the search. 53

I.

The search order of 16 October 1975 - 41 Gs 3313/75 - issued by the Aachen Local Court violates complainant no. 1's fundamental right under Art. 13(1) of the Basic Law in conjunction with the Basic Law's principle of the rule of law. 54

1. As a registered association, complainant no. 1 can be a holder of the fundamental right under Art. 13(1) of the Basic Law. […]. The counselling agency's premises are covered by the protection of Art. 13(1) of the Basic Law; the term 'home' also includes work, commercial and business premises (BVerfGE 32, 54 <69 *et seq.*>; 42, 212 <219>). 55

2. At least in cases where providing such information is entirely feasible based on the results of the investigation and where it does not impede the aims of law enforcement, a written search order issued on the basis of § 102 of the Code of Criminal Procedure that neither contains any factual information about the charge nor indicates the type or possible content of the evidence being sought does not 56

meet the requirements of the principle of the rule of law (BVerfGE 42, 212 <220>). This legal principle also applies in the present case. [...]

57 3. The challenged search order does not meet the minimum requirements arising from the principle of the rule of law. Not only is it missing a specific description of the charge but also any information on the evidence the search was supposed to provide, even though these elements were available according to the results of the investigation and would not have impeded the aims of law enforcement. No other circumstances in this case can be ascertained outside of the search order that could exceptionally take on the function of the principle of the rule of law, which the contents of such an order must normally fulfil (cf. BVerfGE 20, 162 <227 and 228>; 42, 212 <222>).

II.

58 The seizure order of 29 October 1975 issued by the Local Court and the decision on appeal of the Regional Court upholding it violate the fundamental right under Art. 2(1) of the Basic Law of complainant no. 1 and the fundamental rights under Art. 2(1) in conjunction with Art. 1(1) of the Basic Law of complainants nos. 4 to 7; they violate the principle of proportionality in respect of these fundamental rights.

59 1. a) Art. 2(1) of the Basic Law protects the general freedom of action of complainant no. 1 as a registered association (cf. BVerfGE 29, 260 <265 and 266>). This protection encompasses not only the right to establish an addiction counselling agency, but also the right to carry out its intended work in accordance with the law.

60 b) The clients of the counselling agency, including complainants nos. 4 to 7, are holders of the fundamental right to respect of their intimate and private spheres (Art. 2(1) in conjunction with Art. 1(1) of the Basic Law). While the client records kept by the counselling agency, including counsellors' notes on conversations, tests, therapeutic measures and the clients' own written statements, do not belong to the inviolable intimate sphere of the clients, they do belong to their private sphere. Thus, similar to medical index cards (medical records), they are also covered by the protection that the fundamental right under Art. 2(1) in conjunction with Art. 1(1) of the Basic Law affords individuals against intrusions of state authority (cf. BVerfGE 32, 373 <379>).

61 c) Yet intrusions of state authority upon the scope of protection of these fundamental rights are not excluded *per se*. The significance and scope of their protection cannot be determined irrespective of other interests that equally merit protection. Rather, in case of conflict, a balance must be struck with the principle of proportionality serving as the applicable constitutional standard for weighing the conflicting interests. It sets limits to state interference both with regard to the

No. 29 – Addiction Counselling Agency

general freedom of action (Art. 2(1) of the Basic Law) and with regard to the more specific private sphere of individuals (Art. 2(1) in conjunction with Art. 1(1) of the Basic Law), and thus also determines the scope of the fundamental rights in question (BVerfGE 32, 373 <379>; 34, 238 <246> – *Secret Tape Recordings*). Such limits must be set out by balancing the interests at issue. Where the outcome of the balancing suggests that the interests conflicting with the interferences in the specific case are evidently of significantly greater weight than the interests the state measures serve to protect, carrying out [the measure giving rise to] the interference anyway violates the principle of proportionality.

Interferences by way of seizures in criminal proceedings cannot simply be justified on the grounds that the public prosecution office is generally obliged, in accordance with the principle of legality, to take action against all criminal offences that can be prosecuted where there is a sufficiently strong suspicion and, in this regard, to make use of all coercive measures available under procedural law within the limits of the statutory provisions; this is because the constitutional principle of proportionality must also be observed in this respect. 62

2. The challenged decisions in respect of the seizure failed to balance the relevant interests in accordance with constitutional law. 63

a) On the one hand, the balancing must take into account the interest of the public in a properly functioning criminal justice system, including the tasks of prosecuting and punishing criminal offences that breach the Narcotics Act; depending on the specific circumstances of the individual case, the organs of the criminal justice system must be able to make use of the coercive measures set out in the Code of Criminal Procedure to that end. 64

[...] 65-67

b) On the other hand, public health interests, which are also essential to the common good, must be taken into account [in the balancing of interests]; these include providing effective assistance to persons with drug addiction or at risk of addiction and the guarantee that the work of drug counselling agencies will be carried out without disruption. 68

[...] 69-71

c) For the proper weighing of the interests to be balanced against one another, the following general aspects must be stressed: 72

aa) While the seizure of the client records of an addiction counselling agency is a suitable means to investigate drug-related offences, it is only one of several instruments available to law enforcement authorities to investigate such criminal offences. 73

bb) The seizure of records generally does not yield important evidence that could be used to investigate and prosecute illegal drug dealers. [...] 74

75 cc) Generally, the seizure of client records will only have prospects of contributing to the success of an investigation insofar as the investigation concerns the clients' own criminal offences relating to the illegal acquisition and possession of drugs. In this respect, it must be taken into account that when it comes to investigating and punishing offences breaching the Narcotics Act, the legal interests involved are not all of the same weight. Illegal dealers face the most severe punishment, whereas drug users face less severe criminal sanctions […]. Thus, interests of law enforcement have greater weight when it comes to prosecuting illegal dealers than when it comes to enforcing the state's power to punish drug users.

76 dd) Applicable law protects clients' trust in the confidentiality of statements they made in the context of a counselling relationship. […]

77 d) These general considerations show that, in the fight against drug abuse, the interests in a properly functioning criminal justice system do not generally take precedence over the public interest in addiction counselling. If the seizure of client records of an addiction counselling agency in accordance with the requirements set out in the Code of Criminal Procedure were always permissible, it would regularly destroy the relationship of trust required for the work of the affected agency and at the same time jeopardise the work of all other counselling agencies. In the interest of effective public health in the field of addiction counselling, this cannot be tolerated.

78 However, the above-mentioned circumstances do not provide grounds for generally giving precedence to public health interests over the interests of the criminal justice system. Not every addiction counselling agency merits constitutional protection against seizure of its client records, and this privilege cannot be invoked without consideration of the individual case. Rather, whether client records of such a counselling agency can be seized depends not just on those general considerations, but also on the circumstances of the specific case that may give precedence to one interest in one case and to the other interest in another. A violation of the fundamental rights of affected agencies can only be found in this context if the seizure of client records impairs public health interests to such a degree that the damage caused by the interference is disproportionate to the outcome that can reasonably be expected of the seizure. It cannot be definitively decided for all cases what circumstances are to be taken into account in the specific case und what weight they must be given. To make a decision in the present case, the following considerations are sufficient:

79 aa) Only counselling agencies that are officially recognised pursuant to § 203(1) no. 4 of the Criminal Code merit protection against seizure of their client records. Without such recognition, there is a risk that organisations could be established under the guise of counselling agencies with the sole purpose of qualifying for

No. 29 – Addiction Counselling Agency

protection against seizure in order to shield certain information from access by law enforcement authorities.

bb) Yet even the seizure of client records from an officially recognised drug counselling agency does not violate constitutional law *per se*. A counselling agency may only invoke protection against seizure if it has taken all reasonable precautions to avoid the impression that the agency or its staff are suspected of participating in drug trafficking or of condoning it. In particular, this requires that the institution operating the counselling agency carefully select and supervise its staff. 80

[…] 81-82

cc) Accordingly, the seizure of client records from an addiction counselling agency officially recognised pursuant to § 203(1) no. 4 of the Criminal Code violates the principle of proportionality where it is based solely on the general suspicion that clients of the counselling agency have committed criminal acts relating to the acquisition and possession of drugs and have acquired such drugs illegally. 83

3. In the case at hand, the seizure of client records cannot be upheld under constitutional law because the severe detriment arising from the interference with the complainants' fundamental rights is disproportionate to the outcome that can reasonably be expected with regard to the seizure. 84

a) The requirement of official recognition is satisfied given that the Catholic Church recognises the drug counselling agency of the Caritas Association […]. 85

b) In the present case, the seizure of the client records is based only on the general suspicion that clients of the counselling agency committed criminal acts relating to the acquisition and possession of drugs and acquired such drugs from illegal dealers. 86

In its seizure order, the Local Court declared the measure permissible "given that it follows from the records that the persons designated therein have continuously committed offences breaching the Narcotics Act"; it apparently only took into consideration that the clients of a drug counselling agency are addicted to drugs and – because of their addiction – acquire and possess drugs. 87

Likewise, the appellate decision of the Regional Court does not go beyond this suspicion that already arises from the very existence of a functioning counselling agency. […] 88

Regarding the prosecution of illegal dealers, too, the Regional Court limits itself to assumptions that – declared as general experience – do not go beyond general and abstract observations. […] 89

Finally, the Regional Court points out that drug trafficking in a 'tearoom' belonging to a counselling agency could not be prevented and that it could attract dealers without the counselling agency intending to do so; this argument only emphasises a 90 fact that is generally part of the operational risk of any counselling agency that runs a 'tearoom' or a similar contact centre.

91 The challenged seizure orders do not contain any indication that – in the view of the Local Court or the Regional Court – staff members of the drug counselling agency themselves were suspected of criminal offences and that such a suspicion would have justified the seizure of the client records. The public prosecution office based its application for a seizure order only on the grounds that the documents to be seized concerned "persons addicted to drugs". At no point did it attempt to link the suspicion – which, in its opinion, existed initially, but was dropped already before the application for a seizure order was submitted – against "persons responsible" for the drug counselling agency with the client records. In addition, the inspection of the client records would hardly have provided information in this regard because it could not be expected that the "persons responsible" for the drug counselling agency would use these records to confess in writing to criminal acts they committed.

92 4. Thus, the challenged seizure decisions violate the fundamental right to the general freedom of action (Art. 2(1) of the Basic Law) of complainant no. 1 and the fundamental right to the respect for their private sphere (Art. 2(1) in conjunction with Art. 1(1) of the Basic Law) of complainants nos. 4 to 7. A decision as to whether they violate other provisions of the Basic Law is thus no longer required.

D.

93-100 [...]

Justices: Zeidler, Rinck, Wand, Hirsch, Rottmann, Niebler, Steinberger

No. 30

BVerfGE 89, 69 – Mandatory Medical-Psychological Assessment

HEADNOTE

to the Order of the First Senate of 24 June 1993
1 BvR 689/92

On the question under which circumstances cannabis resin consumption may justify an order by the authorities that [the holder of a driving licence] submit a medical-psychological assessment report on their fitness to drive.

FEDERAL CONSTITUTIONAL COURT
- 1 BvR 689/92 -

IN THE NAME OF THE PEOPLE

In the proceedings
on the constitutional complaint of

Mr H...,
– authorised representatives: ...
against a) the Order of the Federal Administrative Court of 19 March 1992
- BVerwG 3 B 28.92 -,
b) the Judgment of the Higher Administrative Court for the *Land* North Rhine-Westphalia of 8 November 1991 - 19 A 1674/91 -
the Federal Constitutional Court – First Senate –
with the participation of Justices
President Herzog,
Henschel,
Seidl,
Grimm,
Söllner,
Dieterich,

BVerfGE 89, 69

Kühling,
Seibert

held on 24 June 1993:

The Order of the Federal Administrative Court of 19 March 1992 - BVerwG 3 B 28.92 - and the Judgment of the Higher Administrative Court for the *Land* North Rhine-Westphalia of 8 November 1991 - 19 A 1674/91 - violate the complainant's fundamental right under Article 2(1) in conjunction with Article 1(1) of the Basic Law. They are reversed. The matter is remanded to the Higher Administrative Court.

[…]

REASONS:

A.

1   The constitutional complaint concerns the question under which circumstances cannabis resin consumption may justify an order that [the holder of a driving licence] submit a medical-psychological assessment report on their fitness to drive.

I.

2   1. Pursuant to § 4(1) of the Road Traffic Act, the authorities must revoke a driving licence if its holder proves to be unfit to drive motor vehicles. Under § 6(1) no. 1 of the Road Traffic Act the Federal Minister of Transport is authorised, subject to the consent of the *Bundesrat*, to issue ordinances and general administrative rules, including on medical examinations, to determine lack of fitness to drive motor vehicles. […]

3-7   […]

8   2. In consultation with the competent highest *Land* authorities, the Federal Minister of Transport enacted administrative directives for assessing the physical and psychological fitness of applicants for and holders of driving licences. […]

9-16   […]

17   3. […]

II.

18   1. The complainant, who is 28 years old, had a driving licence for categories 1 and 3. In January 1990, during a police check carried out at approximately

No. 30 – Mandatory Medical-Psychological Assessment

1:45 a.m., law enforcement officers found the complainant sitting in his parked vehicle together with an acquaintance in a remote car park. The police seized approximately 0.5 g of cannabis resin. The questioning of the two men revealed that the complainant's acquaintance had previously bought approximately 2 g of cannabis resin in Düsseldorf's old town because he wanted to try it out. He ran into the complainant in a restaurant and invited him to smoke a joint together. They did so shortly before the police check. In their report, the police officers stated the following:

A search of the persons and the vehicle for further narcotics did not yield any results.

Both persons displayed obvious signs of drug consumption (slurred speech, slightly unsteady gait).

Following the police officers' orders, the complainant left his vehicle in the car park. During his examination on 21 February 1990, the complainant said it had been his first time trying cannabis resin. The criminal investigation against him was terminated pursuant to § 170(2) of the Code of Criminal Procedure by order of 14 March 1990 since he had only joined in his acquaintance's cannabis smoking, which by itself is not a punishable offence.

2. [...] The Road Traffic Authority informed the complainant that his fitness to drive was in doubt on grounds of his drug consumption, and ordered that he submit a medical-psychological assessment report. Although the complainant underwent the assessment, he did not submit the report. Following this, the Authority set a deadline and announced that it would revoke the complainant's driving licence should he fail to submit the report. After the complainant unsuccessfully remonstrated, the Road Traffic Authority revoked his driving licence. The Authority argued that his cannabis resin consumption had raised reasonable doubts as to his fitness to drive. The only way to dispel these doubts was for the complainant to undergo a medical-psychological assessment. While the required assessment had taken place, the complainant had not submitted the report as proof of fitness to drive despite being notified of the deadline. The Road Traffic Authority found that his refusal to assist in investigating the facts meant that the complainant had to be deemed unfit to drive.

3. After lodging an unsuccessful objection, the complainant brought an action against that decision before the Administrative Court. [...]

4. The Administrative Court reversed the decision on the complainant's objection and the order to revoke his driving licence. [...]

25 5. [...] With the challenged decision, the Higher Administrative Court modified the decision of the Administrative Court and ultimately rejected the complainant's action.
26-27 [...]
28-29 6. [...]

III.

30 In his constitutional complaint, the complainant claims a violation of Art. 3(1) and of Art. 2(2) first sentence of the Basic Law; substantively, he also claims a violation of Art. 2(1) in conjunction with Art. 1(1) of the Basic Law.
31 The complainant argues that the challenged decisions violate the general guarantee of the right to equality since they accept that cannabis and alcohol consumption are treated differently by the road traffic authorities. [...]
32 [...]
33 The complainant argues that Art. 2(2) first sentence of the Basic Law is violated given that individuals, due to the prohibition under criminal law to acquire cannabis products for their own consumption, are pushed towards alcohol, an alternative that is more harmful to health.
34 [...]

IV.

35 Statements on the constitutional complaint were submitted by the Federal Minister of Health on behalf of the Federal Government, several *Land* Governments, the President of the Federal Court of Justice, the Federal Administrative Court, the German Head Office for Addiction Matters (*Deutsche Hauptstelle gegen die Suchtgefahren*) and the defendant in the initial proceedings.
36-47 [...]

B.

48 The constitutional complaint is for the most part admissible. However, the complainant failed to sufficiently demonstrate and substantiate a possible violation of Art. 2(2) first sentence of the Basic Law (§§ 92 and 23(1) of the Federal Constitutional Court Act). [...]

C.

The constitutional complaint is well-founded. The administrative order to submit a medical-psychological assessment report to prove fitness to drive is not compatible with the general right of personality. The challenged court decisions, which found this measure to be lawful, thus violate the complainant's above-mentioned fundamental right.

I.

The court decisions violate Art. 2(1) in conjunction with Art. 1(1) of the Basic Law.
1. a) Art. 2(1) in conjunction with Art. 1(1) of the Basic Law guarantees the general right of personality. This right generally protects individuals against the collection and disclosure of findings about their health, mental well-being and character (cf. BVerfGE 32, 373 <378 *et seq.*>; 44, 353 <372 and 373> – *Addiction Counselling Agency*; 65, 1 <41 and 42> – *Census*; 78, 77 <84> – *Public Announcement of Legal Incapacitation*; 84, 192 <194 and 195>). This protection increases the more closely the data is related to the affected person's intimate sphere, which, as an inviolable part of private life, must be respected and protected by all state authority (cf. BVerfGE 32, 373 <378 and 379>; 65, 1 <45 and 46> – *Census*).
b) The Road Traffic Authority's order that the complainant submit the assessment report involves the disclosure of highly personal information that is protected by the general right of personality. This applies not only to the medical, but to an even greater extent also to the psychological part of the assessment.
Where a medical-psychological assessment is ordered to determine fitness to drive, the medical part of the assessment includes a general health evaluation as well as examinations of the musculoskeletal system, the nervous system, possibly the inner organs, sensory function, psychological well-being, responsiveness and resilience. [...] If drug use is suspected, lab tests of urine samples (drug screening) are used to determine consumption habits. [...]
The psychological part of the assessment begins with an analysis of the personal history of the person under examination: their upbringing, education and training, occupation, marital status, children, illnesses, past surgery, alcohol consumption, smoking, financial situation, leisure interests. If the person under examination has had previous encounters with the law, the psychologist discusses these incidents, including causes and lessons learnt, with them. The psychologist also evaluates performance, including performance under pressure, speed and accuracy of optical perception, ability to react to quickly changing optical and acoustic signals and concentration.

55 These findings are even more closely related to the inviolable part of private life than the purely medical findings obtained in the examination. Therefore, they enjoy greater protection under Art. 2(1) in conjunction with Art. 1(1) of the Basic Law. The findings of the psychological examination relating to the character of the person concerned may affect their self-regard as well as their social standing. They must disclose such details in a setting resembling an interrogation. Moreover, the character assessment is mainly based on a set of exploratory interviews. This method is not as conclusive as lab tests, and uncertainties cannot be ruled out.

56 2. The order to undergo a medical-psychological assessment and to submit the report to the Road Traffic Authority amounts to an interference with the general right of personality.

57 While the complainant was free to decide whether to comply with this order, the Road Traffic Authority had announced that it would revoke his driving licence should he refuse. The announcement of the legal consequences of refusal, which is in line with the established case-law of the administrative courts, is sufficient to make qualify as an interference the Road Traffic Authority's order that the complainant submit the report, based on § 15b(2) of the Vehicle Registration and Licensing Ordinance (cf. BVerfGE 74, 264 <281 *et seq.*>).

58 3. It is true that the protection of the general right of personality is not absolute. Every person must tolerate state measures that serve overriding public interests if these measures have a statutory basis and adhere to the requirement of proportionality, unless they infringe upon the inviolable part of private life (cf. BVerfGE 32, 273 <279>; 65, 1 <44> – *Census*). However, in the present case, the interference is not justified.

59 a) The statutory basis of the challenged decisions does not raise any concerns.

60 [...]

61 [...] Road traffic involves high risks for the life, health and property of numerous individuals. Therefore, fitness to drive must be subject to strict requirements. To ensure fitness to drive, preventive checks of drivers, as provided for in § 4(1) of the Road Traffic Act and § 15b of the Vehicle Registration and Licensing Ordinance, are generally not objectionable under constitutional law.

62 b) Nonetheless, in their interpretation of § 15b(2) of the Vehicle Registration and Licensing Ordinance in the present case, the courts did not sufficiently take into account the general right of personality. In particular, they failed to take into consideration that their interpretation must not result in a disproportionate restriction of fundamental rights.

63 When interpreting § 15b(2) of the Vehicle Registration and Licensing Ordinance in accordance with the general statutory standards for granting and revoking a driving licence, the general right of personality is only sufficiently taken into account

No. 30 – Mandatory Medical-Psychological Assessment

if the authorities base their order to submit a medical-psychological assessment report on deficits which – from a reasonable and realistic perspective – give rise to serious concerns that the person concerned will not display the caution and appropriate behaviour required for driving. Furthermore, not all circumstances potentially indicating a remote possibility that someone may be unfit to drive provide sufficient grounds for ordering a medical-psychological assessment report. Rather, the authorities must base their order on factual findings establishing that the person concerned is likely unfit to drive. Finally, the general right of personality of the person concerned must be taken into account in the decision on what type of assessment is ordered pursuant to § 15b(2) nos. 1 to 3 of the Vehicle Registration and Licensing Ordinance. In all of these respects, the challenged decisions are objectionable.

aa) It is not clearly ascertainable from the decisions which factors, in the courts' view, indicate that the person concerned may be unfit to drive. 64

It was stated that even the one-off consumption of cannabis may lead to echo highs; this could be understood to mean that the authorities and the courts considered even one-off consumption to result in a lack of fitness to drive. […] 65

bb) It would be more plausible if the competent authority, and the courts upholding the administrative decision, merely assumed that a person is unfit to drive in cases of regular cannabis use. It was clearly assumed, by the competent authority and the courts, that at least in these cases, the occurrence of an echo high is likely. […] 66

However, an interpretation of § 15b(2) of the Vehicle Registration and Licensing Ordinance according to which one-off cannabis consumption in itself is a sufficiently compelling reason for ordering a medical-psychological assessment report excessively restricts the general right of personality. Given the far-reaching interference with fundamental rights associated with the ordering of such an assessment, there must be more robust indications that someone is unfit to drive. Based on the current state of knowledge on cannabis use, it cannot necessarily be inferred that anyone who is found with a joint is a regular user. […] In addition, it is by no means certain whether the assumption that regular cannabis users have a tendency to drive while intoxicated is actually true. If there are no sufficiently robust indications of regular cannabis use, the competent authority must at least try to further clarify the circumstances of the case, including by discussing the case with the person concerned, before ordering a medical-psychological assessment report. 67

Measured against these standards, the findings on which the order of a medical-psychological assessment report was based in the complainant's case do not sufficiently support the assumption that he may be unfit to drive. 68

69 In the present case, the fact that the complainant was found smoking a joint on one occasion did not provide sufficient grounds for the suspicion that he is a regular cannabis user; yet such grounds would have been required for ordering a medical-psychological assessment report. [...]

70 cc) Besides, the challenged decisions also violate Art. 2(1) in conjunction with Art. 1(1) of the Basic Law, given that the courts considered the order of a medical-psychological assessment permissible even though, in view of existing screening methods, the question whether the person concerned was a regular cannabis user – which should have been determined first – could already have been answered by means of urine, blood or hair tests. § 15b(2) no. 1 of the Vehicle Registration and Licensing Ordinance expressly provides for the possibility of ordering an examination by a medical specialist. Such an examination would entail a less intrusive interference with the general right of personality. If an alleged lack of fitness to drive hinges on whether the person concerned regularly consumes cannabis, as assumed by the competent authority and the courts in the present case, this must be determined first. Only then may a medical-psychological assessment be ordered, if necessary.

71 [...]

II.

72 Moreover, the challenged decisions raise serious concerns with regard to the general guarantee of the right to equality (Art. 3(1) of the Basic Law). The courts accepted that the Road Traffic Authority, when ordering the assessment report in the present case, applied standards that are stricter than the standards commonly applied by the authorities in cases involving alcohol consumption.

73 1. The more the unequal treatment of persons or situations negatively impacts the exercise of freedoms protected by fundamental rights, the more strictly the right to equality must be observed (cf. BVerfGE 55, 72 <88>; 60, 123 <134>; 82, 126 <146>; BVerfG, EuGRZ 1993, p. 100 <103>). [...]

74 As discussed above, the authorities' order of a medical-psychological assessment considerably impairs the general right of personality, not least because the outcome of the assessment determines whether the person concerned may keep their driving licence. Whether or not someone has a driving licence may considerably affect the exercise of freedoms protected by fundamental rights. This not only applies to the general freedom of action (Art. 2(1) of the Basic Law); depending on the circumstances, it may also apply to specific freedoms, such as occupational freedom (Art. 12(1) of the Basic Law). Therefore, strict standards must be applied to the

reasons that may justify unequal treatment when ordering medical-psychological assessment reports in this context.

2. The practice of the authorities, which has been upheld by the courts, is based on the administrative directives on fitness to drive issued by the Ministry, which are binding on road traffic authorities [...]. These directives state that, except for cases where there is a specific suspicion of alcoholism, alcohol consumption as such can only give rise to doubts as to one's fitness to drive if "repeated traffic offences while driving under the influence of alcohol" have been committed. [...] For drivers found to have violated road safety rules in an alcohol-related incident for the first time, a medical-psychological assessment may be ordered if their blood alcohol content is or exceeds 0.16%, provided that other circumstances in the individual case give rise to the suspicion of regular excessive alcohol consumption. By contrast, the challenged decisions subject cannabis users to considerably stricter standards with regard to the circumstances that give rise to doubts as to their fitness to drive. [...].

3. Sufficient reasons to justify this unequal treatment are not readily ascertainable, even though there are indeed differences between cannabis and alcohol. However, it is not necessary make a conclusive determination on this issue, given that the constitutional complaint is already successful on other grounds.

Justices: Herzog, Henschel, Seidl, Grimm, Söllner, Dieterich, Kühling, Seibert

No. 31

BVerfGE 103, 21 – DNA Fingerprinting

FEDERAL CONSTITUTIONAL COURT
- 2 BvR 1741/99 -
- 2 BvR 276/00 -
- 2 BvR 2061/00 -

IN THE NAME OF THE PEOPLE

In the proceedings
on the constitutional complaints of

1. Mr S...,
– authorised representatives: ...
against a) the Order of the Hanover Regional Court of 4 August 1999
- 46 Qs 193/99 -,
b) the Order of the Hanover Local Court of 3 June 1999
- 234 AR 50201/99 -
- 2 BvR 1741/99 -,
2. Mr P...,
– authorised representative: ...
against a) the Order of the Leipzig Regional Court of 17 December 1999
- 1 Qs 223/99 -,
b) the Orders of the Torgau Local Court of 3 November 1999
- Gs 69/99 -,
c) indirectly: § 2(1) of the DNA Identification Act in the version of 2 June 1999 (BGBl, I p. 1242) in conjunction with § 81g of the Code of Criminal Procedure

[...]
- 2 BvR 276/00 -,

No. 31 – DNA Fingerprinting

3. Mr F...,

– authorised representative: ...

against a) the Order of the Arnsberg Regional Court of 5 October 2000
- 2 Qs 185/00 -,
b) the Order of the Werl Local Court of 1 September 2000
- 3 Gs 239/00 -,
c) indirectly: § 2(1) of the DNA Identification Act in the version of 2 June 1999 (BGBl I, p. 1242) in conjunction with § 81g of the Code of Criminal Procedure

- 2 BvR 2061/00 -

the Third Chamber of the Second Senate of the Federal Constitutional Court with the participation of Justices

President Limbach,
Hassemer,
Broß

unanimously held, on the basis of § 93c in conjunction with §§ 93a, 93b of the Federal Constitutional Court Act in the version of 11 August 1993 (BGBl I, p. 1473):

1. The constitutional complaints are combined for joint decision.
2. The Orders of the Hanover Regional Court of 4 August 1999 - 46 Qs 193/99 - and of the Hanover Local Court of 3 June 1999 - 234 AR 50201/99 - violate complainant no. 1's right under Article 2(1) in conjunction with Article 1(1) of the Basic Law. They are reversed and the matter is remanded to the Hanover Local Court [...]

[...]

3. The constitutional complaints of complainants nos. 2 and 3 are not admitted for decision. [...]

REASONS:

A.

The constitutional complaints concern judicial orders requiring that cell tissue of persons convicted of considerable criminal offences by final judgment in so-called old cases be collected and used in molecular genetic analysis for the purpose of identifying [offenders] in future criminal cases ('DNA fingerprinting').

I.

2   The challenged orders are based on the following provisions:

3   § 81g of the Code of Criminal Procedure

4   (1) If persons are suspected of a considerable criminal offence, in particular of a felony, of a misdemeanour against sexual self-determination, of causing bodily harm by dangerous means, or of aggravated theft or blackmail, cell tissue may be collected from them and subjected to molecular genetic analysis to create their DNA profile for the purpose of identification in future criminal proceedings if the nature of the offence or the way it was committed, the personality of the suspect, or other relevant information provide grounds for assuming that criminal proceedings will be conducted against them in the future in respect of one of the aforementioned criminal offences.

5   (2) The collected cell tissue may be used only for the molecular genetic analysis referred to in section (1); it shall be destroyed without undue delay once it is no longer required for that purpose. The analysis may not be used to retrieve information other than that required to create the DNA profile; examinations seeking to gain information serving other purposes are impermissible.

6   (3) [...]

7   § 2 of the DNA Identification Act

8   (1) The measures authorised in § 81g of the Code of Criminal Procedure may also be carried out if the person concerned was convicted by final judgment of one of the criminal offences listed in § 81g(1) of the Code of Criminal Procedure or was not convicted solely due to exemption from criminal responsibility on grounds of proven or possible incapacity or due to their inability to stand trial on the grounds of mental illness; the same applies in cases where a conviction was not handed down due to proven or possible lack of criminal responsibility under the law on juvenile offenders (§ 3 of the Youth Courts Act) and the relevant entry has not yet been removed from the Federal Central Criminal Register (*Bundeszentralregister*) or the Register on Educative Measures for Juvenile Offenders (*Erziehungsregister*).

9   (2) [...]

No. 31 – DNA Fingerprinting

The law [...] enacting these provisions was promulgated on 21 March 1997 (BGBl I, p. 534). [...]

II.

1. Constitutional complaint 2 BvR 1741/99
a) The creation of the complainant's DNA profile was ordered because he had been repeatedly convicted of criminal offences. [...]
The immediate grounds prompting the measure were complainant no. 1's conviction on 19 April 1995 for attempted aggravated arson, causing bodily harm by dangerous means and threatening the commission of a felony, all committed in a single crime (*Tateinheit*). [...] Most recently, on 29 December 1995, complainant no. 1 was convicted on petty theft charges and sentenced to a fine.
By order of 3 June 1999, the Local Court ordered the collection of cell tissue of complainant no. 1 and its molecular genetic analysis to create a DNA profile [...].
[...]
b) Complainant no. 1 challenged this decision [...].
By order of 4 August 1999, the Regional Court rejected his complaint [...].
[...]
c) In his constitutional complaint, complainant no. 1 claims a violation of his right to informational self-determination under Art. 2(1) in conjunction with Art. 1(1) of the Basic Law. He asserts that the ordinary courts neither took into account the positive social prognosis he was given in the context of the probation decision nor his personal situation. He argues that the remission of his sentence and the time that has passed since he committed a crime and since his last conviction were not sufficiently taken into consideration. The courts failed to base their decisions on a prognosis specifically relating to his personality, he claims. He contends that the challenged decisions amount to schematic decision-making.
d) [...]
2. Constitutional complaint 2 BvR 276/00
a) At the request of the Public Prosecution Office, the Local Court ordered the collection and molecular genetic analysis of cell tissue from complainant no. 2 to create a DNA profile. This order was made because complainant no. 2 was sentenced to a prison term of seven years and six months for attempted murder on 9 June 1995.
[...]
b) The Regional Court rejected as unfounded the complaints filed by complainant no. 2 against the [...] orders of the Local Court. [...]

37 c) Complainant no. 2 claims a violation of his fundamental rights under Art. 2(1) in conjunction with Art. 1(1), Art. 2(2), Art. 3(3) and Art. 19(4) of the Basic Law. He argues that building a DNA database paves the way towards creating "a transparent citizen", which is why a particularly strict standard must be applied to the proportionality assessment. He contends that the statutory provisions [on which the challenged orders are based] do not sufficiently give effect to this constitutional standard. […]

38 The complainant argues that, even assuming that the statutory provisions authorising the measure constituting an interference were constitutional, the measures ordered in his case violate his right to informational self-determination. He submits that the measure is disproportionate given that he has been kept in prison almost without interruption since December 1993.

39 […]

40 3. Constitutional complaint 2 BvR 2061/00

41 a) The measure pursuant to § 2(1) of the DNA Identification Act in conjunction with § 81g of the Code of Criminal Procedure was ordered against complainant no. 3 because he was convicted, by final judgment, of five counts of rape and one count of causing bodily harm, all committed in a single crime (*Tateinheit*) with unlawful deprivation of liberty. […]

42 b) Complainant no. 3 lodged a complaint against this order, which the Regional Court rejected […].

43 c) Complainant no. 3 claims a violation of his right to informational self-determination under Art. 2(1) in conjunction with Art. 1(1) of the Basic Law. […]

B.

44-45 […]

I.

46 The challenged measures are based on § 2 of the DNA Identification Act in conjunction with § 81g of the Code of Criminal Procedure.

47 1. Formally, these provisions are constitutional. They were enacted by the federal legislator based on its concurrent legislative powers for court organisation and procedure in criminal matters. […]

48 […]

49 2. Substantively, § 2 of the DNA Identification Act in conjunction with § 81g of the Code of Criminal Procedure is also compatible with constitutional law.

No. 31 – DNA Fingerprinting

a) The core of personality enjoys absolute protection (cf. BVerfGE 34, 238 <245> – *Secret Tape Recordings*; 80, 367 <373 and 374> – *Diary-Like Notes*; with further references), even against interferences that have a basis in statutory law. However, the challenged provisions do not affect the core of personality. This holds true at least insofar as the statutory provisions authorising the interferences in the case at hand only concern the noncoding part of DNA [...], DNA profiles are created exclusively for the purposes of identifying the person concerned in future criminal cases and the DNA material is destroyed once the DNA profile has been created. Only the DNA profile thus created is stored, and, from a forensic perspective, the code individuality it attains is comparable to that of a fingerprint. The taking and storage of fingerprints does not affect the core of personality. It is irrelevant that the evidentiary value attainable with DNA fingerprinting far exceeds that of conventional fingerprinting, serological procedures (biochemical fingerprinting) or other identification methods [...] and that, in practice, the comparison of DNA patterns offers considerable technical advantages for forensic examinations [...]. What is decisive is that once a DNA fingerprint has been derived from the samples, which must then be destroyed pursuant to § 81g(2) of the Code of Criminal Procedure, it is not permissible to create a personality profile of the person concerned; in particular, the procedure does not allow for any conclusions to be drawn on personality-related characteristics such as genetic make-up, character traits or illnesses of the person concerned [...].

b) However, the creation, storage and (future) use of DNA profiles do interfere with the fundamental right to informational self-determination guaranteed by Art. 2(1) in conjunction with Art. 1(1) of the Basic Law [...]. Based on the notion of self-determination, this fundamental right confers upon the individual the authority to, in principle, decide themselves whether and to what extent to disclose aspects of their personal life (cf. BVerfGE 65, 1 <41 and 42> – *Census*; 78, 77 <84> – *Public Announcement of Legal Incapacitation*). It affords fundamental rights holders protection against the unlimited collection, storage, use or sharing of personal data that is individualised or that can otherwise be attributed to them as individual persons (cf. BVerfGE 65, 1 <43> – *Census*; 67, 100 <143>). This guarantee may only be restricted by law or pursuant to a law if the restrictions serve an overriding public interest and if the principle of proportionality is observed; restrictions may not go beyond what is absolutely necessary to protect public interests (cf. BVerfGE 65, 1 <44> – *Census*; 67, 100 <143>).

§ 2 of the DNA Identification Act in conjunction with § 81g of the Code of Criminal Procedure sufficiently reflects the limits recognised in constitutional law for the right to informational self-determination (cf. BVerfGE 65, 1 <44> – *Census*). The provisions aim to facilitate future investigations of considerable criminal offences;

they thus serve the administration of justice based on rule of law guarantees, to which constitutional law attributes high standing (cf. BVerfGE 77, 65 <76>; 80, 367 <375> – *Diary-Like Notes*).

53 § 2 of the DNA Identification Act in conjunction with § 81g of the Code of Criminal Procedure also satisfies the requirements of legal clarity and justiciability deriving from the rule of law (cf. BVerfGE 47, 239 <252>; cf. also BVerfGE 65, 1 <46> – *Census*). It is sufficient that the provisions allow for a [sufficiently clear] interpretation based on established legal methodology (cf. BVerfGE 65, 1 <54> – *Census*; 78, 205 <212 and 213>); this is especially true with regard to the element of considerable criminal offences, to which the authorised measures must have a sufficient connection. The term 'considerable criminal offences' is also used in other provisions of the Code of Criminal Procedure (cf. §§ 98a(1), 110a(1), 163e of the Code of Criminal Procedure), and has been recognised by the courts as an element that sets limits to the use of investigation methods that are not governed by specific provisions [...]. The existing case-law can serve as a basis for further clarifying the meaning of this term [in the challenged provisions].

54 According to the prevailing legal view, a considerable criminal offence must at least amount to medium-level crime, seriously disrupt the peaceful legal order (*Rechtsfrieden*) and be capable of considerably impairing the sense of security of the general public [...]. While 'considerable criminal offence' is an indeterminate legal concept (*unbestimmter Rechtsbegriff*), the examples of typical offences fitting this element that are listed in the challenged provision further help to delimit this concept, which sufficiently gives effect to the requirement of specificity [...]. Contrary to complainant no. 2's assumption, whether a criminal act qualifies as a considerable offence [within the meaning of the challenged provision] does not depend on the likelihood that the type of criminal offence will produce the type of evidence sought by the measure; rather, this likelihood is a relevant factor for establishing whether the measure is necessary, which must be assessed on a case-by-case basis [...].

55 Precautionary gathering of evidence pursuant to § 2 of the DNA Identification Act in conjunction with § 81g of the Code of Criminal Procedure also does not violate the prohibition of excessive measures (*Übermaßverbot*). Carrying out the measure at issue is only permissible if the person concerned has a prior conviction for a considerable criminal offence, and requires a prognosis indicating, based on specific facts, that criminal proceedings regarding considerable criminal offences will likely be conducted against that person in the future. The measure is thus restricted to special cases. The requirement of prior judicial authorisation (*Richtervorbehalt*) pursuant to §§ 81g(3), 81a(2) of the Code of Criminal Procedure gives effect to the

interest of affected persons in effective fundamental rights protection, as it requires courts to review the circumstances of the individual case.

The interest in rehabilitation of affected persons that could be jeopardised by the risk of social stigmatisation (cf. BVerfGE 65, 1 <48> – *Census*) is sufficiently taken into consideration given that, pursuant to § 2(1) of the DNA Identification Act, the measures may only be carried out as long as entries have not yet been erased from the Federal Central Criminal Register or the Register on Educative Measures for Juvenile Offenders [in accordance with the statutory time limits]; in addition, § 33(2) no. 2 of the Federal Criminal Police Office Act provides that the blocking of data must be ordered, in the individual case, if it is established that knowledge of the data is no longer necessary for the Federal Criminal Police Office (*Bundeskriminalamt*) to perform its tasks.

Furthermore, § 81g(2) of the Code of Criminal Procedure requires that data be subject to a strict purpose limitation and that the entire collected cell tissue be destroyed [after the procedure is completed] […]. This prevents abuse, in particular [impermissible] examinations of coding DNA. The remaining option of storing the DNA profiles at the Federal Criminal Police Office (§ 3(1) of the DNA Identification Act) and the uses and processing measures provided for in § 3(2) of the DNA Identification Act are not objectionable under constitutional law given that they were created by the legislator as precautionary measures that serve a public interest, namely future law enforcement […]. The same applies with regard to the possibility of requesting information from the DNA profile database established by the Federal Criminal Police Office in April 1998 pursuant to § 8(6) of the Federal Criminal Police Office Act (cf. §§ 32, 33 of the Federal Criminal Police Office Act).

II.

The interpretation and application of § 2(1) of the DNA Identification Act in conjunction with § 81g of the Code of Criminal Procedure undertaken by the ordinary courts is only objectionable under constitutional law in the case of complainant no. 1. In the cases of complainants nos. 2 and 3, no violation of specific constitutional law can be found.

1. Where legal challenges concern interferences with the right to informational self-determination, a decision based on sound reasons requires the deciding court to sufficiently investigate the facts of the case (cf. BVerfGE 70, 297 <309>), in particular by requesting and examining available records on criminal proceedings and the enforcement of criminal sentences against the person concerned as well as probation records and recent entries in the Federal Central Criminal Register […];

it also requires that reasons provided for the decision show that the court conducted a balancing of the relevant circumstances. In this context, it is always necessary to make a case-by-case assessment; merely repeating the wording of the law is not sufficient […].

60 a) [The court deciding on DNA fingerprinting measures] is not bound by a social prognosis provided by another court in a decision on suspending a sentence on probation, not least because the reasons provided for the conviction and sentencing decision in the original criminal proceedings, including the findings on the facts of the case, do not partake in the binding effect of the final judgment […]. Moreover, the court ordering the measure pursuant to § 2 of the DNA Identification Act in conjunction with § 81g of the Code of Criminal Procedure must apply different legal standards and decides on different legal consequences than the court deciding on the suspension of a sentence […]. For the same reasons, the court competent to authorise DNA fingerprinting is not bound by the prognosis that the person concerned poses a danger to public security where such prognosis was provided in a prior decision ordering a measure of reform and prevention, like in the case of complainant no. 2.

61 Nonetheless, when the court deciding on measures pursuant to § 81g(1) of the Code of Criminal Procedure conducts its own prognosis of danger, it must take into account some of the same circumstances that are also relevant for the social prognosis that is undertaken by the courts deciding on the suspension of a sentence or the prognosis of danger and that is required for imposing a measure of reform and prevention. These include, for example, how quickly the person concerned has reoffended after a conviction, how much time has passed since the person concerned committed criminal acts […], their conduct during probation or after remission of their sentence, their motives for committing the crime, their life situation […] and their personality. However, the fact that the different frameworks serve different purposes and thus imply different standards of prognosis must be taken into account as well […]. Therefore, in the individual case, it may even be justified to find that the person concerned is likely to reoffend [as part of the prognosis] pursuant to § 2 of the DNA Identification Act in conjunction with § 81g of the Code of Criminal Procedure despite the fact that in a prior court decision their sentence had been suspended on probation […]. Where the prognosis by one court differs from the prognosis issued by another court in a prior decision, the later court decision must generally be based on a more detailed and substantiated reasoning […].

62 b) For ordering the measure pursuant to § 2 of the DNA Identification Act in conjunction with § 81g of the Code of Criminal Procedure, it is necessary, but also sufficient, to establish that there is reason to assume – based on the nature of

the criminal offence for which the person concerned was convicted, the way they committed the offence or the offender's personality, or based on other findings – that criminal proceedings concerning charges of considerable criminal offences will again be initiated against the person concerned in the future. [...] The creation of a DNA profile can only be ordered based on facts that are relevant for establishing that the person concerned is likely to reoffend [...]. Regarding persons that were sentenced a long time ago, the mere assumption that a risk of reoffending "cannot be ruled out with certainty" [...] is not capable of justifying an interference with the right to informational self-determination. Rather, the deciding court must provide reasons related to the individual case that positively establish a risk of repeat offences.

2. The decisions challenged by complainant no. 1 evidently do not meet this standard.

a) In its reasons [for ordering DNA fingerprinting], the Local Court merely lists the prior convictions of the complainant and repeats the wording of the law.

It is not ascertainable from these reasons that the offences that the complainant was convicted of are considerable criminal offences. [...] The fact that [other courts] have repeatedly decided to suspend prison sentences imposed on complainant no. 1 [...] would have called for an assessment of whether the committed offences were indeed considerable. Then, given the differences in nature and weight of the offences, the courts would have had to examine which type of criminal offence the negative prognosis refers to and if that offence, in turn, falls into the category of considerable criminal offences. Such an assessment was not undertaken.

The Local Court in particular failed to provide sound reasons for its negative prognosis. The mere listing of entries from the Federal Central Criminal Register suggests that no further judicial investigation of the facts took place, although such investigation would have been required of the court in light of the favourable social prognosis issued by other courts in their decisions on probation. The challenged decision only makes general references to the "severity of the criminal offence committed", which, according to the Local Court, implies a "high level of criminal motivation", without taking into account the fact that the sentence was suspended on probation; this was not a sufficient basis for forgoing an investigation and assessment of all relevant circumstances, including counter-indications against a negative prognosis. At the very least, the Local Court should have addressed the reasons provided for the prior [positive] prognosis in the probation decision, which differs from its own prognosis. This applies all the more because the complainant's prior conviction already dated back several years at the time the Local Court decided to order the creation of a DNA profile, and because the sentence had been remitted.

67 b) By referring to "the accurate reasons of the [Local Court's] order", the Regional Court failed to remedy the obvious shortcomings of the decision rendered by the examining judge (*Ermittlungsrichter*) in the proceedings before the Local Court. Neither the general references [made by the Regional Court] to "crime statistics" nor its criminological assertions for which no evidence was provided are adequate substitutes for the required assessment of the circumstances of the individual case.

68 3. a) By contrast, the decisions challenged by complainants nos. 2 and 3 adequately give effect to the constitutional requirements that the deciding court sufficiently investigate the facts of the case and provide sound reasons for its decision. The challenged decisions are based on robust evidence and reflect the requirement of a case-by-case assessment. [...]

69 [...]

70 b) DNA fingerprinting measures pursuant to § 2(1) of the DNA Identification Act in conjunction with § 81g of the Code of Criminal Procedure do not give rise to an irresolvable conflict with the requirement to seek social reintegration of offenders, as derived from Art. 1(1) and Art. 2(1) of the Basic Law in conjunction with the constitutional principle of the rule of law, even in cases of long-term imprisonment or confinement as a measure of reform and prevention. Considerable criminal offences, in particular offences against life or limb that tend to generate evidence traceable by way of cross-checking DNA profiles, can still be committed when the person concerned is in prison or confinement, or during times when execution of the prison sentence or the confinement measure is suspended, which cannot necessarily be foreseen at the time a prison sentence or confinement measure is imposed.

71 c) [...]

III.

72 The decisions challenged by complainants nos. 2 and 3 do not violate the constitutional principle of proportionality, which requires that a measure must be suitable and necessary for the purpose pursued and that the interference which it entails not be disproportionate to the importance of the matter and the strength of suspicion. In view of the fact that complainant no. 2 was convicted of several offences against life and limb, it is not ascertainable that the interference with his right to informational self-determination [resulting from DNA fingerprinting] was

No. 31 – DNA Fingerprinting

disproportionate. The same applies with regard to complainant no. 3, who had been convicted multiple times of crimes against sexual self-determination.

IV.

[…] 73

C.

[…] 74

D.

[…] 75-77

Justices: Limbach, Hassemer, Broß

No. 32

BVerfGE 27, 344 – Divorce Files

HEADNOTE

to the Order of the First Senate of 15 January 1970
1 BvR 13/68

Forwarding the files of divorce proceedings to the investigating officer in disciplinary proceedings [initiated against one of the spouses] constitutes an interference with the fundamental right deriving from Article 2(1) in conjunction with Article 1(1) of the Basic Law. Without the affected spouses' consent, such an interference is only permissible if it is justified by overriding public interests and strictly observes the requirement of proportionality.

FEDERAL CONSTITUTIONAL COURT
- 1 BvR 13/68 -

IN THE NAME OF THE PEOPLE

In the proceedings
on the constitutional complaint of

Mr ...,
– authorised representatives: ...

against   the Order of the Hamm Higher Regional Court of 20 November 1967
           - 15 VA 1/67 -

the Federal Constitutional Court – First Senate –
with the participation of Justices

President Müller,
Stein,
Ritterspach,
Haager,
Rupp-v. Brünneck,
Böhmer,

No. 32 – Divorce Files

Brox,
Zeidler

held on 15 January 1970:

The Order of the Hamm Higher Regional Court of 20 November 1967 - 15 VA 1/67 - violates the complainant's fundamental right under Article 2(1) in conjunction with Article 1(1) of the Basic Law. It is reversed and the matter is remanded to the Hamm Higher Regional Court.

REASONS:

A.

1. In 1965, the District Chief Administrative Officer (*Regierungspräsident*) [...] initiated formal disciplinary proceedings against the complainant, who had served as Chief Municipal Director (*Oberstadtdirektor*) since 1961; he was accused, *inter alia*, of having had "a very public adulterous relationship" with his former secretary, "presumably from 1956/57 to the present day". A daughter was born out of this relationship in 1962. As of 31 March 1965, the complainant was sent into early retirement due to incapacity for office.

The complainant, who has been married since 1949, had filed for divorce in November 1963. The action was rejected, whereupon the complainant submitted an appeal on points of fact and law (*Berufung*). He later withdrew the action with the agreement of his wife.

2. The investigating officer in the disciplinary proceedings requested access to the files of these divorce proceedings. In an order addressed to the presiding judge of the competent civil chamber, the President of the Regional Court approved the release of the files, which were then forwarded to the investigating officer.

When the complainant later learned about the release of the files to the investigating officer, he filed objections and eventually requested that the Hamm Higher Regional Court issue a judicial decision, *inter alia*, to reverse the Regional Court President's order.

With the challenged order of 20 November 1967, the Higher Regional Court declared the order of the President of the Regional Court to be lawful. In the reasons attached to this order, the court stated that the application had been admissible pursuant to § 23(1) of the Introductory Act to the Courts Constitution Act.

6-7 [...]
8 3. With the constitutional complaint directed against the order of the Higher Regional Court, the complainant claims a violation of his fundamental rights under Arts. 1(1), 2(1), 3(1), 6(1) and 103(1) of the Basic Law. [...]
9-10 [...]
11-15 4. [...]

B.

16 The constitutional complaint is well-founded.

17 1. a) In its established case-law, the Federal Constitutional Court has affirmed that the Basic Law recognises, for each citizen, an inviolable part of private life which is, in principle, beyond the reach of public authority (BVerfGE 6, 32 <41>; 27, 1 <6> – *Microcensus*). The constitutional requirement to respect the intimate sphere of the individual is based on the right to the free development of one's personality, as guaranteed by Art. 2(1) of the Basic Law. When determining the content and scope of this fundamental right, it must be taken into account that, according to the fundamental precept in Art. 1(1) of the Basic Law, human dignity is inviolable and must be respected and protected by all state authority. Moreover, under Art. 19(2) of the Basic Law, the essence (*Wesensgehalt*) of the fundamental right under Art. 2(1) of the Basic Law may also not be infringed upon.

18 b) However, not the entire domain of private life enjoys the absolute protection afforded by the fundamental right under Art. 2(1) in conjunction with Art. 1(1) and Art. 19(2) of the Basic Law (cf. also BVerfGE 6, 389 <433>; 27, 1 <6 and 7> – *Microcensus*). Rather, as a citizen connected to and bound by the community (BVerfGE 4, 7 <15 and 16>; 27, 1 <7> – *Microcensus*), every person must tolerate state measures that serve overriding public interests and that strictly adhere to the requirement of proportionality, unless these infringe upon the inviolable part of private life. In this respect, the principles which the Federal Constitutional Court has developed in its case-law on the constitutional permissibility of interferences with physical integrity apply accordingly (BVerfGE 16, 194 <201 and 202>; 17, 108 <117 and 118>; 27, 211 *et seq.*). Moreover, the mental and psychological integrity of the person must be protected as a particularly high-ranking value [...].

19 c) It is true that files of divorce proceedings relate to the spouses' private lives. Nevertheless, they do not *per se* belong to the part of private life that is inviolable under all circumstances, which would render any inspection by outsiders impermissible from the outset.

20 As the law stands, spouses may be required to disclose certain information on the innermost part of their lives. Where divorce proceedings lead to the disclosure

of events from private life to the court and the parties to the proceedings, this is done because the court must decide on a conflict of rights and interests within a marriage. However, even in this situation, the disclosure [of private information] is limited in respect of both the group of persons obtaining knowledge – namely the court and the parties to the proceedings – and the purpose pursued – namely to allow the court to reach a decision.

With regard to their contents, the divorce files are subject to confidentiality protection under Art. 2(1) in conjunction with Art. 1(1) of the Basic Law. Both spouses are jointly entitled to this protection. As a rule, the contents of the files can thus only be made available to third parties on the basis of a declaration of consent to disclosure by both spouses. 21

d) It follows from the foregoing that the permission to forward the files of the divorce proceedings to the investigating officer, which is formally based on the inter-agency obligation to provide administrative and legal assistance, constitutes an interference with the spouses' right of personality. Without their consent, forwarding the files is only permissible if it is justified under the principle of proportionality. If this is not the case, the measure violates Art. 2(1) in conjunction with Art. 1(1) and Art. 19(2) of the Basic Law. 22

2. In addition to the aforementioned general balancing of the protection of the private sphere against public interests, the principle of proportionality requires that the measure be suitable and necessary for the purpose pursued by it, and that the intensity of the interference which it entails not be disproportionate to the importance of the matter and the strength of suspicion (BVerfGE 16, 194 <202>; 17, 108 <117>). The authorities and courts must carry out the necessary balancing of the envisaged measures, the grounds prompting them, and the impact of the interference, taking into account all personal and factual circumstances of the individual case. The Federal Constitutional Court cannot review this in detail, it only reviews whether the balancing took place and whether the underlying standards of review are in line with constitutional law (BVerfGE 27, 211 *et seq.*). Measured against these principles, the challenged court order does not stand up to constitutional review. 23

a) It is already objectionable that the release of the files was ordered and declared lawful by the courts although the investigating officer, when requesting the files, failed to demonstrate, in a substantiated manner and based on detailed facts, the significance of the matter and the necessity to inspect the files; as a result, there was no basis for the spouses to submit a statement responding to the request. [...] 24

b) The Higher Regional Court did, in principle, recognise the need to balance the conflicting interests, and set forth theoretical considerations on this issue. It did not, however, sufficiently specify these abstract standards, taking into account all personal and factual circumstances. [...] 25

26 c) In any case, the challenged decision cannot be upheld because it fails to assess the necessity of the investigation measure at issue. It is not ascertainable from the order whether the Higher Regional Court actually examined to what extent the divorce files contained information that could be considered significant for the disciplinary proceedings. [...]

27 Lastly, the Higher Regional Court also failed to consider the necessity of the measure as it did not determine whether other means of evidence would also have been available to investigate the facts of the case [in the disciplinary proceedings]. [...]

28 The Higher Regional Court thus violated the complainant's fundamental right under Art. 2(1) in conjunction with Art. 1(1) of the Basic Law, in part by failing to conduct the balancing of interests required under the Constitution, and in part by conducting the balancing without adequately taking into account the standards applicable under constitutional law.

29 The challenged order is therefore reversed, and the matter remanded to the Higher Regional Court – there was no need to review the complainant's claims concerning the violation of other fundamental rights.

Justices: Müller, Stein, Ritterspach, Haager, Rupp-v. Brünneck, Böhmer, Brox, Zeidler

No. 33

BVerfGE 56, 37 – Bankruptcy Proceedings

HEADNOTE

to the Order of the First Senate of 13 January 1981
1 BvR 116/77

It does not violate fundamental rights that the Bankruptcy Code imposes an unconditional obligation on debtors to provide information in bankruptcy proceedings, which can be enforced by coercive measures. If, in this context, debtors disclose their involvement in criminal acts, their testimony may not be used against them in criminal proceedings without their consent.

FEDERAL CONSTITUTIONAL COURT
- 1 BvR 116/77 -

IN THE NAME OF THE PEOPLE

In the proceedings
on the constitutional complaint of

merchant B...,
– authorised representatives: ...
against a) the Order of the Oldenburg Regional Court of 6 February 1977
- 6 T 62/77 -
b) the Order of the Vechta Local Court of 14 January 1977
- N 23/75 -
the Federal Constitutional Court – First Senate –
with the participation of Justices
President Benda,
Böhmer,
Simon,
Faller,

Hesse,
Katzenstein,
Niemeyer,
Heußner

held on 13 January 1981:

The constitutional complaint is rejected.

[…]

REASONS:

A.

1   The complainant, a debtor in bankruptcy proceedings, invokes the right to refuse to answer questions that might require him to disclose criminal conduct.

I.

2   The debtor's obligation to provide information in bankruptcy proceedings is based on […] provisions of the Bankruptcy Code.

3-6 […]

7   The Bankruptcy Code is silent on whether a debtor's obligation to provide information in bankruptcy proceedings also extends to information through which they would have to disclose that they had engaged in criminal conduct, and whether detention may be imposed to enforce their obligation in such a case. Nor does the Bankruptcy Code contain any express prohibition to use such information against the debtor in criminal proceedings.

II.

8   1. Bankruptcy proceedings were initiated in respect of the complainant's assets. At the request of the trustee in bankruptcy, the complainant was to be questioned on certain asset transfers. He appeared at the evidentiary hearing, but refused to answer questions because criminal investigations into suspected bankruptcy offences were pending in relation to the matters on which he was questioned at the hearing, and he feared that he might incriminate himself by answering the questions.

9   2. Following this, the Bankruptcy Court ordered his detention pursuant to §§ 75, 101(2) of the Bankruptcy Code on the grounds that the debtor's refusal to answer the questions was unjustified.

No. 33 – Bankruptcy Proceedings

The Regional Court dismissed the complainant's immediate complaint (*sofortige Beschwerde*) [...].
3. The complainant lodged a constitutional complaint against these decisions [...].
4. [...]

III.

[...]

B.

The constitutional complaint is admissible but unfounded. The fact that the Bankruptcy Code imposes an unconditional obligation to give testimony on the complainant, which can be enforced by coercive measures, does not in and of itself violate the complainant's fundamental rights. His interests meriting protection are sufficiently accommodated given that any self-incriminating statements fall under a prohibition to use them as evidence in criminal proceedings.

I.

1. Persons who are subject to statutory obligations to provide information may face a dilemma: they must either incriminate themselves, or possibly commit a new offence by making a false statement, or risk coercive measures by choosing to remain silent. Therefore, an obligation to provide information that can be enforced by coercive measures amounts to an interference with the general freedom of action as well as an impairment of the right of personality within the meaning of Art. 2(1) of the Basic Law. Moreover, involuntary self-incrimination affects the human dignity of the persons whose testimony is used against them.
2. As the law stands, it provides for various safeguards protecting against unreasonable (*unzumutbar*) interferences and impairments. [...]
a) The protection against self-incrimination is most comprehensive for witnesses, parties to court proceedings and, most notably, persons charged with an offence in criminal or comparable proceedings. [...]
[Involuntary] self-incrimination constitutes a serious interference given its consequences under criminal law. Therefore, relevant safeguards have primarily been developed in cases where a person is asked to provide information specifically for the purposes of criminal proceedings or similar purposes. [...] According to the applicable case-law, the right to remain silent [...] is regarded as an inherent element of an order based on the rule of law and guided by respect for human

dignity (BVerfGE 38, 105 <113>; [...]). In legal scholarship, the privilege against self-incrimination in criminal proceedings is considered a decision on constitutional values mandated by Art. 2(1) in conjunction with Art. 1(1) of the Basic Law that accords precedence to the right of personality on the part of the accused, which outweighs the interest of the public in law enforcement in this context. The protection of human dignity requires that persons charged with a criminal offence be able to decide freely whether they themselves may be used as a means (*Werkzeug*) for bringing about their own conviction [...]

19 [...]

20 If not even persons charged with a criminal offence and parties to court proceedings are expected to incriminate themselves, witnesses deserve such protection all the more. [...] In the applicable case-law, this rule is considered an inherent element of the right to a fair trial under the rule of law. It protects the witnesses' right of personality, ensuring that other parties to the proceedings cannot treat them as mere objects used for establishing the truth (cf. BVerfGE 38, 105 <111 *et seq.*>; BGHSt 17, 245 <246>).

21 b) As the law stands, it grants witnesses, parties to court proceedings and persons charged with a criminal offence an unconditional right to remain silent and to refuse to answer questions so as to avoid possible self-incrimination. However, this does not necessarily apply to persons who, based on specific legal grounds, are subject to contractual or statutory obligations to provide necessary information to another person or a public authority. In such cases, the interests of the person required to provide information conflict with the need for information on the part of others; the law accommodates these interests in obtaining information in different ways.

22-24 [...]

II.

25 1. The legal order grants a right to remain silent and a right to refuse to answer questions to persons charged with a criminal offence, witnesses and parties to court proceedings in order to protect them against self-incrimination. Yet these rights cannot to the same extent apply to debtors in bankruptcy proceedings. Unlike the testimony given by persons charged with a criminal offence, the testimony given by debtors is not intended to contribute to the debtor's own conviction. [...] In bankruptcy proceedings, debtors are one of the most important sources of information, and creditors and the bodies overseeing the proceedings rely on the information debtors provide to conclude the bankruptcy case properly. The law specifically determines the debtors' rights and obligations in line with the objective

No. 33 – Bankruptcy Proceedings

demands of bankruptcy proceedings. The prevailing opinion in legal scholarship infers from the applicable provisions that debtors in bankruptcy proceedings have an unconditional obligation to provide information and that the interests of creditors must be given priority over the debtor's interest in being protected against involuntary self-incrimination [...].

This interpretation of the applicable provisions set out in bankruptcy law is not objectionable under constitutional law. The legal interests protected by Art. 2(1) of the Basic Law are subject to limits set by the rights of others. Thus, this fundamental right does not merit absolute protection against self-incriminating statements without taking into account whether this would impair interests of third parties that also merit protection. As repeatedly emphasised in the Court's case-law in respect of the fundamental right to general freedom of action (cf. BVerfGE 4, 7 <15>; 8, 274 <329>; 27, 344 <351> – *Divorce Files*), the Basic Law resolves the tension between the individual and the community by endorsing the notion that the individual is connected to and bound by the community. The individual must therefore accept that their freedom of action is subject to limitations imposed by the legislator to maintain and foster social coexistence, within the limits of what is generally reasonable and provided that personal autonomy is upheld. It would be unreasonable and incompatible with human dignity to compel persons to provide information that could lead to their own criminal conviction or similar sanctions. In that respect, Art. 2(1) of the Basic Law, as a defensive right against state interference, affords protection in line with long-established and commonly recognised legal tradition. If, however, the information at issue is necessary to satisfy a legitimate interest, the legislator may undertake a balancing of the various parties' conflicting interests. The legislator may take into consideration that bankruptcy proceedings do not only concern an interest of the state or the public in obtaining information, but also the interests of injured third parties. In this respect, the obligations imposed in bankruptcy proceedings differ from the obligations to provide information imposed under administrative law, which the legislator, in more recent legislation, has supplemented by a right to refuse to answer questions in cases of self-incrimination. An unconditional obligation to provide information is the only way to prevent debtors in bankruptcy proceedings from removing parts of the bankruptcy estate from the legitimate reach of their creditors. In this context, a right to refuse to answer questions would unjustifiably privilege those debtors who have behaved especially reprehensibly to the detriment of their creditors. It does not amount to a violation of human dignity that the legislator holds debtors in bankruptcy proceedings liable to meet the debts owed to their creditors and to assist in settling those debts in the best possible manner by providing the necessary information.

27 Even if, in light of the above, debtors in bankruptcy proceedings have no right to refuse to provide information, compelling them to incriminate themselves would interfere with their right of personality protected under Art. 2(1) of the Basic Law. Thus, imposing coercive measures can […] be disproportionate, and therefore impermissible, in the individual case. In addition, the debtor's obligation to provide information must be supplemented by a prohibition to use the information as evidence under criminal law […]. For the reasons set out above, the obligation imposed on debtors is unconditional only in the context of bankruptcy proceedings where the interests of debtors must stand back behind the interests of creditors. However, the debtor's right of personality would be disproportionately impaired if self-incriminating statements obtained by coercive measures were used for other purposes against the debtor's will and were admissible as evidence in criminal proceedings. This impairment is not justified by objective reasons. For the reasons discussed above, constitutional law requires that debtors be granted a right to remain silent in criminal proceedings; the use as evidence of information obtained by coercive measures in this context is impermissible. Yet this right to remain silent would be meaningless if self-incriminating statements obtained by coercive measures outside the context of criminal proceedings could be used against the debtors for law enforcement purposes against their will. In bankruptcy proceedings, it may be reasonable to impose an unconditional obligation to provide information on debtors in the interest of creditors; this does not, however, mean that it were also justified to require debtors to assist in their own criminal conviction, or to provide law enforcement authorities with means that would not be available to them in other criminal cases.

28 2. While the Bankruptcy Code imposes an obligation to provide information on debtors in bankruptcy proceedings and allows for its enforcement by way of coercive measures, it does so without setting out a prohibition to use such information in criminal proceedings. It is in principle incumbent on the legislator to fill this gap given that only statutory law can define the prohibition to use the information as evidence in more detail and provide for additional safeguards in the form of prohibitions to disclose the information obtained. However, in cases where a provision that predates the Basic Law must be amended for reasons of constitutional law, it also falls to judges to fill legal gaps, following the applicable statutory law as closely as possible and drawing on directly applicable provisions of the Basic Law, until the legislator enacts new provisions (cf. BVerfGE 37, 67 <81>; 49, 286 <301 et seq.> – *Transsexuals I*; additionally BVerfGE 33, 23 <34>).

29 […]

III.

In light of the above, the bankruptcy law provisions imposing an unconditional obligation on debtors to provide information, which is supplemented by a prohibition to use the testimony in criminal proceedings, is constitutionally unobjectionable. The complainant could not invoke a right to refuse to provide information, as claimed by him. Thus, the courts were allowed to order his detention in order to compel him to provide information in the bankruptcy proceedings.
[…]

Justices: Benda, Simon, Faller, Hesse, Katzenstein, Niemeyer, Heußner; Justice Böhmer was unable to attend for signing.

Dissenting Opinion of Justice Heußner

The view of the Senate majority is that the bankruptcy law provisions on the debtor's unconditional obligation to provide information, if supplemented by a prohibition to use the information in criminal proceedings, is constitutionally unobjectionable. I do not believe that it is sufficient to merely supplement the challenged provisions with a prohibition to use the information as criminal evidence. As was correctly stated by the Senate, the debtor's right of personality (Art. 2(1) of the Basic Law) is already impaired "if self-incriminating statements obtained by coercive measures were used for other purposes against the debtor's will and were admissible as evidence in criminal proceedings". However, it does not only follow from this that the legislator can guarantee compliance with a prohibition to use the information in criminal proceedings "by providing safeguards in the form of prohibitions to disclose the information obtained"; it also follows that the sharing of information provided by the debtor in bankruptcy proceedings with law enforcement authorities as such already violates the debtor's right of personality, given that it constitutes an impermissible use of the information for purposes other than the designated one. In this situation, the sharing of information is not necessary – as law enforcement authorities would be prohibited from using it given its inadmissibility as evidence – resulting in an impairment of the debtor's fundamental right under Art. 2(1) of the Basic Law. Where sharing information is not necessary for criminal proceedings, it violates the principle of proportionality and is therefore impermissible (cf. BVerfGE 27, 344 <351 and 352> – *Divorce Files*).

33 Furthermore, only a prohibition to disclose information to unauthorised third parties can fully guarantee that information provided by the debtor in bankruptcy proceedings is not used in criminal proceedings, contrary to constitutional law, for purposes other than the ones provided for in the Bankruptcy Code [...]. This is the only way to avoid – in line with the right to personality – the unnecessary sharing of the debtor's information, which is beyond their control and which would undermine their constitutionally protected right to refuse to provide information [in criminal proceedings].

34 [...]

35 Based on these considerations, the bankruptcy law provisions on the debtor's unconditional obligation to provide information are not objectionable under constitutional law if the courts interpret them to the effect that they must be supplemented by a prohibition to use the information in criminal proceedings and, in addition, a prohibition to disclose the information obtained in such proceedings.

Justice Heußner

No. 34

BVerfGE 113, 29 – Seizure of Electronic Data

HEADNOTES

to the Order of the Second Senate of 12 April 2005
2 BvR 1027/02

1. The Code of Criminal Procedure provides a statutory basis for the securing and seizure of data storage devices and of the data stored on them as evidence in criminal proceedings.
2. When searching, securing and seizing data storage devices and the data stored on them, reasonable efforts must be made to prevent access to information that is irrelevant to the criminal proceedings.
3. At least in cases of serious, deliberate or arbitrary violations of procedure, unlawful searches and seizures of data storage devices and of the data stored on them must result in a prohibition to use the data as evidence.

FEDERAL CONSTITUTIONAL COURT
- 2 BvR 1027/02 -

IN THE NAME OF THE PEOPLE

In the proceedings
on the constitutional complaint of

1. Mr P…, 2. Mr U…, 3. Mr B…, 4. the company R… mbH, represented by the managing directors B… and P…,
– authorised representatives (no. 4): …
against   a) the Order of the Hamburg Regional Court of 25 June 2002
- 618 Qs 52/02 -,
        b) the Order of the Hamburg Regional Court of 20 June 2002
- 618 Qs 54/02 -,
        c) the Order of the Hamburg Regional Court of 14 June 2002

- 618 Qs 52/02 -,
d) the Order of the Hamburg Local Court of 4 June 2002
- 164 Gs 737/02 - 5100 Js 85/02 -,
e) the Orders of the Hamburg Local Court of 7 May 2002
- 164 Gs 737/02 - 5100 Js 85/02 -

the Federal Constitutional Court – Second Senate –

with the participation of Justices

> Vice-President Hassemer,
> Jentsch,
> Broß,
> Osterloh,
> Di Fabio,
> Mellinghoff,
> Lübbe-Wolff,
> Gerhardt

held on 12 April 2005:

1. The Orders of the Hamburg Regional Court of 14 June 2002 - 618 Qs 52/02 -, of 20 June 2002 - 618 Qs 54/02 - and of 25 June 2002 - 618 Qs 52/02 - violate the complainants' fundamental right under Article 2(1) of the Basic Law to the extent that they concern the securing of evidence. They are reversed and the matter is remanded to the Hamburg Regional Court.
2. For the rest, the constitutional complaint is rejected.
3. [...]

REASONS:

A.

1 The constitutional complaint concerns the search and seizure of the electronic data records of a law firm and a tax consultancy firm in the context of criminal investigations against a lawyer-tax consultant, who is a partner in both firms. The current proceedings raise the question to what extent the relationship of trust between the directly affected professionals, who are bound by confidentiality obligations, and

No. 34 – Seizure of Electronic Data

their clients bears on the permissibility of granting authorities full data access in the course of criminal proceedings.

I.

[…]   2-31

II.

1. The Hamburg Public Prosecution Office and the fraud investigation unit of the   32
Hamburg-Neustadt-St. Pauli Tax Office conducted criminal investigations against
complainant no. 2, a lawyer and tax consultant. He is a partner in the joint law firm
of complainants nos. 1 to 3, and authorised signatory and partner of complainant
no. 4, a tax consultancy firm registered at the same address.
The investigating authorities believed that, together with [two] other suspects,   33
complainant no. 2 was involved in payments made to letterbox companies on the
British Island of Jersey by [three] companies […], all with registered headquarters
in Germany, for goods and services that had in fact never been provided. […]
[…] There were grounds for suspecting that the other two suspects, who filed joint   34
income tax returns, had fraudulently reduced their income tax liabilities by a total
of DM 1,390,874.00.
2. a) Against this backdrop, the Hamburg Local Court issued two identically   35
worded search warrants on 7 May 2002 in accordance with § 102 of the Code
of Criminal Procedure for the workplace of complainant no. 2 in the law firm and
for the offices of the tax consultancy firm […]. Complainant no. 2 was suspected of
having devised the tax evasion scheme for the other two suspects, aided by one of
his tax assistants. […].
b) […]   36
3. The search was carried out on 14 May 2002 in the offices of the law firm and of   37
the tax consultancy, which complainant no. 2 at least partially shares with the other
partners of the law firm. Written documents […] were secured, along with "various
data stored on separate devices". This included copies made by the investigating
officers on site of all data stored on the hard drives of the law firm's and the tax
consultancy's computers.
4. […]   38
5. By order of 4 June 2002, the Hamburg Local Court […] upheld the seizure […].   39
[…]   40-50
6. […]   51
7. a) […]   52

53-54 b) [...]
55 c) By separate order [...], the Hamburg Regional Court rejected the complaints of complainants nos. 2 and 4 against the decision upholding the seizure [...].
56 8. [...]
57 9. [...]

III.

58 1. With their constitutional complaint, the complainants claim a violation of their fundamental rights under Art. 2(1) of the Basic Law in conjunction with Art. 20(3), Art. 12(1) and Art. 13(1) and (2) of the Basic Law. [...]
59-63 [...]

IV.

64 [...]

V.

65 Statements on the constitutional complaint and the procedural practice were submitted by the Federal Ministry of Justice, the Public Prosecutor General (*Generalbundesanwalt*), the Federal Criminal Police Office (*Bundeskriminalamt*), the *Länder* Brandenburg, Bremen, Hamburg, Hesse, Mecklenburg-Western Pomerania, Lower Saxony, North Rhine-Westphalia and Saxony as well as the Federal Chamber of Tax Advisers (*Bundessteuerberaterkammer*), the German Association of Tax Advisers (*Deutscher Steuerberaterverband*), the Federal Bar Association (*Bundesrechtsanwaltskammer*), and the German Lawyers Association (*Deutscher Anwaltverein*).
66-70 [...]

B.

71 To the extent that it is directed against the seizure of the complainants' data, the constitutional complaint is admissible.

No. 34 – Seizure of Electronic Data

[...]

C.

The challenged decisions of the Hamburg Regional Court [...] violate the complainants' fundamental right under Art. 2(1) of the Basic Law.

The seizure of the complainants' data must be measured against the fundamental right enshrined in Art. 2(1) of the Basic Law (see I below). In principle, the investigatory powers regime set out in the Code of Criminal Procedure provides a statutory basis for the securing and seizure of data storage devices and the data stored on them (see II below). However, the Hamburg Regional Court failed to consider (see V below) that, in case of seizure of data storage devices and of all data stored on them, the principle of proportionality is particularly significant (see III below). Besides, a blanket seizure of data storage devices and of the data stored on them is only permissible if procedural safeguards are in place (see IV below).

I.

With their constitutional complaint, the complainants challenge, in particular, that the public prosecution office had copied and retained their data in the course of the search and seizure. Thus, the entire data and information stored by the law firm and the tax consultancy was made available to the public prosecution office. The complainants do not object, on grounds of ownership, to being deprived of the physical possession of the data storage devices as such. Rather, the constitutional complaint seeks to prevent the law enforcement authorities from gaining full access to all data belonging to the law firm and the tax consultancy.

1. The challenged decisions must be measured against Art. 2(1) of the Basic Law.

a) Art. 2(1) of the Basic Law does not only protect the core of personality, but all human behaviour. Art. 2(1) of the Basic Law affords individuals a fundamental right to only be affected by intrusive state measures if the measure in question has a statutory basis that is formally and substantively compatible with the Constitution (cf. BVerfGE 29, 402 <408>). Since Art. 2(1) of the Basic Law does not distinguish between different types of activities, this right also protects commercial (cf. BVerfGE 10, 89 <99>) and professional activities; it protects natural and legal persons as well as groups of persons (cf. BVerfGE 10, 89 <99>; 23, 12 <30>).

Searches by law enforcement authorities generally interfere with the inviolability of the home guaranteed by Art. 13 of the Basic Law. To the extent that the authorities, beyond the actual search of the premises, carry out further measures relating to the documents or data found, the general right of personality, which applies subsidiarily, may be affected as well. [...]

81 b) In particular, the seizure of the complainants' entire data records interferes with the right to informational self-determination guaranteed by Art. 2(1) of the Basic Law in conjunction with Art. 1(1) of the Basic Law.

82 aa) The securing and seizure of the complainants' data records allows for automatic processing of the collected data. The increased risk associated with such technical possibilities is reflected in the level of fundamental rights protection afforded in this respect (cf. BVerfGE 65, 1 <42> – *Census*). In the context of modern data processing, the free development of one's personality requires that the individual be protected against the unlimited collection, storage, use and sharing of their personal data. This protection is part of the fundamental right under Art. 2(1) of the Basic Law in conjunction with Art. 1(1) of the Basic Law. This fundamental right confers upon the individual the authority to, in principle, decide themselves on the disclosure and use of their personal data (cf. BVerfGE 65, 1 <43> – *Census*).

83 Beyond the immediate protection it affords, this fundamental right serves to prevent a chilling effect that could arise and impair the exercise of other fundamental rights if individuals were no longer able to tell who knows what kind of personal information about them, at what time and on which occasion. This could greatly impede their freedom to make self-determined plans or decisions.

84 A deterrent effect on the exercise of fundamental rights stemming from the secret knowledge of third parties [regarding one's personal data] must be avoided, not only in the interest of the affected individuals. Such a deterrent effect would also affect the common good because self-determination is a fundamental prerequisite for the functioning of a free and democratic society which relies on the agency and participation of its citizens (cf. BVerfGE 65, 1 <43> – *Census*).

85 bb) In addition, the securing and seizure of the data storage devices and of the data stored on them affects the right to informational self-determination of the complainants' clients.

86 [...]

87 [...] The possibility of unrestricted state access to the data records of a law firm or tax consultancy might deter clients from engaging in confidential communication or even from hiring the lawyer or tax consultant in the first place, including in cases that are completely unrelated to the criminal charges against the suspect under investigation.

88 2. Access to the data also affects the right to a fair trial under the rule of law deriving from Art. 2(1) of the Basic Law (cf. BVerfGE 26, 66 <71>; 38, 105 <111>; 40, 95 <99>; 65, 171 <174>; 66, 313 <318>; 77, 65 <76>; 86, 288 <317 *et seq.*>; 110, 226 <253 *et seq.*>), which gives rise to a right to confidential

No. 34 – Seizure of Electronic Data

communication between defence lawyers and their clients. [...] It is important in this respect as well that unrestricted access to information by law enforcement authorities must not prevent clients from communicating with their defence lawyers in an unfettered, unreserved and trust-based manner (cf. BVerfGE 110, 226 <260>). Due to its scale, access to all data records of a law firm and a tax consultancy severely impairs the legally privileged relationship of trust between clients and their lawyer or tax consultant that is integral to any such consultant-client relationship. 89

3. Although the challenged decisions do not interfere with the complainants' fundamental right to occupational freedom (Art. 12 of the Basic Law), the specific nature of the complainants' professional activities as lawyers and tax consultants must be taken into account in the constitutional review of the measures at issue. 90

[...] 91-96

II.

1. Restrictions of Art. 2(1) of the Basic Law require a statutory basis specifying the underlying prerequisites and scope in a manner that is clear and recognisable for citizens in accordance with the principle of legal clarity deriving from the rule of law. §§ 94 *et seq.* of the Code of Criminal Procedure satisfy these constitutional requirements with regard to the securing and seizing of data storage devices and the data stored on them. 97

2. §§ 94 *et seq.* of the Code of Criminal Procedure provide a statutory basis for the securing and seizure of data storage devices and the data stored on them as evidence in criminal proceedings. 98

a) It is true that the powers to interfere [with fundamental rights] were originally designed for [the search and seizure of] physical objects. [...] 99

b) [Yet] § 94 of the Code of Criminal Procedure can also serve as a statutory basis for the securing of data on storage devices provided by the authorities. The literal meaning of 'object' allows for an understanding that includes non-physical objects. [...] 100

[...] 101

c) It is sufficiently recognisable for persons affected by such data access that §§ 94 *et seq.* of the Code of Criminal Procedure allow for the securing and seizure of data storage devices and of the data stored on them. § 94 of the Code of Criminal Procedure generally covers all objects that could serve as evidence in the investigation. Given the diverse range of possible scenarios, the legislator was not required to differentiate further. Under constitutional law, it is incumbent upon the competent judge to make, to the extent possible, further determinations in 102 the search or seizure warrant issued in the respective criminal proceedings (cf. BVerfGE 42, 212 <220 et seq.>; 44, 353 <371> – *Addiction Counselling Agency*; 45, 82; 50, 48 <49>; 71, 64 <65>).

103 d) The provisions of criminal procedure governing the seizure of objects as evidence also satisfy the requirement, applicable in particular to [interferences with] the right to informational self-determination, that the legislator specify precisely the purposes for which the collected data may be used (cf. BVerfGE 65, 1 <46> – *Census*; 100, 313 <359 et seq.> – *The Article 10 Act*). The legislative framework in which §§ 94 *et seq.* of the Code of Criminal Procedure are embedded (cf. § 152(2), § 155(1), § 160, § 170, § 244(2) and § 264 of the Code of Criminal Procedure) formulates the designated purpose that serves to restrict data access with sufficient precision.

104 While the investigatory powers for obtaining data and their scope are defined rather broadly in the Code of Criminal Procedure, they are strictly limited by the purpose of the investigation. Investigation measures in criminal proceedings are only permissible to the extent necessary to inform the authorities' decisions regarding the criminal charges in question. The powers do not extend to the investigation of other situations and circumstances. […] Therefore, in connection with criminal proceedings, no facts or personal circumstances may be investigated that are irrelevant for determining culpability and assessing the legal consequences of the offence (cf. § 244(3) second sentence, second alternative of the Code of Criminal Procedure). […]

105 With the strict limitation of all investigation measures, including any collection of data, to the purpose of investigating the criminal acts committed, the Code of Criminal Procedure generally restricts interferences with the right [to informational self-determination] regarding one's data to data that is relevant to the specific case under investigation. […]

III.

106 The restrictions of the complainants' fundamental rights not only require a sufficiently specific statutory basis. The principle of proportionality sets [further] limits to state action, especially in the field of criminal procedure. In this respect, it must be taken into account that the securing and seizure of data storage devices and of the data stored on them gives rise to particularly intrusive interferences.

107 1. a) The particular intensity of the interference follows from the fact that this law enforcement measure involves a significant amount of data that is irrelevant to the proceedings, affecting a considerable number of persons who have no connection to the criminal charges and who did not prompt the interference with their conduct (cf.

No. 34 – Seizure of Electronic Data

BVerfGE 100, 313 <380> – *The Article 10 Act*; 107, 299 <320 *et seq.*>). Moreover, the measure affects relationships of trusts that merit special protection against excessive data access. In the individual case, the particularly intrusive interference resulting from access to data storage devices – especially devices belonging to lawyers and tax consultants, who are bound by professional confidentiality – must therefore be subject to especially strict limitations.

b) The principle of proportionality sets limits to state action. It requires not only that the securing and seizure of data storage devices and the data stored on them must have real prospects of success with regard to achieving the statutory purpose of law enforcement. It also requires that use of this specific coercive measure must be necessary for investigating and prosecuting the crime in question; this is not the case if other, less restrictive means are available. Finally, the respective interference must be proportionate to the severity of the charges and the strength of suspicion (cf. BVerfGE 96, 44 <51>). 108

c) Where it has been established that a data storage device does not contain any data relevant to the criminal proceedings, securing the storage device would *per se* be unsuitable. Where data storage devices are presumed to contain information of evidentiary value – albeit to varying degrees –, they will generally also contain a considerable amount of irrelevant data besides the information that has potential value as evidence. [...] 109

d) The prohibition of excessive measures (*Übermaßverbot*) prohibits interferences with fundamental rights that are of such intensity that they are disproportionate to the importance of the affected interests. Fundamental rights and their restrictions must be brought into appropriate balance. In an overall balancing of the severity of the interference on the one hand, and the weight and urgency of the reasons invoked to justify it on the other hand, the limits of what is reasonable (*zumutbar*) must be observed (cf. BVerfGE 67, 157 <173, 178>; 100, 313 <391> – *The Article 10 Act*; established case-law). 110

aa) On the one hand, the state's interest in effective law enforcement must be taken into account. Safeguarding the peaceful legal order (*Rechtsfrieden*) by means of criminal law has always been an important responsibility of the state. [...] The Basic Law accords great importance to the prevention and investigation of criminal acts (cf. BVerfGE 100, 313 <388> – *The Article 10 Act*). 111

bb) On the other hand, the balancing of interests must take into account protected legal interests of third parties that are affected by coercive state measures without having prompted them in any way. According to the principle of proportionality, interferences with the rights of non-suspects require special justification. [By securing data storage devices,] law enforcement authorities might obtain knowledge of data concerning indirectly affected third parties; this often includes excess da- 112 ta that is protected by special confidentiality privileges. Therefore, the right to informational self-determination of third parties and the risks to legally privileged relationships of trust between persons bound by professional confidentiality and their clients must also be taken into account. [...]

113   2. When searching, securing and seizing data storage devices and the data stored on them, there are various ways to give effect to the principle of proportionality.

114   a) If the data storage devices targeted by the measure do contain information of potentially evidentiary value, it must be assessed whether securing the data storage devices and all data stored on them is necessary. [...] Reasonable efforts must be made to avoid the obtaining of excessive and confidential information that is irrelevant to the proceedings.

115   b) To the extent that data can be filtered based on its relevance to the proceedings, the authorities are constitutionally required to consider the possibility of separating the potentially relevant from the irrelevant data. The data relevant to the proceedings could be (partially) copied, and the irrelevant data deleted or returned. [...]

116   c) Depending on the circumstances of the individual case, there are different means that can be used, and possibly combined, to categorise the data in order to limit access. Such means must be exhausted before a definitive decision to seize all data can be considered. [...] For example, the data can be categorised according to subject, time, client or case. It may also be possible to categorise the data according to its relevance to the proceedings by using search terms or programmes.

117   d) It will not always be possible to thoroughly examine and separate the data on site according to their relevance to the proceedings. If, in a particular case, the specifics of the respective criminal charges and the options available to search the data, including the technical means, do not allow for a swift categorisation, the temporary securing of the data storage device for the purpose of determining the relevance of the stored data must be considered.

118   In any event, the examination stage pursuant to § 110 of the Code of Criminal Procedure must precede the final decision on the scope of the seizure (cf. BVerfGE 77, 1 <55>). In line with the purpose of § 110 of the Code of Criminal Procedure, reasonable efforts must be made to only expose data to a permanent and therefore more intrusive interference if it is relevant to the proceedings and admissible as evidence. [...]

119   e) Given the particular technical features of electronic data processing and the often substantial data volume, the problems associated with uncovering and restoring concealed, mixed-up, encrypted or deleted data cannot be ignored. Yet [the decision to] seize the entire data or data processing system may not be based on the generalised assumption that there is a possibility that data might have been concealed. [...]

No. 34 – Seizure of Electronic Data

f) The principle of proportionality, at least under the element of necessity, does not preclude the seizure of the entire data if during the examination stage the law enforcement authorities are, despite reasonable efforts, either unable to identify the data that is relevant to the proceedings, […] or to delete or return the data that is irrelevant. However, it must then be assessed in each individual case whether full data access is compatible with the prohibition of excessive measures.

The resulting interference must be proportionate to the severity of the criminal offence and the strength of suspicion (cf. BVerfGE 96, 44 <51>). This assessment must take into account how important the potential evidence that the search measure aims to obtain is for the criminal proceedings, and how likely it is that evidence relevant to the proceedings will be found. In the individual case, seizure of data may be impermissible where the criminal act under investigation is a minor offence, the evidentiary value of the information that will presumably be found on the data storage device is insignificant, or the basis for presuming that evidence will indeed be found is vague.

IV.

The principle of proportionality […] alone is not sufficient to effectively prevent impermissible interferences with the right to informational self-determination. Fundamental rights protection must also be ensured by adequate procedural means (cf. BVerfGE 73, 280 <296>; 82, 209 <227>). The applicable procedural law must be designed in line with the objective demands of effective fundamental rights protection (cf. BVerfGE 63, 131 <143> – *Right of Reply*).

1. In the context of interferences with the right to informational self-determination, great significance has always been attributed to procedural safeguards. Recognised procedural safeguards include notification, information and deletion requirements and prohibitions to use data as evidence (cf. BVerfGE 65, 1 <46> – *Census*). In addition, the state is in principle required, in view of the right to informational self-determination, to monitor developments in data collection, storage and use and, where appropriate, to consider amending the legal framework (cf. regarding documentation obligations, BVerfGE 112, 304 <320> with further references).

In principle, the purpose limitation applicable to the data collection requires that all copied data that is not necessary to achieve the purpose pursued be deleted. In certain cases, the Basic Law gives rise to a prohibition to use data as evidence, giving effect to the principle of proportionality and to procedural rights (see C IV 3 below).

125 2. The currently applicable law of criminal procedure already contains procedural safeguards that are designed to prevent or minimise interferences with fundamental rights.

126 a) The examination pursuant to § 110 of the Code of Criminal Procedure serves to avoid excessive data collection for long-term storage, and thus to reduce the intensity of the interference with the right to informational self-determination.

127 [...] Nonetheless, to ensure that the interference is proportionate in the individual case, it may be required to involve the owner of the data in question in the examination of whether the secured data is relevant to the proceedings. [In the present case,] specific, comprehensible and verifiable information concerning the data structure and the relevance of the data in question could be provided, in particular, by the law firm partners who are not themselves under suspicion; this could simplify the categorisation of the data and reduce the amount of data to be secured by the authorities. [...]

128 b) The provisions on [law enforcement] databases in §§ 483 *et seq.* of the Code of Criminal Procedure [...] serve to ensure the data protection rights of persons affected by data collection in criminal proceedings. In addition to § 483 of the Code of Criminal Procedure, which limits data collection to the purpose of the criminal proceedings, the provisions on data deletion in § 489 of the Code of Criminal Procedure and the obligation to provide information to the data subjects in § 491 of the Code of Criminal Procedure are of particular importance.

129 aa) § 489 of the Code of Criminal Procedure provides for the correction, blocking, and, most notably, deletion of personal data. According to § 489(2) of the Code of Criminal Procedure, data is to be deleted *ex officio* if its storage is not permissible or if the examination in the individual case shows that knowledge of the data is no longer necessary for the respective statutory purpose. [...]

130 bb) § 491 of the Code of Criminal Procedure governs the obligation to provide information on the storage of their data to persons who are not themselves part of the criminal investigation [...].

131 If it does not jeopardise the purpose of the investigation or contravene overriding protected interests of third parties, persons affected by the data storage must be provided with the relevant information pursuant to § 19 of the Federal Data Protection Act upon request. The request may only be refused if providing the information would specifically jeopardise the purpose of the investigation. [...]

132 3. In principle, when the authorities secure a data storage device, they can obtain knowledge of all information it contains. The large amount of information alone may already lead to a considerable number of coincidental findings within the meaning of § 108 of the Code of Criminal Procedure. The seizure of the entire data belonging to persons bound by professional confidentiality thus necessarily entails

special risks to the integrity of third-party data and thus also to the public interest in the proper administration of justice, for which the privileged relationship of trust between independent lawyers and their clients is crucial.

[…] Nonetheless, securing the data storage device and all available data is permissible if the relevant information cannot be separated from other data during the search by using the available technical means and undertaking reasonable efforts (see C III 2 f above). Even if, as required under constitutional law, the data relevant to the investigation is separated from other data, it cannot be ruled out that the authorities obtain knowledge of irrelevant data. 133

In certain cases, the existing prohibitions to use as evidence data obtained by search and seizure measures, which have already been developed and recognised in the case-law, afford protection against unauthorised interferences with fundamental rights. Yet the question arises whether an additional prohibition to use the data as evidence should be recognised in order to effectively protect the fundamental right to informational self-determination, at least of third parties, and to effectively safeguard the relationship of trust between persons bound by professional confidentiality and their clients. This would strengthen the fundamental right under Art. 2(1) of the Basic Law in conjunction with Art. 1(1) of the Basic Law and the constitutionally protected relationship of trust between lawyers and their clients. 134

At least in cases of serious, deliberate or arbitrary violations of procedure, where the limitation to the investigation purpose prompting the seizure of data storage devices is disregarded deliberately or systematically, the wrongful search and seizure of data storage devices and of the data stored on them must result in a prohibition to use the data as evidence. 135

V.

The decisions of the Hamburg Regional Court do not satisfy these constitutional requirements. 136

1. The Hamburg Regional Court argued that it was not possible to sort the data into different categories because the entire data stored on a data storage device was considered evidence […]. This does not satisfy the constitutional requirements set forth above regarding the securing and seizure of data belonging to persons bound by professional confidentiality. When following the view of the Regional Court, there would be no examination of the particular circumstances of the individual case, yet such an examination is required under constitutional law. The Regional Court disregarded aspects significant to the balancing of interests such as the protected confidentiality of third-party data, the specific criminal charges, the quality of the suspicion, the evidentiary value of the information stored and the probability that 137

relevant evidence will indeed be found. It failed to recognise the high intensity of the interference and the considerable number of third parties affected. [...] The Regional Court accorded absolute priority to law enforcement interests – which may indeed prove to be significant in the individual case – over other legitimate interests that merit special legal protection, excluding them from the requirement of balancing conflicting interests. It failed to examine the relevance of the secured data to the proceedings and the possibility of separating it from irrelevant data, which would have been required. It thus did not even consider any limitation of the excessive data collection measures. [...]

138 2. [...]

VI.

139-140 [...]

Justices: Hassemer, Jentsch, Broß, Osterloh, Di Fabio, Mellinghoff, Lübbe-Wolff, Gerhardt

No. 35

BVerfGE 152, 152 – Right to Be Forgotten I

HEADNOTES

to the Order of the First Senate of 6 November 2019
1 BvR 16/13

1. a) The Federal Constitutional Court reviews domestic law that is not fully determined by European Union law on the basis, primarily, of the fundamental rights of the Basic Law, including in cases where the relevant provisions of domestic law serve to implement European Union law.

   b) The application of the fundamental rights of the Basic Law as the primary standard of review is informed by the assumption that European Union law, where it affords Member States latitude in the design of ordinary legislation, is generally not aimed at uniformity in fundamental rights protection, but allows for fundamental rights diversity.
   This then leads to the presumption that the application of the fundamental rights of the Basic Law simultaneously ensures the level of protection of the Charter of Fundamental Rights of the European Union.

   c) An exception to the assumption in favour of fundamental rights diversity in cases where Member States are afforded latitude in the design of ordinary legislation, or a rebuttal of the presumption that the application of the Basic Law's fundamental rights simultaneously ensures the level of fundamental rights protection of the Charter, should only be considered where there is specific and sufficient indication therefor.

2. a) In respect of the protection against risks to one's personality stemming from the dissemination, in the context of public communication processes, of articles and information relating to one's person, the applicable standard of review under constitutional law derives from the general right of personality in its manifestation as a right protecting against statements affecting one's person, rather than in its manifestation as a right to informational self-determination.

b) Given the realities of Internet communication, time is a specific factor to be considered when deciding on a person's claim for protection. The legal order must protect the individual against the risk of being indefinitely confronted in public with their past opinions, statements or actions. Only when it is possible for matters to stay in the past do individuals have a chance at a new beginning in freedom. The possibility for matters to be forgotten is part of the temporal dimension of freedom.

c) There is no right derived from the general right of personality to request that all information relating to one's person that was disseminated through communication processes be deleted from the Internet. In particular, the individual has no right to filter the publicly accessible information concerning them according to their free discretion and own preferences, thus restricting such information to aspects that they themselves might regard as relevant or appropriate to the self-perceived image of their personality.

d) In balancing the fundamental rights of a media outlet uploading its articles to an online archive with the fundamental rights of a person affected by such articles, it must be taken into account to what extent the media outlet disposes of means to effectively block access to and dissemination of old press articles on the Internet in order to protect affected persons – especially in respect of how these articles are listed in the results of an Internet search for the affected person's name.

3. The right protecting against statements affecting one's person must be distinguished from the right to informational self-determination, which constitutes another separate manifestation of the general right of personality. The right to informational self-determination, too, may bear on relationships between private actors. Its indirect effects on private law relationships differ from its direct effects vis-à-vis the state. Between private actors, it provides the individual the possibility of influencing, in nuanced ways, the context and manner in which their data is accessible to and can be used by others, thus affording the individual considerable influence in deciding what information is available on them.

No. 35 – Right to Be Forgotten I

FEDERAL CONSTITUTIONAL COURT
- 1 BvR 16/13 -

IN THE NAME OF THE PEOPLE

In the proceedings
on the constitutional complaint of

Mr T...,
– authorised representatives: ...
against the Judgment of the Federal Court of Justice of 13 November 2012
- VI ZR 330/11 -,

the Federal Constitutional Court – First Senate –
with the participation of Justices

Vice-President Harbarth,
Masing,
Paulus,
Baer,
Britz,
Ott,
Christ,
Radtke

held on 6 November 2019:

JUDGMENT

1. The Judgment of the Federal Court of Justice of 13 November 2012 - VI ZR 330/11 - violates the complainant's fundamental right under Article 2(1) in conjunction with Article 1(1) of the Basic Law.
2. The Judgment is reversed. The matter is remanded to the Federal Court of Justice.
3. [...]

BVerfGE 152, 152

REASONS:

A.

1   The constitutional complaint is directed against a private law judgment of the Federal Court of Justice. In the challenged judgment, the Federal Court of Justice had rejected the complainant's action seeking injunctive relief against the availability, in an online archive, of press articles from more than 30 years ago; in the respective articles, which cover the complainant's conviction for murder, the complainant is identified by name.

I.

2   1. The complainant was convicted, by final judgment, on charges of murder and attempted murder and sentenced to life imprisonment. He was accused of having shot two persons and of having severely injured another person on board the yacht "A.", which was on the high seas crossing the Atlantic Ocean, in 1981. In 2002, the complainant was released from prison after having served his sentence. [...]

3   In 1982 and 1983, the magazine *Der Spiegel* ran three articles on the case in its print edition, which identified the complainant by name. In 1999, the *Spiegel Online GmbH* – the defendant in the ordinary court proceedings – uploaded the articles to the magazine's online archive, where the articles are accessible free of charge and without any restrictions. When the complainant's name is entered into a common Internet search engine, the articles in question are listed among the top search results.

4   2. In 2009, after learning that the articles were available online, the complainant sent a cease-and-desist letter to the defendant regarding the online articles identifying him. He subsequently lodged an action seeking to enjoin the defendant from disseminating any information on the crime he committed in 1981 containing the complainant's last name. The Regional Court rejected the action, a subsequent appeal on points of facts and law (*Berufung*) to the Higher Regional Court was unsuccessful. [...]

5   [...]

6   3. Following the defendant's appeal on points of law (*Revision*), the Federal Court of Justice, in its judgment of 13 November 2012, reversed the judgment of the Higher Regional Court, modified the judgment of the Regional Court and rejected the action. [...]

[...] 7-8

4. In his constitutional complaint, the complainant claims a violation of his general right of personality. [...] 9

The complainant asserts that the media coverage identifying him results in impairments of his personality right that are disproportionate to the public's interest in obtaining information. He claims that even a felon is entitled to social reintegration. [...] 10

5. Providing the backdrop to these proceedings are provisions of EU law. At the time the challenged decision was rendered, Directive 95/46/EC [...] was in force. This directive obliged Member States to protect the right to privacy of natural persons with respect to the processing of personal data. Art. 9 of Directive 95/46/EC entitled Member States to provide for exemptions under the so-called media privilege. [...] 11

On 25 May 2018, the directive was replaced with the General Data Protection Regulation [...]. In Art. 17, the General Data Protection Regulation contains a right to erasure, which is also referred to as the "right to be forgotten" in brackets. The regulation also affords Member States some leeway in the form of a media privilege (cf. Art. 85 GDPR). 12

II.

Statements concerning the constitutional complaint were submitted by the defendant, the Data Protection Officers of the *Länder* Hamburg and Hesse, the Federal Association of German Newspaper Publishers (*Bundesverband Deutscher Zeitungsverleger e.V.*), the German Federation of Journalists (*Deutscher Journalisten-Verband e.V.*), the association *BITKOM*, the German Association of Law and Information Technology (*Deutsche Gesellschaft für Recht und Informatik e.V.*), Google Germany GmbH, the eco Association of the German Internet Industry (*eco-Verband der deutschen Internetwirtschaft e.V.*) and the German Media Association (*Deutscher Medienverband e.V.*). 13

[...] 14-35

B.

The constitutional complaint is admissible. 36

37-39 [...]

C.

40 The constitutional complaint is well-founded. The challenged decision of the Federal Court of Justice violates the complainant's general right of personality (Art. 2(1) in conjunction with Art. 1(1) of the Basic Law).

I.

41 The standard of review applicable to the constitutional complaint are the fundamental rights of the Basic Law. This applies irrespective of whether in the challenged decision the Federal Court of Justice had to take into consideration provisions of ordinary domestic legislation that constitute an implementation of EU law within the meaning of Art. 51(1) first sentence of the Charter of Fundamental Rights of the European Union.

42 1. The Federal Constitutional Court reviews domestic law and its application against the standard of the fundamental rights of the Basic Law even where the domestic law falls within the scope of application of EU law but is not fully determined by it. This already follows from Art. 1(3), Art. 20(3) and Art. 93(1) no. 4a of the Basic Law. The binding effect of fundamental rights is a corollary of the political responsibility for decisions, and thus corresponds to the respective responsibilities of the legislator and the executive. It falls to the German courts, and in particular to the Federal Constitutional Court, to ensure that fundamental rights are observed in the exercise of this responsibility.

43 2. This does not rule out that in certain cases the Charter of Fundamental Rights of the European Union may also lay claim to applicability. However, this can only be considered to be the case in the context of the EU Treaties and thus in cases where Member States are "implementing Union law" within the meaning of Art. 51(1) first sentence of the Charter. This deliberately limits the domestic scope of application of the Charter: in cases not concerning the implementation of EU law, fundamental rights protection is left to the Member States and their domestic fundamental rights guarantees, on the common basis of the European Convention on Human Rights. Accordingly, the Charter does not provide comprehensive fundamental rights protection for the entire European Union; rather, through the limitation of its scope of application, it acknowledges the diversity (cf. Art. 4(2) TEU, cf. also Art. 23(1) first sentence of the Basic Law) of the fundamental rights guarantees of the Member States. Thus, limits to the simultaneous applicability of EU fundamental rights and the fundamental rights of the Basic Law are set. They

may not be circumvented by an untenably broad interpretation of Art. 51(1) first sentence of the Charter (cf. BVerfGE 133, 277 <316 para 91> – *Counter-Terrorism Database Act I*).

Conversely, the limitation of the Charter's scope of application does not rule out the possibility that domestic provisions may be judged to be provisions implementing EU law within the meaning of Art. 51(1) first sentence of the Charter in cases where EU law affords Member States latitude in the design of such provisions, but also provides for a sufficiently substantial framework for this design, and it is ascertainable that the framework is to be specified in consideration of EU fundamental rights. In such a scenario, the EU fundamental rights are applicable in addition to the fundamental rights guarantees of the Basic Law. This does not fundamentally call into question the binding effect of the Basic Law. 44

3. Even where, pursuant to Art. 51(1) first sentence of the Charter, EU fundamental rights are applicable in addition to the fundamental rights of the Basic Law, the Federal Constitutional Court primarily relies on the fundamental rights of the Basic Law as its standard of review [...]. 45

[...] 46-62

4. [...] 63-72

5. [...] 73

6. [...] 74

II.

The constitutional complaint concerns the protection of fundamental rights in relations between private actors. In such relations, fundamental rights have indirect horizontal effects (*mittelbare Drittwirkung*) (see 1 below). In respect of the complainant, the review must take into account his general right of personality (Art. 2(1) in conjunction with Art. 1(1) of the Basic Law) in its general manifestation as the right protecting against statements affecting one's person (*Äußerungsrecht*) (see 2 below); in respect of the defendant in the ordinary court proceedings, the review must take into account freedom of expression and freedom of the press (Art. 5(1) first sentence and (2) of the Basic Law) (see 3 below). 75

1. The complainant challenges a private law decision rendered in a legal dispute between the complainant and the media outlet he sued. Fundamental rights have a bearing on such disputes between private actors by way of indirect horizontal effects. While fundamental rights do not generally create direct obligations between private actors, they do, however, permeate legal relationships under private law; it is thus incumbent upon the ordinary courts to give effect to fundamental rights in the interpretation of ordinary law, in particular by means of private law provi- 76

sions containing general clauses and indeterminate legal concepts (*unbestimmte Rechtsbegriffe*). The effect of the decisions on constitutional values enshrined in fundamental rights thus comes into play and, in the form of guidelines, permeates private law. In this context, fundamental rights do not serve the purpose of consistently keeping freedom-restricting interferences to a minimum; rather, they are to be developed as fundamental values informing the balancing of the freedoms of equally entitled rights holders. The freedom afforded one rights holder must be reconciled with the freedom afforded another. For this purpose, conflicting fundamental rights positions must be considered in terms of how they interact and must be balanced in accordance with the principle of achieving maximum equilibrium between conflicting fundamental rights of equal weight (*Grundsatz der praktischen Konkordanz*), which requires that the fundamental rights of all persons concerned be given effect to the broadest possible extent (cf. BVerfGE 7, 198 <204 *et seq.*>; 148, 267 <280 para. 32> with further references).

77-78 [...]

79 2. In respect of the complainant, the balancing must take into account his general right of personality following from Art. 2(1) in conjunction with Art. 1(1) of the Basic Law in its manifestation as a right protecting against statements affecting one's person that has been developed by the courts (see a below). This manifestation is to be distinguished from the right to informational self-determination, which constitutes another separate manifestation of the general right of personality that also affects private law (see b below). However, the right to informational self-determination is not relevant here (see c below).

80 a) The general right of personality protects the free development of one's personality; in particular, it also affords protection against media reporting and the dissemination of information relating to one's person, where these are capable of severely impairing the free development of one's personality. Notably, it guarantees protection against statements which could tarnish a person's reputation, especially their public image (cf. BVerfGE 114, 339 <346> – *Stolpe/Stasi Dispute*). This Court has held that different manifestations arise from this fundamental right, including the protection of an inviolable core of private life, the guarantee of the private sphere, the right to one's own image or speech and the right to determine the portrayal of one's person, the right to social recognition and to personal honour (cf. BVerfGE 27, 1 <6> – *Microcensus*; 27, 344 <350 and 351> – *Divorce Files*; 32, 373 <379>; 34, 238 <245 and 246> – *Secret Tape Recordings*; 47, 46 <73>; 54, 148 <153 and 154> – *Eppler*; 99, 185 <193 and 194> – *Helnwein/Scientology*; 101, 361 <384>; 106, 28 <39>; 114, 339 <346> – *Stolpe/Stasi Dispute*; 120, 180 <198> – *Caroline III*). Yet these protective contents are not understood as exhaustive guarantees, distinct from one another; rather, they are to be understood

as manifestations that must be worked out in accordance with the specific need for protection in each individual case (cf. BVerfGE 54, 148 <153 and 154> – *Eppler*; 65, 1 <41> – *Census*).

This case-law was mainly developed in respect of constellations involving indirect horizontal effects, guided by the requirement of achieving maximum equilibrium between conflicting fundamental rights of equal weight. Therefore, the relevant manifestations of the protection of the general right of personality are always determined in each individual case with due regard to the fundamental rights of third parties. Thus, the determination of the protection this right affords and the balancing with conflicting freedoms go hand in hand. The protection afforded by the general right of personality is thus flexible and relativised by viewing a person in the context of their social relationships (cf. BVerfGE 101, 361 <380>; 141, 186 <202 para. 32>; 147, 1 <19 para. 38> – *Third Gender Option*; established case-law [...]). 81

It follows that the general right of personality does not confer upon the individual an exclusive right to determine the portrayal of their person in all respects. It does, however, aim to guarantee the basic conditions enabling the individual to develop and protect their individuality in self-determination (cf. BVerfGE 35, 202 <220> – *Lebach*; 79, 256 <268>; 90, 263 <270>; 117, 202 <225>; 141, 186 <201 para. 32>; 147, 1 <19 para. 38> – *Third Gender Option*). Thus, from its inception, this right protects the right of the individual to decide themselves whether, when and how they enter the public sphere. Accordingly, the general right of personality in principle affords protection against the covert interception of communications, against the dissemination of photos from one's private life or against statements being falsely attributed to one's person (cf. BVerfGE 34, 269 <282 and 283> – *Soraya*; 54, 148 <154> – *Eppler*; 101, 361 <382>; 120, 180 <199> – *Caroline III*). Different burdens of justification apply in view of the tension between protection and freedom with respect to the question of what information that is accessible to third parties or the public may be further communicated in society. The respective burden of justification depends on the constellation at issue. In principle, the case-law distinguishes in particular between the spoken or written dissemination of true facts, which is generally permissible, on the one hand, and the dissemination of images, which generally requires justification, on the other (cf. BVerfGE 101, 361 <381>; 120, 180 <197 and 198> – *Caroline III*; established case-law). However, this is only an initial point of departure from which further diverse – both in terms of procedure and content – balancing rules follow, which are designed to reach a differentiated determination of the specific need for protection and to most adequately take this need into account. Ultimately, there is thus no general rule on which interest takes precedence in the balancing; rather, a differentiated balance 82 must be struck between the presumption of freedom and the right to protection in the individual case.

83 b) The right to informational self-determination is a separate manifestation of the general right of personality (see aa below). This right, too, in principle has a bearing on the relationship between private actors (see bb below). Under the principle of indirect horizontal effects, the decisions on constitutional values enshrined in this right permeate private law and must be balanced against the fundamental rights of third parties. In this respect, its effects differ from those arising when it is invoked directly vis-à-vis the state (see cc below). In relation to the protections against statements affecting one's person deriving from the general right of personality, the right to informational self-determination does not constitute an all-encompassing guarantee of protection; rather, it has a separate content that must be distinguished from those protections (see dd below).

84 aa) According to established case-law, a distinct manifestation of the general right of personality is the right to informational self-determination (cf. BVerfGE 65, 1 <42> – *Census*; 78, 77 <84> – *Public Announcement of Legal Incapacitation*; 118, 168 <184>; established case-law). In the context of modern data processing, the free development of one's personality requires that the individual be protected against the unlimited collection, storage, use and sharing of their personal data. This fundamental right confers upon the individual the authority to, in principle, decide themselves on the disclosure and use of their personal data (cf. BVerfGE 65, 1 <42 and 43> – *Census*; 120, 274 <312> – *Remote Searches*). If individuals cannot, with sufficient certainty, determine what kind of personal information is known in certain areas of their social environment, and if it is difficult to ascertain what kind of information potential communication partners are privy to, this could greatly impede their freedom to make self-determined plans or decisions (BVerfGE 65, 1 <43> – *Census*).

85 bb) Initially, this Court developed the right to informational self-determination in its case-law as a right protecting against data collection and processing measures carried out by the state and its authorities (cf., e.g., BVerfGE 65, 1 <42 and 43> – *Census*; 113, 29 <46> – *Seizure of Electronic Data*; 118, 168 <184>; 133, 277 <320 et seq.* para. 105 *et seq.*> – *Counter-Terrorism Database Act I*; 141, 220 <264 and 265 paras. 91 and 92> – *The Federal Criminal Police Office Act*; 150, 244 <263 and 264 para. 37>). There is no reason, however, why the protection of fundamental rights should not also be extended, in accordance with general rules, to the relationship between private actors, and thus give effect to such protection in the context of private law disputes via indirect horizontal effects. This applies, firstly, to the question under what conditions what types of data must be disclosed in the context of private law obligations (cf. BVerfGE 84, 192 <194>). Yet it also applies

to the conditions on when personal data may be processed and used by private third parties, and to what ends [...]. The impact of the technical possibilities of data processing, too, is becoming increasingly important in the relationship between private actors. In all aspects of life, basic services for the general public are increasingly provided by private companies – often with a strong market position – on the basis of comprehensive personal data collection and data processing measures; these companies play a decisive role in forming public opinion, providing or denying opportunities, allowing participation in social life and basic activities of daily life. It is hard for individuals to avoid disclosing personal data to companies on a large scale if they do not want to be excluded from these basic services. Given that the data can be manipulated, reproduced and disseminated virtually without limit in terms of place and time and that the data can be recombined in unforeseen ways through opaque processing measures by means of incomprehensible algorithms, individuals may become caught in extensive dependencies or severe contractual obligations. Thus, these developments can give rise to major risks to the development of one's personality, which the right to informational self-determination serves to counteract.

cc) The right to informational self-determination has a bearing on relationships between private actors by way of indirect horizontal effects. As a decision on constitutional values enshrined in this right, and as a guideline, it thus permeates private law (see paras. 76 and 77 above). In this respect, its effects differ from the direct protection it affords vis-à-vis the state, where – as a defensive right against state interference – it is determined by the asymmetry of the rule of law, under which citizens are free, whereas the state is subject to limitations. Based on the state's duty to generally justify its actions, the right to informational self-determination, as a defensive right against state interference, ties the constitutional requirements for data processing to a formalised differentiation of the individual steps of data collection and processing, which amount to separate interferences; these interferences then require a sufficiently specific statutory basis that restricts processing measures to specific purposes, and that can, and must, be reviewed as to its adherence to proportionality requirements.

By contrast, the right to informational self-determination, as a decision on values enshrined in the Constitution concerning relationships between private actors, seeks to reconcile conflicting fundamental rights from the outset. In this respect, this right must be balanced against the freedom to gather, process and use information for one's own purposes, including for changing purposes. Unlike the standards applicable vis-à-vis the state, the requirements and burden of justification applicable to relationships between private actors cannot be determined in the abstract but are contingent upon a balancing to assess the need for protection arising between private actors in the various case constellations, which are frequently multipolar. As is the case with the right to determine the portrayal of one's person, the right to informational self-determination does not confer upon the individual a general, let alone an unconditional, right to self-determination regarding the use of their data. It does, however, allow the individual the possibility of influencing, in a differentiated manner, the context and manner in which their data is accessible to and can be used by others. Thus, it guarantees the individual substantial influence in deciding what information is attributed to their person (cf. similarly BVerfGE 120, 180 <198> – *Caroline III*).

88   The permeating effect on private law of the decisions on constitutional values enshrined in this fundamental right does not mean that the requirements this right entails are always less far-reaching or less strict than the ones it entails in its function as a direct right against state interference. Depending on the circumstances, especially where private companies take on a position that is so dominant as to be similar to the state's position, or where they provide the framework for public communication themselves, the binding effect of the fundamental right on private actors can ultimately be close, or even equal to, its binding effect on the state (cf. BVerfGE 128, 226 <249 and 250>). In this respect, strict requirements regarding the structuring of data processing as well as linking and limiting it to a specific purpose – especially in combination with requirements to obtain consent – can constitute suitable, and possibly constitutionally required, means for protecting informational self-determination.

89   dd) In the case-law, the right to informational self-determination was developed as a separate manifestation of the general right of personality, and the protective contents it guarantees are distinct from those of other manifestations, even where the decisions on constitutional values underlying it permeate private law. Thus, it does not constitute a comprehensive right to protection against any and all use of information that would cover the other manifestations of this fundamental right and unify them; rather, it does not bear on the value decisions and balancing rules of these other manifestations.

90   Given that the right to informational self-determination aims to afford protection against the risks arising from novel possibilities of data processing (cf. BVerfGE 65, 1 <42> – *Census*), it must primarily be understood as a guarantee that – besides affording protection against the unintended disclosure of data in private law relationships (cf. BVerfGE 84, 192 <194>) – particularly protects against opaque data processing and use by private actors. It affords protection against third parties appropriating certain data on individuals and instrumentalising it in opaque ways in order to attribute to those individuals personal characteristics, types or profiles over

which they have no control but which significantly bear on the free development of their personality and equal participation in society. [...].

This is to be distinguished from the protection against the dissemination of media reports and information relating to one's person as a result of communication processes. In such cases, the need for protection does not arise from third parties making opaque use of an individual's personal data to attribute personal characteristics or personality profiles, but from the tangible dissemination of certain information in the public sphere. In this context, risks to the free development of one's personality primarily result from the type and contents of the publication itself. The general right of personality in its manifestation as a right protecting against statements affecting one's person affords protection against such risks, whereas the right to informational self-determination is not relevant here. [...]

c) According to the distinguishing carried out above, the right to informational self-determination is not the standard of constitutional review applicable to the legal dispute at hand; rather, it is the protection afforded by the general right of personality in its manifestation as a right protecting against statements affecting one's person that applies. The complainant does not challenge any obligation to disclose data or the opaque use of his data, but rather articles about him that serve to inform the public and are readily accessible to him, too. [...]

3. In respect of the defendant in the ordinary court proceedings, the balancing must take into account the fundamental rights of freedom of expression and freedom of the press.

The dissemination of articles covering events of public life is subject to freedom of expression under Art. 5(1) first sentence of the Basic Law; it protects the dissemination of opinions and facts regardless of their form or the means of communication (cf. BVerfGE 85, 1 <12 and 13>). At the same time, freedom of the press under Art. 5(1) second sentence of the Basic Law is affected. Beyond the freedom to express opinions, this fundamental right also protects the institutional independence of the press. It spans from the obtaining of information to its dissemination (cf. BVerfGE 10, 118 <121>; 62, 230 <243>; established case-law). This also includes the decision of media outlets to make past press articles permanently available to the public in archives. More than being simply about the publication of the contents of an article, this constitutes an important independent decision by a media outlet on the form in which it disseminates its products, and thus on both the effects of its products as well as its own visibility.

By contrast, freedom of broadcasting under Art. 5(1) second sentence of the Basic Law is not affected. [...]

III.

96 The conflicting fundamental rights must be balanced against one another. Such a balancing requires a determination of their respective guaranteed contents. In this regard, particular consideration must be given to the realities of Internet communication.

97 1. The general right of personality affords protection against the dissemination of publications tarnishing the reputation of individuals in a manner that poses risks to the development of their personality. This also applies in respect of the coverage of crimes by the press. Conversely, one of the tasks of the press is to cover crimes and those committing them (cf. BVerfGE 35, 202 <230 et seq.> – *Lebach*). Therefore, whether individuals enjoy a right to protection is determined by the specific conditions of the reporting, such as its type, extent and circulation. Time in particular is a significant aspect to be considered, too.

98 a) There is nothing novel about the significance of the time of publication for the constitutional review of the press coverage of crimes. With regard to current media coverage of crime, the case-law generally accords precedence to the interest in obtaining information and, in principle, finds it permissible that news coverage identifies the offender, at least in cases where a conviction has become final (cf. BVerfGE 35, 202 <231 et seq.> – *Lebach*); at the same time, the applicable case-law has emphasised that the interest in media reporting changes the more time has passed since the crime was committed. The interest justifying such media reporting changes from an interest that is focused on the crime and the offender to an interest in analysing the conditions and consequences of the crime (cf. BVerfGE 35, 202 <231> – *Lebach*). When the interest of the public in obtaining current information on the crime has been satisfied, the 'right to be left alone' of the affected person gains significance (cf. BVerfGE 35, 202 <233> – *Lebach*). It is impossible to determine a general rule stating after how many months or years one would have to draw the line between news coverage, which is in principle permissible, and a later portrayal or discussion, which is impermissible. The decisive criterion is whether the respective coverage might have a significantly new or an added adverse effect on the offender (cf. BVerfGE 35, 202 <234> – *Lebach*). In this respect, the offender's interest in social reintegration can be a particularly significant benchmark.

99 [...]

100 These standards are also set out in the case-law of the European Court of Human Rights. In order to assess the weight of interference of a publication, the European Court of Human Rights, too, expressly considers the time of publication, posing the question whether the dissemination of reports relating to a specific person is in the public interest at the time when the reports are published. In this respect, it also

takes into consideration whether an offender seeks to reintegrate into society after release from prison (cf. ECtHR, *Österreichischer Rundfunk v. Austria*, Decision of 25 May 2004, no. 57597/00).

b) The present day realities of information technology and the dissemination of information on the Internet add a new legal dimension to the requirement that information be considered in the context of time.

aa) Whereas the earlier case-law of the Federal Constitutional Court addressed the question whether past events may be revisited through new coverage, the fundamental problem today is that information is available in the long term on the Internet and on storage media. In the past, information disseminated solely in print media and radio broadcasts was accessible to the public only for a limited period of time beyond which it was largely forgotten. Today, however, information – once it is digitalised and published online – remains available in the long term. The lingering effects of information over time are no longer limited to a fleeting recollection in public discourse; rather, the information can be directly and permanently retrieved by anyone.

bb) Moreover, it can be retrieved at any time and can be combined with other data. For affected persons, this considerably changes the significance of the coverage relating to them. At present, such information can be obtained by complete strangers at any time and without specific reason; it can become the subject of online discussions by groups communicating via the Internet, regardless of whether it concerns issues relevant to the public; it can be taken out of context and presented in a new narrative; and it can be combined with other information to create partial or complete personality profiles, with name-related searches via search engines being widely used for this purpose. This results in far-reaching consequences for public communication processes, which fundamentally change the conditions for the free development of one's personality […].

cc) It is not for constitutional law to halt such trends as a whole or to neutralise any advantages and disadvantages of the consequences they entail. However, where such trends give rise to specific risks to the free development of one's personality, this must be taken into consideration when interpreting and applying the Basic Law. The unlimited availability of information on the Internet warrants such consideration.

(1) Freedom involves forming, developing and changing one's personal beliefs and behaviour in interaction with others on the basis of communication in society. This requires a legal framework that allows the individual to exercise their freedom without intimidation, and offers them the chance to move on from errors and mistakes. Thus, the legal order must protect the individual against the risk of being indefinitely confronted in public with their past opinions, statements or actions.

Only when matters are allowed to stay in the past do individuals have a chance at a new beginning in freedom, because society then forgets past events. The possibility for matters to be forgotten forms part of the temporal dimension of freedom. This applies in particular with regard to the objective of reintegrating offenders.

106 Legal scholars also acknowledge that to safeguard the development of one's personality, such a need for protection exists; figuratively, it is also called the "right to be forgotten" ([...] see also Art. 17 GDPR). This need for protection is also recognised by the European courts. Thus, the European Court of Human Rights acknowledges the offender's interest in no longer being confronted with their acts after a certain period of time has elapsed, with a view to their reintegration in society, which it expressly considers a human rights issue (cf. ECtHR, *M. L. and W. W. v. Germany*, Judgment of 28 June 2018, nos. 60798/10 and 65599/10, § 100). Similarly, the Court of Justice of the European Union holds that in view of Arts. 7 and 8 of the Charter and having regard to the sensitivity of the information in question for their private life or their commercial reputation, affected persons can, under certain circumstances, request that certain events no longer be linked to their name (cf. CJEU, Judgment of 13 May 2014, *Google Spain*, C-131/12, EU:C:2014:317, para. 98; Judgment of 9 March 2017, *Manni*, C-398/15, EU:C:2017:197, para. 63; Judgment of 24 September 2019, *GC and Others*, C-136/17, EU:C:2019:773, para. 77). The inclusion of time as a factor in the assessment of the constitutional requirements for the dissemination of information has arisen as a development resulting from the exchange about fundamental rights in Europe.

107 (2) It must be noted, however, that the general right of personality does not confer upon the individual a 'right to be forgotten' in a strict sense, given that it does not grant the individual an exclusive right to decide what information about them is to be forgotten. One's personality is also formed in communication processes and thus in interaction with the free judgment of third parties and of the public to a greater or lesser extent. It is not for the individual to decide unilaterally what information about them is to be remembered as interesting, admirable, offensive or reprehensible. The general right of personality does not encompass a right to request that all information relating to one's person that is disseminated in the context of communication processes be deleted from the Internet. In particular, the individual does not have a right to filter all publicly accessible information about them based on their free discretion and own preferences, allowing them to restrict such information to aspects that they themselves regard as relevant or appropriate to the self-perceived image of their personality. The Basic Law certainly does not call into question that a permanent examination of crimes and offenders is permissible in cases where the offenders are public persons with an impact on the self-image of the community as a whole. The general right of personality does

not afford protection against events being remembered in a historically responsible manner.

(3) Included in such a balance, the effective protection of the general right of personality is not only significant to individuals, but is also in the public interest. Where individuals can be confronted with their social activities, unusual personal traits, unpopular views or errors and transgressions at any time and these may be used to agitate the public, this not only impairs their possibilities of personal development, but also the common good. This is because self-determination over time is a fundamental prerequisite for the functioning of a free and democratic society which relies on the agency and participation of its citizens. Individuals can only be expected to participate in the state and in society if they are afforded sufficient protection in this respect. This applies not only to the right to informational self-determination (cf. BVerfGE 65, 1 <43> – *Census*), but also more generally to the general right of personality.

dd) Therefore, when assessing and weighing the constitutional significance of reports relating to one's person, their effects must also be assessed in their temporal dimension. It is necessary to consider the circumstances of the individual case, which, in addition to other factors, include the time passed since the events in question occurred. Such an assessment can adhere to previous case-law (cf. BVerfGE 35, 202 <218 *et seq.*> – *Lebach*). Yet it is not sufficient that the publication of a piece of information was initially justified; rather, its dissemination must be justifiable at any point in time during which it is accessible. Even where reporting was initially permissible, its later dissemination may become impermissible – just as it can become permissible again when new circumstances arise.

2. At the same time, the balancing must give appropriate consideration to the protective guarantees of freedom of expression and freedom of the press.

a) Art. 5(1) first sentence of the Basic Law protects the free reporting on events that are of public significance, which generally includes providing complete information to the public on crimes and the events that led to crimes being committed, including information on the offender (cf. BVerfGE 35, 202 <230> – *Lebach*). Limiting media reporting to anonymised information significantly restricts the public's access to information, and requires justification (cf. BVerfGE 119, 309 <326> – *TV Broadcasting from the Courtroom*). These protective contents are also confirmed in the case-law of the European Court of Human Rights. According to this case-law, the inclusion of individualised information in a report on crime is an important aspect of the press's work. Requirements arising from the protection of one's personality must not be designed in such a way that the press is discouraged from publishing individualised reporting (cf. ECtHR, *M. L. and W. W. v. Germany*, Judgment of 28 June 2018, nos. 60798/10 and 65599/10, §§ 104 and 105; on the significance of individualised coverage cf. also ECtHR, *F. v. Germany*, Judgment of 19 October 2017, no. 71233/13, § 37).

112 b) As regards the freedom of the press protected by Art. 5(1) second sentence of the Basic Law, the balancing must take into account the right of the press to make its own decisions on what to report, when, for how long, and in what manner (cf. BVerfGE 101, 361 <389 and 390>; 120, 180 <196 and 197> – *Caroline III*; established case-law). The possibility of archiving unaltered press reports in their entirety, retaining them as reflections of contemporary society, is an important element of this freedom. In this respect, the contents of freedom of the press, too, must be assessed in light of the developments in information technology. Given that they are ubiquitous and available at any time, articles available on the Internet are of great importance for the press – especially as a supplement to print versions, which, on their own, can no longer satisfy the public interest in obtaining information and cannot financially sustain a media outlet.

113 Online archives do not merely serve the interests of media outlets, but are also in the public interest. The general availability of information on the Internet opens up participation in knowledge communication to a broader circle of people and creates new opportunities for citizens to convey and obtain information, including across borders. Online press archives provide easy access to information and are important resources for journalistic research and for research on contemporary society. In this respect, there is considerable interest in archives providing complete and accurate information. Such archives constitute an important source for education and historical research as well as for public debate in a democracy (cf. also, in this regard, ECtHR, *M. L. and W. W. v. Germany*, Judgment of 28 June 2018, nos. 60798/10 and 65599/10, § 90 with reference to ECtHR, *Times Newspapers Ltd v. the United Kingdom*, Judgment of 10 March 2009, nos. 3002/03 and 23676/03, §§ 27 and 45 as well as ECtHR, *Węgrzynowski and Smolczewski v. Poland*, Judgment of 16 July 2013, no. 33846/07, § 59).

IV.

114 The scope of the rights to protection against the dissemination of press reports is determined in the individual case in a balancing of the conflicting fundamental rights with due consideration to the specific circumstances. Having regard to the principles developed in the case-law, such a balancing must take into account the specific need for protection, and in particular assess the circumstances surrounding and the subject matter of a publication, as well as its form, type and reach. This includes both its dissemination on the Internet and the significance of the reporting

over time. In this balancing, the different factors are generally considered in relation to one another.

The proceedings at hand are notable in that the initial lawfulness of the reporting is not disputed. [...] The proceedings only concern the question whether an article that was lawful when it was first published may be further disseminated even though many years have passed and the circumstances have therefore changed. Thus, what is at issue in these proceedings is the significance of the passage of time for the further dissemination of the articles in question.

This requires – as per usual – a comprehensive balancing between the conflicting fundamental rights in the individual case, which primarily falls to the ordinary courts. [...]

1. Firstly, a balance between the interests of a media outlet as the content provider responsible for online publication and the interests of affected persons must be found in respect of when, in procedural terms, new review obligations arise for the content provider.

In principle, the press is responsible for the dissemination of its articles and must review their lawfulness when publishing them. Given that uploading articles to the Internet results in their further dissemination, the press remains responsible for the lawfulness of its articles, including when the relevant circumstances change with the passage of time. However, this cannot give rise to an obligation for the press to regularly review the continued lawfulness of any articles made available online on its own initiative. Such a proactive review obligation would put pressure on media outlets to either omit individualised elements in their reporting or to refrain from keeping such articles in their online archives altogether, which would lead to media outlets no longer fulfilling an important aspect of their role of providing information (cf. [...] ECtHR, *M. L. and W. W. v. Germany*, Judgment of 28 June 2018, nos. 60798/10 and 65599/10, § 104). This would be incompatible with freedom of expression and freedom of the press.

Therefore, a media outlet may assume that an article that was initially lawful may be made available to the public in an online archive unless affected persons challenge its continued publication in a qualified manner. An obligation on the part of the press to take protective measures is only reasonable (*zumutbar*) if affected persons notify the media outlet and specifically demonstrate a need for protection. This is also a reasonable requirement for affected persons; it allows them to assert in which respects they are adversely affected in a plausible manner, thus setting out the framework for review by the media outlet.

2. If publication was initially lawful, and protection is claimed at a later date, the significance of the passage of time must be assessed in consideration of the specific need for protection of affected persons, which must be balanced against

conflicting fundamental rights and the importance of the information in question for the general public.

121 a) Key aspects in this respect are the effects and the subject matter of the article in question. The more the dissemination of news articles on past events impairs the private life of affected persons and their opportunities for personal development as such, the greater the weight that can be accorded to their claim for protection. This is closely related to the subject matter of the article and the reasons for publishing it. The long-term availability of articles covering someone's conduct in the social sphere may be accorded more weight than the availability of articles merely covering private conduct or misconduct that was deliberately not displayed openly. In particular, the public interest in the continued availability of the information is significant in this respect.

122 b) Furthermore, it is also important to consider to what extent the events covered in the article in question subsequently give rise to other related occurrences. Past events are more likely to remain significant in the long term if they form part of a sequence of socio-political or commercial activities or gain new relevance through subsequent occurrences than if they are unrelated to other occurrences.

123 Thus, it may have to be considered if and to what extent affected persons have contributed to keeping alive interest in the events and in their person in the meantime. Where someone has unnecessarily sought public attention and revived public interest in the original articles, their interest in not being confronted with the original news articles may be accorded lower weight. Thus, the chance at being forgotten also requires conduct reflecting the wish to be forgotten.

124 c) The weight of the burden will also depend on the specific circumstances surrounding the communication of the information on the Internet. For instance, it makes a difference whether an event that occurred a long time ago is covered in a personal blog post aiming to scandalise or whether such an event is covered on a review site, where old posts are relativised by newer entries and where the availability of information on long ago events may thus still be permissible. What matters is thus the actual burden on affected persons.

125 The burden on affected persons cannot be determined in the abstract merely on the basis that information is somehow available online; rather, it also depends on whether this information actually reaches a larger audience. One factor that may be significant is whether it is featured among the top search results in search engines. Given that the realities of Internet communication are volatile and differ from case to case, there is no objective standard. However, on the Internet, too, the significance of information hinges upon the context in which it is communicated, and its dissemination and visibility varies. It is thus the overall burden from the perspective of affected persons at the time of the judicial decision on their claim for

protection that must be assessed – and subsequently balanced against the communication-related freedoms [i.e. freedom of expression, information and the press].

d) It is not possible, however, to take schematic rules on the use, publication and deletion of information from other contexts and apply these to determine whether the passage of time has given rise to a right to protection. [...]

e) All in all, a decision on the claim for protection invoked by affected persons and based on changes in circumstances resulting from the passage of time requires a new balancing. According to the general rules, this balancing must fully take into account all currently relevant circumstances. This does not call into question the fact that the initial lawfulness of articles may also be a factor to be considered in the balancing.

3. In striking a balance between the interests of the media and the interests of affected persons, it must be borne in mind that the type of protection to be granted may vary, with different levels of protection corresponding to the changing relevance of information over time.

a) [...]

The press generally has an interest in the full and unaltered documentation of old articles. This interest is accorded great weight under constitutional law. An obligation to permanently delete or alter articles previously published, possibly also applying to print versions, would be generally incompatible with Art. 5(1) second sentence of the Basic Law. The importance of complete archives, not only as a basis for communication and agreement in society, but also as a basis for later research, conflicts with the interest of affected persons in subsequently making permanent and substantive changes to such documents (cf. ECtHR, *M. L. and W. W. v. Germany*, Judgment of 28 June 2018, nos. 60798/10 and 65599/10, § 90 with reference to ECtHR, *Times Newspapers Ltd v. the United Kingdom*, Judgment of 10 March 2009, nos. 3002/03 and 23676/03, §§ 27 and 45 as well as ECtHR, *Węgrzynowski and Smolczewski v. Poland*, Judgment of 16 July 2013, no. 33846/07, § 59). In this regard, both the press and the general public have a significant interest in the availability of old articles on the Internet and thus in rendering them directly accessible to the general public (see para. 112 *et seq.* above). Particularly in regard to older articles, an interest in making these available for research must primarily be recognised where such articles provide a reasonable basis for factual research. Making such articles available as general sources of information relating to the individuals mentioned in them, however, is not justified by a comparable weight.

By contrast, the legitimate interest of affected persons is not so much directed against the availability of initially lawfully published articles for factual research purposes, as against the fact that they are repeatedly confronted with these articles in their daily lives. It is particularly intrusive for affected persons when the old articles can be found via online searches for their name, and thus become known to their personal circle of acquaintances and bear on their social relationships. In comparison, it is less intrusive if such articles only become known to persons who, for particular reasons, are specifically interested in the past events covered in the article.

132 b) These different interests must be taken into account when determining the nature and scope of claims for protection arising after initial publication. In this regard, it must be taken into account to what extent the media outlet operating an online archive disposes of possibilities to ensure the protection of affected persons by influencing access to and the dissemination of old press articles on the Internet. This particularly applies to search engines, which play a key role in determining dissemination on the Internet.

133-135 [...]
136-142 c) [...]

V.

143 The decision of the Federal Court of Justice does not fully satisfy these requirements.

144 1. The starting point of the challenged decision is persuasive in that it balances the relevant fundamental rights of the complainant against those of the media outlet. It correctly finds, in accordance with the case-law of the European Court of Human Rights, that the press, when fulfilling its tasks in relation to the coverage of crime, must not generally be limited to anonymised coverage. It is true that, in principle, violations of the legal order and impairments of the legal interests of individuals or of the general public give rise to a recognised interest in obtaining detailed information on the crime or perpetrator; thus, true statements must generally be tolerated, even if they adversely affect the person concerned. The court also rightly takes into consideration that the article was fact-based and concerned a spectacular capital crime and that the trial in question was a significant event of contemporary history, inextricably linked to the complainant's name and person.

145 2. However, the challenged decision does not sufficiently take into account that the further dissemination of the articles, under the changed circumstances resulting from the passage of time, results in burdens for the complainant. [...]

146-152 [...]

153 3. Furthermore, given that the general availability of the articles seriously impairs the complainant's rights, the challenged decision fails to address nuanced possibilities for protection and thus a compromise that, as a less restrictive means, may

be more reasonable for the defendant than removing the article or altering it by redacting the name. [...] It is true that the necessary measures may not be minor. However, it is not ascertainable that they are, from the outset, unreasonable for the media outlet if they remain restricted to a limited number of cases that are as serious as the present case.

VI.

It is not relevant in the present case that the Charter of Fundamental Rights may be applicable in addition to the fundamental rights of the Basic Law according to Art. 51(1) first sentence of the Charter and the case-law of the Court of Justice of the European Union. The matter at issue concerns legislation that is not fully harmonised under EU law and that seeks to accommodate fundamental rights diversity [...]. There is no indication to suggest that the fundamental rights of the Basic Law do not simultaneously ensure the Charter's level of protection. [...] 154

D.

In light of the foregoing, the challenged decision is to be reversed and the matter remanded to the Federal Court of Justice. 155
[...] 156

E.

The decision was unanimous. 157

Justices: Harbarth, Masing, Paulus, Baer, Britz, Ott, Christ, Radtke

No. 36

BVerfGE 152, 216 – Right to Be Forgotten II

HEADNOTES

to the Order of the First Senate of 6 November 2019
1 BvR 276/17

1. To the extent that the fundamental rights of the Basic Law are inapplicable due to the precedence of EU law, the Federal Constitutional Court reviews the domestic application of EU law by German authorities on the basis of EU fundamental rights. By applying this standard of review, the Federal Constitutional Court fulfils its responsibility with regard to European integration under Article 23(1) of the Basic Law.

2. Regarding the application of legal provisions that are fully harmonised under EU law, the relevant standard of review does not derive from the fundamental rights of the Basic Law, but solely from EU fundamental rights; this follows from the precedence of application of EU law. This precedence of application is subject, *inter alia*, to the reservation that the fundamental right in question be given sufficiently effective protection through the EU fundamental rights that are applicable instead.

3. Where the Federal Constitutional Court applies the Charter of Fundamental Rights of the European Union as the relevant standard of review, it conducts its review in close cooperation with the Court of Justice of the European Union, requesting a preliminary ruling in accordance with Article 267(3) of the Treaty on the Functioning of the European Union where necessary.

4. Just like the fundamental rights of the Basic Law, those of the Charter are not limited to protecting citizens vis-à-vis the state, but also afford protection in disputes between private actors. Thus, in such disputes, the parties' conflicting fundamental rights must be reconciled on the basis of the applicable ordinary legislation. When conducting its review, the Federal Constitutional Court – just as when dealing with the fundamental rights of the Basic Law – does not review the application and interpretation of ordinary legislation but only whether the ordinary (non-constitutional) courts gave sufficient effect to the fundamental rights of the Charter and struck a tenable balance.

5. Where affected persons request that search engine operators refrain from referencing and displaying links to certain online contents in the list of search results, the necessary balancing must take into account not only the right of personality of affected persons (Articles 7 and 8 of the Charter), but must also consider, in the context of search engine operators' freedom to conduct a business (Article 16 of the Charter), the fundamental rights of the respective content provider as well as Internet users' interest in obtaining information.

Insofar as a prohibition of the display of certain search results is ordered on the basis of an examination of the specific contents of an online publication, and the content provider is thus deprived of an important platform for disseminating these contents that would otherwise be available to it, this constitutes a restriction of the content provider's freedom of expression.

FEDERAL CONSTITUTIONAL COURT
- 1 BvR 276/17 -

IN THE NAME OF THE PEOPLE

In the proceedings
on the constitutional complaints of

Ms B...,
– authorised representatives: …
against   the Judgment of the Celle Higher Regional Court of 29 December 2016 - 13 UF 85/16 -

the Federal Constitutional Court – First Senate –
with the participation of Justices

        Vice-President Harbarth,
        Masing,
        Paulus,
        Baer,
        Britz,
        Ott,
        Christ,
        Radtke

held on 6 November 2019:
The constitutional complaint is rejected.

BVerfGE 152, 216

REASONS:

A.

1 The constitutional complaint concerns a claim for injunctive relief demanding that a search engine operator refrain from displaying a search result that appears when the complainant's full name is entered into the search engine.

I.

2 1. On 21 January 2010, the NDR broadcasting corporation aired a segment of the TV show *Panorama* titled "Dismissal: the dirty tricks of employers". Towards the end of the broadcast, the case of a dismissed employee is presented, and the complainant, in her capacity as the managing director of the company, is accused of unfair treatment vis-à-vis that employee after he had tried to establish a works council in her company. The TV show featured an interview with the complainant, which also broached the topic of the dismissal of the employee.

3 Under the title "The dirty tricks of employers", the NDR uploaded a file containing a transcript of the broadcast to its website. When entering the complainant's name into a search engine operated by Google Inc. (now renamed Google LLC), the defendant in the initial proceedings, the link to this content was displayed among the top search results. The complainant requested that the defendant refrain from displaying this link.

4 After the search engine operator had refused to refrain from displaying the link, the complainant lodged an action before the Regional Court. She requested that the operator be ordered to remove the link that appears in the search results when her name is entered into the search engine.

5 2. In its judgment of 22 April 2016, the Regional Court ordered the defendant to remove the link to the NDR website where the transcript of the *Panorama* episode is available, to refrain from redirecting users to the website and to take suitable measures ensuring that, once removed, the link is not displayed in the search results again […]

6 […]

7 3. Following the search engine operator's appeal on points of facts and law (*Berufung*), the Higher Regional Court rejected the action in its judgment of 29 December 2016, which is challenged by the complainant. In its reasoning, the Higher Regional Court states that the complainant could not request the removal of the relevant links (hereinafter: dereferencing), as she could neither establish a claim under § 35(2) second sentence of the Federal Data Protection Act (former

No. 36 – Right to Be Forgotten II

version) nor under § 823(1), § 1004 of the Civil Code in conjunction with Art. 1(1) and Art. 2(1) of the Basic Law. [...]
[...] 8-12
4. With her constitutional complaint, the complainant claims a violation of her general right of personality and her right to informational self-determination (Art. 2(1) in conjunction with Art. 1(1) of the Basic Law). 13
[...] 14-17
5. Providing the backdrop to these proceedings are provisions of EU law. At the time the challenged decision was rendered, Data Protection Directive 95/46/EC was in force. This directive obliged Member States to protect the right to privacy of natural persons with respect to the processing of personal data. On 25 May 2018, the directive was replaced with the General Data Protection Regulation [...]. In Art. 17, the General Data Protection Regulation contains a right to erasure, which is also referred to as the "right to be forgotten" in brackets. 18

II.

Statements on the constitutional complaint were submitted by the Federal Government, the Federal Court of Justice, the Federal Officer for Data Protection and Freedom of Information, the Hamburg Officer for Data Protection and Freedom of Information and Google LLC, as the defendant, as well as by the NDR broadcasting corporation. 19
[...] 20-28

B.

The constitutional complaint is admissible. 29

I.

[...] 30-31

II.

The complainant has standing to bring a constitutional complaint. It is true that the fundamental rights of the Basic Law are not applicable in this case given that the legal dispute in the initial proceedings concerns a matter that is fully harmonised under EU law. However, the complainant can invoke the fundamental rights of the Charter of Fundamental Rights of the European Union. In the constellation 32 under review here, the application of the Charter falls within the jurisdiction of the Federal Constitutional Court.

33 1. As the legal provisions applicable to this legal dispute are fully harmonised under EU law, the Charter of Fundamental Rights of the European Union is in principle the sole standard of review in this case.

34 a) The complainant's claim for dereferencing pursued in the ordinary court proceedings is governed by data protection law, which is comprehensively harmonised under EU law. This holds true with regard to both the law that was applicable at the time of the ordinary court proceedings and the law that is currently applicable.

35-41 [...]

42 b) Regarding the application of legal provisions that are fully harmonised under EU law, the relevant standard of review does not derive from German fundamental rights, but solely from EU fundamental rights; this follows from the precedence of application of EU law [...]. The possibilities of review reserved by the Federal Constitutional Court in the event of a general erosion of such protection remain unaffected [...]

43-49 [...]

50 2. To the extent that the fundamental rights of the Basic Law are inapplicable due to the precedence of EU law, the Federal Constitutional Court reviews the domestic application of EU law by German authorities on the basis of EU fundamental rights (regarding constitutional court review on the basis of the Charter, cf. Constitutional Court of Austria, Judgment of 14 March 2012, U 466/11 *inter alia*, AT:VFGH:2012:U466.2011, sub. 5.5; cf. also Constitutional Court of Belgium, Judgment of 15 March 2018, no. 29/2018, B.9., B.10.5., B.15. *et seq.*; Conseil constitutionnel, Judgment of 26 July 2018, no. 2018-768 DC, paras. 10, 12, 38; Corte costituzionale, Decision of 23 January 2019, no. 20/2019, IT:COST:2019:20, paras. 2.1, 2.3).

51-67 [...]
68-76 3. [...]
77-82 4. [...]

83 5. The complainant's standing is based on a possible violation of Arts. 7 and 8 of the Charter. [...]

84 With her constitutional complaint, the complainant claims a violation of her right to the development of her personality through the challenged court decision. [...] She essentially claims that her fundamental rights to respect for private and family life and to the protection of personal data under Arts. 7 and 8 of the Charter are violated. The fact that, in her submission, she refers to the fundamental rights of the Basic Law, and not to the fundamental rights of the Charter, is immaterial to her legal standing. [...]

III.

It was not necessary to refer this question to the Plenary of the Court pursuant to § 16 of the Federal Constitutional Court Act.

1. A matter must be referred to the Plenary of the Court if one Senate intends to deviate from a legal view put forward in a decision by the other Senate and that legal view was material to that Senate's decision (cf. BVerfGE 4, 27 <28>; 77, 84 <104>; 96, 375 <404>; 112, 1 <23>; 112, 50 <63>; 132, 1 <3 para. 10>; established case-law). [...]

2. In using the Charter of Fundamental Rights of the European Union as the applicable standard for reviewing the judgment of the Higher Regional Court challenged by the constitutional complaint, the First Senate does not deviate from legal views that are material to decisions of the Second Senate.

[...]

C.

The constitutional complaint is unfounded.

I.

1. The complainant challenges a judicial decision in a private law dispute between the complainant and the search engine operator she sued. In the challenged decision, the Higher Regional Court essentially relied on §§ 29 and 35 of the Federal Data Protection Act (former version), which, at the time, implemented Art. 7 lit. f, Art. 12 lit. b and Art. 14 of Directive 95/46/EC in the German legal order. Both the provisions of this directive, which fully harmonises the substantive level of protection, and the domestic provisions implementing it must be interpreted in light of the Charter (cf. CJEU, Judgment of 24 November 2011, *ASNEF and FECEMD*, C-468/10 and C-469/10, EU:C:2011:777, para. 40 *et seq.*; Judgment of 13 May 2014, *Google Spain*, C-131/12, EU:C:2014:317, para. 68; Judgment of 11 December 2014, *Ryneš*, C-212/13, EU:C:2014:2428, para. 29; Judgment of 6 October 2015, *Schrems*, C-362/14, EU:C:2015:650, para. 38; Judgment of 9 March 2017, *Manni*, C-398/15, EU:C:2017:197, para. 39; Judgment of 24 September 2019, *GC and Others*, C-136/17, EU:C:2019:773, para. 53; Judgment of 24 September 2019, *Google [Portée territoriale]*, C-507/17, EU:C:2019:772, para. 45; Vedsted-Hansen, in: Peers/Hervey/Kenner/Ward, The EU Charter of Fundamental Rights, 2014, para. 07.72A).

96 Like the fundamental rights of the Basic Law, those of the Charter are not limited to protecting citizens vis-à-vis the state, but also afford protection in disputes under private law (cf. CJEU, Judgment of 29 January 2008, *Promusicae*, C-275/06, EU:C:2008:54, para. 65 *et seq.*; Judgment of 16 July 2015, *Coty Germany*, C-580/13, EU:C:2015:485, para. 33 *et seq.*; Judgment of 29 July 2019, *Spiegel Online*, C-516/17, EU:C:2019:625, para. 51 *et seq.*; see also Streinz/Michl, EuZW 2011, p. 384 <385 *et seq.*>; Frantziou, HRLR 2014, p. 761 <771>; Fabbrini, in: de Vries/Bernitz/Weatherill, The EU Charter of Fundamental Rights as a Binding Instrument, 2015, p. 261 <275 *et seq.*>; Lock, in: Kellerbauer/Klamert/Tomkin, The EU Treaties and the Charter of Fundamental Rights, 2019, Art. 8 of the Charter para. 5). In particular, this also applies to Arts. 7 and 8 of the Charter, which the Court of Justice of the European Union has repeatedly used, regardless of the type of law applicable to the legal dispute in question, as a basis for interpreting ordinary EU legislation. This also corresponds to the understanding of Art. 8 of the European Convention on Human Rights, which, particularly in relation to disputes between private parties, comes to the fore in the case-law of the European Court of Human Rights. On the basis of the relevant ordinary legislation, the fundamental rights of one party must be reconciled with the conflicting fundamental rights of the other party (cf. CJEU, Judgment of 29 January 2008, *Promusicae*, C-275/06, EU:C:2008:54, para. 68; Judgment of 16 December 2008, *Satakunnan Markkinapörssi and Satamedia*, C-73/07, EU:C:2008:727, para. 53; Judgment of 24 November 2011, *ASNEF and FECEMD*, C-468/10 and C-469/10, EU:C:2011:777, para. 43; Judgment of 29 July 2019, *Spiegel Online*, C-516/17, EU:C:2019:625, paras. 38, 42). Given that the data processor and the affected person are afforded equal freedom under private law, a balancing must determine the extent of fundamental rights protection.

97 In contrast to the German legal order, EU law does not recognise a doctrine of indirect horizontal effects (*mittelbare Drittwirkung*) (cf. BVerfGE 152, 152 <185 paras. 76 and 77> – *Right to Be Forgotten I*). Nevertheless, EU fundamental rights ultimately have similar effects in regard to the relationship between private actors. In individual cases, the fundamental rights of the Charter may have an effect on private law matters.

98 2. In respect of the complainant, the necessary balancing must take into account the fundamental right to respect for private and family life under Art. 7 of the Charter and the fundamental right to the protection of personal data under Art. 8 of the Charter.

99 Art. 7 of the Charter confers upon individuals the right to respect for their private and family life, home and communications; Art. 8 of the Charter confers the right to the protection of personal data. These guarantees correspond to Art. 8 of the

Convention, which protects the right to respect for one's private and family life, one's home and one's correspondence – including in particular protection against the processing of personal data (cf. CJEU, Judgment of 8 April 2014, *Digital Rights Ireland and Seitlinger and Others*, C-293/12 and C-594/12, EU:C:2014:238, paras. 35, 47, 54 and 55; Constitutional Court of Austria, Judgment of 27 June 2014, G 47/12 *inter alia*, AT:VFGH:2014:G47.2012, para. 146; Marauhn/Thorn, in: Dörr/Grote/Marauhn, EMRK/GG Konkordanzkommentar, 2nd ed. 2013, ch. 16, para. 29 *et seq.*; Kranenborg, in: Peers/Hervey/Kenner/Ward, The EU Charter of Fundamental Rights, 2014, para. 08.50; Fabbrini, in: de Vries/Bernitz/Weatherill, The EU Charter of Fundamental Rights as a Binding Instrument, 2015, p. 261 <266 and 267>; Docksey, IDPL 2016, p. 195 <196 *et seq.*>; Meyer-Ladewig/ Nettesheim, in: Meyer-Ladewig/Nettesheim/von Raumer, EMRK, 4th ed. 2017, Art. 8 para. 32 *et seq.*; Kühling/Raab, in: Kühling/Buchner, DS-GVO/BDSG, 2nd ed. 2018, Einführung para. 17 *et seq.*; Lock, in: Kellerbauer/Klamert/Tomkin, The EU Treaties and the Charter of Fundamental Rights, 2019, Art. 7 of the Charter para. 1). The guarantees of Arts. 7 and 8 of the Charter are closely interrelated. At least insofar as the processing of personal data is concerned, these two fundamental rights constitute a uniform guarantee (cf. CJEU, Judgment of 9 November 2010, *Volker und Markus Schecke and Eifert*, C-92/09 and C-93/09, EU:C:2010:662, para. 47; Judgment of 24 November 2011, *ASNEF and FECEMD*, C-468/10 and C-469/10, EU:C:2011:777, paras. 40 and 42; Judgment of 17 October 2013, *Schwarz*, C-291/12, EU:C:2013:670, paras. 39 and 46; Judgment of 2 October 2018, *Ministerio Fiscal*, C-207/16, EU:C:2018:788, para. 51; Constitutional Court of Belgium, Decision of 11 June 2015, no. 84/2015, B.11; *Korkein hallinto-oikeus* [Highest Administrative Court of Finland], Decision of 15 August 2017, no. 3736/3/15, FI:KHO:2017:T3872; High Court of Ireland, Decision of 18 June 2014, [2014] IEHC 310, para. 58). This applies in particular with regard to the protection of affected persons against information relating to them obtained through the results displayed by a search engine (cf. CJEU, Judgment of 13 May 2014, *Google Spain*, C-131/12, EU:C:2014:317, paras. 69 and 80; Judgment of 24 September 2019, *GC and Others*, C-136/17, EU:C:2019:773, para. 44; Judgment of 24 September 2019, *Google [Portée territoriale]*, C-507/17, EU:C:2019:772, para. 45).

Arts. 7 and 8 of the Charter protect against the processing of personal data and call for "respect for private life". Personal data in this sense is understood – just as it is understood in German constitutional law under Art. 2(1) in conjunction with Art. 1(1) of the Basic Law – as any information relating to an identified or identifiable individual (cf. CJEU, Judgment of 9 November 2010, *Volker und Markus Schecke and Eifert*, C-92/09 and C-93/09, EU:C:2010:662, para. 52; Judgment of 24 November 2011, *ASNEF and FECEMD*, C-468/10 and C-469/10,

100

EU:C:2011:777, para. 42; regarding the Basic Law cf. BVerfGE 150, 244 <265 para. 40> with further references). Accordingly, the right to respect for private life is not to be interpreted restrictively; in particular, it is not limited to highly personal or especially sensitive information (cf. CJEU, Judgment of 20 May 2003, *Österreichischer Rundfunk and Others*, C-465/00, C-138/01 and C-139/01, EU:C:2003:294, paras. 73, 75; cf. also Lock, in: Kellerbauer/Klamert/Tomkin, The EU Treaties and the Charter of Fundamental Rights, 2019, Art. 7 of the Charter para. 5). Notably, business and professional activities are not excluded from its scope of application (cf. CJEU, Judgment of 14 February 2008, *Varec*, C-450/06, EU:C:2008:91, para. 48; Judgment of 9 March 2017, *Manni*, C-398/15, EU:C:2017:197, para. 34).

101 Thus, Arts. 7 and 8 of the Charter protect the self-determined development of one's personality against data processing by third parties. At least in principle, under Art. 52(3) of the Charter, the requirements deriving from this protection can also be determined by reference to the case-law of the European Court of Human Rights (cf. CJEU, Judgment of 22 December 2010, *DEB*, C-279/09, EU:C:2010:811, para. 35).

102 3. In respect of the search engine operator, the balancing must take into account its freedom to conduct a business under Art. 16 of the Charter (see a below). However, the search engine operator cannot invoke Art. 11 of the Charter in relation to the search results disseminated by its search engine (see b below). Yet what must be taken into account are the fundamental rights of third parties that may be directly affected by the legal dispute; in the case at hand, this concerns the freedom of expression of content providers (see c below). In addition, users' interest in obtaining information must also be reflected in the balancing (see d below).

103 a) The freedom to conduct a business guarantees the pursuit of economic interests by providing goods and services. The protection afforded by Art. 16 of the Charter covers the freedom to exercise an economic or commercial activity, the freedom of contract and free competition (cf. CJEU, Judgment of 17 October 2013, *Schaible*, C-101/12, EU:C:2013:661, para. 25; Everson/Correia Gonçalves, in: Peers/Hervey/Kenner/Ward, The EU Charter of Fundamental Rights, 2014, para. 16.34 *et seq.*). This also covers the providing of search engines (cf. CJEU, Judgment of 13 May 2014, *Google Spain*, C-131/12, EU:C:2014:317, paras. 81 and 97; High Court of Justice [Queen's Bench Division], Decision of 13 April 2018, [2018] EWHC 799 [QB], para. 34).

104 The search engine operator in question falls within the scope of protection of Art. 16 of the Charter. [...]

105 b) By contrast, the search engine operator cannot invoke freedom of expression under Art. 11 of the Charter in relation to its activities. It is true that the services

it provides and the means used to process search results cannot be considered neutral, as they can have a considerable impact on the formation of users' opinions. However, these services do not serve to disseminate specific opinions. [...]

c) The balancing between the interests of affected persons and search engine operators must, however, also include the fundamental rights of the content providers whose publications are at issue.

aa) Where, in a legal dispute between an individual and a search engine operator, a decision is made to dereference certain contents, this decision will necessarily also entail a restriction of the fundamental rights of third parties, which must also be taken into account in the judicial decision. In such a case, whether the decision vis-à-vis third parties is lawful becomes part of the objective lawfulness requirements that must be met in order to restrict the freedom to conduct a business; the search engine operator can assert these requirements by invoking their own fundamental right under Art. 16 of the Charter. Yet this does not mean that direct effect is given to the fundamental rights of third parties. A search engine operator can thus not be ordered to carry out any measures that violate the fundamental rights of third parties.

bb) A legal dispute concerning the question whether a search engine operator should be prohibited from displaying certain search results often also involves the question of a violation of the fundamental right under Art. 11 of the Charter afforded a content provider as the person making the statement in question. [...]

Where the decision on whether to impose a prohibition on the search engine operator is based on the specific contents of the site in question, for which the content provider is responsible, the impact on the content provider is no mere side-effect of a prohibition imposed on the search engine operator. Rather, the decision is then directly based on the statement at issue and the exercise of freedom of expression (cf. Spiecker genannt Döhmann, CMLR 2015, p. 1033 <1046>; Fabbrini, in: de Vries/Bernitz/Weatherill, The EU Charter of Fundamental Rights as a Binding Instrument, 2015, p. 261 <284>; Peguera, Journal of Entertainment & Technology Law – JETLaw 2016, p. 507 <555 and 556>; Tambou, RTDE 2016, p. 249 <266 and 267>; Jonason, ERPL 2018, p. 213 <219>). Such a decision specifically aims to restrict the dissemination of an article because of its content. In such a case, a decision on the request by the affected person that the search engine operator refrain from referencing search results cannot be made without regard to the question whether and to what extent content providers are entitled, vis-à-vis affected persons, to disseminate the information at issue pursuant to Art. 11 of the Charter.

d) The balancing must also take into account Internet users' interest in having access to the information in question (cf. CJEU, Judgment of 13 May 2014, *Google*

Spain, C-131/12, EU:C:2014:317, para. 81; Judgment of 24 September 2019, *GC and Others*, C-136/17, EU:C:2019:773, paras. 53, 57, 59, 66, 68 and 75 *et seq.*; Judgment of 24 September 2019, *Google [Portée territoriale]*, C-507/17, EU:C:2019:772, para. 45; High Court of Justice [Queen's Bench Division], Decision of 13 April 2018, [2018] EWHC 799 [QB], paras. 133 and 134; *Korkein hallinto-oikeus* [Highest Administrative Court of Finland], Decision of 17 August 2018, no. 3580/3/15, FI:KHO:2018:112; *Hoge Raad*, Decision of 24 February 2017, no. 15/03380, NL:HR:2017:316, paras. 3.5.1 *et seq.*; Article 29 Working Party on Data Protection, Guidelines on the Implementation of the Judgment in Case C-131/12 "Google Spain and Inc v Agencia Española de Protección de Datos (AEPD) and Mario Costeja-González" of 2 November 2014, 14/EN WP 225, p. 6; cf. also Frantziou, HRLR 2014, p. 761 <769>; Spiecker genannt Döhmann, CMLR 2015, p. 1033 <1046>; Fabbrini, in: de Vries/Bernitz/Weatherill, The EU Charter of Fundamental Rights as a Binding Instrument, 2015, p. 261 <284>). In this respect, the Court of Justice of the European Union requires that the interest of the general public in access to information be taken into account as a manifestation of the right to free information guaranteed by Art. 11 of the Charter. The role of the press in a democratic society must also be reflected in the balancing. However, at issue in this regard are not the individual user rights, deriving from Art. 11 of the Charter, to access information on the specific website in question, but rather freedom of information as a principle to be taken into account in the balancing when restricting Art. 16 of the Charter.

II.

111 The Federal Constitutional Court does not review whether ordinary law was applied correctly. Rather, in the context of constitutional complaint proceedings, it limits its review to whether the fundamental rights, in this case EU fundamental rights, have been observed (cf. BVerfGE 18, 85 <92 and 93>; 142, 74 <101 paras. 82 and 83>; established case-law). Therefore, in the case at hand, the Federal Constitutional Court neither reviews whether Directive 95/46/EC, which was applicable at the time the challenged decision was rendered, was applied correctly, nor whether the provisions of the Federal Data Protection Act relevant at the time were applied correctly. It limits its review to whether the decisions of the ordinary courts give sufficient effect to the fundamental rights of the Charter and whether they have struck a tenable balance (cf. regarding the fundamental rights affected here BVerfGE 7, 198 <205 *et seq.*>; 85, 1 <13>; 114, 339 <348> – *Stolpe/Stasi Dispute*; established case-law).

1. Such a review must be based on the consideration that the actions of the defendant's search engine constitute a stand-alone act of data processing, which must therefore also be assessed separately with regard to the fundamental rights restrictions it entails. In particular, the question whether the search engine operator acted lawfully must be distinguished from whether the publication of the article by the content provider was lawful. Given that the rights, interests and burdens that are relevant may be different when affected persons sue the search engine operator from when they sue the content provider, a separate balancing of interests is required. Thus, recourse against the search engine operator is also not subsidiary to recourse against the content provider (cf. CJEU, Judgment of 13 May 2014, *Google Spain*, C-131/12, EU:C:2014:317, para. 83 *et seq.*; Judgment of 24 September 2019, *GC and Others*, C-136/17, EU:C:2019:773, paras. 36 and 37; Judgment of 24 September 2019, *Google [Portée territoriale]*, C-507/17, EU:C:2019:772, para. 44; see also BGHZ 217, 350 <368 and 369 para. 45>). [...]

The ordinary courts give effect to this separate balancing of fundamental rights by setting different requirements for claims for protection against the dissemination of a text vis-à-vis a search engine operator than vis-à-vis a content provider. Thus, for instance, a search engine operator can only be obliged to dereference content based on the principle of notice and take down, i.e. when it receives a request for dereferencing. Unlike when a content provider first uploads an article, the search engine operator does not have to examine the contents of its search results on its own initiative (cf. BGHZ 217, 350 <361 and 361 para. 34>; cf. also CJEU, Judgment of 13 May 2014, *Google Spain*, C-131/12, EU:C:2014:317, para. 94 *et seq.*; Judgment of 24 September 2019, *GC and Others*, C-136/17, EU:C:2019:773, paras. 48, 66, 68 and 77). In substantive terms, too, different liability requirements apply – similar to those developed by the Federal Court of Justice on the basis of, among other things, the distinction between direct liability for persons having caused a disturbance and indirect liability for persons otherwise responsible for the disturbance, which is a distinction that also pervades all other areas of liability law – and can in particular give rise to differing examination and substantiation obligations for different types of data processors (cf. BGHZ 217, 350 <360 *et seq.* para. 32 *et seq.*>). The ordinary courts thus give shape to ordinary law provisions that require specification, reflecting the different situations in which data processors and individuals face one another and specifying the requirements of Directive 95/46/EC – or, today, the General Data Protection Regulation – in light of the conflicting fundamental rights.

2. For the balancing of conflicting fundamental rights, it is necessary to distinguish between the different data processors, even though their actions are somewhat interrelated and the situation of the affected person vis-à-vis the content provider

may also have to be considered when deciding on a claim for injunctive relief vis-à-vis a search engine operator. As set out above, in deciding whether a search result must be dereferenced, it may be necessary to assess specifically whether this entails a restriction of the fundamental right of the content provider to disseminate its articles using available means.

115 a) Merely because it is permissible to upload an article to the Internet, however, does not automatically imply that it is also permissible to reference the same article as a search result. The claim for protection vis-à-vis a search engine operator may be more extensive than vis-à-vis the content provider where, under domestic ordinary law [of some Member States], only the truthfulness of a publication is relevant when balancing the interests of affected persons and content providers, without the effects of its dissemination on the Internet being taken into account, and the need for protection of affected persons arising from the dissemination of the publication is thus not considered at this level. In particular in cases where affected persons did not, or could not, assert changes in circumstances resulting from the passage of time vis-à-vis content providers, recourse against the search engine operator can afford more extensive protection.

116 The case underlying the decision of the Court of Justice of the European Union in *Google Spain* (Judgment of 13 May 2014, C-131/12, EU:C:2014:317) was one such case. [...] The decision of the Court of Justice of the European Union in *GC* (Judgment of 24 September 2019, C-136/17, EU:C:2019:773) arose from equivalent constellations. [...]

117 Accordingly, affected persons can invoke separate claims for protection vis-à-vis a search engine operator if they, from the outset, only challenge a certain search result and its referencing by search engine operators on the grounds that the effects of this information have changed over time. In that case, the initial lawfulness of the uploading of an article to the Internet does not mean that the search engine operator may continue to reference it for any type of search request. If a search engine operator is ordered to dereference a certain article in such a case, this does not automatically also amount to a violation of the content provider's fundamental rights, given that the content provider cannot infer from the initial lawfulness of the publication that it has the right, in relation to affected persons, to continue permanently disseminating the publication (or having it disseminated) in any form (cf. regarding German law BVerfGE 152, 152 <201 and 202 para. 114 *et seq.*> – *Right to Be Forgotten I*).

118 b) By contrast, [in legal orders] where the effects on affected persons arising from the dissemination of an article on the Internet by a content provider are taken into account when assessing lawfulness – as is typically done in German law pursuant to §§ 823 and 1004 of the Civil Code, as applied analogously – (cf. BVerfGE 152,

152 <196 para. 101 *et seq.*> and <201 and 202 para. 114 *et seq.*> – *Right to Be Forgotten I*), the decision on whether such dissemination by the content provider is lawful must generally also inform the decision concerning the search engine operator. If, after taking account both of the realities of Internet dissemination (including the possibility of retrieving information via online searches based on a person's name) and the passage of time, a content provider is entitled to disseminate a publication, the same must hold true for the referencing of such sites by a search engine operator.

c) Regardless, the balancing of the interests of affected persons against the interests of search engine operators will be subject to the tension between the reasonableness (*Zumutbarkeit*) of potential protective measures imposed on the search engine operator and the reasonableness of other possibilities for protection open to affected persons; in this respect as well, the balancing may, and in some cases must, have different outcomes for different data processors. [...]

3. Thus, an assessment whether a claim for protection invoked vis-à-vis a search engine operator is to be granted requires a comprehensive balancing of the conflicting fundamental rights of the person affected by the referencing and of the search engine operator, as well as the fundamental rights of the content provider and the interest of the public in obtaining information. In such a balancing, the weight of the search engine operator's economic interests by itself is generally not sufficient to restrict the claim for protection of affected persons (cf. CJEU, Judgment of 13 May 2014, *Google Spain*, C-131/12, EU:C:2014:317, para. 81; Judgment of 24 September 2019, *GC and Others*, C-136/17, EU:C:2019:773, para. 53; Judgment of 24 September 2019, *Google [Portée territoriale]*, C-507/17, EU:C:2019:772, para. 45). In contrast, greater weight is accorded to the interest of the public in obtaining information and, even more so, to the fundamental rights of third parties that must also be taken into account in the balancing.

In the present case, the balancing must include the freedom of expression of the content provider as a directly affected fundamental right – and not merely as an interest to be taken into account; the content provider is adversely affected by the decision and is holder of the fundamental right in question (cf. on independent public broadcasting organisations as holders of fundamental rights CJEU, Judgment of 26 April 2012, *DR and TV2 Danmark*, C-510/10, EU:C:2012:244, paras. 12 and 57 – regarding Art. 16 of the Charter; Jarass, in: *id.*, EU-Grundrechte-Charta, 3rd ed. 2016, Art. 11 para. 19 - regarding Art. 11(2) of the Charter; ECtHR, *RTBF v. Belgium*, Judgment of 29 March 2011, no. 50084/06, §§ 5 and 94 – regarding Art. 10 ECHR; to the same effect cf. BVerfGE 31, 314 <321 and 322>; 59, 231 <254>; 74, 297 <317 and 318>; 78, 101 <102 and 103>; 107, 299 <310>). Therefore, it cannot be presumed that protecting the right of personality takes precedence; rather, the conflicting fundamental rights must be balanced on an equal basis. Just as it is not for the individual to determine unilaterally vis-à-vis the media what information may be disseminated about them in the course of public communication processes (cf. relating to German law BVerfGE 152, 152 <198 para. 107> — *Right to Be Forgotten I*), neither is it for them to do so vis-à-vis search engine operators.

122 Where affected persons – as in the present case – do not challenge the possibility to search for their name, but rather the effects of specific publications that adversely affect them, the weight of fundamental rights restrictions must be determined on the basis of the effects of the dissemination of these publications. Decisive factors include – as part of the general liability requirements set out by the civil courts on the basis of criteria for reasonableness – the effects of the dissemination of the publication in question on the development of personality that specifically follow from the search results, particularly having regard to the possibility of searches for a person's name. This determination must not be limited to merely appraising the relevant online contents in the context of the original publication, but must also be informed by the easy access to and continuing availability of the information through the search engine. In particular, the significance of the time passed between initial publication and a later search result must be taken into account, as set out in current law under Art. 17 GDPR in the sense of a "right to be forgotten" (cf. CJEU, Judgment of 13 May 2014, *Google Spain*, C-131/12, EU:C:2014:317, para. 92 *et seq.*; Judgment of 24 September 2019, *GC and Others*, C-136/17, EU:C:2019:773, paras. 53, 74 and 77; Judgment of 24 September 2019, *Google [Portée territoriale]*, C-507/17, EU:C:2019:772, para. 45 *et seq.*; regarding how this affects the interpretation of the Basic Law cf. BVerfGE 152, 152 <197 paras. 105 and 106> – *Right to Be Forgotten I*; regarding the "right to be forgotten" cf. Diesterhöft, Das Recht auf medialen Neubeginn, 2014, p. 24 *et seq.*; Frantziou, HRLR 2014, p. 761 *et seq.*; Spiecker genannt Döhmann, CMLR 2015, p. 1033 *et seq.*; Sartor, IDPL 2015, p. 64 ff.; Tambou, RTDE 2016, p. 249 *et seq.*; Auger, RDP 2016, p. 1841 *et seq.*; Jonason, ERPL 2018, p. 213 *et seq.*; Becker, Das Recht auf Vergessenwerden, 2019, p. 49 *et seq.*).

III.

123 According to the above, the challenged decision is ultimately not objectionable.

124 1. The Higher Regional Court correctly considered the name-related finding, indexing, temporary storage and display of the link to the NDR article in dispute to constitute processing of personal data. It also acknowledged that the complainant may have the right to claim for protection and deletion specifically vis-à-vis the search engine operator, which must be determined in a balancing of interests. The

court undertook the necessary balancing, taking into account both the protection of the complainant's right of personality and the defendant search engine operator's freedom to conduct a business; the court also correctly viewed this freedom in conjunction with the freedom of expression on the part of the NDR broadcasting corporation and with Internet users' interest in access to the relevant information. Thus, in its balancing, it recognised and reflected the substantive fundamental rights positions of the parties and the interests of third parties that had to be taken into account. It is irrelevant in this respect whether the court correctly distinguished between the fundamental rights of the Charter and those of the Basic Law. If it duly considered the substantive value decisions under constitutional law, the court satisfies the requirements of fundamental rights protection. In the present case, the Higher Regional Court cited both Art. 2(1) in conjunction with Art. 1(1) of the Basic Law and Arts. 7 and 8 of the Charter in its balancing. Thus, it essentially satisfied the fundamental rights requirements.

2. [...]

a) The Higher Regional Court rightly focused primarily on criteria that determine whether the airing of the NDR broadcast in dispute and its continued availability on the Internet are permissible in relation to the complainant. It was correct in also considering to what extent the broadcast can be found through search engines, in particular through searches for the complainant's name.

Yet the Higher Regional Court did err in finding that the complainant is only affected in her social sphere. In today's reality, given the possibilities for retrieving and combining information via online searches for a person's name, it has become almost impossible to distinguish between the social sphere and the private sphere as regards the effects on the person concerned – a fact that is specifically asserted by the complainant. The Higher Regional Court tenably posited that the broadcast, which concerns the practical effectiveness of protection against dismissal, addresses a topic that is of general public interest. According to the Higher Regional Court, the NDR broadcast relates not to matters exclusively belonging to the complainant's private life, but to her professional conduct, and the conduct of the company she manages, which both have an impact on public life and thus justify the continuing public interest in this information, although this justification diminishes over time. The complainant can be expected to tolerate the resulting burden – including possible effects on her private life – to a greater extent than would be the case for contents that only focused on her as a private person. The distinction between the social and the private sphere does remain relevant for assessing the contents of the online publication in dispute, but not for weighing the effect on the affected person.

129 It was also tenable for the Higher Regional Court to invoke, as an additional consideration, the fact that the complainant agreed to the interview featured in the contested broadcast. […]

130 […]

131 b) The Higher Regional Court also considered time as a relevant factor. Specifically, the Higher Regional Court examined whether the further dissemination of the publication, including the complainant's name, continues to be justified despite the time that had passed since the broadcast was originally published. The passage of time may modify both the weight attached to the interest of the public in this information and the weight of the resulting fundamental rights impairments (cf. BVerfGE 152, 152 <203 para. 120 *et seq.*> – *Right to Be Forgotten I*).

132-134 […]

135 c) […]

136 d) […]

IV.

137 A request for a preliminary ruling from the Court of Justice of the European Union pursuant to Art. 267(3) TFEU is not required. In the present case, the application of the EU fundamental rights neither raises questions of interpretation to which the answer is not already clear from the outset nor questions that have not been sufficiently clarified in the case-law of the Court of Justice of the European Union (as read in light of the case-law of the European Court of Human Rights, which serves as a supplementary source of interpretation in this regard, cf. Art. 52(3) of the Charter).

138-141 […]

D.

142 The decision is unanimous.

Justices: Harbarth, Masing, Paulus, Baer, Britz, Ott, Christ, Radtke

No. 37

BVerfGE 100, 313 – The Article 10 Act

HEADNOTES

to the Judgment of the First Senate of 14 July 1999
1 BvR 2226/94, 1 BvR 2420/95, 1 BvR 2437/95

1. Article 10 of the Basic Law not only provides protection against the state obtaining knowledge of telecommunications. It also protects against information and data processing measures that follow after the state permissibly obtained knowledge of such communications, and against any subsequent use of this data.
2. The territorial scope of protection under the privacy of telecommunications [guaranteed by Art. 10 of the Basic Law] is not limited to the domestic territory. Rather, Article 10 of the Basic Law may also be applicable if telecommunications that take place abroad are intercepted and analysed on domestic territory, which sufficiently links the interference to domestic state action.
3. Article 73 no. 1 of the Basic Law grants the Federation the competence to legislate on the interception, use and sharing of telecommunications data by the Federal Intelligence Service. However, Article 73 no. 1 of the Basic Law does not entitle the federal legislator to confer upon the Federal Intelligence Service powers that are aimed at the prevention or prosecution of criminal acts as such.
4. If the legislator authorises the Federal Intelligence Service to interfere with the privacy of telecommunications, Article 10 of the Basic Law requires that the legislator take precautions against the risks arising from the collection and use of personal data. These precautions include, in particular, that the use of the information obtained be limited to the purpose that justified the collection of the data in the first place.
5. The powers conferred upon the Federal Intelligence Service under § 1 and § 3 of the Article 10 Act to monitor, record and analyse telecommunications traffic data in order to ensure early detection of serious impending danger to the Federal Republic of Germany originating from abroad and to provide

intelligence reports to the Federal Government is, in principle, compatible with Article 10 of the Basic Law.

6. The sharing of personal data obtained through telecommunications surveillance by the Federal Intelligence Service for its own purposes with other authorities is compatible with Article 10 of the Basic Law. It requires, however, that the data is necessary for achieving the purposes pursued by the receiving authority; that the requirements applicable to a change in purpose (BVerfGE 65, 1 <44 *et seq.*, 62> – *Census*) are met; and that the statutory thresholds for data sharing observe the principle of proportionality.

FEDERAL CONSTITUTIONAL COURT
- 1 BvR 2226/94 -
- 1 BvR 2420/95 -
- 1 BvR 2437/95 -

IN THE NAME OF THE PEOPLE

In the proceedings
on the constitutional complaints of

1. Prof. Dr. K...,
   – authorised representative: ...
   against Article 1 § 3(1) first sentence and second sentence nos. 2 to 6, § 3(3), (4), (5), (7) and (8) of the Act of 13 August 1968 on Article 10 of the Basic Law (BGBl I, p. 949), in the version of the Fight Against Crime Act of 28 October 1994 (BGBl I, p. 3186), as amended by the Act of 17 December 1997 (BGBl I, p. 3108),
   -1 BvR 2226/94 -,

2. a) Dr. W...,
   b) Mr S...,
   – authorised representative: ...
   against Article 1 § 1(1), § 3(1), (2) third sentence, § 3(3) to (8), § 7(4), § 9(6) of the Act of 13 August 1968 on Article 10 of the Basic Law (BGBl I, p. 949) in the version of the Fight Against Crime Act of 28 October 1994 (BGBl I, p. 3186), as amended by the Act of 17 December 1997 (BGBl I, p. 3108),
   - 1 BvR 2420/95 -,

No. 37 – The Article 10 Act

3. a) of T... GmbH, b) of Dr. R...,
   – authorised representatives: ...
   against Article 1 § 3(1) first sentence and second sentence nos. 2 to 6, § 3(2) to (8) of the Act of 13 August 1968 on Article 10 of the Basic Law (BGBl I, p. 949) in the version of the Fight Against Crime Act of 28 October 1994 (BGBl I, p. 3186), as amended by the Act of 17 December 1997 (BGBl I, p. 3108),

   - 1 BvR 2437/95 -

the Federal Constitutional Court – First Senate –
with the participation of Justices
>
> Vice-President Papier
> Grimm,
> Kühling,
> Jaeger,
> Haas,
> Hömig,
> Steiner

held on the basis of the oral hearing of 15 and 16 December 1998:

JUDGMENT

1. § 3(1) first sentence and second sentence no. 5, § 3(3), (4), (5) first sentence, (7) first sentence, (8) second sentence, and § 9(2) third sentence of the Act on Article 10 of the Basic Law (the Act) revised by the Fight Against Crime Act of 28 October 1994 (BGBl I, p. 3186), as amended by the Accompanying Act to the Telecommunications Act of 17 December 1997 (BGBl I, p. 3108), are incompatible with Article 10 of the Basic Law. Moreover, § 3(3) first sentence, (4) and (5) first sentence of the Act is incompatible with Article 5(1) second sentence of the Basic Law, and § 3(8) second sentence of the Act is incompatible with Article 19(4) of the Basic Law.
2. For the rest, the constitutional complaints of complainants nos. 1, 2a and 3 are rejected.
3. The constitutional complaint of complainant no. 2b is dismissed as inadmissible.
4. [...]

BVerfGE 100, 313

REASONS:

A.

1 The constitutional complaints concern the powers of the Federal Intelligence Service (*Bundesnachrichtendienst*) to monitor, record and analyse telecommunications traffic and to share the data thus obtained with other authorities. The constitutional complaints also challenge other provisions of the Act on Article 10 of the Basic Law (hereinafter: the Act) as amended in 1994 by the Fight Against Crime Act.

I.

2 1. In its original version, the Act [...] already provided for the possibility of telecommunications surveillance (§ 1 of the Act). Surveillance was permissible in two forms. § 2 of the Act governed the gathering of intelligence on individual persons. According to this provision, surveillance of individuals was permissible if there were grounds for suspecting that someone was planning, committing or had committed certain particularly serious criminal offences that threatened the existence of the Federal Republic of Germany or its democratic order. § 3 of the Act governed so-called strategic surveillance, which served in particular to obtain situation reports on certain impending dangers *(drohende Gefahren)* to the Federal Republic of Germany.

3 The proceedings at hand only concern strategic surveillance. Pursuant to § 3(1) second sentence of the Act (former version), strategic surveillance was originally only permissible to ensure early detection of a danger of armed attacks against the Federal Republic of Germany, and to avert such dangers. [...]

4 An essential feature of the measures restricting the privacy of telecommunications pursuant to § 3 of the Act (former version) was that they did not specifically target individual persons, which in any case would not have been technologically feasible at that time, but served to obtain non-person-related intelligence to provide the Federal Government with information concerning matters of foreign and defence policy. [...]

5 [...]

6 2. The [...] Fight Against Crime Act of 28 October 1994 (BGBl I, p. 3186) provided for several amendments to the Act. [...]

7 The amendments expanded the purposes that could constitute grounds for surveillance measures pursuant to § 3(1) second sentence of the Act. In addition to the danger of armed attacks (no. 1), the amendments added five further categories of danger situations arising from different forms of criminal conduct with an interna-

tional dimension. These categories were as follows: international terrorist attacks (no. 2), international proliferation of military weapons and trading of conventional arms (no. 3), importing narcotics into the Federal Republic of Germany (no. 4), counterfeiting committed abroad (no. 5) and money laundering in connection with the activities set forth under nos. 3 to 5 (no. 6).

Yet, as regards these newly added statutory purposes of intelligence operations carried out under the Act, surveillance is limited to wireless international telecommunications traffic (§ 3(1) first sentence of the Act), for which the necessary technology did not yet exist at the time the original Act was enacted. Wired telecommunications may only be intercepted if there is danger of a war of aggression (§ 3(1) third sentence of the Act). The geographic reach of surveillance was also expanded by the newly introduced categories of relevant dangers under nos. 2 to 6 of the provision. […] 8

Moreover, the amendments expanded the scope of the Act in terms of persons that could be targeted by surveillance. It is true that § 3(2) second sentence of the Act does not allow the targeted interception of specific subscriber lines. Pursuant to § 3(2) first sentence of the Act, subscriber lines are selected for surveillance on the basis of search terms that must serve the gathering of intelligence on the danger situations specified in the warrant [authorising the measure], and which must be suitable for achieving this purpose. However, according to the third sentence of the provision, this does not apply with regard to individual subscriber lines belonging to foreigners in other countries. Their subscriber numbers may [directly] be used as so-called formal search terms. In practice, the number of persons targeted in this manner is much higher today because now – unlike in the past – the technological means exist that make it generally possible to identify the individual subscriber lines involved in telecommunications. 9

[…] 10-11

§ 1(1) of the Act provides the general statutory basis for the powers conferred upon the Federal Intelligence Service to intercept and record telecommunications. […] 12

[…] 13-41

§ 7(4) of the Act governs the destruction of personal data obtained by the measures set forth under § 2 and § 3 of the Act; § 9 of the Act sets out an oversight mechanism while excluding recourse to the courts. […] 42

[…] 43-48

3. […] 49

4. […] 50

II.

51   1. With his constitutional complaint, complainant no. 1 challenges the expansion of the Federal Intelligence Service's powers to interfere with fundamental rights as provided for in § 3(1) second sentence nos. 2 to 6 of the Act; he also challenges the statutory design of the notification requirements in § 3(8) of the Act. [...]

52-65   [...]

66   2. Complainants nos. 2a and 2b additionally challenge the strategic surveillance powers laid down in § 1(1), § 3(1) first sentence, second sentence no. 1 and third sentence of the Act; the envisaged destruction of obtained data without the consent of the affected persons pursuant to § 3(6) and (7) second and third sentence, § 7(4) of the Act; and the exclusion of recourse to the courts set forth in § 9(6) of the Act. [...]

67-76   [...]

77   3. Complainants no. 3 challenge § 3(1) first sentence and second sentence nos. 2 to 6 and § 3(2) to (8) of the Act, claiming that these provisions violate the Basic Law, specifically Art. 10, Art. 2(1) in conjunction with Art. 1(1), Art. 5(1) second sentence, Art. 19(4), Art. 20(2) and Art. 73 nos. 1 and 10 of the Basic Law.

78-84   [...]

III.

85   Statements in the constitutional complaint proceedings were submitted by the Federal Minister of the Interior on behalf of the Federal Government, the Government of the Free State of Bavaria, the Federal Data Protection Officer and the data protection officers of the *Länder* Bavaria, Berlin, Brandenburg, Bremen, Hamburg, North Rhine-Westphalia, Saarland and Schleswig-Holstein.

86-143   [...]

IV.

144   [...]

B.

145   With the exception of the constitutional complaint lodged by complainant no. 2b, the constitutional complaints are admissible.

No. 37 – The Article 10 Act

[...]

C.

The challenged provisions are not fully compatible with the Basic Law.

I.

The standard of review regarding the constitutionality of the challenged provisions derives primarily from Art. 10 of the Basic Law. The right to informational self-determination that follows from Art. 2(1) in conjunction with Art. 1(1) of the Basic Law is not applicable in addition to Art. 10 of the Basic Law since, in the context of telecommunications, Art. 10 of the Basic Law contains a more specific guarantee that supersedes the aforementioned general guarantee (cf. BVerfGE 67, 157 <171>). In addition, Art. 19(4) of the Basic Law is affected regarding the possibility of recourse to the courts against measures taken pursuant to § 3 of the Act and the restrictions of legal recourse pursuant to § 9(6) of the Act. Moreover, the constitutional complaints lodged by complainants nos. 2a and 3 must be measured against Art. 5(1) second sentence of the Basic Law.

1. Art. 10 of the Basic Law protects the privacy of telecommunications.

a) The privacy of telecommunications primarily covers the contents of communications. The state should, in principle, not be allowed to obtain knowledge of the contents of information and thoughts exchanged, orally or in writing, via telecommunications systems. In this context, Art. 10 of the Basic Law does not distinguish between communication of a private nature and other communication, e.g. business or political communication (cf. BVerfGE 67, 157 <172>). Rather, the fundamental rights protection extends to all communication taking place by means of telecommunications technology.

Yet the fundamental rights protection is not limited to shielding the actual communication contents against the state obtaining knowledge thereof. It also extends to the circumstances of a communication, which include whether, when and how often telecommunications traffic occurred or was attempted between whom or between which devices (cf. BVerfGE 67, 157 < 172>; 85, 386 <396>). The state is generally not entitled to obtain knowledge of these circumstances. The confidential use of the telecommunication medium must be ensured in all respects.

By generally shielding individual communications from the reach of the state, the fundamental right is meant to preserve the conditions that are necessary to ensure free telecommunications in general. The inviolability of telecommunications privacy, as guaranteed by fundamental rights, seeks to prevent a situation where communication participants have to expect that state authorities will intercept their communications and obtain knowledge of the relevant communication relations or contents, as a result of which affected persons might cease to exchange opinions or information by means of telecommunications systems altogether, or change how and what they communicate.

165 In addition, the freedom of telecommunications that Art. 10 of the Basic Law safeguards is adversely affected if there is reason to fear that the state will use the knowledge of telecommunications circumstances and contents to the detriment of the communication partners in other contexts (for an overview cf. BVerfGE 65, 1 <42 and 43> – *Census*; 93, 181 <188>). For these reasons, the protection afforded by Art. 10 of the Basic Law applies not only to the state obtaining knowledge of telecommunications that the communication partners wish to keep to themselves, but also to the information and data processing measures that follow after the state has obtained knowledge of protected communications, and to the use of this data (regarding the right to informational self-determination, cf. already BVerfGE 65, 1 <46> – *Census*).

166 b) Art. 10(2) of the Basic Law does permit restrictions of telecommunications privacy. However, such restrictions not only require, like any other fundamental rights restriction, a statutory basis that serves a legitimate purpose in the interest of the common good and satisfies the principle of proportionality for the rest. Art. 10 of the Basic Law also imposes on the legislator particular requirements that are specific to the processing of personal data obtained through interferences with telecommunications privacy. In this respect, the requirements that the Federal Constitutional Court derived from Art. 2(1) in conjunction with Art. 1(1) of the Basic Law in its *Census* decision (cf. BVerfGE 65, 1 <44 *et seq.*>) can largely be applied accordingly to the more specific guarantee of Art. 10 of the Basic Law, too.

167 This includes that the prerequisites and scope of restrictions be clearly set out in the statutory framework so that they are foreseeable for the individual. In particular, the statutory purposes for which interferences with telecommunications privacy are permissible must be specified precisely for each subject matter. Furthermore, the data collected must be suitable and necessary for achieving these purposes. The gathering and retention of data that has not been rendered anonymous for undefined or yet to be defined purposes would not be compatible with these requirements. Therefore, the storage and use of obtained data is, in principle, only permissible for a purpose specified in the law that authorises state authorities to obtain knowledge of the data.

168 The data does not lose the confidentiality protection afforded by Art. 10 of the Basic Law because a state authority has already obtained knowledge of the telecommunications in question; therefore, the requirements deriving from this fundamental

right also apply to the subsequent sharing of data and information that was obtained by measures setting aside the privacy of telecommunications. This holds true all the more as the sharing of data typically not only expands the groups of bodies or persons who have knowledge of the communication but also means that the data becomes available for uses in other contexts; this gives rise to additional, possibly more serious consequences for the affected persons than the original context in which their data was used.

The principle of purpose limitation does not preclude changes in purpose [regarding data use] altogether. However, such changes require a separate statutory basis that is formally and substantively compatible with the Basic Law. This means, *inter alia*, that a change in purpose must be justified by public interests that outweigh the interests protected by the affected fundamental rights. The new purpose must be related to the responsibilities and powers of the authority with which the data is shared, and it must be set out in sufficiently clear statutory provisions. Moreover, the new purpose must not be incompatible with the primary purpose for which the data was originally collected (cf. BVerfGE 65, 1 <51, 62> – *Census*). 169

The required purpose limitation can only be guaranteed if the obtained data subsequently remains identifiable as data stemming from an interference with telecommunications privacy. Therefore, constitutional law requires that the data be labelled accordingly. 170

Moreover, under Art. 10 of the Basic Law the holders of fundamental rights are entitled to be notified of measures of telecommunications surveillance affecting them. This is necessary to ensure effective fundamental rights protection, given that without this information, the affected persons can neither challenge the lawfulness of the interception and monitoring of their telecommunications, nor assert possible rights to have their data deleted or rectified. This right is not necessarily limited to ensuring recourse to the courts under Art. 19(4) of the Basic Law. Rather, it is a specific right to data protection that can be asserted vis-à-vis the authority that processes the relevant information and data. 171

[...] To the extent that the purpose pursued by the measure interfering with the privacy of telecommunications would be frustrated if the affected person were notified, it is not objectionable under constitutional law to limit the notification requirement where necessary. It may be sufficient to only inform the person concerned about the interference at a later stage (cf. BVerfGE 49, 329 <342 and 343>). 172

Affected persons can neither perceive interferences with the privacy of telecommunications nor the subsequent data processing; moreover, the possibility of limiting the notification requirement leads to gaps in legal protection. For these reasons, Art. 10 of the Basic Law requires oversight by state bodies and auxiliary bodies that are independent and not bound by instructions (cf. BVerfGE 30, 1 <23 and 173

24, 30 and 31>; 65, 1 <46> – *Census*; 67, 157 <185>). Yet the Constitution does not specify the details of the oversight regime. The legislator is free to choose the mechanisms it regards as the most suitable as long as the oversight regime is sufficiently effective. To be effective, oversight must extend to all stages of the surveillance process. Oversight mechanisms must assess both whether the interference with telecommunications privacy is lawful and whether legal safeguards protecting telecommunications privacy are adhered to.

174 Finally, given that the interception and recording of telecommunications traffic and the use of the information obtained is limited to specific purposes, the data must be destroyed as soon as it is no longer needed for achieving the specified purposes nor for allowing recourse to the courts.

175 c) The territorial scope of protection under Art. 10 of the Basic Law has not yet been determined in the case-law of the Federal Constitutional Court. [...]

176 Art. 1(3) of the Basic Law defines the general scope of application of fundamental rights and thus provides the basis for determining the territorial scope of Art. 10 of the Basic Law. Under Art. 1(3) of the Basic Law, the legislature, the executive and the judiciary are strictly bound by fundamental rights. However, this constitutional provision does not exhaustively determine the reach of fundamental rights in terms of territorial protection. The Basic Law is not limited to defining the domestic order of the German state, but also determines the essential elements of its relationship with the international community. In this respect, the Basic Law is informed by the necessity to seek a delimitation from and coordination with other states and legal systems. On the one hand, the scope of the competences and responsibilities incumbent upon German state organs must be taken into account when determining the binding effect of fundamental rights (cf. BVerfGE 66, 39 <57 *et seq.*>; 92, 26 <47>). On the other hand, constitutional law must be reconciled with international law. Yet international law does not *per se* rule out that fundamental rights are applicable in matters that have a foreign dimension. Rather, the scope of fundamental rights must be derived from the Basic Law itself, taking into account Art. 25 of the Basic Law. Depending on the constitutional guarantee in question, further modifications and differentiations may be permissible or required (cf. BVerfGE 31, 58 <72 *et seq.*>; 92, 26 <41 and 42>).

177 The protection of telecommunications privacy afforded by Art. 10 of the Basic Law seeks to ensure – in line with international law (cf. Art. 12 of the Universal Declaration of Human Rights of 10 December 1948; Art. 8 of the Convention for the Protection of Human Rights and Fundamental Freedoms of 4 November 1950; in this regard ECtHR, *Klaas and Others v. Germany*, Judgment of 6 September 1978, no. 5029/71, NJW 1979, p. 1755 <1756>) – that telecommunications remain free of unwanted or unnoticed surveillance and that the holders of fundamental

rights can communicate without worry or fear. The protection of telecommunications privacy is tied to the use of a communication medium and aims to counteract the risks to confidentiality that specifically result from the use of such a medium, which makes telecommunications more vulnerable to state interference than direct communication between persons who are physically present (cf. BVerfGE 85, 386 <396>). Modern technology, like satellite and radio transmission, permits access to foreign telecommunications traffic, too, by means of surveillance equipment that is located on the territory of the Federal Republic of Germany.

The interception and recording of telecommunications traffic with receiving equipment of the Federal Intelligence Service that is located on German territory already establishes a technical and informational connection to the respective communication participants and a connection – characterised by the unique nature of data and information – to German territory. Moreover, the analysis of telecommunications thus intercepted is carried out by the Federal Intelligence Service on German territory. These circumstances create a link between the communication undertaken abroad and state action carried out on domestic territory that subjects the latter to the binding effect of Art. 10 of the Basic Law even if one were to assume that a sufficient territorial link was required in this regard. In the case at hand, it is not necessary to decide on intelligence service activities other than the ones governed by the challenged provisions nor on what applies to foreigners participating in telecommunications abroad. [...]

2. In part, the challenged provisions must also be measured against Art. 19(4) of the Basic Law.

Art. 19(4) of the Basic Law guarantees everyone the right to effective judicial review in the event of a possible violation of their rights by acts of public authority. However, Art. 19(4) third sentence of the Basic Law states that this applies without prejudice to Art. 10(2) second sentence of the Basic Law, which specifically exempts interferences with the privacy of telecommunications from the otherwise comprehensive guarantee of legal protection. Yet these provisions do not exempt such interferences from any review whatsoever. Rather, the lack of recourse to the courts must be compensated by a review carried out by bodies and auxiliary bodies appointed by Parliament.

Furthermore, the right afforded by Art. 19(4) of the Basic Law is not limited to judicial review and judicial proceedings. As the guarantee of legal protection aims to safeguard the effective exercise of other, substantive rights, it may require that a person under surveillance be notified of the surveillance measures if notification is a necessary precondition for seeking recourse to the courts (cf. BVerfGE 65, 1 <70> – *Census*), including in cases where Art. 10 of the Basic Law is applicable.

However, Art. 19(4) of the Basic Law does not rule out restrictions of this right, and in any case requires statutory provisions that specify the details of such restrictions.

182 The obligation to ensure that data be in principle destroyed when it is no longer needed must also be read in light of Art. 19(4) of the Basic Law. The guarantee of legal protection under Art. 19(4) of the Basic Law prohibits measures that aim to frustrate legal protection of the affected persons, or are likely to do so (cf. BVerfGE 69, 1 <49>). In cases in which affected persons seek judicial review of information and data processing measures by the state, the obligation to destroy data must be balanced against the guarantee of legal protection so as to ensure that legal protection is not undermined or frustrated.

183-185 3. [...]

II.

186 The challenged provisions allow for interferences with the above-mentioned fundamental rights in several respects.

187 1. The surveillance and recording of wireless international telecommunications by the Federal Intelligence Service interferes with the privacy of telecommunications.

188 Given that Art. 10(1) of the Basic Law serves to protect the confidentiality of communications, any instance where the state obtains knowledge of, records or processes communication data constitutes an interference with fundamental rights (cf. BVerfGE 85, 386 <398>). [...].

189 This means that the interception itself already constitutes an interference, to the extent that it makes the intercepted communication available to the Federal Intelligence Service and is the basis for the subsequent cross-checking with search terms. [...]

190 The interference is perpetuated when the intercepted data is stored, which allows the data material to be accessed for cross-checking with search terms. The cross-checking itself again amounts to an additional interference as it determines the selection of data for further analysis. [...]

191 The examination required under § 3(4) of the Act to determine whether the personal data obtained through telecommunications surveillance is necessary for achieving the legitimate purposes pursued also constitutes an interference. This examination involves a deliberate selection of data, as the recorded data is either cleared for further processing or for storage to allow for future uses, or it is destroyed.

192 When the Federal Intelligence Service, in the context of its obligation to report to the Federal Government, shares personal data obtained through telecommunications surveillance, this also amounts to an interference since it expands the group of those who have knowledge of the relevant communications and can make use

of this information. The transfer of data by the Federal Intelligence Service to the receiving authorities pursuant to § 3(5) and § 3(3) of the Act, and the examination of the data by the receiving authorities pursuant to § 3(7) of the Act, likewise amount to interferences.

The exemptions from the requirement to notify persons under surveillance of the measures restricting their telecommunications privacy pursuant to § 3(8) first and second sentence of the Act also amounts to an impairment of the privacy of telecommunications. 193

2. Moreover, the statutory exemptions from the requirement to notify persons under surveillance pursuant to § 3(8) first and second sentence, and the exclusion of recourse to the courts pursuant to § 9(6) of the Act, impair the guarantee of legal protection under Art. 19(4) of the Basic Law. In addition, the obligation to destroy personal data pursuant to § 3(6), § 3(7) and § 7(4) of the Act can adversely affect the possibilities of judicial review with regard to the measures. 194

3. [...] 195

III.

The powers to monitor and record telecommunications traffic pursuant to § 1(1) and § 3(1) second sentence nos. 1 to 6 of the Act are for the most part compatible with Art. 10 of the Basic Law. However, § 3(1) second sentence no. 5 of the Act is incompatible with this fundamental right to the extent that the provision permits surveillance measures for the purposes of gathering intelligence for the timely detection of counterfeiting committed abroad and for counteracting such counterfeiting. 196

1. Formally, § 1(1) and § 3(1) of the Act do not raise constitutional concerns. The Federation has legislative competence for the subject matters governed by these provisions. This follows from Art. 73 no. 1 of the Basic Law, which confers exclusive legislative competence on the Federation in foreign affairs and defence matters. 197

[...] 198-208

2. § 1(1) and § 3(1) of the Act also satisfy the requirements of specificity and legal clarity deriving from Art. 10 of the Basic Law when conferring statutory powers to interfere with telecommunications. 209

[...] 210

3. Substantively, § 3(1) second sentence no. 5 of the Act disproportionately restricts telecommunications privacy. For the rest, § 3(1) second sentence of the Act satisfies the requirements deriving from the principle of proportionality. 211

212 a) The purpose of ensuring the timely detection of the dangers listed in nos. 1 to 6 of the provision, and of counteracting them, is a legitimate interest of the common good. It is true that the categories of dangers listed in nos. 2 to 6, which were newly added to the Act, do not carry the same weight as the danger of an armed attack, which has been recognised as legitimate grounds for telecommunications surveillance from the outset (cf. BVerfGE 67, 157 <178>). [...] However, they do concern, albeit to differing degrees, high-ranking interests of the common good, the violation of which would result in serious harm to external and domestic peace and to protected legal interests of individuals.

213 b) Surveillance of telecommunications on the basis of § 3(1) of the Act is suitable for achieving the purpose of the law.

214 Its suitability is not called into question merely because the method of data collection indiscriminately affects a large number of persons yet only yields useful intelligence in comparatively few cases. At the legislative level, it is sufficient that there is an abstract possibility of achieving the intended purpose, i.e. that the measures are not unsuitable from the outset but may be conducive to the desired outcome (cf. BVerfGE 90, 145 <172>). This is the case here.

215 The requirement of suitability is also sufficiently reflected at the level of implementation. [...]

216-218 [...]

219 c) The Act is necessary for achieving the purpose pursued. No other means are available that would be equally effective but less intrusive for fundamental rights holders. [...]

220 d) The restrictions of the privacy of telecommunications traffic under § 1(1) and § 3(1) of the Act (intercepting, recording, storing, cross-checking) are for the most part proportionate in the strict sense. Only the restriction of telecommunications privacy for the purposes of detecting counterfeiting committed abroad (no. 5) fails to meet this requirement.

221 aa) The principle of proportionality requires that the curtailing of freedom protected by fundamental rights not be disproportionate to the purposes of the common good that the restriction of fundamental rights aims to achieve. Given that the individual is connected to and bound by the community, they must accept that fundamental rights are subject to restrictions serving overriding public interests (cf., e.g., BVerfGE 65, 1 <44> – *Census*, with further references). However, the legislator must strike an appropriate balance between public interests and the interests of the individual. With respect to the fundamental rights interests, it must be taken into account which and how many holders of fundamental rights are affected by impairments, how intense these impairments are, and on what basis they occur. Thus, relevant criteria include the design of the statutory thresholds for carrying

out the measures constituting interferences, the number of persons affected, and the severity of the impairments. This, in turn, depends on whether the communication participants remain anonymous; on what type of conversations and communication contents can be intercepted (cf., e.g., on the standard deriving from Art. 2(1) in conjunction with Art. 1(1) of the Basic Law, BVerfGE 34, 238 <247> – *Secret Tape Recordings*); and on the disadvantages the holders of fundamental rights might face or have reason to fear on account of the surveillance measures. With respect to the interests of the common good, the weight of the underlying aims and interests that the surveillance measures serve must be determined. This depends, *inter alia,* on the scale and likelihood of the dangers that the surveillance measures aim to detect.

bb) The challenged provisions seriously impair the privacy of telecommunications. Nonetheless, complainant no. 1 errs in claiming that the legislator completely abolished telecommunications privacy protected by Art. 10 of the Basic Law, infringing upon the essence (*Wesensgehalt*) of the fundamental right within the meaning of Art. 19(2) of the Basic Law. The provisions neither allow "global and sweeping surveillance", which would be prohibited by the Basic Law even for gathering foreign intelligence (cf. BVerfGE 67, 157 <174>), nor do they allow the unconditional interception of all telecommunications of individual fundamental rights holders. Rather, surveillance and recording of telecommunications traffic remain subject to legal and factual limitations.

[…]

In determining the intensity of the fundamental right impairments, it must be taken into account that anyone participating in international telecommunications is exposed to the surveillance measures, regardless of whether their conduct has any connection to the surveillance or prompted it. In terms of content, the surveillance extends to any kind of communication in its entirety. Therefore, it cannot be ruled out that staff of the Federal Intelligence Service will obtain knowledge thereof. […]

[…]

In respect of the intensity of the fundamental right impairments at issue, the lack of anonymity regarding the communication participants must be taken into account as well. The linking of gathered intelligence to specific individuals is not limited to the interception and recording stage only, but in practice continues thereafter. […]

The disadvantages that are to be objectively expected or feared [by affected persons] may materialise as soon as the state obtains knowledge of the communication. Even before such knowledge is obtained, the fear of being under surveillance and the risk that communications may be recorded, subsequently analysed, and then possibly shared with and further used by other authorities, may lead to communication being no longer free from fear or worry, to communication disruptions and to changes in communication behaviour, in particular because the communicating parties avoid certain conversation topics or terms. The covert surveillance of telecommunications not only entails individual impairments for a large number of fundamental rights holders, but affects communication in society as a whole. In respect of the right to informational self-determination, which is comparable in this respect, the Federal Constitutional Court has therefore recognised a dimension of this right that serves the common good, going beyond the interest of the individual (cf. BVerfGE 65, 1 <43> – *Census*).

237 cc) However, it is significant that the fundamental rights restrictions at issue serve to protect high-ranking interests of the common good.

238 Surveillance measures under § 3(1) first sentence and second sentence no. 1 of the Act are intended to yield intelligence about facts that are relevant for national defence in order to ensure timely detection if the Federal Republic of Germany is in danger of an armed attack. [...]

239 The proliferation of international organised crime, in particular the illegal trading of military weapons and narcotics as well as money laundering, have resulted in increased dangers in the new fields of surveillance recognised in the challenged provisions. [...]

240 These dangers, which all have in common that they originate abroad and which the powers conferred aim to detect, carry significant weight. The same applies to the danger of armed attacks but also, as has been sufficiently demonstrated by the Federal Intelligence Service, to the dangers of weapons proliferation, arms trading and international terrorism. [...]

241 dd) Based on a balancing of interests that takes these aspects into consideration, § 3(1) second sentence nos. 1 to 4 and no. 6 of the Act are not objectionable under constitutional law.

242 Contrary to the opinion of complainant no. 1, the powers to monitor and record communications and the other measures provided for in the challenged provisions are not disproportionate from the outset because the exercise of these powers is not subject to specific thresholds, such as a specific danger (*konkrete Gefahr*) as traditionally required for public security measures, or sufficient grounds for the suspicion of criminal conduct (*hinreichender Tatverdacht*) as required in the context of law enforcement. The surveillance of telecommunications under the Act is indeed not based on any grounds for suspicion. In this regard, the interference with fundamental rights is not merely limited to the general risk that affected persons might be falsely suspected of wrongdoing. Rather, anyone could easily become the object of surveillance in the course of the measures authorised and carried out under the Act.

243 However, the purposes pursued by the Act differ [from traditional public security and law enforcement purposes]; therefore, it is justified that the statutory prerequi-

sites for interferences with the privacy of telecommunications under the Act are of a different design than those set out in police law [on public security] or the law of criminal procedure. Given that the federal legislative competence for the Act follows from Art. 73 no. 1 of the Basic Law, the purpose of surveillance measures carried out by the Federal Intelligence Service is from the outset limited to gathering foreign intelligence with respect to certain danger situations in the fields of foreign and security policy. [...]

Under constitutional law, even the significant dangers that the telecommunications surveillance measures at issue aim to counter would not justify surveillance powers for the purposes of gathering foreign intelligence if such powers were not subject to any prerequisites or limitations. Yet the legislator actually made sure to specify such prerequisites. The Act does set out certain substantive criteria and procedural safeguards in the first and second sentence of its § 3(1). Substantively, the provision states in particular that intelligence may only be gathered if knowledge of the investigated situation is necessary to ensure the timely detection of dangers. Procedurally, the issuance by the competent ministry of a warrant directing and authorising the surveillance measure requires that the Federal Intelligence Service comprehensively establish, in its application for the warrant, why the targeted telecommunications relations could provide timely information about relevant dangers. 244

Taking into account the safeguards provided for in the Act, the envisaged interception and recording for the purpose of providing intelligence reports to the Federal Government do not appear disproportionate. While the number of intercepted telecommunications relations is far from negligible, it is still relatively low when seen in relation to the total volume of telecommunications, or even just the total volume of relevant international telecommunications. In this respect, it is particularly important that § 3(2) second sentence of the Act prohibits the targeted surveillance of specific individual subscriber lines. Without this prohibition, the principle of proportionality would not be satisfied, given that the surveillance powers do not require any grounds for suspicion, provide for the interception of a large number of telecommunications, and allow for the possibility of identifying the communication participants. [...] It is true that the interception and recording of telecommunications as such could already hamper free communication, which Art. 10 of the Basic Law aims to protect; yet the full extent of this risk only materialises in the subsequent analysis and especially the sharing of intelligence thus obtained. In this respect, however, the risk to fundamental rights can be sufficiently counteracted by the design of the statutory powers concerning data analysis and sharing. 245

246 ee) Nevertheless, § 3(1) second sentence no. 5 of the Act, which sets out the danger of counterfeiting committed abroad [as possible grounds for surveillance], does not satisfy the principle of proportionality in its strict sense.

247 Counterfeiting neither poses a danger that is as serious as the danger of an armed attack, nor does it concern legal interests that are as significant as those affected by the other categories of dangers added to § 3 of the Act by the 1994 Fight Against Crime Act. Nor do the various forms of counterfeiting give rise to the same level of potential danger that characterises the other listed grounds for interference. [...]

248 § 3(1) second sentence no. 5 of the Act could be rendered compatible with the Basic Law if certain limitations were incorporated into the provision. It is therefore not declared void, but only incompatible with the Basic Law. It is incumbent upon the legislator to bring the law in conformity with the Constitution.

IV.

249 § 3(4) of the Act, which requires the Federal Intelligence Service to assess whether the personal data obtained through telecommunications surveillance is necessary for achieving the purposes invoked to justify the measures, is not as such objectionable under constitutional law. It does, however, not sufficiently give effect to the requirement of a purpose limitation, which derives from Art. 10 of the Basic Law, nor to the prohibition of excessive measures (*Übermaßverbot*). In this respect, the provision is incompatible not only with the privacy of telecommunications but also with freedom of the press, which must be taken into account as well.

250 This notwithstanding, § 3(4) of the Act does satisfy the principle of purpose limitation to the extent that this provision requires that the Federal Intelligence Service assess whether the data obtained through the surveillance of telecommunications is suitable for achieving the specified purpose. Moreover, § 3(6) first sentence of the Act reflects the principle of purpose limitation in that it prescribes that data be destroyed or deleted if its examination has shown that the data is not needed for the purposes pursued by the Federal Intelligence Service. However, the Act does not sufficiently guarantee that the use of data which is not destroyed or deleted remains limited to the purpose that justified its collection in the first place. The Act does not exclude possible data uses that go beyond the early detection of the dangers listed in the Act and the corresponding intelligence reports provided to the Federal Government. [...] In addition, § 3(4) of the Act does not give effect to the requirement of labelling the data [as stemming from interferences with telecommunications privacy], which follows from Art. 10 of the Basic Law; without such labelling, it is no longer possible to identify the data that enjoys the fundamental

rights protection afforded by Art. 10 of the Basic Law during later stages of data processing.
Furthermore, the challenged provision does not subject further data analysis to a statutory threshold, as would be required under the prohibition of excessive measures. § 3(3) of the Act, which subjects use of the data to specific requirements, does not apply to the Federal Intelligence Service itself. Instead, the provision concerns use of the data for the purposes of preventing, investigating or prosecuting criminal acts and thus [only] concerns the authorities with whom the Federal Intelligence Service is obliged to share intelligence pursuant to § 3(5) of the Act. The Act does not contain provisions ensuring that the Federal Intelligence Service itself may only analyse data stemming from telecommunications surveillance if the data is sufficiently relevant to the dangers listed in § 1(1) and 3(1) of the Act. The lack of such a statutory threshold is also significant with regard to Article 5(1) second sentence of the Basic Law because this threshold would ensure that the Federal Intelligence Service takes into account the particularly weighty interests of protecting informants and journalistic confidentiality.
It is not possible to interpret the provision in conformity with the Constitution as this would run counter to the requirements of legal clarity and specificity deriving from Art. 10 of the Basic Law. However, as statutory amendments could remedy the constitutional shortcomings of the challenged provision, it is not declared void, but only incompatible with the Basic Law. It is incumbent upon the legislator to bring the law in conformity with the Constitution.

V.

The Federal Intelligence Service's obligation to report to the Federal Government under § 12 of the Federal Intelligence Service Act is only challenged in these proceedings to the extent that, pursuant to § 3(3) second sentence of the Act, this obligation is exempt from the limitations set out in § 3(3) first sentence of the Act. In this respect, the statutory framework lacks sufficient safeguards for protecting the privacy of telecommunications.
Art. 10 of the Basic Law (and Art. 5(1) of the Basic Law to the extent that communication protected by freedom of the press is concerned) also applies to the Federal Intelligence Service's obligation to provide intelligence reports to the Federal Government given that these reporting obligations are one of the purposes for which the Federal Intelligence Service was granted powers to carry out telecommunications surveillance. [...].
It is not objectionable that § 3(3) second sentence of the Act exempts the reporting obligation under § 12 of the Federal Intelligence Service Act from the limitations

on data use pursuant to § 3(3) first sentence of the Act, as the limitations set out in this provision are not suited to the tasks of the Federal Intelligence Service. However, it is incompatible with Art. 10 of the Basic Law that the Federal Intelligence Service is not even subject to the limitation that it may only use the data for the purposes that are recognised as legitimate grounds for telecommunications surveillance in § 1(1) and § 3(1) first and second sentence of the Act. Moreover, the statutory framework violates Art. 10 of the Basic Law as it lacks an obligation to label personal data obtained through surveillance.

256 The statutory framework also lacks sufficient safeguards regarding data use by the Federal Government. The protection afforded by Art. 10 of the Basic Law is not limited to acts of the Federal Intelligence Service, as the authority collecting the data, but also applies vis-à-vis the Federal Government as the authority receiving the data. The holders of fundamental rights have an even greater need for protection vis-à-vis the Federal Government than vis-à-vis the Federal Intelligence Service. The mandate of the Federal Intelligence Service is limited to observing and analysing situations without executive powers to act on that knowledge; by contrast, the Federal Government is a political organ and the head of the federal executive branch and as such has the means to translate the knowledge obtained into action that could entail significant impairments for persons affected by telecommunications surveillance.

257 Therefore, data collected for the purposes of providing intelligence reports to the Federal Government may not be used freely by the latter. Rather, the Federal Government may only obtain knowledge of telecommunications contents or circumstances for the purpose of ensuring timely detection of the dangers listed in § 3(1) second sentence nos. 1 to 6 of the Act, so that measures can be taken to avert those dangers. Thus, it is not permissible for the Federal Government to retain or use the data for other purposes.

258 The challenged provision is not *per se* in conflict with the Constitution, as its constitutional shortcomings can be remedied by statutory amendments; therefore, it is not declared void, only incompatible with the Basic Law. It is incumbent upon the legislator to bring the law in conformity with the Constitution. The Basic Law affords the legislator discretion on how to discharge this responsibility.

VI.

259 § 3(5) first sentence in conjunction with § 3(3) first sentence of the Act obliges the Federal Intelligence Service to share data obtained through telecommunications surveillance with other authorities so that the latter can perform their respective tasks. In this respect, the provision is not fully in line with the requirements

deriving from Art. 10 of the Basic Law, nor with Art. 5(1) second sentence of the Basic Law, which must additionally be taken into account.

1. Nonetheless, the purpose of the provisions is not objectionable under constitutional law. They aim to ensure that data and information obtained by the Federal Intelligence Service through telecommunications surveillance, in the exercise of its functions, can be used for the purposes of preventing, investigating or prosecuting criminal acts in the event that the data obtained implicates certain individuals in a possible crime. The Basic Law accords great importance to the prevention and investigation of criminal acts. The Federal Constitutional Court has therefore repeatedly emphasised the undeniable need for effective law enforcement and the fight against crime; it has also repeatedly stressed the public interest in establishing the truth in criminal proceedings to the greatest extent possible, so as to convict persons guilty of criminal conduct and exonerate the innocent, and has recognised the effective investigation of crimes, especially serious ones, as a fundamental responsibility of society under the rule of law (cf. BVerfGE 77, 65 <76> with further references; 80, 367 <375> – *Diary-Like Notes*). 260

2. The legislator has also satisfied the requirement that the law specify precisely, for each subject matter, the purposes for which the sharing and further use of personal data is permissible (cf. BVerfGE 65, 1 <46> – *Census*). [...] 261

3. [The challenged Act does specify such purposes and] the specified purposes are also compatible with the original purpose that justified the collection of the data and the restriction of [the fundamental right to] the privacy of telecommunications resulting from it (cf. BVerfGE 65, 1 <62> – *Census*). 262

It is true that telecommunications surveillance measures that are not based on any grounds for suspicion may only be carried out by the Federal Intelligence Service for the purposes of strategic surveillance. [...] Only this narrow purpose limitation is capable of justifying the breadth and depth of the resulting fundamental rights interferences. If the surveillance measures could, from the outset, be aimed at preventing or prosecuting criminal acts, the relevant statutory powers would be incompatible with Art. 10 of the Basic Law (cf. BVerfGE 67, 157 <180 and 181>). Where fundamental rights set limits to the use of certain methods of data collection, these limits must not be circumvented by allowing data that was lawfully collected for specific purposes to also be used for other purposes that, by themselves, would not have justified the methods used for collecting the data in the first place. 263

Art. 10 of the Basic Law does not generally rule out any form of data sharing with authorities that otherwise are not or should not be permitted to carry out telecommunications surveillance without any grounds for suspicion. However, it must, in any case, be ensured that the receiving authorities do not have access to the entire data records; this is due to the fact that the Federal Intelligence Service, 264 on account of the methods it is permitted to use, necessarily records large quantities of telecommunications that from the outset have no relevance for the receiving authorities. At the same time, it does not contradict the primary purpose for which the data was originally collected if information that is relevant to the prevention, investigation or prosecution of criminal acts – although it was collected for other reasons – is later shared with the authorities specified in § 3(5) of the Act after a careful examination of the obtained data. The challenged provisions governing data sharing satisfy the constitutional requirements applicable in this context: § 3(5) first sentence and § 3(1) first sentence of the Act both specify certain statutory thresholds and § 3(5) second sentence of the Act subjects the sharing to a special review by an official who must be qualified to hold judicial office.

265   4. By contrast, the challenged provisions are not fully compatible with the prohibition of excessive measures.

266   a) The provisions are suitable and necessary for achieving their purpose.

267-268   [...]

269   b) Yet the legislator did not sufficiently satisfy the requirements deriving from the principle of proportionality in its strict sense with regard to statutory provisions that restrict fundamental rights.

270   aa) The principle of proportionality in its strict sense prohibits interferences with fundamental rights that are of such intensity that they are disproportionate to the importance of the matter and the burden imposed on the individual (cf. BVerfGE 65, 1 <54> – *Census*). To satisfy this principle, restrictions must be appropriate to the importance of the affected fundamental rights. In an overall balancing of the severity of the interference on the one hand, and the weight and urgency of the reasons invoked to justify it on the other hand, the limits of what is reasonable (*zumutbar*) must be observed (cf. BVerfGE 67, 157 <173, 178>; established case-law).

271   [In the present case,] the severity of the interference derives from the fact that the sharing of personal data constitutes an additional encroachment upon telecommunications privacy that could result in even greater impairments than the initial interference. The effects of data sharing are not limited to expanding the group of persons that obtain knowledge of the circumstances and contents of telecommunications. Rather, this knowledge may prompt further measures taken against the persons under surveillance. While the Federal Intelligence Service may not take any measures that directly target individuals, and the political strategies adopted by the Federal Government to counter the danger situations on which the Federal Intelligence Service is required to report are not directed against the respective communicating parties either, the same is not true for the other authorities receiving data shared pursuant to § 3(5) first sentence of the Act. Rather, data sharing will usually prompt the receiving authorities to investigate the persons concerned;

this may lead to further inquiries and, in some cases, to the opening of criminal proceedings.

With regard to the intensity of the impairment, it is also significant that the Federal Intelligence Service obtained the information through a measure that does not require any grounds for suspicion and that has an indiscriminate effect, and thus affects the privacy of telecommunications in an especially profound manner; it must also be taken into account that the relevant powers of the Federal Intelligence Service are only compatible with Art. 10 of the Basic Law because they merely serve the gathering of strategic intelligence, whereas the communicating parties are identified merely to facilitate the interpretation of the gathered information, which will invariably be fragmented and therefore ambiguous. Under these circumstances, sharing the data with other authorities is only proportionate if it serves overriding interests that outweigh the privacy of telecommunications, and if there is a reliable basis for assuming that the data is relevant to these interests and that the persons concerned are, with sufficient probability, involved in criminal conduct. If this basis is lacking, the limits of what is reasonable have been exceeded.

It is therefore imperative that the respective legal interest invoked in this context is of significant weight. It is also imperative that the suspicion that criminal acts are being planned or have been committed be supported by sufficient facts. The greater the weight of the asserted legal interests and the more far-reaching the impairments of these interests that could, or already did, result from the suspected conduct, the more acceptable it becomes to lower the degree of probability required for establishing a violation (or risk thereof) of the respective legal interest, and the degree of certainty required for establishing the facts on which the suspicion is based.

Moreover, the greater the weight attached to the legal interest in question, the more it becomes acceptable to shift the statutory threshold for carrying out data sharing to a purely precautionary stage [before a danger to the legal interest actually arises]. Where the statutory threshold for data sharing merely requires factual indications that certain planning acts that possibly precede criminal conduct are under way, the legal interest must be exceptionally significant (cf. BVerfGE 30, 1 <18>). Accordingly, if the legislator limits the protected legal interests to a few specified high-ranking interests yet the likely damage to these legal interests would be extraordinarily grave, the legislator may set a relatively low threshold for authorising data sharing. If the legislator, by contrast, considerably expands the catalogue of protected legal interests, and the acts it aims to avert include acts that pose a relatively minor threat, it must subject data sharing to a high threshold.

bb) The legislator did not in all respects achieve the necessary balance in the design of the statutory prerequisites for data sharing. § 3(5) in conjunction with

§ 3(3) of the Act is not objectionable to the extent that it permits data sharing regarding persons against whom certain targeted surveillance measures have been lawfully ordered pursuant to § 2 of the Act. However, the constituent elements of the provision are not sufficiently limited in scope with respect to the other statutory grounds for data sharing, namely data sharing based on the suspicion of criminal conduct. This finding follows from an overall assessment of the catalogue of relevant criminal offences, the quality of the factual basis required for establishing the suspicion of criminal conduct, and the temporal scope of what constitutes a threat to the protected legal interests under the statutory regime.

276 The catalogue of criminal offences, based on which the Federal Intelligence Service may share personal data obtained through telecommunications surveillance with other authorities for the purposes of preventing, investigating or prosecuting these crimes, is extraordinarily heterogeneous. It is not limited to felonies but also includes misdemeanours. On the one hand, it includes criminal offences that impair the highest-ranking public interests or even threaten to completely eliminate the ability of the state to protect legal interests. In part, their weight corresponds to, or even exceeds, that of the criminal offences which, pursuant to § 2 of the Act, justify the ordering of targeted surveillance measures against specific individuals. [...] On the other hand, however, some offences listed in the catalogue only constitute medium-level crime [...].

277 Moreover, the statutory framework sets relatively lenient standards for the factual basis establishing a suspicion of criminal conduct, especially when compared to the factual basis that is statutorily required for telecommunications surveillance under § 100a of the Code of Criminal Procedure. [...] Furthermore, by including planning stages that precede the stage of punishable attempt under § 100a of the Code of Criminal Procedure, the challenged provisions expand the grounds for data sharing to mere preparatory acts [by the person concerned] that fall short of punishable criminal conduct; this renders the challenged provisions more or less devoid of any limitation.

278 As a consequence, a distinction must be made between the prevention of crime on the one hand, and the investigation and prosecution of crime on the other hand. This follows from the fact that the urgency of data sharing for the purposes of protecting legal interests differs in these situations. The prevention of crime falls in the domain of averting dangers to public security, seeking to protect the affected legal interest from an impending violation and thus prevent harm, whereas by prosecuting criminal offences, the state seeks to punish a violation of protected legal interests that has already occurred, i.e. can no longer be prevented. [...]

279 Given that criminal prosecution takes places when a violation of legal interests has already occurred and primarily concerns the question of punishment, it is not

No. 37 – The Article 10 Act

justified to lower the statutory threshold for the sharing of personal data obtained through interferences with the privacy of telecommunications pursuant to § 1 and § 3 of the Act to a less strict standard than the one that otherwise applies to law enforcement measures interfering with the privacy of telecommunications pursuant to § 100a of the Code of Criminal Procedure. Given that the interference resulting from data sharing by the Federal Intelligence Service is of comparable severity, it is imperative under constitutional law that the underlying factual basis for the suspicion of a crime be subject to the same standards that apply to measures pursuant to § 100a of the Code of Criminal Procedure. Otherwise, the number of fundamental rights holders affected would exceed the limits of what is reasonable. § 3(3) first sentence of the Act does not satisfy these requirements. [...]

To the extent that the provision [authorises data sharing] for the prevention of crime, it fails to sufficiently accommodate the protected fundamental rights interests. There is a significant imbalance at the expense of the affected fundamental rights as a result of the following combined factors: any factual indication suffices as the basis of suspicion; mere planning acts [below the threshold of criminal conduct] constitute sufficient grounds; and the statutory grounds include less serious criminal offences. In particular, the combination of accepting any factual indication and including the planning stages of possible crimes [as sufficient grounds] means that these powers authorise purely precautionary action in very early stages before an actual danger to legal interests arises. As a result, the challenged provision not only accepts a lower degree of probability and certainty, but also subjects the exercise of the powers to relatively lenient standards as regards the underlying factual basis.

[...]

Moreover, the statutory framework is not fully in line with constitutional law with regard to the procedural safeguards for protecting the privacy of telecommunications. [...] While the provisions do set out obligations to document the implementation of surveillance measures and the destruction and deletion of data, similar documentation requirements are lacking for the sharing of data. As a result, data sharing cannot be properly reviewed by the competent independent [oversight] bodies or the courts.

It is not possible to interpret the provisions in conformity with the Constitution. [...] The legislator must enact new provisions that satisfy the constitutional requirements.

VII.

§ 3(7) of the Act is incompatible with Art. 10 of the Basic Law.

285 The provision is not *per se* objectionable under constitutional law. It obliges the receiving authorities to verify that they need the data shared pursuant to § 3(5) of the Act for the purposes specified in § 3(3) of the Act. […]

286 However, just like the provision governing the corresponding powers of the Federal Intelligence Service, § 3(7) of the Act lacks an obligation to label the data; the legislator must impose this obligation on the receiving authorities as a precaution safeguarding the purpose limitation regarding data use. Without such an obligation the data and information stemming from intelligence measures under the Act could, after their relevance to the purposes for which the data was shared has been verified pursuant to § 3(7) of the Act, be stored or merged with other data and information in such a way that it is no longer identifiable as data obtained through strategic telecommunications surveillance. This would circumvent the purpose limitation set out in § 3(3) of the Act.

287 Again, it is not possible to interpret the provision in conformity with the Constitution. It is incumbent upon the legislator to bring the law in conformity with the Constitution.

VIII.

288 § 3(8) second sentence of the Act, which governs the requirement to notify affected persons of the surveillance measures, is not compatible with the Basic Law.

289 1. It is not objectionable under constitutional law that § 3(8) first sentence of the Act only provides for a limited form of notification of the persons under surveillance. Under Art. 10(2) second sentence in conjunction with Art. 19(4) third sentence of the Basic Law, it is permissible to refrain from notification if the restriction of the privacy of telecommunications serves to protect the free democratic basic order or the existence or security of the Federation or of a *Land*. However, according to the Federal Constitutional Court's established case-law, this only applies on the condition that the person affected be notified *ex post* as soon as it can be ruled out that notification would jeopardise the purpose of the measure or the existence or security of the Federation or of a *Land* (cf. BVerfGE 30, 1 <31 and 32>). […]

290 […]

291 2. By contrast, § 3(8) second sentence of the Act violates Art. 10 and Art. 19(4) of the Basic Law.

292 Pursuant to this provision, the affected persons need not be notified if their data has been destroyed by the Federal Intelligence Service or a receiving authority within three months. […]

No. 37 – The Article 10 Act

[…]

The recording of the data in itself already constitutes an interference with the privacy of telecommunications against which legal protection must in principle be afforded. Yet it is the subsequent use of the data that has particularly severe consequences for the affected persons. Therefore, refraining from notification of the persons affected [by the surveillance measures] would be justified only if the collected data was destroyed immediately due to its irrelevance and if no further steps were taken. As § 3(8) second sentence of the Act is not limited to these cases, it restricts Art. 10 and Art. 19(4) of the Basic Law in a disproportionate manner.

As the provision can be rendered compatible with fundamental rights by means of statutory amendments, it is not declared void but only incompatible with the Basic Law. It is incumbent upon the legislator to bring the law in conformity with the Constitution.

IX.

By contrast, the exclusion of recourse to the courts under § 9(6) of the Act is compatible with the Basic Law.

This provision has a constitutional basis in Art. 10(2) second sentence of the Basic Law, which permits the exclusion of recourse to the courts for measures restricting [the privacy of telecommunications] that serve to protect the free democratic basic order or the existence or security of the Federation or of a *Land*, provided that recourse to the courts is replaced by a review carried out by bodies and auxiliary bodies appointed by Parliament. […]

[…]

X.

The provisions on the destruction of data in § 3(6) and in § 3(7) second and third sentence as well as in § 7(4) of the Act are also compatible with the Basic Law.

They satisfy the requirement following from Art. 10 of the Basic Law that data obtained through interferences with the privacy of telecommunications be destroyed as soon as it is no longer needed for the purposes justifying the interference. It is not ascertainable that the provisions fall short of the required minimum protection.

The provisions are also not objectionable with regard to Art. 19(4) of the Basic Law. The guarantee of effective legal protection does prohibit measures that would essentially frustrate legal protection (cf. BVerfGE 69, 1 <49>). In cases in which it is possible to subject telecommunications surveillance measures carried out by the Federal Intelligence Service to judicial review, the requirement to destroy data that is no longer needed must therefore be reconciled with the guarantee of legal protection in such a way that this guarantee is not circumvented. The provisions are open to such an interpretation.

303 [...]

XI.

304 § 9(2) third sentence of the Act, which subjects the surveillance measures to oversight by the Article 10 Committee (*G 10-Kommission*), is incompatible with Art. 10 of the Basic Law. It does not sufficiently guarantee that oversight extends to the entire process of interception and use of the data. Without such an oversight regime, the challenged provisions granting these powers cannot be upheld as constitutional. [...]

305 [...]

306 In view of the fact that the Fight Against Crime Act has considerably expanded the Federal Intelligence Service's surveillance activities, it must be ensured that the Article 10 Committee is provided with the staff needed to effectively fulfil its mandate. Moreover, it must be ensured that there is sufficient oversight also at the level of *Land* administrations to the extent that data obtained through interferences with the privacy of telecommunications is shared with *Land* authorities pursuant § 3(5) of the Act.

XII.

307-310 [...]

Justices: Papier, Grimm, Kühling, Jaeger, Haas, Hömig, Steiner

No. 38

BVerfGE 115, 166 – Telecommunications Surveillance

HEADNOTES

to the Order of the Second Senate of 2 March 2006
2 BvR 2099/04

1. Telecommunications traffic data stored within the domain controlled by a communicating party after the transmission process has been completed is not protected by [the privacy of telecommunications under] Art. 10(1) of the Basic Law, but by the right to informational self-determination (Art. 2(1) in conjunction with Art. 1(1) of the Basic Law) and, as the case may be, by Art. 13(1) of the Basic Law.
2. §§ 94 *et seq.* and §§ 102 *et seq.* of the Code of Criminal Procedure satisfy the constitutional requirements, also with regard to the securing and seizing of data storage devices and the data stored on them. They meet the requirement, applicable in particular to [interferences with] the right to informational self-determination, that the legislator specify precisely, for each subject matter and in a manner that is recognisable for the affected persons, the purposes for which collected data may be used. This is ensured by the strict limitation of all measures to the purpose of the investigation (cf. BVerfGE 113, 29 – *Seizure of Electronic Data*).
3. When accessing traffic data stored by a communicating party, it must be taken into account that this data merits greater protection. The assessment of proportionality must reflect the fact that this is data which, if it were accessed outside the sphere controlled by the affected person, would enjoy the special protection of telecommunications privacy, and which, if it is stored within the domain controlled by the affected person, is afforded supplementary protection by the right to informational self-determination.

BVerfGE 115, 166

FEDERAL CONSTITUTIONAL COURT
- 2 BvR 2099/04 -

IN THE NAME OF THE PEOPLE

In the proceedings
on the constitutional complaint of

Ms B...,
– authorised representatives: ...

against a) the Order of the Karlsruhe Regional Court of 12 October 2004
- 2 Qs 114/02-,

b) the Order of the Karlsruhe Regional Court of 28 January 2003
- 2 Qs 114/02 -

the Federal Constitutional Court – Second Senate –

with the participation of Justices

Vice President Hassemer,
Broß,
Osterloh,
Di Fabio,
Mellinghoff,
Lübbe-Wolff,
Gerhardt,
Landau

held on the basis of the oral hearing of 23 November 2005:

JUDGMENT

1. The Orders of the Karlsruhe Regional Court of 28 January 2003 - 2 Qs 114/02 - and of 12 October 2004 - 2 Qs 114/02 - violate the complainant's fundamental rights under Article 13(1) and (2) of the Basic Law and Article 2(1) of the Basic Law. They are reversed. [...]
2. [...]

No. 38 – Telecommunications Surveillance

REASONS:

A.

The complainant, who is a local court judge, lodged a constitutional complaint challenging an order for the search of her home based on suspected breach of official secrets [pursuant to § 353b of the Criminal Code]. The purpose of the search was to investigate telecommunications traffic data on the complainant's personal computer and mobile phone, which was believed to contain evidence that the judge had liaised with a journalist.   1

I.

Searches of a suspect's home or possessions are governed by § 102 of the Code of Criminal Procedure. [...]   2
[...]   3-4
The substantive requirements for securing and seizing evidence, which are further specified if evidence is obtained in connection with a search, are set out in § 94 of the Code of Criminal Procedure.   5
[...]   6-19

II.

1. Since mid-July 2002, the local police in H., in cooperation with the *Land* Criminal Police Office (*Landeskriminalamt*), the Federal Criminal Police Office (*Bundeskriminalamt*), and a US police authority, had been investigating P. and E., who were suspected of planning an attack on a US facility in H. or on the city centre of H., based on information received from a witness.   20
All information concerning the investigations of P. and E. was widely shared [among the authorities involved]. [...]   21
On 5 September 2002, in a search of the home of the two suspects, chemicals and components were found that could be used in pipe bombs, together with a picture of Osama Bin Laden and books relating to Islam and to the so-called Holy War. The suspects were taken into custody. E. was interrogated by police officers H. and N.   22
The investigation files were submitted to the complainant as the competent examining judge (*Ermittlungsrichterin*) at the H. Local Court on the morning of 6 September 2002, together with applications for arrest warrants. At approximately 11:00 a.m., lawyer F., acting as P.'s defence counsel, called lawyer N., so that the   23

- 485 -

latter would take on the defence of suspect E. Lawyer N. appeared, without prior notice, for the judicial interrogation of Ms E., which began around 12:00 noon; Ms E. had been brought before the complainant by police officers H. and N. The complainant issued arrest warrants for both suspects. The interrogation ended at about 12:30 p.m.

24 Between 1:30 and 2:30 p.m., K., a reporter for *Spiegel* magazine, called the office of lawyer N., who had not yet returned, to inquire about the investigation proceedings. Differing witness accounts exist as to whether a reporter from *Focus* magazine also phoned that law firm with the same request, and whether this call took place shortly afterwards or a few days later. Between 4:00 and 4:30 p.m. on the same day, journalists from the AP news agency and *Bild* newspaper contacted the press office of the Baden-Württemberg Criminal Police Office with similar inquiries; the police office did not release any information at that time. At 6:00 p.m., the *Deutschlandfunk* radio channel, citing *Bild* newspaper, reported on the investigation proceedings. From 6:15 p.m., the AP news agency – also citing *Bild* newspaper – reported on the matter as well, as did the *n-tv* television station.

25 2. The public prosecution office launched investigations into suspected breaches of official secrets (§ 353b(1) of the Criminal Code). After the public prosecution office learned that the complainant and reporter K. were personally acquainted, it directed the investigation against the complainant as a suspect. An examination of traffic data from the phone lines at the H. Local Court, which were used by the complainant and others, did not indicate any contacts with the reporter. Analyses of traffic data from the phone lines at the H. Police Headquarters, where the investigating police officers had their offices, and from the complainant's private landline also did not reveal any evidence of contact. It was not possible to examine the complainant's mobile phone traffic data because the data had been deleted in the meantime. Interrogations of staff at the court's registries, of another judge at the H. Local Court, of the police officers who had brought E. to the courthouse, and of the secretary of lawyer N. yielded no results. All these persons – who were questioned as witnesses – denied having known or shared the leaked information, and were then ruled out as suspects. The complainant was not questioned.

26 3. a) Search warrants sought by the public prosecution office for the complainant's home and office were denied by the Local Court on 2 December 2002. […]

27 b) Upon a complaint lodged by the public prosecution office, the Regional Court authorised – by way of the challenged order of 28 January 2003, i.e. nearly five months after the event – a search of the complainant's home and office, and the seizure of her computer, of copies of the investigation files, and of the itemised mobile phone bill.

No. 38 – Telecommunications Surveillance

[...]

c) On 5 February 2003, the complainant's private home and her office were searched. The aim of the search was to secure the itemised mobile phone bill, copies of the investigation files, and other data that could possibly indicate contacts with the journalist. The mobile phone was seized to conduct a memory data analysis. The analysis showed that there was no call data for the period during which the suspected criminal acts took place.

d) Following the searches, the complainant filed a complaint against the search order, which was ultimately heard by the courts as an application to reinstate the procedural status *quo ante* on the grounds that her right to be heard had been violated (*Antrag auf Nachholung des rechtlichen Gehörs*). [...]

e) By order of 8 August 2003, the Regional Court rejected a remedy against the search order. [...]

4. The Third Chamber of the Second Senate of the Federal Constitutional Court reversed this order on 5 February 2004 - 2 BvR 1621/03 - [...], finding a violation of the right to be heard (Art. 103(1) of the Basic Law), and remanded the matter to the Regional Court.

5. In the challenged order of 12 October 2004, the Regional Court refused to declare the search unlawful. [...]

III.

With her constitutional complaint, the complainant claims a violation of her rights under Art. 13(1) and (2), Art. 2(1), Art. 3(1), Art. 10(1) and Art. 103(1) in conjunction with Art. 19(4) of the Basic Law.

[...]

IV.

Statements on the constitutional complaint were submitted by the Federal Government, the *Land* Governments of Baden-Württemberg, Bavaria, Lower Saxony and North Rhine-Westphalia, the President of the Federal Court of Justice and the Public Prosecutor General (*Generalbundesanwalt*). In addition, the Federal Criminal Police Office, the Federal Bar Association (*Bundesrechtsanwaltskammer*), the German Lawyers Association (*Deutscher Anwaltsverein*) and the Federal Data Protection Officer were heard on the constitutional complaint.

45-53 […]

B.

54 The constitutional complaint is for the most part admissible.

I.

55-58 […]

II.

59 Although the challenged search order has been rendered moot by its execution, the complainant continues to have a legal interest in bringing proceedings. In cases of serious interferences with fundamental rights – which especially includes state action that the Basic Law itself subjects to the requirement of prior judicial authorisation (*Richtervorbehalt*) – affected persons continue to have a legal interest in bringing proceedings at least where the direct impact of an act of public authority is limited to such a short period that it would hardly be feasible, in the regular course of proceedings, to obtain a timely court decision. This is generally the case regarding searches of private homes (cf. BVerfGE 96, 27 <38 *et seq.*>; 104, 220 <233>).

C.

60 The challenged orders of the Regional Court of 28 January 2003 and 12 October 2004 violate the complainant's fundamental rights under Art. 13(1) and Art. 2(1) of the Basic Law.

61 The complainant's fundamental right under Art. 10(1) of the Basic Law is not affected (see I below); rather, the measures at issue must be measured against Art. 13(1) of the Basic Law (see III below) and Art. 2(1) of the Basic Law (see II below). In the context of search and seizure measures, the principle of proportionality must be observed (see IV below), which the Regional Court failed to do (see V below).

I.

62 The challenged orders do not violate the privacy of telecommunications protected under Art. 10(1) of the Basic Law.

No. 38 – Telecommunications Surveillance

1. The complainant not only objects to the search of her home as such, but also argues that the purpose of the search, i.e. the accessing of traffic data stored on her telecommunications devices, violates her right to the confidentiality of remote communication.

2. The privacy of correspondence, post and telecommunications ensures the free development of one's personality by enabling individuals to conduct communication in private, concealed from the public, and thereby also protects human dignity (cf. BVerfGE 67, 157 <171>; 106, 28 <35>; 110, 33 <53> […]).

Art. 10 of the Basic Law protects private communication at a distance. The privacy of correspondence, post and telecommunications guarantees the confidentiality of individual communications where the communicating parties must rely on transmission by intermediaries because of the spatial distance between them, which makes the communication particularly vulnerable to interception by third parties, including state authorities. The privacy of correspondence, post and telecommunications is an integral part of the protection of the private sphere; it protects against unwanted collection of information, and guarantees privacy despite spatial distance […].

The privacy of telecommunications protects the non-physical transmission of information to individual recipients by way of telecommunications traffic (cf. BVerfGE 67, 157 <172>; 106, 28 <35 and 36>). Its aim is, to the greatest possible extent, to place participants in a position where they can communicate as if they were physically present.

This fundamental right is receptive to new developments, and encompasses not only the forms of telecommunications known at the time of drafting, but also new technologies (cf. BVerfGE 46, 120 <144>). Therefore, the scope of this fundamental right is not limited to the telecommunications services that were historically offered by the *Deutsche Bundespost*, but rather encompasses all transmissions of information by means of available telecommunications technologies. Neither the specific method of transmission (cable or wireless, analogue or digital) nor the form of expression (speech, images, sound, symbols or other data) have a bearing on its scope of protection (cf. BVerfGE 106, 28 <36>).

The privacy of telecommunications protects both the contents and the specific circumstances of telecommunications (see a below). However, where the communication is not part of an ongoing transmission, the contents and circumstances of the communication stored within the domain controlled by a communicating party are not protected by Art. 10(1) of the Basic Law (see b below).

a) The privacy of telecommunications primarily protects the confidentiality of the information that is exchanged, i.e. communication contents, against unauthorised access by third parties.

71 As a consequence of digitisation, any use of telecommunications leaves personal traces that can be stored and analysed. Accessing this data does affect the scope of protection of Art. 10 of the Basic Law, as this fundamental right also protects the confidentiality of the specific circumstances of communications (cf. BVerfGE 67, 157 <172>; 85, 386 <396>; 110, 33 <53>; 113, 348 <365>).

72 In particular, this protection extends to whether, when, and how often telecommunications traffic occurred or was attempted, between whom or between which devices. Otherwise, the fundamental rights protection would be incomplete given that traffic data has its own informative value. In the individual case, traffic data could allow substantial conclusions to be drawn about the communication behaviour and movement patterns of the affected persons. The frequency, duration and time of communication traffic provide insights into the nature and intensity of relationships and allow conclusions to be drawn about the communication contents (cf. in this respect BVerfGE 107, 299 <320>).

73 b) However, the communication traffic data stored within the domain controlled by one of the communicating parties after completion of the transmission process is not protected by Art. 10(1) of the Basic Law. Rather, it is protected by the right to informational self-determination (Art. 2(1) in conjunction with Art. 1(1) of the Basic Law) and, as the case may be, by Art. 13(1) of the Basic Law.

74-75 In this respect, the protection afforded by the privacy of telecommunications ends when the recipient has received the message and the transmission process has been completed [...]. The specific risks of remote communication do not apply within the domain controlled by the recipient, given that at this point they can take their own precautions against unwanted data access.

76 Post and telecommunications enable private communication between persons who are not in the same location, and thereby add a new dimension to the private sphere [...]. Yet they also entail a loss of privacy, because the communicating parties must rely on the particular technical features of a telecommunications medium, and must put their trust in the telecommunications intermediaries involved in the process. Thus, third parties can more easily gain access to the contents and circumstances of the transmitted message. Participants who communicate remotely via technical means and use communication channels provided by intermediaries cannot themselves ensure that their communication remains confidential.

77 Art. 10(1) of the Basic Law serves to compensate for the diminished privacy resulting from the use of technology, and to counteract the risks inherent in the transmission process, including the involvement of a third party (cf. BVerfGE 85, 386 <396>; 106, 28 <36>; 107, 299 <313>). Thus, protection of telecommunications privacy is tied to the use of a communication medium (cf. BVerfGE 100, 313 <363> – *The Article 10 Act*; [...]).

No. 38 – Telecommunications Surveillance

Once the recipient has received the message, it is no longer exposed to an increased risk of interception by third parties – including by the state – that arises from the fact that the communicating parties cannot fully control and monitor the transmission process. From that moment, the stored communication contents and traffic data are no different [in terms of vulnerability] from other data files originally created by the telecommunications users themselves. 78

While communicating parties do not dispose of technical means to prevent or even just influence the generation and storage of traffic data by telecommunications intermediaries, their level of influence changes once the data is within their own sphere of control. Firstly, it is generally not possible for third parties to gain undetected access to the stored data without the knowledge of the communicating party. This removes a key justification for the special need for protection in the context of telecommunications privacy. Secondly, the affected persons themselves have significant control over whether data is stored permanently on their devices. 79

It is true that, generally, electronically stored data cannot be permanently deleted merely by using the delete function on the respective device; according to the expert statements delivered at the oral hearing, permanent deletion can only be achieved by using special software, for example in the case of computer hard drives. However, regardless of the variables and details of whether digitally stored data can be effectively deleted, the fact remains that telecommunications users do have various options of processing and deleting data stored within their sphere of control – including, as a last resort, physical destruction of the data storage device. These options are not available to them during ongoing transmissions or when traffic data is stored by telecommunications intermediaries. Regarding devices within their control, telecommunications users can take a range of measures to protect themselves against third parties gaining access; this includes the use of passwords or other access codes, or – in the case of personal computers – the use of encryption programmes and special data deletion software. […] 80

In determining the scope of protection of Art. 10 of the Basic Law – especially in distinction to Art. 2(1) of the Basic Law – it is not decisive whether users can always reliably delete the traffic data stored within their sphere of control. Rather, the decisive factor is whether the situation is comparable to that of other data stored within the user's private sphere, such as the personal phone directory created by the user on their device, or information stored on the hard drive of a computer. In that case, there are no longer any specific risks associated with a transmission process that are beyond the user's control or influence. 81

The special protection of telecommunications privacy under Art. 10 of the Basic Law compensates for the loss of control over one's private sphere that results from the use of technology as an inevitable consequence of relying on telecom- 82 munications systems operated by third parties; it establishes a particular barrier against the comparatively easy accessing of telecommunications data that the use of telecommunications technology permits. By contrast, the private sphere that individuals can control themselves is protected by other fundamental rights, especially by Art. 13(1) of the Basic Law and the right to informational self-determination (Art. 2(1) in conjunction with Art. 1(1) of the Basic Law).

83 c) The fundamental rights protection afforded [under Art. 10 of the Basic Law] does not always end when the transmission via telecommunications systems reaches the user device (cf. BVerfGE 106, 28 <37>). The confidentiality of telecommunications protected under Art. 10 of the Basic Law may also be jeopardised where third parties directly access the user device. Whether the protection afforded under Art. 10(1) of the Basic Law can be invoked in this respect must be determined by taking into account the purpose of the fundamental rights guarantee and the underlying specific risks (cf. BVerfGE 106, 28 <37>). Surveillance of ongoing telecommunications constitutes an interference with the privacy of telecommunications even if the content of the message is intercepted at the user device. Given that the transmission of telecommunications must be regarded as a uniform process, it is not feasible to draw a distinction based on purely technical categories (cf. BVerfGE 106, 28 <38>). Once the telecommunications process has been completed, however, the communication contents and circumstances now stored on the users' devices are no longer exposed to the same specific risks that arise from the use of a telecommunications device as a communication medium.

II.

84 The challenged orders violate the complainant's right to informational self-determination under Art. 2(1) of the Basic Law.

85 1. In the present case, the right to informational self-determination (Art. 2(1) in conjunction with Art. 1(1) of the Basic Law) does not stand back behind the fundamental right of Art. 13(1) of the Basic Law, which is also affected (see III below). Although Art. 13 of the Basic Law, as the more specific freedom, generally supersedes Art. 2(1) of the Basic Law (cf. BVerfGE 51, 97 <105>; […]), the general right of personality – including in its manifestation as a right to informational self-determination – is not supplanted where its scope of protection only partially overlaps with that of a specific freedom, nor in cases that touch on a separate domain of freedom that has evolved independently and with clearly defined characteristics […].

86 This is the case here. Where a search warrant for a home is issued for the purposes of securing data storage devices or mobile phones on which telecommunications

traffic data is stored, the measure is not limited to intruding on the spatial boundaries of the private sphere. Rather, the interference takes on a different quality by touching on another fundamental rights dimension in that it is intended to reveal information about a communication. As this concerns a special dimension of protection under Art. 2(1) in conjunction with Art. 1(1) of the Basic Law, this means that, by way of exception, this fundamental right does not stand back behind Art. 13 of the Basic Law. This special dimension, which is informed by the distinct characteristics of traffic data and serves to protect the integrity of remote communication, is a manifestation of this fundamental right's supplementary function as a right expanding the protection afforded under Art. 10 of the Basic Law.

2. In the context of modern data processing, the free development of one's personality requires that the individual be protected against the unlimited collection, storage, use and sharing of their personal data. This protection is part of the fundamental right under Art. 2(1) in conjunction with Art. 1(1) of the Basic Law. In this regard, the fundamental right confers upon the individual the authority to, in principle, decide themselves on the disclosure and use of their personal data (cf. BVerfGE 65, 1 <43> – *Census*).

This fundamental right serves to prevent a chilling effect that could arise and impair the exercise of other fundamental rights if individuals were no longer able to tell who knows what kind of personal information about them, at what time and on which occasion. This could greatly impede their freedom to make self-determined plans and decisions.

A deterrent effect on the exercise of fundamental rights stemming from the secret knowledge of third parties [regarding one's personal data] must be avoided, not only in the interest of the affected individuals. Such a deterrent effect would also affect the common good because self-determination is a fundamental prerequisite for the functioning of a free and democratic society which relies on the agency and participation of its citizens (cf. BVerfGE 65, 1 <43> – *Census*).

3. a) Where the protection of telecommunications traffic data is concerned, the right to the privacy of telecommunications and the right to informational self-determination are complementary. Within its scope of application, Art. 10 of the Basic Law contains a specific guarantee protecting telecommunications, which supersedes the general guarantee of the right to informational self-determination (cf. BVerfGE 67, 157 <171>; 100, 313 <358> – *The Article 10 Act*; 107, 299 <312>; 110, 33 <53>; 113, 348 <365>). Yet to the extent that interferences with telecommunications privacy concern the obtaining of personal data, the requirements that the Federal Constitutional Court derived from Art. 2(1) in conjunction with Art. 1(1) of the Basic Law in its *Census* decision (cf. BVerfGE 65, 1 <44 *et seq.*> – *Census*) can, in

principle, largely be applied to the more specific guarantee under Art. 10(1) of the Basic Law, too (cf. BVerfGE 100, 313 <359> – *The Article 10 Act*; 110, 33 <53>).

91 Where Art. 10 of the Basic Law does not apply, personal traffic data stored within the sphere of control of affected persons is protected by the right to informational self-determination under Art. 2(1) in conjunction with Art. 1(1) of the Basic Law. This reflects the fact that the telecommunications circumstances merit special protection, and upholds the confidentiality of remote communications even after the transmission process has been completed.

92 b) Traffic data constitutes personal data with potentially significant informative value; therefore, it requires protection under the right to informational self-determination (Art. 2(1) in conjunction with Art. 1(1) of the Basic Law).

93 The use of digital transmission devices means that telecommunications are no longer transitory in nature but leave permanent traces. Due to digitisation, a multitude of traffic data is not only collected by service providers, but also automatically accumulates on user devices; this data provides information on the lines used in telecommunications, the time and duration of the transmission, and, to some extent, even on the participants' location, and it is regularly stored beyond the duration of the respective communication. The volume and informative value of accumulated traffic data allow the creation of an ever clearer profile of the communicating parties. In the context of telecommunications, the convergence of transmission channels, services, and devices leads to an increasingly concentrated flow of information. Telecommunications devices, especially mobile phones and personal computers, are increasingly used not only for personal conversations but also for everyday transactions, such as shopping or paying bills, for obtaining and disseminating information, and for using various services. More and more areas of life are shaped by modern means of communication. This increases not only the volume of generated traffic data, but also its informative value. This data increasingly allows more conclusions to be drawn about the nature and intensity of relationships, about interests, habits and preferences, and most notably, about the contents of a given communication; depending on the nature and scope of the accumulated data, the resulting conclusions may even amount to the creation of a personality profile.

94 4. The right to informational self-determination affords protection against the collection of one's personal data in any form (cf. BVerfGE 65, 1 <43> – *Census*; 67, 100 <143>). A search order that – as in the present case – is specifically and expressly issued for the purpose of securing data storage devices believed to hold traffic data interferes with the fundamental right under Art. 2(1) in conjunction with Art. 1(1) of the Basic Law (cf. BVerfGE 107, 299 <314> on Art. 10 of the Basic Law).

5. Restrictions of Art. 2(1) of the Basic Law require a statutory basis specifying their prerequisites and scope in a manner that is clear and recognisable for citizens in accordance with the principle of legal clarity deriving from the rule of law (cf. BVerfGE 113, 29 <50> – *Seizure of Electronic Data*). §§ 94 *et seq.* of the Code of Criminal Procedure, and especially §§ 102 *et seq.* of the Code of Criminal Procedure, satisfy the constitutional requirements (see a below); there is no need to subject interferences to further limitations, as proportionality considerations in particular do not merit a stricter standard (see b below). 95

a) In its case-law, the Court has already decided that §§ 94 *et seq.* of the Code of Criminal Procedure satisfy the constitutional requirements, also with regard to the securing and seizing of data storage devices and the data stored on them (cf. BVerfGE 113, 29 <50> – *Seizure of Electronic Data*). The provisions satisfy the requirement, applicable in particular with regard to the right to informational self-determination, that the legislator specify precisely, for each subject matter and in a manner that is recognisable for the affected persons, the purposes for which the data may be used. This requirement is satisfied by the strict limitation of all measures to the purpose of the investigation – especially solving the criminal case under investigation (cf. BVerfGE 113, 29 <51> – *Seizure of Electronic Data*). 96

The same applies to §§ 102 *et seq.* of the Code of Criminal Procedure, which authorise search measures and specify further conditions in this regard. As § 94 of the Code of Criminal Procedure in principle allows for the securing and seizing of data storage devices or the copying of the relevant data, it is also permissible to order and carry out the search measures necessary in this regard. 97

b) Despite the fact that traffic data stored on a personal user device merits special protection and that Art. 2(1) of the Basic Law supplements Art. 10 of the Basic Law in that respect, the principle of proportionality does not require any further limitations on interferences beyond the requirements set out in §§ 94 *et seq.* and §§ 102 *et seq.* of the Code of Criminal Procedure. In particular, collecting traffic data stored on the user device of the person concerned is not subject to the requirements that would usually apply under § 100g of the Code of Criminal Procedure, i.e. it does not require that the investigation concern considerable criminal acts ([…]; BVerfGE 103, 21 <33 and 34> – *DNA Fingerprinting*; […]) or criminal offences included in the catalogue laid down in § 100a first sentence of the Code of Criminal Procedure. 98

aa) The principle of proportionality requires that the measure in question serve a purpose that is legitimate under constitutional law, and be suitable, necessary and proportionate, in the strict sense, for achieving that purpose. The interference must not impose an excessive burden on the affected person, i.e. it must be reasonable (*zumutbar*) (cf. BVerfGE 63, 131 <144> – *Right of Reply*). 99

100 bb) Effective law enforcement is a legitimate purpose with regard to restrictions of the right to informational self-determination. Safeguarding the peaceful legal order (*Rechtsfrieden*) by means of criminal law has always been an important responsibility of the state. The essential functions of the criminal justice system include investigating criminal acts, identifying offenders and deciding on their culpability and punishment, and exonerating the innocent. The criminal justice system thus serves to protect citizens by enforcing the state's power to punish crime in judicial proceedings that are based on uniform standards, satisfy the rule of law and seek to establish the truth. Enacting provisions that impose criminal punishment and applying them in proceedings conducted in accordance with the rule of law are constitutional responsibilities (cf. BVerfGE 107, 104 <118 and 119> with further references). Therefore, the Basic Law accords great importance to the prevention and investigation of criminal acts (cf. BVerfGE 100, 313 <388> – *The Article 10 Act*).

101 cc) §§ 94 *et seq.* and §§ 102 *et seq.* of the Code of Criminal Procedure allow for the accessing of traffic data stored within the domain controlled by the affected person; this is not only a suitable and necessary, but also an appropriate means for achieving this purpose. In particular, neither the fact that traffic data merits special protection nor the fact that Art. 2(1) of the Basic Law supplements Art. 10 of the Basic Law in that regard requires that the afforded level of protection limit interferences with the right to informational self-determination to the prosecution of considerable criminal acts.

102 (1) On the one hand, it must be taken into account in the balancing of the conflicting interests that traffic data merits special protection due to its informative value. In the individual case, such data allows significant conclusions to be drawn regarding communication behaviour and movement patterns. The frequency, duration and time of communication traffic provide insights into the nature and intensity of relationships; depending on the accuracy, quantity and variety of the generated data sets, this may amount to the creation of a personality profile in extreme cases, and even allow conclusions to be drawn about the contents of the communication (cf. in this regard BVerfGE 107, 299 <320>, see also C I 2 a and C II 3 b above). The weight of the interference increases further if the measure also affects the right to informational self-determination of the suspect's communication partners who are not themselves involved in the crime under investigation.

103 On the other hand, it must be taken into account that the increased use of electronic or digital means of communication and their advance into virtually all areas of life has also created new obstacles to law enforcement. Modern communication technologies are increasingly used for committing a wide variety of criminal acts, rendering criminal activities more effective [...].

No. 38 – Telecommunications Surveillance

The necessity that law enforcement keep pace with technological advances goes beyond making a mere practical addition to the traditional arsenal of investigation methods at the disposal of authorities, based on the belief that the existing methods would still be largely effective on their own. Rather, it must be acknowledged that there has been a shift from traditional forms of communication towards electronic communication, which also entails subsequent digital processing and storage of the relevant data.

Given these circumstances, the principle of proportionality does not require that the seizure of traffic data stored on a personal user device be generally limited to the investigation of considerable criminal acts. Such a limitation would result in inappropriate impairments of law enforcement. At the oral hearing and in the written statements, experienced experts familiar with the realities of criminal investigations stated convincingly that there is a great need for the accessing of traffic data stored on user devices even in cases where, based on the applicable range of punishment for the relevant offence, the criminal acts under investigation cannot necessarily be qualified as considerable crime. In this regard, the experts specifically cited as examples the dissemination of pornographic materials, including pornography depicting violence or animal pornography (§ 184 and § 184a of the Criminal Code), certain immigration offences (§ 95 of the Residence Act) and white-collar crime.

(2) In the context of assessing the proportionality of individual measures aimed at obtaining traffic data stored by a telecommunications intermediary, the Federal Constitutional Court held that it was necessary to limit such measures to investigations concerning considerable criminal offences (cf. BVerfGE 107, 299 <321>); yet this finding cannot automatically be applied to the traffic data stored on personal devices, as this data access takes place under different circumstances.

As far as data access is concerned, the measures under review here constitute less intense interferences. This follows from the fact that the data is accessed overtly, rather than covertly; that it does not entail the creation of movement profiles; that it is not necessary to obtain data from third parties – e.g., the telecommunications company – ; and that the affected persons have control over the data stored on their devices.

From the perspective of the communicating parties, the accessing of traffic data stored within the sphere of the affected person is not a covert measure, and thus lacks an essential element that is characteristic for interferences with the privacy of telecommunications; while covertness is not a necessary prerequisite regarding the protection afforded under Art. 10 of the Basic Law, it does significantly increase the severity of the interference. When the measure is carried out overtly, the affected persons can not only adjust their communication behaviour in the context of ongoing surveillance measures, they can in principle also challenge the lawfulness of the measure as such – and seek legal assistance if necessary – on the grounds that it does not meet the applicable legal requirements. Moreover, they can, at the very least, check whether the execution of the measure stays within the limits set out in the search order, including the specific instructions for the authorised seizure, and possibly challenge the execution on the grounds that it exceeds the underlying judicial order.

109 The Code of Criminal Procedure sets out specific safeguards in that respect. § 106(1) first sentence of the Code of Criminal Procedure expressly provides that the affected person must be present during the search. If that person is absent, the overt nature of the measure is to be ensured through the presence of a representative drawn from their family or their neighbours pursuant to § 106(1) second sentence of the Code of Criminal Procedure. If neither the judge nor the public prosecutor is present for the search, § 105(2) of the Code of Criminal Procedure requires, where possible, the presence of a municipal officer or two members of the municipality in whose district the search is taking place.

110 Furthermore, given that the search measure is carried out overtly, affected persons are not *de facto* barred from seeking legal recourse – a risk that could otherwise arise if the state interference was carried out without their knowledge.

111 In addition, the data is not accessed while it is held within the sphere of a third party, most notably the telecommunications intermediary. The specific measure neither requires any technical or organisational arrangements on the part of the telecommunications intermediary, nor does it affect the intermediary's personnel or material resources, nor expose the intermediary to a conflict of interests with its customer. Accordingly, § 102 of the Code of Criminal Procedure sets lower requirements for search measures directed at the suspect than for search measures directed at a third party (§ 103 of the Code of Criminal Procedure).

112 Finally, it must be taken into account that the data which the search aims to collect has already entered the domain controlled by the affected persons, where they have actual means to process, protect or delete the data (see C I 2 b above).

113 While search and seizure measures might entail public stigmatisation of the affected person or severe impairments of their private sphere given that their home is subject to extensive searches, these are not specific to interferences with the right to informational self-determination. §§ 94 *et seq.* and §§ 102 *et seq.* of the Code of Criminal Procedure are designed for precisely this type of interference. Where the interference carries particular weight in the individual case, this must be taken into account in the proportionality assessment of that measure.

114 (3) Due to these differences [between the accessing of communication contents stored on personal devices and telecommunications surveillance as specified in §§ 100a, 100b of the Code of Criminal Procedure], it is not necessary under consti-

tutional law to extend the requirements for exercising the powers set out in §§ 100a and 100b of the Code of Criminal Procedure to the present case. Rather, §§ 94 *et seq.*, §§ 102 *et seq.* of the Code of Criminal Procedure provide a sufficient statutory basis authorising the necessary search and seizure measures as this situation is comparable to, for instance, search and seizure measures in respect of written files containing information that might be relevant as evidence.

III.

The challenged orders must also be measured against Art. 13(1) and (2) of the Basic Law.

115

Art. 13(1) of the Basic Law protects the inviolability of the home. It guarantees individuals a space of private life that is essential to human dignity and the free development of their personality (cf. BVerfGE 42, 212 <219>; 103, 142 <150>). Within their private homes, individuals have the right to be left alone (cf. BVerfGE 51, 97 <107>; 103, 142 <150>). Art. 13(1) of the Basic Law grants a defensive right protecting the sphere of private space within one's home against state interference, and serves to shield private life against intrusions (cf. BVerfGE 89, 1 <12>).

116

The guarantee of this fundamental right is strengthened by the fact that, pursuant to Art. 13(2) of the Basic Law, searches may only be ordered by a judge or, in cases of danger requiring immediate action (*Gefahr im Verzug*), by other organs designated by law subject to the formal requirements set out in the relevant statutory basis. The requirement of judicial authorisation aims to ensure prior review of the measure by an independent and neutral authority (cf. BVerfGE 57, 346 <355 and 356>; 76, 83 <91>; 103, 142 <151>). The Basic Law rests on the presumption that judges can best and most reliably ensure that the rights of the affected person are respected in the individual case (cf. BVerfGE 77, 1 <51>; 103, 142 <151>) due to their personal and professional independence and the fact that they are bound only by the law (Art. 97 of the Basic Law). The judge must independently examine the requested search measure, and ensure that the requirements arising from constitutional and statutory law be strictly observed (cf. BVerfGE 9, 89 <97>; 57, 346 <355 and 356>; 103, 142 <151>). Within the limits of what is possible and reasonable, the judge has the duty to ensure, by formulating the search order accordingly, that the resulting interference with fundamental rights can be measured and reviewed (cf. BVerfGE 103, 142 <151>).

117

IV.

118 1. The considerable interference with both the right to informational self-determination and the right to the inviolability of the home requires justification in accordance with the principle of proportionality in each individual case (cf. BVerfGE 20, 162 <186 and 187>; 96, 44 <51>; 113, 29 <52 and 53> – *Seizure of Electronic Data*).

119 a) In particular, the search must be proportionate to the severity of the criminal offence and the strength of suspicion (cf. BVerfGE 20, 162 <186 and 187>; 59, 95 <97>; 96, 44 <51>; 113, 29 <53> – *Seizure of Electronic Data*). This assessment must take into account how important the potential evidence that the search measure aims to obtain is for the criminal proceedings, and how likely it is that evidence relevant to the proceedings, in the form of physical objects or data, will indeed be found (BVerfGE 113, 29 <57> – *Seizure of Electronic Data*). For the purposes of criminal investigations, the home of a suspect may be entered only if specific charges can be brought against the suspect, which must be expressly set out – in other words, it requires more than just vague indications or mere assumptions (cf. BVerfGE 44, 353 <371 and 372> – *Addiction Counselling Agency*; […]). Moreover, the search must have real prospects of success in light of the purpose for which the search order is sought (cf. BVerfGE 42, 212 <220>; 96, 44 <51>).

120 b) When accessing traffic data stored on a personal device, it must be taken into account that this data merits greater protection (see C I 2 a and C II 5 b cc (1) above). The proportionality assessment must reflect the fact that this data is afforded the special protection of telecommunications privacy if accessed outside the sphere controlled by the person concerned, and the supplementary protection of the right to informational self-determination if accessed within the sphere controlled by the affected person. In this respect, it must be assessed how important the traffic data sought is for the criminal proceedings and how likely it is that relevant traffic data will indeed be found (BVerfGE 113, 29 <57> – *Seizure of Electronic Data*).

121 In the individual case, the measure may be impermissible where the criminal act under investigation is a minor offence, the evidentiary value of the traffic data that will presumably be seized is insignificant, or the basis for presuming that evidence will indeed be found is vague.

122 To the extent that it is possible, under the specific circumstances of the case and without jeopardising the purpose of the investigation, the protection of traffic data must be given consideration in the search order itself, by way of instructions that limit the obtaining of evidentiary material to what is actually necessary. In particular, this may entail narrowing down the relevant time period for which traffic

No. 38 – Telecommunications Surveillance

data may be sought, or limiting the search to specific communication devices if it can be ruled out from the outset that data relevant to the proceedings will be found on other devices of the person concerned.

c) When search and seizure measures are carried out – particularly when extensive electronic data records are accessed –, the constitutional standards that this Court developed in its Order of 12 April 2005 - 2 BvR 1027/02 - (cf. BVerfGE 113, 29 <52 et seq.> – *Seizure of Electronic Data*) must be applied accordingly. In this context, reasonable efforts must be made to avoid obtaining excess data that is irrelevant to the proceedings. The seizure of all data stored on a computer hard drive, or of an entire data processing system, solely for the purpose of obtaining traffic data from, for instance, email correspondence, will generally not be necessary; instead, it will usually be sufficient to inspect the devices at the site of the search in accordance with the purpose of the search, which in any case is limited from the outset.

123-125

V.

The challenged orders of the Regional Court do not satisfy these constitutional requirements.

126

The Federal Constitutional Court does not fully review the lawfulness of the challenged decisions; it merely falls to the Court to review whether the decisions contain an error that is based on a fundamentally incorrect understanding of the significance of a fundamental right, and in particular of its scope of protection, or whether the application of the law no longer appears comprehensible when critically appraising the Basic Law's central notions (cf. BVerfGE 18, 85 <92 and 93>; 95, 96 <127 and 128>).

127

Based on these considerations, the challenged orders of the Regional Court violate the complainant's rights under Art. 13(1) and Art. 2(1) of the Basic Law.

128

1. The challenged decisions do not interfere with Art. 10(1) of the Basic Law. While the search orders did serve to obtain data on the circumstances of telecommunications, specifically the time of communication and call numbers or line identifiers of the communicating parties, they were nevertheless limited to data stored within the complainant's private sphere; moreover, the relevant act of communication had already been completed. Under these circumstances, the data is no longer covered by the scope of protection of telecommunications privacy.

129

2. However, the challenged decisions violate the complainant's right to the inviolability of her home guaranteed by Art. 13 of the Basic Law and her right to informational self-determination (Art. 2(1) in conjunction with Art. 1(1) of the Basic Law) given that they do not give sufficient effect to the principle of proportionality.

130

131 The search order issued by the Regional Court is sufficiently precise, and the court correctly limited the examination of traffic data to the time of the possible crime. There is no need to decide here whether the information on which the order was based actually provided sufficient grounds for suspicion. This is because the suspicion on which the authorities acted, which appears extremely vague at best, could by no means justify the serious interferences with the complainant's fundamental rights – not least in view of the amount of time that had passed and, as a result thereof, the extremely low chances of actually finding relevant evidence.

132 a) The grounds for suspicion implicating the complainant were not very strong. This already follows from the large number of possible suspects in connection with the disclosure of the information. Some of them were ruled out as suspects solely on the basis of their own testimony, whereas the complainant was not given the opportunity to give evidence herself as she was never actually questioned. Others – such as lawyer F. – were not even considered as suspects; rather, the investigations were directed solely against the complainant as a suspect, merely because she had stated in a different context that she knew the *Spiegel* reporter.

133 In the Order of 5 February 2004 - 2 BvR 1621/03 - [...] [which had reversed and remanded an earlier decision by the Regional Court in this matter], the Third Chamber of the Second Senate of the Federal Constitutional Court had already directed the Regional Court to critically assess whether it actually seems probable that the information was disseminated by a journalist working for a weekly magazine, i.e. someone who should have been particularly interested in not making the information public right away. Yet the Regional Court failed to address this question in a substantiated manner. Instead, it only stated apodictically that it cannot generally be assumed that journalists work exclusively for one press medium and would thus refrain from sharing information with other journalists.

134 The now challenged decision of the Regional Court relies on the statement by law office employee S., made in her interrogation on 28 October 2002, that she was not "one hundred per cent sure" that the *Focus* editor did call the law firm on the date of the hearing. In this respect, the court refrained from examining the contradictions between this statement and the earlier statement by lawyer N. (note in the police file dated 23 October 2002), according to which on the afternoon of 6 September 2002 he saw a written note listing calls from both news magazines that day. The court simply assumed that the lawyer must have been mistaken. Yet this assumption seems untenable given that during previous questioning, employee S. was not only able to repeatedly recall the approximate time of the call from the *Focus* editor on 6 September 2002 but was also able to distinguish it from calls made by other journalists the following week (police file note of 23 October 2002).

No. 38 – Telecommunications Surveillance

The Regional Court assumed that these facts did not necessarily exclude the complainant as a suspect. This assumption, however, was evidently not an adequate basis for establishing a sufficiently strong suspicion against the complainant.

b) Furthermore, the Regional Court did not sufficiently take into account that it remains doubtful that the disclosure of official secrets posed a threat to important public interests within the meaning of § 353b(1) of the Criminal Code in the present case.

[…] It appears that the Regional Court, which by its own account did not consult the files of the initial proceedings, simply accepted at face value the vague statement by the police that a "planned" surveillance operation had to be "aborted". The police submitted this statement for the very first time in connection with the investigations against the complainant, and failed to provide any further details even after the statement was challenged by the complainant.

According to prevailing opinion, a specific danger (*konkrete Gefahr*) threatening public interests [as a constituent element of criminal liability] also includes indirect dangers, for instance, situations where the disclosure of official secrets could undermine the public's trust in the impartiality, incorruptibility and proper functioning of public administration […]. However, the Regional Court failed to establish the necessary specific findings in that regard, which would have required the court to carry out an overall assessment of all relevant circumstances of the individual case […].

c) The Regional Court asserted that the original files from the initial proceedings were not consulted because the documents submitted to the court did not indicate any contradictions. This assertion is unconvincing in light of the rather vague suspicion which prompted the Regional Court to order further investigations. Once again, the Regional Court failed to provide a convincing answer as to why the original files were not consulted. An explanation would have been necessary in this regard given that the suspicion against the complainant was vague at most and required further investigations, but also in light of the high standing accorded to the affected fundamental rights and in consideration of the office held by the complainant. Notably, there was no time pressure as the proceedings had been pending for several months already. A comparison of the file contents known to the complainant with the contents reported by the media, most significantly in the *Handelsblatt* article of 8 September 2002, would have shown that the media reports contained information that was not in the original files, and that therefore could not have been known to the complainant. By contrast, the information was in fact part of a confidential preliminary police report that had in the meantime been submitted to the Regional Court […].

140 d) Furthermore, it was doubtful from the outset whether the search was even suitable for finding evidence. At the time of the search order, almost five months had passed since the alleged crime, during which the law enforcement authorities had conducted extensive investigations within the complainant's immediate professional environment. Even if the complainant had been the only one not interrogated about the events, the authorities must have expected that she had become aware of the suspicion against her. The Regional Court should therefore have considered the possibility that the complainant – if there were even grounds for considering her as a suspect in the first place – might have destroyed or deleted evidence of any messages to journalists.

141 e) The interference with the sphere of private space within the complainant's home is serious, including with regard to her professional position. She had emphasised in the proceedings pursuant to § 33a of the Code of Criminal Procedure [application to reinstate the procedural status *quo ante*] that the search of her home significantly affected her professional position as an examining judge. Yet in its subsequent order, the Regional Court merely stated, without any further explanation, that it did not consider the search order to be incompatible with constitutional requirements. Thus, the Regional Court neglected to conduct the required proportionality assessment regarding the interference that would have been imperative given the considerable impairment of fundamental rights. For an examining judge, being accused of a breach of official secrets is particularly stigmatising, which is why caution is generally advised when making such accusations. If investigating authorities and courts signal, by searching the suspect's premises, that they pursue and confirm such a suspicion, the adverse effects of such accusations are further aggravated. In any case, a particularly thorough review must be carried out regarding the grounds for suspicion if the investigation measure in question is not a matter of urgency.

142 f) In addition, the Regional Court's decisions did not take into account the significance of the right to informational self-determination (Art. 2(1) in conjunction with Art. 1(1) of the Basic Law), in that the court ordered search measures to investigate telecommunications circumstances without giving consideration to the weight of the interference resulting from the accessing of traffic data that is afforded special constitutional protection.

143 g) The questionable suspicion, and the substantial doubts regarding the suitability of the search measure, render the measure disproportionate in relation to the interference with the inviolability of the home and the complainant's right to informational self-determination Constitutional law would thus have required the Regional Court to reject the application for a search order.

No. 38 – Telecommunications Surveillance

VI.

1. The orders of the Regional Court are reversed on the grounds that they violate Art. 13(1) and (2) and Art. 2(1) of the Basic Law (§ 95(2) of the Federal Constitutional Court Act). [...]   144
2. [...]   145

D.

[...]   146

Justices: Hassemer, Broß, Osterloh, Di Fabio, Mellinghoff, Lübbe-Wolff, Gerhardt, Landau

No. 39

BVerfGE 115, 320 – Profiling

HEADNOTES

to the Order of the First Senate of 4 April 2006
1 BvR 518/02

1. The type of electronic profiling and searches provided for in § 31 of the 1990 North Rhine-Westphalia Police Act as a preventive police measure is only compatible with the fundamental right to informational self-determination (Art. 2(1) in conjunction with Art. 1(1) of the Basic Law) if there is a specific danger to high-ranking legal interests such as the existence or security of the Federation or a *Land* or life, limb or liberty of the person. Such electronic profiling is impermissible if it serves as a purely precautionary measure before a danger to public security arises.

2. Neither a general threat situation, such as the persistent threat of terrorism since the 9/11 attacks, nor foreign policy tensions constitute sufficient grounds for ordering electronic profiling. Rather, such measures require further facts indicating the existence of a specific danger, such as the danger of a terrorist attack being prepared or carried out.

FEDERAL CONSTITUTIONAL COURT
- 1 BvR 518/02 -

IN THE NAME OF THE PEOPLE

In the proceedings
on the constitutional complaint of

Mr A...,
– authorised representative: ...
against a) the Order of the Düsseldorf Higher Regional Court of 8 February 2002
- 3 Wx 356/01 -,
b) the Order of the Düsseldorf Regional Court of 29 October 2001

- 25 T 873/01 -,
c) the Order of the Düsseldorf Local Court of 2 October 2001
- 151 Gs 4092/01 -

the Federal Constitutional Court – First Senate –
with the participation of Justices

> President Papier,
> Haas,
> Hömig,
> Steiner,
> Hohmann-Dennhardt,
> Hoffmann-Riem,
> Bryde,
> Gaier

held on 4 April 2006:

The Order of the Düsseldorf Higher Regional Court of 8 February 2002 - 3 Wx 356/01 -, the Order of the Düsseldorf Regional Court of 29 October 2001 - 25 T 873/01 - and the Order of the Düsseldorf Local Court of 2 October 2001 - 151 Gs 4092/01 - violate the complainant's fundamental right under Article 2(1) in conjunction with Article 1(1) of the Basic Law. The orders of the Higher Regional Court and the Regional Court are reversed. The matter is remanded to the Regional Court.

[...]

REASONS:

A.

The constitutional complaint challenges judicial decisions on electronic profiling and searches (*Rasterfahndung*) as a preventive police measure.

1

I.

1. Electronic profiling is a special investigation technique that uses electronic data processing for conducting police searches. The police authorities request that other public or private bodies share personal data held by them, which is cross-checked against other data in an automated procedure (profiling). This data cross-checking

2

serves to identify persons that match certain criteria, which must be defined in advance and be considered significant for furthering the investigations.

3 In Germany, electronic profiling was first conceived in the 1970s in connection with the fight against terrorism. […]

4-6 […]

7 2. Following the 9/11 terrorist attacks, information emerged that some of the perpetrators had resided in Germany. The *Land* police authorities, together with the Federal Criminal Police Office (*Bundeskriminalamt*), carried out coordinated nationwide electronic profiling measures in search of Islamist terrorists […]. In particular, these measures were aimed at detecting so-called sleeper terrorists […].

8 […] According to information provided by the Federal Data Protection Officer, the [competent] coordination committee developed a set of profiling criteria for identifying potential Islamist terrorists in Germany. Next, the *Land* Criminal Police Offices (*Landeskriminalämter*) obtained data from universities, residents' registration offices (*Einwohnermeldeämter*) and the Central Register of Foreigners (*Ausländerzentralregister*), which they then filtered based on the following criteria: male, 18 to 40 years of age, student or former student, Muslim faith, born in a country with a majority Muslim population (as specified on a list of relevant countries) or national of such a country […].

9 The data records which yielded positive matches in this cross-checking were transmitted to the Federal Criminal Police Office, which entered the data into the joint national database on sleeper terrorists. According to the Federal Criminal Police Office, it received more than 31,988 data records from the *Länder*. The records were subsequently cross-checked against other data records obtained by the Federal Criminal Police Office. The data used for cross-checking […] included, for example, records kept on holders of pilot licences and records kept on persons requiring special security clearance pursuant to § 12b of the Atomic Energy Act. […] The matches from the cross-checking were compiled in a database which was made available to the *Land* Criminal Police Offices. […]

10 To date, not a single case has emerged in which these electronic profiling measures led to the identification of sleeper terrorists, let alone to charges being brought against one of the profiled persons based on evidence thus obtained – for instance on the grounds that they were members or supporters of a terrorist organisation (cf. §§ 129a, 129b of the Criminal Code).

II.

11 1. The *Land* North Rhine-Westphalia participated in the coordinated nationwide electronic profiling measures.

No. 39 – Profiling

a) By the order challenged in the present constitutional complaint proceedings, the Local Court authorised electronic profiling measures on 2 October 2001 at the request of the Düsseldorf police. The court order compelled all residents' registration offices of the *Land* North Rhine-Westphalia, the Central Register of Foreigners based in Cologne, and all universities, higher education institutions and universities of applied sciences in North Rhine-Westphalia to share [certain personal] data on men born between 1 October 1960 and 1 October 1983. [...]

[...]

b) The court order was based on § 31 of the NRW Police Act in the version published on 24 February 1990 (GVBl p. 70). [...]

[...]

The provision was amended in 2003. In the version published on 25 July 2003 (GVBl p. 441), § 31(1) of the NRW Police Act no longer requires the existence of a present danger (*gegenwärtige Gefahr*). [...]

[...]

2. Based on the challenged court order, electronic profiling was further carried out in North Rhine-Westphalia as follows:

The bodies addressed by the order first transferred approximately 5.2 million data records compiled according to the "criteria for selecting persons of interest". [...]

In an automated procedure, these data records were then cross-checked against the further profiling criteria that had been agreed as part of the nationwide coordination of the measure. According to information by the Ministry of Justice of the *Land* North Rhine-Westphalia, this resulted in 11,004 data records with positive matches. According to the Officer for Data Protection and Freedom of Information for the *Land* North Rhine-Westphalia, the other data records (5,222,717) were deleted by 10 December 2001. The data storage devices provided by the transferring bodies were destroyed.

[...]

III.

1. The complainant, who was born in 1978, is a Moroccan national of Muslim faith. At the time the challenged order was issued, he was a student at Duisburg University. He filed a complaint against the order of the Local Court. [...]

In an order that is also challenged in the present proceedings, the Regional Court rejected the complaint as unfounded. [...]

36-37 [...]
38 2. The complainant filed a further complaint against the Regional Court's order, which was rejected by the Higher Regional Court in an order that is also challenged here. [...]
39-49 [...]

IV.

50 1. The complainant claims that the challenged court decisions violate his fundamental right to informational self-determination under Art. 2(1) in conjunction with Art. 1(1) of the Basic Law.

51-56 [...]

V.

57 Statements on the constitutional complaint were submitted by the Ministry of Justice of the *Land* North Rhine-Westphalia, the Officer for Data Protection and Freedom of Information of the *Land* North Rhine-Westphalia, the Federal Criminal Police Office and the Federal Data Protection Officer.

58-64 [...]

B.

65 The constitutional complaint is admissible and well-founded.

66 The challenged decisions violate the complainant's fundamental right to informational self-determination under Art. 2(1) in conjunction with Art. 1(1) of the Basic Law. While the statutory provision on which the interferences are based is constitutional, the courts have interpreted the provision in a manner that is incompatible with the aforementioned fundamental right; even the legislator could not have enacted statutory provisions with the contents of the courts' interpretation without violating this fundamental right. The application of the provision in the case at hand is based on this [unconstitutional] interpretation.

I.

67 The court order authorising electronic profiling is based on § 31(1) of the 1990 NRW Police Act; this provision is formally and substantively compatible with the Constitution.

No. 39 – Profiling

1. § 31(1) of the 1990 NRW Police Act authorises interferences with the fundamental right to informational self-determination guaranteed by Art. 2(1) in conjunction with Art. 1(1) of the Basic Law.

a) Based on the notion of self-determination, this right confers upon the individual the authority to, in principle, decide themselves whether and to what extent to disclose aspects of their personal life (cf. BVerfGE 65, 1 <43> – *Census*; 78, 77 <84> – *Public Announcement of Legal Incapacitation*; 84, 192 <194>; 96, 171 <181>; 103, 21 <32 and 33> – *DNA Fingerprinting*; 113, 29 <46> – *Seizure of Electronic Data*). It affords fundamental rights holders protection against the unlimited collection, storage, use or sharing of personal data that is individualised or that can otherwise be attributed to them as individual persons (cf. BVerfGE 65, 1 <43> – *Census*; 67, 100 <143>; 84, 239 <279>; 103, 21 <33> – *DNA Fingerprinting*; BVerfGE 115, 166 <188> – *Telecommunications Surveillance*). It is a prerequisite for individual self-determination – especially in light of modern information technology – that the individual be afforded the freedom to decide whether to take or refrain from certain actions, including the possibility to actually conduct themselves in accordance with this decision. If individuals cannot, with sufficient certainty, determine what kind of personal information is known to certain parts of their social environment, and if it is difficult to ascertain what kind of information potential communication partners are privy to, this could greatly impede their freedom to make self-determined plans or decisions (cf. BVerfGE 65, 1 <42 and 43> – *Census*).

Monitoring or surveillance measures by the police can affect the scope of protection of this fundamental right and amount to interferences (cf. BVerfGE 110, 33 <56>). This holds true in particular where personal data is collected and stored for the purposes of electronic data processing. As a consequence, this data can be retrieved at any time within seconds, without distance being an issue. In addition, the personal data in question can be compared with data collected from other sources, especially by creating integrated information systems, allowing for numerous possibilities of using and linking the data (cf. BVerfGE 65, 1 <42> – *Census*). The increased risk associated with such technical possibilities in the context of modern data processing is reflected in the level of fundamental rights protection afforded in this respect (cf. BVerfGE 65, 1 <42> – *Census*; 113, 29 <45 and 46> – *Seizure of Electronic Data*).

b) The authorisation of measures under § 31 of the 1990 NRW Police Act affects the scope of protection of the right to informational self-determination.

The statutory powers concern different types of information that vary in their relevance to the right of personality. There is no need to determine whether the right to informational self-determination affords protection against the collection of each individual data item covered by the measure, since the knowledge of each data item in connection with other data allows for distinct insights into one's personal domain. The combination of the data expressly listed in § 31(2) of the 1990 NRW Police Act – name, address, date and place of birth – with other data such as, in the present case, nationality, religion or field of studies can, and is intended to, provide information on certain behaviours that may be considered suspicious; specifically, this refers to "characteristics increasing potential danger associated with these persons" – as is now explicitly stated in the amended § 31(1) of the 2003 NRW Police Act. The fundamental right to informational self-determination affords protection against the collection and processing of data carried out to this end.

73   c) § 31(1) of the 1990 NRW Police Act authorises interferences with the fundamental right to informational self-determination of the persons whose data is shared [for the purposes of electronic profiling].

74   aa) The court order for the sharing of the requested data constitutes an interference, given that it provides the basis for recording and storing the data and for cross-checking it against other data. The resulting effects on the right to personal self-determination of affected persons show that the order amounts to an interference. It makes the data available to the authorities and is the basis for the subsequent cross-checking with search terms. This qualifies as an interference, unless data is recorded incidentally for purely technical reasons and then deleted immediately and anonymously, without leaving traces and without any interest on the part of the authorities in obtaining knowledge of the data (cf. BVerfGE 100, 313 <366> – *The Article 10 Act*; 107, 299 <328>). [...]

75   Electronic profiling pursuant to § 31(1) of the 1990 NRW Police Act certainly amounts to an interference with respect to persons whose data is subject to further measures, in particular further cross-checking, after the initial cross-checking has been concluded. The order to share data impairs these persons' right to informational self-determination [...] and makes them a potential target of state surveillance measures.

76   In the case at hand, the sharing of data must be considered an interference with fundamental rights regarding the approximately 11,000 persons whose data records were initially selected for further processing measures after they were singled out from the records shared by the *Land* authorities since they matched the criteria agreed in the nationwide coordination of the measure. The records that yielded positive matches were forwarded to the Federal Criminal Police Office for further processing; they were entered into the national sleeper database and cross-checked against further databases. [...]

[...]

bb) The storage of the data – even if it is only temporary – by the receiving body, which retains it and makes it available for cross-checking, interferes with the right to informational self-determination of the persons whose data is subject to further measures after the initial cross-checking (cf. BVerfGE 100, 313 <366> – *The Article 10 Act*).

cc) With respect to these persons, even the cross-checking of the data itself amounts to an interference as it determines the selection of data for further analysis (cf. BVerfGE 100, 313 <366> – *The Article 10 Act*).

2. The authorisation to interfere with fundamental rights laid down in § 31(1) of the 1990 NRW Police Act satisfies the constitutional requirements.

a) The fundamental right to informational self-determination is not guaranteed without limitation. Rather, the individual must accept that this right is subject to restrictions serving overriding public interests (cf. BVerfGE 65, 1 <43 and 44> – *Census*). However, such restrictions require a statutory basis that must be constitutional, satisfying in particular the requirements of proportionality and legal clarity (cf. BVerfGE 65, 1 <44> – *Census*).

b) § 31(1) of the 1990 NRW Police Act, which restricts the aforementioned fundamental right, satisfies the principle of proportionality. This principle requires that the state, in interfering with fundamental rights, pursue a legitimate purpose by suitable, necessary and appropriate means (cf. BVerfGE 109, 279 <335 *et seq.*> – *Surveillance of Private Homes*).

aa) The provision serves the legitimate purpose of averting danger to the existence or security of the Federation or a *Land*, or to life, limb or liberty of the person.

bb) Electronic profiling is also a suitable means for achieving this purpose.

A law is suitable for achieving its purpose if it is conducive to the outcome sought (cf. BVerfGE 67, 157 <173, 175>; 90, 145 <172>; 100, 313 <373> – *The Article 10 Act*; 109, 279 <336> – *Surveillance of Private Homes*). This is the case here. The suitability of the statutory provision is not called into question merely because the method of data collection indiscriminately affects a large number of persons yet only yields useful intelligence in comparatively few cases (cf. BVerfGE 100, 313 <373> – *The Article 10 Act*).

cc) The interference is also necessary for achieving the legislative purpose. There are no less restrictive means that would be equally effective in achieving the purpose pursued.

dd) The statutory authorisation respects the limits of proportionality in its strict sense.

The principle of proportionality in its strict sense requires that the severity of the interference, in an overall assessment, not be disproportionate to the weight of the reasons invoked to justify it (established case-law; cf. BVerfGE 90, 145 <173>; 92, 277 <327>; 109, 279 <349 et seq.> – *Surveillance of Private Homes*). Based on this standard, the review of proportionality may lead to the conclusion that even though a measure protecting legal interests is suitable and necessary as such, it is nevertheless impermissible because the resulting interferences with fundamental rights would outweigh the gain in protection of legal interests, rendering the use of the measure in question inappropriate (cf. BVerfGE 90, 145 <173>). With regard to the tension between the state's duty to guarantee the protection of legal interests and the interest of the individual in upholding their constitutionally guaranteed rights, it is primarily incumbent on the legislator to achieve an abstract balance between the conflicting interests (cf. BVerfGE 109, 279 <350> – *Surveillance of Private Homes*). As a result, certain particularly intrusive interferences with fundamental rights may only be permissible when the suspicion or danger prompting the interference reaches a certain threshold. The relevant thresholds for carrying out the measures constituting interferences must be set out in statutory provisions (cf. BVerfGE 100, 313 <383 and 384> – *The Article 10 Act*; 109, 279 <350 et seq.> – *Surveillance of Private Homes* [...]).

89 In the context of electronic profiling, this requires that the legislator make the measures resulting in interferences with fundamental rights contingent upon the existence of a specific danger (*konkrete Gefahr*) to the legal interests under threat. § 31(1) of the 1990 NRW Police Act meets this standard.

90 (1) The interference authorised by § 31 of the 1990 NRW Police Act serves to protect high-ranking constitutional interests.

91 The existence and the security of the Federation and of the *Länder*, as well as life, limb and liberty of the person, which the provision aims to protect against dangers, are legal interests of significant constitutional weight. The security of the state, as a constituted power of peace and order, as well as the security of the population it is bound to protect – while respecting the dignity and the intrinsic value of the individual – rank equally with other constitutional values that are accorded high standing (cf. BVerfGE 49, 24 <56 and 57>).

92 [...]

93 (2) In order to protect these legal interests, § 31 of the 1990 NRW Police Act authorises particularly weighty interferences with the right to informational self-determination.

94 (a) In the legal assessment of the type of interferences covered by the statutory authorisation, it is significant *inter alia* how many holders of fundamental rights are affected by impairments, how intense these impairments are, and on what basis they occur, in particular whether the affected persons have prompted them (cf. BVerfGE 100, 313 <376> – *The Article 10 Act;* 107, 299 <318 et seq.>;

No. 39 – Profiling

109, 279 <353> – *Surveillance of Private Homes*). Thus, relevant criteria include the design of the statutory thresholds for carrying out the measures constituting interferences, the number of persons affected and also the severity of the individual impairments (cf. BVerfGE 100, 313 <376> – *The Article 10 Act*). The weight of individual impairments depends on whether the persons concerned remain anonymous, what personal information is recorded, and what disadvantages the holders of fundamental rights might face or have reason to fear on account of the measures (cf. BVerfGE 100, 313 <376> – *The Article 10 Act*; 109, 279 <353> – *Surveillance of Private Homes*).

The Federal Constitutional Court has so far primarily developed criteria for assessing the severity of interferences with information-related fundamental rights in decisions concerning the privacy of telecommunications under Art. 10(1) of the Basic Law and the fundamental right to the inviolability of the home under Art. 13(1) of the Basic Law. As these are specific manifestations of the fundamental right to informational self-determination (cf. BVerfGE 51, 97 <105>; 100, 313 <358> – *The Article 10 Act*; 109, 279 <325 and 326> – *Surveillance of Private Homes*), the standards developed in this regard also apply to the more general fundamental right at issue here, unless they are informed by considerations that are particular to the specific guarantees [under Art. 10 and Art. 13 of the Basic Law]. 95

(b) It is true that electronic profiling concerns information that in itself is typically less closely related to one's personality than is the case for information resulting in interferences with the fundamental rights under Art. 10(1) and Art. 13(1) of the Basic Law. Nevertheless, the interferences resulting from electronic profiling are also of considerable weight in view of the general fundamental right to informational self-determination, given the broad substantive scope of the authorisation and the possibilities it creates for the linking of data. 96

(aa) The weight of an interference with the right to informational self-determination depends, *inter alia*, on what information is subject to the interference, in particular how closely related the information is to one's personality, both in itself and when linked to other information, and on the way it is obtained (cf. BVerfGE 100, 313 <376> – *The Article 10 Act*; 107, 299 <319 and 320>; 109, 279 <353> – *Surveillance of Private Homes*). 97

Accordingly, the interference is particularly intrusive where it concerns information obtained in violation of expectations of confidentiality, especially in matters that are afforded special fundamental rights protection, as is the case regarding interferences with the fundamental right to the inviolability of the home under Art. 13 of the Basic Law or the privacy of telecommunications under Art. 10 of the Basic Law (cf. BVerfGE 109, 279 <313 and 314, 325, 327 and 328> – *Surveillance of Private Homes*; 113, 348 <364 and 365, 383, 391>). 98

99 All information covered by electronic profiling relates to individuals and provides insights regarding their personality, given that the information is linked to other data. Information that is particularly closely related to one's personality includes, most notably, information pertaining to matters protected by further constitutional guarantees, such as Art. 3(3) of the Basic Law or Art. 140 of the Basic Law in conjunction with Art. 136(3) of the Weimar Constitution. At the level of statutory law, this is reflected in the recognition of "special categories of personal data" in § 3(9) of the Federal Data Protection Act. These categories include information on racial and ethnic origin, political opinions, religious or philosophical beliefs, trade union membership and data concerning one's health or sex life.

100 (bb) The interference with fundamental rights authorised in the statutory basis for electronic profiling generally has considerable weight in view of the contents of both the data shared for this purpose and the data used for cross-checking. The same applies to further information that can be obtained from linking and cross-checking the different data records.

101 The data shared for the purposes of electronic profiling as such can already be closely related to an individual's personality. Based on the provision's legislative history, electronic profiling primarily focuses on the specifically listed identifying data, i.e. name, address, date and place of birth. Yet the statutory authorisation is not limited to this data. Rather, it also allows "any other type of data, as necessary in the individual case" to be included in the measure (§ 31(2) first sentence, first half-sentence of the 1990 NRW Police Act). The only data that may not be requested is personal data protected by professional confidentiality or special rules of official secrecy (§ 31(2) first sentence, second half-sentence of the 1990 NRW Police Act). Other than that, the provision does not further restrict the type and contents of the data used in electronic profiling. Accordingly, data requests can be extended to include further information on religion, nationality, civil status and field of studies – which occurred in the case at hand. The statutory authorisation thus also covers personal data that individuals may very much want to keep private and that they expect to be treated confidentially, such as one's religious beliefs. This may also be true with regard to the "other data records" against which the shared data is cross-checked. In addition, the compiling and linking of the shared data sets and other data sets, and the mutual cross-checking of the data, may yield a wide variety of new information. The type and contents of this new information may have a particularly close link to one's personality.

102 (c) When an authorisation to share data extends to almost all personal data available at any public or non-public body, like the authorisation under § 31(1) of the 1990 NRW Police Act, it creates the basis for particularly intrusive interferences

No. 39 – Profiling

due to the variety and scope of the data that may be subject to the authorised measures.

Apart from the general requirement of proportionality (cf. § 2 of the 1990 NRW Police Act), the NRW Police Act does not provide for any limitation regarding the scope of data that may be requested for the purposes of electronic profiling. There is no such limitation, not even an indirect one, neither regarding the type of data requested nor regarding targeted persons, given that any public body and any "body outside the public sector" can be requested to share data according to the wording of § 31(1) of the 1990 NRW Police Act. The provision covers all bodies controlling personal data, with the exception of matters for which sector-specific rules set out definitive prohibitions of data sharing. [...] 103

The authorisation thus makes it possible for one body, where that body considers it necessary, to centrally compile and cross-check all data – concerning any person and stored at any public or private body –, subject to the restriction laid down in § 31(2) of the 1990 NRW Police Act and the general limits set by the principle of proportionality. In doing so, it uses the unique possibilities created by information technologies with regard to the processing and linking of data. Therefore, data that by itself appears insignificant may gain new relevance (cf. BVerfGE 65, 1 <45> – *Census*). 104

Consequently, there is a risk that the strict prohibition of collecting data for retention, other than for statistical purposes (cf. BVerfGE 65, 1 <47> – *Census*), is circumvented. [...] 105

Moreover, given the amount and variety of personal data available today on almost any person – when looking at all the data held by public and private bodies combined – the authorisation to access data under § 31 of the 1990 NRW Police Act comes at least close to allowing the linking of data from different data collections to create partial or almost complete personality profiles – which would be impermissible under constitutional law (cf. BVerfGE 65, 1 <42> – *Census*). In particular, the statutory authorisation also applies to all data records held by private bodies ("bodies outside the public sector") [...]. To satisfy constitutional law, the statutory authorisation to access data under § 31 of the 1990 NRW Police Act must be interpreted to the effect that it does not allow for a comprehensive registration and cataloguing of one's personality by means of compiling personality profiles of the citizens concerned on the basis of their biographical and personal data – this would be impermissible even if it were done anonymously for statistical surveys (cf. BVerfGE 165, 1 <53> – *Census*). Nonetheless, the collection and linking of certain data authorised in that provision might come close to the creation of personality profiles, which is why the resulting interference with fundamental rights must be regarded as particularly intrusive. 106

107 (d) The severity of the interference is furthermore determined by other possible consequences resulting from electronic profiling.

108 The weight of information-related interferences with fundamental rights *inter alia* depends on the disadvantages that affected persons might face or have reason to fear on account of the interferences (cf. BVerfGE 100, 313 <376> – *The Article 10 Act*; 107, 299 <320>). The sharing and use of data may expose affected persons to an increased risk of becoming the target of investigation measures by the state, beyond the general risk of being falsely suspected of wrongdoing (cf. BVerfGE 107, 299 <321>). In addition, information-related investigation measures may stigmatise affected persons in the event that these measures become publicly known. This may indirectly increase these persons' risk of being discriminated against in their everyday or professional life.

109 Both these concerns apply to the interferences with fundamental rights linked to electronic profiling.

110 (aa) The fundamental rights holders affected by interferences resulting from electronic profiling face an increased risk of becoming the target of further investigation measures carried out by the authorities. […]

111 (bb) Furthermore, electronic profiling based on certain criteria that is carried out by the police may stigmatise persons who meet these criteria if the measures become publicly known. […] The more closely the attributes determining who is targeted by state measures resemble the grounds listed in Art. 3(3) of the Basic Law, the more strictly the authorities are bound by the right to equality under constitutional law (established case-law; cf., e.g., BVerfGE 92, 26 <51>) and the higher the severity of an interference with fundamental rights linked to unequal treatment – in this case with the fundamental right to informational self-determination –, even if the measure as such does not amount to discrimination based on the grounds of Art. 3(3) of the Basic Law.

112 For instance, for determining the severity of the interference resulting from the electronic profiling measures carried out after 9/11, it is significant that they are directed against foreigners of a certain origin and Muslim faith. Such measures invariably entail the risk of perpetuating prejudice and stigmatising these communities in the public eye. […] This bears on the severity of the interferences under the statutory authorisation of § 31(1) of the 1990 NRW Police Act, which allows for electronic profiling measures that differentiate based on such criteria.

113 (e) The fact that the statutory provision only provides for individual notification of some but not all affected persons, and only upon completion of the electronic profiling measure, also bears on the severity of the interference. Covert measures by the state result in more intrusive interferences (cf. BVerfGE 107, 299 <321>; 115, 166 <194> – *Telecommunications Surveillance*). § 31(5) first sentence of the

1990 NRW Police Act only provides for individual notification of affected persons, once electronic profiling has been concluded, in cases where further measures are carried out against these persons, and only if it does not jeopardise the purpose of further data use. Pursuant to § 31(5) second sentence of the 1990 NRW Police Act, affected persons are not notified if, based on the facts [established during the measure], criminal investigations are launched against them.

It is true that the requirement of a judicial order under § 31(4) first sentence of the 1990 NRW Police Act mitigates the covert nature of the measure, provided that the order is made public – as was the case here [...]. This allows persons potentially affected to realise that they are part of the group of persons targeted by electronic profiling. They may then seek legal protection – like the complainant in the case at hand. However, the law does not require publication of the order. If, unlike in this case, it is not made public, affected persons remain oblivious, unless they are individually notified.

114

(f) It is also significant that persons affected by electronic profiling do not always remain anonymous (cf. BVerfGE 100, 313 <381> – *The Article 10 Act*; 107, 299 <320 and 321>). The anonymity is lifted at least regarding the persons whose data shows up as a match in the final results once the profiling as such has been concluded. The data of these persons is personalised precisely to make it possible to carry out further investigation measures against them.

115

(g) Finally, it is also significant that § 31(1) of the 1990 NRW Police Act provides for interferences with fundamental rights that do not require any grounds for suspicion and indiscriminately affect a large number of persons.

116

(aa) Interferences with fundamental rights are generally particularly intrusive if they do not require any grounds for suspicion and indiscriminately affect a large number of persons, i.e. if the measure affects numerous persons who are neither connected to specific wrongdoing nor prompted the interference with their conduct (cf. BVerfGE 100, 313 <376, 392> – *The Article 10 Act*; 107, 299 <320 and 321>; 109, 279 <353> – *Surveillance of Private Homes*; 113, 29 <53> – *Seizure of Electronic Data*; 113, 348 <383>). The less individuals prompted the state interference, the more severely their fundamental rights are affected. Such interferences may also create chilling effects, which may impair the exercise of fundamental rights (cf. BVerfGE 65, 1 <42> – *Census*; 113, 29 <46> – *Seizure of Electronic Data*). A deterrent effect on the exercise of fundamental rights must be avoided, not only to protect the subjective rights of the individuals concerned. It would also affect the common good because self-determination is a fundamental prerequisite for the functioning of a free and democratic society which relies on the agency and participation of its citizens (cf. BVerfGE 113, 29 <46> – *Seizure of Electronic Data*). People might no longer act without worry or fear if the indiscriminate effect

117

of investigation measures contributes to risks of abuse and a sense of being under surveillance (cf. BVerfGE 107, 299 <328>).

118 (bb) Electronic profiling pursuant to § 31(1) of the 1990 NRW Police Act constitutes an interference that does not require any grounds for suspicion. The provision confers powers to carry out interferences against persons who are not themselves linked to a danger to public security (*Nichtstörer*), as it does not require that the target of the measure constituting an interference be responsible for the danger in question. According to the 1990 version of the law, the measure can be extended to all persons who meet the selection criteria, without setting out any requirements as to the proximity of these persons to the danger or to persons of interest. […]

119 Particularly in cases where electronic profiling serves to uncover so-called sleeper terrorists, it constitutes an "interference for the purposes of identifying suspicious activities or persons of interest" (*Verdachts- oder Verdächtigungsgewinnungseingriff*) […]. Given the presumption that sleepers are characterised precisely by their completely conformist and thus inconspicuous behaviour, there are, by definition, no specific indications of behaviour that might point to them as persons responsible for potential dangers. Therefore, electronic profiling that aims to identify such persons requires that profiles of perpetrators be based on relatively unspecific assumptions and, accordingly, that unspecific search criteria be applied. As a consequence, and in a departure from traditional principles of police law governing public security, the search measures take place on grounds so precautionary in nature that a specific suspicion that someone poses a danger has not arisen yet. This differs fundamentally from a situation where the authorities search for a group of perpetrators who are in principle identifiable through specific behaviour that deviates from the norm. […]

120 Compared to the circumstances typical of earlier electronic profiling measures, the fact that the measure at issue does not require any grounds for suspicion is further aggravated as precisely the inconspicuousness and conformity of behaviour become a significant criterion in the search. This is obvious in the coordinated electronic profiling measures carried out across Germany in the present case. There were no specific indications to suggest even remotely that precisely the persons affected by the measure were so-called sleepers or were in contact with such sleepers; this is true for the approximately 5.2 million persons whose data was transferred to the Düsseldorf police and for the approximately 32,000 persons whose data was included in the nationwide database of sleepers according to information provided by the Federal Data Protection Officer. […]

121 (cc) Moreover, electronic profiling can have indiscriminate effects on an exceptionally large number of persons, as shown by the number of persons affected in the case at hand.

No. 39 – Profiling

(α) As a search method, electronic profiling offers the advantages generally associated with automated, computer-based operations, i.e. the ability to process virtually unlimited and complex information at high speed. This leads to an unprecedented leap of effectiveness in relation to conventional investigation methods, where authorities operate by gradually gathering and connecting more and more relevant information [...]. With regard to fundamental rights, this new quality of police investigation measures results in more intrusive interferences.

(β) To assess the appropriateness of such measures, not only the number of persons affected by electronic profiling in a manner that qualifies as an interference with their fundamental rights must be taken into account, but also the overall number of persons whose data is covered by the measure, due to the objective importance of the fundamental right to informational self-determination (cf. BVerfGE 107, 299 <328>).

If data is compiled according to relatively unspecific criteria, a very large number of persons may initially be affected by electronic profiling who, from an *ex ante* perspective, are neither suspicious nor linked to a danger. Even the group of persons that fit the search criteria used in an initial cross-checking may – as the present case shows – comprise a large number of persons that even from an *ex post* perspective are not linked to a danger, at least in the vast majority of cases.

(3) Given the high-ranking constitutional interests that § 31(1) of the 1990 NRW Police Act serves to protect, the interference resulting from electronic profiling is not disproportionate as such. Nevertheless, the measure constituting an interference is only appropriate if the legislator observes the requirements deriving from the rule of law by subjecting the measure to a threshold in the form of a sufficiently specific danger to the legal interests under threat.

(a) The state may, and must, effectively counteract terrorist threats with the necessary means permissible under the rule of law; these threats include, for instance, endeavours that aim to destroy the free democratic basic order and that use systematic killing as a means to realise this aim (cf. BVerfGE 49, 24 <56>). Yet the Basic Law also requires that state action remain limited to the means permissible under the rule of law.

The Basic Law contains a mandate to avert impairments to the foundations of the free and democratic order, subject to the requirements deriving from the rule of law (cf. BVerfGE 111, 147 <158>; [...]). The strength of the state under the rule of law is reflected precisely in its adherence to general principles, even in the face of its adversaries [...].

This also applies when the state pursues the fundamental aims of ensuring the security and protection of its people. The Constitution requires that the legislator strike an appropriate balance between freedom and security. This does not only preclude the state from seeking to attain absolute security, which in practice could hardly be achieved anyway, at least not without the sacrifice of abolishing freedom. Under the Basic Law, the aim of attaining the highest level of security possible under the given circumstances is subject to restrictions deriving from the rule of law, including the prohibition of inappropriate interferences with fundamental rights in their dimension as rights defending against state interference.

129 This prohibition also limits the state's duties of protection. Fundamental rights serve to protect the sphere of individual freedom against interference by public authorities; they are defensive rights of the citizen against the state (cf. BVerfGE 7, 198 <204 and 205>). Where fundamental rights function as objective principles, giving rise to duties of protection (cf. BVerfGE 96, 56 <64>), this function serves, in principle, to strengthen the normative force of fundamental rights; however, this function still remains rooted in the primary function of fundamental rights as defensive rights (cf. BVerfGE 50, 290 <337>).

130 When choosing the means for fulfilling a constitutional duty of protection, the state is thus limited to using means that are compatible with the Constitution (cf. BVerfGE 115, 118 <160>). Regardless of the weight attached to the constitutional interests the state is bound to protect, interferences with the absolutely protected right of the individual to respect for one's person (*Achtungsanspruch*) (cf. BVerfGE 109, 279 <313> – *Surveillance of Private Homes*) are always prohibited (cf. BVerfGE 115, 118 <152 *et seq.*>). Yet, even where a balancing of interests is required under the principle of proportionality in its strict sense, the duties of protection under the Basic Law must not be invoked so as to render meaningless the prohibition of inappropriate interferences with fundamental rights, with the effect that the principle of proportionality would no longer afford protection except in cases of unsuitable or unnecessary interferences.

131 (b) [...]

132 (c) In the context of electronic profiling pursuant to § 31(1) of the 1990 NRW Police Act, the principle of proportionality does not give rise to an absolute prohibition of interferences with personality-related fundamental rights for investigative purposes. However, the authorisation to carry out electronic profiling resembles measures interfering with the privacy of telecommunications for strategic surveillance purposes to the extent that the aforementioned authorisation also provides for interferences with fundamental rights that do not require any grounds for suspicion and indiscriminately affect a large number of persons. [...]

133 (d). The interferences with fundamental rights resulting from electronic profiling are of considerable weight, especially considering that the prerequisites for such interferences are not narrowly defined in the law. As a result, it is only permissible for the legislator to authorise electronic profiling for the protection of the high-

ranking legal interests set out in § 31(1) of the 1990 NRW Police Act on condition that there is a specific danger to these interests.

When the legislator designs powers to carry out measures constituting interferences, it is not necessarily bound by the limits to interferences deriving from the traditional understanding of the term 'danger' in police law. However, where the severity of interference is as high as in the present case, the legislator may only set a lower threshold if particular proportionality requirements are observed. Yet these requirements are not met if the measure constituting an interference with fundamental rights does not require any grounds for suspicion, which is the case for electronic profiling. Therefore, under constitutional law, electronic profiling may only be carried out in cases of specific danger [as the relevant threshold]. 134

(aa) The Constitution does not generally prevent the legislator from further developing, in line with its prerogative, the traditional requirements deriving from the rule of law in the field of police law on the basis of new or evolving situations of danger and threat. The legislator may readjust the balance between freedom and security, yet it must not fundamentally shift the underlying weighing. 135

With respect to the principle of proportionality in the strict sense, the legislator must maintain a balance between the type and severity of the impairments of fundamental rights on the one hand and the statutory prerequisites for carrying out the measures constituting interferences on the other hand, such as the statutory threshold for interference, the required factual basis and the weight of the protected legal interests (cf. BVerfGE 100, 313 <392 et seq.> – *The Article 10 Act*). The greater the weight of possible or actual impairments of legal interests and the lesser the weight of the interference with fundamental rights at issue, the more acceptable it becomes to lower the degree of probability required for establishing a violation (or risk thereof) of the respective legal interest, and the degree of certainty required for establishing the facts on which the suspicion is based (cf. BVerfGE 100, 313 <392> – *The Article 10 Act*; 110, 33 <60>; 113, 348 <386>). However, the statutory requirements pertaining to the degree of probability and the factual basis of the prognosis must not be lowered arbitrarily; rather, they must be proportionate to the type and intensity of the resulting impairment of fundamental rights and to the prospects of success regarding the intended protection of legal interests. Even where the threats the interference aims to avert concern exceptionally weighty legal interests, the requirement of sufficient probability cannot be dispensed with. In addition, the statutory basis must subject any serious interference with fundamental rights to the requirement that the assumptions and conclusions prompting the interference be based on specific facts (cf. BVerfGE 113, 348 <386>). In particular, the Constitution does not allow interferences with fundamental rights that result from purely speculative investigations (cf. BVerfGE 112, 284 <297>; […]). 136

137 In accordance with the principle of proportionality, the legislator may only provide for particularly intrusive interferences with fundamental rights in the event that certain levels of suspicion or danger are met (cf. BVerfGE 100, 313 <383 and 384> – *The Article 10 Act*; 109, 279 <350 et seq.> – *Surveillance of Private Homes*). [...] The question whether an interference with fundamental rights for the purposes of averting potential future impairments of legal interests, as a purely precautionary measure before a specific danger arises, can be considered proportionate depends not only on its prospects of success (cf. on the requirement of sufficient prospects of success BVerfGE 42, 212 <220>; 96, 44 <51>; 115, 166 <198> – *Telecommunications Surveillance*); it also depends on the requirements laid down in the statutory provision governing the interference regarding the connection between the persons affected by the measure and the threat to the legal interest in question (cf. BVerfGE 100, 313 <395> – *The Article 10 Act*; 107, 299 <322 and 323, 329>; 110, 33 <60 and 61>; 113, 348 <385 et seq., 389>). If the legislator authorises particularly serious interferences but fails to set restrictive requirements pertaining to the probability that the danger will materialise and to a sufficient connection between the affected persons and the threat the measure seeks to avert, it does not satisfy constitutional law.

138 (bb) Based on these standards, electronic profiling is not permissible as a purely precautionary measure before a specific danger arises, since it would result in interferences with fundamental rights that potentially concern highly sensitive personal information without requiring any grounds for suspicion while indiscriminately affecting a large number of persons.

139 Compared to other purely precautionary investigation measures relating to individuals that the Federal Constitutional Court considered not to be impermissible from the outset, electronic profiling under the NRW Police Act differs in that it does not require any facts-based connection between a threat situation and a person specifically responsible for it for that person becoming the potential target of investigation. As a measure to "identify persons of interest", electronic profiling neither serves to further investigate specific persons suspected of criminal conduct (cf. in this respect BVerfGE 107, 299 <314 et seq., 326 et seq.>), nor to further consolidate a suspicion, established by other means, that certain persons pose a threat [to protected legal interests] (cf. in this respect BVerfGE 100, 313 <395> – *The Article 10 Act*; 110, 33 <58 et seq., 61>; 113, 348 <375 et seq., 378 et seq., 383>).

140 The Federal Constitutional Court has emphasised the requirement deriving from the rule of law that in cases where neither a suspicion that a person is responsible for a danger to public security nor a criminal suspicion has been established, it is still necessary to establish a sufficient factual basis showing a connection

No. 39 – Profiling

between persons affected by the measure and possible violations of legal interests. In the case of electronic profiling, this requirement is rendered meaningless, as this measure does not in any way require that a chain of factual evidence be established, pointing to at least somewhat specific grounds for suspicion of criminal conduct relating to an individual. It follows that there are shortcomings in terms of the rule of law, given that electronic profiling typically does not require a sufficiently close connection between the threatened legal interest the measure aims to protect and the persons affected by the interference with fundamental rights resulting from the measure; these shortcomings must be compensated in other ways in order to ensure that the authorisation to carry out this measure does not become devoid of any limitation. In the case at hand, the legislator chose not to define the electronic profiling measures authorised for protecting the relevant legal interests in such a way that possible interferences with fundamental rights resulting therefrom do not result in notable impairments for the persons affected by the measure. Nor did the legislator subject the power to carry out the interferences to strictly limited grounds. This is only compatible with the constitutional requirements if the statutory authorisation at least requires a specific danger to the respective legal interest as prerequisite for carrying out the measure.

(cc) Under constitutional law, the statutory threshold for carrying out electronic profiling measures does not necessarily have to be the requirement of a present danger in the traditional sense; however, as a minimum threshold, the statutory authorisation must at least require the existence of a specific danger. 141

(α) § 31 of the 1990 NRW Police Act sets forth the requirement of a present danger, which is the traditional statutory element [of police law] limiting, in line with the rule of law, the extent to which measures may affect persons that are not themselves responsible for a danger to public security. A danger is qualified as a present one when the damage resulting from a hazardous event has already begun to materialise or when such damage can be expected, in all probability, to occur immediately or in the very near future [...]. This satisfies the constitutional requirements regarding the statutory authorisation of electronic profiling. 142

Nevertheless, the requirement of a present danger in that sense is not a necessary prerequisite under constitutional law [with regard to electronic profiling]. It is true that it cannot be ruled out from the outset that electronic profiling might actually yield results within a short period of time in individual cases. Even so, in light of the efforts regularly required to carry out electronic profiling, the statutory requirement that damage will, in all probability, occur in the very near future means that in most cases where this requirement is satisfied, electronic profiling would be too late to be effective. Given the high standing of the legal interests set forth in 143

§ 31(1) of the 1990 NRW Police Act, such a far-reaching restriction of electronic profiling as a search measure is not necessary to ensure proportionality.

144 (β) Rather, it is sufficient that the legislator ties the permissibility of electronic profiling to the requirement of a specific danger to the legal interests in question. This means that there must be a situation where it is sufficiently likely, in the individual case, that damage to the protected legal interests will occur in the foreseeable future (cf., e.g., § 2(1) no. 1 lit. a of the Lower Saxony Public Security and Order Act). However, under constitutional law, the state bodies responsible for applying such a statutory authorisation are barred from interpreting the term 'danger' under police law in a way that disregards these requirements, which would lower the danger threshold [justifying the interference] to one that is below the constitutionally required minimum threshold for electronic profiling.

145 The probability prognosis required for establishing a specific danger must be based on facts. Vague indications or mere assumptions without tangible grounds relating to the individual case are not sufficient (cf. BVerfGE 44, 353 <381 and 382> – *Addiction Counselling Agency*; 69, 315 <353 and 354>).

146 (γ) A state of permanent danger (*Dauergefahr*) may also fit the elements of a specific danger within that meaning. Such a permanent danger is characterised by a sufficient probability that, over a longer period of time, damage might occur at any point. However, for establishing such a permanent danger, the requirements for establishing a specific danger apply accordingly, namely the requirement of a sufficient probability of damage and the requirement of a specific factual basis for the probability prognosis.

147 Therefore, sufficiently compelling and specific facts are required for establishing a specific permanent danger, for example the danger posed by so-called sleeper terrorists. [...]

148 (δ) Furthermore, making the permissibility of electronic profiling contingent upon the existence of a specific danger is also imperative as it provides the basis for determining the proportionality of electronic profiling in the individual case, and for further specifying the additional procedural and organisational requirements for carrying out the measure, which are not under review here. Without this limitation, it would not be possible to further define these additional requirements in line with the principle of legal specificity deriving from the rule of law.

149 c) The statutory authorisation in § 31(1) of the 1990 NRW Police Act satisfies the constitutional requirement of legal specificity and clarity, provided that its scope of application is understood in the meaning set out here.

150 aa) Authorisations to interfere with fundamental rights require a statutory basis that satisfies the requirement of legal specificity and clarity deriving from the rule of law (cf. BVerfGE 110, 33 <53>). For interferences with the fundamental right

No. 39 – Profiling

to informational self-determination – just as for interferences with the specific fundamental rights of Arts. 10 and 13 of the Basic Law – the legislator must specify precisely, for each subject matter, the purposes for which the data may be used (cf. BVerfGE 65, 1 <46> – *Census*; 110, 33 <70>; 113, 29 <51> – *Seizure of Electronic Data*). Pursuant to § 31(1) of the 1990 NRW Police Act, the sharing of data serves to enable the automated cross-checking of the shared data against other data sets, to the extent that this is necessary to avert certain dangers, namely dangers to the existence or security of the Federation or a *Land* or to life, limb or liberty of the person. Thus, the purpose for which the data may be used is the automated cross-checking of the shared data against other data sets to avert the dangers listed in § 31(1) of the 1990 NRW Police Act. This is sufficient.

Provisions governing the sharing of data must satisfy the requirement that the receiving authorities be designated in a sufficiently identifiable manner, along with rules ensuring that data sharing remain concentrated within the scope of the specific tasks assigned to those authorities (cf. in this respect BVerfGE 110, 33 <70>). This requirement is only satisfied if the term 'danger' serves to limit the statutory authorisation for data sharing. In the case at hand, the police are designated as the receiving authority for the shared data. The purpose for which the data may be used is limited to averting dangers to specifically listed and high-ranking protected interests of public security, i.e. a purpose that is part of the specific tasks assigned to police authorities (cf. § 1(1) first sentence of the 1990 NRW Police Act). 151

Under the above-mentioned conditions, § 31 of the 1990 NRW Police Act is also sufficiently specific regarding not only the types of data expressly listed, but also to the extent that "other data required in the individual case" may be requested and processed pursuant to § 31(2) of the 1990 NRW Police Act. In this respect, the requirements of legal specificity are met, given that the phrase "other data required in the individual case" can be interpreted more specifically – taking into consideration the legislative purpose of averting danger to public security, which also determines for which purposes "necessary" data may be requested – in such a way that the principle of proportionality is satisfied. 152

bb) By contrast, if measures were not limited by the requirement of a specific danger, there would be no sufficient basis for determining, based on the legislative purpose, what data may be covered by the measure, in particular what data constitutes "other data necessary in the individual case". Without the element of a specific danger, it cannot be established in a sufficiently specific manner, as required under constitutional law, under which circumstances data is considered "necessary in the individual case". For instance, if electronic profiling were based on the general threat of terrorism and if this general threat situation thus served as the basis for 153 determining what specific type of data is necessary for the police, the authorisation to use electronic profiling would essentially become devoid of any limitation. [...]

II.

154 The challenged decisions do not satisfy the constitutional requirements. They are based on an expansive interpretation of the term 'present danger' in § 31(1) of the 1990 NRW Police Act that is contrary to the principles set out above. As a result, the statutory authorisation is transformed into an authorisation conferring precautionary powers. This interpretation assigns a meaning to this provision that even the legislator could not have adopted without violating the fundamental right to informational self-determination under Art. 2(1) in conjunction with Art. 1(1) of the Basic Law.

155 1. It is true that the interpretation of statutory law and its application to the specific case fall to the competent ordinary courts and are generally not subject to review by the Federal Constitutional Court (established case-law; cf. BVerfGE 18, 85 <92 and 93>). The interpretation adopted by the ordinary courts, however, must be guided by the affected fundamental rights to ensure that the values enshrined therein are upheld when applying the relevant statutory provisions (established case-law; cf. BVerfGE 7, 198 <205 et seq.>; 101, 361 <388>). When ordinary courts interpret the scope of application of a statutory provision expansively, thereby assigning a meaning to that provision that even the legislator could not have adopted without violating fundamental rights, and the courts then base the application of that provision in the specific case on such an interpretation, they fail to recognise the significance and scope of fundamental rights (cf. BVerfGE 81, 29 <31 and 32>; 82, 6 <15 and 16>).

156 2. This is what the courts did in the case at hand. In the challenged decisions, the courts interpret the term 'present danger' in § 31(1) of the 1990 NRW Police Act in a manner that does not satisfy the constitutional requirements applicable to statutory provisions authorising electronic profiling, specifically the requirement that there be at least a specific danger.

157 a) The electronic profiling measures that were coordinated across Germany after 9/11 required the courts to take decisions in the context of a novel threat situation. This led to uncertainty with respect to handling the statutory basis authorising such measures. Some of the courts deciding on these electronic profiling measures held on to the traditional understanding of the term 'present danger' and found that a present danger did not exist in the cases before them [...]. In light of the magnitude of possible damage, however, other courts lowered the standard establishing the required probability of damage and, based on this standard, found the existence of a

present danger [...]. This is also what the courts in the challenged decisions did. The underlying interpretation of § 31(1) of the 1990 NRW Police Act does not satisfy the constitutional requirements.

b) The challenged decisions do not take into account that ordering electronic profiling is only permissible under constitutional law if it is subject to the existence of at least a specific danger and if the required degree of probability that a violation of legal interests will occur is established by taking into consideration not only the magnitude of possible damage, but also the weight of the interference resulting from the measure carried out to avert the relevant danger as well as its prospects of success. Based on the constitutional standards outlined above, electronic profiling may only interfere with the fundamental right to informational self-determination of a complete non-suspect if the existence of a danger can be established based on specific facts, giving rise to the assumption that measures can be taken on the basis of the investigation of data of a certain group of persons that contribute to averting this danger. 158

[...] 159-160

Contrary to constitutional law, the courts completely dispensed with the requirement that there must be a specific danger, i.e. danger in the individual case and based on sufficient facts, by lowering the threshold of probability to the mere [general] possibility of terrorist attacks. The courts did so by qualifying this [general] threat situation as a 'danger', thus assigning a meaning to this term that under constitutional law is not a sufficient basis for authorising electronic profiling. 161

3. The challenged decisions are informed by these constitutional shortcomings as it can reasonably be assumed that the courts would have reached a different conclusion if they had observed the constitutional requirements for interpreting the term 'present danger' in § 31(1) of the 1990 NRW Police Act. 162

III.

[...] 163

IV.

[...] 164-165

With regard to B II., the decision was taken with 6:2 votes; for the rest it was unanimous. 166

Justices: Papier, Haas, Hömig, Steiner, Hohmann-Dennhardt, Hoffmann-Riem, Bryde, Gaier

Dissenting Opinion of Justice Haas

167 I do not agree with the decision of the Senate majority to the extent that it holds the Higher Regional Court's order to be unconstitutional and reverses it. The Higher Regional Court's interpretation and application of § 31(1) of the 1990 NRW Police Act is not objectionable under constitutional law. [...] I agree with the Senate majority on the finding that § 31(1) of the 1990 NRW Police Act is constitutional, albeit for other reasons.

168 1. The Senate majority and the challenged decision by the Higher Regional Court correctly assume that § 31(1) of the 1990 NRW Police Act interferes with Art. 2(1) in conjunction with Art. 1(1) of the Basic Law. However, this holds true only with regard to data obtained on the basis of § 31(1) of the 1990 NRW Police Act that is not immediately deleted in an automated procedure (cf. BVerfGE 100, 313 <366> – *The Article 10 Act*; 107, 299 <328>). This means that the fundamental rights of the vast majority of persons whose data was used in the electronic profiling measures were not affected.

169 Moreover, the case at hand shows that even for the rest of the persons whose data is obtained and cross-checked, the interference is minor [...].

170 In my view, it is significant for assessing the severity of the interference that the authorisation to obtain and cross-check data on the basis of § 31(1) of the 1990 NRW Police Act only extends to data that has already been disclosed by the affected persons and is stored in databases. In this respect, it must be taken into account that the weight of the interference can only be assessed when considering the criteria on which the profile used in the specific measure was based, given the diversity of threat situations. In addition, information such as sex, place of residence, parenthood, field of study are accessible to anyone anyhow. Anyone can obtain knowledge of these attributes and life circumstances by observing the persons concerned and questioning persons in their social environment. Likewise, it is possible for the state to obtain such knowledge and use it, yet this does not necessarily amount to a particularly serious interference with the individual's general right of personality in each and every case. This holds true all the more where the data concerned has been disclosed specifically to state bodies by the affected persons themselves or where state bodies have recorded the data – in the interest of the affected persons – for other reasons, as is the case here.

No. 39 – Profiling

This also applies to a person's religion, in particular with regard to Muslims, who in general practice their faith openly and, in our free state, do not suffer disadvantages for it. [...] Contrary to the Senate majority's opinion, it cannot be claimed that the affected persons have particular expectations of privacy and confidentiality regarding their place of residence and the religion they practice, as this data is usually made public by the affected persons themselves. Despite what the Senate majority believes, there are no stigmatising effects resulting from cross-checking data on religious affiliation, given that electronic profiling is not carried out in public and thus will generally not become public knowledge. Moreover, we underestimate citizens if we assume that they would perceive the police measure in this way. [...]

The interference cannot be regarded as particularly intrusive merely because data from a large number of persons is obtained and cross-checked. In each case, the interference only affects the respective individual. Therefore, the severity of interference is determined by how intrusive the measure is for that individual. Whether other persons are also affected by the measure neither mitigates nor aggravates the intensity of the interference for the individual person. In addition, and contrary to the Senate majority's opinion, the fact that a large amount of data is used in the cross-checking actually works to the advantage of the affected fundamental rights holders, given that they *de facto* remain anonymous despite their names being entered into the system. Not least due to the overall volume of data, the entirety of the data records is inscrutable. Therefore, the data subjects do not stand out as individual persons and thus *de facto* remain anonymous. It is only when the number of data subjects is narrowed down to a lower figure (less than a hundred in the case at hand) that data subjects are perceived as individual persons in the context of specific checks. This is decisive for determining the severity of the interference. Thus, as long as the group of data subjects affected by electronic profiling is considerably large, the interference can from the outset not be qualified as particularly intrusive.

2. The circumstances of the interference that the Senate majority took into consideration do not suffice, neither separately nor in an overall assessment, to convincingly establish an interference of high intensity; regardless of this, the majority opinion fails to consider one aspect of electronic profiling authorised under § 31(1) of the 1990 NRW Police Act that is absolutely decisive in my view: by merely obtaining data that the state had already collected separately and thus had readily at its disposal anyway, the state safeguards and strengthens freedom, including in particular the freedom of persons affected by the data cross-checking. Therefore, the measure primarily serves to safeguard and strengthen freedom.

The fundamental right to freedom requires that the state guarantee security. Without security, the Basic Law's guarantee of freedom rings hollow. [...] In a democratic state under the rule of law, more security strengthens freedom, thus increasing freedom. This holds true even with regard to citizens whose freedom is affected by state measures serving prevention and protection purposes – state measures touching on their right to decide themselves on the use of their personal data – and who did not themselves prompt the presumption that they seek to impair or destroy the lives of fellow citizens. [...]

175 The state must take seriously the fear for one's life and health. [...] By fulfilling its mandate of protection, the state does not limit the freedom of its citizens; rather, it strengthens and safeguards their right to freedom.

176 When individuals are free from fear, they are free to act in self-determination, to develop their personality and thus their abilities. Contrary to the Senate majority's opinion, the cross-checking of data, carried out in a matter of seconds, does not control or inhibit behaviour. Affected persons will not change their behaviour because of it. [...] The arguments developed in the context of telecommunications surveillance cannot be applied to electronic profiling. This holds true all the more as, given the type of data used, the cross-checking of data carried out in the context of electronic profiling is not repeated on a daily or weekly basis; unlike surveillance of telecommunications, it is not a measure continuously carried out over a certain period of time, targeting the contents of interpersonal communication and thus the confidential sphere from which novel, previously unknown information is gathered.

177 [...]

178 3. It does not raise constitutional concerns that § 31(1) of the 1990 NRW Police Act, which, in conjunction with the principle of proportionality, provides the statutory basis for electronic profiling, requires the existence of a present danger. However, the element of present danger alone would not constitute a suitable criterion for determining when to allow electronic profiling measures. If it were not possible to launch electronic profiling measures until the danger was already present, electronic profiling would simply be a useless investigation method. [...]

179 Art. 31(1) of the 1990 NRW Police Act requires the existence of a present danger. This is compatible with constitutional law if, in accordance with case-law and legal scholarship, the notion of reverse proportionality is taken into account when interpreting the provision. This entails that the principle of proportionality must be taken into account when making the necessary prognosis as to how likely it is that damage will occur; accordingly, a differentiation must be made based on the magnitude of possible damage [...]. Thus, the greater the possible damage, the lower the requirements regarding the probability of damage occurring may be for the purposes of authorising police measures. [...] This enables the police to already take precautionary measures in order to prevent criminal acts and thus

No. 39 – Profiling

avert risks, to which the Basic Law itself accords great importance (cf. BVerfGE 100, 313 <388> – *The Article 10 Act*; most recently BVerfGE 115, 166 <192> – *Telecommunications Surveillance*).

[…] 180-181

4. The Higher Regional Court was right to find the existence of a terrorist threat in the challenged decision based on the factual indications in the present case, which justified electronic profiling. These circumstances were not accorded the significance they deserve by the Senate majority. [...] Given the threat to a large number of innocent people, it was permissible for that court to hold that the complainant's interests and the interference with his right to informational self-determination, which cannot be qualified as serious, carry less weight than the security interests of all citizens and the state's mandate of protection. As citizens connected to and bound by the community, the persons affected by electronic profiling have to tolerate, in the interest of the general public, the interference of minor weight at issue here. 182

5. […] 183-185

Justice Haas

No. 40

BVerfGE 120, 274 – Remote Searches

HEADNOTES

to the Judgment of the First Senate of 27 February 2008
1 BvR 370/07, 1 BvR 595/07

1. The general right of personality (Article 2(1) in conjunction with Article 1(1) of the Basic Law) encompasses the fundamental right to protection of the confidentiality and integrity of information technology systems.
2. The covert infiltration of an information technology system for the purposes of monitoring the use of the system and extracting data stored on its storage media is only permissible under constitutional law if there are factual indications of a specific danger to an exceptionally significant legal interest. Exceptionally significant legal interests are life, limb and liberty of the person or public interests that are of such significance that a threat to them would affect the foundations or existence of the state, or the foundations of human existence. The measure may be justified even if it cannot yet be established with sufficient probability that the danger will materialise in the near future, provided that there are specific facts indicating an impending danger to an exceptionally significant legal interest in the individual case that can be attributed to specific persons.
3. The covert infiltration of an information technology system in principle requires a judicial order. The statutory basis authorising such an interference must include safeguards to protect the core of private life.
4. To the extent that the legislative authorisation is limited to state measures intercepting the contents and circumstances of ongoing telecommunications in a computer network, or analysing data thus obtained, the interference must be measured against Article 10(1) of the Basic Law.
5. Where the state obtains knowledge of the contents of Internet communication by using the normal technical means provided for this purpose, an interference with Article 10(1) of the Basic Law arises only if the relevant state authority was not given permission to do so by one of the communicating parties.

No. 40 – Remote Searches

Where the state obtains knowledge of communication contents that are publicly accessible on the Internet, or participates in publicly accessible communication processes, it generally does not interfere with fundamental rights.

FEDERAL CONSTITUTIONAL COURT
- 1 BvR 370/07 -
- 1 BVR 595/07 -

IN THE NAME OF THE PEOPLE

In the proceedings
on the constitutional complaint of

1. a) Ms W...,
   b) Mr B...,
   – authorised representative: ...
   against § 5(2) no. 11 in conjunction with § 7(1), § 5(3), § 5a(1) and § 13 of the North Rhine-Westphalia Constitution Protection Act as amended by the Act of 20 December 2006 (GVBl NRW 2006, p. 620)
   - 1 BvR 370/07 -,

2. a) Mr B...,
   b) Dr. R...,
   c) Mr S...,
   – authorised representatives: ...
   against § 5(2) no. 11, § 5(3), § 7(2) and § 8(4) second sentence in conjunction with §§ 10, 11 and § 17(1) of the North Rhine-Westphalia Constitution Protection Act as amended by the Act of 20 December 2006 (GVBl NRW 2006, p. 620)
   - 1 BvR 595/07 -

the Federal Constitutional Court – First Senate –
with the participation of Justices

President Papier,
Hohmann-Dennhardt,
Hofmann-Riem,
Bryde,
Gaier,
Eichberger,

BVerfGE 120, 274

Schluckebier,
Kirchhof

held on the basis of the oral hearing of 10 October 2007:

JUDGMENT

1. § 5(2) no. 11 of the North Rhine-Westphalia Constitution Protection Act as amended by the Act of 20 December 2006 (GVBl NRW, p. 620) is incompatible with Article 2(1) in conjunction with Article 1(1), Article 10(1) and Article 19(1) second sentence of the Basic Law, and thus void.
2. [...]
3. To the extent that it challenges § 5a(1) of the North Rhine-Westphalia Constitution Protection Act, the constitutional complaint of complainant no. 1b is rejected.
4. [...]
5. [...]

REASONS:

A.

1   The constitutional complaints concern provisions of the NRW Constitution Protection Act that set out, firstly, the powers of the *Land* Office for the Protection of the Constitution (*Verfassungsschutzbehörde*) regarding various data collection measures, in particular the collection of data from information technology systems, and secondly, the processing of the collected data.

I.

2   [...]
3   1. Both constitutional complaints assert that § 5(2) no. 11 of the NRW Constitution Protection Act is unconstitutional. This provision authorises the *Land* Office for the Protection of the Constitution to carry out two types of investigation measures: covert monitoring and other Internet surveillance measures (first alternative), and covert access to information technology systems (second alternative).
4   a) [...] Covert Internet surveillance is defined as a measure by which the *Land* Office for the Protection of the Constitution obtains knowledge of the contents of Internet communication by using the normal technical means provided for this

No. 40 – Remote Searches

purpose. The *Land* Government of North Rhine-Westphalia refers to such measures as server-related Internet surveillance.

By contrast, covert accessing of an information technology system is defined as technical infiltration, for instance, by taking advantage of vulnerabilities in the target system's security or by installing spyware. The infiltration of the target system makes it possible to monitor its use, to access data on its storage media, and even to exercise remote control over the target system. The *Land* Government of North Rhine-Westphalia refers to such measures as client-related Internet surveillance. [...] 5

b) [...] 6
c) [...] 7
aa) The challenged *Land* provision contains the first and so far the only explicit authorisation of a German state authority to carry out 'remote searches' of information technology systems. [...] 8
bb) 'Remote searches' are designed to respond to the difficulties that arise in the context of criminal investigations where the perpetrators, especially those from extremist and terrorist groups, use information technology, in particular the Internet, for their communication and for the planning and committing of criminal acts. [...] 9
[...] 10-11
d) [...] 12
e) [...] 13
2. [...] 14
3. [...] 15-16
4. [...] 17
5. [...] 18
6. [...] 19
7. [...] 20-115

II.

1. Complainant no. 1a is a journalist [...]. In the context of her work, she visits websites operated by persons and organisations with anti-constitutional aims. She is also a data protection activist and, together with others, operates the website www.stop1984.com. This site allows users to participate in so-called chats; the chat service is also used by right-wing extremists. Complainant no. 1a stores information on chat participants on the hard drive of her computer, which she uses for both private and professional purposes. 116

Complainant no. 1b is an active member of the NRW regional branch of the party *DIE LINKE*, which is being monitored by the NRW Office for the Protection of the 117

Constitution. He also uses his computer, which has Internet access, for his political activities. Like complainant no. 1a, he uses the Internet for private communication as well [...].

118 Complainants nos. 2a and 2b are partners in a law firm. Complainant no. 2a is a lawyer who *inter alia* represents asylum-seekers, including a leading member of the PKK, which is monitored by the NRW Office for the Protection of the Constitution. He uses computer networks that are connected to the Internet, both in his home and on the premises of the law firm. The law firm network is also used by complainant no. 2b, as well as by complainant no. 2c, who is a freelancer at the law firm.

119 2. To the extent that the constitutional complaints challenge § 5(2) no. 11 of the NRW Constitution Protection Act, the complainants claim a violation of Art. 2(1) in conjunction with Art. 1(1), Art. 10(1) and Art. 13(1) of the Basic Law.

120-122 [...]
123 3. [...]
124-125 4. [...]
126-128 5. [...]

III.

129 The Federal Government, the *Land* Government and the *Land* Parliament of North Rhine-Westphalia, the Government of the Free State of Saxony, the Federal Officer for Data Protection and Freedom of Information and the Officer for Data Protection and Freedom of Information of the *Land* North Rhine-Westphalia submitted statements on the constitutional complaint. The parliamentary groups of *Sozialdemokratische Partei Deutschlands* (SPD) and *BÜNDNIS 90/DIE GRÜNEN* in the *Land* Parliament of North Rhine-Westphalia submitted a legal opinion. Furthermore, the Senate obtained written expert statements from Andreas Bogk, Dirk Fox, Professor Dr. Felix Freiling, Professor Dr. Andreas Pfitzmann and Professor Dr. Ulrich Sieber.

No. 40 – Remote Searches

[...] 130-148

IV.

[...] 149

B.

[...] 150-164

C.

To the extent that they are admissible, the constitutional complaints are for the most part well-founded. § 5(2) no. 11 of the NRW Constitution Protection Act is unconstitutional and void regarding the second alternative listed there (see I below). The same applies to the first alternative listed in this provision (see II below). The fact that the provision is void renders moot the complaints directed against § 5(3) and § 17 of the NRW Constitution Protection Act (see III below). [...] 165

I.

§ 5(2) no. 11 first sentence, second alternative of the NRW Constitution Protection Act, which governs the accessing of information technology systems, violates the general right of personality (Art. 2(1) in conjunction with Art. 1(1) of the Basic Law) in its special manifestation as a fundamental right to protection of the confidentiality and integrity of information technology systems. 166

This manifestation of the general right of personality affords protection against the infiltration of information technology systems to the extent that protection is not already guaranteed by other fundamental rights, such as Art. 10 or Art. 13 of the Basic Law, nor by the right to informational self-determination (see 1 below). In the case at hand, the interferences are not justified under constitutional law: § 5(2) no. 11 first sentence, second alternative of the NRW Constitution Protection Act satisfies neither the requirement of legal clarity (see 2 a below), nor the requirements deriving from the principle of proportionality (see 2 b below), nor does the provision set out sufficient safeguards protecting the core of private life (see 2 c below). The challenged provision is thus void (see 2 d below). There is no need for further review of the provision based on other fundamental rights (see 2 e below). 167

168 1. § 5(2) no. 11 first sentence, second alternative of the NRW Constitution Protection Act authorises interferences with the general right of personality in its special manifestation as a fundamental right to protection of the confidentiality and integrity of information technology systems; this manifestation supplements other specific manifestations of that fundamental right such as the right to informational self-determination, as well as the freedoms guaranteed in Art. 10 and Art. 13 of the Basic Law in cases where these do not afford sufficient protection.

169 a) The general right of personality protects aspects of one's personality that are not covered by the specific freedoms of the Basic Law, but are equal to these freedoms in terms of their constitutive significance for one's personality (cf. BVerfGE 99, 185 <193> – *Helnwein/Scientology*; 114, 339 <346> – *Stolpe/Stasi Dispute*). Such a guarantee that fills gaps in protection is in particular necessary in order to respond to new risks [to one's personality], which possibly arise in the context of scientific and technical progress or societal change (cf. BVerfGE 54, 148 <153> – *Eppler*; 65, 1 <41> – *Census*; 118, 168 <183>). Determining what specific legal protection is invoked in relation to the various manifestations of the right of personality is mainly informed by the type of risk to one's personality at play (cf. BVerfGE 101, 361 <380>; 106, 28 <39>).

170 b) The use of information technology has taken on an unprecedented significance for the personality and development of the individual. Modern information technology opens up new opportunities for individuals, but also creates new risks to one's personality.

171 aa) Recent developments in information technology have led to a situation in which information technology systems have become ubiquitous, and their use central to the lives of many people.

172 This applies first and foremost to personal computers, which can now be found in a large majority of households in the Federal Republic of Germany […]. The performance of such computers has increased, as has the capacity of their internal memories and their storage media. Today's personal computers can be used for many different purposes […]. Accordingly, the significance of personal computers for the development of one's personality has increased considerably.

173 […] Additionally, many devices used everyday by large parts of the population involve information technology components. This is increasingly true with regard to telecommunication or electronic devices in homes or motor vehicles, for instance.

174 bb) The functions of information technology systems and their significance for the development of one's personality are amplified where different systems are connected. This is increasingly becoming the norm, not least due to the increase in Internet usage by large parts of the population.

No. 40 – Remote Searches

[...] 175

Most notably, the Internet, as a complex structure linking computer networks, not only provides users of connected computers with access to a virtually limitless wealth of information that is made available by and can be retrieved from other network computers. On the Internet, users have access to numerous innovative communication services, too, allowing them to actively establish and maintain social relations. [...] 176

cc) The increasingly widespread use of networked information technology systems provides individuals with new opportunities for personality development, but also creates new risks to their personality. 177

(1) These risks arise because complex information technology systems such as personal computers allow for a wide range of possible uses, all of which entail the creation, processing and storage of data. This concerns not only data which computer users create or store deliberately. In the context of data processing, information technology systems autonomously create large quantities of further data which, like the data stored by users, can be analysed to determine user behaviour and characteristics. As a consequence, a large amount of data relating to users' personal circumstances, social contacts and activities can be accessed in the working memory and the storage media of such systems. If collected and analysed by third parties, this data allows for far-reaching conclusions regarding the personality of the users concerned, and may even make it possible to compile personality profiles (cf. regarding the risks to one's personality from such findings BVerfGE 65, 1 <42> – *Census*). 178

(2) In a networked system, in particular one connected to the Internet, these risks are aggravated in various ways. Firstly, the network connection expands the possible areas of use, leading to the creation, processing and storage of even larger and more diverse amounts of data in comparison to a stand-alone system. This includes communication contents, as well as data relating to network communication. Extensive knowledge about users' personalities can be obtained by way of storing and analysing data on user behaviour in the network. 179

Above all, the system's network connection gives third parties the technical ability to access it, including for the purposes of spying on or manipulating data stored in the system. Individuals will not always be able to detect such third-party access; in any case, they have only limited powers to prevent it. Information technology systems have now evolved to such complexity that taking effective social or technical measures of self-protection presents a considerable challenge and may not be feasible at least for the average user. [...] 180

c) From a fundamental rights perspective, a considerable need for protection arises given that the use of information technology systems has significance for one's 181 personality development but also entails risks to one's personality. For the sake of the unimpeded development of one's personality, individuals have legitimate expectations regarding the integrity and confidentiality of such systems, and they rely on the state to respect these expectations. The guarantees of Art. 10 and Art. 13 of the Basic Law, like the manifestations of the general right of personality previously developed by the Federal Constitutional Court in its case-law, do not adequately take account of the need for protection arising from advances in information technology.

182 aa) The guarantee of telecommunications privacy under Art. 10(1) of the Basic Law protects the non-physical transmission of information to individual recipients by way of telecommunications traffic (cf. BVerfGE 67, 157 <172>; 106, 28 <35 and 36>); yet its protection does not extend to the confidentiality and integrity of information technology systems.

183 (1) The protection under Art. 10(1) of the Basic Law covers telecommunications, regardless of the method of transmission (cable or wireless, analogue or digital) and the form of expression (speech, images, sound, symbols or other data) used (cf. BVerfGE 106, 28 <36>; 115, 166 <182> – *Telecommunications Surveillance*). The scope of protection of telecommunications privacy thus also extends to Internet communication services (cf. regarding emails BVerfGE 113, 348 <383>). What is more, not only the actual communication contents, but also the circumstances of telecommunications are protected against the state obtaining knowledge thereof. This includes in particular whether, when and how often telecommunication traffic occurred or was attempted between whom or between which telecommunication devices (cf. BVerfGE 67, 157 <172>; 85, 386 <396>; 100, 313 <358> – *The Article 10 Act*; 107, 299 <312 and 313>). In this context, the privacy of telecommunications is faced with both old and new risks to one's personality arising from the increased significance of information technology for the personal development of the individual.

184 Where a legislative authorisation is limited to state measures intercepting the contents and circumstances of ongoing telecommunications in a computer network, or to measures analysing this data, the interference must be measured only against Art. 10(1) of the Basic Law. In this case, the scope of protection of this fundamental right is affected regardless of whether, at the technical level, the measure targets the transmission route or the device used for telecommunications (cf. BVerfGE 106, 28 <37 and 38>; 115, 166 <186 and 187> – *Telecommunications Surveillance*). In principle, this also applies if the device is a networked and complex information technology system that is used for telecommunications but also for various other types of activities.

No. 40 – Remote Searches

(2) Yet the fundamental rights protection afforded by Article 10(1) of the Basic Law does not extend to the contents and circumstances of telecommunications data stored within the domain controlled by a communicating party after the transmission has been completed, to the extent that they can take their own precautions against covert data access. Regarding such data, the specific risks of remote communication, which the privacy of telecommunications aims to avert, no longer apply (cf. BVerfGE 115, 166 <183 et seq.> – *Telecommunications Surveillance*). 185

(3) Likewise, the protection afforded by the privacy of telecommunications does not apply if a state authority monitors the use of an information technology system as such or searches the system's storage media. [...] 186

(4) To the extent that covert access to an information technology system serves to also collect data not protected by Art. 10(1) of the Basic Law, a gap in protection arises, which must be filled by the general right of personality in its manifestation as protection of the confidentiality and integrity of information technology systems. 187

Where the technical infiltration of a complex information technology system is undertaken for the purposes of telecommunications surveillance ('source telecommunications surveillance'), this infiltration is the critical step that makes it possible to spy on the system as a whole. The resulting risks [for one's personality] go far beyond the risks associated with the mere surveillance of ongoing telecommunications. [...] 188

[...] 189

By contrast, Art. 10(1) of the Basic Law serves as the sole standard of review in terms of fundamental rights protection where the authorisation to carry out 'source telecommunications surveillance' is strictly limited to data stemming from ongoing telecommunications. This must be ensured by technical and legal safeguards. 190

bb) The right to the inviolability of the home afforded by Art. 13(1) of the Basic Law guarantees individuals an essential space of private life in light of human dignity and for the development of their personality, where interferences are only permissible subject to the particular requirements set out in Art. 13(2) to 13(7) of the Basic Law; however, it leaves gaps in protection as regards access to information technology systems. 191

This fundamental right protects the sphere of private space within one's home, in which private life unfolds (cf. BVerfGE 89, 1 <12>; 103, 142 <150 and 151>). In addition to private homes, commercial and business premises are also covered by the scope of protection of Art. 13 of the Basic Law (cf. BVerfGE 32, 54 <69 et seq.>; 44, 353 <371> – *Addiction Counselling Agency*; 76, 83 <88>; 96, 44 <51>). The fundamental rights protection is not limited to preventing physical intrusions into the home. Measures that entail the use of technical equipment by state authorities for the purposes of obtaining insights into activities within homes 192 that cannot be naturally perceived from outside the protected space must also be regarded as interferences with Art. 13 of the Basic Law. [...]

193 [...]

194 However, Art. 13(1) of the Basic Law does not generally protect individuals against any infiltration of their information technology system regardless of how the accessing is carried out, not even if the system is located within a private home [...]. The interference at issue can occur regardless of one's location; therefore, a location-specific protection could not counter the specific risks to the information technology system. To the extent that infiltration measures make use of a network connection between the targeted computer and another computer, they do not affect the sphere of private space within one's home. In many cases, the location of the targeted system is irrelevant for the investigation measure, and will frequently not even be known to the authority. This applies in particular to mobile information technology systems such as laptops, personal digital assistants or mobile phones.

195 Nor does Art. 13(1) of the Basic Law afford protection against the collection, by means of system infiltration, of data from the working memory or storage media of an information technology system located within a private home (cf. regarding the equivalence of protection applicable in relation to home searches and seizing of evidence BVerfGE 113, 29 <45> – *Seizure of Electronic Data*).

196 cc) The manifestations of the general right of personality that have previously been recognised in the Federal Constitutional Court's case-law, in particular the guarantees protecting the private sphere and the right to informational self-determination, also do not sufficiently meet the special need for protection of users of information technology systems.

197 (1) In its manifestation as protection of the private sphere, the general right of personality guarantees individuals a [protected] domain tied to certain spaces or subject matters which is to remain, in principle, free of unwanted scrutiny (cf. BVerfGE 27, 344 <350 *et seq.*> – *Divorce Files*; 44, 353 <372 and 373> – *Addiction Counselling Agency*; 90, 255 <260> – *Monitoring of Correspondence*; 101, 361 <382 and 383>). However, the need for protection on the part of users of information technology systems is not limited solely to data attributable to their private sphere. [...]

198 (2) The scope of the right to informational self-determination goes beyond the protection of the private sphere. It confers upon the individual the authority to, in principle, decide themselves on the disclosure and use of their personal data (cf. BVerfGE 65, 1 <43> – *Census*; 84, 192 <194>). It complements and expands the fundamental rights protection afforded freedom of conduct and private life, ensuring that this protection can be invoked against risks to one's personality. Such a risk can already arise before specific threats to identifiable legal interests

No. 40 – Remote Searches

materialise; this applies in particular where personal information can be used and linked in a manner which the person concerned can neither foresee nor prevent. In this context, the scope of protection of the right to informational self-determination is not limited to information that merits fundamental rights protection simply by virtue of its sensitive nature. Depending on the aims pursued by the accessing of data, and in light of the existing possibilities with regard to the processing and linking of data, the use of personal data which by itself has only little informative value may nevertheless affect the private life and freedom of conduct of the person concerned in a manner that is significant from a fundamental rights perspective (cf. BVerfGE 118, 168 <185>).

Risks to one's personality that the right to informational self-determination aims to avert arise from the manifold possibilities for the state, and in some cases also private actors, […] to collect, process and use personal data. By means of electronic data processing in particular, such information may be used to generate further information; this allows conclusions to be drawn, which may both impair the confidentiality interests of affected persons that are protected by fundamental rights and interfere with their freedom of conduct (cf. BVerfGE 65, 1 <42> – *Census*; 113, 29 <45 and 46> – *Seizure of Electronic Data*; 115, 320 <342> – *Profiling*; 118, 168 <184 and 185>). 199

However, the right to informational self-determination does not fully account for risks to one's personality arising from the fact that individuals rely on the use of information technology systems for the development of their personality, entrusting the system with personal data or inevitably generating such data simply by using the system. Third parties accessing the system can potentially obtain extremely large quantities of data with significant informative value without having to resort to further data collection and processing measures. The weight of such data access for the personality of affected persons goes far beyond that of isolated data collection measures against which the right to informational self-determination affords protection. 200

d) To the extent that no adequate protection exists against risks to one's personality arising from the fact that individuals rely on the use of information technology systems for their personality development, the general right of personality applies by virtue of its function to fill gaps in protection; it meets the aforementioned need for protection, which goes beyond the other manifestations of this right recognised so far, by guaranteeing the integrity and confidentiality of information technology systems. This right, just like the right to informational self-determination, is based on Art. 2(1) in conjunction with Art. 1(1) of the Basic Law; it protects the personal and private life of fundamental rights holders against state access in the area of information technology; this protection is not limited to cases where the access 201 concerns individual communication processes or selected stored data, but also applies where access to the information technology system as a whole is concerned.

202 aa) […]

203 The fundamental right to protection of the integrity and confidentiality of information technology systems is applicable where the statutory basis authorising interferences covers systems that may contain, by themselves or due to network connections, personal data of users in such large quantities and of such variety that access to the system facilitates insights into essential aspects of one's personal life or even allows for the creation of a comprehensive personality profile. These possibilities exist, for instance, when personal computers are accessed, regardless of whether they are installed in a fixed location or operated as mobile devices. Regarding both private and business computer use, usage patterns regularly allow conclusions to be drawn regarding personal characteristics or preferences. In addition, the specific fundamental rights protection also covers such mobile phones or electronic assistants that offer a wide range of functions and can collect and store various kinds of personal data.

204 bb) The fundamental right to protection of the confidentiality and integrity of information technology systems primarily protects the user's interest in confidentiality of the data created, processed and stored by information technology systems that falls within its scope of protection. Moreover, it constitutes an interference with this fundamental right if the integrity of the protected information technology system is compromised because the system is accessed in a manner that allows third parties to use its services, functions and storage contents; such access is the critical technical step that enables spying, monitoring or manipulation activities in relation to this system.

205 (1) In its manifestation addressed here, the general right of personality affords protection particularly against covert access through which data available in the system can be spied on in its entirety or on a large scale. This fundamental rights protection extends to both the data stored in the working memory and the data temporarily or permanently kept on the system's storage media. The fundamental right also protects against data collection carried out by means that, even though they are not directly connected at a technical level to the data processing activities of the information technology system in question, nevertheless pertain to the system's data processing. This applies, for example, to the use of so-called hardware keyloggers or to the measuring of electromagnetic radiation from monitors or keyboards.

206 (2) The expectation of confidentiality and integrity is afforded fundamental rights protection regardless of whether the information technology system can be accessed easily or only with considerable effort. Yet the expectation of confidentiality and integrity is recognised from a fundamental rights perspective only insofar as

the affected user regards the information technology system as their own system, so that they can legitimately expect that, based on the relevant circumstances, they have control over the information technology system in a self-determined manner, either alone or together with other authorised users of the system. [...]

2. The fundamental right to protection of the confidentiality and integrity of information technology systems is not guaranteed without limitation. Interferences may be justified both for preventing [dangers to public security] and for law enforcement purposes. Individuals must only accept such restrictions of their right that have a statutory basis in line with constitutional law. The provision authorising the *Land* Office for the Protection of the Constitution to carry out preventive measures, which is under review in the present proceedings, does not satisfy this requirement.

a) The provision at issue does not meet the requirement of legal clarity and specificity.

aa) The requirement of legal specificity is based on the principle of the rule of law (Art. 20 and Art. 28(1) of the Basic Law), including where it concerns the general right of personality in its various manifestations (cf. BVerfGE 110, 33 <53, 57, 70>; 112, 284 <301>; 113, 348 <375>; 115, 320 <365> – *Profiling*). It serves to ensure that the parliamentary legislator, which is democratically legitimated, takes the essential decisions on interferences with fundamental rights and their scope itself; that the law subjects the government and administration to standards that direct and limit their actions; and that the courts can review the lawfulness of their actions. Furthermore, clear and specific provisions ensure that affected persons are able to discern the applicable law and can take precautions against potentially intrusive measures (cf. BVerfGE 110, 33 <52 *et seq.*>; 113, 348 <375 *et seq.*>). The legislator must specify, in a sufficiently clear and precise manner and for each subject matter, the grounds, purpose and limits of the interference (cf. BVerfGE 100, 313 <359 and 360, 372> – *The Article 10 Act*; 110, 33 <53>; 113, 348 <375>; 118, 168 <186 and 187>).

[...]

bb) Based on these standards, § 5(2) no. 11 first sentence, second alternative of the NRW Constitution Protection Act does not satisfy the requirement of legal clarity and specificity insofar as the conditions under which the measures are permissible cannot be derived from the statutory provision with sufficient certainty.

(1) The statutory conditions for carrying out measures pursuant to § 5(2) no. 11 first sentence, second alternative of the NRW Constitution Protection Act are determined by two references to other provisions. Firstly, § 5(2) of the NRW Constitution Protection Act contains a general reference to § 7(1) of the NRW Constitution Protection Act, which in turn refers to § 3(1) of the NRW Constitution Protection Act. These provisions authorise the use of intelligence service methods for the

purposes of gathering information relevant to the protection of the constitutional order. Secondly, § 5(2) no. 11 second sentence of the NRW Constitution Protection Act refers to the more stringent requirements set out in the Act on Article 10 of the Basic Law (hereinafter: the Article 10 Act) for cases in which a measure pursuant to § 5(2) no. 11 of the NRW Constitution Protection Act interferes with the privacy of correspondence, post and telecommunications or is equivalent to such an interference due to its nature and severity.

213 (2) It is not compatible with the requirement of legal clarity and specificity that § 5(2) no. 11 second sentence of the NRW Constitution Protection Act makes the applicability of the Article 10 Act contingent on whether a measure interferes with Art. 10 of the Basic Law. [...] The legislative use of a fall-back clause (*salvatorische Klausel*) does not satisfy the requirement of legal specificity for a provision such as § 5(2) no. 11 first sentence, second alternative of the NRW Constitution Protection Act, which provides for novel investigation measures designed in response to new technological developments.

214 The violation of the requirement of legal clarity is further aggravated by § 5(2) no. 11 second sentence of the NRW Constitution Protection Act, which additionally states that the Article 10 Act also applies if the "nature and severity" of an investigation measure is equivalent to an interference with Art. 10 of the Basic Law. Hence, the conditions under which the accessing [of information technology systems] pursuant to the challenged provision is permissible are contingent upon an assessment comparing the accessing measure to a measure that would qualify as an interference with a specific fundamental right. § 5(2) no. 11 second sentence of the NRW Constitution Protection Act completely lacks any criteria for undertaking such a comparison. [...]

215 (3) Furthermore, the reference to the Article 10 Act in § 5(2) no. 11 second sentence of the NRW Constitution Protection Act fails to satisfy the requirement of legal clarity and specificity insofar as its scope is not sufficiently clear.

216-217 [...]

218 b) § 5(2) no. 11 first sentence, second alternative of the NRW Constitution Protection Act also fails to satisfy the principle of proportionality. This principle requires that an interference with fundamental rights serve a legitimate purpose and be suitable, necessary and appropriate for achieving this purpose (cf. BVerfGE 109, 279 <335 *et seq.*> – *Surveillance of Private Homes*; 115, 320 <345> – *Profiling*; 118, 168 <193>; established case-law).

219 aa) The data collection measures provided for in the challenged provision are designed to aid the *Land* Office for the Protection of the Constitution in fulfilling its tasks [...], and thus serve to protect, as precautionary measures before specific dangers (*konkrete Gefahren*) arise, the free democratic basic order, the existence of

No. 40 – Remote Searches

the Federation and of the *Länder*, as well as interests of the Federal Republic of Germany that concern its international relations. […]

The security of the state as a constituted power of peace and order, as well as the security of the population it is bound to protect against dangers to life, limb and liberty, rank equally with other constitutional values that are accorded high standing (cf. BVerfGE 49, 24 <56 and 57>; 115, 320 <346> – *Profiling)*. The [state's] duty of protection follows from both Art. 2(2) first sentence and Art. 1(1) second sentence of the Basic Law (cf. BVerfGE 115, 118 <152>). In countering dangers from terrorist or other activities, the state fulfils its constitutional mandate. The increased use of electronic or digital means of communication and their advance into virtually all areas of life has created new obstacles for the effective performance of the tasks of the Office for the Protection of the Constitution. Modern information technology also offers extremist and terrorist groups numerous possibilities to establish and maintain contacts, as well as to plan, prepare and commit criminal acts. In particular, legislative measures that allow state investigations to target information technology must be considered against the background of the shift from traditional forms of communication to electronic messaging and the possibilities to encrypt or conceal data files (cf. regarding law enforcement BVerfGE 115, 166 <193> – *Telecommunications Surveillance*). 220

bb) The covert accessing of information technology systems is suitable for achieving these purposes. It expands the possibilities available to the *Land* Office for the Protection of the Constitution to investigate threats. The legislator is granted a considerable margin of appreciation in assessing the suitability of a measure (cf. BVerfGE 77, 84 <106>; 90, 145 <173>; 109, 279 <336> – *Surveillance of Private Homes*). […] 221

[…] 222-223

cc) Moreover, the covert accessing of information technology systems does not violate the requirement of necessity. It was within the legislator's prerogative of assessment to presume that other means for the collection of data from information technology system that would be equally effective but less intrusive for the affected persons are not available. 224

[…] 225

dd) However, § 5(2) no. 11 first sentence, second alternative of the NRW Constitution Protection Act does not satisfy the requirement of proportionality in the strict sense. 226

The principle of proportionality in its strict sense requires that the severity of the interference, in an overall assessment, not be disproportionate to the weight of the reasons invoked to justify it (cf. BVerfGE 90, 145 <173>; 109, 279 <349 *et seq.*> – *Surveillance of Private Homes*; 113, 348 <382>; established case-law). 227

The legislator must appropriately weigh the individual's interest that is curtailed by an interference with fundamental rights against the public interests pursued. An assessment based on these standards may lead to the conclusion that certain means must not be used to enforce public interests because the resulting impairments of fundamental rights outweigh the interests pursued (cf. BVerfGE 115, 320 <345 and 346> – *Profiling*; 118, 168 <195>).

228 § 5(2) no. 11 first sentence, second alternative of the NRW Constitution Protection Act does not satisfy this requirement. The measures set out in that provision result in fundamental rights interferences that are so serious that they are disproportionate to the public investigation interest providing the grounds for interference. Moreover, additional procedural safeguards would be necessary to give effect to the protected fundamental rights interests of affected persons; these are also lacking in the provision.

229 (1) § 5(2) no. 11 first sentence, second alternative of the NRW Constitution Protection Act authorises particularly intrusive interferences with fundamental rights.

230 (a) Where the state collects data from complex information technology systems, there is a considerable potential that the data might be used to spy on the personality of the affected persons. This already applies to measures that only entail one-off and isolated access, such as the seizure or copying of the system's storage media (cf. in this regard BVerfGE 113, 29 – *Seizure of Electronic Data*; 115, 166 – *Telecommunications Surveillance*; 117, 244).

231 (aa) Such covert accessing of information technology systems provides the relevant state authority with access to data records which, in terms of their volume and variety, may by far exceed traditional sources of information. This follows from the fact that complex information technology systems allow for many different possible uses which entail the creation, processing and storage of personal data. In light of today's user habits, such devices are typically also used to deliberately store personal data that is particularly sensitive, for example private text documents, images or sound files. These data records may include detailed information on the personal circumstances and private life of the affected person, their private and business correspondence via various communication channels, or even diary-like personal notes.

232 State access to such comprehensive data records entails the obvious risk that, in an overall assessment, the collected data allows comprehensive conclusions to be drawn regarding the personality of the affected person, which may even include the creation of behaviour and communication profiles.

233 (bb) To the extent that the collected data provides information on communications between the affected person and third parties, the severity of the interference with fundamental rights is aggravated further given that it restricts the freedom of citi-

No. 40 – Remote Searches

zens to participate in telecommunications without being monitored – a freedom that also serves the common good [...]. In addition, such data collection measures indiscriminately affect a considerable number of persons, which increases the weight of interference, since they necessarily also concern the target person's communication partners, i.e. third parties, regardless of whether the statutory grounds for such data access are also met in relation to these third parties (cf. regarding telecommunications surveillance BVerfGE 113, 348 <382 and 383>; furthermore BVerfGE 34, 238 <247> – *Secret Tape Recordings*; 107, 299 <321>).

(b) The interference with fundamental rights is particularly serious if – as provided for by the challenged provision – covert technical infiltration allows for longer-term surveillance of system use and the ongoing collection of the relevant data. 234

(aa) The volume and variety of the data records which can be obtained by such access are considerably higher than in case of one-off, isolated data collection measures. In accessing the target system, the investigating authority also obtains volatile data that is only kept in the working memory, or data only temporarily stored on the storage media of the target system. It also makes it possible to track the entire Internet communication of the affected person over a longer period. Moreover, the indiscriminate effects of the investigation measure can increase if access is extended to a (local) network that the target system is part of. 235

Volatile data or data stored only temporarily can have particularly close links to the personality of affected persons; it can also facilitate access to further, especially sensitive data. This applies for instance to cache data, which is created by software applications such as web browsers; its analysis can provide information on how such applications are used, and may thus indirectly allow conclusions to be drawn on users' preferences or communication patterns. It also holds true for passwords, which allow the user to gain access to technically secure contents on their system or the network. Furthermore, longer-term surveillance of Internet communication, as authorised by the challenged provision, is a considerably more intrusive interference than a one-off collection of data on communication contents and circumstances. Finally, it must be taken into consideration that the possibilities of access set out in the challenged provision serve *inter alia* to circumvent the use of encryption technology and constitute suitable means in this regard. Thus, the individual precautions taken by users to protect themselves against unwanted data access are undermined. The frustration of informational self-protection undertaken by affected persons increases the severity of the interference with their fundamental rights. 236

In addition, there is an increased risk that this will lead to the creation of behaviour and communication profiles given that the provision authorises the comprehensive monitoring of the target system's usage over a longer period. By these means, 237 the competent state authority can extensively spy on the personal circumstances and communication behaviour of affected persons. Such comprehensive collection of personal data amounts to a particularly intrusive interference with fundamental rights.

238 (bb) The severity of the interference stemming from the accessing [of information technology systems] as set out in the Act follows furthermore from the covert nature of the measure. In a state under the rule of law, state interferences through covert measures are the exception and require special justification (cf. BVerfGE 118, 168 <197>). If the persons concerned know about a state measure affecting them prior to its execution, they can defend their interests from the outset. Firstly, they can take legal steps to prevent it, for instance by seeking recourse to a court. Secondly, where data collection measures are carried out overtly, they can actually influence the course of the investigation with their conduct. Excluding this possibility to influence the investigation increases the weight of the interference with fundamental rights (cf. regarding possibilities of legal defence BVerfGE 113, 348 <383 and 384>; 115, 320 <353> – *Profiling*).

239 (cc) The weight of the interference is also informed by possible risks to the integrity of the accessed computer and to legal interests of the persons concerned, or even of third parties, that may result from such access.

240-241 [...]

242 (2) In view of its severity, the interference with fundamental rights stemming from the covert accessing of information technology systems for prevention purposes is only appropriate if specific facts indicate an impending danger (*drohende Gefahr*) to an exceptionally significant legal interest in the individual case; this requirement can be satisfied even if it cannot yet be established with sufficient probability that the danger will materialise in the near future. In addition, the statutory provision authorising such an interference must ensure that the fundamental rights of affected persons are protected, including by suitable procedural safeguards.

243 (a) With regard to the tension between the state's duty to guarantee the protection of legal interests and the interest of the individual in upholding their constitutionally guaranteed rights, it is primarily incumbent on the legislator to achieve an abstract balance between the conflicting interests (cf. BVerfGE 109, 279 <350> – *Surveillance of Private Homes*). As a result, certain particularly intrusive interferences with fundamental rights may only be permissible for the protection of certain legal interests and only when the suspicion or danger prompting the interference reaches a certain threshold. The state's duty to protect other legal interests is further limited by the prohibition of inappropriate interferences with fundamental rights (cf. BVerfGE 115, 320 <358> – *Profiling*). The relevant thresholds for carrying out the measures constituting interferences must be set out in statutory provisions (cf.

No. 40 – Remote Searches

BVerfGE 100, 313 <383 and 384> – *The Article 10 Act*; 109, 279 <350 *et seq.*> – *Surveillance of Private Homes*; 115, 320 <346> – *Profiling*).

(b) Where the interference with fundamental rights is particularly intrusive, the measure may already be disproportionate as such if the grounds for interference set out in its statutory basis are not sufficiently weighty. To the extent that the applicable law serves to avert certain dangers, as is the case here according to § 1 of the NRW Constitution Protection Act, the significance and the nature of the threat to protected interests that the respective provision refers to are essential for determining the weight attached to the grounds for interference (cf. BVerfGE 115, 320 <360 and 361> – *Profiling*). 244

If the interests that the statutory provision authorising interferences aims to protect are as such sufficiently weighty to justify interferences with fundamental rights of that type, the principle of proportionality gives rise to further constitutional requirements regarding the statutory basis, which set the prerequisites for interference. In this respect, the legislator must maintain a balance between the type and severity of the fundamental rights impairment on the one hand and the statutory prerequisites for carrying out the measures constituting interferences on the other hand (cf. BVerfGE 100, 313 <392 *et seq.*> – *The Article 10 Act*). The statutory requirements pertaining to the necessary degree of probability and the factual basis of the prognosis must be proportionate to the type and intensity of the resulting impairment of fundamental rights. Even where the threats the interference aims to avert concern exceptionally weighty legal interests, the requirement of sufficient probability cannot be dispensed with. In addition, the statutory basis must subject any serious interference with fundamental rights to the requirement that the assumptions and conclusions prompting the interference be based on specific facts (cf. BVerfGE 113, 348 <386>; 115, 320 <360 and 361> – *Profiling*). 245

(c) The principle of proportionality sets limits for a statutory provision authorising covert access to information technology systems insofar as it gives rise to special requirements regarding the grounds for interference. [...] 246

(aa) Such an interference may only be authorised if the statutory basis makes it contingent upon the existence of factual indications of a specific danger to an exceptionally significant legal interest. Such exceptionally significant legal interests primarily include life, limb and liberty of the person. They also include public interests that are of such significance that a threat to them would affect the foundations or existence of the state, or the foundations of human existence. These include, for instance, the functioning of essential and vital public infrastructure. 247

For the protection of other legal interests, [...] state measures must be limited to the existing investigatory powers conferred for prevention purposes in the respective field of law. 248

249 (bb) As a prerequisite for covert access, the statutory basis must also require that there be at least certain factual indications of a specific danger to the sufficiently weighty protected interests set out in the relevant provision.

250 α) Given the requirement of factual indications, mere assumptions or conclusions drawn from general experience are by themselves not sufficient to justify covert access. Rather, specific facts must be established that support a prognosis of danger (cf. BVerfGE 110, 33 <61>; 113, 348 <378>).

251 This prognosis must point to the existence of a specific danger. This means that there must be a factual situation where it is sufficiently likely, in the individual case, that certain persons will cause damage to the interests protected by the relevant statutory provision in the foreseeable future, unless the state intervenes. The existence of a specific danger is determined by three criteria: it concerns an individual case; it is foreseeable that the danger will result in actual damage within a certain period of time; and the cause of the danger can be attributed to individual persons. However, the accessing of information technology systems at issue here may already be justified at a time when it cannot be established with sufficient probability that the danger will materialise in the near future, provided that there are already specific facts indicating an impending danger in the individual case with regard to an exceptionally significant legal interest. Firstly, it must at least be possible to determine, based on these facts, the type of incident that might occur, and that it will occur within a foreseeable timeframe; secondly, the facts must indicate the involvement of specific persons whose identity is known at least to such an extent that the surveillance measures can be targeted at and for the most part limited to them.

252 By contrast, the weight of interference resulting from covert access to an information technology system is not sufficiently taken into account where statutory provisions authorise the measure on grounds so precautionary in nature that the existence of a specific danger to the protected legal interests need no longer be foreseeable at all, not even with regard to its basic characteristics.

253 [...]

254 β) Regarding the covert accessing of information technology systems, the constitutional requirements relating to the factual grounds prompting the interference apply to all instances where statutory provisions authorise interferences with fundamental rights that serve the aim of preventing dangers. Since in all these instances, the impairment resulting from the interference for the affected persons is the same, there is no need to set different requirements for different authorities, for instance by differentiating between police authorities and other authorities entrusted with preventive tasks such as offices for the protection of the Constitution. For the purposes of weighing the covert accessing of information technology systems, it is in

No. 40 – Remote Searches

principle irrelevant that the police and offices for the protection of the Constitution have different responsibilities and powers, and that, in consequence, the depth of interference resulting from their measures may differ.
[…]   255-256
(d) Furthermore, statutory provisions authorising the covert accessing of information technology systems must provide for suitable procedural safeguards protecting the interests of the affected persons. […] In particular, such accessing must generally be subject to judicial authorisation.   257
(aa) The requirement of judicial authorisation allows for prior review of a planned covert investigation measure by an independent and neutral authority, which may significantly contribute to effective fundamental rights protection. […]   258
(bb) If a covert investigation measure involves a serious interference with fundamental rights, prior review by an independent authority is constitutionally required because the affected person would otherwise not be afforded any protection. […]   259
The legislator may only entrust a non-judicial authority with exercising this oversight if that authority guarantees the same level of independence and neutrality as a judge. When deciding on the lawfulness of the covert measure, such an oversight authority is also required to state reasons for its decision.   260
This requirement of prior review by a suitable neutral authority may exceptionally be dispensed with in urgent cases, for instance in cases of danger requiring immediate action (*Gefahr im Verzug*); yet it must be ensured that in these cases the neutral authority will conduct an *ex post* review of the measure. In this context, a finding of urgency must meet certain factual and legal conditions informed by constitutional law (cf. BVerfGE 103, 142 <153 *et seq.*> regarding Art. 13(2) of the Basic Law).   261
(3) Based on these standards, the challenged provision does not satisfy the constitutional requirements.   262
(a) According to § 5(2) in conjunction with § 7(1) no. 1 and § 3(1) of the NRW Constitution Protection Act, the use of intelligence service methods by the *Land* Office for the Protection of the Constitution is only subject to the condition that there are factual indications suggesting that these methods allow the gathering of information on anti-constitutional activities. This does not subject the exercise of these powers to a sufficient substantive threshold, neither regarding the factual conditions for carrying out the interference, nor regarding the weight of the legal interests the measure aims to protect. Also, the provision fails to ensure prior review by an independent authority, so that the constitutionally required procedural safeguards are lacking.   263
(b) These shortcomings are not remedied, not even when taking into account – despite its lack of legal specificity – the statutory reference in § 5(2) no. 11 second sentence of the NRW Constitution Protection Act to the more detailed requirements   264

for surveillance measures under the Article 10 Act, and when interpreting this reference broadly, as suggested by the *Land* Government of North Rhine-Westphalia, to the effect that it renders applicable all formal and substantive safeguards set out in the Article 10 Act. While § 3(1) of the Article 10 Act does set out conditions for the use of telecommunications surveillance, covert access to an information technology system pursuant to § 5(2) no. 11 first sentence, second alternative of the NRW Constitution Protection Act is not limited to telecommunications surveillance; rather, the provision generally allows covert access for obtaining all available data from an information technology system.

265 The grounds for interference set out in § 3(1) of the Article 10 Act do not satisfy the constitutional requirements, neither with regard to the threshold for exercising the relevant powers nor with regard to procedural safeguards.

266 (aa) Under § 3(1) first sentence of the Article 10 Act, surveillance measures are permissible if there are factual indications supporting the suspicion that someone is planning, committing or has committed a criminal offence listed in the catalogue set out in that provision. Firstly, the catalogue of criminal offences does not appear to be informed by an overall concept under which all the criminal offences listed in that catalogue would constitute sufficient grounds that could justify measures pursuant to § 5(2) no. 11 first sentence, second alternative of the NRW Constitution Protection Act. Therefore, not all statutory grounds under the Article 10 Act that the challenged provision refers to ensure that the accessing [of information technology systems] in the specific case actually serves to protect one of the aforementioned exceptionally significant legal interests […]. Secondly, the reference to § 3(1) first sentence of the Article 10 Act does not ensure in each case that the covert accessing of information technology systems takes place only if it can be presumed with sufficient probability that relevant legal interests will be endangered […] in the near future.

267 […]

268 (bb) § 5(2) no. 11 first sentence, second alternative of the NRW Constitution Protection Act does not meet the constitutional requirements regarding prior review of covert access to an information technology system, not even when taking into account the reference to the Article 10 Act.

269 § 10 of the Article 10 Act provides that surveillance measures must be authorised by an order issued by the competent *Land* ministry upon request by the *Land* Office for the Protection of the Constitution. This procedure is not sufficient to ensure the prior review required by Art. 2(1) in conjunction with Art. 1(1) of the Basic Law. The foregoing provision sets out neither a requirement of judicial authorisation, nor – given that the prior review exercised by the Article 10 Committee (*G 10-Kommission*) according to § 3(6) of the Act on the Implementation of the Article 10

Act is not included in the statutory reference in question – an equivalent oversight mechanism. […]

c) Finally, there are no adequate statutory safeguards to ensure that measures taken pursuant to § 5(2) no. 11 first sentence, second alternative of the NRW Constitution Protection Act do not interfere with the core of private life, which enjoys absolute protection.

aa) Covert surveillance measures by the state must respect an inviolable core of private life protected under Art. 1(1) of the Basic Law (cf. BVerfGE 6, 32 <41>; 27, 1 <6> – *Microcensus*; 32, 373 <378 and 379>; 34, 238 <245> – *Secret Tape Recordings*; 80, 367 <373> – *Diary-Like Notes*; 109, 279 <313> – *Surveillance of Private Homes*; 113, 348 <390>). Even overriding public interests cannot justify an interference with this core (cf. BVerfGE 34, 238 <245> – *Secret Tape Recordings*; 109, 279 <313> – *Surveillance of Private Homes*). The development of one's personality within the core of private life encompasses the possibility of expressing internal processes such as emotions and feelings, as well as reflections, views and experiences of a highly personal nature, without fear of surveillance by state authorities (cf. BVerfGE 109, 279 <314> – *Surveillance of Private Homes*).

In the context of covert access to information technology systems, there is a risk that the state collects personal data that can be attributed to the core of private life. This is the case, for instance, where the person concerned uses the system to create and store files with highly personal contents, such as diary-like notes, or private video or sound files. Such files may enjoy absolute protection, as may, *inter alia*, written accounts of highly personal experiences (cf. in this regard BVerfGE 80, 367 <373 *et seq.*> – *Diary-Like Notes*; 109, 279 <319> – *Surveillance of Private Homes*). Furthermore, if the system also serves telecommunications purposes, it might be used to transmit contents which may belong to the core of private life, too. This applies not only to voice telephony, but also to remote communications for instance via email or other Internet communication services (cf. BVerfGE 113, 348 <390>). […]

bb) In the event of covert access to information technology systems, special statutory safeguards are required that protect the core of private life of the affected person. Citizens increasingly use complex information technology systems for managing personal matters and for telecommunications, including with persons they are close to. These systems provide them with opportunities for development in the highly personal domain. Compared to other surveillance measures – such as the use of GPS as a technical surveillance tool (cf. in this regard BVerfGE 112, 304 <318>) –, an investigation measure accessing an information technology system, which can be used to collect comprehensive data from the target system, thus gives rise to an increased risk of highly personal data being collected.

275 Because the accessing is carried out covertly, affected persons have no possibility to take steps for ensuring themselves, before or during the investigation measure, that the investigating authority respects the core of their private life. This complete loss of control must be countered by special provisions that afford protection by means of suitable procedural safeguards against the risk of violations of the core of private life.

276 cc) The constitutional requirements regarding the specific design of the framework ensuring protection of the core may differ depending on the method of data collection and the nature of the information obtained by it.

277 A statutory provision authorising a surveillance measure that might affect the core of private life must ensure, to the greatest extent possible, that no data relating to the core of private life is collected. If it is virtually unavoidable that information will be obtained before its link to the core can be determined – as is the case with covert accessing of information technology systems –, sufficient protection must be ensured at the stage of analysis. In particular, where data relating to the core was found and collected it must be deleted without undue delay and any further use must be ruled out (cf. BVerfGE 109, 279 <318> – *Surveillance of Private Homes*; 113, 348 <391 and 392>).

278 (1) In the context of covert access to an information technology system, data collection will be automated for technical reasons, at least in the vast majority of cases. In comparison with data collection carried out manually, this automated process makes it more difficult to distinguish at the stage of collection between data relating to the core and data not relating to the core. […]

279 Even if data is directly accessed manually without relying on prior technical recordings, for instance listening in on voice telephony via the Internet, protection of the core encounters practical difficulties even at the stage of data collection. Typically, when such a surveillance measure is carried out, it cannot be predicted with certainty what the contents of the collected data will be (cf. regarding telecommunications surveillance BVerfGE 113, 348 <392>). It may also be difficult to analyse the contents of the data while the collection process is ongoing. This applies for instance to text files or conversations in foreign languages. In this respect, it is not always possible to assess before or during data collection whether the communications under surveillance relate to the core of private life. However, if there is a risk that the data collection might violate the core of private life, this does not mean that constitutional law precludes the accessing of such information from the outset in these cases, given that the accessing of information technology systems is based on factual indications of a specific danger to an exceptionally significant legal interest.

280 (2) The constitutionally required protection of the core can be guaranteed by a two-tier concept of protection.

No. 40 – Remote Searches

(a) The statutory provision must ensure that the collection of data relating to the core is avoided from the outset as far as this is possible in terms of information technology and investigation technique (cf. regarding telecommunications surveillance BVerfGE 113, 348 <391 and 392>; regarding acoustic surveillance of private homes BVerfGE 109, 279 <318, 324> – *Surveillance of Private Homes*). In particular, safeguards made available by information technology must be used. If there are specific indications suggesting that a certain data collection measure will affect the core of private life in the individual case, it must in principle not be used. The situation is different if, for instance, specific indications suggest that core-related communication contents are deliberately linked to contents targeted by the investigation in order to evade surveillance. 281

(b) In many cases, the extent to which collected data relates to the core of private life cannot be determined before or during collection. The legislator must provide for suitable procedural safeguards to ensure that, where data relating to the core of private life has been collected, the severity of the violation of the core and its impact on the personality and development of the person concerned be kept to a minimum. 282

In this respect, it is crucial that the collected data be examined as to whether it contains information relating to the core of private life. Suitable procedures must be put in place that sufficiently protect the interests of the affected persons. If the examination reveals that data relating to the core was collected, it must be deleted without undue delay. Any sharing or use of this data must be ruled out (cf. BVerfGE 109, 279 <324> – *Surveillance of Private Homes*; 113, 348 <392>). 283

dd) The challenged Act lacks necessary provisions protecting the core. Even if the reference to the Article 10 Act in § 5(2) no. 11 second sentence of the NRW Constitution Protection Act were taken into account despite its shortcomings in terms of legal specificity, this would not merit a different conclusion, given that the Article 10 Act equally lacks safeguards protecting the core of private life. 284

[…] 285

d) The violation of the general right of personality in its manifestation as protection of the confidentiality and integrity of information technology systems (Art. 2(1) in conjunction with Art. 1(1) of the Basic Law) renders § 5(2) no. 11 first sentence, second alternative of the NRW Constitution Protection Act void. 286

e) […] 287

II.

The legislative authorisation of covert Internet surveillance pursuant to § 5(2) no. 11 first sentence, first alternative of the NRW Constitution Protection Act 288 violates the privacy of telecommunications under Art. 10(1) of the Basic Law. In certain cases, measures taken pursuant to this provision constitute interferences with this fundamental right that are not justified under constitutional law (see 1 below). Art. 19(1) second sentence of the Basic Law is also violated (see 2 below). Given that the provision is unconstitutional, it is declared void (see 3 below). Nevertheless, the *Land* Office for the Protection of the Constitution may in principle carry out Internet surveillance measures to the extent that these do not amount to interferences with fundamental rights (see 4 below).

289 1. The covert Internet surveillance provided for in § 5(2) no. 11 first sentence, first alternative of the NRW Constitution Protection Act covers measures carried out by the Office for the Protection of the Constitution to obtain knowledge of the contents of Internet communication via the normal technical means provided for this purpose, for instance by accessing a website on the World Wide Web using a web browser (see A I 1 a above). In certain cases, this may interfere with the privacy of telecommunications. The challenged provision does not justify such an interference under constitutional law.

290 a) The scope of protection of Art. 10(1) of the Basic Law covers ongoing telecommunications conducted via an information technology system that is connected to the Internet (see I 1 c aa (1) above). However, this fundamental right only protects individuals to the extent that they have the legitimate expectation that third parties cannot obtain knowledge of the telecommunications in which they are involved. By contrast, this fundamental rights protection does not extend to the legitimate expectations that communication partners have towards each other. […] Therefore, the fact that the state obtains knowledge of telecommunication contents must only be measured against the privacy of telecommunications if a state authority monitors a telecommunication relationship from the outside without being involved as a communicating party. […]

291 […]

292 Covert Internet surveillance thus interferes with Art. 10(1) of the Basic Law if the Office for the Protection of the Constitution monitors secure communication contents by using access keys obtained without the consent or against the will of the communicating parties. This is the case, for instance, if a password obtained by way of keylogging is used in order to gain access to an email inbox or a private chatroom.

293 By contrast, there is no interference with Art. 10(1) of the Basic Law if for instance a participant in a private chatroom has voluntarily provided a person acting on behalf of the Office for the Protection of the Constitution with their access information, which the authority then uses. An interference with telecommunications privacy can certainly be ruled out where the authority collects generally accessible

contents, for instance by viewing open discussion forums or websites that are not password protected.

b) The interferences with Art. 10(1) of the Basic Law arising under § 5(2) no. 11 first sentence, first alternative of the NRW Constitution Protection Act are not justified under constitutional law. The challenged provision does not meet the constitutional requirements regarding authorisations for such interferences. 294

aa) § 5(2) no. 11 first sentence, first alternative of the NRW Constitution Protection Act does not satisfy the requirement of legal clarity and specificity given that the second sentence of this provision is too vague, failing to set out the prerequisites for interference in a sufficiently precise manner (see C I 2 a, bb above). 295

bb) Furthermore, to the extent that it is measured against Art. 10(1) of the Basic Law, the challenged provision does not satisfy the requirement of proportionality in the strict sense. 296

The interference with telecommunications privacy is serious. Based on the challenged provision, the Office for the Protection of the Constitution could access communication contents which may be sensitive, and which may provide insights into the personal matters and habits of the persons concerned. This holds true not only for the persons who prompted a surveillance measure; the interference may also indiscriminately affect other persons if the information obtained concerns not only persons targeted by the measure but also their communication partners. The covert nature of the accessing increases the severity of the interference. Additionally, given the broad wording of the prerequisites for interference in § 7(1) no. 1 in conjunction with § 3(1) of the NRW Constitution Protection Act, surveillance may also be directed against persons who did not prompt the interference. 297

Even when taking into account the significant weight attached to the pursued aim of protecting the constitutional order, an interference with fundamental rights of such severity in principle requires at least that the statutory basis set a qualified and substantive threshold for interference (cf. regarding criminal investigations BVerfGE 107, 299 <321>). With such a threshold lacking here, § 7(1) no. 1 in conjunction with § 3(1) of the NRW Constitution Protection Act authorises, on a large scale, purely precautionary intelligence service action before specific dangers actually materialise, but fails to take into account the weight of the legal interests, including of third parties, that are potentially violated as a result. Such a far-reaching legislative authorisation of fundamental rights interferences is not compatible with the principle of proportionality. 298

cc) With regard to interferences arising under § 5(2) no. 11 first sentence, first alternative of the NRW Constitution Protection Act, the statutory framework does not contain any safeguards protecting the core of private life. Yet such safeguards are necessary where state authorities are authorised to collect telecommunication 299 contents in a manner that interferes with Art. 10(1) of the Basic Law (cf. BVerfGE 113, 348 <390 et seq.>).

300   2. Finally, to the extent that § 5(2) no. 11 first sentence, first alternative of the NRW Constitution Protection Act authorises interferences with Art. 10(1) of the Basic Law, the provision does not satisfy the requirement that the affected fundamental right be expressly specified (*Zitiergebot*) in accordance with Article 19(1) second sentence of the Basic Law.

301-302   […]

303   3. Given that § 5(2) no. 11 first sentence, first alternative of the NRW Constitution Protection Act violates Art. 10(1) and Art. 19(1) second sentence of the Basic Law, the provision is void.

304   4. However, insofar as Internet surveillance measures do not interfere with fundamental rights, the voidness of the legislative authorisation does not generally bar the authority from taking such measures.

305   Covert surveillance that does not amount to an interference with Art. 10(1) of the Basic Law does not necessarily constitute an interference with the general right of personality guaranteed by Art. 2(1) in conjunction with Art. 1(1) of the Basic Law.

306   a) The confidentiality and integrity of information technology systems guaranteed by the general right of personality is not affected by the Internet surveillance measures pursuant to § 5(2) no. 11 first sentence, first alternative of the NRW Constitution Protection Act, given that these measures are limited to collecting data intended by the relevant system's owner – for instance the operator of a web server – for Internet communication purposes using the normal technical means provided in this regard. For these data collection purposes, the persons concerned themselves have allowed technical access to their systems. Therefore, they cannot legitimately expect that no such measures are taken.

307   b) As a general rule, there is also no interference with Art. 2(1) in conjunction with Art. 1(1) of the Basic Law in its manifestation as a right to informational self-determination.

308   aa) The state is not generally barred from obtaining publicly accessible information. This also applies if this possibility is used to collect personal information in the individual case […]. Therefore, it does not amount to an interference with the general right of personality if a state authority collects communication contents that are available on the Internet and addressed to the general public or to a group of persons that is not further defined. This is the case, for instance, where authorities view a generally accessible website on the World Wide Web, subscribe to a mailing list that is open to everyone or monitor an open chatroom.

309   Yet an interference with the right to informational self-determination may arise if information obtained by viewing generally accessible web contents is deliberately

compiled, stored and, as the case may be, analysed using further data, giving rise to a special risk to the personality of the person concerned. Such measures require a statutory basis authorising this interference.

bb) It does not constitute an interference with the right to informational self-determination if a state authority merely uses a cover identity to build a communication relationship with a fundamental rights holder. However, it does constitute an interference if, in doing so, it exploits that person's legitimate expectations regarding the identity and motivation of their communication partner for the purposes of collecting personal data which the state authority would not receive otherwise [...].

It follows that, as a rule, Internet surveillance as such will generally not amount to an interference with fundamental rights. To a large extent, the communication relationships facilitated by Internet communication services do not merit legitimate expectations regarding the identity and authenticity of one's communication partners since these cannot be verified. This applies even if certain persons – for instance in the context of a discussion forum – participate in communication over a longer time period and thus form a kind of 'online community'. Even in this type of communication relationships, all participants are aware of the fact that they do not know the identity of their communication partners, or are in any case unable to verify the information those partners provide about themselves. Their expectation that they are not communicating with a state authority does thus not merit protection.

III.

[...]

IV.

§ 5a(1) of the NRW Constitution Protection Act is compatible with the Basic Law insofar as its scope of application was expanded to cover activities within the meaning of § 3(1) no. 1 of the NRW Constitution Protection Act. In particular, this provision does not violate Art. 2(1) in conjunction with Art. 1(1) of the Basic Law.

1. The collection of data on bank accounts and transactions provided for in § 5a(1) of the NRW Constitution Protection Act interferes with the general right of personality in its manifestation as a right to informational self-determination.

Such account information can be significant for protecting the personality of the persons concerned, and thus enjoy fundamental rights protection. [...]

316 [...]
317 2. The interferences with fundamental rights authorised by § 5a(1) of the NRW Constitution Protection Act are, however, constitutionally justified with respect to investigating the activities specified in § 3(1) no. 1 of the NRW Constitution Protection Act. In particular, the challenged provision satisfies the principle of proportionality in this respect.
318-332 [...]

V.

333 [...]

Justices: Papier, Hohmann-Dennhardt, Hoffmann-Riem, Bryde, Gaier, Eichberger, Schluckebier, Kirchhof

No. 41

BVerfGE 125, 260 – Data Retention

HEADNOTES

to the Judgment of the First Senate of 2 March 2010
1 BvR 256, 263, 586/08

1. The precautionary retention of telecommunications traffic data by private service providers without specific grounds, for a period of six months, as provided for under Directive 2006/24/EC of the European Parliament and of the Council of 15 March 2006 (OJ L 105 of 13 April 2006, p. 54; hereinafter: Directive 2006/24/EC), is not *per se* incompatible with Art. 10 of the Basic Law; there is thus no need to decide on the possible precedence of the directive over domestic law.
2. The principle of proportionality requires that the statutory framework governing such data retention be designed so as to adequately reflect the particular weight of the resulting fundamental rights interference. This requires sufficiently stringent and clear statutory provisions regarding data security, data use, transparency and legal protection.
3. Under Art. 73(1) no. 7 of the Basic Law, it is incumbent upon the federal legislator to enact provisions ensuring data security and to subject possible data use to a clear purpose limitation, as these elements are inseparable from the statutory provisions imposing obligations to retain data. By contrast, the legislative competence for enacting provisions governing requests for access to the retained data by the authorities, and for specifying the applicable transparency and legal protection regime, lies with the legislator that is competent to legislate on the respective underlying subject matter.
4. With regard to data security, the legislator must lay down particularly high standards in clear and binding provisions. These provisions must ensure that, in principle, the required level of data security is informed by the current state of expertise and incorporates, on an ongoing basis, new research and advances in this field. It must also be ensured that data security may not be freely weighed against general business considerations.

5. Requests for access to and the direct use of retained data are only proportionate if they serve to protect exceptionally significant legal interests. In the domain of law enforcement, this requires that specific facts give rise to the suspicion of serious criminal acts. In the domain of public security and the tasks of the intelligence services, requests for data access and use of the data may only be authorised if there are factual indications of a specific danger to life, limb or liberty of the person or to the existence or security of the Federation or a *Land*, or of a danger to the general public.

6. The mere indirect use of the data by telecommunications service providers to provide information to the authorities on the subscribers of Internet Protocol addresses is permissible for the purposes of law enforcement, public security and the tasks of the intelligence services, even where this is not subject to a narrowly-defined statutory catalogue of criminal offences or protected legal interests. For prosecuting administrative offences [as a law enforcement purpose], such information may only be provided to the authorities in cases of particular weight on grounds expressly set out in the law.

FEDERAL CONSTITUTIONAL COURT
- 1 BvR 256, 263, 586/08 -

IN THE NAME OF THE PEOPLE

In the proceedings
on the constitutional complaints of

I. 1. Prof. Dr. G..., 2. Dr. G..., 3. Mr K..., 4. J... GmbH, represented by its managing director, 5. Mr U..., 6. Mr R..., 7. Mr Z..., 8. Dr. B...,
    – authorised representative: ...
    against §§ 113a and 113b of the Telecommunications Act as amended by the Act Revising the Law on Telecommunications Surveillance and Other Covert Investigation Measures and Transposing Directive 2006/24/EC of 21 December 2007 (BGBl I, p. 3198)

    - 1 BvR 256/08 -,

II. 1. Dr. Dr. h. c. H..., 2. Dr. S..., 3. Ms L..., 4. Mr B..., 5. Ms P..., 6. Mr K..., 7. Dr. L..., 8. Dr. W..., 9. Prof. Dr. S..., 10. Ms S..., 11. Mr F..., 12. Mr S..., 13. Mr V..., 14. Mr W...,

No. 41 – Data Retention

– authorised representative: …
against the Act Revising the Law on Telecommunications Surveillance and Other Covert Investigation Measures and Transposing Directive 2006/24/EC of 21 December 2007 (BGBl I, p. 3198)

- 1 BvR 263/08 -,

III. 1. Ms A…, 2. Ms B…, 3. Mr B…, 4. Ms B…, 5. Ms B…, 6. Mr B…, 7. Mr D…, 8. Dr. D…, 9. Dr. E…, 10. Mr F…, 11. Mr G…, 12. Ms G…, 13. Ms H…, 14. Ms H…, 15. Ms H…, 16. Mr H…, 17. Mr H…, 18. Mr W…, 19. Mr W…, 20. Mr T…, 21. Dr. T…, 22. Mr S…, 23. Dr. S…, 24. Ms S…, 25. Ms S…, 26. Ms S…, 27. Ms S…, 28. Ms P…, 29. Mr N…, 30. Mr N…, 31. Ms M…, 32. Mr M…, 33. Ms M…, 34. Ms L…, 35. Ms K…, 36. Mr K…, 37. Mr K…, 38. Ms K…, 39. Ms K…, 40. Dr. H…, 41. Ms H…, 42. Ms H…, 43. Ms H…,

– authorised representative: …
against the provisions on data retention in the Act Revising the Law on Telecommunications Surveillance and Other Covert Investigation Measures and Transposing Directive 2006/24/EC of 21 December 2007 (BGBl I, p. 3198)

- 1 BvR 586/08 -

the Federal Constitutional Court – First Senate –

with the participation of Justices

>President Papier,
>Hohmann-Dennhardt,
>Bryde,
>Gaier,
>Eichberger,
>Schluckebier,
>Kirchhof,
>Masing

held on the basis of the oral hearing of 15 December 2009:

JUDGMENT

1. §§ 113a and 113b of the Telecommunications Act, as amended by Article 2 no. 6 of the Act Revising the Law on Telecommunications Surveillance and Other Covert Investigation Measures and Transposing Directive 2006/24/EC of 21 December 2007 (BGBl I, p. 3198), violate Article 10(1) of the Basic Law and are void.

2. § 100g(1) first sentence of the Code of Criminal Procedure, as amended by Article 1 no. 11 of the Act Revising the Law on Telecommunications Surveillance and Other Covert Investigation Measures and Transposing Directive 2006/24/EC of 21 December 2007 (BGBl I, p. 3198), violates Article 10(1) of the Basic Law and is thus void to the extent that it permits the obtaining of traffic data retained pursuant to § 113a of the Telecommunications Act.

3. The telecommunications traffic data that was compiled and temporarily stored by providers of publicly available telecommunications services at the request of the authorities but not yet transferred to the respective requesting authority under § 113b first sentence, first half-sentence of the Telecommunications Act in accordance with the preliminary injunction issued on 11 March 2008 in the proceedings 1 BvR 256/08 (BGBl I, p. 659), repeated and extended by Order of 28 October 2008 (BGBl I, p. 2239), last repeated by Order of 15 October 2009 (BGBl I, p. 3704), must be deleted without undue delay. The data may not be transferred to the requesting authorities.

4. [...]

REASONS:

A.

1 The constitutional complaints concern provisions of the Telecommunications Act and the Code of Criminal Procedure that govern the precautionary retention of telecommunications traffic data by the providers of publicly available telecommunications services for a period of six months, and the use of such data.

I.

2 The challenged provisions [...] serve to transpose Directive 2006/24/EC of the European Parliament and of the Council of 15 March 2006 on the retention of data generated or processed in connection with the provision of publicly available electronic communications services or of public communications networks and amending Directive 2002/58/EC (OJ L 105 of 13 April 2006, p. 54; hereinafter: Directive 2006/24/EC).

3 1. All constitutional complaints directly challenge §§ 113a and 113b of the Telecommunications Act, which were inserted into the Telecommunications Act by Art. 2 no. 6 of the Telecommunications Surveillance Revision Act. Furthermore, the constitutional complaints in proceedings 1 BvR 263/08 and 1 BvR 586/08 directly

No. 41 – Data Retention

challenge § 100g of the Code of Criminal Procedure, as amended by Art. 1 no. 11 of the Telecommunications Surveillance Revision Act, to the extent that it permits the authorities to obtain data retained pursuant to § 113a of the Telecommunications Act.

a) § 113a of the Telecommunications Act aims to ensure that for all publicly available telecommunications services traffic data providing information on the lines used in telecommunications, and on the time and location of the communication, be retained for six months and kept available so that it can be used by the authorities in the exercise of their functions. [...]

§ 113a(1) first sentence of the Telecommunications Act obliges providers of publicly available telecommunications services to retain, for a period of six months, the telecommunications traffic data listed in § 113a(2) to (5) regarding phone calls via landlines, the Internet and mobile phones, transmission of text messages, multimedia messages and similar messages, email communications and Internet access. [...] Pursuant to § 113a(11) of the Telecommunications Act, the data must be deleted within one month after the retention period expires. Pursuant to § 113a(8) of the Telecommunications Act, neither the contents of communications nor data on accessed websites may be retained. [...]

In addition to the data retention pursuant to § 113a of the Telecommunications Act, the providers of telecommunications services may continue to store and use telecommunications traffic data pursuant to § 96 of the Telecommunications Act if it is necessary for the purposes specified in that provision. [...]

[...]

b) § 113b of the Telecommunications Act sets out the purposes for which the data retained pursuant to § 113a of the Telecommunications Act may be used. [...]

aa) [...]

[...]

bb) In principle, § 113b first sentence, second half-sentence of the Telecommunications Act rules out the use of data retained pursuant to § 113a of the Telecommunications Act for purposes other than those stated in § 113b first sentence, first half-sentence of the Telecommunications Act. However, it provides for the exception that retained data may also be used by service providers for the purposes of providing certain information to the authorities pursuant to § 113 of the Telecommunications Act.

§ 113(1) of the Telecommunications Act permits the authorities to request the transfer of so-called customer and subscriber data pursuant to §§ 95 and 111 of the Telecommunications Act, in particular telephone numbers, subscriber line identifications, and the names and addresses of subscribers. [...]

45-46	[...]
47	Information pursuant to § 113(1) first sentence of the Telecommunications Act must be provided to the authorities upon request if it is necessary for prosecuting criminal or administrative offences, averting dangers to public security and order, or for the tasks of the intelligence services.
	cc) [...]
48-60	c) § 100g(1) first sentence of the Code of Criminal Procedure sets out to what extent telecommunications traffic data may be obtained for law enforcement purposes. According to this provision, law enforcement authorities may [...] access traffic data stored by telecommunications companies on the basis of § 96 of the Telecommunications Act. Apart from this, § 100g of the Code of Criminal Procedure now also permits authorities to obtain data retained as a precautionary measure pursuant to § 113a of the Telecommunications Act. [...]
61	
62-79	[...]
80-86	2. [...]
87	3. [...]
88	4. [...]

II.

89	1. The complainants in proceedings 1 BvR 256/08 challenge §§ 113a and 113b of the Telecommunications Act. They claim a violation of Art. 10(1), Art. 12(1), Art. 14(1), Art. 5(1) and Art. 3(1) of the Basic Law. [...]
90-116	[...]
117	2. The complainants in proceedings 1 BvR 263/08 challenge §§ 113a and 113b of the Telecommunications Act as well as § 100g of the Code of Criminal Procedure to the extent that it concerns the obtaining of data retained pursuant to § 113a of the Telecommunications Act. They claim a violation of Art. 1(1), Art. 2(1) in conjunction with Art. 1(1), Art. 10(1) and Art. 19(2) of the Basic Law.
118-133	[...]
134	3. The complainants in proceedings 1 BvR 586/08 also challenge §§ 113a and 113b of the Telecommunications Act and § 100g of the Code of Criminal Procedure. They claim a violation of Art. 10(1) and Art. 2(1) in conjunction with Art. 1(1) of the Basic Law.

No. 41 – Data Retention

[…] 135-145

III.

Statements on the constitutional complaints were submitted by the Federal Government, the Federal Administrative Court, the Federal Court of Justice, the Federal Officer for Data Protection and Freedom of Information, and, on behalf of the *Länder*, the Berlin Officer for Data Protection and Freedom of Information.

1. […] 146
2. […] 147-164
3. […] 165
4. […] 166
5. […] 167-170
6. Statements on the Court's technical, factual and legal questions were submitted by Constanze Kurz, Prof. Dr. Felix Freiling, Prof. Dr. Andreas Pfitzmann, Prof. Dr. Alexander Roßnagel, Prof. Dr. Christoph Ruland, the Federal Officer for Data Protection and Freedom of Information, the Berlin Officer for Data Protection and Freedom of Information, the Federal Ministry of Justice with the participation of the Federal Ministry for Economic Affairs and Technology and the Minister of the Interior, the complainants in proceedings 1 BvR 256/08 and 1 BvR 263/08 as well as the Federal Association for Information Technology, Telecommunications and New Media (*Bundesverband Informationswirtschaft, Telekommunikation und neue Medien e.V.*, BITKOM), the eco Association of the German Internet Industry (*Verband der deutschen Internetwirtschaft e.V.*, eco) as well as the Association of Telecommunications and Value-Added Service Providers (*Verband der Anbieter von Telekommunikations- und Mehrwertdiensten e.V.*, VATM). 171
7. […] 172

173

IV.

[…] 174

B.

The constitutional complaints are admissible. 175

176-182 [...]

C.

183 The constitutional complaints are for the most part well-founded. The challenged provisions violate the complainants' fundamental right under Art. 10(1) of the Basic Law. There is no reason to request a preliminary ruling from the Court of Justice of the European Union, since the possible precedence of Community law is not relevant in the present proceedings. The fundamental rights guarantees of the Basic Law do not preclude the transposal of Directive 2006/24/EC provided that the legislator revises the design of the statutory framework.

184 The constitutional complaint of complainant no. 4 in proceedings 1 BvR 256/08 is unfounded to the extent that it claims a violation of Art. 12(1) of the Basic Law.

I.

185-187 [...]

II.

188 The challenged provisions interfere with Art. 10(1) of the Basic Law.

189 1. Art. 10(1) of the Basic Law guarantees the privacy of telecommunications, which protects the non-physical transmission of information to individual recipients by way of telecommunications traffic (cf. BVerfGE 106, 28 <35 and 36>; 120, 274 <306 and 307> – *Remote Searches*) against public authorities obtaining knowledge thereof (cf. BVerfGE 100, 313 <358> – *The Article 10 Act*; 106, 28 <37>). This protection is not limited to the actual communication contents. It also extends to the confidentiality of the specific circumstances of a communication, which include in particular whether, when and how often telecommunications traffic occurred or was attempted between whom or between which devices (cf. BVerfGE 67, 157 <172>; 85, 386 <396>; 100, 313 <358> – *The Article 10 Act*; 107, 299 <312 and 313>; 115, 166 <183> – *Telecommunications Surveillance*; 120, 274 <307> – *Remote Searches*).

190 The protection under Art. 10(1) of the Basic Law applies not only to the initial access, whereby public authorities obtain knowledge of telecommunications activities and contents for the first time. This fundamental right also protects against information and data processing measures that follow after the state obtained knowledge of protected communications, and against any subsequent use of the information thus obtained (cf. BVerfGE 100, 313 <359> – *The Article 10 Act*). Any instance

No. 41 – Data Retention

where the state obtains knowledge of, stores or processes telecommunications data, any analysis of communication contents, and any other use by public authorities constitutes an interference with fundamental rights (cf. BVerfGE 85, 386 <398>; 100, 313 <366> – *The Article 10 Act*; 110, 33 <52 and 53>). Hence, the collection and storage of telecommunications data, the cross-checking with other data, the analysis of the data, its selection for further use, or the transfer to third parties each constitute a separate interference with the privacy of telecommunications (cf. BVerfGE 100, 313 <366 and 367> – *The Article 10 Act*). Consequently, the obligations imposed on telecommunications companies to collect telecommunications data, to retain it, and to transfer it to state authorities all constitute separate interferences with Art. 10(1) of the Basic Law (cf. BVerfGE 107, 299 <313>).

The right to informational self-determination following from Art. 2(1) in conjunction with Art. 1(1) of the Basic Law is not applicable in addition to Art. 10 of the Basic Law since, in the context of telecommunications, Art. 10 of the Basic Law contains a more specific guarantee that supersedes the aforementioned general guarantee and that gives rise to special requirements where data is obtained through interferences with the privacy of telecommunications. Yet the requirements that the Federal Constitutional Court derived from Art. 2(1) in conjunction with Art. 1(1) of the Basic Law can largely be applied accordingly to the more specific guarantee of Art. 10 of the Basic Law, too (cf. BVerfGE 100, 313 <358 and 359> – *The Article 10 Act*).

191

2. a) The obligation to retain telecommunications traffic data imposed on service providers under § 113a(1) of the Telecommunications Act interferes with the privacy of telecommunications. Firstly, this holds true for the obligations to retain data imposed on service providers in § 113a(2) to (5) of the Telecommunications Act, and for the retention obligation that derives from § 113a(2) to (5) of the Telecommunications Act in conjunction with § 113a(6) and (7) of the Telecommunications Act. The data to be retained pursuant to these provisions provides information on whether, when, where and how often connections were established or attempted between which devices. In particular, this also extends to the retention of data concerning email services pursuant to § 113a(3) of the Telecommunications Act, whose confidentiality is equally protected by Art. 10(1) of the Basic Law (cf. BVerfGE 113, 348 <383>; 120, 274 <307> – *Remote Searches*). While intercepting emails may be simple from a technical point of view, this does not alter the fact that such communication is regarded as confidential and merits protection. Retaining data relating to Internet access pursuant to § 113a(4) of the Telecommunications Act also interferes with Art. 10(1) of the Basic Law. It is true that Internet access enables not only communication between individuals, which is protected by the privacy of telecommunications, but also participation in mass communication. How-

192

ever, it is not possible to distinguish between individual and mass communication without determining the contents of the information transmitted in each case, which would actually run counter to the protection the fundamental right seeks to afford; therefore the retention of data relating to Internet access as such must already be regarded as an interference, even where this data does not include any information on accessed websites […].

193 The finding that § 113a of the Telecommunications Act gives rise to interferences is not called into question by the fact that the data retention required by this provision is not carried out directly by the state but by private service providers. This is because the state merely uses these service providers as agents assisting in the exercise of state functions. § 113a of the Telecommunications Act obliges private telecommunications companies to retain data solely so that state authorities can fulfil their responsibilities pursuant to § 113b of the Telecommunications Act, for the purposes of law enforcement, public security and the tasks of the intelligence services. The impairment of fundamental rights resulting from data retention is directly ordered by the state, without affording the companies obliged to retain data any discretion; they are obliged to retain the data in a manner that enables them to comply with information requests by authorised public authorities pursuant to § 113a(9) of the Telecommunications Act without undue delay. Under these conditions, the retention of data must be qualified as a direct interference with Art. 10(1) of the Basic Law that is legally attributable to the legislator (cf. BVerfGE 107, 299 <313 and 314>).

194 b) The data transfers to the authorities set out in § 113b first sentence, first half-sentence of the Telecommunications Act also result in interferences with Art. 10(1) of the Basic Law. It is true that the statutory provision does not directly permit the use of data retained pursuant to § 113a of the Telecommunications Act; instead, reference is made to other, separate legislation, which has yet to be enacted, based on which access to the data may then be requested by the authorities. The aforementioned provision does, however, already contain a basic determination of the purposes for which such data may ultimately be used. […] As the envisaged transfer of data derives from a statutory provision, it is directly based on an act of public authority bound by fundamental rights under Art. 1(3) of the Basic Law; the transfer requires an authorising state order in each individual case; and the recipients of the transfer are state authorities. In legal terms, it must therefore be qualified as a state interference.

195 c) § 113b first sentence, second half-sentence in conjunction with § 113(1) of the Telecommunications Act also gives rise to an interference with Art. 10(1) of the Basic Law. It provides that the authorities may request information from service providers on subscriber and customer data pursuant to §§ 95 and 111 of the

Telecommunications Act, which they can only provide by using the data retained pursuant § 113a(4) of the Telecommunications Act. It is not relevant in this respect whether and to what extent providing information pursuant to § 113 of the Telecommunications Act generally constitutes an interference with Art. 10(1) of the Basic Law or whether, in principle, only the right to informational self-determination under Art. 2(1) in conjunction with Art. 1(1) of the Basic Law is applicable. In any case, an interference with the privacy of telecommunications under Art. 10(1) of the Basic Law arises at least where information is provided on the basis of § 113b first sentence, second half-sentence and § 113(1) of the Telecommunications Act. This is due to the fact that it concerns the use of data retained pursuant to § 113a of the Telecommunications Act, which means it was obtained through an interference with Art. 10(1) of the Basic Law. Where data was originally obtained through an interference with Art. 10(1) of the Basic Law, any subsequent use must be measured against this fundamental right, too (cf. BVerfGE 100, 313 <359> – *The Article 10 Act*; 110, 33 <68 and 69>; 113, 348 <365>). In this regard, it is also irrelevant that the aforementioned statutory provisions require that the retained data be used not by the public authorities themselves, but by private providers seeking to comply with the respective information requests received from the authorities.

d) Lastly, § 100g of the Code of Criminal Procedure also gives rise to an interference with Art. 10(1) of the Basic Law. It enables law enforcement authorities to compel companies obliged to retain data pursuant to § 113a of the Telecommunications Act to transfer this data to these authorities, and to subsequently use it. Thus, both § 100g(1) first sentence of the Code of Criminal Procedure itself and requests for data access based thereon constitute acts of public authority that interfere with Art. 10(1) of the Basic Law.

III.

Formally, there are no objections to the challenged provisions. They satisfy the requirement that interferences be based on a statutory provision in accordance with Art. 10(2) first sentence of the Basic Law, and they fall within the legislative competence of the Federation.

[...]

198-203

IV.

Substantively, interferences with the privacy of telecommunications are constitutional if they serve legitimate purposes in the interest of the common good and also satisfy the principle of proportionality for the rest (cf. BVerfGE 100, 313

<359> – *The Article 10 Act*), i.e., if they are suitable, necessary and appropriate for achieving these purposes (cf. BVerfGE 109, 279 <335 *et seq.*> – *Surveillance of Private Homes*; 115, 320 <345> – *Profiling*; 118, 168 <193>; 120, 274 <318 and 319> – *Remote Searches*; established case-law).

205 Thus, the six-month retention of telecommunications traffic data without specific grounds, as required under §§ 113a and 113b of the Telecommunications Act, serving qualified uses in the domains of law enforcement, public security and the tasks of the intelligence services, is not *per se* incompatible with Art. 10 of the Basic Law. In enacting such a statutory framework, the legislator can pursue legitimate purposes for which the described data retention regime is a suitable and necessary means within the meaning of the principle of proportionality. Nor is such retention unjustifiable from the outset with regard to the requirement of proportionality in its strict sense. Provided that the statutory framework is designed in a way that sufficiently reflects the particular weight of the resulting interference, the retention of telecommunications traffic data without specific grounds is not necessarily subject to the strict prohibition on gathering and storing data for further retention as set out in the case-law of the Federal Constitutional Court (cf. BVerfGE 65, 1 <46 and 47> – *Census*; 115, 320 <350> – *Profiling*; 118, 168 <187>).

206 1. Increasing the effectiveness of law enforcement, public security measures and the tasks of the intelligence services are legitimate purposes, which can in principle justify an interference with the privacy of telecommunications (cf. BVerfGE 100, 313 <373, 383 and 384> – *The Article 10 Act*; 107, 299 <316>; 109, 279 <336> – *Surveillance of Private Homes*; 115, 320 <345> – *Profiling*). [...] Nevertheless, precautionary data retention not based on specific grounds is only ever permissible in exceptional cases. The underlying rationale as well as the design of the relevant framework are subject to particularly strict requirements, especially regarding the purposes for which the data may be used.

207 2. The legislator may recognise the precautionary retention of telecommunications traffic data without specific grounds as a suitable means to achieve the legislative aims pursued, so as to enable a later transfer of retained data – prompted by specific grounds – to the competent authorities in the domains of law enforcement, public security or intelligence. Data retention creates investigation possibilities that, given the increasing relevance of telecommunications, also for preparing or committing criminal acts, are promising in many cases and that would not exist otherwise. [...]

208 3. The legislator may also regard the retention of telecommunications traffic data for a period of six months as a necessary means. Less restrictive means that would allow for similarly comprehensive investigation measures are not ascertainable. [...]

No. 41 – Data Retention

4. Moreover, the retention of telecommunications traffic data for a period of six months, on the scale provided for in § 113a of the Telecommunications Act, is not from the outset disproportionate in the strict sense.

a) This notwithstanding, such data retention constitutes a particularly serious interference, with indiscriminate effects that are unprecedented in our legal system: throughout the entire six-month period, virtually all telecommunications traffic data of all citizens is stored, regardless of whether any culpable conduct can be attributed to them, and regardless of whether there is an – at least abstract – danger or any other qualified grounds prompting the measure. The envisaged data retention concerns everyday behaviour that is a fundamental part of our daily interactions and indispensable for social participation in modern society. [...]

The retained data has extensive informative value. Depending on how the affected persons use telecommunications services, the data may by itself already reveal profound insights into the social environment and the individual activities of individual citizens – this applies all the more if the data serves as a starting point for further investigations. Under the telecommunications traffic data retention regime provided for in § 113a of the Telecommunications Act, only traffic data is stored (including time, duration, connections involved and – in case of mobile phones – location), but not the communication contents. However, a comprehensive and automated analysis of such data could allow considerable conclusions to be drawn about the contents of communications, including contents that fall within the intimate sphere. Where long-term monitoring takes place regarding both the participants of phone conversations (including members of certain professions, institutions or interest groups, or providers of certain services) and regarding the date, time and location of conversations, detailed conclusions can be drawn – by linking data – regarding the persons whose traffic data is analysed; these conclusions may concern social or political affiliations as well as personal preferences, interests and weaknesses of the affected persons. In this regard, no confidentiality protection is provided. Depending on telecommunications practices, and even more so in the future, such data retention may make it possible to create conclusive personality and movement profiles of virtually all citizens. In relation to groups and associations, retained data might also reveal internal influence structures and decision-making processes.

Data retention that makes such data uses in principle possible, and that might even be deliberately used to that end in certain cases, constitutes a serious interference. It adds to the weight of interference that, regardless of how the framework governing the use of retained data is designed, such data retention considerably increases the risk that citizens become the subject of further investigations even where they themselves did not prompt any such investigations. For example, the fact that a person happens to be within a particular cell site or is contacted by a particular person at the wrong time may already suffice to subject that person to wide-ranging investigations and to the pressure of having to explain themselves. In addition, the considerable burden for the persons concerned is aggravated by the potential for abuse arising from such data collection. [...] Furthermore, the retention of telecommunications data is of particular weight because the affected persons are not immediately aware of the data retention as such, nor of the intended use of the retained data; what is more, the measure also covers telecommunications undertaken with expectations of confidentiality. As a result, the retention of telecommunications traffic data without specific grounds is capable of leaving citizens with the diffuse and alarming feeling of being watched, which can impair the exercise of fundamental rights without worry or fear in many areas.

213 b) Even though the obligation to retain data indiscriminately affects an exceptionally large number of people, resulting in an interference of great weight, the legislator is not constitutionally barred, *per se*, from imposing an obligation to retain data for a six-month period, as provided for in § 113a of the Telecommunications Act. This notwithstanding, according to the Federal Constitutional Court's established case-law, the state is strictly barred from gathering personal data for retention, at least where such data has not been rendered anonymous and is gathered for undefined or yet to be defined purposes (cf. BVerfGE 65, 1 <46> – *Census*; 100, 313 <360> – *The Article 10 Act*; 115, 320 <350> – *Profiling*; 118, 168 <187>). However, the precautionary retention of telecommunications traffic data without specific grounds does not necessarily constitute a form of data gathering that would fall under this absolute prohibition. Rather, where data retention actually serves defined purposes, it may satisfy the requirements of proportionality in the strict sense. Yet this requires a statutory design that adequately reflects the resulting interference (see V below).

214 aa) Firstly, it is relevant, in the present case, that the envisaged retention of telecommunications traffic data is not directly carried out by the state; rather, an obligation to retain the relevant data is imposed on private service providers. Therefore, the data is not centrally pooled at the time of retention. Instead, it is held separately by many individual companies, and is not immediately made available to the state in its entirety. In particular, the state is not granted direct access to the data, which must be ensured by appropriate statutory provisions and technical arrangements. Only in a second step may state authorities request access to the retained data, in the event that specific grounds arise; this must be further specified by criteria set out in law. In this regard, the specific design of the provisions governing requests for access to and the subsequent use of retained data can ensure that data retention is not undertaken for undefined or yet to be defined purposes. Thus, where a statutory obligation to retain data is imposed, it can, and must, also

be ensured that the state may only obtain actual knowledge of the data and use it within limits set out in clear legal provisions. These limits must take into account the weight of the extensive data collection and they must restrict requests for data access and the actual data use to that part of the data that is absolutely necessary. In addition, the separation of data retention and access to the data upon request structurally enhances transparency and oversight regarding data use, the details of which must be specified in statutory provisions.

bb) The six-month retention of telecommunications traffic data does not by itself negate the constitutional precepts enshrined in Art. 10(1) of the Basic Law; it neither violates the human dignity core (Art. 1(1) of the Basic Law) enshrined in Article 10(1) of the Basic Law nor the essence (*Wesensgehalt*) of this fundamental right (Art. 19(2) of the Basic Law). Although the data retention is extraordinary in scope, it is still subject to effective limitations. For instance, the retention is limited to traffic data, excluding the contents of telecommunications. In addition, the data may only be retained for a limited time period. In view of the scope and informative value of the retained data, the retention period of six months is very long and just barely within the maximum limit of what can be justified in terms of proportionality. However, citizens can trust that – except for cases where weighty grounds prompted state authorities to exceptionally request data access – their data will be deleted at the end of the retention period and that any later reconstruction is impossible.

cc) Nor does the six-month retention of telecommunications traffic data amount to a measure aimed at the total registration of the entire communications or activities of all citizens. Instead, the measure remains limited in scope, is informed by the special significance of telecommunications in the modern world, and reacts to the particular potential for dangers that may arise in this context. [...]

[...]

Nevertheless, the retention of telecommunications traffic data must not be understood as paving the way for legislation aiming to enable, to the greatest extent possible, the precautionary retention of all data that could potentially be useful for law enforcement or public security purposes. Regardless of how the provisions governing data use were designed, any such legislation would be incompatible with the Constitution from the outset. The retention of telecommunications traffic data without specific grounds will only satisfy constitutional standards if it remains an exception to the rule. [...] It is an integral part of the constitutional identity of the Federal Republic of Germany that the state may not record and register the exercise of freedoms by citizens in its entirety (cf. BVerfGE 123, 267 <353 and 354> on the guarantee of constitutional identity); it is incumbent upon the Federal Republic of Germany to ensure respect for this constitutional identity within the European and international context. With the precautionary retention of telecommunications traffic data in place, there is considerably less leeway for allowing other types of data gathering not based on specific grounds, including for measures originating at EU level.

219 dd) In summary, the six-month retention of telecommunications traffic data on the scale provided for by the legislator in § 113a(1) to (8) of the Telecommunications Act is, at present, not disproportionate from the outset. However, for it to be unobjectionable under constitutional law, it is imperative that the statutory framework governing retention and use of the data be designed in a manner that adequately reflects the particular weight of such a data retention regime.

V.

220 The design of the statutory framework governing the precautionary retention of telecommunications traffic data, as provided for in § 113a of the Telecommunications Act, must satisfy particular constitutional requirements, especially with regard to data security, the scope of permissible data use, transparency and legal protection. The interferences resulting from such data retention are only proportionate in the strict sense if sufficiently stringent and clear statutory provisions give effect to these requirements.

221 1. The retention of telecommunications traffic data on the scale provided for in § 113a of the Telecommunications Act requires particularly high standards of data security laid down in statutory provisions.

222 In view of the scope and the potential informative value of the data sets compiled by means of such retention, data security is of great significance for the proportionality of the challenged provisions. This is particularly true because the data is retained by private service providers, which operate under the realities of profitability and cost pressure with little incentive to ensure data security. […] Thus, it is imperative that a particularly high standard of security be put in place, beyond what would normally be required under constitutional law for the storage of telecommunications data. These data security requirements apply both to the retention and to the transfer of data at the request of authorities; similarly, effective safeguards are necessary to ensure compliance with deletion requirements.

223 […]

224 Constitutional law does not specify the necessary data security requirements in every detail. Ultimately, the adopted standard must ensure a particularly high level of security that specifically takes into account the nature of the data sets compiled by means of telecommunications traffic data retention. […]

No. 41 – Data Retention

It is necessary to enact a qualified statutory framework that outlines at least the basic features of such a particularly high standard of data security in a clear and binding manner. In this respect, the legislator may entrust a regulatory agency with the technical details of the required standard. However, the legislator itself must ensure that the decision as to the type and scope of the necessary data security measures is not ultimately left to the respective telecommunications providers in an unchecked manner. [...] Furthermore, constitutional law requires that compliance on the part of service providers be monitored in a way that is transparent to the public and includes oversight by an independent data protection officer (cf. BVerfGE 65, 1 <46> – *Census*), and that a balanced sanctions regime be put in place that attaches appropriate weight to breaches of data security.

2. The retention of telecommunications traffic data as provided for in § 113a of the Telecommunications Act furthermore requires statutory provisions governing data use. Whether the design of this framework is proportionate determines not only the constitutionality of the respective statutory provisions on data use, which in itself constitute a separate interference with fundamental rights, but is also relevant for determining whether the data retention regime as such is constitutional. According to the case-law of the Federal Constitutional Court, the more serious the interference resulting from data retention, the more strictly the conditions and scope of data use must be defined in the underlying statutory framework. The legislator must specify precisely and clearly, for each subject matter, the grounds prompting the respective interference, its purpose and scope, as well as the threshold for exercising these powers (cf. BVerfGE 100, 313 <359 and 360>– *The Article 10 Act*; 110, 33 <53>; 113, 29 <51> – *Seizure of Electronic Data*; 113, 348 <375>; 115, 166 <191> – *Telecommunications Surveillance*; 115, 320 <365> – *Profiling*; 118, 168 <186 and 187>).

Accordingly, the use of data obtained through the systematic retention of virtually all telecommunications traffic data without specific grounds is subject to particularly strict requirements. [...] Therefore, use of this data is only permissible if it serves exceptionally significant tasks aimed at the protection of legal interests, i.e. if it serves, for instance, the prosecution of criminal offences that threaten exceptionally significant legal interests or the averting of dangers to such legal interests.

a) In the domain of law enforcement, this means that requests for data access require at least the suspicion, based on specific facts, of a serious criminal offence. When imposing the obligation to retain data, the legislator itself must already determine definitively which criminal offences should qualify as serious. In this respect, it is afforded a margin of appreciation. The legislator may either refer to existing statutory catalogues of offences or draw up a new catalogue, for example to include criminal offences for which telecommunications traffic data is particularly relevant. However, the classification of the relevant criminal offence as serious must be objectively reflected in the definition of the crime contained in the underlying provision of criminal law, in particular by the specified range of punishment (cf. BVerfGE 109, 279 <343 *et seq.*, in particular 347 and 348> – *Surveillance of Private Homes*). A blanket clause or mere reference to the notion of considerable criminal offences is not sufficient.

229 In addition to establishing an abstract catalogue of relevant criminal offences, the legislator must ensure that the use of the retained telecommunications traffic data is permissible only if the charges in the specific criminal case also qualify as serious (cf. BVerfGE 121, 1 <26>; on considerable criminal offences cf. BVerfGE 107, 299 <322>; on particularly serious criminal offences within the meaning of Art. 13(3) of the Basic Law, cf. BVerfGE 109, 279 <346> – *Surveillance of Private Homes*) and if the use of the retained data satisfies the principle of proportionality.

230 b) In the domain of averting dangers to public security, the use of retained data must also be subject to effective limitations. Here, it would not actually be a suitable legislative approach to simply make data access subject to catalogues specifying criminal offences which the envisaged data use aims to prevent (cf. BVerfGE 122, 120 <142>). [...] Instead, a suitable approach would be for the statutory framework to directly identify the legal interests whose protection is invoked as grounds to justify the intended data use; the statutory framework should also specify the necessary level of danger to the relevant legal interests that sets the threshold for exercising these powers. Such a framework would be in keeping with the nature of public security as a regime for safeguarding legal interests meriting protection, and ensure that the interference with fundamental rights is directly connected to the aim invoked to justify it.

231 When balancing the weight of the interference resulting from the retention and subsequent use of data against the significance of effective public security measures, it follows that requesting access to retained telecommunications traffic data is only permissible if it serves to avert dangers to life, limb or liberty of the person, to the existence or security of the Federation or a *Land*, or to the general public (cf. BVerfGE 122, 120 <141 *et seq.*>). In this respect, the statutory basis authorising the interference must at least require factual indications of a specific danger (*konkrete Gefahr*) to the legal interests meriting protection. [...] This means that there must be a situation where it is sufficiently likely, in the individual case, that certain persons will cause damage to the interests protected by the relevant statutory provision in the foreseeable future, unless the state intervenes. [...] The existence of a specific danger is determined by three criteria: it concerns an individual case; it is foreseeable that the danger will result in actual damage within a certain time

period; and the cause of the danger can be attributed to individual persons. Nevertheless, requests for access to retained data may already be justified at a time when it cannot be established with sufficient probability that the danger will materialise in the near future, provided that there are already specific facts indicating an impending danger *(drohende Gefahr)* to an exceptionally significant legal interest in the individual case. Firstly, it must at least be possible to determine, based on these facts, the type of incident that might occur, and that it will occur within a foreseeable timeframe; secondly, the facts must indicate the involvement of specific persons whose identity is known at least to such an extent that the measure can be targeted at and focused on them. By contrast, the weight of interference is not sufficiently taken into account where statutory provisions authorise the measure on grounds so precautionary in nature that the existence of a specific danger to the protected legal interests need no longer be foreseeable at all, not even with regard to its basic characteristics.

c) The constitutional requirements relating to the use of retained data for maintaining public security apply to all instances where statutory provisions authorise interferences with fundamental rights to serve the aim of preventing dangers. Therefore, they also apply to the use of retained data by the intelligence services. […]

[…]

The Court is aware that, as a result of these requirements, the intelligence services will likely be excluded from using retained telecommunications traffic data in many cases. Yet this follows from the nature of their tasks, which inherently concern precautionary intelligence operations; it does not, however, constitute an acceptable reason under constitutional law for relaxing the requirements which derive from the principle of proportionality for interferences of this type (cf. BVerfGE 120, 274 <331> – *Remote Searches*).

d) It must also be ensured that data use remains limited to specific purposes even after the data has been requested by and transferred to the authorities; this also requires procedural safeguards. In this respect, it must be statutorily guaranteed that the data is analysed without undue delay following its transfer; where the data proves to be irrelevant to the purposes pursued, it must be deleted (cf. BVerfGE 100, 313 <387 and 388> – *The Article 10 Act*). Moreover, it must be ensured that the data is destroyed as soon as it is no longer needed for the defined purposes, and that this is documented in the files (cf. BVerfGE 100, 313 <362> – *The Article 10 Act*; 113, 29 <58> – *Seizure of Electronic Data*).

Telecommunications traffic data does not lose the protection afforded under Art. 10 of the Basic Law simply because one state body has already obtained knowledge of it. Therefore, the requirement deriving from this fundamental right that use of the data be clearly limited to specific purposes also applies to any subsequent sharing of this data and information with other authorities. However, this does not rule out changes in the purpose for which the data may be used. Yet a change in purpose requires a separate statutory basis, which, in turn, must also satisfy constitutional requirements (cf. BVerfGE 100, 313 <360> – *The Article 10 Act*; 109, 279 <375 and 376> – *Surveillance of Private Homes*). In consequence, the legislator may only provide for the sharing of telecommunications traffic data [obtained through data retention] with other bodies if it serves tasks that would also have justified direct access to this data [by the receiving body] (cf. BVerfGE 100, 313 <389 and 390> – *The Article 10 Act*; 109, 279 <375 and 376> – *Surveillance of Private Homes*; 110, 33 <73>). This must be documented by the body sharing the data (cf. BVerfGE 100, 313 <395 and 396> – *The Article 10 Act*). Here, the required purpose limitation can only be guaranteed if the obtained data subsequently remains identifiable as data initially gathered by means of data retention. Therefore, the legislator must provide for an obligation to label this data accordingly (cf. BVerfGE 100, 313 <360 and 361> – *The Article 10 Act*).

237 e) Finally, further constitutional limitations may arise with regard to the scope of data access that may be requested by the authorities. [...]

238 In principle, the foregoing requirements already set high thresholds for the use of retained telecommunications traffic data. In light of this, the legislator is afforded leeway when further specifying the permissible scope of data use. In particular, the legislator may in principle leave the case-by-case assessment of proportionality to the judge deciding on requests for access to retained data. However, in certain cases it is constitutionally required under the principle of proportionality to recognise an absolute prohibition on granting data access to authorities, at least with respect to a narrowly-defined group of telecommunications that merit special confidentiality protection. These might include, for example, telecommunications with persons, public authorities and organisations involved in social or church work that offer counselling in emotional or social crisis situations, exclusively or predominantly over the phone, to callers who generally remain anonymous, where these organisations or their staff are themselves already bound by confidentiality obligations (cf. § 99(2) of the Telecommunications Act).

239 3. In addition, the retention of telecommunications traffic data without specific grounds and the use of retained data are only proportionate if the legislator puts in place sufficient safeguards to ensure transparency of data use and to guarantee effective legal protection and adequate sanctions for violations.

240 a) For the use of data obtained from data retention to be unobjectionable, certain constitutional requirements, including transparency requirements, must be met. To the greatest possible extent, the use of the data must be limited to overt measures. Where this is not possible, it is in principle necessary that the affected persons

be notified, at least after the measures have been carried out. If, exceptionally, not even *ex post* notification is given, a judicial decision authorising the lack of notification must be obtained.

aa) The retention of all telecommunications traffic data without specific grounds, for a period of six months, constitutes a serious interference, not least because it can generate the feeling of being under constant surveillance; it allows profound and unforeseeable insights into citizens' private life, while they have no immediate knowledge or awareness that their data is being accessed. The individual has no idea which state authority has what kind of information about them; what the individual does know, however, is that the authorities may have extensive and in some cases highly personal information on them. 241

This situation may instil a diffuse sense of threat in relation to data retention, which the legislator must counteract by providing for an effective transparency regime. Statutory requirements to inform the affected persons about the collection or use of their data are among the key instruments of data protection under fundamental rights (cf. BVerfGE 100, 313 <361> – *The Article 10 Act*; 109, 279 <363 and 364> – *Surveillance of Private Homes*; 118, 168 <207 and 208>; 120, 351 <361 and 362>). [...] Without this information, the affected persons can neither challenge the lawfulness of the authorities' use of their data nor assert possible rights to have their data deleted or rectified, or to seek satisfaction (cf. BVerfGE 100, 313 <361> – *The Article 10 Act*; 109, 279 <363> – *Surveillance of Private Homes*; 118, 168 <207 and 208>; 120, 351 <361>). 242

bb) These transparency requirements include the principle of the overtness of the collection and use of personal data. Under constitutional law, the use of personal data without the knowledge of the affected person is only permissible if the purpose of the inquiry for which data access is requested would otherwise be frustrated. The legislator may in principle assume that this is the case where the pursued purpose concerns public security or the tasks of the intelligence services. By contrast, in the domain of law enforcement, it should generally be feasible to collect and use the data by means of overt measures. [...] Accordingly, affected persons must in principle be notified before requests for data access or the transfer of data are carried out. Retained data may only be used covertly if it is necessary in the individual case and authorised by a judge. 243

To the extent that the data is used covertly, the legislator must provide for a requirement to at least notify the affected person *ex post*. In this regard, it must be ensured that the persons whose data was directly targeted – regardless of whether they were classified as suspects, persons responsible for a danger to public security (*Polizeipflichtige*), or third parties – must in principle be informed, at least after the measure has been carried out. [...] 244

245 By contrast, it is not constitutionally required to provide for similarly strict notification requirements vis-à-vis persons whose telecommunications traffic data was only incidentally obtained and who were not themselves targeted by the authorities. While the number of persons incidentally included in the analysis of telecommunications traffic data may be quite high, the mere temporary disclosure of their data to the authorities may not even leave any trace nor does it necessarily have consequences for the affected persons. [...]

246 b) Moreover, the design of the statutory framework for the retention of telecommunications traffic data is only proportionate if it guarantees effective legal protection and an adequate sanctions regime.

247 aa) In order to guarantee effective legal protection, requests for access to and the transfer of this data must generally be subject to prior judicial authorisation (*Richtervorbehalt*).

248 According to the Federal Constitutional Court's case-law, investigation measures which result in serious interferences with fundamental rights require prior review by an independent authority. This applies in particular if the interference with fundamental rights is carried out covertly and cannot directly be perceived by affected persons (cf. BVerfGE 120, 274 <331> – *Remote Searches*). This may be the case regarding authorities' requests for access to and the transfer of telecommunications traffic data. In view of the weight of the resulting interference, the legislator's latitude is reduced in that such measures must in principle be subject to judicial authorisation. As judges must be personally and professionally independent and are bound only by the law, they can best and most reliably ensure that the rights of the affected person are respected in the individual case (cf. BVerfGE 77, 1 <51>; 103, 142 <151>; 120, 274 <332> – *Remote Searches*). Art. 10(2) second sentence of the Basic Law recognises an exception regarding oversight in relation to interferences with freedom of telecommunications by the intelligence services. Here, prior judicial review may be replaced by a review carried out by bodies or auxiliary bodies appointed by Parliament that review the specific surveillance measure in question – like a judge would – in the individual case (cf. BVerfGE 30, 1 <21>).

249 The legislator must set out the requirement of prior judicial review in specific and clear provisions combined with strict standards regarding the content and the reasons of the warrant issued by the court (cf. BVerfGE 109, 279 <358 and 359> – *Surveillance of Private Homes*). This also gives rise to the requirement that requests for access to retained data themselves be sufficiently substantiated and sufficiently limited in scope, so as to enable the courts to exercise an effective review (cf. BVerfGE 103, 142 <160 and 161>). It is only on this basis that the court deciding on the request can and must assess independently whether the intended

use of retained data satisfies the statutory requirements. This entails a careful examination of the statutory prerequisites applicable to the interference, including in particular the statutorily defined threshold for exercising the powers constituting interferences. When issuing the requested warrant, the court must give detailed reasons for its decision. In addition, the principle of proportionality requires that the authorised data access be clearly specified in the warrant and sufficiently selective in scope (cf. BVerfGE 103, 142 <151>), so that the service providers do not have to undertake their own substantive examination. It is only on the basis of a clear warrant that the service providers are permitted, and can be compelled, to transfer the requested data.

Effective review also entails that, based on the warrant, it is incumbent upon the telecommunications companies, in their capacity as third-party entities bound by data retention obligations, to extract and transfer the requested data so that the authorities are not given direct access. This ensures that any use of the data is dependent on the cooperation of several actors and relies on decision-making structures that are informed by mutual checks. 250

bb) It is also required under constitutional law that legal recourse be available to seek an *ex post* review regarding the use of retained data. Where affected persons did not have the opportunity to challenge the use of their telecommunications traffic data in court before the measure was carried out, they must be allowed the possibility of *ex post* judicial review. 251

cc) Finally, the design of the statutory framework is only proportionate if it sets out effective sanctions for violations of rights. If serious violations of the privacy of telecommunications were to ultimately remain without sanction, the protection of the right of personality would be eroded, given that it is non-material in nature even in its specific manifestation under Art. 10(1) of the Basic Law (cf. [...] BGHZ 128, 1 <15>); this would run counter to the duty of the state to ensure that individuals can freely develop their personality (cf. BVerfGE 35, 202 <220 and 221> – *Lebach*; 63, 131 <142 and 143> – *Right of Reply*; 96, 56 <64>), and to protect them against risks to the right of personality originating from third parties (cf. BVerfGE 73, 118 <210>; 97, 125 <146>; 99, 185 <194 and 195> – *Helnwein/Scientology*; [...]). This would in particular be the case if data obtained without authorisation could be used largely unhindered by restrictions, or if affected persons were routinely denied any satisfaction compensating the unauthorised use of their data due to lack of material damage. 252

However, in this context the legislator has broad leeway to design. [...] In determining whether there is a need for more comprehensive legislation, the legislator may choose to first monitor the case-law developed by the ordinary courts under the currently applicable legislative framework; the legislator can thus determine 253 whether, as the law stands, courts already give due consideration to the particular severity of the personality right violations that typically result from unauthorised access to or use of retained data, and thereby satisfy the constitutional requirements.

254   4. Less stringent constitutional requirements apply if the retained data is only used indirectly; this is the case where the authorities are allowed to request information on subscribers of certain IP addresses, which the service providers must then identify by using retained data. Conferring powers on the authorities to request this type of information is generally permissible to a greater extent than requests for access to and direct use of retained telecommunications traffic data by the authorities themselves; therefore, it need not necessarily be limited to narrowly-defined grounds in the form of catalogues listing criminal offences or protected legal interests.

255-257   a) [...]

258-260   b) [...]

261   c) Accordingly, the legislator may permit the authorities to request such information for the purposes of law enforcement, public security and the tasks of the intelligence services, where the authorities exercise general investigatory powers conferred by other legislation authorising interferences; it is not required that such information requests be subject to narrowly-defined catalogues of protected legal interests or relevant criminal offences. [...] However, the applicable statutory thresholds for exercising these powers must exclude purely speculative requests for information; it must be ensured that information requests be based on a sufficient initial suspicion of criminal conduct (*Anfangsverdacht*) or sufficient facts indicating a specific danger in the individual case. In this respect, the requirement of a specific danger based on factual indications applies in all instances where the request for information is made by the intelligence services or by the authorities in charge of averting dangers to public security and order. The legal and factual basis justifying the respective request for information must be documented in the relevant files. It is, however, not necessary to make such requests for information subject to prior judicial authorisation.

262   Nevertheless, making this information available to the authorities constitutes an interference of considerable weight; therefore it would not be permissible to generally allow such information requests without any restriction, including for the purpose of prosecuting or preventing any type of administrative offence. Lifting Internet anonymity is only permissible if a protected legal interest is impaired and the legal order attaches increased weight to that interest, not just in relation to the measure at issue but also in other contexts. This does not completely rule out that information may be requested for the purposes of prosecuting or preventing admin-

istrative offences. Yet the relevant offences must not only be expressly specified by the legislator, they must also be of particular weight – including in the individual case.

Moreover, there is no reason to set aside the principle of transparency (see C V 3 above) regarding the identification of IP addresses. Affected persons may generally assume that their use of the Internet remains anonymous; therefore, they in principle have the right to be informed of the fact that, and for which reasons, this anonymity was lifted. Accordingly, the legislator must provide for a requirement to notify affected persons, unless such notification would frustrate the purpose pursued or interfere with other overriding interests of third parties or of the affected persons themselves. Where the authorities exceptionally refrain from notification in accordance with the applicable statutory provisions, the reasons must be documented in the relevant files. Yet it is not required that judicial confirmation of the decision to refrain from notification be obtained.

5. The constitutionally required guarantees of data security and of clearly defined purpose limitations on data use that satisfy proportionality requirements are inseparable elements of any statutory framework imposing obligations to retain data; enacting such guarantees is therefore incumbent upon the federal legislator as the competent authority to legislate on data retention obligations. By contrast, the legislative competence for provisions governing requests for data access by the authorities, and for specifying the applicable transparency and legal protection regime, lies with the legislator competent to legislate on the respective underlying subject matter.

[…]

VI.

The challenged provisions do not satisfy these requirements. This notwithstanding, § 113a of the Telecommunications Act does not conflict with the fundamental right to the privacy of telecommunications under Art. 10(1) of the Basic Law on the grounds that the scope of the data retention obligations set out in § 113a(1) to (7), (11) of the Telecommunications Act were disproportionate from the outset. Rather, the provisions on data security, on purpose limitations and transparency regarding data use, and on legal protection do not meet the constitutional requirements. In consequence, the design of the statutory framework as a whole fails to adhere to the principle of proportionality. §§ 113a and 113b of the Telecommunications Act, and § 100g of the Code of Criminal Procedure to the extent that it authorises requests for access to data retained pursuant to § 113a of the Telecommunications Act, are therefore incompatible with Art. 10(1) of the Basic Law.

BVerfGE 125, 260

270 1. The scope of § 113a of the Telecommunications Act as such does not render the provision unconstitutional. […] § 113a of the Telecommunications Act cannot be regarded as an attempt by the state to create a precautionary mechanism that generally keeps data available for law enforcement and public security purposes. Its large scope notwithstanding, § 113a of the Telecommunications Act only allows data retention in the form of a limited exception, in an attempt to respond to the particular challenges that modern telecommunications pose to law enforcement and public security.

271 2. However, the statutory framework fails to ensure the particularly high standard of data security that would be constitutionally required for a data collection of this nature. § 113a(10) of the Telecommunications Act merely provides for a general obligation to ensure, by technical and organisational measures, that the retained data can be accessed exclusively by persons who are specifically authorised; yet the provision fails to specify any further details. Other than that, the statutory framework only refers to the general duty of care incumbent upon service providers in the telecommunications sector. Hence, there is no statutory provision giving effect to the particularly strict requirements regarding data security that apply here due to the extensive scope and informative value of the data collection envisaged in § 113a of the Telecommunications Act. §§ 88 and 109 of the Telecommunications Act, which are implicitly referenced [regarding service providers' duty of care] do not sufficiently guarantee a particularly high standard of data security; given their broad scope of application, these provisions recognise various qualifying circumstances that may result in less strict standards. […]

272 […]

273 § 109(3) of the Telecommunications Act does not guarantee sufficient data security either. […]

274 § 9 of the Federal Data Protection Act, in conjunction with the applicable statutory annex, cannot compensate for the lack of adequate data security standards in the Telecommunications Act. On an abstract level, this provision does contain certain high standards for data security. However, § 9 of the Federal Data Protection Act, which in any case only applies subsidiarily, […] is too general to ensure, in a sufficiently specific and reliable manner, the particularly high security standards that would be necessary in relation to the data retained pursuant to § 113a of the Telecommunications Act.

275 All in all, the particularly high standard of data security that would be necessary for the data retained pursuant to § 113a of the Telecommunications Act is not ensured by binding and clear statutory guarantees. […] The framework also lacks a balanced sanctions regime that accords at least as much weight to non-compliance

with data security standards as to non-compliance with the obligation to retain data. [...]

3. The provisions governing the transfer and use of retained data pursuant to § 113b first sentence, first half-sentence of the Telecommunications Act do not satisfy the constitutional requirements.

a) The provisions on the use of retained data for law enforcement purposes are already incompatible with the constitutional standards derived from the principle of proportionality.

aa) Use of the data retained pursuant to § 113a of the Telecommunications Act may only be allowed subject to particularly strict requirements, which § 113b first sentence no. 1 of the Telecommunications Act in conjunction with § 100g of the Code of Criminal Procedure does not meet. [...]

§ 100g(1) first sentence no. 1 of the Code of Criminal Procedure fails to ensure, both in general and in the individual case, that only serious criminal offences constitute sufficient grounds for obtaining the relevant data; it merely states – without providing an exhaustive catalogue of relevant offences – that generally any considerable criminal act provided sufficient grounds. § 100g(1) first sentence no. 2, second sentence of the Code of Criminal Procedure is even less in line with constitutional law; it recognises any criminal act committed by means of telecommunications, regardless of its seriousness and subject only to a general assessment of proportionality, as possible grounds for requesting data access. Under this provision, use of the data retained pursuant to § 113a of the Telecommunications Act could be prompted by virtually any criminal act. Given the increasing importance of telecommunications in everyday life, the use of retained data would thus no longer remain the exception. The legislator no longer limits the use of retained data to the prosecution of serious criminal offences but greatly extends its scope beyond these grounds – in doing so, the legislator also goes far beyond the objective of data retention laid down in EU law, which again is limited to the prosecution of serious criminal offences and does not even concern data retention for the purposes of averting dangers to public security. It is true that retained data could be very useful, specifically for prosecuting criminal offences committed by means of telecommunications; therefore, restricting the use of retained data may in some cases render the successful investigation of criminal offences more difficult or even impossible. However, it is inherent in the guarantee enshrined in Art. 10(1) of the Basic Law, and the corresponding requirements of proportionality, that not every measure that could be useful for law enforcement purposes, and may even be necessary in the individual case, is also permissible under constitutional law. [...]

bb) Furthermore, § 100g of the Code of Criminal Procedure fails to satisfy the constitutional requirements in that it generally permits requests for data access

BVerfGE 125, 260

without the knowledge of the affected person (§ 100g(1) first sentence of the Code of Criminal Procedure). In light of the constitutional requirements regarding transparency of data use, the data retained pursuant to § 113a of the Telecommunications Act may only be obtained covertly where this is necessary for overriding reasons, which must be specified in more detail by the legislator, and subject to judicial authorisation.

281 cc) The design of the provisions governing the notification of affected persons does also not fully satisfy the constitutional standards set out above. This notwithstanding, the envisaged scope of the notification requirement does not raise any constitutional concerns as such. [...] Specifically, it is not objectionable that pursuant to § 101(4) fourth sentence of the Code of Criminal Procedure, affected persons who were not themselves targeted by the requested data access need not be notified in every case but only where a balancing of interests so indicates. This balancing of interests can and must give sufficient consideration to the interests of persons that are indirectly affected by the measure.

282 By contrast, the provisions on judicial review in cases where the authorities may refrain from notification are inadequate. § 101(6) of the Code of Criminal Procedure provides for judicial review only in cases where notification is deferred pursuant to § 101(5) of the Code of Criminal Procedure, but not in cases where notification is indefinitely refrained from pursuant to § 101(4) of the Code of Criminal Procedure. This does not sufficiently reflect the great significance of such notifications for ensuring transparent use of the data retained pursuant to § 113a of the Telecommunications Act. Where requests for data access directly target the traffic data of a specific person, refraining from *ex post* notification requires exceptional grounds, which must be reviewed by a judge. Yet no such judicial review is provided for in cases where notification is refrained from pursuant to § 101(4) third sentence of the Code of Criminal Procedure on grounds of overriding interests on the part of affected persons.

283 dd) By contrast, the challenged provisions do ensure judicial review regarding requests for data access and data use in line with the constitutional requirements. In accordance with § 100g(2) first sentence and § 100b(1) first sentence of the Code of Criminal Procedure, obtaining the data retained pursuant to § 113a of the Telecommunications Act requires a warrant issued by a judge [...]

284 However, the statutory provisions on the formal requirements regarding such warrants are not sufficiently clear [...] The relevant statutory provisions must at the very least require that the warrant define the scope of the data authorised for transfer in a manner that is sufficiently selective, in line with the principle of proportionality, and also unambiguous to the service providers.

b) The challenged provisions also fail to meet the constitutional requirements with regard to requests for access to, and the subsequent use of, data retained pursuant to § 113a of the Telecommunications Act for the purposes of public security and the tasks of the intelligence services. From the outset, the basic concept of § 113b first sentence nos. 2 and 3 of the Telecommunications Act does not satisfy the requirements concerning sufficient purpose limitations on data use. In this provision, the federal legislator merely outlines, in generalised terms, the areas of state action for which data access may be requested; however, it does not specifically delineate the purposes for which the data may be used. [...] Rather, obliging service providers to retain all telecommunications traffic data while allowing the police and intelligence services to use this data in the context of almost all of their tasks leads to the creation of a data pool that is open to diverse and unlimited uses. As the data pool is not subject to limitations other than vaguely defined objectives, the federal and *Land* legislators could independently and freely grant access to this data. The establishment of such an open data pool without specific purpose limitations breaks the required link between the storage of data and the purpose for which the data is stored; this is incompatible with the Constitution [...].

[...]

c) The design of the provisions governing the use of data retained pursuant to § 113a of the Telecommunications Act is also disproportionate in that it provides absolutely no protection against the transfer of retained data relating to relationships of trust. In principle, such protection must be provided at least for a narrowly-defined group of telecommunications connections that merit special confidentiality protection [...].

4. Lastly, § 113b first sentence, second half-sentence of the Telecommunications Act, which allows service providers to indirectly use data retained pursuant to § 113a of the Telecommunications Act in order to fulfil information requests pursuant to § 113(1) of the Telecommunications Act, also fails to fully satisfy the requirements of proportionality.

Yet by the standards set out above, it is not objectionable under constitutional law that in § 113b first sentence, second half-sentence of the Telecommunications Act, the legislator does not subject requests for information on the subscribers of certain IP addresses already known to the authorities to the particularly strict requirements that apply in relation to requests for direct access to data retained pursuant to § 113a of the Telecommunications Act. [...]

[...]

However, § 113b first sentence, second half-sentence in conjunction with § 113(1) of the Telecommunications Act is too broad, in terms of proportionality, in that

292 it generally recognises the prosecution of administrative offences as sufficient grounds justifying requests for data access. […]
5. In summary, neither the statutory provisions on data security nor the provisions on the use of retained data in § 113b first sentence no. 1 of the Telecommunications Act in conjunction with § 100g of the Code of Criminal Procedure, § 113b first sentence nos. 2 and 3 of the Telecommunications Act, and § 113b first sentence, second half-sentence of the Telecommunications Act meet the constitutional requirements. Consequently, the obligation to retain data pursuant to § 113a of the Telecommunications Act as such also lacks sufficient constitutional justification. The challenged provisions are therefore incompatible with Art. 10(1) of the Basic Law in their entirety.

VII.

293-304 […]

VIII.

305 […]

IX.

306 The violation of the fundamental right to the protection of the privacy of telecommunications under Art. 10(1) of the Basic Law renders void §§ 113a and 113b of the Telecommunications Act, as well as § 100g(1) first sentence of the Code of Criminal Procedure, to the extent that these provisions allow the authorities to obtain traffic data retained pursuant to § 113a of the Telecommunications Act. The challenged provisions are therefore found to violate fundamental rights, and are declared void (cf. § 95(1) first sentence and § 95(3) first sentence of the Federal Constitutional Court Act). Accordingly, the telecommunications traffic data that was compiled by service providers at the request of authorities yet – based on the preliminary injunctions of 11 March 2008 and 28 October 2008 – was not transferred to the requesting authorities but temporarily stored instead must be deleted without undue delay. This data may no longer be transferred to the requesting authorities.

307 […]

308 The decision is unanimous with regard to the questions of European law, the formal constitutionality of the challenged provisions, and the question whether the precautionary retention of telecommunications traffic data can as such be compatible with

the Constitution. With regard to the finding that §§ 113a and 113b of the Telecommunications Act are unconstitutional, the decision was taken with 7:1 votes, and with regard to other questions of substantive constitutional law, as indicated in the dissenting opinions, it was taken with 6:2 votes.

The Court decided with 4:4 votes that the provisions must be declared void pursuant to § 95(3) first sentence of the Federal Constitutional Court Act, and not merely incompatible with the Basic Law. Thus, the general rule, as laid down in the law, on the legal consequences attached to a declaration of voidness prevails, namely that the provisions may not continue to apply, not even on a transitional basis or with a limited scope.

Justices: Papier, Hohmann-Dennhardt, Bryde, Gaier, Eichberger, Schluckebier, Kirchhof, Masing

Dissenting Opinion of Justice Schluckebier

I can neither agree with the outcome of the decision nor with large parts of its reasoning for the following considerations.

The Senate majority qualifies the retention of traffic data as a particularly serious interference with the fundamental right under Art. 10 of the Basic Law. In my view, particular weight must indeed be accorded to such an interference; however, it proves to be considerably less serious than surveillance measures targeting communications contents (see I below). Furthermore, the objectives pursued by the legislator include, in particular, the investigation of crimes that, based on the circumstances of the individual case, constitute considerable crime or have been committed by means of telecommunications, and that would otherwise be difficult to investigate; in light of these objectives, I consider the interference resulting from the retention of traffic data and from the provisions on data access in criminal proceedings to be, in principle, justified under constitutional law. In my view, the provisions on which the interference is based essentially meet the requirement of proportionality in the strict sense, particularly in the assessment whether the measure is appropriate and reasonable (*zumutbar*; see II below). The provisions merely fail to satisfy the substantive requirements for ensuring data security in relation to the retention and transfer of telecommunications traffic data; in this respect, I concur with the majority of the Senate and see no need to reiterate the relevant considerations. As regards the legal consequences of the Court's decision, I believe that – even based on the constitutional assessment of the Senate majority – the challenged provisions should not have been declared void; rather, the Court should have ordered that the provisions remain applicable subject to the preliminary injunctions issued by the Court until new provisions are enacted.

I.

312   The Senate majority considers the retention of traffic data by service providers for a period of six months to be a particularly serious interference with the fundamental right under Art. 10(1) of the Basic Law. I do not agree with this assessment.

313   The privacy of telecommunications protects against *the state obtaining knowledge* of the contents and circumstances of communications (cf. BVerfGE 100, 313 <358> – *The Article 10 Act*; 106, 28 <37>; 107, 299 <312 and 313>). The Senate majority argues that the private service providers' obligation to retain data (§ 113a of the Telecommunications Act) amounted to an interference on the grounds that the service providers acted as "agents assisting the state", making the retention carried out by them attributable to the state. Based on this reasoning, it is particularly relevant for assessing the intensity of interference that prior to any potential data access by state authorities, the traffic data remains exclusively in the sphere controlled by the private service providers. The data is in the hands of the very party with whom a contract for telecommunications services was concluded; in this type of contractual relationship, the party using the telecommunications services fundamentally trusts, based on tacit expectations, that their contractual provider will treat data originally collected for technical reasons and billing purposes with strict confidentiality, and ensure data protection in this regard. Furthermore, if an appropriate level of data security is guaranteed based on what is technologically feasible, there is no objective basis for assuming that such data retention might have a chilling effect on citizens, which would intensify the interference, or – as the Judgment puts it – create a "feeling of being under constant surveillance" and a "diffuse sense of threat". Moreover, the data retention is not carried out covertly but on the basis of a promulgated law. The measure does not target the *contents* of telecommunications. Where the traffic data does allow, to a limited extent, to also draw conclusions on the communication contents, or even makes it possible to create movement profiles or profiles of one's social relations, this must be taken into account in assessing the proportionality of the corresponding provisions on data access and in assessing whether the application of the law in practice meets proportionality requirements. While such uses, which are permitted based on sufficiently weighty reasons, may give rise to an intense interference in individual cases, they prove to be limited to exceptional cases overall. Thus, it is not warranted that the assessment of the data retention framework attach crucial

importance to these exceptional cases or that they invariably be relied on as the starting point of the assessment.

[...] It is true that the circumstances of the case at hand are special given the large-scale impact and the precautionary nature of the obligation to retain data. However, the weighing of the interference must still make a noticeable distinction between this type of interference and the particularly serious interferences that arise in connection with the acoustic surveillance of private homes, or the remote searches of information technology systems, but also in connection with the content-related surveillance and analysis of telecommunications *by means of direct interception by state bodies*; those cases – in contrast to the measure at hand – present a particularly high risk that the absolutely protected core of private life could be affected. The collection of the traffic data of all telecommunications is carried out by private service providers, without public authorities obtaining knowledge of the data; the possibility of the authorities to request access to the data constitutes a separate measure, which is subject to strict substantive conditions and procedural safeguards – for instance where the data is obtained by the authorities pursuant to § 100g of the Code of Criminal Procedure – and which in practice must be reviewed and authorised and must also be strictly limited in scope. From the perspective of the affected fundamental rights holders, neither data retention nor the separate possibility of requesting data access amount to an interference with fundamental rights of such weight that it could reasonably be qualified as "particularly serious", which denotes the most severe type of interference conceivable. Ultimately, what remains is an interference that results from the retention carried out by private service providers, and that can be characterised as particularly weighty. This differentiation will become relevant in the assessment of whether the challenged provisions are appropriate [in terms of proportionality].

II.

Contrary to the Senate majority's assessment, the challenged provisions on the obligation to retain traffic data and the possibility of the authorities to obtain this data for law enforcement purposes are not inappropriate; the burdens they impose on the affected persons are reasonable and the provisions are therefore proportionate in the strict sense.

1. The provisions sufficiently reflect the requirement derived from the principle of proportionality that interferences be appropriate and reasonable. In an overall balancing of the severity of the interference with Art. 10(1) of the Basic Law and the weight of the reasons invoked as justification, it becomes apparent that the legislator has respected the limits set by the requirement of proportionality.

317 [...]
318 The assessment of whether the statutory framework is appropriate under constitutional law must first take into account that fundamental rights are not only defensive rights against state interference. They have an objective dimension that gives rise to the duty of the state to protect citizens against infringements. This duty of protection requires the state to take suitable measures to prevent violations of legal interests; to investigate when violations occur; to attribute liability for a violation of legal interests; and to restore the peaceful legal order (*Rechtsfrieden*) disrupted by such violations [...]. In this sense, ensuring the protection of citizens and their fundamental rights and of the foundations of society, and the prevention and investigation of considerable criminal offences, are also prerequisites for peaceful coexistence and the carefree enjoyment of fundamental rights by citizens. Measures for effectively investigating criminal offences, and effectively averting dangers to public security, are therefore not *per se* a threat to the freedom of citizens; they are, however, not permissible without any restraint or limit. Rather, these measures must remain within the limits of what is appropriate and reasonable, ensuring the enjoyment of the fundamental rights as well as the protection of legal interests of the individual. In a state under the rule of law, citizens must be able to rely on effective protection *by* the state just as much as on protection *against* the state [...]. Accordingly, the Federal Constitutional Court has described the state as a constituted power of peace and order; it has recognised the state's duty to guarantee the security of its citizens as a constitutional value that is equal to other constitutional values and an indispensable element for the institutional legitimation of the state (cf. BVerfGE 49, 24 <56 and 57>; 115, 320 <346> – *Profiling*).
319 It is incumbent upon the legislator to create the necessary legal bases for investigating criminal offences and averting dangers to public security; in striking a balance between conflicting interests in this context, it must be taken into account that the individual, who is connected to and bound by the community, can be reasonably expected to tolerate certain impairments that serve the protection of other citizens' legal interests and fundamental rights, but also their own protection (cf. BVerfGE 4, 7 <15>; 33, 303 <334>; 50, 166 <175>). In view of this, the legislator must strike a balance, on the one hand protecting the freedoms of fundamental rights holders, while on the other hand providing an effective statutory framework for ensuring, by appropriate and reasonable means, that the legal interests and fundamental rights of citizens are protected, and criminal offences are investigated; in this respect, the legislator must be afforded leeway.
320 2. The legislator kept within the leeway afforded by the Constitution with regard to designing the obligation to retain telecommunications traffic data for a period of six months; the statutory provisions specifying the purposes for which retained

data may be used; and the provisions permitting authorities to obtain such data in criminal proceedings. In view of the fundamental rights and legal interests these provisions seek to protect, the impairment resulting from the retention of traffic data for the affected communicating parties is neither inappropriate nor unreasonable [...].

a) The leeway granted to the legislator in striking an abstract balance between the respective legal interests and rights involved in the freedom and security conundrum (cf. BVerfGE 109, 279 <350> – *Surveillance of Private Homes*; 115, 320 <346> – *Profiling*) is in part informed by the unique characteristics of the subject matter of the statutory framework and the realities it seeks to address. Therefore, the assessment of whether the challenged provisions are appropriate and reasonable must also take into account the aims and effectiveness of the statutory framework. 321

With the Act Revising the Law on Telecommunications Surveillance and Other Covert Investigation Measures and Transposing Directive 2006/24/EC, the legislator fundamentally reformed the system of covert investigation methods under the Code of Criminal Procedure. [...] This was based on the consideration that in the present day, telecommunications traffic data is either not stored at all, or deleted before a judicial warrant authorising requests for data access can be obtained or even before the information necessary for seeking such a warrant has been ascertained; this is in part attributed to technical advances resulting in the proliferation of flat-rate contracts, which means that telecommunications traffic data is no longer available months later – as used to be the case in the past [...]. Moreover, it is common knowledge that criminal acts are committed on and via the Internet. In other words, social realities, including criminal behaviour, are also reflected in the use of different types of telecommunication. [...] 322

[...] 323

Under these circumstances, the legislator cannot, in principle, be barred from considering the effectiveness of the means it must provide for the purposes of protecting the legal interests of victims of crime, and from adapting to changed circumstances; this may entail imposing an obligation on service providers to store and retain traffic data in their sphere for a certain time period. [...] According to the legislator's assessment, which is not objectionable, the availability of traffic data for a six-month period is of great importance for effective law enforcement and public security measures, not only regarding serious crime, but also for the investigation of crime that, based on the circumstances of the individual case, concerns considerable criminal acts or criminal acts that have been committed by means of telecommunications and are difficult to investigate without access to traffic data (cf. BVerfGE 115, 166 <192 *et seq.*> – *Telecommunications Surveillance*; [...]). 324

325 Accordingly, the Senate majority acknowledges that the increased use of electronic or digital means of communication and their advance into virtually all areas of life has created new obstacles to law enforcement and the averting of dangers to public security. The Senate majority also accepts that modern communication technologies are increasingly used for committing a wide variety of criminal acts, rendering criminal activities more effective. In my view, however, the Senate majority does not attach the necessary weight to this development in its assessment of proportionality in the strict sense.

326 b) Moreover, the Senate majority's decision effectively amounts to an almost complete reduction of the margin of appreciation and leeway afforded the legislator for enacting appropriate and reasonable statutory provisions in the domains of law enforcement and public security that serve to protect the population. Therefore, the Senate majority also fails to sufficiently take into account the requirement of 'judicial self-restraint' [English term used in the original] incumbent upon Constitutional Court Justices in relation to conceptual decisions taken by the democratically legitimated legislator. It provides step-by-step instructions to the legislator, setting out all the details of the envisaged statutory framework, without affording the legislator any margin of manoeuvre for finding a solution that, based on its own assessment, responds best to today's developments in the field of telecommunications.

327 [...]

328-329 3. [...]

330 4. Finally, the Senate majority denies the legislator the possibility of allowing requests for access to traffic data in the investigation of criminal offences that are not listed in the current catalogue laid down in § 100a(2) of the Code of Criminal Procedure but that, based on the circumstances of the individual case, constitute considerable criminal acts, and of criminal acts committed by means of telecommunications (§ 100g(1) first sentence nos. 1 and 2 of the Code of Criminal Procedure). In doing so, the Senate majority also fails to sufficiently take into account the weight of these criminal offences and – to the extent that the legislator considers them difficult to investigate – the significance of the traffic data for effective criminal investigations. [...]

331 According to the Senate majority, access to traffic data retained pursuant to § 113a of the Telecommunications Act should also be excluded in relation to criminal offences committed by means of telecommunications; in this respect, it fails to sufficiently take into account the legislator's assumption that these offences would otherwise be difficult to investigate. These difficulties may render requests for data access appropriate, as is the case where investigations concern criminal acts of particular weight. [...].

Since it is incumbent upon the legislator to guarantee effective law enforcement and to ensure that there are no substantial gaps in protection, the legislator must not be barred from granting the authorities access to traffic data also in cases where criminal acts that, while not necessarily constituting particularly serious offences, still violate legal interests of particular weight, if the legislator considers this the only way to prevent the creation of *de facto* legal vacuums where criminal investigations would largely be pointless. [...]

[...]

5. Similar considerations apply with regard to the threshold set by the Senate majority for granting access to retained data for the purposes of averting dangers to public security. The legal interests recognised by the Senate majority as sufficiently weighty grounds for permitting requests for access to and the use of traffic data should have included the averting of dangers to assets of substantial value the preservation of which is in the public interest, even if the danger in question does not pose a threat to the general public. It does not seem plausible to me to exclude such assets of substantial value given that they in fact enjoy fundamental rights protection (cf. Art. 14(1) of the Basic Law). [...]

6. Lastly, the Senate majority advocates an extension of the requirement to notify affected persons when their traffic data is accessed and demands not only that data access in criminal proceedings be, in principle, limited to so-called *overt* access, but also requires a notification "*before* requests for access to or the transfer of the data are carried out" unless such a requirement jeopardises the purpose of the investigation. This requirement, too, goes beyond the legislative concept, thereby encroaching upon the legislator's leeway to design. [...]

III.

[...]

Justice Schluckebier

Dissenting Opinion of Justice Eichberger

I do not fully agree with the decision of the Senate majority regarding the outcome of the decision and essential elements of its reasoning. In principle, I concur with Justice Schluckebier's criticism, and I largely agree with his conclusion and reasoning. Therefore, I will limit myself to giving a brief summary of the considerations on which my position is based:

338 1. I, too, believe that imposing a statutory obligation to retain telecommunications traffic data is a weighty interference with Art. 10(1) of the Basic Law given that its scope is broad and comprehensive in terms of persons affected and subject matters; given that the data retention is not based on specific grounds; and given that the data is retained for a considerable duration. However, since the obligation to retain data is limited to traffic data and does not concern the contents of telecommunications, and since it is carried out by private service providers in a decentralised manner, the interference arising from data retention is not of such overriding weight as the Senate majority generally assumes. In my view, the concern expressed by the Senate majority that data retention might have a chilling effect on the communication behaviour of the population is [...] unfounded in light of the legislative design of the data retention framework; at any rate, there is no empirical evidence for such a chilling effect.

339 In my opinion, the major burden for citizens with regard to the legal interest protected under Art. 10(1) of the Basic Law, which results from ordering data retention, therefore lies primarily in the potential risks created by such a large data collection in terms of possible abuse by the service providers themselves or by unauthorised third parties, or of excessive use by law enforcement or police authorities. Precautions must be taken to prevent such abuse. I therefore fully agree with the view of the Senate majority concerning the stringent requirements for data security regarding the data retained by the service providers, which must be defined by law. In principle, I also agree with most of the other procedural safeguards regarding data retention, requests for data access and further data use (which concern data deletion and documentation, transparency and legal protection) which the Senate majority considers necessary; however, I find that the requirements which the Senate majority sets out for the legislator in this context are overly detailed in many respects and do not sufficiently take into account the leeway to design that the Constitution affords the legislator in this context.

340 2. Unlike the Senate majority, and concurring with Justice Schluckebier, I think that the legislative design of §§ 113a and 113b of the Telecommunications Act, which divides the legislative responsibility for imposing obligations to retain data and for authorising requests for data access, is, in principle, compatible with the Constitution. Within this legislative design, § 113b of the Telecommunications Act does not constitute a separate interference with Art. 10(1) of the Basic Law that goes beyond the obligation to retain data pursuant to § 113a of the Telecommunications Act. The provision does define the purposes for which traffic data may be retained, as required by the Constitution. Only the separate statutory authorisations to request

access to traffic data, envisaged by § 113b first sentence of the Telecommunications Act, result in a new interference with Art. 10(1) of the Basic Law, and the significance of this interference does go beyond that of the data retention performed pursuant to the former provision. With § 113b of the Telecommunications Act, the federal legislator leaves to federal or *Land* legislation, depending on whether the legislator of the Federation or at *Land* level is competent for the respective subject matter, the authority to decide, based on its constitutional and democratic legitimation, whether and to what extent access to telecommunications traffic data should be permissible for law enforcement purposes, for averting dangers to public security or for the tasks of the intelligence services. When making this decision, the respective legislator is of course responsible for respecting the constitutional boundaries of access to traffic data in line with the principle of proportionality.

This does not amount to an order to collect and retain data for unspecified purposes, which would be impermissible under constitutional law. In § 113a of the Telecommunications Act, the federal legislator imposed an obligation on service providers to retain data, and in § 113b of the Telecommunications Act, it specified the purposes for which the retained data may be used. I agree with the view of the Senate majority that, by ordering the data retention, the federal legislator assumed responsibility for the potential threats to citizens; this requires that at least a minimum threshold for exercising these powers be determined, in addition to the general definition of its purpose [...]. However, in my opinion it is not required under constitutional law that the purposes for which the retained data may be used be already specified in a detailed and definitive manner at the time the obligation to retain data is imposed, as demanded from the federal legislator by the Senate majority.

3. Finally, and above all, I cannot agree with the outcome of the balancing of interests conducted by the Senate majority to the extent that it considers the use of the data retained pursuant to § 113a of the Telecommunications Act for law enforcement purposes, which is governed by § 100g of the Code of Criminal Procedure, to be unconstitutional. Firstly, this is due to the fact that, in my view, the Senate majority from the outset attaches too much weight to the interference with Art. 10(1) of the Basic Law resulting from the ordering of data retention; by contrast, it does not attach enough significance to the justified interests of the general public and of individual citizens in effective law enforcement and in effective public security. Secondly, it fails to sufficiently respect the leeway afforded the legislator in assessing the conflicting protected legal interests and in designing the statutory framework. In this respect, I agree with the remarks made by Justice Schluckebier in his dissenting opinion.

343 Another shortcoming of the proportionality assessment performed by the Senate majority is that, when balancing the conflicting interests, the Senate always assumes that the greatest possible interference will occur, namely that the data will be accessed extensively with the ultimate aim of creating movement profiles of the affected citizens or of profiling their social relations. [...] However, this perspective fails to consider that a large number of requests for data access may concern individual incidents, short time periods and the telecommunications relations of only one or few persons [...]. It is obvious that the weight of interference resulting from such requests for data access is minor and cannot be compared to the weight of interference resulting from access to communication contents [...]. By regarding any kind of data access as a particularly serious interference with Art. 10(1) of the Basic Law, irrespective of its specific scope in the individual case, and thus generally assuming that the legislator is constitutionally obliged to establish very high thresholds for exercising these powers, the Senate majority, in my view, is contradictory in its assessment, – even though it denies this – because the Senate majority does not object to the authorities accessing similar data if the service providers retain the data for technical reasons rather than pursuant to § 113a of the Telecommunications Act.

344 Based on these considerations, and regardless of the different frame of reference for the weighing of interests, I do concur with the standards developed and the requirements set by the Senate majority for permissible use of the traffic data for public security purposes and the tasks of the intelligence services (see C V 2 b and c above); however, I cannot concur with the requirements set by the Senate majority for the use of the data for law enforcement purposes (see C V 2 a and C VI 3 a, aa above). In this respect, I consider the differentiated approach to the obtaining and use of data for law enforcement purposes, as laid down by the legislator in § 100g of the Code of Criminal Procedure, to be constitutional. It is incumbent upon the judge deciding on the permissibility of a request for data access in a given case to adequately take into account the legal interests of the affected persons meriting protection under Art. 10(1) of the Basic Law and the weight of the respective interference, as the legislator specifically requires in § 100g(1) second sentence of the Code of Criminal Procedure with regard to criminal offences committed by means of telecommunications.

345 4. In my opinion, even from the Senate majority's point of view, the Court should have merely declared the challenged provisions incompatible with the Basic Law instead of void. In accordance with the preliminary injunctions issued in this matter, it should have ordered that data can be obtained and retained at least for an interim period until new provisions that are compatible with the Constitution have been enacted. Even though the Senate majority considers requests for data

No. 41 – Data Retention

access which meet the requirements set out in the preliminary injunctions to be in principle constitutional, and even though it can be expected that the enactment of new provisions reflecting these requirements will follow, the Senate majority still chose to declare the challenged provisions void without a transitional period and to impose an obligation to delete the traffic data collected on the basis of the preliminary injunctions. In doing so, the Senate majority tolerates impairments of law enforcement and, above all, puts important protected legal interests in jeopardy. I cannot support this outcome.

Justice Eichberger

No. 42

BVerfGE 129, 208 – The Telecommunications Surveillance Revision Act

HEADNOTE

to the Order of the Second Senate of 12 October 2011
2 BvR 236, 237, 422/08

On the constitutionality of provisions of the Telecommunications Surveillance Revision Act of 21 December 2007 (§ 100a(2) and (4), § 101(4) to (6) and § 160a of the Code of Criminal Procedure).

FEDERAL CONSTITUTIONAL COURT
- 2 BvR 236, 237, 422/08 -

IN THE NAME OF THE PEOPLE

In the proceedings
on the constitutional complaints of

I. 1. Dr. M..., 2. Dr. M..., 3. Dr. G..., 4. Ms M..., 5. Mr M..., 6. Mr B..., 7. Ms H...,
 – authorised representative for nos. 2-7: ...
 against Articles 1 and 2 of the Act Revising the Law on Telecommunications Surveillance and Other Covert Investigation Measures and Transposing Directive 2006/24/EC of 21 December 2007 (BGBl I, p. 3198), to the extent that the complainants assert a violation of fundamental rights by § 100a(2) and (4), § 100f, § 110(3) and § 160a of the Code of Criminal Procedure
 - 2 BvR 236/08 -,

II. Mr H...,
 – authorised representative: ...
 against Articles 1 and 2 of the Act Revising the Law on Telecommunications Surveillance and Other Covert Investigation Measures and Transposing Directive 2006/24/EC of 21 December 2007 (BGBl I, p. 3198),

to the extent that the complainant asserts a violation of fundamental rights by § 100a(2) and (4), § 100f and § 110(3) of the Code of Criminal Procedure

- 2 BvR 237/08 -,

III. 1. Dr. H..., 2. Dr. S..., 3. Mr V..., 4. Dr. L..., 5. Mr K..., 6. Ms P..., 7. Ms L..., 8. Mr B..., 9. Mr S..., 10. Mr F..., 11. Ms S..., 12. Dr. W..., 13. Prof. Dr. S..., 14. Mr W...,

– authorised representative for nos. 2-14: ...

against the Act Revising the Law on Telecommunications Surveillance and Other Covert Investigation Measures and Transposing Directive 2006/24/EC of 21 December 2007 (BGBl I, p. 3198), to the extent that the complainants assert a violation of fundamental rights by § 100a(4) first sentence, § 100f(1) and (2), § 101(4) third to fifth sentence, (5) and (6) and § 160a of the Code of Criminal Procedure

- 2 BvR 422/08 -

the Federal Constitutional Court – Second Senate –

with the participation of Justices

President Voßkuhle,
Di Fabio,
Mellinghoff,
Lübbe-Wolff,
Gerhardt,
Landau,
Huber,
Hermanns

held on 12 October 2011:

[...]

The constitutional complaints are rejected.

REASONS:

A.

The constitutional complaints, combined for joint decision, concern Arts. 1 and 2 of the Telecommunications Surveillance Revision Act, which amends selected provisions of the Code of Criminal Procedure.

1

I.

2-4   1. [...]
5   2. [...]
6   3. a) With the Telecommunications Surveillance Revision Act, [...] the Federal Government intended to create a harmonised comprehensive framework on covert investigation measures in criminal proceedings and to implement several decisions of the Federal Constitutional Court. [...]
7-11 [...]
12-17 b) [...]
18-123 c) [...]

II.

124   1. The complainants in proceedings 2 BvR 236/08 and 2 BvR 237/08 claim [...] that their fundamental rights – like the fundamental rights of all citizens – are directly affected. They argue that – in both their professional and private lives – as lawyers, doctors, secondary school teachers [...] or simply as private individuals [...] they use landlines and have at least one mobile phone as well as Internet access; they trust that their communication via these channels is beyond the reach of the state.
125-130 [...]
131   2. The complainants in proceedings 2 BvR 422/08 – lawyers, members of Parliament, a student and a journalist – assert that their fundamental rights are immediately and directly affected by the challenged provisions because they have to use landlines, mobile phones, the Internet and email in their private lives, in their professional lives as freelancers, or in their political work. They argue that under the new legal framework, they have reason to fear that their data will be accessed by the state, and that even though the framework provides for the *ex post* notification of affected persons, they cannot trust that the authorities will actually observe this requirement in practice.
132-142 [...]

III.

143   Statements on the constitutional complaints were submitted by the Federal Government, the Federal Court of Justice, the Public Prosecutor General (*Generalbundesanwalt*), the Federal Bar Association (*Bundesrechtsanwaltskammer*), the Chamber of Patent Attorneys (*Patentanwaltskammer*), the Federal Chamber of Tax Advisers

No. 42 – The Telecommunications Surveillance Revision Act

(*Bundessteuerberaterkammer*), the German Association of Tax Advisers (*Deutscher Steuerberaterverband*), the Chamber of Public Accountants (*Wirtschaftsprüferkammer*), the German Medical Association (*Bundesärztekammer*), the German Lawyers Association (*Deutscher Anwaltsverein*) and the German Federation of Journalists (*Deutscher Journalistenverband*).
[...] 144-166

B.

[...] 167-174

C.

To the extent that the constitutional complaints are admissible, they are unfounded. The challenged provisions do not violate the complainants' fundamental rights. 175

I.

The Telecommunications Surveillance Revision Act of 21 December 2007 (BGBl I, p. 3198) does not violate the requirement that the affected fundamental rights be expressly specified (*Zitiergebot*) in accordance with Art. 19(1) second sentence of the Basic Law. 176
[...] 177-195

II.

To the extent that the complainants challenge the extension of the catalogue of criminal offences in § 100a(2) of the Code of Criminal Procedure and the lack of clarification of when a criminal offence is considered serious even in the individual case, their constitutional complaints are also unsuccessful. Their claim that the core of private life is not sufficiently protected by § 100a(4) first sentence of the Code of Criminal Procedure cannot be upheld. 196
1. § 100a of the Code of Criminal Procedure authorises the surveillance and recording of telecommunications, thus giving rise to a serious interference with the privacy of telecommunications, which is protected by Art. 10(1) of the Basic Law (cf. BVerfGE 113, 348 <382>). 197
The privacy of telecommunications under Art. 10(1) of the Basic Law covers not only the contents but also the specific circumstances of telecommunications. While telecommunications privacy primarily protects the contents of telecommu- 198

nications, it also extends to the circumstances of communication. These include whether, when and how often telecommunications traffic occurred or was attempted between whom or between which devices (cf. BVerfGE 67, 157 <172>; 85, 386 <396>; 107, 299 <312 and 313>). The state is generally not entitled to obtain knowledge of these circumstances. The fundamental right is meant to preserve the conditions that are necessary to ensure free telecommunications. The confidential use of the communication medium must be ensured in all respects (cf. BVerfGE 100, 313 <358> – *The Article 10 Act*). The inviolability of telecommunications privacy, as guaranteed by fundamental rights, seeks to prevent a situation where communication participants have to expect that state authorities will intercept their communications and obtain knowledge of the relevant communication relations and contents, as a result of which affected persons might cease to exchange opinions or information by means of telecommunications systems altogether, or change how and what they communicate (cf. BVerfGE 100, 313 <359> – *The Article 10 Act*). In this respect, Art. 10(1) of the Basic Law covers any transmission of information by means of telecommunications technologies, irrespective of who operates the relevant transmission and relay networks (cf. BVerfGE 107, 299 <322>).

199 Interferences with the privacy of telecommunications arise where state authorities obtain knowledge of the content or the circumstances of communication transmitted by telecommunications technology without the consent of the communicating parties (cf. BVerfGE 100, 313 <366> – *The Article 10 Act*; 107, 299 <313>).

200 2. When the catalogue of criminal offences in § 100a(2) of the Code of Criminal Procedure was amended by the Telecommunications Surveillance Revision Act, 19 offences were removed and more than 30 new offences were added. With respect to Art. 10 of the Basic Law, there are ultimately no constitutional objections against the legislator categorising the offences added to the statutory catalogue as grounds justifying measures of telecommunications surveillance. According to the legislator, these measures serve the legitimate purpose of providing law enforcement authorities with the necessary means to prosecute serious crimes and crimes that are difficult to investigate (BTDrucks 16/5846, p. 40). In particular, this does not violate the requirement of specificity and the principle of proportionality.

201 a) It was the legislator's intent that the law extend to all newly added criminal offences, all of which concern serious crimes and crimes that are difficult to investigate. [...]

202 b) The legislator satisfied the requirement of specificity by strictly limiting the use of telecommunications surveillance to the purpose of the investigation – in particular investigating the criminal conduct in question and determining the whereabouts of the suspect. In addition, the criminal offences that may prompt investigation measures using telecommunications surveillance are not merely defined by abstract

criteria, but are individually specified in the catalogue. Furthermore, both establishing a suspicion of criminal conduct and extending the surveillance measure to third parties acting as intermediaries in the transmission require a reliable factual basis ("specific facts") (cf. BVerfGE 107, 299 <321 *et seq.*>; 109, 279 <350 and 351> – *Surveillance of Private Homes*; 113, 348 <373, 385 and 386> regarding § 100c(1) no. 3 of the Code of Criminal Procedure). The legislator thus defined the statutory requirements for surveillance measures in a way that is generally comprehensible (cf. BVerfGE 110, 33 <54>).

c) In addition, the extended catalogue of criminal offences set out in § 100a(2) of the Code of Criminal Procedure observes the principle of proportionality. The legislator has a margin of appreciation when assessing the level of wrongdoing reflected in a criminal offence and deciding which crimes should lead to certain criminal investigation measures (cf. BVerfGE 109, 279 <347> – *Surveillance of Private Homes*). Yet interferences with the privacy of telecommunications are only permissible if the relevant offence is categorised as serious; this must be objectively reflected in the definition of the crime set out in the underlying provision of criminal law, in particular by the specified range of punishment (cf. BVerfGE 125, 260 <329> – *Data Retention*). The protected legal interest and its importance for a society based on law may also be significant for this categorisation. 203

All new offences added to the catalogue of § 100a(2) of the Code of Criminal Procedure by the legislator carry a maximum term of imprisonment of at least five years. However, this alone is not sufficient for categorising the offences as serious, which in turn is necessary for ensuring that the resulting interference with Art. 10(1) of the Basic Law is proportionate (cf. BVerfGE 124, 43 <63>; 125, 260 <328> – *Data Retention*). A maximum term of imprisonment of five years is the general standard in the Criminal Code. This maximum term also applies to offences that constitute medium-level crime at best in light of the protected legal interest and given that they are, in part, not subject to increased minimum terms of imprisonment (cf. BVerfGE 109, 279 <348> – *Surveillance of Private Homes*). 204

Nonetheless, the decision by the legislator, which categorises the criminal offences added to § 100a(2) of the Code of Criminal Procedure as "serious", is tenable based on an overall assessment that gives particular consideration to the respective protected legal interests. 205

The criminal offences added to the catalogue in § 100a(2) of the Code of Criminal Procedure that carry a maximum term of imprisonment of only five years either considerably interfere with the functioning of the state or its authorities – such as the offences of bribing members of Parliament (§ 108e of the Criminal Code), restricting competition through agreements in the context of public bids (§ 298 of the Criminal Code), preparatory acts to tampering with official identity documents on 206 a commercial basis or as a member of a gang (§ 275(2) of the Criminal Code) and acquisition of false official identity documents on a commercial basis or as a member of a gang (§ 276(2) of the Criminal Code) – or they significantly interfere with the protected legal interests of individuals – such as the offences of distribution, acquisition and possession of child pornography (§ 184b(1) of the Criminal Code) and assisting in human trafficking (§ 233a(1) of the Criminal Code). Therefore, categorising these criminal offences as serious in qualitative terms is within the legislator's leeway to design.

207 Moreover, the legislator did not simply recognise the suspicion that someone committed or aided or abetted one of the offences listed in § 100a(2) of the Code of Criminal Procedure as generally sufficient grounds for telecommunications surveillance. Rather, § 100a(1) no. 2 of the Code of Criminal Procedure further requires that the criminal act prompting the surveillance measures also be serious in the individual case. Additionally, it is required that without telecommunications surveillance, investigating the facts of the case or determining the whereabouts of the suspect would be significantly more difficult, or even futile (§ 100a(1) no. 3 of the Code of Criminal Procedure). The legislator thus established a protection scheme that satisfies the principle of proportionality.

208 d) Lastly, contrary to the argument put forward by the complainants, the constituent element set out in § 100a(1) no. 2 of the Code of Criminal Procedure that "the offence is particularly serious in the individual case as well" satisfies the requirement of specificity. In its case-law, the Federal Constitutional Court has frequently addressed criteria that may indicate the seriousness of a crime; these include the need for protection of the violated legal interests (cf. BVerfGE 109, 279 <346> – *Surveillance of Private Homes*), the level of the threat posed to the general public (cf. BVerfGE 107, 299 <322>; 113, 348 <388>), the way the offence was committed (cf. BVerfGE 107, 299 <324>; 109, 279 <346> – *Surveillance of Private Homes*), the number of victims (cf. BVerfGE 107, 299 <324>) and/or the extent of damage (cf. BVerfGE 107, 299 <324>). Constitutional law does not require that further details be specified since the determination whether a criminal act fits this constituent element is contingent upon an assessment of the circumstances of the individual case (on the significance of this case-by-case assessment, which adds an additional layer to the protection of freedom beyond the abstract determination of a catalogue listing relevant criminal offences, cf. BVerfGE 125, 260 <329> – *Data Retention*; with further references).

209 3. The safeguards protecting the core of private life in the context of telecommunications surveillance set out in § 100a(4) of the Code of Criminal Procedure satisfy the constitutional requirements both at the stage of data collection and at the stage of data analysis.

a) The constitutional requirements regarding the specific design of the framework ensuring protection of the core may differ depending on the method of data collection and the nature of the information obtained by it (cf. BVerfGE 120, 274 <337> – *Remote Searches*). A statutory provision authorising surveillance measures that might affect the core of private life must ensure, to the greatest extent possible, that no data relating to the core of private life is collected (cf. BVerfGE 120, 274 <337> – *Remote Searches*) […].

However, in many cases it is virtually unavoidable that investigating authorities obtain knowledge of the relevant material before realising that it relates to the core of private life. If there is a risk that the data collection might violate the core of private life, this does not mean that constitutional law precludes the accessing of such information from the outset in these cases (cf. BVerfGE 80, 367 <375, 381> – *Diary-Like Notes*; 120, 274 <338> – *Remote Searches*). The relevant investigation measures may be carried out where specific facts give rise to the suspicion that a criminal offence has been committed, or aided or abetted, or has been attempted […] or has been prepared by means of another crime (cf. BVerfGE 120, 274 <337 and 338> – *Remote Searches*), if the offence is particularly serious, including in the individual case, and the investigations were otherwise considerably more difficult or futile.

In such cases, it is necessary to ensure sufficient protection at the stage of data analysis (cf. BVerfGE 120, 274 <337 and 338> – *Remote Searches* […]). The legislator must provide for suitable procedural safeguards to ensure that, where data relating to the core of private life has been collected, the severity of the violation of the core and its impact on the personality and development of the person concerned be kept to a minimum (cf. BVerfGE 120, 274 <338> – *Remote Searches*; […]). In this respect, it is crucial that the collected data be examined as to whether it contains information relating to the core of private life. If the examination reveals that data relating to the core was collected, it must be deleted without undue delay; any sharing or use of this data must be ruled out (cf. BVerfGE 109, 279 <324, 331 *et seq.*> – *Surveillance of Private Homes*; 113, 348 <392>; 120, 274 <339> – *Remote Searches* […]).

b) § 100a(4) first sentence of the Code of Criminal Procedure provides that the surveillance and recording of telecommunications are impermissible if there are facts indicating that the measures will only yield information relating to the core of private life; this satisfies the constitutional requirements regarding the protection of the core at the stage of data collection.

aa) With the revision of § 100a(4) of the Code of Criminal Procedure, the legislator developed a two-tier concept of protection in order to shield the persons concerned from interferences with the core of private life, which enjoys absolute protection.

§ 100a(4) first sentence of the Code of Criminal Procedure provides that data relating to the core must not be collected in a targeted manner. If the core is nevertheless affected – in cases where this effect was not foreseeable – § 100a(4) second to fourth sentence of the Code of Criminal Procedure provides for documentation and deletion requirements and a prohibition to use the obtained data.

215 bb) There are cases where it can be presumed that the data in question unequivocally relates to the core of private life; this primarily concerns cases where the person under surveillance and their communication partners share a special relationship of trust pertaining to the core of private life – as is the case when communicating with close family members, clerics, phone counsellors, defence lawyers or, in certain cases, doctors as well (cf. BVerfGE 109, 279 <321 *et seq.*> – *Surveillance of Private Homes*). To the extent that such a relationship of trust is ascertainable for investigating authorities, telecommunications surveillance measures must not be carried out.

216 cc) Contrary to the complainants' view, however, the surveillance of telecommunications must not be excluded from the outset merely because the recorded data may also contain information pertaining to the core of one's personality right. Such an absolute prohibition to collect data would restrict telecommunications surveillance to such a degree that effective law enforcement could no longer be ensured, especially regarding serious and most severe crime. Instead, the protection of the core of private life must be ensured by way of sufficient fundamental rights protection at the stage of data analysis.

217 With respect to surveillance of telecommunications, a comprehensive protection of the core of private life at the stage of data collection pursuant to § 100a of the Code of Criminal Procedure would, for various reasons, present considerable practical difficulties, just like in the context of covert access to information technology systems (cf. BVerfGE 120, 274 <337> – *Remote Searches*). [...]

218 Difficulties to ensure comprehensive protection of the core of private life at the stage of data collection in particular result from the fact that telecommunications surveillance is carried out by way of automated recordings of communication contents [...] whereas it is only sporadically possible to (concurrently) have surveillance personnel listen in on the communication in real time.

219 In addition, even if surveillance personnel do screen the telecommunications in real time [...], it is in many cases not possible to eliminate the difficulties regarding an effective protection of the core at the stage of data collection. For instance, the bulk of intercepted telecommunications is conducted in foreign languages [...]. Moreover, there are various other factors that can make it hard to understand the conversations immediately and without prior technical processing [...], for example background noise or bad reception [...].

dd) In the event that a surveillance measure does lead to the recording of data pertaining to the core of private life, the prohibition to use the data pursuant to § 100a(4) second sentence of the Code of Criminal Procedure provides sufficient protection at the stage of data analysis [...]. The statutory framework satisfies the requirements for an effective protection of the core of private life, given that it provides for an absolute prohibition to use the data, requires that the data be deleted without undue delay and sets out corresponding documentation requirements.

c) Contrary to the complainants' view, it is not constitutionally required to establish an independent body that, in addition to the investigating state authorities, reviews whether it is permissible to use the information obtained in the further course of the investigation proceedings.

According to established case-law of the Federal Constitutional Court, it is necessary that procedural safeguards be put in place for ensuring that, where data relating to the core of private life is obtained, such data is not stored, used or shared, but deleted without undue delay (cf. BVerfGE 109, 279 <333> – *Surveillance of Private Homes*; 113, 348 <390 and 391>; 120, 274 <338 and 339> – *Remote Searches*; 124, 43 <70>). In its order regarding the acoustic surveillance of private homes, the Court stated that an independent body must review whether the information obtained may be used in the principal proceedings or as a basis for further investigations in other proceedings (cf. BVerfGE 109, 279 <333 and 334> – *Surveillance of Private Homes*). However, the procedural safeguards necessary under constitutional law do not require, in every type of case, that further independent bodies outside the investigating state authorities be established in order to ensure compliance with the underlying statutory provisions.

In this respect, it must in particular be taken into account that measures pursuant to § 100a of the Code of Criminal Procedure require a judicial warrant, unless there is danger requiring immediate action (*Gefahr im Verzug*); in that case, the measure in question must generally be confirmed by a court afterwards (§ 100b(1) of the Code of Criminal Procedure). The prior involvement of a judge in overseeing surveillance of telecommunications thus ensures that before the measure is executed, the protection of the core of private life is assessed and considered by an independent authority. Moreover, the court authorising the order must be notified of the results after the measure has ended (§ 100b(4) second sentence of the Code of Criminal Procedure). [...]

224 [...]

III.

225 The constitutional complaints are also unfounded to the extent that they challenge the design of the notification requirement in § 101(4) to (6) of the Code of Criminal Procedure.

226 1. In its *Data Retention* judgment, the Federal Constitutional Court stated that the legislator must adhere to transparency requirements in the context of authorising the covert collection of citizens' data. The Court held that the legislator must enact provisions requiring that affected persons be informed about the collection and use of their data, given that such provisions are generally among the key instruments of data protection under fundamental rights. (cf. BVerfGE 125, 260 <335> – *Data Retention*; with reference to BVerfGE 100, 313 <361> – *The Article 10 Act*; 109, 279 <363 and 364> – *Surveillance of Private Homes*; 118, 168 <207 and 208>; 120, 351 <361 and 362>). Effective legal protection can only be guaranteed if the affected persons are notified. [...]

227 The legislator may provide for exemptions from the requirement to notify affected persons, balancing it against the constitutionally protected legal interests of third parties. These exemptions must, however, be limited to what is absolutely necessary (cf. BVerfGE 109, 279 <364> – *Surveillance of Private Homes*; 125, 260 <336> – *Data Retention*). In the context of law enforcement, exemptions from the notification requirement are conceivable, for example, if knowledge of the interference with the privacy of telecommunications would jeopardise the purpose pursued, if the affected person could not be notified without endangering another person's life and limb, or if the notification conflicted with overriding interests of the affected person; this is the case, for instance, where the measure did not have any further consequences and notification of the affected person would only intensify the interference with fundamental rights (cf. BVerfGE 100, 313 <361> – *The Article 10 Act*; 109, 279 <364 et seq.> – *Surveillance of Private Homes*; 125, 260 <336> – *Data Retention*). In addition, it is not constitutionally required to establish similarly strict notification requirements vis-à-vis persons who are only incidentally affected by an investigation measure that is directed against a suspect, and who are thus not themselves the target of state action. If they were subsequently notified, this would frequently even intensify the interference in the individual case (cf. BVerfGE 109, 279 <365> – *Surveillance of Private Homes*; 125, 260 <337> – *Data Retention*; [...]). In such cases, the affected persons need not be notified if they were only negligibly affected by the measure and if it can be

presumed that they have no interest in being notified (cf. BVerfGE 125, 260 <337> – *Data Retention*).

2. Measured against these standards, § 101(4) to (6) of the Code of Criminal Procedure stands up to constitutional review.

[…] The common feature of the investigation measures listed in § 101(4) first sentence nos. 1 to 12 of the Code of Criminal Procedure is that they require that a criminal act was committed and that there are specific leads regarding the identity of the perpetrator or accessories to the crime. Thus, […] the investigation measures do not amount to a gathering of information without specific grounds or without a basis of suspicion, nor do they have an indiscriminate effect (regarding the significance of these criteria for the severity of interferences with fundamental rights cf. BVerfGE 115, 320 <354> – *Profiling*). In addition, all measures require judicial authorisation (*Richtervorbehalt*) – except for § 100h of the Code of Criminal Procedure, which governs the taking of pictures of suspects outside of private homes and the visual surveillance of persons with the aid of technical devices […]

a) Pursuant to § 101(4) third sentence of the Code of Criminal Procedure, a person affected by a covert criminal investigation measure need not be notified if protected interests of another person also affected by the measure outweigh the interest in being notified. […]

By enacting § 101(4) third sentence of the Code of Criminal Procedure, the legislator followed the consideration of the Federal Constitutional Court according to which it is not constitutionally required to provide for similarly strict notification requirements vis-à-vis persons whose data was only incidentally obtained (cf. BVerfGE 125, 260 <337> – *Data Retention*). With respect to this group of persons, it is not required to obtain judicial confirmation of the authorities' decision, based on a balancing of interests, to refrain from notification pursuant to § 101(4) third sentence of the Code of Criminal Procedure (cf. BVerfGE 125, 260 <337> – *Data Retention*). In the context of this decision, it is permissible under constitutional law to leave the balancing of the suspect's interests against the interests of third parties to the public prosecution office, given that the severity of the interference in relation to non-suspects is relatively low.

b) § 101(4) fourth sentence of the Code of Criminal Procedure provides that notification may be refrained from in certain cases regarding the seizure of postal items, telecommunications surveillance and the collection of telecommunications traffic data; in these cases, persons need not be notified if the measures were not directed against them, if they were only negligibly affected and if it can be presumed that they have no interest in being notified. This is not objectionable under constitutional law. […]

233 c) § 101(4) fifth sentence of the Code of Criminal Procedure concerns cases where the identity of persons affected by a covert investigation measure is not known. In this case, the persons could only be notified if further investigations determining their identity were carried out. [...] With respect to this group of persons, such investigations could intensify the interference with fundamental rights, both for the target person and other affected persons (cf. BVerfGE 109, 279 <365> – *Surveillance of Private Homes*; 125, 260 <337> – *Data Retention*; cf. also BTDrucks 16/5846, p. 60). Therefore, it was permissible for the legislator to leave the decision on notification pursuant to § 101(4) fifth sentence of the Code of Criminal Procedure to the investigating authorities, especially because determining the identity of the persons concerned will often require considerable effort (cf. BVerfGE 125, 260 <337> – *Data Retention*).

234 d) § 101(5) first sentence of the Code of Criminal Procedure is also compatible with the Basic Law. It provides that persons affected by the investigation measure should be notified as soon as this is possible without jeopardising the purpose of the investigation, life, limb and liberty of the person, or significant assets; for measures pursuant to § 110a, the foregoing provision also refers to the possibility that notification could jeopardise the continued use of an undercover police investigator.

235 The provision sets out a differentiated statutory regime, striking a balance between the requirement that the affected person be, in principle, notified *ex post* and overriding interests that may, in individual and exceptional cases, conflict with this requirement; this balancing satisfies constitutional law (cf. BVerfGE 125, 260 <353> – *Data Retention*).

236 aa) [...]

237 bb) Where an undercover police investigator is used in the context of surveillance, § 101(5) first sentence of the Code of Criminal Procedure provides that, based on a balancing of interests, notification may be deferred so as to keep open the possibility of using that investigator again; this balancing requirement satisfies the principle of proportionality in its strict sense. The grounds for deferring notification are sufficiently weighty and thus justify statutory limitations of the notification requirement.

238 On the one hand, the state does interfere with the fundamental right to informational self-determination (Art. 2(1) in conjunction with Art. 1(1) of the Basic Law) if officers assume a cover identity to build up communication relationships with fundamental rights holders and to exploit the legitimate expectations of the affected person in order to obtain information about that person's criminal conduct, which they would not otherwise receive (cf. BVerfGE 120, 274 <345> – *Remote Searches*). On the other hand, the interests in ensuring a properly functioning criminal justice system may, and must, be taken into account under the principle of the rule

of law, too (cf. BVerfGE 122, 248 <272>); allowing an undercover investigator to maintain their cover for possible future operations furthers this purpose. The Basic Law accords great importance to the prevention, prosecution and investigation of criminal acts (cf. BVerfGE 100, 313 <388> – *The Article 10 Act*; 113, 29 <54> – *Seizure of Electronic Data*; 115, 166 <192> – *Telecommunications Surveillance*; 122, 248 <270, 272>). Law enforcement authorities are reliant on the use of undercover police investigators; without this option, it would be considerably more difficult or even impossible for them to carry out their tasks, especially with respect to particularly dangerous crime (cf. BVerfGE 57, 250 <284>). [...] With § 101(5) of the Code of Criminal Procedure, the legislator achieved an appropriate balance between the interest of affected persons in being notified about covert investigation measures and the law enforcement interests of the state.

[...] 239-240

e) § 101(6) third sentence of the Code of Criminal Procedure also stands up to constitutional review. According to this provision, the court may authorise the authorities to refrain from notification indefinitely if the conditions for notifying the affected person will, in all probability, also not be fulfilled in the future. [...] 241

It was permissible for the legislator to refrain from imposing an obligation on law enforcement authorities and courts to re-examine, on a recurring basis, the grounds for repeated deferrals of notification if the factual situation precluding notification will in all likelihood not change in the long term. With the constituent element 'in all probability', the provision sets sufficiently strict requirements for the prognosis that the situation will not change in the long term, which effectively bars authorities from jumping to premature conclusions. 242

IV.

§ 160a(1) and (2) of the Code of Criminal Procedure, which governs the protection of persons entitled to refuse to give evidence, does not violate the complainants' fundamental rights. [...] 243

1. a) § 160a of the Code of Criminal Procedure contains a multi-tier system of prohibitions to collect and use evidence in relation to persons bound by professional confidentiality that applies to both [...] overt and covert investigative measures [...]. 244

§ 160a(1) first sentence of the Code of Criminal Procedure imposes an absolute prohibition to collect and use evidence with regard to clerics in their capacity as faith-based counsellors (§ 53(1) first sentence no. 1 of the Code of Criminal Procedure), defence lawyers (§ 53(1) first sentence no. 2 of the Code of Criminal Procedure) and members of Parliament (§ 53(1) first sentence no. 4 of the Code of 245

Criminal Procedure); the legislator extended this prohibition to lawyers in general [...].

246 By contrast, § 160a(2) of the Code of Criminal Procedure provides for a relative prohibition to collect and use evidence in relation to the other groups of persons bound by professional confidentiality listed in § 53(1) first sentence of the Code of Criminal Procedure; this prohibition is contingent on a proportionality assessment in the individual case

247 Based on the right to refuse to give evidence afforded persons that are bound by professional confidentiality, the purpose of § 160a(1) and (2) of the Code of Criminal Procedure is to protect the relationship of trust that these persons are part of. By differentiating between the respective groups of persons bound by professional confidentiality, the legislator takes into account that the Basic Law grants individuals an inviolable part of private life, which is beyond the reach of public authority, and thus also beyond the reach of criminal investigations. Insofar as the legislator determines that an interaction between individuals and persons bound by professional confidentiality typically falls within the inviolable part of private life, it grants absolute protection against the state collecting, using or analysing information in this respect (§ 160a(1) of the Code of Criminal Procedure). In all other cases, it grants only relative protection of the special relationship of trust that exists between individuals and persons bound by professional confidentiality (§ 160a(2) of the Code of Criminal Procedure); this concerns cases where, in the legislator's view, it cannot be ruled out, but it can also not be necessarily presumed, that the information typically relates to the core of private life. To the extent that, in the individual case, the inviolable core of private life is affected with regard to the group of persons § 160a(2) of the Code of Criminal Procedure refers to, the relevant investigation measure must be regarded as impermissible, too [despite the lack of an absolute prohibition] (cf. BTDrucks 16/5846, pp. 36 and 37).

248 b) By limiting the absolute prohibition to collect and use evidence under § 160a(1) of the Code of Criminal Procedure to a few exceptional cases, the legislator takes into account that law enforcement is of great importance (cf. BVerfGE 107, 299 <332>) [...].

249 The Federal Constitutional Court has repeatedly emphasised the constitutional requirement of effective law enforcement, it has also repeatedly stressed the interest in establishing the truth in criminal proceedings to the greatest extent possible, and has recognised the effective investigation of serious crimes as a fundamental responsibility of society under the rule of law (cf. BVerfGE 29, 183 <194>; 77, 65 <76>; 80, 367 <375> – *Diary-Like Notes*; 100, 313 <388 and 389> – *The Article 10 Act*; 107, 299 <316>; 122, 248 <272, 273>). The purpose of law enforcement measures is to investigate crimes and thereby contribute to the enforcement of

criminal law; this could be substantially affected by the right to refuse to give evidence or similar restrictions of law enforcement measures deriving from procedural law (cf. BVerfGE 77, 65 <76>; 107, 299 <332>). Such impairments require a legitimate basis in constitutional law – also in light of the right of the accused to a fair criminal trial under the rule of law (cf. BVerfGE 77, 65 <76>). In the individual case, such legitimation may derive from fundamental rights protection, given that criminal investigation measures regularly interfere with fundamental rights. Therefore, they require justification and must be weighed, in a balancing of interests, against public law enforcement interests.

The statutory framework gives effect to this balancing of interests required under constitutional law, given that for the majority of cases where persons bound by professional confidentiality are entitled to refuse to give evidence, investigation measures relating to these persons are subject to a proportionality assessment in the individual case. At the same time, the statutory framework contributes to the equal treatment of professional groups that are granted a right to refuse to give evidence under § 53(1) of the Code of Criminal Procedure and to which – save for a few exceptions – a prohibition to use evidence applies that is subject to a balancing under § 160a(2) of the Code of Criminal Procedure.

2. [...]

3. The complainants assert that § 160a(1) of the Code of Criminal Procedure should be extended to cover their professional activity [as doctors], too. In this respect, they argue that the differentiation between professional groups under § 160a(1) and (2) of the Code of Criminal Procedure is incompatible with Art. 3(1) of the Basic Law.

The general guarantee of the right to equality of Art. 3(1) of the Basic Law requires the legislator to treat equally matters which are essentially alike and to treat unequally matters which are essentially different (cf. BVerfGE 112, 268 <279>; 116, 164 <180>; 122, 210 <230>; established case-law). The primary purpose of the right to equality is to avoid unjustified unequal treatment of persons; thus, the legislator is generally subject to strict limits where groups of persons are treated differently (cf. BVerfGE 55, 72 <88>; 88, 87 <96>; 89, 365 <375>; 95, 267 <316>). The limits to the legislator's leeway to design are stricter the more the unequal treatment has possible adverse effects on the exercise of freedoms protected by fundamental rights (cf. BVerfGE 60, 123 <134>; 88, 87 <96>; 89, 15 <22 and 23>; 90, 46 <56>; 95, 267 <316 and 317>; 97, 271 <290 and 291>; 103, 172 <193>; 105, 73 <110 and 111>; 107, 27 <46>; 121, 317 <370>; established case-law). This applies in particular if it affects the scope of protection of the freedom to practice one's occupation under Art. 12(1) of the Basic Law, as is the case here given that the applicability of the statutory provision is linked to membership of a certain professional group (cf. BVerfGE 121, 317 <370>). In such cases, the general right to equality is violated if a group of persons addressed or affected by the provision is treated differently from another group, even though there are no differences between the groups that are of such significance or weight that they may justify the different treatment (cf. BVerfGE 55, 72 <88>; 93, 386 <397>; 105, 73 <110>; 107, 27 <46>; 121, 317 <369>; established case-law).

254 With respect to provisions that treat groups of persons differently or adversely affect the exercise of fundamental rights, the Federal Constitutional Court undertakes a detailed review as to whether the differentiation is based on reasons of such significance or weight that they may justify unequal legal consequences (cf. BVerfGE 88, 87 <97>; 95, 267 <317>).

255 4. When measured against these standards, the differentiation between the professional groups in § 160a(1) and (2) of the Code of Criminal Procedure does not violate the general guarantee of the right to equality.

256 a) [...]

257 aa) The absolute prohibition to collect and use evidence set out in § 160a(1) of the Code of Criminal Procedure considerably restricts law enforcement, because it prohibits, from the outset, investigation measures in relation to persons belonging to certain professional groups and it bars the use of any findings that were obtained nonetheless. Such absolute prohibitions are only permissible for narrowly defined exceptional cases; this concerns, in particular, cases where an investigation measure would result in an interference with human dignity given that the protection of human dignity is not subject to any balancing at all. [...] Accordingly, the Federal Constitutional Court held, in the context of acoustic surveillance of private homes, that absolute protection merited by the human dignity dimension of the relationship between the communication partners is required only for conversations with clerics in their capacity as faith-based counsellors and for conversations with defence lawyers (BVerfGE 109, 279 <318 and 319, 322> – *Surveillance of Private Homes*).

258 bb) Regarding the professional groups listed in § 160a(1) of the Code of Criminal Procedure, particularly weighty reasons justify the absolute prohibition to collect and use evidence.

259 (1) The absolute protection afforded both clerics in their capacity as faith-based counsellors and defence lawyers is justified given that their conversations with a suspect are typically linked to Art. 1(1) of the Basic Law: The conversation with clerics in their capacity as faith-based counsellors is part of the human dignity dimension that constitutional law accords to the practice of one's religion under Art. 4(1) and (2) of the Basic Law. Consultations with defence lawyers serve an important function in upholding human dignity, as this contributes to ensuring that the suspect is not treated as a mere object in criminal proceedings (BVerfGE

109, 279 <322> – *Surveillance of Private Homes*). [...] This justifies the general exemption of these two groups from investigation measures.

(2) The legislative decision to extend the absolute protection of § 160a(1) of the Code of Criminal Procedure to lawyers in general [...] can still be justified with regard to Art. 3(1) of the Basic Law.

[...]

Sufficient justification follows from the fact that a different treatment of defence lawyers and other lawyers would in reality hardly be feasible due to the close proximity of the respective areas of practice. [...] From a general point of view, criminal defence is typically an inherent possibility in lawyer-client relationships [...]. Given the connection between criminal defence and the protection of human dignity, the decision to extend the absolute protection afforded under § 160a(1) of the Code of Criminal Procedure to the professional groups that were newly added to this provision is tenable.

(3) The inclusion of members of Parliament in § 160a(1) of the Code of Criminal Procedure is based on a justification that is expressly set out in the Constitution. It is true that the constitutional protection afforded members of the *Bundestag* does not serve to protect the personality right of suspects; rather it aims to protect Parliament as an institution and ensure its proper functioning (BVerfGE 109, 279 <323> – *Surveillance of Private Homes*). For these reasons, the Basic Law affords members of the *Bundestag* the right to refuse to give evidence and prohibits the seizure of documents belonging to them (Art. 47 of the Basic Law). These prohibitions, which are expressly laid down in the Constitution itself, apply even with regard to overt investigation measures, conferring a special status upon members of Parliament compared to other persons entitled to refuse to give evidence; this also justifies that [the challenged provisions] provide special, more extensive protection to this group. [...]

cc) The other groups of persons bound by professional confidentiality listed in § 160a(2) of the Code of Criminal Procedure differ from the aforementioned privileged groups; to that extent, it is justified to make their protection from investigation measures subject to a balancing of interests.

(1) For the professional group of doctors, the Federal Constitutional Court already established that certain aspects, such as doctor-patient consultations, may relate to the core of private life in the individual case (cf. BVerfGE 32, 373 <379>; 109, 279 <323> – *Surveillance of Private Homes*). Where this is the case, access by the state to this information is prohibited, even within the scope of § 160a(2) of the Code Criminal Procedure; this is confirmed by the legislator's intent [...].

Yet while criminal defence, in light of its purpose, invariably relates to the core of private life, in medical settings the core is only affected under particular conditions and in the individual case. Medical records on the patient's medical history, diagnosis or treatment are not necessarily part of the inviolable intimate sphere, but in principle belong only to the patient's private sphere, which may be subject to interferences based on overriding interests of the common good (BVerfGE 32, 373 <379 and 380>). Thus, it does not raise concerns if accessing such information is permitted in cases where the law enforcement interests of the state outweigh other affected interests.

267 (2) The legislator was not required to include representatives of the press or the media in the absolute protection under § 160a(1) of the Code of Criminal Procedure.

268 […] The legislator is neither required nor at complete liberty to accord absolute precedence to freedom of the press and broadcasting over other important legal interests, such as the requirement of establishing the truth in criminal proceedings at issue here (cf. BVerfGE 77, 65 <75 and 76>; 107, 299 <332 and 333>).

269 b) Nor does Art. 12(1) of the Basic Law give rise to an obligation on the part of the legislator to extend the applicability of § 160a(1) of the Code of Criminal Procedure to other groups of persons bound by professional confidentiality listed in § 53(1) first sentence nos. 3 to 3b and no. 5 of the Code of Criminal Procedure.

270 The protection afforded by Art. 12(1) of the Basic Law only applies to legal provisions or acts of public authority that either directly concern occupations or, where this is not the case, objectively have inherent regulatory effects on occupations (cf. BVerfGE 95, 267 <302>; 97, 228 <253 and 254>; 113, 29 <48> – *Seizure of Electronic Data*). This is not the case here, neither for the provisions authorising the investigation measures under the Code of Criminal Procedure, nor for the provisions limiting the general obligation of individuals to cooperate in criminal proceedings against another person (cf. BVerfGE 33, 367 <387>; 38, 312 <324>; 113, 29 <48> – *Seizure of Electronic Data*). Such provisions apply to anyone regardless of their occupation.

271 […]

272 c) There are no constitutional concerns with respect to § 160a(4) of the Code of Criminal Procedure. According to this provision, the prohibitions to collect, use and analyse the data specified in § 160a(1) and (2) do not apply if specific facts give rise to the suspicion that the persons entitled to refuse to give evidence themselves participated in the criminal act under investigation, in assisting the perpetrator in securing the benefits of the crime, in the obstruction of justice, or in the handling of stolen goods. This provision takes into account that the protection afforded relationships of trust between persons bound by professional confidentiality and other persons seeking them out for advice and help does not serve to protect the former from law enforcement measures by the state if they themselves are suspected of having committed a criminal offence (cf. BTDrucks 16/5846, p. 37; […]).

No. 42 – The Telecommunications Surveillance Revision Act

[…] 273

Justices: Voßkuhle, Di Fabio, Mellinghoff, Lübbe-Wolff, Gerhardt, Landau, Huber, Hermanns

No. 43

BVerfGE 133, 277 – Counter-Terrorism Database Act I

HEADNOTES

to the Judgment of the First Senate of 24 April 2013
1 BvR 1215/07

1. The general structure of the counter-terrorism database, a joint database for various security authorities set up for the purpose of combating international terrorism whose function is essentially limited to facilitating inter-agency information requests and whose data may only be used for operational [police] measures in acute and exceptional cases of urgency, is compatible with the Constitution.
2. In light of the fundamental right to informational self-determination, statutory provisions that allow for data sharing between police authorities and intelligence services are subject to more stringent constitutional requirements. Fundamental rights give rise to the principle of separation of police and intelligence data that only permits such data sharing in exceptional cases.
3. Where a joint database for security authorities such as the counter-terrorism database is established, it requires a statutory framework that sufficiently specifies the data to be entered into it and its permissible uses in line with the prohibition of excessive measures. The Counter-Terrorism Database Act does not fully meet these requirements, notably with regard to the determination of the participating authorities, the large number of persons whose data is entered on grounds of potential ties with terrorism, the inclusion of data on 'contact persons', the [direct] use of extended data that is normally concealed from other authorities and the powers conferred upon security authorities to further specify which data is to be stored. The Act also falls short with regard to ensuring effective oversight.
4. The unrestricted inclusion in the counter-terrorism database of data obtained through interferences with the privacy of correspondence and telecommunications and the right to the inviolability of the home violates Article 10(1) and Article 13(1) of the Basic Law.

No. 43 – Counter-Terrorism Database Act I

FEDERAL CONSTITUTIONAL COURT
- 1 BvR 1215/07 -

IN THE NAME OF THE PEOPLE

In the proceedings
on the constitutional complaint of

Mr S...,

– authorised representative: ...

against the Act on Establishing a Standardised Central Counter-Terrorism Database for Police Authorities and Intelligence Services of the Federation and the *Länder* of 22 December 2006 (BGBl I, p. 3409)

the Federal Constitutional Court – First Senate –

with the participation of Justices

    Vice-President Kirchhof,
    Gaier,
    Eichberger,
    Schluckebier,
    Masing,
    Paulus,
    Baer,
    Britz

held on the basis of the oral hearing of 6 November 2012:

JUDGMENT

1. a) § 1(2) and § 2 first sentence no. 3 of the Counter-Terrorism Database Act of 22 December 2006 (BGBl I, p. 3409) are incompatible with Article 2(1) in conjunction with Article 1(1) of the Basic Law.
   b) § 2 first sentence no. 1 lit. b of the Counter-Terrorism Database Act, regarding the element of 'supporting a group that supports a terrorist organisation', and § 2 first sentence no. 2 of the Counter-Terrorism Database Act, regarding the element of 'endorsing' [unlawful violence], are incompatible with Article 2(1) in conjunction with Article 1(1) of the Basic Law.
   c) § 5(1) second sentence no. 1 lit. a of the Counter-Terrorism Database Act is incompatible with Article 2(1) in conjunction with Article 1(1) of the Basic

Law insofar as it provides access to information pursuant to § 3(1) no. 1 lit. a of the Act when a search yields a match in the extended data.

d) § 3(1) first sentence no. 1 lit. b and § 10(1) of the Counter-Terrorism Database Act are incompatible with Article 2(1) in conjunction with Article 1(1) of the Basic Law to the extent that they lack certain supplementary provisions as set forth in the reasons.

e) For the rest, § 2 first sentence no. 2 and § 10(1) of the Counter-Terrorism Database Act must be interpreted in conformity with the Constitution as set forth in the reasons.

2. § 2 first sentence nos. 1 to 3, § 3(1) no. 1, § 5(1) and (2) as well as § 6(1) and (2) of the Counter-Terrorism Database Act are incompatible with Article 10(1) and Article 13(1) of the Basic Law to the extent that they apply to data that is stored in a concealed manner pursuant to § 4 of the Counter-Terrorism Database Act and was obtained through interferences with the privacy of telecommunications and the fundamental right to the inviolability of the home.

3. The provisions held to be incompatible with the Basic Law continue to apply until new provisions have been enacted, but no longer than 31 December 2014, subject to the following conditions: except in acute cases of urgency pursuant to § 5(2) of the Counter-Terrorism Database Act, the use of the counter-terrorism database is only permissible if it is guaranteed that there is no access to data of contact persons (§ 2 first sentence no. 3 of the Act) or to data obtained through interferences with the privacy of telecommunications and the fundamental right to the inviolability of the home, and that data access is limited to information pursuant to § 3(1) no. 3 of the Act in the event that searches of the extended data yield a match; where access to data of contact persons and data obtained through interferences with the privacy of telecommunications and the fundamental right to the inviolability of the home is ruled out, as set forth above, this data may no longer be used, not even under the urgency exceptions set out in § 5(2) of the Act.

4. [...]

5. [...]

REASONS:

A.

1 The constitutional complaint concerns the constitutionality of the Counter-Terrorism Database Act.

No. 43 – Counter-Terrorism Database Act I

I.

The complainant challenges the Counter-Terrorism Database Act enacted by Art. 1 of the Act on Establishing Joint Databases for Police Authorities and Intelligence Services of the Federation and the *Länder* (Joint Databases Act) of 22 December 2006 (BGBl I, p. 3409). [...]

1. The Counter-Terrorism Database Act provides the statutory basis for the counter-terrorism database, a joint database for police authorities and intelligence services of the Federation and the *Länder* that serves to combat international terrorism. This database facilitates and expedites information sharing between the respective police authorities and intelligence services by allowing all participating authorities to more quickly find and more easily access certain information held by the individual authorities in the context of the fight against international terrorism.

a) § 1 of the Counter-Terrorism Database Act provides that the counter-terrorism database is maintained as a joint and standardised central database by the Federal Criminal Police Office (*Bundeskriminalamt*). It also determines the participating authorities, which pursuant to § 1(1) of the Counter-Terrorism Database Act include: the Federal Criminal Police Office and, in conjunction with § 58(1) of the Federal Police Act and § 1(3) no. 1 of the Ordinance on the Competences of the Federal Police Authorities, the General Federal Police Headquarters (*Bundespolizeipräsidium*), as well as the criminal police offices of the *Länder* (*Landeskriminalämter*), the offices for the protection of the Constitution of the Federation and the *Länder* (*Verfassungsschutzbehörden*), the Military Counter-Intelligence Service (*Militärischer Abschirmdienst*), the Federal Intelligence Service (*Bundesnachrichtendienst*) and the Central Office of the German Customs Investigation Service (*Zollkriminalamt*). [...]

b) § 2 of the Counter-Terrorism Database Act provides that authorities must store data already obtained [through other measures] in respect of certain persons or objects in the counter-terrorism database. Data must be stored in this manner if information obtained by the police or intelligence services indicates that the data relates to persons or objects that fall within the categories specified in § 2 first sentence nos. 1 to 4 of the Counter-Terrorism Database Act, and that knowledge of the data is necessary for investigating or combating international terrorism in connection to Germany. Pursuant to § 2 first sentence no. 1 of the Counter-Terrorism Database Act, the data to be stored in the database primarily concerns persons that either belong to or are closely associated with international terrorist organisations or groups. Pursuant to § 2 first sentence no. 2 of the Counter-Terrorism Database Act, data is furthermore to be stored on individuals who unlawfully use, support, prepare, endorse or intentionally incite violence as a means to advance their political or religious interests internationally. § 2 first sentence no. 3 of the Counter-Terrorism Database Act also provides that data be stored on persons who were in contact with the persons laid down in no. 1 and no. 2 [referred to as 'contact persons'], provided that the contact was not merely brief and incidental and that the relevant data can be expected to yield information contributing to the investigation of or fight against international terrorism.

6 c) § 3(1) of the Counter-Terrorism Database Act determines which data is to be stored on the persons and objects specified in § 2 first sentence nos. 1 to 4 of the Counter-Terrorism Database Act. The provision distinguishes between basic data (*Grunddaten*) [...] as provided for in § 3(1) no. 1 lit. a of the Counter-Terrorism Database Act and extended data (*erweiterte Grunddaten*) as provided for in § 3(1) no. 1 lit. b of the Counter-Terrorism Database Act.

7 Basic data must be stored on all persons falling under one of the groups listed in § 2 first sentence nos. 1 to 3 of the Counter-Terrorism Database Act. The provision defines various categories of general personal information as basic data, such as address data, special physical characteristics, languages and dialects spoken by that person, photographs and the respective grounds for storing the data pursuant to § 2 of the Counter-Terrorism Database Act. As regards extended data, § 3(1) no. 1 lit. b of the Counter-Terrorism Database Act provides that such data only be stored in respect of the persons specified in § 2(1) nos. 1 and 2 of the Counter-Terrorism Database Act and in respect of contact persons if there are factual indications that they have knowledge of terrorism-related activities. § 3(1) no. 1 lit. b aa to rr of the Counter-Terrorism Database Act lists the categories of extended data. This data includes, *inter alia*, subscriber lines and telecommunication devices (aa), bank details (bb), ethnic origin (gg), religious affiliation (hh), skills relevant to terrorist activities (ii), information regarding education and training (jj), information regarding work in important infrastructure facilities (kk), information regarding propensity for violence (ll), and locations and areas visited that serve as meeting points for persons suspected of terrorism (nn).

8-9 [...]

10 To the extent that it is mandated by particular confidentiality interests or protected interests of affected persons, § 4 of the Counter-Terrorism Database Act allows for restricted or concealed storage of data. [...]

11 d) § 5(1) of the Counter-Terrorism Database Act governs access to the stored data in standard cases. § 5(1) first sentence of the Counter-Terrorism Database Act allows participating authorities to submit requests in an automated procedure if the information is necessary for carrying out their tasks related to combating or investigating international terrorism. This power to access the database, which is not limited to searches for a particular name, enables these authorities to search all data

sets, which includes both directly accessible data and data stored in a concealed manner as well as both basic data and extended data; it also allows for searches of free text entries [containing additional non-standardised information such as comments or observations]. If a person-related search request yields a match, the requesting authority receives access to the basic data and the information which authority entered the data. Yet pursuant to § 5(1) third and fourth sentence of the Counter-Terrorism Database Act, the authority searching the database only receives access to the extended data in the event of a match if the authority that entered the data specifically grants access in the individual case upon special request in accordance with the applicable data transfer provisions. Regardless of the foregoing, where searches yield a match in the extended data, the corresponding basic data is transferred without any further conditions, independent of a possible accessing of the extended data itself.

Pursuant to § 6(1) first sentence of the Counter-Terrorism Database Act, the authority that submitted the request may only use the data it accessed [in the automated procedure] under § 5(1) of the Counter-Terrorism Database Act to verify whether the match can actually be attributed to the person sought, and to prepare and substantiate a request for an individual data transfer.

e) In urgent cases, § 5(2) first sentence of the Counter-Terrorism Database Act allows the authority that submitted the request to directly access the extended data that belongs to a match. […]

Where the requesting authority directly accessed extended data in an urgent case, this data may, pursuant to § 6(2) of the Counter-Terrorism Database Act, only be used to the extent that it is imperative to avert a present danger (*gegenwärtige Gefahr*) related to the fight against international terrorism. […]

§ 7 of the Counter-Terrorism Database Act provides that the transfer of information following a request pursuant to § 6(1) first sentence of the Counter-Terrorism Database Act is governed by the applicable transfer provisions.

f) § 8 of the Counter-Terrorism Database Act provides that both the authority that entered the data and the requesting authority have a shared responsibility for data protection. The requesting authority is responsible for ensuring that its request is permissible, while the authority that entered the data remains responsible for collecting the data in the first place, for ensuring that entering the data into the database was permissible and for ensuring that the data is correct and up-to-date. § 9 of the Counter-Terrorism Database Act provides for the documentation of any data access for the purposes of oversight in terms of data protection. Pursuant to § 10(1) of the Counter-Terrorism Database Act, responsibility for such oversight lies with the Data Protection Officer of the Federation and – subject to the respective *Land* laws – the data protection officers of the *Länder*.

17 § 10(2) of the Counter-Terrorism Database Act sets out to what extent affected persons must be notified. The provision distinguishes between directly accessible and concealed data. [...]

18 § 11 of the Counter-Terrorism Database Act sets out the requirements for the correction, deletion and blocking of data, and § 12 of the Counter-Terrorism Database Act governs what details the Federal Criminal Police Office has to specify in its order to set up the database. [...]

19 g) [...]
20-33 2. [...]
34-37 3. [...]
38-39 4. [...]
40 5. Various data protection officers performed audits at participating authorities with respect to the counter-terrorism database. The Federal Officer for Data Protection and Freedom of Information audited data processing at the Federal Criminal Police Office, at the Federal Office for the Protection of the Constitution (*Bundesamt für Verfassungsschutz*), and at the Federal Intelligence Service (*Bundesnachrichtendienst*). [...] Further audits were performed by the *Land* data protection officers.

II.

41-51 [...]

III.

52 Statements on the constitutional complaint were submitted by the Federal Government, the Federal Officer for Data Protection and Freedom of Information, the Schleswig-Holstein Independent *Land* Centre for Data Protection (*Unabhängiges Landeszentrum für Datenschutz Schleswig-Holstein*), the Berlin Officer for Data Protection and Freedom of Information, and the Baden-Württemberg Officer for Data Protection.

53-77 [...]

IV.

78 [...]

B.

79 The constitutional complaint is admissible.

No. 43 – Counter-Terrorism Database Act I

I.

The complainant claims a violation of his fundamental right to informational self-determination under Art. 2(1) in conjunction with Art. 1(1) of the Basic Law, of the privacy of correspondence and telecommunications under Art. 10(1) of the Basic Law, of the inviolability of the home under Art. 13(1) of the Basic Law and, in conjunction with these fundamental rights, a violation of the guarantee of legal protection under Art. 19(4) of the Basic Law.
[…]

II.

The complainant is directly, individually and presently affected by the challenged provisions.
1. [For the constitutional complaint to be admissible,] the complainant must be directly affected. This is the case here. A complainant is only directly affected by a statutory provision if the provision as such interferes with the complainant's rights without requiring any further implementation measures. If execution of a statutory provision requires – either by law or based on the practice of authorities – a specific implementation measure that is contingent upon a deliberate decision by the executing authority, complainants must generally challenge this implementation measure and exhaust all available legal remedies before lodging a constitutional complaint (BVerfGE 1, 97 <101 *et seq.*>; 109, 279 <306> – *Surveillance of Private Homes*; established case-law). However, it must be presumed that complainants are directly affected if seeking legal recourse is not possible because they have no way of knowing whether the respective implementation measure was carried out. In such cases, complainants can lodge a constitutional complaint directly against a statute, just as in cases where fundamental rights are affected by a statute without any intermediary implementation measure (cf. BVerfGE 30, 1 <16 and 17>; 113, 348 <362 and 363>; 120, 378 <394>; established case-law). The case at hand fits these conditions. Under the challenged provisions, it is in principle not possible for the complainant to obtain reliable knowledge of the storage or use of his data.
Even though the complainant can request information on the storage of his data pursuant to § 10(2) of the Counter-Terrorism Database Act, and bring an *ex post* challenge before the courts, this does not lead to a different result. On that basis, the complainant could only challenge storage of his data that actually occurred at a certain time; however, he would not be able to challenge the fact that such data storage can occur at any time beyond his control and without him knowing about

it – which is what he actually seeks to challenge with his constitutional complaint. […]

85-87 2. […]

C.

88 There is no need for requesting a preliminary ruling from the Court of Justice of the European Union pursuant to Art. 267 TFEU to clarify the scope of fundamental rights protection under EU law in respect of data sharing among various security authorities through a joint database as provided for by the Counter-Terrorism Database Act. This also holds true with regard to the fundamental right to the protection of personal data under Art. 8 of the Charter of Fundamental Rights of the European Union. The EU fundamental rights laid down in the Charter are not applicable in the case at hand. The challenged provisions must be measured against the fundamental rights laid down in the Basic Law given that the provisions are not determined by EU law (cf. BVerfGE 118, 79 <95>; 121, 1 <15>; 125, 260 <306 and 307> – *Data Retention*; 129, 78 <90 and 91>). Thus, the present proceedings do not concern the implementation of EU law by the Member States, in which case they would be bound by the Charter of Fundamental Rights (Art. 51(1) first sentence of the Charter).

89-91 […]

D.

92 The constitutional complaint is in part well-founded.

I.

93 The challenged provisions interfere with the right to informational self-determination (Art. 2(1) in conjunction with Art. 1(1) of the Basic Law), the right to the privacy of correspondence and telecommunications (Art. 10(1) of the Basic Law) and the right to the inviolability of the home (Art. 13(1) of the Basic Law).

94 1. §§ 1 to 6 of the Counter-Terrorism Database Act govern the storage and use of personal data, and therefore affect the scope of protection of the right to informational self-determination. To the extent that the data stored and used was collected through interferences with Art. 10(1) or Art. 13(1) of the Basic Law, any subsequent use must also be measured against these fundamental rights (cf. BVerfGE 125, 260 <313> – *Data Retention*; established case-law).

No. 43 – Counter-Terrorism Database Act I

2. The challenged provisions interfere with these fundamental rights. First of all, the linking of data from different sources resulting from the obligation to store data imposed in §§ 1 to 4 of the Counter-Terrorism Database Act amounts to an interference. The fact that the data had already been collected by the authorities in other contexts does not lead to a different result; the data is combined and processed based on distinct criteria in order to make it available to authorities other than those that collected the data for their purposes. Further interferences result from §§ 5 and 6 of the Counter-Terrorism Database Act, which govern the use of this data for the purpose of searches in the database; from the possibility to access the basic data in the event of a match pursuant to § 5(1) first and second sentence and § 6(1) first sentence of the Counter-Terrorism Database Act; as well as from the possibility to [directly] access the extended data in urgent cases pursuant to § 5(2) and § 6(2) of the Counter-Terrorism Database Act. 95

II.

Formally, the challenged provisions are compatible with the Constitution. In particular, the Federation has legislative competence. 96
[…] 97-104

III.

The general structure of the counter-terrorism database established by the challenged provisions is compatible with the right to informational self-determination under Art. 2(1) in conjunction with Art. 1(1) of the Basic Law. The principle of proportionality does not *per se* rule out such a database, which, in the context of investigating and combating international terrorism, aims to facilitate requests for information, and, in urgent cases, directly serves to avert dangers to public security. However, the specific statutory design, too, must satisfy the requirements of proportionality. 105

1. The counter-terrorism database has a legitimate aim. It primarily serves to inform security authorities, in a quick and easy manner, whether other security authorities have relevant information about specific persons associated with international terrorism. It thus aims to provide preliminary information, which allows the authorities to request further information from other authorities more quickly and efficiently, and which, in urgent cases, also allows for a preliminary assessment of dangers as the basis for further action. The legislative aim is neither to facilitate the general sharing of personal data among all security authorities nor to eliminate all informational barriers between these authorities; this would undermine the prin- 106

ciple of purpose limitation, and therefore be impermissible from the outset. Rather, the legislative intent behind creating the database is to allow for somewhat easier information sharing within a limited context. This facilitated information sharing does not affect the applicability of the provisions on individual data transfers set out in other areas of ordinary legislation, which remain subject to statutory limitations, and it is limited to the fight against international terrorism. While the term 'terrorism' as such can have different meanings, the Counter-Terrorism Database Act refers to § 129a of the Criminal Code, as follows from § 2 first sentence no. 1 lit. a of the Counter-Terrorism Database Act, which is the central provision determining the persons whose data is included in the database. Accordingly, in the Counter-Terrorism Database Act, the term 'terrorism' refers to specifically defined serious offences that criminalise acts seeking to intimidate the public or targeting the fundamental structures of a state or an international organisation. This understanding of the term does not raise any constitutional objections.

107 2. The challenged provisions are also suitable and necessary for achieving this purpose. The data storage obligations imposed in §§ 1 to 4 of the Counter-Terrorism Database Act create a basic data inventory that is made available to the participating authorities pursuant to § 5(1) and § 6(1) first sentence of the Counter-Terrorism Database Act. It serves to allow those authorities to prepare further requests for information, and to provide them with information needed to avert specific dangers (*konkrete Gefahren*) in particularly urgent cases pursuant to § 5(2) and § 6(2) of the Counter-Terrorism Database Act. Other instruments that would be less intrusive but equally effective in achieving these aims are not ascertainable.

108 3. The general structure of the Counter-Terrorism Database Act is also compatible with the principle of proportionality in its strict sense.

109 The principle of proportionality in its strict sense requires that in an overall assessment, the severity of legislative fundamental rights restrictions not be disproportionate to the weight of the reasons invoked to justify such restrictions. In this respect, an appropriate balance must be struck between the weight of the interference resulting from the statutory provisions and the legislative aim pursued, and between the conflicting interests of the individual and the general public (cf. BVerfGE 100, 313 <375 and 376> – *The Article 10 Act*; 113, 348 <382>; 120, 378 <428>; established case-law).

110 The challenged provisions give rise to interferences of considerable weight (see a below). Yet they also serve weighty public interests (see b below). Based on a balancing of these conflicting interests, the establishment and general nature of the counter-terrorism database are not *per se* objectionable under constitutional law; however, the design of the framework specifying the details of the database must

contain clear and sufficiently restrictive provisions, including for ensuring effective oversight of its application in practice (see c below).

a) The possibilities of information sharing created by the challenged provisions are of considerable weight. [...] It increases the severity of the interference that the database allows for information sharing among a large number of security authorities with very different mandates, including information sharing between intelligence services and police authorities (see aa below). Yet it mitigates the severity of the interference that information sharing is limited to already collected data, that the database is designed as a joint database focusing on facilitating requests for information, and that its sole aim is to investigate and combat international terrorism (see bb below).

aa) It increases the severity of the interference resulting from the counter-terrorism database that it allows for information sharing among a large number of security authorities, including authorities with very different tasks and powers. It is particularly significant here that the database also extends to information sharing between intelligence services and police authorities.

(1) Where personal data is concerned, the powers to collect and process data conferred on the different security authorities are tailored to, and limited by, the respective authority's specific tasks. Under constitutional law, the use of personal data is thus subject to purpose limitations, it cannot readily be shared with other authorities. Security authorities have different remits, depending on their respective domain and role in the federal order; regarding data protection, this division of tasks also has a special fundamental rights dimension. It is not therefore a flaw in the organisational structure of the state that information cannot be shared comprehensively and freely among the various security authorities; rather, this structure is in principle intended and required by the Constitution, as it derives from the principle of purpose limitation in respect of data protection.

However, the constitutional principle of purpose limitation in respect of data does not prevent the legislator from changing the original purpose [for which data was collected] if such a change in purpose is justified by public interests that outweigh the protected fundamental rights interests (cf. BVerfGE 100, 313 <360> – *The Article 10 Act*; 109, 279 <375 and 376> – *Surveillance of Private Homes*; 110, 33 <69>). When assessing whether information sharing between different authorities is proportionate, it is particularly significant whether the different informational contexts are comparable. The more the authorities' tasks, powers and modes of operation differ, the greater the weight accorded to data sharing [in the proportionality assessment]. Therefore, for changes in purpose to be proportionate, it is particularly relevant to what extent the requirements regarding data collection by the transferring authority, or in the present case, the authority entering data into the database, correspond to the requirements under which the requesting authority may collect data. Accordingly, a change in purpose is not permissible if it circumvents fundamental rights-related restrictions regarding the use of certain investigation methods; this is the case where, even on the basis of statutory powers, the information could not have been lawfully obtained for the changed purpose, neither with the investigatory means applied nor by other means (cf. BVerfGE 109, 279 <377> – *Surveillance of Private Homes*; 120, 351 <369>). Accordingly, the Federal Constitutional Court repeatedly held that the further use [for other purposes] of data obtained through interferences with the privacy of telecommunications is only constitutional if the changed purposes could also have justified the original data collection (cf. BVerfGE 100, 313 <360, 389> – *The Article 10 Act*; 109, 279 <375> – *Surveillance of Private Homes*; 110, 33 <73>). The Court found it necessary that procedural safeguards, such as labelling and documentation requirements, be put in place in order to guarantee that these requirements are met (cf. BVerfGE 65, 1 <46> – *Census*; 113, 29 <58> – *Seizure of Electronic Data*; 124, 43 <70>). The same also applies to changes in purpose of data processing measures if data was obtained through interferences with the right to informational self-determination. Constitutional requirements for collecting, storing and processing data must not be circumvented by allowing authorities which, within their remit, are subject to less stringent requirements to transfer data to authorities that are subject to more stringent requirements.

115 (2) Thus, the combination of data held by intelligence services with data held by police authorities is of increased weight and is generally subject to strict constitutional limits, because the tasks of police authorities and intelligence services differ considerably. Therefore, they are subject to fundamentally different requirements with respect to the openness with which they perform their tasks and with respect to data collection.

116 (aa) Intelligence services are tasked with precautionary investigations of threat situations before actual dangers even arise. [...]

117 Given that the mandate of intelligence services largely concerns precautionary measures carried out before actual dangers arise, they have far-reaching powers in respect of data collection; these powers are neither limited to specifically defined areas of activity, nor subject to detailed rules regarding the means that may be employed. [...] Without prejudice to various constitutional requirements that apply in this respect but are not at issue in the present proceedings, these powers reflect the broad mandate conferred upon the intelligence services, and are characterised by relatively low thresholds for carrying out measures constituting interferences. Furthermore, intelligence services generally collect data covertly. They are not subject to the principle of the overtness of data collection and are largely exempt from

transparency and notification requirements vis-à-vis affected persons. Accordingly, indiviudals have few possibilities of legal protection. In part, legal recourse is even entirely replaced by political oversight (cf. Art. 10(2) second sentence of the Basic Law).

At the same time, the permissible investigative aims of measures carried out by intelligence services are restricted in order to compensate for the broad data collection powers. Even though the exact powers of different intelligence services differ, their investigatory mandate is essentially limited to observing and reporting on fundamental threats that might destabilise the community as a whole, in order to allow for an assessment of the security situation at the political level. The overall aim pursued is not to carry out operational measures to avert dangers to public security, but to gather political intelligence. [...]

This mandate of the intelligence services, which is limited to precautionary measures for gathering political intelligence, is also reflected in a restriction of the services' powers in other respects: they do not have police powers, nor may they request that the police carry out measures for which the intelligence services themselves have no authorisation through inter-agency administrative assistance (*Amtshilfe*). [...]

(bb) These tasks and powers differ fundamentally from those of police and security authorities. It is for these authorities to prevent, avert and prosecute criminal acts, and to avert other dangers to public security and order. Their mandate is informed by operative action and in particular includes the power to execute measures against individuals, if necessary by force. At the same time, their tasks are defined in statutory law in a more detailed and restrictive manner and the powers conferred upon them to perform these tasks are subject to a diverse range of substantive and procedural requirements. It is true that some of the tasks assigned to police authorities do fall within the category of purely precautionary action taken before a danger arises. However, their powers to take action against individuals may in principle only be exercised based on specific grounds; they generally require indications of a suspicion of criminal conduct or the existence of a danger. The powers to collect and process data conferred upon the police authorities reflect this mandate. Given that such powers can ultimately be used to prepare and justify coercive measures [against individuals], including interferences with personal liberty, they are more narrowly and precisely defined by law than the powers of intelligence services, and the law distinguishes between different powers in various ways. Where these powers relate to data handling, they also generally require specific grounds, albeit to differing degrees, such as the existence of a danger or the suspicion of a crime. To the extent that the legislator permits, in exceptional cases, data retention not based on specific grounds as a precaution or merely for the purpose of preventing dangers or criminal acts, this requires special justification, and is subject to more stringent constitutional requirements (cf. BVerfGE 125, 260 <318 *et seq.*, 325 *et seq.*> – *Data Retention*).

121 Accordingly, the police generally act overtly, and their handling of data is largely subject to the principle of overtness and transparency. […]

122 Thus, the legal order distinguishes between the police, which generally work overtly, are tasked with operational measures and are subject to detailed statutory regimes, and the intelligence services, which generally work covertly, with powers limited to observation and investigation as precautionary action before a danger actually arises, to provide political intelligence and advice and therefore allowed to act within a less detailed statutory framework. The legal order does not allow for a secret police.

123 (cc) In light of these differences, provisions that allow for data sharing between the police and intelligence services are subject to more stringent constitutional requirements. In this regard, the fundamental right to informational self-determination gives rise to the principle of separation of police and intelligence data (*informationelles Trennungsprinzip*), according to which data may in principle not be shared between the intelligence services and police authorities. Deviations from this principle are only permissible in exceptional cases. If such exceptions are made in relation to operational measures [of the police], they give rise to particularly serious interferences. Data sharing between intelligence services and police authorities that might lead to operational police action being taken must therefore, in principle, serve an exceptionally significant public interest which can justify the accessing of information under the easier conditions normally reserved for the intelligence services. This must be ensured by sufficiently specific and qualified thresholds for carrying out data sharing constituting such an interference, which must be set out in clear statutory provisions; moreover, the data sharing carried out on this basis must not circumvent the thresholds for interferences applicable to obtaining the relevant data in the first place.

124 bb) However, it reduces the severity of the interference resulting from the counter-terrorism database that it is designed as a joint database, which is essentially limited to facilitating requests for information, and which only permits use of the data for operational police action in exceptional emergencies.

125 (1) The challenged provisions set out the counter-terrorism database as an instrument that – except in urgent cases pursuant to § 5(2) and § 6(2) of the Counter-Terrorism Database Act – does not provide information which the respective authorities can use directly in the exercise of their tasks, especially not for operational police purposes; rather, it provides information only as a basis for [requesting] further data transfers. […] Therefore, with regard to the basic data pursuant to § 3(1) no. 1

lit. a of the Counter-Terrorism Database Act, the counter-terrorism database does not authorise the sharing of information for direct use [by the requesting authority] in the exercise of its tasks, but only prepares the basis for such information sharing. This applies all the more to the extended data pursuant to § 3(1) no. 1 lit. b of the Counter-Terrorism Database Act, which the authorities may generally only access subject to the transfer provisions under the respective statutory regimes applicable in the specific case (§ 5(1) fourth sentence of the Counter-Terrorism Database Act). Thus, the Counter-Terrorism Database Act mainly refers to the specific statutory bases for data transfers set out in applicable legislation, upholding the rule-of-law limits deriving therefrom. Ultimately, it ensures that – apart from cases set out in § 5(2) and § 6(2) of the Counter-Terrorism Database Act – data sharing for direct use in investigating and combating international terrorism is permissible only subject to the statutory requirements of the transfer provisions applicable in the specific case. […]

126

(2) The purpose of the counter-terrorism database, which is essentially limited to facilitating requests for information, lessens the weight of interference significantly; yet even in light of this purpose, the weight of interference remains considerable. […]

127

For affected persons, being registered in such a database can be a considerable burden. Once a person has been included in the database, they must expect to be classified as persons associated with terrorism based on [matches] from search requests and – based on further requests for data transfers facilitated by the database – to be subjected to intrusive measures as a result thereof. The consequences of such a classification can be considerable and might put individuals in a difficult situation; at the same time, the persons concerned are not even aware of this classification, nor do they have any feasible options to defend themselves against it. It increases the severity of the interference that the data is entered into the database without background information on its specific context, and may in part be based on mere prognoses and subjective assessments by the respective authority, which are by definition uncertain at best. Ultimately, individuals may face considerable impairments despite not having prompted the measures themselves. Intrusive measures cannot, in principle, directly result from the use of the data from the counter-terrorism database based on the challenged provisions alone, but can only be expected as an indirect effect of these provisions in conjunction with other legislation; however, this does not change the fact that the counter-terrorism database increases the likelihood of such measures.

128

(3) The counter-terrorism database gives rise to interferences of particular weight where it also allows for information sharing between intelligence services and police authorities in urgent cases; in this context, the information may be used

129

directly by the receiving authority to avert a specific danger to public security, i.e. for operational purposes.

130 b) In principle, the establishment of the counter-terrorism database is compatible with the prohibition of excessive measures (*Übermaßverbot*). The weight of interference for affected individuals must be balanced against the public interest in targeted information sharing between the different security authorities for the purpose of investigating and combating international terrorism and allowing more accurate assessments to avert dangers to public security in important and urgent cases.

131 The legislator may attach considerable significance to the establishment of a central joint database for targeted information sharing for the purpose of investigating and combating international terrorism. Given the large number of authorities responsible for these tasks, it is particularly important to ensure that information sharing among them is effective. […]

132 […]

133 When assessing the significance of such a database, it must be taken into account that the effective fight against terrorism carries great weight for a democratic and free society. Criminal acts that qualify as terrorism, against which the Counter-Terrorism Database Act is directed (see D III 1 above), aim to destabilise society and, to this end, comprise attacks on the life and limb of random third parties, in a ruthless instrumentalisation of others. They are directed against the pillars of the constitutional order and society as a whole. Our constitutional order requires that such attacks not be considered acts of war or a state of emergency, which would lead to a suspension of certain requirements deriving from the rule of law, but that they be qualified as criminal acts that must be countered with the means available to the state under the rule of law. At the same time, the proportionality assessment required under the principle of the rule of law must accord considerable weight to the fight against terrorism (cf. BVerfGE 115, 320 <357 and 358> – *Profiling*).

134 c) Given these conflicting interests, an overall assessment does not raise constitutional objections against the general structure of the counter-terrorism database as an instrument for facilitating information requests and as a source of information for assessing dangers in acute cases of urgency. However, the statutory framework governing the database only satisfies the principle of proportionality in its strict sense if the provisions are clear and, in their substantive details, sufficiently limited regarding what data must be stored in the database and the way in which this data may be used, and if qualified oversight requirements are provided for and observed (BVerfGE 125, 260 <325> – *Data Retention*).

135 aa) The general structure set out by the legislator, which establishes the counter-terrorism database as a joint database to facilitate requests for information, is not objectionable under constitutional law. It is not disproportionate in and of itself to

include in the database basic identifying data in respect of specific persons that are likely associated with international terrorism, nor to make this data available to the participating authorities for the purpose of facilitating requests for information. The fight against terrorism justifies the combination of intelligence data and police data in the present case given that the shared data is only used to prepare individual data transfers that are subject to statutory limitations. [...]

However, the database must be designed in such a way that information sharing is governed by clear provisions and sufficiently limited. This also applies with regard to determining the participating authorities, the persons whose data is stored in the database and the scope of data to be stored on them, and with regard to further specifying the statutory regime governing use of this data. Moreover, effective oversight must be ensured (see D IV below). 136

bb) Due to the great importance of preventing terrorist attacks, it is also not objectionable that the legislator intends to provide a source of information in the form of the counter-terrorism database that also allows the participating authorities to conduct a preliminary assessment of dangers as a starting point for further action in acute cases of urgency. [...] 137

IV.

Based on these standards, the challenged provisions fail to satisfy, in various respects, the requirements regarding a sufficiently specific statutory design of the counter-terrorism database that adheres to the prohibition of excessive measures. To this extent, they violate the right to informational self-determination. 138

1. § 1(2) of the Counter-Terrorism Database Act, which provides for the possible participation of other police authorities in the counter-terrorism database, is incompatible with the requirement of specificity. 139

a) The requirement of specificity serves to ensure that the law subjects the government and administration to standards that direct and limit their actions, and that the courts can effectively review the lawfulness of their actions. Furthermore, clear and specific legal provisions ensure that affected persons can take precautions against potentially intrusive measures (cf. BVerfGE 110, 33 <52 *et seq.*>; 113, 348 <375 *et seq.*>; 120, 378 <407 and 408>). [...] The specificity requirements that must be met depend on the severity of the interferences with fundamental rights effected by a provision or measures taken pursuant to that provision. 140

According to these standards, the authorities participating in the counter-terrorism database must be determined either directly by law, or by an ordinance based on a law. The determination which authorities must enter their data into the database, and which authorities may access this data, is decisive for the scope and content 141 of the database as well as for the extent of further use of the data. This is an essential element of the legislative framework that requires a clear, specific and legally binding determination. [...]

142 b) § 1(2) of the Counter-Terrorism Database Act does not satisfy, neither by itself nor in conjunction with § 12 of the Counter-Terrorism Database Act as the provision mandating the establishment of the database, the special requirements relating to the determination in statutory law which other police authorities can participate in the counter-terrorism database.

143 aa) § 1(2) of the Counter-Terrorism Database Act does not provide a sufficiently clear statutory determination from which the participating authorities can be directly derived. [...] If the participating authorities could be derived directly from the law with sufficient specificity, it would not necessarily be problematic that the individual authorities are not listed expressly (cf. BVerfGE 130, 151 <199, 203>). Yet this is not the case here. § 1(2) of the Counter-Terrorism Database Act describes the participating authorities only in broad, general terms that are subject to interpretation. [...]

144 bb) Nor can a sufficiently clear determination of the participating authorities be derived from § 1(2) of the Counter-Terrorism Database Act in conjunction with § 12 no. 2 of the Counter-Terrorism Database Act, as the provision mandating the establishment of the database. It is not, in principle, objectionable to delegate the final determination of these authorities to the executive branch. [...] However, if the legislator chooses to place the decision about the participating authorities in the hands of the executive, Art. 80(1) of the Basic Law requires that this be done in the form of an ordinance.

145 2. The provisions determining the group of persons whose data is included in the database are not compatible with the constitutional requirements in every respect. Some of these provisions violate the principle of specificity and the prohibition of excessive measures. Others require a restrictive interpretation in conformity with the Constitution.

146 a) There are no constitutional objections regarding § 2 first sentence no. 1 lit. a of the Counter-Terrorism Database Act. This provision requires the entering of data on persons suspected of belonging to or supporting a terrorist organisation, i.e. those who are the focus of effective counter-terrorism measures. This provision refers to statutory offences that already criminalise certain conduct long before it results in actual violations of legal interests, and it only requires "factual indications" for the conduct in question – even where it only concerns supporting acts. The provision thus grants authorities substantial discretion with regard to their subjective assessments, which entails many uncertainties [as regards the application in practice]. However, this is acceptable in relation to the counter-terrorism database, which

– apart from acute and exceptional cases of urgency – only serves to facilitate requests for information, and, in that context, to enable participating authorities to refute or corroborate unconfirmed assumptions regarding suspicions of criminal conduct and dangers before formal investigations are even launched. When properly interpreted, the statutory prerequisites are still sufficient to ensure that data is not stored on the basis of mere speculation. [...]

b) § 2 first sentence no. 1 lit. b of the Counter-Terrorism Database Act, which extends the scope of the data stored in the database to data of persons supporting terrorist organisations, is in part incompatible with the prohibition of excessive measures and thus unconstitutional. 147

aa) The provision is not objectionable to the extent that it includes persons who belong to a group that supports a terrorist organisation. [...] 148

bb) However, the provision expands the scope of the database further in that it also includes persons who merely support such a supporting organisation. It is not ascertainable that the provision requires any link connecting the persons in question to terrorism. According to its wording, and the legislative purpose that plausibly derives from it, the provision thus also extends the obligation to store certain data in the database to data on persons who, long before a terrorist act is committed, support what they possibly believe to be an unsuspicious organisation, without being aware of any link to terrorism; an example would be persons supporting a nursery run by a mosque association which the authorities suspect of supporting terrorist organisations. Such an expansive approach, broadening the scope of application to include even persons with only remote links to the environment in which a terrorist organisation operates, violates the principle of legal clarity and is incompatible with the prohibition of excessive measures. [...] 149

c) § 2 first sentence no. 2 of the Counter-Terrorism Database Act is not fully compatible with the Constitution. This provision, which targets individuals who might be associated with terrorism, combines a number of ambiguous and potentially broad legal terms. Following a tie in the Justices' vote, the terms 'unlawful violence' and 'intentional incitement to unlawful violence' cannot be declared unconstitutional. In the opinion of the four Justices who voted against a declaration of unconstitutionality in this respect – and whose view ultimately carries the decision pursuant to § 15(4) third sentence of the Federal Constitutional Court Act – the use of these legal concepts is compatible with the Basic Law as long as they are not interpreted in an overly broad manner (see aa below). In the opinion of the other four Justices, whose position ultimately does not prevail (§ 15(4) third sentence of the Federal Constitutional Court Act), the provision would have to be declared unconstitutional in this regard (see bb below). In the unanimous view of the Court, the mere 'endorsement' of unlawful violence within the meaning 150 of this provision does in any case not provide sufficient grounds justifying the registration of personal data in the counter-terrorism database. To that extent, the provision violates the prohibition of excessive measures and is unconstitutional (see cc below).

151 aa) (1) The provision mainly hinges on the term 'unlawful violence'. This term has a very broad meaning in other parts of the legal order. It is true that based on a broad understanding, the concept of unlawful violence would not be a sufficient basis for classifying persons as being associated with terrorism given that it would not adequately limit the group of affected persons in accordance with the principle of proportionality, and therefore not provide sufficient grounds justifying the data storage under constitutional law. [...] However, in light of the counter-terrorism database's aim to fight terrorist crime, this term must be interpreted to the effect that it only refers to violence immediately directed against life and limb, or characterised by the use of means that endanger the public. When interpreted in this way, the term 'unlawful' in § 2 first sentence no. 2 of the Counter-Terrorism Database Act is not objectionable under the principle of proportionality with regard to determining the group of persons whose data is to be entered in the database.

152 (2) Furthermore, § 2 first sentence no. 2 of the Counter-Terrorism Database Act provides for the registration of both persons who use, support and prepare violence, and those who merely endorse or intentionally incite it with their actions. This would open up disproportionately broad possibilities for interference if mere general criminal intent (*Eventualvorsatz*), within the meaning attached to it in criminal law terminology, were deemed sufficient to establish an intentional incitement to violence. However, if, in this context, the element of intentional incitement to violence is attributed a meaning which only covers acts that deliberately aim to incite violence, this interpretation satisfies the principle of proportionality.

[*Translator's note*: The following sections are highlighted in italics in the German original to denote the opposing view of the four Justices who were in favour of declaring the provision unconstitutional:]

153 bb) *In the opinion of the other four members of the Senate, which ultimately does not prevail pursuant to § 15(4) third sentence of the Federal Constitutional Court Act, § 2 first sentence no. 2 of the Counter-Terrorism Database Act must be declared unconstitutional in its entirety because of its lack of specificity and its overly broad scope. In their view, a narrow interpretation of the terms 'unlawful violence' and 'intentional incitement' that deviates from the established definitions of these terms in criminal law cannot lead to a different result. The attempt to interpret the provision in conformity with the Constitution is inconsistent and undermines the requirements of specificity in respect of data protection law.*

No. 43 – Counter-Terrorism Database Act I

(1) Significant elements of this provision are ambiguous, and are interpreted broadly elsewhere in the legal order – specifically, in criminal law, which is fundamental to the general understanding of legal terms –, to an extent that, in the context of the counter-terrorism database, is incompatible with the requirements of proportionality and the prohibition of excessive measures; the four members of the Senate whose position prevails concur with this finding [...] 154

(2) [Yet in the opinion of the other four members of the Court whose position does not prevail,] the provision cannot be interpreted restrictively and thus brought in conformity with the Constitution. 155

(a) Such an interpretation is already ruled out for § 2 first sentence no. 2 of the Counter-Terrorism Database Act because the central term 'unlawful violence' in that provision was deliberately chosen by the legislator in order to keep the wording broad and open. The vagueness and overly broad scope of this term were explicitly criticised in the legislative process (BTPlenarprotokoll 16/71, p. 7100; Bundestag Committee on Internal Affairs, minutes no. 16/24, p. 55; A-Drucks 16(4)131 D, p. 10; A-Drucks 16(4)131 J, p. 10). Notably, a specific counter-proposal was submitted, putting forward a more restrictive definition based on § 129a(2) of the Criminal Code, according to which unlawful violence was only recognised as grounds for storing data "if such violence was intended to seriously intimidate the population, to unlawfully coerce a state authority or an international organisation, or to destroy or significantly impair the fundamental political, constitutional, economic or social structures of a state or an international organisation, and if the person's actions threatened to inflict serious damage on a state or an international organisation" (cf. BTDrucks 16/3642, pp. 14 and 15). This was an attempt to narrow down the term in line with international and European frameworks on combating terrorism (cf. Council Framework Decision of 13 June 2002 on combating terrorism, OJ L 164/3 of 22 June 2002, Art. 1; Draft of a General Convention on International Terrorism, in: Measures to eliminate international terrorism, Report of the Working Group of 3 November 2010, UN Doc. A/C.6/65/L.10.). The legislator, however, made a deliberate decision to disregard this proposal – apparently in order to grant security authorities more latitude. Such a decision cannot be remedied through an interpretation in conformity with the Constitution. 156

(b) In addition, the provision cannot be interpreted in conformity with the Constitution for reasons deriving from fundamental principles of constitutional law. If the statutory basis for measures that constitute interferences has an open wording, as is the case here, and if, based on recognised definitions, its wording plausibly supports such a far-reaching interpretation, it cannot serve as a basis for the data processing measures at issue here as it fails to satisfy the principles of legal clarity 157

and proportionality in that regard. The principle of legal clarity specifically serves to compel the legislator to make sufficiently clear decisions regarding the statutory prerequisites for interferences with fundamental rights, so as to sufficiently ensure that the prohibition of excessive measures is upheld. If the legislator fails to satisfy these constitutional requirements, the Federal Constitutional Court cannot remedy this failure through an interpretation in conformity with the Constitution. [...]

158 [...] According to the Federal Constitutional Court's established case-law, the requirements of legal clarity and specificity in respect of data protection law are particularly stringent (cf. BVerfGE 65, 1 <46> – Census; 118, 168 <187>; 120, 378 <408>) – and this especially holds true for the counter-terrorism database, given that it governs data sharing among security authorities prior to any formal investigation. As a result, data processing under the Counter-Terrorism Database Act differs, at the level of implementation, from other laws that are implemented by means of ordinary administrative acts: where laws are implemented by means of ordinary administrative acts, the implementing measure is directly addressed to the person concerned, includes a statement of reasons, and allows for judicial review in the individual case; by contrast, under the Counter-Terrorism Database Act, affected persons have no direct knowledge of the data processing measures concerning them. Such data processing measures remain informal, no reasons are provided to the affected individual, and there is generally no possibility of judicial review. [...]

159 The qualified specificity requirements that derive from fundamental rights in respect of data protection are not rooted in excessive mistrust vis-à-vis the security authorities. Rather, these requirements are in place to ensure that the prerequisites for data processing carried out by security authorities are set out in unequivocal terms, especially with regard to [early] stages during which the authorities' activities often involve a significant amount of data processing yet are subject to no or only few formal requirements; it is precisely in these stages that such an unequivocal framework provides the authorities with the clearest possible guidance in performing their demanding tasks, and also eases their burden in cases of doubt.

160 (c) It is also not necessary to undertake an interpretation in conformity with the Constitution out of respect for the legislator. It is true that with the Counter-Terrorism Database Act, the legislator designed a complex and nuanced concept; in various respects, the legislator showed restraint as required under the rule of law and genuinely endeavoured to ensure adequate data protection. However, constitutional review of the specific provisions implementing this concept cannot be based on an overall assessment of the political effort undertaken by the legislator. Rather, the Court must give effect to constitutional standards in all respects regardless of such considerations, and thereby ensure that the notion of the rule of law informing

No. 43 – Counter-Terrorism Database Act I

the general framework is not eroded through overly broad individual provisions incorporated therein. In this regard, respect for the legislator actually requires that the Court refrain from designing a more restrictive data protection arrangement for the challenged provisions, and that it simply declare the provisions unconstitutional instead: Rather than interpreting the provisions [in conformity with the Constitution], and thus imposing an arrangement on the legislator that may seem sensible in light of the legislative aim, but that the legislator clearly did not wish to adopt – at least for the time being –, a declaration of unconstitutionality would again defer to the legislator the responsibility to define, in accordance with its competences, the appropriate limits. Technical or legislative reasons that would have made it particularly difficult for the legislator to accomplish this are not ascertainable.

cc) The element 'endorsement of violence' is especially far-reaching. With this element, the legislator only refers to an attitude without requiring that this attitude must have resulted in activities promoting violence. The use of this element [in § 2 first sentence no. 2 of the Counter-Terrorism Database Act] is incompatible with the Constitution, and the provision is unconstitutional in this respect. This element must generally be considered excessive in scope, which can also not be remedied through an interpretation in conformity with the Constitution. The only example given in the explanatory memorandum to the law is that of hate preachers who publicly incite hatred and violence, an example which in principle does not raise constitutional concerns. However, from the wording of the provision, which generally appears to be further-reaching, it cannot be derived that its scope is limited to such cases. Rather, the wording suggests that the only decisive factor is whether a person's attitude amounts to endorsing violence. According to the wording, it is sufficient that the authorities infer such an attitude from factual indications. The use of such a criterion [in the legislative design], which is directly tied to the *forum internum* and therefore intrudes into an individual's inalienable inner domain, is especially capable of having a chilling effect on the exercise of other fundamental freedoms, in particular freedom of faith and freedom of expression. The challenged provision uses subjective beliefs as such as its decisive element and thus relies on criteria that individuals cannot fully control and that cannot be influenced by law-abiding conduct. The registration of persons in the counter-terrorism database on the basis of such a criterion is incompatible with the prohibition of excessive measures. § 2 first sentence no. 2 of the Counter-Terrorism Database Act is unconstitutional in that respect.

161

d) § 2 first sentence no. 3 of the Counter-Terrorism Database Act is also unconstitutional. It provides for the inclusion of data on contact persons, which is incompatible with both the principle of specificity and the prohibition of excessive measures.

162

163 § 2 first sentence no. 3 of the Counter-Terrorism Database Act provides that even mere contact persons of the persons specified in the preceding numbers of the provision must be included in the counter-terrorism database. [...]

164 The recognition of contact persons as an additional group of persons on whom data can be entered in and shared through the database, including in the form of non-anonymised information, does not satisfy the requirements of specificity. It is impossible to predict on this basis which persons are in fact to be included in the database. [...]

165 In view of the large, almost indeterminable number of persons potentially falling into the category of contact persons, the provision also violates the prohibition of excessive measures. Constitutional law does not generally rule out that data of contact persons, too, is made available in the counter-terrorism database. However, based on the purposes of the database, persons who do not already fall within the categories set out in numbers 1 and 2 of the provision, i.e. who are not regarded as potential supporters of terrorism themselves, are only of interest to the extent that they can provide information about the main target person thought to be associated with terrorism. It would have been imperative that this is reflected in the legal framework. [...]

166 3. The scope of the data to be stored pursuant to § 3(1) nos. 1 lit. a and b of the Counter-Terrorism Database Act is not objectionable under constitutional law. However, supplementary provisions are needed with regard to § 3(1) no. 1 lit. b of the Counter-Terrorism Database Act, in respect of certain further details that the provision leaves for the administrative authorities to determine.

167 a) The scope of the basic data set out in § 3(1) no. 1 lit. a of the Counter-Terrorism Database Act, which is made available as non-anonymised information to the participating authorities without qualified thresholds for interference, is not constitutionally objectionable.

168 The scope and informative value of this data can be considerable. [...]

169 Nevertheless, the provision is compatible with the prohibition of excessive measures. The data is defined in a sufficiently specific manner and, based on an overall assessment, is proportionate in scope. The data is limited to persons who are potentially associated with terrorism (see D IV 2 above), and only used to create a basic profile that allows for a more reliable identification of the persons concerned. While such a profile is indeed informative, it is ultimately limited to external parameters. In view of the importance of combating terrorism, this is not objectionable under constitutional law even if data collected by the intelligence services is included in the database. In this context, it must be taken into account that the data is not newly collected [for the purpose of creating the database], and that the database does not therefore prompt [new] investigation measures with

the aim to create a profile with a complete set of basic data, but merely seeks to combine the existing data already held by the different authorities. [...]

b) The scope of the extended data to be stored pursuant to § 3(1) no. 1 lit. b of the Counter-Terrorism Database Act is also not objectionable under constitutional law with regard to the prohibition of excessive measures; this data is generally only accessible to the participating authorities in the form of searches that keep the actual data concealed, while direct access to the data in its non-anonymised form is only granted in [acute and exceptional] cases of urgency. However, for certain categories of data to be stored, which are listed in that provision, their actual nature only becomes clear once the authorities have specified them further through abstract and general rules; in this regard, the legislator must ensure that such further determinations made by administrative authorities are comprehensibly documented and published. 170

aa) The categories of data to be stored in the database pursuant to sub-clauses aa to ff, jj, ll, mm, oo, pp and qq of § 3(1) no. 1 lit. b of the Counter-Terrorism Database Act are not objectionable under constitutional law. 171

(1) The categories of data to be entered into the counter-terrorism database pursuant to these sub-clauses are sufficiently specific; they do not require, as another step before they can be applied, further determination through abstract and general rules by the administrative authorities. The scope of the obligation to store data is directly ascertainable from the law, and its application in practice can directly be reviewed by oversight bodies and, as the case may be, by the courts. [...] 172

(2) The categories of data to be entered into the database are compatible with the prohibition of excessive measures, including in respect of their scope and informative value. 173

Nevertheless, it must be noted that the potential informative value of this data is extensive. [...] 174

Yet again, it must also be taken into account that the provisions do not authorise the collection of new data, but provide only for a combining of data already held by the different authorities. Most importantly, the weight of interference must be balanced against the exceptionally weighty public interest in the effective investigation of and fight against international terrorism (see D III 3 b above). Given the enormous dangers associated with terrorist crime for the most high-ranking legal interests of individuals and for the legal order as a whole, the combined storage of this data for the legislative aims pursued is compatible with the prohibition of excessive measures in an overall assessment. 175

[...] 176-177

bb) The categories of data to be stored in the database pursuant to sub-clauses gg, hh, ii, kk, nn of § 3(1) no. 1 lit. b of the Counter-Terrorism Database Act are 178 compatible with the Constitution, too. However, the legislator must ensure that the administrative authorities document and publish the rules required for further specifying the application of these categories in practice.

179 (1) These sub-clauses satisfy the requirement of specificity.

180 It is true that these provisions require further determinations [by the administrative authorities] to specify their substantive contents, and that individuals cannot conclusively infer from the provisions themselves what information is actually stored in the database based thereon. [...] According to the legislative intent, the detailed determination of the information to be included in the database is not meant to conclusively derive from the statutory provisions as such, but only from further specifying determinations made by the security authorities through abstract and general rules. In a first step, the authorities must define the information to be included in the order establishing the database [issued by the Federal Criminal Police Office in consultation with the other authorities and with governmental approval] pursuant to § 12 no. 3 of the Counter-Terrorism Database Act, and, in another step, in a standardised computer programme (cf. BTDrucks 16/2950, p. 17). Despite the strictly worded data storage obligations laid down in § 3(1) of the Counter-Terrorism Database Act, the legislator evidently did not intend to conclusively determine in that provision that all information potentially falling into the statutory categories listed there was in fact to be included in the database. Rather, it wanted to leave this decision to the authorities.

181 Despite this broad wording and need for further determination, the provisions satisfy the requirements of legal clarity and specificity in the overall framework of the database. The requirement of specificity does not from the outset preclude the use of indeterminate legal concepts (*unbestimmte Rechtsbegriffe*) (BVerfGE 118, 168 <188>). However, the legislator must draft laws as specifically as possible, taking account of the particular nature of the underlying subject matter and the purposes pursued (BVerfGE 78, 205 <212>; cf. also BVerfGE 110, 370 <396>; 117, 71 <111> – *Life Imprisonment*). [...]

182 The counter-terrorism database primarily serves to facilitate requests for information among various security authorities, and to provide easier access to decentralised intelligence, including unconfirmed findings, from other authorities in order to render counter-terrorism measures more effective. In this context, it is not reasonable to demand that the legislator lay down a more precise statutory definition of the data to be stored in the database. [...] It is not objectionable with regard to the principle of specificity that the legislator works with an open definition of the relevant data categories, which requires further specifying determinations at the level of implementation, and then sets out a tiered procedure for how the authorities are to carry out these determinations in practice in order to further specify and

No. 43 – Counter-Terrorism Database Act I

limit the information that will actually be entered into the database according to technical criteria. Such specifying decisions, even if they entail abstract and general determinations that are of considerable importance, are not a task that is necessarily incumbent upon the legislator itself. Rather, in a state order based on the separation of powers, it is not objectionable under the principle of the rule of law to leave these determinations to the executive. The decisive factor in the present case is that the legislator has not granted a blanket authorisation to the authorities, but has described the relevant data categories in a way that provides a sufficient basis for further determinations [at the level of implementation]. [...]

(2) To compensate for the broad wording of the provisions and the need for their further determination [at the level of implementation], the legislator must ensure that the security authorities comprehensibly document and publish their specifying and standardising determinations that will ultimately govern the application of the provisions in the individual case.

[...]

The current statutory framework does not fully satisfy these requirements [...].

[...] The Counter-Terrorism Database Act does not in a sufficiently clear manner impose on the security authorities an obligation to document and publish their determinations that specify the indeterminate legal concepts set out in § 3(1) no. 1 lit. b of the Counter-Terrorism Database Act. Even the fact that the data to be entered into the database is to be further specified at the level of implementation by means of a standardised IT-based catalogue cannot be directly derived from the law itself, but is revealed only in the legislative materials. [...]

The current statutory framework does not satisfy the requirements for a design in accordance with the rule of law. If the legislator wishes to keep the indeterminate legal concepts in § 3(1) no. 1 lit. b gg, hh, ii, kk, nn of the Counter-Terrorism Database Act, it must enact supplementary provisions that require the security authorities to document and publish, in a comprehensible manner, how they have specified the data categories as provided for in the statutory framework.

(3) With regard to their content, the categories of data to be included in the database pursuant to § 3(1) no. 1 lit. b gg, hh, ii, kk, nn of the Counter-Terrorism Database Act are compatible with the prohibition of excessive measures. Although this data may in some cases reveal highly personal circumstances – especially when linked with other stored data –, the legislator is within its leeway to design given that the database is for limited uses only and given the importance of counter-terrorism (see D III 3 a bb, b above).

This also applies to the data to be stored on ethnic origin and religious affiliation pursuant to § 3(1) no. 1 lit. b gg and hh of the Counter-Terrorism Database Act. However, particularly stringent requirements apply in this regard, given that special constitutional guarantees protect against discrimination on these grounds under Art. 3(3) of the Basic Law, and religious affiliation is specifically protected from an obligation to disclose it by Art. 140 of the Basic Law and Art. 136(3) of the Weimar Constitution. [...] However, in view of the importance accorded to effective protection against terrorism, it is not ruled out from the outset that this type of data, too, may be included in the database. Nevertheless, the Constitution requires restraint. This can be accommodated by ensuring that such information is only included for identification purposes.

190 cc) The possibility of free text entries pursuant to § 3(1) no. 1 lit. b rr of the Counter-Terrorism Database Act is also compatible with the prohibition of excessive measures. It does not amount to a blanket authorisation for arbitrary inclusion of further information in the database; rather, it allows authorities to provide additional comments and assessments which cannot be reflected otherwise due to the standardisation and categorisation of the entries. [...]

191 4. The regime governing data use is not compatible with the prohibition of excessive measures in every respect.

192 a) Nevertheless, § 3(1) no. 1 lit. a of the Counter-Terrorism Database Act, which allows for the request and use of basic data, is not objectionable under constitutional law.

193 aa) § 5(1) first and second sentence of the Counter-Terrorism Database Act provides the participating authorities with direct access to this data in its non-anonymised form. Authorities can both search for names and search in one or more of the categories listed in § 3(1) no. 1 lit. a of the Counter-Terrorism Database Act in order to identify persons not yet known to them. In the event of a match, access is then granted to the entire set of basic data stored on these persons. In this respect, § 5(1) first sentence of the Counter-Terrorism Database Act does not establish qualified thresholds for these measures constituting interferences. According to this provision, searches are generally permissible if they are necessary for the relevant authority's tasks regarding the investigation of and fight against international terrorism. [...]

194 The participating authorities can thus make extensive information requests and searches in the basic data. Yet this does not mean that these powers are unlimited. In particular, one limitation is that § 5 of the Counter-Terrorism Database Act only permits individual searches, but no profiling, bulk searches and searches for general links between persons by combining data fields. Thus, the provision requires a specific investigation basis prompting the search in the individual case. Moreover, every request for information is subject to the requirement of necessity, which must be fully substantiated and assessed in each individual case. [...]

bb) Despite the remaining wide range of possible ways in which authorities can consult the database, resulting in particular from the absence of limiting thresholds, the statutory framework is compatible with the principle of proportionality in this regard. The provisions governing data use are decisive here. Pursuant to § 6(1) first sentence of the Counter-Terrorism Database Act, the accessed data may only be used to identify persons that are relevant to an investigation, and to prepare individual data transfer requests to the authority holding the relevant information. The authorities are not allowed to extract any further information from this data and directly use it as the basis for investigations or [other operational] actions. They may only obtain such information in a further step [by filing an individual information request] under the applicable specific legislation. [...] In relation to the basic data pursuant to § 3(1) lit. a of the Counter-Terrorism Database Act, such a limited, preliminary form of data sharing is not objectionable under the principle of proportionality, given the great importance of protection against terrorism. To that extent, § 5(1) first and second sentence and § 6(1) first sentence of the Counter-Terrorism Database Act are constitutional.

b) § 5(1) first and third sentence of the Counter-Terrorism Database Act allows for searches in the extended data pursuant to § 3(1) no. 1 lit. b of the Counter-Terrorism Database Act; this is compatible with the prohibition of excessive measures to the extent that is concerns searches for specific names.

§ 5(1) first sentence of the Counter-Terrorism Database Act permits search requests in respect of all data included in the counter-terrorism database, and therefore also searches in the extended data. § 5(1) third sentence of the Counter-Terrorism Database Act provides that if a search for the name of a person yields a match in the extended data, the authority does not get access to the extended data as such, but only receives a notification that there is a positive match, together with information on which authority holds the relevant data and the file reference [under which the data is stored there]. Access to the extended data as such is only possible if the authority holding the information releases it following an individual transfer request subject to the applicable specific legislation (§ 5(1) third and fourth sentence of the Counter-Terrorism Database Act). [...]

c) By contrast, the statutory authorisation to carry out searches based on criteria [other than name] in the extended data that provide the authority consulting the database not just with information on how and where to request the [extended] data in the event of a match, but also with direct access to the corresponding basic data pursuant to § 3(1) no. 1 lit. a of the Counter-Terrorism Database Act, is not compatible with the prohibition of excessive measures. In that respect, § 5(1) second sentence no. 1 lit. a of the Counter-Terrorism Database Act is unconstitutional.

199   The informative value of the extended data pursuant to § 3(1) no. 1 lit. b of the Counter-Terrorism Database Act is extensive, and can include highly personal information as well as data that pieces together the biographical background of the data subject (see D IV 3 b aa (2) above). Based on proportionality considerations, access to this type of information must therefore be restricted to a significantly greater degree than access to basic data pursuant to § 3(1) no. 1 lit. a of the Counter-Terrorism Database Act. Accordingly, the law generally only authorises searches that keep the extended data itself concealed [from the authority consulting the database], and makes transfer of the non-anonymised data subject to the transfer provisions under the respective statutory regimes applicable in the specific case. Yet in the event that searches in the extended data yield a match, the law also grants direct access to the corresponding basic data in its non-anonymised form; as a result, it lifts the aforementioned access restriction for searches based on criteria [other than name], i.e. reverse searches, to a significant extent. [...] Thus, authorities can consult the database by searching for one or several criteria – for example, by searching for persons with a certain religious affiliation and training who frequent a certain meeting place (cf. § 3(1) no. 1 lit. b hh, jj, nn of the Counter-Terrorism Database Act) – and thereby obtain, in the event of a match, not just the information which other authorities hold relevant information, but all names and addresses and all other information listed in § 3(1) no. 1 lit. a of the Counter-Terrorism Database Act about all persons matching the search criteria.

200   Such far-reaching data use does not take sufficient account of the fact that the extended data are substantive in scope. [...] The design of the provisions governing use of the database must ensure that, if a search in the extended data yields a match, only the file reference and the authority holding the [concealed] data are displayed, but not the corresponding basic data.

201   d) This notwithstanding, there are no constitutional objections to allowing the [direct] use of extended data in urgent cases pursuant to § 5(2) and § 6(2) of the Counter-Terrorism Database Act, even in the context of reverse searches (see c above).

202   It is true that this constitutes the broadest possible use of the data combined in the counter-terrorism database. In addition to basic data access, it entails direct access to all extended data in its non-anonymised form, and therefore allows [the authority consulting the database] to use the data not just to prepare further transfer requests, but also to directly carry out counter-terrorism measures, for instance if the data is used for assessing a danger as the basis for further operational action (§ 6(2) of the Counter-Terrorism Database Act). As this deviates from the principle of separation of police and intelligence data, it amounts to a particularly serious interference (see D III 3 a aa, bb (3) above).

No. 43 – Counter-Terrorism Database Act I

The statutory prerequisites for such use are, however, sufficiently narrow to justify the interference. The data may be accessed and used only to protect particularly weighty legal interests – which primarily concerns the protection of life, limb, health or liberty of the person. [...] To the extent that the provision additionally lists assets of substantial value as protected interests, it clarifies that this does not entail protection of property or material assets as such, but only applies to assets "the preservation of which is required in the public interest" (§ 5(2) first sentence of the Counter-Terrorism Database Act). In the context of protecting against terrorism, this means significant infrastructure facilities or other sites that are vital for society. The provision also sets out high thresholds for carrying out the measures. It requires a present danger to protected interests, the existence of which must be established not just based on mere indications, but based on specific substantiating facts. The data may then only be accessed and used if this is absolutely necessary and if the relevant data could not be retrieved in time through an individual transfer request. Moreover, direct access to the data is subject to procedural safeguards. [...] 203

5. The principle of proportionality also gives rise to requirements regarding transparency, individual legal protection and administrative oversight. Given the purpose and design of the database, the Counter-Terrorism Database Act only ensures transparency regarding information sharing to a limited extent, thus allowing affected persons only limited possibilities of legal protection; thus, its application is essentially overseen by the data protection officers. This is compatible with the Basic Law provided that the constitutional requirements regarding effective oversight are observed. 204

a) As regards the storage and use of personal data by state authorities in the exercise of their functions, the legislator must also satisfy requirements regarding transparency, legal protection, and administrative oversight in consideration of proportionality aspects (cf. BVerfGE 125, 260 <325 *et seq.*> – *Data Retention*). 205

[...] 206-207

b) The Counter-Terrorism Database Act contains few provisions for ensuring transparency and individual legal protection. In essence, it only recognises rights to information [on the part of data subjects], which are limited in their effectiveness by procedural law and substantive restrictions. Yet in view of the purpose and design of this database, this is not objectionable. 208

aa) To ensure transparency, the Counter-Terrorism Database Act primarily provides for rights to information based on the Federal Data Protection Act (§ 10(2) of the Counter-Terrorism Database Act). However, these rights are subject to restrictions and, in part, considerable procedural hurdles. Yet in view of the purpose pursued by and the function of the Counter-Terrorism Database Act, these limited information rights satisfy the constitutional requirements. 209

210-212 [...]

213 bb) Other than that, the Counter-Terrorism Database Act neither sets out a requirement that data use be in principle carried out overtly, nor a requirement of prior judicial authorisation (*Richtervorbehalt*) nor requirements to notify the affected persons *ex post* beyond the notification requirements already contained in other legislation. Thus, the Act lacks important instruments for ensuring the proportionality of data use. Yet this is justified under constitutional law given the purpose of the counter-terrorism database. It mainly serves to facilitate requests for information in order to prepare further investigation measures in the context of protection against international terrorism. It is evident that this type of investigations cannot generally observe the principle of transparency. As regards the counter-terrorism database, prior judicial authorisation can also not be considered a viable instrument mandated under constitutional law. Given that the statutory framework does not conclusively define all details of the powers set out in § 5(1) of the Counter-Terrorism Database Act, and given that data access pursuant to § 5(2) of the Counter-Terrorism Database Act concerns cases of urgency requiring an expedited procedure, a requirement to obtain prior judicial authorisation would be ineffective for the most part. [...]

214 c) Since the Counter-Terrorism Database Act can only ensure transparency of data processing and individual legal protection to a very limited extent, guaranteeing effective administrative oversight is all the more significant. Therefore, the principle of proportionality places more stringent requirements on the effective design of such an oversight regime both at statutory level and at the level of implementation.

215 aa) Ensuring effective oversight primarily requires oversight bodies equipped with effective powers at both the federal and *Land* level, such as the data protection officers under current law. It is also necessary to comprehensively document any access to and modifications of the data records. In this regard, technical and organisational arrangements must ensure that the data is available to the data protection officers in a form that allows them to conduct effective audits, and that the required documentation provides sufficient information to match the data with the process to be audited.

216 Given the nature of the counter-terrorism database as a joint database used both by federal and *Land* authorities, it must be ensured that effective oversight of the database does not stand back behind optimising data sharing due to uncertainties about the division of competences in the federal order. [...] Regarding the relationship between different oversight authorities, it must be ensured that effective oversight is exercised in respect of data obtained by measures taken under the Article 10 Act [i.e. surveillance measures restricting the privacy of telecommunications under Art. 10 of the Basic Law] – which is of particular importance given that

a significant amount of the data stored in the database is contributed by the Federal Intelligence Service. If the legislator provides for cooperation among security authorities in the form of information sharing, it must also allow for cooperation among oversight authorities to uphold data protection.

Since administrative oversight must compensate for the weak level of individual legal protection, it is particularly significant that audits be performed regularly at intervals not exceeding approximately two years. This must be taken into account when allocating resources to the oversight authorities.

bb) [...]

d) In order to ensure transparency and oversight, the legislator must enact statutory reporting obligations.

Under the Counter-Terrorism Database Act, the data is largely stored and used without the knowledge of affected persons or the public; rights to information can only counteract this to a limited extent. Furthermore, effective judicial review is not sufficiently possible. Therefore, the law must ensure regular reports by the Federal Criminal Police Office to Parliament and the public on what data is included in the counter-terrorism database and how it is used. [...]

6. There are no constitutional objections regarding the deletion arrangements pursuant to § 11(2) and (4) of the Counter-Terrorism Database Act. According to this provision, the maximum duration for which data may be stored depends on the deletion periods set out in the specific legislation governing the respective source data which is entered into the database. This approach is sensible, and it is also tenable under constitutional law.

V.

To the extent that the challenged provisions allow data obtained through interferences with the privacy of telecommunications or with the fundamental right to the inviolability of the home to be included in the database, they violate Art. 10(1) and Art. 13(1) of the Basic Law.

1. Data collected through interferences with the fundamental rights under Art. 10(1) and Art. 13(1) of the Basic Law is generally subject to more stringent requirements, due to the special protection afforded by these fundamental rights. According to the case-law of the Federal Constitutional Court, these more stringent requirements continue to apply to any later transfer and change in purpose of data thus obtained. For instance, the statutory threshold for the transfer of data obtained through the surveillance of private homes for criminal proceedings may not be lower than the threshold applicable to similar interferences for public security purposes, since a change in purpose may not be used to circumvent restrictions set by fundamental

rights regarding the use of certain investigation methods (cf. BVerfGE 109, 279 <377 and 378> – *Surveillance of Private Homes*; cf. also BVerfGE 100, 313 <389 and 390, 394> – *The Article 10 Act*). Likewise, the sharing of telecommunications data, which could only be obtained by the sharing authority subject to particularly stringent requirements, is only permissible if it serves tasks that would [hypothetically] have justified direct access to this data by the receiving authority (cf. BVerfGE 125, 260 <333> – *Data Retention*; similarly already BVerfGE 100, 313 <389 and 390> – *The Article 10 Act*; 109, 279 <375 and 376> – *Surveillance of Private Homes*; 110, 33 <73 and 74>). For the same reasons, data stemming from serious interferences with Art. 10(1) or Art. 13(1) of the Basic Law must be labelled accordingly. Making such data identifiable serves to ensure that the specific restrictions on the use of this data are observed even in the event that the data is transferred to other authorities.

226 2. Full and unrestricted inclusion in the counter-terrorism database of data obtained through interferences with Art. 10(1) and Art. 13(1) of the Basic Law is not compatible with these requirements; the same applies to data obtained through interferences with the fundamental right to protection of the confidentiality and integrity of information technology systems under Art. 2(1) in conjunction with Art. 1(1) of the Basic Law (cf. BVerfGE 120, 274 <302 and 303> – *Remote Searches*), a violation of which was not asserted by the complainant in the present proceedings. Where data is protected by these fundamental rights, it may generally only be collected subject to strict standards, which require, for example, higher statutory thresholds for carrying out measures constituting interferences with these rights, such as the requirement of a qualified danger or a qualified suspicion, a danger to exceptionally significant legal interests, or the prosecution of particularly serious criminal acts. […]

227 3. In the oral hearing, the Federal Government stated that, in the future, such data would only be stored in a concealed manner pursuant to § 4 of the Counter-Terrorism Database Act. This does not, however, lead to a different result in the present proceedings given that no such limitation can be inferred from the Counter-Terrorism Database Act itself. […]

228 This notwithstanding, if the statutory framework were to always require concealed storage of such data pursuant to § 4 of the Counter-Terrorism Database Act, it would be constitutional with regard to the principle of proportionality. With such a design, the statutory framework would ensure that the corresponding information can only be accessed in accordance with the transfer provisions set out in the applicable specific legislation. Those provisions, in turn, can ensure both qualified thresholds for interference, as required under constitutional law, and the protection of sufficiently weighty legal interests. […]

E.

I.

Despite the fact that the challenged provisions are in part unconstitutional, they are not declared void but incompatible with the Basic Law. [...] 229

A mere declaration of incompatibility, combined with an order to temporarily continue the application of unconstitutional provisions, can be issued if the immediate invalidity of the objectionable provision would eliminate the statutory basis for the protection of exceptionally significant public interests, and if a balancing of these interests against the affected fundamental rights requires that the interference be tolerated for a transitional period (BVerfGE 109, 190 <235 and 236>). This is the case here. [...] 230

[...] 231-232

II.

The decision is unanimous with regard to part C; with regard to other parts, there were partial dissents. [...] 233

Justices: Kirchhof, Gaier, Eichberger, Schluckebier, Masing, Paulus, Baer, Britz

No. 44

BVerfGE 141, 220 – The Federal Criminal Police Office Act

HEADNOTES

to the Judgment of the First Senate of 20 April 2016
1 BvR 966/09, 1 BvR 1140/09

1. a) The authorisation of the Federal Criminal Police Office to carry out covert surveillance measures (surveillance of private homes, remote searches of information technology systems, telecommunications surveillance, collection of telecommunications traffic data and surveillance outside of private homes using special means of data collection) is, for the purpose of averting dangers to public security posed by international terrorism, in principle compatible with the fundamental rights enshrined in the Basic Law.

   b) The design of these surveillance powers must satisfy the principle of proportionality. Powers that reach deep into private life must be limited to the protection or defence of sufficiently weighty legal interests; require the existence of a sufficiently specific and foreseeable danger to these interests; ensure that extending the measures to third parties who belong to the target person's contacts but are not themselves legally responsible for the danger is only permissible subject to very restrictive conditions; must be supplemented, for the most part, by specific provisions for the protection of the core of private life as well as the protection of persons bound by professional confidentiality; are subject to requirements of transparency, individual legal protection and administrative oversight; and must be supplemented by deletion requirements regarding the collected data.

2. The constitutional requirements for the use and sharing of data collected by the state are informed by the principles of purpose limitation and change in purpose.

   a) The scope of a purpose limitation depends on the respective statutory basis for the data collection measure in question: the initial purpose of data collection measures is limited to the respective investigation.

   b) The legislator may permit data use beyond the specific investigation that prompted the data collection measure if the envisaged data use is still in line with the purpose for which the data was originally collected (further use). This requires that the use of collected data be limited to the same authority performing the same task and protecting the same legal interests. For data obtained through the surveillance of private homes or through remote searches of information technology systems, any further use must additionally satisfy the prerequisites for establishing sufficient indications of an identifiable danger that were applicable to the original data collection.

c) In addition, the legislator may also permit further use of collected data for purposes other than those for which the data was originally collected (change in purpose).

The proportionality requirements applicable to such a change in purpose derive from the principle of a hypothetical recollection of data. According to this principle, the new use of the data must serve to protect legal interests or to detect criminal acts of such weight that would, by constitutional standards, justify a new collection of the data by means entailing interferences that are comparable in severity [to the original data collection measures]. However, there is generally no need to establish, for a second time, the existence of an identifiable danger, as required for the original data collection; it is necessary but generally also sufficient to require that there be a specific basis for further investigations.

With regard to data obtained through the surveillance of private homes and through remote searches of information technology systems, a change in purpose is only permissible if the prerequisites for establishing sufficient indications of danger that were applicable to the original data collection would also be satisfied in relation to the new purpose.

3. The sharing of data with foreign state authorities is subject to the general constitutional principles of purpose limitation and change in purpose. In this context, the assessment of new data uses must respect the autonomy of the foreign state's legal order. Moreover, it must be ensured that the receiving state will handle the data in accordance with the rule of law.

BVerfGE 141, 220

FEDERAL CONSTITUTIONAL COURT
- 1 BvR 966/09 -
- 1 BvR 1140/09 -

IN THE NAME OF THE PEOPLE

In the proceedings
on the constitutional complaints of

1. Mr B…, 2. Mr F…, 3. Mr S…, 4. Prof. Dr. H…, 5. Dr. N…, 6. Mr H…,
– authorised representatives: …
against § 14, § 20c(3), § 20g, § 20h, § 20k, § 20l, § 20u(1) and (2), § 20v and § 20w of the Federal Criminal Police Office Act in the version of 31 December 2008 (BGBl 2008, p. 3083 *et seq.*)

- 1 BvR 966/09 -,

1. Mr W…, 2. Mr S…, 3. Dr. T…, 4. Ms R…, 5. Mr N…, 6. Mr T…, 7. Ms M…, 8. Ms K…, 9. Mr B…,
– authorised representative: …
against a) § 20g(1) and (2), § 20h(1), (2) and (5), § 20j(1), § 20k(1) and (7), § 20l(1) and (6), § 20m(1), § 20v(4) second sentence and (6) fifth sentence, § 20w(2) first and second sentence of the Federal Criminal Police Office Act,

b) § 20h(5) tenth sentence, § 20k(7) eighth sentence, § 20l(6) tenth sentence of the Federal Criminal Police Office Act,

c) § 20u(1) and (2) of the Federal Criminal Police Office Act in conjunction with § 53(1) first sentence nos. 2 and 3 of the Code of Criminal Procedure

- 1 BvR 1140/09 -

the Federal Constitutional Court – First Senate –
with the participation of Justices

Vice-President Kirchhof,
Gaier,
Eichberger,
Schluckebier,
Masing,
Paulus,

No. 44 – The Federal Criminal Police Office Act

Baer,
Britz

held on the basis of the oral hearing of 7 July 2015:

JUDGMENT

1. § 20h(1) no. 1 lit. c of the Federal Criminal Police Office Act as amended by the Act on the Averting of Dangers from International Terrorism by the Federal Criminal Police Office of 25 December 2008 (BGBl I, p. 3083), and in the later amended versions, violates Article 13(1) of the Basic Law and is void.
2. § 20v(6) fifth sentence of the Federal Criminal Police Office Act violates Article 2(1) in conjunction with Article 1(1), Article 10(1), Article 13(1), each in conjunction with Article 19(4) of the Basic Law, and is void.
3. § 14(1) (excluding first sentence no. 2), § 20g(1) to (3), §§ 20h, 20j, 20k, 20l, § 20m(1) and (3), § 20u(1) and (2), and § 20v(4) second sentence, § 20v(5) first to fourth sentence (excluding third sentence no. 2), § 20v(6) third sentence of the Federal Criminal Police Office Act are not compatible with Article 2(1) in conjunction with Article 1(1), Article 10(1), Article 13(1) and (3) – also in conjunction with Article 1(1) and Article 19(4) of the Basic Law – as set forth in the reasons of this judgment.
4. Until the legislator has enacted new provisions, or until 30 June 2018 at the latest, the provisions that have been declared incompatible with the Basic Law continue to apply, subject to the condition that measures pursuant to § 20g(2) nos. 1, 2 lit. b, 4 and 5 of the Federal Criminal Police Office Act require prior judicial authorisation; in cases of danger requiring immediate action, § 20g(3) second to fourth sentence of the Federal Criminal Police Office Act applies accordingly.
Measures pursuant to § 20g(1) first sentence no. 2, § 20l(1) first sentence no. 2 and § 20m(1) no. 2 of the Federal Criminal Police Office Act may only be ordered if the prerequisites set out in § 20k(1) second sentence of the Federal Criminal Police Office Act, in the interpretation in conformity with the Basic Law as set forth in the reasons of this judgment, are fulfilled.
Further data use pursuant to § 20v(4) second sentence of the Federal Criminal Police Office Act or data sharing pursuant to § 20v(5) and § 14(1) of the Federal Criminal Police Office Act is permissible only in cases of acute danger where data obtained through the surveillance of private homes is concerned (§ 20h of the Federal Criminal Police Office Act); and only in cases of a specific impending danger to the protected legal interests where data obtained through

remote searches of information technology systems is concerned (§ 20k of the Federal Criminal Police Office Act).

5. [...]

6. For the rest, the constitutional complaints are rejected as unfounded.

7. [...]

REASONS:

A.

I.

1 The constitutional complaints are directed against provisions of the Federal Criminal Police Office Act inserted [...] by the Act on the Averting of Dangers from International Terrorism by the Federal Criminal Police Office of 25 December 2008 (BGBl I, p. 3083), effective 1 January 2009. On the basis of Art. 73(1) no. 9a of the Basic Law (BGBl I, p. 2034), as amended in 2006 with this purpose in mind, the federal legislator extended the existing mandate of the Federal Criminal Police Office in the domain of law enforcement by assigning it new tasks in the domain of averting dangers to public security posed by international terrorism, a responsibility that had until then been within the exclusive competence of the *Länder*. The constitutional complaints also challenge a provision in the Federal Criminal Police Office Act that predates the amendment at issue and concerns the sharing of data with foreign state authorities, the scope of which has been extended by the newly attributed tasks.

II.

2 Firstly, the constitutional complaints are directed against various investigatory powers conferred [upon the Federal Criminal Police Office]. The challenged powers include the authorisation to question persons pursuant to § 20c of the Federal Criminal Police Office Act, as well as the use of special means of data collection outside of private homes pursuant to § 20g(1) to (3) of the Federal Criminal Police Office Act including, in particular, the covert interception and recording of non-public communication, covert image recording, the installation of tracking devices, and the use of police informants and undercover police investigators. The constitutional complaints also challenge the powers to carry out visual and acoustic surveillance of private homes pursuant to § 20h of the Federal Criminal Police Office Act, to

conduct electronic profiling and searches pursuant to § 20j of the Federal Criminal Police Office Act, to access information technology systems pursuant to § 20k of the Federal Criminal Police Office Act, to monitor ongoing telecommunications pursuant to § 20l of the Federal Criminal Police Office Act as well as to collect telecommunications traffic data pursuant to § 20m(1) and (3) of the Federal Criminal Police Office Act. To that extent, the constitutional complaints also challenge § 20u of the Federal Criminal Police Office Act, which governs the protection of persons entitled to refuse to give evidence, as well as § 20w of the Federal Criminal Police Office Act, which sets out the requirement to notify affected persons after the surveillance measure has ended.

Secondly, the constitutional complaints are directed against provisions on data use. This concerns the use of data collected by the Federal Criminal Police Office itself [...] pursuant to § 20v(4) second sentence of the Federal Criminal Police Office Act. They also challenge the power pursuant to § 20v(5) of the Federal Criminal Police Office Act – with the exception of third sentence no. 2 – to share this data with other domestic public authorities. Finally, the constitutional complaints also challenge § 14(1) first sentence nos. 1 and 3 and second sentence, § 14(7) of the Federal Criminal Police Office Act, which generally permits the sharing of data with foreign state authorities. By contrast, the present proceedings do not concern § 14a of the Federal Criminal Police Office Act, which additionally establishes special powers to share personal data with EU Member States.

[...]

III.

The complainants in proceedings 1 BvR 966/09 are lawyers, journalists, a doctor and a psychologist, most of whom are active in the field of human rights policy. The complainants in proceedings 1 BvR 1140/09 are former and current members of the German *Bundestag* – acting here as private individuals –, most of whom are also active in the human rights sector and some of whom also work as lawyers or doctors. In substance, they claim a violation of Art. 2(1) in conjunction with Art. 1(1), Art. 3(1), Art. 5(1) second sentence, Art. 10, Art. 12, Art. 13, in part also in conjunction with Art. 1(1), Art. 19(4) of the Basic Law and Art. 20(3) of the Basic Law.

6-40 […]

IV.

41-73 […]

V.

74 […]

B.

75 The constitutional complaints are for the most part admissible.

I.

76 The constitutional complaints are directed against the surveillance and investigatory powers of the Federal Criminal Police Office, including in particular challenges to the inadequate protection of the core of private life and the surveillance of persons entitled to refuse to give evidence, as well as to provisions on data use. […]

II.

77-78 […]

III.

79-85 […]

No. 44 – The Federal Criminal Police Office Act

C.

To the extent that the constitutional complaints are directed against the investigatory and surveillance powers, they are well-founded in several respects.

I.

[…]

II.

The challenged surveillance and investigatory powers authorise interferences with fundamental rights, which, depending on the respective fundamental right and the differing weight of interference, must be measured individually against the principle of proportionality and the principle of legal clarity and specificity. The powers have in common that the potential interferences they authorise are for the most part serious. At the same time, since their purpose is to avert dangers to public security posed by international terrorism, they have a legitimate aim and are suitable and necessary for achieving that aim.

1. The challenged powers authorise the Federal Criminal Police Office to covertly collect personal data for the purposes of averting dangers to public security and of preventing crime. Depending on the power in question, the measures result in interferences with the fundamental rights under Art. 13(1), Art. 10(1) and Art. 2(1) in conjunction with Art. 1(1) of the Basic Law, the latter both in its manifestation as the right to protection of the confidentiality and integrity of information technology systems and as the right to informational self-determination.

All these authorisations provide statutory bases for investigatory and surveillance measures that are usually carried out covertly without the knowledge of affected persons and can constitute deep intrusions into the private sphere. It is true that the challenged powers affect legitimate expectations of confidentiality to differing degrees and that the weight of interference varies significantly depending on the power in question. Yet the interferences they give rise to weigh heavily in any case, with the exception of certain measures set out in § 20g(1) and (2) of the Federal Criminal Police Office Act.

2. The constitutionality of the powers at issue depends on the limits arising from the different fundamental rights affected by them and the requirements deriving from the principle of proportionality, which must be determined individually for each of the powers in question. According to the principle of proportionality, the powers must in any case serve a legitimate aim and be suitable, necessary

and proportionate in the strict sense for achieving this aim (cf. BVerfGE 67, 157 <173>; 70, 278 <286>; 104, 337 <347 *et seq.*>; 120, 274 <318 and 319> – *Remote Searches*; 125, 260 <316> – *Data Retention*; established case-law).

94 Furthermore, the challenged powers must be measured against the principle of legal clarity and specificity, which serves to make interferences foreseeable for citizens, to effectively limit public authorities' powers and to enable effective judicial review (cf. BVerfGE 113, 348 <375 *et seq.*>; 120, 378 <407 and 408>; 133, 277 <336 para. 140> – *Counter-Terrorism Database Act I*; established case-law). With regard to the powers at issue, which concern the covert collection and processing of data and can constitute a deep intrusion into the private sphere, this principle sets particularly strict requirements. […]

95 3. The challenged provisions pursue a legitimate aim and are suitable and necessary for achieving that aim.

96 a) The powers serve a legitimate aim. They provide the Federal Criminal Police Office with means of gathering information that it can use in fulfilling its new task of averting dangers to public security from international terrorism. The term 'international terrorism' is limited to specifically defined criminal offences of particular weight by means of the description of tasks laid down in § 4a(1) of the Federal Criminal Police Office Act and by means of that provision's reference to § 129a(1) and (2) of the Criminal Code, in line with the EU Framework Decision of 13 June 2002 and international terminology (OJ L 164, p. 3; Draft Comprehensive Convention on International Terrorism, in: Measures to eliminate international terrorism, Report of the Working Group of 3 November 2010, UN Doc. A/C.6/65/L.10) and in keeping with the Constitution-amending legislator's intent underpinning the insertion of Art. 73(1) no. 9a into the Basic Law (cf. BTDrucks 16/813, p. 12). Criminal offences characterised as terrorism in this sense aim to destabilise society and, to this end, comprise attacks on the life and limb of random third parties, in a ruthless instrumentalisation of others. They are directed against the pillars of the constitutional order and society as a whole. Providing effective means of gathering information for averting terrorist dangers constitutes a legitimate aim and is of great significance for the free democratic order (cf. BVerfGE 115, 320 <357 and 358> – *Profiling*; 120, 274 <319> – *Remote Searches*; 133, 277 <333 and 334 para. 133> – *Counter-Terrorism Database Act I*).

97 b) The surveillance and investigatory powers in question are suitable for achieving this aim. They provide the Federal Criminal Police Office with the means for gathering information that can be conducive to countering dangers posed by international terrorism. The different powers are, at least in principle, necessary for this task. Each of the powers in question allows the use of specific measures that cannot be replaced by alternative measures, at least not in every case. It is not ascertainable

that there were less restrictive means that could provide equally effective and far-reaching possibilities of gathering information for averting dangers posed by international terrorism. At the same time, it must be ensured, in each individual case, that these powers only be exercised in accordance with the principle of suitability and necessity.

III.

The powers at issue must be sufficiently restricted in accordance with the principle of proportionality in the strict sense. This requires that the surveillance and investigatory powers in question be appropriate to their weight of interference. It is incumbent upon the legislator to balance the severity of the relevant interferences with fundamental rights of potentially affected persons, on the one hand, against the state's duty of protection regarding citizens' fundamental rights, on the other.

1. On the one hand, the legislator must take into account the weight of interference of the powers conferred by the challenged provisions. To differing degrees, depending on the power in question, these allow for far-reaching interferences with the private sphere and can, in individual cases, even intrude upon private refuges, the protection of which is of particular significance for safeguarding human dignity. In its balancing, the legislator must also consider developments in information technology, which increasingly extend the reach of surveillance measures, facilitate their use and enable the linking of data, which can go so far as to create personality profiles. In this regard, the constitutional assessment must distinguish between the different powers as well as the affected fundamental rights.

2. On the other hand, the legislator must ensure the effective protection of [other] fundamental rights and legal interests of citizens. In the constitutional assessment of appropriateness, it must be taken into account that the constitutional order, the existence and security of the Federation and of the *Länder*, and life, limb and liberty of the person are protected legal interests of significant constitutional weight. Accordingly, the Federal Constitutional Court has underlined that the security of the state, as a constituted power of peace and order, as well as the security of the population it is bound to protect – while respecting the dignity and the intrinsic value of the individual – rank equally with other constitutional values that are accorded high standing. In view of this, the Court recognised a duty of the state to protect the life, physical integrity and liberty of the individual, which means in particular that the state must ensure protection against unlawful interferences by others (cf. BVerfGE 115, 320 <346 and 347> – *Profiling*; cf. also BVerfGE 49, 24 <56 and 57>; 90, 145 <195>; 115, 118 <152 and 153>).

101 In assessing appropriateness, it must also be taken into account that the challenged provisions, even though the resulting interferences indiscriminately affect a large number of persons, do not affect the entire population to the same extent. Rather, these are predominantly provisions aiming to enable security authorities to avert, in individual cases, serious dangers threatening constitutionally protected legal interests as well as to prevent serious crime.

102 In light of the dangers posed by international terrorism, the decision to collect certain data is also of particular significance for information sharing between domestic authorities as well as for rendering the cooperation with foreign security authorities as effective as possible. Effective information sharing, which serves the constitutionally mandated protection of the individual, is contingent on the transfer of intelligence gathered domestically [to foreign authorities] and in return relies on intelligence provided by foreign authorities.

IV.

103 With regard to investigatory and surveillance powers constituting deep intrusions into the private sphere, which is the case for most of the powers at issue here, the Federal Constitutional Court has recognised certain general requirements deriving from the principle of proportionality in the strict sense. These requirements address specific large-scale risks to fundamental rights that potentially arise from such powers, including, in particular, risks arising from electronic data processing (cf. BVerfGE 100, 313 <358 et seq.> – *The Article 10 Act*; 115, 320 <341 et seq.> – *Profiling*; 125, 260 <316 et seq.> – *Data Retention*; 133, 277 <335 et seq.* para. 138 et seq.> – *Counter-Terrorism Database Act I*), as well as risks arising where a surveillance measure taken in a particular case results in individuals affected by the measure coming under scrutiny by the authorities involved (BVerfGE 107, 299 < 312 et seq.>, BVerfGE 110, 33 <52 et seq.>; 113, 348 <364 et seq.>; 129, 208 <236 et seq.> – *The Telecommunications Surveillance Revision Act*, BVerfGE 109, 279 <335 et seq.> – *Surveillance of Private Homes*, BVerfGE 112, 304 <315 et seq.>, BVerfGE 120, 274 <302 et seq.> – *Remote Searches*).

104 1. To the extent that covert surveillance measures reach deep into the private sphere, as most of the measures at issue here do, such measures are only compatible with the Constitution if they serve to protect or defend sufficiently weighty legal interests where there are reliable factual indications, in the specific case, suggesting that these interests are violated or at risk of being violated. In this regard, it must generally be established, based on the objective circumstances as examined by a reasonable observer, that the person targeted by a measure is involved in the (potential) violation of protected legal interests. A mere possibility, based primarily

on the intuition-based assumption of the security authorities in charge, that further intelligence might be gained does not provide sufficient grounds for carrying out such measures (cf. BVerfGE 107, 299 <321 *et seq.*>; 110, 33 <56>; 113, 348 <377 and 378, 380 and 381>; 120, 274 <328> – *Remote Searches*; 125, 260 <330> – *Data Retention*). The Constitution thus sets clear limits to the lowering of statutory thresholds applicable to crime prevention measures if the measures in question are carried out covertly and potentially reach deep into the private sphere; in contrast, with regard to measures involving less intrusive interferences with the private sphere, the Constitution affords broader leeway to the legislator in crime prevention matters.

With regard to the specific design of the different statutory powers, the substantive assessment of whether they satisfy the requirements of appropriateness and specificity hinges on the weight of the interference resulting from each measure. The deeper the reach of surveillance measures into one's private life and the more they frustrate legitimate expectations of confidentiality, the stricter the requirements that the measures must satisfy. Among the measures at issue, surveillance of private homes and remote searches of information technology systems result in particularly deep intrusions into the private sphere.

a) Covert surveillance measures must be limited to the protection or defence of sufficiently weighty legal interests.

With regard to the measures that serve law enforcement purposes, and are thus repressive, this assessment depends on the weight of the criminal acts targeted by the measures. The legislator has divided the grounds for carrying out the measures into different categories of crime – considerable, serious and particularly serious – and defined each category in greater detail. For instance, the surveillance of private homes requires the suspicion of a particularly serious crime (cf. BVerfGE 109, 279 <343 *et seq.*> – *Surveillance of Private Homes*), telecommunications surveillance or the use of telecommunications traffic data stemming from precautionary data retention requires the suspicion of a serious crime (cf. BVerfGE 125, 260 <328 and 329> – *Data Retention*; 129, 208 <243> – *The Telecommunications Surveillance Revision Act*), while the collection of telecommunications traffic data based on specific grounds or observation by means of a GPS tracker, for example, requires the suspicion of a considerable crime – for surveillance targeting traffic data, the law furthermore specifies criminal offences that typically qualify as 'considerable crime' in this context – (cf. BVerfGE 107, 299 <321 and 322>; 112, 304 <315 and 316>; with regard to the latter decision, cf. also ECtHR, *Uzun v. Germany*, Judgment of 2 September 2010, no. 35623/05, § 70, NJW 2011, p. 1333 <1336>, regarding Art. 8 ECHR).

108 With regard to measures that serve to avert dangers to public security, and are thus preventive, this assessment depends on the weight of the legal interests that the measures serve to protect (cf. BVerfGE 125, 260 <329> – *Data Retention*). Covert surveillance measures that reach deep into a person's private life are only permissible to protect particularly weighty legal interests. These include life, limb and liberty of the person as well as the existence or security of the Federation or a *Land* (cf. BVerfGE 120, 274 <328> – *Remote Searches*; 125, 260 <330> – *Data Retention*). By contrast, the Federal Constitutional Court has held that the unconditional protection of material assets does not necessarily constitute a sufficiently weighty interest in this context. At the same time, the Court has held that it is generally compatible with the Constitution to allow access to data retained as a precautionary measure (cf. BVerfGE 125, 260 <330> – *Data Retention*) or the surveillance of private homes also on the grounds of a danger to the general public (*gemeine Gefahr*) (cf. BVerfGE 109, 279 <379> – *Surveillance of Private Homes*), or to allow remote searches of information technology systems on the grounds of a danger to assets that affect the foundations of human existence and thus serve public interests (cf. BVerfGE 120, 274 <328> – *Remote Searches*). Based thereon, the legislator is, however, not prevented from laying down uniform grounds, in terms of the protected legal interests, as the statutory threshold for carrying out these surveillance measures.

109 b) For the purposes of public security measures to protect the aforementioned legal interests, the collection of data by means of covert surveillance, which gives rise to very intrusive interferences, is generally only proportionate if there is a sufficiently specific and foreseeable danger to these legal interests in the individual case and the person targeted by these measures appears, from the perspective of a reasonable observer examining the objective circumstances, to be involved therein (cf. BVerfGE 120, 274 <328 and 329> – *Remote Searches*; 125, 260 <330 and 331> – *Data Retention*).

110 The prerequisites applicable to such measures also depend on the type and weight of the respective interference. For the surveillance of private homes, which constitutes a particularly deep intrusion into the private sphere, Art. 13(4) of the Basic Law requires the existence of an acute danger (*dringende Gefahr*). In this respect, the term 'acute danger' qualifies both the extent of possible damage to the legal interests the measure aims to protect and the probability that the damage will occur (cf. BVerfGE 130, 1 <32>).

111 Furthermore, the prerequisites for establishing a sufficiently specific and identifiable danger to the aforementioned legal interests must correspond to the burden imposed on the persons affected by the measure. In general security law, the legal concepts of specific danger (*konkrete Gefahr*), immediate danger (*unmittelbar*

bevorstehende Gefahr) or present danger (*gegenwärtige Gefahr*) are recognised as grounds for public security measures against persons responsible for a danger (*polizeipflichtige Personen*) in relation to one of the protected interests at issue here; these concepts set sufficient standards in line with constitutional law. The term 'specific danger', as traditionally used in police law, requires a situation where it can be assumed, with sufficient probability, that the chain of events that is objectively to be expected will lead, in the individual case and within the foreseeable future, to the violation of an interest protected under public security law if the situation were to unfold without intervention (cf. BVerfGE 115, 320 <364> – *Profiling*; BVerwGE 116, 347 <351>). […]

At the same time, constitutional law does not *per se* prevent the legislator from recognising grounds for interferences that, depending on the type of task and measure in question, differ from the traditional concepts of security law focused on averting specific, immediate or present dangers. Rather, the legislator may subject state action that aims to prevent criminal acts from being committed in the first place to less stringent limits in certain domains by lowering the standard of foreseeability regarding the causal chain [in the respective danger situation]. Yet the statutory basis of the measure constituting an interference must in any case require the existence of a sufficiently identifiable danger (*hinreichend konkretisierte Gefahr*), in the sense that there be at least factual indications that a specific danger to the protected legal interests may emerge. Assumptions based on general experience alone are not sufficient for justifying an interference. Rather, specific facts must be established that, in the individual case, support the prognosis that a chain of events leading to a violation of one of the protected legal interests will occur and that the situation can be attributed [to the person against whom the measure is directed] (cf. BVerfGE 110, 33 <56 and 57, 61>; 113, 348 <377 and 378>). A sufficiently identifiable danger in this sense may already exist even where the causal chain leading to the damage is not yet foreseeable with sufficient probability, provided that there are already specific facts indicating an impending danger (*drohende Gefahr*) to an exceptionally significant legal interest in the individual case. Firstly, it must at least be possible to determine, based on these facts, the type of incident that might occur, and that it will occur within a foreseeable timeframe; secondly, the facts must indicate the involvement of specific persons whose identity is known at least to such an extent that the surveillance measure can be targeted at and for the most part limited to them (BVerfGE 120, 274 <328 f.> – *Remote Searches*; 125, 260 <330 f.> – *Data Retention*). With regard to terrorism, it must be taken into account that terrorist acts are often planned far in advance and carried out by lone individuals who have no criminal record, and that it is often not foreseeable where and how they will be carried out. In this regard, surveillance measures may be authorised even in cases where it is neither possible to determine what type of incident might occur nor to determine the timeframe in which it might occur, provided that the individual conduct of a person establishes the specific probability that they will commit some form of terrorist act in the not so distant future. For example, this might be the case where a person enters the Federal Republic of Germany after having attended a terrorist training camp abroad.

113 By contrast, the weight of interference resulting from covert police surveillance is not sufficiently taken into account where statutory provisions authorise the measure on grounds so precautionary in nature that the existence of a specific danger to the protected legal interests need no longer be foreseeable at all, not even with regard to its basic characteristics. Given the severity of interference, shifting the statutory threshold for exercising the powers in question to a purely precautionary stage is incompatible with the Constitution if it means that such measures could be carried out on grounds of relatively vague indications of possible dangers. [...]

114 c) Constitutional law gives rise to a tiered system of requirements governing the extent to which surveillance measures may be carried out in respect of a target person's contacts where the affected persons themselves are not subject to any special responsibility, neither in the form of responsibility for actions or circumstances causing a danger nor in the form of responsibility as suspect of a crime.

115 Measures involving searches of information technology systems or the surveillance of private homes may only directly target persons that are responsible for impending or acute dangers (cf. BVerfGE 109, 279 <351, 352> – *Surveillance of Private Homes*; 120, 274 <329, 334> – *Remote Searches*). These measures constitute such deep intrusions into the private sphere that they may not be extended to other persons as surveillance targets. Yet it is not constitutionally objectionable for measures targeting the persons responsible to also cover third parties, as long as this is unavoidable (cf. BVerfGE 109, 279 <352 et seq.> – *Surveillance of Private Homes*). Thus, the surveillance of the home of a third party may be authorised if it can be assumed, based on specific facts, that the target person will be present while the measure is carried out, will conduct conversations relevant to the investigation, and the surveillance of the target person's own home would not in itself be sufficient to investigate the case (cf. BVerfGE 109, 279 <353, 355 and 356> – *Surveillance of Private Homes*). Likewise, a remote search may be extended to the information technology systems of third parties if factual indications suggest that the target person uses such systems to store information relevant to the investigation, and that a remote search limited to the target person's own information technology system would not be sufficient for achieving the aims of the investigation.

116 The ordering of other covert surveillance measures directly targeting third parties is not *per se* impermissible. It is conceivable that surveillance measures may be

directed against persons associated with the target person, for instance (selected) persons belonging to the target person's contacts or persons used as messengers. Such surveillance powers can be justified by the purpose of public security as an objective interest, and by the interest in establishing the truth in criminal investigations. Where these surveillance measures are extended to third parties, they are subject to strict proportionality requirements and may only be authorised if there is a special individual link between the affected person and the danger or crime being investigated. [...]

2. In procedural terms, too, the principle of proportionality gives rise to certain general requirements. For the most part, the investigation and surveillance measures in question entail very intrusive interferences, and it is to be expected that they will be carried out covertly and also record highly private information; it is therefore imperative that measures be in principle subject to prior review by an independent authority, for example in the form of a judicial warrant (cf. in this regard ECtHR, *Klass and Others v. Germany*, Judgment of 6 September 1978, no. 5029/71, § 56; ECtHR (GC), *Zakharov v. Russia*, Judgment of 4 December 2015, no. 47143/06, §§ 258, 275; ECtHR, *Szabó and Vissy v. Hungary*, Judgment of 12 January 2016, no. 37138/14,§ 77). For measures relating to the surveillance of private homes, this requirement already results from Art. 13(3) and (4) of the Basic Law (cf. in this respect BVerfGE 109, 279 <357 *et seq.*> – *Surveillance of Private Homes*); for other measures, it directly follows from the principle of proportionality (cf. BVerfGE 120, 274 <331 *et seq.*> – *Remote Searches*; 125, 260 <337 *et seq.*> – *Data Retention*).

The legislator must set out the requirement of independent prior review in specific and clear provisions combined with strict standards regarding the content and the reasons of the warrant issued by the court. [...]

3. In addition to the aforementioned constitutional standards relating to the general prerequisites for exercising such powers, the respective fundamental rights in conjunction with Art. 1(1) of the Basic Law give rise to further requirements for the protection of the core of private life where surveillance measures entail particularly intrusive interferences.

a) The constitutional protection of the core of private life guarantees the individual a domain of highly personal life that is free from surveillance. This protection is rooted in the respective fundamental rights affected by surveillance measures in conjunction with Art. 1(1) of the Basic Law and ensures a human dignity core that is beyond the reach of the state and provides fundamental rights safeguards against such measures. Even exceptionally significant interests of the general public cannot justify an interference with this domain of private life that is absolutely protected (cf. BVerfGE 109, 279 <313> – *Surveillance of Private Homes*; established case-law).

121 The free development of one's personality within the core of private life encompasses the possibility of expressing internal processes such as emotions and feelings, as well as reflections, views and experiences of a highly personal nature (cf. BVerfGE 109, 279 <313> – *Surveillance of Private Homes*; 120, 274 <335> – *Remote Searches*; established case-law). Protection is afforded particularly to non-public communication with persons enjoying the highest level of personal trust, conducted with the reasonable expectation that no surveillance is taking place, which is especially the case in a private home. Persons enjoying this highest level of trust include, in particular, spouses or partners, siblings and direct relatives in ascending or descending line, especially if they live in the same household, and can also include defence lawyers, doctors, clerics and close personal friends (cf. BVerfGE 109, 279 <321 *et seq.*> – *Surveillance of Private Homes*). This group only partially overlaps with the group of persons entitled to refuse to give evidence. Such conversations do no lose their overall highly personal character merely because they concern both highly personal and everyday matters (cf. BVerfGE 109, 279 <330> – *Surveillance of Private Homes*; 113, 348 <391 and 392>).

122 However, communication that directly concerns criminal conduct does not form part of this protected domain, not even when it also touches on highly personal matters. The discussion and planning of criminal acts is not part of the core of private life, but belongs to the social domain (cf. BVerfGE 80, 367 <375> – *Diary-Like Notes*; 109, 279 <319 and 320, 328> – *Surveillance of Private Homes*; 113, 348 <391>). This does not mean that the core protection were subject to a general balancing against public security interests. A highly personal conversation is not excluded from the core of private life simply because it might provide insights that could be helpful for the investigation of criminal acts or the averting of dangers to public security. Notes or statements made in the course of a conversation that only reveal, for instance, inner impressions and feelings and do not contain any indications pointing to specific criminal acts do not simply become relevant to the public because they might reveal the reasons or motives for criminal conduct (cf. BVerfGE 109, 279 <319> – *Surveillance of Private Homes*). Furthermore, despite having some link to criminal conduct, situations in which individuals are in fact encouraged to admit wrongdoing or to prepare for the consequences thereof, such as confessions or confidential conversations with a psychotherapist or defence lawyer, are part of the highly personal domain, which is completely beyond the reach of the state (cf. BVerfGE 109, 279 <322> – *Surveillance of Private Homes*). However, a sufficient link to the social domain does exist where conversations –

No. 44 – The Federal Criminal Police Office Act

even conversations with confidants – directly refer to specific criminal acts (cf. BVerfGE 109, 279 <319> – *Surveillance of Private Homes*).

b) Any type of surveillance measure must respect the core of private life. If the measure in question typically leads to the collection of data relating to the core, the legislator must enact clear provisions that ensure effective protection (cf. BVerfGE 109, 279 <318 and 319> – *Surveillance of Private Homes*; 113, 348 <390 and 391>; 120, 274 <335 et seq.> – *Remote Searches*). Where the powers in question do not entail a risk of core violations, it is not necessary to enact such provisions. Yet when exercising those powers, too, limits directly arising from the Constitution regarding access to highly personal information must be respected in the individual case.

c) The protection of the core of private life is absolute and must not be made conditional upon a balancing against security interests under the principle of proportionality (cf. BVerfGE 109, 279 <314> – *Surveillance of Private Homes*; 120, 274 <339> – *Remote Searches*; established case-law). Yet this does not mean that every instance in which highly personal information is collected amounts to a violation of the Constitution or of human dignity. Given that uncertainties are inherent in measures and prognoses carried out by security authorities in the context of their duties, an unintended intrusion upon the core of private life in the course of a surveillance measure cannot always be prevented from the outset (cf. BVerfGE 120, 274 <337 and 338> – *Remote Searches*). However, the Constitution does require that surveillance powers be designed in such a way that the core of private life be respected as an absolute limit, which cannot be freely circumvented on a case-by-case basis.

aa) Thus, it is absolutely impermissible for the state to make the core of private life a target of investigations and to use information from the core in any way, including as the basis for further investigations. Targeted measures reaching into the highly private sphere – which does not include the discussion of criminal acts (see C IV 3 a above) – are ruled out from the outset, even if such measures could produce information that is helpful for the investigation. The protection of the core may not be subject to a balancing of interests in the individual case.

bb) Furthermore, it also follows that the protection of the core must be taken into account on two levels when carrying out surveillance measures. Firstly, at the stage of data collection, safeguards must be put in place to prevent the unintended collection of information relating to the core where possible. Secondly, at the stage of subsequent data analysis and use, the consequences of an intrusion upon the core of private life that could not be prevented despite such safeguards must be strictly minimised (cf. BVerfGE 120, 274 <337 et seq.> – *Remote Searches*; 129, 208 <245 and 246> – *The Telecommunications Surveillance Revision Act*).

127 d) In this context, the legislator may design the protection of the core of private life differently for different surveillance measures, depending on the type of power and its proximity to the absolutely protected domain of private life (cf. BVerfGE 120, 274 <337>– *Remote Searches*; 129, 208 <245> – *The Telecommunications Surveillance Revision Act*). In doing so, it must, however, provide for safeguards at both stages.

128 At the data collection stage, with regard to measures with a high risk of core violations, a preliminary assessment must ensure that situations or conversations relating to the core are excluded in advance to the extent that this is feasible with reasonable effort (cf. BVerfGE 109, 279 <318, 320, 324> – *Surveillance of Private Homes*; 113, 348 <391 and 392>; 120, 274 <338> – *Remote Searches*). With regard to conversations with persons enjoying the highest level of personal trust, circumstances that typically indicate a confidential setting may warrant the presumption that the communication is part of the core and must not be subject to surveillance (cf. BVerfGE 109, 279 <321 et seq.> – *Surveillance of Private Homes*; 129, 208 <247> – *The Telecommunications Surveillance Revision Act*). In the design of the statutory framework, the legislator may allow for a rebuttal of this presumption, in particular on the grounds of indications, in the individual case, that criminal acts will be discussed. By contrast, the presumption that a conversation is highly confidential cannot be rebutted solely on the grounds that, apart from highly personal matters, everyday matters will be discussed as well (cf. BVerfGE 109, 279 <330> – *Surveillance of Private Homes*). In any case, the measure must be discontinued when it becomes apparent that the surveillance is intruding upon the core of private life (cf. BVerfGE 109, 279 <318, 324, 331> – *Surveillance of Private Homes*; 113, 348 <392>; 120, 274 <338> – *Remote Searches*).

129 At the stage of data analysis and use, the legislator must provide for cases in which it was not possible to avoid collecting information relating to the core. In this regard, the legislator must generally require that the collected data be screened by an independent body that removes information relating to the core prior to use by the security authorities (cf. BVerfGE 109, 279 <331 et seq.> – *Surveillance of Private Homes*; 120, 274 <338 and 339> – *Remote Searches*). However, the procedural safeguards that are necessary under constitutional law do not, in every type of case, require that further independent bodies other than the investigating state authorities be established (cf. BVerfGE 129, 208 <250> – *The Telecommunications Surveillance Revision Act*). The necessity of such a screening depends on the type, as well as, if applicable, the design of the power in question. The more reliable the safeguards for preventing the collection of information relating to the core at the stage of data collection, the more the requirement of a screening by an independent body becomes dispensable, and vice versa. This does not alter the fact that the

No. 44 – The Federal Criminal Police Office Act

legislator may enact the statutory bases necessary to provide the investigation authorities of the state with the means to take action at short notice in exceptional cases of danger requiring immediate action (*Gefahr im Verzug*). In any case, the legislator must provide for the immediate deletion of any highly personal data collected and for mechanisms preventing any use of such data. The deletion must be documented in a manner that makes subsequent review possible (cf. BVerfGE 109, 279 <318 and 319, 332 and 333> – *Surveillance of Private Homes*; 113, 348 <392>; 120, 274 <337, 339> – *Remote Searches*).

4. The combined effect of the different surveillance measures gives rise to distinct constitutional limits. Surveillance taking place over an extended period of time and covering almost every movement and expression of [private] life of the person under surveillance, which could be used as the basis for creating a personality profile, is incompatible with human dignity (cf. BVerfGE 109, 279 <323> – *Surveillance of Private Homes*; 112, 304 <319>; 130, 1 <24>; established case-law). The use of modern investigation methods, especially methods that cannot be perceived by affected persons, requires coordination on the part of security authorities to ensure, with regard to the potential harm inherent in 'additive' interferences with fundamental rights, that the overall extent of surveillance remains limited (cf. BVerfGE 112, 304 <319 and 320>). This applies without prejudice to the limits on data sharing between authorities arising from the principle of purpose limitation (see D I below).

130

5. Based on proportionality considerations, distinct constitutional limits to covert surveillance measures may also arise with regard to certain groups of professionals or other persons whose activities are recognised as meriting special confidentiality protection under the Constitution. The legislator must ensure that the authorities respect these limits when ordering and carrying out surveillance measures.

131

[...]

132-133

6. Moreover, the principle of proportionality sets requirements regarding transparency, individual legal protection, and administrative oversight (BVerfGE 133, 277 <365 para. 204> – *Counter-Terrorism Database Act I*; cf. also BVerfGE 65, 1 <44 et seq.> – *Census*; 100, 313 <361, 364> – *The Article 10 Act*; 109, 279 <363 and 364> – *Surveillance of Private Homes*; 125, 260 <334 et seq.> – *Data Retention*; established case-law [...]). The requirements applicable in this respect are derived from the affected fundamental right in conjunction with Art. 19(4) of the Basic Law (cf. BVerfGE 125, 260 <335> – *Data Retention*; 133, 277 <366 para. 206> – *Counter Terrorism Database Act I*).

134

The transparency of data collection and processing serves to contribute to securing trust and legal certainty, and to ensure that data processing [by the state] remains

135

subject to a democratic discourse (BVerfGE 133, 277 <366 para. 206> – *Counter-Terrorism Database Act I*). […]

136 a) Another requirement for the proportionate design of the surveillance powers in question is a statutory notification requirement. Given that surveillance measures must be carried out covertly in order to achieve their purpose, the legislator must ensure that the affected persons are generally notified, at least *ex post*, of the surveillance measures to allow the possibility of seeking individual legal protection in accordance with Art. 19(4) of the Basic Law. The legislator may provide for exemptions by balancing the interest in being notified against the constitutionally protected legal interests of third parties. The exemptions must, however, be limited to what is absolutely necessary (BVerfGE 125, 260 <336> – *Data Retention*). […] If there are compelling reasons preventing *ex post* notification, this must be confirmed by a judge and reviewed at regular intervals (BVerfGE 125, 260 <336 and 337> – *Data Retention*).

137 b) Given that the affected persons cannot assess with certainty whether and on what scale surveillance measures are carried out against them, the legislator must provide for rights to information [on the part of affected persons] that complement the state's powers to carry out information-related interferences. Restrictions of these rights are only permissible if they serve conflicting interests that outweigh the interest of affected persons in obtaining information. […]

138 c) In light of Art. 19(4) of the Basic Law, a proportionate design of surveillance measures further requires that following notification, affected persons be afforded a reasonable (*zumutbar*) possibility to seek judicial review of the measure's lawfulness (in this respect cf. also Arts. 51 and 52 of the Proposal for a Directive of the European Parliament and of the Council on the protection of natural persons with regard to the processing of personal data by competent authorities for the purposes of the prevention, investigation, detection or prosecution of criminal offences or the execution of criminal penalties, and on the free movement of such data, […]).

139 […]

140 d) With regard to covert surveillance measures, the transparency of data collection and processing as well as individual legal protection can only be ensured to a very limited degree, which is why the guarantee of effective administrative oversight is all the more significant. With regard to surveillance measures that reach deep into the private sphere, the principle of proportionality therefore gives rise to stringent requirements regarding the effective design of the oversight regime both at statutory level and in administrative practice (cf. BVerfGE 133, 277 <369 para. 214> – *Counter-Terrorism Database Act I*).

No. 44 – The Federal Criminal Police Office Act

The guarantee of effective administrative oversight requires the existence of a body vested with effective powers, such as, under current law, the Federal Data Protection Officer (cf., foundationally, BVerfGE 65, 1 <46> – *Census*). [...]
e) [...]
7. The general requirements deriving from the principle of proportionality also entail deletion requirements (cf. BVerfGE 65, 1 <46> – *Census*; 133, 277 <366 para. 206> – *Counter-Terrorism Database Act I*; established case-law). These serve to ensure that the use of personal data remains limited to the purposes justifying the data processing measures, and that data can no longer be used once these purposes have been achieved. The deletion of the data must be documented to ensure transparency and oversight.

V.

The challenged surveillance powers under public security law fail to satisfy, in various respects, the constitutional requirements set out above with regard to the statutory prerequisites for the respective interferences.
1. § 20g(1) to (3) of the Federal Criminal Police Office Act is only in part compatible with the Constitution.
a) § 20g(1) of the Federal Criminal Police Office Act permits surveillance outside of private homes using the special means of data collection defined in greater detail in § 20g(2) of the Federal Criminal Police Office Act. It thus authorises interferences with the right to informational self-determination (Art. 2(1) in conjunction with Art. 1(1) of the Basic Law) on the part of the Federal Criminal Police Office.
[...]
b) With regard to the weight of interference, § 20g(1) and (2) of the Federal Criminal Police Office Act covers a wide spectrum, also encompassing intrusive interferences.
The provision permits surveillance outside of private homes using the means listed in § 20g(2) of the Federal Criminal Police Office Act. These include in particular surveillance for extended periods, covert image recordings, the covert monitoring of non-public communication, the installation of tracking devices or the use of police informants and undercover police investigators.
The weight of interference of these measures can vary greatly. It ranges from interferences of low and medium weight, such as the taking of individual photos or simple observation for a limited time, to serious interferences such as long-term monitoring by means of covert audio and image recordings of a person. Particularly when these measures are combined with the aim to register and audio-visually record as many statements and movements [of the target person] as possible with

	the help of modern technology, they can reach deep into the private sphere and thus constitute interferences of particularly great weight.
152	Like the averting of violations of other weighty legal interests or the prosecution of considerable criminal acts, the public interest in the effective prevention of terrorism can justify such interferences (see C II 3 a above), provided that the powers in question are designed in a proportionate manner. This is not fully the case here.
153-161	c) [...]
162	d) § 20g(1) no. 2 of the Federal Criminal Police Office Act [...] does not satisfy the constitutional requirements. The statutory prerequisites for carrying out the interferences neither satisfy the principle of specificity nor the principle of proportionality in the strict sense.
163	aa) As an addition to § 20g(1) no. 1 of the Federal Criminal Police Office Act, which is limited to averting dangers to public security, § 20g(1) no. 2 of the Federal Criminal Police Office Act extends the grounds for interference. The legislator's intent in creating the latter provision was that the measures should set in at an earlier stage, serving the prevention of crime.
164	Based on the standards set out above, the Constitution neither prevents the legislator from limiting, in principle, the grounds for security measures to the averting of specific dangers – in line with the traditional understanding of this concept –, nor does it require the legislator to stick to these traditionally recognised grounds. However, even measures aimed at preventing criminal acts require a prognosis that is based on facts, rather than merely on general experience, indicating a specific danger. In principle, it must at least be possible to determine the type of incident that might occur, and that it will occur within a foreseeable timeframe (cf. BVerfGE 110, 33 <56 and 57, 61>; 113, 348 <377 and 378>; 120, 274 <328 and 329> – *Remote Searches*; 125, 260 <330> – *Data Retention*). In respect of terrorist acts, the legislator may also recognise alternative grounds for carrying out surveillance measures where the individual conduct of a person establishes the specific probability that they will commit terrorist acts in the not so distant future (see C IV 1 b above). The requirements to this effect must be set out in clear statutory provisions.
165	bb) § 20g(1) no. 2 of the Federal Criminal Police Office Act does not satisfy these constitutional standards. While the provision does require, as grounds for the measure, the possibility that terrorist offences will be committed, the prerequisites for establishing a prognosis to this effect are too lenient. The provision does not prevent the authorities from working with a prognosis based solely on general experience. [...] The provision therefore does not set sufficiently specific criteria for the authorities and courts to work with and could give rise to disproportionately broad measures.

No. 44 – The Federal Criminal Police Office Act

e) [...] 166-169

f) The procedural requirements set out in § 20g(3) of the Federal Criminal Police Office Act do not satisfy the principle of proportionality in all respects. 170

aa) [...] 171

bb) § 20g(3) of the Federal Criminal Police Office Act does not sufficiently give effect to the requirement of prior judicial authorisation (*Richtervorbehalt*) deriving from the principle of proportionality. 172

[...] 173-174

g) Moreover, § 20g of the Federal Criminal Police Office Act fails to satisfy constitutional requirements to the extent that it does not provide for any protection of the core of private life. 175

§ 20g of the Federal Criminal Police Office Act authorises surveillance measures of varying quality and proximity to the private sphere. By also permitting long-term image recordings and long-term interception and recording of non-public communication, the provision authorises surveillance measures that typically intrude deeply into the private sphere. It is true that all these measures concern surveillance taking place outside of private homes. Yet this does not alter the fact that there is a certain risk that these measures will likely result in the recording of highly confidential situations – be it in the car, be it sitting away from the crowds in a restaurant, be it on a secluded stroll – that can be attributed to the core of private life [...]. 176

At least some of the powers laid down in that provision thus have a close link to the core of private life, which requires that protection of this core be guaranteed by an express statutory provision. The legislator must provide for clear safeguards protecting the core both at the stage of data collection and at the stage of data analysis and use (see C IV 3 c bb, d above). Given that such safeguards are lacking, § 20g(1) and (2) of the Federal Criminal Police Office Act is not compatible with the Constitution in that respect either. 177

2. § 20h of the Federal Criminal Police Office Act, too, does not fully satisfy constitutional requirements. 178

a) § 20h of the Federal Criminal Police Office Act permits acoustic and visual surveillance in private homes. It thus constitutes an interference with Art. 13(1) of the Basic Law. 179

By authorising the surveillance of private homes, the provision gives rise to interferences with fundamental rights that are particularly serious. It permits the state to intrude into spaces that are a person's private refuge and that are closely linked to human dignity (cf. BVerfGE 109, 279 <313 and 314> – *Surveillance of Private Homes*). This does not rule out the possibility of surveillance, as set out in Art. 13(3) and (4) of the Basic Law. It is possible to justify such measures for the 180 purposes of averting dangers posed by international terrorism (see C II 3 a above). Yet this is subject to particularly strict requirements, which § 20h of the Federal Criminal Police Office Act does not satisfy in every respect.

181-185 b) [...]
186 c) [...]
187-188 aa) [...]
189-190 bb) [...]
191 cc) The provision is incompatible with Art. 13(1) and (4) of the Basic Law insofar as it authorises the surveillance of private homes directed at a target person's contacts or associates (§ 20h(1) no. 1 c of the Federal Criminal Police Office Act). To this extent, it is disproportionate.
192 The surveillance of private homes is a particularly serious interference that intrudes deeply into the private sphere. The effects of such a measure are inherently more severe than those of surveillance measures outside of private homes or telecommunications surveillance. Its weight of interference is paralleled only by interferences targeting information technology systems. Thus, this type of surveillance only meets the requirement of appropriateness if it is exclusively restricted from the outset to conversations of the target person responsible for the danger in question (cf. BVerfGE 109, 279 <355> – *Surveillance of Private Homes*). In light of the severity of interference, it is disproportionate and impermissible to directly target third parties with this type of surveillance measures (see C IV 1 c above).
193 This does not alter the fact that surveillance of the target person's private home may also affect third parties in cases where this is unavoidable (cf. § 20h(2) third sentence of the Federal Criminal Police Office Act). It may even be permissible, as discussed above, to carry out surveillance of the private homes of third parties where this serves to monitor the target person.
194 d) The procedural design of the powers to conduct surveillance of private homes does not raise constitutional concerns. In particular, the provision contains a requirement that the measure be authorised by a judge. [...]
195 [...]
196 e) However, the protection of the core of private life provided for in § 20h(5) of the Federal Criminal Police Office Act is not fully in line with constitutional law. It does not satisfy the requirements deriving from Art. 13(1) in conjunction with Art. 1(1) of the Basic Law.
197 aa) Since the surveillance of private homes reaches deep into the private sphere and intrudes upon one's personal refuge, which is of fundamental importance for safeguarding human dignity, the constitutional requirements for protecting the core of private life are particularly strict (BVerfGE 109, 279 <313 et seq., 318 et seq., 328 et seq.> – *Surveillance of Private Homes*).

No. 44 – The Federal Criminal Police Office Act

(1) Particular requirements apply at the data collection stage. When assessing whether there is a probability that highly private situations will be recorded, certain presumptions apply in the interest of an effective protection of the core of private life (cf. BVerfGE 109, 279 <320> – *Surveillance of Private Homes*). Accordingly, conversations taking place in private spaces with persons enjoying the highest level of personal trust (see C IV 3 a above) are presumed to belong to the core of private life and may not be the target of surveillance (cf. BVerfGE 109, 279 <321 *et seq.*> – *Surveillance of Private Homes*). Automatic long-term surveillance of spaces in which such conversations are to be expected is therefore impermissible (cf. BVerfGE 109, 279 <324> – *Surveillance of Private Homes*). This presumption can be rebutted when specific indications suggest that certain conversations are, within the meaning of the standards set out above, directly linked to criminal conduct – where such a link exists, it is not cancelled out even when the conversations in question are mixed with highly personal content; the presumption can also be rebutted by indications suggesting that the overall nature of the conversation is not actually highly confidential. The mere expectation, however, that a conversation will concern both highly confidential and everyday matters is by itself not sufficient (cf. BVerfGE 109, 279 <330> – *Surveillance of Private Homes*, see C IV 3 a, d above).

198

Thus, if a surveillance measure is likely to intrude upon the core of private life, the measure must not be carried out. Yet if there are no such indications that there will be an intrusion upon the highly personal domain – also taking into account the above rules of presumption –, the measures may be carried out. However, where the measures, despite no prior indications, result in the recording of highly confidential situations, they must be discontinued immediately (cf. BVerfGE 109, 279 <320, 323 and 324> – *Surveillance of Private Homes*). If it is not clear whether a situation is highly confidential – for example due to language barriers –, or if there are specific indications suggesting that, along with highly private thoughts, criminal acts will also be discussed, surveillance in the form of automatic recordings may be continued.

199

(2) Specific constitutional requirements also arise at the stage of data analysis and use. It must be ensured that the information obtained through the surveillance measure will be screened by an independent body. This screening serves both as a review of lawfulness as well as a filter mechanism to remove highly confidential data, so that – to the greatest extent possible – such data is not disclosed to the security authorities. The independent body must be provided with all data stemming from the surveillance of private homes (cf. BVerfGE 109, 279 <333 and 334> – *Surveillance of Private Homes* [...]).

200

201 Moreover, a prohibition of data use and deletion requirements, together with obligations to document the data deletion, must be put in place for cases where, despite all safeguards, information relating to the core of private life is nonetheless collected (see C IV 3 c bb, d, 7 above).

202 bb) Measured against these standards, § 20h(5) of the Federal Criminal Police Office Act satisfies the constitutional requirements at the stage of data collection, but not at the stage of data use.

203-205 [...]

206 3. With regard to electronic profiling and searches pursuant to § 20j of the Federal Criminal Police Office Act, the statutory prerequisites for interference are constitutionally unobjectionable.

207 [...]

208 4. If interpreted in conformity with the Constitution, § 20k of the Federal Criminal Police Office Act [which governs remote searches of information technology systems] is constitutional with regard to the general prerequisites for interference set out therein. However, the provision lacks sufficient safeguards to protect the core of private life in line with constitutional requirements.

209-210 a) [...]

211 b) If interpreted in conformity with the Constitution, the requirements of § 20k(1) and (2) of the Federal Criminal Police Office Act regarding access to information technology systems satisfy the constitutional requirements.

212 aa) Interferences with the right to protection of the confidentiality and integrity of information technology systems are subject to strict conditions (cf. BVerfGE 120, 274 <322 et seq., 326 et seq.> – *Remote Searches*). Specifically, the measures must be based on factual indications that a specific impending danger (*drohende konkrete Gefahr*) to an exceptionally significant legal interest exists in the individual case. § 20k(1) of the Federal Criminal Police Office Act satisfies this requirement. [...]

213 However, a restrictive interpretation in conformity with the Constitution is merited with regard to § 20k(1) second sentence of the Federal Criminal Police Office Act. That provision opens up the possibility of carrying out measures at a precautionary stage, prior to a specific danger, if specific facts indicate an impending danger of a terrorist act in the individual case; this must be interpreted to the effect that such measures are only permitted if the facts allow a determination as to the type of incident that might occur, and that it will occur in a foreseeable timeframe; the facts must also indicate the involvement of specific persons whose identity is known at least to such an extent that the surveillance measures can be targeted at and for the most part limited to them (BVerfGE 120, 274 <329> – *Remote Searches*). Sufficient grounds for carrying out the measures also exist if neither the type of incident nor the expected timeframe are foreseeable yet, but the individual conduct

No. 44 – The Federal Criminal Police Office Act

of the targeted person establishes the specific probability that they will commit terrorist acts in the not so distant future (see C IV 1 b above).
The wording of § 20k(1) second sentence of the Federal Criminal Police Office Act closely resembles the wording adopted by the Federal Constitutional Court in past decisions (cf. BVerfGE 120, 274 <329> – *Remote Searches*), which is why it can be assumed that the legislator intended to use the Court's case-law as point of reference. Based thereon, it is possible to interpret the provision in conformity with the Constitution. 214

bb) [...] 215
c) [...] 216
d) The safeguards to protect the core of private life, however, do not satisfy the constitutional requirements in every respect. 217
aa) Given that covert access to information technology systems typically entails the risk of recording highly confidential data, and thus bears a particularly close connection to the core of private life, it requires express statutory safeguards for the protection of the core (cf. BVerfGE 120, 274 <335 et seq.> – *Remote Searches*). These constitutional requirements are not in every respect identical to those applicable to the surveillance of private homes, as they shift the protection away from the collection stage to the subsequent stage of analysis and use (cf. BVerfGE 120, 274 <337> – *Remote Searches*). The reason for this lies in the specific nature of access to information technology systems. In this context, [and in contrast to the surveillance of private homes], protective safeguards against violations of the core of private life are not primarily aimed at preventing the recording and storing of a fleeting, highly personal and confidential moment in a private space, but rather at preventing the retrieval of highly confidential information from within an existing comprehensive data pool of digital information that, taken as a whole, is typically not of the same private nature as behaviour or communication in one's home. In this case, surveillance does not take place in the form of a chronological sequence in different locations, but rather in the form of access through spy software, which, as far as access as such is concerned, offers only two alternatives: full access or no access at all. 218

In light of this, the constitutional standards for the protection of the core of private life are somewhat relaxed at the stage of data collection. Nevertheless, even at that stage, it must be ensured that any collection of information attributed to the core is refrained from to the extent that this is possible from a technical and investigative perspective. Available technical means must be used to implement such protection; where it is possible, through technical means, to identify and isolate highly confidential information, access to this information is prohibited (cf. BVerfGE 120, 274 <338> – *Remote Searches*). 219

220 If, however, data relating to the core cannot be filtered out before or at the time of data collection, access to the information technology system is nevertheless permissible even if there is a probability that highly personal data, too, might incidentally be collected. In this respect, the legislator must take into account the need for protection of affected persons by putting in place safeguards at the stage of analysis and use, and by minimising the effects of such access. In this respect, the screening by an independent body that removes information relating to the core before the Federal Criminal Police Office can obtain knowledge thereof and use it is of particular significance (cf. BVerfGE 120, 274 <338 and 339> – *Remote Searches*).

221 bb) § 20k(7) of the Federal Criminal Police Office Act does not fully satisfy these requirements.

222-226 [...]

227 5. § 20l of the Federal Criminal Police Office Act is only in part compatible with the Constitution.

228 a) § 20l of the Federal Criminal Police Office Act governs telecommunications surveillance, providing a statutory basis for interferences with Art. 10(1) of the Basic Law. [...]

229 Telecommunications surveillance entails serious interferences (cf. BVerfGE 113, 348 <382>; 129, 208 <240> – *The Telecommunications Surveillance Revision Act*). Nevertheless, for the purpose of averting dangers from international terrorism, such interferences can be justified (see C II 3 a above) provided that the respective grounds for carrying out the interferences are restricted in a proportionate manner. Yet § 20l of the Federal Criminal Police Office Act only in part ensures that such restrictions are put in place.

230 b) § 20l(1) nos. 1 to 4 of the Federal Criminal Police Office Act provides different grounds for carrying out interferences [in the form of telecommunications surveillance] vis-à-vis different target persons. Not all of these grounds satisfy the constitutional requirements.

231 The authorisation to carry out surveillance measures against persons responsible for a danger under police law pursuant to § 20l(1) no. 1 of the Federal Criminal Police Office Act, which serves to protect qualified legal interests and has the sole purpose of averting acute dangers, does not raise constitutional concerns.

232 However, the extension of telecommunications surveillance pursuant to § 20l(1) no. 2 of the Federal Criminal Police Office Act to persons who, based on specific facts, are believed to be involved in the preparation of terrorist crimes is not compatible with the Constitution given that the grounds laid down therein are not sufficiently restricted. The provision shifts interference powers to a purely precautionary stage of preventing crime, before an actual danger arises; with its vague

and open phrasing, it violates the principle of specificity and is disproportionately broad. [...]

[...] 233

c) [...] 234

d) [...] 235

e) The provisions on the protection of the core of private life pursuant to § 20l(6) of the Federal Criminal Police Office Act are for the most part compatible with the Constitution. 236

aa) Telecommunications surveillance constitutes a serious interference that has a particularly close connection to the core. Given that content-related surveillance measures intercept all kinds of telecommunications-based exchanges, they typically entail the risk of also collecting highly private communication that falls within the protected core of private life. In this respect, special statutory safeguards must be put in place (cf. BVerfGE 113, 348 <390 and 391>; 129, 208 <245> – *The Telecommunications Surveillance Revision Act*). 237

However, in terms of its overall nature, telecommunications surveillance is not to the same extent characterised by an intrusion into the private sphere as the surveillance of private homes or remote searches of information technology systems (cf. BVerfGE 113, 348 <391>). It covers any kind of communication in any situation, as long as it is transmitted by technical means. In fact, only a small part of the contents that could be accessed by this type of surveillance measure qualifies as highly confidential; however, the risk of intercepting highly confidential communication is not an inherent feature of this surveillance measure – unlike in the case of the surveillance of a person's private refuge in a home. In that respect, telecommunications surveillance also differs from remote searches of information technology systems. [...] Its potentially close link to the core of private life mainly stems from the fact that it may also result in the interception of highly personal communication between close confidants (cf. BVerfGE 129, 208 <247> – *The Telecommunications Surveillance Revision Act*). 238

The legislator may reflect these differences by providing for less strict requirements regarding the protection of the core. However, in this case, too, it must be assessed at the collection stage whether it is likely that highly private conversations will be intercepted and, if this is the case, the surveillance of such conversations must be prohibited. Where such conversations cannot be identified in advance with sufficient probability, the surveillance measures may be carried out, including – subject to a proportionality assessment – in the form of automatic long-term surveillance ordered in the individual case (cf. BVerfGE 113, 348 <391 and 392>; 129, 208 <245> – *The Telecommunications Surveillance Revision Act*). 239

240 As for ensuring protection of the core at subsequent stages, the law must provide for prohibitions to use data [relating to the core] as evidence and for deletion requirements, including a requirement that deletion be documented; by contrast, requiring a screening by an independent body is not always necessary in these cases (cf. BVerfGE 129, 208 <249> – *The Telecommunications Surveillance Revision Act*). Regarding telecommunications surveillance, the legislator may in fact make such screening conditional upon whether and to what extent it is likely that the surveillance measures will also touch on highly private information. This may overlap with the safeguards put in place at the data collection stage.

241 In this regard, the legislator has considerable latitude. […]

242 bb) § 20l(6) of the Federal Criminal Police Office Act for the most part satisfies these requirements.

243-246 […]

247-252 6. […]

VI.

253 Measured against the general constitutional standards applicable to all investigatory and surveillance measures, too, the challenged powers are not compatible with the Constitution in several respects (see C IV 4 to 7 above). They require further provisions to ensure respect for the principle of proportionality.

254 1. It is not objectionable, however, that the Act does not contain an express provision that specifies in more detail the prohibition of sweeping surveillance with a view to the combined effect of the different powers (see C IV 4 above). Deriving from the principle of proportionality, the prohibition of sweeping surveillance serves to uphold the constitutionally required protection of the inalienable core of personality that is rooted in human dignity; when exercising surveillance powers, security authorities must observe this prohibition of their own accord (cf. BVerfGE 109, 279 <323> – *Surveillance of Private Homes*; 112, 304 <319>; 130, 1 <24>; established case-law). In this respect, it is not necessary to put in place further statutory provisions. […]

255 2. However, the level of protection afforded professional groups and other persons whose activities and communication merit special confidentiality protection under constitutional law does not satisfy the constitutional requirements in all respects.

256-258 […]

259 3. The provisions governing the guarantees of transparency, legal protection, and administrative oversight do not satisfy the constitutional requirements in all respects either.

260-262 a) […]

b) [...]

c) The design of administrative oversight does not satisfy the constitutional requirements (see C IV 6 d above). While the Federal Data Protection Act provides for oversight by the Federal Data Protection Officer, a body vested with adequate powers in that respect (cf. BVerfGE 133, 277 <370 para. 215> – *Counter-Terrorism Database Act I*), it does not lay down sufficient statutory requirements ensuring that audits are performed at regular intervals not exceeding approximately two years (cf. BVerfGE 133, 277 <370 and 371, para. 217> – *Counter-Terrorism Database Act I*).

[...]

d) [...]

4. The rules governing the deletion of obtained data in § 20v(6) of the Federal Criminal Police Office Act also do not satisfy the constitutional requirements in all respects.

[...]

D.

Insofar as the constitutional complaints are directed against the powers relating to further data uses and the sharing of data with domestic and foreign authorities, the complaints are well-founded in several respects.

I.

The constitutional requirements applicable to further use and sharing of data collected by the state are informed by the principles of purpose limitation and change in purpose (cf. BVerfGE 65, 1 <51, 62> – *Census*; 100, 313 <360 and 361, 389 and 390> – *The Article 10 Act*; 109, 279 <375 et seq.> – *Surveillance of Private Homes*; 110, 33 <73>; 120, 351 <368 and 369>; 125, 260 <333> – *Data Retention*; 130, 1 <33 and 34>; 133, 277 <372 et seq. paras. 225 and 226> – *Counter-Terrorism Database Act I*; established case-law).

Where the legislator permits the use of data beyond the specific grounds prompting the data collection and beyond the reasons justifying this data collection, it must create a separate statutory basis to that end (cf., e.g., BVerfGE 109, 279 <375 and 376> – *Surveillance of Private Homes*; 120, 351 <369>; 130, 1 <33>; established case-law). In this respect, the legislator may, firstly, provide for further use of the data within the purposes for which the data was collected. This approach is generally permissible under constitutional law provided that the legislator ensures that the further use of data adheres to the particular constitutional requirements set by the principle of purpose limitation (see 1 below). Secondly, the legislator may also allow a change in purpose. Given that this amounts to an authorisation for the use of data for new purposes, such a change in purpose is subject to specific constitutional requirements (see 2 below).

278 1. The legislator may allow that data is used beyond the specific investigation that prompted the data collection where this further use serves the same purpose as the original data collection. Such further use may be based on the reasons justifying the data collection in the first place and is thus not subject to the constitutional requirements applicable to a change in purpose.

279 a) The permissible scope of this type of further use depends on the statutory authorisation for the original data collection. The respective statutory basis determines the competent authority as well as the purposes and conditions of data collection, thereby defining the permissible scope of use. Accordingly, the use of the information thus obtained is not only limited to certain abstractly defined public tasks but actually subject to a purpose limitation determined by the collection purpose set out in the relevant statutory basis authorising the respective data collection. For that reason, further use of the data serving the purpose for which the data was originally collected is only permissible to the extent that the data is used by the same authority in relation to the same task and for the protection of the same legal interests as was the case with regard to the data collection. If the original authorisation to collect data is restricted to the purpose of protecting specified legal interests or preventing specified criminal offences, this purpose limits both the scope of immediate data use and the scope of further data uses, even if the data is still being handled by the same authority; other uses are only permissible if there is a separate statutory basis authorising such a change in purpose.

280 b) In principle, the purpose limitations that the same authority must observe, again, in each and every further use of the collected data do not include the relevant thresholds for exercising the data collection powers – this holds true for the threshold of sufficiently specific indications of danger, as traditionally required for public security measures, and the threshold of sufficient grounds for the suspicion of criminal conduct (*hinreichender Tatverdacht*), as required in the context of law enforcement. While the requirement of establishing sufficiently specific indications that an identifiable danger may emerge or a qualified suspicion of criminal conduct determines the permissible grounds of data collection, it does not determine the purposes for which the collected data may be used.

281 For that reason, it does not from the outset run counter to the principle that data be used only in accordance with the purpose for which it was originally collected if the authority in question is allowed to consider the data as mere evidentiary traces used, for the same task, as the basis for further investigations, without having to fulfil additional prerequisites. The authority may use the information thus obtained

– either by itself or in combination with other available information – as a mere starting point for further investigations to protect the same legal interests in the context of the same task. In this regard, and within the limits set out above, the legal order recognises that the gathering of information – not least when aiming to understand terrorist structures – cannot be reduced to an exercise that merely stocks isolated individual data, with formal legal criteria determining which data items may be considered and which ones ought to be disregarded. [...]

The principle of purpose limitation is satisfied if the authority that is authorised to collect data further uses this data while acting within the same remit for the protection of the same legal interests and the prosecution or prevention of the same criminal acts as specified in the statutory provision authorising the data collection. These requirements are necessary, but generally also sufficient, to legitimise further use of the data in accordance with the principle of purpose limitation.

However, more stringent requirements arise from the principle of purpose limitation with regard to data obtained through the surveillance of private homes and remote searches of information technology systems: any further use of such data only satisfies the purpose limitation if it is also necessary to avert an acute danger (cf. BVerfGE 109, 279 <377, 379> – *Surveillance of Private Homes*) or an impending danger in the individual case (cf. BVerfGE 120, 274 <326, 328 and 329> – *Remote Searches*), in keeping with the prerequisites applicable to the collection of such data. The extraordinary weight of interference resulting from this type of data collection is reflected in a particularly narrow limitation of any further use of the obtained data, which is subject to the prerequisites, including the permissible purposes, specified for the original data collection. Information thus obtained may not be used as evidentiary traces providing the basis for further investigations unless there is an acute danger or an impending danger in the individual case.

2. Moreover, the legislator may allow further data uses for purposes other than those for which the data was originally collected (change in purpose). In that case, however, the legislator must ensure that the weight of interference resulting from the data collection is also taken into consideration with regard to the new data uses (cf. BVerfGE 100, 313 <389 and 390> – *The Article 10 Act*; 109, 279 <377> – *Surveillance of Private Homes*; 120, 351 <369>; 130, 1 <33 and 34>; 133, 277 <372 and 373 para. 225> – *Counter-Terrorism Database Act I*).

a) The authorisation to use data for new purposes constitutes a separate interference with the fundamental right affected by the original data collection (cf. BVerfGE 100, 313 <360, 391> – *The Article 10 Act*; 109, 279 <375> – *Surveillance of Private Homes*; 110, 33 <68 and 69>; 125, 260 <312 and 313, 333> – *Data Retention*; 133, 277 <372 para. 225> – *Counter-Terrorism Database Act I*; cf. also ECtHR, *Weber and Saravia v. Germany*, Judgment of 29 June 2006, no. 54934/00, § 79,

NJW 2007, p. 1433 <1434>, regarding Art. 8 ECHR). For that reason, changes in purpose must be measured against the fundamental rights that were affected by the data collection. This applies to any type of data use for purposes other than the purpose for which the data was originally collected, irrespective of whether the data is used as evidence or as a basis for further investigations (cf. BVerfGE 109, 279 <377> – *Surveillance of Private Homes*).

286 b) A change in purpose may only be authorised within the limits of the principle of proportionality. The weight attached to such a change in purpose in the balancing of interests is determined by the weight of interference of the data collection. Information obtained through measures constituting particularly intrusive interferences may only be used for particularly weighty purposes (cf. BVerfGE 100, 313 <394> – *The Article 10 Act*; 109, 279 <377> – *Surveillance of Private Homes*; 133, 277 <372 and 373 para. 225> – *Counter-Terrorism Database Act I*, with further references).

287 aa) In earlier decisions, the Federal Constitutional Court reviewed the proportionality of a change in purpose by determining whether the new use was "incompatible" with the original purpose of the data collection (cf. BVerfGE 65, 1, <62> – *Census*; 100, 313 <360, 389> – *The Article 10 Act*; 109, 279 <376 and 377> – *Surveillance of Private Homes*; 110, 33 <69>; 120, 351 <369>; 130, 1 <33>). This approach has since been developed further and now relies instead on the criterion of a hypothetical recollection of data (*hypothetische Datenneuerhebung*). Where data obtained through intrusive surveillance and investigation measures is concerned, such as the data at issue in these proceedings, it is necessary to determine whether it would hypothetically be permissible, under constitutional law, to collect the relevant data again with comparably weighty means for the changed purpose (cf. BVerfGE 125, 260 <333> – *Data Retention*; 133, 277 <373 and 374 paras. 225 and 226> – *Counter-Terrorism Database Act I*; substantively, this standard is not new as these considerations were already applied in BVerfGE 100, 313 <389 and 390> – *The Article 10 Act* and referred to as a "hypothetical substitute interference" in BVerfGE 130, 1 <34>). The test of a hypothetical recollection of data is not applied rigidly in a schematic manner and does not preclude the possibility that further aspects may be taken into consideration (cf. BVerfGE 133, 277 <374 para. 226> – *Counter-Terrorism Database Act I*). Thus, data sharing between authorities is not, in principle, ruled out simply because the authority receiving the data is – unlike the authority that permissibly collected the data and is now sharing it – not empowered to collect certain data itself as it has a different remit (cf. BVerfGE 100, 313 <390> – *The Article 10 Act*). Furthermore, when creating provisions governing data sharing, legislative objectives such as simplification and practicability can justify the fact that the sharing of data is not subject to every single requirement

applicable to the collection of data. However, the requirement that the new use must serve purposes of comparable weight must in any case be met.

bb) This means that a change in purpose requires that the new use of the data serve the protection of legal interests or the detection of criminal acts of such weight that it would be justified, under constitutional law, to collect the data again with comparably weighty means (cf. BVerfGE 100, 313 <389 and 390> – *The Article 10 Act*; 109, 279 <377> – *Surveillance of Private Homes*; 110, 33 <73>; 120, 351 <369>; 130, 1 <34>). 288

Yet the requirements applicable to a change in purpose are not completely identical to the requirements applicable to the original data collection with regard to the degree of specificity required for establishing the existence of a danger or the suspicion of criminal conduct. Under the principle of proportionality, these requirements primarily establish the direct grounds for the data collection as such but not the grounds for further use of the collected data. An authorisation to use data for other purposes constitutes a separate interference that requires new justification. For that reason, such an authorisation requires its own, sufficiently specific grounds prompting the measure. Under constitutional law, it is thus necessary, but generally also sufficient, that the data – either by itself or in combination with other information available to the authority – creates a specific basis for further investigations. 289

Thus, with regard to the use of data by security authorities, the legislator may in principle allow a change in purpose if the data concerns information that results, in the individual case, in a specific basis for further investigations aiming to detect comparably serious criminal acts or to avert impending dangers that, at least in the medium term, threaten weighty legal interests that are comparable to the legal interests whose protection justified the collection of the relevant data. 290

The same, however, does not apply with regard to information obtained through the surveillance of private homes or through covert access to information technology systems. In view of the significant weight of interference attached to these measures, each new use of such data is subject to the same justification requirements as the data collection itself in that the new use also requires an acute danger (cf. BVerfGE 109, 279 <377, 379> – *Surveillance of Private Homes*) or a sufficiently identifiable danger in the specific case (see C IV 1 b above). 291

cc) These requirements, which must be met for a change in purpose to be permissible, specify and consolidate a long line of case-law developed by both Senates of the Federal Constitutional Court (cf. BVerfGE 65, 1 <45 and 46, 61 and 62> – *Census*; 100, 313 <389 and 390> – *The Article 10 Act*; 109, 279 <377> – *Surveillance of Private Homes*; 110, 33 <68 and 69, 73>; 120, 351 <369>; 125, 260 <333> – *Data Retention*; 130, 1 <33 and 34>; 133, 277 <372 and 373 para. 225> – *Counter-Terrorism Database Act I*). This does not result in stricter standards but 292 cautiously allows more leeway in the constitutional assessment given that the criterion of a hypothetical recollection of the data is not applied in a rigid manner (cf. already BVerfGE 133, 277 <374 para. 226> – *Counter-Terrorism Database Act I*); it means that the traditional requirements regarding statutory thresholds for carrying out interferences, which determine the required temporal proximity of danger, are relaxed to some extent (cf. in particular BVerfGE 100, 313 <394> – *The Article 10 Act*; 109, 279 <377> – *Surveillance of Private Homes*). If, on top of that, the requirement that the change in purpose serve comparably weighty legal interests were waived as well – as suggested in one of the dissenting opinions – the limits set by the principle of purpose limitation, as a core element of data protection under constitutional law (cf. BVerfGE 65, 1 <45 and 46, 61 and 62> – *Census*), would practically be rendered meaningless in the domain of public security (or would only have rudimentary effects as these limits would no longer be applied except to data obtained through the surveillance of private homes or remote searches). This holds true all the more if the requirement of a specific basis for further investigations, too, were rejected as being overly strict.

II.

293   Based on these standards, § 20v(4) second sentence of the Federal Criminal Police Office Act, which governs how the Federal Criminal Police Office may use data it collected itself, does not satisfy the constitutional requirements. The provision is unconstitutional.

294   1. In principle, the use of data for the sole purpose of carrying out tasks serving the averting of dangers posed by international terrorism, as set out in § 20v(4) second sentence no. 1 of the Federal Criminal Police Office Act, is compatible with the Constitution; however, the provision lacks sufficient restrictions regarding the use of data obtained through the surveillance of private homes and remote searches.

295-302   [...]

303   2. § 20v(4) second sentence no. 2 of the Federal Criminal Police Office Act, which concerns the use of data for the purpose of protecting witnesses and other persons, is also incompatible with the constitutional requirements. The provision merely makes a general reference to the tasks assigned to the Federal Criminal Police Office under § 5 and § 6 of the Federal Criminal Police Office Act but does not contain any kind of restriction. Therefore, the provision does not satisfy the requirement of specificity and, for that reason alone, fails to meet the standards set out above.

No. 44 – The Federal Criminal Police Office Act

III.

§ 20v(5) of the Federal Criminal Police Office Act, which governs the sharing of data with other authorities, fails to satisfy the constitutional requirements in several respects. 304

1. § 20v(5) of the Federal Criminal Police Office Act provides various statutory grounds for the sharing of data, collected for the purpose of averting dangers posed by terrorism, with other authorities. With the various authorisations regarding data sharing, the legislator allows the use of that data for a changed purpose in the individual case and based on specific grounds. The legislator thus provides a basis for the use of data by other authorities, which – in accordance with the image of a double door – themselves must also be statutorily authorised to receive and use this data (cf. BVerfGE 130, 151 <184>). Thus, the provision provides for interferences with fundamental rights, which must, in each case, be measured against those fundamental rights that were affected by the collection of the data that is now being shared (cf. BVerfGE 100, 313 <360, 391> – *The Article 10 Act*; 109, 279 <375> – *Surveillance of Private Homes*; 110, 33 <68 and 69>; 125, 260 <312 and 313, 333> – *Data Retention*; 133, 277 <372 para. 225> – *Counter-Terrorism Database Act I*; cf. also ECtHR, *Weber and Saravia v. Germany*, Judgment of 29 June 2006, no. 54934/00, § 79, NJW 2007, p. 1433 <1434>, regarding Art. 8 ECHR). 305

2. [...] 306

3. [...] The challenged powers are unconstitutional to the extent that the statutory prerequisites for data sharing fail to satisfy the standards developed above with regard to the test of a hypothetical recollection of data (see D I 2 b above). 307

a) [...] 308-309

b) § 20v(5) first sentence no. 2 of the Federal Criminal Police Office Act governs the sharing of data for the purpose of averting dangers to public security. For the most part, it satisfies the constitutional requirements. However, the provision is disproportionate to the extent that it generally allows a transfer of data for the purpose of preventing certain criminal offences [without providing for sufficient restrictions].
[...] 310

311-313

c) § 20v(5) first sentence no. 3 of the Federal Criminal Police Office Act, which governs the sharing of data for law enforcement purposes, is [also disproportionately broad and thus] not compatible with the Constitution.
[...] 314

315-318

d) § 20v(5) third sentence no. 1 of the Federal Criminal Police Office Act, which allows the sharing of data with the offices for the protection of the Constitution (*Verfassungsschutzbehörden*) and the Military Counter-Intelligence Service 319

(*Militärischer Abschirmdienst*), is also incompatible with the constitutional requirements.

320 [...]
321 e) [...]
322 4. Finally, with regard to all these data sharing powers, a general statutory framework is lacking that ensures sufficient administrative oversight. [...]

IV.

323 In part, § 14(1) first sentence nos. 1 and 3, second sentence of the Federal Criminal Police Office Act, which governs the sharing of data with foreign authorities – to the extent that § 14a of the Federal Criminal Police Office Act is not applicable, which governs data sharing with EU Member States and which is not challenged in the present proceedings –, also does not satisfy the constitutional requirements.

324 1. Like the sharing of personal data with domestic authorities, the sharing of data with foreign authorities constitutes a change in purpose. In accordance with general standards, this change in purpose must be measured against the relevant fundamental rights affected by the original data collection (see D I 2 a above). At the same time, with a view to ensuring respect for foreign legal orders and values, certain constitutional standards that are specific to the sharing of data with other states apply.

325 a) After data has been shared with other states, the guarantees of the Basic Law can no longer be applied directly and the standards prevailing in the respective receiving state apply instead. Yet this does not generally prevent data sharing with other states. With its Preamble, together with Art. 1(2), Art. 9(2), Art. 16(2), Arts. 23 to 26 and Art. 59(2), the Basic Law binds the Federal Republic of Germany to the international community and programmatically commits German state authority to international cooperation (cf. BVerfGE 63, 343 <370>; 111, 307 <318 and 319>; 112, 1 <25, 27>). This includes interaction with other states even if their legal order and values do not fully conform to the German domestic conception (cf. BVerfGE 31, 58 <75 *et seq.*>; 63, 343 <366>; 91, 335 <340, 343 *et seq.*>; 108, 238 <247 and 248). Such data sharing also aims to maintain both intergovernmental relations in the mutual interest of the participating states and the Federal Government's capacity to act in the context of foreign policy (cf. BVerfGE 108, 129 <137>).

326 However, when deciding on the sharing of personal data with other states, German state authority essentially remains bound by the fundamental rights (Art. 1(3) of the Basic Law); yet the foreign state authority is only bound by its own legal obligations.

No. 44 – The Federal Criminal Police Office Act

Therefore, fundamental rights set limits to data sharing, which serve to uphold data protection guarantees. The limits set by the Basic Law for the domestic collection and processing of data must not be undermined, in terms of their substance, by data sharing between security authorities. The legislator must thus ensure that this fundamental rights protection is not eroded, neither by the sharing of data collected by German authorities with other states and international organisations nor by the receipt and use of data from foreign authorities that was obtained in violation of human rights.

Moreover, limits to data sharing arise with regard to the use of the data by the receiving state if there are concerns about human rights violations. Sharing data with other states is ruled out if there is reason to fear that its use could lead to violations of fundamental principles of the rule of law (cf. BVerfGE 108, 129 <136 and 137>). Under no circumstances may the state be complicit in violations of human dignity (cf. BVerfGE 140, 317 <para. 62>, with further references).

b) Accordingly, the sharing of data with other states must be restricted to sufficiently weighty purposes for which the data may be shared and used (see aa below); moreover, it must be ascertained that the data will be handled in accordance with the rule of law in the receiving state (see bb below). In addition, effective domestic oversight must extend to such data sharing (see cc below). Adherence to these requirements must be ensured through clear foundations in German law (see dd below).

aa) The requirements relating to the purpose of the sharing and use of the data [in the receiving state] derive from the constitutional criteria applicable to a change in purpose under German law (see D I 2 above). Data sharing requires that it were permissible to collect the shared data again, with comparably weighty means, for the purpose for which it is shared (criterion of a hypothetical recollection of data). Thus, data sharing must serve to detect comparably weighty criminal acts or to protect comparably weighty legal interests, depending on what was required for the original data collection. At the same time, data sharing does, in principle, not require sufficient indications of danger or grounds for the suspicion of criminal conduct; it is sufficient that the shared information, or the request by the receiving state, show that there is, in the individual case, a specific basis for further investigations for the purpose of detecting relevant criminal acts or averting impending dangers to relevant legal interests that may emerge at least in the medium term. However, stricter requirements apply to the sharing of data obtained through the surveillance of private homes and remote searches of information technology systems; in these cases, the interference thresholds applicable to the data collection must be fully met (see D I 2 b bb above; cf. also BVerfGE 109, 279 <377, 379> – *Surveillance of Private Homes*; 120, 274 <329 et seq.> – *Remote Searches*).

331 It is therefore necessary, in particular when another state requests that data be shared, to assess the prospective use of data by the receiving state. This assessment must respect the autonomy of the foreign legal order. When determining whether the purpose of data sharing is of comparable weight, it must be taken into account that the German legal order faces another legal order whose parameters, categories and value decisions are not, and do not necessarily have to be, identical to those reflected in the German legal order and the Basic Law. The fact that purpose limitations recognised in the German legal order are not reflected, to the same extent and in an identical manner, in the foreign legal order does not preclude data sharing with that state from the outset. When sharing the data, the receiving authorities must be informed in a clear and express manner of limitations restricting use of the shared data.

332 bb) Furthermore, the sharing of personal data with other states presupposes that the data be handled in accordance with human rights and data protection standards in the receiving state (see 1 below), which must be ascertained by the German state (see 2 below).

333 (1) The sharing of data with other states requires sufficient guarantees that the data will be handled in accordance with the rule of law in the receiving state.

334 (a) In terms of data protection standards, it is, however, not necessary that the receiving state have rules on the processing of personal data that match those within the German legal order, or that the receiving state guarantee a level of protection that is equivalent to the protection afforded by the Basic Law. In fact, the Basic Law recognises and generally respects the autonomy and diversity of legal orders, including in the context of data sharing. […]

335 However, the sharing of personal data with other states is only permissible if the handling of the shared data in these states does not undermine the protection of personal data guaranteed by human rights. […]

336 (b) If there is reason to fear that the use of the data in the receiving state could lead to human rights violations, it must be guaranteed in particular that the data will neither be used for political persecution nor inhuman or degrading punishment or treatment (cf. Art. 16a(3) of the Basic Law). Overall, the legislator must ensure that the sharing of data collected by German authorities with other states or international organisations does not erode the protections of the European Convention on Human Rights and other international human rights treaties (cf. Art. 1(2) of the Basic Law).

337 (2) Ascertaining the necessary level of protection in the receiving state does not always require a comprehensive assessment in each individual case or binding assurances under international law. Instead, the legislator may allow this ascertainment to be based on a generalising assessment made by the Federal Criminal Police

Office of the legal and factual situation in the receiving state. Such an assessment may be relied on unless there are facts to the contrary refuting the generalised assumptions in a particular case (cf. BVerfGE 140, 317 <para. 69>, with further references).

Where such generalised assessments of the situation in the receiving state are not tenable, it is necessary to conduct a fact-based assessment in the individual case; such an assessment must verify that adherence to essential requirements for the handling of data is sufficiently guaranteed (see D IV 1 b bb (1) above). […] 338

[…] 339

cc) In any case, the requirements of effective administrative oversight, including the proper documentation of data sharing activities as well as corresponding reporting obligations, continue to apply in Germany (see C IV 6 d, e above). 340

dd) The standards set out above must be laid down in statutory provisions that satisfy the principles of specificity and legal clarity. This also applies to the design of statutory bases authorising, where permissible, a sharing of data for the purpose of obtaining information by cross-checking this data against data collected by authorities in other states and for receiving additional information on the relevant matter in return; these statutory bases, too, must be designed in line with the principle of legal clarity. 341

2. The prerequisites governing data sharing laid down in § 14(1) first sentence nos. 1 and 3 and second sentence of the Federal Criminal Police Office Act do not satisfy these requirements. 342

[…] 343-354

E.

I.

[…] 355-358

II.

In parts, the decision was not unanimous. […] 359
[…] 360

Justices: Kirchhof, Gaier, Eichberger, Schluckebier, Masing, Paulus, Baer, Britz

BVerfGE 141, 220

Dissenting Opinion of Justice Eichberger

1   I cannot concur with this judgment, as I disagree in several respects with the conclusions regarding the challenged provisions, and with parts of the reasoning.

I.

2   The judgment summarises, consolidates and, in part, further develops the constitutional standards recognised in the Court's case-law regarding the collection of data by means of very intrusive investigation measures, and the sharing of such data, in the domain of counter-terrorism at issue here. I largely agree with the general standards laid down in the majority decision with regard to the different constitutional requirements governing the grounds for such investigation and surveillance measures and with regard to the requirements governing further use of information thus obtained. However, in several respects the Senate majority sets excessive requirements for such data collection and further use of the data. This is the case, in particular, for the obligations the Senate majority imposes on the legislator regarding the design of the statutory framework. As regards the decision on fundamental constitutional values, on the basis of which the Senate majority determines the permissibility of interferences with fundamental freedoms in view of the state's duty to ensure security, and on the basis of which it lays down specific constitutional requirements, the judgment does indeed draw on lines of case-law developed by the Court over the past twelve years. However, in my view, the degree of detail and rigidity of the requirements imposed on the legislator cannot be derived from the Constitution (cf. BVerfGE 125, 380, my dissenting opinion to BVerfGE 125, 260 – *Data Retention*)

3   The standards set out by the Senate majority almost exclusively rely on an assessment of proportionality in the strict sense, that is a balancing of the burdens imposed on persons affected by very intrusive measures interfering with fundamental rights, on the one hand, and the state's duties of protection with regard to averting terrorist dangers, on the other. Yet the Senate does not sufficiently take into account the prerogative of assessment afforded the legislator when appraising the factual basis of dangers and making a prognosis on how such dangers may develop. Moreover, it is primarily for the legislator to weigh the legislative aims pursued. It is true that the Federal Constitutional Court may conduct, as part of the proportionality assessment in the strict sense, a thorough review of the legislator's weighing; however, the Court must not lose sight of its judicial mandate with respect to the legislator's prerogative of assessment and margin of appreciation in weighing the legitimate aim pursued.

With these considerations in mind, my starting point for the required balancing differs from the Senate majority's. This also leads me to different conclusions, in part with regard to the applicable general standards and especially with regard to the specific measures at issue. It is true that even the mere latent risk of covert surveillance and investigation measures exposes fundamental rights holders to burdens associated with the most severe interferences, and directly affects fundamental rights holders where such measures are actually carried out against them. However, in weighing the potential risk posed by covert surveillance and investigation measures, it must be kept in mind that, for the most part, the challenged provisions do not authorise a general collection of data indiscriminately affecting a large number of persons. If, in a specific case, investigation measures affect persons that have not themselves provided grounds for the investigation or have only marginally contributed to such grounds, they may nevertheless be asked to endure the measure as a special sacrifice, as part of their duty as citizens, that serves to maintain public security. [...]

[...] Not all of the requirements imposed on the legislator with regard to provisions governing procedure, transparency and oversight are actually prescribed, in exactly this form, by the Constitution – even if many of these requirements may be sensible and fitting. In my opinion, a significantly higher degree of judicial restraint would have been appropriate in the present case. Instead, though commendable in its attempt to consolidate existing case-law in a general introduction of sorts, the present judgment generalises previous findings in a manner that ultimately results in a problematic affirmation of excessive constitutional requirements in the domain at issue here [...]. Clear statutory provisions are indispensable when it comes to very intrusive surveillance measures. At the same time, the statutory framework should be designed with a significantly higher degree of restraint, in terms of the level of detail, assuming that the security authorities can generally be trusted to take proportionate and lawful action in the individual case unless there are indications to the contrary. [...]

II.

Even though, to the extent set out above, my approach differs from the approach taken by the Senate majority, I agree for the most part with the general standards laid down in the decision with regard to data collection and sharing, including the sharing of data with foreign authorities. I also concur, in large parts, with the conclusions derived from these standards with regard to the challenged provisions. These conclusions are convincing and well-reasoned. The resulting requirements for stringent legislation and obstacles to law enforcement must be tolerated in order to protect the fundamental freedoms concerned. Yet I consider the judgment's approach, though based on past decisions, to be excessive and not prescribed by constitutional law, both with regard to some of the observations made on general constitutional standards and with regard to the conclusions relating to the unconstitutionality of individual challenged provisions. In particular, this concerns the following aspects:

7   1. It is generally imperative that the Court practise more restraint when it comes to setting very detailed requirements for the legislator regarding the design of supplementary procedural and other safeguards; in any case, I think the judgment goes too far in deriving from the principle of proportionality the requirements that persons affected by very intrusive surveillance measures be afforded effective sanctioning mechanisms in addition to the right to seek a judicial review of lawfulness (see judgment C IV 6 c); that the oversight of data collection and use be carried out in regular intervals not exceeding approximately two years (see judgment C IV 6 d); and that reporting obligations vis-à-vis Parliament and the public to ensure transparency and oversight be provided for since the data is collected covertly [...]. It would have been sufficient to simply specify the level of protection that must be ensured by the legislator – anything beyond that constitutes unjustified overreach.

8   2. As for the different challenged investigation and surveillance measures, I believe the constitutional shortcomings to be much narrower in scope than what was found by the Senate majority.

9   a) The Senate majority considers various statutory authorisations to carry out certain investigation and data collection measures for the purposes of crime prevention to lack specificity and to be disproportionate (see judgment C V 1 d bb, 5 b, [...]); in this regard, the Senate needlessly foregoes the possibility of interpreting the relevant provisions in conformity with the Constitution. [...]

10 b) [...]

11 c) Furthermore, I cannot concur with the Senate majority's view that § 20g of the Federal Criminal Police Office Act is unconstitutional for not sufficiently ensuring protection of the core of private life (see judgment C V 1 g).

12 Nevertheless, I do agree with the judgment's basic premise that it is incumbent upon the legislator to provide for safeguards and oversight where statutory provisions authorise surveillance and investigation measures that typically intrude upon the core of private life. This requires the legislator to provide for the various prerequisites set out in the judgment that aim to prevent the collection of data relating to the core in the first place; where the collection of such data cannot be fully prevented, the legislator must provide for screening and filtering at the stage of data analysis and processing, which must not be carried out by the security authority itself (see judgment C IV 3 d). [...]

However, from my point of view, § 20g of the Federal Criminal Police Office Act does not authorise surveillance measures that typically lead to the collection of data relating to the core of private life [...]. Measures taken pursuant to § 20g(2) of the Federal Criminal Police Office Act are generally carried out in public spaces, which contradicts the assumption that the information thus obtained typically includes data relating to the core. [...]

3. If the further use of data obtained through surveillance measures entails a change in purpose, this amounts to a separate interference with the fundamental right affected by the original data collection. This is in line with established case-law, which I agree with. Yet some of the conditions laid out by the Senate majority regarding the permissibility of a change in purpose set the hurdles too high. In this respect, it is not adequately taken into account that the use for other purposes concerns data that has already been lawfully collected.

a) [...]

b) [...] As is the case with other surveillance measures entailing very intrusive interferences, in the context of the surveillance of private homes, too, the real and severe intrusion into the private sphere takes place when the authorities carry out the actual surveillance measure in the protected domain. While any further use, including for changed purposes, does indeed perpetuate this interference, it does not reach the level of severity of the initial interference, not even where the data is obtained through the surveillance of private homes (or remote searches of information technology systems for that matter). The further use, including a change in purpose, of information obtained through surveillance measures should only be measured against the general rules applicable in this regard. The Senate majority has missed the opportunity to correct its case-law accordingly.

Justice Eichberger

Dissenting Opinion of Justice Schluckebier

To the extent that the judgment objects to the challenged provisions under constitutional law, I agree neither with its outcome nor with its reasoning.

The Court's basic premise is correct in that it is incumbent upon the legislator to strike an appropriate balance between the interferences with fundamental rights that might arise, in the individual case, from the statutory provisions in question, and the state's duty to protect the fundamental rights of individuals and legal interests of the public in the context of preventing terrorist acts. However, based on that premise, the Senate majority conducts a proportionality assessment that I believe to be misguided, from a constitutional perspective, in several respects, and sets out excessive specificity requirements in relation to individual provisions. Moreover, the views laid down by the Senate majority have a serious impact on police laws of the *Länder,* yet these implications were not sufficiently addressed in the proceedings. Thus, the judgment restricts both the federal legislator's political latitude and, indirectly, the latitude of legislators of the *Länder* beyond what would have been appropriate. By laying down numerous requirements relating to technical legislative details, the Senate puts its own notion of how the statutory framework should be designed before that of the democratically legitimated legislator, even though it is the legislator that is held politically accountable for the legislative concept and that can adjust the law slightly where necessary; in my opinion, this goes too far.

3 Contrary to what the Senate majority assumed, some of the challenged provisions could in fact have been interpreted in conformity with the Constitution [...]

4 [...]

I.

5 Before going into detail, it should be noted that the legislator, in designing the statutory framework aiming to effectively avert terrorist dangers and prevent crime, has essentially found an appropriate and tenable balance in the complex conflict between the fundamental rights of persons affected by the police measures, and the underlying statutory bases, on the one hand, and the legislator's duty to protect the fundamental rights of individuals and the constitutionally protected interests of the public on the other hand. The legislator thus gives effect to the principle that, in a state under the rule of law, individuals must be able to rely on effective protection *by* the state and on the protection of their freedoms *against* the state (see my dissenting opinion in BVerfGE 125, 364 <369> – *Data Retention*; regarding the state's duty to protect against terrorism and other threats see BVerfGE 120, 274 <319> – *Remote Searches*). It is true that, in the individual case, the measures in question might also affect holders of fundamental rights who are not themselves suspected of terrorism or, as it later turns out, were wrongfully suspected at the time; yet they can be asked to endure the burdens arising from such measures as a special sacrifice demanded of them as members of the community.

6 After laying out general observations regarding the significance and weight attached to the aims pursued by the legislator, the reasoning of the judgment falls short when it comes to reviewing the individual provisions in question; here, the

judgment neither properly assesses the proportionality in the strict sense nor the specificity of the challenged provisions. [...]

As a result, I consider that the Senate majority's assessment of proportionality in the strict sense in relation to several of the challenged provisions is unconvincing and, in part, even fails to satisfy the element of appropriateness. This is confirmed by the fact that the challenged Act, and the statutory authorisations of interferences contained therein, have been in force for more than seven years now, yet, as the oral hearing revealed, the powers in question have only ever been applied in a few cases and, to date, there has been no evidence of shortcomings. [...]

II.

I will now address some of the specific objections raised by the Senate majority:

1. The Senate finds the statutory prerequisites for carrying out the interferences, as set out in some of the challenged provisions, to be lacking on the grounds that the provisions did not subject the interferences to sufficiently stringent requirements and were therefore disproportionate and too unspecific [...]. Yet it would have been possible, based on the considerations set out in the judgment, to interpret the prerequisites designed by the legislator in conformity with the Constitution.

2. The Senate majority held that the surveillance framework lacks an explicit statutory provision ensuring protection of the core of private life with regard to the special methods of data collection set out in § 20g(2) of the Federal Criminal Police Office Act, even where the surveillance measures are carried out outside the home and might differ, in terms of severity and proximity, in how closely they relate to the individual's private sphere. [...]

I do not agree with this conclusion. In cases where technical surveillance measures take place outside the home, they generally do not affect a refuge typically considered private (BVerfGE 109, 279 <320 *et seq.*> – *Surveillance of Private Homes*). [...] Thus, it was not necessary for the legislator to include an express provision protecting the core of private life. Rather, protection in this regard can be ensured when the law is applied in practice.

3. [...]

[...]

4. Furthermore, I cannot support the reasoning by which the Senate majority requires the establishment of an "independent body" tasked with ensuring, in respect of data obtained through the surveillance of private homes and remote searches of information technology systems, protection of the core at the subsequent stages of data analysis and processing. [...]

[...]

16 The rather complicated solution prescribed by the Court hampers the effectiveness of the envisaged measures, especially with regard to the surveillance of private homes, which means that ultimately these powers no longer constitute appropriate means for achieving the legislative aim pursued, namely effective protection against terrorism. […]

17 5. The Senate majority also criticises, based on proportionality considerations, the lack of procedural provisions supplementing the surveillance and investigatory powers to ensure transparency, legal protection and administrative oversight in all respects. Bearing in mind that the powers in question concern action, taken in the individual case, for the purposes of averting dangers posed by terrorism, I again consider the requirements set out in the judgment to be, at least in part, excessive. […]

18 […]

III.

19 I also cannot concur with the Senate majority's finding that the challenged powers concerning further use of the data collected in the context of averting terrorist dangers and the sharing of such data with domestic and foreign authorities were unconstitutional. This applies in particular to the extent that the Senate majority permits the use of lawfully collected data in other contexts solely for the purposes of protecting the same or comparably weighty legal interests. This approach is only tenable in cases where information was obtained through particularly intrusive interferences, for instance, the surveillance of private homes or remote searches of information technology systems. However, in certain other cases where the information in question results from coincidental findings, it would be irresponsible, in my opinion, to leave weighty legal interests, whether of the individual or the public, unprotected due to rigorous doctrine.

20 1. The judgment makes the sharing and further use of the data dependent on whether, after the change in purpose, this data continues to serve the protection of legal interests or the detection of criminal acts of such weight that this could, by constitutional standards, justify collecting the data in question again with comparably weighty means (criterion of a hypothetical recollection of data). This approach may be tenable with regard to information obtained through highly intrusive and particularly serious interferences, which is the case, for example, when methods such as surveillance of private homes and remote searches were used to collect the data. However, with regard to other types of interferences, which result in so-called coincidental findings, this approach, in my opinion, would lead to hardly tolerable results since it requires the legal order, which is committed to the rule of

No. 44 – The Federal Criminal Police Office Act

law, to stand back and ignore impending dangers to other legal interests that are sufficiently weighty, allow crimes to happen and legal interests to be violated. In this scenario, the state fails to fulfil its duty of protection.

[…]	21-24
2. […]	25
3. […]	26-27
4. […]	28
As the real challenge lies in the application of the law in the individual case, the additional statutory provisions, as required by the Senate majority, will not provide a viable solution. Once again, the insertion of additional detailed provisions into the existing legislative framework, as is now required of the legislator, will inflate the legislative text further, rendering the already excessively long statute even less legible and comprehensible – which ultimately leads to the opposite of legal clarity. At the same time, it would not even benefit affected persons, given that it will hardly lead to any measurable strengthening of protection in practice.	29

Justice Schluckebier

No. 45

BVerfGE 154, 152 – Surveillance of Foreign Telecommunications

HEADNOTES

to the Judgment of the First Senate of 19 May 2020
1 BvR 2835/17

1. Under Art. 1(3) of the Basic Law, German state authority is bound by fundamental rights; this binding effect is not restricted to German territory.
   The protection afforded by individual fundamental rights within Germany can differ from that afforded abroad.
   In any event, Art. 10(1) and Art. 5(1) second sentence of the Basic Law, which, in their dimension as rights against state interference, afford protection against telecommunications surveillance, also protect foreigners in other countries.

2. The current legal framework on the surveillance of foreign telecommunications, on the sharing of intelligence thus obtained with other bodies, and on the cooperation with foreign intelligence services violates the requirement that the affected fundamental rights be expressly specified, which is enshrined in Art. 19(1) second sentence of the Basic Law. The legislator deliberately considered fundamental rights not to be affected, yet they are applicable in this context, too. The current legal framework also does not satisfy key substantive requirements arising from fundamental rights.

3. Art. 10(1) of the Basic Law protects the confidentiality of individual communications as such. Persons asserting a violation of their own fundamental rights are not excluded from the protection afforded by the fundamental rights of the Basic Law merely because they act on behalf of foreign legal entities.

4. Legislation on foreign intelligence is covered by the legislative competence for foreign affairs within the meaning of Art. 73(1) no. 1 of the Basic Law. On the basis of this competence, the Federation can confer upon the Federal Intelligence Service not only the task of providing intelligence to the Federal Government with regard to foreign and security policy, but also the separate task of the early detection of dangers with an international dimension that originate from abroad, as long as this does not give rise to operational powers. These dangers must be of such nature and gravity that they can affect the

position of the Federal Republic of Germany in the international community and they must be significant to foreign and security policy precisely for this reason.

5. In principle, the strategic surveillance of foreign telecommunications is not incompatible with Art. 10(1) of the Basic Law. However, given that it is not based on specific grounds and essentially guided and restricted only by the purpose pursued, the power to conduct strategic surveillance is an exceptional power that must be limited to the gathering of foreign intelligence conducted by an authority that lacks operational powers; it can only be justified by the authority's particular tasks and the specific conditions under which it performs them.

   Therefore, the legislator must provide for the removal of telecommunications data of Germans and persons within Germany, limits to data that may be collected, the determination of specific surveillance purposes, the structuring of surveillance based on specifically determined measures, special requirements for the targeted surveillance of specific individuals, limits to traffic data retention, a framework governing data analysis, safeguards to protect confidential relationships of trust, the guaranteed protection of the core of private life and deletion requirements.

6. Sharing personal data stemming from strategic surveillance is only permissible for the purpose of protecting legal interests of particularly great weight and requires indications of an identifiable danger or sufficiently specific grounds for the suspicion of criminal conduct. Reports provided to the Federal Government are exempt from these requirements insofar as they are exclusively intended to provide political intelligence and prepare government decisions.

   The sharing of personal data requires a formal decision by the Federal Intelligence Service and must be documented specifying the applicable legal basis. Before data is shared with foreign bodies, it must be ensured that the recipient will handle the data in accordance with the rule of law; if there is any indication that data sharing could jeopardise an individual affected by it, an assessment of possible risks in the specific case is required.

7. A legal framework on the cooperation with foreign intelligence services only satisfies the constitutional requirements if it ensures that the limits set by the rule of law are not set aside through the mutual sharing of intelligence and that the Federal Intelligence Service essentially remains responsible for the data it has collected and analysed.

   If the Federal Intelligence Service wants to use search terms determined by a partner intelligence service to automatically share any matches with this service without any detailed content-related analysis, these search terms and the resulting matches must be checked thoroughly. The obligations to obtain assurances that are applicable to the sharing of data with other states apply accordingly. The sharing of traffic data in its entirety with partner intelligence services requires a qualified need for intelligence relating to specific indications of an identifiable danger. The Federal Intelligence Service must obtain substantial assurances from the partner services regarding their handling of the shared data.

8. The powers to conduct strategic surveillance measures, to share the intelligence thus obtained and to cooperate with foreign intelligence services are only compatible with the proportionality requirements if they are complemented by independent oversight. Such oversight must be designed as continual legal oversight that allows for comprehensive access to scrutinise the surveillance process.

On the one hand, it must be ensured that the key procedural steps of strategic surveillance are subject to independent oversight resembling judicial review by a body that has the power to make final decisions. On the other hand, the measures must be subject to administrative oversight by a body that conducts randomised oversight of the legality of the entire surveillance process on its own initiative.

Institutional independence of the oversight bodies must be guaranteed. This includes that the oversight bodies have a separate budget, independent personnel management, and procedural autonomy. They must be equipped with the personnel and resources required for the effective performance of their tasks. They must have all powers necessary for conducting effective oversight vis-à-vis the Federal Intelligence Service. It must also be ensured that oversight is not obstructed by the third party rule.

FEDERAL CONSTITUTIONAL COURT
- 1 BvR 2835/17 -

IN THE NAME OF THE PEOPLE

In the proceedings
on the constitutional complaint of

1. *Reporters sans frontières*, represented by its Directeur général D..., 2. Ms I..., 3. Mr G..., 4. Mr N..., 5. Mr Z..., 6. Mr O..., 7. Mr L..., 8. Mr M...,
   – authorised representatives: ...

No. 45 – Surveillance of Foreign Telecommunications

against § 6(1), (2), (3) and (6),
§ 7(1),
§ 9(4) and (5),
§ 10(3),
§ 13(4),
§ 14(1) first sentence and § 14(2),
§ 15(1),
§ 19(1),
§ 24(1) first sentence, § 24(2) and (3)
of the Federal Intelligence Service Act as amended by the Act on the Surveillance of Foreign Telecommunications by the Federal Intelligence Service of 23 December 2016 (BGBl I, p. 3346)

the Federal Constitutional Court – First Senate –

with the participation of Justices

Vice-President Harbarth,
Masing,
Paulus,
Baer,
Britz,
Ott,
Christ,
Radtke

held on the basis of the oral hearing of 14 and 15 January 2020:

JUDGMENT

1. §§ 6, 7, 13 to 15 of the Federal Intelligence Service Act, as amended by the Act on the Surveillance of Foreign Telecommunications by the Federal Intelligence Service of 23 December 2016 (BGBl I, p. 3346), and by the Act to Adapt Data Protection Law to Regulation (EU) 2016/679 and to Implement Directive (EU) 2016/680 of 30 June 2017 (BGBl I, p. 2097), are incompatible with Article 10(1) and Article 5(1) second sentence of the Basic Law.

2. § 19(1), § 24(1) first sentence, § 24(2) first sentence, § 24(3) of the Federal Intelligence Service Act are incompatible with Article 10(1) and Article 5(1) second sentence of the Basic Law insofar as they authorise the processing of personal data collected in the context of strategic telecommunications surveillance pursuant to §§ 6, 7, 13 to 15 of the Federal Intelligence Service Act.

3. The provisions that have been declared incompatible with the Basic Law continue to apply until new provisions have been enacted, at the latest until 31 December 2021.

4. [...]

REASONS:

A.

1   The constitutional complaint challenges the statutory provisions authorising the Federal Intelligence Service (*Bundesnachrichtendienst* – BND) to carry out surveillance of foreign telecommunications, to share the intelligence thus obtained with domestic and foreign bodies and to cooperate with foreign intelligence services in this context. Insofar as they concern cooperation and the surveillance of foreign telecommunications, the challenged provisions were inserted into the Federal Intelligence Service Act through the Act on the Surveillance of Foreign Telecommunications by the Federal Intelligence Service of 23 December 2016 (BGBl I, p. 3346), which entered into force on 31 December 2016. The law was amended in response to findings and discussions by the First Committee of Inquiry of the 18th German *Bundestag* (Committee of Inquiry into NSA Activities, cf. final report BTDrucks 18/12850) and served to clarify the legal framework given that the Federal Intelligence Service had been engaging in these practices prior to the amendment. By contrast, the challenged provisions on data sharing predate the amendment and their wording was not changed by it; however, they now also extend to the sharing of intelligence gathered on the basis of the newly added surveillance powers.

I.

2-3 1. [...]

4   2. Surveillance of foreign telecommunications is solely aimed at intercepting telecommunications of foreigners in other states. It is part of the Federal Intelligence Service's general task of conducting surveillance, which, according to § 1(2) first sentence of the Federal Intelligence Service Act, comprises the gathering and analysis of the information necessary to obtain intelligence on other states that is significant to the foreign and security policy of the Federal Republic of Germany.

5   The Federal Intelligence Service uses different sources of information to fulfil this task. These can be divided into four pillars: gathering and analysing generally accessible information, analysing images – primarily satellite images –, gathering

No. 45 – Surveillance of Foreign Telecommunications

and analysing information obtained through human intelligence, and signals intelligence (SIGINT) collected by the department for technical surveillance. Strategic surveillance of foreign telecommunications, which is at issue in the present proceedings, is part of signals intelligence. […]

The challenged provisions govern strategic telecommunications surveillance. This form of surveillance is characterised by the use of telecommunications transmission channels or networks and applies filtering mechanisms to separate data relevant for intelligence work from the entire telecommunications data transmitted via the networks. By definition, it thus indiscriminately affects a large number of persons and is usually not tied to specific grounds or suspicions. Instead, it is a purely precautionary measure that primarily serves to obtain indications, suspicions, general intelligence and situation reports in relation to matters that the Mission Statement of the Federal Government (*Auftragsprofil der Bundesregierung*; […]) considers significant for the Federal Republic of Germany's actions in foreign and security policy matters. In addition, strategic telecommunications surveillance also allows for and is aimed at the gathering of intelligence relating to specific individuals. 6

Besides the powers to carry out strategic telecommunications surveillance of foreigners in other states, which are challenged in these proceedings, the Federal Intelligence Service has the powers to carry out strategic surveillance of international telecommunications traffic, i.e. telecommunications between foreigners in other states on one side and persons within Germany or German citizens on the other. This is in addition to its powers to carry out measures restricting [the fundamental right under Article 10 of the Basic Law] in the individual case. Those powers, which are not at issue here, are set out in the Article 10 Act […] and are designed differently. Other authorities, in particular the Federal Office for the Protection of the Constitution (*Bundesamt für Verfassungsschutz*) – Germany's domestic intelligence service –, do not have such powers. 7

3. The challenged provisions set out specific rules for collecting data from within Germany and processing it (§ 6 of the Federal Intelligence Service Act), and for further processing data collected from abroad (§ 7(1) of the Federal Intelligence Service Act). […] 8

[…] 9

They provide a basis for collecting any information and data from those networks that are determined by the Federal Chancellery (*Bundeskanzleramt*) in a warrant ('bulk interception warrant' – *Netzanordnung*, cf. § 6(1) second sentence, § 9(1), (3) and (4) of the Federal Intelligence Service Act). […] 10

11 [...]
12 4. §§ 13 to 15 of the Federal Intelligence Service Act set out rules for the cooperation between the Federal Intelligence Service and foreign intelligence services, including the automated sharing of data with foreign bodies. [...]
13 5. Besides these special rules for collecting, processing, storing, deleting and sharing data obtained through the surveillance of foreign telecommunications, the general provisions of the Federal Intelligence Service Act on using, processing, storing, rectifying, deleting and sharing personal data held by the Federal Intelligence Service apply (§§ 19, 20 and 24 of the Federal Intelligence Service Act); these provisions were not modified by the amendment of 23 December 2016. [...]
14 6. [...]
15 7. Even before the challenged powers were enacted, and in the exercise of these powers ever since the enactment, a practice of conducting strategic surveillance of foreign telecommunications has evolved that consists of different steps.
16 a) First, the Federal Intelligence Service gains access to telecommunications data by intercepting signals from telecommunications networks either by using its own equipment or by having telecommunications service providers divert data flows pursuant to § 8 of the Federal Intelligence Service Act. [...]
17-18 [...]
19 b) The data that becomes accessible through the diversion of data or through other interception methods is transmitted to the Federal Intelligence Service's interception systems, initiating a multi-step and fully automated process of sorting and analysis, at the end of which temporarily saved data is stored or deleted. [...]
20 [...]
21 c) The Federal Intelligence Service collects and stores all remaining traffic data [...] (§ 6(6) first sentence of the Federal Intelligence Service Act) without using any selectors, and later performs primarily computer-based analysis through cross-checking and other methods.
22 d) However, pursuant to § 6(2) of the Federal Intelligence Service Act, content data is only stored and analysed beyond temporary storage required for technical reasons if elements of a telecommunications process are identified as relevant during the computer-based cross-checking against predetermined search terms (selectors). [...]
23 The selectors are divided into content-related and formal search terms, yet the Federal Intelligence Service primarily uses the latter (according to the Federal Government, they make up approximately 90% of selectors). These formal search terms are communication parameters, such as telecommunications identifiers or email addresses that can be attributed to persons, entities, groups or phenomena the Federal Intelligence Service considers relevant. The Federal Intelligence Service

No. 45 – Surveillance of Foreign Telecommunications

can use such search terms to identify all telecommunications that are sent to the identifier or address that is used as a search term, are sent from it or contain it, and separate these telecommunications from the rest of the intercepted data for storage. According to the Federal Government, approximately 5% of search terms serve to obtain targeted information on individuals in view of measures to be taken against them; in all other cases, the persons behind the search terms are only sometimes known, and they themselves and their conduct are not the focus of intelligence gathering.
[…] 24
e) Following the selection and storage of content data by means of search terms, the 25 data is subject to further analysis. This step primarily involves manually screening data as to its relevance for the Federal Intelligence Service. […]. According to the Federal Government, it is in this context that the protection of the core of private life required by § 11 of the Federal Intelligence Service Act is implemented in practice […].
f) §§ 13 to 15 of the Federal Intelligence Service Act enshrine the practice of 26 cooperation between intelligence services into law for the first time. […]
[…] 27-29
8. These processes are subject to both specific and general rules on transparency, 30 internal monitoring and oversight. […]
§ 16 of the Federal Intelligence Service Act establishes a special oversight body, the 31 Independent Body (*Unabhängiges Gremium*); its specific oversight powers derive from §§ 6 to 15 of the Federal Intelligence Service Act. General oversight to ensure data protection falls to the Federal Officer for Data Protection and Freedom of Information (§§ 32 and 32a of the Federal Intelligence Service Act). […]. In addition, special oversight competences are assigned to the Article 10 Committee (*G 10-Kommission*) […]. The power to conduct general parliamentary oversight falls to the Parliamentary Oversight Body (*Parlamentarisches Kontrollgremium*) and its Permanent Representative, and this body also has specific powers in relation to the surveillance of foreign telecommunications (§ 6(7) third sentence, § 13(5) second sentence of the Federal Intelligence Service Act).
According to the former chair of the Independent Body and the Federal Officer 32 for Data Protection, oversight by either body is restricted in practice by the need of partner intelligence services to maintain secrecy and by existing confidentiality agreements (third party rule).

II.

33 With their constitutional complaint, the complainants assert that their fundamental right to the privacy of telecommunications under Art. 10 of the Basic Law has been violated. Insofar as they work as journalists, they also claim that their fundamental right to freedom of the press under Art. 5(1) second sentence of the Basic Law has been violated, given that the Federal Intelligence Service Act does not contain special rules for the protection of confidentiality between the press and their sources in the context of strategic surveillance of foreign telecommunications. Finally, complainant no. 1 and complainants nos. 3 to 5 also assert a violation of the general guarantee of the right to equality under Art. 3(1) of the Basic Law because, as a legal entity based in an EU Member State and as EU citizens, they do not enjoy the same protection as German citizens.

34-41 […]

III.

42 In the constitutional complaint proceedings, statements were submitted by the Federal Government, the Government of the Free State of Bavaria, the respective Federal Officers for Data Protection and Freedom of Information and the Sixth Senate deciding on appeals on points of law of the Federal Administrative Court.

43-53 […]

IV.

54 Prior to the oral hearing, the Federal Government, the Federal Officer for Data Protection and Freedom of Information, the eco Association of the German Internet Industry (*eco-Verband der deutschen Internetwirtschaft e.V.*), T-Systems International GmbH and the Chaos Computer Club submitted written statements in response to a list of questions provided by the Federal Constitutional Court regarding the technical aspects of international telecommunications networks and the possibilities and dimensions of intelligence work carried out by the Federal Intelligence Service.

55 In the oral hearing, the Court heard the complainants, the Federal Government, the Federal Intelligence Service, the Parliamentary Oversight Body, the Article 10 Committee and the Federal Officer for Data Protection and Freedom of Information. As experts, the Court also heard the Federal Government's former IT security officer Martin Schallbruch as well as Barrister Dr Tom Hickman QC, Standing Counsel to the Investigatory Powers Commissioner's Office of the United Kingdom. As expert third parties, the Court heard the Judge at the Federal Court

of Justice Gabriele Cirener as the former chair of the Independent Body, the eco Association of the German Internet Industry, T-Systems International GmbH and the Chaos Computer Club.

B.

The constitutional complaint is admissible. 56

I.

The complainants lodged a constitutional complaint against statutes challenging powers to carry out surveillance and to share data which are conferred upon the Federal Intelligence Service for the surveillance of foreign telecommunications. [...] 57

II.

The complainants have standing. 58
1. The complainants assert a violation of their fundamental rights under Art. 10(1), Art. 5(1) second sentence and Art. 3(1) of the Basic Law. [...] 59
[...] 60
2. Complainants nos. 1 to 7 do not lack standing on the grounds that they are a foreign legal entity or foreigners living abroad who are invoking the fundamental rights of the Basic Law. As of yet there has been no definitive answer to the question if and to what extent citizens of other states can invoke the fundamental rights of the Basic Law to challenge measures of the German state in other countries. In its decision of 14 July 1999, the Federal Constitutional Court neither made a positive determination in this regard, nor did it rule this out (cf. BVerfGE 100, 313 <362 et seq.> – *The Article 10 Act*). Thus, a violation of fundamental rights appears at least possible. 61
3. Complainant no. 1 also does not lack standing on the grounds that it is a legal entity based abroad. The complainant sufficiently demonstrates that the extension of fundamental rights protection to legal entities based in the European Union may apply to it [...]. By reason of their nature, the fundamental rights invoked by the complainant meet the requirements regarding the applicability of Art. 19(3) of the Basic Law [...]. 62

63-67 [...]
68-70 4. [...]

III.

71-76 [...]

IV.

77-80 [...]

V.

81-83 [...]

VI.

84 Since the surveillance of foreign telecommunications does not concern the implementation of binding EU law, the assessment of whether the challenged provisions are valid under constitutional law must be based on the fundamental rights of the Basic Law. Thus, the Federal Constitutional Court is competent to decide and the constitutional complaint is admissible in this respect. This applies irrespective of whether EU fundamental rights may also be applicable (cf. BVerfGE 152, 152 <168 para. 39> – *Right to Be Forgotten I*).

85 [...]

C.

86 The constitutional complaint is well-founded. The challenged provisions must be measured against the fundamental rights of the Basic Law; they amount to interferences with Art. 10(1) and Art. 5(1) second sentence of the Basic Law (see I to III below). The interferences are not justified because the challenged provisions are formally unconstitutional (see D below). They also do not satisfy the key substantive requirements arising from Art. 10(1) and Art. 5(1) second sentence of the Basic Law (see E below).

No. 45 – Surveillance of Foreign Telecommunications

I.

The fundamental rights of the Basic Law are binding upon the Federal Intelligence Service and the legislator that sets out its powers, irrespective of whether the Federal Intelligence Service is operating within Germany or abroad. The protection afforded by Art. 10(1) and Art. 5(1) second sentence of the Basic Law also applies to telecommunications surveillance of foreigners in other states.

1. Art. 1(3) of the Basic Law provides that German state authority is comprehensively bound by the fundamental rights of the Basic Law. No restrictive requirements that make the binding effect of fundamental rights dependent on a territorial connection with Germany or on the exercise of specific sovereign powers can be inferred from the provision. In any event, this holds true for the fundamental rights at issue in the present case, which, in their dimension as rights against state interference, afford protection against surveillance measures.

a) According to Art. 1(3) of the Basic Law, the fundamental rights of the Basic Law bind the legislature, the executive and the judiciary as directly applicable law. The provision does not contain an explicit restriction to German territory. There was also no unspoken consensus at the time the Basic Law came into existence from which an exemption could be derived according to which fundamental rights were not applicable to the actions of German state organs abroad ([...]). Rather, particularly in response to the Nazi reign of violence and tyranny, Art. 1(3) of the Basic Law aimed to achieve a comprehensive binding effect of fundamental rights rooted in human dignity; as early as 1949, the provision was embedded in the conviction that the Federal Republic of Germany had to find its place in the international community as a partner that abides by the rule of law ([...]). This is reflected in the Basic Law's Preamble and in particular in Art. 1(2) and Arts. 24 and 25 of the Basic Law. Even though the question whether fundamental rights would be binding outside of German territory was not addressed during the deliberations preceding the adoption of the Basic Law and even though the type of surveillance measures targeting other states that are possible today were unimaginable at the time, it cannot be inferred from the Basic Law's legislative history that fundamental rights protection was always meant to end at the national border. Rather, the Basic Law's aim to provide comprehensive fundamental rights protection and to place the individual at its centre suggests that fundamental rights ought to provide protection whenever the German state acts and might thereby create a need for protection – irrespective of where and towards whom it does so.

b) Under Art. 1(3) of the Basic Law, fundamental rights as rights of the individual against state interference are not only binding in constellations in which the

German state acts vis-à-vis the affected persons as a sovereign power that has the monopoly on the use of force. [...]

91 Rather, state authority is bound comprehensively and universally by the fundamental rights, irrespective of the specific functions, the types of action or the respective object of the exercise of state functions [...]

92 c) The binding effect of fundamental rights on the German state, even when it acts abroad, is not limited to a mere objective legal duty [...]. Rather, it corresponds with a legal right afforded anyone recognised as a protected fundamental rights holder by the fundamental right in question. The Basic Law does not provide for fundamental rights that bind the state vis-à-vis individual fundamental rights holders without also providing the individual with a corresponding subjective right. It is a key part of fundamental rights protection under the Basic Law that fundamental rights are rights of the individual.

93 2. German state authority is bound by fundamental rights even in relation to actions taken vis-à-vis foreigners in other states; this is also in line with Germany's participation in the international community.

94 a) In its Art. 1(2), the Basic Law acknowledges inviolable and inalienable human rights as the basis of every community, of peace and of justice in the world. The Basic Law thus places fundamental rights in the context of international human rights guarantees that seek to provide protection beyond national borders and are afforded to individuals as human beings. Accordingly, Art. 1(2) and Art. 1(3) of the Basic Law build upon the guarantee of human dignity enshrined in Art. 1(1) of the Basic Law. Given this essentially universal nature of fundamental rights protection, in the codification of fundamental rights the Basic Law deliberately differentiates between human rights and rights afforded only German citizens. However, this does not mean that human rights should also be limited to domestic matters or state action in Germany. [...]

95 Furthermore, the terminological distinction between "inviolable and inalienable human rights" in Art. 1(2) of the Basic Law and the "following fundamental rights" in Art. 1(3) of the Basic Law can also not be used as an argument against the integration of fundamental rights into the context of universal human rights. In this respect, too, nothing in the Basic Law's wording and systematic concept suggests that this differentiation ought to be interpreted as relating to territory or as indicating separate territorial scopes of application. On the contrary, the fundamental rights of the Basic Law (Art. 1(3) of the Basic Law) are all linked to the guarantee of human rights; this is also reflected in the Federal Constitutional Court's established case-law, according to which the fundamental rights of the Basic Law must be interpreted in light of international human rights guarantees (cf. BVerfGE 111, 307 <317 and 318>; 128, 282 <306 and 307> – *Coercive Treatment*

in Psychiatric Confinement under Criminal Law; 128, 326 <367 and 368>; 142, 313 <345 para. 88> – *Coercive Medical Treatment*; 148, 296 <351 para. 128>; BVerfGE 152, 152 <176 para. 58> – *Right to Be Forgotten I*). Moreover, the principles enshrined in Art. 1(2) of the Basic Law constitute an absolute limit, within the meaning of Art. 79(3) of the Basic Law, for restrictions of fundamental rights protection by the Constitution-amending legislator (cf. BVerfGE 84, 90 <120 and 121>; 141, 1 <15 para. 34>).

This link between fundamental rights and human rights guarantees is incompatible with the notion that the applicability of the fundamental rights of the Basic Law ends at the national border, which would exempt German authorities from having to adhere to fundamental rights and human rights when they act abroad vis-à-vis foreigners. Such a notion would run counter to the Basic Law's aim of ensuring that every person is afforded inalienable rights on the basis of international conventions and beyond national borders – including protection from surveillance (cf. Art. 12 of the Universal Declaration of Human Rights, Art. 17(1) of the International Covenant on Civil and Political Rights). [...] 96

b) The European Convention on Human Rights, which constitutes a guideline for the interpretation of fundamental rights, also suggests such an understanding of the scope of the fundamental rights of the Basic Law (cf. BVerfGE 152, 152 <176 para. 58> with further references – *Right to Be Forgotten I*). It has not yet been comprehensively determined to what extent its guarantees apply to actions of the Contracting Parties outside of their own territory. The European Court of Human Rights is mainly guided by the criterion of whether a state exercises effective control over an area outside its own territory; on this basis, it has in many cases affirmed the applicability of Convention rights abroad (cf. in summary ECtHR [GC], *Al-Skeini and Others v. the United Kingdom*, Judgment of 7 July 2011, no. 55721/07, §§ 132 *et seq.* with further references; cf. also Aust, AVR 52 <2014>, p. 375 <394 *et seq.*> with further references). However, there has been no final determination as to whether protection is afforded against surveillance measures carried out by Contracting Parties in other states. 97

In a decision that has not become final yet, the First Section of the European Court of Human Rights measured the implementation of surveillance measures targeting persons abroad against the standards of the Convention without any restrictions and found such measures to be in violation of the Convention. The complainants in this case included foreign nationals who were not present or resident in the state against which the applications were directed (cf. ECtHR, *Big Brother Watch and Others v. the United Kingdom*, Judgment of 13 September 2018, no. 58170/13 and others, § 271). Similarly, a Swedish foundation challenged strategic foreign surveillance powers under Swedish law that exclude domestic communications. 98

The European Court of Human Rights reviewed these powers without calling into question the Convention's applicability abroad (cf. ECtHR, *Centrum för Rättvisa v. Sweden*, Judgment of 19 June 2018, no. 35252/08). Both proceedings are now pending before the Grand Chamber.

99 Irrespective of the outcome of these proceedings, the European Convention on Human Rights does not stand in the way of the applicability of German fundamental rights abroad. [...] In any case, the Convention does not rule out further-reaching fundamental rights protection by the Contracting Parties (Art. 53 ECHR).

100 c) In the case at hand, it is also not necessary to seek a delimitation from and coordination with other states and legal systems, which is the only possible reason that could stand in the way of the applicability of fundamental rights to German state authority abroad; this issue was discussed, and left unresolved, by the Federal Constitutional Court with regard to excluding the applicability of Art. 10 of the Basic Law in relation to foreign matters (cf. BVerfGE 100, 313 <362 *et seq.*> – *The Article 10 Act*).

101 The binding effect of German fundamental rights entails accountability and responsibility solely on the part of German state organs. It only applies to autonomous political decisions made by the Federal Republic of Germany and solely limits Germany's own latitude. Accordingly, in other states German fundamental rights – in their dimension as rights against state interference – are only applicable vis-à-vis German state authority and are thus in line with the restrictions arising from the principle of non-intervention under international law. Thus, the binding effect of fundamental rights does not amount to a violation of the principle of non-intervention or to a restriction of other states' executive or legislative powers. It neither imposes German law on other states, nor does it supplant the fundamental rights of other states. In particular, the binding effect of fundamental rights does not extend German state powers abroad, but limits potential courses of action of German state authority.

102 Thus, the applicability of fundamental rights (in this case Art. 10(1) of the Basic Law) has no effect on the legal order of other states; authorisations to carry out surveillance measures that are tied to the applicability of fundamental rights are also not binding within the legal systems of other states. [...]

103 In light of the foregoing, the binding effect of fundamental rights as such does not answer the question whether such measures are permissible under international law. [...]

104 3. The comprehensive binding effect of fundamental rights on German state authority does not alter the fact that the specific protection afforded by fundamental rights can differ according to the circumstances under which they are applied. Just as this

is the case for the different dimensions of fundamental rights within Germany, it is also the case for their scope of protection in other countries. [...]
4. In the present case, the complainants assert a violation of Art. 10(1) and Art. 5(1) second sentence of the Basic Law, which, as rights against state interference, afford protection against surveillance measures carried out in the context of surveillance of foreign telecommunications. It follows from the fact that German state authority is in principle comprehensively bound by fundamental rights that the Federal Intelligence Service and the legislator setting out its powers are also bound by fundamental rights, at least to the extent set out above. Exempting surveillance measures by intelligence services from this binding effect of fundamental rights simply because they are directed at foreigners in other states is alien to the Basic Law, just as exempting them from fundamental rights protection because of their political nature would be. Rather, the comprehensive binding effect of fundamental rights pursuant to Art. 1(3) of the Basic Law creates the framework in which due consideration can be given to the risks to fundamental rights that arise from new technological developments and from accompanying power shifts. This applies particularly to the changing significance of intelligence services that results from advances in information technology, which allow intelligence services a wider reach in other states.

a) The gathering of foreign intelligence by the Federal Intelligence Service has always been of considerable significance for the Federal Republic of Germany's capacity to act in the context of foreign and security policy; yet this significance has increased in recent years. In the course of internationalisation and the development of information technology, the significance and conditions under which foreign telecommunications surveillance, as a key element of foreign surveillance by the Federal Intelligence Service, is conducted have changed profoundly.

In the past, the only purpose of gathering foreign intelligence was the early detection of dangers to avert armed attacks on German territory; measures directly targeting individuals were limited to a small group of persons, as a result of both the technical possibilities and the intelligence interest at the time (cf. BVerfGE 67, 157 <178>). Given today's possibilities of communication and the accompanying internationalisation, potential impending dangers (*drohende Gefahren*) originating from abroad have multiplied. Information technology makes it possible to communicate directly across borders, regardless of physical distance, and to coordinate without any delay. This poses new challenges for the gathering of politically or militarily relevant communications that can be of great significance for the Federal Government's capacity to act. [...]

b) In the context of the tension between freedom and security, the growing importance of foreign surveillance resulting from changed circumstances gives rise to new challenges not only for upholding security, but also for upholding freedom; a balance between these two interests must be struck in accordance with the rule of law and on the basis of fundamental rights.

109 The developments in information technology have led to a situation where data is shared through global channels, where it is randomly routed via satellite or cable according to technical criteria that have no regard to national borders (cf. on this development BTDrucks 14/5655, p. 17). This makes it possible to intercept a considerable number of foreign communications from within Germany. Moreover, communication in society has become increasingly international. […] Given that, under the current realities of information technology, actions and communication relations of all kinds have become increasingly digital, and given the constant increase in data processing capacities, the possibilities for conducting telecommunications surveillance extend to broad areas of all of civil society, even outside a state's own jurisdiction – just as domestic communications are also subject to surveillance by other states (cf. BTDrucks 18/12850, p. 1283 *et seq.*).

110 In light of such developments, an understanding of fundamental rights according to which their protection ended at national borders would deprive holders of fundamental rights of all protection and would result in fundamental rights protection lagging behind the realities of internationalisation […]. It could undermine fundamental rights protection in an increasingly important area that is characterised by intrusive state action and where – in the field of security law – fundamental rights are especially significant in general. By contrast, in binding the state as the relevant actor, Art. 1(3) of the Basic Law accounts for such novel risks and helps bring them into the general framework of the rule of law that is created by the Basic Law.

II.

111 1. The challenged provisions affect the complainants' fundamental rights under Art. 10(1) and Art. 5(1) second sentence of the Basic Law. The provisions authorise the collection of personal data through covert telecommunications surveillance and thus concern the guarantee of the privacy of telecommunications enshrined in Art. 10(1) of the Basic Law. Accordingly, the sharing of data obtained through such measures also affects the protection afforded by the privacy of telecommunications, and such sharing must therefore also be measured against Art. 10 of the Basic Law. The challenged provisions also affect the fundamental right under Art. 5(1) second sentence of the Basic Law of the complainants who work as journalists. They authorise the Federal Intelligence Service to collect, process and share data from telecommunications generated in the context of these complainants' professional activities, including targeted surveillance and analysis of their communications

with journalistic sources (cf. ECtHR, *Weber and Saravia v. Germany*, Decision of 29 June 2006, no. 54934/00, §§ 143 *et seq.*; *Big Brother Watch and Others v. the United Kingdom*, Judgment of 13 September 2018, no. 58170/13 and others, §§ 476, 490 *et seq.*; see also BVerfGE 100, 313 <365> – *The Article 10 Act*).

2. In the present proceedings, there is no need to determine whether the challenged provisions, specifically the distinction made between German citizens and EU citizens, are compatible with equality protections. [...]

112

III.

The challenged provisions give rise to interferences with fundamental rights on various levels.

113

1. § 6(1) of the Federal Intelligence Service Act authorises the Federal Intelligence Service to intercept individual telecommunications from networks determined by a warrant; in particular, this allows for the interception of satellite signals and data transmitted via cable through the Federal Intelligence Service's own systems and also through a diversion order [addressed to telecommunications providers] pursuant to § 8 of the Federal Intelligence Service Act. § 14(1) of the Federal Intelligence Service Act authorises the Federal Intelligence Service to collect personal data in the context of cooperation with foreign intelligence services. [...]

114

115-117

2. § 6(1) to (3) of the Federal Intelligence Service Act gives rise to further interferences with the complainants' fundamental rights as it authorises further analysis of the data. [...]

118

3. A separate interference with fundamental rights lies in the potential sharing of intelligence obtained through surveillance, to the extent that it contains personal data, which is provided for under various separate constituent elements in § 24 of the Federal Intelligence Service Act. [...]

119

4. § 7 of the Federal Intelligence Service Act also gives rise to interferences with Art. 10(1) of the Basic Law and, where applicable, Art. 5(1) second sentence of the Basic Law. While this provision itself does not provide for the collection of data through surveillance measures but merely presumes that such collection takes place [...], § 7(1) of the Federal Intelligence Service Act provides a basis for further processing the data thus obtained, which amounts to a separate interference (cf. BVerfGE 100, 313 <366 and 367> – *The Article 10 Act*). [...]

120

D.

121 These interferences with fundamental rights are not justified under constitutional law. For formal reasons alone, the provisions authorising these interferences do not satisfy the constitutional requirements for statutory bases authorising interferences with the affected fundamental rights. While they are based on a legislative competence that is sufficient, they violate the requirement that the affected fundamental rights be expressly specified (*Zitiergebot*), which is enshrined in Art. 19(1) second sentence of the Basic Law.

I.

122 There are no major constitutional concerns with regard to legislative competence. The federal legislator was competent to enact the challenged provisions on the basis of Art. 73(1) no. 1 of the Basic Law.

123-133 [...]

II.

134 However, the challenged provisions are formally unconstitutional since they violate the requirement that the affected fundamental rights be expressly specified, which is enshrined in Art. 19(1) second sentence of the Basic Law. [...]

135 The legislator violates the requirement that the affected fundamental rights be expressly specified precisely where it considers these fundamental rights to be unaffected based on a certain interpretation of their scope of protection – in this case, the assumption that German state authority is not bound by fundamental rights when acting abroad in relation to foreigners. [...]

E.

136 In substantive terms, too, the challenged provisions are not compatible with the Basic Law. While the Basic Law does not generally preclude the use of strategic surveillance and the cooperation with other intelligence services relating thereto, the challenged provisions do not satisfy the key requirements arising from fundamental rights. [...]

No. 45 – Surveillance of Foreign Telecommunications

I.

1. Like any interference with fundamental rights, interferences with Art. 10(1) of the Basic Law and Art. 5(1) second sentence of the Basic Law must be based on a statutory authorisation that satisfies the requirements of legal clarity and specificity (cf. BVerfGE 65, 1 <44; 54> – *Census*; 100, 313 <359 and 360> – *The Article 10 Act*; established case-law). Provisions authorising the covert collection and processing of personal data are generally subject to more stringent requirements regarding legal clarity and specificity; this is because affected persons are not aware that their data is being processed and these powers can thus not be specified incrementally through individual warrants issued by the relevant authorities combined with judicial review (cf. BVerfGE 141, 220 <265 para. 94> – *The Federal Criminal Police Office Act*; cf. also ECtHR, *Big Brother Watch and Others v. the United Kingdom*, Judgment of 13 September 2018, no. 58170/13 and others, § 306).

Intelligence services are not exempt from these requirements. It is true that they must largely perform their tasks covertly. Especially surveillance carried out abroad must generally be strictly shielded from public knowledge so as to be able to obtain intelligence without jeopardising one's own resources and sources (cf. BVerfGE 30, 1 <18 and 19>; 100, 313 <397 and 398> – *The Article 10 Act*). [...]

However, it cannot be inferred from the need to keep foreign surveillance secret that as little as possible should be known about the Federal Intelligence Service itself or that its statutory bases must largely remain undisclosed. In a democratic state under the rule of law, there can be no general secrecy as to the statutory bases for intelligence activities and the limits of intelligence powers. [...]

The requirement of clear and sufficiently specific statutory powers of intelligence services does not call into question the possibility of keeping the intelligence obtained through such powers secret. Given that the powers only create abstract legal possibilities, they allow no conclusions to be drawn as to whether, how, to what extent and how successfully intelligence services make use of them.

2. To the extent that the challenged provisions authorise interferences with the privacy of telecommunications and freedom of the press, they can only be justified if they satisfy the principle of proportionality. According to this principle, they must have a legitimate purpose and must be suitable, necessary and proportionate in the strict sense for achieving that purpose (cf. BVerfGE 67, 157 <173>; 120, 378 <427>; 141, 220 <265 para. 93> – *The Federal Criminal Police Office Act*; established case-law). The Federal Constitutional Court has specified the standards deriving from proportionality in several decisions concerning covert surveillance measures carried out by security authorities and summarised them particularly in the decision on the Federal Criminal Police Office Act (cf. BVerfGE 141, 220 <268

et seq. para. 103 *et seq.>* – *The Federal Criminal Police Office Act*). These standards also apply to surveillance measures carried out by the intelligence services; they form the basis both for the requirements regarding data collection and processing and for the requirements regarding data sharing. However, the instrument of strategic surveillance as a special means of gathering foreign intelligence is not specifically considered within these standards. Therefore, they must be specified, in line with the decision on strategic surveillance powers under the Article 10 Act (cf. BVerfGE 100, 313 <368 *et seq.>* – *The Article 10 Act*).

II.

142 The powers to collect and process data in the framework of strategic telecommunications surveillance as a special instrument for gathering foreign intelligence are compatible with Art. 10(1) of the Basic Law in principle (see 1 below). Yet the legal provisions must set out sufficient restrictions in relation to these powers (see 2 below).

143 1. Art. 10(1) of the Basic Law does not, from the outset, rule out the creation of powers to gather foreign intelligence by means of strategic telecommunications surveillance. While the use of these powers is not limited to specific and objectively determined grounds and creating these powers thus authorises serious interferences with fundamental rights without any thresholds for their use, these powers, if sufficiently restricted, may still be justified in light of Art. 10(1) of the Basic Law and the principle of proportionality by the aim of foreign surveillance and the special conditions under which it is conducted.

144 a) Strategic telecommunications surveillance serves a legitimate purpose and, in accordance with the principle of proportionality, is suitable and necessary for achieving that purpose. According to the legislative intent, strategic surveillance is meant to yield intelligence on foreign matters that are significant to the foreign and security policy of the Federal Republic of Germany. It thus serves to contribute to the early detection of dangers, to safeguarding the Federal Republic of Germany's capacity to act and to providing information to the Federal Government on matters of foreign and security policy. This constitutes a legitimate aim. Strategic telecommunications surveillance is a suitable means for achieving that aim, because it makes it possible to obtain such information. [...] Strategic surveillance also satisfies the requirements for necessity. Without broad interception and analysis of data that is not based on specific grounds, such intelligence could not be obtained. No less intrusive means that would yield generally comparable intelligence are available.

No. 45 – Surveillance of Foreign Telecommunications

b) Authorising the Federal Intelligence Service to carry out strategic surveillance of foreign telecommunications can, in principle, also be justified in light of Art. 10(1) of the Basic Law with regard to proportionality in its strict sense.

aa) However, strategic telecommunications surveillance results in interferences of particularly great weight.

(1) The interferences are of such great weight because this instrument is used to covertly intrude into personal communications, which are often private and in some cases even highly confidential. Such covert surveillance of telecommunications generally amounts to a serious interference (cf. BVerfGE 141, 220 <264 and 265 para. 92> – *The Federal Criminal Police Office Act*), regardless of whether surveillance is conducted from within Germany or from abroad and whether it targets persons within Germany and German citizens or foreign citizens abroad.

(2) Yet compared to targeted surveillance of individual telecommunications, strategic surveillance gives rise to interferences of less weight given that it relates to data whose informative value cannot be foreseen in detail. [...]

(3) Moreover, its weight of interference vis-à-vis persons abroad is lower because this form of surveillance is not aimed at immediate operational consequences in the same manner as surveillance measures targeting Germans or persons within Germany. [...]

(4) By contrast, the exceptionally broad scope and the indiscriminate effect of strategic telecommunications surveillance is particularly aggravating. Such surveillance can be used against anyone without requiring specific grounds; it is merely restricted by the specific purposes pursued. Objective thresholds for the use of this power are not required, neither with regard to the situations in which surveillance measures are permissible nor with regard to the individuals affected by them. As long as it stays within the boundaries of the purposes of surveillance measures, which are only determined in the abstract, the authority vested with such powers can freely decide which networks, data and individuals it wants to target.

Such powers have an exceptional reach, particularly given the realities of modern information technology and its significance for communication relations. As regards the intensity of interference resulting from these powers, they cannot be compared to the powers [under the Article 10 Act] in respect of which the Federal Constitutional Court rendered a decision in 1999 concerning strategic surveillance measures targeting international communications [where one communicating party is in Germany and the other is abroad] (*Inland-Ausland-Kommunikation*). At the time, telecommunications surveillance was *de facto* restricted to narrowly defined means of telecommunication that were solely used in specific situations (cf. BVerfGE 100, 313 <379 and 380> – *The Article 10 Act*), whereas today the volume of intercepted data alone is exponentially larger. The data flows targeted by surveillance carry an immense volume of electronic telecommunications, which are then analysed. Given the ubiquitous and diverse use of communication services, all forms of activity of individuals and of human interaction are increasingly reflected in electronic signals and thus become a potential target of telecommunications surveillance. Thus, surveillance covers communications reaching deep into everyday life, including highly private and spontaneous communications and the sharing of images or files. [...]

152 (5) Strategic telecommunications surveillance gives rise to interferences of particular weight insofar as it also allows for targeted surveillance of specific individuals. Surveillance thus acquires a new dimension that did not exist with regard to the powers reviewed by the Court in its decision in 1999 [concerning the Article 10 Act]. The strategic surveillance measures examined in that decision used content-related search terms, but were not linked to specific individuals (cf. BVerfGE 100, 313 <384> – *The Article 10 Act*). By contrast, the strategic surveillance measures at issue in the present case mostly use formal search terms such as telecommunications identifiers, which make it possible to target specific individuals. Thus, strategic telecommunications surveillance gives rise to interferences that are fundamentally more far-reaching and more closely resembles targeted telecommunications surveillance.

153 (6) Compared to the previous legal framework, an aggravating factor is that, to a certain extent, strategic surveillance now also allows for traffic data to be retained in its entirety. The analysis of such traffic data – without specific grounds and merely guided by the purpose pursued – can provide deep insights into the communication behaviour and movement patterns of the affected persons, which may go far beyond the content-based analysis of individual communications (cf. regarding the informative value of such data BVerfGE 125, 260 <319> – *Data Retention*; CJEU, Judgment of 8 April 2014, *Digital Rights Ireland and Seitlinger and Others*, C-293/12, C-594/12, EU:C:2014:238, paras. 48, 56). This, too, considerably increases the weight of interference.

154 bb) As specific powers for gathering foreign intelligence, strategic surveillance powers can be justified under constitutional law, despite the particular weight of interference resulting from such surveillance.

155 (1) Yet by refraining from creating specific thresholds for the use of powers, the legislator fails to satisfy a core requirement arising from the rule of law. Such thresholds are indispensable in general, and are of even greater importance in respect of domestic security authorities, even for less intrusive interferences with fundamental rights, but certainly for serious interferences such as telecommunications surveillance (cf. BVerfGE 141, 220 <269 *et seq.* para. 104 *et seq.*> – *The Federal Criminal Police Office Act*; 150, 244 <280 *et seq.* para. 90 *et seq.*>). The

requirement of thresholds tied to specific circumstances ensures that interferences with fundamental rights are restricted, makes them contingent upon objective requirements and allows for oversight based on independent criteria. An authorisation of such interferences that is solely guided and restricted by the purpose pursued is generally incompatible with Art. 10(1) of the Basic Law.

In principle, this also applies to intelligence services. Insofar as surveillance measures extend to domestic communications, reliable thresholds are required in accordance with the general requirements. The same holds true for surveillance measures ordered by targeted warrants against specific individuals – whether they are in Germany or abroad –, for instance telecommunications surveillance measures or remote searches [of information technology systems] (cf. BVerfGE 120, 274 <326 et seq.> – *Remote Searches*; 125, 260 <320 et seq.> – *Data Retention*; 141, 220 <270 et seq.* para. 106 et seq.> – *The Federal Criminal Police Office Act*; [...]).

(2) By contrast, the gathering of foreign intelligence by intelligence services is treated differently insofar as it is aimed at providing general information to the Federal Government or – prior to restrictions of an individual's [fundamental right under Art. 10 of the Basic Law] – at the early detection of dangers. In these areas, the legislator may confer upon the Federal Intelligence Service the power to carry out strategic telecommunications surveillance. The fact that essentially such surveillance is only guided and restricted by the purpose pursued is not from the outset incompatible with the proportionality requirements (on the strategic surveillance of international telecommunications BVerfGE 100, 313 <373 et seq.> – *The Article 10 Act*).

(a) In this respect, the specific tasks that form part of foreign surveillance must be considered. Its primary aim is not to carry out targeted investigations of acts that have already been established and thus to gather information on clearly defined situations; rather, it mainly serves to detect and identify relevant information regarding intelligence interests that can only be defined in abstract terms. Thus, the role of foreign surveillance is to create a comprehensive informational basis, observe a broad range of developments, evaluate the information obtained, assess its relevance and make it available, in a condensed form, to the Federal Government and, as the case may be, other recipients. Given that potential intelligence interests concern the entire field of foreign and security policy, they relate to a wide range of information.

(b) In respect of this task, strategic surveillance without specific grounds that is essentially guided solely by the purpose pursued can be justified under constitutional law. In contrast to measures for the early detection of domestic dangers, it is significant that foreign surveillance is aimed at understanding and providing information about circumstances which cannot be directly perceived on a daily basis by German bodies or the German public. Its purpose is to yield intelligence regarding developments in contexts that are difficult to interpret on the basis of domestically obtained information only and that in part concern countries whose openness in terms of information structures is limited. Yet above all, the special conditions under which this task must be performed are decisive. Foreign surveillance concerns occurrences in other states, where the German state generally has no or only few resources for gathering intelligence and where it is not vested with sovereign powers granting it direct access to information (cf. also ECtHR, *Big Brother Watch and Others v. the United Kingdom*, Judgment of 13 September 2018, no. 58170/13 and others, § 518). […]

160 It must also be taken into account that surveillance is not solely characterised by different intelligence services working against each other; instead, these services also cooperate to gather intelligence on matters concerning both the Federal Republic of Germany and other states. Effective surveillance requires cooperation between intelligence services, particularly where surveillance solely aims to provide information to the Federal Government regarding political or military scenarios, but also where its aim is the early detection of dangers posed by international crime, including international terrorism. However, the Federal Intelligence Service is only able to engage in such cooperation if it also has the powers to examine the intelligence gathered by other services, to use and further analyse foreign intelligence, and if it can use its powers to contribute intelligence as a partner. Based on current knowledge, intelligence services in other states will commonly have powers to carry out surveillance of foreign telecommunications without specific grounds […]

161 (c) The exceptionally significant public interest in the effective gathering of foreign intelligence must also be taken into account.

162 In line with the legislative competence for conferring powers to conduct foreign surveillance […], such surveillance is always aimed at yielding information that is significant for Germany's position and capacity to act within the international community and, in that sense, is significant to foreign and security policy. The provision of information to the Federal Government for its decision-making on foreign and security policy helps it to assert itself in the realm of international power politics and can prevent erroneous decisions leading to potentially serious consequences. This indirectly bears on the safeguarding of democratic self-determination and the protection of the constitutional order – and thus on high-ranking constitutional interests. What is at issue here is an interest of the nation as a whole, which significantly goes beyond the interest in guaranteeing national security as such.

163 It is important to note that threats originating from abroad have increased significantly as part of the advances in information technology and international commu-

nication as well as the closer interconnectedness of living conditions across borders. In this context, the early detection of dangers originating from abroad takes on particular importance for public security. The expansion and internationalisation of the possibilities for conducting communication and the resulting increased politicisation and ability to organise of international criminal gangs mean that domestic situations of danger frequently originate in networks of actors cooperating internationally with foreign and security policy dimensions. [...] Some of these activities seek to destabilise society (regarding international terrorism cf. BVerfGE 115, 320 <357> – *Profiling*; 133, 277 <333 and 334 para. 133> – *Counter-Terrorism Database Act I*; 143, 101 <138 and 139 para. 125>) and can jeopardise the constitutional order, the existence and security of the Federation and of the *Länder* and life, limb and liberty. These are legal interests that are exceptionally significant under constitutional law, and the legislator may consider effective foreign surveillance, circumscribed in accordance with the rule of law, to be an indispensable means for protecting these interests (cf. BVerfGE 115, 320 <358> – *Profiling*; 143, 101 <138 and 139 para. 124 *et seq.*>).

Consequently, the much broader access to data that is permitted in the context of strategic surveillance today is matched by a higher potential for danger than in the case [concerning the Article 10 Act] decided by the Federal Constitutional Court in 1999. For this reason, Art. 10(1) of the Basic Law and the proportionality requirements resulting therefrom in principle do not preclude the use of search terms targeting specific individuals for strategic surveillance measures. In principle, the law may therefore also, within limits, provide for the retention of the entirety of traffic data and for subsequent analysis of this data without requiring specific grounds for doing so.

(d) An important aspect supporting the argument that strategic telecommunications surveillance is justifiable is that the consequences of undertaking such surveillance without specific grounds are somewhat mitigated by the fact that it is conducted by an authority that, in principle, has no operational powers itself. Given the actual circumstances of cases concerning intelligence on persons located in other states, such intelligence can generally not lead to direct follow-up measures against them, as German authorities are not vested with sovereign powers when acting abroad. However, this does not call into question that surveillance measures carried out abroad can also give rise to serious consequences for affected persons, and that such measures also serve to provide a basis for follow-up measures against these persons – either through data sharing or when the persons concerned subsequently cross the border. Yet given that the data is collected by an authority that in principle has no operational powers itself, any further use of this data depends on a screening of the data carried out by persons that have no responsibility for operational action themselves. Therefore, the sharing of this data for operational use can, and must, be subject to qualified thresholds (see para. 220 *et seq.* below).

166 c) Based on the above considerations, the instrument of strategic surveillance, including the use of formal search terms targeting specific individuals and the collection and analysis of traffic data, sometimes in its entirety, is not generally incompatible with Art. 10(1) of the Basic Law or the proportionality requirements resulting therefrom. However, given that they are not based on specific grounds and essentially guided and restricted only by the purpose pursued, the powers to conduct strategic surveillance are exceptional powers that must be restricted to foreign surveillance conducted by an authority that itself has no operational powers for averting dangers to public security. These powers can only be justified by the authority's particular tasks and the specific conditions under which these tasks are performed. In accordance with the principle of proportionality, the specific design of the surveillance powers must be in line with these considerations.

167 2. The legislative design of data collection and processing in the framework of strategic surveillance is subject to further requirements, which must take into account the particular weight of the interferences with fundamental rights and the specific justification provided by the particular task and conditions of foreign surveillance.

168 a) An overarching aim of the requirements arising from the principle of proportionality is to limit strategic telecommunications surveillance by ensuring that it is designed as a sufficiently focused instrument despite its broad scope and indiscriminate effect. The Basic Law does not allow global and sweeping surveillance, not even for the purpose of gathering foreign intelligence (cf. BVerfGE 100, 313 <376> – *The Article 10 Act*).

169 Therefore, the legislator must restrict the volume of data to be taken from the respective transmission channels […] and the geographical area covered by surveillance. Since the technical possibilities for processing data are changing quickly, merely referring to actual capacity limits in this respect is insufficient […]. Yet above all, the legislator must circumscribe the powers in accordance with the rule of law so as to structure and partially restrict data collection and processing. In particular, this includes rules on the use of filtering techniques (see b below), the purposes of surveillance (see c below), the design of the surveillance process (see d below), the focused use of search terms (see e below), the limits of traffic data retention (see f below), the methods of data analysis (see g below), the protection of relationships of trust (see h below) and the protection of the core of private life (see i below), as well as the imposition of deletion requirements (see j below). In addition, the legislator must adhere to requirements regarding transparency, individual legal protection and, above all, comprehensive independent oversight (for general considerations on this, see V below).

No. 45 – Surveillance of Foreign Telecommunications

b) Given that strategic surveillance can only be justified as an instrument for gathering foreign intelligence, further data processing must be based on clear provisions requiring that data stemming from domestic communications be removed. [...]

c) Moreover, the legislator must determine the purposes of telecommunications surveillance and of the use of intelligence thus obtained in sufficiently clear and specific statutory provisions (cf. BVerfGE 100, 313 <372> – *The Article 10 Act*).

aa) Given that telecommunications surveillance is a particularly intrusive instrument for gathering foreign intelligence, it must be substantially restricted to sufficiently limited and precisely defined purposes, for which the legislator is responsible. Within the limits of the relevant legislative competences, the purposes that can be taken into consideration are those that aim to protect high-ranking interests of the common good, the violation of which would result in serious harm to external and domestic peace or to the legal interests of individuals (cf. BVerfGE 100, 313 <373> – *The Article 10 Act*).

bb) In contrast to this, measures carried out in the context of surveillance of foreign telecommunications that are, from the outset, only aimed at providing information to the Federal Government to prepare governmental decisions can be permissible even if they are not aimed at the early detection of dangers. To this end, the legislator may provide for surveillance measures for the entire range of tasks performed by the Federal Intelligence Service. It may, for example, tie these measures merely to orders of the Federal Government – yet the legislator must restrict them, in line with its legislative competences, to measures concerning foreign and security policy. At the same time, the legislator must then ensure that a change in the purpose for which the data may be used is excluded in principle and that the intelligence obtained through such surveillance not be shared with other bodies (see para. 223 *et seq.* below), aside from special exceptions [...].

d) Insofar as strategic surveillance measures are used to pursue the purposes defined by law, the legislator may in principle permit such surveillance measures without requiring specific grounds and does not have to tie them to objective thresholds (see para. 157 *et seq.* above). Yet as the powers to conduct strategic surveillance are only guided by the purpose pursued, the legislator must set out procedural safeguards adequately ensuring that the powers are based on the respective purposes and thus also allow for oversight ([...]).

aa) The granting of such powers must be based on a formal determination of precisely defined surveillance measures. This constitutes a designation of the specific purpose of the measure within the meaning of data protection law. [...]

Under constitutional law, the legislator is not restricted to a specific approach for the internal procedural design of such formal determinations. [...]

181 Yet just as prior judicial authorisation (*Richtervorbehalt*) is required for telecommunications surveillance targeting individuals that is authorised by an individual warrant (cf. BVerfGE 125, 260 <337 and 338> – *Data Retention*; 141, 220 <312 para. 235> – *The Federal Criminal Police Office Act*), the determination of a strategic surveillance measure as such requires oversight that resembles judicial review. While it must in principle be ensured that such oversight is conducted before the measure is carried out, exceptions in cases of urgency are not ruled out.

182 bb) The purposes of the surveillance measures that are defined in this manner must be used to determine the further procedure for data collection and processing, which must subsequently be accessible to independent oversight. […] Rules for the use of coincidental findings made possible by internal changes in purpose are permissible nonetheless (cf. BVerfGE 141, 220 <326 *et seq.* para. 284 *et seq.*> – *The Federal Criminal Police Office Act*).

183-184 dd) […]

185 e) Strategic surveillance gives rise to interferences of particular weight given that it predominantly uses formal search terms and thus also targets specific individuals. This is not generally impermissible under constitutional law. Nonetheless, restrictions are required that, in accordance with the principle of proportionality, take into account the affected persons' need for protection.

186 aa) In line with current practice, the targeted interception of telecommunications of German citizens must be ruled out. […]

187 bb) As a basis for systematically structuring the surveillance process, the legislator must set out the reasons for which strategic surveillance measures may target specific individuals. […]

188 […]

189 cc) For the rest, the possibility of authorising surveillance not based on specific grounds reaches its limits where, by definition, the use of search terms targeting specific individuals – with comparable certainty – results in the targeted surveillance of individual telecommunications that is equivalent to surveillance authorised by a targeted warrant. In that case, the legislator must ensure that the requirements regarding such surveillance authorised by a targeted warrant (cf. BVerfGE 141, 220 <268 *et seq.* para. 103 *et seq.*; 309 *et seq.* para. 228 *et seq.*> – *The Federal Criminal Police Office Act*) are observed and that they are not circumvented through strategic surveillance.

190 dd) The legislator may only refrain from imposing the above-mentioned requirements and restrictions (see para. 187 *et seq.* above) if surveillance measures are solely aimed at providing political intelligence to the Federal Government, and if any sharing of the intelligence with other bodies is ruled out in principle (see para. 177 above).

f) The authorisation to carry out strategic surveillance must also be restricted by law insofar as it permits the retention of traffic data in its entirety. The legislator must ensure that the data flows intercepted to this end are substantially limited and that the data is not stored for more than six months (cf. also BVerfGE 125, 260 <322> – *Data Retention*).

g) It is sufficient that the legislator provides for the basic framework governing the specific steps for the analysis of the intercepted data and tasks the Federal Intelligence Service with creating a detailed structure for analysis in its intelligence service manual, which must be subject to independent oversight (see para. 272 *et seq.* below). This basic framework to be determined by the legislator includes the requirement that the Federal Intelligence Service analyse intercepted data without undue delay (cf. BVerfGE 100, 313 <385 and 386> – *The Article 10 Act*; 125, 260 <332> – *Data Retention*; see also the corresponding provision in § 6(1) first sentence of the Article 10 Act and the accompanying legislative materials BTDrucks 14/5655, p. 13), the applicability of the principle of proportionality to the selection of search terms – which is already provided for in the existing intelligence service manual –, provisions governing the use of intrusive methods of data analysis, in particular complex forms of data cross-checking (regarding the particular need for safeguards applicable to the analysis of strategic surveillance cf. also ECtHR, *Big Brother Watch and Others v. the United Kingdom*, Judgment of 13 September 2018, no. 58170/13 and others, §§ 346 and 347), and adherence to prohibitions of discrimination under the Basic Law (regarding this requirement cf. BVerfGE 115, 320 <348> - *Profiling*; 133, 277 <359 and 360 para. 189> – *Counter-Terrorism Database Act I*; regarding the applicable law in Sweden cf. ECtHR, *Centrum för Rättvisa v. Sweden*, Judgment of 19 June 2018, no. 35252/08, § 29). The legislator may also have to lay down how algorithms may be used, in particular to ensure that their use can generally be reviewed by the independent oversight regime.

h) Confidentiality in relationships of trusts – such as relationships between journalists and their sources, or lawyers and their clients – requires special protection. Such protection already follows from Art. 10(1) of the Basic Law and the proportionality requirements derived therefrom. It corresponds to a greater need for protection that may arise for any of the communicating parties involved in such relationships. For the professions in question, this protection is also guaranteed by Art. 5(1) second sentence of the Basic Law or the fundamental rights that otherwise protect the respective professions – insofar as the scope of protection of these fundamental rights extends to persons affected by foreign surveillance.

aa) The targeted surveillance of communications of professions and groups of persons whose communication relations require special confidentiality protection must be limited. The use of search terms resulting in the targeted interception of telecommunication connections belonging to such persons cannot simply be justified by the assertion that they might serve to obtain potentially relevant intelligence. It is not justified that persons doing journalistic work face a higher risk of surveillance than other fundamental rights holders and that the information which such persons gather from their contacts or research can be siphoned off for the pursuit of security interests (cf. BVerfGE 107, 299 <336>). The same applies accordingly to lawyers. The targeted surveillance of lawyers as messengers must be tied to qualified thresholds, including in the context of strategic surveillance. These thresholds must ensure that the intrusion into relationships of trust is only permissible where it is used to investigate dangers that are deemed serious in the individual case and to investigate particularly serious criminal acts, or to apprehend certain dangerous criminals. This must be based on sound intelligence. For the rest, surveillance and analysis are only permissible where, in a balancing of interests conducted in the individual case, the public interest in obtaining the information in question takes precedence over the affected person's interest in the protection of confidentiality (cf. BVerfGE 129, 208 <258 *et seq*.> – *The Telecommunications Surveillance Revision Act*; 141, 220 <318 and 319 para. 255 *et seq*.> – *The Federal Criminal Police Office Act*). The legislator will have to examine whether and to what extent it must differentiate between different kinds of relationships of trust (cf. § 160a of the Code of Criminal Procedure; BVerfGE 129, 208 <259 and 260> – *The Telecommunications Surveillance Revision Act*). In any case, *ex ante* oversight resembling judicial review must in principle ensure that such relationships are protected.

195 [...]

196 bb) With regard to the protection of professional groups and their activities abroad in the context of foreign surveillance, the legislator can take into account the different conditions under which the press or lawyers operate in other countries. Accordingly, it can limit protection to persons or situations that actually merit protection, which means that their activities are characterised by freedom and independence that justify the special fundamental rights protection afforded such institutions [...]. [...]

197 cc) It is primarily for the legislator to assess whether and to what extent other relationships of trust require protection.

198 dd) Insofar as surveillance measures are exclusively aimed at providing political intelligence to the Federal Government, are not linked to any aim of early detection of dangers and the sharing of intelligence with other bodies is ruled out in principle (see para. 177 above), the legislator can refrain from protecting relationships of trust where necessary.

No. 45 – Surveillance of Foreign Telecommunications

i) Art. 10(1) of the Basic Law in conjunction with Art. 1(1) of the Basic Law gives rise to further requirements for the protection of the core of private life.

aa) The protection of the core of private life guarantees the individual a domain of highly personal life and ensures an inviolable human dignity core that is beyond the reach of the state and provides fundamental rights protection against surveillance. Even exceptionally significant interests of the general public cannot justify an interference with this domain of private life that is absolutely protected (cf. BVerfGE 109, 279 <313> – *Surveillance of Private Homes*; 141, 220 <276 para. 120> – *The Federal Criminal Police Office Act*; established case-law). This also applies to intelligence services (cf. BVerfGE 120, 274 <335 *et seq.*> – *Remote Searches*) and to surveillance measures in other countries.

The free development of one's personality within the core of private life encompasses the possibility of expressing internal processes, reflections, views and experiences of a highly personal nature. Protection is afforded particularly to non-public communication with persons enjoying the highest level of personal trust, conducted with the reasonable expectation that no surveillance is taking place. Such conversations do not lose their highly personal character merely because they combine highly personal with everyday matters (cf. BVerfGE 141, 220 <276 and 277 para. 121; 279 para. 128; 314 and 315 para. 243> – *The Federal Criminal Police Office Act*; established case-law).

However, communications in which criminal acts are discussed and planned do not form part of the core of private life, not even when they also concern highly personal matters. This does not mean that the core protection were subject to a general balancing against public security interests. A highly personal conversation is not excluded from the core of private life simply because it might provide insights that could be helpful for the investigation of criminal acts or the averting of dangers to public security. Statements made in the course of a conversation that only reveal inner impressions and feelings and do not contain any indications pointing to specific criminal acts do not simply become relevant to the public because they might reveal the reasons or motives for criminal conduct. Furthermore, despite having some link to criminal conduct, situations in which individuals are in fact encouraged to admit wrongdoing or to prepare for the consequences thereof, such as confessions or confidential conversations with a psychotherapist or defence lawyer, are part of the highly personal domain (cf. in more detail BVerfGE 141, 220 <276 and 277 paras. 121 and 122> – *The Federal Criminal Police Office Act*; established case-law).

bb) The legislator must enact provisions that expressly protect the core of private life.

204 First and foremost, it must be absolutely impermissible to make the core of private life a target of state investigations and to use information relating to that core in any way or to otherwise base further investigations on it. This also applies to strategic surveillance. In line with the notion of the core of private life set out above, protection of that core must not be limited to situations which exclusively concern highly personal matters.

205 Moreover, the core of private life must be protected both at the stage of data collection and at the stage of data analysis. However, the requirements for how this protection is to be ensured by law differ based on the type of the surveillance measures in question (cf. BVerfGE 141, 220 <279 para. 127> – *The Federal Criminal Police Office Act*).

206 Accordingly, where data collection and the use of search terms for strategic surveillance measures are concerned, legislative safeguards going beyond the prohibition of the targeted collection of data from the core of private life are not required. […]

207 At the stage of manual data screening, the law must ensure that further screening ceases as soon as it becomes ascertainable that surveillance is encroaching on the core of private life; even where mere doubts arise, the measure may only be continued – subject to exceptions for cases of urgency (cf. BVerfGE 141, 220 <280 para. 129> – *The Federal Criminal Police Office Act*) – in the form of recordings that are examined by an independent body prior to analysis (cf. BVerfGE 141, 220 <279 and 280 para. 129> – *The Federal Criminal Police Office Act*; see also § 3a second to eleventh sentence of the Article 10 Act). It must be ensured that intelligence from the highly personal domain must not be used and must be deleted immediately; this must be documented and the deletion logs must be retained for a sufficiently long period so as to allow for oversight under data protection law (cf. BVerfGE 141, 220 <280 para. 129> – *The Federal Criminal Police Office Act*; see also para. 289 *et seq.* below).

208 j) The principle of proportionality also gives rise to deletion requirements with regard to surveillance measures. The purpose of these requirements is to ensure that the use of personal data remains limited to the purposes justifying the data processing, and that data can no longer be used once these purposes have been achieved (cf. BVerfGE 65, 1 <46> – *Census*; 133, 277 <366 para. 206> – *Counter-Terrorism Database Act I*; 141, 220 <285 and 286 para. 144> – *The Federal Criminal Police Office Act*; established case-law).

209 […]

210 The key steps of the data deletion process must be documented, insofar as this is practical and necessary for independent oversight; the deletion logs must be retained for a sufficiently long period to allow for effective oversight (cf. BVerfGE

141, 220 <302 and 303 para. 205> – *The Federal Criminal Police Office Act*; see also para. 291 below).

III.

Personal data stemming from strategic surveillance may only be shared with other bodies if a clear and sufficiently specific statutory basis exists that makes such sharing contingent upon the protection of legal interests and upon certain thresholds that reflect the weight of interference resulting from strategic surveillance. The sharing of personal data stemming from strategic surveillance is only permissible for the purpose of protecting legal interests of particularly great weight and requires, as a threshold, indications of an identifiable danger (*konkretisierte Gefahrenlage*) or sufficiently specific grounds for the suspicion of criminal conduct (*hinreichend konkretisierter Tatverdacht*). This does not apply to reports provided to the Federal Government, insofar as these are exclusively intended to provide political intelligence and prepare government decisions. 211

1. Where an authority makes data collected by it accessible to another body through data sharing, this amounts to a separate interference with fundamental rights (cf. BVerfGE 100, 313 <367> – *The Article 10 Act*; 141, 220 <334 para. 305> – *The Federal Criminal Police Office Act*; established case-law). This interference must be measured against the fundamental rights which the original data collection interfered with (cf. BVerfGE 100, 313 <367> – *The Article 10 Act*; 141, 220 <334 para. 305> – *The Federal Criminal Police Office Act*; established case-law). 212

2. Given that it results in new interferences with fundamental rights, data sharing requires a separate statutory basis that must be clear and sufficiently specific (cf. BVerfGE 65, 1 <46> – *Census*; 100, 313 <389> – *The Article 10 Act*; established case-law). 213

[…] 214-215

3. In substantive terms, both the statutory authorisations for data sharing and the specific data sharing measures must satisfy the proportionality requirements (cf. BVerfGE 65, 1 <45 and 46> – *Census*; 100, 313 <390 et seq.> – *The Article 10 Act*; 141, 220 <327 para. 286> – *The Federal Criminal Police Office Act*). Data sharing must be suitable and necessary for achieving a legitimate purpose. According to established case-law, the determination of whether a data sharing measure is proportionate in the strict sense must be based on the weight of the change in purpose resulting from data sharing compared to the purpose of the original data collection and, on this basis, on the principle of a hypothetical recollection of data. According to this principle, it is necessary to determine whether it would hypothetically be permissible, under constitutional law, to collect the relevant data 216

again with comparably weighty means for the changed purpose (cf. BVerfGE 141, 220 <327 *et seq.* para. 287 *et seq.*> – *The Federal Criminal Police Office Act*).

217 However, special circumstances must be taken into consideration for the constellation at hand. While authorities usually collect data specifically for their own operational purposes and the data is then used for a new purpose when it is shared with other authorities, the Federal Intelligence Service does not collect data for its own operational purposes, but merely with the aim to share it with the Federal Government and, as the case may be, other bodies after having identified and processed the relevant information (cf. § 1(2) of the Federal Intelligence Service Act). Moreover, the powers to collect data in question here are not tied to objective thresholds but are essentially only guided by the purpose pursued.

218 Especially for this constellation, adherence to stringent requirements regarding data sharing is thus of great significance. Data collection for the purpose of foreign surveillance does not require verifiable thresholds so as to allow for the identification of and proactive search for threats and situations of danger as purely precautionary measures long before specific dangers (*konkrete Gefahren*) actually arise. Under constitutional law, this requires that such thresholds must apply at least to the sharing of intelligence thus obtained […]

219 Thus, whether the sharing of data is constitutional depends on whether it were permissible, under constitutional law, to collect the data for the purpose for which the shared data is to be used with comparably weighty means (cf. BVerfGE 141, 220 <328 para. 288> – *The Federal Criminal Police Office Act*). Since it is impermissible from the outset to make an instrument which is as sweeping as telecommunications surveillance that is not based on specific grounds available to domestic security authorities, the constitutional requirements that are also applicable to other particularly severe and intrusive measures, such as the surveillance of private homes or remote searches, apply (cf. BVerfGE 141, 220 <271 para. 110; 273 and 274 paras. 115 and 116; 327 *et seq.* para. 287 *et seq.*> – *The Federal Criminal Police Office Act*), unless measures merely serve to provide reports to the Federal Government (see para. 223 *et seq.* below). This is in line with, and further determines, the requirement of an exceptionally significant public interest and of sufficiently specific and qualified thresholds for data sharing that the Federal Constitutional Court laid down in its decision on the Counter-Terrorism Database Act in relation to the sharing of information obtained by the intelligence services with authorities that carry out operational measures (cf. BVerfGE 133, 277 <329 para. 123> – *Counter-Terrorism Database Act I*).

220 4. In light of the foregoing, requirements must be set both regarding the protection of legal interests and regarding thresholds for the use of powers, in this case thresholds for data sharing. These must distinguish between data sharing for public

security purposes and for law enforcement purposes (cf. BVerfGE 100, 313 <394> – *The Article 10 Act*; 141, 220 <270 and 271 paras. 107 and 108> – *The Federal Criminal Police Office Act*).

In terms of the protection of legal interests, data sharing for public security purposes is only permissible to protect particularly weighty legal interests (cf. BVerfGE 125, 260 <329 and 330> – *Data Retention*; 133, 277 <365 para. 203> – *Counter-Terrorism Database Act I*; 141, 220 <270 para. 108> – *The Federal Criminal Police Office Act*). [...] By contrast, data sharing for law enforcement purposes must be limited to criminal offences of great weight. Based on these criteria, such sharing is only justified if it serves to prosecute particularly serious criminal offences. [...] 221

In terms of thresholds for data sharing, a sufficiently specific and identifiable danger must be established to justify data sharing for public security purposes. The legislator does not have to make data sharing contingent upon the existence of a specific (*konkrete Gefahr*), immediate (*unmittelbar bevorstehende Gefahr*) or present danger (*gegenwärtige Gefahr*) as is traditionally required for public security measures. However, the statutory basis must require sufficient indications of an identifiable danger (*hinreichend konkretisierte Gefahr*) in the sense that there be at least factual indications that a specific danger to the protected legal interests may emerge (cf. in this respect BVerfGE 141, 220 <271 *et seq.* para. 111 *et seq.*> – *The Federal Criminal Police Office Act*). Insofar as data is shared for law enforcement purposes, there must be sufficiently specific facts that give rise to the suspicion that a particularly serious criminal act has been committed. Mere indications that are sufficient to launch initial, general investigations (cf. § 152(2) of the Code of Criminal Procedure) do not suffice here; rather, specific facts are required that give rise to the suspicion that such criminal acts have been committed (cf. BVerfGE 125, 260 <328 and 329> – *Data Retention*), which corresponds to the requirements for the surveillance of private homes pursuant to § 100c of the Code of Criminal Procedure. In this respect, there must be circumstances that have taken specific shape to some extent and support such a suspicion [...]. 222

5. This does not apply to the sharing of intelligence stemming from strategic surveillance with the Federal Government solely in its governmental capacity. Where information is provided to the Federal Government so that it can discharge its responsibility with regard to foreign and security policy and a transfer to other bodies is ruled out, protection of qualified legal interests or thresholds for data sharing are not required under constitutional law. 223

a) Such further requirements are not needed here given that providing information to the Federal Government on matters that are significant to foreign and security policy is the primary purpose of foreign surveillance and the provision of such 224 information constitutes an exceptionally significant public interest even if there are no indications of an identifiable danger.

225 Most notably, where surveillance is only used to provide political intelligence to the Federal Government, its weight of interference vis-à-vis the person under surveillance is generally significantly lower. [...] When intelligence is used as background information for the Federal Government or as a basis for preparing governmental decision-making, the interest in the individuals concerned typically becomes less important; therefore, sharing can be justified regardless of whether specific thresholds for data sharing are observed.

226 [...]

227 b) [...]

228 c) [...]

229-230 6. [...]

231 7. Special requirements apply to the sharing of data with foreign bodies. First of all, this concerns intelligence sharing in the individual case – irrespective of whether this occurs within the context of cooperation (regarding automated data sharing in the context of cooperation see paras. 254 *et seq.* and 262 *et seq.* below).

232 a) The requirements set out above regarding the protection of legal interests and thresholds for sharing data with domestic bodies apply to the sharing of data with foreign bodies, too (see paras. 216 *et seq.* and 220 *et seq.* above). [...]

233 b) In addition, however, a separate requirement when sharing data with foreign bodies is the ascertainment that the foreign bodies will handle the data shared with them in accordance with the rule of law. This reflects the fact that, once shared with foreign bodies, the use of data collected by German authorities is no longer subject to the requirements of the Basic Law since the foreign state authority is only bound by its own legal obligations, yet German state authority is responsible for the sharing of data and remains bound by fundamental rights when sharing data (cf. BVerfGE 141, 220 <342 paras. 326 and 327> – *The Federal Criminal Police Office Act*).

234 According to established case-law, the state receiving the data is required to adhere to guarantees under data protection law (see aa below) and to uphold human rights when using the information (see bb below). Both require clear provisions ensuring that the Federal Intelligence Service sufficiently ascertain that these guarantees will be upheld (see cc below). In addition, adherence to restrictions on the sharing of data collected through strategic surveillance must be ensured by obtaining sound assurances from the receiving states (see dd below).

235 aa) The first requirement serves to uphold the data protection guarantees following from the right of personality. Yet it is not required that receiving states have rules on the processing of personal data that match those within the German legal order

or that they guarantee a level of protection that is equivalent to the protection afforded by the Basic Law. In fact, the Basic Law recognises and generally respects the autonomy and diversity of legal orders, including in the context of data sharing. Value decisions and parameters [in receiving states] do not have to conform to those of the German legal order or the Basic Law.

However, the sharing of personal data with other states is only permissible if the handling of the shared data in these states does not undermine the protection of personal data guaranteed by human rights. [...] What is required is the guarantee of an appropriate substantive level of data protection for the handling of the shared data in the receiving state. [...] The assessment of whether this is the case must be made on the basis of the receiving state's domestic law as well as its international obligations and the implementation thereof in everyday practice (BVerfGE 141, 220 <344 and 345 paras. 334 and 335> with further references – *The Federal Criminal Police Office Act*).

bb) Sharing data with other states is ruled out if there is reason to fear that its use could lead to violations of fundamental principles of the rule of law. Under no circumstances may the state be complicit in violations of human dignity (cf. BVerfGE 140, 317 <347 para. 62>; 141, 220 <342 para. 328> – *The Federal Criminal Police Office Act*). In particular, it must appear certain that the information will be used neither for political persecution nor for inhuman and degrading punishment or treatment in the receiving state (cf. Art. 16a(3) of the Basic Law). The legislator must ensure that the sharing of data collected by German authorities with other states or international organisations does not erode the protections of the European Convention on Human Rights and other international human rights treaties (cf. Art. 1(2) of the Basic Law; cf. BVerfGE 141, 220 <345 para. 336> – *The Federal Criminal Police Office Act*). Given the exceptional nature of surveillance and data sharing measures carried out by intelligence services, which may involve contacts with states not firmly committed to the rule of law, it must be ensured that the information provided is not used to persecute certain ethnic groups, stifle opposition or detain people without due process, kill or torture them in violation of human rights or international humanitarian law. The Federal Intelligence Service itself is responsible for examining and determining which rules of international law have to be observed in this respect. In principle, receiving states must agree to rights to information so that adherence to international human rights standards can be monitored.

cc) To uphold this standard of protection, clear statutory provisions are required that impose an obligation on the Federal Intelligence Service to ascertain the level of protection in the receiving state. Before sharing data, the Federal Intelligence

Service must ascertain that the receiving state adheres to requirements arising from data protection law and from human rights.

239 (1) [...]

240 [...] To the extent that the shared data includes data of journalists, lawyers or other professions meriting confidentiality protection, including to shield them from risks, a separate balancing of interests is required that differs from the balancing conducted to determine whether such data may be used domestically (see para. 193 *et seq.* above); it must generally be subject to *ex ante* oversight resembling judicial review (cf. United Nations Office of the High Commissioner for Human Rights, Letter of the Special Rapporteurs of 29 August 2016, OL DEU 2/2016, p. 7).

241 (2) [...]

242 dd) Given that the data collected by the Federal Intelligence Service in the context of strategic telecommunications surveillance stems from surveillance measures not based on specific grounds, it is especially important that effective limits are observed regarding the sharing of such intelligence with authorities that have operational powers, in particular law enforcement and police authorities or domestic administrative authorities. Insofar as the Federal Intelligence Service shares intelligence with foreign intelligence services, an obligation must be imposed on it – in line with current practice – to generally make such sharing contingent upon the assurance that the foreign service will only share the intelligence with other bodies if the Federal Intelligence Service consents. [...]

IV.

243 The design of a statutory basis for the cooperation with foreign intelligence services in the context of strategic telecommunications surveillance gives rise to special challenges under constitutional law. [...]

244 Such a statutory basis can only satisfy the requirements arising from fundamental rights if it is ensured that the limits to strategic surveillance set by the rule of law are not set aside through the mutual sharing of intelligence and that the Federal Intelligence Service essentially remains responsible for the data it has collected and analysed [...].

245 1. As a constitutional order that is open to international law, the Basic Law permits such cooperation with foreign intelligence services. However, it requires separate statutory provisions ensuring that fundamental rights protection is also guaranteed in the context of international cooperation between intelligence services.

246 a) With its Preamble, together with Art. 1(2), Art. 9(2), Art. 16(2), Arts. 23 to 26 and Art. 59(2), the Basic Law comprehensively binds the Federal Republic of Germany to the international community and programmatically commits German

No. 45 – Surveillance of Foreign Telecommunications

state authority to international cooperation (cf. BVerfGE 141, 220 <341 and 342 para. 325> with further references – *The Federal Criminal Police Office Act*). This also applies to ensuring public security. The Federal Constitutional Court has highlighted that effective cooperation with the security authorities of other states can be especially significant for public security. In the interest of the constitutionally mandated protection of individuals, effective information sharing can require the transfer of intelligence gathered domestically and in return rely on intelligence provided by foreign bodies (cf. BVerfGE 141, 220 <268 para. 102> – *The Federal Criminal Police Office Act*).

Accordingly, the Basic Law is open to cooperation of the Federal Intelligence Service with other intelligence services. Such international cooperation can be essential for protecting Germany's foreign and security policy interests and, in this context, for maintaining public security; it can be based on the Basic Law's openness to international cooperation (cf. also BVerfGE 143, 101 <152 *et seq.* para. 168 *et seq.*>). Thus, the Federal Intelligence Service may be granted the authorisation to use its powers for the intelligence interests of foreign services and states. These interests must be comparable to legitimate intelligence interests of the Federal Intelligence Service and compatible with Germany's foreign and security policy interests. Moreover, the shared data must be used in accordance with the rule of law.

247

b) However, cooperation in the field of telecommunications surveillance must be designed in such a way that fundamental rights protection against covert surveillance measures and the resulting requirements regarding data collection, processing and sharing are not circumvented. This applies in particular to the protection against domestic surveillance, which must not be compromised through the free sharing of intelligence stemming from surveillance measures by foreign intelligence services that target Germany. Such further sharing of data received from foreign partners (*Ringtausch*) is not permissible under constitutional law. This applies accordingly with regard to the fundamental rights requirements that the Federal Intelligence Service must satisfy when conducting surveillance of foreign telecommunications.

248

Foreign intelligence services themselves may only be granted the power to carry out surveillance measures from within Germany and such measures may only be tolerated if there are specific grounds for carrying out the measures and if detailed statutory provisions ensure that fundamental rights protection applies without any reservations, both in substantive and in procedural terms. The protection afforded by fundamental rights entails a duty of the German state to protect individuals under Germany's jurisdiction against surveillance measures conducted by other

249

250 c) In addition, the cooperation with foreign intelligence services requires a separate statutory basis. Firstly, legal provisions are necessary to the extent that the Federal Intelligence Service wants to gain access to surveillance open to foreign intelligence services, and wants to obtain and use the data collected by them. These provisions must cover both the sharing of search terms by the Federal Intelligence Service with a foreign intelligence service for use and analysis by that service and the retrieval or receipt of data made available by a foreign partner for analysis by the Federal Intelligence Service. [...]

251 Secondly, legal provisions are required to the extent that the Federal Intelligence Service is to be granted powers for surveillance and data sharing that it can also use in the interest and under the guidance of other intelligence services. If the legislator wants to allow the Federal Intelligence Service to analyse the data collected by it by means of search terms provided by its foreign partners or to automatically share pre-filtered content data or, as the case may be, even unfiltered traffic data with foreign services, it must create a separate statutory basis for this, as it essentially did when enacting §§ 14 and 15 of the Federal Intelligence Service Act.

252 2. The constitutional requirements applicable to such a statutory basis serve to ensure that the general limits to strategic surveillance arising from fundamental rights are upheld as effectively as possible in the context of cooperation.

253 [...]

254 3. Specific requirements apply insofar as, in the context of cooperation, the Federal Intelligence Service wants to use search terms determined by a foreign intelligence service and then automatically share the resulting matches with the foreign partner without first conducting a content-based analysis. The legislator must create rules for this situation that ensure the Federal Intelligence Service's responsibility with regard to fundamental rights for the data collected by it and its processing.

255 a) First of all, this requires a thorough assessment of the search terms determined by the foreign partner and the resulting matches. The Federal Intelligence Service must assess whether the use of the search terms as such and the data selected through their use is subject to limits arising from fundamental rights.

256 aa) [...]

257 This also applies to persons whose work requires special confidentiality protection under constitutional law, in particular lawyers and journalists meriting protection. However, surveillance measures vis-à-vis these professions are not entirely ruled out even in the context of cooperation. Yet in this context as well, they can only be permissible subject to a protection of qualified legal interests, thresholds and a balancing of interests (see para. 194 *et seq.* above). [...] Insofar as decisions in

this regard are made in the individual case, they must be subjected to oversight resembling judicial review.

bb) The assessment of search terms must be as effective as possible. [...]   258

b) Obtaining substantial assurances by the partner services is particularly signifi-   259
cant with regard to the automated sharing of data that has not been fully analysed. Given that responsibility for the analysis of data collected by the Federal Intelligence Service is placed into the hands of a foreign intelligence service, which is not bound by the Basic Law, specific assurances by this foreign service regarding the further handling of data must be obtained. Given the applicability of fundamental rights abroad, these assurances must be in line with the fundamental rights protection afforded the persons under surveillance.

[...]   260-261

4. Finally, a separate statutory basis is required insofar as an entire set of traffic   262
data is to be shared with foreign intelligence services in the context of cooperation, without prior selection based on specific search terms, allowing the foreign services to retain this traffic data and to analyse it using their own methods.

a) In this scenario, the Federal Intelligence Service hands over the data collected   263
by it without the possibility to exercise any control over content. Therefore, such cooperation must be subject to specific restrictions. The sharing of an entire set of traffic data cannot be authorised continually and merely on the basis of the purpose pursued, but requires a qualified need for intelligence relating to specific indications of an identifiable danger. Certain events beyond the general existence of potential dangers must provide grounds for conducting surveillance measures that counter specific threats and ensure that the Federal Republic of Germany retain its capacity to act. [...]

b) [...]   264

V.

In relation to surveillance measures, the principle of proportionality also sets re-   265
quirements regarding transparency, individual legal protection and oversight (cf. BVerfGE 141, 220 <282 et seq. para. 134 et seq.> with further references – *The Federal Criminal Police Office Act*; established case-law). However, the requirements regarding transparency and individual legal protection are significantly less strict for the surveillance of foreign telecommunications. To compensate for this, the principle of proportionality gives rise to special requirements regarding independent oversight (cf. BVerfGE 133, 277 <369 para. 214> – *Counter-Terrorism Database Act I*; 141, 220 <284 and 285 paras. 140 and 141> – *The Federal Criminal Police Office Act*).

266   1. The requirements regarding transparency of data processing call for rights to information. In principle, this is also the case where intelligence services are concerned (cf. BVerfGE 125, 260 <331 and 332> – *Data Retention*). However, such rights to information can be restricted to the extent necessary to ensure the effective performance of the intelligence services' tasks (cf. BVerfGE 133, 277 <367 and 368 para. 209 et seq.> – *Counter-Terrorism Database Act I*; 141, 220 <283 para. 137> – *The Federal Criminal Police Office Act*). Given that surveillance of foreign telecommunications is largely carried out covertly, the rights to information of affected persons can be significantly restricted. […]

267   2. In principle, notification requirements are a prerequisite for the proportionate design of covert surveillance measures, regardless of whether they are carried out by intelligence services or by other security authorities. In this respect, too, the legislator may provide for exemptions by balancing the interest in being notified against the constitutionally protected legal interests of third parties; these must serve to ensure the effective performance of the intelligence service's tasks. Even though such exemptions must be limited to what is absolutely necessary (cf. BVerfGE 109, 279 <364> – *Surveillance of Private Homes*; 125, 260 <336> – *Data Retention*; 141, 220 <283 para. 136> – *The Federal Criminal Police Office Act*), the notification requirements regarding strategic surveillance are not comprehensive.

268   a) In relation to strategic surveillance concerning persons within Germany, differentiated legal provisions are required that ensure that these persons are notified wherever possible. […]

269   In relation to persons in other states, the legislator may, in principle, refrain from imposing notification requirements for strategic surveillance measures […]. […]

270   Thus, the requirements for transparency of state action are significantly less strict and there are fewer possibilities for obtaining individual legal protection in practice. […]

271   b) […]

272   3. Strategic telecommunications surveillance is only compatible with the proportionality requirements if it is complemented by comprehensive independent oversight that serves to ensure that the law is observed. This concerns, on the one hand, strategic surveillance and the related data use, as well as, on the other, the sharing of intelligence thus obtained and the cooperation with foreign intelligence services. Such oversight must be designed as continual legal oversight that allows for comprehensive access to conduct oversight of the surveillance process. It must be aimed at upholding the fundamental rights of affected persons. Moreover, it must serve to guarantee adherence to the legal limits of state surveillance measures and to ensure the practical effectiveness of these limits.

No. 45 – Surveillance of Foreign Telecommunications

a) In relation to strategic surveillance, the constitutional requirements regarding the design of the oversight regime are particularly strict and detailed. [...]

b) The legislator must provide for two different types of oversight, which must also be reflected in the organisational framework.

aa) Firstly, a body resembling a court must be tasked with conducting oversight. This body must consist of panels with members who must be independent in a way that is equivalent to judicial independence. They must decide in a formal procedure and their decisions must be made in writing and are final and binding on the Federal Government and the Federal Intelligence Service. This type of oversight must provide the protection otherwise afforded through the requirement of prior judicial authorisation or through avenues for *ex post* legal protection, in particular declaratory actions. Thus, it must allow for a review in the individual case which is equivalent to judicial review both in substantive and in procedural terms and is at least as effective, too (cf. BVerfGE 30, 1 <23> on Art. 10(2) second sentence of the Basic Law).

bb) Secondly, independent oversight must also be exercised by a body that is administrative in nature. In this respect, an oversight body must be created that can, on its own initiative, randomly scrutinise the entire process of strategic surveillance as to its lawfulness; this concerns individual decisions, processes, the design of data processing and filtering mechanisms as well as the technical resources used for them. [...]

c) It is incumbent upon the legislator to set out how the competences of the different types of oversight interact. It has considerable latitude in this area, but must adhere to the requirements arising from the principle of proportionality.

aa) [...]

bb) It must be guaranteed that the entire process of strategic surveillance, including the processing and sharing of data based on it and the cooperation with foreign intelligence services, can comprehensively be subjected to oversight when the oversight bodies interact. [...]

cc) With regard to oversight resembling judicial review, the legislator must also assess whether persons who can plausibly demonstrate that they may have been affected by surveillance measures can be granted the right to initiate such oversight measures. [...]

d) It must be guaranteed that oversight can be exercised continually and is institutionally independent. This includes that the oversight bodies must have a separate budget and independent management of their personnel, except where the appointment of the members of the panel resembling a court and the directors of the oversight bodies is concerned. The bodies must be effectively shielded from external influence and must be completely independent in this regard.

282 For the rest, the legislator is afforded wide latitude as regards the institutional structure of the oversight bodies. […]
283 e) Overall, the oversight bodies must be equipped with resources that allow for the effective and independent performance of their tasks.
284 aa) The oversight bodies must be equipped with competent and professional personnel and their composition must be balanced. […]
285-287 […]
288 bb) Sufficient personnel and resources must be made available for both types of oversight. […]
289 f) The oversight bodies must have all the powers necessary for effective oversight vis-à-vis the Federal Intelligence Service.
290 aa) Both oversight bodies must be granted comprehensive access to all documents. […]
291 bb) As part of the constitutional requirements with regard to oversight, the Federal Intelligence Service must document its data processing measures (cf. BVerfGE 133, 277 <370 para. 215> – *Counter-Terrorism Database Act I*; 141, 220 <284 and 285 para. 141> – *The Federal Criminal Police Office Act*; established case-law). […]
292 cc) Oversight must not be obstructed by the third party rule. In designing the oversight bodies and setting out requirements regarding agreements between the Federal Intelligence Service and other intelligence services, the legislator must ensure that the Federal Intelligence Service cannot prevent oversight by invoking the third party rule.
293 Nevertheless, the third party rule is a rule of conduct that is based on agreements with foreign intelligence services and generally recognised by all intelligence services; according to this rule, based on informal arrangements, intelligence obtained from foreign intelligence services may not be shared with third parties without the consent of the intelligence service in question (cf. BVerfGE 143, 101 <150 para. 162; 151 para. 164>). […]
294 The bodies conducting the constitutionally required comprehensive oversight of the Federal Intelligence Service must be designed as independent oversight bodies that are strictly committed to secrecy and not integrated into Parliament and its political communication channels, so as to ensure that the third party rule cannot provide grounds for refusing to cooperate with them. There is no general definition setting out whether an oversight body must be considered a third party within the meaning of the third party rule; rather, this is determined on the basis of its organisational design and agreements between intelligence services (cf. BTDrucks 18/12850, pp. 98 and 99). The third party rule is an administrative practice that is not legally binding, but is merely based on agreements with other intelligence services; it is thus flexible and the Federal Government can influence its practical

No. 45 – Surveillance of Foreign Telecommunications

significance [...]. The Federal Government and the Federal Intelligence Service do remain bound by the assurances they have given. However, in the future, it must be ensured, through the way the oversight bodies are designed and through changes in agreements with foreign services, that the bodies conducting legal oversight are no longer considered to be third parties (cf. also European Commission for Democracy through Law [Venice Commission], Report on the Democratic Oversight of Signals Intelligence Agencies, CDL-AD[2015]011, p. 5 [no. 13]; Council of Europe, Parliamentary Assembly, Resolution 1838 [2011], p. 2 [no. 7]; Council of Europe, Commissioner for Human Rights, Democratic and effective oversight of national security services, 2015, p. 13 [Recommendation no. 16]).

On the one hand, it must be guaranteed that, despite the third party rule, constitutionally required oversight also extends to the Federal Intelligence Service's handling of information obtained from foreign intelligence services; on the other hand, the Federal Intelligence Service must be able to continue to cooperate with other intelligence services (see paras. 246 and 247 above), which is especially important for safeguarding the Federal Republic of Germany's interests with regard to foreign and security policy. The practice of other intelligence services shows that this is possible; their oversight bodies have full access to all documents necessary to scrutinise the intelligence services that are subject to their oversight (regarding the rights to information granted to the Investigatory Powers Tribunal in the United Kingdom cf. ECtHR, *Big Brother Watch and Others v. the United Kingdom*, Judgment of 13 September 2018, no. 58170/13 and others, §§ 250, 379; regarding the Investigatory Powers Commissioner's unlimited rights to information see Annual Report of the Investigatory Powers Commissioner 2017 of 31 January 2019, p. 41). 295

dd) Oversight can in principle be subject to strict secrecy rules. [...] 296

(1) However, open and direct exchange between the oversight bodies must be guaranteed (cf. BVerfGE 133, 277 <370 para. 216> – *Counter-Terrorism Database Act I*). The requirement of effective and coherent oversight calls for such exchange given that these bodies, which are subject to the same confidentiality requirements, are together responsible for oversight of the same measures. [...] 297

(2) Yet the flow of information to the parliamentary sphere and thus also to the Parliamentary Oversight Body can in principle be limited on grounds of secrecy. The legislator may take into account that parliamentary oversight differs (see para. 300 below) from oversight that merely serves to ensure that the law is observed, and that secrecy in the parliamentary and political sphere is subject to factual limits. Nonetheless, under Art. 45d of the Basic Law, the Parliamentary Oversight Body must regularly be informed about oversight activities in a manner that maintains secrecy. In addition, the oversight bodies must also be able to ultimately take their 298

objections and their criticism to Parliament and thus to the public in an abstract manner that guarantees secrecy.

299 (3) The effectiveness of oversight must be continually monitored given that oversight processes largely take place without Parliament and the public obtaining knowledge thereof, but are potentially in conflict with the Federal Intelligence Service's work that is based on secrecy, and given that the conditions under which surveillance measures and oversight take place can change quickly in light of technological developments. The effectiveness of oversight in practice and of its statutory framework must be evaluated at regular intervals (regarding evaluation obligations cf. also BVerfGE 150, 1 <90 para. 176>).

300 g) The design of oversight conducted by the Parliamentary Oversight Body and its Permanent Representative, which exists alongside the other oversight bodies, is also determined by the legislator; this body can become involved in the oversight of surveillance measures (cf., e.g., § 14 of the Article 10 Act). Such oversight is not at issue in the present proceedings. […]

VI.

301 Based on the requirements set out above, the challenged provisions also do not satisfy the constitutional requirements in substantive terms. As with the violation of the requirement that the affected fundamental rights be expressly specified (see paras. 134 and 135 above), the provisions are based on the assumption, which is incorrect from a constitutional law perspective, that fundamental rights are not applicable to the surveillance powers in question. Given that the provisions are unconstitutional for formal reasons alone, the substantive review will only address their key shortcomings. A new legal framework for the Federal Intelligence Service's powers will have to accommodate the fundamental rights of the persons whose telecommunications are under surveillance and will thus have to adhere to the requirements set out above.

302 1. The provisions on data collection and processing in §§ 6 and 7 of the Federal Intelligence Service Act are incompatible with Art. 10(1) of the Basic Law and the proportionality requirements arising from it.

303-309 […]

310 2. The provisions on data sharing do not satisfy the constitutional requirements either. In part, they do not satisfy the requirement of legal clarity. For the rest, the provisions do not sufficiently limit data sharing to the purposes of protecting particularly weighty legal interests and prosecuting particularly serious criminal acts, nor do they make data sharing contingent upon the existence of sufficient

No. 45 – Surveillance of Foreign Telecommunications

indications of an identifiable danger or a suspicion, supported by specific facts, that such criminal acts have been committed.
[…]   311-319
3. The legal framework on cooperation in §§ 13 to 15 of the Federal Intelligence Service Act is also not compatible with the proportionality requirements arising from Art. 10(1) of the Basic Law and is thus unconstitutional in both formal and substantive terms.   320
[…]   321-323
4. Moreover, it is clearly evident that the Federal Intelligence Service Act does not set out a sufficient legal framework for oversight of the aforementioned powers.   324
[…]

VII.

Insofar as the provisions authorise surveillance measures targeting journalists and thus give rise to interferences with Art. 5(1) second sentence of the Basic Law, they are also incompatible with the Constitution, since they do not sufficiently meet the specific needs for protection of independent foreign journalists (cf. in this respect United Nations Office of the High Commissioner for Human Rights, letter of the Special Rapporteurs of 29 August 2016, OL DEU 2/2016, pp. 5 and 6).   325

F.

Contrary to the complainants' view, no further requirements derive from the fundamental rights of the European Union, notwithstanding the question to what extent the competence to conduct such a review in the case at hand falls to the Federal Constitutional Court. Even if, in light of Art. 15 of Directive 2002/58/EC, the challenged provisions were in part considered to be implementing EU law within the meaning of Art. 51(1) first sentence of the Charter of Fundamental Rights of the European Union, there would be no specific and sufficient indication that the fundamental rights of the Basic Law, in the interpretation set out here, do not simultaneously ensure the level of protection of the Charter according to the CJEU's case-law (cf. BVerfGE 152, 152 <180 and 181 para. 67 *et seq.*> – *Right to Be Forgotten I*). […]   326

G.

I.

327 In light of the foregoing, §§ 6, 7 and 13 to 15 of the Federal Intelligence Service Act are unconstitutional. Insofar as they concern data collected on the basis of the aforementioned provisions, §§ 19, 24(1) first sentence, 24(2) first sentence and 24(3) of the Federal Intelligence Service Act are also unconstitutional. They violate the fundamental rights under Art. 10(1) of the Basic Law of complainants nos. 2 to 8 and the fundamental rights under Art. 5(1) second sentence of the Basic Law of complainants nos. 2 to 7. […]

328 […]

II.

329 The finding that a statutory provision is unconstitutional generally results in a declaration that it is void. However, pursuant to § 31(2) second and third sentence of the Federal Constitutional Court Act, the Federal Constitutional Court can choose to declare only that an unconstitutional provision is incompatible with the Basic Law (cf. BVerfGE 109, 190 <235>). It then merely objects to the unconstitutional provision without declaring it void. The Court may combine the declaration of incompatibility with an order to continue to apply the unconstitutional provision for a limited time. This may be considered in cases where the immediate invalidity of the objectionable provision would eliminate the basis for the protection of exceptionally significant public interests and if the outcome of a balancing of these interests against the affected fundamental rights requires that the interference be tolerated for a transitional period (cf. BVerfGE 33, 1 <13>; 33, 303 <347 and 348>; 40, 276 <283>; 41, 251 <266 et seq.>; 51, 268 <290 et seq.>; 109, 190 <235 and 236>).

330 This is the case here. […] In light of the great importance that the legislator may accord to foreign surveillance, an order to continue to apply the unconstitutional provisions for a limited time is preferable to the immediate invalidity of the provisions until new provisions have been enacted, which is expected to happen in the foreseeable future.

No. 45 – Surveillance of Foreign Telecommunications

The legislator must enact new provisions by 31 December 2021 at the latest. The order of continued application is only valid until that date.

331

III.

[…]

332

Justices: Harbarth, Masing, Paulus, Baer, Britz, Ott, Christ, Radtke

Appendix

Basic Law for the Federal Republic of Germany[1]

Preamble

Conscious of their responsibility before God and man,
Inspired by the determination to promote world peace as an equal partner in a united Europe, the German people, in the exercise of their constituent power, have adopted this Basic Law.
Germans in the *Länder* of Baden-Württemberg, Bavaria, Berlin, Brandenburg, Bremen, Hamburg, Hesse, Lower Saxony, Mecklenburg-Western Pomerania, North Rhine-Westphalia, Rhineland-Palatinate, Saarland, Saxony, Saxony-Anhalt, Schleswig-Holstein and Thuringia have achieved the unity and freedom of Germany in free self-determination. This Basic Law thus applies to the entire German people.

I. Basic Rights

Article 1 [Human dignity – Human rights – Legally binding force of basic rights]

(1) Human dignity shall be inviolable. To respect and protect it shall be the duty of all state authority.
(2) The German people therefore acknowledge inviolable and inalienable human rights as the basis of every community, of peace and of justice in the world.
(3) The following basic rights shall bind the legislature, the executive and the judiciary as directly applicable law.

---

[1] Last amended on 29 September 2020
Translated by: Professor Christian Tomuschat, Professor David P. Currie, Professor Donald P. Kommers and Raymond Kerr, in cooperation with the Language Service of the German Bundestag
© Deutscher Bundestag, Berlin, 2021. All rights reserved.
Reproduced with kind permission.

Basic Law for the Federal Republic of Germany

Article 2 **[Personal freedoms]**

(1) Every person shall have the right to free development of his personality insofar as he does not violate the rights of others or offend against the constitutional order or the moral law.
(2) Every person shall have the right to life and physical integrity. Freedom of the person shall be inviolable. These rights may be interfered with only pursuant to a law.

Article 3 **[Equality before the law]**

(1) All persons shall be equal before the law.
(2) Men and women shall have equal rights. The state shall promote the actual implementation of equal rights for women and men and take steps to eliminate disadvantages that now exist.
(3) No person shall be favoured or disfavoured because of sex, parentage, race, language, homeland and origin, faith or religious or political opinions. No person shall be disfavoured because of disability.

Article 4 **[Freedom of faith and conscience]**

(1) Freedom of faith and of conscience and freedom to profess a religious or philosophical creed shall be inviolable.
(2) The undisturbed practice of religion shall be guaranteed.
(3) No person shall be compelled against his conscience to render military service involving the use of arms. Details shall be regulated by a federal law.

Article 5 **[Freedom of expression, arts and sciences]**

(1) Every person shall have the right freely to express and disseminate his opinions in speech, writing and pictures and to inform himself without hindrance from generally accessible sources. Freedom of the press and freedom of reporting by means of broadcasts and films shall be guaranteed. There shall be no censorship.
(2) These rights shall find their limits in the provisions of general laws, in provisions for the protection of young persons and in the right to personal honour.

(3) Arts and sciences, research and teaching shall be free. The freedom of teaching shall not release any person from allegiance to the constitution.

Article 6 [Marriage – Family – Children]

(1) Marriage and the family shall enjoy the special protection of the state.
(2) The care and upbringing of children is the natural right of parents and a duty primarily incumbent upon them. The state shall watch over them in the performance of this duty.
(3) Children may be separated from their families against the will of their parents or guardians only pursuant to a law and only if the parents or guardians fail in their duties or the children are otherwise in danger of serious neglect.
(4) Every mother shall be entitled to the protection and care of the community.
(5) Children born outside of marriage shall be provided by legislation with the same opportunities for physical and mental development and for their position in society as are enjoyed by those born within marriage.

Article 7 [School system]

(1) The entire school system shall be under the supervision of the state.
(2) Parents and guardians shall have the right to decide whether children shall receive religious instruction.
(3) Religious instruction shall form part of the regular curriculum in state schools, with the exception of non-denominational schools. Without prejudice to the state's right of supervision, religious instruction shall be given in accordance with the tenets of the religious community concerned. Teachers may not be obliged against their will to give religious instruction.
(4) The right to establish private schools shall be guaranteed. Private schools that serve as alternatives to state schools shall require the approval of the state and shall be subject to the laws of the *Länder*. Such approval shall be given when private schools are not inferior to the state schools in terms of their educational aims, their facilities or the professional training of their teaching staff and when segregation of pupils according to the means of their parents will not be encouraged thereby. Approval shall be withheld if the economic and legal position of the teaching staff is not adequately assured.
(5) A private elementary school shall be approved only if the education authority finds that it serves a special educational interest or if, on the application of parents

or guardians, it is to be established as a denominational or interdenominational school or as a school based on a particular philosophy and no state elementary school of that type exists in the municipality.
(6) Preparatory schools shall remain abolished.

Article 8 [Freedom of assembly]

(1) All Germans shall have the right to assemble peacefully and unarmed without prior notification or permission.
(2) In the case of outdoor assemblies, this right may be restricted by or pursuant to a law.

Article 9 [Freedom of association]

(1) All Germans shall have the right to form societies and other associations.
(2) Associations whose aims or activities contravene the criminal laws or that are directed against the constitutional order or the concept of international understanding shall be prohibited.
(3) The right to form associations to safeguard and improve working and economic conditions shall be guaranteed to every individual and to every occupation or profession. Agreements that restrict or seek to impair this right shall be null and void; measures directed to this end shall be unlawful. Measures taken pursuant to Article 12a, to paragraphs (2) and (3) of Article 35, to paragraph (4) of Article 87a or to Article 91 may not be directed against industrial disputes engaged in by associations within the meaning of the first sentence of this paragraph in order to safeguard and improve working and economic conditions.

Article 10 [Privacy of correspondence, posts and telecommunications]

(1) The privacy of correspondence, posts and telecommunications shall be inviolable.
(2) Restrictions may be ordered only pursuant to a law. If the restriction serves to protect the free democratic basic order or the existence or security of the Federation or of a *Land*, the law may provide that the person affected shall not be informed of the restriction and that recourse to the courts shall be replaced by a review of the case by agencies and auxiliary agencies appointed by the legislature.

Article 11 [Freedom of movement]

(1) All Germans shall have the right to move freely throughout the federal territory.
(2) This right may be restricted only by or pursuant to a law, and only in cases in which the absence of adequate means of support would result in a particular burden for the community, or in which such restriction is necessary to avert an imminent danger to the existence or the free democratic basic order of the Federation or of a *Land*, to combat the danger of an epidemic, to respond to a grave accident or natural disaster, to protect young persons from serious neglect or to prevent crime.

Article 12 [Occupational freedom]

(1) All Germans shall have the right freely to choose their occupation or profession, their place of work and their place of training. The practice of an occupation or profession may be regulated by or pursuant to a law.
(2) No person may be required to perform work of a particular kind except within the framework of a traditional duty of community service that applies generally and equally to all.
(3) Forced labour may be imposed only on persons deprived of their liberty by the judgment of a court.

Article 12a [Compulsory military and alternative civilian service]

(1) Men who have attained the age of eighteen may be required to serve in the Armed Forces, in the Federal Border Police, or in a civil defence organisation.
(2) Any person who, on grounds of conscience, refuses to render military service involving the use of arms may be required to perform alternative service. The duration of alternative service shall not exceed that of military service. Details shall be regulated by a law, which shall not interfere with the freedom to make a decision in accordance with the dictates of conscience and which shall also provide for the possibility of alternative service not connected with units of the Armed Forces or of the Federal Border Police.
(3) Persons liable to compulsory military service who are not called upon to render service pursuant to paragraph (1) or (2) of this Article may, when a state of defence is in effect, be assigned by or pursuant to a law to employment involving civilian services for defence purposes, including the protection of the civilian population;

they may be assigned to public employment only for the purpose of discharging police functions or such other sovereign functions of public administration as can be discharged only by persons employed in the public service. The employment contemplated by the first sentence of this paragraph may include services within the Armed Forces, in the provision of military supplies or with public administrative authorities; assignments to employment connected with supplying and servicing the civilian population shall be permissible only to meet their basic requirements or to guarantee their safety.

(4) If, during a state of defence, the need for civilian services in the civilian health system or in stationary military hospitals cannot be met on a voluntary basis, women between the age of eighteen and fifty-five may be called upon to render such services by or pursuant to a law. Under no circumstances may they be required to render service involving the use of arms.

(5) Prior to the existence of a state of defence, assignments under paragraph (3) of this Article may be made only if the requirements of paragraph (1) of Article 80a are met. In preparation for the provision of services under paragraph (3) of this Article that demand special knowledge or skills, participation in training courses may be required by or pursuant to a law. In this case the first sentence of this paragraph shall not apply.

(6) If, during a state of defence, the need for workers in the areas specified in the second sentence of paragraph (3) of this Article cannot be met on a voluntary basis, the right of German citizens to abandon their occupation or place of employment may be restricted by or pursuant to a law in order to meet this need. Prior to the existence of a state of defence, the first sentence of paragraph (5) of this Article shall apply, *mutatis mutandis*.

Article 13 [Inviolability of the home]

(1) The home is inviolable.

(2) Searches may be authorised only by a judge or, when time is of the essence, by other authorities designated by the laws and may be carried out only in the manner therein prescribed.

(3) If particular facts justify the suspicion that any person has committed an especially serious crime specifically defined by a law, technical means of acoustical surveillance of any home in which the suspect is supposedly staying may be employed pursuant to judicial order for the purpose of prosecuting the offence, provided that alternative methods of investigating the matter would be disproportionately difficult or unproductive. The authorisation shall be for a limited time. The order

shall be issued by a panel composed of three judges. When time is of the essence, it may also be issued by a single judge.

(4) To avert acute dangers to public safety, especially dangers to life or to the public, technical means of surveillance of the home may be employed only pursuant to judicial order. When time is of the essence, such measures may also be ordered by other authorities designated by a law; a judicial decision shall subsequently be obtained without delay.

(5) If technical means are contemplated solely for the protection of persons officially deployed in a home, the measure may be ordered by an authority designated by a law. The information thereby obtained may be otherwise used only for purposes of criminal prosecution or to avert danger and only if the legality of the measure has been previously determined by a judge; when time is of the essence, a judicial decision shall subsequently be obtained without delay.

(6) The Federal Government shall report to the Bundestag annually as to the employment of technical means pursuant to paragraph (3) and, within the jurisdiction of the Federation, pursuant to paragraph (4) and, insofar as judicial approval is required, pursuant to paragraph (5) of this Article. A panel elected by the Bundestag shall exercise parliamentary oversight on the basis of this report. A comparable parliamentary oversight shall be afforded by the *Länder*.

(7) Interferences and restrictions shall otherwise only be permissible to avert a danger to the public or to the life of an individual or, pursuant to a law, to confront an acute danger to public safety and order, in particular to relieve an accommodation shortage, to combat the danger of an epidemic or to protect young persons at risk.

Article 14   **[Property – Inheritance – Expropriation]**

(1) Property and the right of inheritance shall be guaranteed. Their content and limits shall be defined by the laws.

(2) Property entails obligations. Its use shall also serve the public good.

(3) Expropriation shall only be permissible for the public good. It may only be ordered by or pursuant to a law that determines the nature and extent of compensation. Such compensation shall be determined by establishing an equitable balance between the public interest and the interests of those affected. In case of dispute concerning the amount of compensation, recourse may be had to the ordinary courts.

Article 15 [Nationalisation]

Land, natural resources and means of production may, for the purpose of nationalisation, be transferred to public ownership or other forms of public enterprise by a law that determines the nature and extent of compensation. With respect to such compensation the third and fourth sentences of paragraph (3) of Article 14 shall apply, *mutatis mutandis*.

Article 16 [Citizenship – Extradition]

(1) No German may be deprived of his citizenship. Loss of citizenship may occur only pursuant to a law and, if it occurs against the will of the person affected, only if he does not become stateless as a result.
(2) No German may be extradited to a foreign country. The law may provide otherwise for extraditions to a member state of the European Union or to an international court, provided that the rule of law is observed.

Article 16a [Right of asylum]

(1) Persons persecuted on political grounds shall have the right of asylum.
(2) Paragraph (1) of this Article may not be invoked by a person who enters the federal territory from a member state of the European Communities or from another third state in which application of the Convention Relating to the Status of Refugees and of the Convention for the Protection of Human Rights and Fundamental Freedoms is assured. The states outside the European Communities to which the conditions referred to in the first sentence of this paragraph apply shall be specified by a law requiring the consent of the Bundesrat. In the cases specified in the first sentence of this paragraph, measures to terminate an applicant's stay may be implemented without regard to any legal challenge that may have been instituted against them.
(3) By a law requiring the consent of the Bundesrat, states may be specified in which, on the basis of their laws, enforcement practices and general political conditions, it can be safely concluded that neither political persecution nor inhuman or degrading punishment or treatment exists. It shall be presumed that a foreigner from such a state is not persecuted, unless he presents evidence justifying the conclusion that, contrary to this presumption, he is persecuted on political grounds.

(4) In the cases specified by paragraph (3) of this Article and in other cases that are plainly unfounded or considered to be plainly unfounded, the implementation of measures to terminate an applicant's stay may be suspended by a court only if serious doubts exist as to their legality; the scope of review may be limited, and tardy objections may be disregarded. Details shall be determined by a law.

(5) Paragraphs (1) to (4) of this Article shall not preclude the conclusion of international agreements of member states of the European Communities with each other or with those third states which, with due regard for the obligations arising from the Convention Relating to the Status of Refugees and the Convention for the Protection of Human Rights and Fundamental Freedoms, whose enforcement must be assured in the contracting states, adopt rules conferring jurisdiction to decide on applications for asylum, including the reciprocal recognition of asylum decisions.

Article 17 [Right of petition]

Every person shall have the right individually or jointly with others to address written requests or complaints to competent authorities and to the legislature.

Article 17a [Restriction of basic rights in specific instances]

(1) Laws regarding military and alternative service may provide that the basic right of members of the Armed Forces and of alternative service freely to express and disseminate their opinions in speech, writing and pictures (first clause of the first sentence of paragraph (1) of Article 5), the basic right of assembly (Article 8) and the right of petition (Article 17), insofar as it permits the submission of requests or complaints jointly with others, be restricted during their period of military or alternative service.

(2) Laws regarding defence, including protection of the civilian population, may provide for restriction of the basic rights of freedom of movement (Article 11) and inviolability of the home (Article 13).

Article 18 [Forfeiture of basic rights]

Whoever abuses the freedom of expression, in particular the freedom of the press (paragraph (1) of Article 5), the freedom of teaching (paragraph (3) of Article 5), the freedom of assembly (Article 8), the freedom of association (Article 9), the privacy of correspondence, posts and telecommunications (Article 10), the rights of property (Article 14) or the right of asylum (Article 16a) in order to combat the free democratic basic order shall forfeit these basic rights. This forfeiture and its extent shall be declared by the Federal Constitutional Court.

Article 19 [**Restriction of basic rights – Legal remedies**]

(1) Insofar as, under this Basic Law, a basic right may be restricted by or pursuant to a law, such law must apply generally and not merely to a single case. In addition, the law must specify the basic right affected and the Article in which it appears.
(2) In no case may the essence of a basic right be affected.
(3) The basic rights shall also apply to domestic legal persons to the extent that the nature of such rights permits.
(4) Should any person's rights be violated by public authority, he may have recourse to the courts. If no other jurisdiction has been established, recourse shall be to the ordinary courts. The second sentence of paragraph (2) of Article 10 shall not be affected by this paragraph.

II. The Federation and the *Länder*

Article 20 [**Constitutional principles – Right of resistance**]

(1) The Federal Republic of Germany is a democratic and social federal state.
(2) All state authority is derived from the people. It shall be exercised by the people through elections and other votes and through specific legislative, executive and judicial bodies.
(3) The legislature shall be bound by the constitutional order, the executive and the judiciary by law and justice.
(4) All Germans shall have the right to resist any person seeking to abolish this constitutional order if no other remedy is available.

Article 20a [**Protection of the natural foundations of life and animals**]

Mindful also of its responsibility towards future generations, the state shall protect the natural foundations of life and animals by legislation and, in accordance with law and justice, by executive and judicial action, all within the framework of the constitutional order.

Article 21 [Political parties]

(1) Political parties shall participate in the formation of the political will of the people. They may be freely established. Their internal organisation must conform to democratic principles. They must publicly account for their assets and for the sources and use of their funds.
(2) Parties that, by reason of their aims or the behaviour of their adherents, seek to undermine or abolish the free democratic basic order or to endanger the existence of the Federal Republic of Germany shall be unconstitutional.
(3) Parties that, by reason of their aims or the behaviour of their adherents, are oriented towards an undermining or abolition of the free democratic basic order or an endangerment of the existence of the Federal Republic of Germany shall be excluded from state financing. If such exclusion is determined, any favourable fiscal treatment of these parties and of payments made to those parties shall cease.
(4) The Federal Constitutional Court shall rule on the question of unconstitutionality within the meaning of paragraph (2) of this Article and on exclusion from state financing within the meaning of paragraph (3).
(5) Details shall be regulated by federal laws.

Article 22 [Federal capital – Federal flag]

(1) Berlin is the capital of the Federal Republic of Germany. The Federation shall be responsible for representing the nation as a whole in the capital. Details shall be regulated by federal law.
(2) The federal flag shall be black, red and gold.

Article 23 [European Union – Protection of basic rights – Principle of subsidiarity]

(1) With a view to establishing a united Europe, the Federal Republic of Germany shall participate in the development of the European Union that is committed to democratic, social and federal principles, to the rule of law and to the principle of subsidiarity and that guarantees a level of protection of basic rights essentially com-

parable to that afforded by this Basic Law. To this end the Federation may transfer sovereign powers by a law with the consent of the Bundesrat. The establishment of the European Union, as well as changes in its treaty foundations and comparable regulations that amend or supplement this Basic Law or make such amendments or supplements possible, shall be subject to paragraphs (2) and (3) of Article 79.

(1a) The Bundestag and the Bundesrat shall have the right to bring an action before the Court of Justice of the European Union to challenge a legislative act of the European Union for infringing the principle of subsidiarity. The Bundestag is obliged to initiate such an action at the request of one quarter of its Members. By a statute requiring the consent of the Bundesrat, exceptions to the first sentence of paragraph (2) of Article 42 and the first sentence of paragraph (3) of Article 52 may be authorised for the exercise of the rights granted to the Bundestag and the Bundesrat under the contractual foundations of the European Union.

(2) The Bundestag and, through the Bundesrat, the *Länder* shall participate in matters concerning the European Union. The Federal Government shall notify the Bundestag of such matters comprehensively and as early as possible.

(3) Before participating in legislative acts of the European Union, the Federal Government shall provide the Bundestag with an opportunity to state its position. The Federal Government shall take the position of the Bundestag into account during the negotiations. Details shall be regulated by a law.

(4) The Bundesrat shall participate in the decision-making process of the Federation insofar as it would have been competent to do so in a comparable domestic matter or insofar as the subject falls within the domestic competence of the *Länder*.

(5) Insofar as, in an area within the exclusive competence of the Federation, interests of the *Länder* are affected and in other matters, insofar as the Federation has legislative power, the Federal Government shall take the position of the Bundesrat into account. To the extent that the legislative powers of the *Länder*, the structure of *Land* authorities, or *Land* administrative procedures are primarily affected, the position of the Bundesrat shall receive prime consideration in the formation of the political will of the Federation; this process shall be consistent with the responsibility of the Federation for the nation as a whole. In matters that may result in increased expenditures or reduced revenues for the Federation, the consent of the Federal Government shall be required.

(6) When legislative powers exclusive to the *Länder* concerning matters of school education, culture or broadcasting are primarily affected, the exercise of the rights belonging to the Federal Republic of Germany as a member state of the European Union shall be delegated by the Federation to a representative of the *Länder* designated by the Bundesrat. These rights shall be exercised with the participation of,

and in coordination with, the Federal Government; their exercise shall be consistent with the responsibility of the Federation for the nation as a whole.

(7) Details regarding paragraphs (4) to (6) of this Article shall be regulated by a law requiring the consent of the Bundesrat.

Article 24 [Transfer of sovereign powers – System of collective security]

(1) The Federation may, by a law, transfer sovereign powers to international organisations.

(1a) Insofar as the *Länder* are competent to exercise state powers and to perform state functions, they may, with the consent of the Federal Government, transfer sovereign powers to transfrontier institutions in neighbouring regions.

(2) With a view to maintaining peace, the Federation may enter into a system of mutual collective security; in doing so it shall consent to such limitations upon its sovereign powers as will bring about and secure a lasting peace in Europe and among the nations of the world.

(3) For the settlement of disputes between states, the Federation shall accede to agreements providing for general, comprehensive and compulsory international arbitration.

Article 25 [Primacy of international law]

The general rules of international law shall be an integral part of federal law. They shall take precedence over the laws and directly create rights and duties for the inhabitants of the federal territory.

Article 26 [Securing international peace]

(1) Acts tending to and undertaken with intent to disturb the peaceful relations between nations, especially to prepare for a war of aggression, shall be unconstitutional. They shall be criminalised.

(2) Weapons designed for warfare may be manufactured, transported or marketed only with the permission of the Federal Government. Details shall be regulated by a federal law.

Article 27 [Merchant fleet]

All German merchant vessels shall constitute a unitary merchant fleet.

Article 28 [*Land* constitutions – Autonomy of municipalities]

(1) The constitutional order in the *Länder* must conform to the principles of a republican, democratic and social state governed by the rule of law within the meaning of this Basic Law. In each *Land*, county and municipality the people shall be represented by a body chosen in general, direct, free, equal and secret elections. In county and municipal elections, persons who possess the citizenship of any member state of the European Community are also eligible to vote and to be elected in accordance with European Community law. In municipalities a local assembly may take the place of an elected body.
(2) Municipalities must be guaranteed the right to regulate all local affairs on their own responsibility within the limits prescribed by the laws. Within the limits of their functions designated by a law, associations of municipalities shall also have the right of self-government in accordance with the laws. The guarantee of self-government shall extend to the bases of financial autonomy; these bases shall include the right of municipalities to a source of tax revenues based upon economic ability and the right to establish the rates at which these sources shall be taxed.
(3) The Federation shall guarantee that the constitutional order of the *Länder* conforms to the basic rights and to the provisions of paragraphs (1) and (2) of this Article.

Article 29 [New delimitation of the federal territory]

(1) The division of the federal territory into *Länder* may be revised to ensure that each *Land* be of a size and capacity to perform its functions effectively. Due regard shall be given in this connection to regional, historical and cultural ties, economic efficiency and the requirements of local and regional planning.

(2) Revisions of the existing division into *Länder* shall be effected by a federal law, which must be confirmed by referendum. The affected *Länder* shall be afforded an opportunity to be heard.

(3) The referendum shall be held in the *Länder* from whose territories or parts of territories a new *Land* or a *Land* with redefined boundaries is to be established (affected *Länder*). The question to be voted on is whether the affected *Länder* are to remain as they are or whether the new *Land* or the *Land* with redefined boundaries should be established. The proposal to establish a new *Land* or a *Land* with redefined boundaries shall take effect if the change is approved by a majority in the future territory of such *Land* and by a majority in the territories or parts of territories of an affected *Land* taken together whose affiliation with a *Land* is to be changed in the same way. The proposal shall not take effect if, within the territory of any of the affected *Länder*, a majority reject the change; however, such rejection shall be of no consequence if in any part of the territory whose affiliation with the affected *Land* is to be changed a two-thirds majority approves the change, unless it is rejected by a two-thirds majority in the territory of the affected *Land* as a whole.

(4) If, in any clearly defined and contiguous residential and economic area located in two or more *Länder* and having at least one million inhabitants, one tenth of those entitled to vote in Bundestag elections petition for the inclusion of that area in a single *Land*, a federal law shall specify within two years whether the change shall be made in accordance with paragraph (2) of this Article or that an advisory referendum shall be held in the affected *Länder*.

(5) The advisory referendum shall establish whether the changes the law proposes meet with the voters' approval. The law may put forward not more than two distinct proposals for consideration by the voters. If a majority approves a proposed change of the existing division into *Länder*, a federal law shall specify within two years whether the change shall be made in accordance with paragraph (2) of this Article. If a proposal is approved in accordance with the third and fourth sentences of paragraph (3) of this Article, a federal law providing for establishment of the proposed *Land* shall be enacted within two years after the advisory ballot, and confirmation by referendum shall no longer be required.

(6) A majority in a referendum or in an advisory referendum shall consist of a majority of the votes cast, provided that it amounts to at least one quarter of those entitled to vote in Bundestag elections. Other details concerning referendums, petitions and advisory referendums shall be regulated by a federal law, which may also provide that the same petition may not be filed more than once within a period of five years.

(7) Other changes concerning the territory of the *Länder* may be effected by agreements between the *Länder* concerned or by a federal law with the consent of the

Bundesrat, if the territory that is to be the subject of the change has no more than 50,000 inhabitants. Details shall be regulated by a federal law requiring the consent of the Bundesrat and of a majority of the Members of the Bundestag. The law must provide affected municipalities and counties with an opportunity to be heard.

(8) *Länder* may revise the division of their existing territory or parts of their territory by agreement without regard to the provisions of paragraphs (2) to (7) of this Article. Affected municipalities and counties shall be afforded an opportunity to be heard. The agreement shall require confirmation by referendum in each of the *Länder* concerned. If the revision affects only part of a *Land*'s territory, the referendum may be confined to the areas affected; the second clause of the fifth sentence shall not apply. In a referendum under this paragraph a majority of the votes cast shall be decisive, provided it amounts to at least one quarter of those entitled to vote in Bundestag elections; details shall be regulated by a federal law. The agreement shall require the consent of the Bundestag.

Article 30 [Sovereign powers of the *Länder*]

Except as otherwise provided or permitted by this Basic Law, the exercise of state powers and the discharge of state functions is a matter for the *Länder*.

Article 31 [Supremacy of federal law]

Federal law shall take precedence over *Land* law.

Article 32 [Foreign relations]

(1) Relations with foreign states shall be conducted by the Federation.
(2) Before the conclusion of a treaty affecting the special circumstances of a *Land*, that *Land* shall be consulted in timely fashion.
(3) Insofar as the *Länder* have power to legislate, they may conclude treaties with foreign states with the consent of the Federal Government.

Article 33 [Equal citizenship – Public service]

(1) Every German shall have in every *Land* the same political rights and duties.

(2) Every German shall be equally eligible for any public office according to his aptitude, qualifications and professional achievements.
(3) Neither the enjoyment of civil and political rights nor eligibility for public office nor rights acquired in the public service shall be dependent upon religious affiliation. No one may be disadvantaged by reason of adherence or non-adherence to a particular religious denomination or philosophical creed.
(4) The exercise of sovereign authority on a regular basis shall, as a rule, be entrusted to members of the public service who stand in a relationship of service and loyalty defined by public law.
(5) The law governing the public service shall be regulated and developed with due regard to the traditional principles of the professional civil service.

Article 34   [Liability for violation of official duty]

If any person, in the exercise of a public office entrusted to him, violates his official duty to a third party, liability shall rest principally with the state or public body that employs him. In the event of intentional wrongdoing or gross negligence, the right of recourse against the individual officer shall be preserved. The ordinary courts shall not be closed to claims for compensation or indemnity.

Article 35   [Legal and administrative assistance and assistance during disasters]

(1) All federal and *Land* authorities shall render legal and administrative assistance to one another.
(2) In order to maintain or restore public security or order, a *Land* in particularly serious cases may call upon personnel and facilities of the Federal Border Police to assist its police when without such assistance the police could not fulfil their responsibilities, or could do so only with great difficulty. In order to respond to a grave accident or a natural disaster, a *Land* may call for the assistance of police forces of other *Länder* or of personnel and facilities of other administrative authorities, of the Armed Forces or of the Federal Border Police.
(3) If the natural disaster or accident endangers the territory of more than one *Land*, the Federal Government, insofar as is necessary to combat the danger, may instruct the *Land* governments to place police forces at the disposal of other *Länder* and may deploy units of the Federal Border Police or the Armed Forces to support the police. Measures taken by the Federal Government pursuant to the first sen-

tence of this paragraph shall be rescinded at any time at the demand of the Bundesrat and in any event as soon as the danger is removed.

Article 36 [Personnel of federal authorities]

(1) Civil servants employed by the highest federal authorities shall be drawn from all *Länder* in appropriate proportion. Persons employed by other federal authorities shall, as a rule, be drawn from the *Land* in which they serve.
(2) Laws regarding military service shall also take into account both the division of the Federation into *Länder* and the regional loyalties of their people.

Article 37 [Federal execution]

(1) If a *Land* fails to comply with its obligations under this Basic Law or other federal laws, the Federal Government, with the consent of the Bundesrat, may take the necessary steps to compel the *Land* to comply with its duties.
(2) For the purpose of implementing such coercive measures, the Federal Government or its representative shall have the right to issue instructions to all *Länder* and their authorities.

III. The Bundestag

Article 38 [Elections]

(1) Members of the German Bundestag shall be elected in general, direct, free, equal and secret elections. They shall be representatives of the whole people, not bound by orders or instructions and responsible only to their conscience.
(2) Any person who has attained the age of eighteen shall be entitled to vote; any person who has attained the age of majority may be elected.
(3) Details shall be regulated by a federal law.

Article 39 [Electoral term – Convening]

(1) Save the following provisions, the Bundestag shall be elected for four years. Its term shall end when a new Bundestag convenes. New elections shall be held no

sooner than forty-six months and no later than forty-eight months after the electoral term begins. If the Bundestag is dissolved, new elections shall be held within sixty days.
(2) The Bundestag shall convene no later than the thirtieth day after the elections.
(3) The Bundestag shall determine when its sessions shall be adjourned and resumed. The President of the Bundestag may convene it at an earlier date. He shall be obliged to do so if one third of the Members, the Federal President or the Federal Chancellor so demand.

Article 40 [Presidency – Rules of procedure]

(1) The Bundestag shall elect its President, Vice-Presidents and secretaries. It shall adopt rules of procedure.
(2) The President shall exercise proprietary and police powers in the Bundestag building. No search or seizure may take place on the premises of the Bundestag without his permission.

Article 41 [Scrutiny of elections]

(1) Scrutiny of elections shall be the responsibility of the Bundestag. It shall also decide whether a Member has lost his seat.
(2) Complaints against such decisions of the Bundestag may be lodged with the Federal Constitutional Court.
(3) Details shall be regulated by a federal law.

Article 42 [Public sittings – Majority decisions]

(1) Sittings of the Bundestag shall be public. On the motion of one tenth of its Members, or on the motion of the Federal Government, a decision to exclude the public may be taken by a two-thirds majority. The motion shall be voted upon at a sitting not open to the public.
(2) Decisions of the Bundestag shall require a majority of the votes cast unless this Basic Law otherwise provides. The rules of procedure may permit exceptions with respect to elections to be conducted by the Bundestag.
(3) Truthful reports of public sittings of the Bundestag and of its committees shall not give rise to any liability.

Article 43 [Right to require presence, right of access and right to be heard]

(1) The Bundestag and its committees may require the presence of any member of the Federal Government.
(2) The members of the Bundesrat and of the Federal Government as well as their representatives may attend all sittings of the Bundestag and meetings of its committees. They shall have the right to be heard at any time.

Article 44 [Committees of inquiry]

(1) The Bundestag shall have the right, and on the motion of one quarter of its Members the duty, to establish a committee of inquiry, which shall take the requisite evidence at public hearings. The public may be excluded.
(2) The rules of criminal procedure shall apply, *mutatis mutandis*, to the taking of evidence. The privacy of correspondence, posts and telecommunications shall not be affected.
(3) Courts and administrative authorities shall be required to provide legal and administrative assistance.
(4) The decisions of committees of inquiry shall not be subject to judicial review. The courts shall be free to evaluate and rule upon the facts that were the subject of the investigation.

Article 45 [Committee on the European Union]

The Bundestag shall appoint a Committee on European Union Affairs. It may authorise the committee to exercise the rights of the Bundestag under Article 23 vis-à-vis the Federal Government. It may also empower it to exercise the rights granted to the Bundestag under the contractual foundations of the European Union.

Article 45a [Committees on Foreign Affairs and Defence]

(1) The Bundestag shall appoint a Committee on Foreign Affairs and a Defence Committee.

(2) The Defence Committee shall also have the powers of a committee of inquiry. On the motion of one quarter of its members it shall have the duty to make a specific matter the subject of inquiry.

(3) Paragraph (1) of Article 44 shall not apply to defence matters.

Article 45b **[Parliamentary Commissioner for the Armed Forces]**

A Parliamentary Commissioner for the Armed Forces shall be appointed to safeguard basic rights and to assist the Bundestag in exercising parliamentary oversight. Details shall be regulated by a federal law.

Article 45c **[Petitions Committee]**

(1) The Bundestag shall appoint a Petitions Committee to deal with requests and complaints addressed to the Bundestag pursuant to Article 17.

(2) The powers of the Committee to consider complaints shall be regulated by a federal law.

Article 45d **Parliamentary Oversight Panel**

(1) The Bundestag shall appoint a panel to oversee the intelligence activities of the Federation.

(2) Details shall be regulated by a federal law.

Article 46 **[Immunities of Members]**

(1) At no time may a Member be subjected to court proceedings or disciplinary action or otherwise called to account outside the Bundestag for a vote cast or a remark made by him in the Bundestag or in any of its committees. This provision shall not apply to defamatory insults.

(2) A Member may not be called to account or arrested for a punishable offence without permission of the Bundestag unless he is apprehended while committing the offence or in the course of the following day.

(3) The permission of the Bundestag shall also be required for any other restriction of a Member's freedom of the person or for the initiation of proceedings against a Member under Article 18.
(4) Any criminal proceedings or any proceedings under Article 18 against a Member and any detention or other restriction of the freedom of his person shall be suspended at the demand of the Bundestag.

Article 47 [Right of refusal to give evidence]

Members may refuse to give evidence concerning persons who have confided information to them in their capacity as Members of the Bundestag or to whom they have confided information in this capacity and to give evidence concerning this information itself. To the extent that this right of refusal to give evidence applies, no seizure of documents shall be permissible.

Article 48 [Candidature – Protection of membership – Remuneration]

(1) Every candidate for election to the Bundestag shall be entitled to the leave necessary for his election campaign.
(2) No one may be prevented from accepting or exercising the office of Member of the Bundestag. No one may be given notice of dismissal or discharged from employment on this ground.
(3) Members shall be entitled to remuneration adequate to ensure their independence. They shall be entitled to the free use of all publicly owned means of transport. Details shall be regulated by a federal law.

Article 49 (repealed)

IV. The Bundesrat

Article 50 [Functions]

The *Länder* shall participate through the Bundesrat in the legislation and administration of the Federation and in matters concerning the European Union.

Article 51 [Composition – Weighted voting]

(1) The Bundesrat shall consist of members of the *Land* governments, which appoint and recall them. Other members of those governments may serve as alternates.
(2) Each *Land* shall have at least three votes; *Länder* with more than two million inhabitants shall have four, *Länder* with more than six million inhabitants five and *Länder* with more than seven million inhabitants six votes.
(3) Each *Land* may appoint as many members as it has votes. The votes of each *Land* may be cast only as a unit and only by Members present or their alternates.

Article 52 [President – Decisions – Rules of procedure]

(1) The Bundesrat shall elect its President for one year.
(2) The President shall convene the Bundesrat. He shall be obliged to do so if the delegates of at least two *Länder* or the Federal Government so demand.
(3) Decisions of the Bundesrat shall require at least a majority of its votes. It shall adopt rules of procedure. Its meetings shall be open to the public. The public may be excluded.
(3a) For matters concerning the European Union the Bundesrat may establish a Chamber for European Affairs, whose decisions shall be considered decisions of the Bundesrat; the number of votes to be uniformly cast by the *Länder* shall be determined by paragraph (2) of Article 51.
(4) Other members or representatives of *Land* governments may serve on committees of the Bundesrat.

Article 53 [Attendance of members of the Federal Government]

The members of the Federal Government shall have the right, and on demand the duty, to participate in meetings of the Bundesrat and of its committees. They shall have the right to be heard at any time. The Bundesrat shall be kept informed by the Federal Government with regard to the conduct of its affairs.

Basic Law for the Federal Republic of Germany

IVa. The Joint Committee

Article 53a [Composition – Rules of procedure]

(1) The Joint Committee shall consist of Members of the Bundestag and members of the Bundesrat; the Bundestag shall provide two thirds and the Bundesrat one third of the committee members. The Bundestag shall designate Members in proportion to the relative strength of the various parliamentary groups; they may not be members of the Federal Government. Each *Land* shall be represented by a Bundesrat member of its choice; these members shall not be bound by instructions. The establishment of the Joint Committee and its proceedings shall be regulated by rules of procedure to be adopted by the Bundestag and requiring the consent of the Bundesrat.
(2) The Federal Government shall inform the Joint Committee about its plans for a state of defence. The rights of the Bundestag and its committees under paragraph (1) of Article 43 shall not be affected by the provisions of this paragraph.

V. The Federal President

Article 54 [Election – Term of office]

(1) The Federal President shall be elected by the Federal Convention without debate. Any German who is entitled to vote in Bundestag elections and has attained the age of forty may be elected.
(2) The term of office of the Federal President shall be five years. Re-election for a consecutive term shall be permitted only once.
(3) The Federal Convention shall consist of the Members of the Bundestag and an equal number of members elected by the parliamentary assemblies of the *Länder* on the basis of proportional representation.
(4) The Federal Convention shall meet not later than thirty days before the term of office of the Federal President expires or, in the case of premature termination, not later than thirty days after that date. It shall be convened by the President of the Bundestag.
(5) After the expiry of an electoral term, the period specified in the first sentence of paragraph (4) of this Article shall begin when the Bundestag first convenes.
(6) The person receiving the votes of a majority of the members of the Federal Convention shall be elected. If, after two ballots, no candidate has obtained such a

majority, the person who receives the largest number of votes on the next ballot shall be elected.

(7) Details shall be regulated by a federal law.

Article 55 [Incompatibilities]

(1) The Federal President may not be a member of the government or of a legislative body of the Federation or of a *Land*.

(2) The Federal President may not hold any other salaried office or engage in any trade or profession or belong to the management or supervisory board of any enterprise conducted for profit.

Article 56 [Oath of office]

On assuming his office, the Federal President shall take the following oath before the assembled Members of the Bundestag and the Bundesrat:

"I swear that I will dedicate my efforts to the well-being of the German people, promote their welfare, protect them from harm, uphold and defend the Basic Law and the laws of the Federation, perform my duties conscientiously and do justice to all. So help me God."

The oath may also be taken without religious affirmation.

Article 57 [Substitution]

If the Federal President is unable to perform his duties, or if his office falls prematurely vacant, the President of the Bundesrat shall exercise his powers.

Article 58 [Countersignature]

Orders and directions of the Federal President shall require for their validity the countersignature of the Federal Chancellor or of the competent Federal Minister. This provision shall not apply to the appointment or dismissal of the Federal Chancellor, the dissolution of the Bundestag under Article 63, or a request made under paragraph (3) of Article 69.

Basic Law for the Federal Republic of Germany

Article 59 **[International representation of the Federation]**

(1) The Federal President shall represent the Federation in international law. He shall conclude treaties with foreign states on behalf of the Federation. He shall accredit and receive envoys.
(2) Treaties that regulate the political relations of the Federation or relate to subjects of federal legislation shall require the consent or participation, in the form of a federal law, of the bodies responsible in such a case for the enactment of federal law. In the case of executive agreements the provisions concerning the federal administration shall apply, *mutatis mutandis*.

Article 59a **(repealed)**

Article 60 **[Appointment of civil servants – Pardon – Immunity]**

(1) The Federal President shall appoint and dismiss federal judges, federal civil servants and commissioned and non-commissioned officers of the Armed Forces, except as may otherwise be provided by a law.
(2) He shall exercise the power to pardon offenders on behalf of the Federation in individual cases.
(3) He may delegate these powers to other authorities.
(4) Paragraphs (2) to (4) of Article 46 shall apply to the Federal President, *mutatis mutandis*.

Article 61 **[Impeachment before the Federal Constitutional Court]**

(1) The Bundestag or the Bundesrat may impeach the Federal President before the Federal Constitutional Court for wilful violation of this Basic Law or of any other federal law. The motion of impeachment must be supported by at least one quarter of the Members of the Bundestag or one quarter of the votes of the Bundesrat. The decision to impeach shall require a majority of two thirds of the Members of the Bundestag or of two thirds of the votes of the Bundesrat. The case for impeachment shall be presented before the Federal Constitutional Court by a person commissioned by the impeaching body.
(2) If the Federal Constitutional Court finds the Federal President guilty of a wilful violation of this Basic Law or of any other federal law, it may declare that he has

forfeited his office. After the Federal President has been impeached, the Court may issue an interim order preventing him from exercising his functions.

VI. The Federal Government

Article 62 [Composition]

The Federal Government shall consist of the Federal Chancellor and the Federal Ministers.

Article 63 [Election of the Federal Chancellor]

(1) The Federal Chancellor shall be elected by the Bundestag without debate on the proposal of the Federal President.
(2) The person who receives the votes of a majority of the Members of the Bundestag shall be elected. The person elected shall be appointed by the Federal President.
(3) If the person proposed by the Federal President is not elected, the Bundestag may elect a Federal Chancellor within fourteen days after the ballot by the votes of more than one half of its Members.
(4) If no Federal Chancellor is elected within this period, a new election shall take place without delay, in which the person who receives the largest number of votes shall be elected. If the person elected receives the votes of a majority of the Members of the Bundestag, the Federal President must appoint him within seven days after the election. If the person elected does not receive such a majority, then within seven days the Federal President shall either appoint him or dissolve the Bundestag.

Article 64 [Appointment and dismissal of Federal Ministers – Oath of office]

(1) Federal Ministers shall be appointed and dismissed by the Federal President upon the proposal of the Federal Chancellor.
(2) On taking office the Federal Chancellor and the Federal Ministers shall take the oath provided for in Article 56 before the Bundestag.

Article 65 [Power to determine policy guidelines – Department and collegiate responsibility]

The Federal Chancellor shall determine and be responsible for the general guidelines of policy. Within these limits each Federal Minister shall conduct the affairs of his department independently and on his own responsibility. The Federal Government shall resolve differences of opinion between Federal Ministers. The Federal Chancellor shall conduct the proceedings of the Federal Government in accordance with rules of procedure adopted by the Government and approved by the Federal President.

Article 65a [Command of the Armed Forces]

(1) Command of the Armed Forces shall be vested in the Federal Minister of Defence.
(2) (repealed)

Article 66 [Incompatibilities]

Neither the Federal Chancellor nor a Federal Minister may hold any other salaried office or engage in any trade or profession or belong to the management or, without the consent of the Bundestag, to the supervisory board of an enterprise conducted for profit.

Article 67 [Vote of no confidence]

(1) The Bundestag may express its lack of confidence in the Federal Chancellor only by electing a successor by the vote of a majority of its Members and requesting the Federal President to dismiss the Federal Chancellor. The Federal President must comply with the request and appoint the person elected.
(2) Forty-eight hours shall elapse between the motion and the election.

Basic Law for the Federal Republic of Germany

Article 68 [Vote of confidence]

(1) If a motion of the Federal Chancellor for a vote of confidence is not supported by the majority of the Members of the Bundestag, the Federal President, upon the proposal of the Federal Chancellor, may dissolve the Bundestag within twenty-one days. The right of dissolution shall lapse as soon as the Bundestag elects another Federal Chancellor by the vote of a majority of its Members.
(2) Forty-eight hours shall elapse between the motion and the vote.

Article 69 [Deputy Federal Chancellor – Term of office]

(1) The Federal Chancellor shall appoint a Federal Minister as his deputy.
(2) The tenure of office of the Federal Chancellor or of a Federal Minister shall end in any event when a new Bundestag convenes; the tenure of office of a Federal Minister shall also end on any other occasion on which the Federal Chancellor ceases to hold office.
(3) At the request of the Federal President the Federal Chancellor, or at the request of the Federal Chancellor or of the Federal President a Federal Minister, shall be obliged to continue to manage the affairs of his office until a successor is appointed.

VII. Federal Legislation and Legislative Procedures

Article 70 [Division of powers between the Federation and the *Länder*]

(1) The *Länder* shall have the right to legislate insofar as this Basic Law does not confer legislative power on the Federation.
(2) The division of authority between the Federation and the *Länder* shall be governed by the provisions of this Basic Law concerning exclusive and concurrent legislative powers.

Article 71 [Exclusive legislative power of the Federation]

On matters within the exclusive legislative power of the Federation, the *Länder* shall have power to legislate only when and to the extent that they are expressly authorised to do so by a federal law.

Basic Law for the Federal Republic of Germany

Article 72 [Concurrent legislative powers]

(1) On matters within the concurrent legislative power, the *Länder* shall have power to legislate so long as and to the extent that the Federation has not exercised its legislative power by enacting a law.

(2) The Federation shall have the right to legislate on matters falling within items 4, 7, 11, 13, 15, 19a, 20, 22, 25 and 26 of paragraph (1) of Article 74, if and to the extent that the establishment of equivalent living conditions throughout the federal territory or the maintenance of legal or economic unity renders federal regulation necessary in the national interest.

(3) If the Federation has made use of its power to legislate, the *Länder* may enact laws at variance with this legislation with respect to:
1. hunting (except for the law on hunting licences);
2. protection of nature and landscape management (except for the general principles governing the protection of nature, the law on protection of plant and animal species or the law on protection of marine life);
3. land distribution;
4. regional planning;
5. management of water resources (except for regulations related to materials or facilities);
6. admission to institutions of higher education and requirements for graduation in such institutions;
7. taxes on real property.

Federal laws on these matters shall enter into force no earlier than six months following their promulgation unless otherwise provided with the consent of the Bundesrat. As for the relationship between federal law and law of the *Länder*, the latest law enacted shall take precedence with respect to matters within the scope of the first sentence.

(4) A federal law may provide that federal legislation which is no longer necessary within the meaning of paragraph (2) of this Article may be superseded by *Land* law.

Article 73 [Matters under exclusive legislative power of the Federation]

(1) The Federation shall have exclusive legislative power with respect to:
1. foreign affairs and defence, including protection of the civilian population;
2. citizenship in the Federation;

3. freedom of movement, passports, residency registration and identity cards, immigration, emigration and extradition;
4. currency, money and coinage, weights and measures, and the determination of standards of time;
5. the unity of the customs and trading area, treaties regarding commerce and navigation, the free movement of goods, and the exchange of goods and payments with foreign countries, including customs and border protection;
5a. safeguarding German cultural assets against removal from the country;
6. air transport;
6a. the operation of railways wholly or predominantly owned by the Federation (federal railways), the construction, maintenance and operation of railway lines belonging to federal railways and the levying of charges for the use of these lines;
7. postal and telecommunications services;
8. the legal relations of persons employed by the Federation and by federal corporations under public law;
9. industrial property rights, copyrights and publishing;
9a. protection by the Federal Criminal Police Office against the dangers of international terrorism when a threat transcends the boundary of one *Land*, when responsibility is not clearly assignable to the police authorities of any particular *Land* or when the highest authority of an individual *Land* requests the assumption of federal responsibility;
10. cooperation between the Federation and the *Länder* concerning
    (a) criminal police work,
    (b) protection of the free democratic basic order, existence and security of the Federation or of a *Land* (protection of the constitution), and
    (c) protection against activities within the federal territory which, by the use of force or preparations for the use of force, endanger the external interests of the Federal Republic of Germany,

    as well as the establishment of a Federal Criminal Police Office and international action to combat crime;
11. statistics for federal purposes;
12. the law on weapons and explosives;
13. benefits for persons disabled by war and for dependents of deceased war victims as well as assistance to former prisoners of war;

14. the production and utilisation of nuclear energy for peaceful purposes, the construction and operation of facilities serving such purposes, protection against hazards arising from the release of nuclear energy or from ionising radiation, and the disposal of radioactive substances.

(2) Laws enacted pursuant to item 9a of paragraph (1) require the consent of the Bundesrat.

Article 74   **[Matters under concurrent legislative powers]**

(1) Concurrent legislative power shall extend to the following matters:
1. civil law, criminal law, court organisation and procedure (except for the law governing pre-trial detention), the legal profession, notaries and the provision of legal advice;
2. registration of births, deaths and marriages;
3. the law of association;
4. the law relating to residence and establishment of foreign nationals;
4a. (repealed)
5. (repealed)
6. matters concerning refugees and expellees;
7. public welfare (except for the law on social care homes);
8. (repealed)
9. war damage and reparations;
10. war graves and graves of other victims of war or despotism;
11. the law relating to economic matters (mining, industry, energy, crafts, trades, commerce, banking, stock exchanges and private insurance), except for the law on shop closing hours, restaurants, amusement arcades, display of persons, trade fairs, exhibitions and markets;
12. labour law, including the organisation of enterprises, occupational health and safety and employment agencies, as well as social security, including unemployment insurance;
13. the regulation of educational and training grants and the promotion of research;
14. the law regarding expropriation, to the extent relevant to matters enumerated in Articles 73 and 74;

15. the transfer of land, natural resources and means of production to public ownership or other forms of public enterprise;
16. prevention of the abuse of economic power;
17. the promotion of agricultural production and forestry (except for the law on land consolidation), ensuring the adequacy of food supply, the importation and exportation of agricultural and forestry products, deep-sea and coastal fishing and coastal preservation;
18. urban real estate transactions, land law (except for laws regarding development fees), and the law on rental subsidies, subsidies for old debts, home-building loan premiums, miners' homebuilding and pit villages;
19. measures to combat human and animal diseases which pose a danger to the public or are communicable, admission to the medical profession and to ancillary professions or occupations, as well as the law on pharmacies, medicines, medical products, drugs, narcotics and poisons;
19a. the economic viability of hospitals and the regulation of hospital charges;
20. the law on food products including animals used in their production, the law on alcohol and tobacco, essential commodities and feedstuffs as well as protective measures in connection with the marketing of agricultural and forest seeds and seedlings, the protection of plants against diseases and pests, as well as the protection of animals;
21. maritime and coastal shipping, as well as navigational aids, inland navigation, meteorological services, sea routes and inland waterways used for general traffic;
22. road traffic, motor transport, construction and maintenance of long-distance highways, as well as the collection of tolls for the use of public highways by vehicles and the allocation of the revenue;
23. non-federal railways, except mountain railways;
24. waste disposal, air pollution control, and noise abatement (except for the protection from noise associated with human activity);
25. state liability;
26. medically assisted generation of human life, analysis and modification of genetic information as well as the regulation of organ, tissue and cell transplantation;
27. the statutory rights and duties of civil servants of the *Länder*, the municipalities and other corporations established under public law as well as of the

judges in the *Länder*, except for their career regulations, remuneration and pensions;
28. hunting;
29. protection of nature and landscape management;
30. land distribution;
31. regional planning;
32. management of water resources;
33. admission to institutions of higher education and requirements for graduation in such institutions.

(2) Laws enacted pursuant to items 25 and 27 of paragraph (1) shall require the consent of the Bundesrat.

Article 74a (repealed)

Article 75 (repealed)

Article 76 [Bills]

(1) Bills may be introduced in the Bundestag by the Federal Government, by the Bundesrat or from the floor of the Bundestag.

(2) Federal Government bills shall first be submitted to the Bundesrat. The Bundesrat shall be entitled to comment on such bills within six weeks. If for important reasons, especially with respect to the scope of the bill, the Bundesrat demands an extension, the period shall be increased to nine weeks. If in exceptional circumstances the Federal Government, on submitting a bill to the Bundesrat, declares it to be particularly urgent, it may submit the bill to the Bundestag after three weeks or, if the Bundesrat has demanded an extension pursuant to the third sentence of this paragraph, after six weeks, even if it has not yet received the Bundesrat's comments; upon receiving such comments, it shall transmit them to the Bundestag without delay. In the case of bills to amend this Basic Law or to transfer sovereign powers pursuant to Article 23 or 24, the comment period shall be nine weeks; the fourth sentence of this paragraph shall not apply.

(3) Bundesrat bills shall be submitted to the Bundestag by the Federal Government within six weeks. In submitting them the Federal Government shall state its own views. If for important reasons, especially with respect to the scope of the bill, the Federal Government demands an extension, the period shall be increased to nine

weeks. If in exceptional circumstances the Bundesrat declares a bill to be particularly urgent, the period shall be three weeks or, if the Federal Government has demanded an extension pursuant to the third sentence of this paragraph, six weeks. In the case of bills to amend this Basic Law or to transfer sovereign powers pursuant to Article 23 or 24, the comment period shall be nine weeks; the fourth sentence of this paragraph shall not apply. The Bundestag shall consider and vote on bills within a reasonable time.

Article 77 [Legislative procedure – Mediation Committee]

(1) Federal laws shall be adopted by the Bundestag. After their adoption the President of the Bundestag shall forward them to the Bundesrat without delay.
(2) Within three weeks after receiving an adopted bill, the Bundesrat may demand that a committee for joint consideration of bills, composed of Members of the Bundestag and of the Bundesrat, be convened. The composition and proceedings of this committee shall be regulated by rules of procedure adopted by the Bundestag and requiring the consent of the Bundesrat. The members of the Bundesrat on this committee shall not be bound by instructions. When the consent of the Bundesrat is required for a bill to become law, the Bundestag and the Federal Government may likewise demand that such a committee be convened. Should the committee propose any amendment to the adopted bill, the Bundestag shall vote on it a second time.
(2a) Insofar as its consent is required for a bill to become law, the Bundesrat, if no request has been made pursuant to the first sentence of paragraph (2) of this Article or if the mediation proceeding has been completed without a proposal to amend the bill, shall vote on the bill within a reasonable time.
(3) Insofar as its consent is not required for a bill to become law, the Bundesrat, once proceedings under paragraph (2) of this Article are completed, may within two weeks object to a bill adopted by the Bundestag. The time for objection shall begin, in the case described in the last sentence of paragraph (2) of this Article, upon receipt of the bill as re-adopted by the Bundestag, and in all other cases upon receipt of a communication from the chairman of the committee provided for in paragraph (2) of this Article to the effect that the committee's proceedings have been concluded.
(4) If the objection is adopted by the majority of the votes of the Bundesrat, it may be rejected by a decision of the majority of the Members of the Bundestag. If the Bundesrat adopted the objection by a majority of at least two thirds of its votes, its

rejection by the Bundestag shall require a two-thirds majority, including at least a majority of the Members of the Bundestag.

Article 78 [Passage of federal laws]

A bill adopted by the Bundestag shall become law if the Bundesrat consents to it or fails to make a demand pursuant to paragraph (2) of Article 77 or fails to enter an objection within the period stipulated in paragraph (3) of Article 77 or withdraws such an objection or if the objection is overridden by the Bundestag.

Article 79 [Amendment of the Basic Law]

(1) This Basic Law may be amended only by a law expressly amending or supplementing its text. In the case of an international treaty regarding a peace settlement, the preparation of a peace settlement or the phasing out of an occupation regime or designed to promote the defence of the Federal Republic, it shall be sufficient, for the purpose of making clear that the provisions of this Basic Law do not preclude the conclusion and entry into force of the treaty, to add language to the Basic Law that merely makes this clarification.
(2) Any such law shall be carried by two thirds of the Members of the Bundestag and two thirds of the votes of the Bundesrat.
(3) Amendments to this Basic Law affecting the division of the Federation into *Länder*, their participation in principle in the legislative process, or the principles laid down in Articles 1 and 20 shall be inadmissible.

Article 80 [Issuance of statutory instruments]

(1) The Federal Government, a Federal Minister or the *Land* governments may be authorised by a law to issue statutory instruments. The content, purpose and scope of the authority conferred shall be specified in the law. Each statutory instrument shall contain a statement of its legal basis. If the law provides that such authority may be further delegated, such subdelegation shall be effected by statutory instrument.
(2) Unless a federal law otherwise provides, the consent of the Bundesrat shall be required for statutory instruments issued by the Federal Government or a Federal Minister regarding fees or basic principles for the use of postal and telecommunica-

tion facilities, basic principles for levying of charges for the use of facilities of federal railways or the construction and operation of railways, as well as for statutory instruments issued pursuant to federal laws that require the consent of the Bundesrat or that are executed by the *Länder* on federal commission or in their own right.

(3) The Bundesrat may submit to the Federal Government drafts of statutory instruments that require its consent.

(4) Insofar as *Land* governments are authorised by or pursuant to federal laws to issue statutory instruments, the *Länder* shall also be entitled to regulate the matter by a law.

Article 80a [State of tension]

(1) If this Basic Law or a federal law regarding defence, including protection of the civilian population, provides that legal provisions may be applied only in accordance with this Article, their application, except when a state of defence has been declared, shall be permissible only after the Bundestag has determined that a state of tension exists or has specifically approved such application. The determination of a state of tension and specific approval in the cases mentioned in the first sentence of paragraph (5) and the second sentence of paragraph (6) of Article 12a shall require a two-thirds majority of the votes cast.

(2) Any measures taken pursuant to legal provisions by virtue of paragraph (1) of this Article shall be rescinded whenever the Bundestag so demands.

(3) Notwithstanding paragraph (1) of this Article, the application of such legal provisions shall also be permissible on the basis of and in accordance with a decision made by an international body within the framework of a treaty of alliance with the approval of the Federal Government. Any measures taken pursuant to this paragraph shall be rescinded whenever the Bundestag, by the vote of a majority of its Members, so demands.

Article 81 [Legislative emergency]

(1) If, in the circumstances described in Article 68, the Bundestag is not dissolved, the Federal President, at the request of the Federal Government and with the consent of the Bundesrat, may declare a state of legislative emergency with respect to a bill, if the Bundestag rejects the bill although the Federal Government has declared

it to be urgent. The same shall apply if a bill has been rejected although the Federal Chancellor had combined it with a motion under Article 68.

(2) If, after a state of legislative emergency has been declared, the Bundestag again rejects the bill or adopts it in a version the Federal Government declares unacceptable, the bill shall be deemed to have become law to the extent that it receives the consent of the Bundesrat. The same shall apply if the Bundestag does not pass the bill within four weeks after it is reintroduced.

(3) During the term of office of a Federal Chancellor, any other bill rejected by the Bundestag may become law in accordance with paragraphs (1) and (2) of this Article within a period of six months after the first declaration of a state of legislative emergency. After the expiry of this period, no further declaration of a state of legislative emergency may be made during the term of office of the same Federal Chancellor.

(4) This Basic Law may neither be amended nor abrogated nor suspended in whole or in part by a law enacted pursuant to paragraph (2) of this Article.

Article 82   **[Certification – Promulgation – Entry into force]**

(1) Laws enacted in accordance with the provisions of this Basic Law shall, after countersignature, be certified by the Federal President and promulgated in the Federal Law Gazette. Statutory instruments shall be certified by the authority that issues them and, unless a law otherwise provides, shall be promulgated in the Federal Law Gazette.

(2) Every law or statutory instrument shall specify the date on which it shall take effect. In the absence of such a provision, it shall take effect on the fourteenth day after the day on which the Federal Law Gazette containing it was published.

VIII. The Execution of Federal Laws and the Federal Administration

Article 83   **[Execution by the *Länder*]**

The *Länder* shall execute federal laws in their own right insofar as this Basic Law does not otherwise provide or permit.

Article 84 *[Länder* administration – Federal oversight]

(1) Where the *Länder* execute federal laws in their own right, they shall provide for the establishment of the requisite authorities and regulate their administrative procedures. If federal laws provide otherwise, the *Länder* may enact derogating regulations. If a *Land* has enacted a derogating regulation pursuant to the second sentence, subsequent federal statutory provisions regulating the organisation of authorities and their administrative procedure shall not be enacted until at least six months after their promulgation, provided that no other determination has been made with the consent of the Bundesrat. The third sentence of paragraph (2) of Article 72 shall apply, *mutatis mutandis*. In exceptional cases, owing to a special need for uniform federal legislation, the Federation may regulate the administrative procedure with no possibility of separate *Land* legislation. Such laws shall require the consent of the Bundesrat. Federal laws may not entrust municipalities and associations of municipalities with any tasks.
(2) The Federal Government, with the consent of the Bundesrat, may issue general administrative provisions.
(3) The Federal Government shall exercise oversight to ensure that the *Länder* execute federal laws in accordance with the law. For this purpose the Federal Government may send commissioners to the highest *Land* authorities and, with their consent or, where such consent is refused, with the consent of the Bundesrat, also to subordinate authorities.
(4) Should any deficiencies that the Federal Government has identified in the execution of federal laws in the *Länder* not be corrected, the Bundesrat, on application of the Federal Government or of the *Land* concerned, shall decide whether that *Land* has violated the law. The decision of the Bundesrat may be challenged in the Federal Constitutional Court.
(5) With a view to the execution of federal laws, the Federal Government may be authorised by a federal law requiring the consent of the Bundesrat to issue instructions in particular cases. They shall be addressed to the highest *Land* authorities unless the Federal Government considers the matter urgent.

Article 85 [Execution by the *Länder* on federal commission]

(1) Where the *Länder* execute federal laws on federal commission, establishment of the authorities shall remain the concern of the *Länder*, except insofar as federal laws enacted with the consent of the Bundesrat otherwise provide. Federal laws may not entrust municipalities and associations of municipalities with any tasks.

(2) The Federal Government, with the consent of the Bundesrat, may issue general administrative provisions. It may provide for the uniform training of civil servants and other salaried public employees. The heads of intermediate authorities shall be appointed with its approval.

(3) The *Land* authorities shall be subject to instructions from the competent highest federal authorities. Such instructions shall be addressed to the highest *Land* authorities unless the Federal Government considers the matter urgent. Implementation of the instructions shall be ensured by the highest *Land* authorities.

(4) Federal oversight shall extend to the legality and appropriateness of execution. For this purpose the Federal Government may require the submission of reports and documents and send commissioners to all authorities.

Article 86   **[Federal administration]**

Where the Federation executes laws through its own administrative authorities or through federal corporations or institutions established under public law, the Federal Government shall, insofar as the law in question makes no special stipulation, issue general administrative provisions. The Federal Government shall provide for the establishment of the authorities insofar as the law in question does not otherwise provide.

Article 87   **[Matters]**

(1) The foreign service, the federal financial administration and, in accordance with the provisions of Article 89, the administration of federal waterways and shipping shall be conducted by federal administrative authorities with their own administrative substructures. A federal law may establish Federal Border Police authorities and central offices for police information and communications, for the criminal police and for the compilation of data for purposes of protection of the constitution and of protection against activities within the federal territory which, through the use of force or acts preparatory to the use of force, endanger the external interests of the Federal Republic of Germany.

(2) Social insurance institutions whose jurisdiction extends beyond the territory of a single *Land* shall be administered as federal corporations under public law. Social insurance institutions whose jurisdiction extends beyond the territory of a single *Land* but not beyond that of three *Länder* shall, notwithstanding the first sentence

of this paragraph, be administered as *Land* corporations under public law, if the *Länder* concerned have specified which *Land* shall exercise supervisory authority.

(3) In addition, autonomous federal higher authorities as well as new federal corporations and institutions under public law may be established by a federal law for matters on which the Federation has legislative power. When the Federation is confronted with new responsibilities with respect to matters on which it has legislative power, federal authorities at intermediate and lower levels may be established, with the consent of the Bundesrat and of a majority of the Members of the Bundestag, in cases of urgent need.

Article 87a [Armed Forces]

(1) The Federation shall establish Armed Forces for purposes of defence. Their numerical strength and general organisational structure must be shown in the budget.

(2) Apart from defence, the Armed Forces may be employed only to the extent expressly permitted by this Basic Law.

(3) During a state of defence or a state of tension the Armed Forces shall have the power to protect civilian property and to perform traffic control functions to the extent necessary to accomplish their defence mission. Moreover, during a state of defence or a state of tension, the Armed Forces may also be authorised to support police measures for the protection of civilian property; in this event the Armed Forces shall cooperate with the competent authorities.

(4) In order to avert an imminent danger to the existence or free democratic basic order of the Federation or of a *Land*, the Federal Government, if the conditions referred to in paragraph (2) of Article 91 obtain and forces of the police and the Federal Border Police are insufficient, may employ the Armed Forces to support the police and the Federal Border Police in protecting civilian property and in combating organised armed insurgents. Any such employment of the Armed Forces shall be discontinued if the Bundestag or the Bundesrat so demands.

Article 87b [Federal Defence Administration]

(1) The Federal Defence Administration shall be conducted as a federal administrative authority with its own administrative substructure. It shall have jurisdiction for personnel matters and direct responsibility for satisfaction of the procurement needs of the Armed Forces. Responsibilities connected with pensions for injured persons or with construction work may be assigned to the Federal Defence Admin-

istration only by a federal law requiring the consent of the Bundesrat. Such consent shall also be required for any laws to the extent that they empower the Federal Defence Administration to interfere with rights of third parties; this requirement, however, shall not apply in the case of laws regarding personnel matters.

(2) In addition, federal laws concerning defence, including recruitment for military service and protection of the civilian population, may, with the consent of the Bundesrat, provide that they shall be executed, wholly or in part, either by federal administrative authorities with their own administrative substructures or by the *Länder* on federal commission. If such laws are executed by the *Länder* on federal commission, they may, with the consent of the Bundesrat, provide that the powers vested in the Federal Government or in the competent highest federal authorities pursuant to Article 85 be transferred wholly or in part to federal higher authorities; in this event the law may provide that such authorities shall not require the consent of the Bundesrat in issuing general administrative provisions pursuant to the first sentence of paragraph (2) of Article 85.

Article 87c [Production and utilisation of nuclear energy]

Laws enacted under item 14 of paragraph (1) of Article 73 may, with the consent of the Bundesrat, provide that they shall be executed by the *Länder* on federal commission.

Article 87d [Air transport administration]

(1) Air transport administration shall be conducted under federal administration. Air traffic control services may also be provided by foreign air traffic control organisations which are authorised in accordance with European Community law.

(2) By a federal law requiring the consent of the Bundesrat, responsibilities for air transport administration may be delegated to the *Länder* acting on federal commission.

Article 87e [Rail transport administration]

(1) Rail transport with respect to federal railways shall be administered by federal authorities. Responsibilities for rail transport administration may be delegated by a federal law to the *Länder* acting in their own right.

(2) The Federation shall discharge rail transport administration responsibilities assigned to it by a federal law, above and beyond those regarding federal railways.
(3) Federal railways shall be operated as enterprises under private law. They shall remain the property of the Federation to the extent that their activities embrace the construction, maintenance and operation of the lines. The transfer of federal shares in these enterprises under the second sentence of this paragraph shall be effected pursuant to a law; the Federation shall retain a majority of the shares. Details shall be regulated by a federal law.
(4) The Federation shall ensure that, in developing and maintaining the federal railway system as well as in offering services over this system, other than local passenger services, due account is taken of the interests and especially the transportation needs of the public. Details shall be regulated by a federal law.
(5) Laws enacted pursuant to paragraphs (1) to (4) of this Article shall require the consent of the Bundesrat. The consent of the Bundesrat shall also be required for laws regarding the dissolution, merger or division of federal railway enterprises, the transfer of federal railway lines to third parties or the abandonment of such lines or affecting local passenger services.

Article 87f [Posts and telecommunications]

(1) In accordance with a federal law requiring the consent of the Bundesrat, the Federation shall ensure the availability of adequate and appropriate postal and telecommunications services throughout the federal territory.
(2) Services within the meaning of paragraph (1) of this Article shall be provided as a matter of private enterprise by the firms succeeding to the special trust Deutsche Bundespost and by other private providers. Sovereign functions in the area of posts and telecommunications shall be discharged by federal administrative authorities.
(3) Notwithstanding the second sentence of paragraph (2) of this Article, the Federation, by means of a federal institution under public law, shall discharge particular responsibilities relating to the firms succeeding to the special trust Deutsche Bundespost as prescribed by a federal law.

Article 88 [The Federal Bank – The European Central Bank]

The Federation shall establish a note-issuing and currency bank as the Federal Bank. Within the framework of the European Union, its responsibilities and powers may be transferred to the European Central Bank, which is independent and committed to the overriding goal of assuring price stability.

Article 89 [Federal waterways – Administration of waterways]

(1) The Federation shall be the owner of the former Reich waterways.
(2) The Federation shall administer the federal waterways through its own authorities. It shall exercise those state functions relating to inland shipping which extend beyond the territory of a single *Land*, and those functions relating to maritime shipping, which are conferred on it by a law. Insofar as federal waterways lie within the territory of a single *Land*, the Federation on its application may delegate their administration to that *Land* on federal commission. If a waterway touches the territory of two or more *Länder*, the Federation may commission that *Land* which is designated by the affected *Länder*.
(3) In the administration, development and new construction of waterways, the requirements of land improvement and of water management shall be assured in agreement with the *Länder*.

Article 90 [Federal roads and motorways]

(1) The Federation shall remain the owner of the federal motorways and other federal trunk roads. This ownership shall be inalienable.
(2) The administration of the federal motorways shall be a matter for the federal administrative authorities. The Federation may make use of a company under private law to discharge its responsibilities. This company shall be in the inalienable ownership of the Federation. Third parties shall have no direct or indirect holding in the company and its subsidiaries. Third parties shall have no holdings in the framework of public-private partnerships in road networks comprising the entire federal motorway network or the entire network of other federal trunk roads in a *Land* or significant parts of these networks. Details shall be regulated by a federal law.
(3) The *Länder*, or such self-governing corporate bodies as are competent under *Land* law, shall administer on federal commission the other federal trunk roads.
(4) At the request of a *Land*, the Federation may assume administrative responsibility for the other federal trunk roads insofar as they lie within the territory of that *Land*.

Article 91 [Internal emergency]

(1) In order to avert an imminent danger to the existence or free democratic basic order of the Federation or of a *Land*, a *Land* may call upon police forces of other *Länder*, or upon personnel and facilities of other administrative authorities and of the Federal Border Police.

(2) If the *Land* where such danger is imminent is not itself willing or able to combat the danger, the Federal Government may place the police in that *Land* and the police forces of other *Länder* under its own orders and deploy units of the Federal Border Police. Any such order shall be rescinded once the danger is removed or at any time on the demand of the Bundesrat. If the danger extends beyond the territory of a single *Land*, the Federal Government, insofar as is necessary to combat such danger, may issue instructions to the *Land* governments; the first and second sentences of this paragraph shall not be affected by this provision.

VIIIa. Joint Tasks

Article 91a [Joint tasks – Responsibility for expenditure]

(1) In the following areas the Federation shall participate in the discharge of responsibilities of the *Länder*, provided that such responsibilities are important to society as a whole and that federal participation is necessary for the improvement of living conditions (joint tasks):
1. improvement of regional economic structures;
2. improvement of the agrarian structure and of coastal preservation.

(2) Federal laws enacted with the consent of the Bundesrat shall specify the joint tasks as well as the details of coordination.

(3) In cases to which item 1 of paragraph (1) of this Article applies, the Federation shall finance one half of the expenditure in each *Land*. In cases to which item 2 of paragraph (1) of this Article applies, the Federation shall finance at least one half of the expenditure, and the proportion shall be the same for all *Länder*. Details shall be regulated by law. The provision of funds shall be subject to appropriation in the budgets of the Federation and the *Länder*.

Article 91b [Education programmes and promotion of research]

(1) The Federation and the *Länder* may cooperate on the basis of agreements in cases of supraregional importance in the promotion of sciences, research and teaching. Agreements primarily affecting institutions of higher education shall require the consent of all the *Länder*. This provision shall not apply to agreements regarding the construction of research facilities, including large scientific installations.
(2) The Federation and the *Länder* may mutually agree to cooperate for the assessment of the performance of education systems in international comparison and in drafting relevant reports and recommendations.
(3) The apportionment of costs shall be regulated in the pertinent agreement.

Article 91c [Information technology systems]

(1) The Federation and the *Länder* may cooperate in planning, constructing and operating information technology systems needed to discharge their responsibilities.
(2) The Federation and the *Länder* may agree to specify the standards and security requirements necessary for exchanges between their information technology systems. Agreements regarding the bases of cooperation under the first sentence may provide, for individual responsibilities determined by their content and scope, that detailed regulations be enacted with the consent of a qualified majority of the Federation and the *Länder* as laid down in the agreements. They require the consent of the Bundestag and the legislatures of the participating *Länder*; the right to withdraw from these agreements cannot be precluded. The agreements shall also regulate the sharing of costs.
(3) The *Länder* may also agree on the joint operation of information technology systems along with the establishment of installations for that purpose.
(4) To link the information networks of the Federation and the *Länder*, the Federation shall establish a connection network. Details regarding the establishment and the operation of the connection network shall be regulated by a federal law with the consent of the Bundesrat.
(5) Comprehensive access by means of information technology to the administrative services of the Federation and the *Länder* shall be regulated by a federal law with the consent of the Bundesrat.

Basic Law for the Federal Republic of Germany

Article 91d [Comparison of performance]

With a view to ascertaining and improving the performance of their administrations, the Federation and the *Länder* may conduct comparative studies and publish the results thereof.

Article 91e [Cooperation in respect of basic support for persons seeking employment]

(1) In the execution of federal laws in the field of basic support for persons seeking employment, the Federation and the *Länder* or the municipalities and associations of municipalities responsible pursuant to *Land* law shall cooperate as a rule in joint institutions.
(2) The Federation may authorise a limited number of municipalities and associations of municipalities, at their request and with the consent of the highest *Land* authority, to discharge the tasks pursuant to paragraph (1) alone. In this case, the Federation shall bear the necessary expenditures including the administrative expenses for the tasks which are to be discharged by the Federation in the execution of laws pursuant to paragraph (1).
(3) Details shall be regulated by a federal law requiring the consent of the Bundesrat.

IX. The Judiciary

Article 92 [Court organisation]

The judicial power shall be vested in the judges; it shall be exercised by the Federal Constitutional Court, by the federal courts provided for in this Basic Law and by the courts of the *Länder*.

Article 93 [Jurisdiction of the Federal Constitutional Court]

(1) The Federal Constitutional Court shall rule:
1. on the interpretation of this Basic Law in the event of disputes concerning the extent of the rights and duties of a supreme federal body or of other parties

vested with rights of their own by this Basic Law or by the rules of procedure of a supreme federal body;

2. in the event of disagreements or doubts concerning the formal or substantive compatibility of federal law or *Land* law with this Basic Law or the compatibility of *Land* law with other federal law on application of the Federal Government, of a *Land* government or of one quarter of the Members of the Bundestag;

2a. in the event of disagreements as to whether a law meets the conditions set out in paragraph (2) of Article 72, on application of the Bundesrat or of the government or legislature of a *Land*;

3. in the event of disagreements concerning the rights and duties of the Federation and the *Länder*, especially in the execution of federal law by the *Länder* and in the exercise of federal oversight;

4. on other disputes involving public law between the Federation and the *Länder*, between different *Länder* or within a *Land*, unless there is recourse to another court;

4a. on constitutional complaints, which may be filed by any person alleging that one of his basic rights or one of his rights under paragraph (4) of Article 20 or under Article 33, 38, 101, 103 or 104 has been infringed by public authority;

4b. on constitutional complaints filed by municipalities or associations of municipalities on the ground that their right to self-government under Article 28 has been infringed by a law; in the case of infringement by a *Land* law, however, only if the law cannot be challenged in the constitutional court of the *Land*;

4c. on constitutional complaints filed by associations concerning their non-recognition as political parties for an election to the Bundestag;

5. in the other instances provided for in this Basic Law.

(2) At the request of the Bundesrat, a *Land* government or the parliamentary assembly of a *Land*, the Federal Constitutional Court shall also rule whether, in cases falling under paragraph (4) of Article 72, the need for a regulation by federal law does not exist any longer or whether, in the cases referred to in item 1 of paragraph (2) of Article 125a, federal law could not be enacted any longer. The Court's determination that the need has ceased to exist or that federal law could no longer be enacted substitutes a federal law according to paragraph (4) of Article 72 or item 2 of paragraph (2) of Article 125a. A request under the first sentence is admissible only if a bill falling under paragraph (4) of Article 72 or the second sentence of paragraph (2) of Article 125a has been rejected by the German Bundestag or if it

has not been considered and determined upon within one year or if a similar bill has been rejected by the Bundesrat.

(3) The Federal Constitutional Court shall also rule on such other matters as shall be assigned to it by a federal law.

Article 94 [Composition of the Federal Constitutional Court]

(1) The Federal Constitutional Court shall consist of federal judges and other members. Half the members of the Federal Constitutional Court shall be elected by the Bundestag and half by the Bundesrat. They may not be members of the Bundestag, of the Bundesrat, of the Federal Government or of any of the corresponding bodies of a *Land*.

(2) The organisation and procedure of the Federal Constitutional Court shall be regulated by a federal law, which shall specify in which instances its decisions shall have the force of law. The law may require that all other legal remedies be exhausted before a constitutional complaint may be filed and may provide for a separate proceeding to determine whether the complaint will be accepted for adjudication.

Article 95 [Supreme federal courts]

(1) The Federation shall establish the Federal Court of Justice, the Federal Administrative Court, the Federal Finance Court, the Federal Labour Court and the Federal Social Court as supreme courts of ordinary, administrative, financial, labour and social jurisdiction.

(2) The judges of each of these courts shall be chosen jointly by the competent Federal Minister and a committee for the selection of judges consisting of the competent *Land* ministers and an equal number of members elected by the Bundestag.

(3) A Joint Chamber of the courts specified in paragraph (1) of this Article shall be established to preserve the uniformity of decisions. Details shall be regulated by a federal law.

Article 96 [Other federal courts]

(1) The Federation may establish a federal court for matters concerning industrial property rights.

(2) The Federation may establish federal military criminal courts for the Armed Forces. These courts may exercise criminal jurisdiction only during a state of defence or over members of the Armed Forces serving abroad or on board warships. Details shall be regulated by a federal law. These courts shall be under the aegis of the Federal Minister of Justice. The judges officiating there as their primary occupation shall be persons qualified to hold judicial office.

(3) The supreme court of review from the courts designated in paragraphs (1) and (2) of this Article shall be the Federal Court of Justice.

(4) The Federation may establish federal courts for disciplinary proceedings against, and for proceedings on complaints by, persons in the federal public service.

(5) With the consent of the Bundesrat, a federal law may provide that courts of the *Länder* shall exercise federal jurisdiction over criminal proceedings in the following matters:

1. genocide;
2. crimes against humanity under international criminal law;
3. war crimes;
4. other acts tending to and undertaken with the intent to disturb the peaceful relations between nations (paragraph (1) of Article 26);
5. state security.

Article 97 [Judicial independence]

(1) Judges shall be independent and subject only to the law.

(2) Judges appointed permanently to positions as their primary occupation may be involuntarily dismissed, permanently or temporarily suspended, transferred or retired before the expiry of their term of office only by virtue of judicial decision and only for the reasons and in the manner specified by the laws. The legislature may set age limits for the retirement of judges appointed for life. In the event of changes in the structure of courts or in their districts, judges may be transferred to another court or removed from office, provided they retain their full salary.

Article 98 [Legal status of judges – Impeachment]

(1) The legal status of federal judges shall be regulated by a special federal law.

(2) If a federal judge infringes the principles of this Basic Law or the constitutional order of a *Land* in his official capacity or unofficially, the Federal Constitutional

Court, upon application of the Bundestag, may by a two-thirds majority order that the judge be transferred or retired. In the case of an intentional infringement it may order his dismissal.

(3) The legal status of the judges in the *Länder* shall be regulated by special *Land* laws if item 27 of paragraph (1) of Article 74 does not otherwise provide.

(4) The *Länder* may provide that *Land* judges shall be chosen jointly by the *Land* Minister of Justice and a committee for the selection of judges.

(5) The *Länder* may enact provisions regarding *Land* judges that correspond with those of paragraph (2) of this Article. Existing *Land* constitutional law shall not be affected. The decision in cases of judicial impeachment shall rest with the Federal Constitutional Court.

Article 99   **[Constitutional disputes within a *Land*]**

A *Land* law may assign the adjudication of constitutional disputes within a *Land* to the Federal Constitutional Court and the final decision in matters involving the application of *Land* law to the supreme courts specified in paragraph (1) of Article 95.

Article 100   **[Concrete judicial review]**

(1) If a court concludes that a law on whose validity its decision depends is unconstitutional, the proceedings shall be stayed, and a decision shall be obtained from the *Land* court with jurisdiction over constitutional disputes where the constitution of a *Land* is held to be violated or from the Federal Constitutional Court where this Basic Law is held to be violated. This provision shall also apply where the Basic Law is held to be violated by *Land* law and where a *Land* law is held to be incompatible with a federal law.

(2) If, in the course of litigation, doubt exists whether a rule of international law is an integral part of federal law and whether it directly creates rights and duties for the individual (Article 25), the court shall obtain a decision from the Federal Constitutional Court.

(3) If the constitutional court of a *Land*, in interpreting this Basic Law, proposes to derogate from a decision of the Federal Constitutional Court or of the constitutional court of another *Land*, it shall obtain a decision from the Federal Constitutional Court.

Basic Law for the Federal Republic of Germany

Article 101 **[Ban on extraordinary courts]**

(1) Extraordinary courts shall not be allowed. No one may be removed from the jurisdiction of his lawful judge.
(2) Courts for particular fields of law may be established only by a law.

Article 102 **[Abolition of capital punishment]**

Capital punishment is abolished.

Article 103 **[Fair trial]**

(1) In the courts every person shall be entitled to a hearing in accordance with law.
(2) An act may be punished only if it was defined by a law as a criminal offence before the act was committed.
(3) No person may be punished for the same act more than once under the general criminal laws.

Article 104 **[Deprivation of liberty]**

(1) Liberty of the person may be restricted only pursuant to a formal law and only in compliance with the procedures prescribed therein. Persons in custody may not be subjected to mental or physical mistreatment.
(2) Only a judge may rule upon the permissibility or continuation of any deprivation of liberty. If such a deprivation is not based on a judicial order, a judicial decision shall be obtained without delay. The police may hold no one in custody on their own authority beyond the end of the day following that of the arrest. Details shall be regulated by a law.
(3) Any person provisionally detained on suspicion of having committed a criminal offence shall be brought before a judge no later than the day following that of his arrest; the judge shall inform him of the reasons for the arrest, examine him and give him an opportunity to raise objections. The judge shall, without delay, either issue a written arrest warrant setting forth the reasons therefor or order his release.
(4) A relative or a person enjoying the confidence of the person in custody shall be notified without delay of any judicial decision imposing or continuing a deprivation of liberty.

X. Finance

Article 104a [Apportionment of expenditures – Financial system – Liability]

(1) The Federation and the *Länder* shall separately finance the expenditures resulting from the discharge of their respective responsibilities insofar as this Basic Law does not otherwise provide.
(2) Where the *Länder* act on federal commission, the Federation shall finance the resulting expenditures.
(3) Federal laws providing for money grants to be administered by the *Länder* may provide that the Federation shall pay for such grants wholly or in part. If any such law provides that the Federation shall finance one half or more of the expenditure, it shall be executed by the *Länder* on federal commission. For the granting of benefits for accommodation and heating in the field of basic support for persons seeking employment, the law shall be executed on federal commission if the Federation finances three quarters or more of the expenditure.
(4) Federal laws that oblige the *Länder* to provide money grants, benefits in kind or comparable services to third parties and which are executed by the *Länder* in their own right or according to the second sentence of paragraph (3) on commission of the Federation shall require the consent of the Bundesrat if the expenditure resulting therefrom is to be borne by the *Länder*.
(5) The Federation and the *Länder* shall finance the administrative expenditures incurred by their respective authorities and shall be responsible to one another for ensuring proper administration. Details shall be regulated by a federal law requiring the consent of the Bundesrat.
(6) In accordance with the internal allocation of competencies and responsibilities, the Federation and the *Länder* shall bear the costs entailed by a violation of obligations incumbent on Germany under supranational or international law. In cases of financial corrections by the European Union with effect transcending one specific *Land*, the Federation and the *Länder* shall bear such costs at a ratio of 15 to 85. In such cases, the *Länder* as a whole shall be responsible in solidarity for 35 per cent of the total burden according to a general formula; 50 per cent of the total burden shall be borne by those *Länder* which have caused the encumbrance, adjusted to the size of the amount of the financial means received. Details shall be regulated by a federal law requiring the consent of the Bundesrat.

Basic Law for the Federal Republic of Germany

Article 104b [**Financial assistance for investments**]

(1) To the extent that this Basic Law confers on it the power to legislate, the Federation may grant the *Länder* financial assistance for particularly important investments by the *Länder* and municipalities (associations of municipalities) which are necessary to:
1. avert a disturbance of the overall economic equilibrium,
2. equalise differing economic capacities within the federal territory, or
3. promote economic growth.

By way of derogation from the first sentence, the Federation may grant financial assistance even outside its field of legislative powers in cases of natural disasters or exceptional emergency situations beyond governmental control and substantially harmful to the state's financial capacity.

(2) Details, especially with respect to the kinds of investments to be promoted, shall be regulated by a federal law requiring the consent of the Bundesrat or by an executive agreement based on the Federal Budget Act. The federal law or executive agreement may contain provisions on the shaping of the respective *Land* programmes for the use of the financial assistance. The criteria for the shaping of the *Land* programmes shall be specified in agreement with the affected *Länder*. To ensure that the funds are used for their intended purpose, the Federal Government may require the submission of reports and documents and conduct surveys of any authorities. The funds from the Federation shall be provided in addition to funds belonging to the *Länder*. The duration of the grants shall be limited, and the grants must be reviewed at regular intervals with respect to the manner in which they are used. The financial assistance must be designed with descending annual contributions.

(3) Upon request, the Bundestag, the Federal Government and the Bundesrat shall be informed about the implementation of such measures and the improvements reached.

Article 104c [**Financial assistance for investments in municipal education infrastructure**]

The Federation may grant the *Länder* financial assistance for investments of significance to the nation as a whole, and for special limited-term expenditures on the part of the *Länder* and municipalities (associations of municipalities) directly connected with such investments to improve the efficiency of municipal education infrastructure. The first three sentences and the fifth and sixth sentences of paragraph (2), as well as paragraph (3) of Article 104b, shall apply, *mutatis mutandis*. To ensure that the funds are used for their intended purpose, the Federal Government may require the submission of reports and, where circumstances so warrant, documents.

Article 104d   **[Financial assistance for investments in social housing]**

The Federation may grant the *Länder* financial assistance for investments of significance to the nation as a whole on the part of the *Länder* and municipalities (associations of municipalities) in social housing. The first five sentences of paragraph (2), as well as paragraph (3) of Article 104b, shall apply, *mutatis mutandis*.

Article 105   **[Distribution of powers regarding tax laws]**

(1) The Federation shall have exclusive power to legislate with respect to customs duties and fiscal monopolies.
(2) The Federation shall have concurrent power to legislate with respect to taxes on real property. It shall have concurrent power to legislate with respect to all other taxes the revenue from which accrues to it wholly or in part or as to which the conditions provided for in paragraph (2) of Article 72 apply.
(2a) The *Länder* shall have power to legislate with regard to local taxes on consumption and expenditures so long and insofar as such taxes are not substantially similar to taxes regulated by federal law. They are empowered to determine the rate of the tax on acquisition of real estate.
(3) Federal laws relating to taxes the revenue from which accrues wholly or in part to the *Länder* or to municipalities (associations of municipalities) shall require the consent of the Bundesrat.

Basic Law for the Federal Republic of Germany

Article 106 **[Apportionment of tax revenue and yield of fiscal monopolies]**

(1) The yield of fiscal monopolies and the revenue from the following taxes shall accrue to the Federation:
1. customs duties;
2. taxes on consumption insofar as they do not accrue to the *Länder* pursuant to paragraph (2), or jointly to the Federation and the *Länder* in accordance with paragraph (3) or to municipalities in accordance with paragraph (6) of this Article;
3. the road freight tax, motor vehicle tax, and other taxes on transactions related to motorised vehicles;
4. the taxes on capital transactions, insurance and bills of exchange;
5. non-recurring levies on property and equalisation of burdens levies;
6. income and corporation surtaxes;
7. levies imposed within the framework of the European Communities.

(2) Revenue from the following taxes shall accrue to the *Länder*:
1. the property tax;
2. the inheritance tax;
3. the motor vehicle tax;
4. such taxes on transactions as do not accrue to the Federation pursuant to paragraph (1) or jointly to the Federation and the *Länder* pursuant to paragraph (3) of this Article;
5. the beer tax;
6. the tax on gambling establishments.

(3) Revenue from income taxes, corporation taxes and turnover taxes shall accrue jointly to the Federation and the *Länder* (joint taxes) to the extent that the revenue from the income tax and the turnover tax is not allocated to municipalities pursuant to paragraphs (5) and (5a) of this Article. The Federation and the *Länder* shall share equally the revenues from income taxes and corporation taxes. The respective shares of the Federation and the *Länder* in the revenue from the turnover tax shall be determined by a federal law requiring the consent of the Bundesrat. Such determination shall be based on the following principles:
1. The Federation and the *Länder* shall have an equal claim against current revenues to cover their necessary expenditures. The extent of such expenditures shall be determined with due regard to multi-year financial planning.

2. The financial requirements of the Federation and of the *Länder* shall be coordinated in such a way as to establish a fair balance, avoid excessive burdens on taxpayers and ensure uniformity of living standards throughout the federal territory.

In determining the respective shares of the Federation and the *Länder* in the revenue from the turnover tax, reductions in revenue incurred by the *Länder* from 1 January 1996 because of the provisions made with respect to children in the income tax law shall also be taken into account. Details shall be regulated by the federal law enacted pursuant to the third sentence of this paragraph.

(4) The respective shares of the Federation and the *Länder* in the revenue from the turnover tax shall be apportioned anew whenever the ratio of revenues to expenditures of the Federation becomes substantially different from that of the *Länder*; reductions in revenue that are taken into account in determining the respective shares of revenue from the turnover tax under the fifth sentence of paragraph (3) of this Article shall not be considered in this regard. If a federal law imposes additional expenditures on or withdraws revenue from the *Länder*, the additional burden may be compensated for by federal grants pursuant to a federal law requiring the consent of the Bundesrat, provided the additional burden is limited to a short period of time. This law shall establish the principles for calculating such grants and distributing them among the *Länder*.

(5) A share of the revenue from the income tax shall accrue to the municipalities, to be passed on by the *Länder* to their municipalities on the basis of the income taxes paid by their inhabitants. Details shall be regulated by a federal law requiring the consent of the Bundesrat. This law may provide that municipalities may establish supplementary or reduced rates with respect to their share of the tax.

(5a) From and after 1 January 1998, a share of the revenue from the turnover tax shall accrue to the municipalities. It shall be passed on by the *Länder* to their municipalities on the basis of a formula reflecting geographical and economic factors. Details shall be regulated by a federal law requiring the consent of the Bundesrat.

(6) Revenue from taxes on real property and trades shall accrue to the municipalities; revenue from local taxes on consumption and expenditures shall accrue to the municipalities or, as may be provided for by *Land* legislation, to associations of municipalities. Municipalities shall be authorised to establish the rates at which taxes on real property and trades are levied, within the framework of the laws. If there are no municipalities in a *Land*, revenue from taxes on real property and trades as well as from local taxes on consumption and expenditures shall accrue to the *Land*. The Federation and the *Länder* may participate, by virtue of an apportionment, in the revenue from the tax on trades. Details regarding such apportionment shall be

regulated by a federal law requiring the consent of the Bundesrat. In accordance with *Land* legislation, taxes on real property and trades as well as the municipalities' share of revenue from the income tax and the turnover tax may be taken as a basis for calculating the amount of apportionment.

(7) An overall percentage of the *Land* share of total revenue from joint taxes, to be determined by *Land* legislation, shall accrue to the municipalities or associations of municipalities. In all other respects *Land* legislation shall determine whether and to what extent revenue from *Land* taxes shall accrue to municipalities (associations of municipalities).

(8) If in individual *Länder* or municipalities (associations of municipalities) the Federation requires special facilities to be established that directly result in an increase of expenditure or in reductions in revenue (special burden) to these *Länder* or municipalities (associations of municipalities), the Federation shall grant the necessary compensation if and insofar as the *Länder* or municipalities (associations of municipalities) cannot reasonably be expected to bear the burden. In granting such compensation, due account shall be taken of indemnities paid by third parties and financial benefits accruing to these *Länder* or municipalities (associations of municipalities) as a result of the establishment of such facilities.

(9) For the purpose of this Article, revenues and expenditures of municipalities (associations of municipalities) shall also be deemed to be revenues and expenditures of the *Länder*.

Article 106a   [Federal grants for local public transport]

Beginning on 1 January 1996 the *Länder* shall be entitled to an allocation of federal tax revenues for purposes of local public transport. Details shall be regulated by a federal law requiring the consent of the Bundesrat. Allocations made pursuant to the first sentence of this Article shall not be taken into account in determining the financial capacity of a *Land* under paragraph (2) of Article 107.

Article 106b   [*Länder* share of motor vehicle tax]

As of 1 July 2009, following the transfer of the motor vehicle tax to the Federation, the *Länder* shall be entitled to a sum from the tax revenue of the Federation. Details shall be regulated by a federal law requiring the consent of the Bundesrat.

Article 107 [Distribution of tax revenue – Financial equalisation among the *Länder* – Supplementary grants]

(1) Revenue from *Land* taxes and the *Land* share of revenue from income and corporation taxes shall accrue to the individual *Länder* to the extent that such taxes are collected by finance authorities within their respective territories (local revenue). Details regarding the delimitation as well as the manner and scope of allotment of local revenue from corporation and wage taxes shall be regulated by a federal law requiring the consent of the Bundesrat. This law may also provide for the delimitation and allotment of local revenue from other taxes. The *Land* share of revenue from the turnover tax shall accrue to the individual *Länder* on a per capita basis, unless otherwise provided in paragraph (2) of this Article.

(2) A federal law requiring the consent of the Bundesrat shall ensure a reasonable equalisation of the disparate financial capacities of the *Länder*, with due regard for the financial capacities and needs of municipalities (associations of municipalities). To this end, additions to and deductions from the financial capacity of the respective *Länder* shall be regulated in the allotment of their shares of revenue from the turnover tax. The conditions for granting additions and imposing reductions as well as the criteria governing the amount of these additions and deductions shall be specified in the law. For the purpose of measuring financial capacity, it shall be permissible to consider only part of the revenue from mining royalties. The law may also provide for grants to be made by the Federation to financially weak *Länder* from its own funds to assist them in meeting their general financial needs (supplementary grants). Irrespective of the criteria specified in the first to the third sentence of this paragraph, grants may also be made to such financially weak *Länder* whose municipalities (associations of municipalities) have a particularly low capacity to generate tax revenue (municipal tax-base grants) and, in addition, to such financially weak *Länder* whose shares of the support funds under Article 91b are lower than their per capita shares.

Article 108 [Financial administration of the Federation and the *Länder* – Financial courts]

(1) Customs duties, fiscal monopolies, taxes on consumption regulated by a federal law, including the turnover tax on imports, the motor vehicle tax and other transaction taxes related to motorised vehicles as from 1 July 2009 and charges imposed within the framework of the European Communities shall be administered by federal finance authorities. The organisation of these authorities shall be regulated by a

federal law. Inasmuch as intermediate authorities have been established, their heads shall be appointed in consultation with the *Land* governments.

(2) All other taxes shall be administered by the financial authorities of the *Länder*. The organisation of these authorities and the uniform training of their civil servants may be regulated by a federal law requiring the consent of the Bundesrat. Inasmuch as intermediate authorities have been established, their heads shall be appointed in agreement with the Federal Government.

(3) Where taxes accruing wholly or in part to the Federation are administered by revenue authorities of the *Länder*, those authorities shall act on federal commission. Paragraphs (3) and (4) of Article 85 shall apply, the Federal Minister of Finance acting in place of the Federal Government.

(4) Where and to the extent that execution of the tax laws will be substantially facilitated or improved thereby, a federal law requiring the consent of the Bundesrat may provide for collaboration between federal and *Land* revenue authorities in matters of tax administration, for the administration of taxes enumerated in paragraph (1) of this Article by revenue authorities of the *Länder* or for the administration of other taxes by federal revenue authorities. The functions of *Land* revenue authorities in the administration of taxes whose revenue accrues exclusively to municipalities (associations of municipalities) may be delegated by the *Länder* to municipalities (associations of municipalities) wholly or in part. The federal law referred to in the first sentence of this paragraph may, with regard to collaboration between the Federation and *Länder*, provide that, with the consent of a majority specified in the law, rules for the execution of tax laws will become binding for all *Länder*.

(4a) A federal law requiring the consent of the Bundesrat may provide, in the case of the administration of taxes enumerated in paragraph (2), for collaboration between *Land* revenue authorities and for an inter-*Land* transfer of competence to *Land* revenue authorities of one or more *Länder* by agreement with the *Länder* concerned where and to the extent that execution of the tax laws will be substantially facilitated or improved thereby. The apportionment of costs may be regulated by a federal law.

(5) The procedures to be followed by federal revenue authorities shall be prescribed by a federal law. The procedures to be followed by *Land* revenue authorities or, as provided by the second sentence of paragraph (4) of this Article, by municipalities (associations of municipalities) may be prescribed by a federal law requiring the consent of the Bundesrat.

(6) Financial jurisdiction shall be uniformly regulated by a federal law.

(7) The Federal Government may issue general administrative rules which, to the extent that administration is entrusted to *Land* revenue authorities or to municipalities (associations of municipalities), shall require the consent of the Bundesrat.

Article 109 [**Budget management in the Federation and the *Länder*]**

(1) The Federation and the *Länder* shall be autonomous and independent of one another in the management of their respective budgets.
(2) The Federation and the *Länder* shall jointly discharge the obligations of the Federal Republic of Germany resulting from legal acts of the European Community for the maintenance of budgetary discipline pursuant to Article 104 of the Treaty Establishing the European Community and shall, within this framework, give due regard to the requirements of overall economic equilibrium.
(3) The budgets of the Federation and the *Länder* shall, in principle, be balanced without revenue from credits. The Federation and *Länder* may introduce rules intended to take into account, symmetrically in times of upswing and downswing, the effects of market developments that deviate from normal conditions, as well as exceptions for natural disasters or unusual emergency situations beyond governmental control and substantially harmful to the state's financial capacity. For such exceptional regimes, a corresponding amortisation plan must be adopted. Details for the budget of the Federation shall be governed by Article 115 with the proviso that the first sentence shall be deemed to be satisfied if revenue from credits does not exceed 0.35 per cent in relation to the nominal gross domestic product. The *Länder* themselves shall regulate details for the budgets within the framework of their constitutional powers, the proviso being that the first sentence shall only be deemed to be satisfied if no revenue from credits is admitted.
(4) A federal law requiring the consent of the Bundesrat may establish principles applicable to both the Federation and the *Länder* governing budgetary law, cyclically appropriate budgetary management and long-term financial planning.
(5) Sanctions imposed by the European Community on the basis of the provisions of Article 104 of the Treaty Establishing the European Community in the interest of maintaining budgetary discipline shall be borne by the Federation and the *Länder* at a ratio of 65 to 35 per cent. In solidarity, the *Länder* as a whole shall bear 35 per cent of the charges incumbent on the *Länder* according to the number of their inhabitants; 65 per cent of the charges incumbent on the *Länder* shall be borne by the *Länder* according to their degree of causation. Details shall be regulated by a federal law which shall require the consent of the Bundesrat.

Article 109a [Budgetary emergencies]

(1) To avoid a budgetary emergency, a federal law requiring the consent of the Bundesrat shall provide for:
1. the continuing supervision of budgetary management of the Federation and the *Länder* by a joint body (Stability Council),
2. the conditions and procedures for ascertaining the threat of a budgetary emergency,
3. the principles for the establishment and administration of programs for taking care of budgetary emergencies.

(2) From the year 2020, oversight of compliance with the provisions of paragraph (3) of Article 109 by the Federation and the *Länder* shall be entrusted to the Stability Council. This oversight shall be focused on the provisions and procedures regarding adherence to budgetary discipline from legal acts based on the Treaty on the Functioning of the European Union.

(3) The decisions of the Stability Council and the accompanying documents shall be published.

Article 110 [Federal budget]

(1) All revenues and expenditures of the Federation shall be included in the budget; in the case of federal enterprises and special trusts, only payments to or remittances from them need be included. The budget shall be balanced with respect to revenues and expenditures.

(2) The budget for one or more fiscal years shall be set forth in a law enacted before the beginning of the first year and making separate provision for each year. The law may provide that various parts of the budget apply to different periods of time, divided by fiscal years.

(3) Bills to comply with the first sentence of paragraph (2) of this Article as well as bills to amend the Budget Act or the budget itself shall be submitted simultaneously to the Bundesrat and to the Bundestag; the Bundesrat shall be entitled to comment on such bills within six weeks or, in the case of amending bills, within three weeks.

(4) The Budget Act may contain only such provisions as relate to federal revenues and expenditures and to the period for which it is enacted. The Budget Act may specify that its provisions shall expire only upon promulgation of the next Budget Act or, in the event of an authorisation pursuant to Article 115, at a later date.

Article 111 [Interim budget management]

(1) If, by the end of a fiscal year, the budget for the following year has not been adopted by a law, the Federal Government, until such law comes into force, may make all expenditures that are necessary:
(a) to maintain institutions established by a law and to carry out measures authorised by a law;
(b) to meet the legal obligations of the Federation;
(c) to continue construction projects, procurements and the provision of other benefits or services or to continue to make grants for these purposes, to the extent that amounts have already been appropriated in the budget of a previous year.

(2) To the extent that revenues based upon specific laws and derived from taxes or duties or other sources or the working capital reserves do not cover the expenditures referred to in paragraph (1) of this Article, the Federal Government may borrow the funds necessary to sustain current operations up to a maximum of one quarter of the total amount of the previous budget.

Article 112 [Extrabudgetary expenditures]

Expenditures in excess of budgetary appropriations or for purposes not contemplated by the budget shall require the consent of the Federal Minister of Finance. Such consent may be given only in the event of an unforeseen and unavoidable necessity. Details may be regulated by a federal law.

Article 113 [Increase of expenditures]

(1) Laws that increase the budget expenditures proposed by the Federal Government or entail or will bring about new expenditures shall require the consent of the Federal Government. This requirement shall also apply to laws that entail or will bring about decreases in revenue. The Federal Government may demand that the Bundestag postpone its vote on bills to this effect. In this event the Federal Government shall submit its comments to the Bundestag within six weeks.

(2) Within four weeks after the Bundestag has adopted such a law, the Federal Government may demand that it vote on the law a second time.

(3) If the bill has become law pursuant to Article 78, the Federal Government may withhold its consent only within six weeks and only after having initiated the procedure provided for in the third and fourth sentences of paragraph (1) or in paragraph (2) of this Article. Upon the expiry of this period such consent shall be deemed to have been given.

Article 114   **[Submission and auditing of accounts]**

(1) For the purpose of discharging the Federal Government, the Federal Minister of Finance shall submit annually to the Bundestag and to the Bundesrat an account for the preceding fiscal year of all revenues and expenditures as well as of assets and debts.
(2) The Federal Court of Audit, whose members shall enjoy judicial independence, shall audit the account and determine whether public finances have been properly and efficiently administered by the Federation. For the purpose of the audit pursuant to the first sentence of this paragraph, the Federal Court of Audit may also conduct surveys of authorities outside the federal administration; this shall also apply in cases in which the Federation allocates to the *Länder* ring-fenced financing for the performance of tasks incumbent on the *Länder*. It shall submit an annual report directly to the Bundestag and the Bundesrat as well as to the Federal Government. In other respects the powers of the Federal Court of Audit shall be regulated by a federal law.

Article 115   **[Limits of borrowing]**

(1) The borrowing of funds and the assumption of surety obligations, guarantees or other commitments that may lead to expenditures in future fiscal years shall require authorisation by a federal law specifying or permitting computation of the amounts involved.
(2) Revenues and expenditures shall in principle be balanced without revenue from credits. This principle shall be satisfied when revenue obtained by the borrowing of funds does not exceed 0.35 per cent in relation to the nominal gross domestic product. In addition, when economic developments deviate from normal conditions, effects on the budget in periods of upswing and downswing must be taken into account symmetrically. Deviations of actual borrowing from the credit limits specified under the first to third sentences are to be recorded on a control account; debits exceeding the threshold of 1.5 per cent in relation to the nominal gross domestic

product are to be reduced in accordance with the economic cycle. The regulation of details, especially the adjustment of revenue and expenditures with regard to financial transactions and the procedure for the calculation of the yearly limit on net borrowing, taking into account the economic cycle on the basis of a procedure for adjusting the cycle together with the control and balancing of deviations of actual borrowing from the credit limit, requires a federal law. In cases of natural catastrophes or unusual emergency situations beyond governmental control and substantially harmful to the state's financial capacity, these credit limits may be exceeded on the basis of a decision taken by a majority of the Members of the Bundestag. The decision must be combined with an amortisation plan. Repayment of the credits borrowed under the sixth sentence must be accomplished within an appropriate period of time.

Xa. State of Defence

Article 115a **[Declaration of a state of defence]**

(1) Any determination that the federal territory is under attack by armed force or imminently threatened with such an attack (state of defence) shall be made by the Bundestag with the consent of the Bundesrat. Such determination shall be made on application of the Federal Government and shall require a two-thirds majority of the votes cast, which shall include at least a majority of the Members of the Bundestag.
(2) If the situation imperatively calls for immediate action and if insurmountable obstacles prevent the timely convening of the Bundestag or the Bundestag cannot muster a quorum, the Joint Committee shall make this determination by a two-thirds majority of the votes cast, which shall include at least a majority of its members.
(3) The determination shall be promulgated by the Federal President in the Federal Law Gazette pursuant to Article 82. If this cannot be done in time, promulgation shall be effected in another manner; the determination shall be printed in the Federal Law Gazette as soon as circumstances permit.
(4) If the federal territory is under attack by armed force, and if the competent federal authorities are not in a position at once to make the determination provided for in the first sentence of paragraph (1) of this Article, the determination shall be deemed to have been made and promulgated at the time the attack began. The Federal President shall announce that time as soon as circumstances permit.

(5) If the determination of a state of defence has been promulgated, and if the federal territory is under attack by armed force, the Federal President, with the consent of the Bundestag, may issue declarations under international law regarding the existence of the state of defence. Under the conditions specified in paragraph (2) of this Article, the Joint Committee shall act in place of the Bundestag.

Article 115b [Power of command of the Federal Chancellor]

Upon the promulgation of a state of defence the power of command over the Armed Forces shall pass to the Federal Chancellor.

Article 115c [Extension of the legislative powers of the Federation]

(1) The Federation shall have the right to legislate concurrently for a state of defence even with respect to matters within the legislative powers of the *Länder*. Such laws shall require the consent of the Bundesrat.

(2) To the extent required by circumstances during a state of defence, a federal law for a state of defence may:

1. make temporary provisions concerning compensation in the event of expropriation that deviate from the requirements of the second sentence of paragraph (3) of Article 14;
2. establish a time limit for deprivations of freedom different from that specified in the third sentence of paragraph (2) and the first sentence of paragraph (3) of Article 104, but not exceeding four days, for cases in which no judge has been able to act within the time limit that normally applies.

(3) To the extent necessary to repel an existing or imminently threatened attack, a federal law for a state of defence may, with the consent of the Bundesrat, regulate the administration and finances of the Federation and the *Länder* without regard to Titles VIII, VIIIa and X of this Basic Law, provided that the viability of the *Länder*, municipalities, and associations of municipalities, especially with respect to financial matters, is assured.

(4) Federal laws enacted pursuant to paragraph (1) or item 1 of paragraph (2) of this Article may, for the purpose of preparing for their enforcement, be applied even before a state of defence arises.

Basic Law for the Federal Republic of Germany

Article 115d [Urgent bills]

(1) During a state of defence the federal legislative process shall be governed by the provisions of paragraphs (2) and (3) of this Article without regard to the provisions of paragraph (2) of Article 76, the second sentence of paragraph (1) and paragraphs (2) to (4) of Article 77, Article 78 and paragraph (1) of Article 82.
(2) Federal Government bills that the Government designates as urgent shall be forwarded to the Bundesrat at the same time as they are submitted to the Bundestag. The Bundestag and the Bundesrat shall debate such bills in joint session without delay. Insofar as the consent of the Bundesrat is necessary for any such bill to become law, a majority of its votes shall be required. Details shall be regulated by rules of procedure adopted by the Bundestag and requiring the consent of the Bundesrat.
(3) The second sentence of paragraph (3) of Article 115a shall apply to the promulgation of such laws, *mutatis mutandis*.

Article 115e [Joint Committee]

(1) If, during a state of defence, the Joint Committee by a two-thirds majority of the votes cast, which shall include at least a majority of its members, determines that insurmountable obstacles prevent the timely convening of the Bundestag or that the Bundestag cannot muster a quorum, the Joint Committee shall occupy the position of both the Bundestag and the Bundesrat and shall exercise their powers as a single body.
(2) This Basic Law may neither be amended nor abrogated nor suspended in whole or in part by a law enacted by the Joint Committee. The Joint Committee shall have no power to enact laws pursuant to the second sentence of paragraph (1) of Article 23, paragraph (1) of Article 24 or Article 29.

Basic Law for the Federal Republic of Germany

Article 115f [Use of Federal Border Police – Extended powers of instruction]

(1) During a state of defence the Federal Government, to the extent that circumstances require, may:
1. employ the Federal Border Police throughout the federal territory;
2. issue instructions not only to federal administrative authorities but also to *Land* governments and, if it deems the matter urgent, to *Land* authorities and may delegate this power to members of *Land* governments designated by it.

(2) The Bundestag, the Bundesrat and the Joint Committee shall be informed without delay of the measures taken in accordance with paragraph (1) of this Article.

Article 115g [Federal Constitutional Court]

Neither the constitutional status nor the performance of the constitutional functions of the Federal Constitutional Court or its judges may be impaired. The law governing the Federal Constitutional Court may be amended by a law enacted by the Joint Committee only insofar as the Federal Constitutional Court agrees is necessary to ensure that it can continue to perform its functions. Pending the enactment of such a law, the Federal Constitutional Court may take such measures as are necessary to this end. Determinations by the Federal Constitutional Court pursuant to the second and third sentences of this Article shall be made by a majority of the judges present.

Article 115h [Expiry of electoral terms and terms of office]

(1) Any electoral terms of the Bundestag or of parliamentary assemblies of the *Länder* that are due to expire during a state of defence shall end six months after the termination of the state of defence. A term of office of the Federal President that is due to expire during a state of defence and the exercise of his functions by the President of the Bundesrat in case of the premature vacancy of his office shall end nine months after the termination of the state of defence. The term of office of a member of the Federal Constitutional Court that is due to expire during a state of defence shall end six months after the termination of the state of defence.

(2) Should it be necessary for the Joint Committee to elect a new Federal Chancellor, it shall do so by the votes of a majority of its members; the Federal President shall propose a candidate to the Joint Committee. The Joint Committee may ex-

press its lack of confidence in the Federal Chancellor only by electing a successor by a two-thirds majority of its members.

(3) The Bundestag shall not be dissolved while a state of defence exists.

Article 115i [Powers of the *Land* governments]

(1) If the competent federal bodies are not in a position to take the measures necessary to avert the danger, and if the situation imperatively calls for immediate independent action in particular areas of the federal territory, the *Land* governments or the authorities or representatives they designate shall be authorised, within their respective spheres of competence, to take the measures provided for in paragraph (1) of Article 115f.

(2) Any measures taken in accordance with paragraph (1) of this Article may be rescinded at any time by the Federal Government, or, with respect to *Land* authorities and subordinate federal authorities, by Minister-Presidents of the *Länder*.

Article 115k [Rank and duration of emergency provisions]

(1) Laws enacted in accordance with Articles 115c, 115e and 115g, as well as statutory instruments issued on the basis of such laws, shall suspend the operation of incompatible law so long as they are in effect. This provision shall not apply to earlier law enacted pursuant to Articles 115c, 115e or 115g.

(2) Laws adopted by the Joint Committee, as well as statutory instruments issued on the basis of such laws, shall cease to have effect no later than six months after the termination of a state of defence.

(3) Laws containing provisions that diverge from Articles 91a, 91b, 104a, 106 and 107 shall apply no longer than the end of the second fiscal year following the termination of a state of defence. After such termination they may, with the consent of the Bundesrat, be amended by a federal law so as to revert to the provisions of Titles VIIIa and X.

Article 115l [Repeal of emergency measures – Conclusion of peace]

(1) The Bundestag, with the consent of the Bundesrat, may at any time repeal laws enacted by the Joint Committee. The Bundesrat may demand that the Bundestag reach a decision on this question. Any measures taken by the Joint Committee or by

the Federal Government to avert a danger shall be rescinded if the Bundestag and the Bundesrat so decide.

(2) The Bundestag, with the consent of the Bundesrat, may at any time, by a decision to be promulgated by the Federal President, declare a state of defence terminated. The Bundesrat may demand that the Bundestag reach a decision on this question. A state of defence shall be declared terminated without delay if the conditions for determining it no longer exist.

(3) The conclusion of peace shall be determined by a federal law.

XI. Transitional and Concluding Provisions

Article 116 [Definition of "German" – Restoration of citizenship]

(1) Unless otherwise provided by a law, a German within the meaning of this Basic Law is a person who possesses German citizenship or who has been admitted to the territory of the German Reich within the boundaries of 31 December 1937 as a refugee or expellee of German ethnic origin or as the spouse or descendant of such person.

(2) Former German citizens who, between 30 January 1933 and 8 May 1945, were deprived of their citizenship on political, racial or religious grounds and their descendants shall, on application, have their citizenship restored. They shall be deemed never to have been deprived of their citizenship if they have established their domicile in Germany after 8 May 1945 and have not expressed a contrary intention.

Article 117 [Suspended entry into force of two basic rights]

(1) Law which is inconsistent with paragraph (2) of Article 3 of this Basic Law shall remain in force until adapted to that provision, but not beyond 31 March 1953.

(2) Laws that restrict freedom of movement in view of the present accommodation shortage shall remain in force until repealed by a federal law.

Article 118 [New delimitation of Baden and Württemberg]

The division of the territory comprising Baden, Württemberg-Baden and Württemberg-Hohenzollern into *Länder* may be revised, without regard to the provisions of Article 29, by agreement between the *Länder* concerned. If no agreement is reached, the revision shall be effected by a federal law, which shall provide for an advisory referendum.

Article 118a   [New delimitation of Berlin and Brandenburg]

The division of the territory comprising Berlin and Brandenburg into *Länder* may be revised, without regard to the provisions of Article 29, by agreement between the two *Länder* with the participation of their inhabitants who are entitled to vote.

Article 119   [Refugees and expellees]

In matters relating to refugees and expellees, especially as regards their distribution among the *Länder*, the Federal Government, with the consent of the Bundesrat, may issue statutory instruments having the force of law, pending settlement of the matter by a federal law. In this connection the Federal Government may be authorised to issue individual instructions in particular cases. Unless time is of the essence, such instructions shall be addressed to the highest *Land* authorities.

Article 120   [Occupation costs – Burdens resulting from the war]

(1) The Federation shall finance the expenditures for occupation costs and other internal and external burdens resulting from the war, as regulated in detail by federal laws. To the extent that these war burdens were regulated by federal laws on or before 1 October 1969, the Federation and the *Länder* shall finance such expenditures in the proportion established by such federal laws. Insofar as expenditures for such of these war burdens as neither have been nor will be regulated by federal laws were met on or before 1 October 1965 by *Länder*, municipalities (associations of municipalities) or other entities performing functions of the *Länder* or municipalities, the Federation shall not be obliged to finance them even after that date. The Federation shall be responsible for subsidies towards meeting the costs of social security, including unemployment insurance and public assistance to the unemployed. The distribution of war burdens between the Federation and the *Länder* prescribed by this paragraph shall not be construed to affect any law regarding claims for compensation for consequences of the war.

(2) Revenue shall pass to the Federation at the time it assumes responsibility for the expenditures referred to in this Article.

Article 120a [Equalisation of burdens]

(1) Laws implementing the equalisation of burdens may, with the consent of the Bundesrat, provide that, with respect to equalisation payments, they shall be executed partly by the Federation and partly by the *Länder* acting on federal commission and that the relevant powers vested in the Federal Government and the competent highest federal authorities by virtue of Article 85 shall be wholly or partly delegated to the Federal Equalisation of Burdens Office. In exercising these powers, the Federal Equalisation of Burdens Office shall not require the consent of the Bundesrat; except in urgent cases, its instructions shall be given to the highest *Land* authorities (*Land* Equalisation of Burdens Offices).
(2) The second sentence of paragraph (3) of Article 87 shall not be affected by this provision.

Article 121 [Definition of "majority of the members"]

Within the meaning of this Basic Law, a majority of the Members of the Bundestag and a majority of the members of the Federal Convention shall be a majority of the number of their members specified by a law.

Article 122 [Date of transmission of legislative powers]

(1) From the date on which the Bundestag first convenes, laws shall be enacted only by the legislative bodies recognised by this Basic Law.
(2) Legislative bodies and institutions participating in the legislative process in an advisory capacity whose competence expires by virtue of paragraph (1) of this Article shall be dissolved as of that date.

Article 123 [Continued applicability of pre-existing law]

(1) Law in force before the Bundestag first convenes shall remain in force insofar as it does not conflict with this Basic Law.

(2) Subject to all rights and objections of interested parties, treaties concluded by the German Reich concerning matters within the legislative competence of the *Länder* under this Basic Law shall remain in force, provided they are and continue to be valid under general principles of law, until new treaties are concluded by the authorities competent under this Basic Law or until they are in some other way terminated pursuant to their provisions.

Article 124 [Continued applicability of law within the scope of exclusive legislative power]

Law regarding matters subject to the exclusive legislative power of the Federation shall become federal law in the area in which it applies.

Article 125 [Continued applicability of law within the scope of concurrent legislative power]

Law regarding matters subject to the concurrent legislative power of the Federation shall become federal law in the area in which it applies:
1. insofar as it applies uniformly within one or more occupation zones;
2. insofar as it is law by which former Reich law has been amended since 8 May 1945.

Article 125a [Continued applicability of federal law – Replacement by *Land* law]

(1) Law that was enacted as federal law but that, by virtue of the amendment of paragraph (1) of Article 74, the insertion of the seventh sentence of paragraph (1) of Article 84, of the second sentence of paragraph (1) of Article 85 or of the second sentence of paragraph (2a) of Article 105 or because of the repeal of Articles 74a, 75 or the second sentence of paragraph (3) of Article 98, could no longer be enacted as federal law shall remain in force as federal law. It may be superseded by *Land* law.

(2) Law that was enacted pursuant to paragraph (2) of Article 72 as it stood up to 15 November 1994 but which, because of the amendment of paragraph (2) of Arti-

cle 72, could no longer be enacted as federal law shall remain in force as federal law. A federal law may provide that it may be superseded by *Land* law.

(3) Law that has been enacted as *Land* law but which, because of the amendment of Article 73, could not be enacted any longer as *Land* law shall continue in force as *Land* law. It may be superseded by federal law.

Article 125b [Continued applicability of framework laws – Deviation power of the *Länder*]

(1) Law that was enacted pursuant to Article 75 as it stood up to 1 September 2006 and which could be enacted as federal law even after this date shall remain in force as federal law. The powers and duties of the *Länder* to legislate shall, in this regard, remain unaffected. In the areas referred to in the first sentence of paragraph (3) of Article 72 the *Länder* may enact regulations that deviate from this law; however, in those areas covered by items 2, 5 and 6 of the first sentence of Article 72 the *Länder* may do so only if and insofar as the Federation has made use of its power to legislate after 1 September 2006, in those areas covered by items 2 and 5 beginning at the latest on 1 January 2010, in cases under item 6 beginning at the latest on 1 August 2008.

(2) The *Länder* may enact regulations deviating from federal regulations enacted pursuant to paragraph (1) of Article 84 as it stood up to 1 September 2006; up to 31 December 2008, however, they may deviate from regulations on administrative procedure only if, after 1 September 2006, regulations on administrative procedure in the relevant federal law have been amended.

(3) In the area covered by item 7 of the first sentence of paragraph (3) of Article 72 deviating *Land* law may be taken as a basis for levying taxes on real property for periods beginning on 1 January 2025 at the earliest.

Article 125c [Continued applicability of law within the scope of joint tasks]

(1) Law that was enacted by virtue of paragraph (2) of Article 91a in conjunction with item 1 of paragraph (1) as it stood up to 1 September 2006 shall continue in force until 31 December 2006.

(2) The rules enacted in the areas of municipal transport financing and promotion of social housing by virtue of paragraph (4) of Article 104a as it stood up to 1 September 2006 shall remain in force until 31 December 2006. The rules enacted on municipal transport financing for special programmes pursuant to paragraph (1)

of section 6 of the Municipal Transport Infrastructure Financing Act, as well as the other rules enacted by the Act of 20 December 2001 governing the Federal Financing of Seaports in Bremen, Hamburg, Mecklenburg-Western Pomerania, Lower Saxony and Schleswig-Holstein under paragraph (4) of Article 104a of the Basic Law as it stood up to 1 September 2006 shall continue in force until their repeal. Amendment of the Municipal Transport Infrastructure Financing Act shall be permissible. The fourth sentence of paragraph (2) of Article 104b shall apply, *mutatis mutandis*. The other rules enacted in accordance with paragraph (4) of Article 104a of the Basic Law as it stood up to 1 September 2006 shall continue in force until 31 December 2019, provided no earlier repeal has been or is determined.

(3) The fifth sentence of paragraph (2) of Article 104b shall apply for the first time to regulations that enter into force after 31 December 2019.

Article 126 [Determination about continued applicability of law as federal law]

Disagreements concerning the continued applicability of law as federal law shall be resolved by the Federal Constitutional Court.

Article 127 [Extension of law to the French zone and to Berlin]

Within one year after promulgation of this Basic Law the Federal Government, with the consent of the governments of the *Länder* concerned, may extend to the *Länder* of Baden, Greater Berlin, Rhineland-Palatinate and Württemberg-Hohenzollern any law of the Administration of the Combined Economic Area, insofar as it remains in force as federal law under Article 124 or 125.

Article 128 [Continued authority to issue instructions]

Insofar as law that remains in force grants authority to issue instructions within the meaning of paragraph (5) of Article 84, this authority shall remain in existence until a law otherwise provides.

Basic Law for the Federal Republic of Germany

Article 129 **[Continued authority to issue legal acts]**

(1) Insofar as legal provisions that remain in force as federal law grant authority to issue statutory instruments or general administrative rules or to make administrative decisions in individual cases, such powers shall pass to the authorities that henceforth have competence over the subject matter. In cases of doubt the Federal Government shall decide in agreement with the Bundesrat; such decisions shall be published.
(2) Insofar as legal provisions that remain in force as *Land* law grant such authority, it shall be exercised by the authorities competent under *Land* law.
(3) Insofar as legal provisions within the meaning of paragraphs (1) and (2) of this Article grant authority to amend or supplement the provisions themselves or to issue legal provisions that have the force of laws, such authority shall be deemed to have expired.
(4) The provisions of paragraphs (1) and (2) of this Article shall apply, *mutatis mutandis*, to legal provisions that refer to provisions no longer in force or to institutions no longer in existence.

Article 130 **[Transfer of existing administrative institutions]**

(1) Administrative agencies and other institutions that serve the public administration or the administration of justice and are not based on *Land* law or on agreements between *Länder*, as well as the Administrative Union of South West German Railways and the Administrative Council for Postal and Telecommunications Services for the French Occupation Zone, shall be placed under the control of the Federal Government. The Federal Government, with the consent of the Bundesrat, shall provide for their transfer, dissolution or liquidation.
(2) The supreme disciplinary authority for the personnel of these administrative bodies and institutions shall be the competent Federal Minister.
(3) Corporations and institutions under public law not directly subordinate to a *Land* nor based on agreements between *Länder* shall be under the supervision of the competent highest federal authority.

Article 131 **[Persons formerly in the public service]**

The legal relations of persons, including refugees and expellees, who on 8 May 1945 were employed in the public service, have left the service for reasons other than those recognised by civil service regulations or collective bargaining agreements and have not yet been reinstated or are employed in positions that do not correspond to those they previously held shall be regulated by a federal law. The same shall apply, *mutatis mutandis*, to persons, including refugees and expellees, who on 8 May 1945 were entitled to pensions and related benefits and who for reasons other than those recognised by civil service regulations or collective bargaining agreements no longer receive any such pension or related benefits. Until the pertinent federal law takes effect, no legal claims may be made, unless *Land* law otherwise provides.

Article 132 [Retirement of civil servants]

(1) Civil servants and judges who enjoy life tenure when this Basic Law takes effect may, within six months after the Bundestag first convenes, be retired, suspended or transferred to lower-salaried positions if they lack the personal or professional aptitude for their present positions. This provision shall apply, *mutatis mutandis*, to salaried public employees other than civil servants or judges whose employment cannot be terminated at will. In the case of salaried employees whose employment may be terminated at will, notice periods longer than those set by collective bargaining agreements may be rescinded within the same period.
(2) The preceding provision shall not apply to members of the public service who are unaffected by the provisions regarding "Liberation from National Socialism and Militarism" or who are recognised victims of National Socialism, save on important personal grounds.
(3) Persons affected may have recourse to the courts in accordance with paragraph (4) of Article 19.
(4) Details shall be specified by a statutory instrument issued by the Federal Government with the consent of the Bundesrat.

Article 133 [Succession to the Administration of the Combined Economic Area]

The Federation shall succeed to the rights and duties of the Administration of the Combined Economic Area.

Basic Law for the Federal Republic of Germany

Article 134 [Succession to Reich assets]

(1) Reich assets shall, in principle, become federal assets.
(2) Insofar as such assets were originally intended to be used principally for administrative tasks not entrusted to the Federation under this Basic Law, they shall be transferred without compensation to the authorities now entrusted with such tasks, and to the extent that such assets are now being used, not merely temporarily, for administrative tasks that under this Basic Law are now performed by the *Länder*, they shall be transferred to the *Länder*. The Federation may also transfer other assets to the *Länder*.
(3) Assets that were placed at the disposal of the Reich without compensation by *Länder* or municipalities (associations of municipalities) shall revert to those *Länder* or municipalities (associations of municipalities) insofar as the Federation does not require them for its own administrative purposes.
(4) Details shall be regulated by a federal law requiring the consent of the Bundesrat.

Article 135 [Assets in case of territorial changes between the *Länder*]

(1) If, after 8 May 1945 and before the effective date of this Basic Law, an area has passed from one *Land* to another, the *Land* to which the area now belongs shall be entitled to the assets of the *Land* to which it previously belonged that are located in that area.
(2) The assets of *Länder* or of other corporations or institutions established under public law that no longer exist, insofar as they were originally intended to be used principally for administrative tasks or are now being so used, not merely temporarily, shall pass to the *Land*, corporation or institution that now performs those tasks.
(3) Real property of *Länder* that no longer exist, including appurtenances, shall pass to the *Land* within which it is located, insofar as it is not among the assets already referred to in paragraph (1) of this Article.
(4) Insofar as an overriding interest of the Federation or the particular interest of a region requires, a federal law may depart from the rules prescribed by paragraphs (1) to (3) of this Article.
(5) In all other respects, the succession to and disposition of assets, insofar as it has not been effected before 1 January 1952 by agreement between the affected *Länder* or corporations or institutions established under public law, shall be regulated by a federal law requiring the consent of the Bundesrat.

(6) Holdings of the former *Land* of Prussia in enterprises established under private law shall pass to the Federation. Details shall be regulated by a federal law, which may also depart from this provision.

(7) Insofar as assets that, on the effective date of this Basic Law, would devolve upon a *Land* or a corporation or institution established under public law pursuant to paragraphs (1) to (3) of this Article have been disposed of by or pursuant to a *Land* law or in any other manner by the party thus entitled, the transfer of assets shall be deemed to have taken place before such disposition.

Article 135a [Old debts]

(1) Federal legislation enacted pursuant to paragraph (4) of Article 134 or paragraph (5) of Article 135 may also provide that the following debts shall not be discharged, or that they shall be discharged only in part:
1. debts of the Reich, of the former *Land* of Prussia, or of such other corporations and institutions established under public law as no longer exist;
2. such debts of the Federation or of corporations and institutions established under public law as are connected with the transfer of assets pursuant to Article 89, 90, 134 or 135 and such debts of these bodies as arise from measures taken by the bodies designated in item 1;
3. such debts of the *Länder* or municipalities (associations of municipalities) as have arisen from measures taken by them before 1 August 1945 within the framework of administrative functions incumbent upon or delegated by the Reich to comply with orders of the occupying powers or to terminate a state of emergency resulting from the war.

(2) Paragraph (1) of this Article shall apply, *mutatis mutandis*, to debts of the German Democratic Republic or its institutions as well as to debts of the Federation or other corporations and institutions established under public law that are connected with the transfer of assets of the German Democratic Republic to the Federation, *Länder* or municipalities, and to debts arising from measures taken by the German Democratic Republic or its institutions.

Article 136 [First convening of the Bundesrat]

(1) The Bundesrat shall convene for the first time on the day on which the Bundestag first convenes.

(2) Until the election of the first Federal President, his powers shall be exercised by the President of the Bundesrat. He shall not have authority to dissolve the Bundestag.

Article 137   [Right of state employees to stand for election]

(1) The right of civil servants, other salaried public employees, professional or volunteer members of the Armed Forces and judges to stand for election in the Federation, in the *Länder* or in the municipalities may be restricted by a law.
(2) The election of the first Bundestag, of the first Federal Convention and of the first Federal President shall be governed by an electoral law to be enacted by the Parliamentary Council.
(3) Until the Federal Constitutional Court is established, its authority under paragraph (2) of Article 41 shall be exercised by the German High Court for the Combined Economic Area, which shall make determinations in accordance with its procedural rules.

Article 138   [South German notaries]

Changes in the rules governing the notarial profession as it now exists in the *Länder* of Baden, Bavaria, Württemberg-Baden and Württemberg-Hohenzollern shall require the consent of the governments of these *Länder*.

Article 139   [Continued applicability of denazification provisions]

The legal provisions enacted for the "Liberation of the German People from National Socialism and Militarism" shall not be affected by the provisions of this Basic Law.

Article 140   [Law of religious denominations]

The provisions of Articles 136, 137, 138, 139 and 141 of the German Constitution of 11 August 1919 shall be an integral part of this Basic Law.

Article 141 ["Bremen Clause"]

The first sentence of paragraph (3) of Article 7 shall not apply in any *Land* in which *Land* law otherwise provided on 1 January 1949.

Article 142 [Reservation in favour of basic rights in *Land* constitutions]

Notwithstanding Article 31, provisions of *Land* constitutions shall also remain in force insofar as they guarantee basic rights in conformity with Articles 1 to 18 of this Basic Law.

Article 142a (repealed)

Article 143 [Duration of derogations from the Basic Law]

(1) The law in the territory specified in Article 3 of the Unification Treaty may derogate from provisions of this Basic Law for a period extending no later than 31 December 1992 insofar and so long as disparate circumstances make full compliance impossible. Derogations may not violate paragraph (2) of Article 19 and must be compatible with the principles specified in paragraph (3) of Article 79.
(2) Derogations from Titles II, VIII, VIIIa, IX, X and XI shall be permissible for a period extending to no later than 31 December 1995.
(3) Independently of paragraphs (1) and (2) of this Article, Article 41 of the Unification Treaty and the rules for its implementation shall also remain in effect insofar as they provide for the irreversibility of acts interfering with property rights in the territory specified in Article 3 of this Treaty.

Article 143a [Exclusive legislative power concerning federal railways]

(1) The Federation shall have exclusive power to legislate with respect to all matters arising from the transformation of federal railways administered by the Federation into business enterprises. Paragraph (5) of Article 87e shall apply, *mutatis mutandis*. Civil servants employed by federal railways may be assigned by a law to render services to federal railways established under private law without prejudice to their legal status or the responsibility of their employer.

(2) Laws enacted pursuant to paragraph (1) of this Article shall be executed by the Federation.

(3) The Federation shall continue to be responsible for local passenger services of the former federal railways until 31 December 1995. The same shall apply to the corresponding functions of rail transport administration. Details shall be regulated by a federal law requiring the consent of the Bundesrat.

Article 143b   [Transformation of the Deutsche Bundespost]

(1) The special trust Deutsche Bundespost shall be transformed into enterprises under private law in accordance with a federal law. The Federation shall have exclusive power to legislate with respect to all matters arising from this transformation.

(2) The exclusive rights of the Federation existing before the transformation may be transferred by a federal law for a transitional period to the enterprises that succeed to the Deutsche Bundespost Postdienst and to the Deutsche Bundespost Telekom. The Federation may not surrender its majority interest in the enterprise that succeeds to the Deutsche Bundespost Postdienst until at least five years after the law takes effect. To do so shall require a federal law with the consent of the Bundesrat.

(3) Federal civil servants employed by the Deutsche Bundespost shall be given positions in the private enterprises that succeed to it, without prejudice to their legal status or the responsibility of their employer. The enterprises shall exercise the employer's authority. Details shall be regulated by a federal law.

Article 143c   [Compensation for the cessation of joint tasks]

(1) From 1 January 2007 until 31 December 2019, the *Länder* shall be entitled to receive annual payments from the federal budget as compensation for losing the Federation's financial contributions resulting from the abolition of the joint tasks of extension and construction of institutions of higher education, including university hospitals and educational planning, as well as for losing financial assistance for the improvement of municipal traffic infrastructure and for the promotion of social housing. Until 31 December 2013, these amounts are to be determined by averaging the financial share of the Federation for the years 2000 to 2008.

(2) Until 31 December 2013, the payments pursuant to paragraph (1) shall be distributed among the *Länder* in the form of:

1. fixed annual payments the amounts of which shall be determined according to the average share of each *Land* during the period 2000 to 2003;
2. payments earmarked for the functional area of the former joint financing.

(3) Until the end of 2013, the Federation and the *Länder* shall review the extent to which the financing allotted to individual *Länder* pursuant to paragraph (1) is still appropriate and necessary for the discharge of their tasks. Beginning on 1 January 2014, the earmarking pursuant to item 2 of paragraph (2) of the financial means allotted under paragraph (1) shall cease; the earmarking for the volume of the means for investment purposes shall remain unchanged. Agreements resulting from Solidarity Pact II shall remain unaffected.

(4) Details shall be regulated by a federal law which shall require the consent of the Bundesrat.

Article 143d [Transitional provisions relating to consolidation assistance]

(1) Articles 109 and 115 in the version in force until 31 July 2009 shall apply for the last time to the 2010 budget. Articles 109 and 115 in the version in force as from 1 August 2009 shall apply for the first time to the 2011 budget; debit authorisations existing on 31 December 2010 for special trusts already established shall remain unaffected. In the period from 1 January 2011 to 31 December 2019, the *Länder* may, in accordance with their applicable legal regulations, derogate from the provisions of paragraph (3) of Article 109. The budgets of the *Länder* are to be planned in such a way that the 2020 budget fulfils the requirements of the fifth sentence of paragraph (3) of Article 109. In the period from 1 January 2011 to 31 December 2015, the Federation may derogate from the provisions of the second sentence of paragraph (2) of Article 115. The reduction of the existing deficits should begin with the 2011 budget. The annual budgets are to be planned in such a way that the 2016 budget satisfies the requirement of the second sentence of paragraph (2) of Article 115; details shall be regulated by federal law.

(2) As assistance for compliance with the provisions of paragraph (3) of Article 109 after 1 January 2020, the *Länder* of Berlin, Bremen, Saarland, Saxony-Anhalt and Schleswig-Holstein may receive, for the period 2011 to 2019, consolidation assistance from the federal budget in the global amount of 800 million euros annually. The respective amounts are 300 million euros for Bremen, 260 million euros for Saarland and 80 million euros each for Berlin, Saxony-Anhalt, and Schleswig-Holstein. The assistance payments shall be allocated on the basis of an administrative agreement under the terms of a federal law requiring the consent of

the Bundesrat. These grants require a complete reduction of financial deficits by the end of 2020. The details, especially the annual steps to be taken to reduce financial deficits and the supervision of the reduction of financial deficits by the Stability Council, along with the consequences entailed in case of failure to carry out the step-by-step reduction, shall be regulated by a federal law requiring the consent of the Bundesrat and by an administrative agreement. Consolidation assistance shall not be granted concurrently with redevelopment assistance awarded on the grounds of an extreme budgetary emergency.

(3) The financial burden resulting from the granting of the consolidation assistance shall be borne equally by the Federation and the *Länder*, to be financed from their share of revenue from the turnover tax. Details shall be regulated by a federal law requiring the consent of the Bundesrat.

(4) As assistance for future autonomous compliance with the provisions of paragraph (3) of Article 109, the *Länder* of Bremen and Saarland may receive redevelopment assistance from the federal budget in the global amount of 800 million euros annually from 1 January 2020. To this end, the *Länder* shall adopt measures to reduce excessive debts and to strengthen their economic and financial capacity. Details shall be regulated by a federal law requiring the consent of the Bundesrat. This redevelopment assistance shall not be granted concurrently with redevelopment assistance awarded on the grounds of an extreme budgetary emergency.

Article 143e [Federal motorways, transformation of commissioned administration]

(1) Notwithstanding the provisions of paragraph (2) of Article 90, the federal motorways shall be administered on federal commission by the *Länder* or such self-governing bodies as are competent under *Land* law until no later than 31 December 2020. The Federation shall regulate the transformation from commissioned administration to federal administration under paragraphs (2) and (4) of Article 90 by means of a federal law requiring the consent of the Bundesrat.

(2) At the request of a *Land*, to be made by 31 December 2018, the Federation, notwithstanding the provisions of paragraph (2) of Article 90, shall assume administrative responsibility for the other federal trunk roads, insofar as they lie within the territory of that *Land*, with effect from 1 January 2021.

(3) By a federal law with the consent of the Bundesrat, it may be regulated that a *Land*, upon application, takes over, on commission of the Federation, the function of administering plan approval and planning permission for the construction and alteration of federal motorways and other federal trunk roads for which the Federa-

tion has assumed administrative responsibility under paragraph (4) of Article 90 or paragraph (2) of Article 143e and on what conditions this function may be transferred back.

Article 143f [Financial relations within the federal system of government]

Article 143d, the Act regulating Revenue Sharing between the Federation and the *Länder* (Financial Equalisation Act) and other laws enacted on the basis of paragraph (2) of Article 107 as it stands from 1 January 2020 shall expire if, after 31 December 2030, the Federal Government, the Bundestag or at least three *Länder* acting jointly have requested negotiations on a restructuring of financial relations within the federal system of government and, when five years have elapsed since the Federal President was notified of the negotiation request made by the Federal Government, the Bundestag or the *Länder*, no statutory restructuring of financial relations within the federal system of government has entered into force. The expiry date shall be published in the Federal Law Gazette.

Article 143g [Continued applicability of Article 107]

For the regulation of the distribution of tax revenue, of financial equalisation between *Länder* and of federal supplementary grants, Article 107 as it stood until the entry into force of the Basic Law Amendment Act of 13 July 2017 shall continue to be applied until 31 December 2019.

Article 144 [Ratification of the Basic Law – Berlin]

(1) This Basic Law shall require ratification by the parliaments of two thirds of the German *Länder* in which it is initially to apply.
(2) Insofar as the application of this Basic Law is subject to restrictions in any *Land* listed in Article 23 or in any part thereof, such *Land* or part thereof shall have the right to send representatives to the Bundestag in accordance with Article 38 and to the Bundesrat in accordance with Article 50.

Article 145 [Entry into force of the Basic Law]

(1) The Parliamentary Council, with the participation of the members for Greater Berlin, shall confirm the ratification of this Basic Law in public session and shall certify and promulgate it.
(2) This Basic Law shall take effect at the end of the day on which it is promulgated.
(3) It shall be published in the Federal Law Gazette.

Article 146 [Duration of the Basic Law]

This Basic Law, which, since the achievement of the unity and freedom of Germany, applies to the entire German people, shall cease to apply on the day on which a constitution freely adopted by the German people takes effect.

Extracts from the German Constitution of 11 August 1919 (Weimar Constitution)

Religion and Religious Societies

Article 136

(1) Civil and political rights and duties shall be neither dependent upon nor restricted by the exercise of religious freedom.
(2) Enjoyment of civil and political rights and eligibility for public office shall be independent of religious affiliation.
(3) No person shall be required to disclose his religious convictions. The authorities shall have the right to inquire into a person's membership of a religious society only to the extent that rights or duties depend upon it or that a statistical survey mandated by a law so requires.
(4) No person may be compelled to perform any religious act or ceremony, to participate in religious exercises or to take a religious form of oath.

Article 137

(1) There shall be no state church.

(2) The freedom to form religious societies shall be guaranteed. The union of religious societies within the territory of the Reich shall be subject to no restrictions.
(3) Religious societies shall regulate and administer their affairs independently within the limits of the law that applies to all. They shall confer their offices without the participation of the state or the civil community.
(4) Religious societies shall acquire legal capacity according to the general provisions of civil law.
(5) Religious societies shall remain corporations under public law insofar as they have enjoyed that status in the past. Other religious societies shall be granted the same rights upon application, if their constitution and the number of their members give assurance of their permanency. If two or more religious societies established under public law unite into a single organisation, it too shall be a corporation under public law.
(6) Religious societies that are corporations under public law shall be entitled to levy taxes on the basis of the civil taxation lists in accordance with *Land* law.
(7) Associations whose purpose is to foster a philosophical creed shall have the same status as religious societies.
(8) Such further regulation as may be required for the implementation of these provisions shall be a matter for *Land* legislation.

Article 138
(1) Rights of religious societies to public subsidies on the basis of a law, contract or special grant shall be redeemed by legislation of the *Länder*. The principles governing such redemption shall be established by the Reich.
(2) Property rights and other rights of religious societies or associations in their institutions, foundations and other assets intended for purposes of worship, education or charity shall be guaranteed.

Article 139

Sunday and holidays recognised by the state shall remain protected by law as days of rest from work and of spiritual improvement.

1919 Weimar Constitution

Article 141

To the extent that a need exists for religious services and pastoral work in the army, in hospitals, in prisons or in other public institutions, religious societies shall be permitted to provide them, but without compulsion of any kind.

INDEX

addiction 94–96, 98, 358, 360, 362, 363, 365, 366, 370, 375, *see also* substance abuse
arbitrariness 5, 22, 277, 346, 401, 413, 523, 654
armed forces 71, 83, 213, 220
art 85, 203, 206, 266–272, 274, 278, 279, 281, *see also* freedom of the arts
– artist 202–204, 206, 264, 267–271, 273–276, 278–280, 282, 283, 285–288
– literary work 262, 266–288
autonomy, personal 74, 123, 137, 140, 141, 143, 147–150, 152–155, 157–162, 164, *see also* self-determination

balancing of interests 10, 12, 13, 15, 19, 20, 38, 69, 70, 75–77, 80, 83, 90, 91, 109, 110, 122, 135, 136, 140, 152, 156, 162, 171–173, 199, 200, 207–209, 215–221, 227, 229–231, 233–241, 247, 248, 255–259, 268, 271–273, 275, 277, 284, 286, 288, 292, 294, 296–298, 303, 305, 307, 314, 315, 328, 329, 348, 352–355, 357, 362–364, 384, 391, 392, 396–398, 409–414, 416, 422–428, 431–436, 438, 439, 444, 446–454, 463, 466, 468, 470, 476, 477, 496, 514, 521–523, 550, 552, 553, 582, 588, 592, 597–599, 603, 604, 616–619, 621–623, 636, 637, 642, 651, 661, 671, 678, 679, 682, 696, 705, 707, 728, 742, 743, 750, 752, 754, 760, *see also* proportionality
bankruptcy 393, 394, 396–400
Basic Law
– amendment 307, 310, 312–316, 327, 333–336, 670, 725
– constitutional identity 579

– constitutional order 10, 147, 153, 158, 164, 247, 268, 548, 561, 642, 670, 671, 736, 737, 750
– history 723
– interpretation *see* interpretation
– system of values 3, 17, 18, 24, 25, 77, 81, 158, 164, 336, 422, 704

capacity 96, 98, 120, 124, 136, 378, *see also* coercive treatment; confinement; criminal responsibility
– best interest 121, 129, 134
– consent to medical treatment 120–124, 126, 129–131, 134, 135, 137, 138, 148, 155, 158
– custodianship 120, 127, 129–133, 135–138
– free will 122, 129, 132, 134–138, 140, 147–155, 162–164, 181, 205
– guardianship 88, 95, 98
– legal capacity and agency 94–99, 123
– legal incapacitation 95–99
– limited contractual capacity 95, 98
– mental ~ 116, 120–124, 126, 127, 129, 132–136, 138
– natural will 116, 120–123, 127, 130, 132–138
– ~ for insight 116, 122, 123, 126, 129, 132–136
case-law 10, 16, 18, 20, 22, 24, 194, 199, 292, 304, 413, 422, 427, 428, 432, 437, 532, 587, *see also* judicial development of the law
– administrative courts 372, 375
– civil courts 11, 14, 15, 17, 18, 20, 21, 33, 37, 80, 93, 129, 173, 208, 209, 224, 234, 236, 257, 259, 269, 276, 352, 356, 449, 452
– Constitutional Court 10, 32, 37, 38, 44, 52, 53, 55, 57, 59, 74–76, 91, 107,

172, 182, 192, 199, 206–208, 224, 232, 235–237, 255, 256, 258, 266, 268, 269, 272, 277, 278, 283, 292, 295, 305, 313, 347, 390, 395–397, 422–424, 426, 429, 431, 462, 464, 470, 475, 480, 493, 495, 501, 515, 542, 544, 573, 576, 578, 581, 586, 608, 612, 615–617, 620, 622, 638, 648, 659, 689, 696, 697, 704–707, 721, 724, 726, 731–734, 737, 745, 746, 748
- Court of Justice of the European Union 430, 443–452, 454, 734, 759
- criminal courts 304, 305, 382, 396
- European Court of Human Rights 137, 138, 161–163, 223, 224, 230–232, 234, 235, 238–240, 428, 430, 431, 433, 435, 436, 444, 446, 451, 454, 464, 673, 677, 695, 699, 725, 726, 729, 731, 736, 741, 757

celebrities *see* contemporary society: figures of ~; fundamental rights holders: celebrities; media

censorship 268

census 1–5, 41–68

change
- constitutional ~ *see* Basic Law: amendment
- legislation *see* legislator: legislative reform
- societal ~ 22, 23, 25, 44, 55, 56, 59, 63, 98, 181, 411, 425, 429, 494, 540–542, 549, 557, 591, 599, 600, 728, 733, 734, 737
- technological ~ 44, 55–57, 61, 63, 228, 312, 337, 406, 411, 425, 426, 429, 432, 458, 459, 465, 489, 490, 494, 496, 497, 511, 517, 521, 537, 540–542, 548, 549, 557, 565, 576, 579, 590, 591, 599, 600, 671, 727, 728, 733, 734, 736, 758
- ~ in purpose (data) *see* data

child, best interest 86, 87, 90–92, 179, *see also* family and partnership

chilling effect 56, 208, 257, 258, 330, 406, 462, 469, 471, 493, 519, 578, 585, 596, 602, 610, 649

civil procedure
- action for damages 14–25, 167, 250, 256, 350–352, 354–357
- burden of proof 34, 36, 39, 40, 209, 252, 257, 259
- burden of substantiation 40, 209, 210, 260
- evidence 36, 39, 40, 170, 209, 210, 253, 259, 394–398
- injunctive relief 21, 34, 167, 168, 202, 204–207, 209–211, 223, 225–227, 250–253, 255–258, 266, 275, 276, 418, 440, 450
- non liquet 36, 39, 259
- obligation to cooperate 34, 40
- retraction 15, 21, 209, 250, 256

civil register 26–33, 42, 46, 50, 51, 66, 177, 179, 182, 187–192
- third gender option 185–195

civil status 26–33, 181, 183, 185, 187–194, 338, 340, 343–349, 516
- change in ~ 27, 29, 32, 182, 193, 339–341, 346

coercive treatment 116–139

communication 57, 74, 124, 171, 218, 230, 245, 292, 304, 305, 314, 317, 319, 329, 330, 406, 407, 415, 416, 423, 424, 426–430, 432, 434, 435, 444, 452, 461, 465, 470, 490, 493, 532, 546, 549–551, 563, 608, 614, 618, 622, 678, 689, 691, 692, 712, 727, 728, 733–736, 756
- contents 169, 302–305, 318, 320, 329, 335, 461, 462, 469, 489, 490, 494, 534–536, 541–543, 551, 557, 560–562, 569, 572–574, 577, 579, 595, 596, 602, 604, 609, 610, 614, 718, 728, 734, 743, 752
- free ~ 77, 208, 461, 465, 469, 471, 551, 610
- mass ~ 245, 573

Index

- non-public ~ 310, 317–320, 322, 323, 328–330, 334, 335, 560, 666, 678, 683, 685, 743
- remote ~ *see* telecommunications

computer *see* information technology system

confidentiality 48, 49, 60, 61, 64, 65, 207, 290, 293, 295, 297, 300, 304–306, 314, 354, 391, 410, 413, 462, 465, 466, 489, 490, 492, 494, 503, 515, 516, 531, 545, 546, 572, 573, 577, 578, 584, 596, 610, 630, 669, 673, 681, 685, 687, 689, 691, 719, 731, 733, 740, 742, 756–758
- clerics 614, 619, 622, 678
- confession 678, 743
- confidential sphere 317–319, 324, 334, 335
- conversations 11, 219, 317–320, 322–325, 328, 330, 334, 335, 406, 489, 490, 532, 577, 622, 678–680, 687, 743
- correspondence 300–306
- counselling 360, 364, 614, 619, 622
- diary 289–299
- doctor-patient 320, 614, 678
- journalists 473, 720, 729, 741, 742, 750, 752
- lawyer-client 219, 320, 403, 406, 407, 409, 410, 413, 614, 619, 622, 623, 678, 741–743, 750, 752
- professional ~ 318–320, 323, 325, 335, 402, 407, 409, 410, 412, 413, 485, 486, 516, 584, 619–621, 623, 624, 662, 681, 692, 750, 752
- relationship of trust 304–306, 317–319, 324, 334–336, 364, 402, 407, 409, 413, 593, 614, 620, 624, 678, 680, 687, 713, 738, 741–743
- therapy 678, 743
- ~ of computer devices *see* information technology system
- ~ of telecommunications *see* telecommunications: privacy of ~

confinement (in an institution) 124, 130, 132, 138, 386
- criminal offenders 110, 118, 121, 291
- medical treatment 116–127, 129, 131, 138
- psychiatric ~ 110, 116, 118, 120–124, 126, 291

Constitution *see* Basic Law

Constitutional Court (Federal ~)
- case-law *see* case-law
- dissenting opinion 149, 154, 267, 270, 271, 276, 277, 283, 333, 336, 399, 530, 595, 601, 698, 704, 707, 708
- oral hearing 52, 142, 309, 325, 491, 497, 660, 709, 720
- Plenary 443
- relationship with the ordinary courts 17, 20, 33, 36, 40, 73, 84, 85, 92, 132, 170, 171, 206, 235, 236, 239, 242, 256, 262, 267, 269, 270, 272, 277, 278, 294, 296, 383, 391, 420, 421, 433, 438, 448, 501, 528
- tied vote 294–298, 595, 645–649, 661

constitutional jurisdiction
- constitutional complaint against court decision 7, 17, 20, 30–33, 36, 71, 73, 87, 104, 119, 167, 187, 197, 202, 206, 213, 223, 227, 251, 252, 262, 264, 291, 302, 341, 351, 360, 371, 377, 390, 395, 405, 418, 440, 443, 485, 507
- constitutional complaint against statute 43, 52, 53, 143, 310, 458, 460, 536, 568, 570, 607, 628, 629, 633, 666, 716, 721
- declaration of incompatibility (legal provision) 163, 194, 333, 349, 472–474, 481, 594, 595, 604, 645, 646, 649, 661, 665, 760
- declaration of voidness (legal provision) 68, 126, 146, 163, 194, 243, 248, 472–474, 481, 539, 559, 560, 562, 594–596, 604, 661, 665, 760

- 853 -

Index

- judicial referral *see* judicial review of statutes (specific)
- judicial review of statutes (specific) 2, 95–97, 127, 131, 176, 242, 244
- order containing transitional rules 128, 184, 333, 349, 595, 661, 665, 760
- preliminary injunction 71–73, 196–200, 568, 594, 596, 604, 605

contemporary society 231, 237, 240, 432
- figures of ~ 19, 200, 216, 235–237, 269, 430
- significance for ~ 83, 199, 216, 217, 431, 436

core of private life (~ of one's personality) 3, 4, 37, 121, 151, 179, 228, 241, 274, 275, 279, 292, 293, 297, 314, 315, 317–321, 323–326, 328, 334, 335, 342, 381, 405, 534, 539, 557–559, 561, 609, 612–615, 620, 623, 662, 668, 677–680, 685–692, 706, 707, 709, 713, 719, 738, 743, 744
- inviolability 10, 11, 32, 69, 74, 80, 179, 272, 279, 292–295, 297, 298, 307, 314–318, 320, 321, 323, 324, 327, 334, 371, 372, 381, 390, 422, 557, 597, 613, 620, 649, 677–680, 687, 692, 743, 744

court hearing 216, 217
- broadcasting 196–200, 212–221
- criminal trial 196–200, 212–221
- measures to maintain order 196–200, 212–221
- non-public 13

covert measures 60, 317, 406, 423, 463, 470, 497, 518, 519, 534, 536, 537, 543, 546, 549–562, 584–586, 592, 596, 614, 616, 633, 638, 640, 641, 648, 658, 659, 731, 733, 751, 754, *see also* surveillance
- law enforcement 307–337, 606, 608, 617–619

- notification 331, 333, 411, 518, 519, 585, 586, 589, 592, 601, 617–619, 632, 639, 658, 667, 682
- public security 662–711
- warrant *see* warrant

criminal justice 12, 13, 197, 213, 214, 217, 218, 293–298, 314, 315, 326, 328, 363, 364, 382, 496, 618, 624
- custodial sentence 70, 71, 81, 83, 108, 110, 111, 143, 146, 163, 291, 300–302, 305, 379, 380, 385, 386, 611
- juvenile delinquency 378, 383
- life imprisonment 71, 100, 103–105, 107–113, 290, 418
- probation 72, 83, 102, 104, 105, 107–111, 379, 383–386
- punishment 80, 81, 106–108, 143, 144, 151, 157–159, 164, 290, 295, 301–303, 305, 363, 364, 383, 384, 386, 418, 478, 496, 497, 582
- recidivism 82, 103, 104, 110, 297, 378, 379, 381, 382, 384, 385
- reintegration into society 70, 81, 84, 85, 107, 108, 115, 218, 379, 383, 385, 386, 418, 419, 428–430
- remission of sentence 379, 384, 385
- truth *see* truth: establishment of ~
- victims of crime 79, 83, 172, 216, 218, 296, 599, 612

criminal law
- administrative offences 146, 151, 163, 375, 566, 570, 588, 589, 594
- catalogue of offences 310, 316, 321, 328, 382, 478, 495, 556, 566, 581, 582, 588, 591, 600, 609–612, 673
- criminal offences 7, 11–13, 71, 72, 81, 103, 107, 110, 111, 121, 140, 141, 143, 144, 146, 150–154, 156, 157, 159–161, 163, 164, 172, 213, 220, 290, 294–297, 300, 303, 305, 306, 310, 315–317, 321, 326, 328, 358, 363–366, 369, 370, 377–379, 381, 382, 385, 386, 395, 408, 411, 418, 458, 470, 472, 478, 479, 485, 486, 495, 497, 503, 570, 581, 582, 588,

Index

591, 595, 598, 600, 604, 609–613, 624, 636, 642, 644, 660, 670, 673, 678, 687, 747
- culpability (principle of) 80, 105–107, 111, 218, 290, 294–296, 298, 408, 496, 577
- intent 646
- offences against life and limb 12, 71, 72, 83
- particularly aggravated guilt 100, 102–109, 112, 113
- terrorist offences 459, 470, 537, 642, 645, 646, 651, 670, 675, 684, 690, 736

criminal procedure
- admissibility of evidence 6, 10–12, 289, 290, 293–298, 321, 323–325, 335, 382, 393–395, 397–401, 407–411, 413, 414, 615, 619–622, 692, 696
- conviction 80, 103, 256, 300–303, 306, 377–380, 382, 384–386, 397, 398, 418, 428, 475
- defence 114, 218–220, 290, 320, 407, 614, 619, 622, 623, 678, 743
- exculpating evidence 12, 13, 295, 297, 298, 475
- lay judge 196, 220
- presumption of innocence 80, 218
- prohibition to collect evidence 293, 297, 321, 323–325, 335, 361, 382, 411, 619–622, 624, 744
- right to refuse to give evidence 319, 320, 324, 335, 394, 396, 398–400, 619–621, 623, 624, 667, 668, 678
- right to remain silent 298, 395, 396, 398, 400
- rights of suspects 12, 80, 200, 217, 218, 220, 289, 295, 296, 298, 315, 319, 320, 323, 324, 328, 393–398, 400, 407, 617, 621–623
- self-incrimination 12, 66, 393–400
- sentencing 71, 109, 290, 291, 294, 295, 302, 379, 383, 384, 408, *see also* criminal justice

- suspicion, grounds of 294, 295, 298, 310, 311, 316, 317, 324, 335, 358, 361–363, 365, 366, 386, 403, 409, 411, 413, 471, 475, 477–479, 500, 502, 504, 514, 519–525, 552, 556, 566, 581, 588, 611–613, 617, 624, 639, 645, 660, 673, 676, 694, 697, 713, 745, 747, 759
- trial 6, 84, 196–200, 212–221, 289–291, 293–298
- violations of procedure 401, 413
- witness 217, 218, 319, 395, 396, 485, 486, 698

criminal responsibility 118, 296, 298, 378, *see also* capacity

custodianship *see* capacity; family and partnership

damages 18, 167, 209, 250, 256, 350–352, 354–357, 585, 587, *see also* civil procedure
- non-pecuniary 15–17, 20, 21, 24

danger 49, 106, 111, 113, 114, 135, 157, 296, 305, 384, 458, 459, 467–474, 476, 479, 499, 512, 514, 520, 521, 523, 524, 526, 527, 549, 552, 553, 570, 577, 579, 581, 582, 585, 588, 591, 600, 601, 603, 635, 638–640, 642, 651, 662, 669, 670, 672, 674, 676, 677, 686, 690, 711, 712, 727, 735–737, 739, 742, 743, 746, *see also* public security
- categories of dangers 310, 458, 459, 468, 470, 472–474, 525–527, 552, 554, 555, 583, 615, 660, 662, 663, 674–676, 681, 688, 690, 694, 695, 697, 713, 714, 727, 745, 747, 753, 759
- present danger 509, 525, 528, 529, 532, 631, 657, 675
- prognosis of ~ 110, 111, 113–115, 384, 385, 523–526, 528, 529, 532, 534, 552–554, 556, 558, 635, 641–643, 645, 656, 657, 662, 663, 672, 674–676, 679, 684, 688, 694, 697,

698, 704, 713, 714, 745, 747, 748, 753, 759
- specific danger 295, 470, 503, 506, 514, 521, 523–529, 534, 548, 553, 554, 558, 561, 566, 582, 583, 588, 636, 642, 662, 674–676, 684, 746, 747

data
- access 49, 51, 56, 59, 60, 63, 365, 389, 391, 401, 403, 405–413, 416, 424, 425, 427, 455, 458, 461–463, 465–467, 469, 474–476, 483, 489–493, 495–498, 500, 501, 504, 508, 511, 512, 516, 517, 530, 534, 536, 537, 539, 541–546, 548–558, 560–562, 565, 566, 569, 570, 572–575, 578, 579, 581–597, 599–604, 608, 610, 613, 614, 624, 626, 629–632, 635–637, 640, 641, 643, 651, 652, 654–658, 660, 674, 679, 687, 689, 690, 697, 718, 736, 737, 745, 752
- anonymous ~ 4, 41, 58, 60–62, 64, 65, 67, 169, 219, 221, 329, 431, 436, 462, 469, 512, 515, 517, 519, 531, 578, 588, 589, 650, 651, 654, 656
- automated processing 44, 55–59, 98, 406, 410, 424, 426, 493, 507, 509, 511, 517, 521, 527, 558, 577, 614, 630, 672, 718, 748, 752
- change in purpose 456, 463, 584, 637, 638, 659, 662, 663, 693–701, 707, 710, 739, 740, 745, 746
- collection 41, 42, 44, 50, 54–65, 307, 317, 320–324, 332, 334, 371, 377, 379, 381, 382, 401–414, 424–427, 455, 458, 459, 462–472, 474, 475, 477, 481, 486, 487, 489, 493–496, 498, 501, 508, 511–513, 515–517, 521, 530–532, 534, 536, 541–546, 548–552, 555–563, 573, 575, 576, 585, 589, 590, 596, 602, 603, 605, 609, 612–617, 620, 624, 626, 629, 631, 634, 635, 637–640, 650, 651, 659, 660, 662, 666, 667, 669, 670, 672–674, 677, 679–683, 685, 687–

701, 704–707, 709, 710, 713, 716–719, 727–729, 731–740, 742, 744–746, 750–752, 758, 760
- confidential ~ *see* confidentiality
- cross-checking 42, 46, 50, 51, 56, 62, 66, 386, 466, 468, 507–509, 511–513, 516, 517, 519, 521, 527, 530–532, 573, 631, 654–656, 703, 713, 718, 741, 752
- data protection officer 96
- database 378, 380, 383, 385, 508, 512, 520, 530, 626–661
- deletion 58, 60, 65, 307, 317, 321, 323–326, 332, 378, 383, 410–412, 416, 430, 452, 459, 460, 463, 464, 466, 467, 472, 479–481, 486, 491, 498, 509, 512, 530, 558, 559, 568, 569, 579, 580, 583, 585, 594, 599, 602, 605, 613–615, 632, 659, 662, 681, 683, 688, 692, 693, 713, 718, 738, 739, 744
- hypothetical recollection (test) 660, 663, 696–699, 701, 710, 745, 746
- linking 56–59, 62–64, 68, 425, 426, 429, 453, 469, 480, 508, 511, 512, 515–517, 521, 525, 531, 545, 563, 577, 635, 651, 653, 656, 671
- personal ~ 2, 4, 41, 44, 48, 49, 56–62, 64–68, 97, 98, 332, 360, 371, 381, 406, 412, 418, 419, 424–427, 441, 442, 444, 445, 452, 455, 458, 459, 462, 466, 467, 472, 474, 475, 478, 493, 494, 507, 511, 512, 515–517, 519, 530, 532, 544–546, 550, 552, 557, 562, 563, 569, 574, 578, 585, 630, 634, 635, 637, 644–646, 649, 650, 653–657, 667, 669, 681–683, 690, 700, 702, 713, 718, 728, 729, 731, 744, 745, 748, 749
- processing 41, 58–61, 64, 65, 322, 325, 332, 383, 406, 410, 424–426, 441, 444–446, 449, 451, 452, 455, 458, 462, 463, 465–467, 469, 471, 473, 487, 490, 491, 493, 497, 498, 501, 507, 511, 512, 517, 521, 534,

Index

536, 541, 542, 545, 546, 550, 558, 563, 572, 573, 577, 583, 586, 612–615, 620, 624, 632, 635, 637–639, 647, 648, 658, 670, 679–683, 685, 687, 690, 701, 702, 706, 709, 713, 716, 718, 728, 729, 731, 732, 734, 736–741, 744, 746, 750–756, 758
- protection 58, 60, 61, 64, 65, 332, 410, 412, 419, 424, 426, 440–446, 448, 449, 451, 452, 463, 498, 508, 516, 520, 537, 581, 585, 590, 596, 616, 631, 632, 634, 637, 646, 648, 649, 657–660, 682, 683, 693, 698, 701, 702, 719, 739, 744, 748–750
- purpose limitation 41, 58, 59, 65–67, 332, 378, 383, 399, 400, 408, 410–414, 425, 426, 455, 462–464, 472, 474–476, 480, 483, 495, 527, 565, 569, 574, 576, 578, 583, 584, 589, 591, 593, 603, 610, 636–638, 640, 642, 653, 654, 660, 662, 663, 681, 683, 693–696, 698, 702, 739, 740, 744, 758
- retention 58, 59, 462, 474, 517, 565–605, 639, 673, 674, 713, 737, 738, 741
- right to be forgotten *see* personality, protection
- security 537, 541, 543, 545, 546, 549, 551, 560, 565, 570, 580, 581, 589, 590, 594–596, 602
- sharing 41, 42, 44, 48, 56, 58, 59, 61, 65–67, 97, 321, 322, 332, 381, 399, 400, 406, 424, 455, 456, 458, 463, 466, 467, 469, 471, 473–480, 482, 493, 507–509, 511, 512, 516–518, 527, 568–570, 573–575, 583–589, 591, 593–595, 601, 613, 615, 626, 629, 631, 634–638, 640–643, 645, 648, 650, 652, 654–660, 662, 663, 666–668, 672, 681, 693, 696, 699–705, 710, 712–714, 716, 718, 721, 728–730, 732, 737–740, 742, 745–758
- statistical ~ 1, 2, 4, 5, 41–68, 517

- storage 41, 48, 49, 56, 58–60, 62, 98, 322, 325, 381, 383, 401–403, 405–413, 424, 429, 452, 459, 462, 463, 466, 468, 480, 483, 489–497, 501, 508, 509, 511–513, 517, 530, 534, 537, 540, 541, 543, 544, 546, 550, 551, 557, 563, 565, 568–570, 573–581, 589, 593, 594, 596, 599, 600, 603, 615, 626, 629–631, 633–636, 638, 642–646, 649–654, 657, 659, 660, 676, 677, 689, 718, 719, 741
- traffic ~ 455, 458, 461, 483, 485, 486, 489–491, 493–497, 500–502, 504, 534, 542, 543, 551, 565–605, 609, 610, 617, 662, 667, 673, 713, 714, 718, 734, 737, 738, 741, 752, 753, *see also* telecommunications
- use 41, 44, 56–59, 61, 62, 64, 66, 67, 97, 99, 307, 317, 321–326, 332, 333, 335, 377, 381, 383, 399, 401, 406, 408, 411, 424–427, 455, 462–464, 466, 472–475, 480–482, 493, 511, 518, 519, 531, 545, 550, 558, 565, 566, 568, 569, 572–585, 587–589, 591–594, 596, 601–604, 613–616, 620, 624, 626, 631, 633–635, 637–643, 650, 653–660, 662, 663, 667, 668, 673, 679–681, 683, 685, 687, 688, 690, 692–698, 701, 702, 704, 707, 710, 718, 719, 736, 739, 744, 746, 748, 750, 752, 754

defamation 202, 207, 252, 260, *see also* freedom of expression

democracy 56, 215, 240, 320, 337, 406, 431, 432, 448, 547, 682, 708, 731, 736
- democratic order 12, 19, 20, 75, 77, 79, 458, 480, 481, 519, 521, 531, 548, 642, 670
- role of free media *see* media

disability 129, 133
- persons with disabilities 123, 137

discrimination 173, 185, 187, 189, 192, 193, 516, 518, 531, 654, 741

Index

DNA 376–387
- database 377, 380, 381

equality 5, 33, 123, 131, 132, 185, 187, 192, 193, 302, 370, 374, 375, 380, 390, 422, 427, 516, 518, 621–623, 654, 667, 720, 721

eternity clause 307, 312, 313, 315, 316, 333–337, 725

European Convention on Human Rights 80, 119, 137, 138, 147, 161, 162, 224, 229–232, 234–236, 239, 420, 430, 444, 451, 464, 673, 696, 699, 702, 725, 726, 749

European Court of Human Rights 137, 138, 161–163, 223, 224, 230–232, 234, 235, 238–240, 428, 430–433, 435, 436, 444, 446, 451, 454, 464, 725

European Union 580, 667, 700, 720, 721
- Charter of Fundamental Rights 415, 420, 421, 430, 437–439, 441–448, 451, 453, 454, 634, 722, 759
- Court of Justice 430, 437, 438, 443–452, 454, 572, 634
- EU law 63, 415, 419–421, 437, 438, 441–444, 448, 454, 565, 568, 591, 594, 634, 647, 670, 682, 722, 759
- European integration 438
- precedence of application 438, 442, 565, 572

excessive measures, prohibition 5, 21, 77, 110, 111, 114, 115, 135, 156, 208, 247, 347, 373, 382, 409, 411, 412, 414, 472, 473, 476, 495, 602, 626, 642–651, 653–655, 684, 691

family and partnership 264, 302, 317, 319, 321, 322, 324, 329, 335, 352, 390, 444, 445
- adoption 348
- children 3, 86, 87, 90, 91, 167, 172, 229, 265, 275, 281, 284, 348, 351, 352, 354–356, 371, *see also* child, best interest

- civil partnership 180, 183, 338–345, 349
- custody 87, 88, 90, 91
- divorce 28, 33, 352, 354, 388–392
- family 82, 88–92, 95, 144, 167, 173, 224, 225, 229, 238, 265, 285, 302, 304, 319, 340, 343, 356, 442, 614, 678
- foster care 86–93
- guardianship 88
- legally protected partnership 175, 176, 178, 180, 183, 184, 338, 341, 343–345
- marriage 28, 32, 177, 180–184, 224, 226, 229, 240, 265, 275, 305, 319, 339, 340, 343–345, 352, 355, 371, 390, 391, 678
- parent-child relation 33, 87, 90, 91, 115, 167, 172, 229, 238, 275, 348, 349
- parents 86, 87, 90, 91, 264, 348, 350–352, 354–357, 530
- paternity (biological) 351, 352, 354–356
- paternity (legal) 350–352, 354–357
- same-sex relationship 177, 180, 181, 183, 184, 338, 340, 341, 343–346

fine (sanction) 2, 5, 61, 71, 143, 146, 163, 252, 302, 379

foreign states 701–703, 712, 717, 727, 736, 737, 742, 749, 752
- authorities 663, 666, 667, 672, 693, 700, 710, 712–714, 716, 718, 719, 729, 730, 736, 748–754, 756, 757
- citizens 716, 717, 720, 721, 723–725, 727, 733, 737, 759
- law 442, 445, 448, 663, 700, 702, 725, 726, 741, 748, 749

freedom of action, general 37, 146, 149, 151, 163, 189, 358, 362, 363, 366, 374, 395, 397, 544, 545

freedom of assembly 56

freedom of association 56

Index

freedom of broadcasting 69, 74–85, 172, 198, 199, 212, 214, 215, 220, 246, 247, 427, 624

freedom of conscience 37, 160

freedom of expression 24, 37, 55, 75, 166, 168–173, 206–209, 211, 229–231, 235, 239, 252, 255–259, 261, 288, 300, 302, 303, 306, 421, 427, 431, 433, 435, 439, 446–448, 451, 453, 649
- ambiguous statement 250, 256, 257, 261
- calumny 207, 257, 273, 281, 288
- defamation 202, 207, 255, 260, 274, 282, 288
- insult 15, 282, 300–303, 305, 306
- legitimate interests 36, 207, 255, 258, 259
- opinion *see* opinion
- profanity 207, 257
- truthfulness 34, 207–210, 244, 246, 252–254, 257, 259–261, 423, 436, 450, *see also* truth, establishment of ~

freedom of occupation 146, 163, 374, 404, 407, 439, 446–448, 453, 621, 624, 667, 741

freedom of religion 39, 51, 54, 320, 321, 649

freedom of the arts 85, 262, 266–288

freedom of the press 18–21, 24, 25, 51, 54, 75, 168, 170, 199, 225–227, 229, 231–235, 237–240, 421, 427, 431–433, 435, 460, 461, 472, 473, 475, 624, 667, 712, 720–723, 727–729, 731, 741, 759, 760

fundamental rights
- applicability abroad 455, 464, 700, 712, 721, 723–728, 730, 733, 735, 742, 748, 749, 753, 758
- binding effect 33, 420, 421, 426, 464, 465, 574, 700, 712, 723–728, 730, 748, 751, 753
- core protection 268, 275, 307, 315, 579, *see also* core of private life; human dignity
- defensive rights against state 57, 120, 133, 206, 267, 292, 312, 397, 405, 416, 424–426, 438, 499, 522, 545, 598, 708, 712, 723, 726, 727, 743
- duty of protection 19, 106, 127, 132–138, 140, 147, 152–154, 157, 158, 161, 162, 164, 206, 208, 254, 260, 357, 514, 521, 522, 532, 549, 552, 587, 598, 671, 704, 707, 708, 711, 751
- essence 3, 7, 10, 20, 57, 75, 76, 109, 292, 390, 391, 469, 579
- EU fundamental rights 415, 420, 421, 430, 437–439, 441–454
- exercise of ~ 56, 121, 122, 134, 141, 150, 151, 156, 157, 160, 171, 208, 246, 257, 259, 270, 374, 406, 429, 447, 493, 519, 578, 579, 598, 621, 622, 649
- gap in protection 18, 189, 274, 325, 398, 463, 473, 490, 540, 542–545, 601, 701, 728
- horizontal effects (between private actors) 18, 206, 235, 267, 270, 416, 421, 423–426, 438, 443, 444, 447
- interpretation *see* interpretation
- objective values 17, 73, 77, 133, 154, 207, 255, 267, 313, 330, 336, 396, 422, 424–426, 453, 522, 704
- permeating effect (on private law) 17, 38, 69, 73, 75, 81, 92, 172, 207, 229, 235, 254, 255, 416, 421, 422, 424–426
- procedural rights 51, 80, 89, 112, 113, 119, 125, 246, 253, 411, 460, 461, 463, 465–467, 480, 481, 487, 587, 633, 681, 682, 749, 751, 755
- requirement that legislator specify affected rights 560, 562, 609, 712, 730, 758

fundamental rights holders 39, 81, 120, 122, 123, 134, 145, 149, 154, 171,

227, 322, 327, 329, 330, 362, 381, 422, 451, 463, 464, 468–470, 474, 479, 511, 514, 515, 518, 531, 545, 563, 597, 598, 705, 708, 724, 742
- celebrities 19, 223–226, 228, 232–241, 269
- children 88, 90, 91
- criminal offenders 60, 69, 74, 82, 100, 104, 172, 173, 218, 289, 293–298, 305, 313, 377, 379, 380, 383, 385, 386, 418, 419, 428–430
- doctors 143, 160, 608, 614, 621, 623, 667
- foreigners 465, 518, 712, 720, 721, 723–725, 727, 728, 737, 758, 759
- journalists 461, 473, 537, 608, 624, 667, 720, 728, 741, 742, 750, 752, 759
- lawyers 143, 220, 403, 405, 407, 538, 608, 614, 619, 622, 667, 741, 742, 750, 752
- legal persons 197, 213, 214, 224–227, 238, 267, 275, 276, 278, 361, 362, 364, 405, 427, 432, 433, 436, 437, 439, 440, 446, 447, 451, 453, 721
- politicians 35, 239, 251, 255, 537, 608, 619, 667
- soldiers 220

fundamental rights, interference
- consent 60, 120–122, 124, 126, 134, 135, 137, 180, 388, 391, 426
- statutory basis 18, 41, 57, 65, 125, 151, 307, 313, 315, 316, 321–323, 325, 333, 335, 353, 357, 372, 380, 381, 401, 405, 407, 408, 425, 459, 462, 463, 466, 467, 471, 473, 475, 495, 499, 510, 513, 514, 516, 522–526, 528, 532, 534, 546, 547, 552–555, 561, 563, 565, 575, 578, 580–584, 586, 587, 589, 598, 613, 629, 647, 648, 669, 675, 676, 681, 683, 684, 690, 693–695, 699, 703, 709, 730, 731, 735, 745, 747, 750, 752, 753
- threshold (for carrying out measures constituting interferences) 316, 326–328, 456, 468, 470, 471, 473, 475–479, 496, 500, 502, 514, 515, 521, 523, 525, 526, 552, 553, 555, 556, 561, 566, 577, 581, 582, 587, 588, 601, 603, 604, 638–640, 650, 654, 657, 659, 660, 673, 674, 676, 688, 690, 694, 698, 732–735, 738, 739, 742, 745–748, 752
- weight and severity of interference 11, 12, 21, 63, 69, 78, 79, 83, 92, 110, 112, 116, 120–123, 125, 135, 151, 156, 157, 171, 173, 207, 234, 255, 260, 262, 267, 270–272, 275–281, 284, 285, 316, 327, 329–331, 347–349, 354, 356, 365, 373, 374, 391, 395, 406–412, 414, 424, 428, 435, 436, 452, 454, 463, 469–471, 474, 476, 477, 479, 481, 488, 493, 496–498, 500, 502, 504, 513–519, 521–524, 529–531, 533, 545, 548–555, 559, 561, 565, 576–580, 582, 583, 585, 586, 588, 595–597, 599, 602–604, 609, 613, 616–618, 636–638, 640–643, 651, 656, 660, 663, 669, 671–674, 676, 677, 681–686, 690, 691, 695–697, 704–707, 709, 710, 728, 732–734, 737–741, 745, 746, 748

fundamental rights, justification of interference 10, 11, 13, 19, 20, 32, 61, 65, 74, 84, 109, 111–113, 116, 121–125, 135, 136, 140, 141, 147, 150, 151, 157, 161, 179–181, 189, 192, 193, 207, 208, 219, 235, 238, 268, 270, 275, 276, 280, 283, 293, 307, 314, 316, 347, 363, 366, 372, 375, 385, 388, 391, 398, 409, 423, 425, 431, 435, 453, 454, 471, 472, 475, 479, 481, 500, 502, 534, 539, 547, 549, 552–554, 556, 557, 561, 564, 576, 579, 582–584, 594, 595, 597, 610, 611, 618, 621–623, 636, 639, 640, 643, 646, 657, 660, 663, 675,

Index

677, 683–685, 690, 693, 694, 696, 697, 710, 713, 722, 730–733, 735, 737–739, 742–744, 747, 748, *see also* fundamental rights, limits; proportionality

fundamental rights, limits 54, 57, 170, 206, 229, 255, 268, 296, 303, 307, 313, 315, 316, 381, 513, *see also* fundamental rights, justification; balancing of interests; proportionality
- common good 4, 57, 74, 81, 97, 106, 152, 156, 292, 293, 298, 315, 334, 390, 397, 462, 468–470, 533, 575, 624, 739
- constitutional order 170, 206, 229–231, 255
- general laws (Art. 5) 18, 20, 25, 76, 77, 170, 206, 229, 230, 255
- moral law 10, 31, 32
- public interests 6, 10–13, 19, 32, 41, 57, 62, 69, 70, 74, 97, 106, 109–112, 121, 151, 179–181, 193, 230, 259, 292–298, 314, 328, 363, 364, 372, 381, 388, 390, 391, 396, 397, 409, 413, 432, 463, 468, 475, 477, 478, 503, 513, 523, 533, 534, 549, 550, 553, 557, 566, 579, 581, 582, 588, 601, 636, 637, 640, 651, 657, 671, 674, 677, 679, 684, 707, 708, 736, 737, 743, 745–748, 752, 754, 758, 760
- rights of others 10, 19, 69, 70, 74, 76, 77, 80, 109, 114, 121, 151, 152, 161, 192, 206, 207, 229–231, 247, 255, 257–259, 268, 270–273, 275, 278, 284, 292, 293, 296, 298, 303, 315, 328, 334, 372, 397, 409, 410, 412, 413, 423–425, 428, 432–435, 438, 444, 446, 447, 449–453, 468, 472, 598, 636, 651, 657, 671, 674, 707, 708, 737, 739, 754

fundamental rights, scope of protection 11, 17, 36–41, 54–57, 73–85, 90, 92, 120, 140, 143, 147–150, 166, 168–170, 172, 173, 179, 185, 189, 193,

199, 201, 205, 206, 208, 211, 215, 217, 227–233, 236, 246, 254, 266–269, 271, 272, 274, 278, 283, 286–288, 292, 293, 295, 296, 300, 303–307, 312–315, 317–319, 321, 322, 334, 335, 342, 348, 350, 353–355, 361, 362, 364, 371, 372, 381, 390, 397, 405, 406, 420–432, 438, 441, 444–446, 448, 450, 455, 461, 462, 464, 466, 473, 483, 488–494, 500, 501, 511, 512, 515, 516, 534, 539, 540, 542–546, 560, 562, 563, 572, 573, 583, 596, 609, 610, 621, 624, 634, 659, 660, 678, 712, 723, 726–728, 730, 733, 741–744, 751

GDR (East Germany) 197, 251–253, 255, 258–260
- Ministry of State Security 251–253, 255, 258–260
- unofficial collaborator 251–253

gender 27, 29, 31, 33, 176, 179, 182, 184, 185, 191, 192, 340, 342–344, 346, 348, 349
- third gender *see* civil register: third gender option
- ~ identity 28, 30, 31, 175, 179–185, 188–193, 338, 340–349
- ~ reassignment surgery 26, 28, 30, 31, 33, 176–184, 339, 340, 343–345, 347

government 9, 24, 44, 50, 58–60, 62, 332, 420, 456, 458, 466, 471–474, 476, 547, 643, 660, 713, 735, 736, 739, 740, 742, 745–748, 756
- defence policy 458, 470, 736
- foreign policy 458, 471, 506, 549, 700, 712, 713, 716, 717, 727, 732, 735–737, 739, 747, 751, 757
- security policy 470, 471, 712, 713, 716, 717, 727, 732, 735–737, 739, 747, 751, 757

guardianship *see* capacity; family and partnership

- 861 -

Index

health 2, 3, 129, 130, 132, 200, 371, 516, 532, 657, *see also* capacity: consent to medical treatment; coercive treatment
- addiction counselling 358, 366
- advance healthcare directive 129, 136
- freedom 'to be ill' 122, 134, *see also* coercive treatment
- medical assessment 31, 130, 133–136, 164, 367–369, 371–375
- medical records 360, 362–366, 624
- medication 118, 120, 121, 124, 125, 130, 160
- mental health 32, 89, 91, 93, 118, 123, 167, 171, 200, 296, 304, 348, 371, 390
- mental illness 60, 95, 96, 118, 121, 123, 124, 129, 130, 133, 155, 162, 265, 285, 378
- psychological assessment 367–369, 371–375
- psychotherapy 27, 290, 291, 360
- public health 158, 159, 161, 164, 358, 363, 364
- treatment 116, 118–121, 124, 125, 127, 129, 130, 132–136, 138, 148, 149, 346, 360
- ~ impairments 32, 91–93, 107, 116, 120–124, 126, 127, 130, 132–135, 137, 138, 143, 149, 154, 155, 158, 161, 162, 164, 224, 225, 238, 275, 284, 343, 347, 348, 371, 381
- ~ risks 87, 89, 108, 118, 121, 123, 124, 132, 133, 135, 138, 200, 343, 347, 370, 372

history 431
- constitutional ~ *see* Basic Law
- contemporary ~ 199, 200, 216, 217, 436, *see also* contemporary society
- interpretation *see* interpretation
- research 432, 435

human dignity 3, 4, 15, 18, 31, 37, 41, 51, 55, 62, 74, 75, 77, 83, 91, 100, 105–108, 113–115, 147–151, 158, 162, 179, 207, 257, 268, 272, 275, 279, 295, 296, 298, 307, 313– 315, 317–320, 323, 333–336, 342, 395–397, 489, 499, 514, 543, 579, 622, 623, 671, 677, 679, 681, 685, 686, 692, 701, 723, 724, 743, 749
- inviolability 3, 4, 10, 108, 147, 292, 307, 315, 316, 334, 390, 622
- object theory 3, 59, 106, 147, 246, 313, 314, 320, 396, 622
- objective constitutional value 25, 75, 81, 106, 158, 313, 396

human rights 313, 428, 430, 431, 433, 435, 446, 634, 667, 702, 724, 725, 748–750
- policy 667
- treaties 80, 119, 122, 136–138, 147, 161, 162, 224, 229–232, 234–236, 239, 420, 444, 451, 464, 673, 696, 699, 702, 725, 726, 749
- violations 701, 702, 749

information
- access to ~ 44, 49, 51, 53, 56, 58, 62, 64, 65, 69, 75, 79, 81, 98, 99, 172, 199, 200, 207, 215, 216, 219, 232, 233, 237, 252, 292, 294, 297, 298, 365, 389, 391, 393–401, 405–407, 409, 410, 412, 415, 416, 418, 422– 424, 426–436, 439, 445–448, 450– 454, 461, 467, 530, 532, 535, 541, 560, 562, 635–637, 640–643, 645, 652, 658, 660, 682, 689, 714, 716, 727, 732, 735, 736, 740, 742, 747, 749, 754, 756, 757
- freedom of ~ 75, 199, 215, 231, 237, 257, 439, 446–448, 452
- interest of the public 19, 20, 69, 72, 79–84, 200, 207, 215–221, 227, 230– 241, 259, 397, 419, 427–432, 434, 436, 448, 451, 453, 454, 742, 758
- media *see* media

information technology system 56, 410, 486, 491, 494, 511, 517, 614, 662, 663, 667, 673, 674, 676, 686, 688– 691, 695, 697, 709, 710
- access to ~ 597

- 862 -

Index

- confidentiality and integrity of ~ 534–564, 660, 669, 688
- inhuman and degrading treatment 108, 119, 702, 749
- intelligence 458, 459, 468–473, 477, 480, 513, 626, 640, 652, 712
  - foreign ~ 467, 469, 471, 712–761
  - oversight *see* oversight
  - political ~ 456, 458, 473, 474, 639, 640, 712, 713, 736, 739, 740, 742, 745, 746, 748
  - strategic ~ *see* surveillance
  - ~ service 455, 456, 458–460, 465–467, 469–482, 534–564, 566, 570, 574, 576, 583, 585, 586, 588, 593, 603, 604, 626, 629, 637–641, 643, 650, 659, 700, 712–761
- international law 80, 119, 122, 124, 132, 136–138, 147, 161, 162, 224, 229–232, 234–236, 239, 420, 428, 430, 431, 433, 435, 444, 446, 451, 464, 647, 670, 673, 696, 699, 702, 725, 726, 748–750, 757, 759, *see also* European Convention on Human Rights; human rights
  - international organisation 636, 647, 702, 749
  - openness to ~ 230, 235, 464, 700, 723, 724, 750, 751
- Internet 416, 418, 419, 425, 427, 429, 430, 432–437, 439, 440, 445–453, 535–538, 540, 541, 551, 560, 562, 563, 569, 573, 574, 588, 589, 593, 599, 608
  - communication 416, 428, 429, 434, 534, 536–538, 541, 542, 551, 557, 558, 560, 562, 563, 569, 573, 608
  - device *see* information technology system
  - search engine 416, 418, 429, 434, 436, 439–441, 443, 445–447, 449–453
  - surveillance *see* surveillance

- interpretation 22, 159, 162, 421
  - comparative ~ 23, 344, 442, 445, 448, 757
  - drafting history 4, 18, 23, 24, 50, 62, 91, 160, 182, 489, 516, 647, 649, 653, 670, 723
  - dynamic ~ 22, 23, 25, 37, 55, 63, 228, 312, 406, 424–426, 429, 430, 489, 511, 540, 542, 544, 545, 727, 728, 733, 734, 737
  - error of ~ 36, 92, 501, 529
  - guided by fundamental rights 17, 18, 25, 36, 73, 76, 84, 90, 92, 170, 171, 199, 207, 229, 235, 255, 303, 304, 372, 373, 421, 422, 449, 510, 528
  - historic ~ 312, 723
  - in conformity with European law 443, 446, 454
  - in conformity with international law 122, 136, 137, 161, 235, 236, 239, 444, 670, 724, 725
  - in conformity with the Constitution 25, 32, 77, 86, 89, 90, 93, 105, 126, 146, 163, 248, 324, 326, 328, 336, 337, 349, 398, 400, 473, 479, 480, 482, 517, 527, 529, 644–649, 688, 689, 706, 708, 709
  - legal gap 17, 18, 22–24, 33, 189, 398, 540, 542–545
  - legislative intent 33, 62, 105, 160, 163, 164, 182, 312, 527, 645–647, 652, 670, 689, 732
  - methodology 24, 113, 382
  - spirit and purpose 23, 77, 192, 306, 312, 320, 334, 336, 406, 425, 471, 490, 492, 543, 545, 574, 723, 725
  - statutory ~ 170, 199, 207, 229, 255, 325, 328, 352, 372, 373, 382, 383, 397, 438, 510, 526, 528–530, 547
  - systematic ~ 315, 336, 382, 647, 723, 724
  - wording 21, 33, 62, 75, 90, 316, 324, 335, 336, 382, 407, 517, 561, 636, 645–647, 649, 652, 670, 689, 724

Index

intimacy *see* sexuality and intimacy; personality, protected spheres: intimate sphere

judicial authorisation, requirement of ~ 130, 330, 331, 361, 382, 384, 407, 488, 499, 509, 534, 555, 556, 584–586, 588, 592, 604, 615, 617, 658, 677, 685, 686, 740, 755, *see also* warrant

judicial development of the law 11, 15–25, 33, 76, 163, 283, 350, 352, 353, 356, 398, 413, 422–424, 449, 587, 600

judicial referral *see* constitutional jurisdiction: judicial review of statutes (specific)

judicial review 111, 113, 115, 130, 208, 330–333, 383, 385, 386, 389, 391, 392, 407, 434, 447, 459–461, 463–467, 481, 488, 497, 499, 547, 552, 555, 584–587, 589, 592, 615, 617, 633, 643, 648, 651, 659, 682, 706, 714, 731, 740, 742, 750, 753, 755
- effective ~ 383, 384, 465, 586, 587, 670

justice 22, 24, 217, 218, 293, 295, 313, 724, *see also* rule of law
- administration of ~ 12, 13, 217, 218, 220, 293–295, 382, 413
- criminal ~ *see* criminal justice
- substantive ~ 23

law enforcement 12, 13, 74, 80, 81, 197, 213, 214, 218, 290, 293–298, 305, 307, 310, 311, 313–318, 325–329, 335, 359, 361–365, 369, 377, 378, 381–385, 393–396, 398–403, 405–414, 455, 470, 471, 473, 475–479, 486, 496, 497, 503, 508, 519, 520, 537, 547, 552, 556, 566, 570, 574–576, 579, 581, 585, 588, 590, 591, 594, 595, 597–605, 609–622, 624, 639, 645, 646, 659, 660, 666, 673, 678, 682, 684, 694, 695, 699, 705, 713, 742, 743, 745, 747, 750, 758
- police raid 360, 361
- search 9, 359–362, 369, 401–403, 405, 407, 410, 411, 413, 485–489, 492, 494, 495, 498–502, 504
- seizure 9, 290, 358–366, 401–413, 483, 485, 486, 488, 495, 497–499, 501, 550, 617, 623
- surveillance *see* surveillance
- undercover investigator 331, 618, 619

lawyer 217–220, 251, 402, 403, 405–407, 409, 412, 413, 486, 538, 608, 619, 620, 622, 623, 667, 678, 741, 742, 750, 752
- defence ~ 111, 114, 320, 485, *see also* criminal procedure

legal certainty 22, 33, 62, 66, 325, 681

legal clarity 4, 41, 57–59, 62, 66, 67, 116, 125, 193, 316, 353, 382, 407, 463, 467, 473, 495, 513, 526, 539, 547, 548, 561, 565, 579–581, 586, 589, 590, 592, 609, 637, 640, 642–645, 647, 648, 652, 669, 670, 677, 679, 684, 685, 703, 705, 711, 731, 739, 745, 748, 749, 758

legal gap 23, 24, 33, 189, 193, 352, 356, 398, 540, 543, 545, *see also* interpretation

legal positivism 20, 22–24, 29, 32

legal protection 51, 53, 58, 124, 125, 268, 325, 352, 459, 460, 463, 464, 466, 481, 488, 498, 499, 519, 552, 555, 565, 580, 584–587, 589, 602, 616, 633, 639, 641, 648, 657–659, 662, 681, 682, 692, 710, 731, 738, 753–755
- right to effective ~ 51, 101, 214, 307, 331, 332, 380, 460, 461, 463, 465–467, 480, 481, 487, 633, 667, 681, 682, 755

legal recourse *see* legal protection

Index

legal scholarship 16, 18, 19, 24, 33, 76, 80, 81, 110, 236, 304, 396, 397, 430, 532

legislator 5, 16, 22, 24, 25, 33, 41, 44, 57–59, 63–66, 98, 110, 121, 122, 133, 136, 153–161, 180, 182, 184, 194, 246, 247, 313, 324–328, 342–348, 356, 357, 380, 383, 397–399, 407, 408, 420, 455, 462, 468, 469, 471, 473, 475–477, 480, 481, 483, 495, 510, 514, 521–526, 528, 552, 553, 559, 565, 574, 576, 578, 580–582, 584–586, 588, 589, 591–593, 597–604, 610–613, 616, 618–621, 624, 642, 644, 648, 649, 651–653, 657, 659, 662, 666, 671, 673–675, 677, 679–682, 690, 693–695, 697, 702, 704, 706–708, 712, 713, 723, 727, 734, 735, 737–743, 749, 752, 754–757, *see also* separation of powers
- Constitution-amending ~ 313, 316, 327, 335, 725
- democratic legitimation 547, 600, 603, 708
- inaction 23, 24, 133, 164, 193, 323
- latitude 5, 32, 133, 135, 152, 157, 158, 164, 194, 247, 327, 349, 357, 415, 419, 421, 464, 468, 474, 477, 523, 549, 580, 581, 584, 586, 587, 598–603, 611, 612, 619, 621, 653, 673, 684, 691, 692, 704, 708, 739, 755, 756, 760
- legislative intent 33, 62, 153, 180, 184, 335, 527, 595, 610, 623, 635, 636, 645, 647, 649, 652, 670, 684, 689, 732
- legislative reform 23, 30, 32, 50, 51, 61, 126, 128, 135, 143, 144, 183, 191, 310, 333, 335, 337, 349, 357, 411, 441, 442, 448, 458, 460, 472–474, 479–481, 509, 512, 568, 572, 596, 599, 605, 607, 610, 629, 666, 670, 708, 716, 718, 719

liberty of the person 100, 105–111, 114, 115, 120–122, 146, 163, 506, 513, 514, 527, 534, 549, 553, 566, 582, 618, 639, 657, 671, 674, 737
- deprivation of ~ 103, 106–114, 122, 305, 380, 394, 399, *see also* confinement; criminal justice

life 111, 121, 132, 133, 135, 140, 141, 144, 146–149, 151, 153–159, 161, 162, 164, 275, 372, 521, 532, 749
- right to ~ 133, 134, 137, 138, 152

margin of appreciation 137, 152, 162, 234, 238, 241, 327, 549, 581, 600, 611, 704

marriage *see* family and partnership

media 75, 79–81, 172, 197, 203, 208, 209, 215, 217, 230–235, 237–242, 245–247, 260, 267, 320, 415, 416, 419, 421, 422, 427, 429, 431, 452, 624
- broadcasting 69, 71, 74–76, 167, 196–200, 212–221, 242–244, 246–248, 251, 429, 440, 451–454, 486, *see also* freedom of broadcasting
- celebrity pictures 222, 241
- commercial interests 17, 21, 232, 432
- correction 16, 17
- duty of care 21, 208, 246, 259
- entertainment media 16, 19–25, 75, 76, 78, 81, 222–227, 232–234, 240
- fabricated interview 16, 19–21, 38
- journalists 197, 199, 219, 320, 432, 667, 720, 728, 741, 742, 750, 752, 759
- mass ~ 217, 232, 233, 245
- online archive 416, 418, 427, 432, 433, 435, 436
- press 16, 21, 75, 78, 167, 199, 202, 203, 206, 209, 210, 213, 219, 224, 225, 227, 231–235, 237–242, 260, 418, 427–429, 431–437, 486, 487, 624, 720, 742, *see also* freedom of the press
- reporting on criminal cases 69–85, 196–200, 212–221, 418, 419, 428, 431, 436
- right of reply 242–249

- 865 -

- role in democracy 19, 75
- television 69, 70, 74–85, 167, 173, 197–200, 212–214, 217–221, 243, 244, 247, 251, 440, 453
- true crime documentary 69, 71, 72, 78, 79, 82, 83, 85

occupational freedom *see* freedom of occupation

opinion 55, 79, 168, 169, 209, 215, 229, 231, 235, 246, 250, 251, 257, 304, 334, 416, 427, 429, 447, 462, *see also* freedom of expression
- formation of ~ 19, 20, 55, 75, 84, 168, 209, 215, 232–235, 239, 257, 258, 425, 447
- public ~ 19, 20, 39, 84, 168, 206, 215, 231–235, 237, 239, 246, 252, 270, 425, 432
- statement of ~ 255, 256, 271, 304

oversight 58, 65, 126, 325, 459, 463, 464, 476, 479, 482, 555–557, 579, 581, 586, 615, 626, 631, 632, 637, 642, 643, 651, 657–659, 677, 682, 683, 705, 706, 714, 719, 735, 738–742, 744, 750, 753–759
- administrative oversight 657–659, 662, 681–683, 692, 693, 700, 703, 710, 714, 755
- judicial oversight 467, 481, 499, 555, 586, 592, 615, 682
- parliamentary oversight 465, 481, 482, 556, 586, 659, 719, 757, 758
- political oversight 639

Parliament 50, 51, 251, 320, 547, 586, 611, 619, 623, 659, 667, 706, 716, 719, 756–758

peaceful legal order 80, 382, 409, 496, 598

personal autonomy 134, 136

personality, free development of 6, 9, 10, 12, 15, 18, 31, 37, 56, 74, 75, 83, 91, 106, 134, 135, 148–150, 158, 164, 171–173, 179, 189–192, 205, 227, 228, 254, 269, 294, 296, 304, 314, 315, 343, 390, 406, 422–425, 427–431, 434, 442, 446, 452, 489, 493, 499, 532, 540–543, 545, 557, 587, 678, 743

personality, protected spheres *see also* core of private life
- closer personal sphere 21, 37, 151, 179, 228, 245, 254, 268, 272, 297, 342, 371, 372, 515, 516
- intimate sphere 4, 10, 11, 31, 37, 57, 175, 179–181, 184, 207, 275, 279, 280, 284, 285, 296, 314, 315, 319, 334, 337, 342–345, 350, 354, 355, 362, 371, 390, 577, 624
- private sphere 18, 19, 21, 37, 38, 69, 75, 78, 81, 151, 207, 228, 234, 239, 241, 272, 294, 300, 303–306, 322, 343, 350, 354, 355, 362, 363, 366, 391, 422, 453, 489–493, 498, 501, 544, 624, 669–674, 676, 679, 682, 684–686, 691, 707, 709, 733
- social sphere 434, 453, 678

personality, protection 37, 38, 296, 415, 416, 540, 544
- personal honour 38, 170, 207, 254, 255, 268, 303, 422
- portrayal of one's person 38, 39, 74, 77, 79, 205, 228, 230, 231, 234, 246, 254, 268, 269, 271–274, 278, 280, 281, 285, 415, 416, 419, 421–424, 426–431
- reputation 205, 206, 252, 255, 422, 428
- respect for one's person 3, 75, 106, 147, 150, 158, 189, 191, 192, 200, 313, 314, 522
- right to be forgotten 416, 419, 428–431, 433–436, 441, 449–454
- right to one's name 166, 169, 170, 175–184
- right to one's own image 6, 10, 38, 74, 76, 200, 217–219, 228, 231, 233–241, 271, 422, 423

Index

- right to one's own speech 6, 10, 11, 38, 74, 422
- social image 34, 38–40, 78, 170, 172, 201, 205, 246, 252, 254, 255, 268, 372, 422

physical integrity 89, 91, 93, 108, 121, 130, 132, 133, 200, 347, 348
- right to ~ 10, 116, 119–121, 133–138, 295, 343, 347, 348, 370, 390, 671

political persecution 702, 749
politics 59, 630, 757
- international ~ 736
- political affiliation 516, 577
- political campaign 35
- political oversight *see* oversight
- political parties 35, 50, 251, 537
- politicians 35, 197, 203, 239, 251, 252, 255, 320, 537, 608, 611, 619, 623, 667

pre-constitutional law 24, 398
prejudice 60, 79, 82, 169, 218, 518
press *see* media
private home 54, 62, 229, 307–337, 444, 485, 487–489, 492, 500, 504, 531, 538, 543, 544, 617, 662, 663, 666, 673, 674, 676, 678, 685–687, 689, 691, 695, 697, 698, 707, 709, 710, 746, 747
- inviolability 51, 54, 312, 322, 361, 404, 405, 483, 488, 490, 492, 493, 499–501, 504, 515, 527, 538–540, 542–544, 626, 633, 634, 659, 660, 667, 669, 674, 677, 686
- mixed use of premises 318
- non-residential building 318, 329, 334, 361, 403, 405
- surveillance *see* surveillance

private life 3, 11, 32, 55, 80, 81, 137, 138, 161, 162, 222–224, 226, 228, 230–235, 237, 238, 240, 268, 292–295, 307, 312, 314, 354–356, 371, 390, 391, 423, 430, 434, 442, 444–446, 453, 543–546, 550, 585, 662, 674, 734
- core *see* core of private life
- right to be left alone 18, 74, 81, 229, 304, 312, 314, 322, 428, 499

procedural safeguards 12, 41, 42, 57, 58, 60, 61, 64, 65, 108, 111–113, 116, 124–126, 135, 136, 138, 164, 307, 313, 316, 323–325, 330–333, 405, 411, 412, 460, 463–465, 467, 471, 472, 474, 479–481, 498, 526, 534, 539, 550, 552, 555, 556, 558, 559, 561, 580, 583–585, 588, 589, 597, 602, 612–616, 631, 638, 652, 653, 657, 658, 660, 677, 679–682, 685–688, 690, 692, 703, 705, 706, 709, 710, 713, 714, 738–741, 744, 751, 753, 754

profile
- communication and behaviour ~ 334, 490, 494, 496, 541, 550, 551, 734
- DNA ~ 377–386
- movement ~ 320, 490, 496, 497, 577, 596, 604, 734
- personality ~ 4, 41, 44, 56, 59, 62, 290, 297, 298, 320, 334, 381, 427, 429, 494, 496, 517, 541, 546, 550, 577, 596, 671, 681

profiling, electronic 506–533, 579, 667, 688

proportionality 4, 5, 10, 12, 41, 57, 62, 63, 66, 69, 77, 80, 97, 100, 105, 108–111, 113, 122, 123, 125, 126, 140, 151, 152, 159, 161, 207, 216, 219, 247, 248, 276, 292, 296, 297, 307, 310, 311, 315, 316, 321, 324–330, 333, 335, 358, 362–365, 372, 373, 380, 381, 386–388, 390, 391, 398, 399, 405, 408–414, 419, 425, 456, 462, 467, 468, 470, 471, 477, 481, 483, 488, 495–498, 500, 501, 504, 513, 517, 521–524, 526, 527, 532, 539, 548, 550, 553, 561, 564–566, 575, 576, 579–584, 586, 587, 589,

Index

591–593, 596, 597, 603, 604, 610–612, 620, 621, 635, 637, 642, 646–648, 650, 655–658, 660, 662, 663, 669, 674, 677, 679, 681–686, 690–692, 696, 697, 699, 705, 706, 708–710, 714, 731, 732, 735, 737, 738, 740, 741, 744, 745, 753–755, 758, 759
- legitimate aim 58, 63, 152–154, 156, 158, 181, 192, 247, 326, 346, 348, 386, 391, 397, 462, 466, 468, 475, 495, 496, 513, 548, 575, 576, 610, 635, 651, 669, 670, 704, 710, 731, 732, 745
- necessity 4, 12, 57–60, 63, 64, 66, 68, 80, 97, 98, 107, 110–112, 114, 116, 124, 133, 136, 152, 153, 156, 181, 192, 197, 219, 247, 248, 294, 316, 326, 327, 343, 374, 381–383, 386, 391, 392, 399, 408–412, 453, 462, 466, 468, 472, 476, 495, 496, 513, 514, 522, 548, 549, 576, 636, 654, 657, 669, 670, 731, 732, 745
- suitability 58, 63, 66, 97, 98, 124, 152, 156, 161, 181, 192, 247, 294, 326, 327, 363, 386, 391, 409, 462, 468, 476, 495, 496, 504, 513, 514, 522, 548, 549, 576, 636, 669, 670, 731, 732, 745
- ~ in the strict sense (appropriateness) 9, 80, 98, 99, 106, 107, 111, 115, 116, 124, 126, 152, 153, 156, 160, 181, 192, 219, 247, 294, 328–330, 409, 411, 468, 472, 476, 495, 496, 513, 514, 521–523, 548, 549, 552, 561, 576–578, 580, 595, 597–600, 618, 619, 636, 642, 670–673, 684, 686, 704, 709, 731, 733, 745

public security 49, 79, 103, 106, 107, 109–113, 305, 331, 382, 384, 455, 470, 471, 506, 507, 514, 520–525, 531, 534, 547, 552–554, 566, 574, 576, 579, 582, 583, 585, 588, 590, 593, 598–604, 612, 626, 629, 634, 635, 637, 639, 646, 659, 674, 675, 677, 679, 683, 694, 698, 705, 727, 728, 731, 734, 735, 737, 742, 743, 746, 747, 750, 751
- averting dangers 305, 458, 467, 471, 474, 476, 513, 514, 524–529, 532, 552–554, 558, 570, 581, 582, 588, 591, 598, 600, 601, 603, 631, 635, 636, 639, 642, 645, 651, 656, 657, 660, 662, 666, 669–672, 674, 675, 678, 681, 684, 686, 688, 690, 695, 697–699, 704, 708, 713, 727, 738, 742, 743, 745, 753
- existence and security of the Federation and the Länder 458, 470, 480, 506, 513, 514, 527, 534, 549, 553, 566, 582, 671, 674, 736, 737
- life and limb, protection 372, 386, 506, 513, 514, 521, 527, 532, 534, 549, 553, 566, 582, 616, 618, 642, 646, 657, 670, 671, 674, 737, *see also* physical integrity
- prevention of crime 79, 82, 105, 121, 293, 296, 297, 305, 409, 455, 467, 468, 473, 475–479, 496, 532, 556, 588, 598, 619, 639, 640, 669, 672, 673, 675, 682, 684, 690, 694, 695, 697, 699, 706, 708, 736, 742
- purely precautionary action 477, 479, 506, 520, 523, 524, 528, 532, 548, 554, 561, 583, 588, 590, 638–640, 648, 676, 688, 690, 717, 746

reasonableness, limits 5, 21, 44, 63, 92, 126, 140, 150–152, 156, 161, 181, 197, 247, 342, 344–347, 354, 395, 397, 398, 409, 410, 433, 437, 451, 452, 476, 477, 479, 495, 595, 597–600, 682, *see also* proportionality

religion 54, 365, 516, 531, 630, *see also* freedom of religion
- clerics 320, 614, 619, 622, 678
- cults 203, 204
- faith-based counselling 320
- free practice of ~ 320, 622

Index

- religious affiliation 44, 47, 54, 67, 206, 508, 509, 512, 516, 518, 531, 630, 653, 654, 656
- religious or ideological community 44, 46, 47, 54, 67, 206, 251

residence, residential building *see* private home

rule of law, principle of 4, 41, 51, 57, 101, 106, 108, 112, 215, 253, 293, 295, 296, 307, 328, 331, 336, 337, 351, 361, 362, 382, 386, 395, 404, 406, 407, 420, 425, 475, 495, 496, 521–526, 532, 547, 552, 598, 619, 620, 641, 642, 648, 653, 663, 667, 701, 702, 708, 711, 713, 723, 728, 731, 734, 737, 738, 748–751
- fair trial 80, 119, 217, 218, 295, 296, 396, 406, 621
- judges bound by law 18, 21, 22, 33, 499, 586
- right to be heard 89, 277, 308, 331, 390, 487

scientific research 27, 31, 42, 50, 63, 67, 91, 107, 156, 157, 179, 180, 182, 183, 342, 343, 373, 435, 565
- medical 32, 122, 134, 182

Scientology 147, 192, 201–204, 206, 210, 211, 422

security *see* public security

self-determination 4, 31, 38, 55, 56, 106, 120–123, 129, 134–137, 140, 147–150, 152–154, 158, 159, 161, 162, 164, 189, 191, 192, 258, 268, 292, 298, 342, 343, 347, 381, 387, 406, 411, 416, 422–425, 431, 446, 493, 511, 512, 519, 532, 547, 736
- informational ~ 4, 41, 42, 55–68, 97–99, 350, 352, 354–356, 379–381, 383, 385, 386, 406, 408, 410–413, 415, 416, 422, 424–427, 431, 441, 461, 462, 470, 483, 488, 490, 492–496, 498, 500, 501, 504, 506, 510–515, 518, 521, 527–530, 532, 533, 539, 540, 544, 545, 551, 562, 563, 573, 575, 618, 626, 633–635, 638, 640, 643, 669, 683
- life and death 137, 140, 143, 146–162, 164, *see also* suicide
- medical treatment *see* coercive treatment; health: freedom 'to be ill'
- private life 4, 18, 19, 32, 38, 74
- sexual ~ 179, 344, 345, 348, 378
- suicide *see* suicide
- ~ of the media 76, 227, 233, 246, 432

separation of powers 21, 22, 25, 327, 398, 600, 601, 643, 644, 648, 649, 651–653, 704–706, 708

sex (biological) 26, 44, 46, 47, 179, 181, 182, 185, 187, 188, 190–194, 338, 340–342, 344, 346–348, 530
- assigned at birth 27, 31–33, 187, 189–191, 340, 341, 346, 348
- civil status 28, 29, 31
- intersex persons 29, 31, 188, 189, 193, 194
- third gender *see* civil register: third gender option
- ~ assigned at birth 176, 180

sexual abuse 167, 168, 170–172

sexual orientation 175, 179, 180, 183, 341–345, 349

sexuality and intimacy 179, 180, 264, 265, 272, 275, 276, 279–281, 284, 285, 288, 314, 315, 319, 334, 342, 345, 350, 352, 354–356, 516

sharks 418

social state, principle of 59, 81, 98

specificity (legal) 58, 62, 67, 112, 113, 116, 125, 163, 310, 323, 382, 462, 467, 471, 473, 475, 483, 495, 526, 527, 547, 548, 555, 559, 561, 578, 581, 586, 589, 590, 610, 612, 626, 643, 644, 646, 648–653, 669, 670, 673, 677, 684, 691, 698, 703, 706, 708, 709, 731, 739, 745

statistics 1–5, 41–68, 517, *see also* data

stigmatisation 59, 79, 81, 82, 84, 169, 172, 173, 218, 383, 498, 504, 518, 531, 641

substance abuse 165, 370
- alcohol 94–96, 98, 265, 285, 371, 374, 375
- drug abuse 60, 98, 358, 360, 363–365, 368–371, 373–375

suicide 27, 130, 140, 141, 143–164, 302
- assistance 140–165
- prevention 153, 158, 161

surveillance 307, 316, 329, 423, 511, 512, 520, 557, 585, 596, 658, 662–711
- acoustic ~ 307–337
- foreign ~ 465–467, 469, 471, 712–761
- informant 473, 666, 683
- information technology system 534–564, 614, 662, 663, 667, 673, 674, 676, 686, 688–691, 695, 697, 698, 709, 710, 735, 746
- Internet 534–564, 608
- notification 331, 333, 460, 463, 465, 467, 480, 481, 608, 616–619, 667, 682, 754
- oversight *see* oversight
- private home 54, 307–337, 543, 597, 615, 622, 659, 662, 663, 666, 673, 674, 676, 677, 685–687, 689, 691, 695, 697, 698, 707, 709, 710, 746, 747
- strategic ~ 458, 460, 475–477, 522, 712–761
- telecommunications 327, 455, 456, 458, 459, 462–482, 492, 497, 532, 534, 542, 543, 556, 560, 586, 595, 597, 606–625, 662, 667, 673, 686, 690–692, 712, 716–723, 727–729, 732–736, 738–740, 742, 746, 750, 751, 753, 754
- tracking device 666, 673, 683
- undercover investigator 666, 683

telecommunications 327, 455, 458, 459, 461, 462, 465–472, 476, 483, 485,
486, 489–498, 500, 501, 504, 541–543, 549, 551, 557, 558, 565, 566, 568–570, 572–581, 584, 588, 590, 591, 593, 595, 599, 600, 604, 608, 614, 630, 660, 686, 690–692, 713, 717, 718, 727, 728, 733, 734
- communication contents 461, 462, 469, 489–491, 494, 534, 542, 543, 557, 560–562, 569, 572, 573, 577, 579, 595, 596, 602, 604, 609, 610, 614, 691, 718, 728, 734, 752
- devices 228, 461, 462, 465, 485–487, 489, 491, 492, 494, 495, 497, 500, 501, 538, 540, 542, 544, 546, 572, 573, 608, 630
- international ~ 465, 466, 469, 713, 716–722, 727, 728, 733, 736, 751, 753, 754
- privacy of ~ 455–483, 488–493, 497, 500, 501, 515, 522, 527, 534, 538–540, 542, 543, 548, 556, 560, 562, 565, 572–576, 579, 587, 589, 591, 594–597, 602, 604, 609–611, 616, 626, 633, 634, 638, 658–660, 667, 669, 690, 712, 713, 717, 720–723, 726–729, 731–733, 735, 737, 738, 741, 743, 758–760
- surveillance *see* surveillance
- traffic data *see* data

terrorism 244, 485, 508, 520, 526, 527, 529, 533, 537, 549, 636, 641, 642, 675
- 9/11 attacks 506, 508, 518, 528
- counter-terrorism 508, 521, 549, 626–661, 670, 684, 686, 690, 704
- international ~ 459, 470, 626–711, 736
- Islamist ~ 508
- threat of ~ 506

transparency 58, 60, 565, 579–581, 584, 585, 589, 592, 602, 616, 639, 640, 657–659, 662, 681–683, 692, 705, 706, 710, 719, 738, 753, 754

Index

transsexual persons 26–33
- civil status 182–184, 191, 338, 340, 342, 346–349
- hormone treatment 27, 348
- marriage and partnership 32, 176, 177, 180, 338
- name 27, 30, 31, 175–184, 340, 341, 344, 345
- surgery 26, 30, 33, 176–184, 338–349

truth 48, 54, 60, 169, 172, 207, 208, 210, 218, 246, 252, 253, 257, 259–261, 275, 281, 285, 288, 319, 395, 396, 423, 432, 436, 450
- establishment of ~ 35, 39, 40, 208–210, 217, 218, 259, 293, 295, 314, 475, 496, 620, 624, 677
- false statements 16, 21, 34, 38, 78, 201, 205–210, 244, 254, 259, 274

UN Convention on the Rights of Persons with Disabilities 122, 123, 136, 137

violence 71, 72, 83, 107, 110, 118, 213, 285, 290, 291, 296, 378–380, 386, 418, 630, 645–647, 649, 727, 749
- incitement of 629, 645, 646, 649
- sexual 103, 110, 291, 380

vulnerable persons 27, 86, 87, 89, 122, 132, 133, 136–138, 155, 161, 363

warrant 499, 529, 740
- arrest 485
- judicial 310, 316, 330, 331, 360–362, 377, 403, 485, 486, 498, 499, 502, 509, 510, 512, 519, 534, 555, 584–587, 592, 599, 604, 615, 617, 677
- law enforcement 310, 316, 360–362, 403, 408, 485, 486
- search 360–362, 403, 408, 486, 488, 494, 498–502, 504
- surveillance 310, 316, 459, 471, 556, 586, 717, 729, 731, 735, 740